THE PHILOSOPHY OF
MICHAEL DUMMETT

THE LIBRARY OF LIVING PHILOSOPHERS

PAUL ARTHUR SCHILPP, FOUNDER AND EDITOR 1939–1981
LEWIS EDWIN HAHN, EDITOR 1981–2001
RANDALL E. AUXIER, EDITOR 2001–

Paul Arthur Schilpp, Editor
THE PHILOSOPHY OF JOHN DEWEY (1939, 1971, 1989)
THE PHILOSOPHY OF GEORGE SANTAYANA (1940, 1951)
THE PHILOSOPHY OF ALFRED NORTH WHITEHEAD (1941, 1951)
THE PHILOSOPHY OF G. E. MOORE (1942, 1971)
THE PHILOSOPHY OF BERTRAND RUSSELL (1944, 1971)
THE PHILOSOPHY OF ERNST CASSIRER (1949)
ALBERT EINSTEIN: PHILOSOPHER-SCIENTIST (1949, 1970)
THE PHILOSOPHY OF SARVEPALLI RADHAKRISHNAN (1952)
THE PHILOSOPHY OF KARL JASPERS (1957; AUG. ED., 1981)
THE PHILOSOPHY OF C. D. BROAD (1959)
THE PHILOSOPHY OF RUDOLF CARNAP (1963)
THE PHILOSOPHY OF C. I. LEWIS (1968)
THE PHILOSOPHY OF KARL POPPER (1974)
THE PHILOSOPHY OF BRAND BLANSHARD (1980)
THE PHILOSOPHY OF JEAN-PAUL SARTRE (1981)

Paul Arthur Schilpp and Maurice Friedman, Editors
THE PHILOSOPHY OF MARTIN BUBER (1967)

Paul Arthur Schilpp and Lewis Edwin Hahn, Editors
THE PHILOSOPHY OF GABRIEL MARCEL (1984)
THE PHILOSOPHY OF W. V. QUINE (1986, AUG. ED., 1998)
THE PHILOSOPHY OF GEORG HENRIK VON WRIGHT (1989)

Lewis Edwin Hahn, Editor
THE PHILOSOPHY OF CHARLES HARTSHORNE (1991)
THE PHILOSOPHY OF A. J. AYER (1992)
THE PHILOSOPHY OF PAUL RICOEUR (1995)
THE PHILOSOPHY OF PAUL WEISS (1995)
THE PHILOSOPHY OF HANS-GEORG GADAMER (1997)
THE PHILOSOPHY OF RODERICK M. CHISHOLM (1997)
THE PHILOSOPHY OF P. F. STRAWSON (1998)
THE PHILOSOPHY OF DONALD DAVIDSON (1999)

Lewis Edwin Hahn, Randall E. Auxier, and Lucian W. Stone, Jr., Editors
THE PHILOSOPHY OF SEYYED HOSSEIN NASR (2001)

Randall E. Auxier and Lewis Edwin Hahn, Editors
THE PHILOSOPHY OF MARJORIE GRENE (2002)
THE PHILOSOPHY OF JAAKKO HINTIKKA (2006)
THE PHILOSOPHY OF MICHAEL DUMMETT (2007)

In Preparation:
THE PHILOSOPHY OF ARTHUR C. DANTO
THE PHILOSOPHY OF MARTHA NUSSBAUM
THE PHILOSOPHY OF HILARY PUTNAM
THE PHILOSOPHY OF RICHARD M. RORTY

Michael Dummett

THE LIBRARY OF LIVING PHILOSOPHERS
VOLUME XXXI

THE PHILOSOPHY OF
MICHAEL DUMMETT

EDITED BY

RANDALL E. AUXIER

AND

LEWIS EDWIN HAHN

SOUTHERN ILLINOIS UNIVERSITY CARBONDALE

CHICAGO AND LA SALLE, ILLINOIS • OPEN COURT • ESTABLISHED 1887

To order books from Open Court, call 1-800-815-2280, or visit our website at www.opencourtbooks.com.

THE PHILOSOPHY OF MICHAEL DUMMETT

Open Court Publishing Company is a division of Carus Publishing Company.

Library of Congress Cataloging-in-Publication Data

The philosophy of Michael Dummett / edited by Randall E. Auxier and Lewis Edwin Hahn.
    p. cm. -- (The library of living philosophers ; v. 31)
    Includes bibliographical references and index.
    ISBN-13: 978-0-8126-9621-9 (cloth : alk. paper)
    ISBN-10: 0-8126-9621-2 (cloth : alk. paper)
    ISBN-13: 978-0-8126-9622-6 (trade paper : alk. paper)
    ISBN-10: 0-8126-9622-0 (trade paper : alk. paper) 1. Dummett, Michael A.
E. I. Auxier, Randall E., 1961- II. Hahn, Lewis Edwin, 1908-
    B1626.D854P49 2007
    192--dc22

                                        2007019943

The Library of Living Philosophers is published under the sponsorship of Southern Illinois University Carbondale.

GENERAL INTRODUCTION
TO
THE LIBRARY OF LIVING PHILOSOPHERS

Since its founding in 1938 by Paul Arthur Schilpp, the Library of Living Philosophers has been devoted to critical analysis and discussion of some of the world's greatest living philosophers. The format for the series provides for creating in each volume a dialogue between the critics and the great philosopher. The aim is not refutation or confrontation but rather fruitful joining of issues and improved understanding of the positions and issues involved. That is, the goal is not overcoming those who differ from us philosophically but interacting creatively with them.

The basic idea for the series, according to Professor Schilpp's general introduction to the earlier volumes, came from the late F.C.S. Schiller's essay "Must Philosophers Disagree?" While Schiller may have been overly optimistic about ending "interminable controversies" in this way, it seems clear that directing searching questions to great philosophers about what they really mean or how they might resolve or address difficulties in their philosophies can produce far greater clarity of understanding and more fruitful philosophizing than would otherwise exist.

To Paul Arthur Schilpp's undying credit, he acted on this basic thought in launching the Library of Living Philosophers. The general plan for the volumes has sometimes been altered to fit circumstances, but in ways that have well served the mission of the series. The intellectual autobiographies, or, in a few cases, the biographies, shed a great deal of light on both how the philosophies of the great thinkers developed and the major philosophical movements and issues of their time; and many of our great philosophers seek to orient their outlook not merely to their contemporaries but also to what they find most important in earlier philosophers. The critical perspectives of our distinguished contributors have often stood on their own as landmark studies, widely cited and familiar not only to subsequent specialists, but frequently discussed in their own right as pieces of great philosophy. The bibliography helps to provide ready access to the featured scholar's writings and thought.

There is no reason to alter our historical format or mission for the present century. We are pleased that the success of the Library of Living

Philosophers has led to a wider appreciation of the need for dialogue of the type our format creates. We respect the efforts of other academic publishers to employ versions of our format to facilitate pluralistic, meaningful, sharp, constructive, and respectful exchange in philosophical ideas. We are fortunate to have such support from the Open Court Publishing Company, the Edward C. Hegeler Foundation, and the Board of Trustees, College of Liberal Arts, and the Department of Philosophy of Southern Illinois University Carbondale, as to permit us to carry out our purpose with a degree of deliberate thoroughness and comprehensiveness not available to other academic publishers, and we have rededicated ourselves to maintaining the highest standards in scholarship and accuracy anywhere to be found in academic publishing. In recognition of the permanent value that has been accorded our previous volumes, we are committed to keeping our volumes in print and available, and to maintaining our sense of the long-term importance of providing the most reliable source for scholarly analysis by the most distinguished voices of our day about the most important philosophical contributions of the greatest living thinkers.

The Library of Living Philosophers has never construed "philosophy" in a narrow and strictly academic sense. Past volumes have been dedicated both to the leading academic philosophers and to the most visible and influential public philosophers. We renew with each volume our historical orientation to the practice of philosophy as a quest for truth, beauty, and the best life, and we affirm that this quest is a public activity and its results a public possession, both for the present generation and in the future. We seek, with the sober judgment of our Advisory Board, to bring forth volumes on the thought of figures whose ideas have made a genuine difference to the lives of people everywhere. Ideas truly do have consequences, and many of the ideas that have had the broadest impact were indeed best articulated by the figures to whom we have dedicated past volumes. The selfless work of Paul Arthur Schilpp and Lewis Edwin Hahn in realizing this mission stands among the most important scholarly contributions to twentieth-century philosophy. Their judgment regarding how best to pursue the purposes of the Library of Living Philosophers has found constant and continuous confirmation in the reception and ongoing importance accorded this series. Let us continue in their footsteps as well as we may.

RANDALL E. AUXIER

DEPARTMENT OF PHILOSOPHY
SOUTHERN ILLINOIS UNIVERSITY CARBONDALE

FOUNDER'S GENERAL INTRODUCTION*
TO
THE LIBRARY OF LIVING PHILOSOPHERS

According to the late F.C.S. Schiller, the greatest obstacle to fruitful discussion in philosophy is "the curious etiquette which apparently taboos the asking of questions about a philosopher's meaning while he is alive." The "interminable controversies which fill the histories of philosophy," he goes on to say, "could have been ended at once by asking the living philosophers a few searching questions."

The confident optimism of this last remark undoubtedly goes too far. Living thinkers have often been asked "a few searching questions," but their answers have not stopped "interminable controversies" about their real meaning. It is nonetheless true that there would be far greater clarity of understanding than is now often the case if more such searching questions had been directed to great thinkers while they were still alive.

This, at any rate, is the basic thought behind the present undertaking. The volumes of the Library of Living Philosophers can in no sense take the place of the major writings of great and original thinkers. Students who would know the philosophies of such men as John Dewey, George Santayana, Alfred North Whitehead, G. E. Moore, Bertrand Russell, Ernst Cassirer, Karl Jaspers, Rudolf Carnap, Martin Buber, et al., will still need to read the writings of these men. There is no substitute for first-hand contact with the original thought of the philosopher himself. Least of all does this Library pretend to be such a substitute. The Library in fact will spare neither effort nor expense in offering to the student the best possible guide to the published writings of a given thinker. We shall attempt to meet this aim by providing at the end of each volume in our series as nearly complete a bibliography of the published work of the philosopher in

---

*This General Introduction sets forth in the founder's words the underlying conception of the Library. L.E.H.

question as possible. Nor should one overlook the fact that essays in each volume cannot but finally lead to this same goal. The interpretive and critical discussions of the various phases of a great thinker's work and, most of all, the reply of the thinker himself, are bound to lead the reader to the works of the philosopher himself.

At the same time, there is no denying that different experts find different ideas in the writings of the same philosopher. This is as true of the appreciative interpreter and grateful disciple as it is of the critical opponent. Nor can it be denied that such differences of reading and of interpretation on the part of other experts often leave the neophyte aghast before the whole maze of widely varying and even opposing interpretations. Who is right and whose interpretation shall he accept? When the doctors disagree among themselves, what is the poor student to do? If, in desperation, he decides that all of the interpreters are probably wrong and that the only thing for him to do is to go back to the original writings of the philosopher himself and then make his own decision—uninfluenced (as if this were possible) by the interpretation of anyone else—the result is not that he has actually come to the meaning of the original philosopher himself, but rather that he has set up one more interpretation, which may differ to a greater or lesser degree from the interpretations already existing. It is clear that in this direction lies chaos, just the kind of chaos which Schiller has so graphically and inimitably described.**

It is curious that until now no way of escaping this difficulty has been seriously considered. It has not occurred to students of philosophy that one effective way of meeting the problem at least partially is to put these varying interpretations and critiques before the philosopher while he is still alive and to ask him to act at one and the same time as both defendant and judge. If the world's greatest living philosophers can be induced to cooperate in an enterprise whereby their own work can, at least to some extent, be saved from becoming merely "desiccated lecture-fodder," which on the one hand "provides innocuous sustenance for ruminant professors," and on the other hand gives an opportunity to such ruminants and their understudies to "speculate safely, endlessly, and fruitlessly, about what a philosopher must have meant" (Schiller), they will have taken a long step toward making their intentions more clearly comprehensible.

With this in mind, the Library of Living Philosophers expects to publish at more or less regular intervals a volume on each of the greater among the

---

** In his essay "Must Philosophers Disagree?" in the volume of the same title (London: Macmillan, 1934), from which the above quotations were taken.

world's living philosophers. In each case it will be the purpose of the editor of the Library to bring together in the volume the interpretations and criticisms of a wide range of that particular thinker's scholarly contemporaries, each of whom will be given a free hand to discuss the specific phase of the thinker's work that has been assigned to him. All contributed essays will finally be submitted to the philosopher with whose work and thought they are concerned, for his careful perusal and reply. And, although it would be expecting too much to imagine that the philosopher's reply will be able to stop all differences of interpretation and of critique, this should at least serve the purpose of stopping certain of the grosser and more general kinds of misinterpretations. If no further gain than this were to come from the present and projected volumes of this Library, it would seem to be fully justified.

In carrying out this principal purpose of the Library, the editor announces that (as far as is humanly possible) each volume will contain the following elements:

First, an intellectual autobiography of the thinker whenever this can be secured; in any case an authoritative and authorized biography;
Second, a series of expository and critical articles written by the leading exponents and opponents of the philosopher's thought;
Third, the reply to the critics and commentators by the philosopher himself; and
Fourth, a bibliography of writings of the philosopher to provide a ready instrument to give access to his writings and thought.

PAUL ARTHUR SCHILPP
FOUNDER AND EDITOR, 1939–1981

DEPARTMENT OF PHILOSOPHY
SOUTHERN ILLINOIS UNIVERSITY CARBONDALE

ACKNOWLEDGMENTS

The editor hereby gratefully acknowledges his obligation and sincere gratitude to all the publishers of Michael Dummett's books and publications for their kind and uniform courtesy in permitting us to quote—sometimes at some length—from Professor Dummett.

RANDALL E. AUXIER
LEWIS EDWIN HAHN

Added to Board after the subject of this volume was chosen.

TABLE OF CONTENTS

PREFACE

Professor Sir Michael Anthony Eardley Dummett, longtime Fellow of All Souls' College and New College, and Wykeham Professor of Logic at Oxford, has lived an extraordinary life. Most who know his major philosophical works will learn much they have not even suspected in the pages of this volume. In working with Sir Michael (for such is the way he is cheerily greeted in Oxford, since he was knighted on New Year's Day, 1991) over recent years, a more general question has arisen in my thinking: what lifts a philosopher from ordinary prominence in the profession into the realm of undying and permanent contribution to the enterprise of human thought? In thinking specifically of Michael Dummett, I have come to believe that one indispensable feature of such a rise is, as Goethe, speaking of Plato and Aristotle, once said: "they had the fortune to educate themselves fully, to utter their education completely, not in short laconic sentences like oracular sayings but in exceptional, extensive, numerous works." While Goethe rightly credits good fortune, we should read this as a necessary but insufficient condition for the move beyond mortality and into the lasting annals of human thought. No one rises without fortune's good nod, but many who receive it fail to employ the opportunity it affords. Michael Dummett acknowledges both good fortune and providence, but the present task is to address what may be termed the "natural" and "moral" causes, those which bring necessary conditions to sufficiency.

In addressing the natural causes of Sir Michael's achievement, we should consider native gifts, and he possesses an astonishing array of them. Most of these seem to be connected in one way or another with an unusual command of language in general and languages in particular, but as I will suggest, these abilities make up only a portion of the natural endowment.

If I have rightly counted, Sir Michael has at some point in his life gained facility and something approaching full reading or spoken fluency with at least six languages, apart from his native English: Greek, Latin,

Japanese, German, Italian, and French. Given his experiences living among the people in India, Malaysia, and Ghana, and his extensive travels elsewhere, his formal studies have been supplemented with an experiential knowledge of many other tongues. Sir Michael treats all this rather casually, as though anyone similarly situated could have done what he did. While an endearing comradery may flow to those of us who are so treated, it is, to say the least, a charming overestimation of most. Thus we discover one natural feature of Dummett's mind which has made him the preeminent philosopher of language of his generation: his theories are grounded in broad, detailed knowledge of natural languages. Hence, his judgment and intuitions about how language functions, and why, are simply more informed than most of his interlocutors.

Sir Michael's command of other languages has also played no small role in his near perfect mastery of the English language. His style of writing is adaptable to any subject, any audience, and the economy of expression, wit, and fluidity of his English has led us to leave almost untouched his contributions to this volume, including his British spelling. We have thought that the literary value of his writing stands alongside his thought in an appealing complementarity and have not wished to alter its tone or flow in any way. It is true that for the sake of exactitude Dummett has often sacrificed some of the literary concerns he might have wished to preserve in the more technical works in his corpus, but even these are dotted with not infrequent jewels of expression and examples of his dry wit. Those who have examined his more popular writings, and those who go on to examine the autobiographical essay in this work, will be left with no doubt at all regarding his command of his native language. It is unfortunate that his book, *Grammar and Style for Examination Candidates and Others* (1993) finds no mention in the contributions to this volume, but it was ever before the editor's mind, for the writing wants no improvement at all.

Among the other natural causes of Sir Michael's achievement we find his facility in mathematics and logic, what I would call together the formal structures of thinking. Dummett has not only a great aptitude in applying these formal structures, but an accompanying power to step back from them and understand the foundations of their operation. Those who can apply mathematical and logical principles are perhaps not so terribly uncommon, although persons who can use the most technical among these tools, as Dummett can, are not to be found on every corner, even in Oxford. But persons who possess the combination of applied and theoretical excellence in the formal structures of thinking are exceedingly rare, even in the most exalted seats of learning, for, as Emerson phrased it, "men more easily transmit a form than a virtue." The best among us seem to reach the ceiling of our native gifts in mathematics and logic, irrespective of our exertions, before Sir Michael so much as begins to *sense* that there is any barrier at all. In considering (to the extent anyone can) Dummett's native gifts, I think he could learn anything he decided to learn. One would expect him to deflect this suggestion as nonsense, but our purpose here is not to appease his modesty, however genuinely felt it may be. Many of our readers will be surprised to learn that Dummett's efforts relating to applied and theoretical formal structures of thinking have been important not only to the philosophy of mathematics and mathematical logic, but also to the theory and practice of voting procedures.

The combination of intellectual capabilities I have so far described might have sufficed to make Sir Michael one of the pre-eminent thinkers of his generation. Yet, it would be an inexcusable injustice were we to give no notice to at least three more natural gifts, although one could enumerate several others that may be equally as deserving of mention.

First among these is that Sir Michael has not only the practical and theoretical command of languages and formal systems, he has the mind and temper of an historian. Those who observe the qualities of the human mind closely will know that fine historians have a particular sobriety of judgment, a caution with inference, a quality of patience, and a respect for what evidence truly shows and fails to show—altogether making for a critical sense which is both heightened beyond the ordinary and further disciplined by the tedium and rigors of close research. It is difficult to convince the historical mind of an inference with anything short of genuinely conclusive evidence. This sort of patience and sobriety is a native intellectual gift. By contrast, the typical philosophical mind runs from one inference to the next at a dizzying pace, deeming whatever evidence it needs as "possible to come by" (so long as some other person does the actual digging). These two competing temperaments are rarely combined in a single individual, for the presence of the historical sense generally kills the willingness to speculate, but we may note that David Hume and G. W. Leibniz possessed both tempers, grounding the speculations in the particulars of common life, while elevating their grasp of the meanings and implications of those particulars. And these giants of Western thought are fair templates against which to assess the historical and philosophical mind of Michael Dummett. He is their equal in this combination, I would argue. Nearly all professional philosophers will be aware of the very close scholarship in Dummett's books on Frege and his work on the origins of analytic philosophy, and they will review their sources with utmost care before challenging him on a point of history. For this reason his views on the *philosophy* of history are also held in great esteem, even though they are quite controversial. And here the pattern in his success becomes evident—it is a balance of and excellence in practical as well as theoretical understanding, what Aristotle called *nous*, each side complementing the other where most of us experience the division as a limitation. In language, in the formal structures of thinking, and in the balance of speculation and weighing particular evidence, Dummett finds complementarity. With respect to history, our readers may be surprised to learn in the succeeding pages that his knack for particular history has been so fully documented in his several books on Tarot cards. Although he regards this as a hobby, it is clear to me that Dummett could have been one of the finest pure historians of his generation had he chosen that path, and it is unclear whether we ought to be grateful he did not, for great historians change the world as surely as do great philosophers; it is not easy to choose between Plato and Thucydides.

The last two natural qualities of mind may be taken together, for they introduce what I take to be the moral causes of Sir Michael's achievement. It has seemed to me that Michael Dummett possesses both his sense of justice and his religious faith as natural endowments. I will not pursue these impressions in any detail, except to note that it is not obvious to everyone from an early age that racism is wrong, that true justice is *not* the advantage of the stronger, or that there is surely a God. Several contributions to this volume attest to a life dedicated to the synthesis of these three sensibilities. Perhaps some will say that the autobiography here contained reads, in places, like Michael Dummett's Christian witness, and it does. Should a person of faith, although he be a philosopher, not bear witness? God forbid. And equally for the sense of justice, should a philosopher not do whatever is within his personal power to fight injustice with the best of his energy? Let it never be so, even where such a philosopher can secure neither his faith nor his sense of justice by any conclusive philosophical demonstration. Philosophical doubt has found its place and has done its appointed work in due course over the reach of Dummett's life and work, but it has made no serious dent in either his native faith or his sense of justice. It is greatly to be hoped that Dummett will expend his energies in these later years doing in ethics and political and religious thought what he has already done for our thinking on language, formal thinking, history, and time. For Dummett has done the particular work necessary for the same degree of insight in our moral thinking as he has done for the excellence of particular understanding in the other areas. What, we may beg of him, *is* justice, what *is* faith? If you do not tell us, Sir Michael, the task will surely devolve upon someone less able. The forthcoming publication of his Gifford Lectures are certainly to be greeted as an important contribution toward the fulfillment of such a hope. And such, I hold, are some of the natural causes of his philosophical achievement.

If these natural endowments are those of a polymath, and they are, one may still note that precious few polymaths live such balanced, productive, and even blessed lives as Sir Michael. He has noted in his autobiography that the Lord has not chosen that he should suffer the traumas of rejection, but if providence has spared him that especial strain of adversity, it has not spared him many others that accompany the human lot. Having already presumed much in the foregoing comments, it would be still more unfitting to place myself in the position assessing what may be the secret behind the happiness of another. Some mysteries are best left unspoken, even if they could be discovered. And yet, surveying as I have for the past five years, the living legacy of Michael Dummett, taken more or less whole, I cannot withhold a few remarks about the moral causes to be gleaned, and must beg his pardon for making both the observations and the remarks, but I will speak in more general terms so as to preserve some sense of caution.

However immense Sir Michael's natural gifts are, what has actuated them is an indomitable spirit, issuing in a genial reception of life's possibilities and a decisive determination not to allow them to pass unaccosted by tireless effort. I think of how Mark Twain was led into the darkest recesses of despair by the loss of his children and by what he called "the insults of old age." He could find no explanation short of blind necessity itself for the injuries life had inflicted, and could not resist the urge to universalize his particular miseries as the inevitable lot of all humankind. He was not correct in this, for I know of a philosopher who might offer a similar list of misfortunes (and blessings) and bear up under them with an equanimity not allowed in Twain's broodings on the subject.

If death comes too soon, is unmet, ill deserved, or ill timed, it is called tragic; if old age harbors hardship and decline in oneself or one's dearest companions in life, then many may speak of it as something merely to be endured. But one man's irreparable *grief* is only another's *sorrow*, for the difference is, as Josiah Royce said, that in grief we are imprisoned in insisting that the tragic event never should have been, while in sorrow we see that the tragedy is part and parcel of the joy and blessing of having shared life with those whom we have lost. Wisdom teaches us sorrow, while fear is the true teacher of grief. I observe much wisdom in Michael

Dummett, and were it not ridiculous to envy the tested steel that has been forged in the furnace of another's particular sorrows, I should want that shiny thing for myself. He has been jailed in his life, but not by grief; rather, it was by the police, and for a just cause. We should all seek such prisons.

Similarly, in the matter of endurance, I think about the golden moment in *The Republic* when Socrates quiets the boisterous and self-forgetful gathering so that they may pay due homage to what Cephalus, their host, might say—for he is on the threshold of the old. And here we learn that one man's "insults of age" can be another's liberation. Sir Michael has remarked in this volume that writing replies to the contributions herein is like being afforded the impossible opportunity of writing thank-you notes to favorable obituaries. Perhaps so, but I suppose one ought not take favorable obituaries lightly; even granting that their favorability is the universal form, not all are equally merited, and it is the degree of merit which warrants their truth and the name "eu-logy," or "good words." There are not less than three robust generations of students, several individuals being represented in this volume, whose testimonials come in the form of critique, extension, and even rejection of Dummett's ideas; there is no hagiography here. Teachers who leave their students unafraid to think for themselves will not justly be concerned about the merit of the name "eulogy," for the good words are the true ones. Michael Dummett's students think for themselves.

Such are the moral causes of Sir Michael's achievements, so far as I am capable of estimating them. At the risk of offending the partisans of Solon, I think we can count this philosopher happy while he is very much alive. I do not fear contradiction on this point, for there are a thousand pages of evidence in your hands.

On behalf of everyone at the Library of Living Philosophers I thank Professor Dummett for his beneficent tolerance during the rather long and ponderous gestation period which brings this volume into the world. If anything has really tested his endurance, this volume must surely be on that list. A number of highly technical contributions to this volume have required us to take close care with the text. We have done all we can, but for the errors that remain we assume responsibility and solicit pardon. We want to thank the distinguished contributors for their excellent offerings, and we hope that our efforts in their behalf have adequately repaid their time and creativity.

The LLP staff is happy to acknowledge once more the warm support, encouragement, and cooperation of our publisher, Open Court Publishing

Company, especially M. Blouke Carus, André Carus, David R. Steele, and Kerri Mommer. And we also very much appreciate continued support, understanding, and encouragement from the administration of Southern Illinois University Carbondale, especially the College of Liberal Arts, its former Dean, Shirley Clay Scott, and its present Acting Dean, Alan Vaux. As always, we are grateful for the friendly and unfailing help in a variety of ways from the staff of Morris Library at SIUC. It is invaluable for our work and that of our fellow scholars. Without the unflagging support of the Department of Philosophy at Southern Illinois University Carbondale, and its Chair George Schedler, these volumes could not be published. As Editor, my warm gratitude also goes to Jeletta Brant and the Philosophy Department secretariat for help with numerous projects; to Frances Stanley, the LLP Technical Editor, who does nearly everything related to these volumes, such as creating the camera-ready proofs, helping with manuscripts, catching many editing points I have missed, and keeping the constant correspondence with contributors moving and well-ordered. I would also like to thank James Russell Couch, Jason Hills, Brett Carroll, Tony Giambusso, Aaron Fortune, Chesna Braniger, and Alejandro Strong, graduate students at SIUC, for their excellent research, library work, and tireless efforts in tracking down and verifying quotations and citations.

RANDALL E. AUXIER
EDITOR

DEPARTMENT OF PHILOSOPHY
SOUTHERN ILLINOIS UNIVERSITY CARBONDALE
FEBRUARY 2007

PART ONE

INTELLECTUAL AUTOBIOGRAPHY OF MICHAEL DUMMETT

During 1951 I settled down to read everything that Frege had written. His writings had not yet been collected, let alone translated, so I had to read the articles in the original journals. I had had a year of German at school, so I had a backbone of grammar, but very little vocabulary: I read with a dictionary at my side. One result was that I became to learn mathematical logic and mathematics at least up to Finals standard, I asked the then Warden of All Souls', Humphrey Sumner, if I could take an undergraduate degree in mathematics, but he refused me on the ground that it would disgrace the College if I failed to obtain a First. As an alternative, John Hammersley very kindly agreed to give me tutorials in the subject. As far as mathematical logic, there was no one to teach me. The subject did not flourish then in Oxford: most mathematicians thought it should not exist, as not being real mathematics; most philosophers thought it probably should exist, but that it was no business of theirs.

Michael Dummett

INTELLECTUAL AUTOBIOGRAPHY

To write my autobiography has always seemed to me a nearly impossible task. To be of interest, it ought to be completely honest, as surely very few autobiographies are. If it were completely honest, it would necessarily expose me as having often acted very stupidly or made myself ridiculous; these are things of which we can live with the memory, but would squirm to tell others about. Worse, it would involve describing others and their behaviour, which would violate their privacy and often could not be done without putting them in a bad light. But now I have to write one. I have been told that it need not be a purely intellectual autobiography. Still, in the context of this book, it must principally be that; this fact makes the task much easier. I will record here some episodes of my life that have an interest apart from my intellectual work; I shall not attempt the all-encompassing autobiography I could never write. But I shall confess to some foolish actions, and shall not put everyone I mention in a favourable light.

My father was a businessman—a silk and rayon merchant. My mother was the daughter of a former head of the Indian Forestry service, and had taken up the breeding of Alsatians. My school career was a patchwork. I went as a scholar to Winchester in September 1939, just after the war had started. In those days my parents paid a derisory sum for my education there—I believe that it was £30 a year, though it may have been £30 a term: things are utterly different now. College at Winchester could not be claimed as a socially egalitarian system, however: to get a scholarship to Winchester a boy had then to have a substantial amount of Latin—I began Latin at eight —and a fair amount of Greek: only those whose parents could afford the fees of a private preparatory school could acquire either. I am very conscious of the advantage I gained from being educated at Winchester; I do not know how I should have made out if I had not been. The upper forms at Winchester were divided into the A or classical ladder, the C or science ladder and the B or history and modern languages ladder. All scholars had to spend their first year on the A ladder. After my first year, I opted for the C ladder. Before reaching Winchester, I had read many of the works of popular science by Jeans and Eddington, and had been fascinated by them;

science, I thought, was the most exciting subject there was. My year on the C ladder was deeply disappointing. My so-called experiments always came out wrong; I found phrases such as "Take a copper calorimeter" profoundly boring. It so happened that I was taught history that year by the senior history master, Harold Walker, an inspired teacher. History had previously seemed to me a dull subject: now I thought it was what I really wanted to do. I applied to transfer to the B ladder. There was great opposition: scholars simply did not go on to the B ladder; but I gained my way. I obtained a history scholarship to Christ Church, Oxford, in 1943. There was at that time a scheme under which one could take a six-month university "short course" before entering the army, but this seemed to me pointless; so, being eighteen in that year, I went into the army, at first into the Royal Artillery.

During my time at Winchester, my religious opinions underwent a radical swing. Initially, I had an atheist and scientistic outlook; in company with many others in College (the scholars' "house"), I declined to receive an Anglican confirmation at the designated age. My parents protested mildly; neither was a practising Christian, and I think their objection was to any unconventional behaviour rather than to religious dissent. Then my opinions started gradually to shift. From a diffuse pantheism I came to believe in God, as understood in the Semitic religions. (I use "Semitic" in place of the "Judaeo-Christian" which seems to me inaccurately to ignore Islam.) I was much influenced by a heterogeneous set of Catholic writers —G. K. Chesterton, Eric Gill, Christopher Dawson. One by one, I came to accept the tenets of the Christian faith. That which I found it hardest to swallow, and which was the last I came to accept, was that of life after death. I do not think that I understood at that time that this rested absolutely on the belief in that, on the face of it, bafflingly unlikely event, the general resurrection: I think I had then a dualist conception of our souls as naturally capable of existing separated from our bodies. I should probably have been puzzled if I had learned of St. Thomas's dictum *"Anima mea non est ego"* ("My soul is not me").

It never occurred to me to think otherwise than that the Church of Rome was the only institution with a plausible claim to be continuous with the Church founded by Christ and enjoying that protection of the Holy Spirit from deviation in belief that was promised by Christ. It appeared to me plain from the New Testament that it was the duty of followers of Jesus Christ never to do anything to disrupt the unity between them. All the other ecclesiastical bodies—even the Orthodox churches—owed their origins to an act of disunity, of deliberate separation from the unified mother church: only those who belonged to the church in union with the Pope had not separated themselves. I realised very well that those who had broken away had often received great provocation; but I thought—and indeed still think—that it was the duty of a Christian to endure whatever persecution by other Christians was visited upon him—even to the extent that St. Joan was called upon to do—rather than himself break the unity it was his duty to preserve. Hence, long before I became convinced of the truth of the Christian faith, I had no doubt that, if I were to become a Christian, I should become a Catholic. By the time I left school in the summer of 1943, I had determined to become one.

My first six months in the Royal Artillery were spent in Edinburgh. Having been rejected for the navy on account of (mild) colour-blindness, I had not paid much attention to the process whereby I joined the army. I suppose now that I was a member of a group of ex–public schoolboys, earmarked for officerhood, attending at Edinburgh University, under the auspices of the R. A., one of those six-month university short courses which I had declined to do at Oxford, but in subjects not of our choosing. These included a course on surveying and one on the internal combustion engine. I passed the latter examination successfully, but my knowledge was all theoretical: faced with a jeep that had broken down, I should have had no idea what to do. Even during the war, the army was still influenced by the British class system: having attended a public school made it likely that you had officer-like qualities. I contacted the University Catholic chaplaincy, which was then run by the Dominicans, and, having announced my wish to become a Catholic, underwent a long series of instructions by the chaplain, Father Ivo Thomas.

I was received into the Church in February 1944. My parents were very upset, not, I think, because my action was unconventional, but because of a deep prejudice against Catholicism which had been instilled into them in childhood and survived their loss of all religious faith. Apart from three distant cousins, all female and two of an older generation, whom I very much liked, I had never known any Catholics, and had never attended a Catholic service; I now went to two nearby churches, and found the forms of worship strange, and fascinating. I later learned much more about my religion, and became critical in various ways and a strong advocate of liturgical reform; but my faith was deeply rooted, and it was not for twelve years or more that the first doubts assailed me about whether it was all true.

I have undergone several periods when I have been overcome by such doubts; during them, I have not ceased to attend Sunday Mass, but have abstained from the sacraments. My doubts have always been global rather than local; my reasons for believing in God are philosophical rather than affective; they can suddenly strike me as unconvincing. The liturgy enables those who take part to feel themselves present at the long-past events of Christ's life; something similar is a feature of all religions, I think. But during such periods I am oppressed by the thought that all that is *actually* happening is the present performance of the liturgy. But most usually my doubts have been engendered by what troubles everyone: can a world in which such suffering occurs be one made by a God who is said to be love? "What a tender love was His, Who from realms of highest bliss Came into a world like this" the Christmas hymn exclaims: well, it was the world He created. That world *looks* as if governed by uncaring forces. The pain of animals is a good example; I once saw on television a sloth carried off by some bird of prey and then devoured alive. As for human pain, it is not its mere occurrence that has usually troubled me: after the Cross, no one can say to God, "You don't know what it is like." After the great cry of dereliction, no one can say this even about the feeling that the Sicilian heroine Rita Atria had, that God had abandoned her. What troubles me most is the way some people die. Some deaths are too devoid of dignity or peace to allow any self-surrender; how can they be the means by which anyone's soul is supposed to pass into eternity? I have no answer to these questions; they trouble me continually. It has been only sporadically, and not for a long time now, that they have overwhelmed me and prevented me for a period from being a whole-hearted believer. When the period has ended and my faith in God has been restored, it has not been because I have found the answers, but because I have become able to live with the agony of not knowing them, confident that they are to be found.

Edinburgh was succeeded by six weeks' Basic Training in Catterick, which was horrible; also, having long held Socialist principles and sympathised with the working class, I was dismayed by the foul-mouthed speech of the other conscripts. I escaped having to undergo Basic Training a second time only by being tagged as potential officer material. There followed a period of training on field guns (25-pounders) at Shoeburyness; because of the impending invasion of France, no one was allowed out of or into Essex. During this period I went for three days to a War Office Selection Board, and was rejected as unsuitable to be given a commission. My mother said, "It is your first failure"; I was glad I was not to become an officer. While many of my companions went off to be trained as officers, I went to an artillery camp for specialist training; the atmosphere was pleasant, and we learned how to plot trajectories, which was interesting. I have never discovered why, in the midst of this, I received an order to report to a house in Bedford; the C.O. called me in and demanded whether I had been applying for things behind his back, which I had not. At Bedford I was given a test and asked whether I should like to learn Japanese; thinking it would be more interesting still than the mathematics of gunnery, I said "Yes." I then spent six months attending a Japanese course in the house in Bedford, billeted on a local family. We were a mixed bunch of soldiers, sailors, and civilians; I was transferred to the Intelligence Corps. We spent every morning and every afternoon and evening, except Sundays, learning Japanese; we were taught only to read and write the language, not to speak it. Our instructors were Captain Ceadle, who later became University Lecturer in Japanese at Cambridge; David Hawkes, who later became Professor of Chinese at Oxford and a good friend; and a retired Naval Captain whose name I forget, who had a great love of Japanese literature and showed us many haiku. Among the other students were Mike Screech, who many years later became a Fellow of All Souls' as an expert on Rabelais, and Mary de Turville, a Catholic whose husband was in the army in India and who particularly befriended me.

After some more training at the Intelligence Corps depot in Rotherham, I was sent out by ship to India; the war in Europe was drawing to a close, but no one knew how long it would take to defeat the Japanese. After some weeks of being messed about, I ended up in what was misleadingly called the Wireless Experimental Centre outside Delhi. There I found Dominic de Turville, Mary's husband; he became my principal friend at the Centre. He had a great love of the liturgy, a dislike of the rosary, and an interest in Eastern-rite churches; when I met him again after the war, he was obsessed by schemes for joining one of the Eastern rites of the Catholic Church and becoming a married priest. Our work was intensely boring: translating Japanese—mostly wireless messages intercepted in Burma—for eight hours at a stretch, on an insane schedule, to which it was impossible to adjust, of eight hours on, 24 hours off, eight hours on, incessantly. I formed a great liking for Indians and a love for India (where in fact my mother had been born and brought up), but I missed seeing parts that I longed to see: in the whole time I was in India—about nine months—I was never given as much as six hours' leave, and so I never even saw Agra. I sympathised greatly with the Indian nationalist demand for independence, but not with Subhas Chandra Bose, the founder of the Indian National Army that fought alongside the Japanese: he is now ranked an Indian patriotic hero, but to my mind, then and now, he was a Fascist traitor to the Indian cause.

Before the first atomic bomb was dropped on Hiroshima, we had been expecting the war to continue for at least two more years. Dominic and I both thought that we could not in conscience remain in the forces of an alliance that could commit so atrocious a crime. We went to some Franciscans whom we knew for advice about declaring we could no longer serve in the army. The Franciscans told us that the Pope was sure to declare that Catholics could no longer serve in the Anglo-American forces, and that we should wait until then: we naively believed them. Then the second atomic bomb was dropped on Nagasaki, the war ended, and we decided that it was pointless at that stage to make the gesture we were contemplating.

The W.E.C. was disbanded, retaining only those who knew Chinese or
Russian, so that we could spy on our allies. I was sent to Karachi, and from
there to Singapore, to join a Field Security section. Originally I was
supposed to join one in Saigon, but, after being messed about for some
time, I was sent to join one in Malaya, at first in Khota Bharu and then in
Taiping. The official task of Field Security was to supervise the security of
messages, documents, arms, and munitions in army units; in practice, it did
a variety of odd jobs, mostly semi-political, that there was no one else to do.
In Malaya we were in effect a minor branch of the military government
which, during most of my time there, ran the country very well; we sent in
weekly reports of the economic, political, and general situations in our
areas. I was very happy in Field Security. People often think we must have
had to do with combating the Communist insurrection, but the so-called
Emergency did not begin until well after I left the country; when I was
there, the Communists were very much more our friends than the
Kuomintang, having organised the guerilla war against the Japanese during
the occupation, which British officers had been dropped by parachute to
assist. Field Security was not very like being in the Army: we were divided
into small detachments, and almost all our time was spent with the local
inhabitants. With no determinate place in the social hierarchy, we could
meet almost everyone. I greatly enjoyed the cultural, and indeed racial,
diversity of the country: the three main cultures—Malay, Chinese, and
Indian—hardly intermingled, but there was at that time no tension between
them. Knowing that I was to return home, I made no effort to retain a
connection with the British culture in which I had been brought up, but
immersed myself in what surrounded me.

I think it must have been in Malaya that a passionate hatred of racism
was first born in me. I learned of the means by which the British masters of
pre-war colonial Malaya had maintained and acted out the myth of white
racial superiority: how no white person would lower his dignity by riding
on a bus; how no white person earning less than a certain minimum was
allowed to live in the country; how the clubs guarded their racial purity;
how Europeans were paid far more highly than "natives." Then, before I
left, the military government came to an end, and the civilian colonial
government was restored, in large part staffed by those who had run it
before the Japanese invaded. Many of these people had suffered greatly
from the Japanese, imprisoned and mistreated in Changi jail. But with utter
lack of imagination, they plainly expected to return to the status quo. The
British had ignominiously fled before the Japanese invaders, leaving their
Asian subordinates no instructions or advice how to behave towards their
new masters. The Japanese had subjected the population to much propaganda about Asia for the Asians. The Chinese had been their enemies from

the start; many of the Indians had been their enthusiastic supporters (although those who were not had often been sent to the Burma-Siam death railway); the Malays had played for safety. After those experiences, things could not be the same as before; there could be no more acquiescing in the acting out of the myth of white superiority. It was not that these returning colonialists stupidly supposed that they could get away with reinstating the racial myth: they had internalised it; they believed that they *were* superior.

I arrived back in Britain for demobilisation in September 1947, just in time to go up to Christ Church in October. I decided to read P.P.E. (Philosophy, Politics, and Economics) rather than the History which I should inevitably have read had it not been for the war. Those seemed to me interesting subjects, and I had read a very little philosophy—Whitehead, Maritain, Gilson, and an excellent double Pelican introduction by Olaf Stapledon; but my chief reason was that, after four years in the army, I had forgotten much of the history I once knew. I was soon captivated by philosophy. My tutors in Christ Church were Michael Foster, Antony Flew, and James Urmson; but a tutor outside the College who influenced me far more was Elizabeth Anscombe, the literary executor and translator of Wittgenstein, who also became a personal friend. She was always especially critical when I wrote things with which I expected her to agree. I later learned much from her husband, Peter Geach, despite his utterly different style in philosophy. I chose to take a special paper in Finals that had been invented by John Austin: it required the study of about twelve texts that one would not otherwise have read, starting with Plato's *Theaetetus* and ending with Frege's *Die Grundlagen der Arithmetik*, which Austin had translated specifically for that paper. I was bowled over by the *Grundlagen*: I thought, and still think, that it was the most brilliant piece of philosophical writing of its length ever penned. It was written before Frege developed the ideas of his middle period for which he is most renowned; it is a great pity that, during that middle period, although his intellectual power retained its strength, he lost the brilliance of performance that made his early writing scintillate. In my last year as an undergraduate, Wittgenstein's *Blue and Brown Books*, and the notes of his seminar on philosophy of mathematics, arrived in Oxford. There being no photocopiers then, everyone who bought them arranged with a typist to make four more copies, which he then sold on to people who had not yet obtained copies. We had known that there was this genius in Cambridge, but we had not known until then what he was saying. The impact on me was immense: for about three months, everything I tried to write came out as a *pastiche* of Wittgenstein.

I took Finals in 1950, obtaining a First. I next took the Civil Service examination; in those days, it was possible to get into the civil service, as in imperial China, by taking written examinations in academic subjects. One was marked out of 300 for an interview, and out of 700 for the written papers; I did badly on my interview, but since I was able to take six papers in philosophy, I still got in. In October I sat for the Fellowship examination at All Souls' College, and was lucky enough to be elected. It has proved that my rejection by my W.O.S.B. was my *last* failure of the kind. This is not meant as a boast, but as an acknowledgement of my extraordinary good fortune in this regard; the Lord has not chosen that I should suffer from traumas of rejection.

I could not benefit immediately from my Prize Fellowship, which was to last for seven years, since I had obtained a one-year assistant lectureship at Birmingham, where, having had no training as a teacher, I gave what I now realise must have been terrible philosophy lectures. I had to keep rushing between Birmingham and Oxford, since All Souls' required "pernoctation": half the nights in each term must be spent in the College. During 1951 I settled down to read everything that Frege had written. He lacked Wittgenstein's insight into views he rejected, and Wittgenstein's sympathy for the confusions in our minds; but what attracted me to him were the almost complete lucidity of his writing and the almost complete rigour of his arguments. His works had not yet been collected, let alone translated, so I had to read the articles in the original journals. I had had a year of German at school, so I had a backbone of grammar, but very little vocabulary: I read with a dictionary at my side. One result was that I became anxious to learn mathematical logic and mathematics at least up to Finals standard. I asked the then Warden of All Souls', Humphrey Sumner, if I could take an undergraduate degree in mathematics, but he refused me on the ground that it would disgrace the College if I failed to obtain a First. As an alternative, John Hammersley very kindly agreed to give me tutorials in the subject. As for mathematical logic, there was no one to teach me. The subject did not flourish then in Oxford: most mathematicians thought it should not exist, as not being real mathematics; most philosophers thought it probably should exist, but that it was no business of theirs.

In that year I became engaged to Ann Chesney, who had been at Somerville since 1948, reading history: we were married on the very last day of the year, and spent our honeymoon in Dublin. She has been my constant support and delight throughout my life. She has taken her own part in the fight against racism, and, until her recent retirement, she has worked for several anti-racist organisations in turn. She has no interest in abstract thought, but she has a keen intelligence, which has often enlightened me.

Humphrey Sumner died unexpectedly in office during my second year as a Fellow, and the College was thrown into a Wardenship election; this was for me an initiation into life as the Fellow of a College. I read C. P.

Snow's *The Masters* at the time, and thought it tame in comparison with the hysteria taking place around me; the Fellows could speak of nothing else, and split into groups of supporters of the various candidates (about eight of them), often accusing other groups of underhand behaviour. The economist Sir Hubert Henderson was elected. He would have been a very good Warden, but he immediately had a stroke and resigned; a second stroke then killed him. Another Wardenship election followed, the egotistical historian A. L. Rowse and the witty but reactionary lawyer John Sparrow the only candidates: Sparrow won. Rowse ludicrously cast me as the architect of his defeat, and for some years cut me dead whenever we met. I found it more amusing than upsetting.

Since All Souls' then paid its Fellows no marriage allowance, housing allowance, or children's allowance, and, unlike other colleges, had no houses to rent to Fellows on preferential terms, I had, once married, to do a great deal of undergraduate teaching for other colleges in order to earn enough for us rather meagerly to live on. I once complained to John Sparrow, when Warden, that the College had houses for servants but not for Fellows: he replied that it was difficult to get servants.

I became acquainted with Robin Farquharson, a brilliant undergraduate who, long before social choice theory had become a fashionable branch of economics, had become interested in the theory of voting. From him I acquired a lifetime's interest in the subject. Farquharson brought me a conjecture which I was pleased to be able to prove: together we published a joint article in *Econometrica*, in which we conjectured in passing that there was no voting procedure under which no one could ever gain an advantage by voting tactically. Farquharson's life was a tragic one. He sat the All Souls' examination, and would quite certainly have been elected had he not suffered the first of successive attacks of manic-depressive psychosis between the examination and the election. His subsequent academic career was frustrated by these psychotic episodes; he dropped out to live as a hippy, and was burned to death when an oil stove overturned.

I determined to go to Berkeley to learn mathematical logic, and in 1955 was awarded a Harkness Fellowship to do so; Berkeley was the only American university where logic flourished both in the mathematics and in the philosophy departments. I went on my own, because the Harkness Foundation gave only three months' allowance for spouses to join Fellows during their year in America; by skimping severely, we later stretched it to seven months. I travelled by ship, which was then much cheaper than flying. At that time the United States was the most racist country in the world after South Africa; I was greeted on arrival by news of the murder of Emmett Till, a black youngster from the North who, visiting relatives in the South, had been killed for supposedly looking impertinently at a white woman. Quine, who had spent the year before that in Oxford, and whom I had got to know very well, kindly invited me to spend a week with him at his home; he then gave me letters of introduction to all the logicians of his acquaintance so that I could call on them on my way to Berkeley. I called both on Church and on Kleene, who very kindly put me up for a night; I did not dare to call on Gödel. On the long train ride from Chicago to San Francisco, I enjoyed the scenery, but grew to dread the frequent requests of other passengers to "visit with" me. Experience taught that, sooner or later, they would make some racist remark which I should feel obliged to repudiate, causing umbrage to be taken.

At Berkeley I learned a great deal of mathematical logic, as well as some more mathematics, from Leon Henkin, Raphael Robinson, John Myhill, Paul Halmos, and others; I also met Donald Davidson, who was teaching philosophy at Stanford, and who became my friend for the rest of my life and one with whom, despite much disagreement between us, I have found it easier and more rewarding to talk about philosophy than with anyone else. Ann joined me, with our then two small children, Christopher and Andrew, in the New Year, after a terrible journey; one feature of it—not the worst—had been that the ship's clocks had been put back one hour each day, so that the children kept waking up one hour earlier by ship's time. Social status in Berkeley is measured by the height of your house above sea level: we rented a small house in the flat part, inhabited to a large extent by Chinese- and Japanese-Americans. We heard a great deal of jazz in San Francisco, and much enjoyed the entertainments it offered. We also joined the N.A.A.C.P. and heard Dr. Martin Luther King speak at a meeting in the city. We followed the racial news closely and were shocked by a series of poisonous articles by Alistair Cooke in the *Manchester Guardian Weekly* about black protest in the United States: particularly outrageous were two about Montgomery, Alabama, where the bus boycott was in progress; Dr. King was described as a "pretty smooth operator." I wrote to the *Guardian* to complain; my letter was not printed, but I received a sarcastic response from Alistair Hetherington, saying that he preferred to trust their eyewitness reporter to anyone living in California. Since I knew I should later be in Montgomery, I resolved to check Cooke's articles on the spot.

One of my duties as a Harkness Fellow was to spend the three summer months travelling round the country, enlarging my knowledge of it. I had meant to take Ann and the children as far as New York, but we made a late start because our car had to be repaired after a careless driver had crashed into it from behind, so we got only as far as Chicago before they left me by train to return home. I decided to devote the rest of my tour to black Americans. In Chicago I contacted two young black men I had met on the train going across; I also heard Billie Holiday sing, in person, in a small bar on the South Side. I flatter myself that I must be one of the few people in Britain who ever heard Billie Holiday in the flesh. She did not appear until midnight. At that time her career was at its nadir. Her voice was often harsh, but I was enraptured: she still cast a spell, with her charm and her strong emotion.

From Chicago I went to New York, and stayed in Harlem with a Nigerian friend. At that time everybody was very friendly. The only odd incident occurred in a cinema I was in: the police burst in, to arrest some youth in a front seat, and the entire audience rose to its feet and pressed hastily as far back as possible. From New York I drove down to Washington; having resolved never to stay at a segregated hotel, I stopped for a few days in what was advertised in the yellow pages as an "interracial" hotel, soon realising that that was code for "Negroes only." From there I went to Montgomery. The previous year I had made friends in Oxford with John Anderson, a black American who taught at a segregated college in that city. The bus boycott had not started then, and he had invited me to stay with him in Montgomery. Total segregation was an uncanny experience: the only public place in which it was possible for black and white people to sit down together was the army base, which admitted us freely. A liquor store had a chain running down from the counter: when, accompanied by some black friends, I attempted to buy something, I was told, "I can't serve you there." I stepped over the chain, received my bottle, and stepped back across the chain. All the black people whom I met were very nice to me. Some supposed me to be a very light-coloured Negro (that was the word favoured at that time by African-Americans); others explained that British attitudes differed greatly from those of white Americans. I attended a rally about the boycott in a black church, and had a personal meeting with Dr. King, whom I admired greatly: through his leadership of the bus boycott he was just coming into national prominence. He discussed Alistair Cooke's articles in the *Guardian* with me, and said that nothing so vicious had been printed in the white Southern press; he asked me, when I returned to England, to expose their falsehood, and I promised to do so. Accordingly, I did as much fact-finding as I could. I looked at the transcript of the trial of Mrs. Rosa Parks, the lady whose refusal to give up her seat had sparked the boycott. When I asked for it, the official said in a loud, hectoring voice, "*Rosa* Parks, not *Mrs.* Parks," and everyone looked up; I repeated, "The trial of Mrs. Rosa Parks," and for a moment I thought he was going to hit me, but he gave it to me with no more words. I came to the conclusion that Mr. Cooke had interviewed these officials in his hotel, without making any further investigation; the articles had contained a vivid "eyewitness" description of a street in the black part of town which seemed to bear no relation to reality whatever. There had also been a confused story, suggesting corruption, about a garage; no one knew anything about this, and I never discovered its origin.

From Montgomery I visited Oxford, Mississippi; Memphis, Tennessee; and New Orleans. In Memphis I met two very nice black girls, who professed to like my accent. (One set off on a plane for the North, and left her cardigan behind; I was very pleased to be able to run up the steps—airports being much less regimented in those days—and hand it to the attendant saying, "The young lady left this behind.") When, having sold my car, I left the South and boarded the plane at New Orleans to go to New York to catch my ship home, I felt as if I were being released from prison.

Back in England, I attempted to keep my promise to Dr. Martin Luther King. I had had little experience then, and realise that I went about it very stupidly. I first wrote an article, correcting Cooke's inaccuracies and deflecting his prejudices, and sent it to the *Guardian*: it was rejected. I then wrote a much shorter letter to the *Guardian*; it was not printed. Next, I wrote an even shorter letter, but that, too, was turned down. The letters editor wrote to ask me why I was so concerned about the matter. Then, considering that no other newspaper would print anything criticising a rival, I wondered about a broadcast. At that time the B.B.C. broadcast frequent talks about philosophy on its Third (radio) Programme. The organiser of these talks called on me to ask if I would do one: I replied that I would if he would arrange for me to give a talk on Montgomery, and sent him a script. I waited and heard nothing until he called again: he had forgotten all about my request and had mislaid my script. I was angry and drove him away; I made no further effort to set the record straight, and so broke the promise I had made.

Within philosophy, I followed up an interest I had long had in the philosophy of time, and gave a seminar on the subject in collaboration with Elizabeth Anscombe. The chief fruit was a pair of articles on backwards causation. I observed that the standard argument that one cannot affect the past, in the sense of doing something neither fruitless nor redundant to make it the case that something should have happened, is isomorphic to the commonly rejected argument for fatalism. The conclusion I reached was (roughly) that there is nothing intrinsically absurd in doing something in order that something else should previously have happened. I began a book about Frege, meaning to cover all aspects of his philosophy. I also became interested in deviations from the law of excluded middle, lectured and even wrote a book about the subject. It was accepted by John Austin on behalf of the Oxford University Press, but he told me that the style needed improvement. Though this annoyed me at the time, I am very glad he did: while trying to revise it stylistically, I became dissatisfied with it and did not resubmit it. I should be ashamed of it now if it had been published.

This led me to study intuitionistic logic and the intuitionist philosophy of mathematics, to which I felt strongly drawn. This may seem inconsistent with my devotion to Frege, who was a determined realist. It was not his realism that attracted me, however, for which, I thought, he never really argued, but which he simply took for granted, but the clarity of his thought: much of his thinking was perfectly compatible with a constructive view of mathematics. I reflected on the rationale underlying intuitionistic mathematics. It appeared to me that it was independent of the solipsism which constantly threatened Brouwer's thought, and of the psychologism which infected it. Mathematical thought was, if anything, *more* communicable than thought of any other kind, and the meanings of mathematical statements would be better explained in terms of operations that all can understand and carry out than of any executed within a private mental world. What was essential to these meanings, as conceived by intuitionists, was that they reflected only the *use* that we learn to make of mathematical statements, not a conception of their truth-value, determined by abstract reality whether apprehensible by us or not. The use of a mathematical statement consists in what is needed to prove it and what can be proved from it; probably also, as Frege insisted, in how it can be applied, although intuitionists paid little attention to that.

The logical aspect led to the only article I have ever published in the *Journal of Symbolic Logic*, about the logic resulting from adding "(P → Q) ∨ (Q → P)" as an axiom to those of intuitionistic logic. It also led to a collaboration with John Lemmon on the modal systems between S4 and S5 corresponding to logics intermediate between intuitionist and classical, which resulted in a joint article. We studied the work of Tarski and McKinsey. I was very happy to discover that the distributive lattices known to be jointly characteristic for intuitionist logic IC could each be represented as composed of closed sets in a topology defined on a partially ordered set. These were in effect Kripke models, which made their first appearance in our joint article; for models of modal logic, we needed quasi-orderings in place of partial orderings. We put no semantic interpretation on them, however; for us the lattices simply supplied an algebraic characterisation of IC, and the topological models merely a way of representing finite lattices by much smaller posets; restrictions on the orderings yielded extensions of IC and corresponding extensions of S4. What blocked us from hitting on a semantic interpretation of our topological models was that they were (intuitively) upside down. This was because we had been following Tarski and McKinsey, who had chosen closed sets instead of open sets as their elements, and hence made union correspond to conjunction and intersection to disjunction, so that, to arrive at a semantic interpretation, we should have had to make points in the set assigned to any sentence-letter those at which it was *not* true. We also did not know how to handle the quantifiers in these terms: Kripke's idea of variable domains did not occur to us. But we did establish some worthwhile results, and for a short time our article was cited in many papers, the technique of our topological interpretation proving useful to many students of intermediate and modal logics.

My first daughter Susanna was born in 1957. In that year I was elected for a further seven years at All Souls'. The system then in force allowed a Prize Fellow to apply for the next grade of Fellowship when he reached the end of the first, but with no guarantee of success: if not elected, he had quickly to find a post elsewhere. I was lucky. In 1958 I went on my own for a term as Visiting Lecturer to the University of Ghana, where I lectured on the philosophy of time. While I was there, a glimmering of the semantic interpretation of our topological models (still the wrong way up) dawned on me, but an "unidentified fever" took me into hospital—and, as I later learned, in danger of my life—and obstructed me from thinking the matter through. I did not revert to the matter after I recovered; possibly, if I had, what are now called Kripke models might have been called Dummett-Lemmon models, though I doubt if we should have thought what to do about the quantifiers. After Ghana, I joined my wife for a holiday in Siena and Assisi, the first we had had since our honeymoon. Arriving first at the hotel, I told the staff, my Italian as yet being very poor, that I was expecting my *sposa* (bride), instead of my *moglie* (wife): when Ann arrived, seven months pregnant with twins, her appearance caused great hilarity. I had received, in Ghana, an invitation to a post in Berkeley, which, after postal consultation with Ann, I had accepted. As soon as the matter was raised between us in Siena, it was obvious that we had both thought better of it: so, although after the deadline for a decision, we sent a cable withdrawing the acceptance. We neither of us wanted our children to grow up in an environment alien to us which we did not truly understand. The twins, Tessa and Judith, were born in August 1958. Judith had been brain-damaged at birth, and suffered distressingly from epilepsy. Given large doses of cortisone to control the fits, she contracted pneumonia and died aged a year and nine months. Our son Paul was born in 1960. Later, we had another son, Philip, who was also brain-damaged at birth and died after a few days. After that, we determined to have no more children.

A few years after my re-election at All Souls', I applied for and was fortunate to obtain the University Readership in Philosophy of Mathematics in succession to Dr. Friedrich Waismann, the first holder. I remained a Fellow of All Souls', but at a nominal stipend. John Crossley, the University Lecturer in Mathematical Logic, and I together persuaded the university to establish a new honours school in Mathematics and Philosophy. We kept the pure mathematics part of the Mathematics syllabus, excising the applied part, and invented new philosophy papers. As bridge subjects we included in the curriculum the philosophy of mathematics and a very large component of mathematical logic, including an optional paper on intuitionism. To fulfil the teaching requirements, we both carried out at least twice the number of lectures and tutorials required of us. After two years, John Crossley left for Australia; Robin Gandy, then Professor at Manchester, applied for his post on condition that it was upgraded to a Readership. It was, and he came, to the enormous benefit of mathematical logic in Oxford; he and I then for some years laboured under the double load of teaching, until others took much of the weight from our shoulders.

Reflecting on my rationale for intuitionistic mathematics as an exemplification of Wittgenstein's dictum about meaning as use, it struck me that the metaphysical conceptions accompanying both Platonist and constructive conceptions of mathematics were not the *foundations* of those conceptions: they were merely pictures illustrating them. One could not argue from the metaphysical pictures, because there was no independent ground for accepting one or the other. The core of the different conceptions lay in the divergent views of what the meanings of mathematical statements must consist in: to adopt one or the other view was to make one or other picture natural. Given that the metaphysical picture was not the foundation of the rationale for doing mathematics in this way, and for accepting a non-classical logic as formalising the reasoning to be used in mathematics, the rationale did not rest upon any specifically mathematical feature of the subject-matter. It was highly general, and could be applied with the same cogency to discourse about other subject-matters.

These and other thoughts led to one of my earliest articles, and probably the best, "Truth." One fundamental idea, at odds with views recently expressed by Timothy Smiley, was that falsity and truth do not have equal rights, so that one might specify the meaning of a statement by laying down that it was to be considered true in a certain case and false in a certain other case: either falsity must be whatever precludes a statement from being true, or truth must be the absence of anything that could make it false; given one, the other is fixed. The fundamental notion of the truth of a statement is the condition for an assertion of it to be correct, in the sense of unerroneous—a sense I believe can be filtered out from all other notions of a mistaken utterance, such as being tactless or impolite. When you know what one learns from the statement's having been correctly asserted, you know what it is for it to be true in the fundamental sense. Fully to know its meaning, one must know more, namely how it contributes to the senses of sentences of which it is a component or in which it is subject to an operator: it is to explain this that complicated systems of truth-values or notions of temporal or modal status are employed. But of course the leading idea was a generalisation of the intuitionistic notion of the truth of mathematical statements. The conception of truth-values determined by reality independently of us should be abandoned. The notion of a statement's *being* true should be replaced by that of its being shown to be true: the content of a statement consists in what is needed to show it to be true.

I became interested in the different varieties of realism. One could be a realist about one or another subject-matter; but the arguments for and against different varieties of realism are remarkably, although not totally, similar in form. I read a paper to the Oxford Philosophical Society (printed as "Realism" in *Truth and Other Enigmas*) which in effect announced as a research programme a comparative study of different varieties of realism, with the aim of determining which arguments for and against them were valid. I held that in all cases in which some variety of realism was disputed, what was at issue was the correct account of the meanings of statements of a certain class (statements about the past or the future, theoretical statements of science, etc.). I concluded that well-known theories repudiating realism about one or another subject-matter, such as phenomenalism and behaviourism, erred for one of two reasons. They attempted to *reduce* statements about the given subject-matter to statements of some other class; and they either continued to accept a classical logic—in particular, the principle of bivalence—for statements of the former category or assumed that to reject bivalence entailed acceptance of an intermediate truth-value. Mathematical intuitionism was not only the sole fully worked out example of an anti-realist theory: it was the only one that avoided both these errors. My subsequent interest therefore concentrated ever more on the question whether a global anti-realism, modelled after intuitionist mathematics, was sustainable. I was at first disappointed at the poor response to my manifesto; since then these ideas have received much discussion. I aimed to crown my career by writing a book, which now I shall never write, surveying every variety of realism and of denial of realism. A preliminary version was contained in a course of lectures I gave in 1964 at Stanford.

All this was to come to an abrupt end. In Stanford, with a black friend, John Howard, who said we formed the Stanford civil rights movement, I had joined the Congress On Racial Equality, and taken part in some picketing. Back from Stanford in the autumn of 1964, Ann and I decided that the time had come for organised resistance to the swelling racism in England. From that moment, while keeping up with my heavy teaching load, I devoted every moment I could spare to the fight against racism. I abandoned my book on Frege; I gave no more time to thinking about philosophy. This condition lasted until the summer of 1968, when I had accepted an invitation to teach for a semester at the University of

Minnesota—a visit bracketed by the assassinations of Martin Luther King and of Robert Kennedy; after I returned from there, I was still substantially involved with local and national anti-racist groups, but not with quite the same intensity. Those years seem in retrospect to have lasted much longer than in fact they did, so hectic was the activity. I thought at the time that I had wrecked my career, as did Ann; but I was content that the sacrifice was worth it, the enemy being so evil. Some years later I discovered that I had not after all wrecked my career.

We formed what became the Oxford Committee for Racial Integration, joining forces with Evan Luard, the Labour M.P. for the city, who had undertaken a similar initiative. O.C.R.I. was remarkably successful in its first year. Pressed Steel had banned the employment of Asians, while Morris's would employ Asians and West Indians only in the cleansing department: we induced both car factories to stop discriminating. There was no law against racial discrimination in those days, but firms were nervous of bad publicity; and O.C.R.I. had some powerful Trade Unionists in its ranks.

A national organisation, the Campaign Against Racial Discrimination, had been founded about the same time as O.C.R.I., which affiliated to it. I went as one of two delegates to its annual convention and was elected to its national council; thereafter my activity was more with C.A.R.D. than with the local group. C.A.R.D. had some notable successes, above all the drafting of the forthcoming race relations legislation; but its principal importance lay in its being accepted for what it professed, but largely failed, to be: a focus of the entire anti-racist movement. Journalists, glad to have a number they could telephone for a comment on any matter involving race, accepted it as such; the government-sponsored National Committee for Commonwealth Immigrants also accepted it as such and was scared to do anything to offend it. C.A.R.D. was primarily a federation of local and national community organisations. Its members differed widely in political opinion, cultural background, and race; but the leadership failed to appreciate the delicacy with which so diverse a body needed to be handled. As a result it was constantly rent by dissension, and important bodies like West Indian Standing Conference disaffiliated. The leadership blundered, and blustered when criticised; the principal mistake was for the chairman, Dr. David Pitt, and his vice-chairman to have accepted co-option to the N.C.C.I. without consulting the organisation they represented. 1967 seemed calmer, but only because so many critics had defected. The late Vishnu Sharma, a leading member of the Indian Workers' Association, Southall, was appointed a paid organiser. Sharma was a life-long Communist, who had been on the run from the British Raj, and became a good friend of mine. However, West Indians were poorly represented in the top ranks of

C.A.R.D. David Pitt, himself West Indian, relied largely on the highly unrepresentative Johnny James, a Maoist who believed there would soon be a revolution in the Caribbean, and that all West Indians in Britain, if properly prepared for it, would return home to take part. (Johnny James made one funny remark by referring to "Her Majesty's Communist Party.")

Meanwhile, in Oxford, O.C.R.I. decided in 1967 to picket a hairdresser's which, despite repeated pleas to change its policy, refused to serve Asian or Caribbean people. Ann, who was then O.C.R.I.'s one paid officer, notified the police of our intention. Soon after our picket had begun, a huge band of policemen burst, like Keystone cops, from a tiny police box across the street. Most of those taking part in the picket, including a Methodist minister, a respected lady city councillor who later became Lord Mayor of Oxford, and myself, were arrested and taken to the police station, where we were harangued by a senior police officer who accused us of inflaming the populace; we were then placed in police cells. Together with my wife, we were later charged with public order offences and tried before three magistrates. We did not know what the outcome would be, but we heard that the Director of Public Prosecutions had recommended that we should be bound over to do nothing of the kind again; since none of us was likely to accept this condition, that would have meant our all being sent to prison. I was told by David Pitt that the Community Relations Commission disapproved of our action. My old friend from undergraduate days, Peter Weitzman, generously offered his services as a barrister free. His conduct of the case was brilliant: from a police witness, whom he had asked whether pedestrians could pass freely along the pavement and who had replied that they could not, he succeeded in eliciting the answer, "Because there were so many policemen," when he asked him why not. The outcome was a triumph for us. Our counsel submitted that there was no case to answer, and the magistrates agreed. The City Council rebuked the police for their conduct, and the Home Secretary, Roy Jenkins, summoned us to his office to give us his personal apology.

An initiative I took independently of C.A.R.D. was to attempt to found a Council of Faiths, with local branches. My idea was that through such bodies all the religious groups would co-operate on social problems, and especially on religious discrimination; with Anglican participation, they would be generally respected. I was immensely proud of having persuaded representatives of different Sikh bodies, of all branches of both the Muslim and Jewish faiths, as well as Buddhists, Hindus, a delegate of the Cardinal Archbishop of Westminster, and members of the Orthodox and of all Protestant churches, including Pentecostal ones especially favoured by West Indians, to sit together round a single table. When the Government-appointed Community Relations Commission had been formed, the

Archbishop of Canterbury, Archbishop Ramsey, was named its chairman. He agreed to chair the meetings of the tentative founders of the Council of Faiths, and accordingly allowed us to use the C.R.C. offices for them; with him presiding, it seemed otiose to invite any other Anglican representative. However, each time we assembled, we were told that the Archbishop was unable to be present, but wished us well. We thrashed out a constitution and set of objectives. After our final meeting, I was informed that the Archbishop wished to see me in Lambeth Palace. I am about to tell of the second series of stupid actions on my part. I protested that several members of our group should go: I ought to have insisted, and have demanded that we should meet him on our ground, not on his; I did neither, but meekly presented myself at Lambeth. The Archbishop then proceeded to lecture me on why the Church of England could take no part in a Council of Faiths. His ground was that the C. of E. disbelieved in religious syncretism. I vainly tried to explain that all we were after was co-operation in practical matters, not a merging of doctrine or even worship; he did not take in, or even listen to, anything I said, but, whenever I spoke, kept up a disconcerting "H'm, h'm, h'm" throughout, impatient for me to fall silent. I failed to ask him why he had allowed us to go so far, with his pretended blessing, if that had been his mind all along; I came away with his flat refusal to allow the Church of England to participate. I was immensely depressed, thinking that without the participation of the C. of E. the Council of Faiths could come to nothing. I did nothing—not even to consult my variegated committee, which was informed of the debacle by the C.R.C. staff: I allowed the venture to die.

At that time, there were no entry clearance certificates: people simply arrived at the airport and were put back on the next plane if the immigration officer refused them. It was possible, however, to intervene and "make representations" on a refused immigrant's behalf if one could do so before he was put on the plane; local community organisations sent someone to do this when they knew of an impending arrival. The process was often successful. Inspired by my wife's triumph in gaining readmission for a young boy who had been refused on the basis of false information given by the Oxford police, I of my own initiative, but acting always in the name of C.A.R.D., took up this work. I set up a network of informants at Heathrow, who would telephone me at any hour of the day or night to tell me of someone refused and with no one to speak for them. I would then have first to telephone the Chief Immigration Officer, which took a long time to get through, say I wished to make representations and then dash to the airport as quickly as possible. There I had to find out what I could about the case and say whatever I could on the refused person's behalf; he was then often admitted. This was the most exhausting period of my life.

In the spring of 1967 a small group, including Vishnu Sharma and myself, some of us members of C.A.R.D., others not, planned the formation of a new federation. Our idea was that ideological differences would not obstruct co-operation if it were on a narrow sector of the front rather than against all forms of racism, and involved practical help to individuals. We chose immigration as the sector to be tackled: the new federation would organise representation for refused immigrants, but also campaign for juster immigration laws—immigration being at the core of the British response to the "coloured" presence. The racists' demand was to "Stop Immigration," and successive governments yielded to it as a coded message that "we don't want such people here." During the summer Vishnu and I travelled all over England, urging local organisations to send delegates to the inaugural meeting. Just as this was about to take place on September 23 at the Dominion Cinema, Southall, Sir Geoffrey Wilson, the chairman of a committee reporting on a possible tribunal to hear appeals against refusal of entry, expressed the hope in his report that voluntary bodies concerned for the welfare of immigrants would combine to provide representation at such appeals: just what we were doing. The founding meeting was attended by representatives of something like 170 organisations: the new body was launched, with great enthusiasm, as the Joint Council for the Welfare of Immigrants. Over the next few years, most of my activity was centred on J.C.W.I., whose history I shall not give here, except to say two things. It organised the first anti-racist march in London, against the disgraceful Commonwealth Immigrants Act of 1968, which denied entry to our own citizens from East Africa. And it is still active today, thirty-three years after its foundation.

In December 1967 the postponed annual convention of C.A.R.D. was held, and lasted three days. It took the form of a triumphant coup by Johnny James and his allies. Many organisations—Maoist, Trotskyite, and Black Power groups and a disaffected splinter from I.W.A., Southall—had affiliated only on the eve of the convention, but were entitled under the constitution to attend and vote. An unbelievable hysteria was incited. The principal accusation was that Asians and whites had conspired to run C.A.R.D. to the exclusion of West Indians; shamefully, racial epithets like "coolie" were bandied about. Whites were said to be taking part only to forward their careers. Many ordinary decent West Indian rank-and-file members were infected by the hysteria and believed these accusations. It was the practice to put forward resolutions prepared by the executive committee, and I was asked to present one on Rhodesia, calling for "one man, one vote" (we weren't scared of the word "man" in those days). The madness engendered by the hysteria is illustrated by the fact that the delegates from both ZANU and ZAPU opposed the resolution, on the ground that "one man, one vote" was a colonialist slogan; it was defeated. I attempted a speech explaining why whites might detest racism; I was jeered. The chairman, abandoning all those who had believed themselves his allies, sided with the rebels, who swept to power in the elections. Boarding the train for home, I felt inexpressibly depressed: they have rejected us, I thought. Most of those who were dismayed by the takeover resigned from C.A.R.D. I did not, and O.C.R.I. did not disaffiliate; I even found myself on the executive committee once more. But it was hopeless: those who had taken over C.A.R.D. did not want to do anything with it. It was effectively dead. Its death was the worst thing that ever happened in the fight against British racism.

In the midst of all this, I formed a new interest in the history of Tarot games. This began casually on holiday in France, where I bought a Tarot pack *avec règles du jeu*; my son Andrew found a pamphlet with a rather clearer explanation. We played the game in the family, and found it a good one. Back in England, I came across an Austrian pack, also with rules: the game was very different, although plainly related. I wanted to discover how the game was played in other countries, and wrote to card-game experts to ask, but none of them could tell me. I then embarked on my own enquiries, which gradually grew into a serious piece of research into the whole history of this great family of card games. I read *Collecting Playing Cards* by Sylvia Mann, the leading British playing-card collector. I got to know her well. She knew nothing about the games, but had an immense store of knowledge about the history of playing cards, which she freely imparted; in the case of Tarot, the history of the games and of the cards are especially closely intertwined. I very soon realised that the pack was invented, in early fifteenth-century Italy, for play, not for divination; the latter was a French accretion of the late eighteenth century. It may seem odd that I could pursue this new interest in the midst of involvement in the struggle against racism. It was a solace. It provided difficult intellectual problems whose solution, unlike those of philosophical ones, had no serious import: it relieved the anxiety that always accompanied thinking about the racial situation or the problems of individuals entangled in it.

By the early 1970s I was still involved with J.C.W.I., but my activity had eased off sufficiently to allow me to give substantial time to other things. Colin Haycraft of Duckworth's wrote to ask me if I knew anyone who could write a book on Frege. I told him that I had begun to do so, but had abandoned it; he encouraged me to start again, which I did, from scratch. The result was *Frege: Philosophy of Language*, which he published in 1973; I doubt if I should ever have written it without Colin Haycraft's support. It had grown too long to include anything about mathematics; it was therefore addressed to that part of Frege's philosophy which in 1906 he believed to have survived the collapse of his attempt to construct the foundations of arithmetic. I believe that the book helped to revive interest in Frege. I now realise that I paid insufficient attention to the intellectual context of Frege's work. I was much more interested by the extent to which the problems he posed remain live issues, which have had other responses; as a result, the book contained many reflections with no very immediate relevance to Frege. Frege's great achievement, in my eyes, was to have been the first to have fashioned a genuine theory of meaning; he constructed the first semantic theory and, by distinguishing sense from semantic value (*Bedeutung*), explained how an account of meaning, as the content of linguistic understanding, should rest on a semantic theory as base.

Just before I published my first book, Ann published hers, under the title *A Portrait of English Racism*. I would rather have written that book than any of the many I have written. Often very moving, it is a deadly accurate portrait; I believe it to be the best book on the subject yet to have appeared.

At the instigation of Dana Scott, then Professor of Mathematical Logic at Oxford, in 1975 I wrote a book on intuitionistic logic and foundations of mathematics; it came out in 1977. The first part was composed by my lecturing on the subject; Roberto Minio took notes and wrote them up, which I then corrected when, infrequently, necessary. The later chapters I wrote on my own. I approached Beth and Kripke trees via the Dummett-Lemmon topological models, turned the right way up. I also surveyed the literature on the completeness of intuitionistic first-order logic, including Kreisel's proof that an intuitionistic proof of it would imply a form of Markov's principle, surely not acceptable intuitionistically. I also surveyed in detail the work of the Nijmegen school on Beth trees on which absurdity was allowed to hold at some node. To my great pleasure, this led to an intuitionistic proof of completeness for negation-free formulas, showing that there is something quite special about negation. I later learned that Harvey Friedman had arrived at the same result at much the same time by an entirely different method.

In 1975, wanting to concentrate on philosophy instead of logic, I resigned my Readership and applied for one of two Senior Research Fellowships at All Souls' which had been advertised for open competition, and was fortunate to be elected. At the beginning of 1976 I went to Harvard to give the William James lectures on "The Logical Basis of Metaphysics." I arrived without anything written, and had to compose each lecture in the week before it was delivered. The lectures developed my idea that metaphysical pictures illustrated theses about meaning; they were meant as an introduction to the book on realism I still hoped to write. I left copies of them behind at Harvard. Later, in Oxford, I gave a set of lectures developing, in a manner that may not have pleased him, Dag Prawitz's idea of a proof-theoretic justification of logical laws, with the introduction rules treated as specifying the meanings of the logical constants; I experimented with the opposite procedure, treating the elimination rules as definitive of meaning. The main substance of these lectures I later incorporated into the book version of *The Logical Basis of Metaphysics*, composed in 1988 at the Stanford Center for Advanced Study in the Behavioral Sciences. It is a very odd experience to revise a text one has written twelve years before.

In 1979, having become Wykeham Professor of Logic, I moved from All Souls' to New College, since in Oxford each Chair is attached to a particular college. Earlier that year I had undertaken my last major task in race relations. In April there had been a disturbance in Southall, arising out of a so-called election meeting held by the racist National Front in the town hall; one demonstrator against the National Front, Blair Peach, had actually been killed. There were calls for an official enquiry, which the government ignored; so the National Council for Civil Liberties set up its own enquiry, conducted quite independently of the Council, and I was asked to be chairman. Patricia Hewitt, then General Secretary of the N.C.C.L., acted, with the greatest assiduity, as secretary of the enquiry. We interviewed a great many witnesses, although the police refused to meet us; we learned their account from the numerous court cases against people charged with wrongful behaviour. We published our report in 1980, following it with a supplement on the death of Blair Peach. In the report we established that, while there had been some violence on the part of protestors, the police themselves had acted with utterly uncalled-for violence, as well as manifesting racist attitudes by displaying National Front symbols and in other ways. Blair Peach was killed by a blow to the head by one of a small number of policemen, though we never established which.

Also in 1980 my lengthy book, *The Game of Tarot*, appeared, beautifully produced, under Duckworth's imprint. It contained, among much else, rules for all the Tarot games, obsolete or presently played, of which I then knew; and I flattered myself that I had for the first time set the history of Tarot cards and games on a sound basis, the key to directions of influence being the different orders of the trump subjects originally characteristic of Milan, Ferrara, and Bologna. I cannot now understand how I could have done so much work, reading countless old card-game books in German, French, Italian, and other languages: without the devoted help of Deborah Blake of Duckworth's, daughter of Lord Blake who had taught me Politics at Christ Church, I should never have sorted out my notes. My sources were not only from books but from field work: I had learned the

Hungarian game from some Hungarians in New York, who were very kind to me, and had visited Bologna, Ljubljana, and Sicily to observe and take part in play in those places; my friend John McLeod had done similar field work elsewhere and communicated the results to me. The field work in Sicily was the most fascinating. The game had once been popular all over the island; now it had been forgotten save in four widely separated towns—rock pools after the tide had ebbed. Marcello Cimino, a journalist on *L'Ora* who had bravely published the results of his investigations of the Mafia, gave me indispensable help in tracking down players in these four localities. Despite our different opinions—he was a staunch Communist, though very much a Eurocommunist—he became perhaps my closest and dearest friend. After he died of cancer in 1989, his widow Giuliana also became a very dear friend; unhappily, she has now also died of cancer. I am strongly of the view that games, including card games, and their history are worthy of academic study. Games are an essential ingredient of popular culture; devising and playing them require creative imagination, and their history exhibits the directions of cultural currents better than anything else can do. This is generally understood on the Continent; but in British minds there is an indissoluble connection between games and frivolity. *The Game of Tarot* did not do well commercially. In a specialist games shop I discovered a copy in the small occult section, where anyone interested in the occult would have returned it to the shelf at once, while no one interested in card games would ever see it. It is fatal to include the word "Tarot" in the title of a book in English: all but one in 100,000 will assume it to be about divination or the occult.

In 1983 I went back to the theory of voting, and published *Voting Procedures* in 1984. My object was to convey to those practically concerned with how to carry out a vote all that it was essential for them to know from the social choice theory whose results had been being published in the economics journals. It seemed to me catastrophic that a mathematical theory should have been developed that remained unknown to those concerned in real life with what it was a theory of. I had retained my interest in voting and its theory ever since my work with Robin Farquharson, but had not troubled to keep up with all the published theorems in social choice theory; so I made use of an excellent survey of the field kindly lent to me by Professor Amartya Sen. From it I discovered that the conjecture Farquharson and I had made, that no voting procedure could always deny an advantage to tactical voting, had been proved by Alan Gibbard. Without looking up Gibbard's article, I devised a proof of my own of this result, which I included in the book; I later found that my proof was quite different from Gibbard's. I was more annoyed than pleased by this, thinking—perhaps wrongly—that I could have found my proof at any time, even just after our *Econometrica* article; I had never attempted a proof of our conjecture before I learned that it was possible to prove it, wrongly believing that a proof would be immensely hard. My book failed to accomplish what I had aimed at. I rightly emphasised that addition and multiplication were the only mathematical concepts anyone would need before reading it; but I had expected readers to be willing to *think* mathematically. What I had overlooked was that hardly anyone would have that willingness. I much later wrote *Principles of Electoral Reform* to correct my error. In that book I spoke only of elections of representatives to Parliament or local councils, since it is quite falsely but generally assumed that only these raise any problem about the voting system to be used. I included no formulas or diagrams and defined no technical terms; I proved nothing, but only asserted it. It was not an exposition of social choice theory, only of maxims I had formulated on the basis of my knowledge of it, but it had greater success than *Voting Procedures*, and was studied by Lord Jenkins's committee on electoral reform.

In 1984 I contributed to the volume *Objections to Nuclear Defence*, edited by Nigel Blake and Kay Pole. I argued that the policy of nuclear deterrence is immoral: a conditional intention to do something terrible cannot be defended on the ground that the condition will probably not be fulfilled, nor on the ground that announcing it will have a good effect; it is to be condemned as giving one's will to the terrible act. I reverted to the topic in an article published in *The Canadian Journal of Philosophy* in 1986. These essays, together with an article on contraception published long before in the *Clergy Review*, form my principal published incursions into ethics.

In 1985–86 an interesting problem came up, which led to my undeservedly appearing as co-author of an article in the *Bulletin of the London Mathematical Society*. I was working on my *Frege: Philosophy of Mathematics*, the long delayed sequel to my book on Frege of 1973. I had long ago been, and was now again, troubled by an independence problem that arose in his (uncompleted) formal theory of real numbers. Frege's theory of real numbers is largely neglected. Believing that mathematical entities are characterised by their applications, he thought that there were only two kinds of number, those answering the question "How many?" and those answering the question "How great?" Hence negative and rational numbers were not to be defined separately, but together with real numbers, which must be constructed directly from the natural numbers rather than from the rationals as an intermediate stage. The strategy was therefore to define the general notion of a quantitative domain, exemplified by the domain of distances, that of masses, and so on, and then to define real numbers as ratios between elements of some quantitative domain. Frege's theory of real numbers was not nearly so elegant or convincing philosophically as his theory of cardinal numbers had been, but its formal development in volume II of his *Grundgesetze* is extremely interesting mathematically. On the way to defining a quantitative domain, Frege defines the notion of what he calls a positival class. This, in effect, consists of the positive elements of an ordered group of permutations; Frege never uses the word "group," though he must have known the concept. Unknown to Frege, Otto Hölder had partially anticipated him in an article of 1901, which also did not use the word "group." Frege lays down four conditions for a set of permutations to form a positival class; the first three imply that the ordering, right-invariant from its definition, is upper semi-linear (branches below but not above); the fourth implies further that it is linear and left-invariant. Frege is worried that he cannot show whether the fourth condition is independent of the first three, and proves as much as he can without invoking it. The proof that the Archimedean law follows from the completeness of the ordering is credited in all the reference books to Hölder; Frege proves it from much weaker assumptions. Hölder also first derived commutativity from the Archimedean law; Frege did the same, but without assuming left-invariance. Frege thus made notable contributions to group theory, of which hardly anyone is aware, presumably because most have been reluctant to work their way through his eccentric and difficult symbolic notation.

I did not think I ought to publish a book on Frege's philosophy of mathematics without solving his independence problem, which I tried in vain to do. I therefore took the problem to Dr. Peter Neumann, a mathematician in Queen's College, Oxford, and an expert on group theory. He solved the problem by showing, by means of an ingenious construction, that the fourth condition *was* independent of the others; his young Nigerian collaborator Dr. Samson Adeleke showed that it was *not* independent of the other conditions governing Frege's more restricted notion of a positive class. All this appeared as an article in the *Bulletin* of the L.M.S. in 1987, with my name as a co-author.

To a volume of essays in honour of Basil Mitchell, published in 1987, I contributed one on "The Intelligibility of Eucharistic Doctrine." The author of the hymn "Adoro te devote" wrote:

> In cruce latebat sola deitas,
> At hic latet simul et humanitas.

("On the Cross only your divinity was concealed, /Here your humanity is concealed, too." "Here" means "in the Sacrament.") But the cases are not analogous. In my essay I invoked the concept of deeming; an adopted son is deemed to be the son of his adoptive parents. We cannot rightly say, "He is not their son," but we can say, "He is not biologically their son" and even "He is not really their son." For something to be deemed to be X is for it to be treated, as far as it is possible, as if it were X. The consecrated Host is deemed to be the Body of Christ; such a change could therefore not occur if no one were aware of it, or otherwise than in the course of a communal re-enactment of the Last Supper. Since Christ said that it *was* his Body, we cannot say that it is not *really* so; but we can say something like, "It is his Body sacramentally, not corporeally." Jesus in agony on the Cross is not *deemed* to have been God: in Christian belief, he was God in an unqualified sense.

In October 1987 I became embroiled in a controversy in the pages of the Dominican monthly, *New Blackfriars*, which ran until the end of the following year. I published an article on reunion with the Orthodox, in which I cited, as an obstacle to such reunion, what had been described by Professor Thomas Sheehan as a "liberal consensus" among Catholic scholars and seminary teachers, rejecting the Virgin Birth, the Resurrection in bodily form, Christ's having claimed to be the Messiah, and his having founded a church. On this I commented that it "might be combined with some religious belief in which Jesus played an important role, but not with anything recognisable as the Christian religion." The article provoked a reply from Professor Nicholas Lash, a Cambridge theologian, and many subsequent articles, none of which showed the least concern with reunion with the Orthodox; I replied to some of them, since all save one, by Fr. Brian Davies, O.P., were hostile to me. I was struck by how greatly many of the participants would have benefited from a short course in philosophy. I had maintained that it could not reasonably be believed that Jesus Christ was God without supposing him to have known this and imparted the knowledge, since otherwise we could have no reason to believe it. Professor Lash responded that in that case only those who knew themselves to be holy should be canonised, apparently seeing no difference in character between a judgement that someone displayed heroic virtue and the astonishing judgement that a particular man was God. Dr. Eamon Duffy wrote that "the divinity of Jesus is not a 'fact' about him, like the facts that he was male and Jewish. . . . To confess his divinity is not to admit something extra about him, over and above his humanity, but to adopt a particular stance towards his humanity." I agree with Frege that a fact is simply a true thought, and belongs to the realm of sense rather than being a constituent of the external world. However this may be, every true statement states a fact. Dr. Duffy was presumably in the grip of the fallacious distinction between factual judgements, with objective truth-conditions, and value judgements, which only express attitudes. In addition, he was surely following Wittgenstein's account of religious statements; that is the account of a sympathetic unbeliever, to which a believer cannot subscribe without nullifying his belief. The editor of *New Blackfriars* wanted to reprint the whole series of twelve articles as a booklet, which would have been instructive to theology students, but Professor Lash vetoed this by refusing to allow his own article to be reprinted.

I retired in 1992; since then I have given many lectures, though not in Oxford, and attended many conferences. In 1993 I published a revised version, in English, of my *Origins of Analytical Philosophy*, which had had some success in its original German edition of 1987, beautifully translated by Joachim Schulte; it had been based on lectures which, at the invitation of Professor Eva Picardi, I had given (in English) at the University of Bologna. I had supervised Eva when she wrote her doctoral thesis at Oxford, and she has remained a good friend ever since. She is one of the leading Italian exponents of analytic philosophy, and has stoutly defended many of my views, as well as translating books of mine into Italian. The principal theme of *Origins* was that, at the time when he published his *Logische Untersuchungen* in 1901, Husserl's views were close to Frege's, so that no one at the time would have judged them to belong to different schools; and yet the two men were the founders of two traditions of philosophy, phenomenological and analytic, which were to diverge so far as to lose all communication with one another. I strove to discern what seeds of this divergence were present at that early date. I identified one such seed as Husserl's later introduction of the notion of "noema," as a generalisation of that of "sense." For Frege the notion of sense was incapable of generalisation; it could be expressed only linguistically or symbolically, although in principle able to be grasped independently of its expression (though not by us). I did not confine myself to this question: I discussed the reasons for the linguistic turn, the features of Frege's philosophy that pointed towards attending to language rather than directly to the thoughts expressed by means of it, and the relation between thought and language in general. I labelled as the fundamental axiom of analytical philosophy the thesis that a philosophical account of thought can be attained through a philosophical account of language, and that a comprehensive such account can only be so attained. And I discussed whether the thoughts we express in words can be ascribed to creatures without language, concluding that they cannot, but that such creatures could have some imperfect simulacra of thoughts which I called "proto-thoughts."

Throughout the 1990s I have been much exercised over the subject on which I had published an article in 1969, the reality of the past. That article had been designed to determine whether anti-realism about the past was a coherent doctrine; I hoped, if it proved not to be, thereby to have found a fallacy in the general anti-realist argument. The outcome had been the worst possible: anti-realism about the past was coherent but unbelievable. An anti-realist about the past could agree that a statement made in a year's time about a state of affairs as obtaining a year previously will be true if there is *now* evidence for its truth; but he will also concede that if, in a year's time, such evidence has irretrievably dissipated, he will then deny that the statement is true. Moreover, he will claim that he will be right to deny it. How does he avoid contradicting himself? He holds that a statement is true only if there is something in virtue of which it is true; but he thinks that, immersed in time as we are, we shall not be able in a year's time to mean by "there is something in virtue of which it is true" what we *now* mean by it. I do not think this position can be confuted; but I cannot bring myself to subscribe to it. What notion of truth, then, is proper to an anti-realism that does not deny the reality of the past? If the same logical laws are to hold for past-tense as for present-tense statements, the anti-realist cannot identify the truth of a statement with our possession of evidence for it, but only with our having had an effective means of obtaining such evidence, even if we did not avail ourselves of it. Thus large concessions to realism must be made; is it possible to make such concessions without adopting a full-fledged realist notion of truth?

In 1996 Ronald Decker, Thierry Depaulis, and I put out *A Wicked Pack of Cards*, reviewing the origins and development of Tarot occultism in France up to the early twentieth century. Though I had once resolved never to write on this subject, I had formed a collaboration with Don Laycock, an Australian anthropologist, to use the chapter on it from *The Game of Tarot* and bring the story up to date (which he was to do). This was to be done while I was at the Stanford Center in 1988–89. But when I returned early in 1989 from a trip to England and Sicily, I found waiting for me a pathetic letter from Laycock, saying that he had contracted leukemia and could no longer work; the letter I wrote him arrived after he died. Thinking at first that the book had died with him, I found two new collaborators; there will be a sequel, by myself and Ron Decker.

In 1997 I gave four Gifford lectures at the University of St. Andrews. My aim was to describe the conception of the world—of reality—that would be proper to one who accepted the version of anti-realism that has been associated with me, namely a generalisation to all language of the intuitionist understanding of mathematical language, which I have never for long more than provisionally accepted. It turned out very Berkeleyan, with a strong asymmetry between past and future, something to which I am temperamentally averse. Told that publication of the lectures was not a requirement but a usual practice, I have not yet published them because I am unsatisfied with them, and have found no time to revise them in between all the other things I have to do; but I mean to do so. I suppose most philosophers want at times to make their own Tennyson's words:

> So runs my dream; but what am I?
> An infant crying in the night,
> An infant crying for the light,
> And with no language but a cry.

In 1998 Ann and I spent a month at the Rockefeller Foundation Research Center at Bellagio, on Lake Como. In that beautiful spot I tried to think up alternatives to the conception of time on the model of the classical continuum of real numbers. I hope the article I am soon to publish on the subject will persuade a few people of the need for such an alternative, of which I have long been convinced, even if they do not like mine.

I have celebrated my seventy-fifth birthday. I remain a Catholic, and hope to die one. In Winchester College chapel we used to sing, "The days of our age are threescore year and ten; and though men be so strong that they come to fourscore year, yet is their strength but as labour and sorrow, so soon passeth it away and we are gone." I of course do not know whether I shall come to fourscore year, fall short of them or pass them. In every case, wish me well, readers.

AFTERWORD

I wrote the foregoing in the year 2000. The process of producing a volume of the Library of Living Philosophers is so slow that the autobiography is now out of date at several points, which I indicate here.

To my great distress, my friend Donald Davidson died unforeseeably in August 2003, while in hospital for an operation on his knee; he was 86, but had been expected to live for many years yet.

J.C.W.I. remains active, thirty-nine years after its foundation.

A Wicked Pack of Cards: The Origins of the Occult Tarot, by Ron Decker, Thierry Depaulis, and myself, was published in 1996. The sequel to it, *A History of the Occult Tarot, 1870–1970*, by Ron Decker and myself, came out in 2002.

I have at last lightly revised my Gifford Lectures of 1997; they will come out under the title *Thought and Reality*.

My article "Is Time a Continuum of Instants?" appeared in *Philosophy* 75 (2000): 497–515.

I am now a month off my eighty-first birthday, to the relief or chagrin of the editors of the Library of Living Philosophers.

27TH MAY 2006

PART TWO

DESCRIPTIVE AND CRITICAL ESSAYS WITH REPLIES

1

Brian McGuinness

COMING TO TERMS WITH WITTGENSTEIN

Michael Dummett says more than once, in different words, that analytic philosophy still has to come to terms with Wittgenstein. Indexes show that his own works refer to Wittgenstein oftener than to any other philosopher except Frege. He at first considered himself a follower of Wittgenstein. In the early 1950s that was not so exclusive an allegiance as it has perhaps become: all felt that they had much to learn from this star that was just then making its cosmic rising. Dummett, like Bernard Williams, had indeed been a pupil of Elizabeth Anscombe, but neither could be called her follower. In early papers Dummett discusses very fruitfully her interpretation of Wittgenstein's views on time and memory, a discussion prolonged in later reflections on realism with regard to the past. But he was not a member of a party. In fact I think at that time there was a sense not of distinct parties but of a common enterprise, for which much could be learnt from Wittgenstein. Ryle's obituary of Wittgenstein and Strawson's review of his *Philosophical Investigations* give a good idea of this attitude.[1] To this common enterprise it was at once clear that Dummett, fresh from his military service and still boyish—a young Apollo golden haired—was to make an important contribution. This was not to depend only on his scrupulously acquired knowledge of mathematical logic and of the writings of Frege, published or unpublished (even the former were difficult of access at the time), but on his arguments, often heterodox, on themes regarded as central. In the year that Quine spent in Oxford as Eastman Professor, a year that showed much of the strength and weaknesses of philosophy as then practiced at Oxford, Dummett was among those who had contact with the visitor. That he learnt much from Quine he himself acknowledges and in the indexes to his works Quine's name is often the third most frequently cited, but he was not regarded in the 1950s as having been won over by Quine. On the contrary, his criticisms of central Quinian notions such as holism were regarded as part of the "Oxford" reply to Quine, who had survived, if not won, many jousts during his Oxford year. It is pleasant to record that when Dummett delivered his William James Lectures in Harvard in 1976,[2] Quine, already very senior, was among the more assiduous attenders from the Harvard faculty. A criticism Dummett made in 1955 against Goodman (but also against Quine) will illustrate a tendency in his thought. He took exception to the practice, common to Quine and Goodman at the time, to refer not to letters or words but to "inscriptions" as being more clearly concrete objects, pointing out that the only obviously material objects involved were the chips excised by the graver. In the printed version of Dummett's remarks[3] these have become the lumps of ink, but the Aristotelian point, that even concrete things have a form, remains. It was not party spirit but aversion to a materialist program that inspired him in such interventions, as also in a remarkable solo performance at a class of J. J. C. Smart's on the material nature of the soul, a rather tendentious class, as some thought. An occasional piece, Dummett's intervention was, as far as I know, not published.

My own impression was that a sense of estrangement from "Oxford philosophy," which he acknowledges, came to Dummett rather later, perhaps at the end of the 1950s, though of course his own account is authoritative. By then the hostility particularly of Miss Anscombe to that style of philosophy had become overt. Wittgenstein himself had always spoken ill of it, though hardly knowing it. This was a Cambridge habit—we find it in Russell—and had many roots: the larger size of discussion groups at Oxford, the professionalism and flavor of a joint enterprise that Ryle favored, though himself very much a private worker. There was a sense too of a lack of seriousness in Oxford, an unwillingness to confront the real difficulties. Certainly Wittgenstein thought that he saw these in Austin, for example, which is to some extent surprising. When Austin gave the paper to the Moral Sciences Club in Cambridge that occasioned this remark of Wittgenstein's, its theme was that there were some utterances, later called "performative," regarding which we should resist the temptation to call them true or false, a theme that might be thought attractive to Wittgenstein, but the Club's secretary commented: "A not very successful attempt was made to separate philosophical from linguistic considerations." It may be that Austin's deadpan manner masked what can fairly be called the profundity of his ideas. As regards Ryle, for example, there were also (as so often with Wittgenstein) questions of priority: he thought his ideas had been not only borrowed but distorted.[4] Dummett's treatment of contemporaries and near-contemporaries is admirably impersonal but it is worth saying that when obliged to touch on the matter he understands, without at all sharing, this sensitiveness of Wittgenstein's, whose very conception of philosophy required him to disown and reject the efforts of most other professionals, however well-meaning they may in fact have been.[5]

Friends of Wittgenstein have told me that, while there were pupils who adopted more or less unconsciously his gestures and mannerisms, the philosopher that most resembled him was Dummett, who had hardly glimpsed him. It is not hard to imagine what gave them this impression: the behavior referred to is that of a thinker, the concentration and the seriousness, the unwillingness to be distracted manifesting themselves also physically. They manifest themselves again in the written style: at least in my opinion this is true of Dummett's work, where each sentence that follows is clearly there for the sake of the argument and the reader is never at a loss to know how he is meant to move from one step to the next. It is no hyperbole to say that at its best this resembles the style of Frege, "first clearly stating the problem, then considering various proposed solutions and demonstrating their inadequacy, and finally setting out a satisfactory one" (this is Dummett's own description).[6] But let either style be compared with Wittgenstein's! Who yet says, at one point, "The style of my propositions is extraordinarily strongly influenced by Frege. And if I wanted to, I could establish this influence where at first sight no one would see it."[7] But note that the claim is at the level of *Sätze,* propositions,[8] that is to say the remarks or *aperçus*, which seem to have been Wittgenstein's natural form of writing and out of which he would compose, in a sort of mosaic, the drafts for publishable works (as most of them remained for his lifetime). The volume *Zettel* (literally "slips") represents a collection (perhaps no more than a miscellany) of such remarks—many being deliberate excisions in the course of preparing the *Philosophical Investigations.*

We can see from occasional comments of Wittgenstein on his own work that he did indeed put much effort into trying to write these remarks in the correct (sic: *der richtige*) style: the carriage must be set plumb upon the rails, nothing must be rickety or forced.[9] This will have been the feature of Frege's style that he most wanted to reproduce. He had to bring his thoughts to the point where they themselves dictated the most natural and incontestable formulation. The difficulty of doing this over a longer composition will be clear and he felt that he would perhaps only produce remarks for his heirs to publish. This was nearly, but not quite, what in fact happened. Not quite, because some of his drafts were substantially complete, in that he had set the stones of his mosaic in what he thought the best arrangement if they

were to have the effect aimed at. It is for this reason that Dummett is right
to stress the great difference between the *Remarks on the Foundations of
Mathematics*, relatively raw material, and the *Philosophical Investigations*,
which had gone through a long and complex process of composition.[10]

Wittgenstein's affinities with Frege, but no less his divergence from
what Frege expected of him, throw light on the difficulties that Dummett
finds in coming to terms with the former, while with the latter he has less
difficulty than any living man. From the very fact of the meetings in Jena
before the First World War and from Frege's affectionate, paternal, and
patriotic letters during that war,[11] it is obvious that Frege had great esteem
for Wittgenstein. Perhaps for that very reason the typescript of what was to
be the *Tractatus* was a disappointment and a puzzle to him.[12] "I find it hard
to understand," he wrote, "you put propositions side by side mostly without
giving grounds for them, or at any rate without giving sufficiently detailed
grounds," and later (after having received a reply from a depressed but not
surprised Wittgenstein), "[it seems that] the book's achievement will be on
the artistic level rather than as a contribution to knowledge: what is said in
it takes second place to the way it is said."[13] These remarks were accompanied by shrewd and detailed questions and objections, which, however,
revealed to Wittgenstein that Frege had missed the whole point of the book,
which was meant to be, as Wittgenstein said to Ficker (as if in answer to
Frege), "strictly philosophical and at the same time literary."[14] And indeed
it is highly literary in that it refers the whole time to its own form—it is
deliberately cast in the form of a text book, definitions seem to follow upon
definitions, yet in the end we recognize two things (or two aspects of the
same thing). The whole is circular, each definition depends upon all the
others (this of course Frege points out in further parts of his correspondence) and (the other thing or aspect) what the book is saying is that such
definitions are indeed impossible. I have suggested this elsewhere as
regards arguments in the *Tractatus*. When one seems to be offered, as at
Tractatus 2.0211–2 ("If the world had no substance [i.e., if there were no
simple objects], then whether one proposition had sense would depend on
whether another proposition was true.—In that case we could not sketch
any picture of the world, true or false."), it begs the question, because
determinacy of sense, which for Wittgenstein means bivalence, is assumed.
The lessons for ethics, religion, aesthetics, and for logic itself that
Wittgenstein thought could be won from this disclosed circularity do not
fall to be discussed at the moment. Frege does not advert to them, while
Russell was shocked. I do not think they are relevant to Dummett's
difficulties with Wittgenstein.

Frege was, however, open-minded enough to see that there might yet be something for him in what Wittgenstein was saying. In a remarkable tribute, he writes:

> In long conversations with you I have got to know a man who is in search of the truth like myself, though in part on a different route. But precisely this last point leads me to hope that I may find through you something that will complement or even correct what I have found for myself. So in trying to teach you to see with my eyes I expect to learn to see with yours. I will not so readily give up the hope of a mutual understanding with you.[15]

This impression of Frege's had the same source as Russell's conviction that the next big step in philosophy would be taken by Wittgenstein. Both saw the younger man as an ally in the project of providing a justification of the laws of thought, precisely not of the laws of psychology but, as Frege said, those of truth itself. The *Tractatus* was initially to be called *Logic* and was to be a substitute for the first chapters of *Principia Mathematica*. As such it would also, so Wittgenstein believed, solve problems raised by Russell's paradox, for which indeed he had thought he had a solution as early as 1909. Now he was convinced that the solution of all problems in the foundations of mathematics followed fairly easily from his fundamental insight, itself far from easily won, into the nature of a proposition: in German *der Satz* (also used by him as a title for his work) or, coming closer still to Frege's terminology, *der Gedanke* (not "thought" in the psychological sense but that which is or is fit to be the object of a completed act of thinking).

In Wittgenstein's belief, and in his terminology, once he has established that all the logical constants are implicit in the elementary propositions and that the general form of proposition so given is the "one and only primitive sign in logic,"[16] then he will have shown that the apparatus or symbolism that we have to employ, consciously or not, for affirming the simplest proposition is also adequate to establish any of the propositions of logic. Thus he will be well on his way to providing the foundations required for the logic of *Principia Mathematica* precisely by showing that none is required. All this comes by formulating in a persuasive manner the conditions for any proposition whatsoever to be true-or-false. Such is indeed the content of what I believe to have been the first version of his *Abhandlung* or *Tractatus*, which ended with the remark that logic was not a theory but the mirror-image of the world.[17]

In this way, what set out to be an account of logic in a realist mode, a contribution to heroic philosophy like the works of Russell and Frege, giving an account of all that was thinkable, turns out to be a way of showing (Wittgenstein frequently stresses this word) totally inside language what the logical features of reality are. Thus questions such as whether numbers are objects or whether classes exist do not arise. Perhaps this is what is behind the strange fact that, as may be inferred from a reply of Frege's, Wittgenstein (while not subscribing to idealism) had suggested that there were profound reasons (*tiefe Gründe*) underlying it.[18]

Now my question is whether the later Wittgenstein does not disappoint a reader like Dummett in a similar way. He seems to be attacking the same problems as such a reader, but his final treatment is so divergent as to be unsatisfying. And if this is so, where does the truth lie? Or does the divergence represent an irresoluble difference over what a philosopher should be doing?

In some measure the very development that led Wittgenstein to his later philosophy is relevant to this theme. Of great importance here is the figure of Ramsey. He was the first to visit Wittgenstein in his mountain village and to get him to give an account of the *Tractatus*. Ramsey too filled out the theory of mathematics adumbrated in that work and claimed in his *Encyclopædia Britannica* article more triumphantly than in his paper to the London Mathematical Society[19] that Wittgenstein's work enabled one to show that mathematics consists entirely of tautologies and that there is no need for the axiom of reducibility: the program of *Principia Mathematica* was complete![20] Here he was going beyond his mentor, since Wittgenstein in fact believed that mathematics consisted of equations, but not that these were tautologies. Ramsey discussed Wittgenstein's work with other mathematicians and philosophers, even when his own relations with him for a while broke down. He represented Wittgenstein, no doubt accurately enough, as a semi-intuitionist. He developed a method of overcoming Wittgenstein's objections to the definition of identity and the use of the equals sign—a method communicated to the Vienna Circle and haughtily criticized there by Wittgenstein. In the last year of his short life relations with Wittgenstein (now back in Cambridge) were fully restored and there took place what Wittgenstein describes in the preface to *Philosophical Investigations*: those "innumerable conversations" during which he learnt so much from Ramsey's "unerring and forceful" criticism of his ideas—those in particular of his first book. Wittgenstein's notebooks, which are particularly rich in notes of a personal nature during that year, show him reacting with alternate joy and despair to Ramsey as a thinker and a friend. The two "papers" that Wittgenstein delivered in that year—the printed "On Logical Form" and the paper on the Infinite that he read in its place[21]—both resulted from their discussions.

Discussion as such was of the greatest importance to Wittgenstein: he comments how valuable to him these meetings with Ramsey were: "There is something erotic and chivalrous about them. They educate me into a degree of courage in thinking. . . . In science I do not like to [or I only reluctantly] go for a walk on my own."[22] This is, as far as I can determine, the last occasion on which Wittgenstein refers to his own activity as "science," if one may use that word as a translation of *"Wissenschaft."* Nor is this fact unrelated to Ramsey. Ramsey's criticisms were indeed telling but their aim was to produce a systematic work out of Wittgenstein's ideas, or to point out that the *Tractatus* had not yet attained that status. Discussions with members of the Vienna Circle in that city and the work of Waismann who was trying to produce a compendium of Wittgenstein's philosophy, beginning with the rewriting of the *Tractatus* as a set of *"Thesen"* were pushing Wittgenstein in the same direction. He began to resist and described Ramsey as "a bourgeois thinker." He himself found more inspiration in what Ramsey called the Bolshevist ideas of the intuitionists, as later in Sraffa's general way of thinking, Sraffa whose economics was subtly related to the ideas of Marx and Gramsci. In the preface quoted above Wittgenstein indeed puts his debt to Sraffa above that to Ramsey (just as in the preface to the *Tractatus* Frege's great works are implicitly rated above "the writings of my friend Mr. Bertrand Russell"). At one point he ranks Sraffa and Spengler alongside Frege and Russell, as if they were the Muses of his later as these of his earlier philosophy.

From Michaelmas Term of 1930 onwards (nine months after the death of Ramsey) there were, with some interruptions, getting on for 240 meetings between Sraffa and Wittgenstein, scheduled in their respective pocket diaries.[23] These were intended precisely for discussion of all sorts of topics. On one occasion in a letter (recently come to light) Wittgenstein mentions vivisection as a topic on which more has to be said. Sometimes Sraffa, sometimes Wittgenstein found these discussions too taxing. On one occasion when Wittgenstein begged Sraffa to continue—they could talk about anything Sraffa chose—Sraffa replied, "yes, but in your way." This was the point: they were meeting to exercise and develop their dialectic skills and now one, now the other would learn something or feel he was being bullied. There were to be many other discussion partners in Wittgenstein's later life, some definitely disciples, others more independent, such as Georg Kreisel, but Sraffa seems to have had the strongest intellectual effect. It is consonant with this that, when asked, long after Wittgenstein's death, what his contribution had been, he replied that he had only said what was perfectly obvious.

The change in Wittgenstein that I would characterize as the move from Ramsey to Sraffa was the abandonment of a kind of dogmatism. He insists on such abandonment in his conversations with Waismann (in December 1931) and, indeed, the word "dogmatism" first appears in his writings at this time. He associates it with taking an object of comparison, which we use to understand and describe a range of phenomena, as being instead a rule that they must follow. This form of criticism of a method in philosophy derives from the reading of Spengler (whom Wittgenstein mentions in this context) and is reminiscent of the morphological approach to explanation, which both Wittgenstein and Spengler adapted from Goethe, from whom perhaps the word "dogmatism" is borrowed. But it is altogether of a piece with Sraffa's hostility to general theories: Sraffa, whose own account of the production of commodities is of considerable conceptual and even mathematical complexity, regarded his own theory as a technical matter in which perfection should be required but that it would be idiotic to take anything like it as a rule for ordinary life or even day-to-day economics.

The working out of this insight, if we may call it such, took Wittgenstein some time. What we know as *Philosophical Remarks* and *Philosophical Grammar* are compilations that still smack of a systematic philosophy. In *Blue and Brown Books* and other results of dictation or note-taking in the first half of the 1930s, there is no clear awareness of the change that has taken place. That we do find, however, in the excursus on the nature of philosophy that occupies §§89–133 of *Philosophical Investigations* as we have it today. The contribution of Sraffa and Spengler demonstrably dates from the beginning of the 1930s but a full realization of its importance comes, I believe, in a pocket notebook of 1937 (MS 157b), where Wittgenstein is clearly collecting his thoughts for the first version (so to speak) of *Investigations*, which we have in MS 142—a determined rewriting, a new approach decided on and executed in his Norwegian retreat. In one passage of MS157b[24] he says that the idea of the family (he means that of family resemblance, derived from Spengler) and the realization that understanding was not a pneumatic process were two axe strokes against his previous doctrine—that, I infer, of the crystal clarity of logic in itself. Sraffa showed him that he had to accept as a sign something for which he could not give the rules and grammar.[25] He saw in a flash that no rules or grammar lay behind this sign or transaction between speakers. All we could say about it was how it was received in the language. So also in general there was not such a thing as a meaning, a sense, which we, unskillfully and unwittingly yet unerringly, managed to express. There was only a set of reactions found appropriate—in the early 1930s, the period of the verification principle, these might typically have been the measures necessary to establish the truth or falsity of something said but they should not be limited to that.

Wittgenstein associates this immediately with the realization that there was no essence of language, no realm of meaning to be tapped into. That was (as he called it now) the pneumatic theory of thought, misrepresented in the English of §109 as "the conception of thought as a gaseous medium." The word "gaseous" is used by Wittgenstein in English but is an inept translation and he himself says that the word "ethereal" would be better. Pneuma is certainly not gas. The pneumatic theory was the idea that behind our understanding and meaning there was some structure (something concrete) that we could perhaps only glimpse but on which we depended for our thoughts or utterances to have sense. This substructure or skeleton now vanished. He describes the theory also as one that supposes that sense is something that we give life to, like a child, and it then has a life of its own, which we can only follow and examine. Not so with sense or understanding, for it is only our activity that gives life to sense or language—shown above all (in the earlier period) in the propositions that we accept as following from the one we are concerned with or in the propositions from which it follows.

The move towards the verification principle was an ingenious modification of the *Tractatus* system but was not the whole of the lesson learnt at the beginning of the 1930s. Looking back in 1937 he thought that the realization that the pre-existence of a set of rules is an illusion. We invent or abstract rules later as a kind of model or ideal case for our actual practice. And that practice includes a whole variety of things, a family whose members resemble one another to various degrees in various ways. And there came very naturally the realization that there was not one thing (not even one chief thing) that language always (or nearly always) did. Understanding and hence sense itself were not "spiritual" processes behind language because language itself was a family of practices, not just the operation of pneuma. Any one practice would be, as any one member of a family is, only a rough guide to what the others would be like. (The terminology and approach here is determined by Wittgenstein's understanding and modification of Spengler.)

This does not mean, as Sraffa in one of his rare "philosophical" notes points out, that the rules of a language can be constructed only by observation. If that were so there could never be any nonsense said. This identifies the cause and the meaning of a word. (He goes on to say that in that case birdsong and the talk of metaphysicians will have a meaning.) On a true view (I interpret) grammatical speech would be not what people actually say but what we allow them to say without criticism. This was the crucial turn away from the *Tractatus*: we do not find grammar inside language, we impose it from outside. It is our set of models that we apply—of course not rigorously.

In doing this we have to be very careful about generalization. General theories are models that we use to indicate what we are about, but we constantly go wrong when we do not think of the individual cases. Here (in *Philosophical Investigations* and elsewhere) Wittgenstein repeats exactly what Sraffa says in a fragment of his on language preserved in Trinity College Library: we should give up generalities and take particular cases from which we started.

That is why we find in §109 of *Philosophical Investigations* the warning that our activity is not a scientific one. The philosopher (grammarian) is not investigating how much it is possible to imagine, as if efforts of fancy might extend the realm of the possible. (This is something that Ramsey thought possible, when he talked about imagining a row of trees that went on for ever.) In fact, and here we come to another connection with Sraffa, Wittgenstein is not investigating any interior thing. It does not matter what people feel when they say something, what matters—and this is what grammar tells us—is what it amounts to, as we have seen before, what follows from it, what we can do with it. From 1930 on (I imagine under Sraffa's influence or goading) Wittgenstein says he is interested in the account books, *die Geschäftsbücher*, of the mathematicians or of the philosophers. In the case of mathematicians this will mean being interested in what use they make of their results in mathematics—and he is not interested in what they say about it to the man in the street. But the philosopher must in the end be able to talk to the man in the street.

So the move away from all speculation was a Sraffa-inspired one and was executed with tools derived from Spengler, and the move included turning one's back on the bourgeois philosophy of Ramsey. There was not one system that we had to respect and shore up but lots of different rulebooks towards which we had different attitudes and reactions. The change involved a further devaluation—an *Abhandlung* in an unusual sense but one which Wittgenstein used—of logic. While the *Tractatus* had shown that logic was absolute but had no content, now we see that it is a form (or a set of forms) that we apply, more or less loosely, to areas of our language. For this reason Wittgenstein was always happy to find some feature of our ordinary language that (as he thought) escaped the logic of the logicians, for example, what has been called Moore's Paradox—the logical oddity of saying "p but I do not believe that p," although anyone who says it is not uttering a contradiction. Of course it may be said that Wittgenstein's satisfaction at this inadequacy of existing logic was to be short-lived because it is usually possible in such cases to produce a logic that will prohibit the sort of expression in question, but I suppose him to have thought that there will always be new oddities or inconsistencies or implications that will require us to invent new logics, which may or may not be successful.

A logic of belief, a logic of questions, a modal logic, like the one von Wright extracted from the *Tractatus*, are they not simply sophisticated examples of Wittgensteinian language games[26]—we imagine for a while that this fragment is the entire language of the participants or that we allow it to be so? They serve as models to illuminate some of our practices, but we do not normally think that they mirror exactly or exhaust the nature of those practices, save indeed for the case where we determine to use that artificial language to define a set of practices, as in mathematics or chess. For such languages we can indeed have a scientific theory, hypotheses about what is possible, but (Wittgenstein maintains) for language as a whole we cannot. Anything that, when taken together with its full context, is compatible with a recognizable human social life (*die gemeinsame menschliche Handlungsweise*) must be permissible and we have no means of determining that in advance.

It is fair to see Wittgenstein as an analytic philosopher, if that term designates one whose approach to philosophy is through considerations of language (though to be true a very wide conception of language in his case, absorbing so much of the social and institutional background).[27] He ruefully said of the effects of his teaching that these consisted in his getting the tag "and Language" added to many book or article titles. But, after the change or *Wende* we have sketched, it seems wrong to call him a philosopher of language, for that seems to demand a systematic character that his philosophy plainly does not possess. Humanly speaking it is natural enough that, having once tried to develop a theory of language and having failed, he should now try something else. But in fact a theory was not at all the aim. What he wanted to convey was that "way of talking about" things which when poured out incessantly had irritated Sraffa. On nearly every topic, he thought, people began thinking in the wrong way, always grasping the wrong end of the stick. That was what irritated him and he tried to put together a manual of imaginary corrective conversations—for *Philosophical Investigations* is a carefully crafted book. Followed through it should give a sense of the approach. It is needless to stress again—Dummett recognizes better than most—what philosophical pearls are to be found in these depths—the discussion of rules, of private language, of the transparency of language (which needs no interpreter), and many more. But what cannot be summarized is the cumulative effect of the style of reasoning, the openness to human weaknesses and aspirations, the awareness of possibilities, the tolerance, if I may put it so, of contradiction but not of absurdity. It is the sort of work, the sort of approach that could only be presented in this way: if a knockdown theory had been presented, it would simply be that, namely, another theory, which might be exemplary in its area but would not provide, so to speak, a paradigm of paradigms. Undoubtedly part of the aim of Wittgenstein's philosophical work is to illustrate the variety of activities and considerations that determine our conscious life. He is also aware (even if it is not the first concern of *Philosophical Investigations*) of the variety of cultures that there have been or might yet be.

It is often thought a limitation of Wittgenstein's methods that they lead only to the solution of problems or puzzles, which moreover, if the method is successful, are shown to be trivial: some problems about other minds—the question, for example, whether the color red is "the same" when experienced by you and by me—may be thought to be of this kind. Here it is important to see that problems and paradoxes are a natural way into philosophy, if they are not the only way. The subject would not exist if one were confined to asking questions to which there was a clear path to an answer—though it is difficult to imagine such a ban being enforced. Pilate's question and the sort of remark that gives rise (shades of W. C. Fields!) to books on children's philosophy are of some use. But of course we should not (in a useful phrase of Dummett's) go bald-headed at them.[28] Some context, some conception of the grammar or rules of such questions must be provided or inferred. Then the solution or some general idea of how to talk about the matters involved will be developed, typically by a more suitable model of discourse in this area, a schematic description of the particular language game in question. This has been the method of philosophy since Aristotle if not before: the solution of *aporiai* is the discovery of truth.[29] This is clear to philosophical critics of Wittgenstein. What raises some doubt is the piecemeal nature of the models or paradigms used to solve problems. It is, however, not altogether clear why this is an objection. If this method resolves some problems and gives an idea of how to solve others by the application of similar feats of imagination and rethinking, is it not doing much? It is true that some of the notions used by Wittgenstein are not strictly defined—his notion of criterion would be one example, but this is not an objection if the structures or assumptions that we are imagining to be embedded in our common language are in any case applicable only within the limits of common sense (*der gesunde Menschenverstand*).

How this method, if it may be called such, relates to more systematic approaches is not altogether clear. Wittgenstein had strong disagreements with all three of Carnap, Waismann, and Popper, the first two of whom produced structured accounts either of an alternative to his own approach or of his own approach itself, while the difference with the third seems to have consisted in the question whether the problems were properly called philosophical. With literary quarrels it is almost axiomatic that both parties are in the wrong, and indeed it is hard to see why both a systematic and an unsystematic approach should not be tolerated. There is obvious interest in a philosophy of language on Fregean lines, such as Dummett lays the foundations for in *The Logical Basis of Metaphysics*. One wants to see how far it gets: the Wittgensteinian rejection of theory would apply to it only if some linguistic practice were excluded a priori or if an unsubstantiated claim was made to have covered all uses of language. The question about which of the two is the better approach may be left to individual choice and to the judgment of time. The mere fact that one is a more scientific approach than the other is not decisive.[30] A parallel to consider would be that of medicine. I adduce this not on the assumption that philosophical difficulties are like illnesses and need therapy, but just on the basis that medicine is a field of activities aimed at certain results. Now these results first of all may themselves be questioned: what exactly is the aim of medicine? Even assuming certain aims, to some extent these can be produced by scientific means, though there may even be conflicting sciences, but there may also be important psychological factors; evidence-based medicine is in one sense nonscientific, so are alternative therapies, and clinical judgment. If there exists in principle a complete map of the human being and of the biochemical basis of his health problems, it is so remote as to be practically irrelevant. It is the doctor who has to (as the first Lord Horder proudly claimed to have done) "bring the laboratory to the bedside."

There are of course difficulties for the unsystematic approach in philosophy, one being the question of criteria. How can it be judged that a linguistic practice is legitimate when each range of practice has to be judged by its own standards?[31] Is the religious believer secure within his own belief system, which only he can judge? The same problem arises over the writings of the nonsystematic philosopher. Is he simply someone parroting the words or copying the mannerisms of a sage such as Wittgenstein (supposing him to be such)?[32] These questions seem telling ones because they demand an exact standard, mechanically applicable, in matters, which are precisely ones of judgment, as they might be in literature or in history. The wise man is the one who can see the human dimension or the lack of it in the proposed language game and who can make its presence felt in his discussion or description of it.

A caveat must be entered as regards the subject of mathematics, and is perhaps especially owed to Dummett. Much editorial and expository work is required before we shall have a satisfactory account of the Wittgensteinian point of view on mathematics. He spent much of his working life on it without reaching a clear position, whereas I think we have the material to see what he thought about what is now called philosophy of language and philosophy of mind. His position seems to be in principle that the mathematician may do what he likes in his own subject (*urbi*) but should not make pronouncements (*orbi*) on the content or truth-value of what he has done. The difficulty is that the preference Wittgenstein shows for constructivist systems is hardly intelligible unless he takes up a position on the existence of mathematical objects or at least on the objectivity of mathematical truth.[33] Perforce leaving this matter to be dealt with by the excellent scholars concerned,[34] I mention it to point out the possibility that a *prima facie* incompatibility may arise (and of course not here only) between Wittgenstein's theory and the practice of philosophy.

BRIAN McGUINNESS

UNIVERSITY OF SIENA
FEBRUARY 2005

NOTES

1. Gilbert Ryle, a Third Programme talk (obituary of Wittgenstein), reprinted in *Analysis* 12, no. 1 (October 1951): 1–9; P. F. Strawson, "Critical Notice," a review of Wittgenstein's *Philosophical Investigations*, in *Mind* 63 (1954): 70–99.

2. Published (with revisions) as *The Logical Basis of Metaphysics* (Cambridge, MA: Harvard University Press), 1991.

3. Michael Dummett, *Truth and Other Enigmas* (London: Duckworth, 1978), 32.

4. Letters to G. E. Moore, 3 December 1946, to R. Rhees, 30.4.1947. All letters quoted are available in the Innsbruck Electronic Edition (CD-ROM and Internet) *Ludwig Wittgenstein: Complete Correspondence* published in the InteLex *Past Masters* series (Charlottesville, VA: InteLex, 2004).

5. See Michael Dummett, "What It Was Like to Be Wittgenstein" in *The Tablet* 6 (August 1988): 901. "He thought that they uniformly misunderstood the nature of their subject, believing it to be one amenable to exposition of the standard kind, with problems stated and solved: their utterances therefore in no way competed with his work, but, at best, would provide useful illustrations of the conceptual disorders for which philosophy, as he conceived it, should provide the treatment."

6. Ibid.

7. "Der Stil meiner Sätze ist außerordentlich stark von Frege beeinflußt. Und wenn ich wollte, so könnte ich wohl diesen Einfluß feststellen, wo ihn auf den ersten Blick keiner sähe." *Zettel* §712 (originally in MS 112, fo.1r, entry for 8.10.1931, where the context gives us little clue as to the occasion of the remark).

8. The Anscombe translation "sentences" is inappropriate here, unless we are to think of the *Sentences* of Peter Lombard.

9. "Den richtigen Stil schreiben heißt, den Wagen *gerade* auf's Geleise

setzen." MS 117.225 (1940) "Wackelig" and "geschraubt" come from MSS 119.91 and 118.89 (both 1937).

10. Dummett, *Truth and Other Enigmas*, 166. For the compositional history of the *Investigations* see Ludwig Wittgenstein, *Philosophische Untersuchungen: Kritisch-genetische Edition*, ed. J. Schulte (Frankfurt: Suhrkamp Verlag, 2001).

11. "Gottlob Frege: Briefe an Ludwig Wittgenstein," ed. Allan Janik, *Grazer Philosophische Studien*, vol. 33/34 (1989), 5–33.

12. Typescript 204, now in the Austrian National Library: we know that this was the actual typescript sent to Frege because he at first complained that page 10 was missing and here page 10 is in fact supplied in manuscript and in the handwriting of Wittgenstein's companion in captivity Ludwig Hänsel.

13. Letters of 28.6.1919 and 16.9.1919 respectively. For Wittgenstein's implied reply to the second charge (his work is strictly philosophical and at the same time literary) see my "Philosophy and Literature in the *Tractatus*," in *Wittgenstein: The Philosopher and his Works*, ed. Alois Pichler and Simo Säätelä (Working Papers from the Wittgenstein Archives at the University of Bergen [WAB] no. 17 [Bergen: WAB, 2005], 326–40).

14. Letter to Ficker of 7.10.1919. His actual answer to Frege is lost.

15. Letter of 16.9.1919.

16. *Tractatus Logico-Philosophicus* 5.47, 5.472. This last point is equivalent to Wittgenstein's idea that one symbolic rule will suffice for recognizing all the logical propositions of the first eight chapters of *Principia Mathematica*, an idea formulated in a letter to Russell of November 1913. There are two forms of such a rule, truth tables and Wittgenstein's bracket notation (*TLP* 4.442 and 6.1203 respectively).

17. See "Some pre-*Tractatus* Manuscripts," in my *Approaches to Wittgenstein* (New York: Routledge, 2002), 259–69 and my "Wittgenstein's 1916 'Abhandlung'" in *Wittgenstein and the Future of Philosophy*, ed. R. Haller and K. Puhl (Vienna: Öbv and Hpt, 2002), 272–82.

18. Letter from Frege 3.4.1920. This seems to have been one of Wittgenstein's objections to Frege's "Der Gedanke."

19. Printed as the title essay in Frank Plumpton Ramsey's *Foundations of Mathematics and Other Logical Essays*, ed. R. B. Braithwaite (London: Routledge and Kegan Paul, 1931), 1–61, and all later collections.

20. *Encyclopædia Britannica*, 13th ed., new vol. 2, pp. 830–32.

21. I believe I have been able to identify a sheet of notes in German among Ramsey's papers as being intended for this occasion: it contains ideas on the infinite, clearly Wittgenstein's, and (on a more daring hypothesis) perhaps dictated for purposes of translation.

22. "Es ist etwas Erotisches und Ritterliches darin. Ich werde dabei auch zu einem gewissen Mut im Denken erzogen. Ich gehe in der Wissenschaft nur gern [*quaere* nur ungern *or* nicht gern] allein spazieren" (Wittgenstein Papers 105 4 15 Feb 1929). The appended sentence is puzzling as written and requires the amendment suggested (either that of Wolfgang Kienzler or my own) to give a natural

sense. The thought that Ramsey helped Wittgenstein to overcome a cowardly preference for solitude is too convoluted; nor did Wittgenstein exhibit such a preference, as I shortly show. Ramsey ("Frank") was one of the few exceptions to Wittgenstein's practice of referring to friends by their surnames.

23. Miss Alexandra Marjanovic has kindly provided me with a schedule of these.

24. An elliptical passage that I have had to fill out in my text.

25. The reference is to the famous "Neapolitan gesture" for which Sraffa rhetorically demanded the "grammar" (the version of his demanding its "logical form" is not authentic). The gesture incidentally is not a particularly Neapolitan but a common Italian one, and immediately intelligible in context, sometimes meaning that there is nothing more to be said because the point should already be clear. In this sense its use by Sraffa may have been self-referential.

26. To be sure Wittgenstein preferred the horny-handed builders: one of his favorite cartoons was a sketch of construction workers manoeuvering huge girders to the accompaniment of cries of "Let her go!" or "Easy does it!" and the like, observed by two professors one of whom says, "Isn't it remarkable, Herr Kollege, that so precise a task can be carried out by means of such inexact language?" Assuming the license of a *raconteur* he told Kreisel that this actually occurred when he was building a house for his sister in Vienna.

27. For this theme see Dummett's "Can Analytic Philosophy be Systematic and Ought it to Be?" in *Truth and Other Enigmas*, 437–58.

28. Advice given to him and his wife by a plumber: *The Logical Basis of Metaphysics*, 19.

29. *Nicomachean Ethics* VII.4 (1146b7). In *From Wodehouse to Wittgenstein* (Manchester: Carcanet, 1998), Anthony Quinton points out how epistemologists intent on refuting a skepticism that no one ever seriously held have contributed much to the study of scientific methodology.

30. Both Quinton (*From Wodehouse to Wittgenstein*, 339 ff.) and Dummett ("Can Analytic Philosophy be Systematic?" 437ff.) put Carnaps's influence on later philosophy above Wittgenstein's. But they are speaking of influence within an environment designed to favor systematic research.

31. Quinton makes a suggestion like this (ibid., 354).

32. Wittgenstein himself feared he might simply generate a sort of philosophical jargon. Speaking of Kierkegaard and Hamann (both of whom he revered), he said they encouraged presumption in their own editors (meaning, I suppose, expositors). These say they know nothing but give themselves much credit for doing so (MS 183.98: a diary entry for 22 February 1931).

33. Dummett makes a related point in the introduction to his *Elements of Intuitionism* (Oxford: Clarendon Press, 1977).

34. I am thinking of Juliet Floyd, Pasquale Frascolla, and Mathieu Marion.

REPLY TO BRIAN McGUINNESS

Brian McGuinness opens his essay with a sketch of a period of Oxford philosophy; I will comment briefly on this. He is right, I think, to say that in the 1950s there was a general sense that we were engaged in a common enterprise. I recovered that sense when (in hospital with a painful back) I wrote "Is Philosophy Systematic?" thinking rather of the school of analytical philosophers in general than of Oxford philosophy in particular. I foolishly imagined that we could all co-operate to decide the correct form of a theory of meaning, and go on to fill in the detail. Philosophers simply do not behave as though engaged in a common enterprise. Quine's first visit to Oxford must, I think, have been in the academic year 1954–55. I met him several times to discuss different topics. He was very kind to me, and invited me to stay with him for a week on my first trip to the United States in the following year. While I was there he wrote letters of introduction for me to present to all the great logicians in the course of my voyage to California. I did use them to call on Church and Kleene, but, being very junior and quite unknown, I thought it would be going too far to try the patience of Gödel. I thought at the time that Quine was a great philosopher of language; since then I have realised that his influence extends beyond that area, and have been repelled by his behaviourism, his scientism, and his advocacy of philosophical naturalism. Quine surely won most of the many jousts he had with Oxford philosophers. Few of the latter had read much of Quine's work; most expected him to be easy prey to their refutations of him. I remember a meeting of the joint seminar run by Peter Strawson and Paul Grice at which Quine was present. Grice read a paper attacking Quine's views, which he finished with a triumphant glint in his eye. Quine replied to him with a subtle and crushing retort; Grice took on a very disconcerted expression. The only one who took the measure of Quine was John Austin, who read a paper to the Philosophical Society criticising a minute point Quine had made in a footnote. I much regret that my joke about inscriptions has been mutilated in the book version: the point of it was that inscriptions, in the literal sense, are read from the bits of stone that aren't there.

McGuinness is probably right that it was not until towards the end of the 1950s that I began to feel an alienation from the "ordinary language" school that reigned over Oxford philosophy; perhaps it coincided with the rise of Austin to dominance. Before that Ryle had been dictator, not merely of Oxford philosophy but of British philosophy more generally. Although I acknowledged that *The Concept of Mind* provided the starting-point for much philosophical discussion in the period following its publication, I never greatly cared for Ryle; he tried to make us narrower and narrower, scorning not only Heidegger, whom he had once reviewed respectfully, but Carnap as well. I remember him complaining that a portrait of him made him look like a drowned German general: but that was exactly what he did look like. Ryle was very hostile to me; I heard that in a seminar he had said that "Dummett said that" was equivalent to "It is false that." I do not think that I had allowed my dislike of Ryle to show, and could not account for this enmity; perhaps it resulted from Ryle's propensity to approve of other philosophers to the degree to which they agreed with him. Austin was entirely the opposite: he despised his disciples, but respected those who stood up to him, provided that they were clever. When Wittgenstein's *Philosophical Investigations* came out, Ryle said that he could kick himself for all the things that he had missed and Wittgenstein had seen. Austin's attitude was far less respectful: I heard that at one of the Saturday morning sessions at which Austin gave the troops their marching orders, and which I, not being a Fellow of an undergraduate college, happily never attended, he referred to "poor old Witters."

McGuinness tells us that Wittgenstein claimed that his style resembled Frege's; he was fantasising. The comparison is not like that between Frege's style and Husserl's. At his best, as in *Die Grundlagen der Arithmetik*, Frege wrote beautifully; I do not think that his greatest admirer could maintain that Husserl wrote at all well. Frege and Wittgenstein were both great stylists; but their styles differed sharply. In his essay, Brian McGuinness concentrates particularly upon Wittgenstein's growing, and in the end total, opposition to system and general theory; this opposition totally determined his later manner of writing.

As McGuinness quotes me as saying, Frege proceeded by first clearly setting out the problem, then showing the inadequacy of proposed solutions, and then lucidly expounding his own solution. If you do not believe that philosophical problems have solutions, at least not solutions that can be stated, or that there are any philosophical conclusions that can be expressed by propositions, you cannot proceed in this way. What, on such a view, are the conclusions they believe themselves to have arrived at, the propositions they take themselves to have arrived at? They can be no more than exemplifications of the conceptual confusions it is the task of philosophy to disentangle. The self-styled Wittgensteinians make this the whole principle of their philosophical activity: much of their effort is devoted to demonstrating that what other philosophers, of the present time or of the past, have said is nonsense. But it does not read very like Wittgenstein. Why not? Because, if they have interpreted the other philosophers aright, they are enunciating what is trivially nonsense, and hence rather boring nonsense. The neo-Wittgensteinians write as though engaged in a process of debunking: once you realise that all would-be philosophical propositions must be nonsense, you can see nonsense everywhere. Wittgenstein hardly ever cited what another philosopher had said without treating it with great respect; it was because it exerted so strong a pull upon our intellects that it demanded such skill to unravel. For all that, I have never been able to swallow the contention that there are no genuine philosophical arguments, arriving at genuine conclusions. In this respect, Frege is my exemplar, not Wittgenstein.

What would a comprehensive theory of meaning for a natural language such as English be like? I take a theory of meaning to embody an account of the functioning of the language. A theory of meaning for a natural language would be of vast complexity. It would have to encompass all idioms of the language; though systematic, it would have many exceptions to every principle. No one will ever construct one. But the possibility of such a thing appears unquestionable. Wittgenstein, however, would not have thought it possible; he would have condemned the conception of such a theory of meaning as a phantasm engendered by the misguided search for a general theory and the misguided belief in the possibility of systematisation.

Now consider Wittgenstein's language-games. The term "language-game" is used in two ways in Wittgenstein's writings. Sometimes it refers to a restricted component of our language or of our use of it—the use of a circle of expressions or a distinctive use of sentences. But when it is first introduced in the *Investigations*, it is explained as referring to an imaginary miniature language that Wittgenstein describes. This miniature language is to be thought of as all the language that its speakers have. Such a language-game is in complexity to a natural language as a clockwork toy to a space rocket. What is the point of these language-games? To show us what meaning is, or at least the meanings of expressions of some particular type. But they are comprehensive descriptions of the functioning of miniature languages. Apparently, if the language is restricted enough, with a small enough vocabulary and a narrow enough range of uses, a systematic account *is* possible. So just where, in a progression from Wittgenstein's language-games through ever more complex imaginary languages, all the way to natural languages, does the boundary lie, beyond which systematic description ceases to be even in principle possible? Does increase in complexity eventually produce a difference in kind? At what point does it do so? And if there is a difference in kind between a natural language and a Wittgensteinian language-game, what justification or point was there in setting up the language-games as objects of comparison? It would be a false comparison. But if there is not a difference in kind, then there can be no objection in principle to a systematic theory describing how the language functions.

It appears to me that there was indeed no principle underlying Wittgenstein's hostility to theory and to system, just a prejudice. One might almost say a mood: a prejudice of this kind is simply a mood wilfully sustained through life. But the avoidance of systematic handling makes Wittgenstein's writing very hard to read, and goes to explain why we have not fully come to terms with him yet. Often, in reading him, one has the feeling "I don't know where we are going." In some cases it is clear where we are going; in others it eventually becomes clear. But often the answer is, "We are not going anywhere: we are just observing the scenery and making comments on it." It is still very worth while persisting, because many of the comments, ironic or sardonic, bite very deep; occasionally, however, they seem to miss the point. I should like to come to terms with Wittgenstein; I am sure I have not yet. I hope that eventually we shall.

M. D.

2

Jan Dejnožka

DUMMETT'S BACKWARD ROAD TO FREGE AND TO INTUITIONISM

This essay addresses Michael Dummett's paper, "The Context Principle: Centre of Frege's Philosophy" (1995), in which Dummett revises his thinking on Frege. I shall argue that Dummett's semantic program for Frege rests on a scholarly and philosophical mistake. Namely, it takes what Bertrand Russell calls the backward road from reference to sense. Since Dummett endorses the backward road, I must show that the mistake is genuine. But I need not enter the murky waters of "On Denoting" to do so, if I can make the mistake independently clear. After arguing that no senses are objects or functions, I show how we can keep Frege's context principle from bifurcating into one principle for senses and another for references.[1] I conclude by showing that intuitionism is a form of the backward road and shares in the mistake.

1. DUMMETT'S SEMANTIC PROGRAM FOR FREGE

Dummett (1995) in effect now agrees with me that there is abundant evidence that Frege actively uses the context principle in *Grundlagen*, and that the principle plays a key role in his arriving at his definition of Number. I advanced these views in my "Frege: Existence and Identity" (1979), which remains the most detailed treatment of these matters I know of.[2] We now also agree that the principle is implicitly in *Grundgesetze* (my 1996/2003, 279–87).

Dummett says, "The context principle is not concerned with principles of *definition*, however, but with how the *primitive* symbols of the system are to be explained: by what means should the semantic theory stipulate their *Bedeutungen* and thereby their *Sinne*?" (1995, 14–15). Dummett is openly saying Frege's context principle requires that Frege's semantic theory take the backward road from references "and thereby" to senses. But Dummett's question is apparently rhetorical, because he then says that no stipulations should be needed, since the theory ought to explain how to derive all references, except for our knowledge of the two truth-values, from truth-conditions. Dummett interprets Frege's semantic program as follows:

> I interpret [Frege] as follows. A *theory of **Bedeutung*** for a language must of course be stated in some language; if it is concerned to lay down the interpretation of the object-language, it must necessarily be stated in a metalanguage disjoint from the object-language, since the latter cannot yet be understood. *Now if the theory is to display the existing or intended **Sinne** of the expressions of the object-language, it must embody only what anyone who has a mastery of the object-language will know.* As far as possible, therefore, it must refrain from exploiting what can be known only by understanding the metalanguage. There is an inescapable exception to this. Anyone who makes a judgment knows what the two truth-values are; but this knowledge cannot be stated. Only one who can grasp a thought can make a judgment, and, among human beings, only one who can speak a language can grasp a thought; nevertheless, we can say what is known by someone who is master of a language only by presupposing the two truth-values as known.
>
> Our theory may accordingly specify outright the conditions for a sentence *of a given form* to be true or false, that is, to have one or other truth-value as its *Bedeutung*; but it cannot fix the *Bedeutung* of any term by specifying that it is to be any other object namable in the metalanguage. *A mastery of the object-language consists in grasping the condition for each of its sentences to be true. It is only in doing so that one who knows that language knows the **Bedeutungen** of its terms; hence to stipulate in the metalanguage that certain terms are to denote certain objects is at best to take as understood what the theory should be explaining.* The only way in which a speaker of the object-language can specify the *Bedeutung* of one of its terms is by using some co-referential term, *which he recognises as such by his grasp of statements of identity.* This is but part of his knowledge of what determines the truth or falsity of sentences containing the term; it is the content of that knowledge which the theory of *Bedeutung* must exhibit. (1995, 16–17, emphasis mine)

In this puzzling passage, it looks for all the world as if Dummett is saying that it is by specifying the truth-conditions of a "sentence of a given form," and "only [by] doing so," that we can explain the references of its subsentential terms, and thereby also the "intended *Sinne*" expressed by those terms. The sole exception noted is that we must presuppose knowledge of what the truth-values are, though not of which sentences are true and which are false. These objects are Frege's sentential references. But they are also subsentential references. We can use "the True" to refer to the

True. It might seem from the phrase "any *other* object [than a truth-value]" that Dummett is allowing us to fix the *Bedeutung* of "the True" as the True. This seems to contradict the aim of the program. But the phrase's grammatical reference is unclear to me, and I shall charitably assume Dummett does not mean that. In any case, the passage states the semantic program Dummett interprets Frege as having. I shall call it "Dummett's program."

Dummett is saying that for Frege, there is a backward road from reference to sense. This departs from Dummett's earlier books in which he held Russell is right that there is no backward road for Frege (1981a, 87, 95; 1981, 267), and amended Frege's theory because the no backward road thesis is a "problem" (1981a, 87–88, citing 1981, 268). My view is that the earlier Dummett is right that for Frege there is no backward road, and the 1993 Dummett is right that the context principle is actively used in *Grundlagen* and implicit in *Grundgesetze*. But the 1993 Dummett is interpreting the context principle too strongly, so that it permits and even requires a backward road in Frege's theory of sense and reference.

2. PROBLEMS WITH THE PROGRAM

Dummett's program has at least seven problems.

The first problem is a dilemma based on an ambiguity. Dummett says, "Our theory may accordingly specify outright the conditions for a sentence *of a given form* to be true or false. . . . " But when we are given the form of a sentence, does he mean that we are given (1) *that* the form of sentence S *is* the form of, say, an identity statement? If so, then we are not given *which* subsentential name in S refers to the identity relation or *which* subsentential names in S are the logical subject names. Even if S is "$a = b$," we have no right to assume that the subsentential expressions are what they usually are. How can we derive references and senses for subsentential names if we do not even know how to parse a sentence into names, that is, if we do not know which physical portions of the sentence to count as names? We would be lost before we started. We have only a list of complete sentences of the object language to work with, and not a list of subsentential names. Or does he mean that (2) we are given (1) *plus* which portion of an identity statement to count as the name referring to the identity relation and which portions to count as the logical subject names?

It might seem that Dummett has option (1) in mind, since he continues, "that is, to have one or other truth-value as its *Bedeutung*," which would not give us any clue as to how to parse sentence S into names. And he further continues, "but it cannot fix the *Bedeutung* of any term by specifying that it is to be any other object namable in the metalanguage." This seems to rule out option (2) expressly. But if so, it is puzzlingly worded. For the *Bedeutung* of the term for identity is not an object but a relation. In fact, every sentence must have at least one term, namely its logical predicate, whose *Bedeutung* cannot be an object. Surely Dummett's program aims to derive references and senses for all primitive names, not just for primitive object names.

On option (2), Dummett would be illicitly appealing to our prior understanding of the term for identity. That term is not only subsentential but primitive, and he has ruled out our prior understanding of precisely such terms as "to take as understood what the theory should be explaining." But if he does take option (2), his motive is obvious. As Dummett knows, grasping "statements of identity" is key to specifying the reference of a subsentential expression (1995, 17). We cannot know which two terms in an identity statement are the co-referential ones, i.e., the logical subject names, unless we also know which term is the identity name. And the name for identity is one of the primitive names the reference of which Dummett's program is trying to derive. The whole point of the program is to show how to derive references "and thereby" senses for all primitive names from truth-conditions alone.

Frege admits eight primitive logical names, including that of identity, in *Grundgesetze* vol. 1, §31. There Frege proves that all eight primitive logical names refer. But how do we come to grasp their senses? Does Frege state any procedure for deriving or grasping their senses in §32? That is, do we look to statements in which primitive names occur, treat the thoughts the statements express as the thoughts that the statements' truth-conditions are fulfilled, then logically derive the references of the primitive names, and then identify the senses of the primitive names as the contributions those names make to the expression of this thought? Do we, perhaps, look to the truth-conditions for identity statements *about* identity[3] and the other primitive logical entities in order to determine which names refer to them and thereby the names' senses?

Absolutely not. That would be a magical procedure, like pulling a rabbit out of a hat. For Quinean problems of inscrutability of reference and indeterminacy of translation implicitly abound in Frege as early as 1884 in *Grundlagen* §22, where one card pack is also many cards, and as late as the permutation of red and green in "The Thought." Dummett says, "In *Grundgesetze*, Volume I, §10 . . . Frege uses a permutation argument to show that the *Bedeutungen* of value-range terms have not yet been fixed. This appears to imply that he had ceased to believe that questions of reference are internal to language" (1995, 13). Indeed, the card pack and duality of geometry permutation arguments in *Grundlagen* appear to imply that Frege did not believe that questions of reference are internal to language as early as 1884.[4] All this applies to purely logical names as well. Thus the sense and reference of the identity name must be assumed prior to any derivations of sense and reference for any other subsentential names —purely logical or otherwise—in the object language (Frege's formal notation) from the truth-conditions of statements in the object language. Otherwise we beg the question of the identity of identity. Similarly for all the other primitive logical names. I think Dummett knows this. And I think that is why he is smuggling in our prior knowledge of the references and senses of all eight of Frege's primitive logical names under the guise of their belonging to the logical form of statements. But their belonging to logical form scarcely hides their being subsentential names which express senses and refer to references. Elsewhere, Dummett says that the context principle "must apply to the logical constants as much as to other words" (2000, 252). Thus I think he must have option (2) in mind after all.

The second problem is that of referential inscrutability of nonlogical terms. Even on option (2), i.e., already fixing the senses and references of all eight primitive logical names in the object language, which eliminates the permutation problem for those eight names, and for all complex logical names defined in terms of them, the permutation problem remains for all nonlogical names, such as names of card packs and of figures subject to dual geometrical theorems. That is, we cannot transcendentally deduce the world of references from pure logic plus truth-conditions alone. For primitive logical names are not the only primitive names. And even within pure logic, as we just saw, Dummett admits that in *Grundgesetze*, Frege uses a permutation argument to show that value-range terms do not yet have references. And that is with the eight primitive logical names' already expressing their senses and referring to their references.

For Frege and Quine, having a referential apparatus ("logical form") alone, even including identity, is not enough to preclude systematic permutations. That is why Frege would require explications of some nonlogical terms, and why Quine requires references to rabbits in a home language. Quine says it is not the logical identity term, but sortal terms such as "rabbit," that do the real work of individuation (1981, 12; 1975, 91, 116). Surely Frege would agree, using sortal concepts such as *card pack*. I call this the permutation problem for references.

More deeply, the problem is this. The truth-conditions of identity statements cannot be understood unless we already understand (the identity conditions of) the objects they are about. These are so interdependent, they are distinct only in reason. This might seem to give Dummett's program at least a Pyrrhic victory. But Frege starts with explications of names as opposed to statements. Thus for Frege, Dummett's program presupposes what it purports to derive.

Third, senses have the same problem. Frege says, "the thought itself does not yet determine what is to be regarded as the subject" (1971d, 49; see 46 n.*). Thus, since "a thought can be split up in many ways," so that many things can appear as the subject (1971d, 49; see 46 n.*), there is a permutation problem even for the *senses* of logical subject names. I call this the permutation problem for senses, or the problem of sensial inscrutability.

The fourth problem is that as Dummett says, "according to Frege, the sense of an expression determines its reference" (1981, 266). He even says that "sense determines reference but not conversely" (1981, 274). This is the forward road from sense to reference. But on Dummett's program, reference determines sense. This is a problem of circularity.

The fifth problem is that the senses of the primitive logical names are underdetermined by their references. Thus even if Dummett's program magically succeeded in deriving the references of all subsentential names from the truth-conditions, each reference can be presented in indefinitely many ways. Even the identity relation can be presented to us in many ways. Thus it is magical to suppose that we can derive intensional senses from truth-conditions, which consist of extensional references, even if we assign truth-conditions to all statements in the object language. I call this the problem of sensial underdetermination.[5]

Whitehead and Russell distinguish four classic senses of the word "intension." (1) There are propositional functions that are not truth-functional, e.g., "*A* believes that *p*" (1950, 8; see 187 for a derivative sense of "intensional proposition"). (2) There are propositional functions that lack extensional identities—"the same class of objects will have many determining functions" (1950, 23). Such functions are called formally equivalent (1950, 21, 72–73). We may say more generally that different ways of presenting a thing are intensional in this sense. (3) There are intensional functions in the sense that their values need not be specified for them to be specified (1950, 39–40). This sense is inimical to intuitionism. (4) Where extensional classes ("extensions") are identical just in case their members are identical (1950, *20.31, *20.43), by implication a class is intensional if it is not extensional. (Whitehead and Russell use only extensional classes.)

There are four corresponding senses of "extension." For Frege, senses (2) and (4) are logically tied. That is because for him, all functions are extensional in sense (2) and all classes are extensional in sense (4). Functions correspond one-one with their courses-of-values, where a course-of-values is the class of ordered pairs of arguments and values mapped by the function. For a function and its course-of-values represent each other via the representation function. The representation function is formally well-defined as mutual and is therefore one-one (Frege 1964, 92–94). We may say that functions which have the same course-of-values are representatively identical. Representatively identical functions are not different functions, though due to the "peculiarity" of predicative language we cannot directly say so (Frege 1971d, 46). Since functions are incomplete, they cannot directly stand in the identity relation. A function cannot even be directly said to be identical with itself. For "in view of its predicative nature, it must first be . . . represented by an object" (Frege 1971d, 46). It is the representing object that stands in the identity relation. We representatively say that functions are identical when we say that their representing objects are identical. Since mutual representation would be impossible if there were not a one-one correspondence between functions and their courses-of-values, the representative identity conditions of functions are exactly as sharp as the identity conditions of the objects that represent them. That this one-one correspondence obtains is the famous extensionality thesis (Furth 1964, xl–xliv), whose name we may honor by saying that for Frege, functions are always extensional in sense (2). A function is definable as any equivalent function (Frege 1971c, 80). Functions are equivalent if and only if their courses-of-values are identical (Frege 1964, 43–44). Thus equivalence is the relation of representative identity. The equivalence relation and the identity relation represent each other, as do their respective relata. But the identity relation itself is indefinable, for a technical reason: since a definition is a stipulated identity, all definitions presuppose identity (Frege, 1971c, 80–81). More precisely, a definition of a function is a stipulated representative identity.

When Dummett contrasts intensionality with truth-functionality, he has sense (1) implicitly in mind. When he discusses senses as different ways of presenting one object, he has sense (2) implicitly in mind. And when he discusses our inability to traverse infinitely many objects which might fall under a concept, he has sense (3) implicitly in mind. But I cannot recall that he ever expressly distinguishes these three *Principia* senses of "intension." I doubt even more that he distinguishes the corresponding three *Principia* senses of "extension." In his Frege books, he introduces a single notion of extension in terms of both truth-functionality and opacity, blurring senses (1) and (2). The slip from sense (1) to sense (2) is subtle:

> . . . *are* . . . *extensional: that is,* provided that the truth-value of a complex sentence depends only on the truth-values of the constituents. . . . What happens, then, in a case in which a method of sentence-formation is used which is *not extensional, that is,* when a sentence is formed which contains an opaque context? (Dummett 1981, 189–90, emphasis mine; see 1981a, 155)

But he does clearly identify intension in sense (2) in discussing intuitionism (2000, 16–17).

For Frege, all sentential contexts, even opaque contexts, are extensional in sense (1). To preserve truth-functionality in opaque contexts, Frege introduces a systematic reference shift from customary references to senses. Thus senses are extensional in sense (1). But senses are intensional in sense (2). That is the whole point of Frege's explanation of informative identity statements. Namely, different names expressing different senses can refer to the same reference.

All senses are intensional in sense (2), while all customary, i.e., direct, references are extensional in sense (2). For any customary reference, there are indefinitely many senses containing modes of presentation of that reference. Insofar as a reference is informatively identifiable indefinitely many times, there are indefinitely many senses through which it can be identified. Thus in general, the relation of a reference to the senses which are ways of identifying it is one-many. Thus it is magical to suppose that starting from any given set of references, i.e., objects and functions, we can work back so as to determine any one sense in particular as the sense expressed by a name of any one of those references in a given sentence.

The same goes for truth-conditions. For a truth-condition consists of extensional in sense (2) references. It is the extensional in sense (2) references of the subsentential names, in some extensional in sense (2) order, which make a customary statement true or false.

We must not beg the question by using descriptions of truth-conditions to identify them prior to the promised derivation of subsentential references and thereby subsentential senses from them. For such descriptions are intensional in sense (2), while the truth-conditions themselves are extensional in sense (2). Truth-conditions do not contain modes of presentation of truth-values. Thoughts do. Truth-conditions are not intensional in sense (2) because they are not ways of presenting or identifying anything. They are presented or identified in different ways by thoughts. I think Dummett would agree with this (1981, 5, 634, 642; 1981a, 252–53).

The sixth problem is that Dummett's program discusses only Frege's semantic stage of stipulative regimentation, and entirely ignores Frege's initial semantic stage of explication.

How can we convey the senses of primitive names? Is it by stipulation, as I quoted Dummett as saying? No. Stipulation has all the advantage of theft over honest explicative toil, as Russell might say. For Frege, stipulations cannot be made for primitive names except in the sense of stipulated regimentations of reference to ensure logical determinacy. Regimentations can be highly artificial. But if a regimentation of a primitive name which already has a sense is intuitively correct—notably, regimenting the identity name so that an object is truly said to be identical with itself but not identical with anything else (*Grundgesetze* vol. 1, §7)—Frege calls it an *analysis* (1979f, 210). Frege's only other stipulations are his definitions. For Frege, all definitions are stipulations which fix sense and reference for the defined names (*Grundgesetze* vol. 1, §27; 1979f, 207–8, 210, 211), and as stipulations, they are neither true nor false (1980c, 36; 1971f, 24; 1971e, 50–51). Of course, explications are not true or false either. But there is an important sense in which stipulations logically cannot fail, and are thus scientifically certain. Namely, they are stipulations! This is very different from explications.

Frege's view in *Grundgesetze* is that we cannot figure out subsentential references unless we already grasp as primitive the apparatus of identity and quantification, much as in Quine, and also negation, material implication, and some other functions. In particular, Frege's stipulation of logical determinacy for the identity relation in vol. 1, §7 is not a definition, since Frege lists "$\xi = \zeta$" as a primitive name in vol. 1, §31, and argues elsewhere that identity is indefinable because every definition is an identity (1971c, 80). Thus §7 can only be a regimentation of identity merely to ensure its logical determinacy. Frege says he has been talking about identity all along, i.e., prior to its regimentation (*Grundgesetze* vol. 1, §7; compare 1979f, 210).

Some terms need less regimentation than others, since some explications are more determinate than others to begin with. It is a short jump from the ordinary sense of "gleich" to the regimented sense of the formal identity sign. The case is the same for negation. But notoriously, truth-functional "or" is a big regimentation. And the horizontal stroke is a big regimentation that prevents any well-formed sentence from lacking a truth-value for categorial reasons. For example, "5 is pink" is arguably an indeterminate statement, but prefixing the horizontal stroke imposes falsehood on it.

For Frege, explications (*Erläuterungen*) are not stipulative definitions, or even stipulated regimentations. Explications are hints. Frege says right in *Grundgesetze* vol. 1, §0 (last para.) that he must indicate what he intends by his primitive names by "hints," since not everything can be defined. For Frege, communication *always* begins with hints, metaphors, or suggestions, and thus with an element of uncertainty.[6] Thus explications logically can fail. This is essentially different from regimentations and definitions. This is why Frege requires explications to occur in a propaedeutic, while definitions, and perhaps also regimentations, occur within the scientific notation. Before we can start a formal notation at all, "we must be able to count on a meeting of minds."[7] Thus explications are always prior to the object language. Thus Dummett is wrong when he says Frege "was setting out what [the formal notation's] formulas were to mean . . . not . . . from without but from within" (1995, 16). This is true of definition and perhaps of regimentation, but not of the key stage of explication. In fact, the meeting of minds is precisely what leads Frege to require extralinguistic, extramental objective entities, so that the minds have something they can agree or disagree about in his private language arguments, though of course those arguments are scarcely limited to cases of explication.

I suspect that regimentation occurs outside the object language as well. For regimentation is a process, and only its end results, primitive names which are "proved" to have references, are permitted into the formal notation. And unlike definition, Frege has no sign for regimentation in the formal notation, no way of indicating within the notation that he is regimenting anything. On the other hand, regimentations have the same stipulative certainty as definitions, and can occur in the formal notation as safely as definitions do. But it does not matter for us here, since either way Dummett's program omits the whole stage of explication.

Some explications must be not only prescientific but prelinguistic, on pain of vicious regress of metalanguages (compare Dummett 1981, 231). At least some hints, if not metaphors or verbal suggestions, must be prior to language altogether for first-time language learners. The very first hinter and hintee are both outside language until their minds meet. Thus not every propaedeutic can be a metalanguage. We all start language as outsiders, *pace* Dummett (1995, 16; see 10–11). There are no born insiders. Insiders and outsiders alike must *ultimately* start teaching or learning a language by explications from outside the language. Adults often use a metalanguage to learn a new language by translation, but for Frege they must always start from prelinguistic explications at some point. They can even follow the path of children, starting as outsiders by taking a course of prelinguistic explications directly of the language they wish to learn.[8]

For Frege, references are conveyed only via senses. Frege says "it is *via* a sense, and only *via* a sense that a proper name is related to an object" (1979c, 124). Thus explications convey references only via senses. Thus every explication is first and foremost an explication of a sense.

Frege says that the regimentation process in §31 "also" fixes senses:

> Not only a denotation [i.e. reference], but also a sense appertains to all names correctly formed from our signs. Every such name of a truth-value *expresses* a sense, a *thought*. Namely, by our stipulations it is determined under what conditions the name denotes the True. The sense of this name—the thought—is the thought that these conditions are fulfilled. (*Grundgesetze* vol. 1, §32)

This is the text Dummett bases his program on. But Frege says references and *also* senses, not references and *thereby* senses. That fits his primary focus on proving references for the names. And we cannot stipulate (regiment) any primitive names until we first explicate them, on pain of there being nothing to regiment. And every explication is first and foremost a conveyance of a sense. Thus there is no transcendental deduction of senses from references in the regimentation process. It is merely unregimented senses in, regimented senses out, not magical, but sensible. There is no reversal of Frege's thesis that references are conveyed only via senses. When compounded into thoughts, the explicated senses present the truth-conditions, not the other way around. Regimentation merely ensures their logical determinacy.

Thus the order of logical priority for Frege is: (1) explications of the senses and thereby the references of the primitive names; then (2) regimentations of the senses and thereby the references of the primitive names into logical determinacy, "proving" that they have references, and regimenting thoughts and thereby truth-conditions in the process, thus satisfying the context principle for senses and thereby for references; then (3) definitions of any defined names. §32 implies no backward procedure for identifying senses given the truth-conditions of statements. On its face, it is merely a general statement of what senses essentially do and thereby are.

Dummett seems to think Frege's regimentation of primitive names fixes truth-conditions first, then subsentential references and thereby sub-sentential senses. This is backwards. He might as well say Frege's thesis is that senses are conveyed only via references. But if we regiment unexplicated blank names, we obtain blank truth-conditions. *Ex nihilo, nihil fit.* We really need that first stage of explication!

Frege's context principle can never be interpreted so strongly as to destroy Frege's theory of language as beginning with explication. And it would make a mockery of explication as the start of language learning to suggest that it must be done in accordance with an already assumed list of the truth-conditions for any sentences. I do not see how we could have even the concept of a truth-condition, much less the concept of a stipulation, prior to the use of explication to get language started by conveying some undefined senses and thereby some undefined references. In the lexicon of Wittgenstein, explication is Frege's rock bottom. It is what we do to start language at all. Dummett discusses explication elsewhere, but his program ignores it completely.

We can, of course, explicate a name in the metalanguage, e.g., "gleich," and then stipulate that a certain sign in the object language—say "="—is to express the same sense as the explicated metalinguistic name. Perhaps that is what Dummett has in mind. But this only postpones the problem to the metalanguage. On pain of vicious regress of metalanguages, some names for Frege's eight primitive references must be explicated before we can stipulate that any names in the object language refer to those references. Thus even if Dummett wins the battle on the object language, he loses the war on language in general.

The seventh problem is that since references are conveyed only via senses, regimentation regiments references only via senses. Thus regimentation is first and foremost regimentation of senses (compare Dummett 1981, 626). And for Frege, everything is regimented at once. This resolves the problem of double *oratio obliqua* (in ordinary language, the *obliqua* chips fall where they may). Since all opaque contexts and all senses, however indirect, are regimented at once, it is always determinate which sense is expressed in which context. But if we start with blank terms, each will take in all other's washing.

Definitions stipulate references only via senses, but Dummett's program rightly does not concern them. For Frege, definitions are never needed to say what we want to say. They merely abbreviate.

3. DOES THE PROGRAM WORK?

Dummett never attempts an example of how his program works. I have already argued that it does not work even if we pump it up with advance knowledge of which portions of sentences to count as subsentential names, and of the senses and references of all primitive logical names, in the object language. But an example may help.

Suppose the vocabulary of object language L is already given as four blank object names, "a," "b," "c," and "d," one blank concept-name, "$F(\ )$," "blank" meaning without their senses or references, plus Frege's eight primitive logical names with their senses and references. We are then told the truth-conditions of all atomic sentences of L. That can be done only via thoughts, but we can then disregard the thoughts in a sleight of hand in place of the magical start the program demands. Now, if we knew which objects in the world were a, b, c, and d, and that they were the only four objects in the world, and (3) that only a, b, and c fall under the concept F, then there would be no permutation problems for the object names (e.g., cards or decks), and we could enumeratively define "$F(\ )$" as referring to the function that maps the arguments a, b, and c, but not d onto the True. But we are not entitled to know these things on Dummett's program. Knowing them would amount to knowing the truth-values of the sentences, and we were only supposed to know their truth-conditions.

But let us pretend that we magically succeeded in defining the reference of "$F(\ )$" in the enumerative manner suggested. Can we thereby derive the sense expressed by "$F(\ )$" as the same as that expressed by "$(\ )$ falls under the purely extensional in sense (2) mapping-function which maps the arguments a, b, and c, but not d onto the value the True"? I cannot think of what else Dummett might have in mind. But the reference of "$F(\ )$" can be presented in indefinitely many ways, for example, as the reference now under discussion. Thus there can be indefinitely many object languages L_1 ... L_n that agree on the reference but differ on the sense of "$F(\ )$."

Suppose that all and only a, b, and c are red and round. How can we tell whether speakers of L are using "$F(\ )$" to express the sense '$(\ )$ is red', '$(\ )$ is round', '$(\ )$ is red and round', or '$(\ )$ is red or round'? Or in a world in which all and only red objects are round, and in which infinitely many objects are red, so that $F(\ )$ must be intensional in sense (3), how can we identify the sense expressed by "$F(\ )$"? By hypothesis, the only senses "$F(\ )$" could possibly express for us are: '$(\ )$ is red', '$(\ )$ is round', '$(\ )$ is red and round', or '$(\ )$ is red or round'. Which sense is it? How can we identify which sense it is without already grasping the senses expressed by "red" or "round"? Since a is an object and concept F is merely a mapping function, the truth-condition, Fa, is purely extensional in sense (2), and leaves us clueless as to which sense is expressed by "Fa." What kind of ideal language is it in which we cannot even distinguish colors from shapes?[9]

Is L perhaps too small? It seems large enough to refute Dummett's program. And we can always add more names.

Appealing to "All red things have color" or "All round things have shape" will not do. Where all and only red things are round, these two statements have the same extensional in sense (2) truth-condition. We cannot even say "Red is a color" in Frege's notation. The closest we can come is "If anything is red, then it has a color." And L has only one nonlogical predicate! But it would not help even if we could say it, since there would be a Quinean compensatory adjustment of "color" and "shape" as well.

Are not the concepts *red* and *round* differently principled and therefore different mapping functions? The premise is true but the conclusion does not follow. They are differently principled by the senses expressed by "red" and "round." More precisely, incomplete senses contain modes of presentation which are the mapping principles of functions.

Dummett's program fails even if we provide truth-conditions for all possible sentences of L as used to describe all possible truth conditions. Even if such a procedure were correct in principle, it would be unworkable in practice. No human can learn that "is red" expresses the sense of a color by working through all possible sentences of English as used to describe all possible truth conditions. Dummett would be the first to tell us that we cannot even work through all actually used sentences of English, but must be able to use only a finite fragment of a language to learn senses and references. Yet his view implies just the opposite:

> Suppose, then, that we have two sentences which are analytically equivalent, but have different senses. Since they have different senses, they must, on a view of Frege's kind, have different truth-conditions. Since they are analytically equivalent, the world cannot be so constituted that one is true and the other false: the set of possible worlds in which the one is true is the very same set as that of those in which the other is true. How can there be room for Frege to distinguish the truth-conditions of the one from those of the other? (1981, 588)

Here Dummett adduces a nonexistent problem from a strange view of Frege's truth-conditions. If Dummett thinks that difference in sense implies difference in truth-conditions, then perhaps that is why he thinks his program will work! For then sameness of truth-condition implies sameness of sense, which is the backward road. The implication is really that truth-conditions are as intensional in sense (2) as senses are. But does that make any sense? Do not truth-conditions consist of references? Are then all customary references intensional in sense (2)? Or can we truth-functionally compose intensional in sense (2) truth-conditions out of extensional in sense (2) customary references? Or perhaps the implication is that senses are as *extensional* in sense (2) as truth-conditions are!

One might suggest that all analytic truths have the same truth-condition, for example, "2 + 2 = 4" and "$(x)(x = x)$." Is that not so? Their truth-condition is true under any condition! Would not Frege agree (1979d, 187–88; 1979f, 208 on $x = x$)? *Pace* Dummett (1995, 12), Frege adopts a theory of logical necessity as purely general truth, i.e., as invariance of interpretation, and holds it for at least twenty-seven years, from 1879 *Begriffsschrift*, §4 to 1906 "Introduction to Logic" (1979d, 187, 188, 189). Frege even uses the word "vary" twice (1979d, 187, 188).[10]

On this suggestion, if Frege really makes logical equivalence the criterion for the identity of thoughts (1971d, 46 n.*), *contra* Dummett's view the test is their *given* identity (1981, 632)—Dummett's test contradicts the last two sentences of Frege's note n.*—this would provide only limited help to Dummett's program. Yes, all logical truths would then slice up the same thought and slice up the same truth-condition, true under any condition. Then in a formal notation consisting only of logical truths, we could always derive one and the same thought from one and the same truth-condition, no matter what the logical truth. The case is the same for logical falsehoods, and for all sets of statements which are true in exactly the same possible worlds. But the problems of referential and sensial inscrutability of subsentential names would remain. And Frege rejects possible worlds. For him, there is no such thing as a merely possible object, *Grundgesetze* (1971a, 222). As Dummett puts it perfectly, Frege's intended model is the actual world (1995, 12 n.5). And in the actual world there are clearly many pairs of logically nonequivalent predicates expressing different senses yet referring to the same extensional in sense (2) mapping function. Our world of four objects logically could be the actual world. Thus even if logical equivalence were Frege's criterion for the identity of thoughts, the problem of sensial underdetermination would remain for indefinitely many logically contingent statements in an ideal scientific language (compare Dummett 1981, 228, 636).

But I reject the suggestion and I accept Dummett's view that sensial identity is given. Perhaps all analytic truths have the same *general* truth-condition, true under any condition. But even if necessary truth is the same as purely general truth for Frege, the *specific* or *proper* truth-conditions of "2 + 2 = 4" and "$(x)(x = x)$" are different, consisting of different specific functions and objects in different specific relationships. Strictly, even "2 + 2 = 4" and "4 − 2 = 2" have different truth-conditions and express different thoughts. As to sensial identity, Frege's plea that we must allow transformations of the same thought in logical inference can be substantially preserved by glossing transformations as changes to new thoughts which are substantially the same and differ only holistically in their slicing. But on pain of vicious cognitive regress, it is essential that all senses *logically can* be directly given, no matter how indirect the sense. Dummett is absolutely right that given sensial identity is fundamental and trumps transformations (1981, 631–37). But then even sameness of truth-condition does not imply sameness of sense, since Frege's specific truth-conditions are extensional in sense (2), exactly like the customary references they consist of, while his given senses are intensional in sense (2). This is why Frege would reject even a definition of a predicate's intension as the class of all possible objects satisfying it (compare C. I. Lewis). For on that definition, the senses of " = (1 + 1)" and " = (4 − 2)" are the same.

The actual world is only the actual set of *compossible* truth-conditions. But even if we knew all possible truth-conditions as composed of all possible customary references in all possible worlds, why assume that the problem of sensial underdetermination would somehow magically vanish? Even if to give all possible customary references is to give all their possible modes of presentation via each other (I waive the possibility of presentations of customary references via their relationships to names, senses, forces, tones, and ideas), where is the one-one correlation between all possible customary references and all possible customary senses?

Even assigning all the truth-*values* of all possible sentences of L would leave us clueless, since truth-values are extensional in sense (2), just as truth-conditions are, and there is no backward road. For example, add all the truth-values of all the atomic sentences to my example. Namely, "*Fa*," "*Fb*," and "*Fc*" refer to the True and "*Fd*" refers to the False. How could that help? We simply cannot squeeze any intensions in sense (2) out of extensions in sense (2), even if we include all truth-value assignments as well as all truth-conditions among the extensions. There is always sensial underdetermination. This intimates the consequences for intuitionism.

We must distinguish the truth-condition of a statement from a statement of the truth-condition. The former is extensional in sense (2). The latter is intensional in sense (2), even if it describes a definitional enumeration of a mere set by its members. And it expresses a thought whose component senses, intensional in sense (2), refer to the extensional in sense (2) references which compose the extensional in sense (2) truth-condition (compare Dummett 1981a, 80). This might be called a logically indirect relationship in virtue of the mediating roles of the component senses and component references. Frege's semantic schema is not truth-describes-fact, but function-maps-value-onto-argument(s).[11] An extensional in sense (2) truth-condition is just that a certain concept does map its argument(s) onto the True as asserted. But even the previous sentence expresses an intensional thought in sense (2). And although that thought reflects or mirrors the essence of concepts (my 2003, xix, 31, 217, 272, 301), it is only one way of many to present the truth-condition in question. Thus there is no backward road from the truth-condition to it.

Certainly we do not understand the thoughts expressed by statements if we have no idea of the conditions which would make them true or false. But those very thoughts of the truth-conditions are intensional in sense (2), and the truth-conditions are graspable only via such thoughts. Indeed, the thought we grasp *is* the "idea" we have of the truth-condition.

One might be tempted to say that where "$F(\ )$" expresses the sense '( ) is red', the truth condition of "*Fa*" is *a*'s being red. That is what most of us would say. But can Frege say it? Our world of four objects shows that for Frege, the ontological locus of objective redness as opposed to objective roundness is the realm of sense. And as this is a categorial matter this is so in every possible world. Is the ontological locus of the truth-condition of "*Fa*" then the realm of sense? Is it senses, not references, which make our sentences true? Except for cases of indirect reference, no.[12]

If we enrich L so as to include sentences expressing propositional attitudes, then thoughts would be logical parts of the truth-conditions of L, since thoughts are the indirect references of such sentences for Frege. And while only thoughts can be believed, and subsentential senses cannot be believed, presumably the subsentential senses composing believed thoughts must also be indirect references by parity of reason. But Dummett's program would still fail for infinitely many languages L* which lack such sentences, and he gives no indication that he is thinking of this limited way out. And there is no backward road to the indirect senses which occur in cases of indirect reference. We would have to include sentences expressing second-order beliefs about beliefs so as to make first-order indirect senses into second-order indirect references, and so on for any n-level order of beliefs. Thus we would have to admit an infinite series of orders of indirect sense and reference. I think Frege allows and requires that (Dummett agrees, 1981a, 87).[13] But Dummett's program would fail for infinitely many more languages L**, which lack various higher orders of propositional attitudes, and again, Dummett gives no indication that he is thinking of this limited way out.

That senses are truth-functional, i.e., extensional in sense (1), does not make a backward road possible. To the contrary, it is precisely because senses are truth-functional that the problem of permuting the obviously different senses expressed by "red( )" and "round( )" arises *within* the confines of truth-functionality. For Frege, the problem of opacity arises, and can be solved by a reference shift in opaque contexts, *because* things are presented in different ways. That things are presented in different ways is not a problem but the pre-philosophical truth grounding the sense-reference distinction, implying the "no backward road" thesis as its *alter ego*, and underlying both the problem of opacity and Frege's solution. This is why senses (1) and (2) of "extensional" must not be blurred. It is also why Dummett's emendation of accepting Frege's shift of reference from customary reference to customary sense (indirect reference) in opaque contexts, but omitting Frege's shift of sense from customary sense to indirect sense, logically concerns only the problem of *oratio obliqua*, and is too shallow to touch the general "problem" of no backward road, *pace* Dummett (1981a, 87). For things are presented to us in different ways even if our language has no opaque contexts.

Of course, Dummett could insist on his interpretation and say the problems are Frege's. But my interpretation avoids the problems. Frege can easily construct L by explicating his eight primitive logical names, explicating "*a*," "*b*," "*c*," and "*d*" as primitive names of concrete objects, and by either explicating "*F*( )" as expressing a primitive sense, say, that of "red," or defining "*F*( )" as expressing a complex sense, say, that of "red and round," or defining "*F*( )" extensionally as the concept under which *a*, *b*, and *c*, but not *d*, fall. On any of these options we ensure the determinacy of all names by ensuring that every statement in which they occur has a determinate truth-value. Since we introduced only names which can occur in sentences, and since we ensured that all statements of L have a determinate truth-value, the context principle is satisfied for senses and references alike. The only thing that even appears to resemble Dummett's program is the option—I say again, *option*—of defining "*F*( )" extensionally. But even this would be impossible unless the senses of the object names were explicated first.

How could a language come into being at all? Could it be by our first collecting the truth-conditions for all or some of the statements and grasping the two truth-values, and then deriving the references and thereby the senses expressed by subsentential expressions?

I think Frege would hold that children learn the senses of subsentential expressions of their language not by being handed two truth-values plus the bundle of truth-conditions for all or some sentences of that language and being told to go figure out all the subsentential references and thereby the subsentential senses (they would not even understand what they were handed, much less the instruction), but by being given prelinguistic explications of names of perceived objects, followed by a process of comparing those objects and abstracting imperceptible concept-senses and concepts.[14] And sense-perception is intensional in sense (2). Of course, the children would not use these senses *as* linguistic senses at first, and in that functional sense, these senses would not yet *be* linguistic senses, i.e., they would not yet be expressed by any names. They would still be mere modes of cognitive presentation, and would become linguistic senses containing modes of presentation only when used in language according to the context principle. I think that is the essential role of the principle, and the difference Frege is concerned to distinguish is between a sense and the mode of presentation it contains, *pace* Dummett (1981, 227).[15]

The problems with Dummett's program seem so obvious and so many that it is natural to wonder if I understood it correctly. In particular, I am criticizing what might be called the pure, ideal, or radical backward road, and insisting that Dummett adhere rigorously to it. But Dummett does not take the pure backward road. He says we are to take that road only "as far as possible" (1995, 16). He assumes knowledge of the truth-values. I concede that this objection is a fair one. Pure or ideal theories often have problems which more subtle "compromise" programs avoid. Nonetheless, I am criticizing what is surely Dummett's ideal theory, which he is trying to approach as best as he thinks we logically can. And criticizing ideal theories can be illuminating of radical problems.

4. THE BACKWARD ROAD

Russell says "there is no backward road" from reference to sense (1971, 50). There has been no consensus on exactly what Russell's main argument against a meaning-denotation distinction is.[16] Only its conclusion is clear: generally speaking, whenever we try to refer to a sense, we succeed only in referring to a reference.[17] But the "no backward road" closure clause Russell adds at the end of the argument is also clear. Dummett beautifully states what I call Russell's explicit "no backward road" thesis as having two conjuncts: "Russell points out that, on Frege's own principles, 'there is no backward road' from reference to sense: sense determines reference, but reference does not determine sense" (1981, 267; see 159). But surely Russell is implicitly raising a many-one problem in his "no backward road" thesis. Namely, the backward road requires a one-one reference-sense correspondence; but there are many ways a reference can be given. That seems the most natural reason for his thesis. In fact, it is the only reason I can think of. Why else would he hold it? Indeed, he is well aware that Frege's many-one sense-reference correlation is precisely how Frege explains informative true identity statements (Russell 1971, 46). Thus I shall also call the thesis of sensial underdetermination Russell's implicit "no backward road" thesis.

Russell holds that propositional attitudes are essentially not truth-functional. And as we saw, Dummett treats truth-functionality as the key to understanding extensionality and opacity. Thus for Russell and Dummett, the thesis of sensial underdetermination concerns intensions in both senses (1) and (2). But for Frege, the thesis of sensial underdetermination concerns only intensions in sense (2), since he rejects intensions in sense (1) when he makes senses truth-functional.

Dummett also beautifully states what I call Russell's implicit "no backward road" thesis: "Since different senses may correspond to the same reference, the reference of an expression does not determine its sense" (1981a, 245). Perhaps due to his preoccupation with double *oratio obliqua*, he does not recognize this as being Russell's implicit "no backward road" thesis, much less as being his own acceptance of that thesis. The thesis implies the second conjunct of Russell's explicit "no backward road" thesis as Dummett states it, which conjunct in turn implies double *oratio obliqua*. In fact, the implicit thesis is a logically necessary and sufficient condition of the second conjunct of the explicit thesis. But I think the order of ontological priority is this: Different senses correspond to any given reference. Therefore no reference determines any one sense as being or containing the way that reference is given. Therefore the reference of an expression does not determine its sense. And that fact explains the phenomena of *oratio obliqua* and double *oratio obliqua* for Frege, but it does not imply those explanations, since other explanations are available, such as Russell's theory of descriptions. Thus Dummett's emendation does not imply the denial of any of the "no backward road" theses. Things are presented in different ways even if our language has no opaque contexts at all.

If I am wrong about Russell, it remains the case that we cannot work backward from references to senses because of the sensial underdetermination problem. Thus we need not enter the murky waters of "On Denoting" in order to see why Dummett's mistake is genuine.

I think Frege would agree that there is no backward road for this very reason. Frege says that a sense "serves to illuminate only a single aspect of the reference," and that we cannot achieve "[c]omprehensive knowledge of the reference" unless we can already "say . . . whether any given sense belongs to it" (1971i, 58). Nor can we pick out an aspect, i.e., property, i.e., concept under which the reference falls, except via a sense.

In *Frege: Philosophy of Language*, Dummett admits Russell is right that there is no backward road in Frege (1981, 267–68). Nonetheless, he offers the following argument against Russell's explicit "no backward road" thesis, and by implication the implicit thesis as well:

> The sense of an expression is the mode of presentation of the referent: in saying what the referent is, we have to choose a particular way of saying this, a particular means of determining something as the referent. In a case in which we are concerned to convey, or stipulate, the sense of the expression, we shall choose that means of stating what the reference is which displays the sense: we might here borrow a famous pair of terms from the *Tractatus*, and say that, for Frege, we say what the referent of a word is, and thereby show what its sense is. (This is the correct answer to Russell's objection in 'On Denoting' to Frege's theory, considered generally, rather than apropos of oblique reference, that there is 'no backward road' from reference to sense.) (1981, 227)

I call this *the forced choice argument*. Dummett is arguing as follows. A reference must be given in some way. And a sense is a way of giving a reference (if any). Therefore we can fix a sense by simply choosing it as the way we choose to fix the reference (if any). Therefore we can fix a reference and thereby fix a sense. The implied conclusion is that this removes the sensial underdetermination problem with Dummett's program. The argument seems supported by Frege: "in saying something about the meaning [i.e., reference] of the sign '3 + 5', I express a sense" (Frege 1980b, 149). But the argument gets things backwards. Dummett might as well say that Frege introduces references to explain how we can identify senses.[18] That we talk about reference "only *via* a sense" (Frege 1979c, 124) does not support Dummett's argument. Quite the opposite. If a reference must be given in some way, so that fixing a sense for an expression is a necessary condition of fixing the reference (if any) of that expression, then the logical priority is that of fixing the sense over fixing the reference. And this is the forward road from sense to reference. I can convey a reference to you via a sense of my choice only if I have already singled out the reference via some sense. And you will grasp the reference via the sense I choose, not the sense I choose via the reference. I think the (1980b, 149) text merely indicates that senses are required in addition to references in order to explain informative identity statements.[19]

In *Frege: Philosophy of Language*, there is a passage that seems to anticipate, and even to call for, Dummett's program as a theoretical ideal explaining Frege's "whole theory of meaning," but finding the program too problematic to succeed (1981, 652–53). The forced choice argument seems to be what carries us from references to senses (1981, 653). If the forced choice argument is Frege's, there is no need for Dummett's emendation, since the argument implies a forced choice of all senses, including indirect senses. But be that as it may, the first problem for Dummett is that Frege "failed almost completely" to provide "an account of the other means that exist, besides definition, . . . for introducing expressions into the language" (Dummett 1981, 652–53). The answer is explication; there is also explanation. (Frege is indeed brief on these matters.) The second problem for Dummett seems to be that truth-conditions do not determine a "unique solution" of subsentential references (1981, 653). This is the permutation problem for references.

Dummett says, "The references of the component expressions constitute their respective contributions to the determination of its truth-value; and the sense of any one of them constitutes the particular way in which its reference is given to one who grasps the thought" (1991, 193). He takes this from *Grundgesetze* vol. 1, §32 almost word for word, and it is perfectly correct. But it is a vast jump from this point to the thesis that a sense can be *cognitively identified* via *cognitively identifying* the reference first. Not only is the jump a logical non sequitur, but the point is not even evidence for the thesis. If you choose to present a reference in a certain way, I must grasp your way first, then via that, your reference; and you must have grasped some way first as well. In fact, the second part of the quote states the *forward* road from senses to references.

Dummett says that "the systematic theory of *Bedeutung* provided a basis for explaining in what the *Sinn* of an expression should be taken to consist, namely the way in which its *Bedeutung* is given to a competent speaker of the language" (1995, 4–5). I agree, if this is merely the explanation of what senses are in terms of how they function. I believe that is the explanation behind the explanation in *Grundgesetze* vol. 1, §32. But Dummett's program makes it sound for all the world as if §32 implies that given the truth-conditions of L, references are *cognitively identified* (said) and senses then are *cognitively identified* derivatively (shown when references are said), or at least can be if we choose our senses right. This suggests that the following definition (not explanation) of senses is basic to Dummett's program:

> [In] the sense of expression "A" = Df the way in which the reference of "A" is given to a competent speaker of the language, or the way the reference of "A" would be given to such a speaker if "A" had a reference.

This takes the backward road. Senses are mentioned only in the definiendum, and references only in the definiens. Given the reference of "A" we can define the sense of "A." But there are two problems. First, there would be no primitive senses, since all senses would be defined. This is wrong because Frege holds that not every sense can be defined. That is precisely why Frege says that primitive names—including both the senses they express and the references they refer to—need explication. And second, since reference is given "only *via* a sense" (1979c, 124), the application of this definition in particular cases would always presuppose our grasping some sense, since the reference of "A" can only be given to us via some sense in the first place. And that is circular.

On the face of it, *Grundgesetze* vol. 1, §32 describes what senses essentially are in terms of how they function in relationship to references, but without trying to define sense in terms of reference, and without suggesting that senses can be derived from references. I think the circularity of the attempted definition of sense is the underlying reason why. Thus, to apply Frege's threefold distinction among definition (*Definition*), explanation (*Erklärung*), and explication (*Erläuterung*) (see my 2003, 73), §32 may only be understood as stating Frege's explanation (not definition) of what senses are. (An explanation states what a thing is, but without technically being a definition; Frege's sole explanation is of identity as indiscernibility.) And saying that senses are the ways references are given is the explanation underlying the explanation. Thus the difference between what Dummett seems to think §32 says and what §32 actually says is as little— and as great—as the difference between definition and explanation.

In *The Interpretation of Frege's Philosophy*, Dummett revisits his *Frege: Philosophy of Language* rejection of the "no backward road" argument. He admits there is "no backward road" in "Frege's unamended theory" (1981a, 95). He does not "attempt to examine the details of Russell's argument" (1981a, 131; see my 2003, 275–77 for the details). He is very clear on the conclusion of the argument: whenever we try to refer to a sense, we succeed only in referring to a reference (1981a, 131). But this is a red herring. The explicit "no backward road" thesis is not a premise of the argument or its conclusion, but a closure clause at the end of the argument. Yet if Dummett rejects it, he is committed to rejecting the argument as futile, since we can then backwardly single out senses after all.

Recalling the forced choice argument, Dummett says his saying-showing gloss is merely a "suggested . . . possible retort to Russell" (1981a, 131, citing 1981, 227). The retort is that even if Russell is right that we cannot refer to a sense, it may still be the case that when we "say" a reference, we thereby "show" the sense we choose to use. Again, Dummett might as well say that Frege introduces references in order to explain how we can identify senses. Surely the opposite is true: when we "say" or express a sense, we thereby "show" how to identify the reference (if any); compare Dummett (1981a, 132).

Dummett suggests that Russell's argument is more plausible if what he really has in mind is not objects of reference but objects of apprehension. Now, Russell does begin and end "On Denoting" with early statements of his distinction between knowledge by description and knowledge by acquaintance (1971, 41, 56). But Russell's argument against Frege concerns only denoting phrases, and knowledge by denoting phrases is precisely what Russell is distinguishing from acquaintance (1971, 56). Thus the suggestion is not what Russell has in mind. But it does reveal what Russell's argument is logically most deeply about. It is deeply perceptive of what the argument should have been, but was not. Whether we can single out senses at all is what Russell's argument is logically most deeply about, though Russell's focus is on denoting, in keeping with Russell's linguistic turn in "On Denoting." I would rewrite Russell's argument this way. Frege distinguishes his categories of references, senses, forces, and tones in terms of how the entities essentially function, so as to explain basic features of language. It is because modes of presentation do not function as objects of presentation that they, and thereby senses, cannot be customary references. The moment they are treated as objects of presentation, they are no longer functioning to present something else, and in that sense they *are* no longer modes of presentation (compare Dummett 1981a, 132). Thus whenever we try to single out a sense, we must single out an object instead. Frege would reply that we directly grasp only modes (or senses), but can grasp them only as modes (or senses). It is a subtle issue. My theory of qualified objects goes between the horns of the dilemma (2003, xxvi, 47, 61, 73).

Phenomenologists hold that an intentional act cannot be identified independently of the object of the act. If we equate such an act to a Fregean sense, and such an object to a Fregean object, this might seem to support the backward road. But a Fregean sense is not an act, and a Fregean object is not a phenomenal object, but an object in itself. For Frege, an act of judgment, query, or command cannot be identified independently of its *force* and its *sense*, and there may be no object to single out.

There are two orders of determination in Frege: the order of cognition, and the order of being.

The order of cognition or cognitive dependence is the order of what must be singled out first, in order for something else to be singled out. Namely, senses must be grasped first, and references can be grasped only via senses.

The order of being or ontological dependence is the order of what must be capable of existing first, in order for something else to have an ontological function or reason for being. Namely, customary references are the primary beings and comprise what we ordinarily consider the world, and senses function merely as modes of presentation. The reference determines what all its essential modes of presentation are and what its accidental modes of presentation can be. This is why the reference cannot backwardly determine any single mode as "the" mode of its presentation.

If we remain within the realm of senses alone, or within the realm of references alone, the two orders are the same, if we cognize independent or simple beings first. But when we consider senses and references together, so as to discuss their interrelationships, the two orders must go in opposite directions as just described. The paradox is trivial. It is precisely because senses ontologically function as mere modes of presentation that they are first in the order of cognition. Thus the order of cognition takes the forward road from senses to references, and the order of being takes the backward road from references to senses.

The explicit and the implicit "no backward road" theses assert the order of cognition. *Grundgesetze* vol. 1, §32 asserts the order of being, namely, that senses *are* nothing but ways of presenting references and thereby of helping present truth-conditions. But Dummett is treating §32 as if it belongs to the order of cognition, that is, as if it inverts Russell's "no backward road" thesis, which belongs to that order. I think this is why Dummett interprets §32 as implying and virtually saying there is a backward road. Indeed, there is a backward road implicit in §32, but it is not the backward road Russell is denying. It is in the order of being, and does not permit senses to be singled out, cognitively determined, or cognitively derived via references.

At least within the realm of senses, Dummett has it perfectly. He says that to reduce Frege to a slogan, "in the order of *explanation* the sense of a sentence is primary, but in the order of *recognition* the sense of a word is primary."[20] This beautifully states the order of being and the order of cognition respectively for that realm.

Again, I may have misunderstood Dummett's program. He sketches it very briefly, and the problems I am finding with it seem obvious. But the program as I quoted it seems quite clear, and my interpretation of it is supported by his rejection of the explicit "no backward road" thesis in his paper (1995, 14–15). If Dummett had the order of being in mind instead of the order of cognition as the *locus* of the backward road, then he should have said he was giving a "*general* explanation" of the semantics in which he is deriving the *general* notion of a sense from the *general* notion of a reference, and the *general* notion of a thought from the *general* notion of a truth-condition, per his 1981 (5). But instead he speaks of "*primitive* symbols [and] their *Bedeutungen* and . . . *Sinne*," as if we could derive the senses of *specific* names such as "red" from *specific* truth-conditions in the order of cognition.

Dummett's thesis that all senses are ways of identifying references, if conjoined with his thesis that all senses are identified by means of truth-conditions, which consist of references, creates a vicious circle in the order of cognition. But I think his interpretation conflates the orders of cognition and being.

The two orders form an ancient pattern. After we cognitively ascend from Plato's Cave to the Sun, we can look back to see the true place of the Cave in the order of being as participatively dependent on, but also as a distorted way of apprehending, the world of forms. On this deep ontological level, I do not see Frege as departing from tradition. This deepens my 2003 thesis.

Dummett's program appears to be an idealization of a more concrete interpretation Dummett has of Frege which I shall call "Dummett's project." I quoted Dummett's program from near the end of Dummett's 1995 paper. Dummett's project is stated by Dummett's 1995 paper as a whole, which I shall now briefly summarize in my own way.

In *Grundlagen*, a fundamental principle is always to separate the objective (mind-independent) from the subjective (mental). The admission of mind-independent entities is Frege's basic realism. Frege argues for it using a permutational private language argument (duality of geometry). Namely, we cannot communicate private ideas because they can be permuted across speakers. In *Grundlagen*, the objective world divides into objects and (if you please) functions. There they are *Inhalten* or contents, which the later Frege splits into senses and references. Thus contents are strictly neither senses nor references. But that is because they are both, only not yet differentiated. If we were to try to differentiate them, we would find fluctuations in Frege's talk of contents in *Grundlagen*. So to speak, sometimes he has references more in mind, sometimes senses. But the sense-reference distinction would in any case occur entirely on the objective side of the house in *Grundlagen*. The later Frege gives a general theory of sense and reference. This allows him to see a second problem of realism which is entirely on the objective side of the house. Namely, there might exist only senses, but no references. The existence of senses by themselves establishes basic realism (objectivism), since they are mind-independent entities. But the second problem of realism reveals a second core notion of realism: we are realists only if we hold the things we refer to are mind-independent, as opposed to the thoughts we express, however mind-independent our thoughts may be (compare Dummett 1981a, 133).

This raises a second problem of permutation, this time on the objective side of the house. To communicate, we must avoid permutations of senses and of references just as much as we must avoid permutations of ideas. (I believe Frege's solution is explication. Dummett believes Frege's solution is translation—basically the same as Quine's solution of translation into a home language, *pace* Dummett 1995, 16, n.8; both rely on identity.)

The context principle's role remains the same even as we shift from the first problem of realism to the second, i.e., from *Grundlagen* to *Grundgesetze*, from ideas to senses. Namely, whether objects are *Grundlagen* contents or *Grundgesetze* references, we have perceptual evidence of concrete objects, but not of abstract (noncausal) objects such as numbers. The ontological role of the context principle is to establish realism for abstract objects, even though its more general semantic role is to establish that (in some sense) all terms, concrete and abstract alike, have meaning (be it content, sense, or reference) only in the context of statements. In *Grundgesetze*, this devolves to the determinacy requirement: a name refers to a reference only if it conforms to the law of excluded middle, i.e., only if every statement in which it occurs has a determinate truth-value. Making names conform by specifying truth-conditions for the statements is what I call regimentation. So far, I think we both agree.

Dummett's project is to understand what Frege is specifically doing in *Grundgesetze*. We start with Frege's primitive terms, given as ostensibly referring names, and wish to explain how Frege thinks he proves they do in fact refer, thereby establishing realism of the second kind for abstract objects. So we already know which terms are ostensibly names of identity, negation, and so on. Following *Grundgesetze*, we limit the objects of concern to truth-values and courses-of-values (the Moon is an object in the preface). We must take truth-values as understood because Frege's proof procedure, regimentation, cannot be understood if we do not. Thus for objects, the only permutation problem of interest would be for courses-of-values. Here I think we are still in basic agreement.

If by "deriving" subsentential references from truth-conditions, Dummett merely means proving that ostensible names refer by ensuring that every statement in which they occur has a determinate truth-value, I agree this is Frege's project. Frege's principles of importance here are that every true or false sentence must have a denoting logical subject, and that every such statement can be sliced in different ways into a logical subject or subjects and a logical predicate. But I believe this does not amount to identifying which terms refer to which references. For we already know not only which marks are the ostensible names, but what their ostensible references are. And that is because they were explicated as expressing certain as-yet-unregimented senses prior to the regimentation. Dummett says the terms are translated, as from metalinguistic German "gleich" to the formal identity sign. This is fine if the explication of the sense is not swept under the rug. The explication would be of "gleich," whose sense we then transfer to the formal sign. Again, I doubt that regimentation ("derivation") of reference is internal to the formal language, but it does not matter much for me, since explication is ultimately language-external.

The problem of sensial underdetermination remains. Dummett writes as if he thinks *Grundgesetze* vol. 1, §32 states or implies the forced choice argument. But senses are *merely* regimented by regimentation. Senses are not proved, derived, or identified via proving the references of the primitive names through regimentation, because only senses can guide us on how to regiment references in the first place. This is just what the second problem of realism is: Given senses, are there references?

5. ARE SENSES OBJECTS OR FUNCTIONS?

The most direct way to derive senses from references would be to show that some senses *are* references. That would not only kill Russell's main argument that whenever we try to refer to senses we refer instead to references, but would make the explicit and the implicit "no backward road" theses pointless as well. Dummett's argument that senses are objects is simple and seemingly convincing. Namely, we can refer to a sense by a name such as "Fermat's Last Theorem," or by a definite description such as "the sense of expression 'A'" (1981, 226–27; see 190; 1981a, 132). But I think it does not follow that senses are objects. In fact, I think that "the sense of expression 'A'" does not refer to an object.

On its face, Frege's discussion in "On Concept and Object" of the

singular definite article as indicating reference to an object is a discussion
of references as opposed to senses (1971d, 46–47). He confines his first
mention of senses to a note (1971d, 46 n.*), introducing the sense-reference
distinction in the main text only after the discussion of objects and the
singular definite article (1971d, 47). He then uses that distinction to
explicate objects in terms of reference as opposed to sense in the same
paragraph (1971d, 48). His main discussion of senses is at the end of the
paper (1971d, 54–55). There is nothing here to show that "the sense of
expression 'A'" refers to an object. If anything, his opposition of reference
to sense suggests the opposite.

Let us turn to "On Sense and Reference." Frege says, "In order to speak
of the sense of an expression 'A' one may simply use the phrase 'the sense
of the expression "A"'" (1971i, 59). Now, this is the first sentence of the
second of two paragraphs discussing indirect sense and indirect reference
in reported speech (1971i, 58–59). I think this sentence is not an anomalous
break in the discussion of reported speech, that is, is not an odd shift of
topic to customary sense and customary reference. I think this sentence is
a continuous, not to say integral, part of the two-paragraph discussion of
indirect sense and indirect reference. In other words, I think this sentence
indicates an exception to Frege's rule that expressions beginning with the
singular definite article refer to objects. The exception is precisely for
reported speech, i.e., indirect quotation, which by definition refers to senses,
as opposed to direct quotation, which refers to names (1971i, 59, 65; 1980c,
149). Senses are indirectly tied to quotation because they must be garbed in
language; thus for Frege, the identity of a sense is never directly given to us,
but ultimately only via names, as functionally opposed to customary
references.

I think this is obscured by the fact that the two paragraphs in question
mainly discuss the reported speech of a speaker, while in "the sense of
expression 'A'," 'A' is a piece of speech not being attributed to a speaker.
But "A" would not be an expression at all unless someone could use it, and
in that general sense "the sense of expression 'A'" does report speech.
There is no doubt that words are being quoted here. We often quote words
without quoting a speaker. We simply surround the words with quotation
marks, for example, "Fermat's Last Theorem," which is just an "A".

Dummett is right that singular definite descriptions of the form "the *F*"
customarily refer to objects, because *customarily* they logically function as
object names. But if I am right, Frege classifies "the sense of expression
'A'" as indirect quotation, and therefore it *has* no customary reference, but
only an indirect reference, which is its sense. Unless Dummett has
independent evidence that some senses are objects, there is nothing here to
show that some senses are objects. Indeed, on my reading it follows that no

senses can be objects, since senses are essentially indirect references. By parity of reason, "the thought that A" refers to a thought as opposed to an object. The test is precisely that it "designates" a thought (Frege 1971i, 66; see 59), and the mark is precisely that we are "concerned" with thought as opposed to reference (1971i, 63, 67). At best, it could only refer to an object which represents the thought. But Frege rules out that possibility, since he holds that it refers to the thought.[21]

On Dummett's view, Frege's sentence about the sense of expression "A" is even odder than I have indicated. For I assume that "A" can be any expression, including function names such as "$F( )$" as well as object names such as "b." But the sense of expression "$F( )$" is essentially incomplete, while all objects are essentially complete. Therefore, if "the sense of expression '$F( )$'" must refer to an object, then it cannot refer to the sense expressed by "$F( )$." On my reading, the absurdity vanishes. "The sense of expression '$F( )$'" refers to an incomplete sense, not to an object, because it makes an indirect quotation.

My assumption might be wrong. Frege's capital "A" looks like a function name, but it marks no argument-place. But surely Frege is using "A" to range at least over all names. And even if he is not, the problem of the sense of expression "$F( )$" remains.

Dummett is part of a crowd. Gustav Bergmann, Rulon S. Wells, Howard Jackson, and Charles Caton all hold that senses are objects (my 2003, 65). Michael Beaney argues that they are or ought to be (1997, 28–36; see 29 n.67).

Caton argues that all senses are objects because "the sense of expression 'A'" always refers to an object. He admits both that all objects are complete and that some senses are incomplete. He admits that this implies the formal contradiction that some objects are both complete and incomplete. He does not propose to address the problem in his paper (1968).

In *Frege: Philosophy of Language*, Dummett says, "The sense of a predicate is indeed to be considered an object" (1981, 294). For Dummett, the only other option is that it is a function, which he rejects (1981, 291, *pace* 442). He then suggests that it is "incomplete only in that it would be necessary" to grasp it as the sense of an incomplete expression (1981, 291). That is, he thinks all senses are really complete.

I think this way out makes nonsense of the metaphysical gap-and-binding Frege requires to unify the thought as an entity. Frege says he cannot explain the unity of a thought without admitting unsaturated senses (1971d, 54), as Dummett is well aware (1981, 265). And if unsaturated senses are not really unsaturated, they cannot really unify thoughts. On the face of it, Frege's texts expressly make saturation a transcategorial bond applying in the realm of references and the realm of senses alike. Frege's arguments and his language are equally serious in both realms.[22] Frege says that if we allow the same thing to "occur now as object, now as concept . . . the difficulty . . . is only shifted" because *thoughts* need to "hold together" (1971d, 54; see 55), implying that functions and incomplete senses face the very same metaphysical difficulty. Indeed, he says, "The words 'unsaturated' and 'predicative' seem *more* suited to the sense than the meaning [i.e. reference]; *still*, there must be something on the part of the meaning [i.e. reference] which *corresponds* to this" (Frege 1979e, 119 n.*, emphasis mine). This implies that the unsaturatedness of incomplete senses is primary and that of functions derivative. Thus if incomplete senses are really complete entities with gaps in a merely nominal sense, then functions are too, and even more so, since their incompleteness is derivative.[23]

Frege states his metaphors of incompleteness and unsaturatedness for incomplete senses and functions alike. On Dummett's view, why would Frege even bother with these metaphors in the case of incomplete senses? There would be nothing real for them to be metaphors *of*. On Dummett's view, perhaps Frege should have said that incomplete senses are *not* like functions because incomplete senses are really complete. Perhaps Frege should have offered metaphors of their real completeness. Perhaps Frege should have said an ostensively incomplete sense only seems like a cloak, and is really like a body that fills out a cloak, unlike functions, which are really like cloaks. But Frege says the opposite.

Thus Dummett's way out vitiates Frege's thesis that expressions, senses, and references stand in a modeling relationship such that all mirror each other (Frege 1971h, 123). Surely it is unrewarding to hold that the mirroring merely implies "there is a so-called incomplete sense," and not also that it has a gap needing completion. In language, sense, and reference alike, surely Frege intends gaps in whatever is incomplete! If Dummett wants to make a function's sense into a complex of an objectual sense that is really complete and a merely nominal gap or argument-place that is external to the sense per se, this is emendation, not scholarship. If anything, it is the mode of presentation which is the complete constituent the incomplete sense contains. Modes of presentation need no binding because cognition per se is nonpropositional. Modes of presentation are the cognitive core of linguistic senses. The context principle governs senses, not modes of presentation. Frege's containing modes of presentation within senses is his synthesis of cognition with thoughts expressible in language. The extension of this synthesis to entities which can only be grasped in the context of a statement, e.g., to numbers, is Frege's subtle contribution.

The root of Dummett's dilemma is his belief that for Frege every entity is either an object or a function (Dummett 1981, 257, 248–54). Dummett is convinced Frege actually says this, citing *Grundgesetze* vol. 1, §2, "I count as *objects* everything that is not a function" (1981a, 235 n.1). But Frege restricts the paragraph to the "domain of arguments," and Frege never expressly takes senses as arguments. Absent independent evidence that senses are objects or functions, there is nothing here to show that any sense is an object or a function. We do not even need to know what the restriction is, in order to know that not all entities are objects or functions. *Any* restriction would be pointless if all entities were objects or functions. On its face, the restriction is of all *customary* references to objects or functions. In fact, just two paragraphs earlier, which sets the context, Frege distinguishes senses in general from references in general,[24] and seems to be mentioning senses only to set them aside until §5. We see the same pattern in "Function and Concept." Frege says, "An object is anything that is not a function," but he starts the paragraph by restricting it to the domain of "arguments and values" (1971b, 32). And three pages earlier, he distinguishes senses from references only to set senses aside for the rest of the paper (1971b, 29). Thus I have never read these texts as saying that all entities are objects or functions, though they obviously seem to say that if they are read out of context.

In *The Interpretation of Frege's Philosophy*, Dummett is still convinced Frege actually says that all entities are objects or functions, citing *Grundgesetze* and "Function and Concept" (Dummett 1981a, 235, 235 n.1). He speaks of "Frege, with his classification of what exists into objects and functions" (1981a, 429). He admits that senses are entities. And he still rejects Peter Geach's thesis that incomplete senses are functions (1981a, 251–53). These three points collectively imply that Dummett still holds that all senses—even incomplete senses—are objects. He says that Frege "distinguish[es] various kinds of object: logical objects; physical objects; ideas and other mental contents; rational beings; thoughts and other senses. . . ." (1981a, 429).[25] The rest of the paragraph confirms he means thoughts and *all* other senses (1981a, 429, "Still less. . . ."). Dummett (1981a, 393, "But, in general . . .") also confirms this. He duly discusses again in what way senses are incomplete (1981a, 265–70), and seems to take the same way out (1981a, 270).

In light of all this, Dummett's positive statement that incomplete senses are objects is surprisingly weak: "on a non-Fregean use of the word 'concept' [to mean incomplete sense], it *might* be held that 'the concept of citizenship' stood for the sense of the word 'citizen'," where the singular definite article indicates an object (1981a, 90, emphasis mine). The most he is willing to argue is that:

> Since the phrases "the sense of the name 'Mont Blanc'," "the thought that the Earth is larger than the Moon," and "Pythagoras's Theorem" do appear to

function as what Frege called "proper names," there is, for Frege, no question that *at least some* senses are objects." (1981a, 132, emphasis mine)

He does not mention that "the sense of the incomplete name 'ξ is a card deck'" functions exactly as much as a proper name as do his examples. This proper name is complete; the "'ξ'" is not used but only mentioned as part of the indirectly quoted incomplete name.

Montgomery Furth makes complete senses objects and incomplete senses functions (1968, 9). Perhaps the 1993 Dummett agrees, since he says a concept is "a component of a thought" (1993, 61, 105, 129; see my 2003, 65); but perhaps this is his "non-Fregean use" of "concept" again. If Dummett is no longer insisting that all senses are objects, this rescues him from the dilemma of admitting incomplete senses either as complete objects or as incomplete objects. But he still faces the deeper dilemma. If he still insists that for Frege all entities are either objects or functions, his only other options are that incomplete senses are either functions—*pace* his rejection of Geach—or not entities. The 1993 Dummett also says, "All things are *Bedeutungen*" in the sense of being "a possible object of reference" (1995, 8), facing the deeper dilemma.

Dummett criticizes Geach for saying incomplete senses are functions because they map other senses onto thoughts. I agree with Dummett that they are functions only functionally speaking. They do not belong to Frege's category of functions. But in virtue of their being indirect references, incomplete senses might be called indirect functions. I think we may accept Geach's innocuous mapping observation, which is not the same as the harmful conclusion he draws from it that incomplete senses are customary functions. If his mapping observation sheds no light on the ultimate nature of senses, *pace* Dummett (1981a, 268), so what? We might also harmlessly note that assertoric force in effect maps thoughts onto assertions. Would anyone conclude that forces are functions, or that this sheds any light on the nature of forces? In this innocuous sense, we can even use objects to map functions onto truth-values! But on Frege's view that sentence, thought, and truth-condition are structural models of each other, sense-mapping is just what we should expect. The mapping of senses onto thoughts by incomplete senses innocuously models the mapping of references onto truth-conditions by incomplete references.

Dummett criticizes Geach's view that incomplete senses are unsaturated functions for destroying Frege's major atoms-and-molecules metaphor of how thoughts are composed of senses (1981a, 263–66). I face the criticism too, since I find incomplete senses unsaturated in their own right. I think Dummett has it backwards. Saturation is a basic *part* of Frege's atoms-and-molecules metaphor. Frege studied chemistry. And when I described

Frege's functions and concepts to him, the chemist Stephen Richardson immediately identified the basis of the metaphor as chemical saturation. An unsaturate is an atom having electron-spaces available for electrons from another atom to fill, binding the two atoms together into a molecule. Thus the mapping is of electrons onto molecular compounds by unsaturates. Polyadic functions and polyadic incomplete senses are like polyunsaturates. The greater the number of binding completions needed to form the compound, the more unsaturated—and existentially unstable (volatile!)—the compound is. Thus Frege seems to be explicating the metaphysical bond of the unity of a thought as a valency bond. And valency bonds are just what bind atoms into molecular compounds. Now how could saturation, which is the basis of molecular theory, go against molecular theory?[26]

Dummett argues further that if senses are removed from thoughts to yield incomplete senses, then we must know thoughts first, and cannot learn new thoughts by "atomically" compounding them out of senses (1981a, 267). If so, this is no special problem about senses, since by parity of reason we could not learn new truth-conditions by "atomically" compounding them out of references either. And Dummett still has Frege's saturation metaphor backwards. It is precisely through saturation that we compound chemicals out of atoms. Dummett is confusing the order of cognition with the order of being. In the order of cognition, we can and generally do cognize new thoughts by compounding them out of senses. We can do so precisely because in the order of being, thoughts are parsed in many ways into incomplete senses by removing complete senses.

The truth is that the difference between decomposing thoughts into senses and composing senses into thoughts is as little as the difference between *immortal* and *lives forever* (Frege 1971h, 125). The distinction is only in reason, *pace* Dummett (1981a, 290–91). Frege says:

> The mental activities leading to the formulation of a definition may be of two kinds: analytic or synthetic. This is similar to the activities of the chemist, who either analyzes a given substance into its elements or lets elements combine to form a new substance. In both cases, we come to know the composition of a substance. (1971e, 61; see 1979, 202; 1979f, 208–9; 1971d, 42, 43 on chemistry; *Begriffsschrift*, §9)

Indeed, statements *are* definable names for the later Frege, since they are always composed of simpler logical subject- and predicate-names.

Thus Frege's context principle for senses can easily permit and require that subsentential senses be logically derivable as remainders from the thoughts they are parts of, *pace* Dummett (1995, 14). Here we must not be confused by Frege's statement that "the whole reference [of a statement] and one part of it do not suffice to determine the remainder" (1971i, 65). Frege is right. The True minus the concept *iron* does not tell us which object is said to be iron. Nor would the True minus the Eiffel Tower tell us which concept the Eiffel Tower is said to fall under. But this is a red herring. A *thought* and one part of it *do* suffice to determine the remainder. The thought that the Eiffel Tower is iron minus the sense of "the Eiffel Tower" yields the sense of "( ) is iron." Similarly for any sense. This is why definitional composition and decomposition are distinct only in reason for Frege. For definitions can fix references only by fixing senses. Again, for the later Frege, statements are definable names composed of simpler logical subject- and predicate-names.

We must also not be confused by Frege's statement that "I call anything a proper name if it is a sign for an object" (1971d, 47 n.*). Dummett is wrongly converting this to "If anything is a proper name, then it names an object." The conversion is restricted to customary references.

Dummett himself cites a text that "an object such as Mont Blanc cannot be part of a thought"(1981a, 533n). Indeed, Dummett knows as well as anyone it is Frege's famous view that "the object is not . . . itself a constituent of the thought," and that an object such as a mountain "is not the sort of thing that can be a constituent of a thought" (1981a, 130; see 137–38, 177, 533n). Yet Dummett insists just two pages later that "at least some senses are objects" (1981a, 132). Dummett's way out is to say that it is only *wirklich* or concrete objects that cannot be senses (1981a, 393). I disagree. Frege's terminology is misleading. What we would normally call his realism, he calls objectivism. It is objective entities as such that are logically mind-independent, i.e., exist and are as they are independently of the manner in which we think of, regard, conceive, or speak of them. "*Wirklich*" ordinarily translates as "actual" or "real." Frege's "*wirklich*" is best translated as "causal." He has in mind a causal activity or capacity that has nothing to do with the issue of metaphysical realism. Senses are not *wirklich*; they can act on us only in the passive sense of being sometimes grasped by us, and thus affecting how we regard things. That is a *special but secondary* reason why concrete objects cannot be senses. The general and primary reason is that to allow any object, *wirklich* or not, to be a part of a thought would destroy the objectual realism implicit in Frege's sense-reference distinction. It is not just our accompanying subjective idea, but even our objective sense via which we think about a mountain, that must be distinguished from the mountain itself. Frege says, "When we say 'the Moon', we do not intend to speak of our idea of the Moon, *nor are we satisfied with the sense alone, but we presuppose a reference*" (1971i, 61, emphasis mine). And Frege applies this realism, which he calls his objectivism, with the strictest sameness to abstract objects.

If senses were objects, would not Frege have said so? That is a huge category question. What, if anything, does Frege say about it?

Frege says right in "On Sense and Reference" that senses are not objects: "*A truth value* cannot be a part of a thought *any more than*, say, the Sun can, *for it is not a sense but an object.*"[27] This is the key text. It is the only text in which Frege says whether senses are objects. Frege says that a truth-value—an abstract object   is not a sense, because it is an object. Note the level of generality of this category exclusion. He does not say, "for it is not a sense but a *truth-value*." He does not say, "for it is not a sense but an *abstract* object." He does not say, "for it is not a sense but a *customary* object," as if senses were objects after all—indirect objects. (Senses are, of course, indirect *references*; this is what indirect reference is all about.) He says, "for it is not a sense but an object." And if no objects are senses, then no senses are objects. The context does not even appear to suggest a qualification. He is saying that the True cannot be a sense, not because it is the True, not because it is an abstract object, and not even because it is a customary reference (on my view there is no other kind of object; functions are the other kind of customary reference), but for the same reason the Sun cannot be a sense: because it is an object. This is close to Aristotle's principle that the true reason is the most general one; "because it is a customary reference," which is suggested by other texts which distinguish customary references in general from senses, is more general but is not what Frege says here. Nor is this "smoking gun" text in some obscure writing. It is in *the* paper on sense and reference.

Can we sweep this plain and forthright text under the rug of esoteric argument? The only way out the text allows is to admit some senses as objects which "cannot be a part of a thought." And that is no way out. All senses must be parts of thoughts, due to the context principle in its application to senses; even thoughts are parts of compound thoughts.

Frege wrote "On Sense and Reference," in which he says that a truth-value is not a sense because it is an object, and therefore that in general an object is not a sense because it is an object, almost at the same time as "Function and Concept" and *Grundgesetze* vol. 1, in which, Dummett believes, Frege says that every entity is either an object or a function, and "On Concept and Object," in which, Dummett believes, Frege says that the singular definite article always indicates an object in every possible context, including even contexts which shift reference to indirect reference. Frege never suggests that these four works contradict each other in the least on whether senses are objects or functions. To the contrary, Frege presents the works as being all of one piece. This is easily explained on my interpretation. Looking to the context of each text Dummett cites, Frege is saying only that all *customary references* are either objects or functions, and only that in contexts of *customary reference*, the singular definite article always indicates an object. But how can Dummett reconcile the texts?

The problem of the sense of expression "A," which Frege never mentions, is subtler than the problem of the concept *horse*. For there is a tension here between the fact that the singular definite article indicates reference to a complete entity in the case of customary reference, and the fact that directly quoted incomplete names are mentioned not used, so that their incompleteness is not an incompleteness of any expression containing the quoted name. The dilemma is that indirect reference and indirect quotation lie in between customary reference and direct quotation. Or more simply, senses lie in between customary references and names. There are two options. First, if we assimilate indirect reference to customary reference, then "the sense of expression '*horse*( )'" refers not to a complete *object*, but to a complete *sense* which represents the intended incomplete sense. For indirect quotation is of senses (1971i, 65), and no senses are objects (1971i, 64). Second, if we assimilate indirect quotation of senses to direct quotation of names, then "the sense of expression '*horse*( )'" can and therefore must refer to the intended *incomplete* sense. For we can and must refer to an intended incomplete *name* if we directly quote it using the singular definite article, since its incompleteness is mentioned not used. The second option is correct. For while incomplete senses are literally and metaphysically incomplete, their incompleteness is mentioned not used in indirect quotation of them. That is, their incompleteness is not a literal, metaphysical incompleteness of or within any sense containing them, if they are being indirectly quoted. For if they are indirectly quoted, they are not literally, metaphysically contained in any accompanying customary sense in the first place. For example, in "The sense of '*horse*( )' is an incomplete sense," the gap in the sense expressed by '*horse*( )' is not a gap in the thought the sentence expresses. The thought is complete and has no gap. Thus the second option trumps the first. Ironically, the solution is that due to the mentioning nature of indirect quotation, there *is* no problem of the sense of expression "A" like the problem of the concept *horse*. And perhaps that explains why Frege never mentions the problem.[28]

Twelve years later Frege repeats virtually the same text in a letter to Russell: "*Truth* [i.e. the True] is not a component part of a thought, *just as* Mont Blanc . . . is not . . . " (1980, 163, emphasis mine). The text is so much the same that surely we must impute the "for it is not a sense but an object."

As Frege explains in a third text in another letter to Russell:

> Now a class cannot be the sense of a sign, but only its meaning [i.e. reference], as Sirius can only be the meaning of a sign, but not its sense. Hence a class

cannot be the indirect meaning of a sign, *any more than* Sirius can. . . . Can any class whatever be a component part of a thought? *No more than* the planet Jupiter can. A class . . . can be defined in different ways. . . . If the class was part of the thought that an object *p* belonged to it, then the change in the sense of the class name would not affect the thought, provided that the class itself remained unchanged. . . .

Or does a proposition have a meaning [i.e. reference], and this is a thought? If the latter, then the propositions '$2^3 > 7$' and '$3^2 - 1 > 7$' would have to designate the same thought [for they have the same reference]. Now the thoughts contained in those propositions are evidently different. . . . We are thus compelled to regard a thought as the sense of a proposition. (1980a, 157, emphasis mine; see 158)

Note that logical equivalence is not the test of identity of thoughts. The natural reading is that since objects are customary references, and customary references remain the same across changes in sense, no objects are senses. That is, the reason why objects are not senses is that objects are extensional in sense (2) and senses are intensional in sense (2). Frege is telling us that we do not understand his solution to his puzzle about informative identity statements unless we understand that no senses are objects or functions.

Frege repeats this in a fourth text in "[Notes for Ludwig Darmstaedter]":

The object and concept are not constituents of the thought expressed. . . . A distinction has to be drawn between the sense and meaning [i.e. reference] of a sign. . . . If an astronomer makes a statement about the moon, the moon itself is not part of the thought expressed. The moon itself *is the meaning* of the expression 'the moon'. Therefore *in addition to* its meaning this expression *must also* have a *sense*, which *can* be a constituent of a thought. . . . This is what makes it *possible* for a sentence of the form 'A = B' to express [an informative identity]. (1979g, 254–55, emphasis mine)

The natural reading is that there must be senses *in addition to* objects and concepts. For Frege's expression "object and concept" indicates that he makes the sense-reference distinction generally for all customary references. Some functions, such as *the capital of* ξ, are not concepts, but I see no reason for them to be an exception to the general distinction.

In a fifth text in "Introduction to Logic," Frege asks very generally, "Now what has the object got to do with the thought?" Mont Blanc is the example, but his argument applies to abstract objects as well, since there can be thoughts about the axis of a fictitious planet or about the odd and even integer, even though such abstract objects do not, and in the latter case cannot, exist. Frege then says that "the same point can be approached" by explaining in general how informative identity statements are possible (1979d, 191–92; see 187).

Frege adds in a sixth text that numbers cannot be parts of thoughts: "while the sense of a number sign can be part of a thought, a number itself cannot" (1980a, 158; see 163 for a seventh text on the number 7).

Thus Frege denies that three kinds of abstract objects—truth-values, classes, and numbers (numbers are classes of classes for the later Frege)—are senses. If that were all, Dummett's view that senses are abstract objects would emerge as Ptolemaic, with truth-values, classes, and numbers as big epicycles. Dummett could still say that senses are a special class of abstract objects, namely, objects that are indirect references. He might say that in all the works in which to all appearances Frege is introducing senses as a unique category to do a job objects cannot do, Frege is really distinguishing objects which are not senses from other objects which are, but without ever telling us his secret meaning. He might even say that while a *truth-value* is not a sense but an object, a *sense* is both a sense and an object. But all this is curiouser and curiouser. Frege's plain meaning is that senses and objects are different categories. A sense is not an object but a sense. An object is not a sense but an object. And Frege is most naturally read in all these texts as arguing for the even more general thesis that *no* customary references are senses.

Frege rarely argues that concrete objects in particular cannot be senses. He says "one can see Etna, but one cannot see the thought that Etna is higher than Vesuvius" (1979f, 225). He says "the sense of the word 'sun' is not somewhere in space, nor does it have mass" (1980e, 128). We can see why he has little interest in giving such arguments: they are shallow and overkill.

"On Sense and Reference" and "[Comments on Sense and Meaning]" read so much more easily when we think of senses as a unique category that we can see how badly Dummett is bewitched by his belief that Frege says every entity is a function or an object. For example, Frege explains objects as the customary references of proper names. Frege says, discussing only the customary reference of a proper name, "I call such a meaning [i.e., customary reference] an object" (1979c, 119). Is that the role of any senses? Quite the opposite. Senses are introduced precisely because the category of objects is inadequate to explain the possibility of informative identity statements. Frege says "it is *via* a sense, and only *via* a sense that a proper name is related to an object" (1979c, 124); the word "object" is used without qualification. This implies that if senses are objects, they are named only via senses. If, then, senses *are* objects, is there not a vicious regress of objects? Or is the category of objects then adequate to explain the possibility of informative identity statements after all?

This is not to mention the diagram in Frege's letter to Husserl with all the senses on one line and all the references on another. Frege says:

The following schema should make my view clear:

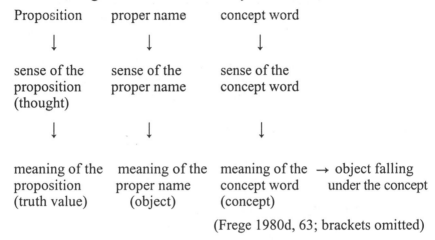

(Frege 1980d, 63; brackets omitted)

Frege places objects on only one line, the line of references.[29] Dummett is placing objects on both lines. If senses are objects, why does Frege not write "object" for the three senses on the line of senses? Or if only complete senses are objects, why does Frege not write "object" for the two complete senses? The answer is in "On Sense and Reference": for they are not objects but senses.[30]

This pulls the realm of senses out of the realm of customary references, *pace* Dummett (1981, 680). In fact, Frege's distinction between senses in general and references in general already does that. This answers the question, Just how tightly does Frege tie linguistic function to ontological category (Dummett 1981a, 384)? Namely, tightly enough to pull the whole category of senses out of the category of customary references. And by parity of reason, tightly enough to pull tones and forces out of that realm too (Frege never calls them objects or functions). For if anything, they function even less like customary references than senses do. Ideas never were in the realm of customary references. Frege's private language arguments require that *all* references, customary and indirect alike, be objective, that is, mind-independent. (As indirect references, senses do belong to the realm of *all* references. Thus when Frege distinguishes senses from references, he can only be distinguishing them from the realm of customary, i.e., direct, references.)

How can we refer to the tone T or the force F, if they are not objects? Assimilating reference to tones or forces to direct quotation of names or other expressions seems too implausible to consider. But there are three other models of reference in Frege: reference to functions, to ideas, and to senses.

First, "the function F" refers to an object, a course-of-values, which technically represents the function. We might say that in *saying* something about the object, we *show* something about the function it represents. Can objects represent tones or forces?

Second, we can "take" an idea "as" an object. We might say that in *saying* something about the ostensible object, we *show* something about the idea. Can we "take" a tone or force "as" an object?

Third, we talk about the sense of expression "A" as an indirect reference in indirect quotation. Here we say an indirect sense, showing the indirect reference. Indirect references are presented only via indirect senses. Is reference to tones or forces part of indirect speech?

All three models anticipate the early Wittgenstein on saying and showing; I think the first model might have influenced him.

I think the first model is inappropriate. Granted, tones and forces need something to apply to. But if Frege thought they were incomplete, then his notation would have argument-places for their arguments. That is, if they were incomplete, I think Frege would have said or at least shown so. Of course, there is the innocuous sense in which items in any two or more related categories can map each other onto something. Sad tones can map utterances onto sad utterances, and assertive force can map utterances onto assertions. But in that innocuous sense, truth-values can map functions onto objects, reversing the metaphysical order of completeness, and reversing arguments and values as well. Of course, on an ontologically serious mapping reversal, objects and functions must be "converted . . . or, speaking more precisely, represented" as appropriate (Frege 1971d, 46).

The other two models may seem inappropriate as well. Tones and forces are neither wholly objective nor wholly subjective on my view, and they are not ways to identify anything. But I shall argue that the second model is workable, and that the third model is best.

Are ideas, tones, and forces objects because "the idea my assertion of 'A' produces in you," "the tone of assertion 'A'," and "the assertoric force of assertion 'A'" must always refer to objects? The quick answer is no, since objects are essentially and wholly objective.

As we saw, Dummett lists ideas as a subcategory of objects (1981a, 429). That would be a quick way to rescue idealist intuitionism from psychologism (Dummett 1981, 684)! Indeed, it would rescue psychologism from psychologism. For it makes nonsense of Frege's twelve private language arguments (my 2003, 289 n.1) and his cautious verdict that ideas can at best be "taken as" objects (1971i, 60; see 1968a, 510). The verdict implies that ideas are *not* objects. Why would Frege suggest that ideas can be "taken as" objects, if Dummett is right that ideas already *are* objects? On Dummett's account, should not Frege be suggesting that ideas—or *private* objects—can be taken as *public* objects? But Frege speaks of objects without qualification. The verdict also implies that the arguments aim to show not just that our thoughts are objective, but that the things we talk about, i.e., our references, are objective. This double aim merges in indirect reference. Even in *Grundlagen*, ideas are not objects. Frege makes ideas *subjective Vorstellungen* and objects *objective Vorstellungen*; these are mutually exclusive categories (§27, n.1), *pace* Dummett (1991, 225). Why would Frege place ideas and objects in mutually exclusive categories, if Dummett is right that ideas are objects? Frege is saying that objects are objective and ideas are subjective. Splitting these *objective Vorstellungen* (*Inhalten*) into senses and references, the later Frege's objects are just as totally excluded from being ideas. The later Frege says to Husserl, "objects and concepts have the same objectivity" (1980d, 63). Do ideas have this same objectivity too?

This pulls "the realm of the purely mental" out of the realm of reference, *pace* Dummett (1981, 680). This completes our separation of three realms (references, senses, the mental) Frege repeatedly distinguishes (1971i, 60–61; 1968a, 523–24), but Dummett commingles.[31]

Making tones into objects would spare Dummett the difficulty of having to argue that tones can be objective (1981, 84–89). For they would all be objective as a matter of course. But Frege says, "Such colouring and shading are not objective," and insists they are really ideas belonging to art (1971i, 61; 1979e, 145). If so, tones cannot be objects, functions, or senses. But in other texts he discusses the objective aspects of language which give rise to the ideas, such as choice of word, tone of voice, and onomatopoeia (1979e, 127–28; 140; 1968a, 514–15), and even seems to call tones "constituents of sentences" (1968a, 514). I think the best view is that tones necessarily involve both objective aspects of language use (or, more generally, of behavior), and subjective ideas the aspects cause in us. A very plausible gloss would be that tones are really groups (extensions of classes) of (normally resembling) subjective ideas (across persons), namely groups of moods or feelings caused by certain objective language uses. This is plausible because Frege seems to say tones are really ideas. That would place tones on the subjective side of the house. But if so, my criticism of Frege is that this only sweeps the emergent nature of tones under the rug. Taken by themselves, neither the objective language behaviors nor the subjective ideas they cause are (successful) conveyances or expressions of mood or feeling. Conveyance or expression is essentially relational and clearly an emergent property. Thus tones are or ought to be emergent entities with objective and subjective components. If so, they cannot be objects, functions or senses, insofar as objects, functions, and senses are wholly objective; and they cannot be ideas, insofar as ideas are wholly subjective. This may seem to violate Frege's principle always to separate the objective from the subjective. But the components are separate. And if there can be no relations among entities in different categories, we will all be in trouble, except for kind-monists. This is not to mention how tightly Frege ties linguistic function to ontological category. Thus the best gloss is that tones are emergent entities for Frege. And if tones are special kinds of emergent entities, this would provide an excellent explanation of why they are a unique category. It would also remove the mystery about their nature. For the concept of an emergent entity is a merely logical concept. An emergent entity is merely an entity that has at least one property none of its logical constituents has.

Similarly for forces. Frege says assertion is the *objective* communication of a judgment, where a judgment is an indefinable sort of *inward* recognition (1979e, 139; 1968a, 513; see 1971i, 65; 1971h, 126, 126 n.*). A very plausible gloss would be that forces are really kinds of objective speech acts, namely acts which communicate inward states such as recognition or query. This is plausible because the assertion sign (judgment stroke) is part of the objectively communicable formal notation. That would place forces on the objective side of the house. But if so, my criticism of Frege is that this only sweeps the emergent nature of forces under the rug. Taken by themselves, neither the objective nor the subjective components of assertions are outward communications of inward recognitions. Such communication is essentially relational and clearly an emergent property. Thus the best gloss is that forces are emergent entities for Frege. But we already know assertion cannot be an object or a function. For Frege says the assertion sign (judgment stroke) cannot function as a name, on pain of reducing assertions to suppositions (*Grundgesetze* vol. 1, §5; see 1968a, 514); and we have seen how tightly he ties linguistic function to ontological category.

Thus tones and forces are unique categories; they are irreducible to each other. But we can "take" them "as" objects by first "taking" their subjective components "as" objects, and thus refer to them as easily as we can refer to ideas. I call this a "double take" (pun intended). Thus the second model seems workable for tones and forces, if Frege's single take works.[32]

The third model is best. Tones, forces, and explications are part of speech as much as senses are. They have no use outside of speech, and their use is what they are. Even a happy humming or a commanding look is expressive in some sense. Thus we should, after taking their subjective components as objects (a single take), construe reference to the tone T, the force F, or the explication E as indirect reference by analogy to indirect reference to the sense S. In contrast, reference to objects we double take such entities to be on the second model is direct reference.

To sum up, Frege provides reasons why senses, ideas, tones, and forces cannot function as—and so cannot be—objects or functions. Yet Dummett reduces Frege to two categories, objects and functions. Because he honestly believes Frege actually says this, he is constrained into pounding square and triangular pegs into round holes, and reducing Frege's jungle to a desert.

Dummett is steering a heroic course in the face of great difficulties, pursuing a mirage of Frege as an austere dualist with two categories, objects and functions. Frege's austerity lies deeper, in his severe tie of ontological category to linguistic function. This results in a profusion of categories due to the profusion of linguistic functions. The textual difficulties vanish. We also see the whole linguistic turn. Dummett is right to pinpoint the turn in Frege's requirement that for objects to be named, a criterion for their identity must be provided. But objects are just the tip of the iceberg.

6. THE PROBLEM OF BIFURCATION

A chief problem for Dummett is how to keep Frege's later context principle from bifurcating into one principle for senses and another for references (Dummett 1995, 10, 14). Dummett links them backwardly in the cognitive order by deriving senses from references.

I double-link them. Senses are logically tied to references by being ways of presenting references. This links them on the forward road in the cognitive order, and on the backward road in the ontological order. Due to the ontological dependence of modes on objects and functions, senses and references are not wholly distinct from each other as categories, even though there may not always be a reference. For surely a reference is not wholly distinct from the ways in which it can be given. Not every distinction in reason involves symmetric dependencies. This is not to mention that on the descriptivist theory of senses, every definite description expresses a sense which is essentially descriptive of an extensional in sense (2) concept under or within which its reference, if any, falls.[33]

The leap from sense to reference is especially transparent for primitive logical entities such as the identity relation. Here the leap is between not wholly distinct entities in the strong sense that primitive references cannot fail to exist if the senses reflecting their nature do, entailing symmetric ontological dependencies. This is the later Frege's implicit atomistic version of the Parmenidean thesis that the rational is the real and the real is the rational, though Frege has a more general and somewhat different version in his thesis that every true or false sentence must have a referring logical subject (1971i, 62). It is in any case the later Frege's implicit version of his own earlier thesis that even some complex logical entities, namely numbers, are transparent to the reason (*Grundlagen*, §105).[34]

7. THE CONSEQUENCES FOR INTUITIONISM

By parity of reason, there is no backward road from truth to propositional sense.[35] This is fatal to intuitionism, and to strong verificationism. It does not matter whether a propositional sense describes a truth-condition, or whether it is logically tied to a truth-condition at all. What matters is that the truth-value, truth, is propositionally presented in indefinitely many ways in the order of cognition. Thus there is no backward road from truth to propositional sense in the order of cognition, any more than there is from truth-conditions. We cannot squeeze an intension in sense (2) out of all the extensions in sense (2) in the world, even including *assignments* of truth-values among the extensions. My point is so general, it does not even matter if the assignments of truth-values are based on proofs or not. We may say that the truth of a statement underdetermines the thought it expresses.

A second problem of intensionality in sense (2) arises more specifically for intuitionism in that there can be many different proofs of the same thesis, so that there is no backward road from the truth of a thesis to any one proof as the sense the thesis expresses. As Frege says, "Frequently several routes for a proof are open" (*Grundgesetze*, p. 3; see Dummett 1981, 634). Thus we may say the truth of a thesis underdetermines its proof.

We cannot need to be guaranteed we will discover an object in order to understand the sense its name expresses, since we cannot need to single out that object in order to understand that sense. For an objectual inquiry to be genuine, it must be at least zetetically, i.e., investigationally, possible for the object to turn out to have properties other than those we think it has, or not to exist at all. By parity of reason, we cannot need to know how to prove that a statement is true in order to understand its sense, because we cannot need to have the truth in order to understand its sense. For the inquiry to be genuine, it must be at least zetetically possible for the statement to turn out to be false. These two points coalesce for Frege, for whom truth *is* an object. I need not add that the order of investigation is a form of the order of cognition.

This is the problem of Plato's *Meno*. How can it make sense to inquire about anything if the object of inquiry must already visibly contain the answer? What would we be discovering?

The problem of how informative inquiry is possible is more generally the problem of how informative identity statements are possible. Thus the *Meno* problem is more generally Frege's puzzle. And for Frege, for a statement "to be informative—to have 'cognitive value'—it is necessary that a mere knowledge of its sense be insufficient to guarantee a recognition of its truth" (Dummett 1981, 228). The burden is on the intuitionist to explain why the *Meno* problem and Frege's puzzle are not genuine puzzles.

Can an intuitionist find any sense of discovery in moving from having an effective means for obtaining a proof ("informal proof" or "demonstration") to obtaining a proof ("canonical proof") (Dummett 2000, 270–71)? No, this is illegitimate on intuitionism's own showing. For the expressions "an effective means" and "a proof" are existential generalizations. And according to intuitionism, the only way to prove an existential generalization is to prove that there is an instance.[36] Thus the only way to prove "*There is a* proof," "*There is an* effective means to *a* proof," or even "This is an effective means to *some* proof," so that these assertions have meaning, is to produce an actual proof. Thus there can be no sense of informative inquiry for intuitionists, since for them a statement can have no meaning until we have already proved (or disproved) it. Thus intuitionists cannot discover whether intuitionism is true or false. This is not a problem of recognition or of circularity, but an application of the intuitionist rule for proving an existential generalization. If there is no actual, specific proof or disproof of intuitionism, then intuitionism is neither true nor false, on intuitionism's own showing.

Dummett says, "From an intuitionistic standpoint . . . , an understanding of a mathematical statement consists in the capacity to recognize a proof of it when presented with one; and the truth of such a statement can consist only in the existence of such a proof" (Dummett 2000, 4; 1978, 8). But "a proof" is an existential generalization, and so is "the existence of such a proof"; and the intuitionist always requires an instance. Thus for the intuitionist, a mathematical statement has neither sense nor truth-value until an actual, specific proof or disproof is found. Nor has any actual, specific proof been given of the general intuitionistic thesis just quoted. What proof could there be? Certainly not a mathematical one!

Dummett defines intuitionist ¬A as its being provable that there is no proof of A (Dummett 2000, 11). But if I have just proved that there is no proof of intuitionism, then ¬(Intuitionism).

If the general intuitionistic thesis needs no proof to be meaningful, why do mathematical statements need proofs to be meaningful? Both involve generalizations; and if anything, the general thesis is more general.

Can intuitionists informatively move from nonintuitionistic meaning to intuitionistic meaning? If so, then our interest in intuitionism is destroyed. For then mathematics has nonintuitionistic meaning after all (see Dummett 2000, 250–51; ix).

Can intuitionists informatively move from mere strings of symbols to intuitionistic meaning? If so, then intuitionism is a mere appendage or post-script to formalism. And if proof-strings have formalist meaning-in-use, then mathematics has nonintuitionistic meaning after all.

It seems, then, that intuitionism cannot explain away our sense of mathematical discovery even as a mere appearance. I mean that if what is proved is meaningless until it is proved, we cannot meaningfully *look for* anything. Phenomenologically, the intentionality is gone. Is not human creation, such as intuitionists take mathematics to be, normally a teleological process with an end in mind? Is not trying to prove a thesis a paradigm of having an end in mind?[37]

If different proofs provide or constitute different meanings for a theorem (see Dummett 1981, 674–75), the question arises whether they prove the same theorem, or whether the theorem is ambiguous. But this question is meaningless for the intuitionist unless there is an actual, specific second-order proof of sameness of the theorem. But if there are different second-order proofs of sameness of the theorem and so on, then there is a vicious regress involved in proving whether different provers are ever proving the same theorem.

Perhaps Dummett's belief in intuitionism has influenced his interpretation of Frege, or vice versa. Perhaps his own contextualism and his forced choice argument have influenced both. Dummett makes it clear that Frege is no intuitionist (1981, 586–87, 589).[38] But intuitionism and Dummett's program have something essential in common. Namely, both take the backward road. Intuitionism holds that only a proof of the truth or falsehood of a mathematical theorem can provide a thought for the theorem to express. Dummett's program holds that for Frege, the truth-condition of a statement wholly determines which thought the statement expresses.

In any case, Dummett takes the backward road in all three traditional areas of logic: terms (senses via references), statements (propositional senses via truth-conditions), and inferences (theorem senses via proofs of truth), in his Frege scholarship and/or his philosophy.[39]

It may not seem so, but I agree with most of Dummett's views on Frege. Whatever merit this paper has is largely due to Dummett. For over a quarter of a century, I have regarded him as my Frege teacher from afar. I owe more to him for my understanding of Frege than to anyone except Frege himself. He will always be the world's best Frege scholar to me. I want to thank him for over fifty years of wonderful service not only to the community of Frege scholars, but to the world of philosophy at large. Thanks to his devotion and integrity, and his ability to bring out the huge volumes of thought implicit in Frege, he has done more than anyone to bring Frege to his rightful place in philosophy.

JAN DEJNOŽKA

RESEARCH FELLOW, UNION COLLEGE
JANUARY 2005

NOTES

1. Dummett prefers the term "referents" (1981, 94; 1981a, 2).
2. See my 1979 (59–85), summarized in my 1982 (2–5), and updated in my 1996 (104–9) / 2003 (104–9). All three provide a specific analysis explaining why Frege's formally explicit definition of Number is implicitly and functionally a contextual definition, in contrast to Dummett's general and conclusory paragraph (1995, 4–5). The heart of the analysis is that once we see that parallel completions of (A) identity statements about numbers, (B) statements of the equinumerosity of certain concepts, and (C) identity statements about the extensions of those concepts, are logically equivalent, the mediation of (B) can drop out and the identification of numbers with the extensions can take on a life of its own (and this takes us to the later Frege). The end result is an explicit definition, just as Dummett says, but this is just a husk covering up the contextual work of (B)'s mediation. I mailed a copy of my 1979 to Dummett in 1979. He never replied. I wonder if he ever received it. Imagine if he had recanted in 1979!
3. Strictly, about the object that represents identity, namely, a double course-of-values.
4. The geometry permutation is also a private language argument (compare Dummett 1981, 638–42). In *Grundlagen*, Frege uses private language arguments to show that numbers are mind-independently objective long before he uses the context principle to define numbers.
5. This is not Quine's sense, which involves a fact of the matter (Gibson 1987, 147; Quine 1987, 155).
6. *Grundgesetze* vol. 1, §§0, 30; Frege 1980c, 36–37; 1971d, 42–43; 1971i, 59–61.
7. Frege 1979j, 271; see 1980c, 37; 1979f, 209; 1971e, 53, 59; Kluge 1971, xxvii.
8. Thus the Heijenoort-Hintikka critique of Frege's distinction between metalanguage and object language is misplaced. For Frege, the distinction has nothing to do with whether his quantifiers range over names as well as objects. For him, the key issue is that science must begin with explications, on pain of vicious regress of definitions. Frege demands that explications occur in a propaedeutic because they are too uncertain to belong to rigorous science. This is what requires and justifies his use of metalanguage. Even if Frege's quantifiers range over names

as well as objects, he can still make the distinction by using predicates such as "x is a name of y" and "z explicates name x." The quantifiers would then be the vehicles for general statements about explication (my 2003, 82; compare Dummett 1981, 226). Indeed, what better way is there to talk about general relationships among names and objects, in object languages *or* metalanguages? In Neurath's metaphor, formal object languages and formal metalanguages are rebuilt ships at sea, built from the timbers of a natural language. Thus to call an object language level 0 and its metalanguages levels 1 . . . n is to go in the wrong direction. It is the natural language which is the level 0 starting point, and the object language is the level n result. Any formalization of a natural language ought to preserve its capacity for referring to object languages and metalanguages alike, as well as to their relationships. And "Carnap . . . has . . . shown that a language can without self-contradiction be used in the analysis of itself" (Ayer 1952, 71; see Carnap 1959, xiv, 53). That is, a language can function as, and so be, both an object language and a metalanguage. Within a universal logic, it is not only possible but necessary to discuss itself as an object language metalinguistically. Of course, we can *also* discuss a universal logic from without, i.e., from within another logic.

What reason is there to suppose that Frege's quantifiers do range over both names and objects? Frege seems to use German as a metalanguage to explicate the semantics of his eight primitive terms informally as object language, then to formalize their use through regimentation; and all his defined terms are mere abbreviations. He knows the use-mention distinction, and his formal notation seems only to *use* names. But I think he may admit three systematic shifts of his referential use of names. First, I argue elsewhere that for Frege, identity statements assert that two names refer to the same reference (my 2003, 42–65; 1981, 31–36; 1979, 34–50). If so, Frege's identity statements are metalinguistic, yet occur within the formal notation; he has a formal identity sign. My view implies that Frege quantifies over names as objects in $(\exists x)x = a$. In my 2003 (54), I see this as a formal oddity, a systematic shift of reference in identity contexts, and technically harmless for doing proofs. Now, the identity sign is one of the eight primitive terms. That is because definitions are identity stipulations that two names express the same sense and refer to the same reference, so that definition always presupposes identity (Frege 1971c, 80–81). And Frege has a formal definition sign as well. Second, then, all definitions in the formal notation are metalinguistic. Thus on my view, both asserted identities and stipulated identities are metalinguistic, yet within the formal notation. Third, Frege says "there are two wholly different cases [where] we speak of existence. . . . In the one case the question is whether a proper name designates . . .; in the other, whether a concept takes objects under itself" (Frege 1971, 104). Surely it would be odd if Frege could not state his own first kind of legitimate existence-talk in his own notation by a systematic reference shift, or simply by introducing names of names and a name for designation.

Frege's quantifiers do not presuppose names or objects. Frege is very clear on which eight logical names are primitive. They include the universal quantifier and negation, and he defines the existential quantifier directly in terms of them. One must not be confused by the regimentations. They are not definitions. He provides them precisely for his primitive names, which already have explications.

Is there any circularity in the informal *explications* of Frege's primitive logical names? Due to the logically contingent nature of explication, the answer must be no, even if some terms which are or later become defined terms are used or presupposed in the explication of a primitive term. Thus I am not even bothering to check for that. As Frege would say, we must begrudge him a pinch of salt. As Whitehead and Russell say, "a preliminary explanation of the notation [can] place lucidity before correctness" (1950, 1). Indeed, after distinguishing the order of discovery (or of pedagogy) from the order of logic (Russell 1985, 16), Russell adds that for primitive terms, "it must be strictly impossible to *say* what they mean, except by a tautology, for it is with them that language begins" (1985, 26). And Russell is not even discussing contingent explications such as Frege's.

Since there is no circularity in Frege's series of definitions either, circularity is not the cause of Russell's paradox in Frege. The assumption that every concept determines a class is an assumption (*Grundlagen*, §§69 n. 1, 107), and Basic Law 5 is an axiom. The assumption and the axiom may be false, but they are not circular. Whitehead and Russell say the assumption "is perhaps the most fundamental case, of the vicious-circle principle" (1950, 39). This is strictly incorrect. Certain viciously circular *terms*, such as "class of classes not members of themselves," appear to *falsify* the assumption. But many innocent terms have "self-reference or reflexiveness" (1950, 61), and "generate a totality containing members defined in terms of itself" (1950, 64). Thus circularity in this sense is not a sufficient condition of viciousness, and it remains to explain the viciousness of any viciously circular terms. To say the problem is viciousness is merely to pose it. There is at present no definition of viciousness which is neither too broad nor too narrow, or even a specific explanation of Russell's paradox which is any deeper than the mere fact of the paradox (compare Jean van Heijenoort).

I turn from diagnosis to prevention. Self-referential circularity is a necessary condition of Russell's paradox. Ramified type theory eliminates the paradox, and much else, by eliminating all such circularity. Is then such circularity the cause of Frege's *failure to prevent* the paradox? Dummett says, "The stipulations governing the primitive functors . . . could be determinate only if the domain, consisting wholly or largely of value-ranges, was determinate; but the domain was in process of being determined by fixing the *Bedeutungen* of the value-range terms, and so the procedure went round in a circle" (1995, 18; see Dummett 1991, 215, 233, 239, 318; 1981, 529–41). "That is to say, a function is not a well-defined function unless all its values are already well-defined" (Whitehead 1950, 39). But regimentation does not involve such circularity. Regimentation starts with the primitive terms, and thereby all terms, already explicated as expressing fairly clear senses. Regimentation merely aims to make these senses logically determinate, so as to ensure that all terms have logically determinate references. Now, without knowing the cause of the paradox, the only way to regiment without overkill or underkill may seem to be not principled or general, but individually for each sentence in which any paradoxical term occurs, an infinite task not in our power to complete. But in theory, Russell's paradox can be prevented by regimenting each sense so as to impose a determinate truth-condition on each sentence, thereby ensuring a reference for each term. There would be *mutual determination* of all references by their being regimented in terms of each other, but no circularity, due to the explications. Regimenting is like using scissors to make rough pieces fit in a jigsaw puzzle, or using a saw to make rough planks fit in Neurath's ship, or training civilians into a regiment of soldiers. Any paradoxical sensial guidance from a sense would be individually regimented, and any innocent sensial guidance would remain. Or second, we could generally stipulate that every sense meta-determine that if it determines a paradoxical class, then that class is a member of itself. Or third, we could generally stipulate that every paradoxical sense is barred from the notation, and thereby every paradoxical function along with its paradoxical totality of values. In any of these three ways, every concept named in the notation will determine a class. Frege's paradox is that he should have shown more faith in his commitment to classes as abstract entities. This commitment is established in the *Grundgesetze* preface by his private language argument, long before he tries to prove in vol. 1, §29 that his names refer. The proof is a mere question of slicing up the objective realm into determinate entities; and Frege permits our slicing it as arbitrarily as we please. Thus Frege need not provide any principled solution to Russell's paradox in order to preserve logicism. See my (2003, 100), *pace* Dummett (1991, 211). Of course, my second and third suggestions are principled in preventive ways. Note that explication, used as sensial guidance on how to regiment senses and thereby references *truth-functionally*, is extensional in sense (1). Frege regiments extensional in sense (1) references via extensional in sense (1) senses. Senses and references alike are extensional in sense (1); senses are intensional in sense (2).

The Heijenoort-Hintikka critique seems based on the assumption that for Frege, names *are* objects. And that might be based on the assumption that for Frege, every entity is an object or a function. Now, Frege's names are very plausibly glossed as signs (physical objects) expressing immaterial senses. Thus it might seem that they are not wholly objects, since their component senses are not objects. And it might seem to follow that if we can directly refer to them as signs expressing senses, we can also indirectly refer to them as senses expressed by signs, and that either way, they are not strictly objects, so that strictly objectual quantifiers should not range over them. But Frege makes it clear that all signs are objects (1971, 194). Even the equality (identity) sign is an object (1971, 194). Thus names cannot be a class of signs, namely signs expressing senses. For all signs are objects, and all objects are complete; but many names are incomplete, including the name for equality. (Their incompleteness can only be due to their sense.) Thus names are not objects. The charitable gloss is that names are emergent entities. Their emergent property is that of explaining the possibility of an informative identity statement. Neither mere signs (nor names considered as mere labels) nor mere senses have that property. Making names objects by making them a class of signs would sweep their emergent nature under the rug.

9. As Dummett says, most of the objects Frege names in his formal notation are value-ranges (1995, 18). But Frege is talking about an ideal language for science in general—a *lingua characteristica*—not a *calculus ratiocinator* (*Begriffsschrift*, 6–7; see 2–3). And he uses statements such as "All men are mortal" to explicate quantification.

10. See Haaparanta 1985, 38–40, 46 n.26; my 1999, 116; my 2001, 26.

11. Dummett says Frege rejects facts as a category (Dummett 1981a, 176–77) until 1918, when Frege assays facts as true thoughts in "The Thought" (Frege 1968a, 531; Dummett 1981, 659, 662). If so, this makes facts emergent entities with a thought and an object—the True—as components. There is nothing like this in Russell or Wittgenstein. But it might be better to say that Frege is merely analyzing an ordinary sense of the word "fact."

12. The following four items in Frege must not be confused with each other: (a) the abstract (noncausal) extensional in sense (2) concept *red*; (b) the abstract intensional in sense (2) sense expressed by "red"; (c) a concrete (causal) extensional in sense (2) red object in the physical world; and (d) an extensional in sense (2) mental sensation of red, normally had by one when one perceives a red object. Now, if (d) is concrete (causal), or even has normal or lawlike patterns of occurrence, then to that extent (d) is objective, *pace* Frege's classification of ideas as subjective and in flux, and *pace* his sharp separation of the objective from the subjective. Frege allows, and I think requires, at least resemblances across different persons' ideas even to explain how art is possible (1971i, 61).

13. Thus Frege would reject Dummett's solution of the *oratio obliqua* problem. Dummett is very clear that his solution is "emendation," not scholarship (1981, 267, 268; 1981a, 87).

14. Dummett says Frege found that the traditional concept of abstraction is irrelevant to the notion of sense, and does not use it in his final account; but Dummett admits that this final account concerns the formal notation and not ordinary language (Dummett 1981, 676–78). This is consistent with my view that Frege never retracts his early paper (1972) on the basic role of abstraction in learning ordinary language.

Frege denies that traditional abstraction can yield a logically adequate concept of number (*Grundlagen*, §§34, 44; 1971c, 84–85). But in *Grundlagen*, §89, he does not repudiate altogether Kant's principle that concepts without percepts are blind, which is the heart of abstraction, but only for numbers. Indeed, he calls this "the mistake of supposing that a concept can *only* be acquired by direct abstraction from a number of objects" (§49, emphasis mine). This implies he thinks some concepts *are* acquired by abstraction. Late in life, he indicates that we use abstraction to teach and learn our first "kindergarten numbers" in ordinary language (1979h, 276; see 1979a, 280); perhaps he thinks such teaching is a type of explication (1979j, 271). Perhaps the best view is that from 1884 on, he thinks that not every concept can be acquired by abstraction, but that some must be. This is parallel to Dummett's distinction between primary and secondary objects. See my 2003 (240–42).

15. One might object that modes in general are ontologically dependent, and that thus perhaps modes of presentation contained by incomplete senses are incomplete too. If so, the chief difference between such senses and the modes of presentation they contain is simply that the former have a linguistic role and the latter are their cognitive components. But surely the modes of presentation contained by complete senses are just as dependent, yet are complete. Thus I see no need for incomplete senses to contain incomplete modes of presentation.

16. My interpretation is in my 2003 (275–77).

17. The conclusion is clear enough to show that Russell interprets Frege the

same way I do. For Russell is criticizing Frege precisely for *not* holding that every denoting phrase denotes a denotation (reference) as opposed to a meaning (sense). That is, Russell is agreeing with me that Frege holds that some denoting phrases denote meanings (senses) *as opposed to* denotations (references).

18. Dummett is well aware that difference in reference implies difference in sense.

19. Dummett is right that references are singled out only via senses; Frege expressly says so (1979c, 124). But I criticize Frege in the following limited sense. If dogs can single out the Moon without the use of imperceptible concepts in *Grundlagen*, §31, then dogs can single out the Moon without the use of imperceptible senses in *Grundgesetze*. Of course, the Moon is not a linguistic reference for dogs, but merely a physical phenomenon for them (see my 2003, 86, 94, 240–42; *Grundlagen*, §31).

20. Dummett, 1981, 4; see 9–12, 240, 334, 557, 576, 677–79.

21. This is a retraction of my 1996 (65–73). My 2003 corrects my mistake. See note 28.

22. On functions, see 1971d, 47, 47 n.†; 1971b, 31, 38–39; on incomplete senses, see 1971c, 54; 1971f, 134; 1968, 538.

23. See also Frege (1979g, 254–55) on the correspondence of sense- and reference-incompleteness.

24. William Marshall notices this (1968a, 300). This by itself does not imply that senses are not objects; indeed, Marshall holds that senses are objects. But it does pull the realm of senses out of the realm of customary references, *pace* Dummett (1981, 680). Thus Marshall can only admit senses as indirect objects. But what content does "indirect object" add to the content of "sense"?—Can indirect objects be incomplete?

25. Dummett omits tones and forces from his list of Frege's objects. On his own showing, his only other options are that they are functions or nonentities.

26. I thank Richardson, who was then a graduate student in chemistry, in my (1979, ii). The chemistry metaphor is, of course, realist in import.

Dummett speaks of "logical valency" (1981, 32, 62, 43). But Frege wants *metaphysical* valency to unify the thought, resolving—not dissolving—Bradley's regress, *pace* Dummett (1981, 174–75). Frege is a realist on universals. Frege's concepts are *ante rem* universals, *pace* Dummett (1981, 257–58). A concept name always refers to literally the same concept regardless of how many objects are truly said to fall under that concept, and even if no objects fall under it. Predicative senses are *ante rem* universals too. They remain literally the same across different thoughts. And assertoric force is a universal, since it remains literally the same across assertions; the judgment stroke always indicates the same force. Insofar as tones concern particular acts of utterance and mental ideas, they are particulars; but *tone* is a universal. Thus while all concepts are universals, not all universals are concepts. We must not confuse the object-concept distinction with the particular-universal distinction. This is not a difficulty. Consider that ideas are particulars and *idea* is a universal.

Even if Frege has another sense of "saturation" in mind, such as solubility (*Grundlagen*, §80), surely it would still be a physical sense, and consistent with molecular theory. I doubt he has in mind, say, the saturation of a poetry reading with emotion. Marshall shows the limits of several physical senses of Frege's other main metaphor, "incomplete" (1968, 253–58, 262–65). As Dummett notes, metaphors necessarily have limits (1968, 277). Frege agrees (1979c, 137), and adds that any bodily metaphor has limits when applied to immaterial senses (1971h, 134). Thus even the valency metaphor has limits, though the filling of electron-spaces by electrons is remarkably apt. Indeed, Frege's logical atomism is more aptly called his logical chemistry.

Molecules can be *conceptually* sliced in different ways, *pace* Ramsey (Dummett 1981a, 264). For Frege, anything complex can be conceptually sliced in different ways merely by regarding something different as the subject. Water is sliced as H_2O (dihydrogen oxide) or as HOH (hydrogen hydroxide, or hydronium hydroxide); HOH is physically more perspicuous. Frege's example is that it is "more appropriate to represent . . . hydrogen . . . by . . . H [and hydroxil by OH] than . . . to designate hydrogen as de-oxidized hydroxil" (1979b, 37; see 36; 1979d, 194 on chemistry).

Dummett says mathematical functions provide the "really important" metaphor of Frege's functions (1968, 296). I agree, but only as to mapping values. Frege expressly generalizes the mathematical notion into his notion, but circularity is not a problem at the level of explication. The problem is illuminating the problem of metaphysical unity. I see no illumination of the metaphysical problem, regardless of the clarity of the formal notation for function names, and regardless of whether mathematical functions are themselves instances of the functions to be explicated. What literal incompleteness of mathematical functions would be the basis of the metaphor illuminating the literal incompleteness of Frege's functions in general? What would be metaphorical about it?

27. Frege 1971i, 64, emphasis mine; quoted twice in my 2003, 65, 68. "Ein Wahrheitswerth kann nicht ein Theil eines Gedankens sein, sowenig wie etwa die Sonne, weil er kein Sinn ist, sondern ein Gegenstand" (Frege 1892, 35). Literally, "A truth-value cannot be a part of a thought, as little as for example the Sun, because it is no sense, but rather an object." Or according to *Cassell's*, "it is no sense, but on the contrary, an object."

28. Thus I was wrong to suggest that senses should be assimilated to the first model, with "the sense of 'A'" referring to an object which represents the sense (my 1996, 68–73; 1982, 13; 1981, 36–37). For Frege openly says it refers to the sense (my 1996, 69; 1981, 36). My earlier idea was feasible by "converting" senses to objects, but the representation would not be mutual, i.e., one-one, due to sensial underdetermination (*pace* my 1996, 118; 1982, 13). My 2003 corrects my mistake. Of course, we could arbitrarily *posit* a representative object that corresponds one-one to the sense, but Frege clearly does no such thing, since he says we refer to the sense.

29. In the schema, "meaning" means reference. Truth-values, of course, are objects.

30. Nor does Frege write "concept" for the incomplete sense, for it is not a concept but a sense.

If senses are objects, why does Frege fail to say so in his schema of his view?

Frege says, "The . . . schema should make my view clear." If senses are objects, how could the schema possibly make his view clear?

Does Frege, perhaps, fear confusing Husserl by explaining the additional complexity that the senses too are objects, though none is the object the proposition in question is about? I would think that if senses were objects, *not* saying so would be confusing. Indeed, the schema should eliminate any such confusions. Otherwise it would not be making Frege's view clear. This is exactly the sort of thing Frege should be labeling in the schema and explaining in the letter. It would have been easy to do. I explained it very easily myself just now. He could even have said "indirect object."

Does Frege feel it is too obvious to mention that senses are objects? Other things in the schema are far more obvious, such as that proper names refer to objects. And how obvious is it that senses are objects?

Does Frege feel it is too unimportant to mention that senses are objects? The omission of such a basic categorial relationship would be monumental.

31. Frege says persons are objects (1971b, 31), making them customary references. Perhaps he thinks of persons as perceptible and bodily. Perhaps persons are a class of bodies, namely bodies having minds. But then persons ought to be emergent entities on the double take, since they or their minds are also the homes of ideas. Their emergent properties would include public acting and speaking.

32. Explications seem best glossed as emergent entities on the doubletake as well, since they aim at meetings of private minds on public references via public senses.

Senses might be emergent entities too. Frege describes only one constituent, the mode of presentation each contains. But they have a linguistic property of being expressible by names that this nonlinguistic, merely cognitive constituent lacks. I would like to say that the other logical constituent of senses is their completeness or incompleteness in conformity with the context principle. Their emergent property would be that of explaining how informative identity statements are possible.

I do not know what Frege would have thought of my glosses of emergence. He should be familiar with the concept of emergence. Numbers (classes of classes) have emergent properties, such as being odd or even, which their constituent classes lack. Whether these properties are ultimately purely logical does not matter to this point. There is also his statement that definitions can result in something new (1974, 100–101); and definition implies logical complexity, i.e., logical constituents. But Frege never says that senses, forces, tones, persons, names, or explications are emergents; and if they are, that would be a most important generalization to communicate. Nor does he define them, though he often seems to state their constituents and the relationships among their constituents. He may say so little about them because he knows they are mere logical emergents, or because he does *not* know and finds them mysterious, or because he takes them to be primitive categories, or because he takes them to be what they do. Of course, there are other possibilities; he may simply be laconic. Opinions may also differ on how much these entities' being emergents would remove the mystery about them. At least they would be not *deus ex machina sui generis*, but relational states of affairs logically composed of reasonably familiar constituents.

33. Dummett rejects Saul Kripke's thesis that every sense is descriptive, since Frege says that without some use of contextual cues, we could not convey where or when anything is (Dummett 1981a, 84; see 85–128; Frege 1979f, 213). But this confuses the sense with the conveyance of the sense—with "the conditions of utterance" (Frege 1968a, 517). Indexicality concerns only the linguistic garb of senses. In ordinary language, explications are the norm. They can convey references only via senses. Their indexicality is fourfold: *I* must guess what *you* mean *here* and *now*. Surely they are often ostensive. Kluge says Frege does not discuss this (Kluge 1971, xxviii). But Frege mentions "the pointing of fingers" (1968a, 517). Frege divorces senses themselves from indexicality of any kind. They are timeless and placeless. Surely they are logically tied many-one to equally timeless and placeless concepts under or within which the references (if any) fall. Consider Frege's example, "the pupil of Plato . . ." (1971i, 58 n.*). Dummett is right that in practice, not every "sense can be conveyed by means of a definite description" (1981a, 85). But the operant sense of "can" is logically can. Also, a sense can always be conveyed by a description used referentially in Donnellan's sense.

34. The sense-reference distinction is not so basic to logic that Frege could not have completed his formal logicism in 1884, *pace* Dummett (1995, 8). Even a "mere label" name-theorist can define numbers as classes of classes. And Frege distinguishes contents from ways of presenting contents in *Begriffsschrift*. Thus he had a "glimmering" of the distinction after all, *pace* Dummett (1995, 7). Indeed, his earlier ways of presenting contents would seem to be what later mutate into senses. I agree with Dummett that *Grundlagen* would be clearer if it expressly used the distinction, and that a philosophy of logic, as opposed to a formal logicist system, ought to make some such distinction.

35. This is directly so for Frege, since his truth-values *are* referential objects.

36. Frege's implicit nod to intuitionism is his requirement of existence-proofs. He says that to prove a concept's consistency, we must produce an object falling under the concept (*Grundlagen*, §§74, 95 n.1); and we cannot existentially quantify over an inconsistent concept to yield a truth.

Frege even says "*F*'s exist" *means* that there is at least one *F* (*Begriffsschrift*, §12 n.15), i.e., that there are not zero *F*'s (*Grundlagen*, §53). But this is no general theory of intuitionistic meaning. It is merely his analysis of the single word "exist," and his informal analysis at that. Frege formally defines the existential quantifier in terms of the universal quantifier and negation, and he makes it clear that we understand "all *F*'s" even if we do not know every *F*. Both quantifiers express universal senses and refer to universal concepts.

37. One need not be a phenomenologist to agree that: "By saying that we do not or cannot understand [impossible] suppositions, we can only mean that we find what they suppose unthinkable, inconceivable. For, of course, we do not literally mean that we do not or that we cannot understand them; what we mean is that we cannot *think* what we do understand them to suppose. . . . Inability to understand, in the sense in which philosophers appeal to it when determining the absolute impossibility of something, is the *unthinkability* of what, in a sense, is *understood* to be described by the proposition, not the literal nonunderstanding of that proposition" (Butchvarov 1970, 81). Frege agrees, analyzing thinkability in terms

110   JAN DEJNOŽKA

of references, and understanding in terms of senses (1971i, 58). But intuitionists are constrained to literal nonunderstanding of nonintuitionistic mathematics, on pain of its being as literally meaningful as intuitionistic mathematics.

38. Neither Frege nor Russell says so, but probably they both believed that every truth of logic is either an axiom or a provable theorem. Certainly the Frege-Russell camp was stunned by Gödel's incompleteness proof. But neither Frege nor Russell makes proof/disproof a requirement of meaningfulness. Frege says it may not always be in our power to apply a concept, and Russell expressly rejects intuitionism.

39. The pre-sense-reference Frege says, "That a concept contains a contradiction is not always obvious without investigation; but to investigate it we must first possess it and, in logic, treat it just like any other" (1974, 87). Frege adds, "The concept 'fraction smaller than 1 and such that no fraction smaller than one exceeds it in magnitude' is quite unexceptionable: in order, indeed, to prove that there exists no such fraction, we must make use of just this concept, despite its containing a contradiction" (1974, 87 n.1). On the sense-reference split, the point applies not only to the concept, but to the sense as well. For Frege we must first possess the sense, and in order to prove that there exists no reference, we must make use of just this sense (1971i, 58). Ironically, it is the question whether any mathematical objects exist that leads Dummett to hold that we must first possess the reference in order to prove that there exists any sense to our inquiry.

If I were to defend intuitionism, I would look to Parmenides' view that nothing can be said or thought about nothing. This implies that we must first possess the reference. But that reduces Parmenides to taking the backward road. Also, like the verification principle, Parmenides' view violates itself. It says something about nothing. And the sense-reference distinction is Frege's reply to Parmenides.

                                    REFERENCES

Ayer, Alfred Jules. 1952. *Language, Truth and Logic*. 2nd ed. New York: Dover. 1946.
Beaney, Michael. 1997. "Introduction to Frege." In Gottlob Frege, *The Frege Reader*, ed. and trans. Michael Beaney. Oxford: Blackwell.
Butchvarov, Panayot. 1970. *The Concept of Knowledge*. Evanston, IL: Northwestern Univ. Press.
Carnap, Rudolf. 1959. *The Logical Syntax of Language*. Routledge and Kegan Paul.
Caton, Charles. 1968. "An Apparent Difficulty in Frege's Ontology." In Klemke, 1968. (Original printing 1962).
Dejnožka, Jan. 2003. *The Ontology of the Analytic Tradition and Its Origins: Realism and Identity in Frege, Russell, Wittgenstein, and Quine*. Reprinted with further corrections. Lanham, MD: Littlefield Adams. (Original printing 1996).
————. 2001. "Origin of Russell's Early Theory of Logical Truth as Purely General Truth: Bolzano, Peirce, Frege, Venn, or MacColl?" *Modern Logic* 8/3–4: 21–30.

————. 1999. *Bertrand Russell on Modality and Logical Relevance*. Aldershot, U.K.: Ashgate.

————. 1996. Original printing of 2003.

————. 1991. "Russell's Seventeen Private-Language Arguments." *Russell* 11/1: 11–35.

————. 1982. "Frege: Existence Defined as Identifiability." *International Studies in Philosophy* 14: 1–17.

————. 1981. "Frege on Identity." *International Studies in Philosophy* 13: 31–41.

————. 1979. "Frege: Existence and Identity." Ann Arbor, MI: University Microfilms International. Doctoral dissertation, The University of Iowa, Iowa City.

Dummett, Michael. 2000. *Elements of Intuitionism*. 2nd ed. Oxford: Clarendon Press.

————. 1995. "The Context Principle: Centre of Frege's Philosophy." In *Logik und Mathematik: Frege-Kolloquium Jena 1993*, ed. Ingolf Max and Werner Stelzner. Berlin: Walter de Gruyter. Presented in 1993.

————. 1993. *Origins of Analytical Philosophy*. London: Duckworth.

————. 1991. *Frege: Philosophy of Mathematics*. Cambridge, MA: Harvard Univ. Press.

————. 1981. *Frege: Philosophy of Language*. 2nd ed. Cambridge, MA: Harvard Univ. Press.

————. 1981a. *The Interpretation of Frege's Philosophy*. Cambridge, MA: Harvard University Press.

————. 1968. "Frege on Functions: A Reply." In Klemke 1968. 1955.

————. 1968a. "Note: Frege on Functions." In Klemke 1968. 1956.

Frege, Gottlob. 1980. Letter to Bertrand Russell dated November 13, 1904. In Frege 1980f.

————. 1980a. Letter to Bertrand Russell dated May 21, 1903. In Frege 1980f.

————. 1980b. Letter to Bertrand Russell dated October 20, 1902. In Frege 1980f.

————. 1980c. Letter to David Hilbert dated December 27, 1899. In Frege 1980f.

————. 1980d. Letter to Edmund Husserl dated May 24, 1891. In Frege 1980f.

————. 1980e. Letter to Giuseppe Peano, undated. In Frege 1980f.

————. 1980f. *Philosophical and Mathematical Correspondence*, ed. Gottfried Gabriel et al., trans. Hans Kaal. Oxford: Basil Blackwell.

————. 1979. "A Brief Survey of my Logical Doctrines." In Frege 1979i. 1906.

————. 1979a. "A New Attempt at a Foundation for Arithmetic." In Frege 1979i. 1924/25.

————. 1979b. "Boole's logical Calculus and the Concept-script." In Frege 1979i. 1880/81.

————. 1979c. "[Comments on Sense and Meaning]." In Frege 1979i. 1892–1895.

————. 1979d. "Introduction to Logic." In Frege 1979i. August 1906.

————. 1979e. "Logic." In Frege 1979i. 1897.

————. 1979f. "Logic in Mathematics." In Frege 1979i. Spring 1914.

————. 1979g. "[Notes for Ludwig Darmstaedter]." In Frege 1979i. July 1919.

————. 1979h. "Numbers and Arithmetic." In Frege 1979i. 1924/25.

————. 1979i. *Posthumous Writings*. Ed. Hans Hermes et al., trans. Peter Long and

Roger White. Chicago: Univ. of Chicago Press.

———. 1979j. "Sources of Knowledge of Mathematics and the Mathematical Natural Sciences." In Frege 1979i. 1924/25.

———. 1974. *The Foundations of Arithmetic*. (*"Grundlagen"*). Trans. J. L. Austin. Evanston, IL: Northwestern Univ. Press. 1884.

———. 1972. "On the Scientific Justification of a Conceptual Notation." In *Frege, Conceptual Notation and Related Articles*, ed. and trans. Terrell Ward Bynum. Oxford: Clarendon. 1882.

———. 1971. "A Critical Elucidation of some Points in E. Schroeder's *Algebra der Logik*." Trans. Peter Geach. In Frege 1971j. 1895.

———. 1971a. "Frege Against the Formalists." In *Grundgesetze der Arithmetik* vol. 2, §§86–137, trans. Max Black. In Frege 1971j. 1903.

———. 1971b. "Function and Concept." Trans. Peter Geach. In Frege 1971j. 1891.

———. 1971c. Illustrative Extracts from Frege's Review of Husserl's *Philosophie der Arithmetik*. Trans. Peter Geach. In Frege 1971j. 1894.

———. 1971d. "On Concept and Object." Trans. Peter Geach. In Frege 1971j. 1892.

———. 1971e. "On the Foundations of Geometry." In Frege 1971g. 1906.

———. 1971f. "On the Foundations of Geometry." In Frege 1971g. 1903.

———. 1971g. *On the Foundations of Geometry and Formal Theories of Arithmetic*. Trans. Eike-Henner W. Kluge. New Haven, CT: Yale Univ. Press.

———. 1971h. "On Negation." Trans. Peter Geach. In Frege 1971j. 1919.

———. 1971i. "On Sense and Reference." Trans. Max Black. In Frege 1971j. 1892.

———. 1971j. *Translations from the Philosophical Writings of Gottlob Frege*. Ed. Peter Geach and Max Black. 2nd ed. Oxford: Basil Blackwell. 1960.

———. 1968. "Compound Thoughts." Trans. R. H. Stoothoff. In Klemke 1968. 1923.

———. 1968a. "The Thought." Trans. A. M. Quinton and Marcelle Quinton. In Klemke 1968. 1918/19.

———. 1967. *Begriffsschrift, a formula language, modeled upon that of arithmetic, for pure thought*. Trans. Stefan Bauer-Mengelberg. In *From Frege to Gödel: A Source Book in Mathematical Logic, 1879–1931*, ed. Jean van Heijenoort. Cambridge, MA: Harvard Univ. Press. 1879.

———. 1964. *The Basic Laws of Arithmetic*. (*"Grundgesetze"*). Ed. and trans. Montgomery Furth. Berkeley: Univ. of California Press. Vol. 1, 1893; vol. 2, 1903.

———. 1892. "Über Sinn und Bedeutung." *Zeitschrift für Philosophie und philosophische Kritik* 100: 25–50.

Furth, Montgomery. 1968. "Two Types of Denotation." In *Studies in Logical Theory*, ed. Nicholas Rescher. American Philosophical Quarterly Monograph Series, no. 2. Oxford: Blackwell.

———. 1967. Editor's Introduction. In Frege 1967.

Gibson, Roger F., Jr. 1987. "Translation, Physics, and Facts of the Matter." In Hahn and Schilpp 1987.

Haaparanta, Leila. 1985. *Frege's Doctrine of Being*. Acta Philosophica Fennica, vol. 39. Helsinki.

Hahn, Lewis Edwin, and Paul Arthur Schilpp, eds. 1987. *The Philosophy of W. V. Quine*. The Library of Living Philosophers, vol. 18. La Salle, IL: Open Court.

Klemke, E. D., ed. 1968. *Essays on Frege*. Urbana: Univ. of Illinois Press.

Kluge, Eike-Henner W. 1971. Introduction. In Frege 1971g.

Marshall, William. 1968. "Frege's Theory of Functions and Objects." In Klemke 1968. 1953.

———, 1968a. "Sense and Reference: A Reply." In Klemke 1968. 1892.

Quine, Willard Van Orman. 1987. "Reply to Roger F. Gibson, Jr." In Hahn and Schilpp 1987.

———. 1981. "Things and Their Place in Theories." In *Theories and Things*. Rev. ed. Cambridge, MA: The Belknap Press.

———. 1975. *Word and Object*. Cambridge, MA: The M.I.T. Press. 1960.

Russell, Bertrand. 1971. "On Denoting." In *Logic and Knowledge*, ed. Robert C. Marsh. New York: Capricorn. 1905.

———. 1957. "Knowledge by Acquaintance and Knowledge by Description." In *Mysticism and Logic*. Garden City, NY: Doubleday Anchor Books. 1910/11.

Whitehead, Alfred North, and Bertrand Russell. 1950. *Principia Mathematica*, vol. 1. 2nd ed. London: Cambridge Univ. Press. 1927.

REPLY TO JAN DEJNOŽKA

Jan Dejnožka's concluding statement that I am for him the best Frege scholar makes me truly proud, but I agree with him that you would never guess he thought so from reading the rest of his essay.

Although Jan Dejnožka makes clear that by the expression "Dummett's program" he does not mean the programme that I myself would adopt for a theory of meaning for a language, he uses it so frequently that I feel impelled to reiterate that it is very much not my own programme, but my interpretation of Frege's programme. Specifically, it is my interpretation of the programme Frege follows in Part I of his *Grundgesetze der Arithmetik*.[1] There is no indication of such a programme in his other writings, but Part I of that book gives so strong an impression of being a full-dress, authoritative, if concise, statement of his views on semantic matters that it commands special attention.

I have from the beginning of my study of Frege been aware that the sense of an expression, as Frege understands the notion, determines its reference (*Bedeutung*) but that its reference does not uniquely determine its sense. Thus, if we know that a singular term refers to the planet Venus, we do not know its sense: it may have the sense of "the second planet from the Sun," or of "the planet which appears in the early morning as a bright star," or many other senses. Hence, there is no backward road from reference to sense. Dr. Dejnožka argues that to define the sense of an expression as the way its reference is given to a competent speaker of the language is to take the backward road, since it involves holding that, given the reference of an expression, we can define its sense. This appears to confuse "defining the sense of the expression **A**" with "defining 'the sense of the expression **A**'." If we know of a certain expression only that it refers to the planet Venus, we cannot infer its sense, which would be attempting to take the backward road, but we can characterise its sense as being the way Venus is given by that expression to any competent speaker of the language.

In Part I of his *Grundgesetze*, Frege sets out a semantic theory for the formal language he uses throughout that book. In view of there being no backward road from reference to sense, we might expect that Frege would first stipulate or explain the senses of the primitive expressions of the language and of combinations of them: from these their references would be determinable. But this is not at all what he does. In §2 of vol. I he first explains his understanding of the word "*Bedeutung*" (reference); he does so for names of truth-values and singular terms only, although earlier in the section he had spoken of "function-names." (By a "name of a truth-value," Frege means what we should call a "sentence." In §5 he requires what he is willing to call a [formal] "sentence" to be preceded by the judgement-stroke; what we are left with when the judgement-stroke is removed is a name of a truth-value.) Towards the end of the section he makes a very cursory mention of the notion of sense (*Sinn*), as follows: "But I distinguish the *sense* of a name from its *reference*. '2^2' and '2 + 2' do not have the same sense, nor do '$2^2 = 4$' and '2 + 2 = 4' have the same sense. The sense of a name of a truth-value I call a *thought*. I say further that a name *expresses* its sense and *refers to* (*bedeute*) its reference." And that is all the mention of the notion of sense for another thirty sections. To understand this passage we must be aware that in *Grundgesetze* Frege calls every semantically significant expression, saturated or unsaturated (containing argument-places), a "name." A reader would grasp from the passage no more than that Frege was using the term "sense" in more or less its ordinary meaning.

It is not until the celebrated §32 that Frege mentions the notion of sense again. Because it is crucial, I shall quote it in full.

It has thus been shown that our eight primitive names have a reference, and thereby that the same also holds good for all names properly constituted out of them. But not only a reference but also a sense attaches to all names properly formed from our symbols. Every such name of a truth-value *expresses* a sense, a *thought*. That is, by means of our stipulations (*Festsetzungen*) it is determined under what conditions it refers to the True. The sense of this name, the *thought* is that these conditions are fulfilled. Now a formal sentence consists of the judgement-stroke and a name, or a Latin mark, of a truth-value. Such a mark is, however, transformed into the name of a truth-value by the introduction of German letters, prefixed by a concavity, in place of the Latin ones, in accordance with §17. If we think of this as carried out, we have only the case in which the sentence is composed of the judgement-stroke and the name of a truth-value. Now such a sentence asserts that this name refers to the True. Since it at the same time expresses a thought, we have in every correctly formed formal sentence a judgement that a thought is true; and so a thought cannot by any means be lacking. It is the task of the reader to make clear to himself the thought of every formal sentence that occurs, and I will take the trouble to cast as much light on this as possible in advance.

Now the simple or already themselves composite names out of which the name of a truth-value is composed contribute to expressing the thought, and this contribution on the part of a particular one is its *sense*. If a name is part of the name of a truth-value, the sense of that name is part of the thought which the whole expresses.

A "Latin mark" is an expression containing Roman letters, which Frege uses as free variables with universally quantified significance. Thus "$x = x$" signifies "For all **a**, **a** = **a**." Frege explains this in §17, and he lays down a rule of derivation allowing the transformation of a Latin mark by replacing the Roman letters with the German ones he uses as bound variables, with an initial universal quantifier, for which Frege uses a horizontal line with a concavity in the middle, surmounted by the bound variable, and the converse transformation.

Just as there had been nothing about sense before §32 since §2, so very little is said about sense after §32. In §§5–13 Frege gives a series of explanations of the reference he intends his primitive symbols to have. Dr. Dejnožka makes much of the notion Frege elsewhere employs of explications (*Erläuterungen*) of expressions that cannot be defined, and applies it to Frege's explanations of the primitive symbols. But Frege does not use the word "*Erläuterungen*" of these explanations in *Grundgesetze*: he calls them "*Festsetzungen*" (stipulations) and "*Bestimmungen*" (specifications). The difference is surely this: We can give only explications of expressions that are absolutely indefinable. But here Frege is giving a semantic theory in German for a formal language. The primitive symbols of that formal language are indefinable *in that formal language*: that does not prevent them from being completely explained in the natural language which is serving as the metalanguage of the theory.

Dejnožka says, "Frege says right in *Grundgesetze* vol. 1, §0 (last para.) that he must indicate what he intends by his primitive names by 'hints,' since not everything can be defined." By "§0," Dejnožka means what Frege calls the Introduction (not part of Part I), and in the last paragraph of that, Frege indeed says, "The following may be remarked at the outset. It will not always be possible to give a principled definition of everything. Because it must be our endeavour to reduce all to the logically simple, which, as such, is not properly definable. I must then content myself with indicating what I mean by hints." I do not think Frege here had in mind his specifications of the references of the primitive symbols of his formal notation; he certainly does not say so. I think, rather, that he was thinking of his initial explanations in Part I of the terms "concept," "relation," and "function," expressions he had elsewhere classed as indefinable; that it was they he had in mind is made likely by his having been discussing the notions of concept and relation in the preceding paragraph, the last sentence of which says that they are the foundation stones of his structure.

Dr. Dejnožka accuses me of assuming that we have a prior knowledge of the senses and references of the primitive symbols of Frege's formal language, indeed of "smuggling in" such knowledge. He does this on the basis of my speaking of "a sentence of a given form." He asks whether I mean that we are given that the form of a particular sentence is that, say, of an identity statement. But the form of a sentence is a syntactical feature. Frege gives a very clear exposition of the syntactical formation of sentences of his formal language. From it we are enabled to pick out proper names (singular terms), expressions for first-level functions of one argument, expressions for first-level functions of two arguments, and expressions for second-level functions whose one argument is a first-level function. We are also in possession of a knowledge of several particular symbols with their syntactic types. We can therefore pick out a range of sentences by their (syntactic) form. We can, for example, refer to sentences of the form "$s = t$," where s and t are singular terms. In doing so, we are not assuming it as known that "=" is a sign of identity, or that we even yet have the concept of identity. We are, I should like to say, picking out such sentences by their form alone, were it not that this expression appears to mislead Dr. Dejnožka. An objection might be made to my speaking of "sentences," on the ground that in *Grundgesetze* sentences are not syntactically distinguished from any other singular terms. Very well, I make an emendation: for "sentence" read "expression preceded by the horizontal stroke."

In §10 Frege gives a permutation argument to show that he has not yet fully determined the references of terms for value-ranges. He resolved the difficulty by an application of the context principle: their references will be determined if the value of every function for a value-range as argument is fixed. If this is secured, then the reference of every more complex expression of which a term for a value-range is part will be determined, including that of sentences (names of truth-values) in which such a term occurs. In the process of fixing the values of the functions that are references of function-names formed from his primitive symbols, Frege evades the Julius Caesar problem by identifying the two truth-values with their unit classes. (It will be recalled by readers of Frege's *Grundlagen* that the Julius Caesar problem becomes, in this context, that of determining the truth-value of statements of identity in which a term for a value-range stands on one side and a term of some other kind on the other.) He justifies this as a solution of the problem by saying that the truth-values are the only objects not explicitly given as value-ranges in the formal language; that language has no means of referring to Julius Caesar. Dejnožka denies that for Frege the reference of expressions is internal to the language to which they belong, but this argument has no force unless that assumption is made.

The oddity is that Frege's solution to the problem of fixing the references of terms for value-ranges does not resolve the permutation problem which was supposed to have prompted it. What, then, is the significance of a permutation argument? Dejnožka very pertinently refers to the permutation argument in §26 of *Die Grundlagen der Arithmetik*. I will again quote the relevant passage *in extenso* (in Austin's translation):

> What is objective in [space] is what is subject to laws, what can be conceived and judged, what is expressible in words. What is purely intuitable is not communicable. To make this clear, let us suppose two rational beings such that projective properties and relations are all that they can intuit—the lying of three points on a line, of four points on a plane, and so on; and let what the one intuits as a plane appear to the other as a point, and vice versa, so that what for the one is the line joining two points for the other is the line of intersection of two planes, and so on, with the one intuition always dual to the other. In these circumstances they could understand one another quite well and would never realize the difference between their intuitions, since in projective geometry every proposition has its dual counterpart; any disagreements over points of aesthetic appreciation would not be conclusive evidence. Over all geometrical theorems they would be in complete agreement, only interpreting the words differently in terms of their respective intuitions. With the word "point," for example, one would connect one intuition and the other another. We can therefore still say that this word has for them an objective meaning, provided only that by this meaning we do not understand any of the peculiarities of their respective intuitions. And in this sense the axis of the Earth too is objective.[2]

When he wrote *Grundlagen*, Frege did not yet have his mature theory of sense and reference, but he had the distinction between objective and subjective he was to hold all his life. In his mature theory a thought was something objective; different people could grasp, and dispute over the truth of, one and the same thought; Frege equated the intersubjective with the objective. The senses that compose a thought—the senses of the component expressions of a sentence expressing the thought—were therefore also objective. The moral of the permutation argument in §26 of *Grundlagen* is that a permutation argument is always irrelevant to the senses and references of the words to which it relates. Perhaps this is the answer to those who regard the existence of a non-trivial automorphism of the complex numbers as a challenge to Frege. A permutation argument concerns only the subjective associations different individuals may have with the words, not their senses as used in the language common to many, nor, therefore, to their references. This conclusion makes Frege somewhat disingenuous in using a permutation argument to show that the references of terms for value-ranges had not yet been fixed: the real point was that it had not yet been laid down what was to be the truth-value of an identity-statement in which a term for a value-range stood on one side and one for a truth-value on the other. Perhaps he used the permutation argument, though it was in fact irrelevant, because it seemed more convincing and less pedantic.

In §§ 29 and 30 of *Grundgesetze*, vol. I, Frege explains under what conditions expressions of different types are to be said to have a reference, and in §31 he offers a proof that all well-formed expressions of his formal language have a reference, a proof that, after he learned of Russell's antinomy, he conceded to have been defective. And so we come to §32.

How, then, are we to understand §32? Jan Dejnožka contends that the section concerns only the order of being, not the order of cognition. That is, there being such a thing as the sense of a word, symbol, or other subsentential expression consists in its making a particular contribution to the thoughts expressed by sentences in which it occurs, but we do not arrive at a grasp of that sense by considering that contribution. But on this interpretation of Dejnožka's observation, Frege seemingly supplies no account of that in which the existence of a thought expressed by a sentence consists. In §32, Frege is concerned first to explain what thought is expressed by a sentence of his formal language, and only then to explain what constitutes the sense of a component expression within such a sentence. Does Dejnožka think that the existence of such a thought is constituted by the fact that by means of Frege's stipulations it is determined under what conditions the sentence refers to the True, but that it is not by considering what conditions those are that we come to grasp the thought it expresses? If so, this takes no account of the fact that Frege offers no other explanation of how we arrive at a grasp of that thought.

Section 32 provides the first and only explanation Frege gives in *Grundgesetze* of the notion of sense: it is surely intended to explain not just in what there being such a thing as the thought expressed by a sentence or the sense of a subsentential expression consists, but also how we know what it is and, in particular, how we are to know what the senses of the primitive symbols of the formal language are. We can arrive at the thought expressed by a formal sentence by working out, from the stipulations governing the references of the primitive symbols, under what conditions that sentence would refer to the True. If Frege's account in §32 were not so intended, there would be lacking any explanation of what the senses of the formal sentences of Frege's symbolism are; there would be only an account of how their references are determined, and this would not yield any explanation of their senses. If this were so, it would be an extraordinary omission.

Dejnožka has indeed a point in respect of the senses of subsentential expressions. I do not think that Frege means that we apprehend such a sense by considering different sentences in which the expression occurs and abstracting the common contribution made by that expression from the various thoughts expressed by those sentences. He thinks that we must look to the stipulations made concerning the references of the components of the expression to determine its sense. The sense is the way in which the reference is given, and Frege's stipulations display the way we are to take the reference of each expression as being given. These stipulations will, however, always have been made with an eye to their contributions to the determination of the truth-value of sentences in which they occur, as was explicitly done for value-range terms in §10. This is because, first, determining the reference of a component of a complex expression constitutes that step in determining the reference of the whole that corresponds to that component and, secondly, because the reference of any expression depends upon how it contributes to determining the reference of any more complex expression of which it is a component. The argument of §10 would be beside the point if it were not so.

Frege's procedure in §32, as thus understood, is not to determine the senses of expressions from their references, taking the backward road. It is to determine the sense of an expression from the particular way in which its reference has been specified. One and the same reference can be specified in different ways. For Frege the sense of an expression is the way in which its reference is given to one who knows the language, in virtue of his knowing the language. His idea in *Grundgesetze* is that his stipulations *say* what the reference is and, by the particular manner in which they say that, *show* what the sense is. That idea is shared, I believe, by many people. It is not my own idea, but it is the only way I can see to interpret Part I of *Grundgesetze*. It does not involve treading the backward road, the existence of which Frege no more believed in than did Russell: it requires us to take what he believed was a short path from the way the reference of an expression is specified to the sense it is intended to bear.

Dr. Dejnožka makes great play with the notion of truth-conditions. The notion echoes Frege's talk in §32 of the conditions (in the plural) for a sentence to refer to the True. It is a useful notion for characterising a certain type of theory of meaning, which, so far as I know, Frege was the first to propose. But it is a treacherous notion, which we should take care in using. Truth-conditions are not entities. We say, "In the circumstances, . . ."; but it would be foolish for a philosopher to ask, "What is a circumstance?" Likewise, the question, "What is a truth-condition?" is misbegotten. We can assign a truth-value to a particular sentence/statement/proposition, but when we are concerned with a type or range of sentences or statements, we have to lay down the condition for each of them to be true. In such a context truth-conditions lie, I suppose, within the realm of reference. But when truth-conditions are regarded as determining sense, then they of course belong to the realm of sense. They are not entities, however: they are not inhabitants of the realm of sense.

Dejnožka, on the other hand, holds that truth-conditions are always extensional and belong to the realm of reference. He goes so far as to infer from this that " '2 + 2 = 4' and '$(x) (x = x)$' have the same truth-condition," for, he argues, "their truth-condition is true under any condition!" How, if he had understood "condition" in such a way, could Frege have cited the conditions under which a sentence referred to the True as determining the thought expressed by that sentence, as he did in §32? Frege's formal language is a purely logical one, in which logical objects are the only objects that can be referred to; every sentence that can be framed in it is either analytically true or analytically false. All true sentences of the language would therefore have the same truth-condition, on Dejnožka's understanding of "truth-condition," as would all its false sentences. This would make nonsense of what Frege says in §32. The way to arrive at the condition for the truth of a sentence **A**, as determining the sense of **A**, and as Frege, in §32, intends the notion to be understood, is to ask, not "How must the world be for **A** to be true?" but "How might we come to recognise the sentence **A** as true?" By contrast, Dejnožka takes the *specific* truth-condition to be, in effect, a tree whose terminal nodes are the references of the simple component expressions of **A**, and the *general* truth-condition how, given this, the world must be for **A** to be true. But this general condition surreptitiously invokes the senses of the expressions. We are not, for example, given functions extensionally, as mappings of arguments on to values: we are given them by the senses of the words that denote them.

I am puzzled by what Dejnožka says about Frege's theory of logical necessity, which he takes Frege to regard "as purely general truth, i.e., as invariance of interpretation." The passage from "Einleitung in die Logik" he cites in support appears to be completely irrelevant. That from *Begriffsschrift* is concerned with "apodeictic judgements," such as "President Bush must be mortal." Frege says that there is no need to represent the apodeictic form in his formal language (the *Begriffsschrift*) because that form merely gives a hint as to the speaker's grounds for the judgement (the judgement expressed by the assertoric form "President Bush is mortal"). He also says more explicitly that the apodeictic form indicates that a general judgement from which the proposition can be derived holds good. In our example, this might be "All American Presidents are mortal," "All politicians are mortal," "All Protestants are mortal," or any of many others. These observations of Frege's certainly do not concern *logical* necessity in particular, and can scarcely be said to amount to a *theory*. Frege gives his definition of an a priori truth in *Grundlagen*, namely, as a proposition derivable by logical means alone from general truths that neither need nor admit of proof, and he also defines analytic truth, namely, as an a priori truth which derives from such general truths as are of a purely logical character. Being analytic is the only notion admitted by Frege that can count as one of logical necessity. It is true that he never later repeated this characterisation of the a priori and the analytic, but there is no reason to suppose that he ever departed from it to any serious degree. It has nothing to do with invariance of interpretation.

Are senses objects? There are for Frege three realms of reality: the inner world of sensations and mental images, the outer world of physical objects, and the third realm of senses and thoughts. Does the distinction between objects, concepts, and relations (and other functions) apply only within the outer world, or does it apply in all three realms? There seems no reason why it should not. Those who believe that the sense of a predicate is a function mapping the sense of a name on to a complete thought—say the sense of "the Earth" on to the thought that the Earth moves—certainly suppose that it does.

The idea is, however, erroneous. To grasp, or to specify, a function, we must know in advance what it is that we apprehend, or are laying down, as its value for any given argument: To recognise a function as mapping a certain sense on to a certain thought, we must already understand what that thought is. To grasp the thought expressed by "The Earth moves," we must know the sense of "ξ moves"; to know merely that it is a function that maps the sense of "the Earth" on to the thought expressed by "The Earth moves" will get us nowhere. The sense of "ξ moves" is a *part* of the thought that the Earth moves, which we must know before we can grasp that thought; as a part, it cannot be a function. A function cannot be a part of one of its values. The incompleteness of the sense of a predicate cannot consist in its being itself a function, but only in its being the sense *of a predicate*, something of which we must be aware if we are to grasp that sense. Thus, the notion of a function does not seem to have application within the realm of sense. But are senses objects? It certainly seems that thoughts must be objects: we can even name them, as "the theorem of Pythagoras," "the labour theory of value," "the second law of thermodynamics," and the like. But to conceive of senses as objects tends to produce a misconception. It causes us to think of the form of words as being directed towards an object in the third realm and, from this halfway station, being sent on to the reference. But this is a false picture: the sense is not a halfway station; it is the route from the form of words to the reference.

Thus, I recant my earlier view and am now in full agreement with Jan Dejnožka that senses—even thoughts—cannot be objects. He deserves credit for perceiving this. If there are no objects in the realm of sense, there can be no functions either, if only because a function requires objects to serve as arguments and values. The whole apparatus of objects, concepts, and functions is inapplicable in the realm of sense. Dr. Dejnožka perceives this, too; he says that there is nothing in §2 of *Grundgesetze*, vol. I—nor, I suppose he believes, anywhere else in Frege—to show that any sense is an object or a function. It therefore puzzles me that he disputes my claim that the incompleteness of the sense of a predicate or functional expression is of a different nature than that of a concept or function. If it is of the same nature, then such a sense must be a function, and, if some senses are functions, then other senses (the senses of complete expressions) must be objects. There seems a tension here between different ingredients of Dr. Dejnožka's thinking. I am not fully convinced from his quotations that Frege had a firm view that thoughts are not objects; I think now that he ought to have held that view, and I applaud Dr. Dejnožka's recognition of this.

How, then, do the parts of a thought hold together? Dejnožka pertinently refers to the passage in "Über Begriff und Gegenstand" in which Frege says that at least one part of every thought must be unsaturated or predicative since otherwise the parts of the thought would not hold together. So what effects the unity of a thought? The subject-term and the predicate of a sentence hold together because they are made for each other. Indeed, if we accept Frege's view of the predicate as formed in the first instance from a complete sentence by removing one or more occurrences of some term, filling the argument-place of that predicate is simply refilling the gaps by the same term or another like it: it is unproblematic that the result has a unity. It is somewhat different at the level of reference. The concept and the object are indeed made for each other. The concept, as understood in *Grundgesetze*, is a function from objects to truth-values; the object is simply an argument of that function, and it is of the being of functions to have arguments. Indeed, the values of a function that is the reference of a predicate are given as the truth-values of sentences whose argument-places are filled by terms referring to the objects serving as the arguments of that function. So there is again no mystery about the truth-values yielded by the reference of the predicate when applied to the reference of the subject. The corresponding point holds good when the sentence is formed from an expression for a function of second level and one for a first-level function inserted in its argument-place.

How is it, then, at the level of sense? The parts of a thought do not need to hold together. To speak of them as holding together is to think of the thought as an object, which it is not. The thought expressed by a sentence is a complex of paths from the parts of the sentence to their references. It is enough if the parts of the sentence hold together and if their references fit together as functions and their arguments. The references of the parts of the sentence are functions and objects understood as to be taken as their arguments, and perhaps also second-level functions with first-level functions understood as to be taken as *their* arguments. I suspect that Frege never fully thought this matter through. If he had, he might have abandoned the whole philosophical mythology of the third realm. That is why I do not offer my revised view that senses are neither objects nor functions as what I think that Frege believed, as Dejnožka does, but only as what I think that he ought to have believed in consistency with his other doctrines.

What follows from a denial that thoughts are objects? Certainly that they neither fall within the domain of ordinary first-order bound variables nor lie within the range of application of ordinary first-level predicates. Do they then form a domain of quantification of their own, and can special predicates be defined over this domain? This is to regard them as objects of a different *sort* from physical objects, numbers, and the like. It is a very un-Fregean idea: he never countenanced distinct sorts of objects with distinct domains of quantification. If he had, then surely he would have taken numbers and human beings to be of different sorts, and the Julius Caesar problem, in that form, would never have arisen. We are not, however, bound by Frege's ideas in this context because we are not attempting faithful exegesis; we do not know for sure what Frege would have answered, asked whether thoughts were objects.

The late John Myhill's paradox, modelled on Russell's, concerning thoughts, of which Professor William Demopoulos reminded me, at first sight provides us with a reason for rejecting the view of thoughts as a separate sort of objects. Consider the thought that every thought p, if it is to the effect that every thought falls under some particular concept F, then p does not fall under F; let us call this thought q. The thought q is itself a thought to the effect that every thought falls under a certain concept, namely the concept of p's being such that if it is a thought to the effect that every thought falls under some particular concept F, then p does not fall under F: let us call this concept W. It is now easy to see that, just as with Russell's paradox, if q, the thought that every thought falls under W, itself falls under W, it does not fall under W, and, if it does not fall under W then it does fall under W.

One solution is to deny that thoughts are objects, even objects of a different sort from physical objects and numbers, for the statement of the paradox required only quantification over thoughts and over concepts under which thoughts fall. What is the price of this denial? If thoughts are not objects of any sort, they cannot be quantified over; nor can we define predicates over them. Is this not contrary to reason? Can we not say of certain thoughts that they are malicious, of others that they are kindly, and of yet others that they are brilliant? These are not really predicates of thoughts, but of mental acts. It is malicious to entertain particular thoughts, kindly to dwell on others: the thoughts themselves do not have these characters, but the acts of thinking them.

Other predications cannot be similarly dismissed, however; it would be wrong to contend that one can say nothing about thoughts. We can attribute to them features arising from what is intrinsic to them. It is intrinsic to them that they have content and that they have structure. It is also intrinsic to them that they can be grasped by human beings and by other rational creatures, if any; it is intrinsic to them, again, that they can be expressed in words. We can therefore speak of conditional (hypothetical) thoughts and of thoughts about poetry, for example; we can also think or say such things as that there are some thoughts that it is impossible to express in words, or deny that there can be any such. Within the limits of predications of these kinds, we can undoubtedly quantify over thoughts. Our denial to them of the status of objects can be understood not as ruling out quantifying over them but rather as excluding them from the domain of objects of the usual kinds, concrete and abstract.

Thoughts, then, though they are not objects in the ordinary sense, are objects of a special sort, to which we can refer and over which we can quantify within a vocabulary tailored to them and not to ordinary objects. This, therefore, leaves the Myhill paradox unresolved since it speaks only of thoughts that are of a certain form (universal) and about a certain subject-matter (other thoughts). It seems that we must fall back, as Demopoulos suggests, on a solution of Russell's type, namely by distinguishing orders among thoughts: a thought about first-order thoughts will be of second order, and so forth. This is a clumsy necessity, needed to resolve a tiresome paradox, but as Demopoulos observes, such a paradox will always arise in any domain of objects of some sort if we can construct a many-one mapping on to those objects of concepts under which those objects fall. The mapping which takes a concept into the class of objects falling under it is such a mapping; the mapping which takes a concept under which thoughts fall on to the thought that all thoughts fall under it is another. In conceding to thoughts the status of objects of a special sort, and in specifying the admissible predications applicable to thoughts, we did not bar the construction of such a mapping; and so Myhill's paradox cannot be killed at birth; it necessarily arises, and can be blocked only by such a device as a distinction of orders among thoughts.

To say that thoughts are objects of a special sort does not mean merely that a different range of predicates can intelligibly be applied to them, as we normally take different predicates to be applicable to human beings and to numbers: it means that they are not full-fledged objects, even though we can intelligibly quantify over them. This is not because they are not sharply demarcated from one another. We can frame a criterion that determines whether or not a given thought is the same as another. If the answer to either of the following questions is "Yes," then the two thoughts are distinct:

(1) Does either of the thoughts involve a concept that the other does not involve?

(2) Does it make sense to judge one of them to be true but not the other?

If the answer to both is "No," the thoughts are the same. What disqualifies thoughts from being full-fledged objects is that they are not self-subsistent: a thought could not exist unless at least one human being or other rational creature grasped it. Thoughts, therefore, do not form, as Frege may well have supposed, a determinate domain containing every thought that ever will or ever could be grasped or expressed, some waiting in vain because they never will be expressed or grasped. The domain of thoughts is indeterminate and constantly expanding. Quantification over it, therefore, cannot be explained in the classical manner as the outcome of scrutinising each element of the domain to determine whether it satisfies the predicate or not. It can be explained only in the intuitionist fashion, under which an existential statement is justified only by the production of an instance, and a universal one by a demonstration of its necessitation from the very notion of a thought.

Jan Dejnožka's attempted refutation of intuitionism is based on an erroneous interpretation of the intuitionist conception of the understanding of a mathematical statement. Intuitionists do not think, as Dejnožka supposes, that such a statement acquires a meaning only when it is either proved or disproved. How could anybody set about trying to prove or to disprove a conjecture if he did not know what it meant? Rather, for intuitionists, one understands a mathematical statement if one is able to recognise a proof or a disproof of it: its meaning consists in an effective classification of mathematical constructions into those that are proofs of it and those that are not. When meaning and understanding are interpreted in this way, Dejnožka's attempted rebuttal fails.

I thank Dr. Dejnožka for his patient examination of my interpretation of Frege, though I agree with only one of his conclusions, that thoughts and their component senses are neither objects nor functions.

M. D.

NOTES

1. Gottlob Frege, *Grundgesetze der Arithmetik* (Hildesheim, Germany: Georg Olms, 1962). All translations are by M. Dummett, save one by J. Austin.

2. Gottlob Frege, *Foundations of Arithmetic*, 2nd rev. ed., trans. J. L. Austin (Evanston, IL: Northwestern University Press, 1980).

3

James W Allard

REALISM, ANTI-REALISM, AND ABSOLUTE IDEALISM

At the conclusion of his discussion of asymmetrical relations in *Principles of Mathematics*, Russell summarized one of his reasons for advancing a new theory of relations. He writes,

> We have now seen that asymmetrical relations are unintelligible on both the usual theories of relation. Hence, since such relations are involved in Number, Quantity, Order, Space, Time, and Motion, we can hardly hope for a satisfactory philosophy of Mathematics so long as we adhere to the view that no relation can be "purely external." As soon, however, as we adopt a different theory, the logical puzzles, which have hitherto obstructed philosophers, are seen to be artificial.[1]

Besides encapsulating Russell's grounds for rejecting competing philosophies of mathematics, this passage also captures Russell's reasons for rejecting the then dominant form of British philosophy, absolute idealism. Absolute idealism, Russell charged, was incapable of offering solutions to problems of mathematical philosophy and of philosophy in general because it treated all relations as internal. But this, Russell thought, meant that absolute idealism was unable to account for the existence of asymmetrical relations. As Russell saw it, this inability was in turn the result of its adherence to the traditional view that all propositions have subject-predicate form. Like other previous philosophers, absolute idealists had, in Russell's opinion, made a mistake about logical form. Russell took his realization that it was a mistake, that not all propositions have subject-predicate form, to be a major discovery, one that refuted absolute idealism and opened the way for his own pluralistic realism.[2]

None of the British idealists had the requisite mathematical knowledge to counter Russell's criticism within the philosophy of mathematics, and the leading absolute idealist, F. H. Bradley, confessed himself "incompetent utterly to sit in judgment on Mr. Russell's great work (*Principles of Mathematics*)."[3] But even though the body of *Principles of Mathematics* was never subjected to criticism from absolute idealists, the more general aspects of Russell's realism came under attack. Prime among them was the account of truth that he had presupposed, apparently without deeply considering it, in *Principles of Mathematics* and in his essays on Meinong. According to this account, truth is a simple property of some propositions. It can be apprehended, but apprehension does not otherwise affect the propositions apprehended.[4] This view of truth was vigorously challenged by H. H. Joachim. After subjecting Russell's view to sustained criticism, Joachim proposed an idealistic theory of truth, the coherence theory of truth. According to this theory, truth is systematic coherence within a significant whole.[5] Since individual judgments for Joachim are abstractions from such wholes, it is the whole itself rather than the individual judgments that, properly speaking, are true or false. In the face of Joachim's criticisms, Russell abandoned his previous view of truth and adopted a correspondence theory of truth while rejecting Joachim's view that the nature of truth is coherence. In the process Russell came to see the nature of truth as *the* fundamental question of philosophy.[6] The aspect of the coherence theory that formed Russell's primary target was Joachim's holism or "logical monism" as Russell called it.[7] By aligning holism with idealism and rejecting holism, Russell rejected absolute idealism.

Holism has not, however, always stood on the side of idealism against realism. In a more recent and continuing controversy, holism has been aligned with realism against idealism, or at least against anti-realism of which idealism is presumably a species.[8] The person most responsible for this debate is Michael Dummett. In a series of books and essays Dummett has surveyed a number of metaphysical disputes in philosophy. They include disputes between realists and anti-realists about the reality of the external world, about the existence of theoretical entities in science, and about the reality of the past. He has argued that all of these debates share a common feature: they concern the meanings of statements of a certain class, a class he calls "the disputed class." Dummett proposes that these debates can be resolved by constructing meaning theories for the statements in the disputed classes. For Dummett, a meaning theory is realistic if it accepts the principle of bivalence and anti-realistic if it does not.[9] So if the most satisfactory meaning theory for statements in one of the disputed classes employs the principle of bivalence, then the realistic interpretation of the statements in that class is correct. If the meaning theory does not accept bivalence, then the anti-realistic interpretation of them is correct.[10]

In addition to characterizing metaphysical disputes, Dummett has also been a party to them. In this role he has advanced general doubts about the coherence of realistic meaning theories, and he has sketched the outline of an alternative, anti-realistic meaning theory based on intuitionistic logic. A key component of his anti-realistic theory is his rejection of holism. As he puts it in his rejection of a realistic philosophy of mathematics, "The path of thought which leads from the thesis that use exhaustively determines meaning to an acceptance of intuitionistic logic as the correct logic for mathematics is one which rejects a holistic view of mathematics, and insists that each statement of any mathematical theory must have a determinate individual content."[11] Because his argument does not rest on any particular mathematical notions, it can be applied to any body of statements. As a result, for Dummett holism is in general aligned with realism. By rejecting holism, Dummett rejects realism.

Comparing Russell's defense of realism with Dummett's defense of anti-realism reveals two significant features of the recent debate between realists and anti-realists. The first is that holism is capable of being aligned either with or against realism. The second is that aligning holism with realism effectively prevents absolute idealism from playing any role in the debate. Absolute idealism is in some respect an alternative to realism, but its reliance on holism prevents it from being a form of anti-realism. As a holistic alternative to realism, it fits neither side in the current debate. This elimination of absolute idealism from the debate seems to me to be unfortunate. Absolute idealism formed the opposition against which both realism and analytic philosophy initially defined themselves. Even if it had been decisively refuted by Russell, it should still occupy a recognizable position in the contemporary controversy between realists and anti-realists. My aim in this essay is to place absolute idealism in its proper position in this controversy. I will do this by first considering the way in which holism can be used in support of absolute idealism. In doing this I will not further consider Russell's criticisms of holism but rather examine Bradley's use of holism in one of his arguments for absolute idealism. Next, I will consider in more detail Dummett's reasons for aligning holism with realism. I will conclude by describing more fully the role of holism in Bradley's semantics and the implications it might have for any view about meaning theories that might reasonably be attributed to him. These views determine the position of absolute idealism in the current controversy between realism and anti-realism.

I

Bradley's argument for absolute idealism as he presents it in *Appearance and Reality* does not obviously depend on semantic theses of which holism is obviously one. Nevertheless, a significant part of his argument, the one that I will sketch, does depend on semantic considerations. This argument has its roots in Bradley's *Principles of Logic*. Bradley's primary concern in that book is to solve a problem in deductive logic, a problem popularized by Mill: how can deductive inferences be both legitimate and useful? In order to solve this problem, Bradley provides a semantic analysis of truth bearers, which for him are judgments. According to his analysis, all judgments refer to reality (this accounts for their objectivity), and all judgments are in one respect or another conditional.[12] Unlike contemporary logicians, Bradley takes counterfactual judgments as his model for interpreting conditionals. He treats them as abbreviated inferences. The premises of the abbreviated inference are the relevant laws of nature, judgments describing the circumstances under which the law holds, and the antecedent of the conditional provisionally asserted or supposed to be true. If the consequent of the conditional follows from these premises, then the conditional judgment that the inference abbreviates is true.[13] This analysis of judgments allows Bradley to justify deductive inference. He does this by arguing that deductive inferences are legitimate if their conclusions follow from their premises and useful when what is asserted in their conclusions has not been asserted in their premises. Inference can satisfy both conditions, Bradley claims, because neither the antecedent nor the consequent of a conditional is asserted by the conditional judgment in which they are components. So the contents of the conclusion may be necessitated by the premises of an inference without being asserted in those premises. Treating judgments as conditionals thus explains how legitimate and useful deductive inference is possible.[14]

Having thus given his semantics credibility, Bradley examines its implications for metaphysics. One significant implication arises from the fact that for Bradley all judgments are semantically ambiguous. Bradley reaches this conclusion on the basis of his semantic analysis of judgments. He claims that because all judgments are conditionals and all conditionals are abbreviated inferences, judgments are true if the inferences they abbreviate are sound. But for an inference to be sound its premises must be true, and this in turn requires the arguments they abbreviate to be sound, and so on *ad infinitum*. A consequence of this regress is holism because the truth of a single judgment depends on the truth of an indefinite number of others. Since there is no way for this series to be completed, it follows that all judgments are incomplete or semantically ambiguous.[15] This conclusion provides Bradley with an argument for absolute idealism that rests on his semantics.

This argument is summarized in the introduction to the second edition appendix of *Appearance and Reality*, and it provides Bradley with a solution to what he calls "the great problem of the relation of Thought to Reality."[16] The problem has the form of a dilemma. One horn is that thought, understood as the totality of all true judgments, is not identical to reality. This seems tolerably obvious in itself, but Bradley makes a point of it to voice his opposition to his more Hegelian contemporaries who happily identified thought and reality. In fact, the reasons he gives in his appendix for asserting that thought is not identical with reality consist entirely of criticisms of various arguments for their identity.

The other horn of the dilemma is that thought, again understood as the totality of all true judgments, is identical to reality. This is a much more contentious claim, and Bradley's argument for it is very condensed. It turns on his claim that to assert that there is a difference between thought and reality "seems somehow impossible without somehow transcending thought or bringing the difference into thought, and these phrases seem meaningless."[17] I take his point here to rest on the idea that true thought in some way grasps reality.[18] Now it is natural, and it has been part of the philosophical tradition since Aristotle, to understand this grasping as a kind of correspondence. According to Aristotle, "To say of what is that it is not, or of what is not that it is, is false, while to say of what is that it is, and of what is not that it is not, is true."[19] This suggests that truth consists in a relation between what is said, an assertion, proposition, judgment, or other truth bearer, and what is, a fact, a state of affairs, or some other sort of entity. This relation has usually been understood as some sort of correspondence.[20] Bradley's argument for the second horn of his dilemma is a rejection of this claim. His reason is that to assert that truth consists in correspondence requires comparing thought with reality. The problem is that there seems to be no intelligible way to do this. One cannot transcend thought and compare it to reality externally. But it is also unclear how to effect such a comparison in a manner internal to thought. If these comparisons cannot be made, then the view that truth consists in correspondence has unacceptable consequences, and this is a ground for rejecting it.

This brief criticism of the correspondence theory of truth is backed by Bradley's much more elaborate criticism in *The Principles of Logic*. His argument there sprawls through the entire book. The basic idea behind it is that judgments containing logical particles do not correspond with fact. "Has every negation I choose to invent a real counterpart in the world of things?" Bradley asks. "Does *any* logical negation, as such, correspond to fact?"[21] So if there is a correspondence between thought and reality, it is either between simple judgments and reality or between systems of judgments and reality. Bradley rejects both of these possibilities. There is no correspondence between simple judgments and reality because there are no simple judgments. There is no correspondence between systems of judgments and reality because systems of judgments are formed in part by treating judgments as abbreviated inferences and inferential relations do not correspond to reality. If these arguments are correct, then true thought does not correspond to reality.[22] From this Bradley concludes that if thought grasps reality but does not correspond or stand in some similar relation to reality, then it must be identical to reality, and this conclusion forms the other horn of the dilemma. So thought must then, it would seem, both be and not be identical to reality. This is the dilemma.

Bradley claims that his resolution of the dilemma is "the only one possible" and that it brings his view of reality with it. It has two parts. The first consists in identifying reality with experience. This allows Bradley to treat thought as an aspect of reality, one that consists in abstracting features of experience to form ideas and using these ideas to refer to objects. By itself, however, this does not resolve the dilemma. That requires a second step. This step consists in holding that thought, as conditional and essentially incomplete, is different from reality. This difference can be expressed using Church's notation for functions (which is also used for property abstracts). Where P is a predicate, an object a is incomplete if and only if for some P, a does not have $(\lambda x)(Px)$ or its complement $(\lambda x)(\sim Px)$.[23] For Bradley reality is complete in this sense, and thought, because it is abstract, is not. Because thought consists of features abstracted from reality, these features are removed from their contexts within experience, that is, within reality, and it is this removal that is responsible for thought being conditional. But, Bradley continues, were thought, *per impossibile*, able to complete itself, it would then become identical to reality. This solution goes between the horns of the dilemma by distinguishing between incomplete and ideally completed thought and then affirming one horn of each. It allows Bradley to affirm his monistic and idealistic metaphysical conclusion that at its limit, in its ideally completed form, thought is made true by reality, which is identical with it.[24] Thought in its completed form, as an interlocking system of judgments, is a whole in which every judgment is related to every other judgment. Ontological monism is thus a consequence of Bradley's semantic monism, and his holism thus plays a significant role in one of his arguments for absolute idealism.

II

At the same time, holism may also function as a support for realism, at least if Michael Dummett is correct. His treatment of holism grows out of his concern with a number of traditional metaphysical debates concerning such topics as the existence of the external world. In Dummett's characterization these debates turn on the proper interpretation of specific classes of statements, the disputed classes. He proposes that these debates can be resolved by constructing meaning theories for these disputed classes of statements.

The project of constructing a meaning theory for a natural language or for a fragment of it originates with Donald Davidson. Dummett's reflections on meaning theories presuppose some understanding of the general idea behind Davidson's theory. This theory takes as its starting point the fact that understanding a language requires the ability to interpret the words of another speaker of the language. Because the speaker whose words are to be interpreted might utter any of an infinite number of sentences, and because it would seem that an interpreter's knowledge of meaning must take finite form, a meaning theory must be a recursive theory. Such a theory will take meaning to depend on a finite number of features of sentences. A model for such a meaning theory, Davidson suggests, is found in Tarski's definition of truth for formal languages. This definition fixes the extension of the predicate "true sentence" in a particular language by entailing the set of all biconditionals in the language of the form "s is true if and only if p," where "s" is the name of each sentence and "p" is a structural description, in effect a translation, of the sentence in the metalanguage. Tarski thus assumes a knowledge of translation and uses it to define truth. Davidson assumes that it is possible to identify the truth conditions for sentences in a language independently of a knowledge of their translations into the metalanguage. His proposal for a meaning theory is that a knowledge of the truth conditions of all of the sentences in a language, constructed on the model of a Tarski style definition of truth, would enable interpreters to determine the translation or interpretation, and hence the meaning, of all sentences in the language.

According to Dummett, this sort of meaning theory is a realistic one. His reason for saying this is that in such a theory the meaning of a statement is determined by the conditions under which the statement is true. That the statement has a particular truth condition can be known by someone who lacks the ability to recognize whether the condition actually holds, that is, whether the statement is actually true or false. In this respect the meaning of the statement is independent of what would constitute knowing that it is true. Since on this account a statement is false if it is not true, every statement on this account will be true or false independently of what would count as recognizing that it is in fact true. Such a theory, then, takes truth to be independent of whether true statements can be recognized as true, and in this respect it treats truth as independent of mind. It is thus a realistic theory. By contrast, in an anti-realistic meaning theory, the meaning of a statement consists in the conditions under which it would be recognized as being true or false.[25] Its meaning is therefore not independent of what would constitute knowing that it was true or false. Since there are operations that allow the formation of sentences that transcend a capacity to recognize them as true (e.g., the operation forming subjunctive conditionals), for anti-realists some of the sentences formed by these operations will be neither true nor false.[26] Consequently, the distinction between realism and idealism, often expressed by means of conflicting answers to the question of whether reality is independent of human knowledge, can be captured as a distinction between the meanings attached to a class of statements. The distinguishing feature of the realistic position, Dummett claims, is an insistence on the principle of bivalence, that every statement is determinatively true or false.[27] This is required by a realistic account of meaning. An anti-realistic account will reject the principle of bivalence. If this characterization of these disputes is correct, then they can be resolved, Dummett suggests, by constructing a meaning theory for the statements in the disputed class. If the meaning theory requires the principle of bivalence, then realism for that class of statements is true. If it does not, then realism, for that class of statements, is false.[28]

Dummett associates holism with realism in his account of the general form of argument employed by anti-realists. The argument has two basic parts. The first is a rejection of realism. This part of the argument builds on the idea that the meaning of a statement is determined by its role in communication, in other words, by its use. Dummett incorporates this idea into his argument by focusing on speakers' knowledge of meanings. In order to communicate successfully, speakers must know the meanings of their statements. Sometimes this knowledge will be explicit in the sense that speakers will be able to verbalize the rules according to which words and statements are used. Much of the time, however, it will remain implicit. If understanding the use of an expression required speakers to be able to state the rule governing its use, then learning the use of an expression would presuppose a considerable knowledge of language, so much that it would be difficult or impossible to explain how a speaker could learn a language. Granting that a portion of speakers' knowledge of their language is implicit raises a new question: On what basis is this implicit knowledge attributed to them? It would seem that the answer to this question has to be that it only makes sense to attribute implicit knowledge to speakers if this knowledge is capable of being fully manifested in their behavior. The meaning of a word consists in its role in communication and speakers cannot communicate anything that they cannot manifest in their behavior. Dummett concludes from this that the knowledge speakers have of the meanings of their statements must be capable of being fully manifested in their behavior, including, of course, their linguistic behavior.[29]

For Dummett the difficulty with realistic meaning theories is that they are unable to meet this requirement. They are unable to do this because they are truth-conditional meaning theories. In other words, they explain knowledge of meaning in terms of truth. Now, any meaning theory will require some notion of truth in order to conform to the principle of compositionality, that is, to explain the meaning of an expression in terms of the contribution that expression makes to the truth conditions of sentences that contain it. What distinguishes realistic meaning theories is that they do not explain truth by means of any other notions, e.g., that of verification or that of the acceptability of its consequences. In realistic meaning theories truth is the central notion in the strong sense that semantic value consists in being true or in not being true. Thus bivalence requires that speakers' implicit knowledge of the truth conditions of sentences must be capable of being fully manifested in their behavior. That is, there will be an observable difference between the behavior of someone who knows the truth conditions of a sentence and someone who does not. This difference will manifest itself in situations where the speaker who knows the truth condition of the sentence recognizes that it obtains and behaves accordingly. The problem, Dummett claims, is that speakers cannot in general fully manifest their knowledge of the truth conditions for sentences. For there are many sentences (of which mathematical ones are the most obvious) that speakers are not in a position to recognize as true. And if they are not in a position to recognize them as true, then it would seem that their knowledge of the truth conditions of these sentences will not be capable of being fully manifested in their behavior. If this is the case, then truth is not suitable as the central notion of a meaning theory in the strong sense.

On the basis of this criticism of taking truth as the central notion of a meaning theory, Dummett suggests that a more appropriate notion will focus on the ways in which speakers recognize statements as true. Here the central notion of the meaning theory in the strong sense is verification rather than truth. The notion of verification is essential in formulating the second part of Dummett's argument for anti-realism. This part of the argument proceeds on the assumption that individual sentences have contents that are determined by their components independently of sentences lacking these components. If the meanings of individual sentences are determined in this way, then meaning theories are subject to another requirement, one that concerns the different ways in which expressions are used. The two most important aspects of use are the conventions governing the conditions under which a statement is justifiably asserted and the logical consequences of asserting a statement that hold in virtue of the inferential relations between it and other statements. The additional requirement is that a meaning theory show these two aspects of use to be in harmony. This is required because a language that lacks this sort of harmony will be incapable of being systematized. There is, of course, no a priori reason for thinking that all languages exhibit this sort of harmony. But the failure of this kind of harmony to obtain in the linguistic practice of a language provides a ground for criticizing that practice. For example, it is possible to have two different justifications for asserting observation statements. They can be justified directly because of certain sensory stimulations, or they can be justified indirectly by virtue of having been deduced from more theoretical statements. These two aspects of the use of observation statements will clearly be in harmony if it is not possible to deduce justified observation statements from which speakers of the language dissent on the basis of their sensory stimulations. If it is possible to make such deductions, then the practice of the language is out of harmony, and this provides a ground for criticizing and reforming it.

This requirement can be made even stronger, and indeed must be if there are to be genuine observation statements, statements justified on the basis of sensory observations. For labeling statements as observation statements requires that it be possible for speakers to occupy situations in which these statements will be justified on the basis of sensory evidence. If there are such statements, then the stronger requirement is that any observation statement that is capable of being indirectly justified is also capable of being directly justified. This can perhaps be expressed by adapting the notion of a conservative extension of a formal theory. A formal theory closed under logical consequence can be extended by the addition of new terms, predicates, rules of inferences, or other means of forming new sentences, that is, theorems. An extension is conservative if none of the new theorems was expressible in the language of the formal theory prior to its extension.

An important application of the idea of a conservative extension for Dummett's purposes concerns statements containing logical constants. Such statements can be justified either directly by means of introduction rules or indirectly by means of elimination rules. On a molecular view of language, the meaning of logical constants will be determined by means of statements lacking them. For example, the meaning of the sentence "A or B" will be determined by means of the component sentences "A" and "B." This amounts to treating the meanings of the logical constants as determined by introduction rules.[30] If this is the case, then the use of statements containing logical constants will be in harmony if the addition of elimination rules is a conservative extension of the fragment of the language that lacks them. This requires that statements logically less complex than the premises used in deriving them by means of elimination rules be capable of being established by introduction rules alone. Where verification is the central notion of a meaning theory, understanding the meaning of statements containing logical constants is dependent on the capacity to recognize derivations of these statements by means of the introduction rules alone. But such a meaning theory reveals a lack of harmony in the direct and indirect means of justifying theorems in classical mathematical reasoning as represented by means of introduction and elimination rules for logical constants. For in classical mathematics negation elimination can be used to establish statements of lesser complexity that are incapable of being established using introduction rules alone. This lack of harmony can be removed, however, by giving an intuitionistic interpretation of the logical constants. This allows the language to be systematized in a way not possible using the classical interpretation and so provides a ground for rejecting the classical interpretation and hence for "repudiating, within mathematical reasoning, the canons of classical logic in favour of those of intuitionist logic."[31] One of these canons is the law of bivalence. It is in virtue of abandoning the law of bivalence that intuitionism is a form of anti-realism. Since nothing in this argument rests on any peculiarly mathematical notion, it becomes a general argument for anti-realism. In virtue of abandoning bivalence, intuitionism is a version of anti-realism, so Dummett's argument makes a case for anti-realism based on theory of meaning.

This argument assumes a molecular view of language according to which each statement has a determinate individual content. To deny this assumption is to accept some form of holism, the view that it is language as a whole rather than individual sentences that have determinate content. To understand a sentence on a holistic view is to understand the place of that sentence in the language as a whole. This is the view called "semantic holism." As a result, Dummett's argument can be countered by rejecting a molecular view of language and thereby affirming a holistic one. This move undermines his argument because on a holistic theory each statement will lack determinate content. Consequently, no questions can arise about the harmony between direct and indirect ways of recognizing a statement's truth value, and there will therefore be no grounds for criticizing the existing practice of a language. In particular, the meanings of logical constants will be fixed not by introduction rules alone, but by elimination rules as well, and no justification of them by reference to their antecedently given meanings will be possible. There will be no antecedently given meanings. The truth values of sentences containing logical constants will be a function of the place of these sentences in the language as a whole. As a result, there will be no lack of harmony in the use of sentences containing logical constants that can serve as a ground for criticizing linguistic practice. Because current linguistic practice accepts the principles of classical logic and because classical logic accepts bivalence, an identifying feature of realism, holism functions as a support for realism.[32]

III

What emerges from this analysis is that holism, understood as the general thesis that to understand a sentence is to understand the larger whole of which it is a part, can function as a support for realism or for idealism. It is able to function as a support for realism by countering Dummett's anti-realist argument and by preserving bivalence for meaning theories. But as Bradley showed and as Russell recognized, holism is also able to function as a buttress for idealism, which is in some respect a rejection of realism. This raises a new question: if we follow Dummett in distinguishing between realism and anti-realism by way of meaning theories that incorporate or fail to incorporate the law of bivalence, what place does absolute idealism occupy in contemporary debates about realism?

It is not immediately obvious how to answer this question. This is in part because Bradley and his fellow idealists did not put forward meaning theories. But even though Bradley did not address issues arising in meaning theories, his semantics, taken with his general account of the development of thought, suggests the sort of view he might have held of meaning theories. These views would require an immediate divergence from a Davidsonian meaning theory, but one that Dummett explicitly allows. In a Davidsonian theory, Dummett writes, "we fasten on some feature of the speakers' linguistic behavior which can be described at the outset, before any understanding of the language has been gained, and try to use it as the basis for the entire interpretation."[33] Bradley would, I think, reject this requirement. A viable meaning theory cannot, of course, rely on notions that presume an understanding of the language to be interpreted. But this view does not require that the basis for the meaning theory be a feature of linguistic behavior that can be described from the outset. As Bradley recognizes, language acquisition proceeds in stages, and there is no reason why a meaning theory cannot do likewise. Such a theory would explain the beginning state of a meaning theory in terms of features of linguistic behavior that could be described at the outset. It would then explain more advanced features of language, the use of subjunctive conditionals, for example, in terms of simpler features of the language that require prior mastery and are explained by the first level of the theory.[34]

I attribute this view to Bradley because it accords with the account he gives of moral development in *Ethical Studies*. As Don MacNiven has shown, Bradley thinks that morality develops through a series of stages in which later stages overcome difficulties in earlier ones. These stages roughly parallel those described by Piaget and Kohlberg.[35] Bradley does not identify his stages with any degree of rigor, but as MacNiven points out, he recognizes at least four stages: egotistical hedonism, institutionalism, personalism, and a final stage that MacNiven labels "metaphysical mysticism." In the first, a proto-utilitarian stage, the child is concerned with the hedonistic consequences of actions for him or herself. In the second the child accepts the conventional morality of his or her social group. This is the stage Bradley describes in Essay V of *Ethical Studies*, "My Station and Its Duties," an essay often and wrongly thought to express Bradley's final view. In the third stage the child identifies universal moral principles that he or she may use in criticizing the morality of the social group. Bradley describes this stage in Essay VI of *Ethical Studies*, "Ideal Morality." In the final stage the child becomes critical of morality itself as a coherent body of thought and incorporates principles of religion into morality. Bradley describes this stage in the "Concluding Remarks" that bring *Ethical Studies* to a close.[36]

Although *Ethical Studies* contains Bradley's only detailed description of any form of cognitive development, he sees each stage in moral development as a stage in the development of mind in general. "It is better," he writes, "to treat the mind as a single phenomenon, progressing through stages. . . ."[37] In accordance with this view Bradley identifies three fundamental laws of mind that constitute his alternative to the laws of association.[38] He then uses these laws to explain the development of all mental processes, including perception, will, feeling, and thought.[39] His account of the development of thought is much sketchier than his account of moral development, but MacNiven has identified four stages in it that proceed in harmony with Bradley's account of the stages in moral development. They are, first, the preconventional or practical instrumental stage, a stage that Bradley finds in the earliest beginnings of human intelligence and in animal intelligence as well. The second is a conventional stage in which the child accepts as true a conventional body of knowledge. The third is a critical stage in which the child appeals to universal principles in criticizing conventional knowledge. The fourth is a stage in which the child sees the universal principles of stage three as true only to a degree.

Even though these stages are not well marked in *The Principles of Logic*, MacNiven finds evidence of all of them in that work.[40]

The first stage is nonlinguistic, and it has no bearing on meaning theories. I can find no difference as far as meaning theories are concerned between stages two and three. Bradley introduces his main criteria for truth, coherence and comprehensiveness in stage three, and this suggests that he thinks of the concept of truth as emerging only at this stage.[41] Because meaning theories require a concept of truth, it is at this stage, stage three, that a meaning theory can be given. If this is correct, then any meaning theory that Bradley might have is to be located at stages three and four. Bradley explicitly notes the presence of at least two stages, a lower and a higher one, in the course of his analysis of the logical forms of categorical and hypothetical judgments in chapter 2 of *The Principles of Logic*.[42] These stages do correspond, at least roughly, to stages three and four in his account of the development of thought. So I take Bradley's semantic theory to have two stages.[43]

Most of his semantic theory is concerned with the lower stage. His project here is to identify the truth conditions of affirmative categorical judgments and to explain the truth conditions of more complex judgments in terms of them. Bradley introduces this project in chapter 2 of book I by noting that judgments, if true, are made true by fact or reality. Reality, however, can make judgments true either directly or indirectly.[44] In most of book I Bradley takes a particular class of affirmative singular categorical judgments to state facts directly.[45] He calls these judgments analytical judgments of sense, and he takes them to be about the presently judged contents of sense perception. His project is to determine how the truth of categorical judgments, usually exemplified by analytical judgments of sense, determines that of more complex judgments, judgments that do not state facts directly. An example is provided by his analysis of disjunctive judgments. According to Bradley disjunctive judgments do not state facts directly because "no real fact can be 'either-or.'"[46] Bradley's task in his discussion of disjunctive judgments is to explain how they state facts indirectly. He does this by explaining how their truth or falsity is determined by categorical judgments. This same concern is present in his treatment of negative judgments, modal judgments, universal categorical judgments, and judgments of probability. Because they do not state facts directly, he needs to explain how facts determine their truth or falsity. He does this by giving their truth conditions in terms of categorical judgments and often in terms of analytical judgments of sense.

Bradley's semantics at this level supports a truth-conditional and hence a realistic meaning theory. Should this seem too tenuous a connection, Bradley's realism is also apparent at this level in his acceptance of bivalence. This is clear in some of his examples. The judgment "Socrates is not sick," Bradley states, may be true either because Socrates is well or "because there is now no such thing as Sokrates [sic]."[47] The same is true of the judgment "The King of Utopia died on Tuesday." This may be false because there is no such place, because it never had a king, because the king is still alive, or because he died on Monday.[48] If the acceptance of bivalence is the mark of realism, then Bradley's semantics at this level supports realism. Notice, however, that Bradley's distinctive form of holism plays no role at this lower level.

It is at the higher level that Bradley introduces his distinctive form of holism. Bradley reaches this level when he reconsiders his initial analysis of analytical judgments of sense. Bradley initially treated the grammatical form of these judgments as a guide to their logical form. That is, he treated them as having the truth conditions of affirmative singular categorical judgments. So, for example, the analytical judgment of sense "This tree is green" is, on this analysis, true if and only if the object referred to by the subject term, "this tree," falls into the class of things that are green. In reconsidering his analysis Bradley assumes that there are judgments in this class that are in some sense true, and he confines his discussion to these judgments. His question is whether they are true when they are construed as having the logical form of affirmative singular categorical judgments.

Bradley's surprising answer is that, construed in this way, such judgments are all false. In giving this answer he proceeds, as he does through most of *The Principles of Logic*, by assuming that true judgments correspond with facts.[49] But facts are individuals, while the ideas from which judgments are constructed are universals. Because no conjunction of universals ever describes one and only one individual, he concludes that no judgments of this class ever describe a fact. Such judgments refer to fact only by means of a sort of demonstrative reference. But this reference, Bradley thinks, is not selective, and so any judgment that refers to any fact must correspond to all facts. Because no judgment can do this, it follows that if analytical judgments of sense are construed as affirmative singular categorical judgments, then they are all false. Because Bradley assumes that analytical judgments of sense are in some sense true, he concludes that they are not properly construed as categorical. That is, they do not state fact in an unqualified way. Rather, they state fact subject to a qualification, to a condition—in which case they are conditional judgments. The result of Bradley's reconsideration of analytic judgments of sense is thus to construe them as conditionals.

This move introduces his holism. For if analytical judgments of sense are conditionals and if all other judgments are either constructed from analytical judgments of sense or conditionals in their own right, then all judgments are conditionals. They are true if the arguments they abbreviate are sound. But if this is so, then all judgments are incomplete. To determine the truth of any one of them will require evaluating the soundness of the argument it abbreviates. But this argument will be sound only if its premises are true. Since these premises will be conditionals, they will be true only if the arguments they abbreviate are sound, and so on *ad infinitum*. This incompleteness is a consequence of Bradley's distinctive form of holism, and it provides a basis for the argument for absolute idealism he gives in the appendix to *Appearance and Reality*.

Bradley's form of holism is also a basis for the account of truth he employs in this argument for absolute idealism. The account of truth arises from his holism in the following way. In his reconsidered and deeper analysis of analytical judgments of sense, Bradley assumes the truth of the correspondence or copy theory of truth. As a result, when he parses analytical judgments of sense as conditionals, he assumes them to be true provided the inference they abbreviate corresponds with reality. It is only at the conclusion of his discussion of the validity of inference that he finds himself compelled to abandon this assumption. He does so on the basis of the fact that inferences depend on logical principles that have no counterpart in reality. Again, Bradley assumes that there are judgments that are in some sense true. But since no judgment understood as an abbreviated inference corresponds with fact, it follows that truth cannot consist in correspondence with fact. This is the conclusion with which *The Principles of Logic* ends. Bradley's holism thus requires him to abandon the correspondence theory of truth and to search for another theory of truth. The theory he finds is an identity theory, and it is embodied in his solution to "the great problem of the relation of Thought to Reality."

The two levels of Bradley's semantic theory reveal the position of his version of absolute idealism in the contemporary debate between realism and anti-realism. At the lower level Bradley's theory is realistic. He accepts bivalence and explains the truth conditions of logically complex judgments in terms of the logically simple judgments from which they are constructed. Bradley's logically simple judgments, at this level, are categorical and hence either determinately true or determinately false. At the higher level Bradley finds his lower level theory, and hence the realism it supports, inadequate. The reason is that the concept of truth by means of which logically simple judgments can be seen to be categorically true is inapplicable. In order to make judgments of this supposedly simple class true, these judgments need to be parsed as conditionals. It is this construal of them that introduces Bradley's distinctive form of holism according to which all judgments are incomplete. This, however, requires Bradley to abandon the principle of bivalence and hence the semantic basis for realism. The incompleteness of judgments renders them semantically ambiguous and neither determinately true nor determinately false. So Bradley's semantic theory at the higher level is not realistic.

But neither is it anti-realistic. By construing judgments as semantically incomplete, Bradley has in effect denied that it is possible to construct a theory of meaning of the kind envisioned by Dummett as required for anti-realism. Because of the incompleteness he finds in all judgments, he concludes that it is not possible to state their truth conditions fully. As a result, their truth or falsity does not depend on a finite number of linguistic features. This, in effect, is an argument against the possibility of a theory of meaning of the kind envisioned by either Davidson or Dummett. It is this impossibility that underlies Bradley's semantic argument for absolute idealism. In more general terms, it is the result of Bradley's insistence that there is a difference between thought and reality. Absolute idealism, at least in Bradley's form, thus takes its place in the contemporary debate by containing elements of both realism and anti-realism by virtue of its two-level semantics and by denying that a meaning theory of either form can be complete. Absolute idealism in this form results from a principled denial of the adequacy of either realistic or anti-realistic theories. This is its position in the contemporary debate.

It has sometimes been said that the views expressed by the absolute idealists are too vague, obscure, and confused to be worth discussing. I do not believe that this is the case. But I do believe that in order to discuss their views productively, the vocabulary they used in expressing them needs to be sharpened. In my attempt to do this, I have drawn heavily on the work of Michael Dummett. No one in our time has contributed as much as he has to the sharpening, enlarging, and deepening of metaphysical debate.[50]

JAMES W. ALLARD

MONTANA STATE UNIVERSITY
AUGUST 2005

NOTES

1. Bertrand Russell, *Principles of Mathematics*, 2nd ed. (New York: W. W. Norton, 1964), 226. The first edition of *Principles of Mathematics* was published in 1903.

2. Peter Hylton, *Russell, Idealism and the Emergence of Analytic Philosophy* (Oxford: Clarendon Press, 1990), 154–58

3. F. H. Bradley, *Essays on Truth and Reality* (Oxford: Clarendon Press, 1914), 280.

4. Bertrand Russell, "Meinong's Theory of Complexes and Assumptions," in *Essays in Analysis* (New York: George Braziller, 1973), 75–76. This essay was originally published in *Mind* 13 (1904): 204–19, 336–54, 509–24.

5. Harold H. Joachim, *The Nature of Truth* (New York: Greenwood, 1969), 67–68.

6. Bertrand Russell, "William James's Conception of Truth," in *Philosophical Essays* (London: George Allan & Unwin, 1966), 114.

7. Russell, "The Monistic Theory of Truth," in *Philosophical Essays*, 131.

8. Dummett occasionally uses the term "idealism" as a replacement for "anti-realism," as, for example, when he writes, "So regarded [as a form of constructivism] intuitionism is the most thoroughly thought-through presentation of idealism in modern philosophy." *The Interpretation of Frege's Philosophy* (Cambridge, MA: Harvard Univ. Press, 1981), 66. But this is not his usual practice. The term "idealism" serves as a label for any philosophy that contrasts either with realism or with materialism. For Dummett's purposes, the latter contrast is irrelevant. See "Realism and Anti-Realism," in *The Seas of Language* (Oxford: Clarendon Press, 1993), 464.

9. I will qualify this claim below.

10. Michael Dummett, "The Reality of the Past," in *Truth and Other Enigmas* (Cambridge: Harvard Univ. Press, 1978), 358–61.

11. Dummett, "The Philosophical Basis of Intuitionist Logic," in *Truth and Other Enigmas*, 220.

12. F. H. Bradley, *The Principles of Logic*, 2nd ed., rev. (Oxford: Oxford Univ. Press, 1928), 106.

13. Bradley, *The Principles of Logic*, 85–90.

14. I have discussed this in more detail in *The Logical Foundations of Bradley's Metaphysics: Judgment, Inference and Truth* (Cambridge: Cambridge Univ. Press, 2005), 156–65.

15. F. H. Bradley, *Essays on Truth and Reality*, 252; see also *The Principles of Logic*, 89.

16. F. H. Bradley, *Appearance and Reality*, 2nd ed. (Oxford: Clarendon Press, 1930), 492.

17. Bradley, *Appearance and Reality*, 492.

18. This is part of the meaning of his assumption that "the object of metaphysics is to find a general view which will satisfy the intellect, and . . . that whatever succeeds in doing this is real and true" (*Appearance and Reality*, 491).

19. Aristotle, *Prior Analytics,* trans. A. K. Jenkinson, in *The Complete Works of Aristotle*, vol.1, ed. Jonathan Barnes, (Princeton: Princeton Univ. Press, 1984), 1011b 26–27.

20. Until Bradley criticized it, Aristotle's description of truth had generally been regarded as a truism and not as a matter for philosophical reflection.

21. Bradley, *The Principles of Logic*, 46.

22. Ibid., 589.

23. Gordon G. Brittan, Jr., "Transcendental Idealism, Empirical Realism, and

the Completeness Principle," in *Kant und die Berliner Aufklärung: Akten des IX Internationalen Kant-Kongresses*, ed. Volker Gerhardt, Rolf-Peter Horstmann, and Ralph Schumacher (Berlin: Walter de Gruyter, 2001), 543–44.

24. Stewart Candlish, "The Truth about F. H. Bradley," *Mind* 98 (1989): 338–39.

25. Anti-realism will also involve at least a weak claim about the reducibility of statements in the disputed class to statements of some other class, and realism may also involve such claims. I have ignored this complication here. See Dummett, *The Logical Basis of Metaphysics* (Cambridge: Harvard Univ. Press, 1991), 322–23 and "The Reality of the Past," in *Truth and Other Enigmas*, 358–61.

26. Dummett also includes quantification over infinite totalities and references to inaccessible regions of space and time among these operations. "What Is a Theory of Meaning? (II)," in *Seas of Language*, 60.

27. In his later work Dummett specifies another condition that theories must meet in order to count as realistic: they must accept a classical two-valued semantics as applying across the board where this requires taking apparent singular terms as referring to objects within the domain of quantification. See Dummett, "Realism and Anti-Realism," 468; see also *The Logical Basis of Metaphysics*, 325.

28. Dummett, "The Reality of the Past," 358–61.

29. Dummett, "The Philosophical Basis of Intuitionist Logic," 216–17.

30. This view will be the case when verification is the central notion of a meaning theory. It is also possible to take the central notion as the immediate consequences of a statement for one who accepts it as true. In this case the meanings of logical constants are determined by elimination rules. See Dummett, *The Logical Basis of Metaphysics*, 280–81.

31. Dummett, "The Philosophical Basis of Intuitionist Logic," 215.

32. Although there are a number of variations in Dummett's treatment of holism, he always treats it as aligned with realism and as a counter to anti-realism. For these variations, see Neil Tennant, "Holism, Molecularity and Truth," in *Michael Dummett: Contributions to Philosophy*, ed. Barry Taylor (Dordrecht, The Netherlands: Martinus Nijhoff, 1987), 31–58; Sanford Shieh, "Some Senses of Holism: An Anti-Realist's Guide to Quine," in Richard Heck, Jr., *Language, Thought, and Logic* (Oxford: Oxford University Press, 1997), 71–103.

33. Dummett, "What Does the Theory of Use Do for the Theory of Meaning?" in *The Seas of Language*, 115.

34. Dummett, "What Does the Theory of Use Do for the Theory of Meaning?" 114–15.

35. For a summary of these stages see Don MacNiven, *Bradley's Moral Psychology* (Lewiston, PA: Edwin Mellen Press, 1987), 179–85, 246–48.

36. MacNiven, *Bradley's Moral Psychology*, 150–79; 246–48.

37. Bradley, *The Principles of Logic*, 29.

38. For a succinct statement of these laws, see F. H. Bradley, "Association and Thought," in *Collected Essays* (Oxford: Clarendon Press, 1969), 208–12.

39. For details see MacNiven, *Bradley's Moral Psychology*, 125–43.

40. Don MacNiven, "F. H. Bradley on Logic and Psychology," *Bradley Studies* 8 (2002): 136–43.

41. MacNiven, "F. H. Bradley on Logic and Psychology," 140.

42. Bradley, *The Principles of Logic*, 106–7. Bradley calls these stages "points of view."

43. Bradley takes thought to be prior to language. While this distinguishes his semantic theory in terms of its foundation from the theories of many recent philosophers, this is not a difference that plays itself out in the details of his theory. On this general issue, see Michael Dummett, "Truth and Meaning," in *The Seas of Language*, 152.

44. Bradley, *The Principles of Logic*, 41–42.

45. Ibid., 48–49.

46. Ibid., 129.

47. Ibid., 124.

48. Ibid., 124–25.

49. Ibid., 591–92, n1.

50. I would like to thank Gordon Brittan, W. J. Mander, and the participants in the 2005 Idealism Today conference at Harris Manchester College, Oxford, for helpful comments on earlier versions of this paper.

REPLY TO JAMES W. ALLARD

Professor Allard's contribution to this volume is of real importance, since we need, as he has done, to go back to before Frege and Russell if we are to orient ourselves correctly in the historical context of the development of modern philosophy after Kant, for, as Allard very truly says, "Absolute idealism formed the opposition against which both realism and analytic philosophy initially defined themselves"—at least in Britain.

I had better start with some autobiographical remarks about the origin of my obsessive interest in realism, since, as Allard says, in addition to characterising metaphysical disputes, I have been a party to them. My original interest was aroused by my noticing a structural similarity between the arguments used by opponents of realism concerning different subject-matters. Thus phenomenalists argued that the basis of our judgements about the material world consisted always and only in our sense-data; behaviourists argued that the only basis of our knowledge of the mental states and processes of others consisted in what they said and how they behaved; those who denied that the past was a separate realm which determined the truth-values of statements in the past tense observed that judgements about the past were always based, and could only be based, on our present memories, presently existing records, and present traces of prior events. The argument seemed always to start in the same way, although sometimes a transformation of the syntactic form of statements of the disputed class was used to undercut the realist interpretation. Russell certainly conceived his theory of descriptions as thus undercutting Meinongian realism about possible objects. I coined the colourless term "anti-realist" to cover the opponent of realism in the various cases. I did not want to call the generic opponent of realism an "idealist" because, although idealism is one form of rejection of realism, the term plainly could not be applied to all theories opposed to realism concerning a particular subject-matter: behaviourism, for example, was evidently not a species of idealism. The rejection of materialism was far from being an essential ingredient of philosophical opposition to this or that form of realism.

Realists countered these attacks in different ways. A common response was to declare the anti-realist's interpretation of statements in the "disputed class" a distortion of their true meanings; here of course we have an explicit connection of the dispute over realism with conceptions of meaning. Sometimes the realists could claim a syntactic principle as tenable only on a realist understanding, as with an appeal to the truth-value link as requiring belief in the independent reality of the past: it is, for example, a requirement of the truth-value link that it will be true in a year's time that the Queen was alive a year previously just in case she is alive now.

I thought that this presented a programme for philosophical research. For each dispute over realism concerning a particular subject-matter, the abstract structure of that dispute could be described, and a comparison made between the structures of all the various such disputes. From such a comparison, it might then be possible to discern in which cases the defenders of realism, and in which cases its opponents, were, objectively, the winners.

The salience of bivalence to the defensibility of realism became apparent from consideration of an objection of Isaiah Berlin's to phenomenalism. Berlin observed that, on a phenomenalist account, the truth of statements about the material world which were unsupported by any actual sense-data would reduce to that of counterfactual conditionals, but that that required some counterfactual conditionals to be, in the terminology I introduced, barely true, which they could not be. This argument presupposes that the phenomenalist assumes bivalence for statements about material objects. If the phenomenalist drops this assumption, he no longer has any reason for supposing that there are any barely true counterfactual conditionals. He may adopt an intuitionistic logic, and assume the truth of only those counterfactual conditionals for which there are compelling grounds available to us.

Although Allard is inclined to represent me as taking acceptance of bivalence as sufficient for realism, he acknowledges in his note 27 that I do not believe that whether a theory of meaning incorporates the principle of bivalence is the only criterion on which it is to be judged realist or otherwise. To be a realist theory, it must treat the syntactic form of sentences at face value, and in particular treat every expression apparently a singular term as genuinely such, denoting an individual object. It must then apply to the language so understood a classical truth-conditional semantics.

Thus one who would render the numerals in arithmetical equations, not as singular terms but as signifying numerically definite quantifiers ("There are just two . . .", and so on) does not strictly speaking understand elementary arithmetic realistically, however much he may believe its statements to be subject to bivalence. In the same way, as already remarked, Russell's theory of descriptions constitutes a rejection of realism concerning possible objects, because it does not take definite descriptions at face value as singular terms. Frege's position in this regard is equivocal. It is correct to regard him as holding strongly realistic views both of the physical world and of mathematics. He was a strong adherent of bivalence, but nevertheless did not take it as holding for propositions—which he called "thoughts"—expressible in natural language. He believed that sentences of natural language containing empty proper names or definite descriptions nevertheless expressed thoughts: after all, we know what it would have been for there to have been such a man as Odysseus. He treated empty proper names and definite descriptions as genuine singular terms, and as having a sense; but he regarded them, not as referring to possible but non-existent objects, but as not referring to anything at all. He regarded thoughts expressed by sentences containing them as neither true nor false; but he should not for this reason be classified as anti-realist, since he regarded it as a defect of natural language that it contained such terms and allowed the formation of such sentences: a purified language suited to the requirements of science would do neither, he believed.

I became a party to the disputes over realism by abandoning the idea of a research programme and coming to conceive of a global anti-realism. I thought that the reductive forms of anti-realism—those that maintain that statements of the disputed class are translatable into statements of some other (the reductive) class—were all untenable; there was, however, a general form of argument for a form of anti-realism that could be applied quite generally. Such a global anti-realism—modelled on the intuitionist interpretation of mathematics—would reject bivalence and would demand the replacement of classical by intuitionistic logic, but it would eschew any reductionist claims.

The argument for such a global anti-realism—in particular, for the use of intuitionistic logic—demanded a compositional theory of meaning: the meaning of every sentence must be given in accordance with its composition, that is, in terms of the meanings of its component expressions; and such an account of the meanings of sentences of the language must be non-circular. That is, there must be a relation of dependence among expressions and forms of sentence-formation of the language: the understanding of some expressions might depend on, in other words, presuppose, the understanding of others; but this relation of dependence must be well founded. It must not be possible for an expression to be dependent upon another that was ultimately dependent upon it. Thus the understanding of an expression **E** might presuppose the prior understanding of some segment of the language, the understanding of which did not in turn presuppose the understanding of **E**. Such a segment would constitute a language, in the sense that it could in principle be the entire language of a community of speakers, even if very impoverished and very unlikely to be so. In this sense Wittgenstein's dictum, "To understand a sentence is to understand a language," would be satisfied. This conception indeed allows that the acquisition of a mastery of the language must of necessity proceed by stages, as Allard interprets Bradley as believing. Indeed, it is quite obvious that this is so: consider a child's gradual grasp of the sense of the word "father." This "molecular" conception of the semantic structure of a language does not exclude the existence of local holisms, that is, of small sets of expressions whose senses must be acquired simultaneously.

I first heard Professor Allard's contrast between my attitude to holism and that of Bradley in a paper that he gave at a conference I attended. The contrast is this: for Bradley, holism, in which he believed, was an essential step towards the absolute idealism which he espoused, and thus to the rejection of realism; whereas for me holism is to be rejected if a coherent argument for the global anti-realism I put forward for consideration is to be given. My first reaction to Allard's contrast was that these were two different holisms: Bradley's holism was a holism of truth, whereas the Quinean holism I was attacking was a holism of meaning. Bradley held that every truth depended on another truth, which must be made explicit if the former truth was genuinely to accord with reality, whereas Quinean holism maintained that no sentence of a language could be fully understood without a knowledge of the entire language (which of course no one has). The Quinean holist thus compares a language to a game. We do not know the significance of a move in the game of Go unless we know all the rules of the game, including how the winner is determined: the *same* piece of knowledge is required for a grasp of the significance of *every* move. But reflection quickly showed me that my distinction was invalid: *any* holism regarding language and thought must be *both* a holism of meaning (or content) and a holism of truth.

The only substantial quarrel I have with anything Allard says in his essay is to do with whether a holist should be considered a realist. Allard more than once suggests that I believe that he should be. In his section II he says, "Dummett associates holism with realism." The last sentence of the section reads, "Because current linguistic practice accepts the principles of classical logic and because classical logic accepts bivalence, an identifying feature of realism, holism functions as a support for realism." And the attached note 32 begins, "Although there are a number of variations in Dummett's treatment of holism, he always treats it as aligned with realism and as a counter to anti-realism."

I protest that I have never characterised the holist as a realist or holism as a defence of realism: as a counter to (global) anti-realism, yes; as a support for realism, never. It is a counter to global anti-realism because it undercuts the principle of compositionality on which the argument for the use of intuitionistic logic rests. The intuitionist mathematician takes the meaning of a mathematical statement to be characterised in terms of proof, and infers that the meanings of the logical constants must likewise be characterised in terms of proof; it is on this ground that he rejects the law of excluded middle. The holist makes no such inference, because he does not respect compositionality; he may explain the meaning of a mathematical statement in general in terms of proof, but he sees no reason why that should imply anything about how the logical constants are to be explained. For him, they are to be explained, if at all, in terms of the rules governing their use in standardly accepted proofs, which are the rules of classical logic. The holist will presumably subscribe to bivalence, if he takes that principle to be acknowledged by most speakers of the language; but that is not enough to make him a realist. For me, realism must rest on a full classical two-valued semantics; a realist theory of meaning must be a truth-conditional theory.

Allard understands Bradley as tacitly regarding a theory of meaning as ultimately unfeasible. If Allard is right, then in this respect Bradley was a true holist: as I said in my lecture "The Justification of Deduction" of 1973, "Holism is not . . . a theory of meaning: it is the denial that a theory of meaning is possible" (*Truth and Other Enigmas*, 309). Holism renders a theory of meaning impossible, because when the relation of semantic dependence is not well founded, the provision of a recursive specification of sense is blocked: no theory of meaning can then be constructed. As Allard says of Bradley, the holist is neither a realist nor an anti-realist.

Consider a holist view of mathematics. The holist starts out by agreeing with the intuitionist that a mathematical statement is true only if there is a proof of it. But it quickly turns out that they understand the word "proof" in very different ways. The holist understands it as covering any proof that the mathematical community at large (which does not include constructivist mathematicians) agrees to be valid. The intuitionist takes it as covering a very restricted type of proof that he calls "canonical." The divergence occurs because the intuitionist wants to conform to the principle of compositionality: for him the understanding of any expression can depend only on the understanding of simpler expressions, including those that compose it; the holist appeals to mathematical practice as currently observed. That is why the intuitionist requires each logical constant to be explained by specifying what would constitute a canonical proof of a statement of which it is the principal operator, the meanings of the subsentences being assumed as already known. The holist, by contrast, regards a logical constant as explained by its role in proofs accepted by the mathematical community.

It is for this reason that holism blocks the argument for adopting intuitionistic logic in place of classical logic, an essential ingredient of global anti-realism as characterised above. Holism does not supply a defence of realism: rather, it presents an obstacle to anti-realism (in the global sense). The holist, by contrast to the intuitionist, is content to abide by conventional methods of reasoning involving the logical constants. He does not require the meaning of a complex statement to be explained in terms of those of simpler statements: he does not ask for it to be explained at all. If we ask the holist in what the understanding of an as yet unproved mathematical statement consists, he must answer that it consists in knowing all of mathematics, since there is no saying what might not be used in a proof of it: he may mean all the mathematics that is currently known, or he may mean the totality of mathematical knowledge that will eventually be acquired. In either case, no one (or virtually no one) can be said fully to understand the statement. The holist does not think a grasp of the logical constants and of addition and exponentiation suffices to confer an under-standing of the statement of Fermat's last theorem; he believes that it requires a knowledge of at least enough mathematics to follow Wiles's proof, including the theorems to which that proof appeals. The holist cannot give any specific answer to the question in what the meaning of a particular mathematical statement consists; for him, fully to know the meaning of any such statement demands a knowledge of the whole of mathematics. As I already remarked, it is like the significance of a move in a board game. To understand any such move you must know all the rules of the game; beyond that, you have only to distinguish that move from others.

The holist is not a realist. Quine may have believed himself to be a realist, but he was not. The holist does not have a realist theory of meaning; rather, he holds a view that rules out any theory of meaning whatever as impossible. True, he accepts bivalence; but he means little by it. The principle of bivalence is in place within a semantic theory, and the holist does not have a semantic theory. He may have a characterisation of truth, as did the mathematical holist; it will amount to a statement's being true if it is accepted by those best qualified to judge as conforming to the normal canons for being assertable. The holist does not mean by bivalence that, for each statement, either it or its negation is or will be so accepted: he means no more than that the law of excluded middle holds generally, and is therefore to be accepted, and hence that classical logic governs acceptable reasoning. His acceptance of bivalence is a mere part of his acceptance of standard linguistic practice.

On my original use of the term "anti-realist," as applied to any view that involved the repudiation of realism; the holist is an anti-realist; but more substance has accrued to the term than that. The holist does not repudiate realism on the basis of any argument that in the slightest degree resembles other arguments against realism, and in particular not that which underlies global anti-realism of the kind sketched above. The Quinean holist is therefore not an anti-realist in this sense. Like Allard's Bradley, he is neither a realist nor an anti-realist; like him, he rejects a theory of meaning as in principle unfeasible. Both these agreements between him and Bradley spring from the same source, the holism that they have in common.

In other respects they are quite different; the Quinean holist is nothing like an absolute idealist. On the account of Bradley's thought given by Professor Allard, which I should not dare to challenge, Bradley's absolute idealism did not originate from his holism alone, but also from his ideas about the relation between thought and reality, which Quine was very far from sharing. My conclusion is that Allard is completely right in situating absolute idealism in a position off to the side in the argument between realists and anti-realists, but that, to find philosophers to locate in that position, he did not need to go so far back as Bradley or as idealists of any kind.

M. D.

4

Hilary Putnam

BETWEEN SCYLLA AND CHARYBDIS: DOES DUMMETT HAVE A WAY THROUGH?

Like Quine's essays, starting with "On What There Is" and "Two Dogmas of Empiricism," and like Donald Davidson's essays, starting with "Meaning and Truth," and like Kripke's lectures published as *Naming and Necessity*, Michael Dummett's essays and books blazed entirely new paths in philosophy of language, construed not narrowly, but as absolutely central to the whole of metaphysics and epistemology. In all three of these cases, the reverberations still continue to be felt, and they will go on being felt for a long time to come. In my own case, it was hearing Dummett's William James Lectures delivered in 1976[1] at my own university that exerted a profound influence. Even if my own orbit has carried me some distance away from the point of closest approach to Michael Dummett's philosophical planet, I continue to feel his gravitational attraction, and I feel tremendously enriched by our interactions, personal as well as philosophical.

THE PROBLEM DUMMETT SEES WITH REALISTIC SEMANTICS

The difficulty Dummett sees with realistic semantics is summed up in his famous "manifestation argument," to the effect that if we *did* have a conception of "realist" truth, truth as fully independent of all possibility of verification, then there would be would no way in which we could "manifest" our conception in our behavior, and hence no way in which we could teach our realist conception of truth to others, determine which others really *have* this concept of truth, and so forth.[2] But one all-important remark: although Dummett has concentrated for many years on arguing that there are (apparently insuperable) difficulties with realism, there is a sense in which the "anti-realism" or "justificationism" that Dummett regularly treats as the alternative to realism is not precisely *advocated* by Dummett. Instead, Dummett (admirably, in my view) sees himself as *exploring* a philosophical issue, or exploring a philosophical dialectic (with, to be sure, a predilection to one side of the debate). As he himself puts it in the preface to *Truth and the Past*,[3] "I do not think anyone should interpret everything that a philosopher writes as if it was just one chapter in a book he is writing throughout his life. On the contrary, for me every article and essay is a separate attempt to arrive at the truth, to be judged on its own."

If the "anti-realist" position Dummett proposes as the alternative to realist semantics remains in this way "work in progress," the manifestation argument against realism has remained a constant in the many years Dummett has been making his "separate attempts to arrive at the truth" in this area.[4] A pithy statement of the manifestation argument occurs, in fact, in an essay titled "Truth: Deniers and Defenders" that he added to the lectures that make up the body of *Truth and the Past*. Dummett writes:

> What prompts [justificationist] theories of truth is a thought similar to that of Rorty in concluding that justification is the goal of inquiry: namely that when we acquire the practice of using language, what we learn is what is taken to justify assertions of different types. We learn what is accepted as entitling us to make those assertions; we learn also whether what justifies us in doing so is conclusive or whether it is defeasible, that is, capable of being overthrown by subsequent counterevidence. We do *not* learn what it is for those assertions to be true independently of any means we have for establishing their truth. How could we? If we are not in a position either to assert or to deny a given proposition, we cannot be shown what nevertheless makes it true or false. So, according to a theory of this kind, to grasp the meaning of a statement is to know what would justify asserting it or denying it. (114)

REDEFINING "REALISM"

What I hope to do in this essay is to make clear how it was that I came to see what I regard as insuperable difficulties with anti-realism. In this way, I hope to open yet another page in the dialogue that Michael Dummett and I have been having for forty years.

The term "realism" occurs quite often in my essays prior to 1975.[5] In those essays, it means one thing and one thing only: the rejection of logical positivism, operationalism, and related positions. As I explained in one of those essays, "A Philosopher Looks at Quantum Mechanics":

> All attempts to *literally* "translate" statements about, say, electrical charge into statements about so-called observables (meter readings) have been dismal failures, and from Berkeley on, all *a priori* arguments designed to show that all statements about unobservables must ultimately reduce to statements about observables have contained gaping holes and outrageously false assumptions. It is quite true that we "verify" statements about unobservable things by making suitable *observations*, but I maintain that without imposing a wholly untenable theory of meaning, one cannot even *begin* to go from this fact to the wildly erroneous conclusion that talk about unobservable things and theoretical magnitudes *means the same* as talk about observations and observables. [6]

Although I pointed out in that essay that Carnap had given up the attempt to reduce statements about unobservables to "observation language," I criticized him in "Explanation and Reference," for an "idealist" tendency manifested in the fact that according to the theory of the meaning (or "partial interpretation") of theoretical terms in science he defended in his late writings, every change in the total scientific theory amounted to a change in the reference of every one of those terms, so that theoretical terms were not treated as names of, say, unobservable things and forces concerning which scientists change their minds, but as merely parts of a machine for predicting "observations," parts which have no meaning in themselves apart from their role in the particular theory. [7]

The term "idealism" in those essays was virtually synonymous with "phenomenalism." Prior to my reading Dummett's William James Lectures, the only "idealism" I knew was Berkeley's, and the only "anti-realism" I knew was anti-realism about unobservables (and, in the case of phenomenalism, about "middle sized dry goods," which were treated as unobservables by phenomenalists). Thus it was an eye-opener that "realism" and "anti-realism" could be understood as positions about the nature of truth itself, and not simply as positions about the reducibility or nonreducibility of "theoretical terms" to "observation terms" or of "thing-language" to "sense-datum language."

What I then called "idealism" is better called *reductionism*, Dummett taught me. [8] Reductionism, with respect to a class of statements, is the philosophical theory that statements in that class are 'made true' by facts described by statements in what is claimed to be some epistemologically or metaphysically more 'basic' class. For example, the phenomenalist view that statements about tables and chairs and other ordinary 'material objects' are made true by facts describable in a sense-datum language is a reductionist view of the kind I called "idealist."

If a view is reductionist with respect to assertions of one kind only to insist on a "correspondence" notion of truth for statements in the reducing class, then that view is, according to Dummett, metaphysically realist at base. A truly nonrealist view is nonrealist all the way down.

I say that this redefinition of realism (and anti-realism) was an "eye-opener" because it seemed to open a way out of the difficulties I had been having in thinking about the model theoretic argument against metaphysical realism—an argument that had occurred to me *before* Dummett's William James Lectures, but that I could not see my way clear either to accepting or rejecting at that time, which is why I did not present it publicly until 1976.[9]

Not surprisingly, Dummett's redefinition of "realism" and "anti-realism" was contested: most vehemently, perhaps, by Michael Devitt.[10] According to Devitt, the realism issue is simply, "Is there a mind-independent reality or not?" (*thump*) and *that* question has nothing to do with semantics.—This short way with the issue reminds one of Lenin's (disastrously incompetent) polemical book against Machian positivism.[11] Lenin simply claimed that positivists, since they took human sensations as the class of truth-makers for all propositions (I am using present-day terminology, not Lenin's, of course), could not accept the statement that the solar system existed before there were human beings.[12] This argument simply assumes—what positivists of course deny[13]—that the positivists cannot *interpret* "the solar system existed before there were human beings" in their rationally reconstructed "language of science."

But what of the word "independent" in "the behavior of the stars is independent of human sensations and thoughts and beliefs"? (This is what Devitt portrayed anti-realists as *denying*.)

Well there are many kinds of independence. Presumably causal independence is what Devitt was talking about, since *logical* independence is a property of *statements* (or, perhaps, of events *under a description*), and whether statements are or are not logically independent is certainly a question about their *semantics*, which Devitt claimed to be irrelevant to the realism issue. But then Devitt's argument once again simply assumes— what anti-realists of course deny—that the anti-realist cannot *interpret* the sentence "the behavior of the stars is independent of human sensations and thoughts and beliefs" in a "justificationist" way, interpret it so that it is 'true' (in the anti-realist sense). Devitt cannot, after all, say "but that's not what the sentence *means*!" without engaging in a discussion of— guess what?—semantics.

I remain convinced that Dummett has made a truly lasting contribution to our appreciation of the *depth* of the realism anti-realism issue, just as

Berkeley did at an earlier time. Devitt's dismissive attitude is as unphilosophical as Samuel Johnson's stone-kicking.

THE ANTI-REALIST TRIES TO STEER BETWEEN SCYLLA AND CHARYBDIS

But can one really develop a defensible anti-realist account of the semantics of our language? When I reread what I wrote in *Reason, Truth and History* (especially in chapters 3 and 5), I see my former self as trying to steer between the Scylla of solipsism and the Charybdis of metaphysical realism, and when I read Dummett's *Truth and the Past*, I find that I have the same feeling. But this takes some explanation, I know.

In §16 of *Experience and Prediction*[14] Reichenbach considered and rejected a form of verificationism that he described as "the choice of an egocentric language" (a language in which things can meaningfully be said to exist only when observed to exist by the subject, and can meaningfully be said to have only the properties they appear—to that same subject—to have). According to this form of verificationism (Reichenbach is clearly thinking of a position held by members of the Vienna Circle at a certain point), all cognitively meaningful assertions that seem to be about times or places the speaker never observes are to be reinterpreted as asserting that if the speaker were to do so-and-so, then she would experience such-and-such. Reichenbach argued that even if such a reinterpretation faced no other difficulties, it would certainly not be able to express the rationale for certain practical decisions (ibid., 150):

> The insufficiency of a positivist language in which talk of events after my death is construed as a device for predicting my experiences while I am alive is revealed as soon as we try to use it for the rational reconstruction of the thought processes underlying actions concerned with events after our death, such as expressed in the example of [purchasing] life insurance policies.

One obviously does not buy life insurance so that one will oneself have certain experiences if one does so (or if one has the experience of doing so)! Let us see now how a similar difficulty might confront a "justificationist" philosopher.

Suppose that this philosopher maintains that what it is for a statement (*any* statement) to be true is for the statement to be justified by experiences she has or will have in *her* lifetime. If what makes the statement true is also supposed to be what the statement "means"—what it asserts to be the case —she is a solipsist. If not, an unacceptable gap seems to open between what a statement *says* and what *makes it true*. In either case, Reichenbach's observation has force: she cannot intelligibly rationalize buying a life insurance policy.

A verificationist who denies that there is such a thing as logically conclusive verification of an empirical proposition may nonetheless face a similar problem. If my understanding of my own sentences is alleged to consist in my ability to assign them a degree of verification on the basis of my own experiences, then, in particular, my *understanding* of the prediction that my family will be better off after my death if I buy life insurance now consists in the knowledge that certain experiences I have or could have in my lifetime justify asserting that sentence to this, that, or the other degree. Again, if the justificationist says, "Oh, but I didn't claim that the sentence is *about* those experiences," she creates a gap between the semantics of the sentence—since what makes her a *justificationist* philosopher, in Dummett's sense, is precisely that her program is to give the semantics of the sentence in terms of justification—and what she claims sentences *mean*. But how can *semantics* not be about what sentences *mean*?

AVOIDING SCYLLA: STEP ONE

The first step in avoiding the Scylla of solipsism is one that Dummett and I both took at different times. That step was simply to insist that the justificationism or verificationism[15] that we advocated was *social* and not *individualistic* in nature. Dummett puts it very clearly in *Truth and the Past* (41): "What is the concept of truth appropriate to a justificationist theory of meaning? Plainly it must turn on the notion of our being justified in asserting a statement. It is evident at the outset that the word 'our' must be taken in a collective, not a distributive, sense."

AVOIDING SCYLLA: A SECOND STEP

In chapter 3 of my *Reason, Truth and History*, this first step was combined with a further one: replacing talk of verification with *idealized* verification:

> Truth is an *idealization* of rational acceptability. We speak as if there were such things as epistemically ideal conditions, and we call a statement "true" if it would be justified under such conditions. "Epistemically ideal conditions," of course, are like "frictionless planes"; we cannot really attain epistemically ideal conditions, or even be absolutely certain that we have come sufficiently

close to them. But frictionless planes cannot really be attained either, and yet talk of "frictionless planes" has "cash value" because we can approximate them to a very high degree of approximation.

Perhaps it will seem that explaining truth in terms of justification under ideal conditions is explaining a clear notion in terms of a vague one. But "true" is *not* so clear when we move away from such stock examples as "Snow is white." . . .

The simile of frictionless planes aside, the two key ideas of the idealization theory of truth are (1) that truth is independent of justification here and now, but not independent of *all* justification. To claim a statement is true is to claim it could be justified. (2) Truth is expected to be stable or "convergent"; if both a statement and its negation could be "justified," even if conditions were as ideal as one could hope to make them, there is no sense to thinking of the statement as *having* a truth-value.[16]

THE ROAR OF CHARYBDIS IS HEARD IN THE NEAR DISTANCE

The foregoing account of truth made use of the counterfactual conditional as well as of the notion of epistemically ideal (or "close to ideal") conditions. S is true, according to this view just in case the following counterfactual is true:

(1) S would be justified if epistemic conditions were good enough.[17]

But how is this counterfactual to be understood? As I put the difficulty in my Dewey Lectures,[18] explaining my reasons for giving up the whole approach:

Unlike Dummett's "global antirealist," I did not suppose that empirical propositions could be *unalterably* verified or falsified.[19] And I was bothered from the start by the excessively "idealist" thrust of Dummett's position, as represented, for example, by Dummett's flirtation with strong antirealism with respect to the *past*, and I avoided that strong antirealism by identifying a speaker's grasp of the meaning of a statement not with an ability to tell if the statement is true now, or to tell whether it is true under circumstances the speaker can actually bring about . . . but with the speaker's possession of abilities which would enable [any] sufficiently rational speaker to decide if the statement is true in sufficiently good epistemic circumstances.

To the objection that this is still an "idealist" position, I replied that it certainly is not, on the ground that while the degree of confirmation speakers actually assign to a sentence may simply be a function of their sensory experiences . . . the notion of *sufficiently good epistemic circumstances* [was] a "world involving" notion. That is why the totality of actual human sense

experiences does not, on this position, determine the totality of truths, even in
the long run.

. . . On my alternative picture (as opposed to Dummett's), the world was
allowed to determine whether I actually am in a sufficiently good epistemic
situation or whether I only seem to myself to be in one—thus retaining an
important idea from commonsense realism—[but] the conception of an
epistemic situation was, at bottom, just the traditional epistemological one. My
picture still retained the basic premise of an interface between the knower and
everything "outside." But while the need for a "third way" besides early
modern realism and Dummettian idealism is something I feel as strongly as
ever, such a third way must . . . *undercut* the idea that there is an "antinomy,"
and not simply paste together elements of early modern realism and elements
of the idealist picture.

As mentioned above, the "idealization theory of truth" was presented
in chapter 3 of *Reason, Truth and History*. In chapter 5, the problem of the
understanding of counterfactuals like (1) was addressed, however, by
adopting a verificationist account of how we understand counterfactuals. I
said simply that:

A non-realist or "internal" realist regards conditional statements as statements
which we understand (like all other statements) in large part by grasping their
justification conditions. This does not mean that the "internal" realist *abandons*
the distinction between truth and justification, but that truth (*idealized
justification*) is something we grasp as we grasp any other concept, via a
(largely) implicit understanding of the factors that make it rationally acceptable
to say that something is true. (122–23)

The dilemma I faced (but was not aware that I faced at that time) was this:
let us suppose, as seems reasonable, that whatever makes it rational to
believe that S makes it rational to believe that S would be justified were
conditions good enough. If my understanding of the counterfactual "S
would be justified if conditions were good enough" is *exhausted* by my
capacity to tell to what degree it is justified to assert it, and that is always
the same as the degree to which it is justified to assert S itself, why did I
bother to mention the counterfactual at all? Why did I not just say that my
understanding of S is just my capacity to tell what confirms S to what
degree, *full stop*? It seems that the whole appeal to "idealized" verification,
to counterfactual verification, was an unnecessary shuffle. But then the jaws
of the Scylla of solipsism close on me! On the other hand, if I repudiate the
justificationist account of our understanding of counterfactuals, the
Charybdis of the metaphysical realism I was trying to avoid sweeps me into
its whirlpool. It was the impossibility, as I now think it to be, of steering an

anti-realist course between the Scylla of solipsism and the Charybdis of metaphysical realism that led me to develop and defend what I believe to be an unmetaphysical version of realism in *The Threefold Cord: Mind, Body and World*. It is time now for us to see if Michael Dummett has found a way where I failed, to steer between Scylla and Charybdis.

DUMMETT'S WAY

As was already said, the first step in avoiding the Scylla of solipsism was simply to insist that the justificationism we both advocated was *social* and not *individualistic* in nature, or as Dummett put it, that the word "our" in "our being justified in asserting a statement" must be taken "in a collective, not a distributive, sense." Whether this is something that Dummett *can* say without doing violence to his own justificationist principles, and what it means when understood in a justificationist way, is what we must now ask.

The question is important because of its connection with another question, the question to which, indeed, *Truth and the Past* is devoted: how to avoid anti-realism about the past. I referred above to Dummett's "flirtation with anti-realism about the past"; he himself says that this is a topic that troubled him for years, and that this new book is an attempt to see if a justificationist can repudiate "the view that statements about the past, if true at all, must be true in virtue of the traces past events have left in the present."[20] He still does not find that view incoherent, but he does say it is "repugnant."[21] The way in which Dummett proposes to reject anti-realism about the past involves simply counting past observers as fully on a par with present observers. The details of this proposal are complex, and it would take a much longer essay that this to examine them in detail. But the essential ideas are (1) that the semantically crucial verification of a statement about the past is not the present "indirect" verification, via a memory, or, in the case of the distant past, via a historical trace, that the statement is true, but the verification by a witness at the time ("Dying does not deprive anyone of the status either of an observer or of an informant" [p.68]); and (2) that while that "direct" verification may be transmitted to us via a trace, it counts as a verification whether it is transmitted or not ("For all the messages that have been lost, it remains that statements about the past must count as having been directly established, and therefore as true, if someone observed them to be true at the, or an, appropriate time" [p. 68]).

The problem, however, is that while language is indeed social, *competence* is individual. Earlier I quoted Dummett as asking (rhetorically) how we could learn what it is for assertions to be true independently of any means we have for establishing their truth; but one can also ask "How could" an individual language learner learn to understand Dummett's "we." Dummett, indeed, tells us that:

> A child who had learned only when he was right to come out with simple assertoric utterances, such as "Doggie" when a dog was in sight, would serve as an extension of adults' range of observation, but could not yet be credited with saying that anything was so; he can be credited with that only when he has learned to treat the utterances of others as extending *his* range of observations. It is intrinsic to the use of language that we accept the testimony of others: to believe what we are told is the default response. Language binds us into society. (41)

I agree that it does, of course. But Dummett moves too rapidly from the child's acquisition of the practice of accepting the testimony of others—an idea the justificationist seems clearly entitled to—to the child's "treating the utterances of others as extending his range of observations," where this "treating" must amount to something quite different from a mere disposition to accept sentences that the child hears if it is to account for the child's grasp of the thought that a statement about the past may be true even though *no* testimony is available (to the child). (Dummett also speaks of the child's forming a mental "grid" that shows the relations of other places and times to one another and to the child's present location.)

THE ALTERNATIVE TO ANTI-REALISM

In *The Threefold Cord: Mind, Body and World*, discussing the anti-realism about the past that Dummett once defended (or experimented with), I wrote:

> If we accept it that understanding the sentence "Lizzie Borden killed her parents with an axe" is not simply a matter of being able to recognize a verification in our own experience—accept it, that is, that we are able to conceive of how things that we cannot verify *were*—then it will not appear as "magical" or "mysterious" that we can understand the claim that that sentence is *true*. What makes it true, if it is, is simply that Lizzie Borden killed her parents with an axe. The recognition transcendence of truth comes, in this case, to no more than the "recognition transcendence" of some killings. And did we ever think that all killers can be recognized as such? Or that the belief that there are certain determinate individuals who are or were killers and who cannot be detected as such by us is a belief in magical powers of the mind?[22]

I believe that today Michael Dummett would agree with this. But I think that he would still say that we cannot *rest* with the commonsense thought that being able to think about past events that we cannot verify (being able to locate them in our mental "grid") is an ability that we acquire as we acquire language and all the skills that language brings with it. He believes that we need to show that that ability can be accounted for in a "justificationist" way. (Perhaps he thinks this because he thinks that anti-realism about the past is only "repugnant" and not actually "incoherent.") But, first, I don't see that he *has* accounted for that ability in a justificationist way, for the reasons I have just briefly laid out, and, secondly, I *do* think that antirealism about the past is incoherent.[23] I look forward with very great interest to whatever Michael Dummett will respond.

HILARY PUTNAM

THE UNIVERSITY OF CHICAGO
NOVEMBER 2004

NOTES

1. Michael Dummett, *The Logical Basis of Metaphysics: The William James Lectures 1976* (Cambridge, MA: Harvard Univ. Press, 1991).

2. Michael Dummett, "What is a Theory of Meaning? (I)" collected in his *Seas of Language* (Oxford: Clarendon Press, 1993).

3. Michael Dummett, *Truth and the Past* (New York: Columbia Univ. Press, 2004).

4. However, I don't wish to give the impression that it was the manifestation argument that was responsible for what I described as a close approach of our philosophical orbits around the time of Dummett's William James Lectures (and for a number of years subsequently). If anything it was because of a different argument, my model-theoretic argument against metaphysical realism, that I was prepared to accept the claim that "we have no means" for acquiring the realist notion of truth. The model-theoretic argument is set out in a lecture titled "Realism and Reason" to the American Philosophical Association reprinted as the last chapter of my *Meaning and the Moral Sciences* (London: Routledge and Kegan Paul, 1978), and set out at more length in my *Reason, Truth and History* (Cambridge: Cambridge Univ. Press, 1981). I explain what I think is wrong with it in *The Threefold Cord: Mind, Body and World* (New York: Columbia Univ. Press, 2000).

5. I am thinking in particular of the essays I collected in the first two volumes of my *Philosophical Papers*, which were published in 1975 by Cambridge University Press. (A third volume, *Realism and Reason*, published in 1983, represents my subsequent "internal realist" position—a position I now regard as a false start to dealing with the very real problem of the normativity of language use.)

6. "A Philosopher Looks at Quantum Mechanics," in my *Philosophical Papers*, vol. 1, *Mathematics, Matter and Method*. The quotation in the text is from p. 131.

7. "Explanation and Reference," in my *Philosophical Papers*, vol. 2, *Mind, Language and Reality*.

8. The views I am referring to were those in the William James Lectures (see n. 1, above). They were set out more briefly in "What Is a Theory of Meaning? (I), (II)" in *Truth and Other Enigmas* (Cambridge, MA: Harvard Univ. Press, 1980).

9. See n. 4 for details.

10. Michael Devitt, *Realism and Truth* (Princeton, NJ: Princeton Univ. Press, 1984); see Drew Khlentzos, *Naturalistic Realism and the Anti-Realist Challenge* (Cambridge, MA: MIT Press, 2004) for a convincing criticism of Devitt's response to Dummett.

11. V. I. Lenin, *Materialism and Empirio-Criticism* (Moscow: Foreign Languages Publishing House, 1952).

12. Indeed, Devitt seems to have read Lenin extensively—at least his first published attack on my "internal realism" was titled "Realism and the Renegade Putnam," a play on the title of Lenin's famous article "Marxism and the Renegade Kautsky."

13. For example, Carnap discusses this sort of statement—his example is "If all minds (or all living beings) should disappear from the universe, the stars would still go on in their courses"—(in "Testability and Meaning," Part II, *Philosophy of Science*, vol. IV, 1937, 37–38), and concludes that it is both cognitively meaningful and well confirmed.

14. Hans Reichenbach, *Experience and Prediction* (Chicago: Univ. of Chicago Press, 1938).

15. Dummett uses the term "justificationism" in *Truth and the Past*; I spoke of "verificationist semantics" in my first internal realist writing, my American Philosophical Association (Eastern Division) Presidential Address of 1976, collected in my *Meaning and the Moral Sciences* (London: Routledge and Kegan Paul, 1978).

16. *Reason, Truth and History*, 55–56.

17. I employed a similar counterfactual in *Representation and Reality* (Cambridge, MA: MIT Press 1988), 115.

18. "The Dewey Lectures 1994: Sense, Nonsense, and the Senses: An Inquiry into the Powers of the Human Mind" (Special Issue of *The Journal of Philosophy* 91, no. 9, September 1994); these are collected as part I of *The Threefold Cord*. The quotation is from p. xxx.

19. Although Dummett is not unaware that the verification of an empirical statement is typically corrigible, as a rule, he tends to prescind from this fact. This tendency may spring from his expressed desire to carry Brouwer's intuitionist logic, a logic designed by Brouwer in connection with an anti-realist philosophy of mathematics, over to empirical language. The simplest possible way to make such a carry-over is to extend the notion of "proof," which is the basic notion in the intuitionist semantics for mathematical language, to a bivalent predicate "verified" applicable to mathematical and nonmathematical language alike, and this is what Dummett does.

20. *Truth and the Past*, ix.

21. Ibid. I believe that Yuval Dolev has successfully argued that, contrary to Dummett, anti-realism about the past *is* incoherent. See Dolev's "Dummett's Antirealism and Time," *European Journal of Philosophy* 8, no. 3 (Dec. 2000): 253–76.

22. *The Threefold Cord: Mind, Body and World*, xxx.

23. See the paper by Yuval Dolev cited in a previous note. Dummett himself pointed out that if one holds the ant-realist view that statements about the past, if true at all, "must be true in virtue of the traces past events have left in the present," then it must be that the semantics of every empirical statement about the past changes every time the reference of "the present" changes—that is to say, must change at every moment. But, as Dolev points out, any attempt to say what a statement about the past meant *a moment ago* must then likewise be semantically unstable—indeed, the change in question will be *indescribable*.

REPLY TO HILARY PUTNAM

I by no means wish to be dashed on the rocks of Scylla—an ignominious fate for a solipsist; but I have little taste for being sucked into the whirlpool of metaphysical realism, either: the terrestrial counterpart to a black hole.

If an ant could philosophise, could it be a solipsist, or even conceive of solipsism? We are not ants; but we are not butterflies, either.

Hilary Putnam thinks that I am in danger, on the one side, of falling into solipsism. Solipsism has never exerted any attraction on me. How could I—how can anyone—be a solipsist? I learned my language from other people; without it I could form only inchoate thoughts about the immediately present. I might be quite cunning in dealing with the immediately present, but I should barely be rational. I am what I am only because I belong to the human race, and am surrounded by its members, with whom I interact in various ways.

But may not what I call "other people" be merely items in my experience? Who gives me this experience? No one: not God, nor a crazy scientist—the solipsist cannot believe in either. But these phantasms, these items of my experience, can do all sorts of things to me; they can amuse me, they can show me kindness and love, they can caress me, they can insult me, they can hit me. They could shoot me, and that would be the end of my life. Do we all, when the ordained ends of our lives arrive, fantasise the circumstances of our deaths? I was forgetting—the others do not die, because they do not have lives to end: they are merely deleted from my experience. But if it is all a product of my imagination, how does it come about that my imagination is so fertile? How could I have imagined *King Lear*? And if I did, why cannot I write a play one twentieth as good? *I* cannot have imagined my whole experience: it must have come to me from without. But from where? I use language; the meaning of what I say is determined by the circumstances in my experience that I take as warranting this assertion or that. So what I call "other people" must be other people, according to the sense in which I use the words "other people." But does it follow that they have lives—that they have experiences as I do? Well, they behave as if they do: I cannot make any sense of the way they act and of what they say if they do not. Are we back with that's being what, as I use my language, I *call* "other people's having experiences"? No: it is a matter of what I can and cannot believe. I think that solipsism is like anti-realism about the past: it is coherent—you cannot force the solipsist to contradict himself; but you would have to be mad, and rather unpleasantly mad, to believe it.

When I began writing "The Reality of the Past," I did not know what the outcome would be. I thought that, if anti-realism about the past proved to be coherent, I must accept that it is a consequence of the general anti-realist argument, whereas, if it proved to be incoherent, it would point to some fallacy in the general anti-realist argument. In the event, it appeared to me to be coherent, but implausible and, I decided after efforts to believe it, repugnant. In the article, I naturally presented the anti-realist position as strongly and plausibly as I could. Hilary Putnam believes anti-realism about the past to be incoherent, and, for proof, refers me to an article by Yuval Dolev in the *European Journal of Philosophy.*

Dolev treats anti-realism about the past as my personal view, which is fair enough; I did *try* to believe it. He says that it involves "solipsism of the present moment," which is doubly false. There is no overt trace of solipsism in the article; my anti-realist does not think that a statement is true only if there is now a ground known by *him* for accepting it as true, or warranting its assertion; he does not even think it to be true only if there is a ground known by someone. He thinks that a statement is true if there is now a ground available to us for accepting it as true. Here the "now" does not refer to a durationless moment; I do not even believe in durationless moments, as I said in my article "Is Time a Continuum of Instants?"[1] Dolev appears to think that the anti-realist would have difficulty about saying, "What a pretty tune," on the ground that a tune cannot exist at a moment, but takes time to play and to hear. In general, the word "now" refers to whatever length of time what is referred to takes to exist; but of course when we are speaking of grounds for supposing something to have existed or to have happened, it refers to whatever length of time it takes to register those grounds—in the case of a complex argument, perhaps a considerable length of time. What the anti-realist's view of time amounts to is *presentism*—the belief that only the present is real. The realist about time believes that a statement about the past, if true, is rendered true by a past event, and that a statement about the future, if true, is rendered true by a future event. He therefore believes that past and future events enjoy a shadowy existence. The presentist, by contrast, believes that there is only what there *is*.

If Henry sees John board a plane whose destination is Montreal, and sees the plane take off, he has, by anyone's standards, ample ground for believing the statement, "John left today for Canada," to be true. My anti-realist is anxious to preserve the truth-value link which, in this situation, requires that if, in exactly ten years' time, Henry says, "John left for Canada ten years ago to the day," what he says will be true. The anti-realist believes that statements are true or false according to the grounds that exist *now* for asserting them. So if presented with the hypothesis that Henry will make that statement in exactly ten years' time, he can happily accept that it will be true: true in exactly the same sense that the statement, "John left today for Canada," is now true, namely that there are *now* grounds for assigning it the value *true*. There are now grounds for the truth of the statement, made today, "John left today," and there are *now* grounds for the truth of the statement, which will be made in ten years' time, "John left exactly ten years ago."

We are trying to get the anti-realist—let us call him "Arthur"—to acknowledge another sense of "true," one which applies on the strength of grounds for assertion which may exist, or have existed, at a time other than the present. Simple appeal to the truth-value link has not brought this about. We try the following: "Suppose that in ten years' time Henry meets John at the airport off a plane from Toronto, will he not be right to say, 'John has returned from Canada.'?" Arthur sticks to his guns and replies, "Of course I grant your conditional, which I interpret as meaning that if there were at any time grounds for thinking that in ten years' time from now Henry would meet John at the airport off a plane from Toronto, there would then be grounds for thinking that he would be right to say, 'John has returned from Canada', which would mean that that statement was true." Exasperated, we say, "Suppose that in ten years' time everyone has forgotten the exact date of John's departure, and that all the passenger lists have been destroyed, would not Henry be right to say, 'It is neither true nor false that John left for Canada exactly ten years ago.'?" Arthur replies, "No, because that would be a contradiction: if a statement is not true, it is false. To say that it was not true would be to say that no ground for it would ever be found, and you could not be sure of that unless you knew independently that it was false." "What should he say, then?" we ask. "Just that it is not known whether that statement is true or false. Would that not be correct even by your standards?" answers Arthur. "Yes, it would," we reply, "but ought he not to say that it is not *now* known?" "He could," the answer comes, "but the 'now' would be redundant: the tense is carried by the 'is'." "Well, you spoke of the hypothetical possibility that Henry might at some time be right to say a certain thing, which would therefore be true at that time," we say; "so you admit that we can speak of a statement's being true at a time other than the present, on the basis of evidence available at that time." "Yes," Arthur replies, "but such a possibility is that of there *now* being grounds to suppose that there would then be such evidence."

We cannot trap the anti-realist in this way, and Dolev does not attempt to do so. His refutation turns, rather, on the notion of truth-conditions. The anti-realist acknowledges that the meaning of the word "true," as it is now used, changes when it is used at a later time. For "true," as used now, is understood as subject to the principle that a statement can be true only if there is (that is, *is now*) something in virtue of which it is true; when the word "true" is used later, it will be subject to the principle that a statement can be true then only if there is *then* something in virtue of which it is true. Dolev argues that, over and above the difference in the meaning of "true," there is also a difference in the meaning of "truth-condition," and that *this* difference cannot be explained. It should seem obvious that, if the word "true" changes in meaning, the meaning of the expression "condition for a statement to be true" will change with it. Dolev disallows this plea, on the score of circularity: the change in meaning of the word "true" has been explained because of the change in truth-conditions, and so we cannot now explain the change in truth-conditions by appeal to the change in meaning of the word "true." I cannot see the justice of the charge of circularity. Suppose I say that the English word "doctor" has two different senses, and that therefore the phrase "the condition for truly saying 'That person is a doctor'" has two different senses. I am asked the difference in the two senses of "doctor," and I reply by explaining the difference between what someone has to have done to be a doctor in the one sense and what someone has to have done and to do to be a doctor in the other. Am I guilty of circularity? I am not, it may be said, because I have explained the difference between the application-conditions of "doctor" independently of the two senses of that word. But then the anti-realist can explain the difference in the truth-conditions of any given statement at one time and at another independently of the change in meaning he ascribes to the word "true" from one time to the other. The condition for its truth at one time is the existence *at that time* of something in virtue of which it is true; the condition for its truth at the other time is the existence *at that other time* of something in virtue of which it is true. No circularity is involved. Nor is the sentence "A solar eclipse is occurring now," thought of in relation to future conditions, nothing but a string of marks on paper for the anti-realist, as Dolev claims.

It is true, as Dolev says, that in "The Reality of the Past" I saddled the anti-realist with the view that we "cannot by any means at all express" what someone—even a fellow-presentist—means by "true" at a time other than the present. That seems inconsistent with professing to explain the condition he will at a later time require for a statement to be true. So I softened this doctrine. The anti-realist takes the word "true" to be like the word "today"; there is a general principle governing its use at different times, but what it *says* changes. This idea can be expressed by saying that one cannot *mean* by "today" what anyone meant by it yesterday; but this is not to say that the dictionary-meaning of the word "today" changes. It is, rather, that I cannot today think the very thought that I expressed yesterday by saying, "How beautiful the park looks today." In just the same sense, if someone says to me, "I am in terrible pain," I cannot myself either express or think the very thought he expressed. But, although I cannot think that thought, I know what thought he is expressing, and that entitles me to say that I both understand and sympathise with him. I put all this in "The Reality of the Past" as follows:

> The anti-realist need not hang on to the claim that the meaning of the expression ["There *is* something in virtue of which . . . "] alters: he may replace it by the explanation that he cannot now *say* what he will in a year's time be saying when he uses it. Even if "now" *means* the same whenever it is used, I cannot now *say* by means of it what I will later be able to say by means of it: to adapt an example of Prior's, if I am glad that the pain will be over in five minutes, this is not the same thing I shall be glad about in five minutes' time when I say, "Thank God it's over now!"[2]

Thus I do not see any reason why the anti-realist about past and future may not enunciate the general principle governing what he will at any time take as the condition for the truth of a statement. Of course, when he entertains some hypothesis about the circumstances prevailing at any time other than the present, he is supposing that there is now some ground for thinking that such circumstances will prevail or have prevailed at that time; but this does not prevent him from making the supposition, and saying what bearing the hypothetical circumstances would have or would have had upon judgements of truth and falsity at that time. Dolev writes, "The way the world *is* is identified with the way it is *now*. If this is not an empty tautology, then the phrase 'The world as it is' must designate all that we can meaningfully think or speak of, and if you can't think or speak of it, then you can't whistle it either."[3] There is no more reason why the anti-realist cannot think of what is not than there is that none of us can. In any case, the anti-realist can think of the past, as embodied in his and other people's memories and the traces it has left. He is aware of time, that is, of the fact that the world changes: what there is is not what there will be. The anti-realist does not agree with Dolev that what he (the anti-realist) "cannot say, what he denies the very possibility of saying . . . , is that what was present *was* real and that what will be present *will be* real in the way that what is present *now* is."[4] He can say that, all right: what he will not say is what the realist is committed to saying, that what is past and what is future are real enough by themselves—that is, independently of the traces the one has left in the present, and the present indications that foreshadow the other—to render our past- and future-tense statements true or false. He might challenge Dolev to explain his phrase "in the way that"; it needs some explaining.

So I think that both Hilary Putnam and Yuval Dolev are wrong. The position of the anti-realist about the past is perfectly coherent and free of self-contradiction. It is just difficult, and not very pleasant, to believe (though Łukasiewicz found it consoling).

Why does Hilary Putnam believe me in danger of falling into solipsism? Because he thinks that a justificationist theory of meaning is naturally individualistic. I thoroughly disagree. Human beings are bound together in a net of knowledge which we communicate to one another. This ought to be more obvious in the information age than it has ever been; but it has always been so—always, though more saliently than before the invention of writing; before that, however, tribal tradition was passed down orally through the generations. Admittedly, information is very inequitably distributed between individuals; but what would any of us know of the world were it not for what, from childhood onward, we have been told? Language serves to communicate knowledge from one of us to others of us. Provided that testimony is truthful, those who receive it receive the knowledge it conveys; they then possess that knowledge as genuinely as the one who testified. Language is a social phenomenon; and no plausible theory of meaning can ignore its social character. There is direct evidence for the truth of some statements, and indirect evidence for that of others. There is not direct evidence for an event only when I personally have witnessed it, but when someone has witnessed it; if he testifies to it, he puts it into the common pool of knowledge available in principle to all of us. It is by appeal to this common pool of knowledge that a plausible justificationist theory of meaning needs to appeal, not to the knowledge possessed by a single speaker. There are no private languages; and there is not really any private knowledge, either.

Putnam remarks that while language is social, competence is individual. This is of course true: we are not ants. Ants have no individuality; I doubt if there is any difference in ability to perform their allotted tasks between any one ant and another. Putnam is concerned with competence, not in speaking, but in understanding: he asks how a child can come to understand the communal "we," and rebukes me, probably rightly, for being too quick in *Truth and the Past* in passing from a child's learning to accept the testimony of others to his grasping "the thought that a statement about the past may be true even though *no* testimony is available (to the child)." It surely comes about in ways such as the following. The child wants to know what happened on a certain occasion long ago. He asks his mother, who says, "Ask your grandfather." He does so and his grandfather replies, "I don't know; I wasn't there. Your great uncle Joseph was there, but he is in Australia, so we can't ask him." Or in reference to another occasion he answers another such question by saying, "I don't know; I wasn't there. Your great-aunt Edith, whose funeral we went to last Friday, was there, but she would never tell me what happened." It is in such ways that the child learns that a statement may be true even though no one can tell him that it is.

What is wrong with anti-realism about the past? Despite the anti-realist's quite sincere disavowal of solipsism, his view is subtly individualistic. We cannot travel into the past, the anti-realist argues, so all that remains of the past, and hence all that there is to the past, are the traces it has left in the present. The argument is based on an analogy to, or disanalogy with, what we may say concerning what there is at another place, and this is an individualistic notion: another place than what? The anti-realist thinks that we—any one of us—will obtain a direct justification for a statement that some event is occurring in some place other than where we are by travelling to that place and observing that event if it is still going on or otherwise obtaining grounds for thinking that it recently happened. He is using an individualistic notion of justification. Rather, direct evidence for the occurrence of an event at a given place and time consists in the observation of it by someone suitably placed in space and time to observe it. And we often have testimony to such direct evidence for events in the past, in the form of the recorded testimony of people so placed. That we cannot travel into the past is beside the point. People now dead can have been direct observers, and they have often left testimony to having been so, either by what they have written or by what they have told others. Of course, of events sufficiently remote in time, since there were no intelligent observers of them, we can have only indirect evidence.

Putnam's fear that I might fall into the whirlpool of metaphysical realism has more justification than his warning that I might be dashed on the rocks of solipsism, because in *Truth and the Past* I did indeed teeter on the brink of realism. I expressed the view that the meaning of a statement that some event occurred or that some state of affairs obtained at some particular place or time had two components: what evidence would justify its assertion, and what it *said*; and I allowed that the admission of this second component involved a lurch towards realism. I now think that this was a mistake, due to my thinking too much about the evidence obtainable by an individual. I did so because I had started by treating of a child's acquisition of the conception of an event's occurring or a state of affairs as obtaining in another place—a place other than where he is. Thinking in that way, it is natural to feel that some essential element is missing: I decided that that was what was *said* by making the statement. From this I inferred that the evidence available to an individual, when he was not at the time and place referred to (including when he was considering a statement about a previous event), was indirect evidence, and that the only direct evidence is that obtained by an observer at the right time and place. That conclusion was correct; but it shows that it was unnecessary to make a detour through the obscure notion of what the statement *says*. It is sufficient to insist on the communal conception of direct evidence for its being right to assert such a statement, as against the best evidence obtainable by an individual speaker.

Thus Putnam's doubts about whether my position is truly justificationist are laid to rest. I believe I can navigate between Scylla and Charybdis. I do not even have to be tied to the mast in order not to succumb to the siren voices of realism. I have never actually declared myself an opponent of realism, though those who have taken an interest, hostile or friendly, in my work usually believe that that is what I am. I have merely pressed arguments to show that realism is incoherent. I should not mind being brought to accept realism; I just do not see how I can accept it. Many philosophers nowadays give voice to resounding declarations that they are realists. This is unobjectionable when they have arguments to show that realism can be defended, or even that it is necessary; on the part of those who have no such arguments, it is mere prejudice.

There are many local realisms and anti-realisms. One may be a realist or an anti-realist about the past; about mathematics (platonism versus constructivism); about mental events and states (this anti-realism is called behaviourism); about the external world (anti-realism in this case is phenomenalism); about other minds (this anti-realist is a solipsist); about propositions (think of Frege's third realm); about possible objects (concerning which Meinong was a realist); about possible worlds (concerning which David Lewis was a realist); about the future (about which C. D. Broad, among many others, was an anti-realist). My interest in the subject was first prompted by my noticing that the arguments for different such local anti-realisms often resembled, or paralleled, one another, as did the arguments against them. The term "global anti-realism" was perhaps badly coined. My global anti-realist did not embrace all these local anti-realisms. He did not, for example, attempt to combine phenomenalism with behaviourism. Both these are reductive anti-realisms, and the "global anti-realist" is typically not a reductionist. He is better called a justificationist. His distinctive thesis is global in that he applies to all statements the account of their meanings that many local anti-realists apply to the statements of some restricted class: that their meanings are determined by what constitutes direct evidence that it would be correct to assert them. Opposed to him is one who might be called a "global realist." Again, he need not endorse realism concerning all the topics I listed above (although Meinong came very close to doing so). He is better called a truth-conditionalist: his distinctive thesis is that the meanings of all statements are determined by the conditions for them to be true. Typically, he endorses the principle of bivalence, that every statement is determinately either true or false, and he accepts classical logic. The justificationist will reject bivalence, on the ground that for some statements there is no justification either for asserting or for denying them. He is therefore likely to favour intuitionistic logic.

As thus characterised, justificationism and truth-conditionalism are semantic doctrines. But they carry with them different accounts of the notion of truth. The justificationist explains truth in terms of the notion, that of the justification of an assertion, that he has made central to his theory of meaning. Very often, the truth-conditionalist leaves the notion of truth unexplained, taking it as "primitive"; this was essentially Frege's attitude. Frege thought that anyone who makes a judgement possesses the concept of truth, at least implicitly. Well, whether or not this is so, we have to learn what the word "true" means, and it must be possible to give an account of what we learn when we learn that. It would not do to replace the word "true" in a Davidsonian truth theory by some otherwise meaningless technical term, and explain that the term derived its meaning from its role in the theory: it would not *have* any role in the theory. It would no more have a role than the term "trump" would have in the rules of a certain card game if the rules specified that in that game such-and-such cards were trumps, but the notion of a trump card were no further mentioned in the rules. That is, it would have no role unless the rules presupposed that we brought with us a knowledge of the function of trump cards in other card games; and we can understand a Davidsonian truth theory as a theory of meaning only if we bring to it a prior understanding of what "true" means. What is needed in order to see it as a theory of meaning, or as the basis of one, is an account of how the conditions for the truth of a statement go to explain the use of the sentence expressing that statement in converse. That will constitute the account of the notion of truth that is part of a truth-conditional theory of meaning. Admittedly, adherents of such a theory of meaning usually shirk this essential part of their task. It is not enough that they should say that the condition for the truth of a statement differs according to its form: that a statement of the form "$F(\mathbf{a})$," such as "The Earth spins," is true if the predicate $F(x)$ is true of the denotation of $\mathbf{a}$, and so on for other forms. It is essential to a truth-conditional or realistic theory that truth-values of statements are independent of our knowledge of them and our capacity to know them, and this needs to be spelled out as part of the theory. Adherents of such a theory do not usually expound their conception of truth; but they have a cloudy picture of external reality as determining our statements as true or as false, regardless of whether *we* can decide this. They may waver when it comes to mathematical statements; but the more dogged may press on, and conceive of an objective mathematical reality as determining *their* truth-values independently of our knowledge.

It is through their divergent accounts of truth that different semantic theories obtain their metaphysical overtones. Different accounts of truth will affect what truths there are thought to be; and this is a metaphysical consequence, because reality consists in the totality of facts, not of things. The justificationist is, metaphysically, an anti-realist, because he rejects bivalence and does not accept classical logic. The adherent of a truth-conditional semantics, by contrast, is likely to be a realist; he thinks that a statement may be true independently of whether we have or could have any grounds for thinking it to be true.

In *The Threefold Cord* Hilary Putnam repudiates bivalence. He mentions two types of exception to it. One consists of vague statements, and in this he does not diverge much from realists of the usual type: they usually formulate the principle of bivalence as being that every unambiguous, definite statement is determinately either true or false; "definite" may be glossed as "sufficiently definite in the context" (compare the example of the word "flat" cited by Putnam in *The Threefold Cord*).[5] The other category is more perplexing. It occurs when there occurs a "failure of the world to behave the way it should if the terms [the statement] employs are to work"[6] (Putnam's example is simultaneity in the face of Special Relativity). He denies that "linguistic intuition" is adequate for perceiving an instance of this. Do we here a revival of the thesis that logic is empirical? How *can* a logical law such as that of excluded middle be found by empirical enquiry to fail?

As relativity is explained in popular expositions, the fact that simultaneity is relative to the frame of reference can be realised by considering, given that the speed of light is a constant within every frame of reference, how we determine the simultaneity of spatially separated events: a consideration more congenial to the justificationist than to the realist. If a statement lacks a needed explicit or tacit relativisation, such as "He is a cousin," said in no relevant context, of course it has no determinate truth-value as it stands: it acquires one when the relativisation is supplied, as in "He is Angela's cousin." Now it is true that empirical investigation can discover whether a physical relation is absolute or relative to a frame of reference. This is not discovering that *logic* depends on how the world is: the law of excluded middle was never intended to hold for statements lacking a needed relativisation.

In his essay Putnam claims that in *The Threefold Cord* he embraced and expounded a *non*-metaphysical realism. What, then, is metaphysical realism? In *The Threefold Cord* he says, what he had often said before, that traditional forms of realism assume that "there is one definite totality of objects."[7] This may be part of what Putnam means by "metaphysical realism"; but I cannot see why a realist should be saddled with this assumption. A philosopher may be determinedly realist, and yet recognise that how we slice the world up into discrete objects depends upon the sortal concepts we use, and recognise that we might have used, or other rational creatures might use, quite different ones. For instance, if we all had not only believed in reincarnation but had means by which we thought we could identify newly born babies with people recently dead, we should have quite a different notion of an individual human person. It might be objected to this example that not only realists but others may think there is an objective right and wrong to the way individual human beings are identified; but then we may imagine these beliefs transferred from human beings to dogs. One who recognises all this may yet hold that, given the sortal concepts we have, statements about the objects we accordingly regard as existing are determinately true or false independently of our knowledge or means of knowledge. If so, he is a realist, even if, in Putnam's eyes, an untraditional one.

More to the point is what Putnam writes about truth:

> What makes the metaphysical realist's response [to me] *metaphysical* is its acceptance of the idea (which it shares with the Dummettian antirealist) that our ordinary realism—for example, about the past—presupposes a view of truth as a "substantive property." The metaphysical realist, in wanting a property that he can ascribe to all and only true sentences wants a property that corresponds to the assertoric force of a sentence. But this is a very funny property. To avoid identifying this property of "truth" with that of assertibility, the metaphysical realist needs to argue that there is something we are saying when we say of a particular claim that it is true over and above what we are saying when we simply assert the claim. He wants Truth to be some thing that *goes beyond* the content of the claim and to be that in virtue of which the claim is true. This forces the metaphysical realist to postulate that there is some single thing we are saying (over and above what we are claiming) whenever we make a truth claim, no matter what sort of statement we are discussing, no matter what the circumstances under which the statement is said to be true, and no matter what the pragmatic point of calling it true is said to be.
>
> The right alternative to thinking of truth as a "substantive property" *à la* the metaphysical realist is *not* to think of our statements as mere marks and noises that our community has taught us to associate with conditions for being conclusively verified (as in the account of Dummett's "global antirealist"). . . . The right alternative is to recognize that empirical statements already make claims about the world . . . whether or not they contain the words *is true*.[8]

A striking feature of this passage is its strong resemblance in places to a piece from 1915 in Frege's *Nachlass*, of which the following is part:

The word "true" thus makes no essential contribution through its sense to the thought. When I assert, "It is true that seawater is salt," I assert the same as when I assert, "Seawater is salt." We must recognise here that the assertion lies not in the word "true" but in the assertoric force with which the sentence is uttered. From this one might think that the word "true" has no sense. But then a sentence in which the word "true" occurred would have no sense. We can only say: the word "true" has a sense that contributes nothing to the sense of the whole sentence in which it occurs as a predicate.

But it is precisely through this that this word seems suited to indicate the essence of logic. . . . Thus the word "true" seems to make the impossible possible, namely to make what corresponds to the assertoric force appear as a contribution to the thought.[9]

What Frege says that the word "true" seems to do is what Putnam says the metaphysical realist wants to do—convert the assertoric force which is attached to an utterance into a property; but they both agree that it cannot be done. Now if I say, "The statement 'Seawater is salt' is true," am I saying anything "over and above" what I say when I say simply, "Seawater is salt"? Well, consider the following fragment of a dialogue between two people discussing whether to instruct the doctors to turn off the life-support system from a relative of theirs in a persistent vegetative state:

A: He is either alive or dead.
B: How can you say that? We're not even sure what it *means* to say that he is alive or that he is dead.
A: I didn't say that to say that he is alive is either true or false. I meant that however you fix the criteria for being alive, it will come out that he's either alive or dead.

To say, "The statement 'Seawater is salt' is true," *is* to say something "over and above" what I say when I say simply, "Seawater is salt." It is true enough that the sentences "Seawater is salt," and "The statement 'Seawater is salt' is true," or "It is true that seawater is salt" have the same assertoric content. The assertoric content of a sentence is what is conveyed by an utterance of it on its own to make an assertion—what is added to the picture of the world of a hearer who accepts the assertion as correct. But it is a fallacy, committed by Frege and by many others, to infer from two sentences' having the same assertoric content that they are equivalent; Frege even thought that it proved that they had the same sense. For the assertoric content of a sentence does not exhaust its meaning. It also has an *ingredient sense*, which determines the contribution it makes to the sense of a more complex sentence of which it is a subsentence. The identity of the assertoric contents of two sentences by no means implies that they have the same ingredient sense. It therefore does not at all follow that an instance of what

Donald Davidson always used to call Convention T, in our case:

The statement "Seawater is salt" is true if and only if seawater is salt

is true, since this involves the ingredient senses of both "The statement 'Seawater is salt' is true" and "Seawater is salt," as subject to the logical constant "if and only if."

Putnam rightly says on page 56 of *The Threefold Cord* that if I assert that "it is true that p," then I say the same thing as if I simply assert p; that is, I convey the same in both cases, and so the assertoric contents of both sentences are the same. But on page 51 he has me conceding that "the statement that (1) is true is equivalent to (1) itself" (where (1) is of course a sample declarative sentence). This looks very like an endorsement of the truth of all T-sentences. It has become a Pavlovian reaction among analytic philosophers to the mention of truth to avow a belief in the truth of all T-sentences (one even wrote that no one who does not believe this can be talking about *truth*). Whether a T-sentence is true or not depends upon the semantic theory within which truth is to be characterised. That semantic theory affects the ingredient senses of sentences containing the word "true," not only their assertoric contents. The easiest way to see this is to consider a theory under which sentences in the future tense have no truth-value: they may become true or false at the time when it is right or wrong to assert their present-tense transforms. (The theory would have been acceptable to C. D. Broad, according to whom reality comprised past and present, but not the future.) One who holds this view may allow that one can *believe* a statement about the future, and that the word "true" may be used in avowals of such beliefs; but such a statement is neither true nor false until the time to which it relates. You may not share this view; but it undoubtedly embodies a conception of truth. One who holds it may well agree that "There will be a thunderstorm tomorrow," and "The statement 'There will be a thunderstorm tomorrow' is true" have the same assertoric content; but he will not accept the T-sentence "The statement 'There will be a thunderstorm tomorrow' is true if and only if there will be a thunderstorm tomorrow," because that would imply the biconditional "The statement 'There will be a thunderstorm tomorrow' is not true if and only if there will not be a thunderstorm tomorrow." He holds, after all, that the statement "There will be a thunderstorm tomorrow" is not true; but he is by no means committed to believing that there will not be a thunderstorm tomorrow.

The concluding remarks in the lengthy passage I cited from *The Threefold Cord* suggest a hostility to the very idea of semantics or of a theory of meaning that I feel sure was only a passing mood. When I see words written in a script with which I am very familiar, say the Roman alphabet, I cannot help seeing them as carrying some sound I can utter; if I know how the letters are pronounced in the language in which they are written, I may even see them as carrying the intended sound. But if I see words written in a script I do not know—Arabic or Tamil—I see them *only* as marks. There is an intermediate case, such as when the words are written in Cyrillic, and I do not see them as carrying such a sound, but can pick it out by reading the letters one by one—"P-r-e-s-i-d-e-n-t—it says 'President'." Likewise, when I see or hear words in a language I know, I see or hear them as bearing a certain meaning, as Husserl and Wittgenstein both insisted. But when I hear people speaking in a language of which I am quite ignorant, I associate no meanings with them at all: I hear them only as sounds of a certain kind. I know that the conversants are reporting facts, commenting on them, trying out explanations, expressing reactions to them, perhaps making jokes, doing some of the many things that can be done by people communicating with one another by means of language. If anyone hears them and is of a philosophical bent, he may start to wonder what makes it possible for them to do such complicated things just by uttering noises of that kind. In the case of written words seen as carrying sounds of just that kind, the solution is easy: we all know of the association of sounds with letters in a given language which you have to master when you learn to read. But how is it with understanding a spoken language, as compared with reading (without necessarily understanding) written words? Can we speak of an association between words and meanings, as we spoke of an association between letters and sounds? Well, we can; but how far does that get us? What *are* meanings? We know what sounds are, but *what are meanings*?

Putnam's remark that we ought not to think of our statements as mere marks and noises that our community has taught us to associate with something or other, but to recognise that they already make claims, reads to me like a prohibition on asking such questions. Of course empirical statements make claims about the world: if we know the language, we hear them as making such claims. If we do not know the language, we hear them as no more than noises. We know that the speakers are making statements that express claims, probably about the world, because we know that they are speaking a language and that is what one does with language. But when we hear non-human creatures emitting sounds of a quite different sort—dolphins, say—it is not immediately obvious whether they are using a language or not, whether they are making claims about the world. What is it to know a language? What exactly do we know when we know a language? A semantic theory is intended to be a basis—no more than a basis—for an answer to these questions; a whole theory of meaning gives the whole answer for a particular language—a sample answer for a sample language from which we can see what the answers for other languages would look like. In doing so, a semantic theory must at the outset treat the words and sentences of the language as marks and noises, for that is what they are, considered independently from their significance and expressive power, and the whole point of the theory is to explain what this significance and this expressive power are. I confess that I do not understand what Putnam's "right alternative" amounts to. It looks like an admonition to give up philosophy of language and have nothing to do with anybody who speaks a language other than your own. It obviously cannot be this; but to divine what it is defeats me.

I noted that in his essay Putnam claims that in *The Threefold Cord* he embraced and expounded a *non*-metaphysical realism. For me, realism is in the first instance a semantic doctrine which, in virtue of the conception of truth it implicitly involves, and particularly in virtue of the principle of bivalence, yields a metaphysical doctrine. It is for me an intrinsically metaphysical doctrine. So I have been very puzzled to know what Hilary Putnam could have been claiming to have achieved in propounding a *non*-metaphysical realism. I have here attempted to discover that by examining what he describes as essential to *metaphysical* realism. Two doctrines are ascribed by him to metaphysical realism: that there is a definite totality of objects; and that truth is a substantive property. The first I cannot see as essential to realism. About what the second means I feel uncertain. I applauded his sketch from *The Threefold Cord*, on pages 52–54, of the metaphysical realist's response to the deflationist's account of truth, and found myself in large part agreeing with it, though not, of course, with its distinctively realist slant. But then Putnam says on page 54 that there is nothing wrong with the metaphysical realist's response to the deflationist save his calling truth a "substantive property"; so this gets us very little further in understanding what it means to call it that. I think that truth is a semantic notion, and that a semantic theory must include a characterisation of it that goes beyond a Tarskian truth-definition. If this is believing truth to be a substantive property, then that belief does not distinguish between the metaphysical realist and the anti-realist. Perhaps the answer lies in what the characterisation is; but I can speculate no further.

When we look at the positive views put forward in *The Threefold Cord*, we find: a direct or naive realism about perception, as opposed to the causal theory allied to a phenomenalist or other representationalist account; realism about the past; and an opposition to reductionism concerning the mental. These are all local realisms, with which I largely agree but will not here discuss. I do not see that they together add up to a general commitment to a truth-conditional semantics, which I take as essential to "global realism." Putnam has doubts about the principle of bivalence; but I suspect that he could be brought to agree to a small list of features that cause statements to be exceptions to it. I remain perplexed about what non-metaphysical realism can be.

I agree with Hilary that appealing to the idealisation of evidence justifying the assertion of a statement is an unnecessary shuffle. Some statements admit of a conclusive justification (always allowing for mistakes of perception and memory and for dishonesty). Is idealisation necessary in order to prescind from such mistakes and from deceit? We allow for them in practice, judging as best we can whether they have occurred. Should we define idealised justification to be that which we should obtain if such distorting factors were absent, and explain the meanings of statements of this class as determined by such idealised justification? There is no need. The meanings are given by what counts as a conclusive justification; whether that is what we have is up to us to judge, and we do not need to write the criteria we go by into the theory of meaning. This is what Hilary means when, quoting his own Dewey Lectures, he says that for him "the world [is] allowed to decide whether I actually am in a sufficiently good epistemic situation or whether I only seem to myself to be in one." Reality determines whether I am in a sufficiently good epistemic condition, that is, whether what appear to be adequate grounds for asserting a statement really are adequate grounds for doing so. We do not always investigate possible reasons for doubt, when they seem unlikely, even when we could do so with comparative ease. A justificationist semantics does not explain the meanings of statements in terms of the judgements we actually make, but in terms of genuine grounds for asserting them.

Other statements do not admit of conclusive justification: any justification we may have for asserting them may always be overturned by subsequent counter-evidence. (It is for a cognate reason that many philosophers have maintained that a statement about the future, as long as it remains a statement about the future, cannot be true, or at least cannot be known to be true, since, however well founded, the evidence for it can always be refuted by things turning out otherwise at the relevant time.) If a statement is of this second class, that goes to characterise its meaning; no amount of idealisation can alter this feature of it.

Finally, a few passing observations about remarks in Hilary Putnam's essay. I was surprised by his quoting with apparent approval from an early essay on Carnap that "theoretical terms were not treated [by Carnap] as names of, say, unobservable things and forces . . . , but as merely parts of a machine for predicting 'observations,' parts which have no meaning in themselves apart from their role in the particular theory." I of course agree that a theory serves not only to ground predictions, but to *explain*; but is it not just what it is for a word to be a theoretical term, for it to have no meaning apart from its role in the theory to which it belongs? Theoretical terms are to theories as technical terms used in games are to the rules of the games: "checkmate" has no meaning apart from its role in the rules of chess, and "trump" (in that sense) no meaning apart from its role in the rules of card games. I suppose that, properly speaking, we cannot observe forces, but only their effects; but care needs to be taken to distinguish *things* that are in principle unobservable from those that we are as yet unable to observe; genes have passed from a hypothetical to an observable status, and we must take care not to classify as a theoretical term one which is merely hypothetical.

I very much enjoyed Hilary Putnam's criticism of Michael Devitt's attempted refutation of anti-realism, and thought it wholly to the point. Of course the behaviour of the stars is causally independent of human sensations, desires and beliefs. I suspect that Devitt meant "logically independent," in which case, as Putnam says, he must have been concerned, properly speaking, with statements or propositions about the behaviour of the stars. Well, there may be other intelligent creatures in the galaxy (or in other galaxies); but, as Putnam also observes, the question surely belongs to semantics. A justificationist semantics does not make the meanings of statements turn on human sensations, desires, or beliefs: it makes them turn on what, for any rational beings, are grounds for asserting those statements. We seem to have here a severe case of *ignoratio elenchi*.

M. D.

NOTES

1. Michael Dummett, "Is Time a Continuum of Instants?" *Philosophy* 75 (2000): 497–515).

2. Michael Dummett, "The Reality of the Past," *Proceedings of the Aristotelian Society* 69 (1969): 239–58.

3. Yuval Dolev, "Dummett's Antirealism and Time," *The European Journal of Philosophy* 8, no. 3 (Dec. 2000): 253–76.

4. Ibid., emphasis added.

5. Hilary Putnam, *The Threefold Cord: Mind, Body and World* (New York: Columbia Univ. Press, 2000), 89.

6. Ibid., 65.

7. Ibid., 7.

8. Ibid., 55–56.

9. Gottlob Frege, *Nachgelassene Schriften*, ed. Hans Hermes, Friedrich Kambartel, and Friedrich Kaulbach, Hamburg, 1983, 271–72 (my translation).

5

Ernie Lepore and Kirk Ludwig

THE REALITY OF LANGUAGE: ON THE DAVIDSON/DUMMETT EXCHANGE

> *I conclude that there is no such thing as a language, not if a language is anything like what many philosophers and linguists have supposed. There is therefore no such thing to be learned, mastered or born with.*
>
> (Davidson 1986, 446)
>
> *The occurrence of the phenomena that interests Davidson is incontrovertible: but how can an investigation of them lead to the conclusion that there is no such thing as a language?*
>
> (Dummett 1986, 465)

Michael Dummett and Donald Davidson, two of the most important and influential philosophers of the latter half of the twentieth century, were engaged in an ongoing debate, in and out of print, for two decades. They disagreed about the role of convention in communication and about whether knowledge of linguistic conventions is essential to interpretive success. Prior knowledge of conventions of linguistic usage is typically thought to play a significant role in communication. We know something about the conventions with which our words are used, and this prior knowledge evidently plays a significant practical role in interpreting them. In the face of this commonplace wisdom, Davidson insisted that such knowledge is neither necessary nor sufficient for communication (Davidson 1994, 3). Dummett protested against this, and, further, responded to Davidson's claim that there is no such thing as a language (in the epigraph above) by arguing that Davidson's own program in the philosophy of language would be undercut if his argument were to succeed (Dummett 1986).[1]

For many readers the debate remains elusive; Dummett and Davidson often seemed at cross-purposes, and it was unclear whether in the end serious disagreement separated them. In this paper we will discuss and evaluate two rounds of their exchange, the first constituted by "A Nice Derangement of Epitaphs" (Davidson 1986)[2] and "A Nice Derangement of Epitaphs: Some Comments on Davidson and Hacking" (Dummett 1986), and the second by "The Social Aspect of Language" (Davidson 1994) and Dummett's reply (Dummett 1994).[3] We will argue that, once it is understood exactly which thesis Davidson was attacking, it is hard to see how it undermines anything he had previously maintained and that it is, in a certain sense, just a further articulation of the consequences of his basic methodological stance. We will also argue that there is no reason for him to have suspended his use of the notion of a language in a perfectly respectable sense (distinct from the one he attacks) that comports with his theoretical aims. Indeed, it may be doubtful whether the argument undermines any beliefs any reasonably sophisticated philosopher or linguist has ever held, including Davidson. After clearing away some of the misunderstandings which separate them, we will argue that it is unclear that there is in the end much substantive disagreement between Dummett and Davidson on the role of convention in communication. However, we will also isolate one issue on which there may remain, if not an outright disagreement, a difference of emphasis of some importance.

We will begin by clarifying Davidson's argument against the "reality of language." Sections 1 and 2 identify Davidson's target. Section 3 considers his argument against it. We will not follow precisely the development in his hands, partly to try to elicit more clearly what is going on in his argument, partly to make the discussion more tractable, and partly to position ourselves to register, we hope, illuminating comments about it. This discussion will serve as a foil for raising general questions about our understanding of conventions in communication. In section 4, we will consider Dummett's responses to Davidson's argument, in the light of our exposition, and try to determine where there is agreement despite initial appearances, and where disagreement over fundamental matters may remain. We hope this will set the stage for further clarification of the role of conventions in communication, both in principle and in the case of linguistic beings who share our epistemic limitations. Section 5 provides a brief conclusion.

1. First (Literal) Meaning, Speaker Meaning, and Conventional (Dictionary) Meaning

Davidson's denial of "the reality of language" is motivated by examples of language use which are incompatible or at odds with dictionary (or customary) meaning, but which do not impede communication. The title of his paper "A Nice Derangement of Epitaphs" is an example of this, taken from a line spoken by Mrs. Malaprop in Sheridan's play, *The Rivals*. A malapropism, of which this is an instance, is a ludicrous misuse of a word by a speaker mistaking one word for another similar in sound which *does* express the meaning he intends. For this reason, it is usually easy to determine what a speaker intends to convey when guilty of a malapropism, as in Mrs. Malaprop's attempt to convey that something was a nice arrangement of epithets.

But mistakes of this kind are not the only occasions on which we take another to have intended, in some sense, something other than what the words he used literally meant in his community's language. Words may be used with a nonstandard meaning when a speaker knows it will be clear to an interpreter exactly how he intends them to be understood. Hearing Mrs. Malaprop, we may reuse her misused words in fun, saying, "And that's a nice derangement of words," intending them to be understood as meaning what they were *misunderstood* to mean—and then meaning them ironically—without falling into misunderstanding ourselves.

This phenomenon prompted Davidson to distinguish between literal meaning (or what he called "first meaning") and conventional (or dictionary) meaning. Our imagined utterance is understood to mean "And that's a nice arrangement of words," but only ironically, that is, we are taken to mean, by so meaning with our words, that it was *not* a nice arrangement of words. Here we find the familiar separation of literal and speaker meaning, even though the words were not used with conventional meanings. This distinction between first and conventional meaning is one key to Davidson's rejection of one conception of the role of convention in communication, and one conception of a language, according to which language consists of conventional meaning bearers—and how that is understood is important—knowledge of which is necessary and sufficient for communication.

First meaning is what a speaker intends his words to be understood to have so as to form the basis for subsequent effects achieved by his using those words as he does. As Davidson put it, it is the meaning he intends to be "first in the order of interpretation" (Davidson 1986, 435). Various forms of nonliteral meaning always play off of the literal (or first) meaning of an utterance. Grasping a metaphor or literary figure involves first understanding what the words literally mean. The image in these lines from Shakespeare's Sonnet 73

> That time of year thou mayst in me behold
> When yellow leaves, or none, or few, do hang
> Upon these boughs which shake against the cold,
> Bare ruin'd choirs, where late the sweet birds sang.

would be lost if we did not understand what these words literally meant (their first meaning as intended by Shakespeare). It would be lost if we did not understand *inter alia* that 'choir' designates that part of the church, the chancel eastward of the nave, screened off from the rest of the church and the audience, which is appropriated to the singers, and where the services are performed. Understanding the intent involves understanding first what these words literally mean, which together with their use in application to a person, prompts us to see certain analogies, and to make certain associations, as we are intended to.

Usually we take for granted that what words literally mean is determined by public norms governing them in a speaker's linguistic community. But the distinction between literal and speaker meaning survives nonstandard uses of words, and so this important distinction must be relativized to a speaker. When a speaker uses his words in accordance with public norms, his literal, that is to say, his first meanings, will correspond to their dictionary meanings. Yet the two can and do come apart. They coincide when the competent speaker intends any further meaning attached to his words to be arrived at by first interpreting the words in accordance with public norms. They diverge when he intends the words he utters to be interpreted in the first instance in a way that does not correspond to their dictionary meanings, whether intentionally or inadvertently. (One could insist that "literal meaning" be reserved for dictionary meaning or conventional meaning, but this would be a verbal quibble, for we would still need the distinction between first meaning and speaker meaning, where first and dictionary meaning need not coincide.)

The reason it is important to distinguish first meaning from conventional meaning is that the former is essential to all communication, and, indeed, to all linguistic uses of language. If we misidentify the two, we will be led to suppose conventional meaning is also essential to all linguistic communication. Davidson did not explicitly draw this connection, but seeing that it is there helps to throw into better definition the thought underlying his argument.

2. DAVIDSON'S TARGET

Dummett remarks (in the epigraph of this essay), "The occurrence of the phenomena that interest Davidson is incontrovertible: but how can an investigation of them lead to the conclusion that there is no such thing as a language?" (Dummett 1986, 465). We believe the answer to his question can be uncovered through careful attention to Davidson's remarks about the following three "plausible principles concerning first meaning in language" (Davidson 1986, 436).

(1) *First meaning is systematic.* A competent speaker or interpreter is able to interpret utterances, his own or those of others, on the basis of semantic properties of the parts, or words, in the utterance, and the structure of the utterance. For this to be possible, there must be systematic relations among the meanings of utterances.

(2) *First meanings are shared.* For speaker and interpreter to communicate successfully and regularly, they must share a method of interpretation of the sort described in (1).

(3) *First meanings are governed by learned conventions or regularities.* The systematic knowledge or competence of the speaker or interpreter is learned in advance of occasions of interpretation and is conventional in character.

Davidson's target is principle (3), in particular, when interpreted as saying that first meanings are governed essentially by learned conventions or regularities. (3) is equivalent to identifying first meaning, conceived of in its role as what words are intended in the first instance to be interpreted as meaning, with conventional meaning of the sort expressed by dictionary definitions.

What is the connection between (3) and Davidson's claim that there is no such thing as a language? It is made as follows. First, we plausibly hold that to interpret another, we must know which language he is speaking on that occasion of interpretation. Second, we identify his language as determined by what he intends the first meanings of his words to be at that moment. Third, we identify first meanings, as in (3), with conventional meanings of the words in his linguistic community. Thus, we arrive at a conception of language as something essential to interpretation, because knowledge of a speaker's first meanings is essential to interpretation, and such knowledge consists (by the identification of first with conventional meaning) in mastery of conventions determined by community practices, mastery which must be acquired prior to interpretation. On this conception, a language is (a) a vocabulary and set of rules determined by conventions in a linguistic community which (b) is mastered by members of the community, and mastery of which is both (c) necessary and (d) sufficient for interpreting its speakers.[4]

It is evident that the denial of a "language" in this sense does not commit one to there not being languages in *any* respectable sense. For convenience, when we speak of a language as characterized by (a)–(d), we will write "language." Henceforth, we will restrict "language" for use to characterize a meaningful vocabulary and set of rules which determine the meanings of sentences formed using it. Every language is a language the meanings of whose words are determined by linguistic conventions in a community mastered by its members, and mastery of which is both necessary and sufficient for interpreting its speakers. Though Davidson does not draw this distinction, it is nonetheless implicit in his discussion, and it will aid us in discussing the implications of his argument, and determining the extent to which there is a genuine conflict between Dummett's position on the role of language in communication and Davidson's.

3. DAVIDSON'S ARGUMENT

We have already anticipated an important part of Davidson's argument against the reality of languages, but we shall fill in the details in this section. Here is what needs to be established:

(1) That knowledge of the conventional meanings of the words that a speaker uses (henceforth, "knowledge of conventional meanings") is insufficient for interpreting him.

(1) can be understood in both a stronger and a weaker sense. (a) In a weak sense, (1) is the claim that knowledge of conventional meanings does not guarantee correct interpretation, so that on occasion, perhaps quite often, additional facts must be adduced to arrive at a correct interpretation of a speaker. (b) In a stronger sense, (1) is the claim that we must always bring to bear other knowledge in addition to knowledge of conventional meaning to interpret a speaker correctly. We shall consider how the evidence bears on both (a) and (b).

(2) That knowledge of the conventional meanings of words that a speaker uses is unnecessary for interpreting another.

(2) also can be taken in a stronger and a weaker sense. (c) The weaker interpretation is that in principle, if not in fact, given our limited epistemic capacities, knowledge of conventional meanings can be discarded. (d) The stronger claim is that as a matter of fact, speakers being as they are, no knowledge of conventional meanings is required for them to succeed in interpretation.

(1) The argument against sufficiency appeals to facts we previously surveyed to motivate distinguishing conventional from literal (or first) meanings, where the latter are necessary for all communication. The data establish that people do speak misusing words relative to public norms without preventing their audience from figuring out, as we might put it, what they would have said had they used their words in conformance with the public norms. What this comes to is that their audience correctly interprets their words to mean what the speaker intended them to think he meant. We will come to some worries about this below, but for now we are interested in the consequences of accepting it.

If this is the right way to interpret the data, it follows that knowledge of conventional meaning is insufficient in sense (a) for interpretation. In these cases our knowledge of conventional meanings plays a role in our coming to interpret the speaker's words correctly, since it is in part by recognizing their inappropriateness interpreted in accordance with their conventional meaning in the context that we come to assign a different literal or first meaning to them. However, we also rely on knowledge that it is unlikely the speaker in those circumstances would have wanted to say what his words literally say, and knowledge of certain kinds of errors we know people are liable to make in speaking and in learning public norms for the use of words. This seems obvious and incontrovertible. It is very likely that every speaker has at least once misused a word relative to his community's norms, and yet still has been understood. This happens whenever we are corrected, the right word being supplied, since such correction requires knowing what we intended to say. Misuse of words relative to public norms is an occupational hazard of speaking, as understanding people despite their linguistic foibles is a routine exercise of charity.

It is not as obvious that claim (b) is correct, nor is it clear Davidson ever meant to argue for (b) rather than just (a). (At least one sympathetic commentator has suggested Davidson's target is [in effect] (b), which of course entails (a), though not *vice versa* [Pietroski 1994, 105].) The case *against* (b) can be run as follows: While people do make mistakes from time to time, or use words deliberately with a nonstandard meaning, often they do not. And even if no one is an ideal speaker, say, of English, in the sense of grasping completely the entire vocabulary of English with all its variants and specialized suburbs, surely there are competent, dull, and responsible English speakers who are paragons of erudition and who do not misuse what words they deploy in speech either intentionally or unintentionally. And it is at least plausible that on many occasions there is no call for reinterpreting what another says by assigning nonstandard meanings to his words. In these cases, it is just plain false that any knowledge must be brought to bear in addition to knowledge of the conventional meanings of the words uttered. Thus, while knowledge of conventional meanings does not guarantee interpretive success, sometimes it is all that is needed.

A counterargument rests on the observation that the possibility a speaker has not used his words in conformity with public norms is ever-present. Thus, in interpreting a speaker as meaning with his words exactly what we understand those words to mean according to public norms, we must believe that he is using those words in accordance with public norms, that is, that he is not mistaken and does not intend us to recognize that he intends us to interpret his words in a nonstandard way. In order for our interpreting him thus to be justified, our belief must also be justified. But since this justification will invoke more than knowledge of the conventions for the use of words and even that the speaker is a member of the appropriate linguistic community, it follows that knowledge of conventional meaning is never sufficient for interpretive success.

There is truth in both the objection and its response. It does seem obvious, once we turn our attention to the matter, that deploying our knowledge of conventional meaning to interpret a speaker *does* require our supposing, and believing justifiably, if our interpretation is to be justified, that he is speaking in conformity with public norms.[5] And this requires knowledge of more than just conventional meanings. At the same time, it also seems clear that we routinely and successfully interpret others successfully on the basis of taking them to mean what their words mean according to public norms. We do so because we often have good reason to think that others, particularly our intimates, in most circumstances, are using words in conformance with public norms, and we are adept at noticing when they are not. Acknowledging these facts, the question whether (b) is justified boils down to *what we intended by saying that knowledge of conventional meanings is sufficient for interpretive success.* If we meant simply that sometimes, even often, we are not called upon to revise our view that the speaker speaks with the majority, then (b) should be rejected. If we meant simply that knowledge of conventional meanings all by itself sometimes suffices for interpreting another as speaking in accord with public norms, then, since this is not so, we should accept neither (a) nor (b). Indeed, in this case, (b) follows simply from the observation that human beings are in general fallible.

Our discussion can be recast in terms of Davidson's distinction between a speaker's and an interpreter's *prior* and *passing* theories, and it will be useful to do so in anticipation of later argumentation (Davidson 1986, 441–42). We begin with the more central distinction between an *interpreter's* prior and passing theories. The theories in question are *not* ones the interpreter is actually supposed to hold, but rather ones a theorist uses in characterizing the interpreter's dispositions to understand a particular speaker. In a communicative exchange, an interpreter always stands ready to modify how he is disposed to understand a speaker in light of information provided by the context and what the speaker has already said.

The prior theory for the interpreter is one that characterizes his dispositions to interpret the speaker prior to the onset of a communicative exchange.

The passing theory for the interpreter is one that characterizes his dispositions to interpret the speaker's utterances in the midst of the communicative exchange.

(In the limit, the passing theory is the theory applied to each distinct utterance in the conversation by the speaker.) Prior and passing theories for interpreters are always relativized to particular speakers and times (or time intervals).

As with the interpreter, the prior and passing theories for the speaker are to be thought of as relativized to interpreters and times.

The prior theory of the speaker is "what [the speaker] *believes* the interpreter's prior theory to be . . ." (Davidson 1986, 442).

The passing theory of the speaker "is the theory he *intends* the interpreter to use" (ibid.), the one, then, which expresses what the words in his mouth mean while he is talking to the interpreter.

Davidson says the passing theory for the speaker is the theory he *intends* the interpreter to use, but in light of his own admonishments that we are not to take seriously the idea that communicators hold full-blown meaning theories (438, 441), it seems appropriate to interpret him to mean that the passing theory for the speaker is what characterizes his dispositions to speak during a communicative exchange, and expresses how he intends to be interpreted.

Dummett points out that there is an asymmetry in the distinction between prior and passing theories for interpreter and speaker (Dummett 1986, 460). For the interpreter, the prior and passing theories are representations by the theorist of how the interpreter is disposed to interpret the speaker prior to and during a communicative exchange. For the speaker, the prior theory is *what* the speaker *believes* the interpreter's prior theory is. This is not exactly the same as how the speaker is disposed to interpret the interpreter prior to the interpretive exchange, which would be parallel to the interpreter's prior theory.

Dummett is right about the asymmetry. However, we believe that he makes a mistake about the content of the speaker's prior theory. He says it is a *second-order theory*, a theory about a theory, presumably because Davidson describes the speaker's prior theory in terms of the speaker's beliefs about what the interpreter's prior theory is. However, it is a mistake to suppose Davidson assumes the speaker has formulated a meaning theory that he explicitly believes to be held by the interpreter. This would, if Davidson is right, make both the theorist and the speaker wrong. So, his remark about what the speaker believes must be a shorthand and misleading way of saying something which could be captured from the theorist's perspective without attributing detailed beliefs about semantic theories to the speaker. What is it, though?

The prior theory for the speaker is *a first-order theory* that characterizes the speaker's dispositions to use words *conditional on* his wanting to use those words in accordance with how he would suppose the interpreter to interpret them by default. So, it is not, as Dummett says, a second-order theory. In part, the mistake arises from an ambiguity in the passage: in the locution "what the speaker believes the interpreter's prior theory to be," the theory being denoted is the theory x such that x is believed by the speaker to be the interpreter's prior theory. This theory is first order. Its content is not given by the content of the speaker's beliefs about the interpreter.

What then are these theories theories of? They are theories of languages; they aim to model dispositions of interpreter and speaker. For the interpreter, the prior and passing theories model his dispositions to interpret the speaker prior to and during the communicative exchange. For the speaker, the prior and passing theories model, respectively, his dispositions to speak as his interpreter would by default understand him, conditional on his wanting to be so understood *prior to* the communicative exchange and his dispositions to speak *during* the communicative exchange. At any given time determinate facts about the speaker's dispositions to use words fix what they mean. Thus, the speaker's dispositions determine, at a time in question, a meaning for each of the infinity of sentences which can be grammatically formed from words to which he then has dispositions attached. In the sense of "language" at the end of section 2, then, they are theories of languages the speaker can speak at a time. Prior and passing theories for both interpreter and speaker are theories about the speaker's language (specifically about the language he intends to use in speaking to the interpreter). The difference is that for the interpreter they characterize his dispositions to interpret the speaker (these theories may not work for his own dispositions to speak to the speaker), while for the speaker they characterize his dispositions to speak, conditionally for the prior, and actually for the passing, theory. (Davidson suggests we think of these theories as cast in the form of truth theories for the speaker. However, nothing hinges on his way of thinking of the form of such theories.)

Let us recast the issue about whether there is any such thing as a language in terms of the distinction between prior and passing theories. The thesis that Davidson argues against is that successful communication requires both an interpreter's and a speaker's prior theories (at least the portions relevant to the communicative exchange) to capture correctly the conventional meanings of the speaker's words, and to coincide with their passing theories. This identifies first meaning with conventional meaning. His objection, then, is that successful interpretation depends solely upon an interpreter's and speaker's passing theories coinciding. The prior and passing theories of the interpreter can differ with respect to one another, as can those of the speaker; and the prior theories of interpreter and speaker need not be identical, even when they succeed in communication, because they can converge on a passing theory. Prior and passing theory may both diverge from a correct theory of the meanings of words according to public norms. Passing theories are often modifications of prior theories in light of inferences about what the speaker really means in the context (or for the speaker about how the interpreter is understanding and will understand him), and prior theories for particular speakers may themselves diverge from public norms, that is, they may not treat the speaker as speaking in perfect conformity with those norms.

How is knowledge of conventional meaning in fact related to prior and passing theories? We typically suppose members of our linguistic community will speak for the most part in accordance with public norms, as we do, though we recognize there will be deviations from public norms (of course, we may also deviate unknowingly from public norms, as most of us recognize, though we are not in a position to do anything about it). We might be said to have dispositions characterizable using a generalized prior theory, which can be thought of as generalizing over members of the linguistic community. The dispositions this theory characterizes or models are conditioned by what we believe words in our linguistic community to mean according to public norms. This theory would aim to capture what would usually be thought of as our competence in the public language, the language of our community.

This answers a question Davidson asks in "A Nice Derangement of Epitaphs" (444) when he despairs of identifying prior and passing theories for particular speakers with linguistic competence: "Is there any theory that would do better?" Yes, the theory that characterizes our dispositions to interpret someone as, so far as we can tell, an ideal speaker of the public language. This theory characterizes our competence in the public language. To the extent that it corresponds to the public norms, we can be said to be competent in the public language. This is obviously not what Davidson calls a framework theory, "a basic framework of categories and rules, a sense of the way English (or any) grammar may be constructed, plus a skeleton list of interpreted words for fitting into the basic framework" (Davidson 1986, 444).

When we encounter a speaker (or interpreter) for whom we have no clues to idiosyncratic usage, we are apt to treat him by default as in perfect accord with public norms. The prior theory for us will then be the instantiation of the generalized theory to the individual. As we learn more about the speaker's or interpreter's idiosyncrasies (or flights of fancy), our dispositions to interpret or speak will be modified. This shows up in the prior and passing theories as their characterizing the speaker's language as distinct from the language determined by public norms.

How are these facts, then, related to repudiating languages? Clearly, nothing in any of these considerations would lead us to deny a speaker is speaking a language when interpreted. In fact, the account *presupposes* it, for otherwise prior and passing theories would lack a subject matter. One can speak a language, though, without speaking a language. A language is a language that meets certain additional conditions, chief among which is that it play a certain role in communication, namely, (i) that it be learned prior to communicative exchanges, (ii) that it be all one need know for successful interpretation, (iii) that knowing it be necessary for successful communication, and (iv) that it be identical with what one learns in learning which public norms attach to words (in the relevant linguistic community), namely, that it be the public language. Given (i)–(iv), to deny that knowledge of public norms for the use of words is sufficient for successful communication is to deny there are languages.

It is a bit odd, however, to cast the thesis in this form, and that may be why commentators have been misled about its import. It is doubtful anyone ever thought all of (i)–(iv) were necessary for something's being a language. The position that the public language *plays* the relevant roles is one we can *imagine* someone holding. But then the more natural way to put the contrary thesis would be to say that knowledge of the public language is not sufficient or necessary for successful communication. This way of framing the thesis renders it more plausible if less exciting.

We have characterized the thesis under attack as that speakers communicate successfully by bringing to bear identical (or overlapping) competencies in speaking and interpreting public languages. Davidson often puts the thesis in a more general form, as the claim that speakers and interpreters bring to a communicative exchange an identical competence which is necessary and sufficient for communicative success. "The problem we have been grappling with depends on the assumption that communication by speech requires that speaker and interpreter have learned or somehow acquired a common method or theory of interpretation—as being able to operate on the basis of shared conventions, rules or regularities" (Davidson 1986, 446). This would be so only if shared prior theories, however derived, were both necessary and sufficient for communication. If the argument we have surveyed here is correct, then this view is mistaken, and the denial of the more general thesis, which would have been seen as founded, in any case, on the more specific, is established as well.

Does any of this undermine the idea that many actual speakers share a language in a fairly robust sense that accounts for the ease with which they communicate with one another? Presumably not. The thesis being attacked requires prior and passing theories be both shared and exactly alike. It is doubtful anyone ever wanted to claim anything so strong. So, the denial of this claim leaves plenty of room for thinking that the prior and passing theories for many interpreters and speakers in a linguistic community share a lot in common, certainly enough to make sense of the idea that they share a language. We can think of this simply as the shared subset of the axioms that characterize their prior or passing theories: given any overlap, they share a language. Of course, this will never be the whole of what is thought to be the public language: but none of us is a master of that, and no one could ever seriously have thought otherwise.[6]

(2) We now turn to the second thesis Davidson defends, namely, that prior knowledge of conventional meanings is unnecessary for successful communication. Since the thesis Davidson attacks claims that prior knowledge of conventional meaning is both necessary and sufficient, his attack on its sufficiency alone is enough to refute it. However, it is clear that he thinks knowledge of conventional meanings is unnecessary as well, and this looks in any case to be the more substantive thesis. We distinguished a strong and weak version of the claim. The strong version is that, given our cognitive abilities, we can interpret someone without prior knowledge of any conventional meanings attached to his words. The weak version is that it is in principle possible to interpret another without prior knowledge of conventional meanings.

The thesis that knowledge of conventional meanings is unnecessary for communication is clear in "Communication and Convention": "Knowledge of the conventions of language is . . . a practical crutch to interpretation, a crutch we cannot in practice afford to do without—but a crutch which, under optimum conditions for communication, we can in the end throw away, and could in theory have done without from the start" (1984, 279). It is not entirely clear whether Davidson thinks that without expanding our cognitive powers we could in fact interpret others without relying upon shared knowledge of prior conventions or established regularities, interpreting deviancies in light of the standard practice. What we could do in theory may require suspending certain of our current limitations. We take first, then, the question whether shared knowledge of prior conventions is in principle necessary for interpretive success.

In asking this question, it is important *not* to require speaker and interpreter to use the same conventional meaning bearers in speaking. All that is required is that they share prior knowledge of the conventional meanings of the words each uses, whether the same or not, with the same conventional meanings or not. One party to a conversation might speak Mandarin and the other French and yet understand each other perfectly well.[7]

The question whether it is in principle possible to interpret another without an appeal to prior knowledge of conventions can be put usefully this way: Is there knowledge an interpreter can in principle access, leaving aside natural limitations of knowledge and perspicacity, which would enable him to interpret correctly a speaker at a time of whom he had no prior knowledge? Setting aside natural limitations of knowledge and cognitive abilities, this is equivalent to asking whether there are facts independent of linguistic conventions that determine (or could determine) what a speaker means by his words. If Davidson's basic methodological stance on matters of meaning is correct, the answer is clearly affirmative.

A speaker's dispositions to use words, as he is disposed to in his environment, fix their meanings. More cautiously, if the speaker does not intend his words' meanings to be determined by conventions in his linguistic community, then what his words mean is determined by his dispositions to use them. If we grant an interpreter knowledge of a speaker's dispositions to use words in his environment, then the interpreter knows everything he must in order to interpret correctly the speaker's words. Indeed, if knowledge of a speaker's dispositions plus knowledge that he is of the same psychological type as oneself is sufficient for correctly determining what his words mean, it is in principle possible to interpret another speaker without relying on prior knowledge of any conventions or regularities for the use of words. Two gods could speak to each other, each relying on knowledge that the other knew all of his dispositions without any need to appeal to knowledge of how either had used or understood his words in the past.

It is much more difficult to decide whether *we* could succeed without the crutch of conventions and established regularities. *We* clearly cannot know what someone's dispositions to use words are without either having observed him over a period of time or locating him within a linguistic community whose regularities in word use we have antecedently learned. Even with his complete physical description and a correct theory of physics, the computational problem would be intractable. There is no prospect for us of knowing what someone means by his words at a time with no grounds whatsoever to think that prior to the communicative interchange he uses them one way rather than another. The role that participation in a speech community plays in actual communicative practice is to provide us with grounds for thinking a speaker is disposed to use words in a certain way. It is, perhaps, imaginable that two speakers could interact, and by mutual consent converge, on a changing passing theory which deviates further and further from public norms, and perhaps in some systematic way that does not leave any words with stable meanings. But even this, clearly something not within our powers, would rest on prior knowledge of public conventions.

It might be objected that in fact field linguists do break into alien languages all the time. Of course, this is correct. But they do so by figuring out which regularities there are in the use of words by their subjects, which is a matter of coming to see by which conventions their words are governed in their linguistic community. Knowledge of conventions for word use seems, for us at least, to be essential for communicative success, even if it is unnecessary that we always interpret words in accordance with public conventions.[8] We suspect, and will suggest below, that one locus of the disagreement between Davidson and Dummett comes down to the question of the importance of our epistemic limitations and consequent reliance on prior learned conventions to our understanding of the nature of *our* communicative abilities.

So far, we have been concerned with whether knowledge of public conventions for word use, or prior knowledge of conventions, even if adhered to only by individuals involved in a particular communicative exchange, is either necessary or sufficient for communicative success. In practice, it is insufficient; in principle, it is unnecessary. But it might be maintained that nonetheless in a sense conventions are necessary for communication. This depends on how we understand what it is to participate in a convention, or understand words in accordance with one. In "Communication and Convention," Davidson argues conventions are unnecessary for communication. His conclusion rests on both of the kinds of considerations we have so far reviewed and also on a certain conception of what a convention is that derives from work by David Lewis.[9]

For Lewis, the most important component in a characterization of *convention* is the notion of a regularity. In particular, he says:

> a regularity R in the behavior of members of a population P when they are agents in a recurrent situation S is a *convention* if and only if it is true that, and it is common knowledge in P that, in almost any instance of S among members of P,
>
> (1) almost everyone conforms to R;
> (2) almost everyone expects almost everyone else to conform to R;
> (3) almost everyone has approximately the same preferences regarding all possible combinations of actions;
> (4) almost everyone prefers that any one more conform to R, on condition that almost everyone conform to R;

> (5) almost everyone would prefer that any one more conform to R', on
> condition that almost everyone conform to R',
>
> where R' is some possible regularity in the behavior of members of P in S, such
> that almost no one in almost any instance of S among members of P conforms
> both to R' and to R. (Lewis 1969, 78)

If we take Lewis to mean here, as is natural, an *actual* regularity in
behavior, then his account requires there to be instances, presumably many,
of the behavior constitutive of the convention in order for there to be a
convention of the kind in question. If this is a necessary feature of
convention, then conventions are neither sufficient nor in principle
necessary for communicative success however important a role they play
in actual communicative success.

An actual regularity, however, is not a necessary feature of a convention. We can establish conventions that have not yet been followed, for
instance, when explicitly establishing conventions for governing forms of
behavior we already engage in. When a group of nations agree upon
conventions to govern the treatment of prisoners of war, or noncombatants
in war zones, these conventions are in effect from the time of the agreement
whether there is any immediate scope for their application. If we agree to
the conventions, and dispose ourselves to follow them, then they, in effect,
exist, even before anyone's behavior is governed by them. Indeed, we could
have conventions for governing behavior in situations which *never* arise, for
example, governing contact with an extraterrestrial intelligence.[10]

What, then, is necessary for conventions? For present purposes, we
would like to slightly modify Lewis's characterization to apply to conventions that hold in a community, though no particular behavior has yet been
governed by them. This characterization does not require explicit agreement: During a time interval t, a *convention* obtains in a population P to
behave in accordance with a rule R in a situation type S if and only if it is
true that, and it is common knowledge in P that, in almost any instance of
S among members of P,

(1) almost everyone conforms to R;[11]
(2) almost everyone expects almost everyone else to conform to R;
(3) almost everyone has approximately the same preferences regarding
   all possible combinations of actions;
(4) almost everyone prefers that any one more conform to R, on
   condition that almost everyone conform to R;
(5) almost everyone would prefer that any one more conform to R', on
   condition that almost everyone conform to R'

where R' is some possible rule governing the behavior of members of P in
S, such that almost no one in almost any instance of S among members of
P would conform both to R' and to R.

This modified characterization differs from Lewis's by being about the conditions under which a convention obtains to behave in accordance with a rule, rather than being a condition on when a regularity is a convention. We might say the relation between them is that a regularity in behavior in a community is a convention when it arises because of a convention to behave in accordance with a rule. This provides a plausible characterization of when a convention obtains in a community which does not require past regularity of behavior.[12] It does not require future regularity of behavior either, since the situation the rule governs may never occur, and also because it does not require members of the community to adhere to the convention in the future for it to qualify as a convention now.

If convention is understood in this sense, it is crucial to couch Davidson's point in terms of prior knowledge of established conventions. For the speaker and the hearer in a communicative exchange understand the speaker to be intending to use words in accordance with certain rules: these rules will meet the conditions for there being conventions to behave in accordance with them. Only the speaker and interpreter are required. The conventions which govern their communication need not be stable. But since the speaker and interpreter need to converge on a passing theory for successful communication, they must converge on a common set of rules governing the speaker's use of words, that is, on shared conventions. In this sense, conventions are necessary for communicative success, at least insofar as it is linguistic communication.[13]

Does this undermine any of Davidson's conclusions? So far as we can see, no serious damage is done. Some re-expression of his conclusion is required if what we have said about convention is correct. But when we say conventions are required for communication, given what we mean by that, we do not say anything which conflicts with anything Davidson maintains. And in fact in our discussion, looking ahead, we worded things in a way that avoids the difficulty.

This characterization of convention, which countenances them in the absence of antecedent regularities in a community, or on a speaker's and interpreter's part, helps render more palatable a claim Davidson makes at the end of "Communication and Convention," namely, "philosophers who make convention a necessary element in language have the matter backwards. The truth is rather that language is a condition for having conventions" (1984, 280). If we are right, there is a sense in which we can have our cake and eat it too. Convention is essential to language. But *prior* shared conventions are not. We cannot, however, quite stretch this to sanction the claim that language is a condition for having conventions, though it is clear why Davidson should think this so, since he is committed to language being necessary for thought, and clearly thought is necessary for conventions (Davidson 1984).

Suppose we are mistaken about what is expressed by "convention" in English, and that, as Lewis thinks, nothing is a convention unless it is a regularity. Would this be significant? We do not think so. This would mean that there is a historical component to the common notion of convention. It would not show that a central part of this historical notion is neither necessary nor sufficient for linguistic communication. Though people who think language is necessarily conventional have probably not carefully distinguished between the historical and ahistorical conceptions of convention, it seems most likely they have thought that language must be conventional roughly because (in the relevant community) its vocabulary is governed (in a certain sense) by arbitrary rules which everyone expects, and wants, everyone else to obey.[14] Clearly, we miss something important if we flatly deny communication must rely on conventions because we believe convention has an historical component that requires that the rules have been followed in the past. Here what is needed is a further distinction marking the difference between the historical and ahistorical conceptions. The observation that language is not necessarily conventional because the historical requirement may not be met in possible communicative situations appears, then, to be less damaging to traditional views about the relation of convention to linguistic communication.

With this discussion in the background, we turn now to a closer look at Dummett's response to Davidson's argument(s) and position.

4. DUMMETT'S REACTION

Dummett has criticized Davidson's thesis that "there is no such thing as a language, not if a language is anything like what many philosophers and linguists have supposed." If our take on Davidson's argument and its import is right, then Dummett's critical reaction has in part been based on a mistake about what Davidson was arguing for. Before discussing the two rounds of exchange between them (to repeat, the first constituted by Davidson 1986 and Dummett 1986, and the second by Davidson 1994 and Dummett 1994), we want to consider and then distinguish the view we just sketched from a view Davidson attributes to Dummett according to which conventions govern speech acts.

The doctrine Davidson attacks is expressed by Dummett as follows: "there is a general convention whereby the utterance of a sentence, except in special contexts, is understood as being carried out with the intention of uttering a true sentence" (Dummett 1981, 298). Davidson objects that no such convention can attach to the utterance of declarative sentences, because no convention can guarantee someone has intentions requisite for assertion. This issue is not the same as whether shared (prior) knowledge of conventions is required for communication, for that could be true even if his attack against Dummett's doctrine here is completely successful.

On the doctrine itself we make a brief digression. We agree with Davidson that there is no convention attaching to declarative sentences that makes it the case that someone who utters one, except in certain circumstances, has thereby made an assertion. It is not so clear to us that some utterance acts do not count as performances of certain sorts of speech acts in certain circumstances even if the speaker does not intend them to. For example, saying "I do" absent mindedly at an appropriate point in a wedding ceremony would not be grounds for denying after the ceremony that one had contracted in marriage to someone else. But in any case, in most circumstances we could beg off having asserted something by saying that we were just rehearsing, or pretending, or practicing elocution, or the like. It may be that in some cases, when we are well aware that by uttering a certain sentence we give our audience license to think we intend to assert something, we will be treated as if we had asserted it. For in such cases, if we utter it anyway, and give no warning that we do not intend to assert something, it is quite likely we will be held responsible for any untoward consequences just as if we had asserted it. However, in this case, we might wish to distinguish between having asserted it and having undertaken an obligation to have asserted it, so that for purposes of praise or blame we are treated as if we had asserted it, though we did not. Let us say an official at the United Nations charged with emergency response for flood victims is asked by a subordinate where the rain has been falling. Well aware of the question and effect of what he is about to utter, he continues disdainfully practicing his elocution: "The rain in Spain falls mainly in the plain." Arguably this is not an assertion, but he will be held responsible as if he had asserted it because he has in the circumstances licensed his interlocutor to take it as one.

In any case, it is not clear that Dummett ever wanted to maintain the strong thesis that Davidson is attacking. His words are certainly compatible with a significantly weaker thesis, namely, that there is a convention that one use declarative sentences standardly to make assertions, just as there is a convention in the United States to drive on the right on a two-lane road. Such a convention does not guarantee that when one utters a declarative sentence, one makes an assertion, any more, unfortunately, than the convention to drive on the right guarantees one will. But if one does not, and it is what is recognized as a standard context, it follows that one is not following the convention.[15] We need not take a stand about whether there are such conventions. But whether there are or not, it is clear there is nothing conceptually problematic about it.

These sorts of conventions govern forms of activity which can occur without conventions governing them. Constitutive conventions bring into existence kinds of behavior that would not exist otherwise. Conventions governing games are like this. There would not be any moves in chess without the conventions that define chess. It may be that Davidson is mainly concerned to deny that whatever conventions there are governing the use of declaratives to make assertions are constitutive conventions. This implies that it is possible to make assertions without following those conventions, which indeed seems possible.

Let us now return to the main debate. We will concentrate on the more recent exchange between Dummett and Davidson, since it gets past obvious misunderstandings in their first exchange (for example, whether Davidson intended to be attributing to interpreters and speakers knowledge of the content of prior and passing theories, and, to some extent, about whether he meant to deny we learn and use public languages in communication—he did not). In "The Social Aspect of Language," Davidson characterizes the issue between himself and Dummett as about whether the idiolect or language (in the sense of public language) is conceptually primary. In more detail, he locates the disagreement between them as follows:

> What bothers Michael is . . . my failure to appreciate that the concept of a speaker meaning something by what he says depends on the notion of a shared language and not the other way around. My mistake, in his eyes, is that I take defining a language as the philosophically unimportant task of grouping idiolects, whereas he thinks I have no non-circular way of characterising idiolects. (Davidson 1994, 3)

To adopt the view that the idiolect is primary is not to deny language is social. But it is to raise a question about what constitutes its essential social element.

The connection between Davidson's thesis that prior shared knowledge of public conventions for the use of words is neither necessary nor sufficient for communication and the thesis that the idiolect, not the public language, is conceptually primary, is that if prior knowledge of the (or a) public language is not necessary or sufficient for communication, then our core understanding of linguistic communication is independent of our conception of a prior shared public language. We understand what linguistic communication is even in the absence of an enduring public language; consequently, our conception of it derives from our conception of something prior to it, namely, overlap of idiolect: Stable overlap of idiolect, then, summons the idea of an enduring public language.

Davidson imagines three critical responses. The first is that taking the idiolect as basic fails to account for our holding ourselves to a public norm in speaking. The second is that in practice we cannot get along without prior knowledge of a public language. The third is that without the public language we have no answer to Wittgenstein's question about what makes the way we go on the right way.

To the first, Davidson protests that there is no obligation to speak as others do, and that the reason we hold ourselves to a public norm is adequately explained by its utility. There could arise a responsibility to speak to others in conformity to public norms, where an antecedent responsibility to cooperate in certain enterprises is in place, and where speaking the same as others is important for success: but this is a derived, and not an original, obligation and it is not *to* public norms but to those to whom one is speaking. Davidson takes Dummett to be his target here. Dummett, however, declines the role, and rather adopts a view similar to the one we have been sketching (Dummett 1994, 266), claiming that Davidson has misinterpreted him.

To the second response, Davidson says that it is irrelevant to the theoretical issue. In a sense, this seems right, though we will ask below whether there is still not an important issue here that is being overlooked. Davidson's response to the third is not as clear. Consider this passage:

> My proposal takes off from this observation: what matters, the point of language or speech or whatever you want to call it, is communication, getting across to someone else what you have in mind by means of words that they interpret (understand) as you want them to. . . . The intention to be taken to mean what one wants to be taken to mean is, it seems to me, so clearly the only aim that is common to all verbal behavior that it is hard for me to see how anyone can deny it. . . . If it is true, it is important, for it provides a purpose which any speaker must have in speaking, and thus constitutes a norm against which speakers and others can measure success of verbal behavior. (Davidson 1994, 11)

His suggestion appears to be that the norm that determines correct or incorrect interpretation is provided by a speaker's intentions in using words, though he adds that this does not imply a speaker's words mean whatever he wants or intends them to mean. It does not, because for his words to mean what he intends, it must be possible to succeed in communicating with a reasonable interpreter when he uses them in accordance with his intentions. In this sense, communication is the source of meaning, though intending is essential to meaning, and provides its normative element.

There is one more point Davidson advances, which may be connected with the last, though it is unclear to us whether this is so, namely, an answer to Wittgenstein's question about what makes it the case that we go on in the same way as we have before. Wittgenstein intended this question to be equivalent to the question what makes it the case that we follow one rule rather than another. This looks as if it should be essentially the same question as the one we have just addressed, since to mean something by one's words is to have used them in accordance with a rule. The question of whether we are going on in the same way is just the question whether we are following the same rule. Intending to mean the same thing by the same word, then, should supply the answer. But Davidson goes on to give a different answer.

So far as we can tell, his answer is that one goes on in the same way provided one is a member of a social group minimally consisting of two people who have correlated each other's reactions to some common stimuli with the stimuli. One goes on in the same way if one does not frustrate the other's natural inductions about one's behavior. This is supposed to be the minimal social element in answering the question what it is to go on as before.

It is unclear to us how this answer is connected with identifying intentions as providing the guide to whether one has interpreted another correctly. The proposal does not in fact seem sufficient to account for someone's going on the same as before, at least if this means responding in the same way to the same stimuli. If two people make the same mistake about a stimulus, e.g., and have the same reaction, which they have come to expect in the light of what they mistook the stimulus for, on Davidson's proposal they would have gone on in the same way. But in a clear sense they did not: they reacted differently from usual, assuming they usually get it right. But neither detected the error.

In any case, this would not be sufficient for following a rule. Suppose something consistently amuses both A and B, and they notice this about each other, and enter into the relevant natural deductions. This has so far nothing to do with following a rule or speaking a language. So, whatever question Davidson's answer addresses does not seem to be the question Wittgenstein was posing.

We suspect there is no informative answer to the question what is it to go on as before in the sense of following the same rule. To suppose that there is is to suppose rule following can be reduced to something else. But there is no reason to think that this is so. Thus, Davidson's first answer, that it is in virtue of our intending to go on as before, is likely to be as informative an answer as is possible.

Dummett, in his reply to Davidson, concedes, straight off, "Davidson is quite right that sharing [a language in the sense he has characterized] is neither necessary nor sufficient for communication, and he is right for the right reasons" (Dummett 1994, 257). Dummett disclaims ever having held the view criticized. However, he denies this is central in the debate about whether the common public language or idiolect is conceptually primary.

That knowing a common language, in the usual sense, is neither necessary nor sufficient for communication, Dummett says, does not show it is unimportant for our philosophical understanding of linguistic communication.

However, Dummett does not make clear what he takes the question about the primacy of the common language over the idiolect to be. He clearly does not think the primacy of the common language requires that knowledge of it be both necessary and sufficient for communication. It is not sufficient, because we can succeed in communication even though we do not know the same things about the public or common language. It is not necessary for the same reason: mistaken about the common language, a speaker may still be successfully understood. In what sense, then, could one maintain that a common language is central to an investigation of linguistic communication?

One suggestion might be that although shared knowledge of a common language is neither necessary nor sufficient, without *some* prior shared knowledge of conventions for the use of words, linguistic communication would be impossible. If our discussion in section 3 is correct, however, not even this constraint is required in principle.

Dummett, however, takes the issue to hinge apparently on whether two speakers could communicate using different vocabularies (Dummett 1994, 263). He says, granting its possibility, it would still be the case that the two speakers shared a language, for though each speaks using different words, each presumably could speak using the other's words given that he can interpret the other.[16]

But true or not, this is not the issue. The real issue is whether speaker and interpreter must have prior knowledge of shared conventions. For this, it would suffice, as we noted, that they learn a prior language one speaks and the other interprets, though neither speaks the other's language.

Because of this misunderstanding, it is unclear whether Dummett disagrees with Davidson over the central issue. The reason is that Dummett does not raise the question whether *prior* shared knowledge of rules governing meaning bearers is essential to communication rather than simple shared knowledge at the time of communication of rules governing meaning bearers. Furthermore, the question (at least as Davidson understands it) is not whether such prior knowledge is in fact required, but whether it is in principle required.

It may well be that Dummett's insistence on the importance of a public language is really an insistence on the importance of there being shared mastery of a common set of rules governing meaning bearers for linguistic communication to take place. If this is so, then it does not conflict with any doctrine Davidson has advanced—if we are right. For, this would be merely to hold that on the ahistorical conception of convention, shared mastery of conventions is necessary for communication. Moreover, even if Dummett holds that for actual speakers, prior knowledge of a public language (not necessarily complete overlap) by participants is necessary for communicative success, this would not yet constitute a conflict, since it is doubtful Davidson would deny this. Thus, in the end, it remains, as Dummett says, "obscure . . . how far apart Davidson and I really are on the strictly philosophical issues" (Dummett 1994, 265).

If there is a remaining disagreement, it may attach not to the question whether prior knowledge of shared conventions is necessary for any communication in principle, nor to the question whether we must use conventions as a crutch given our epistemic position, but rather to the question whether discounting it in a philosophical account of specifically human communication, or, more broadly, communication among linguistic beings of our epistemic type, leads to a serious distortion of our understanding of our own nature as linguistic agents. By linguistic beings of our epistemic type we have in mind linguistic beings whose cognitive abilities do not enable them access to dispositions of others without induction on past behavior and whose computational abilities are not equal to figuring out rapid shifts in systematic and wholesale use of words. For such beings, knowledge of prior shared convention is necessary. God may dispense with prior knowledge of shared conventions. We cannot. We have no reason to think that Dummett and Davidson do not agree that some prior knowledge of linguistic conventions is essential for communication for linguistic beings of our epistemic type. However, because it is not in principle necessary, Davidson would hold that it is not essential for understanding the nature of communication among even such limited epistemic agents, and that there is no sense in which the public language is conceptually prior to the idiolect.

It may be on precisely this point that Dummett disagrees with Davidson. Communicating like the gods is not an option for us. *We* must master a public language in order to communicate at all. A philosophical understanding of *our* communicative practices and communicative successes may well then have to locate a central place for mastery of a public language, on pain of distorting our understanding of what makes communication possible *for us*. If so, then we should not, in fact, have given up "the attempt to illuminate how we communicate by appeal to conventions" (Davidson 1986, 446).

An analogy may be appropriate. Philosophical understanding of the epistemic position of an omniscient being, a being with direct knowledge of everything (assuming it is possible), has no need for an account of how such a being could come to know things about its environment on the basis of sensory experience. So, one might say, an account of how sensory experience plays a role in our knowledge of our surroundings should not be thought of as pertaining to the essence of knowledge. It is for us merely a crutch, in principle dispensable. Suppose all of this is true. Nonetheless, we would not have an adequate philosophical understanding of *our* epistemic position if we did not pay attention to the central role sensory experience plays *for us* in gaining knowledge of the world. Similarly, we would not have an adequate philosophical understanding of *our* communicative abilities if we did not pay attention to the central role that mastery of public languages plays *for us* in enabling us to communicate with one another successfully.

This lays the ground for a version of the thesis that the public language is conceptually prior to the idiolect. It is not an option for us to think of knowledge of idiolects as coming first, and the public language as being constructed out of their overlap. For us the public language, even if it is an abstraction from the overlapping practices of different speakers, comes first, and we must think of the various idiolects of public languages as deviations from them. That is, when we approach others as interpreters of their speech, we must accept that it will depend upon establishing shared conventions for interpretation of public signs, and that interpretation will then proceed by accepting default interpretations based on the picture we have built up of our shared conventions, deviation from which must be justified. Even in the case of another speaker who does not share our public language, and whom we do not have the opportunity to see in his linguistic community, our interpretation of him will be conceived of as the project of discovering or developing a public language, in the sense of settled conventions for the use of words which are taken as giving the default interpretation in communicative exchanges. Communication for us, then, goes essentially through knowledge of a public language. Idiolects are thought of by us as deviations from shared conventions. In precisely this sense we can say that the public language is conceptually prior to the idiolect for us.

We are not sure to what extent Davidson would have disagreed with this picture if it had been presented to him, for it is not in conflict with the denial that conventions are in principle necessary—abstracting away from our epistemic type. We suspect that Dummett may well have something of the sort sketched in mind in arguing that the public language is conceptually prior to the idiolect. If there remains a dispute, though, we would urge that both sides have got hold of an important truth. Linguistic communication *in principle* does not presuppose prior shared knowledge of conventions, and in that sense the public language is not prior to the idiolect. But linguistic communication for linguistic beings of our epistemic type does require prior shared knowledge of conventions, and in that sense the public language is conceptually prior to the idiolect.

5. CONCLUSION

Our purpose has been to sort out the issues in the debate between Dummett and Davidson on the role of conventions in linguistic communication and the importance of public language in our understanding speech. On its face, Davidson's astonishing claim that "there is no such thing as a language, not if a language is anything like what many philosophers and linguists have supposed" looks to be plainly set against the view that conventions are central, and flatly to deny that there are public languages. Against this Dummett has argued that the public language in fact is conceptually prior to the idiolect and pointed out that Davidson's position looks to be incompatible with much of his own program in semantics. We have argued that appearances are misleading here, and that Dummett and Davidson are closer on matters of substance than might have been thought. Davidson does not deny that there are languages in a perfectly intelligible sense. He rather denies that prior knowledge of shared conventions is necessary or sufficient for communication *in principle*. This falls out of his taking the stance of the radical interpreter as methodologically basic in understanding meaning. For the radical interpreter can focus attention on an individual in isolation from his linguistic community. The radical interpreter wishes to gain access to the individual's dispositions to use words. So it is the individual's dispositions which determine, on this view, his meanings. Thus it will appear that participation in conventional practices is not essential for being a speaker or for communication, however important it is in practice. But this is not to deny, in the sense of convention as rule following we introduced, that speaker and interpreter share conventions, for this is what it is to share passing theories, and this Davidson sees as essential to linguistic communication.

The dispute between Dummett and Davidson, in light of these clarifications, seems to some degree to be a matter of mutual misunderstandings. It is unclear that they differ on whether conventions in the sense we have articulated are required for linguistic communication, or even on whether prior knowledge of shared conventions can be dispensed with in principle. On the matter of the priority of the public language to the idiolect, we suggested a way of understanding that thesis, as applied to epistemically limited agents, which looks to capture an important truth about the role of public languages for us in communication. For us, the idiolect is conceived as a deviation from a set of shared conventions, rather than the shared conventions being conceived as an abstraction from independent idiolects. This is still compatible, however, with the claim that in principle, for beings of a different epistemic type, a public language is not necessary for linguistic communication, and so in that more abstract sense is not conceptually prior to the idiolect. There then seems room both for the traditional emphasis on the importance of understanding the role of conventions in linguistic communication which Dummett defends, and for Davidson's claim that there is a sense in which the public language is not fundamental to an understanding of linguistic communication as such.

ERNIE LEPORE   AND   KIRK LUDWIG
CENTER FOR COGNITIVE SCIENCE   PHILOSOPHY DEPARTMENT
RUTGERS UNIVERSITY   UNIVERSITY OF FLORIDA
JULY 2004   JULY 2004

NOTES

1. Dummett is not alone. Ian Hacking observed, "'True-in-L' is at the heart of Davidson's philosophy. What is left, if there is no such thing as an L?" (Hacking 1986, 447). Dorit Bar-On and Mark Risjord wrote: "Unless Davidson's radical claim is a departure from his developed views, the Davidsonian program appears to have undermined itself" (Bar-On and Risjord 1992, 163). They go on to say that the thesis "in an important sense . . . robs the [Davidsonian] program of subject-matter and empirical content" (164), and they point out that Davidson does not in fact abandon the use of the notion of a language after "A Nice Derangement of Epitaphs" (187).

2. Davidson's paper "Convention and Communication" (Davidson 1984), though its primary focus is not the same as "A Nice Derangement of Epitaphs," already, if more briefly and with milder rhetoric, announces its main theme, and advances essentially the same reasons for it. We will focus however on the latter, since it will position us to state more precisely what Davidson's target is, and also to see what motivated the picture he aimed to oppose when he wrote that there is "no such thing as a language" (446), in a sense which undermines what many philosophers and linguists have wanted to maintain.

3. Dummett's papers "Language and Communication" (Dummett 1989) and "Meaning, Knowledge and Understanding" (Dummett 1991) are also of some relevance for this debate, but we will focus on his two papers mentioned in the main text above.

4. "I take for granted, however, that nothing should be allowed to obliterate or even blur the distinction between speaker's meaning and literal meaning. In order to preserve the distinction we must, I shall argue, modify certain commonly accepted views about what it is to 'know a language', or about what a natural language is. In particular, we must pry apart what is literal in language from what is conventional or established" (Davidson 1986, 434).

5. This might be challenged on the grounds of a general rejection in

epistemology of the need to justify what might be called default assumptions. That is, it might be maintained that when it comes to our beliefs about what others in our community mean by their words and actions, they are justified by default: unless circumstances depart in some way that we should notice from the norm, the beliefs we automatically have are justified without appeal to anything. They must be actively justified only when circumstances depart in certain specific ways from the norm. Perhaps this would motivate a rejection of (b). But to pursue this issue in epistemology would take us too far afield, and is not likely to shed much additional light on the issues of direct concern to us here.

6. It is doubtful Davidson would want to quarrel with any of this. In Davidson 1994 (3), he says, "I am happy to say speakers share a language if and only if they tend to use the same words to mean the same thing, and once this idea is properly tidied up it is only a short uninteresting step to defining the predicate 'is a language' in a way that corresponds, as nearly as may be, with ordinary usage."

7. Within some linguistic communities, there are systematic differences in the vocabulary used by subgroups. In Japanese, men and women are supposed to use systematically different forms for certain grammatical particles and pronouns. It is easy to imagine extending this social arrangement so that two groups in the same linguistic community used entirely nonoverlapping vocabularies.

8. Suppose you encounter someone in a context where there is no reason to think he is a member of your speech community and he utters words that sound like English. Suppose you interpret them as English with success. Is this an instance of interpreting someone correctly without prior knowledge of shared conventions? The question is whether you know that you have interpreted him correctly without acquiring knowledge of which conventions he intends his words to be governed by. Guessing correctly is not knowledge, though you may quickly become assured you have guessed correctly by his reaction to what you say and do in response to his utterances. In this case, it looks as if speaker and hearer do adhere to like conventions, and a trial at communicating on this assumption quickly confirms it. But knowledge of correct interpretation succeeds the trial rather than precedes it. But see the discussion below in the text on convention.

9. Davidson does not quote Lewis's final version of his analysis of convention, but a preliminary, although in a relevant respect they are identical, i.e., in treating a convention as a regularity.

10. Although Lewis's characterization is strictly about the conditions under which *a regularity* in behavior in a community is a convention, and not of what *a convention* is, it is clear that he thinks only regularities are conventions. He says as much flatly at one point, e.g., "A convention is a regularity in behavior" (Lewis 1969, 51), and it is presupposed in much of his discussion.

11. This does not require everyone actually to engage in behavior in accordance with R in situations of type S, but only that they are disposed to do so, since S may not occur. For our purposes, all that is important in calling R a rule is that it is a statement of a pattern of behavior in situation type S; one conforms to the rule if one's behavior in the situation type exemplifies the pattern.

12. We are not concerned with whether this is exactly right. What is important for our point is just that it is close enough that any refinement will yield the same results for our interests, namely, that convergence on a passing theory amounts to mutual agreement on conventions.

13. It might be thought that the requirement that everyone conforms to the rules will require speaker and hearer to speak in the same way. But the formulation is not so restrictive, since the rule can be that everyone interpret the speaker in accordance with a certain set of rules, including the speaker.

14. Consider a remark by Alston, which probably represents the attitude of many philosophers: "What really demarcates symbols is the fact that they have what meaning they have by virtue of the fact that for each there are rules in force, in some community, that govern their use. . . . Henceforth, we shall feel free to use the term 'conventional' purged of misleading associations, as shorthand for 'on the basis of rules'" (Alston 1964, 57–58).

15. See Lewis's remarks on conventions of truthfulness (Lewis 1969, 148f).

16. Is this clearly true? It is easy to imagine someone who has the capacity to understand a language spoken to him, but who cannot speak it; otherwise, those who are dumb but not deaf could not master a language to the extent of understanding others when they were spoken to, a manifest falsehood. Certainly, to survive these sorts of cases, the claim would have to be carefully qualified.

REFERENCES

Alston, W. 1964. *Philosophy of Language.* Englewood Cliffs, NJ: Prentice-Hall.

Bar-On, D., and M. Risjord. 1992. "Is There Such a Thing as a Language?" *Canadian Journal of Philosophy* 22: 163–90.

Davidson, Donald. 1984. "Communication and Convention." *Synthese* 59: 3–18. Reprinted in *Inquiries into Truth and Interpretation*, D. Davidson, 265–80. New York: Clarendon Press, 1984.

———. 1986. "A Nice Derangement of Epitaphs." In *Truth and Interpretation: Perspectives on the Philosophy of Donald Davidson*, ed. E. Lepore, 433–46. Cambridge: Blackwell.

———. 1994. "The Social Aspect of Language." In *The Philosophy of Michael Dummett*, ed. B. McGuinness and G. Oliveri, 1–16. Dordrecht: Kluwer.

Dummett, Michael. 1981. *Frege: Philosophy of Language*, 2nd ed. Cambridge, MA: Harvard Univ. Press.

———. 1986. "'A Nice Derangement of Epitaphs': Some Comments on Davidson and Hacking." In *Truth and Interpretation: Perspectives on the Philosophy of Donald Davidson*, ed. E. Lepore, 459–76. Cambridge: Blackwell.

———. 1989. "Language and Communication." In *Reflections on Chomsky*, ed. A. George. Oxford: Oxford Univ. Press. Reprinted in *The Seas of Language*, M. Dummett, 166–87. Oxford: Oxford Univ. Press, 1993.

————. 1991. "Meaning, Knowledge and Understanding." In *The Logical Basis of Metaphysics*, M. Dummett, 83–106. London: Duckworth.

————. 1994. "Reply to Davidson." In *The Philosophy of Michael Dummett*. B. McGuinness and G. Oliveri, 257–67. Dordrecht: Kluwer.

Hacking, Ian. 1986. "The Parody of Conversation." In *Truth and Interpretation: Perspectives on the Philosophy of Donald Davidson*. ed. E. Lepore, 447–58. Cambridge: Blackwell.

Lewis, David. 1969. *Convention*. Cambridge: Boston, MA.: Harvard Univ. Press.

Pietroski, Paul M. 1994. "A Defense of Derangement." *Canadian Journal of Philosophy* 24: 95–117.

REPLY TO ERNIE LEPORE
AND KIRK LUDWIG

I bitterly regret the loss of the late Donald Davidson; he was a very good friend, and also, though we disagreed about much, the person to whom I found it easiest to talk to about philosophy; we always understood both what the other said and what he was driving at. Donald came to the conclusion that "there is no such thing as a language, not if a language is anything like what many philosophers and linguists have supposed." It is not a good idea to make an aggressively paradoxical assertion, and immediately to temper it with an ungraspably imprecise qualification: we cannot tell just what has been asserted. This was not at all a common practice on Donald's part; why did he resort to it on this occasion? Did he have a precise thought, and, if so, why did he choose not to formulate it precisely? Or was it only a fuzzy thought, which he could not succeed in capturing in words?

Suppose my wife and I were on a bus, and we overheard some people talking together. I ask her, "What language is that?" and she replies, "I don't know: it sounds like some Slav language." Peter Geach, who unexpectedly turns out to be sitting behind us, tells us, "They are speaking Polish." Now were our common assumptions that "Polish" is the name of a language, that there are several Slav languages, that when people are talking together, there must be some particular language or dialect which they are speaking (or possibly some mixture of languages), based on the conception of languages held by "many philosophers and linguists" and spurious according to Davidson? Or were we all employing some concept of a language that was legitimate in Davidson's eyes, and hence distinguishable from the one held by all these philosophers and linguists? If so, how should it be distinguished? We cannot answer these questions from Davidson's manifesto. To answer them, we need, as Lepore and Ludwig have done, to scrutinise the reasons Davidson had for declaring that there is no such thing as a language.

Lepore and Ludwig (henceforward L&L) address themselves, for the bulk of their essay, to Davidson's paper "A Nice Derangement of Epitaphs." In this part of their essay they are principally concerned with exegesis of Davidson's paper, and say hardly anything about my reply to it in the same volume. They open their discussion by distinguishing three types of meaning: first meaning; dictionary or conventional meaning; and speaker's meaning. Dictionary meanings are those which words conventionally have in the language; it was to the dictionary meaning that Alice was appealing when she told Humpty-Dumpty, "But 'glory' does not *mean* 'a nice knock-down argument'." First meaning is what a speaker intends his hearers in the first instance to understand him as conveying; L&L somewhat confusingly also call it "literal meaning." First meaning diverges from dictionary meaning in cases of malapropism and other misuses of words under a misapprehension of their dictionary meanings. It also diverges when someone speaks ironically: he means his hearers to understand him as saying the opposite of what his words conventionally mean. Speaker's meaning is what a speaker intends the hearers to understand *through* their understanding of the first meaning of what he says. It is exemplified by metaphor.

We should all of course recognise that conventional meaning is fluid: words come to have conventional meanings different from those they formerly possessed. One way in which this happens is through a widespread misapprehension of the conventional meaning of a word, such as the use of the verb "to meld" as a portmanteau of "weld" and "merge," rather than as meaning "to announce a scoring combination of cards in a card game." There is an intermediate stage at which it is indeterminate whether the new use is a widespread mistake or an example of a newly acquired conventional meaning. But this fact does not call in question the legitimacy of the notion of conventional meaning.

I confess myself somewhat confused by L&L's classification, in which they are seeking to follow Davidson. Irony and metaphor are two of what we were told at school to recognise as "figures of speech"—uses of language to convey something other than what the words conventionally mean. I do not see why they should be treated differently. There seem to me to be only two types of meaning, which we may call "first" and "second." The first type can be subdivided into three subtypes, thus:

(a) the conventional meaning of the speaker's words;

(b) the conventional meaning of the words the speaker intended to use;

(c) the conventional meaning of the words he would have used if he had known the language better.

We need to invoke (b) when the speaker has made a slip of the tongue; we need to invoke (c) in cases of malapropism and other misuses of language.

Second meaning is what the speaker intends his hearers to understand.

I see no merit in appealing to a distinction between the first and second instances. Whenever a figure of speech is used, the speaker is playing on the first meaning, and intends his hearers both to grasp that first meaning and to grasp what he intends to convey, which differs from the first meaning, but is to be apprehended through it. There seems to me no sense in which one who speaks ironically intends his hearers to understand him in the first instance as doing so, but one who speaks in metaphor intends them to grasp the metaphorical character of his words only in the second instance. A metaphor may itself exploit, not a conventional meaning, but a figure. An example is given by Isaiah Berlin's *The Hedgehog and the Fox*. People are classified as hedgehogs and foxes not by allusion to the actual characteristics of those animals, but to a fanciful description of them, as knowing many things or just one big one; this must itself be termed figurative. If this description had not been cited at the outset, no one would have had any idea what Berlin meant—what his second meaning was.

L&L's notion of first meaning seems to me an unhappy amalgam of conventional and what I should call second meaning. Their motive for distinguishing between first and conventional meaning is apparent from the following passage from the end of their first section: "The reason it is important to distinguish first meaning from conventional meaning is that the former is essential to all communication, and, indeed, to all linguistic uses of language. If we misidentify the two, we will be led to suppose conventional meaning is also essential to all linguistic communication." The argument fails. Of course, to understand what someone is saying, the hearer must apprehend not only the first meaning of his utterance—subtype (c) when things have gone wrong with it—and its second meaning, where this differs from the first. But our grasp of these depends upon our knowledge of conventional meaning, as L&L's examples show. To advance from an interpretation of a speaker in accordance with type 1(a) to one in accordance with type 1(b) or 1(c), one must know the conventional meanings of the words he actually uttered, judge that he was unlikely to have intended to be understood in accordance with them, and, from a knowledge of the conventional meanings of other words, guess what he ought to have said to convey his meaning.

A knowledge of conventional meaning *is* therefore essential to communication. The discussion to this point has proceeded on the assumption that speaker and hearer are aiming to communicate in the same language. It may happen that the hearer knows, or, while listening to him, comes to suspect that the speaker is using a dialect different from his own. In such a case the hearer must guess, from various clues, at the conventional meanings in the speaker's dialect of some of the words he uses; among such clues are a knowledge of systematic consonantal and vowel differences between his dialect and the speaker's, and a knowledge of other languages, as when an Englishman correctly interprets a Scotsman's uses of "kirk" and "ken." Something similar happens when the hearer has an imperfect knowledge of the speaker's language. But these details in no way impugn the importance of conventional meaning for communication.

It may seem that I commit the primordial sin against Davidson's conception of understanding another speaker, as L&L interpret him: I identify first meaning with conventional or dictionary meaning. I certainly think that what a speaker *says* is determined by the conventional meanings of his words in the language he is intending to speak: it is what his words mean. But understanding him is a matter of apprehending what he is intending to convey; and here I allow that he may misspeak, either by uttering different words from those he meant to utter, or by using words wrongly, taking them to have conventional meanings different from those they in fact have. I have also allowed that quite often we may correctly guess what he intended to convey—what he should have said; though it should not be forgotten that sometimes we guess wrongly, or can make no guess at all—something of which L&L make no mention. I insisted that such estimates of what a speaker intended, when he obviously did not mean what he actually said, depend upon a knowledge of the conventional meanings both of the speaker's words and of other words. Is this enough to excuse my emphasis upon conventional meaning, or do I remain a primordial heretic against Davidsonian orthodoxy?

The exegesis of Davidson's declaration that there is no such thing as a language proposed by L&L is that in it the word "language" is to be understood as embodying a requirement that a knowledge of the conventional meanings of a speaker's words in the language he is speaking is both sufficient and necessary for understanding his utterances. This seems a surprisingly mild interpretation of a bold and paradoxical statement; but certainly it leaves the conversation on the bus which I imagined unimpugned. L&L observe that both theses, of the sufficiency and of the necessity of a knowledge of conventional meanings, admit of weaker and stronger denials. Such knowledge certainly suffices for knowing what the speaker said—what his words meant; but the two theses relate to the hearer's apprehending what the speaker intended to convey. The weak denial of the sufficiency thesis is that a knowledge of conventional meanings is sometimes insufficient for apprehending this. In view of the occurrence of slips of the tongue and mistakes about the conventional meanings of words this weak denial is incontrovertibly true, and it has never occurred to me to controvert this. The strong denial of the thesis states that a knowledge of conventional meanings is *never* sufficient, on the ground that to know what the speaker intended to convey, one must know that he has made no slip of the tongue and is under no illusion about what any of his words mean in the language. I accept the epistemological thesis mentioned by L&L in their note 5, that, for someone to know something, it is unnecessary that he have specific reason for making default assumptions unless he has specific reason for doubting them. But in any case understanding what someone is meaning to say does not require knowledge in any heavy sense: it is merely a matter of catching hold of what he was aiming to convey, which is surely all that is necessary for him to have succeeded in communicating. So the strong denial of the sufficiency thesis is certainly false, despite L&L's efforts to confer on it a partial endorsement.

I am not discussing these issues in terms of Davidson's apparatus of prior and passing theories: I do not find it helpful. I acknowledge that the speaker's prior theory does not need to be understood as a theory about a theory. Davidson's *mise en scène* resembles an audience at a lecture (or a congregation listening to a sermon) more than a conversation: there is always only *one* speaker (and one hearer or interpreter). In an actual conversation, one participant may ask the other what he means, and be given an explanation. The same can happen in a lecture, but not during a sermon.

The denial of the necessity thesis raises deeper problems than that of the sufficiency thesis. L&L provide it, too, with a weaker and a stronger version. The weak version they take to be that it is in principle possible, for a being with greater cognitive powers than ours, to understand another such being without knowing the conventional meanings of the words of the language he is using (supposing him to be using a language whose words have conventional meanings). I doubt whether Donald Davidson was much interested in beings with superior cognitive powers, and am sceptical that he was concerned to advance any theses about them. L&L's strong denial of the thesis is that it is in practice possible for us to understand another without knowing the conventional meanings of the words of the language he is using.

L&L argue in favour of their weak version. What a speaker means by his words, they say, "is determined by his dispositions to use them." So, if superhuman beings—L&L call them "gods"—can discern one another's dispositions to use their words in particular ways, they can each tell what another means without adverting to, or even knowing, the conventional meanings of his words in his language.

This is a very bizarre fantasy. By knowing the disposition of another being B to use a particular word in a certain manner in certain contexts, one of these beings A can, according to L&L, know what B means by it. How does A know B's disposition? Can he look into B's mind and read off from it all his dispositions to use the words he employs? In that case A will know all the meanings B attaches to all the words in his vocabulary. To understand B's utterances, A must also know by the same means the syntax of B's language, since in different languages words are put together in very different ways to form sentences with determinate meanings. A is therefore able to grasp all the thoughts B can express in his language. Well, if A can read all this from B's mind, why is it necessary for B actually to utter any words? Could A not read B's mind and tell from it what B was intending to convey? If A can read dispositions, and hence meanings, can he not also read actual thoughts?

There are several reasons. For B to have any dispositions to use his words in particular ways, and hence to mean anything by them, he must actually use them. Moreover, we must suppose that A *cannot* read all B's thoughts, only those he expresses in words; B needs to be able to conceal some of the thoughts he has, and even to dissemble by asserting what he does not believe to be true.

Now all this is nonsense. The only way in which it is possible—in principle, not just in practice—to discover people's dispositions to act or speak in certain ways is by observing their actions or verbal utterances and noting the relevant regularities. This is what we ourselves commonly do in getting to know another person's behavioural dispositions, though few of us pick up another's language by this means alone. The foregoing interpretation of the manner in which L&L's "gods" came to understand one another was prompted by their characterisation as having cognitive abilities surpassing our own; but, to discover anyone else's dispositions, these are not needed and would be of no help. L&L make explicit that they are appealing to supposedly superior cognitive powers when they say of their "gods" that one could know all the other's "dispositions without any need to appeal to knowledge of how" the other "had used or understood his words in the past." There can be no such magical knowledge of another person's dispositions. So the fantasy may perhaps be taken as illustrating the stronger denial of the necessity thesis, namely as a manner in which we might understand one another without appeal to conventional meanings. We may therefore imagine the scene as taking place just after the punishment for building Babel was imposed on us. Here is a collection of human beings each of whom speaks a language, but no two of whom speak the same language. This is undoubtedly very inconvenient for them; but according to Davidson (as interpreted by L&L, I think correctly) it does not prevent them from understanding one another's speech. We need attribute to them no powers that we, their degenerate descendants, lack; but we may suppose them able to go about things a good deal faster than we can. Let us call these people "Babelonians."

One of these Babelonians will come to understand the speech of another by observing his utterances and accompanying behaviour for long enough to establish what he means by his words and the syntax of his language. Of course, we need not suppose that he does this solely by passive observation; he will surely engage in a good deal of interaction with the other. In so doing, he will be putting himself in the position of learning his language by the direct method. Probably in the process he will teach the other a considerable part of his own language.

But have we not supposed that each Babelonian speaks a private language? Initially each addresses the others in his own language, specific to him, at first to their mutual incomprehension. But as they study each other's verbal behaviour, they become multilingual in as many languages as they have friends and frequent acquaintances; and so, for each language, a little circle is formed of people who all know that language. At the very earliest stage, when the curse first takes effect on them, they each speak a private language in the sense of one that no one else knows. But it is not essentially private in Wittgenstein's sense of being a language that only the speaker *can* understand. Nevertheless, as long as they *are* private, these *de facto* private languages have the fundamental defects of an essentially private language. They cannot be used incorrectly, because there is no criterion for their correct use; there is no distinction between its seeming to the speaker right to apply a particular word and its being right to do so. Since it is integral to something's being a genuine language that there be an objective distinction between what it is right and what it is wrong to say, they are not genuine languages as long as they remain private. But since they are inessentially private, they may be called potential languages; they become genuine languages as soon as they are spoken by many people, indeed by more than one. At that stage, there comes about an agreement, for the most part tacit, about how the language should be used, how sentences should be constructed and in what circumstances they should be accepted as true. To come to know the language will require a grasp of these conventions, and, as with all languages, it will be on the basis of such conventions that utterances in that language will normally be understood.

L&L arrive at the same conclusion more briefly: they mistakenly accept the weaker version of the denial of the necessity thesis—that it is in principle possible that intelligent beings might understand one another's speech without any knowledge of the linguistic conventions the other was following; but they repudiate the stronger version, that *we* are capable of doing this. They do this on the ground that we cannot know another's dispositions without observing his behaviour, including his linguistic behaviour, which they wrongly take to be a human limitation. Having amended David Lewis's characterisation of a convention so that a convention may be in force although the situation that calls for its implementation has never yet arisen, they conclude that "conventions are necessary for

... linguistic communication" if it is to be successful. This is because, even if the speaker uses some words idiosyncratically, the hearer (interpreter) must apprehend the rules or conventions governing the speaker's use of those words if he is to grasp what the speaker is aiming to convey. This conclusion contradicts Davidson's statement, which they quote, that "philosophers who make convention a necessary element in language have the matter backwards." I am one of those philosophers, but I have the matter the right way round. To grasp what someone means to convey when he misuses some word is like guessing what he said when you did not hear a word. You go on what he has said before and what he goes on to say; your knowledge of the common language is essential. Sometimes you guess wrongly, sometimes you cannot guess at all. But if a speaker misused almost all the words he uttered, you could not understand him at all.

I conclude that the contention that it is unnecessary in principle, and perhaps even in practice, to know the conventions governing the language or dialect of the speaker and determining the meanings of its words, in order to understand what he seeks to convey, is completely false. It belongs in the realm of fantasy.

Donald Davidson's picture of human communication by means of language seems to have resembled my vision of the Babelonians. Were it not that I know that he travelled far more widely than I, I should have thought that someone could have such a picture only if he had never spoken to anyone who did not speak some dialect of his own mother tongue; I remember Donald telling me of the difficulty he had had in understanding Scottish speech when he had made a visit to Scotland seeking his roots. In this matter I feel far away from his thought; much less so from that of L&L.

In their final section L&L turn to discuss my views on the topic; this is something of a new beginning to their essay, and my comments will be a new beginning of this reply. There will be some overlap, but I hope no inconsistency. They first spend some pages on a remark of mine in *Frege: Philosophy of Language* concerning a linguistic convention governing what Frege called the force of a whole sentence uttered rather than the meanings of individual words, namely: "there is a general convention whereby the utterance of a sentence, except in special contexts, is understood as being carried out with the intention of uttering a true sentence." I should explain that in making this remark, my concern was with the concept of truth rather than with the linguistic indications of the making of an assertion. In Davidson's early writings, when he put forward his thesis that a theory of truth could serve as a theory of meaning, the notion of truth was taken as given. Obviously no one could derive from such a theory the meanings of the words and sentences of the language unless he brought to it a prior understanding of the concept of truth. I thought, and continue to think, that, in order plausibly to present a Davidsonian truth theory as a theory of meaning, what it was required to know about truth in order to derive the meanings of those words and sentences must be stated explicitly as part of the whole theory of meaning. Now one thing must certainly be known: the connection between truth and assertion. If that was not known, the word "true," as used in the truth theory, might just as well mean "false." The notion of truth indeed takes its origin from the practice of making assertions. It is essential to that practice that we distinguish between correct and incorrect assertions; the primordial concept of truth is that of a sentence that could be used to make a correct assertion. I used a crude way of characterising assertions, but adequate to indicate the conceptual connection between the notion of truth and the practice of assertion.

Thus I was not particularly interested in an exact characterisation of the way we signify, and the way we recognise, that an assertion is being made. I was not far off the mark, nevertheless. We have in English a mark of the interrogative, namely an inversion of the order of the main verb and its subject (in the absence of any other syntactic reason for the inversion). Most languages have some (often very different) interrogative mark, although some, such as Italian, freely allow questions to be asked in speech without using it. But English lacks an assertoric mark; declarative sentences have the same form when standing alone to make an assertion and when forming a co-ordinate or subordinate clause. (I do not know of any natural language that has an assertoric mark, but I am not a comparative linguist.) By the proviso "except in special contexts," I meant to exclude cases of the kind L&L list; quotation and mimicry are others. But I think of the matter more simply than do L&L. Their analogy with driving on the right is misplaced: I do not signify anything by driving on one or other side of the road. I think that when someone utters a declarative sentence, addressing some hearer or group of hearers, and there is not any evident special context, then he is asserting whatever that sentence says, unless he has indicated a special context by his immediately preceding remark or indicates one by his immediately following remark. This applies even if he had no intention of making that assertion. I do not see that there is any room for a notion of licensing one's hearer to take what one says as an assertion, distinct from that of making an assertion. In this sense I think that the convention we observe concerning the utterance of a declarative sentence on its own is a constitutive convention: unless there was some way of recognising that someone was making an assertion, there would not be such a thing as assertion. It might be argued that the assertoric use of sentences is the primal employment of language: we therefore need only indications of when someone is using language in some other way. I will not contest this: it remains a convention that, except when otherwise indicated, our utterances aim at truth. That is part of what is taken as given when the concept of truth is taken as given.

L&L now turn to an examination of Davidson's paper in *The Philosophy of Michael Dummett* (1994) and my reply to it; in this section professedly about my views, they devote at least as much space to Davidson's remarks as to mine. They open by crediting Davidson with characterising the dispute between us as being over whether the primary notion, in the order of philosophical explanation, is that of a shared common language or an idiolect. I had raised just this question, without express reference to Davidson, in my *Origins of Analytical Philosophy* (first published in English in *Lingua e Stile* in 1988, in book form in German in the same year, and in book form in English in 1994).

After summarising Donald Davidson's essay L&L turn to my response. They begin by quoting my acknowledgement that Davidson was right that sharing an ability to operate in accordance with a set of syntactic and semantic rules is neither necessary nor sufficient for communication, and right for the right reasons. They do not note that I gave a deeper reason for its insufficiency than the malapropisms and slips of the tongue we have considered so far. Observing that human discourse is not to be explained on a stimulus/response model like the responses of a computer (and increasingly nowadays of a telephone), but was the interaction of rational agents, I said that understanding the utterances of another involves not only apprehending *what* he says but assessing *why* he said it, and that the latter is not, or very little, governed by convention. Was his last remark supposed to be relevant to what had been being discussed, or was he changing the subject? Was it meant as an illustration or example of what he had said before? Or was it supposed to follow from it? Was it to be taken literally, or was it meant ironically? Was it meant as a joke? A hearer must be able to answer these and other questions before he can be said to have understood what the speaker was driving at, what was the *point* of his having said what he did. For the most part, the answers he would give will be based on the ordinary means we use for judging another's intentions in his actions, not on any special conventions governing the use of language.

In conceding that a knowledge of conventional meanings is not necessary for communication, I gave a trivial reason, that a wrong use of a word may still be understood by the hearer, who correctly guesses what the speaker intended to convey (or misunderstands the word in the same way). I failed to grasp the radical nature of Davidson's contention, well brought out by L&L. I came somewhat closer in my speculations, based on the distinction between a passive and an active knowledge of a language, about people who converse, each speaking his own very different language. But this does not get to the heart of the matter.

What would? Perhaps this. Children are brought up speaking quite distinct languages. Davidson says that there could not be anything *like* a language without more than one person; thus far he is in agreement with what has always been my view. So let us suppose the children are brought up in pairs, one language to each pair; up to a certain age they meet no child save the other member of the pair. The adults they meet all address them in their special language; those adults have invented that language and taught it to those children. So we have a large number of tiny linguistic communities. Since each community has two members, there are right and wrong uses of words, true and false statements. Perhaps correct use sometimes has to be negotiated; but it must be established, otherwise communication will be in danger. At the given age, the children are allowed to meet other children. They try to talk to them, but the responses are all in other languages. Nevertheless, if prior knowledge of the other's language is not necessary for communication, they will be able to communicate.

How can they do this? Well, for every two conversants, not members of the same original pair, at least one must teach the other his language, or a fragment of it. This may be difficult, but we know that it is possible. So what is the problem?

There is no problem. Does this not prove that, to communicate, one does not need any *prior* knowledge of the language in which the other is speaking? No, because communication does not begin until the hearer has learned the speaker's language, something which requires instruction, not just listening to his speech. Of course, the hearer does not need to learn the *whole* of the speaker's language, only so much as to understand what he chooses then to say; he does not need all at once to learn as much as he will need during the conversation, only enough to understand the next remark. Most of us know what it is to have a partial knowledge of a language. It remains that the hearer must acquire a knowledge of the meanings of the speaker's words *before* he can understand what he says. Nothing can alter the fact that you can understand what someone says only if you have acquired a sufficient knowledge of his language; according to what he says, this may be a very exiguous knowledge of it.

Davidson would not have denied this; he would have seen it as agreement with him. He required, for successful interpretation, a reasonably adequate passing theory held by the interpreter. Talk of its not being necessary to have a prior knowledge of the speaker's language gives the impression that the formation of such a passing theory by one who comes to the conversation knowing nothing of that language is a process essentially like that of the formation of a passing theory by adjusting for the speaker's idiosyncratic use of certain words or syntactic forms in a language shared by speaker and hearer. It is in fact quite different—different in essence; teaching a language is a process quite unlike conducting a conversation.

So, it is agreed that the interpreter must know the language that the speaker is using. But must he know the common language he is using (or misusing)—French, Arabic, or whatever—or does he not rather need to know the speaker's idiolect? The inadequacy of the idiolect for this role is that it is nothing like a language, since there is by definition no more than one person who speaks it. What is an idiolect? An individual has as many idiolects as there are languages he can at least partially understand or speak; as before, each bifurcates into an active and a passive idiolect. The idiolect is determined by the fragment of the given language which that individual knows, and incorporates all his misunderstandings of words as well as his correct understanding of them. It is also determined by any dialect which the individual understands or aims to speak, any slang expressions and any words which he believes, even wrongly, to be part of the language or dialect. It is impossible to explain the notion of an idiolect save by reference to a common language. Certainly it cannot be explained as a language, a private language known to only one individual. There is no such thing.

Davidson in his essay devotes some space to attacking my supposed claim of an obligation to speak one's language correctly. I did not speak of an "obligation." I said that a speaker must hold himself responsible to the accepted meanings of the words he uses. The exclusive concentration of both Davidson and L&L upon the hearer's efforts to discern what the speaker is intending to convey diverts attention from the question what he actually *says*. What the speaker *says* is determined by the meanings of his words in the common language he is using, and by the syntactic construc-tions proper to it; what he says is what his words mean in the common language. A speaker must hold himself responsible to this; if what he says is not what he intends to convey (his first meaning), and this is brought to his attention, he is bound to correct himself. If he refuses to do so, but nevertheless does not deny that he said what he did, that is, that his words meant that in the language, it can only be concluded that he did intend to convey just what he said.

L&L correctly report Donald Davidson's three imagined objections to his view: that he does not recognise that a speaker holds himself responsible to the conventions of the common language; that it is pointless to consider communication between speakers who do not share a language, since this, though theoretically possible, never occurs in practice; and that no answer has been given to Wittgenstein's question what distinguishes using words correctly and merely thinking that one is doing so. Enough has already been said about the first two points. Concerning the third, Davidson says that what is needed is a norm, a standard by which a speaker can judge that he has gone wrong. He wishes, of course, to avoid locating this in the judgement of other speakers of the common language; he locates it in a hearer's understanding the speaker as he intended to be understood. (He here remarks that "it is understanding that gives life to meaning, not the other way around"; having always insisted that a theory of meaning must be a theory of understanding, I can only applaud this.) L&L appear to me to misinterpret Davidson here, saying that his "suggestion appears to be that the norm that determines correct or incorrect interpretation is provided by a speaker's intentions in using words." The norm Davidson is seeking is not one that governs the hearer's interpreting the speaker correctly, but the speaker's using words correctly. His intention will not serve the purpose, since the question will arise whether he has succeeded in carrying out his intention. (L&L allow that a speaker's words will not always mean whatever he intends them to mean, because, for them to do so, it must be possible for him "to succeed in communicating . . . when he uses them in accordance with his intentions." The relevant intention, however, was that the hearer should interpret him in a certain way, not that he himself should use the words in a certain way.) Davidson's proposal would have some odd consequences; it would turn out that, most of the time, both Mrs. Malaprop and Dr. Spooner spoke correctly. In any case, what is the criterion for the hearer's having understood the speaker as he meant? He might find a way of paraphrasing what the speaker said; if the speaker agreed that that is what he meant, then the hearer understood him aright. But now there is the question whether the speaker understood the hearer's paraphrase as the hearer intended; clearly such questions can continue indefinitely. I do not think that the norm can be found outside the shared practice of using the common language.

L&L drive towards an eirenic conclusion that the difference between Davidson and me was due to our talking past each other. Davidson, they think, was concerned with what is in principle possible for beings with greater cognitive powers than our own, I with what is possible for us with our restricted powers. I think the difference greater than this; and I do not believe that Donald Davidson was much interested in science-fiction fantasies of superior beings. As always, readers have to decide.

M. D.

6

Peter Simons

WHAT NUMBERS REALLY ARE

INTRODUCTION: FREGE AND THE PHILOSOPHY OF ARITHMETIC

No one puzzling about arithmetic can avoid Frege. If only Frege's logicism had worked, there would now probably be little dissent about the nature and status of numbers and arithmetic truths. It was not to be, and we are still living with the consequences. Frege's philosophy of arithmetic has been analyzed by Michael Dummett in a series of writings which are indispensable for all who try to understand how and why Frege's heroic attempt to show arithmetic to be extended logic came unstuck. If there is dissent about the reasons for Frege's failure and more dissent about the correct philosophy of arithmetic, it is not for want of efforts on Dummett's part. Like many others I learned from *Frege: Philosophy of Language* how crucial Frege's context principle was to his approach to defining the numbers and grounding arithmetic. I have lost count of how often I have worked through chapter 14, "Abstract Objects," of that book. I later retraced the oft-followed story of *Die Grundlagen der Arithmetik* with new insight, having worked through it with *Frege: Philosophy of Mathematics* in hand. Dummett's intimate appreciation, exposition, and analysis of Frege have irreversibly cemented the latter's position as the greatest of all philosophers of mathematics, as well as the unwitting architect of modern analytical philosophy. It is scarcely possible now to imagine a time when Frege was regarded as an unfruitful outsider, an oddball, a *"Sonderling,"* as Husserl cruelly but accurately described him to Scholz in 1936. No matter how much one agrees or disagrees with Frege, he can no longer be ignored, and that is one of Michael Dummett's undeniable achievements, for which all philosophers of mathematics may be grateful.

The sections of *Grundlagen* which remain the greatest challenge and at the same time the crux of Frege's logicism are §§62–69,[1] in which Frege outlines his own view as to how numbers can be given to us cognitively, despite being neither physical nor mental. Dummett has analyzed these sections on numerous occasions and has shown how subtly crafted Frege's arguments are. Yet it is not Dummett's fault that this crucial transition remains enigmatic and disputed. Frege is drawn first to attempt to show how statements of number can be understood if we see how numbers figure in identities. If we can understand and in principle assign truth-values to identity statements, then we can fairly say we know all there is to be known about numbers as objects. We may find out some facts later than others, but in this regard numbers will be just like flowers and stars, and no more mysterious. The crucial transition comes when Frege explains that a statement of equinumerosity, that there are as many *a*s as there are *b*s, has the same content as a statement of numerical identity, that the number of *a*s is the same as the number of *b*s. In view of Frege's later distinction of content into the two factors of sense and reference, one may wonder whether the sameness of content is closer to sameness of sense or sameness of reference. Sameness of reference, that is, for clauses, truth-value, is a very weak condition, so sameness of sense appears much closer to Frege's intentions. Let us assume it is so. Then in

EQU   The number of *a*s = the number of *b*s ↔ there are as many *a*s as there are *b*s

the equivalence here signified by '↔' would have to be sameness of sense, propositional equality, or synonymy.[2] There are difficulties with all these interpretations but that is not my concern. Rather I am concerned that for Frege the transition from one side of EQU to the other is direct and immediate. Frege talks metaphorically of cutting up (*zerspalten*) the content of the right-hand side in a different way, and so gaining a new concept, that of the number of …, to be understood in the context of the whole proposition.[3] What happens next is well known. Having raised the question how an identity can be understood when only one side has the given form "the number of *x*s," Frege notes that the truth-value of an identity statement about numbers in which at least one side does not have the particular form is not determined by EQU. Thus the equivalence does not pronounce on whether a certain number is or is not identical with Julius Caesar or any other object not given in that way—the "Caesar Problem." From this problem Frege sees no way out and proceeds instead—with more than a tinge of regret, one suspects—to an explicit definition of "the number of *x*s" as "the extension of the concept *equinumerous with the xs*," a definition which led to extensions, *Grundgesetz* V, and ruin. The decision, turning on what seemed such a minor point, takes on the proportions of a Greek tragedy.

Having introduced his explicit definition schema for numbers, Frege goes on to show that there are infinitely many of them, by a procedure I call "Frege's Bootstrap." Taking 0 to be the number belonging to the necessarily empty concept *not identical with itself*, he then has one object, viz., 0, and the concept "identical to 0" yields a different number, 1, and so on. This ensuing part of *Grundlagen* has an economical genius that continues to inspire wonder. The kernel of the Bootstrap is the ability to take concepts and return objects as the numbers they determine, in such a way that no empirical assumptions are made, thus safeguarding the logicist claim.

In the light of the inconsistency of Frege's conception of extensions of concepts, many subsequent theories of number have attempted to rescue what can be rescued of Frege's ideas without lapsing into contradiction. Of those attempts, I shall mention three which take numbers seriously as entities in our ontology: the quantifier view, the set view, and the neo-logicist view.

The quantifier view goes back to Frege's claim, set out in advance of the *Grundlagen*'s crucial transition, that an applied statement of number is an assertion about a concept. There are twelve months in the year. Parsing this as Frege indicated, this asserts of the concept *month of the year* that it has the property that twelve things fall under it. That this account does not presuppose we already have the numbers and so become circular is a main thrust of the context principle, which it becomes unnecessary to stress when Frege makes such moves not in German but in his symbolic system, where the order of introduction of defined symbols is under his full control.

The quantifier view is preserved in Whitehead and Russell's *Principia Mathematica*, though it is there placed in the complex setting of the ramified theory of types. In the context of a simple type theory it becomes the view that numbers are second-order properties, properties of properties (or of propositional functions). The two problems with this view are well known. The first is that because of the restrictions of type theory there has to be not one sequence of numbers but one for every type above the second. The second and more serious problem is that to guarantee that there be infinitely many numbers Whitehead and Russell are forced to adopt an uncertain empirical assumption, the Axiom of Infinity, that there are infinitely many individuals. This means that arithmetic no longer rests for its truth on logical principles alone and so logicism is not maintained. Despite this, the quantifier view has been maintained as a species of logicism by David Bostock.[4]

The set view is the most commonly held one among mathematicians and philosophers of mathematics. It is that numbers are to be conventionally identified with certain sets in the context of an axiomatic set theory. Typically the sequence chosen is that suggested by von Neumann. The existence of an infinity of natural numbers is guaranteed by the much stronger existence assumptions of axiomatic set theory. One problem with this view, highlighted by Paul Benacerraf,[5] is that because of the conventionality attaching to the definition of the numbers, no sets can be definitively and unproblematically identified as *the* numbers. Most mathematicians are insouciant about this. They tend to be concerned about structure only, and not about the possibly spurious philosophical problem *which* objects the numbers are. They might indeed be right about this, though I do not think they are. They also by and large do not carry any torches for logicism, so the fact that the axioms of the various set theories are not logical does not worry them. Whether philosophers of mathematics should accede in mathematicians' insouciance is a much debated question. I shall not debate it here, but simply continue to worry.

The neo-logicist view, associated with Wright and Hale,[6] attempts to return to the simplicity of EQU and Frege's rejected direct transition from statements of equinumerosity to numerical identities, seeing Frege's problems as having begun with the introduction of extensions. The attractiveness of this view is that it preserves Frege's insights about the epistemological order in which we can come to cognize numbers. However, it faces a number of difficulties. One disadvantage is that it does not solve the Caesar Problem, and the neo-logicist view is that this is an unavoidable fact of life. Another disadvantage is that the use of related principles to set up objects for other parts of mathematics runs into more serious indeterminacy of reference. The complex numbers, as has been pointed out by Robert Brandom,[7] cannot be uniquely identified by an equivalence principle because complex conjugation is a nontrivial automorphism. There is thus no fact of the matter, of any object specified by an equivalence as a complex number, whether it is z or z^*, so to speak.

All the theories mentioned have their advocates and these advocates naturally defend their views against the standard objections, sometimes at great length and with great ingenuity of argument. I cannot here go into their various defenses because I am concerned to put another view, which is that all three views are wrong because they are mistaken about what numbers in fact are, so the ingenuity and arguments are beside the point.

NUMBERS AS PROPERTIES OF MULTITUDES

When we learn how to count as small children, we are instructed in the presence of small groups of objects, often but not invariably graphically presented all at once in an array. A child's counting book may contain pictures of three hens, five geese, twelve cars, and so on. More concretely, we are asked how many marbles are in a jar, or how many times the clock strikes, or how often the cat has miaowed. Careful instructors will vary the examples in as many ways as possible so that children grasp that things counted need not all be physically of one kind, and need not all be present together, for example, they may ask how many things a child has in her pencil case, or how many Kings and Queens of England there were between 1065 and 1486. Later we learn how to count or otherwise determine the number[8] of more abstract things, such as the months in a year, or the number of solutions of an equation. There is no reason to assume that this gradual induction into numbers and counting forces us to adhere to the extreme view of Mill, which Frege rightly criticizes,[9] that numbers are properties of physical aggregates. Nevertheless, that we are always counting several things—except in the cases of 0 when there are no objects and 1 where there is only one—and this strongly suggests that number, as an entity, is closely linked with these several things, and is in fact a certain kind of property of several things taken together. To have a word for such a collection I shall use the old term "multitude,"[10] stipulatively dissociating it from its usual connotations of large size or crowding together,[11] so it is possible to have a multitude of one.

My view is that numbers are certain nondistributive formal properties of multitudes. 'Nondistributive' means that just because the multitude has the property, it does not follow that its parts, or submultitudes, in particular its members, have it. Contrast the properties of being located in Europe, and of being owned by John. If a multitude of cities is (i.e., several cities are) in Europe, then so is each city; if John owns two thousand books, he owns each book singly. By contrast, if there are twelve apostles, then Peter, James, John, and so on are not each twelve apostles, nor are any group of four, for example. Each apostle is just one apostle, each group of four is four and not twelve, and so on. "Formal" means that the property is topic-neutral, not confined to any limited domain of discourse, but has application as long as we are in the business of counting, that is, as long as we are not dealing with mass terms or other nonsortal terms where the question "How many?" makes no sense. We have the properties of being one object, being two objects, and so on (the null case will be dealt with later). Of the apostles, or the months, we say, using the plural, that they *are* twelve, or that there are twelve *of them*. This form of speech is wholly natural and unforced, and is I think excellently suggestive.

Observe the difference between this account and the others mentioned above. When Frege says that a statement of number ascribes a property to a concept, this property cannot be the property of *being two*, *being three*, and so forth. For the concept *moon of Mars* is not itself two: it is one, a single concept. The property it has is not that of *being two* but of having two objects falling under it. Likewise a set with two members is not itself two things: it is one thing with two members, notwithstanding the name "pair" standardly used of it. The set {Whitehead, Russell} is a pair set in that its members, Whitehead and Russell, *are* a pair, but it is one thing just as much as each of them is. Finally, since any object denoted by a genuine singular term is not something of which a number other than *one* can be predicated, so whatever the status of the numerals and other numerical expressions used in arithmetic, if they stand for single objects which furthermore are not properties, they *a fortiori* do not stand for numbers taken as properties of multitudes. To take the numbers as abstract objects introduced by EQU is to take them as ones, and therefore if the term "number" is used of each of them it is used equivocally.

This conception of number is not new: it can be found in variant forms in Husserl's *Philosophie der Arithmetik* of 1891 and in Russell's *The Principles of Mathematics* of 1903, where Husserl and Russell call multitudes, respectively, "Vielheiten" and "classes as many." What is surprising is not that it is old, but that it is not more popular. I shall suggest a reason for this unpopularity later in the general neglect of plural terms.

Before proceeding to outline how the natural number properties may be defined, it is worth indicating how the properties-of-multitudes conception of numbers relates to the other three views. Take as an example the number three. This, I claim, is the formal property applying to any trio of things, no matter how diverse, just as Frege required. No restriction to physical or concrete collections is implied. Nor need the three things be gathered together, whether in space or time, as Mill imagined, or "in thought," as Brentano and Husserl imagined. Obviously we never arrive at a determination of a certain group as being three things unless we gather them in thought, but they do not become three by our thinking of them together. On the contrary, they are or were three independently of any particular act of thinking: all that is required for them to be three is that they be different from one another, and fail to include any other thing. As Jevons put it, in a passage quoted by Frege, "Any means of differentiation can be a source of multiplicity."[12] Frege's requirement that numbers presuppose concepts comes into the way in which a multitude is determined. A multitude is a plurality of individuals, each of which is an individual in virtue of falling under some sortal concept or other, of being a thing of some kind, a *tode ti*. There need not be a single general concept under which they all fall and nothing else does, except *per accidens*, but in specifying which multitude it is in any concrete case we are constrained to use general concepts, spatio-temporal restrictions, disjunctions, and any other means that we can lay our hands on, and a determinate answer to a "How many?" question can only be guaranteed when the basic concepts we need to use in such a case can be guaranteed to divide their reference neatly as Frege indeed required. Where vague concepts and/or vague boundaries are in play, a determinate answer to the "How many?" question will generally be lacking, as when I ask "How many gas molecules are there in this room now?," which has no determinate answer for a variety of reasons, albeit that a well-informed person could give a fair estimate with upper and lower bounds. Sometimes the concepts we invoke to throw a cognitive lasso around several things will be artificial or gerrymandered, but there are also naturally occurring unities from stars to subatomic particles whose unity and individuality we recognize *a posteriori* and which do not wait on us or our concept use to be individualized. For such things, the numerical properties apply independently, so that to the extent that such natural unities exist independently of mind and language and there are more than one of them, to that extent the numerical properties also exist independently of mind and language. Getting the strength of this realism just right is difficult, but I would personally sooner give up almost any philosophical proposition rather than be forced to deny the mind-independence of the plurality of things.

The connection with set theory is now obvious. Any set has a certain number of members. Not it, but *they*, collectively, have the relevant number-property. Finally, if numbers as abstract objects are introduced via an abstraction equivalence such as EQU, then they will be different entities from the number-properties, but obviously related in a similar way the properties are related to sets. Two multitudes determine the same abstract number object if and only if they are equinumerous, that is, if and only if they have the same number-property. We can thus see the sense in which each of these three (classical) theories taking numbers as entities shares aspects with the properties-of-multitudes theory.

DEFINING THE NUMBERS

We now show how to define the numerical properties, but in outline only, not in full formal detail. Standard logical languages in the twentieth and twenty-first centuries do not contain plural terms, terms for multitudes. This is in large part because of Frege's influence, and I shall return to it at the end. To introduce expressions for numbers as properties of multitudes we need predicates for the properties and nouns to denote multitudes, in the way that plural terms denote several things at once in a natural language. Rather than carry the inconveniences of the Indo-European singular/plural syntactic distinction with us into logic, let us have a run of terms which are not inflected for number even logically, and also allow terms to be empty, that is, fail to denote anything. For variables for such terms I shall use the lower-case Italic letters a, b, and c, and for predicates true or false of such terms I shall use upper-case Italic letters. In addition we shall need a two-place predicate saying that an individual specified by one term name is one of several specified by another, as Andrew is one of the apostles. I shall simply co-opt the English "is one of" for this purpose. Lest it be thought this is smuggling in the concept of "one" and therefore of number into the whole discussion, let me say that the concept of being one of can be defined in terms of existence, term conjunction, and term-binding quantification. In any case, we are using semi-English and it pays to be mindful of the context principle. With symbols the problem is pushed to the side. To make readings more idiomatic I shall often write "is a" instead of "is one of."

Let us have two constant terms, 'V' and 'Λ'. The former is, in any context in which a domain of discourse has been specified, the universal term, "object," standing equally for every individual in the domain. The latter is an *a priori* empty term, axiomatically specified as standing for nothing, or definable in terms of a contradictory condition such as being all non-self-identical things. We assume an extensional account of multitudes, that is, multitudes are the same when they have the same members. This is in fact how we use plural terms away from intensional contexts. The Beatles are the four most famous Scousers, and they are John, Paul, George, and Ringo. Whitehead and Russell are the authors of *Principia Mathematica*, and the inhabitants of Stockholm are the inhabitants of Sweden's capital city.

Let us have an existence predicate and its contradictory, nonexistence. "as exist" means that one or more as exist, while "as do not exist" means that no a exists, there is or are no a. Obviously it is a theorem that no Λ exists. I call this "Heidegger's Law." Its dual, that some object exists, is not a theorem, since it encapsulates the metaphysically nonneutral thesis that there is something rather than nothing. There is thus no empty multitude, and by extensionality we can say, with a pinch of salt, "all empty multitudes are the same": the unicorns are the centaurs, the wyverns, and the dragons, because there are none of any of them.

Let us avail ourselves of the usual truth-functional connectives and a pair of quantifiers "for all" and "for some," which will be allowed to bind term-variables and predicate variables and be subject to the usual principles. Such quantifiers cannot carry existential import when binding term-variables, because it is a theorem following Heidegger's Law that for some a, there are no a.

The following equivalences connect the binary predicate "is one of"/"is a" with existence, nonexistence, and other concepts. In all stated theses, free variables are understood to be invisibly bound with wide scope by universal quantifiers. All the stated theses may be understood as definitions of the new expressions on their left-hand sides in terms of "is a" together with logical constants.

a exist (there is at least one *a*) iff for some *b*, *b* is an *a*

a do not exist (there is no *a*) iff for all *b*, not (*b* is an *a*)

b is the same object as *a* (*b* = *a*) iff *a* is a *b* and *b* is an *a*

b are the same objects as *a* (*b* are *a*) iff for all *c*, *c* is an *a* iff *c* is a *b*

Notice that this last sameness predicate does not require there to be an *a* or a *b*. We now introduce some further numerical predicates.

There is at most one *a* iff for all *b* and *c*, if *b* is an *a* and *c* is an *a* then *b* = *c*

There is exactly one *a* iff there is at least one *a* and there is at most one *a*

An object is an *ab* iff it is an *a* and also a *b*

An object is a non-*a* iff there is exactly one of it but it is not an *a*

There are at least two *a* iff for some *b* and *c*, there is an *ab* and there is an *ac* but there is no *bc*

There are at most two *a* iff for all *b* *c* and *d*, if there is an *ad*, an *ac* and an *ad*, then there is either a *db* or a *dc*

There are at least three *a* iff for some *b* *c* and *d*, there is an *ab* and an *ac* and an *ad* but no *bc*, no *cd* and no *da*

We could go on introducing new constant numerical predicates such as "there are at least seven" or "there are between four and fifteen," but there is little theoretical point once we see how to proceed. The question is how to generalize from here.

The first thing we need is equicardinality or equinumerosity. We can define this in the standard way:

There are as many *a* as *b* iff there is a one-one correspondence between the *a* and the *b*.

Now let us define a *cardinality property* as one which, if it holds of any multitude *a* holds of all and only multitudes equicardinal with *a*:

F is a cardinality property iff for all *a* and *b*, if *Fa* then *Fb* iff there are as many *a* as *b*

It might be thought that this definition fails to capture what we mean by cardinality or how-manyness. For example, suppose all and only five-membered multitudes had some nonnumerical property *P*. Then we would be wrongly defining *P* as a cardinality property, when it might have to do with something other than number. There are two reasons why we need not

worry greatly about this. The first is that it is extremely hard to see, in a
universe of more than a tiny handful of individuals, what properties could
satisfy the condition for being a cardinality except cardinality properties.
And secondly, provided we are happy to understand properties as the same
when they are coextensional, there cannot be such a nonnumerical property
P. Any property coextensional with a cardinality property *is* a cardinality
property. These are perhaps not definitive refutations of the objection but
they reduce its suasive force considerably.

It is immediate to show that the nonexistence and exactly-one properties
are cardinality properties, and easy to show that no multitude has more than
one cardinality property. But can we assert that every multitude has a
cardinality? We cannot, for two reasons. The first is that we should need to
build into the assumptions behind the use of terms that for all a, there are
as many a as there are a. This sounds like a platitude, but it is not: it
assumes that everything over which we can quantify (at first level) can be
numbered or counted. If the world consists in part of masses of stuff or
other noncountables, and I believe it does, then universal countability is not
true. Secondly, and also in connection with the way in which the problem
is framed, we made a tacit assumption that we had a determinate domain of
discourse for the term variables to take values in. As Michael Dummett has
pointed out most graphically,[13] one of the lessons we have to take from
Frege's failure is that we cannot uncritically assume the existence of
universal domain of quantification, even if we allow universal countability
within particular domains. What this suggests is not that principles may fail
because quantifiers may vary over masses as well as individuals, but rather
that we cannot universally quantify at all except in some set context. Now
I am by no means so sure we cannot avail ourselves of a universal context,
but the matter is rather deeper than I can fathom, so for current purposes let
me simply concede the point and say that we cannot prove that every
multiplicity has a cardinality unless we make two nontrivial assumptions,
a single universal domain and universal countability on that domain.

No matter how things stand, it can be shown that the cardinality
properties "there are no" and "there is exactly one" are different in all
circumstances in which they make sense at all, since in all worlds (even one
with no objects at all) it is true that there is no Λ, and in all worlds it is false
that there is exactly one Λ. So now we may feel modestly justified in
notating these two properties as "0" and "1" respectively. We have that 0Λ
and that $1a$ for all individual objects a.

Let us now say that b has the cardinality-property-belonging-to-(the
multitude) a if and only if there are as many a as b. This defines the
parametric functorial expression "the cardinality-property-belonging-to a."

Assuming for present purposes universal countability for our term variables (or universal within a pregiven domain), we can easily concoct a predicate-analogue of Russellian definite descriptions for properties and show that the cardinality-property-belonging-to a as just parametrically defined is indeed definable coextensively with the unique cardinality property F (as previously generally defined) such that Fa, thus retrospectively justifying the hyphenated English verbiage. From this we may prove the equicardinality principle. Note that this is then a nonlogical principle resting on those two framework assumptions.

We can say there is one more b than a if and only if, for some c, c is a b and there are as many a as there are b which are not c. A *successor-property* of a property F applies to the multitude a if and only if, for some c, c is an a, and F applies to the a which are not c. It cannot be shown a priori that if F is a cardinality property then so is its successor property, because if the universe is finite, then for some cardinality property F, we have FV, but the successor of F fails to apply: it is the null property, never applying at all, not even to Λ.[14] If F applies to infinitely many objects, it is its own successor (note: a successor need not be a cardinality property). It is *not* a priori true that every cardinality property has a successor: for that to hold we need there to be one infinite multitude. This is guaranteed if we assume Whitehead and Russell's Axiom of Infinity. Given the Axiom of Infinity, or some other principles guaranteeing that every cardinality has a successor, the Peano axioms follow, and we can define a natural number (property) as a cardinality property which is either 0 or bears the ancestral of successor to 0. Mathematical induction is then the *third-order* principle

IND: For all P, if $P0$ and P applies to the successor of every cardinality property to which it applies, then P applies to every natural number property.

One may then go on, assuming Infinity, to define sum and product in much the way Whitehead and Russell did in *Principia Mathematica*, and show that the usual laws apply, but the details are complex and inappropriate here, where the point is only to indicate that the development can be made rigorous.

The sketch just given (and it is only a sketch) uses a slightly regimented semi-English, but the exact medium in terms of which it can most easily and naturally be developed is the logical system called "ontology" by Stanislaw Lesniewski. Lesniewski was one of the handful of logicians before the Second World War to have unequivocally recognized and trumpeted the greatness of Frege, and it is a great shame that his work is so marginalized in modern logic.

The Existence of the Natural Numbers

It would be nice now to be able to operate Frege's Bootstrap and conjure up an object for each cardinality property, getting something for nothing. While cardinality properties as defined conform closely to what we ordinarily understand by "number," they are incapable of providing such objects as they stand. We have no way to input properties and get objects. Frege's way of doing so is inconsistent. Could we use the Equicardinality Principle to do so? The answer is that as things stand we cannot, because the version of the Equicardinality Principle which can be proved (assuming Universal Countability) uses the definite article *the cardinality property belonging to a* as a description not of an object but of a property, the description being a type-shifted version of Russell's descriptions, one type higher. Unless we can somehow reduce the type by one this is incapable of delivering the object needed to start the Bootstrap. The force of contextual abstraction principles such as those which Frege rejected in *Grundlagen* and which are embraced by the neo-logicists is to provide new objects for the cardinality properties. Hume's Principle as understood by the neo-logicists can thus be seen as the combination of the relatively unproblematic Equicardinality Principle with the much more questionable assumption that we can lower the type by one. Such type-lowering is not in general possible because of Cantor's Theorem, and Frege's inconsistency arose because Frege tried to provide as many distinct objects as sets of objects.

If some such lowering were possible in this limited context, then Equicardinality would allow the Bootstrap to work, but the argument is by no means straightforward. At all events, the patency Frege required of his principles cannot be ascribed to Hume's Principle, so the success of the neo-logicist project is shakier than is desirable for anything like logicism to be established.

Singular Terms

The account of the ontology of arithmetic that I have outlined here depends on rejecting two linked doctrines of Frege about names or terms. Frege considered, for methodological reasons, that every term fit for use in science must denote one and only one object. He acknowledged that natural languages frequently use grammatically singular terms which do not denote, but he proposed banishing such terms from science, if need be by conventional stipulation of a default denotatum. This has some bizarre consequences, such as his needing to find a denotatum for complex functional terms such as "2 + the Moon." The other respect in which he deviated from tradition was in ignoring or evading terms which denote more than one object. These had been the mainstay of term logic from Aristotle to Schröder, and Frege gives no argument for their inadmissibility, he simply does things another way, from *Begriffsschrift* onwards, using predicates true of several objects rather than terms denoting several. This way to deal with plurality is now rarely questioned orthodoxy. But as we have seen, it gets in the way of taking plural subjects to be the bearers of numerical or cardinality properties. In *The Principles of Mathematics* Russell was still sensitive to plural terms, but by *Principia Mathematica* he had abandoned it and acceded to Frege's emphasis on the singular. Almost all post-Fregean logic and analytical philosophy has shared Frege's unargued anti-plural prejudice, and this has not been to its advantage. An honorable exception is Lesniewski.

It is a cornerstone of the neo-logicist project that numbers are objects, denoted by genuine singular terms. Grammatically singular definite descriptions of the form "the number of xs" are said to behave syntactically and inferentially sufficiently like grass-roots descriptions such as "the British Prime Minister elected in 1997" to overcome any qualms one might have about their status, and therefore to persuade us that they have denotata. With this assured, the Bootstrap may be operated and arithmetic justified a priori.

This is not the strongest part of the neo-logicist position, because any sophisticated modern language abounds in abstract singular terms, some of which, such as "the average British family," obviously and notoriously do not denote anything at all, while many others, such as "the property of having four wives," "the discrepancy between his declared and his actual income," seem to be in use because of a general paucity of robust and easily manipulated linguistic machinery for managing higher-order concepts. We seem as a linguistic species to prefer to concoct new singular terms and use them in familiar subject-predicate type sentences rather than wrestle with various orders and types of adverb, conjunction, and so on. A not insignificant indicator of this is the distaste with which mathematicians view type theory by comparison with set theory as a general expressive framework. Frege's move in *Grundgesetze*, fatal though it was, to replace predicates true of concepts by predicates true of value-ranges, which are his object-surrogates for properties and relations, certainly goes with the linguistic grain.

Since we have good if somewhat scattered reasons to suppose that expressions of the form "the number of xs" do not in fact stand for objects but for properties, and should be logically regimented not as ground-floor singular terms but as predicative, there is some onus on those taking them to denote objects to show that these reasons are deceptive or that the terms are equivocal. I do not intend to show all possible arguments against the numbers-as-properties-of-multitudes view are wrong, only to advertise its plausibility. It is true that this view falls well short of providing a guarantee that all the standard truths of arithmetic are a priori, or indeed all literally true. This means we have to balance the theoretical desirability of a certain epistemology of arithmetic with an ontological opinion as to the nature of numbers. Linguistic facts help but are not decisive. Unlike Michael Dummett, I do not regard metaphysics and ontology as generally secondary to the philosophy of language: our account of how language works is sensitive to assumptions about what there is as well as the other way around. For that reason I am willing to place some weight on the robustness of ontological intuitions, while accepting their fallibility and corrigibility. The intuition that numbers are not abstract objects is set against the desirability of a rationalist epistemology of arithmetic.

THE ULTIMATE ONTOLOGY OF NUMBER

In standard predicate logic the work done in our theory by plural terms and predicates attached to them has to be done by first- and second-level predicates respectively. The quantifier view of numbers, which is Frege's stripped of the reduction of quantifiers to objects, accepts this. But the difference seems to be merely one of linguistic framework and means of expression, so, provided both are equally expressively powerful, why should one associated ontology (numbers as properties of multitudes) be preferable to the other (numbers as second-order properties)? Surely we should need to give arguments that one of these frameworks is definitively better than the other, cuts reality with the grain while the other does not. This would entangle ontology with semantics again, and I already said I was in favor of disentanglement where possible, and I shall certainly not try and argue for the preferability of the plural terms framework in this context, as I do not think there is any such decisive argument.

   If we are not able to use a plural term "*a*" we can still avail ourselves of the monadic predicate "is one of *a*" and get at the objective fact about how many *a* there are by recourse to a quantifier. If we are not allowed

   P The Beatles are four

then we can say instead

   Q There are four things, each of which is a Beatle.

Given a language allowing both forms of expression, these must be logically equivalent. The local linguistic impoverishment of a language without plural terms can be compensated by ascending to a higher type. If this is so, then taking numbers as properties of multitudes and taking them as properties of properties ought to be somehow equally acceptable, which looks like a return to Carnapian ontological tolerance—or indifference—which again goes against most of what I have been saying about robust ontological intuition.

So *what* is the fact both equivalent statements differently get at? Is it about a property of a quartet, or about a property of a property of the members of the quartet? Neither, or both equally. Putting this in terms of an idiom which often throws unexpected new light on ontological puzzles, what *makes it true* that the Beatles are four (and not, e.g., three or five), what *makes it true* that there are four Beatles (and not that there are three or five Beatles)?

To answer this, first break down both P and Q into conjoined truths:

P≥ The Beatles are four or more

P≤ It is not the case that the Beatles are five or more

Q≥ There are at least four things, each of which is a Beatle

Q≤ It is not the case that there are at least five things, each of which is a Beatle

Now re-pose the truthmaker question for each of these. P≥ and Q≥ both have a truthmaker, or truthmakers: John, Paul, George, and Ringo jointly make each of P≥ and Q≥ true.[15] Between them, *they* (note the plural) make it true that there are not fewer than four Beatles. They have no need of a further, superadded property of fourness to help them make this true. Just by existing, just by being who they essentially are, they make it true. Their differences (the Scholastics would have said, "numerical differences") one from another are not additional facts over and above their existences, since each is who he is, and not another thing. So their being four is an internal, essential fact to them and requires no addition of being.

That there is no fifth Beatle is a truth without a truthmaker,[16] which does not make it any less true or objective. It is true because its contradictory would require someone other than one of the Fab Four to be a Beatle; it would need a truthmaker to be true, and there is none.[17] So its opposite is true by default. So P≤ and Q≤ are also true, and so P and Q are true. Neither of the conjuncts in either case requires there to be an extra entity called the property of being four, or the higher-order property of having four objects falling under one.

So I take it back that numbers are properties, if by that is meant that they are items additional to, over and above, the various other things rendering propositions of number true or false, or helping to do so. To get the numbers, all you need is enough objects, and nothing else. To put it as William of Ockham would have done, God could not have created lots of objects while withholding the creation of their attendant number properties. Therefore, since God can create or not create separately anything that can exist at all, number properties are not part of the furniture of the world. In that sense, the correct answer to the question "What are numbers, really?" is "Nothing at all." Does that mean that numerical propositions have no sense, or no truth-value? Not at all. There are vast numbers of numerical truths and falsehoods, most of them contingent, and they are true or false in general because of what things are in the world. But they require no special ontology of number-entities. The difference between there being four Beatles and five Beatles rests not on the inherence of a property of first or second order, but on the things, four or five persons as the case may be. Even the talk about properties of multitudes, suggestive as it is, is provisional, what Carnap called pseudo-material mode.

This outcome appeals to my Ockhamist sentiments. Michael Dummett is a recorded opponent of nominalism, which he sees as a manifestation of philosophical confusion.[18] Obviously I cannot argue this here, though I will say my nominalistic tendency is methodological and revisable, not dogmatic. To undergird it properly requires much work, including giving a proper and detailed account of the semantics of nominalization, which no one has yet come close to doing.

THE STATUS OF ARITHMETIC

If the truthmakers for applied statements of number are the sundry items otherwise needed anyway in our ontology, this helps explain our justified view that numbers are logical constants in just the same way that identity and difference are, the latter being sufficient to define the finite numbers with the help of other logical constants. Indeed on Tarski's account of what it is to be a logical constant,[19] namely a concept invariant under all permutations of any domain, all constant number-concepts are logical constants *par excellence*.[20]

But what about the truths of arithmetic? In particular, what about the principle that every number has a successor that is different from it, $n \neq n + 1$? If there were fewer than n actual things, this would be false, since n and $n + 1$ would apply to no multitude and so be the same, by extensionality. It looks as though we are running dangerously close to Mill's empiricism here, and that cherished theorems of arithmetic could be false *per accidens* because of a paucity of objects in the world. This after all is what logicism, neo-logicism, and many though not all versions of constructivism strive to avoid. With our view that numbers are not any addition of being, we offer no solace to them. So, against the whole history of mathematics, could it be false that $n \neq n + 1$? Taken strictly and literally, I am forced to admit that it could. There might be too few objects for all the theorems of Peano arithmetic to be literally true. Even if there are infinitely many objects, there will be cardinalities too large to be exemplified among real things. How then does arithmetic manage to remain such that its theorems are immune from refutation, as nearly everyone would accept?

My answer is: by fiat. We humans have collectively, over the millennia, elected to treat $n \neq n + 1$ and the like as valid, immune to counterexample, and so lifted out of the hurly-burly of empirical investigation. We may console ourselves with the thought that in another possible world there could be more objects than we have, but that just tells us that the theorems are not necessarily false, and would seem to require our mathematics to be steeped in hidden modality if we are to accept them as genuinely true. Suppose the postulationist idea is right. Then that means that the propositions of arithmetic, such as $n \neq n + 1$, change their status, so they are no longer literally true at face value, but have some other truthlike status. That would not require us to change what we mean by "number," "2," "+," and the like. We have a good grasp of those on the basis of the facts we learned at our teachers' knees. So I can stand by my view of number. But it does mean that we must treat pure mathematics as something a little more like fiction and a little less like physics.

PETER SIMONS

UNIVERSITY OF LEEDS
DECEMBER 2004

NOTES

Though never a student or colleague of Michael Dummett's I have benefited from his encouragement and support over the years, for which I here express my heartfelt thanks. At our infrequent meetings the common interest in Frege and the foundations of mathematics was uppermost. I was also delighted when he later "found" Husserl and Brentano. The problem of the nature and status of the natural numbers is one I have fretted about for thirty years, often literally with his books in hand, so while this is not a direct commentary on his work, it concerns our common problem, and not a thought in it has not in my mind's eye been held up to his views.

1. I refer to Frege's *Grundlagen* by section number, to enable any edition to be used.

2. EQU, or something close to it, is usually now called "Hume's Principle." As an inspection of Hume shows, it is not close to any principle actually formulated by Hume, and the name follows a somewhat misleading historical footnote to Hume's *Treatise* in *Grundlagen*, §63. In fact the principle, which can be called the Equicardinality Principle, is clearly stated by Cantor in 1895: cf. Cantor 1932, 283.

3. *Grundlagen*, §64.

4. Bostock 1974.

5. Benacerraf 1965.

6. Hale and Wright 2004.

7. Brandom 1996.

8. For brevity I shall call all cases of determining a number "counting," whether or not they involve a procedure of counting upwards one by one.

9. *Grundlagen*, §7 f.

10. Cf. Luke 2, 13: "And suddenly there was with the angel a multitude of the heavenly host," from the Latin "ultitudo militiae caelestis." Here Luther suggestively has "die Menge der himmlischen Heerscharen."

11. In the past I have also used the words "manifold," "plurality," "collection," and "Vielheit." None is ideal, all are suggestive.

12. Jevons 1874, p. 126, quoted in *Grundlagen*, §40.

13. E.g., Dummett 1973, 455 ff.

14. In the empty universe, only the cardinality property 0 is realized: all others are null.

15. For present purposes I am assuming that the Beatles just *are* John, Paul, George, and Ringo, and that there is no additional truthmaker beyond John for the truth that John is a Beatle, etc., no further Beatlehood-fact. This may be a slight simplification but only because of the choice of example. There *is* a further fact requiring an account for John's being a Liverpudlian. The difference is that being one of these four is formal, while being a Liverpudlian is material.

16. I accordingly reject truthmaker maximalism, according to which every truth has a truthmaker.

17. For present purposes neither Stu Sutcliffe nor Pete Best counts (note the word!) as a Beatle.

18. Dummett 1956.

19. Tarski 1986.

20. Though not necessarily the same across all domains. A large number is the null constant on small enough domains but not null on larger ones.

REFERENCES

Benacerraf, P. 1965. "What Numbers Could Not Be." *Philosophical Review* 74: 47–73.

Bostock, D. 1974. *Logic and Arithmetic: Natural Numbers*, vol. 1. Oxford: Clarendon.

Brandom, R. 1996. "The Significance of Complex Numbers for Frege's Philosophy of Mathematics." *Proceedings of the Aristotelian Society* 96: 293–315.

Cantor, G. 1932. *Gesammelte Abhandlungen mathematischen und philosophischen Inhalts*. Berlin: Springer.

Dummett, M. 1956. "Nominalism." *Philosophical Review* 65: 491–505.

———. 1973. *Frege: Philosophy of Language*. London: Duckworth.

———. 1992. *Frege: Philosophy of Mathematics*. London: Duckworth.

Hale, R., and C. Wright. 2001. *The Reason's Proper Study: Essays towards a Neo-Fregean Philosophy of Mathematics*. Oxford: Clarendon.

Jevons, W. S. 1874. *The Principles of Science: A Treatise on Logic and Scientific Method*. London: Macmillan.

Tarski, A. 1986. "What are Logical Notions?" *History and Philosophy of Logic* 7: 143–54.

REPLY TO PETER SIMONS

I am grateful to Peter Simons for the kind words he accords to my work on Frege at the opening of his essay. When, as an undergraduate, I read, in Austin's translation, Frege's *Die Grundlagen der Arithmetik*, I was bowled over by it: no work of philosophy I had previously read possessed such power and precision. So when, later, I started to write about Frege, it was not with any intention of reviving the reputation of a forgotten genius; I simply thought it obvious that his work merited close attention.

Peter Simons believes that cardinal numbers are properties of multitudes. He is a nominalist. I confess to feeling little patience with this species of philosophical puritanism. For one thing, it is so difficult to communicate with the nominalists as they would wish to be addressed. You cannot say that there are 26 letters in the English alphabet: you have to say that there are 26 letter-tokens in every English-alphabet-token. You cannot ask how many words there are in a particular book. You cannot even ask how many word-tokens there are in every copy of that book, because for the nominalist there are no books for there to be copies of. You have to ask how many word-tokens there are in every book-token equiform with the one you are now holding in your hand—though only those in the same room as you can tell what book-token that is. (Book-tokens are to be distinguished from book tokens, which are cards entitling the owner to purchase a book up to the price printed on the card. Do they exist in English-speaking countries other than Britain? I suppose a nominalist would not countenance languages, such as English, nor prices, such as £20.) But, in his essay, Simons does not make a great deal of his nominalism. He ranges over several different topics, making it hard to catch his main thrust.

In *Grundlagen*, Frege insists that (cardinal) numbers are objects, falling in the domain of first-order quantifiers. Granted, they are abstract, not concrete objects; but Frege thought it a vulgar mistake (as I do) to suppose that the only objects there are are concrete ones. Numbers must be objects if the numerical operator "the number of . . ." is to be the *same* expression, and not merely an analogous one, in "the number of prime numbers less than 30" and in "the number of giraffes in the London Zoo." It is intuitively plausible that the very same operator is used in these two terms. This was important to Frege, since it allowed him to prove the infinity of the sequence of natural numbers by means of the proof Peter Simons so greatly admires, but does not accept, calling it "Frege's Bootstrap." Frege points out that the answer "Nought" to a question "How many?" is an answer to the question, not a rejection of it like "No one" and "Never"; it does not lead to the paradoxes that result from treating "No one" and "Never" as if they were specifications of a person and a time. Hence 0 is to be treated as a cardinal number; the number of moons of Mars is 2, of moons of the Earth is 1, and of moons of Venus is 0. So, for any natural number n, the number of numbers $\leq n$ is 1 greater than n: every natural number has a successor distinct from it, and so there are infinitely many natural numbers, a result attained by pure logic.

Peter Simons does not believe that natural numbers are objects. This denial is one of the principal theses of his essay. Simons takes the natural numbers as cardinal numbers, as Frege did, but thinks that cardinal numbers are properties, not objects. If one accepts plural terms, as Peter Simons does, and as the late George Boolos also did, one can take them as properties of what plural terms denote, which Simons calls "multitudes." He sometimes speaks of plural terms as denoting many objects severally, but sometimes as each denoting what appears to be a single thing, a multitude: of a multitude, each of many single objects is one of those that make it up.

So, for Simons, cardinal numbers are properties of multitudes. Multitudes, for him, are entities of the same type, type 0, as individual objects, in the sense of "type" that occurs in "the theory of types." So properties of multitudes are of type 1. Plural terms must undoubtedly be recognised in the grammar of natural language; but, as Simons observes, Frege refused to countenance them from a logical standpoint, and in this he has been followed by the great majority of modern logicians (Lesniewski being the commendable exception).

If one does not accept plural terms in one's logic, then the plural terms of natural language must be represented by predicates. In this case, if natural numbers are properties, they must be properties of what predicates denote, namely first-level properties or concepts in Frege's terminology. In this case they will be of type 2, analogous to what quantifiers denote, or concepts of second level as Frege would have it. Whether we take cardinal numbers to be properties of multitudes or properties of properties, we shall be unable to allow that the same operator is used in speaking of the number of giraffes in the zoo and of the number of primes less than 30. In the one case we should be speaking of the number of objects of a certain kind, in the other of the number of (first- or second-level) properties of a certain kind: the difference in type of the operator "the number of . . ." used in speaking of the number of giraffes and of the number of primes would import a difference in type of the two terms and hence of the numbers referred to. Frege's proof of the infinity of the sequence of natural numbers would be blocked.

Worse than that, we have no ground of assurance that, when interpreted in this way, the sequence of natural numbers is infinite. If the universe is finite and has finite complexity, and we take the natural numbers to be properties of collectives of concrete objects, whether multitudes comprising them or properties possessed by them, then the sequence of natural numbers will *not* be infinite, whatever concrete objects we consider as belonging to the domain.

But we cannot say with assurance that the sequence of natural numbers is not infinite. Even if it is the prevailing opinion that the universe is finite, we cannot be sure that it is not infinitely complex. The idea of infinite complexity upwards is easy to grasp: planets belong to stellar systems, stars to galaxies, galaxies to groups, groups to clusters, clusters to superclusters: might this not go on indefinitely? But the idea of infinite complexity downwards is much harder to comprehend. Leibniz's *Monadology* states that if there are complexes, there must be simple substances. A chain is made up of links; each link may in turn be a chain made up of smaller links. Could this go on indefinitely? No, because chains are made by human beings, and human beings must start somewhere. But does God have to start somewhere? Atoms have structure; surprisingly, protons and neutrons have structure. Might not quarks prove to have structure? Might this not go on indefinitely? Perhaps everything has structure. Or does a lower bound on meaningful size rule this out? Perhaps there are reasons in principle why the universe must be both finite and finitely complex. Or perhaps again, physicists and cosmologists do not know as much as they think they know.

What is a multitude? Simons equates a multitude with what Russell called a "class as many"; and he tells us of several other words he has in the past used in place of "multitude." The singular nouns "multitude" and "class" suggest that a multitude is a single entity consisting of individual objects—perhaps none, perhaps one, perhaps many—which has a status intermediate between a concrete and an abstract object. Like an individual object, a multitude can have a property; it seems to be a sort of abstract object, but one not abstract enough to offend a nominalist. And what exactly is this curious relation that a multitude may have to individual objects of "consisting of" them? Simons does not intend to convey that a multitude is a single entity; he does not intend us to ask these questions. The term "multitude" is for him a collective noun like "audience" and "congregation." We can do without collective nouns; and Simons would do better to dispense with the word "multitude" or any word corresponding to it, and use instead a plural expression. A singular term stands for or denotes a single object; and a plural term stands for or denotes several individual objects (in some cases only one, in the extreme case none). Instead of speaking of a property of a multitude, we can speak of a property that several things have. Let us call this, for short, a "collective property." Now collective properties are of two kinds, distributive and non-distributive. The distributive ones provide no motive for admitting plural terms; several objects have a distributive property only if, and only because, each of those objects has it individually. The non-distributive properties are much more interesting. They are properties possessed by two or more objects together, but by none of them individually. Thus: Russell and Whitehead wrote *Principa Mathematica* (together); Castor and Pollux were twins; the island of Skye and the Scottish mainland are connected by the Skye Bridge; Mars, Deimos and Phobos form a planetary system (and a great many things form the solar system); the points a, b, and c are collinear; Guy Fawkes and several others conspired to blow up the Houses of Parliament; at any one time two kings (together) ruled Sparta. Collaboration, kinship, connection, membership of a system, shared relationship to a particular object are among the relations that bring about the possession of a non-distributive property by several individuals.

At first sight, non-distributive properties of several objects, taken together, give a reason for allowing the use of plural terms in logical symbolism. All these statements *can* be expressed without the use of plural terms, but, when the sense does not determine how many objects are involved, rather clumsily. When the number of objects is so fixed, there is no difficulty: being a twin is a symmetrical relation, and a bridge always connects two places, so that we simply need a ternary relation. The appearance that an assignment of a non-distributive property to several objects when the number of such objects is not fixed by that property is difficult to express without the use of a plural term is illusory, however. We simply need to have a different relation from that we usually employ. Thus, instead of the relation of writing a book, we need that of contributing to the writing of a book. "Russell and Whitehead wrote *Principia Mathematica*" then becomes "Russell contributed to writing *Principia Mathematica* and Whitehead contributed to writing *Principia Mathematica* and no one else did." Similarly for membership of a system and participation in a conspiracy. I therefore do not think that there is a strong case for the use of plural terms from the considerations adduced by Simons in this essay.

I do not believe in truth-makers. I am glad that Peter Simons has the grace to allow that not all true statements have truth-makers; but I do not care at all for John, Paul, George, and Ringo as the truth-makers of "There were four Beatles." The example is tendentious, in any case. Suppose the statement "There are presently four M.P.s who have become Catholics since their election" were true. Would those four individuals by themselves constitute truth-makers of that statement? Obviously not. It would also matter that they had become Catholics, when they did so, and whether there were any other M.P.s who had done so. Simons is anxious to limit the totality of objects in the world and to extrude properties and relations from it. But the world is the totality of facts, not of things: to know what God created, we must know *how* the world is, not just what objects it contains. In echoing the *Tractatus*, I am not campaigning for an ontology of facts, which, with Frege, I identify with true propositions.

Are numbers objects? If they are, they are abstract objects: they cannot be perceived by the senses, they have no causal powers, they even lack a position in time or in space. But an object does not need to be capable of being shown to us: one of Frege's examples was the Equator. The classification of things as objects is a semantic classification, that is, a classification of expressions referring to them as singular terms. To know what a given such object is, we must know what kind of things can be said about it, and what are the criteria for their truth. That is all we need to know: that is what Frege meant by saying that a word has meaning only in the context of a sentence. There can therefore be no principled reason for repudiating reference to abstract objects—objects that have no causal powers. Simons rightly remarks that we readily form what are grammatically abstract singular terms such as "the discrepancy between his declared and his actual income" that it would be absurd to think of as denoting abstract objects. Frege may have been too impressed by appearances in this regard; in later life he complained that he had been misled by expressions of the form "the extension of the concept . . ." into believing that they had a denotation. Our propensity to form abstract singular terms of the kind mentioned by Simons is due to the demands of the grammars of our languages. (I do not know nearly enough languages to be confident that this holds good in all of them, but it is certainly true in those I know.) If I am asked what I am thinking about, a grammatical answer must be a noun-phrase; so I may answer, "The appropriateness of Elisabeth's gift" (although I could have said, "How appropriate Elisabeth's gift was"). To take an abstract singular noun-phrase as denoting an object, we must be able to say what kind of object it is, and what is the criterion of identity for things of that kind, and there must be a vocabulary of predicates and relational expressions applicable to things of that kind. These conditions are satisfied by colours—we can say of a colour that it is warm, bright, primary and so on, and of two colours that they clash or are complementary. It is unnecessary to illustrate the vocabulary we can use for talking about natural numbers. But, asked what an appropriateness is, we can only say, lamely, that it is an instance of a quality, and, asked what a discrepancy is, we can only say that it is a relation. Qualities and relations are expressed by one- and two-place predicates: abstract noun-phrases incorporating such nouns go proxy for whole sentences, and are not seriously meant as denoting an object of any kind.

So *are* numbers objects? It is hard to resist the conviction that when I say that there are ten primes less than 30, I mean the very same thing by "ten" as when I say that there were ten lost tribes of Israel, or that I have ten fingers. If so, numbers must be objects—at least as much objects as tribes are. (Are tribes multitudes for Simons? If so, to say that there are ten of them, he must allow of a multitude of multitudes. But I doubt whether multitudes of multitudes figure in his ontology, his syntax, or his seman- tics.) It is equally hard to resist the conviction that arithmetical sentences and formulae are to be taken at face value, rather than being viewed as disguised forms of statements involving entities of a higher type. But, if the numbers of arithmetic are to be taken as the same as those spoken of in empirical statements, what can justify treating them as objects? It is evident that the correct analysis of what Frege called "statements of number," such as the (false) statement "There are just four moons of Jupiter" or "Jupiter has just four moons," is as involving numerically definite quantifiers (standing for what Frege called concepts of second level): the tendentious rendering "The number of Jupiter's moons = 4" obviously distorts the logical form.

Any range of systematically connected first-level properties, such as colour properties, gives birth to a corresponding range of abstract objects, such as colours; the relation, between coloured objects, of matching in colour becomes the criterion of identity for colours. We make this transition easily, and it does not occur to us to be troubled by the Julius Caesar problem—whether we need to stipulate that the colour green is not Julius Caesar, and, if so, how to do it. (This problem will arise only in a logical symbolism with a single sort of bound individual variables; it will not arise in a many-sorted notation.) Frege thought that the totality of *all* properties gives birth to a corresponding totality of objects, the extensions of those properties or classes of objects possessing them. Even this would have been harmless if he had not taken the abstraction operator to be reflexive, so that there could be classes of classes at the same level as classes of other objects, and so was led into contradiction.

Now the numerically definite quantifiers and their kin (at-least and at- most quantifiers, etc.) are systematically connected; so it is natural for us to make the transition to speaking of numbers as objects. But the case is different from that of colours and directions: not only are we at a different logical level, but the numerical operator is reflexive; it was in order to speak of the number of numbers which . . . that we particularly needed to treat numbers as objects. If we are to be able to speak of numbers of numbers, then, it seems, numbers must be treated as of the same sort as any other objects that we can count. But we can count objects of all sorts, and thus, it seems, we can acknowledge only one sort of object, just as Frege believed; and then we cannot resolve the Julius Caesar problem by having recourse to a many-sorted logic.

The equicardinality principle to which Frege appealed seems the obvious source for our move from using numerical adjectives to using numerical substantives; but we have become aware how much justification appeal to such an abstraction principle requires. As generating abstract objects, abstraction principles in which the operator is to be applied to a singular term, such as Frege's "direction" example, are evidently harmless for two reasons. First, they are not reflexive: there are numbers of numbers, but directions do not have directions, nor do colours have colours. Secondly, given this, there can be no more of them than there are objects of the kind to terms for which the operator is applied. At first sight, taking numbers as properties of multitudes offers hope that the relevant version of the equicardinality principle will be similarly harmless, as the operator will be of first level, like "the direction of. . . . " But this hope is short-lived. If the universe is finite and contains n individual objects, there will be 2^n multitudes. If there are denumerably many objects, the same relation will hold, so that there will be non-denumerably many multitudes, if we allow multitudes to be infinite in size. If we rule that multitudes can only be finite, then there will be only denumerably many multitudes, so things will be better: but we are still relying on a non-logical assumption about the size of the universe.

What, then, can be the justification for regarding numbers as objects; that is, for treating words or signs for numbers and other numerical terms as singular terms rather than as components of quantifiers, and thus allowing ourselves to speak of the number of numbers satisfying a given condition as a number on the same level as those numbers? A justification need not in all cases take the form of a deductive inference. In this case the justification is to be seen as lying in the first instance in Frege's Bootstrap rather than in the equicardinality principle. The Bootstrap guarantees that there is no end to forming ever newer initial segments of the natural numbers. When a child asks, "What is the largest number?" we usually answer that there isn't one, because, for any number, you can always conceive of one that is greater than it by 1. But this answer is not compelling, because "conceive of " may be understood to mean "imagine that there was." The observation that the number of numbers from 0 to n (less than or equal to n) is greater than n by 1 *is* compelling. Taking the natural numbers as finite cardinals involves that they can be the numbers of objects of any sort, and this seems to force us to conceive of a dizzyingly large totality. But, by appealing to the Bootstrap, we see that we can make do, in envisaging the totality of natural numbers, with an appeal to a restricted and conceptually manageable base—initial segments of the natural numbers themselves, which can be generated successively by invoking only the segments previously generated. This manageable base is of course not at all the same as the base of colour-predicates on which we rest the colours taken as objects. But it is equally serviceable as avoiding the impredicativity that confuses the attempt to justify treating numbers as objects by appeal to the equicardinality principle. Once the natural numbers are conceptually in place, we can treat them as giving the cardinalities of (finitely many) objects of all sorts; that is what we do when we count, starting with 1 rather than 0. Similar remarks of course apply if we take the natural numbers to be finite ordinals, which I think is truer to the conceptual order.

The equicardinality principle of course gives the criterion of identity for cardinal numbers. In our ordinary conceptual development, we are no more worried by the Julius Caesar problem for numbers than by that problem concerning colours. Numbers cannot be identical to human beings, or objects of other sorts, because their criterion of identity is quite different. This is the thought which induces those whom Simons calls "neo-logicists" to treat the Julius Caesar problem as trivial, although one to which they have no logical solution. But I see no obstacle to a many-sorted logical symbolism, with one sort for cardinal numbers, in which the cardinality operator "the number of . . ." is allowed to be applied to predicates of every sort.

Thus, if this justification be accepted, we may remain assured of the truth of arithmetic, even before we have a full analysis of the grounds on which its axioms rest and of our implicit grasp of those grounds.

What is the intention underlying Simons's essay? He cannot be urging that number theory ought to be carried out on the assumption that there may or may not be a largest natural number. Obviously number theory would be crippled if we could not take for granted that the ordinary arithmetical functions such as multiplication and exponentiation were always well defined. It is indeed of interest whether strict finitism, according to which the natural numbers are closed under the successor operation but not under exponentiation, can be made coherent. On the strict finitist theory, the domain will consist of the "feasible" numbers, say those up to which it is in actual practice possible to count. It seems plain that such a domain is closed under successor: if it is possible to count to n, it is possible to count to $n + 1$. But, equally plainly, it is not closed under exponentiation: we can count up to 1000, but not up to 1000^{1000}. Induction, if universally valid, would allow us to argue that, if it is possible to count up to the successor of any number up to which it is possible to count, and it is possible to count up to 1, then it is possible to count up to 1000^{1000}.

Evidently, induction is not universally valid. It is of philosophical interest to have a clear analysis of the extent of its validity, more precise than that it fails when applied to vague predicates. Induction fails when the induction step is, by however small a degree, less than totally rigorous: what account is to be given of the notion of rigour, in this sense? It is also of philosophical, though perhaps not of mathematical, interest to construct a theory which acknowledges both the palpable truth of the principle that if it is possible to count to n, it is possible to count to $n + 1$, and the palpable falsity of the statement that it is possible to count up to 1000^{1000}. But only a very few would think that such a theory ought to replace number theory as ordinarily practised.

Peter Simons is not a strict finitist. He is an agnostic about whether there are infinitely many natural numbers. What, then, *is* the intention underlying his essay? He wants to persuade us that natural numbers, while they are indeed finite cardinal numbers, are not what Frege believed them to be. They are not abstract objects; Simons does not really believe that there are any abstract objects. If there are no abstract objects, there are no mathematical objects: natural numbers, real numbers, complex numbers, transfinite ordinals and cardinals—none of them can be what we are accustomed to regard them as being. They are properties masquerading as objects, according to Simons; we must be content to leave it in question whether every natural number, so understood, has a successor. But we are not to drop that assumption from mathematics as we practise it.

What status, then, does the mathematics that Simons urges us to continue to practise have? Its propositions can no longer claim, in general, to be true: they "have some other truth-like status." We "must treat pure mathematics as something a little more like fiction and a little less like physics." Some of its propositions are to be constituted "by 'fiat'," otherwise known as postulation. But Simons's postulationist does not say, "I am laying it down that . . .", he says, "Let's pretend that . . ." For Simons insists that the terms "number," "+," "2," etc., as used in number theory, are to retain the same meanings as they have in empirical contexts. We are not giving them new meanings, drawn from their role in the postulated theory; we are employing them with their meanings as established from their use in empirical statements, but with false or dubious assumptions governing them. It is worse than that. If arithmetic deals with numbers as Simons understands them, namely as properties of multitudes, then it systematically misrepresents the logical form of its statements by displaying what are in fact reference to and quantification over properties as reference to and quantification over objects. In practice this does no harm. As already observed, the standard form of arithmetical statements makes it appear that we can speak of the number of numbers below a given bound that satisfy a certain condition, and be thereby referring to an element of the domain of numbers of which arithmetic treats, whereas in fact we shall be referring to a number of a higher logical type. But this is no serious matter, for we can, for example, define the number of primes $\leq n$ as the sum of $\varphi(i)$ for from $i = 1$ to $i = n$, where $\varphi(i) = 1$ if i is prime and 0 if i is composite.

Faced with what Simons understands the natural numbers to be, we might say with Frege, "Arithmetic crumbles!" It might well be thought a *reductio ad absurdum* of an analysis of the notion of number that it calls into question the truth of arithmetic. If Simons is right, mathematicians are not amassing a treasury of truths more solid than any other: they are playing a game of pretending that what may in fact very well not be so is known to be so. I do not believe that mathematics is a game of make-believe; and I think that anyone who thinks it is owes us an explanation of what point it has or what use it is.

M. D.

7

Anat Matar

RADICALLY DIFFERENT:
ON DUMMETT'S METAPHILOSOPHY

> *Philosophy must be of some use and we must take it*
> *seriously; it must clear our thoughts and so our*
> *actions. Or else it is a disposition we have to check,*
> *and an inquiry to see that this is so; i.e. the chief*
> *proposition of philosophy is that philosophy is non-*
> *sense. And again we must then take seriously that it is*
> *nonsense, and not pretend, as Wittgenstein does, that*
> *it is important nonsense!*
>
> Frank P. Ramsey

Michael Dummett is a rare bird among the philosophers acting within the analytical philosophy scene. On the one hand, he is acknowledged as one of the tradition's most eminent figures; on the other, it is hard to find analytic philosophers following in his footsteps and adopting the radical logic that characterises his metaphysics. In this essay I account for this by presenting Dummett's position as combining an "analytical" frame of reference with a metaphilosophical view that is usually taken to be "continental." This position is hard to digest by both contemporary philosophical traditions.

I. METAPHILOSOPHY: THE BASIS

Dummett declares himself to be an analytical philosopher. For him, that means roughly, adhering to the belief, "first, that a philosophical account of thought can be attained through a philosophical account of language, and, secondly, that a comprehensive account can only be so attained" (*OAP*, 4).[1] Dummett's preliminary assumption here is that a philosophical account of the fundamental structure of our thought, and hence of the way we represent the world in our thought, is what philosophy aims at. From these points of departure, Dummett deduces not only that philosophers should construct a theory of meaning, an account of what it is that we know when we know a language, but also that they should pave their way in philosophy "from the bottom up"; that is, they should defer the more pictorial metaphysical disputes and concentrate upon building a theory of meaning proper. Once the disputes in this logico-linguistic realm are settled, the result will directly reflect our conception of reality and of thought. Metaphysics is embedded in logic, but it is the realm of logic that is primarily accessible to us.

Dummett reminds us at this point that in adopting the "bottom up" method he is no different from Hegel.[2] Hegel too regarded logic as the appropriate starting point for philosophy, precisely because it is the most purely *self-conscious* discipline. "*Logic therefore coincides with metaphysics, the science of things set and held in thoughts*—thoughts accredited able to express the essential reality of things."[3] There are significant differences between Hegel's and Dummett's conceptions of logic and metaphysics, as we shall see below; but it is important to emphasize that Dummett's agreement with Hegel is not a mere agreement in methodological principle, since for both philosophers, there are no "merely methodological principles." Indeed, the main difference between the two concerns precisely the question whether this anti-formalism entails full-fledged holism, and that, in turn, affects their views on the finality of philosophical results. Like Hegel, Dummett holds the view that for philosophy to be philosophy, it cannot be based on suppositions. Its disputes can, in principle, be settled; since what is at stake is self-consciousness, the overall understanding of understanding (and not merely the appearance of understanding), the truth of the results has to be absolute:

> It may seem as if philosophy, in order to start on its course, had, like the rest of the sciences, to begin with a subjective presupposition. The sciences postulate their respective objects, such as space, number, or whatever it be; and it might be supposed that philosophy had also to postulate the existence of thought. But the two cases are not exactly parallel. *It is by the free act of thought that it occupies a point of view, in which it is for its own self, and thus gives itself an object of its own production.* Nor is this all. The very point of view, which originally is taken on its own evidence only, must in the course of the science be converted to a result—the ultimate result in which philosophy returns into itself and reaches the point with which it began. In this manner philosophy exhibits the appearance of a circle which closes with itself, and has no beginning in the same way as the other sciences have.[4]

Thus the truth of philosophy is not only absolute—its very existence is unassailable. It is "by the free act of thought"—or of language, as Dummett would have it—that it creates for itself an immanent viewpoint, a *metalanguage* that gains its particular meaning from its being self-conscious. Once such a metalevel of self-consciousness is acknowledged, it is clear that as long as there are disputes regarding its content, it has not yet been "converted to a result"—for the ultimate result of self-consciousness should be indisputable.

Hegel, famously, claimed that by acknowledging this much, and by delineating the procedure leading to this result, he has *already* arrived at the deepest level of self-consciousness. His philosophy reached the long-awaited final truth of philosophy, and no *essential* development is conceivable from this point onwards. This claim has to do with the special holistic character of Hegel's logic. Logic is everywhere: it is not merely formal, and does not serve just as a *method* on the way to metaphysical truth. Since everything is, by its nature, thought, then a comprehensive formulation of the reflective laws of thought is equivalent to expressing reality itself.

It is at this point that the similarities and differences between Hegel and Dummett are most crucial. As the introduction to *The Logical Basis of Metaphysics* makes clear, Dummett also does not take logic, in its broad sense (which includes the theory of meaning), to be merely a formal device. Like Hegel, he regards its aim as that of providing us with an overall theory, a comprehensive metaphysical system. Yet his view of this system is less holistic and more structured than that of Hegel. It is precisely here that his being an analytic philosopher comes into play. Since metaphysical disputes are deeply rooted in disputes about meaning, what we need in order to solve them, according to Dummett, is a firm *basis* consisting of "a set of general principles governing the formulation of a meaning-theory" (*LBM*, 16). Only upon this ground will we be able to draw up the complete meaning-theory, or metaphysical system, itself. This is why Dummett cannot yet envisage finality in philosophy. He denies that full self-consciousness has *already* been achieved: it is only on a *programmatic* level that we have come closer to it. He does however believe that we are at long last on the right path towards the resolution of philosophical controversies (*TOE*, 458). What hindered philosophers from taking it before was the diversity of conceptions of the aim of philosophy and its method (*TOE*, 457), but Frege's *metaphilosophical* insight about the linguistic turn that metaphysics should put us on the right track. Now the road to metaphysical system is paved. Dummett's interpretation of Frege included his famous claim that in order to achieve what he did, Frege had to break with Hegel's idealism. But in the heat of the debate about the right interpretation of *Frege*, it has gone unnoticed that, in the manner he proffered his case, Dummett virtually acknowledged *his own* overwhelming debt to idealism. This is particularly evident in the last page of the second edition of *Frege: Philosophy of Language*, where the overthrow of Hegelian idealism is introduced as a historical necessity, a dialectical stage on the way to achieving the conception of a systematic theory of meaning. Frege's chief contribution was to enable us to reformulate the antithesis between realism and idealism "as an opposition between two accounts of what, in general, an understanding of our *language* consists in" (*FPL*, 684, my emphasis); for that linguistic turn to occur, Frege needed to diverge from Hegel's homogeneous, non-structured conception of metaphysics. But now that this has been achieved, Dummett brings idealism back to the foreground, reintroducing it in a linguistic guise.

II. HOW IS PHILOSOPHICAL TRUTH POSSIBLE?

The question of the possibility of truth in philosophy has haunted modern philosophical literature. In the last 200 years there has been a constant uneasy feeling that the notion of philosophical truth is intrinsically paradoxical, and at least two parallel formulations attempted to expose this paradox. One has dominated the so-called "continental" tradition, and was originally raised by Fichte; the other, directed specifically to the analytical tradition, is connected with the name of Moore, but can be traced back at least as far as Husserl.

Fichte's problem of Identity-Thinking may be summed up as follows: The notion of self-consciousness, which defines philosophy, seems to be inconsistent, since it necessarily involves the conceptualization of subjectivity, while at the same time demanding that it be retained as it is, subjective, immediate. By trying to form a concept of itself, the subject unavoidably takes a step back, thus making itself into an object; but he thereby surrenders the privileged position from which he was supposed to conceive of himself as the antecedent source of all objectification. However, the mark of the understanding sought by philosophy is precisely this privileged subjective location of the source of knowledge—that which distinguishes it from *scientific* attempts to objectify this source. In other words, the privileged perspective philosophy aims at attaining is untenable, since the wanted subjectivity constantly evades its objectification, or conceptualization. Now this formulation of Fichte's paradox, which leans heavily on the demand for immediacy, may seem to be redolent of traditional epistemology, and hence as easy to overcome after the philosophy of consciousness has been superseded by philosophy of language.

However, it reappears in linguistic attire as forcefully as before.

The question raised in Moore's version of the puzzle regarding philosophy's striving after truth is how it can be possible for philosophy, being a study of what is by definition the most *trivial* realm, that of logic and language, to achieve *knowledge* at all. For either its results are trivial, or, if they do convey knowledge, they are empirical. It is this version which attracts Dummett's attention. Dummett poses the question variously. Sometimes (as in MV), he confronts the challenge of triviality, and phrases the paradox as a need to explain how nonempirical statements like those of philosophy can nevertheless advance our knowledge. At other times, it is the second horn of the dilemma that is treated critically, by admitting that "the philosopher seeks not to *know* more but to *understand* what he already knows" (*LBM*, 240, my emphases). In this case the question is how we can dub the results of such a self-search "true." At any rate, it is clear to Dummett that the linguistic turn, while relieving us from the myths of platonism and mentalism, has at the same time imposed severe threats on philosophy. Both these traditional positions explained the notion of philosophical truth by positing special realms for philosophy to represent and special means enabling it to do so. The transcendental realm and the private one were taken to yield the required spheres for privileged representation, which could be carried out through either reflection or introspection. With the incoherence of these positions exposed through an attention to the primary role of language in philosophy, it is not at all clear whether there remains any truth for philosophy to represent—whether, and how, it can represent at all. But as Dummett candidly confesses: "Philosophy would interest me much less if I did not think it possible for us eventually to attain generally agreed answers to the great metaphysical questions" (*LBM*, 19). How, then, does he deal with the problem of philosophy's access to truths?

In "Frege and the Paradox of Analysis," Dummett offers the following account. Philosophical analysis involves definitions, that is, analytic equations. Our task is, then, to show how these equations may be nonempirical, yet true and informative. What has to be ensured is a sort of epistemological gap between the two sides of such analytic equations. This means that our theory of meaning should guarantee, on the one hand, the possibility of equations whose truth values could be known on the basis of reflection alone, but on the other hand, their being modeled on informative equations rather than on the notion of synonymy. It is this notion, the notion of synonymy, which summons the accusation of triviality. But, Dummett notes, this very conception of synonymy is a direct result of a purely subjectivist assumption, according to which, understanding always comes in a flash and is gained by an immediate contact between the subject and its apprehended object. This is precisely how the classical paradoxical split is created: the object of apprehension is alienated from the subject, but can nevertheless be miraculously taken in in a single act. However, such relics of empiricism and psychologism, embedded in the notion of synonymy, are no longer conceivable after Frege's context principle had been introduced. Understanding becomes a more complex matter, and, according to Dummett, a more active and creative one. Both these features—complexity and creativity—serve as Dummett's springing board towards the possibility of true and informative philosophical statements.

It is easy to see how the complexity of what is involved in understanding takes away the threat of triviality.

> An understanding of an expression is manifested in a range of interconnected abilities; and one who has these abilities may well not have apprehended the connections [between] them. . . . That is why conceptual analysis can bring to light connections that we have failed to notice [between] different components of the complex linguistic practices that we have mastered, and even abilities that we have failed to observe that we possess. (*FOP*, 51f.)

But this part of Dummett's solution is still insufficient to rescue philosophy from *both* horns of the dilemma. According to the present suggestion, philosophical analyses do, indeed, yield novel understandings, by furnishing us with a perspicuous representation of what was only blurred, confused, too complicated to grasp without any amount of reflection. Philosophy is not trivial, since it uncovers a systematic network of connections among our various linguistic practices. But it is here that our problem reappears. For it may now seem as if the achievement of philosophy were simply a passive representation of an *objet trouvé,* which has already been "given"—our linguistic practices—and hence that there was no significant difference between philosophical representations of these data and theories of empirical science. By portraying conceptual analyses simply as systematic accounts of our uses of language, how do we distinguish them from similar accounts given by linguists and anthropologists? How, in other words, do we avoid the *exterior* nature of our account—how can these scientifically oriented objectifying explanations satisfy us as *philosophical* explanations? It seems as if Dummett's solution of the paradox of analysis was achieved through substituting the traditional, psychologistic model of understanding, according to which it represents an internal state, by one that adopts the stance of *empirical* psychology, where what is represented is a complicated network of our linguistic practices. But now we see that such a solution only escapes the *triviality* accusation, to fall prey to the second horn of the dilemma.

However, this is not the full story. What was lacking in my account of

Dummett's solution was a direct reference to the *creative* facet of analysis. The substitution just mentioned is actually much more thoroughgoing. It is not merely that instead of representing one realm, we actually have to represent another. Rather, the whole notion of *representation* as what should be achieved by philosophy is revised. In this revision, Dummett leans heavily on the insights of the later Wittgenstein.

A linguistic formulation of scruples similar to those of Fichte, regarding the antinomic demand to conceptualize in philosophy, may be found in several paragraphs of Wittgenstein's *Philosophical Investigations* (§§ 120–122):

> In giving explanations I already have to use language full-blown (not some sort of preparatory, provisional one); this by itself shews that I can adduce only exterior facts about language.
> Yes, but then how can these explanations satisfy us? . . .
> Your questions refer to words; so I have to talk about words. You say: the point isn't the word, but its meaning, and you think of the meaning as a thing of the same kind as the word, though also different from the word. Here the word, there the meaning. The money, and the cow that you can buy with it. (By contrast: money, and its use.)[5]

Read with Fichte's paradox in mind, this paragraph shows us the problem ensued by trying to reflect philosophically in, and about, language. Any conceptualization of the *reflexive* power of language itself is nonsensical, since it objectifies, and hence *splits*, what ought to remain one. ("The money, and the cow . . ."; language, and the thought that is supposed to "accompany" it, or hide behind it.) Philosophers adopt an "exterior" approach, while at the same time renouncing such approaches as scientific objectification. They aim both at representing (the representational power of language) and not-representing (since representation brings us back to the empirical sphere).

Wittgenstein's suggested alternative is hinted in the parentheses at the end of the paragraph, and Dummett's solution of the paradox of analysis builds upon this very insight. His understanding of understanding cuts across the objective/subjective dilemma by doing away with the old concept of representation altogether. We are offered no extensional—objectifying—conception of understanding, like the one endorsed by Frege, and attacked as such by Husserl. Neither do we opt for a Husserlian subjectivist account of understanding, according to which conceptual equations form "an obvious circle," by equating senses, which (as synonymies should) are present to the mind. Dummett's conception differs from both because it conceives of our target not primarily as a passive representation (either of internal or external facts about our practices) at all, but as an active, creative process. It is here that we realize Dummett's *anti-realism* is needed in order to secure the very intelligibility and fruitfulness of philosophy. The difference between "the money—and the cow" and "the money—and its use" is that the latter conception—of meaning, of course—is intensionalist: the object forms part of the subject, or better, of *intersubjective* thought, as it is manifested in practice. The philosophical viewpoint "thus gives itself an object of its own production," in Hegel's words. Rather than striving for an objective description of practice, we should understand that it is shared practice that gives the object life, and thus that the latter should no more be captured as an alienated entity to be passively represented. Truth-conditional semantics stems from (and betrays) a realist conception of world-thought relationship. As a result, it condemns itself to submit to the paradoxes of philosophy's self-consciousness, as the *Tractatus* of course acknowledges. It was to this erroneous conception that Wittgenstein alluded in the paragraphs quoted above.

In "Language and Communication," Dummett takes us one step forward, by spelling out why Wittgenstein's radical insights about understanding and meaning must be combined within a systematic approach. He brings to light the connection between realist, representational truth-conditional semantics and the unintelligibility of philosophy, and thus shows why it is that to grasp the full implications of Wittgenstein's radical move what is needed is a firm anti-realist logic and theory of meaning. A resolution of the paradox of self-consciousness in philosophy turns out to be conceivable in light of a revolutionary metaphysics, founded on a new logical basis, which would *finally* liberate us from the platonist and mentalist myths. This revisionist logic should enable us to reformulate the relationship between object and subject, in such a way that self-consciousness would no longer depend on an impossible demand. Thus it is precisely because logic is not merely a formal method but forms a metaphysical system, that the paradoxical nature of philosophy is subdued.

In Hegel's view, Fichte's paradox may be resolved only when a dialectical relationship is bestowed among subject and object. In order to achieve the knowledge sought by philosophy, our notion of experience should change from passive to active. And although what we aim at is the way we represent the world in our thought—our way of knowing reality—we eventually understand that it is also the way we construct reality, the way which renders unintelligible the notion of a reality which is independent of thought, or one that transcends it. "Everything turns on grasping and expressing the True, not only as *Substance*, but equally as *Subject.* At the same time . . . substantiality embraces the universal."[6] What we try to capture in philosophy is a dialectical procedure, which manifests itself in self-developing life, originating from thought but also grasped by thought. Only when substance is seen as generated out of thought, and thought itself is substance rather than an alienated ghostly procedure, are its subjective moments also taken into an objective account and its estranged nature mitigated.

Dummett's guidelines for a theory of meaning are delineated according to this vision of philosophy. This is the understanding which gives rise to his insistence on the incomprehensibility of the notion of an existing lifeless universe (DR, 351ff.; MV, 146f.). The material universe exists *in virtue of* the experience that we have of it. "It exists because we exist" (DR, 352). Like Hegel, and in many respects following Kant, Dummett conceives of a materialist and determinist conception of the world as a philosophy that did not overcome the pitfalls of unjustified analogies from ordinary, objectifying experience. It is based on a strong realist and alienating assumption, which Dummett sees "every reason to reject" (DR, 353). And it is indeed only this assumption that renders philosophy as incapable of gaining truth.

III. PHILOSOPHICAL TRUTH: INDEFINITELY EXTENSIBLE?

But Dummett does not pave an explicit way from such considerations back into their logical source. Although he pronounces his metaphysical creed occasionally, he regards it as "no more than a picture." His preferred direction, as we have seen, is the opposite one: from the principles governing the logical basis to the full metaphysical picture. Here, he believes, is where our situation is better than that of Aristotle and Hegel, his acknowledged predecessors in stressing the immense importance of an appropriate logical basis for metaphysics.

> Where modern analytical philosophy differs is that it is founded upon a far more penetrating analysis of the general structure of our thoughts than was ever available in past ages, that which lies at the base of modern mathematical logic and was initiated by Frege in 1879. (*LBM*, 2)

In order to represent world-thought relationship correctly, an appropriately sophisticated portrayal of the notion of thought is needed. Frege's analysis of thought, based on the notation of quantifiers and variables, sets up for Dummett the logical framework, thus enabling him to build a firmer foundation for metaphysics. Yet Dummett is far from adopting Frege's logic in its entirety. Actually, he diverges from it in one of its most essential components, believing that Frege misunderstood the far-reaching consequences of his own achievements: for a genuine linguistic turn to occur, the logic underlying it cannot be platonist. It is here that Hegelian thought returns to the front of the stage, having been shelved until it could be rephrased in more appropriate terms. Dummett's way of overcoming Frege's cardinal flaw is, famously, by introducing *intuitionist* logic at the basis of metaphysics. It is crucial to see that this move, far from being a "borrowing" of a somewhat debatable technical instrument into philosophy, is motivated rather by the metaphilosophical consideration brought above. Intuitionist logic at the basis of metaphysics yields a whole array of deep revisions. Its repercussions resonate throughout Dummett's work, shaping not only his views of language and of mathematics, but also those of the constitution of reality, the past, vagueness, and phenomenal qualities. It would be too long an excursion to go into a detailed account of how intuitionism, taken as a logical foundation of the theory of meaning, creates the sought-after metaphysical system for Dummett. Yet one detour is indispensable in the present context. It has to do with the notion of the theory of the creative subject—a notion that occupied many logicians in the post-Brouwer intuitionist tradition, and which is thoroughly discussed in Dummett's *Elements of Intuitionism* (335–59).

Following Brouwer, Dummett holds that "a mathematical statement is rendered true or false by a proof or disproof, that is, by a construction, and constructions are effected in time" (*EI*, 336). A new sentential operator, '$\vdash_n$', is introduced, indicating time segments, where '$\vdash_n A$' means 'At the n-th stage we have a proof that A'. This step, as Dummett remarks, involves us in a nonextensional context and hence bears comprehensive results on the nature of logic. Under extensionalist and holist assumptions, the new operator '$\vdash_n$' leads to a self-referential paradox;[7] but if we replace these assumptions by their opposites, that is, divide time into stages punctuated by our effecting constructions and impose a hierarchy upon these constructions, the paradox is avoided. Deliberating on the results of this move, Dummett reaches the following insight:

> To suppose that we can ever arrive at a range of statements closed under the application of this operator is to invoke an intolerably impredicative notion. The introduction of choice sequences defined effectively in terms of the notion expressed by '$\vdash_n$' . . . represents an *extension* of the notion of a construction or a lawlike sequence: although it is a legitimate extension, we have no right to pretend that we have a grasp of any domain of sequences or functions closed under the application of this device. (*EI*, 347)

The theory of the creative subject thus denies the existence of ranges of statements closed under intensionalist operations. The time factor, the inherent appeal to the notion of proof as a way of explaining the truth of statements and the temporal hierarchy imposed upon proofs rule out any final extension of any lawlike (i.e., intensional) sequence. Later in the book, under the heading "Concluding Philosophical Remarks," Dummett spells out for us what this formal result boils down to. It is here where we fully grasp the radical implications intuitionism has on our notions of mathematics, logic, and—since the latter serves as its basis—metaphysics, or philosophy in general.

> The totality of the methods of proof, within a given mathematical theory, is likely to be an indefinitely extensible one: certain methods of reasoning intuitively acceptable to us can be carried out only after we have achieved a formulation of some range of methods of proof not including them. This means, of course, that mathematics undergoes a continual process of evolution. This remark is in itself banal, and would be interpreted by a platonist as meaning that we constantly make advances in our knowledge of the unchanging mathematical reality which we are describing. On any constructivist view of mathematics, on which its subject-matter is our own mathematical activity, and meaning is given to our statements by reference to the methods of proof that we possess, this evolutionary process must be understood more radically, as entailing that the very meanings of our mathematical statements are always subject to shift. (*EI*, 401)[8]

There is of course no strict analogy between the above claims about the mathematical realm and claims about the nature of philosophy. However, one should not be too quick to dismiss the genuine similarity between the two reflective discourses either. In particular, Dummett himself is rather *forced* to such a comparison, because of his own professed use (as opposed to Hegel's) of a structured hierarchy in his conception of metaphysics, where a *formal* consideration of logical principles serves as a basis, outlining the most general features of the theory of meaning. The fact that our model is taken from mathematics rather than pure logic should not hinder us: Dummett frequently derives significant consequences from the mathematical case onto logic.[9] For a constructivist, any kind of truth (and hence philosophical truth as well) is closely related to the notion of proof, or justification. This means that in order to gain insight on philosophical truth, a study of methods of proof *must* be relevant.

As we have seen, Dummett's solution of the paradox of philosophy's self-consciousness consisted in his adoption of anti-realism. Both the complexity and the creativity of philosophical statements, which render them not only trivially true but full of content, result from his fusion of Hegel's understanding of the nature of philosophy, Frege's formal contribution to the analysis of thought, Wittgenstein's insights about meaning, use and representation, and Brouwer's creative conception of mathematics. However, reading carefully the results of the mathematical theory of the creative subject, one cannot but conclude that one important principle of Dummett's must be given up: the finality of philosophical results, and our ability ever to reach the *final* truths of metaphysics. Read with philosophy, instead of mathematics, in mind, the quoted paragraph makes it clear that wherever discursive thought obtains, methods of justification are likely to form an indefinitely extensible totality, evolving in time. The subject matter of philosophy is our own thought, as it manifests itself in our activities, and these are naturally prone to be shaped and reshaped as a result of previous activities and our reflection upon them. Since the meaning and the truth of philosophical statements could not be given them by reference to any unchanging reality, it must be bestowed on them by our ever developing forms of life and of thought.

There is hence for Dummett no alternative but to acknowledge the results of his own revolutionary logical basis of metaphysics: philosophical truth itself is an indefinitely extensible concept. Whatever philosophical achievements we may have gained up to a certain stage in time form only a legitimate extension of the open notion of philosophical truth. It should be noted that this does not affect the *objectivity* of the results. Intuitionistic logic is Hegelian in its intensional emphasis, its serious treatment of time and evolvement, its conception of the subject's role in creating truth, and also in the objectivity of the mathematical results. But once a hierarchy is imposed within the logical basis of metaphysics—once Hegel's holism is substituted by a structure whose elementary layer is more formal[10]—we get a metaphilosophy closer to that of pre-Hegel Fichte, or better even, to that of post-Hegel Collingwood. Both these philosophers understood the metaphilosophical implications of giving a crucial role to the creative subject in forming reflexive, nonempirical truth. For them, philosophical truth is gained by a historical chain of overlapping self-positing acts and is hence under a continuous process of envelopment. After all, "the whole point of our being in time is that we do not have *one* point of view; our point of view is constantly shifting. We do not merely have an experience of succession, but a succession of experiences" (DR, 360). It is inconceivable that such a profound metaphysical insight should not bear on the nature of metaphysics itself.

IV. Meaning as Use; Metaphysics as Radicalism

Frege regarded his notation of quantifiers and variables less as a means of analysing language as we have it than as a device for *replacing* it by a symbolism better designed for carrying out rigorous deductive reasoning, insisting that he had provided not merely a means of representing thoughts but a language in which they could be expressed. (*LBM*, 2)

Dummett undoubtedly takes after Frege here. Far from regarding logic (in particular) and philosophy (in general) as representing, and thus passively accepting, any ongoing practice, he sees them as criticizing our ways of thinking by providing us with a means of expressing the principles governing them. Thus, the role of the logico-metaphysical language has to do directly with its autonomy, its *remoteness* from any "ordinary" discourse. In his conception of the role of logic and metaphysics as of active, creative endeavors, Dummett aligns with Frege, whereas he stands in a diametrical opposition to Wittgenstein, early and late. Wittgenstein's Tractarian move of encapsulating Frege's "ideal," transcendent logic within our ordinary language, and his consequent assertion that "all propositions of our colloquial language are actually . . . logically completely in order,"[11] led directly to his later attack on the very "ideal" nature of logic, and to his well-known, often quoted adage that "philosophy may in no way interfere with the actual use of language; it can in the end only describe it. For it cannot give it any foundation either. It leaves everything as it is."[12] What Dummett seems to suggest is that like Frege, Wittgenstein has not grasped the full consequences of his own ingenious move. Wittgenstein justly replaced the transcendental model of meaning with an immanent one, but then went too far in maintaining that this step entailed the inconceivability of any split between levels within language. Dummett contends that this conclusion confuses the new ideas with some vestiges of the old, Tractarian model of meaning as representation. Logic was empty of content in the *Tractatus* because representation was a necessary condition for having meaning, and being internal to language, logic had nothing to represent. But this condition for meaningfulness should now disappear. To say that logic provides a language in which the basic principles that govern our thoughts are expressed is to see it, indeed, not as representing anything, but as an active procedure of creatively *establishing* these principles. Here lies its meaningfulness. It is undoubtedly to this sharp contrast between the attitudes of Frege and Wittgenstein that Dummett alludes when he regards Frege's work, rather than that of Wittgenstein's, as "a solid foundation for future work in philosophy" (*TOE*, 452). Wittgenstein, says Dummett,

> wished to replace the philosophical study of phenomena by the study of the kind of statement we make about phenomena. But such a study, if it is to yield illumination, cannot accept whatever is normally or frequently said as immune to criticism: statements do not in general acquire authority from the frequency with which they are made. We need, rather, to distinguish what is merely customarily said from what the principles governing our use of language and

determinative of the meanings of our utterances require or entitle us to say...
The distinction does not draw itself, but requires some theoretical apparatus.
(*SL*, 183)

And this theoretical apparatus requires—and indeed, enables—distance.
Giving this distance its proper place within Dummett's thought is substantial for seeing correctly his interpretation of the principle that meaning is to
be analyzed in terms of use, or practice. As we have seen, the replacement
of the representational model of meaning by one that renders meaning in
terms of human activity stems from Dummett's recognition that this is the
only way to overcome the paradoxes of self-consciousness which threaten
the meaningfulness and truth of philosophical statements. Only thus can
metalanguage be conceived as immanent to language, and the subject-object
estrangement be mitigated. However, precisely for this reason, the creative
component of philosophical activity should not be overlooked: this change
of model yields also a change from seeing philosophy as essentially passive,
descriptive, primarily faithful to the level of an "ordinary" *object*-language,
to seeing it as active, imaginative, critical. Dummett says of his metaphysical idea of gaps in reality that it "goes against the grain of our whole way
of thinking," but that "that intuitive repugnance is no ground for rejecting
it" (MV, 146). The same is true of his counterintuitive views of the past and
backward causation. Thus the 'meaning as use' slogan, in its Dummettian
guise, is far from bidding allegiance to "normal" people's intuitions or ways
of speaking. Logic and metaphysics rather form an antithesis to common
sense and "ordinary language":

> Philosophers need make no presumption that the views which, in their
> particular age, make up the common sense of the day are in some fundamental
> sense the true ones, subordinate to which any other conception, whether of
> scientific or of philosophical origin, must find a place if it can. . . . Common
> sense views enter our understanding of the words we use in everyday speech.
> . . . An abandonment of a common-sense view may therefore require a certain
> shift in the understanding of words, a shift rendered more palatable by a
> philosopher's effort to bring the common-sense view to light and to analyse the
> change of meaning demanded. (*SL*, 393)

If the gist of Dummett's metaphilosophy were to be captured in one short
term, this would certainly be "anti-pragmatism." It is clear that whoever
knows "nothing but the present," as pragmatists do, cannot feel the least
sympathy or understanding for his attitude.[13] This precisely is the reason
why Dummett refuses to justify philosophy in pragmatic terms.

> For someone to whom it was of no concern if we had no clear idea of what we
> were doing—who was content with an assurance that what we are agreed on

was true, even though we did not know what it meant, what made it true, or on what basis we believed it—all enquiry into these matters is vanity. (*LBM*, 240)

There is no point in trying to convince pragmatists that "philosophy must be of some use and we must take it seriously," for that would only be taken by them as a confirmation of their own stance, a reduction to practical vocabulary, hence as a surrender. A reform that is motivated by a radical, metaphysical break with our normal ways of thinking, pragmatists regard as dogmatism ("into which we fall so easily in doing philosophy"[14]), since it does not come out of practical, real needs, but rather of "a preconceived idea to which reality *must* correspond."[15]

Ramsey understood that we face two basic rival positions. In the present context they may be regarded as reflecting the two opposing attitudes towards philosophy and practice. According to the first view, any logical or metaphysical proposition should convey a basic loyalty to ongoing practice as a limiting "given." It is, I believe, the position to which the vast majority of analytic philosophers adhere. Analytic philosophy is traditionally conceived as lying between two poles. Its terrain was first outlined by the differences between Russell and Moore, and later by the opposite attitudes of Quine and of Austin. But despite the huge disagreements between these philosophers, there is a lot in common to them, a lot that is shared throughout the wide field of analytic philosophers. I think it would be fair to say of most analytic philosophers that one of their chief goals is to trim metaphysical "nonsense" on the basis of prevalent practice. The differences between the poles are drawn according to the practice they see as primary: natural science, or everyday routines, including "ordinary language."

Although Dummett acts within the traditional analytic agenda, makes use of the analytic logical organon, and is engaged in polemics with prominent analytic figures, he holds the other position regarding philosophy's relationship with practice. His metaphilosophical beliefs in this respect can only find a home on the "continental" side of the philosophical scene. The continental tradition follows the agenda set to it by Hegel, an agenda according to which it is only a "slothful mind" who would say that "logic must be sure to leave us as we were before."[16] Philosophy's remoteness involves freeing us from the hold of ordinary conceptions: "the problem is to become acquainted with them in a new way, quite opposite to that in which we know them already."[17] The reform philosophy offers, then, is radical, and not merely a "pragmatic" correction. What is at stake here is, in Herbert Marcuse's words, the preservation and protection of

the right, the *need* to think and speak in terms other than those of common usage—terms which are meaningful, rational, and valid precisely because they are other terms . . . an irreducible difference exists between the universe of everyday thinking and language on the one side, and that of philosophic thinking and language on the other.[18]

The rival positions cited by Ramsey were presented here as revolving around the metaphilosophical issue of philosophy's relationship with practice. This opposition resonates of the one that is seen by Dummett as the most fundamental in contemporary philosophy, the one between realism and anti-realism. Dummett is never tired of stressing that both sides are, as of yet, sketched merely programmatically, and that it is the most urgent task of contemporary philosophers to work them out. Logic, he believes, will eventually determine in favor of one of these views. I must say that I am much more skeptical. Every philosopher's decision regarding practice and metaphysics, passivity and creativity, realism and anti-realism, is deeply rooted in subjective tendencies. Dummett's own inclination towards metaphysics as a radical means of critique is so basic, that no logical theory contradicting it could be found by him convincing.[19]

ANAT MATAR

DEPARTMENT OF PHILOSOPHY
TEL AVIV UNIVERSITY
OCTOBER 2000

NOTES

I am indebted to Daniele Moyal-Sharrock and Zvi Tauber for their helpful comments on a previous draft of this article.

1. I have used the following acronyms for Dummett's works:

DR: "Dummett's Replies," in *The Philosophy of Michael Dummett*, ed. B. McGuinness and G. Oliveri (Dordrecht: Kluwer, 1994).

EI: *Elements of Intuitionism* (Oxford: Oxford Univ. Press, 1977), first edition.

FOP: *Frege and Other Philosophers* (London: Duckworth, 1991).

FPL: *Frege: Philosophy of Language* (London: Duckworth, 1973), second edition 1981.

LBM: *The Logical Basis of Metaphysics* (London: Duckworth, 1991).

MV: "The Metaphysics of Verification," in *The Philosophy of A. J. Ayer*, ed. L. Hahn (Chicago: Open Court, 1992).

OAP: *The Origins of Analytical Philosophy* (London: Duckworth, 1993).

SL: *The Seas of Language* (Oxford: Oxford Univ. Press, 1993).

TOE: *Truth and Other Enigmas* (London: Duckworth, 1978).

2. See *LBM*, 2.

3. G. W. F. Hegel, *Logic* (1830), trans. W. Wallace, 3rd ed. (Oxford: Oxford Univ. Press, 1975), 36. The emphasis is Hegel's.

4. Ibid. 22f., my emphasis.

5. Ludwig Wittgenstein, *Philosophical Investigations*, trans. G. E. M. Anscombe (Oxford: Blackwell, 1953), ## 120–22.

6. G. W. F. Hegel, *Phenomenology of Spirit*, trans. A. V. Miller (Oxford: Oxford Univ. Press, 1977), 10.

7. The paradox has been brought up by A. S. Troelstra. It is presented and discussed in *EI*, 345f.

8. Note that these quotes are taken from the first edition of EI. In the second edition, the discussion of the creative subject remains the same, but the concluding philosophical remarks are slightly altered and shortened.

9. See, e.g., *EI*, 340 and 402.

10. Not formalistic, though: the logical principles are not devoid of content!

11. Ludwig Wittgenstein, *Tractatus Logico-Philosophicus*, trans. C. K. Ogden (London: Routledge and Kegan Paul, 1933), # 5.5563.

12. Wittgenstein, *Philosophical Investigations*, # 124.

13. The phrase is taken from a remark made by J. M. Keynes regarding the conservative nature of such an attitude.

14. Wittgenstein, *Philosophical Investigations*, # 131.

15. Ibid.

16. Hegel, *Logic*, 27.

17. Ibid., 25f.

18. Herbert Marcuse, *The One Dimensional Man* (Boston: Beacon Press, 1964), 145.

19. This basic assumption is, for Dummett, strongly connected with his belief in God. The linkage is especially evident in his explicit endorsement of idealism in MV and DR. I have determined not to investigate it, and questions relevant to it, in this essay.

REPLY TO ANAT MATAR

When I was still functioning as part of the teaching body of Oxford University, I had the pleasure, and the embarrassment, of supervising Anat Matar's thesis on my philosophy. Normally, I greatly dislike reading other people's writings about my work or listening to their comments on it. But in this case the pleasure greatly outweighed the embarrassment. Anat Matar's perceptiveness, and her agility in connecting apparently disparate things, opened my eyes to facts about my own thinking which I had never explicitly perceived. She understood me very well; she greatly helped me to understand myself better.

I should be happy to think that my work provided a bridge between the analytic and so-called 'continental' schools of philosophy, as is hinted in Anat Matar's concluding remarks, but I doubt that I deserve this tribute. It does not seem to me fair to characterise a principal goal of most analytic philosophers as being "to trim metaphysical 'nonsense' on the basis of prevalent practice." This of course well describes a preoccupation of earlier analytic philosophers, notoriously those of the Vienna Circle; but present-day analytic philosophers do not have the horror of metaphysics that some of their forebears had. That horror might well have evolved into an aversion from cosmologists' speculations—multiverses and the like—which are metaphysical in the pejorative positivist sense if anything is; probably a fear of criticising scientists has inhibited this. Nor is it right to play down the divergence "according to the practice [different analytic philosophers] see as primary: natural science, or everyday routines, including 'ordinary language'." Notoriously, there are those who look forward to a radical reform of everyday psychological terminology: terms such as "motive," "belief," "jealous," "amused," and so on, will be excised from our vocabulary in favour of a new system of terms yet to be supplied by scientists. Clearly, these enemies of "folk psychology" must have a very different conception of the role of philosophy from those who seek patiently to devise a clear account of such a concept as that of intention.

It is true that many analytic philosophers nowadays appear to take realism as axiomatic: they read papers beginning, "I want to develop a realist theory of . . . " or "I want to put forward a realist account of . . . ," without saying why they want to do this, let alone offering a defence of realism. This habit may in part go to vindicate Anat Matar's characterisation of analytic philosophers in general. She is entirely right that I utterly repudiate Wittgenstein's idea that philosophy can change nothing—nothing in our language, in our way of thinking (except when doing philosophy) or, presumably, in our manner of living (though it can induce us to leave of our own accord what we had thought to be a paradise). Human languages are wonderful things, but they can have defects—features that hinder them from fulfilling their purpose; we have only to consider the trouble arising from the lack in English of a pair of words corresponding to "homo" and "vir" to recognise this. Ambiguity—the existence of ambiguous words and ambiguous constructions—is an obvious defect, common to all languages. Gross ambiguity merely prevents us from being certain that we have communicated the thought we meant to express or have apprehended the thought intended; it is only when we all fail to perceive that a word or expression has distinct senses that ambiguity becomes an obstacle to clear thought. In my view, the most serious defects are what in *The Logical Basis of Metaphysics* I called disharmony and instability. These arise when the accepted grounds for using a given form of words fail to match the customary consequences drawn from a use of it. In the book I discussed harmony and stability as applied to the logical constants; but they apply also to many other types of expression, and accepted practice may violate one or the other. A linguistic practice may easily be marred by the twin defects of disharmony and instability. If it is, it needs to be reformed; until this is done, our thinking will go awry.

These considerations supply one of many convergent reasons for replacing classical by intuitionistic logic, insofar as the former is the logic of everyday reasoning. For the classical introduction and elimination rules for negation are in palpable disharmony. This fact points, in my view, to a strong ground for doubt whether classical negation, which has so tight a grip upon our thinking, is genuinely intelligible. (There is something mysterious even about intuitionistic negation. We can give an intuitionistic proof of the completeness of negation-free intuitionistic first-order logic, but demonstrably cannot do the same for the full system with negation. What is it about negation that causes this difference?)

The explanation of what is wrong with classical logic in terms of disharmony between its rules of inference, while thin for those who from the start have their eye on metaphysical consequences, overlooks disharmony in other sectors of language. Wittgenstein was strongly opposed to criticising past societies on the ground that their members reasoned wrongly; his idea was presumably that the way they thought it correct to reason went to determine the meanings of their words, and this they had the right to confer on them as they wished. But the question stands open whether a practice of reasoning in certain ways genuinely conforms as a whole to any coherent set of assignments of meanings to the words involved: there is no reason in principle why it must. Thinking as I do that we ought to replace classical by intuitionistic logic, I am committed to holding that, so far as we do reason in accordance with classical logic, we customarily reason wrongly, as, presumably, Brouwer thought that Hilbert reasoned wrongly.

Towards the end of her most interesting essay, Anat Matar claims that I ought to give up the principle of "the finality of philosophical results, and our ability ever to reach the *final* truths of metaphysics." Her argument is modelled on some remarks of mine about whether the meanings of mathematical statements, intuitionistically interpreted, remain fixed. If the meaning of a statement is given by what would justify asserting it, she argues, it cannot remain fixed, because "methods of justification are likely to form an indefinitely extensible totality, evolving in time." Followers of Lakatos are likely to applaud the thesis that the meanings of mathematical statements do not remain fixed. His excellent examples were based on changes in our understanding of specifically mathematical terms; but the general question is better approached by asking after the fixity of the meanings of the logical constants. A proof of a conditional statement is an operation of which we can recognise that it will transform any proof of the antecedent into a proof of the consequent; since it is required of a proof that we can recognise it as such, the clause "of which we can recognise" cannot be omitted. But in the course of time we can envisage new types of operations, and can come to recognise their effects with greater assurance. Thus the meaning of the sentential connective "if . . . , then . . ." may be said to broaden as we acquire greater mathematical knowledge and insight.

But, while the meanings of mathematical statements do not remain fixed, no mathematician need fear that any theorem he has proved will forfeit its status. He need not think, "What I have done counts as a proof of the theorem now, but may no longer count as one in later years." Provided that his proof was not open to challenge at the time it was presented, it will not be repudiated; for the constructivist as for the classical mathematician, whatever has once been genuinely proved stays proved. For if we have an effective method of transforming a proof of A into a proof of B, we shall always have one, no matter what new operations come to be recognised as effective. The meanings of mathematical statements may change; the truth of mathematical theorems remains inviolate. It may be found advisable to rephrase or reformulate them; they cannot lose their status as established truths. Now there are thousands of theorems, and very few definitive philo-sophical results; but what holds for the former surely also holds for the latter. Philosophy does make some secure advances. Virtually no one would now argue that properties are real, but relations ideal; nor would anyone contend that St. Anselm's version of the ontological argument was valid as it stands. Nevertheless, most philosophical problems remain unresolved. If someone came up with a treatment of the question of free will that struck practically all philosophers of the time as unassailable, the likelihood is that within twenty years someone else would demonstrate grave flaws in it. But it is conceivable that this accustomed sequel would not occur: that the celebrated handling of the problem would continue to be unchallenged. If so, the problem of free will would have at last been resolved.

Doubtless it is true that, to a far greater extent than with mathemati-cians, what a philosopher finds convincing depends upon his intellectual character and general outlook. All the same, I hope that philosophy can be ranked with the sciences rather than with the arts. It would be nonsense to speak of music or of poetry as having come to an end, all that there was to be done having been done. It will not happen, of course, but I do not think it is nonsense to envisage philosophy as coming to an end, all philosophical problems having been resolved. It is in the nature of a piano concerto that it cannot be the piano concerto to end all piano concertos, one that would make it pointless to write any new piano concerto. But it is not in the nature of a treatment of a philosophical problem that there should always remain more to be said about that philosophical problem. If I believed that it was an intrinsic feature of philosophy that none of its problems could be definitively resolved, the subject would for me lose almost all its interest; the point of slogging away at them would be largely lost.

Anat Matar is right to say that I believe that philosophy may call on us to make a radical break with our normal ways of thinking. She is right, too, to say that I do not believe that the alternative to realism that she has induced me to call "justificationism" rather than by the colourless term "anti-realism" has come anywhere near to being fully worked out; especially is this so in regard to its application to the past. It is equally true that philosophers disposed towards realism have made no effort to delineate the limits of realism. Does it, for example, allow us to entertain the possibility that we inhabit only one of a huge, perhaps infinite, number of universes, with no other of which we can have any contact? Although we may most naturally think in realist terms, philosophers of a realist cast have largely failed to address the difficulties that stand in the way of a philosoph-ical justification of realism, difficulties I have been at pains to expound; I have yet to see a convincing defence of realism. I hope that this is not merely because, in Anat Matar's concluding words, no defence of it could be found by me convincing. No doubt our philosophical inclinations are, as she says, "deeply rooted in subjective tendencies." But I should be loth to think that every graduate student is, ineradicably, either a little realist or a little idealist. The opposition between realism and justificationism needs to be rationally resolved, or, if not, dissipated in some manner. I believe that it can be rationally resolved. I do not think that my interest in the question is due only to a subjective tendency; in fact, I think I have an inherent tendency towards realism as strong as most people's. If I had not believed that the problem could ultimately be resolved, I should not have spent so much time on it.

M. D.

8

John Campbell

IF TRUTH IS DETHRONED, WHAT ROLE IS LEFT FOR IT?

Michael Dummett's investigation of a speaker's grasp of meaning, the role that this plays in grounding the validity of logical laws, and the relation of that role to realism, is one of the great works in the canon of twentieth-century philosophy. In this essay I want to sketch out some of his main lines of argument, express some reservations and very briefly suggest some alternatives.

Dummett has recently protested against the idea that a philosopher should be taken to be "writing one long book" all his life. Nevertheless, in setting out what I take to be the main lines of his central arguments here, I have gone back and forth across his work. Dummett is an unusually systematic thinker, and it seems to me that the argument of one piece is often illuminated by the remarks in something else he has written. Nevertheless, I leave it to the reader to judge how far I have put together quite disparate ideas in setting out Dummett's main lines of thought.

I begin by endorsing Dummett's argument that a truth-conditional theory of meaning, thought of as giving the content of a speaker's knowledge of language, should take the form of a properly semantic theory rather than a truth theory. Then I look at the alternative, use-based account of meaning that Dummett recommends instead. This, I argue, ultimately provides us with an unrecognizable picture of our understanding of language. So I go back to look at the prospects for a properly semantic theory as giving the content of speaker knowledge. The prospects, I suggest, are better than Dummett allows.

I. Truth Conditions and the Epistemology of Inference

In *The Logical Basis of Metaphysics*,[1] Dummett distinguishes between two types of truth-conditional theories of meaning. First, a theory may state the conditions for the truth of a complex sentence in terms of the truth of its constituents. A Davidsonian truth theory does exactly this. In contrast, a properly semantic theory shows how the truth, or lack of truth, of the complex statement is determined by the truth or otherwise of its constituents. Simple examples of such a semantic theory are the ordinary truth table explanations of the propositional constants. The general strategy of the book is to force the proponent of a truth-conditional theory to accept the properly semantic account, rather than, as many have attempted to do, clinging to the less ambitious description of meaning by truth theory. Once the truth-conditional theorist is forced into this more exposed position, the approach is subjected to a withering attack, and an alternative approach developed, one that describes meaning by describing the use to be made of statements.

At first the distinction between two types of truth-conditional theory can seem difficult to grasp. Suppose we characterize the meaning of a propositional constant by means of a truth theory. Then we will have, "'A and B' is true if and only if A is true and B is true." What is the difference between this characterization of meaning and that given by a truth table? I think the key point here is that on Dummett's view, the rules of inference governing the sign "and" in the object language cannot be explained by the truth theory. If the rules of inference for the language in which the theory is stated are classical, for instance, then the rules of inference for the object language will be classical too. The truth theory simply projects the logic of the metalanguage onto the object language. Therefore, the description of meaning provided by the truth theory cannot give any insight into why the rules of inference of the object language are right or wrong. In contrast, a truth table describes the meaning of the constant as given by a function from the truth values of the constituents to the truth values of the whole. Whether an elementary introduction rule in the object language is correct will depend on whether it is the least demanding introduction rule that preserves truth from input to output. Whether an elementary elimination rule is correct will depend on whether it is the strongest possible rule that preserves truth from input to output. This kind of approach to the validation of inferences in the object language does not depend on projecting inferences from the metalanguage into the object language. In fact, on this approach, the logic of the object language might be quite different to the logic of the metalanguage.

The distinction between the two types of truth-conditional theory seems vivid when we consider modals. We can in a truth theory state the truth condition of "Necessarily, A," by saying that it is true if and only if necessarily, A is true. That states the condition for the truth of "Necessarily, A" in terms of the truth of A. But evidently it does not show that the truth or otherwise of "Necessarily, A" is determined by the truth or otherwise of A. To show how A's being true or otherwise depends on the semantic values of its components we need a semantic theory which assigns to A a semantic value, such as a set of possible worlds at which it is true, and the stipulation for "Necessarily, A" that it is true if and only if A is true at all worlds. From the truth-theoretic stipulation that "Necessarily, A" is true if and only if necessarily, A is true, we gain no understanding of the inferential link between "Necessarily, A" and "Possibly, A," considered as governed by the stipulation that it is true if and only if possibly, A is true. If a grasp of the metalanguage already provides a grasp of the inferential link, then it will indeed be recognized by the truth theorist, but only the semantic theory will explain why the link exists.

The key point here again is that on a truth-theoretic approach the logic of the object language is maximally sensitive to the logic of the metalanguage. The logical links that exist in the object language will be exactly those that exist in the metalanguage. If the link between "Necessarily" and "Possibly" exists in the metalanguage, it will be inherited by the object language; otherwise not. A semantic theory does not have this sensitivity. A semantic theory for a language with modal operators need not be stated in a language containing modal operators. A semantic theory stated in a classical metalanguage need not ascribe a classical logic to the object language. A Kripke-tree semantics for intuitionistic logic may be stated in a classical metalanguage.

This contrast between a truth theory and a semantic theory is forcefully drawn, but it does not yet explain why, if I am trying to characterize what a speaker knows when he knows a language, I should not settle for what a truth theory has to offer, while acknowledging that it falls short of being a semantic theory. Dummett says that if the notion of truth is to play an important role in a meaning theory, then it seems reasonably clear that the meaning theory must incorporate a semantic theory, then he draws the above contrast between a truth theory and a semantic theory. But it is not yet clear why the contrast matters. Perhaps it is true that a comprehensive account of "how a language functions" will at some point have to include a semantic theory in order to explain why certain inferential patterns obtain in the language, but it is not immediately obvious that anyone who knows that language must have that degree of insight into the functioning of the language. Perhaps this is simply one point at which an account of the functioning of language comes apart from a theory of understanding.

One way to fill out the argument is this: One reason why grasping a language is described as "knowledge" is that it increases one's cognitive powers in a number of ways. For example, having learned a language, it becomes possible to find out things from the testimony of others, and this greatly increases the range of one's knowledge. But learning a language also makes deductive reasoning possible. It makes it possible to get from premises which one knows already to new knowledge, knowledge of conclusions which one did not know already. An account of a speaker's knowledge of language has to explain how it confers this epistemic ability on the speaker. How does the speaker know which sentences are and which are not logical consequences of others? If we describe the speaker's understanding by using a truth theory, we get no understanding of how the speaker has this knowledge. The speaker is ascribed knowledge of the theorems of the truth theory, using a metalanguage in which various inferential connections are assumed to hold, so the knowledge of the theorems of the truth theory may be supposed to be sufficient for grasp of certain inferential connections, in that the speaker would not be said to grasp the theorems of the truth theory unless he recognized those inferential connections. But this tells us only what the speaker knows, and gives us no insight whatever into how he knows it. In contrast, if we assume that the speaker knows the semantics of his language, we can see how it is that the speaker knows which inferential relations obtain. The knowledge depends on the speaker's having some understanding of why those inferential relations obtain, and that just requires that the speaker should know a semantic theory for his language, rather than having his understanding exhaustively characterized by the truth theory.

I think that this line of thought must, indeed, be in the background in Dummett's discussion of the informativeness of deduction, the fact that deduction can yield new knowledge (*LBM*, 195–99). Dummett's point here is that recognition of the validity of an inference often involves an ability to spot new patterns in a sentence one has already grasped as structured in one way. For example, one might grasp, "If you do government business with the chairman, then the chairman will pay your bill" as having the structure "If A then B." So one will be able to infer "the chairman will pay your bill" from "you do government business with the chairman." But one might as yet not realize that it is the same people being referred to in the antecedent as in the consequent. So one will not be in a position yet to grasp the inferential connection between "If you do government business with the chairman, then the chairman will pay your bill" and "Anyone who has his bill paid by someone with whom he is doing government business will be severely reprimanded." These two imply that if you do government business with the chairman then you will be severely reprimanded. To grasp this inferential relation, you have to spot that it is the same people who are being referred to in the antecedent as in the consequent of the conditional. So inferences of the first type are trivial, but inferences of the second type, involving a capacity to spot new patterns in a structure already grasped, can be genuinely informative. This makes perfect sense if we suppose that the speaker grasps a semantic theory for his language. But on a truth-theoretic characterization of understanding, it is very hard to see what this distinction comes to. All that we know about the inferential patterns which the speaker ought to recognize in the object language is that they are the very patterns which obtain in the metalanguage, and since we are given no account of how the speaker knows these inferential patterns to obtain, an ability to spot new patterns in familiar sentences is being given no work to do. So this account of how deduction can be informative, which actually does seem compelling, demands that the subject be thought of as grasping a semantic theory for his language.

If we accept that a truth-conditional meaning theory ought to take a semantic theory rather than a truth theory as its base, is there any objection to the resulting position? The fundamental question here is whether the semantic theory is correct. There is a broad sense in which, given any syntactically characterized set of patterns of inference, we can find some model-theoretic characterization or other of logical consequence that validates all and only those inferences. This is what Dummett calls a "purely algebraic" definition of logical consequence, and the key point here is that such a model theory has no tendency to show that the patterns of inference that it validates are actually correct. The condition on the correctness of a semantic theory is that it should be possible to extend it to a meaning theory for the language. And Dummett's central point is that a classical semantic theory, which takes the semantic value of a sentence to consist in its being true or not, and so is committed to bivalence, cannot be extended to an adequate meaning theory.

Dummett's fundamental point here is that we cannot say what it is to have the conception of a statement being, determinately, true or not true. It cannot, in general, be explained as a matter of our being able to give a verbal explanation of meaning of the statement. But nor could having such a conception be a matter merely of being able to use the statement appropriately in response to the evidence of observation, even when reasoning from observation is needed to confirm or falsify the statement

(*LBM*, 301–21). I will return to this argument in §IV below. For the moment, having indicated what I take to be the main destructive thrust of Dummett's argument, I want now to sketch his positive picture.

II. HARMONY

Dummett proposes an alternative approach to the justification of logical laws, one that will again, though Dummett does not highlight the point, be rooted in the speaker's knowledge of language. The guiding idea here is that our use of language has ends which it may attain more or less successfully, and that we can criticize a way of using language on the grounds that it does not attain those ends (*LBM*, 210). And the primary reason why a use of language can be defective is that our total linguistic practice involves a multiplicity of principles for getting from one state to another, a multiplicity of transition rules. There are principles that we use in verifying statements, and principles that we use in drawing consequences from statements. And for the linguistic practice to be in order, all the various principles we use must be in harmony with one another.

It is important to emphasize that what gives the demand for harmony its normative status is its relation to our objectives in using language. A truth-conditional semanticist might have made a similar claim about his way of validating the use of particular rules of inference. The "mythology of truth conditions" was attempting to describe the objectives we have in our use of language. Our knowledge of what it is for a proposition to be true was thought to define the objective at which our ways of establishing the proposition aim. On the face of it, though, when Dummett describes the approach in terms of harmony, he describes it as one that tries to determine whether our ways of using language do indeed achieve our objectives in using language, without appealing to semantic notions at all. We can ask and answer the question whether our ways of using language achieve our objectives, without using the notion of truth.

The question of harmony comes up in many ways. For example, we can ask whether there is harmony between what we might call different evidential perspectives. On the face of it, if you say "I see a tree," you do so on a quite different basis from that on which I say of you, "You see a tree." And the question arises whether these different ways of finding out are correctly related to one another. Or again, if on one day I say "Today it's raining," I do so on a quite different basis than that on which I say, the following week, "A week ago it rained," and again we can ask about the harmony between these different evidential perspectives. And even if we stay with a single evidential perspective, we can ask whether there is harmony between the perceptual basis on which one makes a judgment, and the consequences for action that one takes the judgment to have.

In *The Logical Basis of Metaphysics*, Dummett's concern is with a still further aspect of harmony: the demand for harmony between the introduction and elimination rules for a logical constant. Given a particular set of introduction rules, we do not want the elimination rules to allow us to derive unwarrantedly strong conclusions, but we do want them to allow us to derive all the conclusions to which we are entitled. What is striking about Dummett's approach is that he attempts to give a proof-theoretic approach to harmony. The central question this raises is whether we can explicate harmony in syntactic terms; again, as I said, without appealing to the notion of truth at all. On the face of it, indeed, there is a straightforward way to get this effect. Suppose we have an introduction rule for each logical constant. This tells us when a statement with that constant as its principal operator is justified, in terms of the conditions under which the sub-sentences are justified. Call an argument canonical if it begins with atomic sentences as premises and uses only these introduction rules. Then we can say an arbitrary argument, perhaps with complex premises, is valid if, given canonical arguments for its premises, we could construct a canonical argument for its conclusion. Using this procedure, we could justify the elimination rules for the logical constants. For example, given the introduction rule for "A&B," any canonical argument for "A&B" will let us derive a canonical argument for A and a canonical argument for B, so the elimination rules are justified. We can also have a procedure that takes the elimination rules as basic. An arbitrary argument will then be valid if any atomic consequence that could be drawn from its conclusion, using only the elimination rules, could already be drawn from its premises, using only the elimination rules. We can use this idea to evaluate proposed introduction rules. For example, suppose we have the usual or-elimination rule, taken as given. Consider now the usual or-introduction rule. The upshot of any application of the introduction rule will be a statement with "or" as its principal operator, to which we can apply the elimination rule. But any conclusion that we get by applying elimination rules here could also have been obtained by applying elimination rules to the premises of that application of the introduction rule; and that validates the introduction rule.

Consider now the case of classical negation. The elimination rule is, from not-not-A to infer A. That will validate the introduction rule, that from A we can infer not-not-A, and that is all; it does not show how to validate any other introduction rule. The introduction rule we want, for classical negation, is that if, from A as hypothesis, we can derive not-A, then we may discharge the hypothesis that A and conclude not-A. Can we take that introduction rule as given, and use it to justify the elimination rule?

Evidently not: to obtain the premise of an application of the elimination rule, not-not-A, we need to derive not-not-A from the hypothesis that not-A. But that does not of itself give us a way of deriving A by use of the introduction rules alone. So it does seem that by this criterion, the classical rules for negation are not in harmony with one another.

All that we have supplied so far, though, is the point that we cannot see from the rules themselves that classical negation is harmonious. So a speaker who simply grasps those rules does not thereby have the right to use them. The conclusion Dummett draws is only that these rules cannot be regarded as giving a meaning to classical negation. It remains a possibility that there are some empirical facts, relating to the meanings of the particular sentences to which negation is applied, in virtue of which it could be seen to be harmonious. In that case, a speaker who knew the rules and knew those empirical facts would indeed have the right to use classical negation, though it would have lost its status as a logical constant. But this is only an abstract possibility. It is not easy to see, even in outline, what the relevant empirical findings might be.

What exactly does this point establish? Does it show that classical negation should be abandoned? Conservativeness really does matter if we plan on giving only a syntactic explanation of a logical constant, if we are only going to give introduction and elimination rules for it in order to explain it, with no semantic foundation. A logical constant so understood is really just a trick to facilitate inference, and what we want to be sure of is that its use will do no harm; at the same time, we would like to be sure that we are getting as much as we can out of the device. The proof-theoretic account explains how to secure that. But this applies only to the case in which we are trying to rest with a purely syntactic account of the functioning of a constant.

One way of trying to rescue classical negation would be to find a purely proof-theoretic definition of harmony on which something like the classical rules can be seen to be after all harmonious. But the more fundamental question is whether we really can define our objectives in using negation in purely syntactic terms. What makes it seem compelling that classical negation is intelligible is not our shaky grasp of the possibilities for various types of proof-theoretic approaches, but the apparent intelligibility of the classical truth-table. The basic question here is whether it really can be right to think that our objectives in using language are properly described as merely a demand for harmony, without any appeal being made to the notion of truth. If we can dispense with the notion of truth in describing our objectives in using language, then the demand for harmony really does have the global significance that Dummett ascribes to it. If classical negation is not harmonious, then it cannot be explained in purely syntactic terms;

everyone should agree to that. It is a more far-reaching claim to say that if classical negation is not harmonious, then it should not be used at all. This claim depends on the idea that our objectives in using language can indeed be explained in purely syntactic terms.

It is difficult to see how Dummett can avoid making this claim, that the normative demands of language can be characterized in purely syntactic terms. It seems to follow from the abandonment of truth-conditional theories and the consequent insistence on an absolute demand for harmony in the rules of inference for logical constants. It is also quite difficult to see how Dummett can be right about this, for reasons that he more than anyone else made vivid. In a famous early discussion of the notion of truth, Dummett said, "It is part of the concept of truth that we aim at making true statements."[2] The question here is how much weight that remark will bear. Does the appeal to the notion of truth do any work whatever in describing the objectives that we have in using language? If so, then it cannot be right to give a syntactic conception of harmony the overpowering force that Dummett gives it in determining whether our uses of language serve their objectives, and we cannot dismiss the use of a logical constant simply on the grounds that it is not harmonious. On the other hand, suppose that the appeal to the notion of truth does no work in characterizing our objectives in using language. That is, suppose that we can give a complete normative description of the whole enterprise without appealing to the notion of truth. In that case the demand for harmony, syntactically characterized, can indeed be sustained. But we have lost what seemed to be one of Dummett's central insights on the notion of truth. It does not seem too strong to say that we have deprived language of its point.

III. AIMING AT TRUTH

How does Dummett see the role of the notion of truth in an account of the functioning of language? He raises the question whether a statement, for a given language, of the conditions under which each of the sentences of that language is true, constitutes an explanation of the notion of truth for that language. He remarks that one might know all the clauses of a truth definition of this type for a language, and still have no idea how to go about speaking the language. So it must be possible to explain how the truth of a sentence is related to the use we ordinarily make of it. A first response is to say that in assertion we aim at making true statements. But it must be possible, Dummett says, to explain why we go in for the practice of assertion at all; it must be possible to say what we are about in making assertions. And a theory of the functioning of language, of this most general type, may be taken to explain what truth is.

This problem was first raised in Dummett's early article, "Truth." When we make a statement, we are characteristically trying to tell the truth. This means that an explanation of truth has to do more than simply assign every statement to one of two classes, the truths and the rest. It is not enough for the explanation to get it right about the extension of the concept of truth. It also has to make comprehensible the point of the concept, the way in which the classification relates to our interests. The beginning of the explanation is that we aim at truth in assertion. But we can further ask why that is what we do, why we engage in that activity of assertion.

There is a use of the notion of truth, in remarks such as "Everything Bill said was true," which does seem capable of being explained by a Tarskian truth definition, which simply specifies, for each sentence of the language, what it is for that sentence to be true. This use of the notion of truth does not involve any picture of the functioning of language; it is when we go beyond that use, and ask in general how the truth of a statement relates to the use we make of it, that we need the richer account of truth envisaged by Dummett.

In *Frege: Philosophy of Language*, the response Dummett gave to his question, "What is the point of the practice of assertion?" emphasizes the role of assertion in communication. He holds that there are features of the assertions in any given language which are, by convention, the features that make them assertions, and the convention in question is "to utter such sentences with the intention of uttering only true ones."[3] However, he continues, this description of the convention

> did not make clear the point of this convention, which can be stated in a general way as follows: we learn to react to the statements of others in the same way that we react to various observed features of our environment. . . . It is thus essential to the activity of assertion that the making of an assertion will in general modify the behaviour of those to whom it is made. (*FPL*, 355)

So far as I know, this is the only place where Dummett gives a direct reply to his famous question about the point of engaging in assertion. The problem with a disquotational theory was said to be that it did not characterize the point of our practice of assertion; that it missed the importance of the fact that in making assertions we aim at truth. This comment, that "we learn to react to the statements of others in the same way that we react to various observed features of our environment," is what we are to use to fill in what the disquotational theory missed.

The striking thing about this comment is how little the appeal to truth now seems to contribute to the normativity of language use. Suppose that we have two speakers of individual idiolects. We can describe the way each of them uses language as a pattern of use of sentences in response to observation. We can suppose that this pattern of use is described in entirely syntactic terms—at any rate, without having to appeal to semantic notions. And we can suppose that each speaker individually meets the normative conditions of harmony in use of the idiolect. So far, there has been no appeal to the notion of truth in characterizing the point of their practice. Suppose that now we introduce a disquotational notion of truth for each idiolect, and add the condition that each speaker is to aim at making only true assertions. This will not actually affect what either speaker does, since the pattern of use for sentences not involving the word "true" will be exactly as it was before. All that has been added is that each idiolect now has a communicative function, and presumably that the speakers should individually be aware that they will each be reacting to the statements of the other in the same way that they each react to "various observed features" of the environment. If before the introduction of the notion of truth each speaker was operating simply as a manipulator of syntax, it is difficult to see that there has now been a radical change in the situation.

The pressure Dummett puts on the question, "In what does knowledge of language consist?" inevitably leads to the view of the individual speaker as the determinant of the meanings of the signs. Certainly the syntactic account of harmony does not acknowledge any essential place for the social character of language. Suppose we ask just what is being conserved when we conservatively extend our practice. Well, what more is there to the practice than the rules governing the logical constants? A further factor is the connections that the sentences have to perception and action. Ultimately, what the proof-theoretic justification procedures are checking is that the use of a particular set of introduction and elimination rules will not disturb those connections that our sentences have to perception and action: that we will not be able to derive excessively strong consequences for action from a given range of perceptions, and that we will be able to derive all the appropriate consequences for action from those perceptions, rather than some unduly weak set. The presupposition here is that the connections between perception and action in our practice are all in order as they stand, and that the task of deduction is merely to respect them, while letting us see them more readily in particular cases. On this view of harmony, one's own perceptions and actions provide a basic perspective, which has to be conservatively extended by any new modes of thought.

Once we have dethroned the notions of truth and falsity from their fundamental place in the theory of meaning, and have argued that the normative constraints on the use of sentences are provided by the syntactic criteria of harmony, we seem to be driven to this kind of picture of the functioning of language. Dummett is more alive than most to just how alien this picture of language use is to our ordinary understanding of the situation; I do not think that he would want to endorse this account. The trouble is that we face a dilemma at this point. One possibility is that we should return to the picture on which our understanding of the sentences of our language consists in knowledge of what it is for them to be true or not true, knowledge derived from our knowledge of the references of their parts. This would mean that we do not face the threat of having to suppose that our understanding of language is a matter entirely of syntactic manipulation. Alternatively, we can persist with the dethronement of truth and falsity, and describe merely the use that we make of sentences. But what role shall we find for the dethroned? The trouble is to see how there can now be any significant role for the notions of truth and falsity in setting the norms of language use. The best we can do is to consider the attenuated role envisaged by Dummett, on which they have to do merely with management of the social aspect of the use of language. There is no reason why a single speaker of an individual idiolect could not meet the criteria of harmony in use of that idiolect; talk about the notion of truth merely signals that we are envisaging the possibility of communication and the responsibilities it brings with it.

This does not seem to do justice to how fundamental the practice is of aiming at truth in assertion. I can bring this out by returning to Dummett's original talk of explaining how the practice is connected to our interests. One way of trying to give the explanation is to insist that aiming at truth is instrumental for other concerns that we have; another approach is to say that it is something we do "for its own sake," something which we can understand by locating it in a broader perspective of interdependent objectives we have, of which aiming at truth is one. At first sight these approaches seem to exhaust the alternatives, and the problem with them is that they leave it seeming that aiming at truth is simply one among many interests that we have. On these approaches, someone who did not go in for aiming at truth at all might be a bit deviant, like someone with no interest in music or in playing games, and we might try various ways of getting him or her to take up this life-enhancing practice. But if we failed, our subject would be, as it were, otherwise normal. The problem is that this does not really seem to be an intelligible scenario: there would be nothing left in respect of which our subject could be said to be "otherwise normal." The problem is really to articulate that datum: to explain why aiming at truth is so fundamental to human life that without it, no distinctively human interests would be left.

In section I, I set out Dummett's case for a truth-conditional theory of meaning to be a properly semantic theory, rather than merely a truth theory. It seems to me that this case is compelling. I think therefore that we have to look again at the prospects for a properly semantic truth-conditional theory of meaning. The syntactic conception is not recognizable as an account of our ordinary understanding of language, and it does not seem to be possible to patch it up by finding supplementary supporting roles for the notions of truth and falsity.

IV. THE OBJECTION TO A TRUTH-CONDITIONAL MEANING THEORY

Could not our grasp of a classical conception of truth be displayed by our use of classical reasoning? Could it not be that the reason we ascribe a grasp of a classical conception of truth to people is exactly that we want to explain their use of classical reasoning? So far as I have been able to see, Dummett does not explicitly address this natural response in *The Logical Basis of Metaphysics*. I think, though, that an answer is implicit. The fullest and most illuminating presentation of the line of thought here comes in an earlier article, "The Justification of Deduction":

> The model of meaning in terms of truth-conditions can be vindicated only by reference to the whole language. If we consider a fragment of natural language lacking the sentential operators, including negation, but containing sentences not effectively decidable by observation, it would be impossible for that fragment to display features embodying our recognition of the undecidable sentences as determinately true or false. (*TOE*, 316)

The key point to notice here is that the conditional claim is persuasive. Suppose we did have a logic-free fragment of language. What would that fragment look like? Would it contain structured sentences? Typically when we discern structure in language we are discerning inferential structure; but here there are, on the face of it, no inferences to demand structure. It is hard to see how we could even discern singular reference in such a fragment: no complex predicates, no negation. We seem to be describing a "feature-placing" fragment of language, containing only various unstructured ways of responding to the environment, various cries with which to greet the various features that occur, "Hot!" "Foggy!" and so on. Consider someone who has only this unstructured language, and suppose for the moment, for the sake of argument, that some of these feature-placing sentences are not effectively decidable by observation. Could there be anything about such a speaker that would persuade you that the speaker understands those sentences in such a way that they are, determinately, either true or not true? It seems immediately evident that there could not be. Once you try to spell out why not, though, you are liable to be charged immediately with reductionism or behaviorism about meaning. The natural question to ask is:

"What could there be in the use that someone made of an unstructured sentence such as 'Frosty!' that could make it so that he was understanding the sentence as not effectively decidable, and yet bound to be determinately, either true or not true?" The idea that the speaker is interpreting the sentence as subject to bivalence seems evidently a fantasy, even though it is hard to spell out why without seeming to appeal to a behaviorist conception of understanding. Suppose, for the moment, we give Dummett the conditional claim, that the speaker grasping a logic-free fragment of language cannot understand these sentences as subject to bivalence. What follows from this? Evidently, we now have to concede that "The assumption of bivalence for such sentences shows itself only in the acceptance of certain forms of inference, classically but not intuitionistically valid" (*TOE*, 316). The classical truth-conditional semantics cannot be demanded for the logic-free fragment of language. It is not as if we can suppose that bivalence is already established for the atomic sentences of a language and then look at what constraints this puts on the introduction of logical constants:

> Even if the two-valued semantics, the realist model of meaning in terms of truth-conditions, is required for the extended language, it was not required for the original fragment. So far as our use of the original, logic-free language was concerned, there was no need to invoke a notion of truth going beyond the recognition of truth. The model in terms of truth-conditions indeed supplies a representation of the content of the atomic sentences, to which the classical logical laws are faithful; but it is a representation which was not called for by the linguistic practices which existed before the logical constants were introduced. A very clear case would be that of the past tense in a language in which there were no compound tenses, and in which the past tense, considered as an operator, could not be subjected to any of the ordinary logical constants: in such a language nothing could reveal the assumption that each statement about the past was determinately either true or false. (*TOE*, 317)

Again, the conditional claim here seems compelling. Suppose we do consider someone using a fragment of language in which he has only simple past-tense statements, such as "Rained," and no complex tenses, no logical constants. Would there be anything in this person's understanding of such a fragment that could constitute grasp of bivalence for those simple statements? It again seems evident that this is a fantasy; any argument on this simply laboring the obvious. So why should we ever appeal to the truth-conditional semantic theory in which it is taken that every statement is determinately either true or not true? "It thus becomes conceivable that a certain model of meaning is required *only* in order to validate certain forms of inference the employment of which is part of our standard practice"

(*TOE*, 317). And now Dummett claims his conclusion:

> It is just this which an opponent of a realist model of meaning finds incredible: he cannot believe that a grasp of a notion of truth transcending our capacities for its recognition can be acquired, and displayed, only by the acceptance of certain forms of reasoning. He concludes, instead, that these forms of reasoning, though generally accepted, are fallacious. (*TOE*, 318)

The idea is that the notions of semantic theory to which we appeal in explaining the validity of inferences should not be allowed to become posits, invoked to explain inference without having any independent grounding. It is not hard to sympathize with this concern. If we resist the idea of a purely algebraic approach to validity, on which any inference we like can be regarded as valid because there will be some notion of model available to underwrite it, do we not have to explain in what sense we can be said to know the semantic theory that validates correct inferences, otherwise than merely by making those inferences?

Nonetheless, it seems to me that the focus on a logic-free fragment of language pushes the point too far. The following pair of claims seems consistent:

(a) There is such a thing as grasp of a classical semantic theory for one's language, and it is one's grasp of a classical semantic theory that explains the correctness of the inferences in which one engages.

(b) Grasp of a classical semantic theory can be exercised only in connection with reasoning and inference. A subject who possessed only a logic-free fragment of language would have no use for semantic notions, and could not put them to work.

This way of putting the point does immediately invite the three questions on which Dummett focuses in *The Logical Basis of Metaphysics*. These are:

(1) What is it to grasp a semantic theory for your language? This cannot be identified with the capacity to engage in suitable reasoning; it is rather to be what makes it right for you to engage in those patterns of reasoning. Dummett's claim is that there is nothing we could find to constitute grasp of the references of the expressions of our language; all we find are ways of using sentences in response to experience.

(2) Once we have characterized what it is to grasp the truth conditions of sentences, we face the problem of explaining how the capacity to use those sentences can be derived from that grasp of truth conditions. And, Dummett says, there evidently is no way in which the ability to use a sentence could be derived from a grasp of truth conditions.

(3) Even if we get this far, we shall find that there is no way in which we could, ordinarily, know that you and I are associating the same references with the same signs. All we can observe is the use that we make of the signs. The alleged grasp of truth-conditions, lying behind the use that is made of the signs, cannot itself be observed; it is ultimately unknowable. (See *LBM*, 301–21.)

We do have to answer those questions if we are to sustain the roles of truth and falsity as central to the theory of meaning.

V. Experience as Acquaintance

I will not here try to give a comprehensive response. I will try to indicate what I think the promising lines are. For the moment, though, I hope it is enough if I have indicated why I think we should persevere with truth-conditional semantic theories, and that Dummett's objections should be viewed as helpful impositions of constraints rather than as indicating fatal errors in the approach.

I think that a key point is one that generally goes unremarked: the role of experience in our understanding of language. Dummett, like almost everyone except Russell who writes on meaning, implicitly takes it that the only role experience can play in our understanding of language is to allow us to verify sentences about our surroundings. But the role of experience may be to acquaint us with the references of our terms, just as Russell thought. There seems to be no obvious reason why the fundamental role of experience in understanding should not be to provide us with knowledge of reference, and ultimately knowledge of truth conditions.

As I said, moreover, it does press Dummett's point too hard to insist that it must be possible to display grasp of the semantic theory in relation to grasp of a logic-free fragment of language. It may be that grasp of the references of the parts of a sentence can be exercised only in connection with reasoning and inference; that does not of itself mean that grasp of references has to be exhausted by engagement in a particular style of reasoning.

The same point applies when Dummett develops his second argument against the truth-conditional conception. Assuming that we associate classical truth conditions with the sentences we use means, he says, that we cannot explain how the ability to recognize the truth of statements is derived from knowledge of their truth conditions (*TOE*, 306–11). However, an opponent may respond by putting pressure on the kind of "derivation" in question here. What is required is not that the speaker should, without using any principles of reasoning or evidence, somehow extract the right principles to use in confirming a statement, from a grasp of the truth-condition of that statement. That would indeed be an impossible task, analogous to the task of providing what Dummett calls a "suasive" justification of deduction (*LBM*, 202). Rather, all that can be asked is that the speaker's grasp of truth conditions should provide what Dummett calls an "explanatory" justification of those principles of confirmation. A truth-conditional theorist need not work with a picture on which the speaker is simply given knowledge of the truth conditions of statements, with no idea how to verify them or draw implications from them, and then left to get on with it. Rather, we should think of the speaker as being provided with a mass of techniques for reasoning, confirming, and acting on the basis of statements, together with a grasp of the truth conditions of those statements. So long as the grasp of truth conditions provides the speaker with an explanation of the point of those techniques, that is all the "derivation" that is required.

Is the situation here that I am postulating various patterns of reasoning as being absolutely constitutive of conceptual thought, and that the notions of truth and reference have to be regarded as being indeed mere posits that we invoke to try to justify our use of these patterns of inference? Certainly not. It is part of the general picture I am recommending that there is a role for experience in our understanding of basic concepts. And the role of experience is to acquaint us with the semantic values of those concepts; truth and reference are not here mere posits. Our encounters with the references of our terms are as direct as any encounter could be.

This is particularly vivid in the case of perceptual demonstratives. There are some basic patterns of inference in which we use demonstratives, such as those involving identity and complex predicates, or existential generalization:

This thing is F
This thing is G
Hence, this thing is both F and G.

This thing is F
Hence, something is F.

The reference of the term "this" is not a mere posit invoked to explain the validity of the inference; it is an object with which you are directly confronted. You understand the term "this" only because you have experience of the object. And this provides you with an explanatory justification of the validity of the arguments above.

If we take the full force of Dummett's argument that I outlined in section IV above, though, we would have to regard these patterns of inference as being justified by the fact that they provide conservative extensions of a more primitive, feature-placing level of language. Dummett does indeed begin to sketch how such a program might go (*FPL*, 570–83). But from our present perspective this aim seems misplaced. We begin in the middle. There are certain patterns of reasoning we regard as fundamental, and we are acquainted with the semantic values of various basic concepts. This acquaintance with semantic values supplies an explanatory justification of the patterns of reasoning. There is no need to attempt to reconstruct the whole enterprise by asking whether it conservatively extends some more basic fragment of language.

The second line of response I want to suggest to Dummett's argument against a truth-conditional semantic theory begins by remarking a certain solipsism implicit in the approach in terms of harmony. One way to bring this out is to consider what I earlier called the demand for harmony between different evidential perspectives. This comes up most sharply when we consider statements involving indexicals. For example, we want there to be harmony between the basis on which Jack says "I see a tree," and the basis on which someone else says of Jack, "He sees a tree." And we want there to be harmony between the basis on which one says on one day, "It is raining," and the basis on which one says, a week later, "A week ago it rained." To understand how there can be harmony here, we need the conception of a single world on which there are many evidential perspectives: a single world on which one's current evidential perspective is simply one among many. And it is not just that this conception has to be something that the theorist can formulate: it must be available to the subject, if the subject is to have any grasp of what is going on in the coordination of his current evidential perspective with his own past evidential perspectives and other people's current evidential perspectives.

What allows us to transcend this solipsism is that we each have the conception of our own causal relation to the world, to each other and to our own past and future selves. We are not simply agents who intervene in the world; we know what we are doing and what is being done to us. This reflective grasp of agency provides us with an understanding of what we are about in our actions. It means we have an understanding of why we act as we do, and why in particular we observe the things that we do. We grasp that what we observe depends in part on what is there, waiting to be observed, and in part on our own position in the world, our own relation to it. Dummett has often stressed that having this idea of the world as there, waiting to be investigated, is an ingredient in our ordinary notion of truth. But this is not something to which we have to win our way by means of increasingly tenuous extensions from the primitive fragment of language in which there is no distinction between truth and verification. Rather, this reflective understanding of our own causal relation to the world is part of our most primitive grasp of concepts. Grasp of our causal relation to the world is constitutive of the capacity for conceptual thought.

Let me relate this line of thought to the project of explaining the point of our interest in truth; explaining why we aim at truth. Dummett's challenge was to explain the way in which the concept of truth relates to our interests. How should we do that?

It seems to be a precondition of our having any desires whatever that we also have some beliefs or other; desiring something would have no impact on our behavior unless we had some beliefs about how to bring it about. And surely the formation of beliefs involves aiming at truth. One might suggest that this gives a kind of transcendental account of the point of aiming at truth. It is not that it is connected with some interests that we happen to have, but rather that it is a precondition of our having any interests whatever. But if aiming at truth is given a role only as the necessary complement to desire in the mediation of perception and action, the point of aiming at truth is still being explained in terms only of the mediation of perception and action.

It seems to me that this notion of truth is actually all that we need for the judgments and beliefs of creatures that have only first-order desires and no way of criticizing or correcting their desires. But this is not the ordinary human case. We do tell ourselves stories about what we are up to in our actions, stories which articulate a picture of our causal relations to the environment and each other, and which we use to explain, justify, and correct our motivations. This capacity for causal narrative construction is really basic to ordinary human motivation. I want to suggest finally that we see the point of the ordinary notion of truth as its being something aiming at which is a precondition of this kind of narrative construction. So the point of the notion of truth is not that it meets some particular desires we have, nor that aiming at truth is a precondition of desire in general, but that it is a precondition of the kind of motivational structure that separates us from many other animals; the kind of motivational structure which makes us free agents.

At one point in *The Logical Basis of Metaphysics* Dummett speaks of himself as leading a mountaineering expedition which he plans to take no further than the foothills. I have been arguing that it is possible to complain about the direction in which we are being taken, that we are missing the best routes, and so on. It is consistent with that to acknowledge that the whole topography with which we are grappling—the mountains and the lakes, the glaciers and the swamps—all sprang into being in response to his probing.

JOHN CAMPBELL

UNIVERSITY OF CALIFORNIA, BERKELEY
FEBRUARY 2005

NOTES

1. Michael Dummett, *The Logical Basis of Metaphysics* (London: Duckworth, 1991), hereafter *LBM*.

2. Michael Dummett, "The Justification of Deduction," in *Truth and Other Enigmas* (London: Duckworth, 1978), 2. Hereafter *TOE*.

3. Michael Dummett, *Frege: Philosophy of Language* (London: Duckworth, 1973), 354. Hereafter *FPL*.

REPLY TO JOHN CAMPBELL

I applaud John Campbell's opening exposition of, and support for, my view that what we need is a genuine semantic theory rather than a mere truth-theory in the style of Davidson; Campbell has grasped the point of the opposition I posed between theories of these two kinds and has expounded it brilliantly. Why should I not be content with a truth-theory for which the metalanguage was governed by intuitionistic rather than classical logic? Such a truth-theory would be perfectly practicable, and would spare me from the charge of wishing to dethrone truth. But it would be inadequate because, as Campbell makes clear, it would be helpless to explain why intuitionistic logic was the right choice. Pitted against a Davidsonian truth-theory based on classical logic, there would be no argument in its favour—at least no argument derived from the truth-theory itself; correspondingly, Davidson would have had no argument that his version of the truth-theory was preferable.

Do I wish to dethrone truth? Well, what is truth?

There are many different kinds of thought one may have. And as Wittgenstein insisted, there are many different things one can do with language: blessing, cursing, telling jokes, recounting anecdotes, describing one's symptoms to a doctor, writing poetry, presenting prizes, appealing for funds, and so on and so on. But all the different uses of language employ words; and they rely on those words' having meanings. What is it for a word to have a meaning? We shall not get very far if we say just that it contributes to the effect of a string of words of which it is one in accomplishing one of the multifarious purposes of which a sample was listed above. How does it come about that a word can subserve all these different purposes? That is not because the word has a variety of different functions. It may do, but that is not here to the point. It is not that it has a different meaning according to the different purpose it contributes to effecting: the word can subserve quite different purposes even though it has just *one* meaning—the word "seldom" for example.

How are we to explain this? Here is a more or less universally accepted explanation. The use of sentences—sentences of different kinds—can usually be explained by taking them to be related in different ways to states of affairs which those sentences delineate. (It would be wrong to say that the sentences *describe* those states of affairs: rather, they identify them, they present them.) It is because the meanings of most sentences can be (partially) characterised in this way that Donald Davidson was able to get away with the claim—to my mind the preposterous claim—that a truth-theory of the type he advocated could constitute the entire theory of meaning for a language. It is natural to allow a description of the different relations that sentences of different types have to the states of affairs they specify. (That is, the different forces—assertoric, interrogative, etc.— attached to them.) It remains that there is a core of meaning common to sentences of the various types—the delineation of a state of affairs. And it is to the delineation of that state of affairs that most words in the sentence contribute. That is why a word can have a constant meaning in so many different sentences.

But what then is truth? For the most part we apply the word "true" as a tribute to only one class of utterances—those that serve to assert that the state of affairs delineated obtains. Such an utterance was true if that state of affairs *does* obtain. If it does not obtain, the utterance was false. Any specific state of affairs either obtains or does not obtain, a realist will aver.

But, now, what is it for a state of affairs to "obtain"? Well, the realist might reply, it is just for there to be such a state of affairs: obtaining is for states of affairs what occurring is to events and existing for types of objects. Surely that must be wrong. There is such a state of affairs as there being fewer than ten and more than seven people in a certain room at a particular time, while there is no such state of affairs as there being fewer than ten but more than nine people in the room at that time: but this is surely not the contrast that the realist intended.

Infuriated, the realist says that this spurious difficulty was caused by the introduction of the phrase "state of affairs," which he proposes to abandon. He suggests that we should say that what most sentences have in common is that they delineate a way things may or may not be. Either things are that way or they are not, he says: if the speaker was making an assertion, then what he said was true if things are that way, and false if they are not.

Well, the only thing I want to quarrel with in what the realist has now said is his dictum that either things are a provided way or they are not— given that the way in question is anything at all that we may intelligibly assert to be so. But has the realist really escaped the difficulty about what obtaining is by descending to this more commonplace mode of expressing himself? We were wanting to know what truth is, and have been told that an assertion that things are a certain way is true if things are that way. We are entitled to ask what it *is* for things to be a certain way. Perhaps the progress of such an enquiry is best presented in dialogue form.

Q: What is it for things to be a certain way?

R: I can explain only by example, of which there are many sorts. Let me take one of the simplest. You go out of your front door and see and feel that it is snowing. You have recognised that things are a particular way, namely that it is snowing here now.

Q: Yes, that is how those of us who live where snow commonly falls first learn what it means to say that it is snowing at some place and time. But surely we can tell when it snowed at some other time, or that it is snowing at some other place.

R: Yes, of course. You may remember seeing it snow a week ago, and you might be told—say over the telephone—by someone at a different place that it was snowing there.

Q: Yes, indeed. Memories first introduce us to the use of the past tense, while we are trained to understand and to accept what others say. But cannot we know that things were that way—that it was snowing at some place and time—even though there was no one to observe that it was so?

R: Certainly. We learn to reason according to certain canons, both deductively and inductively, and we may sometimes be able by this means to conclude that it must have snowed at a certain place and time.

Q: I understand all this perfectly well, and agree to it. But why do you insist that either things are a given way or they are not?—for example that either it snowed at a certain place on the earth's surface at some given time or it did not snow there then, even in the absence of anyone to witness it or any reason to think it occurred or that it did not?

R: Well, if someone had been suitably placed, he would either have observed it snowing or he would have observed that it was not snowing.

Q: Indeed he would. But are you not committing a logical fallacy? You cannot validly argue from "If someone had been there, he would have seen it snowing or not snowing" to "Either it is the case that if someone had been there, he would have seen it snowing, or it is the case that if someone had been there, he would have seen that it was not snowing." In symbols, you are inferring from an undoubtedly true statement of the form

$$P \mathbin{\square\!\!\rightarrow} (Q \vee R)$$

to a statement of the form

$$(P \;\square\!\!\rightarrow Q) \lor (P \;\square\!\!\rightarrow R),$$

and that is an invalid inference.

R: So you are saying that it may be neither snowing nor not snowing at a given place and time?

Q: I am saying that we have no right to assume that it is determinately either snowing or not snowing at any given place and time.

R: But whenever we observe the weather anywhere, we always see that it is either snowing or not snowing there. We never see it in an in-between or half-and-half state.

Q: And you'll never see Schrödinger's cat half alive and half dead, either —I mean half in perfect health and half stone dead.

R: Oh, well, if you're going to appeal to quantum mechanics, and dubious quantum mechanics, at that. . . .

Q: I'm not appealing to quantum mechanics; I'm just saying that it's what we should expect. Whenever we observe anything, we always observe it as in a determinate state. That is no ground for assuming that everything is always in a determinate state, even when unobserved.

Q has here argued against a thesis about truth—that it is bivalent. Implicitly, he is maintaining a particular conception of truth, namely that a statement is true only if there is a ground, direct or indirect, for taking it to be true. What is his reason for doing so? He thinks that what grounds warrant accepting a given statement is what we learn when we learn language, together with the consequences that should follow upon our acceptance of it. He does not think that these need to be represented as distinct components of meaning, because in a well regulated language, there should be harmony between them: either will then determine the other. Admittedly, our language may prove not to be well regulated. In that case, our linguistic practice is to that degree incoherent: it is not the task of a theory of meaning to describe an incoherent practice. Of an incoherent practice there can be no coherent description.

So Q's conception of meaning is that someone knows the meaning of a statement if he knows what counts for speakers of the language as a justification for asserting the statement. R, on the other hand, thinks that one knows the meaning of a statement if one knows the way things must be for the statement to be true; he adds that every definite statement—one that can be judged either true or false—is, determinately, either true or false: things either are the way it says they are or they are not.

So have I dethroned truth? Q, in the foregoing dialogue, of course represented my views; but *he* surely was not pulling truth off her throne. Campbell's argument that I have tried to do so centres on the notion of harmony. More exactly, on the twin notions of harmony—our not deriving unwarrantedly strong conclusions from a statement, given what we have accepted as admissible grounds for asserting it—and what I called "stability" —our allowing ourselves to derive all the conclusions we are entitled to, given the grounds on which we asserted it. Campbell brackets these together as "harmony," which is perfectly legitimate. In *The Logical Basis of Metaphysics*, I spoke of both of these as requirements upon a language if it was to function as it ought—if it was to serve faithfully the purposes for which we use language. I illustrated both notions in detail for the logical constants; but I intended this as illustrative of a general demand upon all expressions of a language. I had in mind harmony between grounds and consequences in all cases; Campbell mentions other varieties of harmony, for instance, between different grounds for accepting a statement. These are perhaps legitimate subjects of enquiry, though I cannot see how one would set about it. Certainly it does not seem feasible in the logical case: what would it mean even to ask whether there was harmony between the two introduction rules for "or"—to infer "A or B" from A and to infer "A or B" from B?

Campbell observes, quite truly, that my demonstration of harmony for the intuitionistic logical constants in *The Logical Basis of Metaphysics* was purely syntactic: it did not invoke the notion of truth or any other semantic notions. It is this that prompts him to conclude that I wish to dethrone truth. Now it is quite true that my discussion of the logical constants was purely syntactic; but I did not intend this as a precedent for the treatment of harmony in respect of all other expressions. The logical constants are a special case in that grounds and consequences of statements in which they are the principal operators can both be represented as rules of inference—introduction and elimination rules respectively (thanks to the natural deduction formalisation of logic due to the genius of Gerhard Gentzen). Given this, a syntactic treatment of harmony lies to hand. The essential point in the case of harmony proper is the eliminability of an application of an introduction rule governing the logical constant in question immediately followed by an application of an elimination rule governing the same logical constant. If the elimination rule enabled us to infer more than the introduction rule entitled us to do, we should not be able to dispense with its use; but if we could have arrived at the conclusion of this application of the elimination rule without making the detour consisting of an application of the introduction rule immediately followed by an application of the elimination rule, then harmony prevails between them: the elimination rule does not allow us to infer more than the introduction rule entitled us to infer.

The fundamental principle of the converse of harmony, which I labelled "stability," is equally simple. Suppose we have assumed the standard introduction rules for "or," to infer "A or B" from A and to infer "A or B" from B. And suppose the only elimination rule for "or" that we recognise is the restricted version of the standard rule that does not admit side premisses in the two subordinate deductions. This rule is that we may infer from "A or B" whatever follows from A on its own and also follows from B on its own. The rule holds in quantum logic, whereas the full, unrestricted standard rule does not; the restricted rule does not allow derivation of the distributive law, which accordingly fails in quantum logic. Now this restricted rule is in harmony with the two introduction rules; but the unrestricted rule is also in harmony with them. Hence there is instability in our logical practice: we do not allow ourselves to infer from a disjunctive statement as much as the introduction rules we employ would entitle us to infer.

Both harmony and stability in respect of a logical constant can thus be established by purely proof-theoretic arguments: semantic considerations do not need to be invoked. But it does not in the least follow that in cases other than the logical constants the demonstration of harmony and stability will not appeal to semantic notions. Very often the grounds for a given form of statement will not be expressible as rules of inference—for reports of observation, for instance; even more often the consequences of accepting a given form of statement will not be so expressible, but will consist in certain types or courses of action. Moreover, in *The Logical Basis of Metaphysics* I had another interest than expounding the notions of harmony and stability: I wanted to explore the idea that we give the meaning of a logical constant by laying down the rules of inference that govern it. This involved asking for which rules of inference we are entitled to *lay down* that they shall hold. I tried to discover syntactic criteria to answer this question. In no way was the proof-theoretic enquiry that I carried out intended to teach the moral that we could do without the notion of truth and without a semantic theory.

Even though Campbell has misunderstood me in this matter, he proceeds to develop an argument about the role of the concept of truth in an account of our use of language, intended to support a truth-conditional theory of meaning. The argument runs as follows: Suppose that we consider two speakers of a language. We may first regard them as employing idiolects—their own personal versions of the language. And suppose for the sake of argument that these idiolects conform to the requirement of harmony and stability, and that these can be formulated without appeal to the notion of truth or of other semantic notions. Now what use is there for the notion of truth in an account of these two speakers' use of language? Well, first, when they utter sentences in accordance with a certain convention—when they engage in the practice of assertion—they do so aiming to make only true statements. Why, then, do they engage in this practice? Each does so with the intention that the other, understanding him and accepting what he says, will be able thereby to build up the picture of the world that he has formed by means of his own observations—that he will be able to use what his colleague has told him as if he had himself observed or inferred that it was so. Here for the first time we encounter the social aspect of language: the two speakers are not just employing idiolects, but conversing in a language shared between them. But does this account of the role of truth in an account of our use of language suffice to make clear the centrality of the notion of 'aiming at truth'? Suppose that one of the two speakers chose not to go in for making assertions. It could not be said that he was like someone who did not care for music or saw no point in playing games, but was otherwise normal. Although Campbell does not do so here, we could bring this out by asking whether, in refraining from making assertions, he also refrained from making judgements: if he did not, surely he would aim at making only true judgements. If he did refrain from making judgements, in what respect would he be normal? How, then, can we explain why truth is so central a notion?

In response to this question, Campbell first concentrates on the principle of bivalence. He is right to do so: it is bivalence that principally distinguishes a truth-conditional theory of meaning from a justificationist one, just as it is the law of excluded middle that principally distinguishes classical from intuitionistic logic. Campbell first considers my argument in *The Logical Basis of Metaphysics* that the acceptance of the principle of bivalence cannot be considered as manifested simply by the use of classical logic. The recognition as valid of principles of inference must be grounded on our understanding of the logical constants involved, and, if also on our understanding of the sentences to which they are applied, then on features of those sentences which they could be recognised to possess independently of the application of those very principles of inference. But if the sentences were, as far as possible, used just as we use them, but were part of a language not containing any logical constants, there is no way in which a recognition that they were determinately true or false independently of our knowledge could be manifested. The acceptance of the principle of bivalence can therefore be manifested solely in the use of rules of inference that can be validated only by appeal to that principle itself; and this is a circular procedure not entitled to serve as justifying either those rules of inference or that semantic principle. Such was my argument. A glance at Ian Rumfitt's essay in this volume will allow us to add that using classical logic does not unequivocally manifest acceptance of bivalence; in a falsificationist semantics it can be validated without appeal to that principle.

Campbell objects that this argument, from considering a logic-free language, goes too far. Is it not consistent to hold that someone might grasp the classical (two-valued) semantics, and on its basis reason classically, although his grasp of it could be manifested only by his so reasoning, since one whose language was logic-free would have no use for semantic notions and could not put them to work? Whether it is consistent or not depends on whether it really is possible to grasp the classical semantics.

In the chapter on truth-conditional meaning-theories in *The Logical Basis of Metaphysics* (301–21), on which John Campbell comments, I criticised such theories for their treatment of two classes of expression: words expressing basic notions and statements admitting no effective method for deciding their truth or falsity. A word expresses a basic notion if we cannot state the condition for its application without circularity, and we do not determine that it applies *by* anything (in the sense in which we determine the application of "square" by verifying or judging that the sides are equal and at right angles one to the next): I gave the examples of "yellow" and "pain." The truth-conditional theorist must hold that one who understands such a word must grasp a condition for its application: it is because we all grasp the same condition that we agree by and large when the word applies. Such a condition would be incommunicable and a grasp of it private; postulating it is idle and fails to explain anything. What is significant is the fact of general agreement on the application of such a term; it is a speaker's participation in this agreement that is the criterion for his understanding it. This argument was my attempt to capture the core of Wittgenstein's attack on private ostensive definitions.

If there is no effective method for deciding the truth-value of a statement, but the statement must be either true or false, then it may be true even when we are unable to recognise that it is. The whole thrust of a truth-conditional theory of meaning is to sunder understanding from knowledge of truth: to understand a statement is to know the condition for it to be true, independently of whether we know its truth-value, or can know this, or how we might know it if we can. This is very clear in Frege's writings, not only in his proclamation that being true has nothing to do with being taken to be true, but in his repeated enunciation of the condition for the definiteness of sense of a predicate. For a predicate to have a definite sense, he says, it must be determined for every object whether or not it falls under the concept for which that predicate stands. He always hastily adds that this does not mean that *we* can determine this: reality determines it, one might say, whether we are able to do so or not.

It is unclear in what the knowledge of a condition that cannot be recognised as obtaining whenever it obtains can consist. It appears that the truth-conditional theorist wishes to explain a speaker's grasp of the proposition expressed by a statement as consisting of his knowledge of another proposition—the biconditional giving the condition for the statement to be true. But knowledge is idle unless the knower can make use of it; in *The Logical Basis of Metaphysics* I pressed the question how the speaker's knowledge of the condition for the truth of the statement was supposed to be delivered. It seems impossible to explain this; as I said, the alleged knowledge is ascribed all the properties of a piece of explicit, statable knowledge save that it is not explicit. It has all the marks of a creature of philosophical mythology.

Campbell quite rightly attributes to me the view that grasping a semantic theory cannot consist just in reasoning in accordance with it; it is a conception that justifies those modes of reasoning. But, even if we interpret "reference" to mean "semantic value," I am not happy with his ascription to me of the thesis that "there is nothing we could find to constitute a grasp of the references of the expressions of [the] language; all we find are ways of using sentences in response to experience." This makes it sound as though I do not believe in semantic theories at all. On the contrary, I think a good semantic theory is a means of making explicit the speakers' inchoate grasp of the way their language functions. But this grasp is manifested in their linguistic practice—in their ways of using sentences in response to experience. Only an erroneous semantic theory will attribute to the speakers a grasp of conceptions that cannot be so manifested.

The second problem cited by Campbell in his summary of my chapter is how a speaker can use his supposed grasp of the truth-conditions of statements in his language to determine the use he makes of them. The salient features of this use are what he takes as justifying the assertion or acceptance of a statement, and the consequences he takes to follow from such acceptance—both what can be inferred from it and the actions it mandates. A justificationist theory of meaning treats the meaning of a statement as determined by the former; a pragmatist theory takes it as determined by the latter. Assuming harmony between grounds and consequences, either is fixed by the other. Such theories of meaning take the meaning of a statement to be determined by a central feature of its use. Truth-conditional theories, by contrast, are at pains to sever meaning from these aspects of use: how, then, can someone who has mastered the truth-conditions of statements that can be made in the language come to know, from their meanings, how those statements are to be used? Being true is indeed distinct from being taken to be true: we frequently take to be true what subsequently proves to be false or groundless. We can, and constantly do, make mistakes: we reason wrongly and misestimate probabilities. But there is a connection between being true and being taken to be true. Our canons of reasoning, deductively and inductively, are aimed at arriving at the truth, and are justified only insofar as they are rightly so aimed; our reports of observation are based on training to give true reports of what we perceive. That we frequently misapply those canons and stumble in assessing the information provided by our senses does not annul the connection between truth and our methods of attaining truth; and this connection needs to be explained on the basis of a sound theory of meaning. A truth-conditional theory is well placed to justify our canons of deductive reasoning, provided that it first be agreed that every definite statement is determinately either true or false: but on what grounds can this assumption be based?

The third question Campbell elicits from my chapter is how it can be known what conception of meaning another speaker has. What one speaker can observe about another is that he uses the language in the same way as himself. But according to a truth-conditional theory each speaker's grasp of the meanings of a statement made in the language consists of associating with them a condition for it to be true. How can it be known by anyone else what condition a speaker associates with each statement? Much can be told from his use of the language. But of a statement for which we do not have an effective means of determining its truth-value, how can we know what truth-condition that other speaker associates with it? This association of truth-conditions with statements is an internal state of mind, however it is to be explained. So far as we have been given any reason to believe, it is not uniquely determined by the use the speaker makes of the language. Hence, so far as we know, the meanings the other speaker attaches to the statements of a language which he uses just as I do may be different from those I attach to them. Of what use is a theory that allows of such a possibility?

I experience some difficulty in replying to Campbell's response to my criticisms of truth-conditional theories of meaning, since I find myself agreeing with very much of what he says, and yet cannot see it as fatal, or even greatly damaging, to my position. He opens by saying that he will not try to give a comprehensive response. If he had, I should doubtless have had other, perhaps greater, difficulty in answering him. He then proceeds to emphasise the role of experience in our understanding of language: only Russell comes well out of this. I applaud Campbell's work in connecting the phenomenon of attention with our grasp of reference; I do not want to discard the notion of reference, and give no weight to Davidson's permutation argument to show that we should dispense with it in favour of that of truth. There is a difference between the justificationist and the truth-conditionalist accounts of reference. For the justificationist, a grasp of the reference of a term consists in an ability to recognise the referent or, failing that, an effective procedure for identifying it; this seems to fit Campbell's ideas very well. If the object no longer exists, it must be known how, when it existed, it could have been recognised or identified. For the truth-conditionalist, a grasp of reference consists in the knowledge of the condition something must satisfy in order to be the referent. If someone is able to recognise the referent upon perceiving it, I do not know that we can characterise his ability as knowledge of such a condition. Campbell sees no reason why the "role of experience in understanding should not be to provide us with knowledge of reference, and ultimately knowledge of truth-conditions." The gulf between knowing the reference of singular terms and knowing the truth-conditions of statements seems to me too broad for leaping.

Campbell questions my use of "derived" when I asked how the use of statements could be derived from their truth-conditions. He says that we learn their use *together with* their truth-conditions. We then see that their truth-conditions give the point of the use they have learned: "that is all the 'derivation' that is required." I could be content with that if I could be convinced that our learning the practice of using our language could be faithfully described as learning the truth-conditions of our statements, classically understood as determinately either obtaining or not obtaining. Perhaps it could for a restricted segment of the language. I do not see that it could quite generally.

Campbell criticises my justification of rules of inference as conservatively extending a primitive "feature-placing" language by objecting that we do not in fact begin with such a language, but "in the middle." Well, a child's first stage in learning language closely resembles a "feature-placing" one; but indeed the child does not have the concept of a conservative extension. I have never used the term "rational reconstruction," but it could be said that that is what I was about here. It is not philosophically out of place to consider the most primitive part of a practice, and explain the rest as growing out of that, without suggesting that this is an empirical description of the actual process of learning and adopting the practice. No doubt in fact "we begin in the middle"; this does not invalidate a consideration of how things would stand if the logically prior had been the temporally prior.

Campbell proceeds to give an excellent account of how we come by a conception of the world as something of which we are parts, but only parts. I might object that he is here doing what he rebukes me for doing, by showing how we may build up from an initial solipsism to a conception of the objective world: do we not begin in the middle in this case, too? I do not in the least wish to deny that we have such a conception. The question is whether it need be a conception of a world in which each detail is objectively filled in or whether it can be one under which some details are left undetermined. Possibly which of them seems more natural depends on whether you believe in God or not. I have had people say to me that belief in God hangs together with the realism I am disposed to reject. Quite the contrary. If you think of the objective world as the work of a creator, it is perhaps easier to understand how that creator may have left some details indeterminate, just as a human "creator" may do with the imaginary world he fashions, than to think likewise if you believe the world is uncreated.

A justificationist of the sort I describe is no solipsist. He takes the truth of a statement to rest on there having been grounds justifying its assertion available to any rational creature, if suitably placed, living or dead. Truth, for him, depends on there being or having been a means of knowing—not in *his* knowing, but in its being known. He thus sidesteps Campbell's demands for a demonstration of harmony between one person's grounds and another's, perhaps at a different time. I confess I am unclear whether and how this can be demonstrated.

Campbell asks, finally, *why* we aim at truth. A preliminary answer is that to have desires and any means of satisfying them requires also having beliefs, and the formation of beliefs involves aiming at truth. This is all the notion of truth needed to account for the judgements and beliefs of creatures that have only first-order desires and no way of criticising or correcting them. But we are not such creatures. We can reflect on our knowledge, scrutinise our motivations, consider our plans and our way of life. We can confess our sins; we can ask others to forgive our faults. We "tell ourselves stories about what we are up to," Campbell says, and he claims that the point of the notion of truth lies in its being a precondition of this narrative construction that we aim at truth. Aiming at truth, he concludes, is a precondition of the structure of motivations that separates us from other animals and makes us free agents. I do not want to contest Campbell's claim, nor to endorse it. If our having first-order beliefs and desires makes truth central, I do not see that our having second-order ones can make it more central, or central in a different way; but perhaps he sees further than I do. I rejoiced at Campbell's hymn to truth. But I have a complaint to make.

The tenor of Campbell's justification of our aiming at truth suggests that he conceives of himself as defending truth from *me*. What he says does not go to defending the classical two-valued conception of truth, but, rather, to defending truth itself. Campbell really does seem to believe that I want to jettison the notion of truth. I do not: I believe it to be indispensable. I think we need it as what is preserved from premisses to conclusion of a valid deductive inference. We need it as what holds good of the content of an objectively correct assertion. It is what we aim at in making an assertion, or in forming a belief. It is what we search for in any enquiry. Philosophy, mathematics, physics, history would all be pointless if there were not truths to be discovered. Where I differ from Campbell is in my conception of what truth is. For me only what is knowable can be true: of a true statement we can have no sound reason to believe for sure that we can never know it. Campbell does not need to defend truth from me. He needs, rather, to make clearer how he conceives of truth, and to defend that conception.

M. D.

9

Wolfgang Künne

TWO PRINCIPLES CONCERNING TRUTH

Principles C and K are the topics of this essay. This announcement bears spelling out, I suppose. In his 1976 essay "What is a Theory of Meaning? (II)" Michael Dummett used 'Principle C' as a nickname for the correspondence intuition which is expressed by

(C)   *If a statement is true,*
       there must be something in virtue of which it is true,[1]

and 'Principle K' served him as the title for an epistemic constraint on truth:

(K)   *If a statement is true,*
       it must be in principle possible to know that it is true.[2]

In Part I of my paper ("Varieties of Making True") I try to get clear about Dummett's understanding of Principle C by comparing and contrasting it with similar principles endorsed by other philosophers from Aristotle to Armstrong (§§1–4). In the course of expounding Dummett's conception I register a feature which I find confusing (§5). In Part II ("Vagaries of Knowledge") I first relate the varieties of making true to the issue of alethic realism (§6), and finally, after bracketing "ideal verificationism" (§7), I comment on a surprising move, surprising to me at any rate, which Dummett recently made with respect to Principle K (§8). For alethic realists (like myself) this move has a gratifying aspect, but all things considered they would be well advised, so I shall argue, not to accept it.

I. VARIETIES OF MAKING TRUE

1. *Aristotle and the Principle C*

Here is the passage in which the first principle was given its name:

(D-1)   "If a statement is true, there must be something in virtue of which
         it is true. This principle underlies the philosophical attempts to
         explain truth as a correspondence between a statement and some
         component of reality, and I shall accordingly refer to it as the
         principle C. The principle C is certainly in part constitutive of our
         notion of truth." (WTM II, 52)

Aristotle is generally regarded as the initiator of all "attempts to explain
truth as correspondence between a statement and some component of
reality," and he appears to make a claim to the effect that a truth owes its
truth to something, is true in virtue of something, is rendered or made true
by something, when he says:

> It is not because of (διά) our having the true thought that you are pale, that you
> are pale; rather it is because of your being pale that we who say so have a true
> thought.

> It is because of (τω) the thing's being, or not being, thus and so that the
> statement is said to be true or false.[3]

On one interpretation of this remark (the other readings will have to wait for
a while) the intended message is best conveyed if we replace the preposition
"because of" by the connective "because" and accordingly substitute a
sentence for the gerund phrase. Then we obtain: "The statement that you are
pale is true, because you are pale," and the general point can be captured by

(SCHEMA P) If *the statement that p* is true, then *it* is true because p.

Is Aristotle's contention (thus understood) plausible? Certainly it would be
ridiculous to answer the question "Why is Socrates pale?" by saying:
"'Because it is true (to think or say) that he is pale." We would rather expect
answers like "Because he is ill" or "Because he has just received bad news."
But do things really look better the other way round? If our question is
"Why is it true that Socrates is pale?", we would normally be annoyed if we
were told: "Because he is pale." (This looks more like an answer to
questions like "Why does Xanthippe feel sorry for Socrates?".) Again we
would rather expect answers like "Because he is ill" or "Because he has just
received bad news." The reason for this is, I think, that 'It is true that p' and
'p' are cognitively equivalent. But then, how *are* we to understand the
question 'Why is it true that p?', if 'Because p.' is supposed to be a *proper*
answer? Roderick Chisholm once called the Aristotelian answer "Aristotle's
basic insight" concerning truth, but unfortunately he did not pause to
explain it.[4]
     One might be tempted to explain this alleged insight by an argument
which invokes (an instance of) the Denominalization Schema:

(Den)   It is true that p, if and only if p.

After all, Aristotle himself was very well aware that "if it is true to say that so-and-so is pale . . . , then necessarily he is pale; and if he is pale . . . , then it was true to say that he is."[5] This is clearly meant to generalize, and if we do so we obtain (the universal closure of) the (modally strengthened) Denominalization Schema. Jean Buridan calls this principle *regula Aristotelis*.[6] Let "s" abbreviate "Socrates is pale." Why is it true that s? An appeal to Aristotle's Rule and a look at the man would seem to deliver the answer:

(1)	It is true that s if (and only if) s.	Aristotle's Rule
(2)	s.	perceptual judgment
(3)	Therefore, it is true that s.	1, 2 *Modus Ponens.*

But this immaculate little deduction does not really capture Aristotle's alleged insight. The following argument appealing to the other direction of Aristotle's Rule is equally sound:

(1*)	It is true that s (if and) only if s.	Aristotle's Rule
(2*)	It is true that s.	perceptual judgment
(3*)	Therefore, s.	1, 2 *Modus Ponens.*

Certainly this reasoning does *not* answer the question why s. But if the soundness of the second argument does not rationalize the bizarre claim, 's because it is true that s', it is hard to see why the soundness of the first argument should legitimize the contention 'It is true that s, because s'.

By endorsing Principle C, Dummett seems to confirm Aristotle, and he clearly distinguishes this principle from the Denominalization Schema when he writes:

(D-2)   "The correspondence theory expresses one important feature of the concept of truth which is not expressed by the law 'It is true that *p* if and only if *p*' . . . : that a statement is true only if there is something in the world *in virtue of which* it is true." ("Truth," 14)

As we just saw, (Den) really fails to capture this alleged feature of the concept of truth. For the same reason, (Den)'s sibling, the Disquotation Schema

(Dis)   'p' is true if and only if p,

does not capture it either. Quine thinks otherwise:

> Truth should hinge on reality, and it does. No sentence is true but reality makes it so. The sentence 'Snow is white' is true, as Tarski has taught us, if and only if real snow is really white.[7]

Surely this will not do. Predicates like 'x is made true by y' or 'x is true in virtue of y' signify asymmetrical relations, so we cannot preserve the point of a slogan like "No sentence is true but reality makes it so" by using a "symmetrical" (commutative) connective, even if we embellish the right-hand side of the biconditional by a generous use of "real(ly)." The Disquotation Schema is no substitute for the principle which that slogan encapsulates.[8]

Elizabeth Anscombe finds talk of "making true" intelligible only if one truth is said to be made true by a different truth. Logical Atomists have presented one kind of example which meets this condition. Suppose somebody asserts that either Socrates or Seneca drank the hemlock. Then the question may arise who did, and if somebody answers that Socrates did, he can intelligibly be said to have told us what makes that disjunction true.[9] By contrast, Anscombe finds a statement to the effect that a certain proposition is made true, but *not* by the truth of any other proposition, hard to understand:

> A proposition can't make itself true: we have to gloss the statement and say '[the proposition that] p is made true by the *fact that p*'. If we have a Tractatus-like metaphysic of facts this would be possible: we would have reached an elementary proposition, made true by the existence of an atomic fact. But without such a metaphysic we are only saying [that the proposition that] p is made true by its being the case that p, or by its being true! That is an empty statement, with only a false air of explanation. And so in the end we'd have to accept . . . propositions which are true without being made true. If this seems shocking, that is because of a deep metaphysical prejudice.[10]

Now we are in a quandary. Does Aristotle give voice to a basic insight or to a deep prejudice?

And there is a further question which needs to be considered: Does Principle C really articulate Aristotle's alleged insight if we take the latter to be captured by Schema P? Consider the locution "true in virtue of something" in Principle C. There are uses of "something" in which it does not subserve quantification into singular term position ("There is something that Solomon and Socrates both are, namely wise"), but in Principle C the prepositional phrase "in virtue of" enforces such a reading: The open sentence ". . . is true in virtue of . . ." is, so to speak, a singular-term hungry on both sides. It goes well with this that in some of his formulations of the principle Dummett expands "something" into "something in the world" or "some component of reality." So apparently the point of Principle C can be conveyed by

(SCHEMA X) If *the statement that p* is true, then for some x, x makes *it* true.

By contrast, Schema P does not contain any quantification over objects in the world or components of reality. Davidson seems to contest Principle C and Schema X when he writes: "Nothing, no thing, makes sentences and theories true: not experience, not surface irritations, not the world, can make a sentence true."[11] But does he thereby deny "Aristotle's basic insight"? One would hope not, if the latter deserves its laurel. But if not, then there must be at least two varieties of making true.

2. A Propositional Reading of "Making True"

In order to clear the ground for an attempt at explaining the first variety of making true, let us stand back for a while and ask: how are sentences of the type 'x makes y such-and-such' to be understood? Often we use them to ascribe a *causal connection:* "Sunshine makes the flowers grow." "Sandra's arrival made Alec happy, her departure will make him sad." Some ordinary applications of 'x makes y *true*' are also to be understood causally: "She had announced in advance that she would visit him, and yesterday she made her announcement true." Here something is made true by the efforts of an agent.[12] Perhaps the Almighty, by a remarkably efficient illocutionary act, made it true (brought it about, saw to it) that there was light. But obviously this use of "making true" is far away from the philosopher's use: By assenting to Aristotle's, or to Dummett's, tenet one is not committed to endorsing any, let alone each, instance of the schema: 'If it is true that p, then some agent or other brought it about that p'. (Surely one does not incur a commitment to theism by subscribing to Schema P, or to Schema X, for that matter.)

But then, sentences of the type 'x makes y such-and-such' are not always to be understood causally. Look at the following example: "This molecule consists of two hydrogen atoms and one oxygen atom, which makes it a water molecule." We might just as well say: "This is a water molecule because it consists of two H-atoms and one O-atom." This is not the "because" of causal explanation but rather that of *theoretical reduction:* chemical theory tells us that being water is having a certain molecular structure. But obviously the "because" in Schema P is not that of theoretical reduction either. So we are still in want of a model for understanding it.

Happily, talk of x's making y such-and-such is not confined to these two kinds of uses. Consider

(R)   He is a child of a sibling of one of your parents,
        which makes him your first cousin.

In other words,

(R*)   He is your first cousin
        because he is a child of a sibling of one of your parents.

This is the "because" of *conceptual explanation:* the second part of (R*) elucidates the sense of the first part. If we take the use of "make" which is

exemplified by (R) as our model for understanding philosophical pronouncements like

(S)   The fact that snow is white makes the statement that snow is white
        true,

then they do not affirm a relation of any kind between a truth vehicle and
something in the world.[13] There is no reason to ban claims of type (S), but
their point can be made without mention of facts:[14]

(S*)   The statement that snow is white is true, because snow is white.

And we can understand (S*) along the same lines as (R*): Why is it correct
to say of him that he is your first cousin? The second clause of (R*) gives
the answer. Why is it correct to say of the statement that snow is white that
it is true? The second clause of (S*) gives the answer. Of course, there are
differences as well: Unlike the sense of "first cousin" that of "true" can be
elucidated (at least partially) by a sentence which contains *no* component
expressing it. And by contrast with the "first cousin" case, (S*) does not
give us a *full* account of the sense of "true." To be sure, Schema P, whose
consequent is instantiated by (S*), is equally hospitable to all propositionally revealing truth ascriptions, but as it stands it does not elucidate propositionally unrevealing applications of "true" ("The Pythagorean Theorem
is true," "Everything the witness said was true").

The intelligibility of sentences like "It is true that either Socrates or
Seneca drank the hemlock, because Socrates did" or "It is true that
somebody drank the hemlock, because Socrates did" is conceded on all
sides. Will Anscombe's doubts concerning the comprehensibility of substi-
tution-instances of 'It is true that p, because p' be allayed by pointing out
that one can make sense of (S*) without invoking a "Tractatus-like
metaphysic of facts"? Presumably not, for she thinks that (apart from a few
"quite particular situations") ascribing truth to the proposition that snow is
white, or even to the sentence "snow is white," comes to the very same
thing as saying that snow is white, and if these identity claims are correct
then one might think that (S*) is, as Anscombe puts it, "an empty statement,
with only a false air of explanation."[15] Elsewhere I have argued against both
identity claims.[16] Apart from those identifications Anscombe offers no
reason for her harsh verdict on statements like (S*). Furthermore, even if
two sentences 'p' and 'q' have the same conventional linguistic meaning,
uttering 'q because p' with assertoric force may *not* be making an empty
statement, with only a false air of explanation: Examples like (R*) above
show this.[17]

So much for the first variety of making true.

3. *An Ontic Reading of 'Making True'*

In my attempt at spelling out the Aristotelian insight along the lines of Schema P, I took for granted that the same sentence can be used both in the specification of what *is* true and in the specification of what *makes* it true. No such presupposition is visible in Principle C or in Schema X. David Armstrong implicitly denies that presupposition when he says:

> Every truth has a truthmaker. The truthmaker for a particular truth is that object or entity in the world in virtue of which that truth is true. . . . The truthmaker is the "correspondent" in the Correspondence theory of truth, but with the repudiation of the view that the correspondence involved is always one-one. The discovery of what are in fact truthmakers for a particular truth can be as difficult and controversial as the whole enterprise of ontology. . . . A truth-maker must . . . necessitate the truths that it is a truthmaker for. It must not be metaphysically possible for the truthmaker to exist and the truths not to be true.[18]

This reading of "making true" is common among Australian and Austrian (self-styled) realists. What renders a truth-candidate true they are prone to call a "truth-maker."[19] I shall model my discussion on the Austrian variant of the theory. According to this theory, no truth-maker is a fact, and all truth-makers for empirical truths are parts of the natural (spatio-temporal causal) order.[20] Suppose the statement that p is an atomic empirical statement which is true. Then you specify its Truth-Maker, if you answer the following question:

(TM)   Which part of the natural order, x, is such that

   (i)   the existence or occurrence of x ensures that the statement that p is true, and

   (ii)   x is what that statement is about or what it reports on?

Let me first run through some examples before I try to motivate the details of this formulation. Substituting for the sentence letter in (TM) (a) 'Caesar was assassinated', (b) 'Philip of Macedonia begot Alexander, (c) 'Alexander was angry', (d) 'Bucephalus is a horse', (e) 'Bucephalus is an animal', (f) 'Hesperus is Phosphorus' and (g) 'Venus exists', reasonable answers to that question will specify the following truth-makers: for (a) Caesar's assassination, for (b) the pertinent royal procreation, for (c) the king's anger at the contextually relevant time, for (d) and (e), the king's war horse (being essentially a horse and an animal), and, for (f) and (g), the planet Hesperus (alias Phosphorus alias Venus). In the last two pairs two different truths are made true by the same thing. And the truth-maker is never specified by means of a sentence, let alone by means of the same sentence which is, or expresses, what is made true. The schematic letter 'x' in (TM) is a place-holder for singular terms, and the same holds for its role in Schema X. So let us call this interpretation of "making true" the *non-propositional*, or *ontic*, reading.

The truth-maker for the statement that Caesar was assassinated is an event.[21] In the case of events one feels more at ease with "*occurrence*" than with "*existence*," so I have formulated clause (i) of (TM) accordingly. 'The existence or occurrence of x ensures (guarantees, necessitates) that . . .' is equivalent with 'That x exists or occurs entails that . . .' (where "entails," as I shall soon argue, is best read as "relevantly implies"). As to the disjunction in clause (ii), let aboutness be tied to identifying reference, so statements (a) to (c) are about the persons referred to, whereas (a) and (b) report on an event and (c) reports on someone's state.[22] Clause (ii) as a whole restricts the range of claimants for the title "truth-maker." Take (a), the statement that Caesar was assassinated. Someone's witnessing Caesar's assassination could not occur if Caesar had not been assassinated, hence that witnessing ensures the truth of (a). But it does so only indirectly, as it were, in virtue of the event witnessed, and it is shut out by clause (ii). Thanks to this clause neither the History of the Universe nor the (slightly less colossal) totality of events which consists of Caesar's assassination and everything that happened before, nor the sum of all events that occurred at the time of his assassination, is the truth-maker of (a). Or consider (g), the statement that the planet Venus exists. Clause (ii) prevents the Universe and the (less gigantic) collection of all heavenly bodies from playing the role of the truth-maker for (g). If one drops the second clause, the remaining question has a truly global (if boring) answer: "the world," or "world-history."

How is the question posed in (TM) to be answered if we replace the sentence letter with (h) "Socrates is wise" or any other property attribution which, unlike (c), cannot be read as a report on a thing's state? According to the Austrian theory I am outlining, the statement that (h) is made true by the wisdom of Socrates. The definite description in this answer is not meant to refer to a shareable quality (for that would exist even if Socrates were a fool), nor to a fact, of course, but to an individual accident or a particular-ized quality. Thus understood, Socrates's wisdom cannot be identical with Solomon's, since Solomon is not identical with Socrates; his wisdom is subject to change, and it can no more survive Socrates than the grin of the Cheshire cat can linger on after the Cheshire cat has died.[23]

Notice that this provides us with an alternative interpretation of Aristotle's claim that the statement that you are pale is true because of your being pale. Perhaps we are to take the gerund as designating an individual accident, your paleness, something which is different from my paleness even if I am just as pale as you are. (For the purposes of this paper it is not important to decide this exegetical issue.[24])

A truth expressed by a substitution-instance of 'If it is true that p, then x makes it true' does not have to be knowable a priori, let alone be self-evident. If I am now putting salt on my omelette, then that statement is made true by WK's currently putting sodium chloride on his omelette, but nobody can know this conditional truth a priori. If physicalism is correct then every empirical truth is made true by something which can be specified in the language of (an ideally completed?) physics, but the correct physical specifications of those truth-makers would not be a matter of a priori knowledge.

When a truth-maker theorist claims that the statement that Caesar was assassinated is true because of Caesar's assassination, the "because" is neither that of causal explanation nor that of theoretical reduction nor that of conceptual explanation. It could be called the "because" of *ontological grounding*. (The reader may be pleased to hear that this intimidating unexplained phrase will not occur again on the following pages.)

Using 'T' and 'M' as short for "It is true that" and "makes it true that" respectively, we can abbreviate our

SCHEMA X: If Tp, then $\exists x \, (x \, M \, p)$.

To be on the (comparatively) safe side, let us preserve the restriction of the substitution-class of 'p' to singular non-compound empirical statements. Additional intuitively plausible schematic principles governing 'M' will include

(P1)   If $\exists x \, (x \, M \, p)$, then Tp

(P2)   If $a \, M \, p$ and that p entails that q, then $a \, M \, q$.

According to (P1), the operator 'M' is factive: if a proposition is made true by something then it is true. From Schema X and (P1) as premises we obtain

(T1)   Tp iff $\exists x \, (x \, M \, p)$

as a theorem. From (P1) it follows that if a proposition is made true by something then nothing makes its negation true:

(T2)   If $\exists x \, (x \, M \, p)$, then $\neg \exists y \, (y \, M \, \neg p)$.

For suppose that for some x and some y, x makes a certain statement true whereas y makes its negation true. Then, by (P1), both the statement and its negation are true, which is absurd. Therefore (T2).[25]

According to the entailment principle (P2) different atomic truths can have the same truth-maker. Intuitively, the truth that this book page is less than 30 centimeters wide entails the proposition that it is less than 31 centimeters wide, and so on, for all n greater than 30. Hence the truth-maker of the former proposition makes all the latter propositions true at one fell swoop. Now if we endorse the conception of entailment which underlies both classical and intuitionistic logic, (P2) has a consequence which may be less easy to swallow. Suppose that a certain event X makes some empirical truth true. Then whatever that truth may be, each logical truth is entailed by it, according to classical and intuitionistic logic. Hence, by (P2), X makes each logical truth true. The death of Socrates, for example, makes it true that a rose is a rose, that nobody is both married and unmarried, and so forth. This very consequence may stimulate the search for a different conception of entailment.[26] One will look for the formal implementation of such a conception in systems of Relevant Logic, for they contain no theorems of the form A→B where A and B do not share any parameter, and consequently they do not validate the claim that a logically necessary propositions is entailed by every proposition. Let us suppose that our truth-maker theory is supplemented by a conception of entailment which absolves us from maintaining that the death of Socrates, or any other particular, makes any conceptual truth (whether logical or not) true.

As a result of this supplementation, our truth-maker theory, as it stands, does not answer the question what it is for a truth candidate, *any* truth candidate, to be true. (The Austrian variant on which my sketch was based did not aspire to answer this question in the first place.) But eventually an adherent of such a theory has to face the question whether conceptual truths are made true by anything, and if so, by what. Let me hint at one way he could begin to answer it.[27] Take atomic conceptual truths like the propositions (h) that beauty is an excellence, and (j) that ten is even. If we refrain from identifying the world with the natural (spatio-temporal causal) order and subscribe to Platonism,[28] we can easily specify the truth-makers for (h) and (j). Remember Bucephalus: since he is essentially a horse, his existence ensures the truth of the statement that he is a horse. Similarly, or so the Platonist truth-maker theorist could say, beauty is essentially an excellence, hence its existence guarantees the truth of (h), and the number ten cannot fail to be even, so its existence entails that (j) is true.

This outline of a truth-maker theory goes some way, I hope, to give substance to Principle C under the ontic reading captured by Schema X, and it may suffice to highlight its difference from the conception of making true conveyed by Schema P. But of course, it invites questions. One of them concerns the whole enterprise. Is the concept of truth essentially involved in Schema P? Take any particular claim to the effect that the existence or occurrence of x ensures that the statement that p is true (and that x is what the statement that p is about or what it reports on). We would save breath without losing anything essential to this claim if we were to say instead:

'The existence or occurrence of x ensures that p'. So to all intents and purposes we can, as it were, subtract truth from Schema X:

(SCHEMA X–)   If p then for some x, the existence or occurrence of x (topic-specifically) ensures that p.

The use of "true" in Principle C allows us to subscribe to all instantiations of (Schema X–) in one breath (without using higher-order quantification). It seems to have fallen into oblivion that some early Australian truth-maker theorists saw this clearly:

> What the Truthmaker axiom [says] is this: Whenever something is true, there must be something whose existence entails that it is true. . . . The term "truth" makes its appearance here largely to facilitate generality of exposition. If we focus on just one particular truth, then the guts of Truthmaker can be stated without even using the term "truth" or any equivalent.[29]

(The general point that truth talk provides us with expressive facilities is due to Quine, of course.) Other questions invited by the truth-maker theory sketched above point at various kinds of recalcitrant empirical truths: What are the truth-makers for general statements, for example, or for negative existentials? In view of the controversy between Russell and Wittgenstein concerning general statements, it is worth mentioning that the truth-maker theory supports the view Russell took in 1918. For the sake of the example he used let us assume that mortality is not written into the concept of a human being. An advocate of the theory sketched above has to maintain that the many human deaths which occur in the history of the universe do not jointly ensure that all humans are mortal, for there *could* exist a Methuselah who successfully refuses ever to die. But then, what makes that general statement true? Furthermore, what about negative existentials?[30] Which part of the natural order, if any, makes it true that dragons do not exist, or that Faffner does not exist? Such truths do not seem to owe their truth to the existence of any veri-ficr, but rather to the non-existence of any falsi-fiers. (If it were true that there is nothing, no contingent thing, rather than something, then that truth would certainly not be due to the existence or occurrence of something.) So we are back with instances of Schema P: If the statement that there are no dragons is true, then it is true because there are no dragons. This claim explains why "true" is correctly applied to a certain statement if it applies to it all, but truth-maker theorists are not aiming at conceptual explanation. And it is a claim about a particular truth in which "true" occurs essentially, for surely "There are no dragons because there are no dragons" does not pass muster as an explanation in any sense of this word.

4. *Another Propositional Reading*

Dummett's formulations of Principle C strongly suggest that he agrees with the Austr(al)ian realists in favoring an ontic reading of "true in virtue of" or of "made true by." But perhaps the agreement is merely verbal.

(D-3)   [The principle] that a thought can be true only if there is something in virtue of which it is true . . . is not easily explained, particularly in the absence of any ontological realm of facts to constitute that in virtue of which thoughts may be true. (*FPL*, 464[31])

By itself, this only excludes an ontic reading in terms of *facts,* but Dummett not only denounces facts as truth-conferrers,[32] he never argues in favor of any other kind of entities as better equipped for this role (be they continuants, events, states or particularized qualities). So what is the point he attempts to make by invoking Principle C? I suspect that the difficulty of explaining this principle in the way Dummett wants it to be understood ultimately stems from an infelicity of phrasing: he talks of "something (in the world)" or of "some component of reality," he asks "what sort of things count as rendering a given type of statement true,"[33] and all this inevitably suggests quantification into singular term position, as represented in Schema X. But that is precisely what is not intended. This becomes obvious as soon as one considers Dummett's distinction between truths that are "barely true" and those that are not:[34]

(D-4)   Let us say of a true statement that it is "barely true" if there is no other statement or set of statements of which we can say that it is true in virtue of their truth. This formulation suffers . . . from reliance on the obscure, if compelling, notion of a statement's being true in virtue of the truth of another. [Here is] one way of avoiding this. . . . We may call a class of statements "irreducible" if there is no disjoint class such that a necessary and sufficient condition for the truth of any statement in the first class is that of some set of statements of the second class. It is then clear that any specific way of construing the notion of a statement's being true in virtue of the truth of other statements will require that *some* true statements be barely true. (*LBM*, 328)

Notice that (at least) in the case of truths that are not "barely true" Dummettian truth-donors are themselves *truths.* So in this respect Dummett's conception resembles Anscombe's. But Dummett does subscribe to the unrestricted Principle C: For *every* truth there is a correct affirmative answer to the (somewhat misleadingly phrased) question, "In virtue of what is it true?". So Dummett's understanding of that principle may be best captured by something like

(SCHEMA Q)   If the statement that p is true, then for some q, the statement that p is true, because q.

(The quantification into sentence position can be understood substitutionally.) Sometimes the answer to the question in virtue of which truth a certain truth is true is bound to be lame, since it can only be given either in the homophonic manner, 'The statement that p is true, because p', or by an instance of 'The statement that p is true, because q' in which 'q' just paraphrases 'p'. ("It is true that Kaa is a serpent, because Kaa is a snake" would be an example of allophonic lameness.) Whenever we are in this predicament, the truth in question is "irreducible." If we do not go in for phenomenalism nor for physicalism, we will take the truth that *this here* is a book to belong to such a class. True disjunctions are not barely true, of course.[35] And the true counterfactual conditional that this sugar cube would have begun to dissolve if it had been immersed in water is true in virtue of the truth of an (at least *prima facie*) categorical proposition to the effect that this sugar cube has such-and-such a molecular structure. In this case, too, the homophonic answer would not be incorrect, *pace* Anscombe, but it can be superseded by a more informative answer. The "truth-free" variant of a homophonic answer is always incorrect, since "because" is not commutative. So our Schema Q really is about truth.

There is a difference between my two examples for non-lame answers, which is relevant for assessing appeals to the theory of linguistic understanding in determining truth-conferrers. Such appeals are as alien to the "directly" metaphysical project pursued by Austr(al)ian realists,[36] as they are essential to Dummett's project of settling, or dissolving, metaphysical issues by first constructing a systematic account of linguistic understanding. Important though the difference in logical form between Schemata X and Q is, the fundamental contrast between the projects associated with these schemata comes to the fore when Dummett says:

(D-5)   The theory of meaning determines what makes a statement true, if it is true. (*IFP*, 446)

          The specific content of any assertion is given by what is taken as rendering . . . true the sentence used to make the assertion. (*LBM*, 166)

Thus a meaning-theory for a given language L would have to determine, among other things, which class of sentences of L is such that understanding its members is not based upon understanding sentences which belong to a disjoint class: they are the sentences which are barely true (if true at all). Now recall my two examples for reducible truth candidates. If somebody does not know that the truth of "Either Socrates or Seneca drank the hemlock" is due to the truth of one of the disjuncts, his or her knowledge of English is deficient. But in the case of our counterfactual conditional no such claim could be upheld: Here the "reductive" answer does *not* "reflect the way we do, or the only way in which we can, acquire an understanding of statements of the given class."[37] Or take statements to the effect that it is true that a certain vessel contains some F, because it contains some G, where 'F' is a non-scientific mass noun like "water" or "salt" and 'G' specifies the chemical composition of the F-stuff: certainly such statements do not show that our comprehension of 'F'-sentences rests upon our understanding of 'G'-sentences. Several of Dummett's own examples clearly exemplify reductions which are in this sense hermeneutically sterile. He describes such cases always in a non-committal way: Some philosophers (might) think, we are told, that statements about a person's character, linguistic abilities or mental acts, if true, are rendered true by neurophysiological truths about that person.[38] Still, one wonders whether such examples (however plausible or implausible they may be in themselves) are at all compatible with the following tenet:

(D-6)   It is . . . essential that the reductive thesis be advanced, not as a mere observation concerning a connection between the truth-conditions of statements of the two classes, but as part of an account of the meanings of statements of the given class: the proponent of the thesis holds that an understanding of those statements involves an implicit grasp of their relation to statements of the reductive class. ("Realism," 242)

This worry does not affect Dummett's observation that reducibility does not imply eliminability. Sometimes truths in the "reductive class" will contain truths of the "given class" as constituents. Take intrafictional truths: In virtue of what is it true that Anna Karenina committed suicide? It seems to be reasonable to answer: Well, it is true because *in Tolstoy's novel* Anna Karenina committed suicide. Quite generally, I would suggest, whenever 'p' expresses an intrafictional truth, it is true that p because there is a work of fiction according to which p.[39] So the expression of what makes true contains an expression of what is made true as a subordinate clause. (By contrast, Meinong takes intrafictional truths to be barely true.) One of Dummett's own examples is mathematical constructivism: In virtue of what is Lagrange's Theorem true? It is true, constructivists maintain, because *we possess a proof that demonstrates that* every natural number is the sum of four squares. (Platonists disagree, of course.) In the constructivists' answer an expression of what is made true is embedded in the expression of what makes it true.[40] If non-eliminativist reductionism of this type holds for the sentences of a given class, one's understanding of an assertion made by uttering a sentence *s* of this class is deficient unless one knows that this assertion, if true, owes its truth to the truth of what is expressed by the appropriately prefixed counterpart of *s*.

Let us take stock. I have distinguished sharply between *ontic* and *propositional* readings of "making true." Austr(al)ian realists favor the ontic reading. I have argued, as others did before, that many empirical statements are true without the benefit of a "truth-maker" and that "truth-maker" principles are at bottom not really about truth. Aristotle, on one interpretation, and Dummett both opt for the propositional reading. But Aristotle, understood along the lines of Schema P, can be seen as making an attempt at illuminating the *sense of* "*true*" as applied to given truth candidates, while Dummett takes substitution instances of Schema Q to be contributions to a meaning-theory for a given language. Those instances, when they are not lame, throw light on the *sense of the truth candidates* mentioned in their antecedents, and so does the fact that sometimes those instances are bound to be lame.[41] I have remarked on a certain tension between this role of Schema Q and some of Dummett's examples for full-fledged reductionism.

II. VAGARIES OF KNOWABILITY

5. *Correspondence and the Issue of Alethic Realism*

As far as I know, all advocates of the ontic reading wave the flag of *realism*, that is why I have referred to them by their favorite name. But the philosophical use of the term "realism" is, to put it mildly, underconstrained. Let me use the term "*alethic realism*"[42] to designate the following tenet: Not every true proposition we can grasp is such that in principle we could recognize its truth. Truth, alethic realists contend, outruns knowability. Now does the claim that certain, or all, truths are true in virtue of something commit one to alethic realism? I cannot see that it does. First, one can consistently maintain both that all (non-pathological) substitution instances of Schema P are true and that in principle all truths are epistemically accessible to us. Second, somebody who thinks that every true empirical statement is made true by one or more parts of the natural order severally or jointly may also believe that in principle we can always know whether something is true: an Austr(al)ian alethic *anti*-realist may be an unlikely figure, but his position could scarcely be accused of inconsistency. Thirdly, one can consistently maintain that no irreducible truth and no reducible truth is in principle beyond our ken. (In particular, the truth-donors in our examples for non-eliminativist reductionism are not recognition-transcendent: we can find out whether according to a certain novel things are thus and so, and constructivists say the same about the question whether we have a proof for a certain mathematical theorem.) Thus one can accept the Correspondence Intuition in *any* of the varieties I took pains to distinguish without thereby incurring an obligation to embrace alethic realism.

Dummett disagrees, or rather, he disagreed for a while. In his classic paper of 1959, immediately after his introduction of Principle C, he goes on to say:

(D-2, cont.) Although we no longer accept the correspondence theory, we remain realists *au fond*; we retain in our thinking a fundamentally realist conception of truth. ("Truth," 14)

This is obviously meant to give voice to a conviction shared by all advocates of Principle C, and in his first book on Frege Dummett calls this principle a "realist thesis."[43] One might suspect that this divergence results from a fundamentally different understanding of the slippery term "realism." But that does not seem to be the case, for a few pages later he says:

(D-7)   The fundamental tenet of realism is that any sentence on which a fully specific sense has been conferred has a determinate truth-value independently of our actual capacity to decide what the truth-value is. (*FPL*, 466)

To be sure, there are subtle differences between this characterization of realism and my definition of "alethic realism." But we do not have to go into them here, for the question recurs: why should a philosopher who adopts Schema P, X, or Q not *reject* realism as characterized in (D-7)? Each of these principles permits, of course, that some sentences on which a fully specific sense has been conferred may have a determinate truth-value independently of our actual capacity to decide what the truth-value is, but none of those principles *requires* that there are such sentences. So Dummett's retraction is to be welcomed:[44]

(D-8)   It is . . . [a] mistake to regard the principle that, if a statement is true, there must be something in virtue of which it is true, as peculiar to realism. On the contrary, it is a regulative principle which all must accept. (*LBM*, 331)

One does not even incur an obligation to endorse alethic realism if one accepts a *definition* of truth in terms of correspondence. Of course, such an explanation of the concept of truth *tolerates* truths beyond verifiability. But it does not *require* that there are such truths. An advocate of Object-based Correspondence is not committed to deny that in principle we can always find out whether the object a proposition is about really is as it is said to be by someone who expresses that proposition. An adherent of Fact-based

Correspondence can consistently maintain that in principle each fact can be recognized by us. And a partisan of Event-based Correspondence would not be convicted of inconsistency if he were to claim that in principle we could always come into the possession of information which would justify accepting a true statement to the effect that such-and-such an event occurred (will occur).[45]

We are not moving here in the realm of mere possibilities. Nobody will suspect William James of subscribing to alethic realism, and yet he maintains:

> Truth, as any dictionary will tell you, is a property of certain of our ideas. It means their "agreement," as falsity means their disagreement, with "reality." Pragmatists and intellectualists both accept this definition as a matter of course. They begin to quarrel only after the question is raised as to what may precisely be meant by the term "agreement," and what by the term "reality," when reality is taken as something for our ideas to agree with.[46]

His ally John Dewey, too, is "concerned not with denying, but with understanding" the characterization of truth in terms of agreement or correspondence.[47] Substituting "fact" for "reality," he proudly proclaims: "[Pragmatists] supplied (and I should venture to say for the first time) an explanation . . . of the nature of fact and idea, and of the kind of agreement or correspondence between them which constitutes the truth of the idea."[48] The explanation supplied by James is clearly anti-realist (and in this respect it is congenial to Dewey): "What does agreement with reality mean? It means verifiability. Verifiability means ability to guide us prosperously through experience."[49] I am not sure I understand the last statement,[50] and for reasons which will soon demand our attention, I am not willing to accept alethic anti-realism. By presenting it at this juncture I only want to make the point that a philosopher who accepts a definition of truth in terms of correspondence can consistently *reject* alethic realism.

Is there a commitment in the other direction? Davidson thinks there is: "The realist view of truth, if it has any content, must be based on the idea of correspondence."[51] But if Dummett is right about Frege, he has managed to refute this claim long before it was made: "Frege, although a realist, did not believe in [a] correspondence theory of truth."[52] If Frege was an alethic realist it is plain which content his view has: The concept of truth is not definable in terms of correspondence (or of anything else), and truth is not epistemically constrained. Was Frege an alethic realist? In the course of his attack on psychologism (and the idealism which is consequent upon it), he declares: "Being true is something different from being taken to be true, whether by one, by many or by all, and is in no way reducible to it. . . . Being true does not depend on being recognized by anyone." He also says that "thoughts . . . can be true without being grasped by a thinker."[53] I am hesitant to join Dummett in calling this declaration "a classic pronouncement of the realist faith,"[54] for would not every sane alethic *anti*-realist admit that, as a matter of contingent fact, many a true proposition which we are able to comprehend will never become the content of a non-committal thought, let alone of a judgment? There are ever so many decidable yes/no questions which we understand but which nobody ever bothers to ask, let alone to answer. (The question whether the letter A occurs more than 23,456 times in my copy of *Frege: Philosophy of Language* would have been such a question, I guess, had I not wasted a bit of this paper by posing it.) The sanity of sane alethic anti-realists consists in their refusal to embrace what Dummett describes as extremist constructivism:

(D-9)   [To deny] that there are true statements whose truth we do not at present recognize and *shall not in fact ever* recognize . . . would appear to be to espouse a constructivism altogether too extreme. One surely cannot crudely equate truth with being recognized . . . as true. ("Wittgenstein on Necessity," 446)[55]

But alethic anti-realists do maintain that every true proposition we can grasp is such that in principle we can recognize its truth. Frege's declaration allows for rejecting this tenet without implying its rejection.

6. *A Trojan Horse*

I have spelled out the alethic realist slogan, "Truth outruns knowability," in such a way that 'it is knowable that p' abbreviates "it is in principle possible for *human beings* (and other beings with our modes of sensory awareness and our conceptual resources, if there are any) to know that p." Let me now motivate this anthropocentrism by considering a non-standard feature of Dummett's portrayal of the realist. According to Dummett the principles of correspondence and of knowability come in a package:

(D-10) If a statement is true, it must be in principle possible to know that it is true. This principle is closely connected with the first one: for, if it were in principle impossible to know the truth of some true statement, how could there be anything which *made* that statement true? I shall call this second principle the principle K: its application depends heavily upon the way in which "in principle possible" is construed. (*WTM* II, 61)

Apparently assuming that the rhetorical question has secured his readers' consent to the "connection thesis," Dummett immediately goes on to offer a superhuman yet subdivine construal, as it were, of "knowability in principle."[56] The God of the Philosophers cognitively surpasses us so much that He literally knows *everything*. But nowadays hardly any anti-realists rest their case on theism: The epistemic constraint is always in terms of "recognizability by cognitively *finite* beings." But even cognitively finite beings might be much superior to us, and this possibility is relevant for the way Dummett conceives of alethic realism. He maintains that *even a realist* has to concede that the concept of truth is governed by the principle of knowability. A realist is bound to reject Principle K, of course, if "in principle possible" is supposed to mean: in principle possible for beings with our modes of sensory awareness and our conceptual resources. But his attitude towards the principle of knowability will change, Dummett contends, as soon as it is taken to cover also hypothetical beings endowed with superhuman (yet finite) perceptual and conceptual abilities. Why is the realist's attitude towards Principle K supposed to change if it is given this reading? Dummett challenges him to explain how we can understand answers to questions which we do not know how to decide, and the hypothesis of a superhuman verifier seems to enable the realist to give such an explanation:[57]

(D-11) The realist holds that we give sense to those sentences of our language which are not effectively decidable by appealing tacitly to means of determining their truth-values which we do not ourselves possess, but which we can conceive of by analogy with those which we do. ("Truth" [Postscript 1972], 24)

(D-12) [The realist] concedes the absurdity of supposing that a statement of any kind could be true if it was in principle impossible to know that it was true. The anti-realist's mistake, he thinks, is to apply this proposition in such a way that "impossible" is taken to mean "impossible *for us*." Our . . . observational and intellectual faculties are, contingently, limited, so that there is no reason to suppose that any true statement will be able to be known to be true by us. All that is necessary is that there could be a subject capable of knowing it, if only one with greater perceptual or cognitive powers than ours. (*LBM*, 345)

In the case of questions we do not know how to decide, the realist is supposed to think of a superhuman but not omniscient verifier, of a being with cognitive abilities which transcend our own, but which we can conceive of by analogy with those we do possess. This being, just to mention a few of its most remarkable achievements, is *per hypothesin* able not only to inspect each cup in his or her cupboard individually but also all elements of an infinite totality, and it can "directly see" into the remote past, the future, and your soul. Dummett then goes on to reject this appeal to a hypothetical superhuman cognitive subject as an *obscurum per obscurius*.

After all, what is dubious is whether the realist correctly ascribes to *us* an ability to understand answers to questions we do not know how to decide. How could this ascription be legitimized by appealing to the idea of an ability which we—undoubtedly—do not possess?[58] Realists will be well advised to lock out this Trojan Horse before Dummett can jump out with the sword of his criticism.[59] But then they must find a more plausible way of answering Dummett's Hermeneutical Challenge: how can we understand sentences that allegedly express truths beyond knowability?

7. *The Demise of Principle K*

According to the Gospel of St. Matthew (10: 30), "the very hairs of [my] head are all numbered," but let us suppose that the Gospel, taken literally, is wrong here. Although I am rather thin on top, I beg you to concede that I am definitely not bald (when writing this). Furthermore, let us make the (sadly counterfactual) assumption that whatever grows on my head is a paradigm case of a hair. Undisturbed by vagueness worries we can now say: Either it is true that the number of hairs now on my head is odd, or it is true that the number of hairs now on my head is even. (By maintaining this one does *not* incur any obligation to subscribe to the general principle that of any two contradictory propositions one must be true.) Now *as a matter of contingent fact,* nobody ever bothers to count. But in the case at issue knowledge depends, let us assume, on someone's counting. Hence nobody ever knows whether the number in question is odd. Therefore one of the following two sentences:

(Σ_O)   The number of hairs now on my head is *odd*,
            but nobody ever knows that this is so

(Σ_E)   The number of hairs now on my head is *even*,
            but nobody ever knows that this is so

expresses a truth.[60] Sane anti-realists who wisely abstain from claiming that every truth is known at some time or another are ready to concede this. They only claim that every truth, including the first conjunct of either Σ_O or Σ_E, *can* in principle be known. But now consider the conjunctions: can anybody ever know that things are as they are said to be in one of these conjunctions? At this point anti-realists run into trouble.

But let us not be too quick here. In arguing that one of the two Σ-sentences expresses a truth we took for granted that these sentences make sense. But are Σ-sentences comprehensible at all? (This is part of what I called Dummett's Hermeneutical Challenge.) Nonsense is not always patent nonsense, sometimes it masquerades as sense, so the impression of intelligibility can be deceptive. As a sufficient condition of being significant we

can lay down this: If a type-sentence under standard readings of its constituents can be used to make a warranted assertion, then it *is* significant.
Surely neither of our Σ-sentences is warrantedly assertible. So how can they
be cleared from the charge of being cases of disguised nonsense? Here is
one way of achieving this goal. Suppose that I am alone in the desert, and
I am well aware of this fact. In a fit of desperation I have just pulled out a
bunch of my hair, I am presently going to do so again, and in the meantime
I do not seize the opportunity to determine the number. Then I can
warrantedly assert

(EQ)   ∃n (The number of hairs now on my head is n, but nobody ever
        knows that n is the number of hairs now on my head).

So this sentence is significant, and it is very likely that what I say by
uttering it in that situation is true. But (EQ) cannot express a truth about me
unless some number between 20 and 200,000 is such that *it* is the number
of my hairs at the time in question.[61] (Remember your kind concessions as
to the state of my scalp.) So a sentence that is obtained from (EQ) by
deleting the quantifier and substituting a designator of that number for the
variable in the matrix must also be significant. But that number is either
even or odd. So our understanding of (EQ) ensures, "top-down" as it were,
that our Σ-sentences are significant. This answers the Hermeneutical
Challenge.

Therefore the anti-realist has to face the question posed above: Can
anyone ever know that Σ_O (or that Σ_E)? Far from brushing this question
aside, Dummett has recently conceded, in what may very well be the
shortest paper he ever published, that the answer must be *No*.[62] Not even a
superhuman yet subdivine knower could know that Σ_O (or that Σ_E).
Dummett christens the theorist "with an epistemic notion of truth" who
"carelessly" subscribes to the unrestricted Principle K "Victor." In view of
the passages presented above I cannot help thinking that "Michael" would
have been at least as appropriate a name for that theorist. In Dummett's
lesson for Victor the unrestricted Principle K appears under the guise of
schema (*), and Σ- sentences are represented by the schema 'B & ¬K(B)'.

(D-13) Victor grants that he is committed to the schema:

   (*) If A, then ◇ K (A),

   where A is any sentence, 'K' abbreviates "it is known that" and the
   possibility operator '◇' is suitably interpreted. Can Victor allow
   that some statement B might be true, and yet it was not and never
   will be known that B? He does allow this: that was the whole point
   of his inserting the modal element in his characterization of truth.[63]
   But now substitute 'B & ¬ K(B)' for 'A' in (*). It is obviously

impossible that anyone should know both that B and that it will never be known that B. By contraposition, Victor should infer that it cannot ever hold good both that B and that it will never be known that B. This is the paradox of knowability. ("Victor's Error," 1)

The so-called paradox is that by accepting a sane form of alethic anti-realism, sc. (*), one incurs a commitment to collective omniscience, a rather insane form of alethic anti-realism.[64] Dummett recommends Victor to give an inductive (recursive) characterization of truth, with

(BASIC) If A is a basic statement, then: it is true that A, iff $\diamond$ K(A)

as one of seven base clauses. The other clauses specify truth conditions for the results of applying the truth-operator to a conjunction, a disjunction, a conditional, a negation, or an existential or universal quantification, and in each case the logical operator on the right-hand side of the biconditional is to be understood as "subject to the laws of intuitionistic logic." Dummett concedes that now "there is a good deal of work for Victor to do, particularly in specifying what is to count as a basic statement." For the time being we are only given a necessary condition for a statement's being basic: it has to be free of logical connectives and quantifiers. Now suppose 'B' abbreviates a basic statement. If Victor subscribes to the inference rule, "Given A as premise, we may derive 'It is true that A' as conclusion," (which is not a matter of course, but we are authoritatively told that "Victor is likely to accept it"[65]), then he is committed by his inductive characterization of truth to infer from

(Σ)   B, and it is not the case that K(B)

both that someone could know that B and that nobody ever does know that B. But "there is now no contradiction in this; that was precisely the type of situation he wished to envisage." By laying down (Basic), the *provisoed* principle of knowability, as one might call it, Dummett avoids what "led Victor into the trap posed by the paradox."

So far this has a pleasingly pacificatory air about it, but the pleasure should not seduce us into embracing Dummett's inductive characterization of truth. First of all, there is the general worry whether all operations used in natural languages to form complex sentences can be covered by the clauses of the inductive characterization and by supplementary clauses of the same kind. A second worry concerns the question of how the notion of a basic statement is to be defined, for it has to subsume all sentences not taken care of by the other clauses. (Dummett frankly acknowledges both problems as "work for Victor.") One reason for not endorsing the inductive characterization of truth as stated by Dummett concerns his clause for disjunctions:

(Disj)   It is true that (A or B) iff (it is true that A ∨ it is true that B).

Remember, the operator on the right-hand side is to be understood intuitionistically. Now the intuitionistic rule for '∨' is something like this:[66]

(Int-∨)   You may assert 'A ∨ B' iff you are warranted in asserting 'A', or you are warranted in asserting 'B' (or at least you know of a standard strategy which, if applied, is guaranteed to provide you with a warrant for asserting 'A' or with a warrant for asserting 'B').

Roughly put, the 'only if' part of (Int-∨) conveys the injunction not to assert 'A ∨ B' unless one can tell which. But in our empirical enquiries we often have good reasons for asserting a disjunction without any guarantee that we will ever be able to tell which disjunct is true. The following story illustrates this point nicely: "A house has completely burnt down. The wiring was checked the day before, and two, independent, grave electrical faults [call them 'X' and 'Y'] were noted. Other possible explanations having been ruled out, we can (it seems) assert confidently 'Either fault X caused the fire, or fault Y did.' But this violates (Int-∨), as it is impossible to tell which fault caused the fire."[67] So (Int-∨) jars with a cognitively essential feature of our use of disjunction. (Elsewhere Dummett himself concedes this when he says that the "ordinary use [of 'or'] in natural language could not be captured by a straightforward intuitionistic explanation."[68])

A closely related reason for resistance against the inductive characterization of truth as stated by Dummett concerns his clause for existential quantifications:

(E.Q.)   It is true that something F iff ∃x (it is true that Fx).

The intuitionistic rule for '∃' is something like this:[69]

(Int-∃)   You may assert '∃x (Fx)' iff you are warranted in asserting a substitution instance of the open sentence 'Fx' (or at least you know of a standard strategy which, if applied, is guaranteed to provide you with a warrant for asserting a substitution instance).

The "only if" part of (Int-∃) conveys the injunction not to assert '∃x(Fx)' unless one is entitled to assert some substitution instance 'Fa'. This does not capture our use of existential quantifications, any more than (Int-∨) captures our use of disjunctions, and, unsurprisingly, the incendiary story again serves to make the point: We can justifiably assert, "Some electrical fault caused the fire," although we are not warranted to blame any particular electrical fault (and do not know of any strategy for removing this ignorance).[70] Furthermore, recall Thomas Gray: "Some flower that is born to blush unseen is never referred to singly." So even apart from the (admittedly) largely programmatic character of Victor's reformed position, there are reasons not to adopt it if one wants to elucidate our workaday concept of truth, for this concept is expressed in the same language as (those) disjunctions and existential quantifications which do not comply with the intuitionistic rules.

WOLFGANG KÜNNE

DEPARTMENT OF PHILOSOPHY
HAMBURG UNIVERSITY
JUNE 2002

NOTES

Earlier versions of (parts of) this paper were delivered at the Philosophy Reading Group in St. John's College, Oxford, the Philosophy Department of University College, London, and the Moral Sciences Club, Cambridge. On all these occasions I benefited from the discussion. Special thanks are due to Bill Brewer, Jonathan Dancy, and Ian Rumfitt.

1. "What is a Theory of Meaning? (II)" (henceforth: WTM II), in Michael Dummett, *The Seas of Language* (Oxford: Oxford Univ. Press, 1993), 52; cf. "Truth," in Michael Dummett, *Truth and Other Enigmas* (Cambridge, MA: Harvard Univ. Press, 1978), 14; and Michael Dummett, *Frege: Philosophy of Language* (henceforth: *FPL*) (London: Duckworth, 1973), 464.

2. WTM II, 61; cf. "Truth," 23–24; *FPL* 465; Michael Dummett, *The Logical Basis of Metaphysics* (henceforth: *LBM*) (Cambridge, MA: Harvard Univ. Press, 1991), 345.

3. The first quotation is from *Metaphysics* Θ 10: 1051 b 6–9, the second from *Categories* 5: 4 b 8–9.

4. Roderick Chisholm, *Theory of Knowledge* (Englewood Cliffs: Prentice Hall, 1966), 1st ed., 113; 1977, 2nd ed., 101.

5. Aristotle, *De Interpretatione* 9: 18 a 39 – b 2. Cf. *Cat.* 12: 14 b 14–18.

6. Jean Buridanus, *Sophismata*, ch. VIII (ed. and trans. G. E. Hughes as *Buridan on Reference*, Cambridge: Cambridge Univ. Press, 1982), 2nd Soph., 45, 47.

7. W. V. O. Quine, *Philosophy of Logic* (Englewood Cliffs: Prentice Hall, 1970), 10.

8. Nor can it do duty for the sentential counterpart of Schema P: If 'p' is true, then 'p' is true because ('p' means that p, and p).

9. G. E. M. Anscombe, "'Making True'," in *Logic, Cause and Action*, ed. R. Teichmann (Cambridge: Cambridge Univ. Press, 2000), 1–2. Cf. the third of

Russell's 1918 lectures on "The Philosophy of Logical Atomism."

10. Anscombe, "Making True," 8. I took the liberty of inserting the material in brackets in order to restore grammaticality. Anscombe's use of 'p' is not coherent.

11. Donald Davidson, *Inquiries into Truth and Interpretation* (New York: Oxford Univ. Press, 1984), 194. He might have included in his negative list "cosmic distributions of particles over space-time"; which are said by Quine to make sentences true (*Philosophy of Logic*, 4).

12. In Schiller's drama *Don Carlos* (IV, 21) the best friend of the heir to the throne expects him to "make the bold vision of a new State true" (*'er mache . . . das Traumbild wahr, / Das kühne Traumbild eines neuen Staates'*). In Annette von Droste-Hülshoff's novelette *Die Judenbuche* we are told about the boastful negative hero that he sometimes tried hard to "to avoid possible exposure by making true what had originally only been vain pretence on his part (*um durch Wahrmachung des Usurpierten möglicher Beschämung zu entgehen*)." Compare Henry James, *The Wings of the Dove* (Bk. X, ch. i):' "If I had denied you," Densher said with his eyes on [Kate], "I'd have stuck to it." . . . "Oh you'd have broken with me to make your denial a truth? You'd have 'chucked' me"—she embraced it perfectly—"to save your conscience?"

13. See Bede Rundle, *Grammar in Philosophy* (Oxford: Clarendon Press, 1979), 345–48. I disagree with him, however, at one point. In claiming that the fact that p makes it true that p, Rundle contends, we affirm "no more than a deductive connection between one proposition and another" (348). This cannot be the whole story, for the entailment between 'p' and 'It is true that p' runs in both directions whereas 'makes true' signifies an asymmetrical relation.

14. As Davidson says, "*That* experience takes a certain course, *that* our skin is warmed or punctured, *that* the universe is finite, these facts, if we like to talk that way, make sentences and theories true. But this point is put better without mention of facts" (Davidson, loc. cit.). Unfortunately he then goes on to claim that the point can be made by saying, e.g., "The sentence 'My skin is warm' is true if and only if my skin is warm" (loc. cit.). This repeats Quine's mistake.

15. Anscombe, "'Making True,'" 4–5; see Dummett's critique: "Sentences and Propositions," in Teichmann, 14–17.

16. In chs. 2 and 4 of my *Conceptions of Truth* (henceforth: *CT*) (Oxford: Oxford Univ. Press, 2003).

17. Contrast "He is your first cousin because he is your first cousin."

18. David Armstrong, "Difficult Cases in the Theory of Truthmaking," *Monist* 83 (2000): 150.

19. The Austrian contributions I have in mind (which are Austrian by inspiration rather than by nationality) are Kevin Mulligan, Peter Simons, and Barry Smith, "Truth-Makers," *Philosophy and Phenomological Research* 44 (1984): 287–321, and Simons, "How the World Can Make Propositions True," in *Sklonnosci Metafizyczna*, ed. M. Omyta (Warsaw: Warsaw Univ. Press, 1998), 113–35. In Australia the basic idea was first presented in print, as far as I know, by

John Fox in "Truthmaker," *Australian Journal of Philosophy* 65 (1987): esp. 189, 204–7; and in John Bigelow's *The Reality of Numbers* (Oxford: Clarendon Press, 1988), esp. 122–34. The most elaborate antipodean version is to be found in Armstrong's book *A World of States of Affairs* (Cambridge: Cambridge Univ. Press, 1997). It is not only the use of the hyphen which separates Austrians and Australians. Incidentally, to my ear, for what it is worth, "truth-donor" (designed after the model of "blood-donor") or "truth-conferrer" would be stylistically less unpleasant. "*Wahrmacher*" in German is acceptable, "*Wahrheitsmacher*" sounds discordant. Is the English counterpart any less cacophonous?

20. By contrast, Armstrong takes facts (which he calls states of affairs) to be truth-makers. This is not easy to reconcile with Armstrong's naturalism according to which the world consists of, and is exhausted by, whatever stands in spatio-temporal and causal relations. Facts, being abstract (non-extensional) entities, are not parts of the natural (spatio-temporal causal) order. (I could not discover a rebuttal of this objection in the passage in which Armstrong faces it: *A World of States of Affairs*, 135–38.) At any rate, not all truth-makers can be facts. Certainly there are entities which are not facts (even if they were somehow constituents of facts). So the truth that there are non-facts is made true by those non-facts severally. See David Lewis, "Forget about the 'Correspondence Theory of Truth'," *Analysis* 61 (2001): 278.

21. "I believe that Caesar was assassinated; the verifier of this belief is the actual event which happened in the Senate House long ago." Thus Bertrand Russell, in *An Inquiry into Meaning and Truth* (1940) (Harmondsworth: Penguin, 1967), 227. "Verifying" here is, of course, "making true" latinized. (I comment on Russell's view(s) on truth in ch. 3 of *CT*.)

22. As far as temporally extended events and states are concerned, one could, perhaps, regard states as monotonous events (or events as variegated states).

23. The term "individual accident" is borrowed from Leibniz (who inherited it from the scholastics), and "particularized quality" is Peter Strawson's term. The entities in question have been variously named "modes" (Descartes, Locke, Lowe), "*Adhärenzen*" (Bolzano), "*individuelle Momente*" (Husserl, Mulligan et al.), "abstract particulars" (Stout, Campbell) or "cases" (Wolterstorff). Nowadays the least appropriate title of all, "tropes" (due to D. C. Williams), has become the common coin.

24. If we paraphrase "because of your being pale" as "because of the fact that you are pale" and then refrain from taking the latter to be a verbose variant of "because you are pale," we hit on a third interpretation of Aristotle's remark. Unsurprisingly, this is the way Armstrong reads Aristotle when he enrolls him as an early advocate of a "factualist" truth-maker theory (*A World of States of Affairs*, 13). The evidence Armstrong himself provides is just a bad translation of *Categories* 12: 14 b 14–22. (In ch. 3 of *CT* I argue that one should not invoke the category of facts when trying to understand Aristotle's conception of truth.)

25. In Mulligan et al., "Truth-Makers," §6, principles (P1) and (P2) are

registered under (1) and (14). In Simons, "How the World Can Make Propositions True," 120, they are given as (1) and (4), and what is given as (2) follows from theorem (T1), hence from principles C and (P1).

26. As several authors have pointed out: see Greg Restall, "Truthmakers, Entailment and Necessity," *Australian Journal of Philosophy* 74 (1996): 331–40 (who pleads for a conception of entailment which is close to, but not quite as restrictive as, relevant implication). The passing appeal to "the entailment of Anderson and Belnap" in Mulligan et al., "Truth-Makers," 313, may be similarly motivated, and Simons explicitly rejects a truth-maker theory according to which logical truths are made true by something in the natural order ("How the World Can Make Propositions True," 114). By contrast, Quine argues: "Any sentence logically implies the logical truths. Trivially, then, the logical truths are true by virtue of any circumstances you care to name—language, the world, anything" (*Philosophy of Logic,* 96). Quine takes this to demonstrate that the doctrine that logical truths are true by virtue of meaning is vacuously true. But is the doctrine not rather that logical truths are true by virtue of meaning *alone*? So if his "anything you like" thesis were correct it would show the doctrine to be *false*. One also senses a certain tension between this thesis and the invocation of Tarski's paradigm in our earlier quotation from the same book: There Quine's suggestion seemed to be that every truth is true in virtue of its satisfied disquotational truth condition.

27. I took my cue for this move (which down-to-earth Austrians would hardly approve of) from Strawson: see his "Universals," as reprinted in his *Entity and Identity* (Oxford: Clarendon Press, 1997), 61–62.

28. By opposing naturalism the Platonist also rejects physicalism, of course, but a naturalist does not have to be a physicalist.

29. Bigelow, *The Reality of Numbers*, 125, 127. Exactly the same tenet is upheld by Fox: see "Truth-maker," 189. It must be due to oblivion that David Lewis makes the point that "truth is mentioned in the truth-maker principle only for the sake of making a long story short" with an air of novelty: "Forget about . . . ," 278–79, "Truthmaking and Difference-Making," *Noûs* 35 (2001): 604–6.

30. See David Lewis, "Armstrong on Combinatorial Possibility" [1992], in his *Papers in Metaphysics and Epistemology* (Cambridge: Cambridge Univ. Press, 1999), 204; "Truthmaking and Difference-Making," 610–12. Hilary Putnam also presents negative existentials as evidence when he maintains that the principle, "if a statement is true there must be a *something* which 'makes' it true," is a "picture" which does not fit all empirical statements, let alone all statements. He does think that it fits some empirical statements, but his advice is to "[break] free of the grip of the picture." (The wording of this advice comes as no surprise in a paper "On Wittgenstein's Philosophy of Mathematics," *Proceedings of the Aristotelian Society*, SV 70, 1996, 251–52.) The problem is recognized as such in Mulligan et al., "Truth-Makers," 315.

31. Cf. Dummett, *The Interpretation of Frege's Philosophy* (henceforth: *IFP*), 444.

32. Provided that they are regarded as different from truths! Dummett often mentions Frege's tenet that facts are nothing but true thoughts, but as far as I can see he never raises any objection to it. (I cast some doubt on that tenet in chs. 1 and 3 of *CT*.) If he accepts the Fregean identification, then his occasional reference to facts as truth-donors (e.g. in "The Reality of the Past," in *Truth and Other Enigmas*, 361, or in "Realism" [1982], in *The Seas of Language*, 248) are compatible with the dismissal of facts, as *different* from truths, in (D-3) and, as we shall soon see, in perfect harmony with his understanding of Principle C.

33. Dummett, *The Logical Basis of Metaphysics*, 328.

34. See Dummett, "Realism" [1963], in *Truth and Other Enigmas*, 148–50; "The Reality of the Past," 360; *FPL*, 464; WTM II, 52–57, 66–67; *IFP*, 447–48; "Realism" [1982], 247–48.

35. "On the explanation given," Dummett says, "no universal statement can be barely true. . . . A true universal statement will be true in virtue of the truth of all its instances (WTM II, 67). But in which sense does the truth of all instances of a general statement S "determine" S "as true"? Of course, the statement that all instances of S are true entails that S is true. But it is possible that these instances are all true although S is not true, and does not this refute the determination thesis?

36. "Truthmakers are one thing, meanings are quite another" is the war cry of Austr(al)ian realists against approaches to metaphysics that are driven by semantics (Armstrong, "Difficult Cases," 153).

37. Dummett, *Truth and Other Enigmas*, Preface, xxxiv.

38. See Dummett, "Realism" [1963], 148–50; "The Reality of the Past," 359; WTM II, 53–57; "Realism" [1982], 245–47; *LBM*, 324.

39. I call the example "intrafictional" as opposed to (a) interfictional statements ("Anna Karenina did not live in the same country as Madame Bovary"), (b) transfictional statements ("Many readers pity Anna Karenina") and (c) "ontological" statements ("Anna Karenina never existed"). A Fregean approach to this minefield is pursued in my "Fiktion ohne fiktive Gegenstände" in *Metaphysik - neue Zugänge zu alten Fragen*, ed. J. Brandl et al. (Sankt Augustin: Academia, 1995), 141–62.

40. See Dummett, "The Reality of the Past," 361; "Realism" [1982], 243–45; *LBM*, 324.

41. Strictly speaking, this requires replacing the sentence-nominalizations in Schema Q by quotational designators of sentences, for what has a sense is not the statement that snow is white, say, but the sentence "Snow is white." But then, sentences are not true (or false) *simpliciter*, so some relativizations would have to be put in. Although these issues are important (and receive a lot of attention in chs. 4–6 of my *CT*), I do not think that they matter for the contrasts which I wanted to emphasize in this essay.

42. Borrowed from William Alston, *A Realist Conception of Truth* (Ithaca: Cornell Univ. Press, 1996). As to the doctrine associated with this term, Alston's definition (see pp. 1, 6, 231) differs widely from my own explanation in the text

above.

43. Dummett, *Frege's Philosophy of Love*, 464.

44. Actually he retracted already in his "Postscript (1972)" to "Truth," 23.

45. For the distinction, just alluded to, between different kinds of correspondence theories see ch. 3 of *CT*.

46. James, *Pragmatism*, in *Works*, vol. 1 (Harvard: Harvard Univ. Press, 1975), 96.

47. Dewey, *Essays in Experimental Logic* (Chicago: Univ. of Chicago Press, 1916), 236.

48. Dewey, ibid., 24; 231.

49. James, *Pragmatism*, 8. Cf. Dewey, *Essays in Experimental Logic*, ch. XII.

50. I make an attempt at explication and evaluation in *CT*, ch. 7.

51. Davidson, "The Structure and Content of Truth," *Journal of Philosophy* 87 (1990): 304. Since Davidson takes correspondence theories to be hopeless, one can understand why he sees "no point in declaring oneself a realist, or, for that matter, an anti-realist" ("Is Truth a Goal of Inquiry?", in Donald Davidson: *Truth, Meaning and Knowledge*, ed. U. Zeglen [London: Routledge, 1999], 17).

52. Dummett, *FPL*, 442; cf. 464, and *LBM*, 331.

53. The first quotation is from the preface to volume I of *Grundgesetz*, xv–xvi, the second from the bottom of the final page of "The Thought." In *Nachgelassene Schriften,* 133 (*Collected Papers*, 144, trans. corrected) Frege makes both claims in one breath: "In order to be true, thoughts . . . not only do not need to be recognized by us as true: they do not even have to be thought by us at all." Cf. also *Nachgelassene Schriften*, 206 (*Collected Papers*, 223).

54. *LBM*, 325 (on the slightly weaker claim in *Grundgesetze*). Cf. *IFP*, 433; 511: "The crux of the dispute concerning realism is precisely where Frege locates it, . . . namely in the relation between truth and our recognition of truth. . . . In drawing his distinction between being true and being taken to be true, Frege hits the very centre of the issue concerning realism." Unfortunately the preface to *Grundgesetze* does not contain a convincing argument for alethic realism: Frege seems to think that alethic realism follows immediately from the premise that a (non-indexical and non-ambiguous) sentence expresses the same proposition to all who understand the language. Dummett takes him to task for this (*IFP*, 65).

55. As reprinted in *The Seas of Language*. On pp. 458–60 of the same paper Dummett unambiguously declares extremist constructivism to be "totally implausible."

56. Similarly in *FPL*, 465: "The two theses are closely connected. To describe what would make a statement true is to describe what it would be to recognize it as true, *even if the means of recognition are not available to us*" (my italics).

57. See also *FPL*, 465–67.

58. See *FPL*, 467–68, WTM II, 62, and especially *LBM*, 346–48.

59. Gareth Evans cautioned realists against "ideal verificationism" in *The Varieties of Reference* (Oxford: Oxford Univ. Press, 1982), 94–100.

60. Of course, this contention does not depend on acceptance of the general principle either: It is possible that our Σ-propositions are *both* false, so they do not make up a contradictory pair. Resistance motivated by the intuitionistic understanding of disjunction will be faced towards the end of this paper.

61. I am not assuming here that an existential quantification can *never* be true when no instance of it is. This general assumption is rebutted by examples like "∃x (x is an anonymous pebble in the dark unfathomed caves of ocean)."

62. All Dummett quotations which follow in this subsection are from "Victor's Error," *Analysis* 61 (2001): 1–2.

63. Perhaps one should prefix "It is true that" to the first occurrence of 'A' in (*), in order to make explicit that it is a "characterization of truth."

64. The argument to which Dummett alludes was first published in 1963 by Frederic Fitch (and attributed to the anonymous referee of a paper he submitted to the *Journal of Symbolic Logic*, but did not publish, in 1945). It received the title Dummett uses in a paper by Dorothy Edgington ("The Paradox of Knowability," *Mind* 94, 1985), and was recently carefully defended by Timothy Williamson (in the last chapter of his book, *Knowledge and Its Limits* Oxford: Oxford University Press, 2000). I discuss some of the literature and present my own version of the argument in ch. 7 of *CT*.

65. It is not a matter of course, because by accepting Truth Introduction, Contraposition and Transitivity of 'if-then' one is committed to conceding that lack of truth is truth of negation (which excludes truth-value gaps): By T-Intr. (1) If p then Tp, so by Contr. (2) if not-Tp then not-p. Now, again by T-Intr. (3) if not-p then T not-p. Therefore, by Trans. (4) if not-Tp then T not-p.

66. See Dummett, "Truth," 17; *Elements of Intuitionism* (Oxford: Oxford Univ. Press, 1977), 12–21.

67. Edgington, "Meaning, Bivalence and Realism," *Proceedings of the Aristotelian Society* 81 (1981): 157, with a bow to Ian Hacking. (I have relabeled the rule.) Actually, Dummett himself gives an example that serves the same dialectical purpose: "Hardy may simply not have been able to hear whether Nelson said, 'Kismet, Hardy' or 'Kiss me, Hardy', though he heard him say one or the other" (*LBM*, 267).

68. Dummett, "The Source of the Concept of Truth," in *The Seas of Language*, 194. (He goes on to suggest tentatively a "more complicated explanation" which implies that one understands 'or' only if one has mastered *modus tollendo ponens*. Ian Rumfitt has shown that this proposal does not work because it fails to validate ∨-elimination: see his "Unilateralism Disarmed: A Reply to Dummett and Gibbard," *Mind* 111 [2002]: 305–21.)

69. See note 66.

70. Dummett himself points out that our use of existential quantifications as antecedents of conditionals is not captured by (Int-∃).

REPLY TO WOLFGANG KÜNNE

I first enunciated principles C and K in my early article "Truth." I was prompted to propound principle C by reflecting on the theological notion of *scientia media* and on the phenomenalists' explanation in terms of counterfactuals of statements about the physical world not backed by observation. *Scientia media* is the knowledge that is supposed to motivate God not to create certain people. This knowledge is of what those people would do if He created them. It is not based on determinist grounds: it is not that they would be programmed to commit certain actions. Rather, God's *scientia media* is knowledge of what these putative individuals would *freely* do if they were to come into existence.

The whole notion seemed to me patently absurd. What made it absurd? Why, the fact that, if there were such knowledge, there would be nothing in virtue of which the propositions known would be true. Likewise, phenomenalists frequently explained a statement about an unobserved locality as tantamount to a counterfactual to the effect that if anyone were to go to that locality he would observe the state of affairs in question. Now if only those statements about the physical world were true that were either based upon observation or were translatable into counterfactuals for which grounds could be given by appeal to what was already known to be true about the physical world, this position would not be absurd on its face. But if statements about the physical world were all assumed to be determinately true or false, there would necessarily be many true counterfactuals for which no such grounds could be given: they would, in the terminology I later adopted, be *barely true*, like the items of the *scientia media*. What refuted both classical phenomenalism and the theory of the *scientia media* was the princple that subjunctive conditionals cannot be barely true.

The idea of a true statement's being or not being barely true still seems to me a reasonably intuitive one. Wolfgang Künne gives the natural example of existential and disjunctive statements as ones that cannot be barely true: you cannot drink tea or coffee without drinking a particular one of them. "John and James are brothers" is not barely true: it is true in virtue of their both being male and having the same parents. "John and James have the same parents" is not barely true: it is true in virtue of a certain particular pair being their parents. But I suppose that if "The flag of the U.S.A. has thirteen stripes" is barely true, it would be ridiculous to ask, "Which stripes are they?"

Künne remarks that the presupposition "that the same sentence can be used both in the specification of what *is* true and in the specification of what *makes* it true" (or, as I should much prefer to say "of that in virtue of which it is true") is not visible in principle C. He quotes Elizabeth Anscombe as scorning this presupposition. But, insofar as he is concerned to treat of my views, it must be obvious to him that I do make that presupposition, since he discusses my notion of being barely true. I willingly acknowledge that, in framing principle C, I neither had nor wanted any precise conception of the kind of thing in virtue of which, in general, a statement is true. As Künne remarks, I specifically rejected the notion of facts as serving this role; facts, to my mind, are true propositions, not that in virtue of which propositions are true. I think, if asked, I should have said that that in virtue of which a statement is true varies in kind, even in category, according to the statement in question. Künne is right to say that in natural language "something" and "everything" may express second-order rather than first-order quantification. But I think they may express something vaguer than either. If I say, "There is something mysterious about this," I do not specifically mean that there is a mysterious object involved in the situation, nor that there is a mysterious feature that the situation possesses: anything, of any category, might constitute the mysterious something.

I am allergic to the notion of "truth-makers," and do not much like to talk about what makes a statement true, rather than that in virtue of which it is true, although Künne has turned up a passage in which I did use the former expression. It was to evade the difficulty of specifying what *in the world* it is in virtue of which a statement is in general true that I switched to speaking of a statement's being true in virtue of the truth of other statements (or, in the case of a barely true statement, of its own truth); after all, "It is true in virtue of . . ." is most naturally completed by a phrase with a gerund. Künne cites this alternative means of formulating the principle. On the basis of it, he classifies me as adhering to a propositional reading of "making true," as opposed to the ontic reading favoured by miscellaneous Austrian and Australian philosophers. I am content with this classification; certainly I should not endorse the idea that all true statements have objects as what make them true.

I think that Künne is right to agree with my later denial that adherence to principle C is a step in the direction of realism, as I had earlier suggested. It is not: it is a principle that should be endorsed as much by opponents of realism as by those who support it. He is also right that, in my view, a sentence expressing a statement in virtue of whose truth another statement A is true may incorporate A itself: the example from the constructivist account of the meanings of mathematical statements is apt, and is one that I have used myself. It is one reason why principle C is not a reductionist thesis.

Künne raises a difficulty about the relation between a statement A and the set of statements in virtue of whose truth A is true. The true counterfactual conditional that if a particular cube of sugar had been immersed in water, it would have dissolved, is, he says, true in virtue of the molecular structure of sugar. This, he argues, conflicts with my claim that it is the meaning of any statement A that determines that, if a certain set of statements were true, A would be true in virtue of their truth. To understand the conditional about the sugar cube's dissolving, we do not have to know anything about the molecular structure of sugar; we do not even have to know that sugar *has* a molecular structure; we need not as much as have the concept of a molecule.

What is it for me to know what a counterfactual conditional means? It is not, surely, for me to be able to think of all the possible considerations which, if sound, would validate it. There may be some that have never occurred to me; there may be some which it would take a great deal of explanation for me to come to understand. It is enough for me to *be able to recognise* any particular set of circumstances as establishing the truth of that counterfactual when they are presented to me if it does in fact establish it—and to recognise various other circumstances as failing to establish it. I need not know anything about the molecular structure of sugar in order to understand the counterfactual conditional about the sugar's dissolving in water; it is enough that, were it explained to me, I should accept that that showed the conditional to hold good. This is not a feature of counterfactual conditionals in particular: it is a feature of linguistic understanding in general. I know that the statement, "There is someone at the door," if true, must be true in virtue of some particular person's being at the door. I do not have to be able to name or otherwise pick out every living person in order to understand the statement, so as to be able in principle to say, "If true, it may be true in virtue of the Pope's being at the door, or Andy Warhol's being at the door, or the Prime Minister's being at the door, or . . . "; I just have to be able to recognise whatever will render the statement as true as doing so (and whatever will *not* render it true as not doing so).

When he comes to discussing principle K, Künne very naturally fastens on the paradox of knowability, widely believed to refute principle K. If we symbolise that principle by the schema (*):

$$A \rightarrow \Diamond K(A)$$

where "K(A)" means "it has been, is, or will be known that A," then the substitution of "B & ¬K(B)" yields

$$\neg \, [B \, \& \, \neg K(B)]$$

for every B, since it is obviously impossible to know that B and that it is never known that B. This is regarded as a refutation of (*), since it amounts to what I apparently once called "extremist constructivism": it is taken as undeniable that there are true statements which are never known to be true.

I do not stand by the resolution of this paradox I proposed in "Victor's Error," a piece I wrote in a mood of irritation with the paradox of knowability. I much prefer the proposal of Bernhard Weiss, that principle K should be formalised by (#):

$$A \rightarrow \, \neg\neg K(A),$$

where the negation sign is to be understood intuitionistically. The double negation of any statement C, so understood, does say, in a clear sense, that it is possible that C. That is, it says that it is not possible to prove that not C, or, in other words, that it always remains open that C. The idea is that it can never be ruled out, of any statement that has not been shown to be false, that it may eventually be shown to be true, however unlikely that may appear. Schema (#) of course implies that for no statement B can it ever hold that B & ¬K(B): the supposedly absurd consequence is embraced. We here tread on the divergence between realist and constructivist conceptions of truth. It is not being asserted that there cannot be a true statement which will not *in fact* ever be known to be true: this "in fact" expresses a realist understanding of universal quantification as infinite conjunction and is therefore not constructivistically intelligible. What is being said, rather, is that we cannot have any ground to assert that it will never be known that B: there is no obstacle to its coming to be known. In Künne's example, that it will never be known whether the number of hairs on his head at a certain time was even or odd would seem to be the safest of predictions: if we can say anything about the future with virtual certainty, surely we can say this. But, when the point is pressed as hard as possible, we cannot absolutely rule out that some means of deciding the question, now wildly unexpected, may come to light: say some physiological condition proves to be correlated with the parity of the number of hairs on the head, and it can be determined whether Professor Künne was in that condition at the time.

I indeed believe that it can never be wholly ruled out, of any statement that has not been shown to be false, that it may eventually be shown to be true. But I doubt if bizarre speculations are necessary. Strictly speaking, in the intuitionistic semantics of mathematical statements, we have a canonical proof of 'A ∨ B' only if we have a canonical proof either of A or of B; but we are entitled to assert 'A or B' within an ordinary mathematical demonstration if we merely have an effective procedure of which we know that it will yield a canonical proof either of A or of B. So in particular we may assert that either A or not A, for instance, that some large number is either prime or composite, if we have a means, effective in principle, for deciding whether A or not. The statement A is then true if our decision procedure would yield an affirmative answer if it were to be carried out.

Similarly, if B is an empirical statement, we shall, from a constructivist viewpoint, be entitled to assert 'B or not B', and to regard it as true, if we have an effective method of determining whether B or not, even if we do not use it. The statement B will be true if this method, had we used it, would have yielded an affiirmative result. But now, does the fact that, in such cases, the law of excluded middle may be asserted imply that the mathematical statement A or the empirical statement B is determinately true or false? The truth of each is tantamount to the truth of a counterfactual conditional. But we know very well that it does not follow from the truth of the conditional 'If it had been the case that P, then it would have been the case that either Q or R' that one or other of the conditionals 'If it had been the case that P, then it would have been the case that Q' and 'If it had been the case that P, then it would have been the case that R' must hold good: which is true may depend upon some factor not mentioned or implied. Let us call this the "fallacious inference." So how can bivalence follow from the truth of these instances of the law of excluded middle?

I am disposed to think that, in an instance of this kind, it does follow in the mathematical case, but not in the empirical case: it is determinately either true or false that A, but it is not determinately either true or false that B. The reason is that the outcome of the mathematical decision procedure is determined entirely internally, but that of the empirical procedure is not. Each step of the mathematical procedure is determined from the previous steps by how the procedure is laid down, and there is no room for choice how to apply it: so the fallacious inference is valid in the mathematical case. We possess a method that is effective in principle, even if unfeasible in practice, to decide whether a given natural number is prime or composite. For any natural number N, either it holds good that, if the decision procedure were applied, it would yield the result that N was prime, or it holds good that, if it were applied, it would yield the contrary result. Hence the proposition that N is prime is determinately either true or false.

The "fallacious inference" is, however, truly fallacious in the empirical case, because the outcome of the empirical procedure will not be determined solely by the rules of the procedure: it will depend upon what we observe and what results when we make this test or that. We cannot claim that one or other of the pair of counterfactuals, "If the hairs on Künne's head were counted, they would prove to be even in number" and "If those hairs were counted, they would prove to be odd in number," must hold good. This cannot be inferred from the unquestionable truth that, if Künne's hairs were counted, they would be found to be either even or odd in number.

If this is right, we may rightly say that the number of hairs on Professor Künne's head is either odd or even, without supposing that there is any truth of the matter which it is. A constructivist theory of meaning for empirical statements allows that there may be gaps in reality; I am arguing that these gaps may occur betwen two conditions of which we may truly say that one or other holds. Wolfgang Künne relies on assuming bivalence in order to provide an example of a true statement that will never be known to be true—more exactly, of a pair of statements one of which is true. He has to. If he could instance a specific true statement, he would know that it was true. This illustrates how important the principle of bivalence is in the controversy between supporters and opponents of realism.

If what I have argued here is right, from a justificationist/constructivist/anti-realist standpoint, the schema (#) is more readily defensible, without invoking implausible scenarios, than it may at first have seemed. I think that is a better response to the paradox of knowability than that which, in a mood of irritation, I offered to Victor.

M. D.

10

John McDowell

DUMMETT ON TRUTH CONDITIONS AND MEANING

I

Michael Dummett has long argued that a conception of meaning centered on the idea of truth conditions cannot be adequate when not all sentences are effectively decidable. His argument is supposed to recommend conceiving meaning in terms of conditions, not for truth, but for justification in accepting and rejecting sentences. In this essay I shall consider Dummett's argument one more time, in a recent and streamlined version. I shall argue that it is not convincing.

II

But first I need to say something to set up the version of the truth-conditional approach I want to defend.

I shall assume a (nearly enough) Davidsonian view of meaning theories.[1] Specifications of truth conditions take the form "s is true if and only if p," where "if and only if" is the so-called material biconditional. Of course that form by itself suggests no interesting connection between truth and meaning. As is well known, "Snow is white" is true if and only if grass is green. We can eliminate unintended truths, at least of that sort, by considering finitely axiomatized theories that entail a truth of that form for every sentence in a language; the derivations would need to exploit the way the sentences are composed out of repeatable elements. But that still leaves us without a guarantee that our specifications of truth conditions will capture the meanings of sentences.[2] The best thing is simply to stipulate the connection up front. What we want is a truth theory for a language that is usable in making sense of the language's speakers, in a way exemplified by this condition: if a speaker were to utter a sentence in a stand-alone speech act intelligible as an assertion, her action would be intelligible as saying that . . . , assertorically expressing the thought that . . . , where what fills the blank is the specification of a truth condition that the theory yields.

In a case in which when we say how we understand speakers, we use the language they speak, it is easy to know what our target specifications of truth conditions should look like. Apart from complications involving indexicality, and ignoring cases where to make sense of a speaker we need to exploit idiosyncrasies in her understanding of the language she speaks, "disquotational" specifications of truth conditions will clearly do.[3]

If we focus exclusively on this case (the "homophonic" case), we may miss how much goes into the condition that our theories are to be usable to make sense of people. But when we consider dealing with one language in another (the "heterophonic" case), it becomes clear that a full understanding of the condition brings in the whole substance of our understanding of what is involved in finding people's actions, including their linguistic actions, intelligible as manifestations of rationality. This is the context in which Davidson's reflections about radical interpretation belong. It will be important later in my argument.[4]

III

Writing about how common sense conceives truth, Tarski quotes Aristotle's remark that to say of what is that it is, or of what is not that it is not, is true.[5] The specifications I have been considering give truth conditions for *sentences*, but that means conditions under which people would speak the truth by uttering the sentences. In a less archaic formulation than Aristotle's, the commonsense conception of truth is that if one says that things are thus and so, what it is for what one says to be true is for things to be thus and so. That things are thus and so is what one says, but it is also what is the case if what one says is true. That brings out why this conception of truth—the one Tarski finds in Aristotle and credits to common sense—has been called "the identity theory of truth." (I would not myself dignify it with the title "theory"; it is a truism.) If one thinks or speaks truly, what one thinks or says is—is no other than—something that is the case.[6]

Suppose we say the identity conception captures what "is true" means in our specifications of truth conditions. We cannot spell out this conception of truth except by exploiting the concept of what one can use a sentence to say. So there is no question here of explaining the concept of meaning—of sentences being usable to say things, to express thoughts—in terms of a prior understanding of the concept of truth.

Should we envisage an explanatory movement in the opposite direction, with truth explained in terms of an independent understanding of thought-expression? No. There is no reason to suppose that something recognizable as an idea of expressing the thought that things are thus and so could be intelligible in advance of the idea that if things are indeed thus and so, such a performance constitutes speaking the truth.

So on this view there is no priority in either direction between the concept of truth and the concept of expressing thoughts. To do justice to the conception I have outlined of how truth theories might serve as meaning theories for languages, we must suppose that the concept of truth that would be employed in any such theory, on the one hand, and, on the other, the concept of thought and thought-expression that one employs when one summarizes what it is for such a theory to be usable as a meaning theory by saying that its specifications of truth conditions are to capture what the sentences in question can be used to say—what thoughts they can be used to express—are intelligible only together.

IV

That is how Dummett says we must see things if we are to respect "Frege's insight . . . that the concept of truth plays a central role in the explanation of sense."[7] But I do not believe the conception I have outlined ever comes clearly into Dummett's view as a way of respecting the insight.

A truth theory of the relevant sort would be usable as if it set out to specify what sentences in the language it deals with can be used to say. It would show how a sentence's having its truth condition depends on the semantical properties of the parts of the sentence and how they are put together. Thereby it would helpfully link the sentence's availability for thought-expression to its composition out of simpler linguistic elements.

I think something on these lines fits how Frege conceives the relation between truth and thought. Frege typically places truth in relation to sense by talking not about saying but about judging, advancing from a thought to the truth value True. But that difference is not important for my purposes here. In the framework of the linguistic turn, of which Frege is at least a precursor, the first thing to say about judging is that our understanding of it is to be modeled on our understanding of making claims.[8] Focusing on saying, as I have done, and focusing on judging, as Frege does, are interchangeable ways of conveying the same picture.

I am suggesting that for Frege the concepts of sense and truth are interdependent. In spite of the remark I cited at the beginning of this section, Dummett puts this in question by a reading he gives of how Frege explains senses and references in the first volume of *Grundgesetze der Arithmetik*.[9] Frege first specifies references; he states the references of simple expressions and explains how the references of simple expressions determine the references of complex expressions, up to the case of sentential formulae, whose references are truth values. Only then does he start to attribute senses to expressions. He explains the sense of a sentential formula as the thought that the condition for its truth value to be the value True is fulfilled. And finally he explains the senses of subsentential expressions as their contribution to the senses of sentential formulae in which they occur. Now Dummett argues that this order of explanation is inconsistent with Frege's official doctrine that truth values attach primarily to thoughts and only derivatively to sentences. According to Dummett, Frege's procedure implies that "we must know what it is for a *sentence* to be true before we can know what it is for it to express a thought."[10] That is, it implies that the concept of truth for sentences is prior to the idea of their having a sense.

But what could be the content of a conception of a sentence's being true that would be available to someone who did not yet have the idea of a sentence's being usable to say something, to express a thought? Surely the order in which Frege specifies references and senses need not have the implication Dummett finds in it. Surely when Frege explains the references of expressions in his formal language, he must be presupposing that the formulae for which the specifications of reference determine truth conditions—that is, sentences—can be used to make claims, to express thoughts. Otherwise it would be mysterious what might be meant by talking of conditions for formulae to have the truth value True. When Frege goes on to explain how to derive an expression's sense from what he has stipulated about reference, he cannot be introducing completely new conceptual apparatus. He is saying how conceptual apparatus that must have been, implicitly and in a general way, on the scene from the start, in a background needed for it to be intelligible that the formulae of the language have truth values at all, applies in detail to the expressions whose references he has been explaining.

I suspect what moves Dummett here is that he thinks Frege's official doctrine that truth values attach primarily to thoughts is backsliding from the linguistic turn, like the idea that we can contemplate beings who have no need to clothe thoughts in language. The thesis that truth for sentences must be in view before thoughts are would definitely avoid such backsliding. But any merit it might have on those grounds is compromised if the thesis employs no intelligible conception of truth, as I have suggested. And in fact there is no threat to the linguistic turn if we take Frege's view to be that knowing what it is for a sentence to be true and knowing what it is for it to express a thought come together. The official doctrine can be put by saying that truth values attach primarily to things one can say, in the sense in which what one says is, schematically, that things are thus and so. That poses no challenge to the linguistic turn; language is centrally in view when we say what we need to say in order to connect the concepts of truth and of thoughts. Frege's official doctrine about the primary bearers of truth values should not seem to be of a piece with the idea of beings who have thoughts but not language.

<h1 style="text-align:center">V</h1>

Dummett thinks a truth-conditional conception of meaning cannot be acceptable for any language with sentences for which there is no effective means of determining their truth or falsity. There are, he says, problems about how the understanding of such a language, as conceived in a truth-conditional account, could be manifested, and how it could be acquired. But though he continues to hold that those problems—around which his earlier criticisms of the truth-conditional conception revolved—are serious, Dummett now urges that "the central objection" to a truth-conditional conception of meaning is that it is circular.[11]

The accusation of circularity depends on a claim Dummett puts like this: "On a truth-conditional account of meaning, the understanding of a sentence cannot be equated with an ability to *do* anything: neither with an ability to set about determining the truth or falsity of the sentence, nor with an ability to recognise it as being true or false in suitable circumstances."[12] Understanding is a variety of knowledge. Dummett's claim is that according to a truth-conditional conception, the knowledge that understanding a sentence consists in would need to be "irredeemably propositional knowledge—theoretical knowledge which, if we have it at all, we can have only in virtue of being able to express it."[13] The truth-conditional conception of meaning is supposed to explain what it is to grasp a proposition as expressed by a sentence of some language that one understands. But because the truth-conditional conception represents knowing the meaning of a sentence as knowing a proposition, which one would need to be able to express, its answer to the question what it is to understand a sentence presupposes an ability to grasp a proposition as expressed by a sentence one can produce about that sentence: the proposition that gives the content of the irredeemably propositional knowledge in which one's understanding of the original sentence is supposed to consist. So no explanation is provided of what it is, in general, to understand a sentence. What the truth-conditional conception affords in this area presupposes what was to be explained.[14]

This alleged circularity applies only to languages with undecidable sentences. If all sentences were effectively decidable, it would not be the case that understanding a sentence, on the truth-conditional conception, could not be equated with an ability to do anything, and we would not be stuck with its needing to be irredeemably propositional knowledge. Understanding a sentence could be equated with being able to put into practice the *ex hypothesi* available effective means for deciding whether the sentence is true or false, and to accept or reject it according to the results.

And Dummett takes this as a pointer towards how we should conceive understanding when, as in our natural languages, there are sentences for which there is no effective means for deciding their truth value. The condition for avoiding circularity is that we can equate understanding a sentence with an ability to do something, as opposed to knowledge that something is the case. From the fact that there is no effective means for deciding whether a sentence is true or false, it does not follow that there is no such thing as accepting or rejecting the sentence in a way that is rational in the light of how one understands it. Indeed, as Dummett says: "Of a sentence such that we could in no circumstances correctly judge, in accordance with its sense, that an utterance of it was true or was false, it would unquestionably be dubious in the extreme that we had conferred a sense on it at all."[15] So we should see understanding a sentence as consisting in the ability to recognize circumstances that justify acceptance or rejection of it, and to accept or reject it accordingly.[16]

VI

This argument starts from the claim that a truth-conditional conception of meaning cannot equate understanding a sentence with being able to do anything. That is what is supposed to force a theorist of truth conditions to identify understanding with knowledge that is purely theoretical. But if a truth-conditional conception is spelled out in the way I have outlined, the claim is false, and the argument cannot get started. Certainly understanding a sentence cannot be equated with being able to decide its truth or falsity if there is no such ability. But understanding a sentence can be equated with being able to use it so as to express a thought—the thought it is enabled to express, given the way the language works, by the expressions that compose the sentence and how they are put together.[17]

Mastery of a language is in the broadest sense a practical capacity, knowing how to use the language. That does not rule out the obvious thought that actualizations of mastery of a language on specific occasions involve bits of knowledge that . . . , knowledge of what is being done in the relevant performances, in speech of one's own intentionally and therefore knowingly undertaken and in comprehending the speech of others. The content of this knowledge that . . . , occasion by occasion, is at one's disposal by virtue of one's mastery of the language. So, as Dummett urges, mastery of a language is not a *mere* practical ability, on a level with the ability to swim, for which detailed knowledge of what the ability is an ability to do is available to people who do not possess it just as much as to people who do.[18] The first-hand knowledge of what is being done on specific occasions that is the cognitive aspect of exercises of mastery of a language is itself an actualization of the capacity that mastery of the language is. People who do not know the language can have such knowledge only at second hand, as in communication through interpreters.

According to Dummett, it is only after we discard a truth-conditional conception of meaning that we can "represent a knowledge of the meaning of a sentence or word as knowing how to use that sentence or word."[19] But knowing how to use sentences is knowing what thoughts one can express by using them, and knowing how to use words is knowing what difference their presence in a sentence makes to the thoughts that can be expressed by using it. And if we constrain specifications of truth conditions in the way I have outlined, we secure that what a theory gives as a truth condition for a sentence specifies precisely what one can say, what thought one can express, by uttering that sentence. Such a theory, treated as a meaning theory, would be perfectly suited to represent knowing the meanings of expressions as knowing what thoughts they can be used to express, which is knowing how to use them in order to express thoughts. It would compendiously capture the content of all the potential knowledge that . . . —knowledge of what one would be saying oneself, or of what others would be saying, in making assertoric utterances of sentences—that would be the cognitive aspect, occasion by occasion, of those exercises of mastery of the language.

The supposed problems about manifestation and acquisition of mastery of a language similarly have no purchase against a truth-conditional conception of the sort I have sketched.

Speakers must be able to make manifest to one another, not a matter for guesswork or hypothesis, what thoughts they are expressing. But to specify what thoughts speakers are expressing on specific occasions just is to specify conditions under which the sentences they utter are true. This equation is completely general; its correctness is not sensitive to whether or not there is an effective means of deciding whether a sentence is true or false. So there is no problem about manifesting a grasp of truth conditions for sentences. One manifests it by using the sentences to express the thoughts they are enabled to express, in the language they belong to, by the way they are constructed.

As for acquisition, Dummett asks: "By what means could we possibly come to know in what a statement's *being* true consists, when we have no means of telling that it is true? What could constitute our having such a piece of knowledge?"[20] But to learn a statement's truth condition in the relevant sense—to learn what its being true consists in—is just to learn what thought it can be used to express. We learn what a statement's being true consists in by coming to understand the statement, which we do by learning the language in which it can be made. Again, this is quite general; it makes no difference whether or not there is an effective means of deciding whether the statement is true or false.

VII

It may seem captious to respond to Dummett's argument as I have done. I have urged that the truth-conditional conception does not represent understanding as purely theoretical knowledge. This undercuts Dummett's charge of circularity. But the charge of circularity is only a way of pressing an underlying complaint: that the truth-conditional conception does not explain what it is, in general, to grasp a proposition as expressed by a sentence of a language one understands. As I have outlined it, the truth-conditional conception exploits, unanalyzed, the notion of using a sentence in order to express a thought. So I have interpreted the truth-conditional conception in such a way that it does not even aim at the explanation that Dummett argues it cannot deliver. And now it looks as if, even without the circularity objection, Dummett is right in his fundamental complaint.

This shifts attention to the question what sort of illumination a theory of meaning *should* aim to afford. Dummett thinks meaning theories must not "take as already given any notions a grasp of which is possible only for a language-speaker."[21] That certainly rules out taking as given the notion of using a sentence in order to express a thought. The prohibition expresses Dummett's conviction that such concepts must be explained by connecting them with a description of the practice of speaking a language given from outside the conceptual space they constitute.

Now one way to query this requirement is *ad hominem*. Does Dummett's own favored apparatus conform to his prohibition? Dummett's "justificationism" takes as given the notion of acknowledging the truth of a sentence, or rejecting it as false, in the light of recognizable evidence. On a natural construal, a grasp of that notion is possible only for a language speaker, no less than the notion of using a sentence in order to express a thought, and indeed in a way that depends on its connection with the latter notion. How could a speaker conceive herself as acknowledging the truth of sentences if she did not have the idea that sentences can be used to express thoughts? What conception of truth could be operative here?

It may be suggested that none needs to be. Perhaps the notion of accepting or rejecting sentences can be interpreted so that its application does not presuppose that the person who accepts or rejects sentences grasps the notion of truth, and with it the notion of thought-expression. Dummett sometimes hyphenates "accepting-as-true" and the like, and perhaps the point of this is to express a concept whose application to a person's behavior does not presuppose that the person has the notion of truth.[22]

But if we described the practice of speaking a language in such thinned-down terms, would the description contain enough to reveal moves in the practice as meaningful? If our apparatus for saying what people do with sentences does not include concepts whose possession presupposes the idea that sentences are usable to express thoughts, is there anything to ensure that our description represents the practice as a *language*-game? Interpreted in the thinned-down way, Dummett's apparatus would depict a practice in which one responds to certain circumstances with certain vocalizations. Within the game there is reason for the vocalizations; these are the moves that the game licenses in these circumstances. But if we are not allowed to spell out the legitimacy of the moves in terms of grounds for saying that things are thus and so, are the vocalizations marked out as meaningful? If we describe what is in fact the practice of using a language in a way that does not reveal its performances as expressing thoughts, why should we suppose we can cast light on the concept of meaning by lining it up with the description?[23]

So Dummett's alternative faces a dilemma. On a natural interpretation, appealing to the concept of responding to a justification by accepting a sentence is just as illegitimate, by Dummett's official lights, as appealing to the concept of using a sentence to express a thought. On this construal Dummett's alternative does not promise an explanation, from outside, of the very idea of grasping a proposition as expressed by a sentence, any more than the truth-conditional conception does. But if we reinterpret the concept of accepting a sentence on the basis of a justification, thinning the concept down so that using it does not presuppose that sentences can be used to express thoughts, we put in doubt whether a description of linguistic practice in terms of such a concept would reveal what it describes as meaningful. And that threatens the promise of an explanation in a different way.

I have expressed this doubt about Dummett's picture by exploiting a connection between the concepts of truth and thought-expression to whose attractions he is evidently immune. Recall how he finds in Frege a priority of the concept of truth for sentences over the idea that sentences can be used to give expression to thoughts. As I remarked, he is not deterred from that reading of Frege by the question what conception of truth could be involved in such a claim of priority. He thinks it could seem a good project to give substance to the notion of truth by using it in a description of the practice of speaking a language that does not employ notions only a language speaker could understand.[24] Such a project would not presuppose the notion of giving expression to thoughts. So the resulting explication of the notion of truth could figure in an explanation of the notion of thought-expression, given from outside the conceptual space constituted by concepts available only to language speakers—if only the envisaged description of the practice of speaking a language were possible. What prevents that, in Dummett's view, is that there are undecidable sentences. If that were not so, the project would be a good one.

Given this conception of what a truth-conditional conception of meaning needs to provide in the way of an explanation of the notion of truth, and this diagnosis of why the project cannot succeed, it would be natural to suppose, as Dummett does, that though the notion of a sentence's *being* true cannot be explained in terms of how it would figure in a description of the practice of speaking a language from outside ways in which only a speaker of the language could conceive performances in it, the notion of a sentence's being *accepted*-as-true can.

But this line of thought focuses on the wrong reason for rejecting the project of explaining truth from outside concepts available only to a language speaker. The real trouble with the project is that there is no recognizable notion of truth that can be understood independently of a notion of saying things, of expressing thoughts. This is indifferent to whether sentences the notion is applied to are decidable or not. The project would not be a good one even if there were only decidable sentences. And this puts Dummett's alternative in a different light. Moving to the concept of accepting-as-true does nothing to correct the real defect in the idea that the concept of being-true can be explained from outside the concept of giving expression to thoughts. Not focusing on the real defect, Dummett does not see the parallel point that applies to his favored alternative, at least on the most natural construal of it.

VIII

In any case, casting light on the notion of grasping a proposition as expressed by a sentence need not require that we prohibit the use of such notions in our meaning theories, as in Dummett's rule.

In one sense it is true that the truth-conditional conception of meaning "takes as given" the notion of using a sentence to say something. There is no attempt to explain the notion in terms of other notions, regarded as independently available.

But it is not that the notion is baldly invoked by itself, without any background. Saying things figures, in the sketch I offered, as the central case of exploiting language in actions that are rationally intelligible. To decide whether a performance makes sense as a case of saying some specified thing—perhaps that there is a bear in some indicated thicket—we would need to satisfy ourselves that the construal can be intelligibly integrated into a story about the speaker's psychological life that has a rational fit with her behavior, linguistic and otherwise, and with her situation in the world and her opportunities to find things out. And because a sentence uttered on one occasion contains words that also figure in different sentences uttered on different occasions, accepting interpretations is not a matter of satisfying oneself that linguistic performances taken one by one have this rational fit with larger stories about speakers. The interpretation of a language would need to be tested as a whole.

A complete warrant for a truth-conditional interpretation for a language would thus be very extensive, and it would need to use a rich battery of concepts. Exploitations of the concept of saying things would need a background involving such concepts as those of believing things, being in a position to know things, making mistakes, informing others of things, having a motive to mislead others about certain things, and so forth.

Dummett's rule ignores the light that can be cast on concepts, not by explaining them in terms of antecedently understood other concepts, but by locating them in a context with other concepts that are not supposed to be independently available.

About interpretation, Davidson writes: "What makes the task practicable at all is the structure the normative character of thought, desire, speech, and action imposes on correct attributions of attitudes to others, and hence on interpretations of their speech and explanations of their actions. . . . The way to improve our understanding of such understanding is to improve our grasp of the standards of rationality implicit in all interpretation of thought and action."[25] This improved grasp of what is involved in making sense of thought and action would be improved insight into the sort of shape a rationally intelligible biography must take. For this purpose, the richer the conceptual apparatus we envisage as employed in such a biography, the better. It is seeing more clearly how applications of the concepts must hang together for intelligibility that improves our understanding of them, and it would not contribute to that, in the case of the linguistic members of the collection, if we tried to reframe our descriptions of action so as to do without them, with a view to bringing them back into the picture only later.

Notice that the wider context we need includes the conceptual material made central by Dummett's "justificationism." Typically when one makes sense of someone as saying something, one takes her to believe it. And it does not make sense to suppose someone believes something if she is not suitably responsive to evidence that bears on the question whether that is how things are. So a due sensitivity to grounds for accepting and rejecting sentences must figure in the warrant for supposing that a truth-conditional meaning theory for a language has the connection it needs to have with the linguistic behavior of those who speak the language.

But this is a far cry from a recommendation for "justificationist" meaning theories. There is nothing about the concept of responsiveness to evidence that would license singling it out from the range of concepts that I am insisting needs to figure in connecting a truth-conditional meaning theory for a language with the facts about its speakers. There is no reason to suppose understanding of sentences can be correctly represented as *consisting in* behavioral propensities characterizable in terms of a restricted subclass of the conceptual background that I am insisting truth-conditional accounts of meaning would require.[26]

IX

Dummett will not allow a proponent of the truth-conditional approach to meaning to characterize truth as what a thought enjoys when things are as one says they are if one gives expression to the thought—as in the Aristotelian conception that Tarski attributes to common sense. This reflects the fact that he imposes on the truth-conditional approach his rule about what concepts a meaning theory may "take as given." It follows that the truth-conditional approach needs a conception of truth explicable from outside concepts only language speakers can have, in particular the concept of saying that things are thus and so. What might seem to fit the bill is a certain kind of correspondence theory of truth, in which truth is supposedly explained in terms of correspondence to "states of affairs," with the idea of states of affairs supposedly explicable independently of the idea of capacities to give expression to thoughts. (A very peculiar notion of states of affairs.)[27]

But for all its capacity to fascinate philosophers, the correspondence idea in that form yields nothing genuinely recognizable as a conception of truth. Dummett suggests we could conceive truth like this if there were only decidable sentences. But that is not so. Truth is what Aristotle said it is, for decidable sentences no less than others. And Aristotle's formulation makes vivid how the concept of truth—the only one we really understand—comes together with, not in advance of, the concept of saying that things are thus and so.

Not that there is anything wrong with the idea that sentences are true, when they are, by virtue of the obtaining of states of affairs. But properly understood, that is just another wording for the Aristotelian conception of truth. A state of affairs is something that is the case. And if one truly says that things are thus and so, that things are thus and so is something that is the case. For thinking about that by virtue of which a sentence is true, we need the apparatus of the identity conception of truth, not the correspondence theory's fantasy of putting truth in place from outside an understanding of the idea of saying things.[28] And there is no warrant for excluding the truth-conditional conception of meaning from this insight.

In the work of his I know, Dummett does not formulate his thinking about truth-conditional and "justificationist" meaning theories in terms of a clash between representational and inferential conceptions of meaning. But if one thinks the meaning of a sentence can be specified by giving its truth conditions, one is seeing meaning in broadly representational terms. Dummett's treatment of the truth-conditional approach is an instance of a genre, in which representational conceptions of meaning are caricatured as offering to explain meaning in terms supposedly intelligible independently of the concepts we need for describing the rationally structured context in which we place linguistic performances when we understand them.[29] The obvious unsatisfactoriness of such an approach is then supposed to motivate explaining meaning in terms of a prior understanding of the rational situatedness of speech acts. (Another, more egregious instance of the genre is Robert Brandom's recommendation for inferentialist semantics.)[30]

In fact there is no reason to suppose an understanding of the rational situatedness of speech acts—what justifies acceptances of sentences, in Dummett's version of the genre—is available ahead of an understanding of their representational significance—their potential for thought-expression, in Dummett's version. And properly understood, the truth-conditional approach, which we can see as exemplary of a conception of meaning in broadly representational terms, already accommodates the importance of the concepts of rational situatedness that are supposed to provide the materials of the competing approaches. These competitions between representational and broadly inferential conceptions of meaning are misconceived from the start.

JOHN MCDOWELL

UNIVERSITY OF PITTSBURGH
APRIL 2004

NOTES

1. See several of the essays collected in Donald Davidson, *Inquiries into Truth and Interpretation* (Oxford: Clarendon Press, 1984).

2. See J. A. Foster, "Meaning and Truth Theory," and Brian Loar, "Two Theories of Meaning," both in *Truth and Meaning*, ed. Gareth Evans and John McDowell (Oxford: Clarendon Press, 1976). If all that matters is truth in a theory's consequences, there is no reason to prefer a theory that yields the statement that "Snow is white" is true if and only if snow is white to a theory that yields the statement that "Snow is white" is true if and only if snow is white and the earth orbits the sun—using a perverse, but not false, specification of the condition under which "is white" is true of something.

3. How central a position we should accord to the cases I am here ignoring is a point of dispute between Davidson and Dummett. For Davidson, see, e.g., "The Structure and Content of Truth," *Journal of Philosophy* 87 (1990): 310–11; for Dummett, see, e.g., *Origins of Analytical Philosophy* (Cambridge, MA: Harvard Univ. Press, 1994), 148–57. In ignoring the cases, I am agreeing with Dummett that the first concern for philosophical reflection about meaning ought to be meaning expressed in shared languages. (In a different context this point would need more attention.)

4. Charles Travis has repeatedly argued that truth theories of the sort I am envisaging cannot do what I am suggesting they can do. Travis's point is that what is being said, on different occasions when someone says, say, that something is green, can be different, in ways that a truth theory cannot capture. (What it is even for an apple to be truly said to be green can differ from occasion to occasion.) This is not the sort of ground on which Dummett attacks truth-conditional approaches to meaning, and this is not the occasion to try to deal with it properly. But note that on all the various sorts of occasions envisaged in this case of Travis's point, something is being said (or hypothesized, or . . .) *to be green*, and a truth theory might capture that much. Of course it is not to be expected that a general theory could capture the variations in what it can come to for something to be green that Travis points to. Detailed understanding of speech in a language could not result from mere application of a general theory. It is not clear why this should seem to undermine the hope that reflection about truth theories for languages might yield something illuminating—so far as it goes, and Travis rightly points to limits—about meaning in general.

5. For Aristotle, see *Metaphysics* 1011b26–7. Tarski cites this in a number of places; see, for instance, "The Concept of Truth in Formalized Languages," in *Logic, Semantics, Metamathematics* (Oxford: Clarendon Press, 1956), at 155, n. 2.

6. See Jennifer Hornsby, "Truth: The Identity Theory," *Proceedings of the Aristotelian Society* 97 (1996–7).

7. Dummett, *Origins of Analytical Philosophy*, 19.

8. For Frege as a precursor of the linguistic turn, see ibid., 4–14.

9. Frege, *Grundgesetze der Arithmetik*, vol. 1 (Darmstadt: Wissenschaftliche Buchgesellschaft, 1962 [reprint of Jena, 1893]).

10. Dummett, *Origins of Analytical Philosophy*, 9. See also "The Relative Priority of Thought and Language," in Dummett, *Frege and Other Philosophers* (Oxford: Clarendon Press, 1991), 317: "Frege here explains the notion of sense in terms of the notion of reference, taken as antecedently understood."

11. Dummett, "Meaning and Justification" (Coimbra Lecture, 1997), in *Language, Logic and Formalization of Knowledge*, ed. Brian McGuinness (Gaeta: Bibliotheca di Gabriele Chiusano, 1998), 15.

12. Dummett, "Meaning and Justification," 16.

13. Ibid., 18.

14. This is a paraphrase of Dummett's formulation of the alleged circularity, at "Meaning and Justification," 16. Dummett's formulation is complicated by the fact that he directs his argument also at a truth-conditional conception of the content of thought, conceived as prior to an account of the understanding of language.

15. Dummett, "Meaning and Justification," 19.

16. See Dummett, "Meaning and Justification," 19. Note that the justifying circumstances need not be conclusive. Where they are not, understanding a sentence will consist in "an ability to recognise evidence for it when presented with it, and to judge correctly whether or not it is outweighed by any given piece of counter-evidence."

17. Of course it may be that the only actions one is in a position to perform in which one expresses the thought in question are statements that that is not how things are, or statements saying how things would be if that were how things are.

18. See Dummett, "Meaning and Justification," 15–16.

19. Ibid., 17.

20. Ibid., 22.

21. Michael Dummett, *The Logical Basis of Metaphysics* (Cambridge, MA: Harvard Univ. Press, 1991), 13.

22. See, e.g., Dummett, "Meaning and Justification," 23.

23. Note that Davidson's "holding-true," the model for Dummett's "accepting-as-true" and the like, is not supposed to be applicable to speakers in a way that avoids presupposing that they have the concept of truth, and with it the concept of thought-expression. Its applicability is supposed to be antecedent only to particular hypotheses about *what* propositions, or thoughts, speakers take to be expressed by the sentences they hold-true.

24. This must be how he envisages the explanation of the concept of truth that a truth-conditional theorist would give by using the concept in a description of the practice of speaking a language, at "Meaning and Justification," 14–15.

25. Davidson, "The Structure and Content of Truth," 325. What Davidson says here is exactly right. It undercuts the need he feels for a single, extra-propositional starting point for interpretation: holding-true in his earlier formulations, preferring-true in this work. It is no more plausible about preferring-true than it was about holding-true that applications of it can be *known* independently of knowing what the sentences in question mean, as Davidson claims (322–23). But it does not matter at all that there is no independently knowable foundation for interpretation

such as Davidson seeks. That should be clear when we see how an interpretation of a language rests on the totality of the behavior of its speakers in a way that is mediated by those standards of rationality.

26. The position of responsiveness to proofs in a plausible conception of what it is to understand mathematical sentences is quite special; there is no reason to expect an analogue in the case of understanding extra-mathematical language. For some discussion of this, see "Mathematical Platonism and Dummettian Anti-Realism," in my *Meaning, Knowledge, and Reality*, especially at 353–54.

27. The correspondence theory Dummett appears to envisage would be a special case in that the supposed conception of that in virtue of which sentences are true, though not explicable in terms of concepts that only language speakers can have, is supposed to be such that it could be explained in terms of a characterization of the practice of speaking a language that did not use such concepts, if only the presence in languages of undecidable sentences did not bar the way.

28. Compare *Origins of Analytical Philosophy*, 164, where Dummett suggests that "the very notion of a state of affairs is called into question" by a view that discards the supposed idea of states of affairs as conceivable independently of understanding a language. See also "Realism and Anti-Realism," in *The Seas of Language* (Oxford: Clarendon Press, 1993), where (at 466) Dummett is willing to single out, from among statements in the most general sense, a special category called "affirmations," on the basis that they have "truth-conditions independent of the knowledge or abilities of the speaker." By the lights of the Aristotelian conception of truth, the very idea of a truth condition requires invoking abilities of speakers, and this distinction misfires. Dummett's own thinking about truth is shaped, to its detriment, by the correspondence idea. (For a remark about this, see Hornsby, "Truth: The Identity Theory," 8–9.)

29. Dummett's version is special. He allows the truth-conditional conception of meaning to offer to explain truth in terms of its role in a description of the practice of speaking a language. (What he argues is that the offer cannot be discharged where there are sentences that are not decidable.) But the description is constrained to avoid the concepts under which speakers of the language themselves make sense of their behavior as rational. That is what saddles proponents of a truth-conditional conception with a correspondence theory of truth.

30. See Robert B. Brandom, *Making It Explicit: Reasoning, Representing, and Discursive Commitment* (Cambridge, MA: Harvard Univ. Press, 1994), especially ch. 2.

REPLY TO JOHN McDOWELL

I

I am grateful to John McDowell for revisiting an old subject of disagreement between us. I assume that he has done his best to set out the case for truth-conditional theories of meaning as convincingly as possible. I shall do my best to set out the case against them as convincingly as possible. If I succeed this may become a *locus classicus* for the debate on the issue.

I confess that reading defences of truth-conditional theories of meaning often produces on me the same sensation as listening to a conjuror's patter. I ask John McDowell's forgiveness if he is offended by my saying that his essay has had that effect on me. I hope he will not be, but merely put it down to my invincible ignorance.

II

McDowell's essay falls into two parts. Of the first, from section II to section VI, he says, at the beginning of section VII, that it may seem captious. Part Two, from section VII to the end, is a more temperate and detailed exposition of his argument. I shall reply to the captious Part One first, then turning to the temperate Part Two, in the belief that Part One contains the essence or nub of his defence of truth-conditional theories of meaning. In both parts, McDowell avoids the complexities of formulation arising from the phenomenon of indexicality; for convenience, so shall I. I shall also, for the most part and for the same reason, follow him in speaking of sentences rather than of utterances of them or of statements made by uttering them.

III

Part One of McDowell's essay is a dance with the concept of expressing a thought. McDowell requires of a truth-conditional theory of meaning for a language that the condition it specifies for the truth of a sentence S be that which a speaker who uttered S on its own in a manner intelligible as making an assertion would be (intelligibly understood as) saying that the condition was fulfilled or, equivalently, (intelligibly understood as) assertorically expressing the thought that the condition was fulfilled. That is, if the theory tells us that S is true if and only if P, such a speaker would be assertorically expressing the thought that P. McDowell does not explicitly say whether an enunciation of this principle is to be embodied in a theory of meaning of the kind he favours, or whether it is merely an external guide to a formulation of such a theory, like what Davidson always called "Convention T" in Tarski's truth-definition. If it were the former, some substantial concepts would need to be explained in the theory, or taken by it as given. But I shall assume that it is the latter.

The passage to which I have just alluded is the only time that McDowell qualifies the phrase "express the thought" by the adverb "assertorically"; but there is a big difference between asserting something and merely expressing the thought which is the content of the assertion. The verb "say" is of course ambiguous. Sometimes it is synonymous with "assert," as in "That is not consistent with what you said before"; sometimes it merely amounts to "utter a sentence with such-and-such a meaning," as (probably) in "I could not bring myself to say that." In section III McDowell equates the concept of meaning with that of "sentences being usable to say things, to express thoughts." To express a thought is to utter a sentence as having a certain meaning. To make an assertion is to advance a thought as being true. It is beside the point to discuss whether or not there is such a thing as uttering a sentence on its own solely to express a thought: the distinction remains essential. It is above all essential when we are considering as a theory of meaning one whose core—or perhaps one the totality of which—consists of a semantic theory issuing in a specification of the truth-conditions of sentences of the language.

The notion of assertion is intimately linked with that of truth. There is no chance that anyone should derive an understanding of a language from a specification of the conditions for sentences of that language to be true unless he brought to it a prior understanding of the word "true." If he did not, the word would be for him a meaningless label: he could not see any reason to prefer that theory to one that attached the same label to the conditions for them to be false. Only when he has grasped the practice whereby an utterance of a sentence is taken as correct only if the thought thereby expressed is true can the truth-theory have a chance of conveying the meanings of the sentences to him. The notion of truth is born out of that of the correctness of an assertion. (For Frege, out of that of an act of judging; McDowell sets aside the distinction between judgement and assertion as beside the point. Whether it is or not depends upon whether judging is an interiorisation of assertion, as I think, or assertion an outer avowal of judgement, as it is more usual to say.) McDowell does not say whether a description of the speech-act of assertion will form part of a theory of meaning of the sort for which he is arguing, or whether the matter will be left tacit. Davidson, in his early phase, was insistent that a truth-theory needed no further addition to constitute a theory of meaning. I argued that it needed supplementation by a statement of what it assumed concerning the concept of truth and its connection with the use of the language in converse. In the present essay, McDowell is not explicit about whether his truth-theory requires supplementation or not.

Of course, we do not—and could not—learn language from a theory of meaning for a particular language. One might in principle come by an understanding of a second language in that way; but then many notions could be taken as already understood—one does not expect a *Teach Yourself Italian* book to explain the distinction between verbs and nouns. In practice, we do not first learn the meanings of sentences and only then the practice of using them to make assertions. Rather, we pick up the meanings of sentences by hearing them used as assertions and commands, and learn the distinction between what it is correct and what incorrect to say from our infant attempts to imitate their assertoric use; so that distinction is with us from the start. That is beside the point. A theory of meaning for a language is not intended to recapitulate the process of learning it, but to display, for philosophical purposes, what constitutes the practice of speaking it, and, in particular, in what the meanings of its words and sentences consist.

As McDowell rightly says, I believe that the central defect of truth-conditional theories of meaning is that they are circular. My argument, McDowell says at the beginning of his section VI, starts from the claim that a truth-conditional conception of meaning cannot equate understanding a sentence with being able to *do* anything. The claim is false, he says. Understanding a sentence can be equated with being able to use it so as to express a thought. "Isn't that doing something?" he tacitly asks. He goes on to quote me as arguing that it is only after we abandon truth-conditional theories of meaning that we can represent the knowledge of the meaning of a word or sentence as knowing how to use it. He retorts that one who knows the meanings of the sentences of a language knows what thoughts can be expressed by using them, and that this *is* knowing how to use them;

likewise knowing what difference the presence of a word in a sentence makes to the thought that can be expressed by using it *is* knowing how to use the word.

Understanding a sentence is knowing what it means. This is not an explanation but the statement of a synonymy: "understand" and "know the meaning of" are synonyms when applied to linguistic items. McDowell's explanation of what it is to understand a sentence, that is, to know what it means, is that it is to be able to use the sentence to express a particular thought. What is it to express a thought by using a sentence? It is to utter that sentence in the knowledge of its meaning. I express a thought by uttering a sentence only if I understand that sentence. Could there be a neater instance of circularity than that?

The circle goes:

understanding a sentence → knowing how to express a thought with it
expressing a thought with a sentence → uttering the sentence knowing what it means

knowing what a sentence means → understanding the sentence

This is not the circle to which I was originally referring, but it shows just as well how truth-conditional theorists argue.

IV

What are we trying to explain? The use of a language is a practice. To engage in the practice, you must know the meanings of the words. In what do their meanings consist, and what is it to know them? That is a philosopher's question; and he will do well to accept from the outset Frege's principle of the priority of sentence-meaning over word-meaning: the sense of a word is its contribution to the sense of a sentence in which it occurs, just as McDowell holds in the passage I quoted above. (The priority is in the order of systematic explanation; in the order of recognition, we understand a sentence by understanding the words that compose it.) A theory of meaning attempts to answer the question in what the meanings of a sentence, and of a word of any particular kind, consist, and either to explain what it is to understand a sentence or a word, or to provide the materials from which such an explanation can be constructed. It must at least do the latter, since understanding is essential to participating in the practice of using the language; a theory which assigned meanings of a certain form to the words and sentences of the language, but left no clue to what a knowledge of them would consist in or how such knowledge could be manifested, would do little to make explicit the practice of using the language. To make that explicit, the theory must show how the use of sentences in converse flows, or is derivable, from the meanings that the theory assigns to them.

I hope to have indicated that McDowell's explanation of understanding is of no use: it simply takes us round in a circle. The most obvious explanation of the understanding of a sentence for a truth-conditional theorist to offer, correlative to his account of its meaning, is that it consists in a knowledge of the condition for the sentence to be true. It was against this that I lodged my original charge of circularity. For it seems that the knowledge can only be full-blown knowledge-that, theoretical or proposi-tional knowledge. And this explanation of understanding begs the question spectacularly. If he is to be able to use the sentence to express whatever thought it does express, the speaker must on this account grasp a more complex thought; if he is to be said to know the condition for the truth of the sentence, must he not be able to state that condition and say what it is a condition of? Understanding a sentence—grasping the thought it expresses—has been explained as having a piece of knowledge about that thought, knowledge involving the concept of truth; knowing something of course requires grasping the thought that is the content of the knowledge. It may be objected that a statement of the condition for the sentence to be true need be no more complex than the sentence itself: in fact that very sentence is the most straightforward means of formulating the condition for its own truth. And is the circularity not now blatant?—even if we refrain from pointing out that what is known is not *that the condition holds*—it may not—but *that the sentence is true if and only if the condition holds*.

I should not put forward the same objection if it were explained that a speaker understands a statement if he would be able, when presented with it, to recognise whatever we should count as substantiating it (certain observations, a piece of deductive or inductive reasoning, or both together), and would be able, when presented with it, to recognise whatever we should count as refuting the statement. (I have switched from "sentence" to "statement" only because of the awkwardness of the former in these contexts.) How can a speaker manifest his ability to recognise either of these circumstances? By accepting the statement in the one case and rejecting it in the other. What is it to accept a statement? To act on it, if there can be such a thing, to draw inferential conclusions from it, to avow it when asked or advance it when it is otherwise relevant to do so. What is it to reject a statement? To deny it, or, in general, to accept its negation. Note that, on an account of this kind, nothing is assumed about the speaker's *having in mind* the circumstances that would substantiate or refute the statement—he may or may not have: what is required is that, when circumstances of either kind occur, he reacts appropriately. That sort of thing is what I meant by urging that the understanding of a statement must consist in the ability to *do* something.

Such an explanation does not presume bivalence. Under a theory of meaning that assumes bivalence, such as I take a truth-conditional theory to be, a speaker must conceive of the condition for a statement to be true as one that determinately either obtains or does not obtain, independently of whether we know or can know which. When truth-conditions are thought of in this way, a grasp of them cannot be fully manifested by a readiness to accept a statement when it is substantiated, and to reject it when it is refuted: the speaker must grasp the condition for it to *be* true even when there is nothing to indicate whether that condition obtains or not, and no means to secure such an indication. It is on this conception that understanding a statement must be represented as an intellectual capacity to *conceive* the condition for its truth; and it is that which renders the theory circular.

There is much that I should expect to find in a defence of truth-conditional theories of meaning that I do not find in McDowell's essay. Such a defence ought to show why we need to base our account of meaning on the notion of a sentence's being true; to do that, it must show we cannot give it a different basis. Suppose, for example, that, in surveying the immensely complex practice of using a language, we were to observe that assertoric utterances have to be evaluated as correct or incorrect, and to hit on the idea of taking the utterance of a declarative sentence as the making of a claim that needs to be vindicated when challenged. The difference between the condition for vindicating a claim and that for the truth of an assertion, as understood by the truth-conditional theorist, is that, unless the assertion relates to the speaker, what the speaker does or can do is irrelevant to the condition for its truth; whereas the justification of a claim always consists in something that the speaker can indicate, say or do. Thus if the speaker utters an existential sentence, he will, on this theory, be claiming to be able to give an instance; if instead he comes out with the negation of that statement, he will be claiming to be able to give a compelling reason why there can be no such instance. Clearly bivalence will not hold on such a theory; the speaker may not be in a position to make either claim.

A defence of truth-conditional theories must show why we cannot interpret assertoric utterances as making claims rather than as stating impersonal truths: it must show why, in order to represent how our language functions, we need the notion of objective truth rather than that of justifying a claim. McDowell's remarks at the end of his section III and the beginning of his section IV seemed to me at first an expression of what I have repeatedly emphasised, that the concepts of truth and of meaning must be explained *together*. But subsequently I have wondered: does he offer any explanation of the concept of truth at all, or does he just use it to explain meaning? Any theory of meaning must explain the notion of truth—that conception of truth proper to that theory; and the explanation will bear the heaviest burden in a theory that has explained meaning in terms of truth.

A truth-conditional theory of meaning must show how the condition for the truth of a statement determines what we are to count as evidence for it, conclusive or otherwise, and what arc conventionally regarded as the consequences of asserting it and of accepting it. All this will enter into the account of the concept of truth within the theory; it will at the same time show what makes the theory a theory of *meaning*. It is not enough for the proponent of a theory to say, "Well, that is what meaning is in my eyes"; the theory must be plausible as an analysis of those meanings of which we acquire a grasp in learning to engage in the practice of using the language. It must therefore yield a description of the salient features of that practice.

But this is not yet enough. Why should a theory of meaning take the form of explaining meaning in terms of the concept of truth, rather than of something directly descriptive of features of linguistic practice such as accepting or rejecting a statement? A defence of a theory of this kind must show why we *cannot* faithfully describe our practice of using language save by invoking a notion of objective bivalent truth. And since it must represent understanding a statement as a conception of the condition for it to be true, a defender must argue that anyone who masters the language thereby obtains at least a tacit grasp of the concept of truth.

I should very much like to see a defence of truth-conditional theories of meaning that fulfilled what seem to me essential requirements for such a defence; I should not put it beyond possibility that it would even convert me, though I doubt it. But I regret to say that McDowell's essay does not seem to me to embody what is needed for an adequate such defence.

V

Before going on to respond to Part Two of McDowell's essay, I shall pause to comment on some other interesting matters touched on in his Part One. I found an incompatibility between Frege's procedure in *Grundgesetze*, where he first lays down in detail the conditions for a sentence to refer to the True (have the value *true*) and only then explains the notions of sense and of the thought expressed by a sentence, and his official doctrine that it is to thoughts that a truth-value is to be ascribed in the first instance, and only derivatively to the sentences that express them. McDowell gently objects to my doing so. We can only know what truth is, he argues, if we understand the connection between judgement or assertion and truth. This is therefore a tacit background to the semantic theory Frege sets out in *Grundgesetze*, and, when brought to the foreground, dissolves the alleged incompatibility. In "Über Sinn und Bedeutung," Frege says that anyone who makes a judgement knows, at least implicitly, what objects the True and the False are. In *Grundgesetze*, on the other hand, he simply takes for granted that the reader knows what the True and the False are, without spelling out how the activity of forming judgements bears upon this knowledge. It is strange that, in a full-dress exposition of his theory such as occurs in *Grundgesetze*, though without any argument for its correctness, Frege should have left so important a point unstated. But I acknowledge that, once it is made explicit, the tension I once perceived between his official doctrine and his actual procedure is greatly mitigated. Indeed, for reasons like McDowell's, I had ceased to feel that tension.

McDowell refers to the thoughts I have expressed about knowledge of a language. Is this theoretical knowledge, knowledge *that* the words of the language have the meanings they have? Or is it practical knowledge, knowledge how to engage in the practice of speaking the language? Neither: it is a kind of knowledge that falls between the two. I have frequently illustrated this by a joke from one of P. G. Wodehouse's novels. A lady is asked whether she can speak Spanish; she replies, "I don't know: I have never tried." Knowledge of a language is mastery of a practical ability, although it usually has some propositional components; but it is an ability which confers on its possessors a knowledge of what it is an ability to do, a knowledge which those who lack the ability cannot have. In this it contrasts with a straightforward practical ability such as knowing how to swim: those who cannot swim can know perfectly well what it is to swim. Someone who had never been taught to swim might find to his surprise that, when forced to try to swim, he could do it. I think that John McDowell agrees with this; he makes of it something in favour of truth-conditional theories of meaning by his usual juggling with the notion of expressing a thought.

VI

Expressing a thought continues to figure largely in Part Two. In the first paragraph of section VII McDowell declares that in Part One he had used as unanalysed the notion of employing a sentence to express a thought. If so, that undercuts my charge that his argument was circular. But how can that notion remain unanalysed? In what I said above, I took expressing a thought to consist in uttering a (declarative) sentence, conscious of its sense. For Frege, a thought is the sense of a sentence (with due allowance for indexicality, whereby different thoughts can be expressed on different occasions by means of the same sentence). We have, for him, no access to thoughts save through a language by means of which we can express them. So on his account, expressing a thought just is uttering a sentence whose sense is that thought, knowing what sense it has. Does McDowell demur from Frege's view that *we* can grasp thoughts only as expressed in language? It seems, rather, that he goes further than Frege, rejecting his claim that there is no contradiction in supposing the existence of beings who grasp the same thoughts as we do, but not clothed in words. But, even if he did demur, what bearing would that have upon our *expressing* thoughts by means of sentences? McDowell gives the impression that he thinks that the concept of our expressing a thought is far deeper than that of merely uttering a sentence (assertorically or not) which has the appropriate sense, by a speaker aware of what that sense is. But, then, what, for him, does the capacity of a sentence to convey a given thought consist in? Does he not think that the meaning borne by a sentence, as specified by his truth-conditional theory of meaning, suffices to endow it with that capacity? If not, is not his theory of meaning seriously defective? He later says that if we do not presuppose that sentences can be used to express thoughts, we put in doubt whether our description of linguistic practice will reveal that which it describes as being meaningful. Why must a theory of meaning *presuppose* that sentences can be used to express thoughts? Surely that notion should be *explained* by a theory of meaning. I confess myself baffled to comprehend McDowell's view.

McDowell uses an *argumentum ad hominem* against me. If using the notion of expressing a thought violates my constraint on using, in a theory of meaning, any concept available only to a language-user, then so do the notions of accepting and of rejecting an assertion, which I want to employ in place of those of being true and being false. Without the idea that sentences can be used to express thoughts, he asks, how could a speaker have the conception of acknowledging the truth of a sentence? What conception of truth could be operative here?

Of course, the constraint ought to be on using a concept available only to a language-user that has not already been explained in the theory. Noting that I have sometimes hyphenated "accepting-as-true," McDowell offers me a way out—one that he later finds as objectionable as the position from which it was an escape route. This is to take the concept of accepting a statement as not presupposing the concept of truth, "and with it the notion of thought-expression." Well, of course, he is here in part right. The point of using the notion of accepting a statement as true was to avoid presup-posing—indeed, invoking at any stage—the conception of a statement's simply *being* true. It was *not*, however, intended as a means of setting aside the notion of expressing a thought. It was a proposal for how to construct a non-truth-conditional theory of meaning. If we have a satisfactory theory of meaning, it will explain what it is for a declarative sentence to have the sort of meaning it has, and thereby to express a thought. The notion of accepting a statement *is* attainable without forming a concept of the statement's *being* true. A theory of meaning that aims to make explicit the whole practice of using the language must explain the assertoric use of sentences. In doing so, it will need to distinguish between a speaker's being entitled to make an assertion, and there being an entitlement to be had. The theory will attribute to each sentence the condition for a speaker's being entitled to assert it. This condition may consist in his making certain observations, or being reliably informed that others have made them; it may, as with mathematical statements, consist in carrying out or being presented with a chain of reasoning; usually it will consist in a mixture of the two. One who is in one of the relevant such positions accepts the sentence as one he will be justified in asserting; he may also draw conclusions from it, and will also act on it if it bears on what he should do. It is integral to the practice of assertion that the hearers may accept what is said, or may decline to do so. When they are in doubt, they will ask the speaker for his grounds. As with the original speaker, to accept a statement involves being ready to draw inferences from it, to assert it if questioned and to act on it if that is in place. To act on a statement is to act as one would if one had oneself had the grounds for the assertion that the speaker had. (Perhaps it would be necessary to explain the difficult notion of integrating a newly accepted statement into a coherent conception of how things are.) No doubt these are extremely difficult matters to describe comprehensively; but that is not what is at issue here. What is in question is whether the notion of accepting a statement can be arrived at without calling upon the concept of its being true independently of our knowing it to be true or of having evidence or grounds for it. I maintain that it obviously can. Converse between people involves the making of assertions and the responses to them by accepting them or declining to do so: a description of linguistic practice must make that one of its primary components. Such a description does not need to invoke the notion of a statement's being true, independently of our having good reason to make it.

John McDowell wishes to deprive me, in advancing the proposal for what I have called a justificationist theory of meaning in place of a truth-conditional one, of the notion of expressing a thought. He has no right to do so. He also, rather oddly, denies me the right "to spell out the legitimacy of the moves" in the language-game "in terms of grounds for saying that things are thus and so": the whole point of the proposal was to specify the meanings of sentences of the language in terms of the kinds of ground that would justify their assertion.

How would a truth-conditional theory of meaning stand, for me, if applied to a language all of whose sentences were effectively decidable? Such a language would be meagre indeed: it would have no past tense; no quantifiers like "everywhere" and "at some (possibly remote) future time"; no subjunctive conditionals; perhaps no statements of comparison between quantities that can never be subjected to a direct comparison. But if there were such a language, it would be easy to explain the notion of a grasp of the condition for the truth of a statement. To know that, a speaker would need only to know how to carry out the relevant decision procedure and how to recognise its result. It may be said that he would have to do more than that to be said to know the meaning of the statement; for instance, he must know how to convey the result of that decision procedure by asserting the statement, how to act on the truth of the statement if that comes to be in question, and how to draw consequences from it. All that is true: the specification of the truth-conditions of sentences will only be a part of the theory if it is to amount to a comprehensive description of the practice of using the language. It remains that an account of a grasp of those truth-conditions would be unproblematic.

McDowell says that, in arguing that it is the presence in our language of sentences whose truth or falsity we have no effective means of deciding that makes it difficult to give a clear content to or a non-circular explanation of the notion of grasping the truth-condition of a sentence, I have failed to focus on the real defect. The real defect arises from there being "no recognizable notion of truth that can be understood independently of a notion of saying things, of expressing thoughts."

Let us see how this works. A truth-conditional theory of meaning specifies the meanings of sentences of the language by laying down the various conditions for them to be true. (I set aside the question how far it can do this without circularity.) Now either a novice in the theory of meaning confronted with these stipulations already understands what truth is or he does not. If the former, then this novice must have had an explanation of the procedure of making assertions on a promissory note of an as yet forthcoming set of specifications of the content of assertions made by using various sentences: he has, as it were, a programmatic conception of truth, one that is, indeed, connected with the notion of expressing a thought, a thought determined by the meaning of the sentence uttered. An assertion will then be justified if the sentence used is true; but this notion of justification will apply in cases in which neither the speaker nor anyone else had or could have an entitlement to make that assertion. Suppose, now, that the latter case obtains for another novice: he does not bring to the theory a prior grasp of the concept of truth. Then he will be presented with the specifications of truth-conditions before there is available to him any genuine notion of truth. These specifications may be regarded as being in terms of a condition for a sentence to be T, where T is a term of the theory with which he has no prior acquaintance. The interest of being T will not be made plain until later, when the procedure of making assertions is explained and the condition for an assertion's being justified equated with that for the sentence used to be T. At that point the second novice will acquire a genuine notion of truth. For both novices, the notion of truth comes as bound up with that of expressing (and endorsing) a thought.

I do not of course believe in truth-conditional theories of meaning. I do not believe that there is a coherent notion of truth under which a statement may be true although there is nothing that would entitle anyone to assert it. The truth-conditional theorist does. But I am not pursuing this disagreement at this point. I am here interested in McDowell's notion of "the real defect." Both of the novices being instructed in a truth-conditional theory whom I considered above—the first one who starts with a notion of truth connected with assertion, but has yet to learn the truth-conditions of sentences of the language, and the second one who learns the T-conditions of sentences, and only then acquires the notion of truth, again as connected with assertion—have come to have a conception of expressing a thought. They therefore do not appear to violate McDowell's precept that there is no recognisable notion of truth that can be understood independently of a notion of expressing thoughts.

They do violate a precept of McDowell's all the same. This is because, so far at least, they have come to their partial understanding of a truth-conditional theory of meaning "from outside," that is, without invoking any concepts that they already had in virtue of being language-users. *That* is what upsets John McDowell. The concept of being-true cannot be explained, he says at the end of section VII, "from outside the concept of giving expression to thoughts." You can understand a theory of meaning only by deploying certain concepts which you already had because you were already a speaker of a language. If you do not come to it in this way—from the inside—then you cannot *really* understand the theory of meaning. Our two novices *acquired* the conceptions they have of expressing a thought from explanations they were given. But they should have *presupposed* a notion of expressing a thought that they already had, and should have been content to leave it unexplained. So their understanding exhibits the "real defect," and risks continuing to do so.

I cannot share this attitude of McDowell's at all. He thinks I suffer from an inability to see what light can be thrown on a range of interconnected concepts by displaying the relations between them, rather than by attempting to define them all by appealing, for the initial definitions, only to concepts outside that range. I don't think I am unaware of this way of shedding light, when there is good reason to think it impossible to do better, or simply when one cannot see how to do better. But in the case in point

—the range of concepts having to do with the way language functions—I think there is good reason to believe that it must be possible to give a description of the—admittedly extremely complex—practice of using a language without presupposing notions we have in virtue of our already engaging in that practice. I don't think philosophers should be in the business of presupposing; being forced to resort to it is a confession of failure. We are not born with a knowledge of a language. We *acquire* such knowledge. If we *were* born with a knowledge of a language, I should be prepared to believe that McDowell was right. As it is, we are inducted into a complicated practice, and what we learn to do we must be capable of describing without presupposing anything. It is indeed much harder to arrive at a satisfactory and convincing such description than it was to acquire the practice in the beginning. As we attempt to do so, we are more or less bound at initial stages to employ concepts we have by being language-users, trusting that we shall eventually be able to dispense with such props by explaining those concepts without presuppositions: that is, that we shall be able to say accurately just what it is that we learn to do. That means describing it "as from the outside." We are ourselves inside; but, as philosophers, we want to be able to say just what it is to be inside. At least, I do: and I do not see that there can be any obstacle in principle to our doing so, difficult as the task may be.

VII

In his section VIII, McDowell mentions a large number of things that must enter into a comprehensive description of the practice of using language. He sees these as figuring in a "complete warrant for a truth-conditional interpretation." I see them, rather, as being comprised in the theory of meaning itself, considered as providing a description of the practice of using (speaking, hearing, writing, reading) the language. McDowell evidently thinks of the theory of meaning as consisting solely in the specification of the meanings of individual words and sentences; the rest is contained only in the warrant for such a theory. This probably reflects no deep disagreement between us, but is a mere boundary dispute. McDowell argues against me that there "is nothing about the concept of responsiveness to evidence that would license singling it out from the range of concepts that . . . needs to figure in connecting a . . . meaning-theory for a language with the facts about its speakers," and that there "is no reason to suppose understanding of sentences can be correctly represented as *consisting in* behavioral propensities characterizable in terms of a restricted subclass of the conceptual background that . . . accounts of meaning would require."

Well, given a theory of meaning of the general shape on which

McDowell and I agree, there will be a narrower and a wider sense of "understanding." In the narrower sense, someone may be said to understand a sentence if he grasps that feature of it which is said by the theory to constitute its meaning—in McDowell's case, its truth-condition, in mine what would entitle a speaker to assert it. This feature is that used in the part of the theory—in McDowell's classification, the theory proper—that serves to specify the meanings of individual sentences and words. But there is a wider sense, used in common discourse, in which understanding demands a grasp of many other features of the use of the sentence. Suppose that a child has been taught how to count objects of a given kind. He can therefore count up the lamb chops to be cooked, and say, "There are seven chops": he knows the canonical ground for making such an assertion, and, I suppose, knows its truth-condition: so, for both McDowell and me, he understands the sentence in the narrow sense. But suppose that, there being eight at table, he cannot understand what is meant by saying, "There won't be enough to go round." In the wide sense, he does not fully understand the sentence "There are seven chops": he does not know its connection with one-one correlation. Suppose a child knows how to recognise stupidity, and the condition for a sentence ascribing it to someone to be true. But he does not understand that stupidity is a defect, and perhaps has not the concept of a defect: so he does not grasp that saying, "Jane is very stupid," to Jane's mother, is grossly tactless. He understands the sentence in the narrow sense, but not in the wider. Understanding cannot be explained in terms of grounds for assertion in more than the narrow sense; nor can it be explained in more than that sense in terms of truth-conditions.

If we are to have a theory of meaning embodying—or consisting in—a recursive specification of the meanings of sentences, they must be specified in terms of *something*; we have then to explain our employment of those sentences by reference to their meanings, considered as so given. I believe that this can be done when the meanings are specified in terms of the conditions that justify assertion. So far as I can see, McDowell has supplied no reason for thinking that the concept of truth-conditions should be singled out to play this role. The supplementary explanation of our linguistic practice is surely harder to give when truth-conditions are made to play it than when a feature more directly connected with our practice, such as grounds for assertion, is chosen for the role.

I presume that in McDowell's theory of meaning, classical logic holds good in the metalanguage (as also in the object-language). And I presume also that no distinction is drawn between a statement's not being true and its being false. If these presumptions are right, McDowell's conception of truth incorporates the principle of bivalence.

For McDowell, the notion of using a sentence to express a thought is essentially linked to his conception of truth, that is, of a condition for the sentence (or the thought) to be true. This condition determinately either obtains or does not obtain, independently of our knowing or having any means to know which. This, of course, is the essence of the metaphysical doctrine of realism. McDowell believes that you cannot have the notion of expressing a thought unless you connect it to this conception of truth, and subscribe to this doctrine. I have tried to explain why I do not think that is correct; one with a different conception of truth may possess a vivid notion of expressing a thought. The notion of expressing a thought, understood as he understands it, is for McDowell a magical one. It must be presupposed, not explained; it is the breath of life for meaning-theories, which without it dwindle into mechanical language-games which soulless beings, who cannot be credited with having thoughts, let alone with expressing them, may be trained to play. I think it is superstition to attribute to any notion such astonishing powers. Other defenders of truth-conditional theories of meaning do not, so far as my limited experience goes, make such play with the notion of expressing thoughts, except for Frege, probably the first proponent of a truth-conditional theory of meaning; but he explains the notion, rather than presupposing it, and ascribes no magical potency to it. So perhaps such theories of meaning can be defended in a different style; I feel fairly confident that any such defence will be no more cogent than John McDowell's appears to me to be. But I thank him for taking such pains to examine my views and to explain why he thinks his approach far superior to mine. Though we are no nearer agreement than we were before, I feel that much has come to light from this exchange.

M. D.

11

Akeel Bilgrami

PURSUING AN ANALOGY

I

In a well-known passage in an early paper entitled, simply, "Truth," which prompted many philosophers to rethink, if not repudiate, their instinctively realist assumptions about the nature of truth, Michael Dummett says this:

> Let us compare truth and falsity with the winning and losing of a board game. . . . It is part of the concept of winning a game that a player plays to win, and this part of the concept is not conveyed by a classification of the end positions into winning ones and losing ones. . . . Likewise, it is part of the concept of truth that we aim at making true statements; and Frege's theory of truth and falsity . . . leaves this feature of the concept of truth quite out of account.[1]

The point Dummett makes in drawing this analogy between truth and falsity and winning and losing, viz., that we aim at winning and at truth and aim at avoiding losing and aim to avoid falsity and error, is a point with far-reaching and significant implications. To pursue those implications for the debate that Dummett and Donald Davidson had for over thirty years is the main preoccupation of this essay.

The point and the analogy from which it derives speak to nothing less than the value of truth, to the normative nature of truth. One would have thought that this aspect of truth is obvious—one cannot understand the concept of truth if one leaves this aspect of it out, the aspect of its value, in other words, that in some sense, truth is a goal we have (as is avoiding error or falsity). But the fact, one explicitly mentioned by Dummett in that passage, that Frege did not see the point shows that it is not such an obvious point after all. And the fact that other well-known philosophers since Frege, such as Davidson (and more recently Rorty)[2], have explicitly opposed it shows that it is not only unobvious, it is not an uncontroversial point either.

A closer look at what Davidson has had to say about it over the years will be useful. In a paper, entitled "Communication and Convention,"[3] Davidson focuses on a formulation of the analogy where Dummett says that "there is a general convention whereby the utterance of a sentence, except in special contexts, is understood as being carried out with the intention of uttering a true sentence."[4] Focusing on passages like this, Davidson interprets Dummett's analogy between truth and winning as being a point wholly about the concept of truth as it surfaces in *communicative* contexts.

With that highly specific focus, he is able to say that there is no such convention to speak the truth in uttering declarative sentences because when we do so, we at least as often as not speak lies, metaphors, ironies, jokes, and so on. These are so pervasive, says Davidson, that we cannot make any claims with confidence about the intentions or goals with which declarative or indicative sentences are uttered. The only thing that we can perhaps say with any confidence is that when a declarative sentence is uttered to make an assertion (which it often need not be), the speaker (merely) *represents himself* as speaking the truth. There is no closer tie between speaking a declarative sentence and aiming at speaking the truth.

This very point surfaces again in his elaboration of the method of radical translation or interpretation. One does not have to spell out the details of this method to convey the point. In collecting evidence for his eventual project of devising a theory of meaning, a radical interpreter seeks first (by Mill's methods) to correlate recurring circumstances in the world with the recurring utterance of or assent to declarative sentences containing indexical elements, by native informants. To take just one example, he might note that "Es regnet" is uttered by native informants in a certain linguistic community under the circumstance that it is raining whenever it is uttered. But a question arises as to how one knows that the native informants are not lying (or speaking metaphorically, or ironically, or jokingly, etc.) when they make or assent to these utterances. Lies, metaphors, ironical remarks, jokes, and so on, are so frequent in communicative contexts that this question is undismissable. If a radical interpreter relied on those occasions in which the native informants were lying, speaking metaphorically, and so on, the correlations he makes might well turn out to yield bad and misleading evidence upon which to construct a theory of meaning.

Now, as a point of philosophy, Davidson could, right at this point, appeal to just the close tie Dummett claims between uttering a declarative sentence and speaking the truth. But he explicitly refuses to do so, saying that that would be going against the facts since there is no such tie or "convention." It is not part of our understanding of either declarative speech or the concept of truth that there is such a tie or convention. Instead, he proposes the following much more complicated idea. The radical interpreter should use his wits by looking at clues of various kinds having to do with the context in which speech occurs and on this basis make *hypotheses* as to which cases of the native informant's speech are cases of aiming to speak sincerely and truthfully and which not. It is the nature of the method of radical interpretation that this way of accumulating the evidence is itself a kind of hypothesis-making rather than anything firmer as the word "evidence" might misleadingly suggest.[5] So, we may not *assume* that (due to the existence of a convention of the form that Dummett claims) the informant is aiming to say something true, but we may *hypothesize* in this or that case that he is and on the basis of that accumulate the requisite evidence correlating specific utterances or assents with some rather than other circumstances in the world. And if the theory of meaning built on this evidence is a good one, if it effectively accounts for the speakers' linguistic behavior, then we can return and *retroactively* say that these initial hypotheses that formed the evidence for the theory were correct hypotheses.[6] Thus the evidence is the basis of the theory, even as it is fortified, qua evidence, by the success of the theory that is built on it. This complicated and radically holistic[7] methodological approach to theory-construction is forced on Davidson by the fact that he finds it necessary to deny Dummett's point of the close tie between declarative speech and aiming to speak the truth.

As I said, Davidson is able to say these critical things about Dummett because he views the entire point of the analogy in Dummett as a point about the concept of truth as it surfaces in communicative contexts. Perhaps he does so because in the first passage we cited from Dummett in the opening paragraph of this paper, where the analogy is first drawn by him, Dummett goes from saying that it is part of the concept of winning in a game that we aim to win, to saying that it is part of the concept of truth that we aim to make true *statements*. And there is no doubt that, quite generally, Dummett does want to make the point connecting truth with linguistic acts such as the utterance of declarative sentences in communication. This is also evident in the passage cited above in which he formulates the convention which Davidson criticized.

All the same, the analogy drawn by Dummett makes a prior and more fundamental point that need not be seen as necessarily invoking, right at the outset, a communicative context for truth. As subjects who think and inquire (and who are also of course necessarily speakers of a language) we aim in our inquiry and thought to avoid error and seek truth. It is a further point, perhaps necessitated by the close links between thought and language (about which Dummett has written much and illuminatingly, as has Davidson) that leads Dummett to express the analogy in specifically communicative linguistic terms. But there is no denying that the point of the analogy can be made and made truly and without obscurity, as being first and foremost about inquiry and its deliverances. This point should remain unaffected by anything Davidson says against the convention that thinking subjects are said to have to *speak* the truth.

The term "inquiry" as it is used here should not give any impression that what is intended by it is to talk specifically of a "scientific" enterprise. Rather it is meant merely to be coextensive with the much more general fact that subjects capable of thought are, in a loose and informal sense, essentially involved in an activity that is governed by (and assessed for) being true and false, rational and irrational, in the light of evidence and other sorts of grounds that are available to them. They are involved with it whether they are studying the nature of quarks, whether they are wondering if they will be hurt if they jump from a certain height, or whether there is a fly in front of them or a black spot, or so on. The range of inquiry is not restricted to science but to all of commonsense thought. In this broad sense, there is inquiry where there is thought in the sense of belief, where there is thought that is capable of being true or false.

Now, thought of the kind that sophisticated creatures like human beings possess no doubt has essential links with linguistic capacity and expression. And the relations between the two are difficult and important to get right. But however we think of the relations and the conceptual priorities between thought and language, we must for many purposes of philosophy keep them apart and notice differences in philosophical points as they apply to each of them, even as we notice philosophical points of commonality. Often, terms such as "contents," "propositions," and even "statements" (in the sense of "what is said" as opposed to the sentences whose utterance is used to say it) fall on the side of thoughts as much as they fall on the side of linguistic communication, and different things must be said of them depending on which side they fall. So the next thing I want to do is to proceed with some care and make some distinctions about Dummett's analogy between truth as it applies to thoughts and as it applies to utterances in communicative contexts. We can then see whether the deep point that Dummett wants to make is so easily unsettled by Davidson's critical remarks that we registered above.

In thought and inquiry (in this broad sense), we aim at the truth and we seek to avoid error. That is what is most generally meant by talk of the normative aspects of truth, of truth as a value. The assessment of beliefs as true or false is not just to place them in two innocuous categories. One says "*assessment*" and means it. It is considered a *good* thing when it falls into one category and not the other, and that is why we aim at one and aim to avoid the other. There is no understanding thought and inquiry without this normative understanding of the nature of truth. And there is no understanding the notion of truth which leaves this normative aspect out.

None of this talk of truth being the goal of inquiry should give the impression that we are obsessively seeking to acquire more and more truths, nor that we are constantly vigilant and on the lookout for error and falsehood in out thinking. The normative understanding of truth as it relates to thought does not require that. One may, of course, often have other (and by one's lights) better or more pressing things to do with one's time and resources. But that does not cancel the fact that truth is an aim of inquiry nor that that aim is constitutive of thought. One, in general, can be committed to a norm or a goal and then one can put it aside when the costs are too high to pursue it. This general point about norms applies to truth as a norm or goal. What is important is that acknowledging this is not to concede in any way that the normative aspect of truth is wholly voluntary, that some subjects capable of thought may have it and others may lack it, having cast it away. Even at the times when we are not pursuing truth and have put aside that pursuit because we have other things to do and therefore the costs of pursuing it are high, it does not lose its status as a norm or goal of inquiry. Seeking truth does not become a norm that is entirely conditional, something one pursues when and if one wants to but which has no more unconditional status than that. If that were so, it would be quite wrong to say that it constitutes the very notion of thought and inquiry—and Dummett's analogy would have run to waste.

There are, in general, two ways of thinking of norms. One is to say that there is no norm in place until someone decides to adopt it as a norm with a view to pursuing specific interests. This is the wholly voluntarist notion of norm. Applied to our present topic, this would mean that truth does not constitute thought and inquiry, we just aim at the truth whenever we have an inclination or an interest in doing so. On such a way of thinking of norms, norms can be viewed as (or as generating) imperatives or goals of the form, "If you find it useful or interesting or . . . , do x or seek x." Such a way of thinking of norms accommodates the phenomena we have acknowledged (viz., that we often put aside the goal of seeking truth, as for instance when we are too busy with other things) in a very specific way: by making the norm itself conditional on our interests and inclinations at given times. But there is a quite different way of formulating norms, which accommodates the acknowledged phenomena in a quite different way. In this other way of thinking of norms, they are (or they generate) imperatives or goals of the form "Do x or seek x, unless the costs (costs, broadly conceived, of course) are too high." Here the norms are in place first, as a prior, as it were, and the acknowledged phenomena are accommodated only as falling under an excusing condition for something *already in place*. It is in this sense of norm that truth as a norm governs thought and inquiry. We aim to seek truth in this sense in inquiry and this is what is intended by Dummett's analogy at its most basic level.

We still have to say what the relation of this notion of truth and the analogy with winning has to do with aiming at the truth in speech in communicative contexts. So far we have restricted the focus to truth aimed at inquiry in the broad sense of that term, which is involved in any thought capable of truth and falsity. How does it relate to truth as an aim in the context of communicative speech that Davidson has explicitly criticized? Let us approach the question of this relation by asking: would all that we have just said about the analogy and the notion of truth as something we aim for in thought and inquiry, be spoiled if Davidson's criticism of Dummett is correct? Suppose it is indeed the case that, as Davidson says, we, in our declarative speech, just as often do not aim to speak the truth as we do aim to speak it. Does that undermine anything we have just said about truth as something we aim at?

The answer is surely no.

First of all, Dummett could simply say that the fact of the statistical frequency of our failing to speak the truth does not mean that the convention he had claimed, the convention to speak the truth with the declarative sentences we utter, which Davidson is criticizing, does not exist. He could make a point parallel to the one we have just made about norms and say that the convention is indeed in place as a prior, even if it is often violated. It is not that we just speak the truth when and if it serves our interest, rather there is the convention to speak the truth in our declarative utterances—it is just that we sometimes put it aside for one reason or another. And these reasons are to be viewed just as we viewed the excusing conditions mentioned above in the second formulation of the nature of norms, they merely come in to excuse one from something that is *already in place*, the convention to speak the truth.

This will seem like dogmatic assertion to those who take the Davidsonian view. Communication, they will say, is for all sorts of things, so why should we think that something is in place as a prior and as a more fundamental aim of communication? They may even grant that assertion as a speech act, that is, utterances made with assertoric *force*, are basic in some way as opposed to, say, asking a question or giving an order. And they may grant (a different point) that the indicative *mood* of a sentence is more basic than other moods, such as interrogatives and imperatives. They may grant, that is, that there may be good reasons for both these claims in order to understand the nature of language. But, they will insist, neither of these granted claims requires that we see utterances made with assertoric force as being made with the aim or intention of speaking the truth. That is a further claim quite different from the ones that have been granted, and it is not obvious, they will say, that anything in the study of language is advanced by elevating this particular intention above others. Even if we have a truth-conditional or verification-conditional account of meaning (in which sentences in a certain mood and utterances with a certain force have to be viewed as central because the predicates "is true" and "is verified" attach more suitably to such things than to others), that does not mean that we have to see such things as being spoken with the intention of telling the truth. Granted that we would not be able to correlate (truth or verification) conditions in the world with sentences very well if we did not fasten on uttered sentences that were uttered with this intention of speaking the truth rather than with the intention to lie, or to speak metaphorically, and so forth. But Davidson has already shown that that problem can be solved by adopting the radically holistic method of interpretation of another's speech, as briefly outlined above. The problem does not need one to announce a convention of speaking the truth, it will be said.

Let us, for the moment, even grant that this is so. That is, let us grant that the fact of the statistical frequency in communication of the violations of the so-called convention to speak the truth puts into doubt that there is such a convention. The point is that the convention is about communication. It is about speaking or *telling the truth*. What do these doubts about it have to do with the value of *truth*, what does it have to do with the analogy with winning, whose first point is to connect truth with a value or goal of attaining it, just as we aim at winning? Can we not at least cleave to the idea that we aim at the truth, even if Davidson has put into doubt that we aim at telling the truth in communication? Why should the latter doubt cast doubt on the former idea, why should it utterly spoil Dummett's analogy? All that Davidson could show with his doubts is that we need to be clearer and distinguish the *value of truth* from the *value of telling the truth*. These are two distinct values.

Davidson, actually, does not deny that there is a value to truth-telling, in some sense. All he wants to deny is Dummett's claim that, qua value, truth-telling has any relevance to the nature of thought and language, that it has any relevance for the philosopher in these regions of philosophy. On this picture of value, the only values there are are moral values, aesthetic values, even perhaps the norms of rationality. But Davidson (in his later work) is explicit in claiming that there is *no cognitive* value attaching to *truth* because truth is not a value or a goal at all; and moreover he thinks there are very good and important reasons to deny that it is a value. Truth-telling, therefore, will be admitted by him (as it should by anyone) to be a value, but, he will insist, that it is only a moral value. Somebody who tells the truth has or exemplifies a value of a kind that we are familiar with, just as someone who is kind or considerate or generous does. What Davidson (and following him, Rorty) denies is that there is something more abstract, a cognitive value that is to be found not in telling the truth, but in truth itself. The only value there is surrounding the notion of truth is the value of truth-telling and that is a moral value of no relevance to the study of language and thought.

But this seems wrong. There is a value that truth has which is quite distinct from the value of telling the truth. Where does the difference lie, exactly?

There must be a difference because the person who violates or shuns the one need not be violating or shunning the other. The person who violates or shuns the value of truth-telling is the liar. But a liar most likely *does* value *truth*. Why would he want to conceal it or invent it, if he did not in some sense value it?

What is this sense, then? Part of the difficulty is this: We seem to be able to get a glimmer of the value of truth and its distinction from the value of truth-telling by noticing, as we just did, that those who do not value truth-telling might well value truth. But if even someone who does not value truth-telling, who violates the value of truth-telling, values truth, that is if *even the liar* values truth, it is not clear that anyone *fails* to value truth. And if no one can fail to value truth, how can it be a value? Surely there cannot be a value that no one can fall afoul of. That seems to put into question that there is a value there at all.

This is a good difficulty to raise, but there is an answer to it. It is possible to violate the value of truth and there is indeed a kind of person who violates it, it is just not the liar. Rather it is another sort of person who, in America, is called a "bullshitter,"[8] not someone who uses declarative speech to lie, but rather uses it to just sound off—to make an impression, say, or to have someone hear what he wants to hear, or with any of a number of other motives. Sounding off of this kind has no regard to get things right. It is effects of these kind that matter and their mattering does not require the speaker to even try and get things right in what he says. "Getting things right" is, no doubt, not a very precise form of expression to convey what is meant by the value of truth, but it conveys enough to show the difference between the liar and the bullshitter. The liar cares about what is right, what is the truth; for one or other reason, he just does not tell the truth. The bullshitter may even tell something that is true, he just does not care that it is the truth; truth is not something that he values or that motivates him. But not caring about it does not make him a liar. He does not violate the value of truth-telling as the liar does. He violates the value of truth. What makes truth a value more abstract than truth-telling, then, is precisely what makes it a cognitive rather than a moral value. If even the (moral) truth-teller and the (immoral) liar value truth, then we are forced to *abstract away* from the moral domain of values such as truth-telling and locate the *cognitive* not moral value, which is truth itself.

I have been trying to argue that whatever side one takes on the question as to whether there is or is not a convention to speak the truth in our declarative speech, the analogy between truth and winning is not undermined at its deepest level. Even if Davidson is right on the matter of whether there is such a convention, so long as we understand how truth as a value differs from truth telling, the analogy holds. Even if he is right, all it shows is that in the context of communication, the idea that we aim for the truth surfaces not in aiming to speak the truth, but in aiming to make one's speech reflect what one does aim for (the truth, getting things right), in other words, it surfaces in the fact that, in one's speech, one does not "bullshit."

I am not here taking a stand on whether Davidson is right or not. It may well be that truth and truth-telling are more closely related than I have just proposed, in the sense that to value truth does require one to understand oneself as being governed by a convention regarding truth-telling in communicative contexts. That is not an issue I will explore here in detail because I want to go on in the space I have left to talk about what underlies Davidson's failure to see any point in the analogy and why he does not view truth as a value and a goal at all. But I will just say that it may well be possible to give support to the idea of such a convention by invoking the distinction between the two formulations of norms mentioned earlier, and arguing that the statistical frequency of violations of the convention need not undermine the idea of such a convention if we had good reasons to formulate our understanding of the convention along the lines of the second more unconditional and nonvoluntarist version of norms mentioned earlier, and thereby see the violations as accommodated by the excusing conditions. What those good reasons might be is the question that I will not pursue here.

II

Why does Davidson not see the point of the analogy as I have been expounding it—as having a life even outside of the convention to speak the truth in communicative contexts?

It is not until fairly late in his writing that we are given explicit statements about truth not being a goal of any kind at all. There is nothing in his work until just a few years ago which suggests that he took such a view. In fact, I must confess that in an article, "Meaning, Holism and Use,"[9] written twenty years ago in which I first discussed the debate on truth between Davidson and Dummett, much of my defense of his views against Dummett was based on an understanding of his views which assumed that he did think that truth was something we aimed at in inquiry, even if we did not as speakers and communicators subscribe to a convention to speak the truth in our declarative utterances. And so, there I had criticized Dummett for interpreting Davidson in a way that made him out to be more realist than he was, and at the time I wrote it I had no reason to think that Dummett was right in his interpretation. But Davidson's later writing on the subject changes all of this in a very significant way and in fact explains some of the anomalies in his earlier writing. Let me turn to these issues now.

In a recent paper, "Truth Rehabilitated,"[10] Davidson explicitly concluded that truth is not a norm, that it cannot be something we aim for and therefore cannot be a goal of inquiry. He does not mention Dummett's analogy as the target of this criticism because in this paper he was considering the epistemological doctrine of pragmatism. Even so, its relevance to Dummett and the analogy is obvious and rather direct. Davidson's argument for this conclusion is quite straightforward. It cannot be a goal we aim for because truth is not something we can ever know we have achieved. For any given belief (at any rate beliefs about empirical matters), we can have great confidence in it but we can never know that it is true because—for all our confidence in it—it may turn out to be false.

It must be said that if the premise is true (viz., that we never can know that any belief is true), it is very plausible to conclude that truth is not a goal of inquiry. Davidson does not say very much about what makes for its plausibility but it is not hard to see what does. It is very peculiar to think that one should be pursuing something that one can never know has been achieved. Perhaps this is not as peculiar as intending to do something that is impossible to do, but it is peculiar enough because it makes inquiry akin to sending messages out in a bottle to sea, which is a very peculiar way to think of inquiry. If all my cognitive pursuits were pursuits about whose success I were completely blinded, it would make inquiry a kind of "hoping for the best" and that is not how we think of inquiry.

So the surprise is not with Davidson's reasoning, which seems impeccable, but with the premise. For someone who has so often repudiated Cartesian ways of thinking about truth and knowledge, it is indeed surprising that Davidson should accept the premise that we can never know when any given belief of ours is true. To put it in other words, it turns out that Davidson's repudiation of Descartes is really quite selective. He merely rejects the claim that, for all we know, *all* our beliefs (staying with empirical beliefs) can be false, something that Descartes was prepared to assert on the basis of familiar epistemological arguments invoking dreams and demons that make comprehensive the fact of occasional illusions. Davidson does not reject the claim that, for all we know, any given belief of ours may be false. He rejects the Cartesian fantasies of *comprehensive* illusion because he thinks that there are good philosophical reasons having to do partly with the principle of charity and partly with a doctrine in the philosophy of mind and language known as "externalism," to deny that all or even most of our beliefs can be false. So, since he accepts that any given belief could, for all we know, be false, but not all our beliefs, he thinks that the fallacy in Descartes lies in going from the correct claim that any given belief can always be false, for all we know, to the incorrect claim that all might be. This last claim is incorrect because it falls afoul of a certain version of the principle of charity and the doctrine of externalism and so Descartes is guilty of an illicit transition from an uncontroversial claim to his incorrect skeptical conclusion.

The allegedly uncontroversial claim, as I said earlier, is the basis of Davidson's dismissal of the most basic point underlying Dummett's analogy. I have already said that the dismissal would be perfectly plausible if its basis were true. But the fact is that from Dummett's point of view and from the point of view of a credible epistemology, one might well question the uncontroversialness of the claim that forms the premise. Cartesian skepticism is not just the view that all our (empirical) beliefs, for all we know, might be false. It is equally and more interestingly (and more challengingly) the view that for any given (empirical) belief, we can never know that it is true and amounts to knowledge. This last and fundamental aspect of Cartesianism is something that apparently Davidson is fully prepared to accept as uncontroversial. To use his own term in that paper, he thinks it is essential to viewing truth as "objective." Once one accepts this residual Cartesianism, Dummett's analogy of truth with winning (that establishes truth as a goal and norm), cannot stand.

But why should one accept it? It is true that standard opposition to Descartes usually proceeds by labeling his position on truth, from which his skepticism is supposed to flow, as the "absolute conception of reality" and this is usually characterized in terms of a picture of truth which is so ulterior that it allows for *all* of our beliefs about the world to be false. On this standard picture, opposition to Cartesian skepticism only requires what Davidson tries to provide with his version of externalism and his argument against the very idea of a conceptual scheme. But in fact an earlier tradition of philosophizing against skepticism, going back to G. E. Moore and found in Wittgenstein and Austin as well, battles more ambitiously against a quite different picture of Cartesian epistemology. On this picture, skepticism consisted of the idea that for any given belief, we have no guarantee that it is true and no guarantee that it amounts to knowledge. We may have a great deal of confirmation, but no assurance of the real thing: truth. It is this skepticism that Moore opposed not by general arguments appealing to principles of charity or an externalist semantics, but by trying to provide specific counter instances to the skepticism, such as the belief expressed in the utterance "This is a hand" said under certain specified conditions characterized as "normal." Now, it is true that if Moore was right about this, he would have refuted not just the skepticism that consists in saying that, for all we know, any given belief of ours can turn out to be false but also the skepticism which consists in saying that, for all we know, all our beliefs can turn out to be false. But one should not be misled into thinking that just because a Moorean "refutation" (if indeed it is a refutation) would refute both versions of Cartesian skepticism that I have distinguished, that the two skepticisms should not be distinguished. I am not here concerned to say that Moore's specific strategy against this skepticism is the right one. I am only registering that there are two different understandings of what Cartesian skepticism amounts to: (1) the claim that it is possible that all our beliefs can be false; and (2) the claim that of any given belief, we can never know that it is true, however convinced we are of its truth. Davidson is complacent (at any rate, too unambitious) in thinking that only (1) needs to be opposed in order to formulate a credible epistemology.

So once again, the question arises, "Why should one accept (2)?" It cannot be that the *logical possibility* that any given (empirical) belief of ours is false forces on us an understanding of truth as it is found in (2). Why should such logical possibility make a difference to epistemology? Why should we take it seriously in inquiry? Inquiry takes seriously something that makes a difference to inquiry. It can treat all other possibilities as idle, from its point of view, that is, by the lights of its concerns. And why should something matter epistemologically if inquirers are not moved by it for anything that they pursue? What matters in inquiry is the particular belief one has is put into doubt by some counterevidence or reason that is relevant to *it in particular*. (And, of course, it must be allowed that there are local connections between beliefs; when reason is provided to doubt one belief some other related beliefs are also put into doubt.) But an inquirer cannot and does not put any particular belief in doubt on the completely *general* grounds that *any* given belief might be false. That is why (2) makes no difference to the inquirer's deliberations at all. Just as the preface-paradoxical acknowledgment of one's fallibility is not something that makes a difference to the author's convictions in his inquiry, acknowledgments of the logical possibility of a belief's being false may be granted by an inquirer and yet he would proceed just as he would have, had he not granted it. Its granting is idle to his enterprise. It puts nothing in particular in doubt. It does not give him pause in his inquiry.[11]

All these points about the irrelevance of some possibilities *to the inquirer* come to the surface only because, by making his analogy between truth and winning, Dummett has brought onto center stage the point of view of the inquirer. For it is the inquirer in us that aims for truth and the inquirer in us who, when he speaks, does not bullshit. The analogy implies that the notion of truth is tied to such a point of view and not to the person who has no such enterprise and who, when he communicates, is simply sounding off in his speech. But Davidson, who is not impressed by Dummett's analogy, is not only unimpressed by it in the context of communication (the subject of the last section), he is unimpressed by it even from the point of view of thought and inquiry because, as he says in the later writing that we are now discussing, bringing the point of view of the inquirer into the study of truth would lead inevitably to a surrender of what he describes as the "objectivity" of truth, which, he says, is to be found in (2). Anxious that we should not give up the objectivity of truth, he abandons the point of view of the inquirer as being relevant to epistemology and refuses to allow that we aim for the truth at all.

Some philosophers who have been influenced by Dummett (such as Hilary Putnam) have seen the importance of bringing in the point of view of the inquirer in this way, in a way that Davidson refused to do. It will be interesting and illuminating to say just a word here about how Putnam develops the claim which I have said is implicit in Dummett's analogy (viz., the relevance of the point of view of inquiry to our understanding of truth), because the way he develops it fails to come to full grip with the strengths of the claim. Though Putnam sees the relevance of the inquirer's point of view, he is also anxious to save something of the objectivity that one instinctively locates in (2). As a result he revives a certain Peircean understanding of the relevance of the point of view of inquiry to truth.[12] Realizing that (2) is not really compatible with stressing the point of view of the inquirer he abandons (2)—but nevertheless, in order to find an alternative way to save the "objectivity" of truth, he so *idealizes the notion of inquiry*, that it is not clear that the notion of truth which emerges can make a difference to any *actual* inquiry. "Truth" is characterized by him as the omnibus outcome of an ideal limit of inquiry at the limit of time; and the hankering for the objectivity found in (2) is located instead in the idea that any actual inquirer at any given time will acknowledge that any given belief of his (even if the logical possibility of its falsity is irrelevant) might be false by the lights of the ideal limit of inquiry at the limit of time. But this view, despite its acknowledgment of the importance of bringing on to the stage an inquirer's point of view, spoils the point of the analogy of truth with winning. Putnam's notion of truth makes no difference to the inquirer any more than the one found in (2). The inquirer is given no instruction for his deliberations by the caution that, at the ideal end of inquiry, one's current belief might be false. Putnam's is not a conception of truth that allows us to aim for truth. We aim for things we know we might achieve at the time we aim for them and with the inquiry with which we aim for them, not in some ideal limit of time and inquiry. We may, of course, sometimes aim for truth in a collective enterprise, knowing that some others might continue and do better after we stop, but this still does not amount to any idealization of the kind that Putnam is envisaging. It is in fact not an idealization, it is a sense of dynamic continuance of our *present* inquiry by others after us. It makes no appeal to the ideal limit of inquiry.

If the effect of the analogy with winning and of stressing the fact that we aim for truth is to bring onto center stage in discussions of truth, the point of view of those who aim for it, in other words, inquirers, we will need to do better than Putnam does in describing the stage. This is a very large subject and needs a treatment all its own. But even in giving a very crude picture of what is needed in a few words, the crucial point to be stressed is that the beliefs that inquirers hold without doubt (the belief, to use Moore's example, that they have hands, or that Oxford University is in England, or that the earth is not flat, and so forth) are considered to be true, and not short of true or merely justified, verified, and the like. The deliberation of inquiry which lead to beliefs of this sort, *beliefs that are doubt-free* (or to use Wittgenstein's term "beliefs of which we are 'certain'"), has the full prestige of *truth*, nothing less.

Beliefs of this kind form the background for inquiry's further deliberative efforts to investigate whether other sorts of beliefs—of which inquirers are far less certain and consider to be more controversial, namely, *hypotheses and conjectures*—are the kinds of things that they should admit to the set of certain beliefs or reject and place in the set of beliefs that they take to be certainly false. All inquiry therefore begins *in medias res*, assuming some beliefs without doubt and using them in the background to provide the standard by which one will assess other beliefs that are held without certainty as hypotheses, in the light of incoming evidence. Since these other beliefs are not doubt-free, the question of justification arises seriously for them and them alone, as far as inquirers are concerned at any given time. Being certain of the others, they do not consider the matter of their justification, they take them for granted in their inquiries.

At any given time, then, there are beliefs which form the background and about which the question of justification is not relevant. These "truths" in the background set the standard by which inquirers will deliberate as to whether the beliefs of which they are not certain are justifiably to be admitted to the set of beliefs held with certainty or justifiably to be omitted from them. This is what the notion of justification primarily applies to: whether or not *to change* the set of beliefs of which one is certain by *adding* to them some of the beliefs of which one is not certain (hypotheses) and also whether or not sometimes, if evidence and grounds exist, to *subtract* from the beliefs held with certainty.[13] That is to say, inquirers in the midst of their inquiry need justification (and the question of justification arises for them) only for whether they should *change* their minds about what to count as truths. And whether they are justified or not in changing their minds will depend on their deliberations, which always proceed with a background of "truths" and ask whether to add or subtract from this class of truths.[14] In this picture, it is evident not only that aiming for truth is at the heart of inquiry, but that that aim is often achieved because there is no inquiry possible without a background of *truths*. Truth as a goal cannot, by its nature, transcend inquiry in the form of a goal whose achievement is unseen by the inquirer as in Davidson's residual Cartesian picture.[15]

There are several questions that arise. What sort of objectivity does this notion of truth have, if it is always something that is understood from the point of view of inquiry? Does Davidson's picture, which explicitly aims to capture the "objectivity" of truth, not succeed in capturing it far better? It is quite right that once we see truth as something that inquiry aims for, we cannot retain Davidson's residual Cartesian conception of the objectivity of truth as found in (2), since, as Davidson rightly points out, truth cannot be aimed for in that conception. Does this mean that we have given up on the objectivity of truth?

There is no reason to think so. There is no reason to think that all notions of objectivity must take such ulterior form. After all, we revise our beliefs (held with certainty) from time to time and take ourselves to have improved on our past inquiry in doing so, so we are committed to objectivity. We are committed to the idea that it is not simply the case that whatever an inquirer judges to be true is true because *his* lights sanction its truth. Truth has not been reduced to truth from a point of view. Nothing in this picture requires one to say that truth is dependent on our beliefs, in that way. If "objectivity" requires that what is true is true independent of what we believe, this picture of truth *is fully able to meet that requirement*. Nothing about bringing in the point of view of the inquirer prevents one from meeting this demand.

What gives the impression that any rejection of Davidson's way of thinking of objectivity is bound to land us with no objectivity at all, is the fact that we are not only saying that truth is *judged* from the point of view of inquirers by the lights of their current doctrine, but we are also claiming that truth is something that we can aim for and achieve as inquirers. Does saying this make truth lose all objectivity? No, because even though we, as inquirers, judge something to be true by the standards provided by the point of view of one's background beliefs held with certainty, we will also be saying that were we to judge something true that is not judged true by these standards, we would be wrong. Thus the truth of a belief that is judged by one's standards is not at all threatened, if one were to believe something inconsistent with it. This last belief would be false. This shows that if, as a result of one's applying one's standards given by one's current commitments, one believed that p, p would be true; and if one supposed that one did not believe that p (and believed something inconsistent with it), one would be wrong, and p would still be true. Thus, on this picture of truth, p is true if one believes it and p is true even if one does not believe it (and believes something inconsistent with it). *In other words, p is true, whether one believes it or not.* This amounts to one clear sense of the "independence" of truth from one's belief and if independence from belief is what defines "objective" truth, then we have just demonstrated that, on this picture, truth is objective in that sense. This notion of independence from one's belief and of objectivity is not the same as the notion of independence and objectivity that Davidson aspires to in his commitment to (2), but it has the advantage over his notion that one does not give up on the idea that we aim for truth, which is the fundamental point of Dummett's analogy.

Davidson makes much of the fact that one cannot define truth and he is right and insightful to do so. Dummett has not claimed to be defining truth in anything he has said. And certainly nothing said in this paper has been said by way of claiming a definition of truth. If one were *defining* truth from the point of view of the inquirer and what he believes, then presumably one would be landed with the Euthyphro-like view that truths are what inquirers believe. But no such commitment flows from bringing in the point of view of the inquirer. There is no commitment to the idea that because we think truth is something we aim for and often achieve, we must be *defining* truth in terms of what the inquirer achieves. This is because, quite simply, even though what inquiry delivers or assumes as certainties are indeed truths and nothing short of truths, there are lots of truths, presumably, that inquiry has not and will not deliver. So the Euthyphro-like position is not a consequence of making the inquirer's point of view central to the study of truth and allowing truth to be something that is aimed for and achieved by inquirers. There is no reason to think that objectivity (in a thoroughly non-Cartesian sense that falls short of the demands of [2] that Davidson embraces) is threatened by stressing the inquirer and his point of view and his aims towards truth. The fact that there are truths not achieved by inquiry is proof of that. And the Euthyphro-like position (or any view that truth is *defined* in terms of the deliverances of inquiry) requires not only that what inquirers believe with certainty is true but also that what is true is what inquirers believe with certainty. This latter, I am saying, is no part of the picture of truth that allows us to see truth as something that we aim for in inquiry. And if it is not part of the picture, the picture does not make truth depend on inquirers, let alone define truth in terms of what inquirers achieve.

III

I have focused wholly on truth, independent of its relation to meaning. Even when I commented on Davidson's focus on the aspect of Dummett's analogy that related truth as a goal to *speaking* the truth as a convention of communication, the relation between truth and meaning was not discussed explicitly. This is because truth as it relates to communication is not the same as truth's relationship to meaning per se, since meaning (at any rate literal or sentence meaning) is an abstraction from what is conveyed in communication. If that were not so there would be no distinction between semantics and pragmatics.

There are (at least) two reasons for insisting on this abstraction.

First: Truth (or verification or justification) conditions give not only the contents of one's indicative sentences, they give the contents of one's beliefs, which we express when we (sincerely and nonmetaphorically) utter those sentences. In saying that meaning is an abstracted core of what gets communicated, I am not denying that the contents of our beliefs are what are expressed in our communicative utterances of indicative sentences when they are uttered sincerely, nonmetaphorically, and so forth. And so, I suppose, to the extent that one has commitments in having a belief with a certain content, one is making commitments *to others* when one expresses the beliefs to others in communication. But expressing one's commitments to others does not mean—as some philosophers like Richard Rorty have claimed—that something essential to the expressed belief and to epistemology and to meaning in this abstracted sense, is dependent on others with whom we are communicating. For instance, just because I express the commitments contained in my beliefs to others in communication, I do not—as Rorty says—have to *justify* myself *to others*, when they challenge my beliefs. I may do so, but it is not part of the concept of belief or meaning that I must do so. Rorty's idea is that audiences are the watchdogs in epistemology and inquiry, and that justification is addressed to them and is responsible to them. It is that idea which is quite uncompulsory. Justification is not intrinsically a social or communicative phenomenon.[16] I do not justify myself to others when I do not take their views seriously. If someone challenged my belief that the earth is not flat, I would not, in the normal course of things, justify myself to him. I do not take flat-earthers seriously. Communication with others is not intrinsic to justification, even if people often do justify their commitments to others when challenged. When people justify things to others, it is because of specific purposes they might have: to convey information to them, to convince them if they disagree and their disagreements are to be taken seriously, to advance causes, to advance their careers, and the like. If one holds a certain sort of theory of meaning, justification is essential to our understanding of the meanings of sentences and the contents of our beliefs which sentences with meaning express when they are uttered in communication, but someone subscribing to such a theory is not required to say, with Rorty, that meaning and justification are constituted by our address to others with whom we communicate.

Second: When one utters sentences in the indicative mood in communication, there is often a failure of match among three relevant elements: the meanings of sentences, the contents of our beliefs, and what is conveyed and intended to be conveyed in communication. Just to give two types of examples, take the utterance of indicative sentences in metaphorical speech and in lying. I do not express the belief that men are wolves when I say "Man is a wolf," nor do I express the content of what I believe about someone's lecture, when I am being merely polite in saying to him after his lecture, "That was an interesting lecture." In the second example, what I believe is not the same as what the words mean nor the same as what is communicated and intended to be communicated, though what is intended to be communicated and is communicated (if I am a good enough actor) is the same as what the words mean. In the first example what I believe is again not the same as what the sentence means nor the same as what is communicated, but (unlike as in the second example) what the sentence means is not the same as what is communicated (unless the listener is obtuse) and it is certainly not what is intended to be communicated. All this shows that the links between communication and meaning (and belief) are not simple at all.

For both these reasons, when philosophers thinks of meaning in terms, say, of truth conditions, something they have been doing ever since Frege, they have been thinking of meaning in a sense that is an abstracted core of what is conveyed in communication. And that is the sense of truth's relation to meaning that I have ignored so far in my discussion of both Dummett and Davidson. But it is this relationship that is essential to their lifelong interest in truth and it is time to turn to that before closing. Though this relationship has not been the explicit topic of discussion so far, what I have been saying so far about Davidson's notion of truth, which is not shared by Dummett, has a great bearing on the relationship.

Dummett's argument against Davidson on this particular subject is well known and I have written about it in a previous paper of some years ago, which I mentioned earlier. But in these closing remarks of the present paper,

I want briefly to discuss the same subject—the relation between truth and this abstracted core of communication that is meaning—by a slightly different route than a direct discussion of Dummett's own specific anti-Davidsonian argument. The defense I had tried to provide in my earlier paper of Davidson's account of meaning in terms of truth conditions was *not* a defense of meaning in terms of truth conditions understood along the lines that I now know to be what Davidson understood by truth. Given all that I have been saying against Davidson's understanding of truth in his later work, I could not possibly defend Davidson's views about the relationship between truth and meaning. The idea that meaning is in some sense given by conditions of truth (where "truth" is understood as characterized by [2] above) is not a defensible idea. It is not defensible because it is hard to see how it could cope with the puzzles about identity raised by Frege and Kripke. In those puzzles, a subject who fails to know the identity of a planet or a city, can land in contradictions, if one (a) assumes a certain referential understanding of the meaning of proper names or the nature of singular concepts, and (b) assumes certain basic principles of substitutivity (and in the case of the Kripke puzzle, certain basic principles of disquotation and of translation as well). He can, for instance, end up with the thoughts that Hesperus is bright and Hesperus is not bright or that London is pretty and London is not pretty. But since we know in advance that it is uncharitable to take these subjects to be irrational, in other words, since we know that merely being ignorant of the world, namely, of astronomy or geography, does not amount to irrationality, we have to treat them as rational. And there is no way to do so without introducing a notion of meaning which does not merely relate terms to things or objects in the world, but also is tied to a subject's *conceptions* of those things or objects in the world. ("Senses," "modes of presentation," etc., are the words philosophers have used ever since Frege to speak of these conceptions of things.) And so it would seem that the right way to think of meaning in terms of truth conditions is to think of the latter as being conditions of truth, *as subjects conceive of the truth*, and not truth that transcends an agent's conceptions of things.

This account is perfectly of a piece with how a notion of truth, which is geared to an inquirer's point of view that aims at truth, would relate to the notion of meaning. If truth is something that is aimed at and often achieved by inquiry, and if these achieved truths form the background that guide the further ongoing pursuits of inquiry, it *cannot* be that the truth conditions of sentences are outside the scope of how thinking subjects conceive of the world. A notion of meaning tied to such a notion of truth and truth conditions cannot allow for what (2) claims or what Davidson demands for truth to be objective. A notion of meaning that is forced on one by Frege's elementary but profound insight that underlies his puzzle about identity (viz., that mere ignorance does not amount to irrationality) is simply not going to be captured in a notion of truth or truth conditions that thinks of truth as Davidson has declared himself to be thinking of it.

It is a remarkable fact that Davidson, the cornerstone of whose philosophy of language was a notion of meaning elaborated in terms of truth conditions, was never really worried by Frege's puzzle about identity. Since this puzzle is posed precisely to raise a question about what is the right notion of truth and truth conditions to illuminate Frege's own ambition for the linking of meaning and thought with truth conditions, one would expect that Davidson, who inherited Frege's ambition, would have been exercised by it too. But he was not. His reasoning behind this neglect was roughly as follows: Unlike Frege, he had situated the meanings of words and sentences in a context where such meanings are arrived at in the form of assignments of truth conditions by an interpreter (a radical interpreter, though that is not what I am stressing at the moment) to the words and sentences of speakers *in tandem with a set of assignments of beliefs to speakers*. (In his last work, seeing meaning as an essential supplement to the larger framework of making sense of people's actions quite generally as decision theory does, Davidson even saw assignment of truth conditions to sentences as being in tandem not only with an assignment of a set of beliefs but also a set of assignments of desires to a speaker.) This was crucial to the enterprise. Meaning and belief were two closely related components (and desire, a third) of an overall theory that made sense of a speaker's words (and actions). The meaning component assigned truth conditions to speakers' sentences (and these were seen in a now familiar project of viewing them as theorems derived from axioms of a kind of theory made familiar by Tarski, which assigned conditions of "satisfaction" to the parts of sentences). The belief component, which was an essential second element in the overall theory, assigned to the speakers a set of beliefs. Together they made sense of speakers' words (and when desires were also assigned in a third component, they made sense of their actions, including their linguistic actions). Now, Davidson's unconcern about the difficulties raised by the Fregean and Kripkean puzzles about identity, was a result of his conviction that a double-barreled theory of meaning *and belief* would resolve these puzzles quite satisfactorily, without having to appeal to senses or to how a speaker conceives of things. Appealing to senses or to truth as the speaker conceives of the truth would be to appeal to something that would affect *the meaning component that assigned truth conditions*. There is no need to do this, no need to mess with the notion of truth and truth conditions in this way, according to Davidson.

The meaning component should give the truth conditions for speakers' sentences derived from the reference and extension of speakers' terms. When one looked to this component *only*, Davidson concedes that the Frege and Kripke puzzles are indeed very troublesome. "Hesperus" and "Phosphorus" get the same assignment and so it looks as if a subject who thinks and says "Hesperus is bright" and "Phosphorus is not bright" is contradicting himself blatantly. But, says Davidson, there is no real worry raised by this puzzle (at least for the relation between truth and meaning) and things only *seem* troublesome because we are looking *only* at the meaning component of the theory. The overall theory has *two* components, however, and if we turn to the other component, the belief component, the trouble disappears. How so? The belief component assigns beliefs to a speaker. When one notices that among the beliefs assigned to the speaker by the belief component, the belief (about a worldly identity) that Hesperus is Phosphorus is missing, the trouble disappears. In other words, on Davidson's picture of things, there is no need to worry with Frege and bring *into the meaning component* a conception of truth that is tied to speakers' conceptions of things. As I said, there is no need at all to mess with the notion of truth and truth conditions as they are characterized in the meaning component. All that needs to be done is to point out that there is a belief component in the overall theory and that component is an *essential* supplement of the meaning component in the overall theory, and so long as it does not contain the crucial belief in the relevant identity the Fregean anxieties should not arise since it is this failure of worldly knowledge that gives rise to the puzzle. That source of the puzzle can be captured, therefore, by *looking to the belief component*.

But this way of thinking of the relation of truth to meaning, which sees it as having these intrinsic ties to the notion of belief (and desire)—though subtle and fascinating on its own terms—is simply not able to cope with the absolutely fundamental difficulty raised by Frege's puzzle. Suppose one puts the question to the protagonist in the Frege puzzle, "Is Hesperus, Phosphorus?" He would presumably say "No" since the belief component does not assign the belief in the identity to him in its list of assignments of beliefs to him. But in this dissent he *must* be understanding the *meanings* of the two terms of the sentence from which he is dissenting, *differently*. If so these meanings are not being captured by the assignments of meanings to his words by the meaning component because we have been instructed by Davidson not to mess with the meaning component and bring in a speaker's conceptions of things. It is only by messing with it and bringing in such conceptions that we can assign different meanings to his two terms in the meaning component. Thus Davidson's own solution to the puzzle makes no clear sense if he sticks with a notion of truth and truth conditions that does not appeal to subjects' conceptions of the truth and how they conceive of things. There is no getting away from the fact that any notion of meaning that deals satisfactorily with Frege's insight via the puzzles is going to be a notion of meaning that relates to truth only as agents conceive of the truth, and will not be a conception of truth that transcends their conceptions. Such a notion of truth cannot be the sort of thing about whose achievement we are blinded as (2) implies. The sort of realism that is inherent in (2) is thus no part of truth as it relates to meaning, or at any rate a notion of meaning that squares with any satisfactory solution to Frege's puzzle about identity.

This does not mean that we have to discard the use of Tarski-style theories of truth in the rendering of an account of meaning. We just have to be clear that the notion of truth that is deployed by it is a notion of truth that has nothing to do with (2), but is rather a notion of truth that is normative and that inquirers can aim for and achieve and know that they have achieved. For a sentence, say the sentence, "Indian Independence was achieved in 1947" to be true, is for it to be correctly utterable to assert that Indian independence was achieved in 1947. This is what the instances of the Tarski schema—the theorems derived from the axioms of a Tarski-style truth theory—capture. The idea of "correctness" as it occurs above is just the idea of normativity that is contained in the notion of truth. True utterances or assertions of this kind express true beliefs that inquirers aim for and achieve and then take for granted in their further inquiries—and theories of meaning formulated in Tarski-style theories of truth can capture this normativity along the lines just mentioned, *so long as it is clear that the notion of truth involved is not transcendent of our conceptions of things.* That is, it must be clear that the right-hand side of the Tarski-style theorems express facts that fall within our conceptions of things and are not supposed to be capturing elements in the world beyond our conceptual and recognitional reach.

I should quickly connect what I have just said with the notion of inquiry mentioned in the last section by pointing out the answer to the question: What constitutes our conceptions of things *from within which* the facts described by the right hand sides of these theorems are conveyed? The answer is: Those very beliefs that are held with certainty in inquiry and that form the background from which inquiry is conducted.

In a recent work,[17] Dummett says that the right approach to the study of the relation of meaning and truth does not take truth for granted and solve for meaning (and translation), reversing what Tarski did. *It rather solves for meaning and truth together.* Davidson often spoke as if he was reversing Tarski's procedure and taking truth for granted to solve for meaning. This is precisely to fail to solve for them together. Dummett points this out and says that Davidson makes this mistake in his *early* work.

But that is not quite right if by "early" Dummett means the papers Davidson wrote on truth and meaning before situating those two notions in the project of radical interpretation. The fact is that one can find the view Dummett is criticizing explicitly in a paper such as "Radical Interpretation,"[18] whose entire point was to so situate it. In this paper Davidson writes: "What I propose is to reverse the direction of explanation: assuming translation, Tarski was able to define truth; the present idea is to take truth as basic and to extract an account of translation or interpretation" (134). But it should be obvious that a sympathetic reading of Davidson's radical interpretation project (one which is hinted at by Dummett's restricting the criticism to Davidson's early work), would try and improve on his own self-understanding of it and take the point and ideal of radical interpretation to be precisely an attempt to solve for meaning *and truth* by constructing them *both* from evidence of the patterns of assent and dissent (and generally of the behavior of linguistic agents) in the circumstances of the world around them. The concept of truth, on this sympathetic Dummettian reading, would itself emerge out of the assignments of meaning-giving conditions to a speakers' sentences via the method of radical interpretation. However, such a sympathetic reading of the point of radical interpretation is exactly what Davidson does not allow us when, in his last writings, he commits himself to a notion of truth that is characterized by the overweening realism implied by (2).

Does it follow from this that the characterization of truth which shuns (2) and allows it to be something we aim for, as Dummett's analogy demands, amounts to an *anti*-realism? Or to put it more fully, does the relationship of the notion of truth, so characterized, to meaning, amount to an anti-realist theory of meaning? These are questions that will turn eventually on terminology. In giving an argument that opposes Davidson's understanding of the relation between truth and meaning by appealing to considerations of how he will cope with Fregean puzzles about identity, I have not taken up the kinds of considerations *Dummett* appeals to in his well-known argument against Davidson. And, as a result, I have avoided using Dummett's own favored terms "verification" or "justification" as explicit markers for the notion of meaning that might replace Davidson's. Nor have I made appeal to Dummett's qualms about the principle of bivalence or about the doctrine of holism in order to argue against the kind of realism found in (2) and against the usefulness for the theory of meaning of the notion of truth which is assumed by (2). What I have done instead is to pursue the implications of his analogy, with which I began, and to see in its implications a picture of truth and its relations to meaning that simply does not square with the sum of Davidson's writing on the subject. If this amounts to an anti-realism, when the more detailed implications of such a picture are elaborated—something I cannot possibly do here—then that is what it is. But I do not yet see why any elaboration of it should be in terms of the explicit marks of anti-realism that are found in such notions as our capacities for recognition and such notions as verification and justification. I have certainly tried to show how, by mobilizing what is implied by Dummett's analogy, we cannot and should not follow Davidson's later ideas and his commitment to (2) there, which allows truth to go beyond all justification and our powers of recognition. But this is not the same as saying that notions of justification or of our powers of recognition are the terms in which truth and meaning have to be elaborated.

AKEEL BILGRAMI

COLUMBIA UNIVERSITY
FEBRUARY 2005

NOTES

1. "Truth" in Michael Dummett, *Truth and Other Enigmas* (Cambridge, MA: Harvard Univ. Press, 1978), 2.

2. Richard Rorty, "Is Truth a Goal of Enquiry: Davidson versus Wright" in *Philosophical Quarterly* 180 (1995); Donald Davidson, "Truth Rehabilitated" in *Rorty and his Critics*, ed. Robert Brandom (Oxford: Blackwell 2000).

3. "Communication and Convention" in Donald Davidson, *Inquiries into Truth and Interpretation* (Oxford: Oxford Univ. Press, 1984), 267.

4. Michael Dummett, *Frege: Philosophy of Language* (London: Duckworth, 1973), 298.

5. In fact, Davidson even says that the attribution to the native informants of declarative speech and assent to declarative sentences is itself a series of hypotheses. We do not have any firm knowledge but only make hypotheses as to which of their utterances or behavior are declarative speech or assent behavior. In this way we sift out such speech from other sorts of speech that is not declarative and other sorts of behavior that is not assent behavior.

6. This is also exactly what happens with the hypotheses about declarative speech and assent mentioned in the last note. These too are retroactively confirmed if the theory constructed on the evidence that they supply is a successful theory.

7. It should be clear that by "holistic" here I mean not (or perhaps, not just) the sense of the term which conveys that the meaning of one sentence depends on the meaning of others. Rather this "holism" is of a piece with the holism generated by the idea of the theory-ladenness of observation and the image of Neurath's boat.

8. This bit of American slang and this point about the distinction between the liar and the bullshitter is the subject of a philosophical article by Harry G. Frankfurt, "On Bullshit," *The Raritan Review* 6 (1986) [and later his book, *On Bullshit*

(Princeton Univ. Press, 2005)]. Frankfurt is not, however, thinking of the kinds of issues that Dummett is pursuing in his analogy.

9. "Meaning, Holism and Use" in *Truth and Interpretation*, ed. Ernest Lepore (Oxford: Blackwell, 1986).

10. See note 2 for the reference to the relevant paper by Davidson.

11. It is natural to protest: "But why is Philosophy itself not part of inquiry?—and if it is, Cartesian skeptical questions about the logical possibility of each belief we hold being false is not an idle question for that sort of inquiry." But the protest is misguided. When one says of such doubt, "It makes no difference to inquiry, so philosophers should stop taking it seriously because inquirers do not take it seriously," one is assuming something like this: Nothing that makes a difference to inquiry makes a difference to Epistemology. And this assumption is, of course, a special case of the pragmatist ideal that what does not make a difference to practice, does not make a difference to Philosophy, inquiry being the crucial form of *cognitive* practice relevant to the epistemological themes of this paper. Now in pragmatist assumptions of this kind, it is implicitly taken for granted that philosophy itself is not to be regarded as an inquiry. Points about only things relevant to inquiry being relevant to philosophy are points that presuppose that inquiry and philosophy are two separate things, and that what is relevant to one alone is relevant to the other. The whole point of such a criterion of relevance would be lost if we allowed Philosophy itself to be inquiry. This is, in any case, a sensible view to take on things because, as Wittgenstein points out repeatedly in his mature work, there is only confusion and muddle to be had if one takes philosophy to be inquiry. The contamination of ordinary (or scientific) thought by philosophy done at a distance from it and the unnecessary cognitive dust that raises, is a central theme of his later thinking and this qualm is of a piece with our resistance to the protest we are considering in this note. In this sense, Wittgenstein's later thinking was quite proximate in its sympathies to pragmatism, though with real differences as well. I discuss the relation between Wittgenstein's later thinking and pragmatism in the volume on Wittgenstein mentioned in the references cited at the end of note 13.

12. See, among other places, Hilary Putnam, *Reason, Truth, and History* (Cambridge: Cambridge Univ. Press, 1981).

13. We should not conclude from the fact that we might revise our beliefs by rejecting in the future beliefs that are held with certainty now, that beliefs that are held with certainty now should not be counted as true. I have discussed this and other related matters such as why we should not conclude from the fact that truth is something to be discussed from an inquirer's point of view, that we will end with a relativism about truth, in my paper, "Realism and Relativism" in a special volume edited by Ernest Sosa and Enrique Villanueva on *Realism and Relativism* in *Philosophical Issues*, vol. 12 (Oxford: Blackwell, 2002). For more on all these themes, see also my "Scepticism and Pragmatism" in *Wittgenstein and Scepticism*, ed. Denis McManus (London: Routledge, 2004) and "Is Truth a Goal of Inquiry: Rorty and Davison on Truth" in *Rorty and his Critics*, ed. R. Brandom (Oxford: Blackwell, 2000).

14. This picture of truth and inquiry, though very distant from the Peircean view that Putnam has revived and which I mentioned earlier, is very close to the picture to be found in Peirce's seminal essay "The Fixation of Belief" in *C. S. Peirce, Collected Papers* (Cambridge, MA: Harvard Univ. Press, 1931). It is much honed and developed by Isaac Levi in his book, *The Enterprise of Knowledge* (Cambridge, MA: MIT Press, 1980) and I owe a great deal to Levi for my own arrival at a conviction in such an epistemological position.

15. Again, talk of "inquiry" and the description of beliefs held with uncertainty as "hypotheses," may give the impression that by "inquiry" one means something scientific. But that is not so. As I said, even the most common sense and everyday thinking is pervaded by thoughts that are uncontroversial and free of doubt and thoughts that are not, and calling the latter hypotheses, though perhaps misleadingly scientific in tone, should not convey the impression that something very specialized is meant by "inquiry."

16. For Rorty's views on the social nature of justification and its relevance to truth and meaning, see the paper mentioned in note 2.

17. Michael Dummett, in chapter 6 of his recent book, *Truth and the Past* (New York: Columbia Univ. Press, 2004).

18. Donald Davidson, "Radical Interpretation" in *Inquiries into Truth and Interpretation* (Oxford: Oxford Univ. Press, 1984).

REPLY TO AKEEL BILGRAMI

There is something not quite right in saying that assertion is governed by a convention that, as far as we manage, the statements we make shall be true. There could not be a linguistic community within which the convention governing assertion was that the speakers should aim at uttering false statements. Suppose we were given a truth-and-falsity theory for a language we did not know, set out in a metalanguage which, for the most part, we did know, save that we did not know the words used in it for "true" and "false"; say that these are "orev" and "oslaf." We guess that one means "true" and the other "false": but which means which? We could discover this only by observing the linguistic behaviour of the speakers. If they tend, by and large, to utter sentences (more exactly, make statements) that are 'orev' according to our truth-and-falsity theory, then very probably "orev" means 'true' and "oslaf" means 'false'; especially will this be so when the frequency of this happening increases when the condition laid down by the theory for a statement to be 'orev' is rather easily recognised as obtaining. Truth is what we aim at.

We are not, of course, in the situation of first learning in what circumstances a declarative sentence, considered as uttered by a particular person at a particular time, is true, and subsequently learning the practice of making assertions. The first utterances we hear are either assertions or orders addressed to us. Later, we are told stories, which we have to learn are not intended to be true. Quite soon, it occurs to us to exploit the practice of assertion by lying; after a while it also occurs to us to suspect others of lying, and we sometimes discover that our suspicions were justified. As we grow up, we learn more sophisticated uses of language, such as irony and sarcasm; and of course we learn to tell jokes. Davidson rejected the thesis that there is a convention of using declarative sentences with the aim, understood by the hearer, of saying what is true, on the ground that there are so many utterances of such sentences made, and understood to be made, with a different intention. One who constructs a truth-theory for the language must form *hypotheses* about when an utterance by one of its speakers was made with the intention of saying something true.

Well, how do we, as speakers, judge whether someone is making a straightforward assertion, or using irony, or being sarcastic, or making a joke? Do we form *hypotheses*? Hardly. After all, the other speaker is trying to communicate with us; so he gives us indications of what he is at —by inflection, tone of voice, expression of face, gesture, and the content of what he says. We have learned that there are different uses of declarative sentences; we need, and usually receive, a clue as to which use a speaker is intending to employ. These clues are not always successful: misunderstandings occasionally occur; but by and large we have the means to judge when a serious assertion is being made. The non-assertoric uses are governed by convention: there could not be such a thing as irony if there was not a general rule governing how an ironic utterance was to be understood.

The thesis was not that all utterances of declarative sentences are aimed at truth, but that all *statements*—assertoric utterances of declarative sentences, which we can usually recognise as such—are aimed at truth; more exactly, that the convention governing assertoric utterances is that we aim at uttering true sentences. This does not rule out lying, any more than the rules of a game make it impossible to cheat. Davidson's argument thus fails.

Non-assertoric utterances are not aimed at being literally true; they are subject to different conventions. So we may legitimately say that the convention governing assertion is that we should aim at saying what is true. That remark does not, of course, exhaust the conventional requirements on assertion. Naturally, if we are aiming to say what is true, we will tend to say only what we have reason to think is true; but there is also a social necessity to do this. Any assertion is open to the challenge, "How do you know?" or, "Why do you think so?", and we admit to having transgressed the norms of linguistic intercourse if we cannot produce some at least moderately plausible reason for what we have said.

Bilgrami is of course quite right to say that it is more obvious that we aim at truth in *judgement* than in assertion. The object of enquiry is to arrive at true judgements. I have the greatest respect for Donald Davidson's work; but his argument that, in enquiry, we cannot be said to be aiming to discover the truth, on the ground that we can never know whether we have found it, strikes me as little short of fatuous. This view implies that we never know anything. Like G. E. Moore and Akeel Bilgrami, I believe that we do know some things; there are some of our beliefs that we can be quite certain are true. But even concerning that of which we can never be quite certain, the argument is quite fallacious. A murder has been committed; do the police set about to discover the murderer? Common sense answers, "Yes"; a follower of Davidson must say, "No", because neither they nor anyone else can be certain that they have identified him correctly. Judgements of evidence by the police are not infallible; judges and juries can make mistakes. So should we say that the police are merely trying to identify the man whom they most strongly suspect? No: that is not what they are trying to do. They are seeking to bring it about that they arrest the man who has committed the murder. They know that they may not succeed, even when they think they have done so. But that is what they are *trying* to do, not anything less than that. The fact that you cannot ever be sure that you have succeeded has no bearing on what it is that you are trying to do. What goes for the police investigation goes also for an enquiry of any kind.

In saying this, I am disagreeing with Bilgrami when he says that "if the premise is true (viz., that we never can know that any belief is true), it is very plausible to conclude that truth is not a goal of inquiry." I agree with him, however, that the premiss is false: we can sometimes know that our beliefs are true. Apparently Davidson thought that premiss essential in order to guarantee the objectivity of truth. I strongly agree with Akeel Bilgrami that it is not. The identity of the murderer is an objective fact. That we can never be sure that we have identified the murderer shows it to be objective: that everyone agrees that Bentley was the murderer does not make him the murderer. What the victim died from is also an objective fact; but it is one that the autopsy can establish for certain. That something may hold good even though we can never know for sure that it does demonstrates its objective status. But an objective status also attaches to what can be agreed by all, and what can be demonstrated to all as holding good: the intersubjective is ordinarily the objective. When is it not? When it can be demonstrated, or reasonably conjectured, that we are all so positioned, or so constituted, that we each receive a false or distorted impression. In the absence of any such hypothesis, what we all take to be so can reliably be assumed to be objectively so.

Is Bilgrami right to say that Putnam's Peircean conception of truth as that on which our judgements will converge, or would in ideal circumstances converge, rules out truth as the aim of enquiry? Bilgrami says that it is not clear that the notion of truth which emerges from Putnam's idealisation of the notion of enquiry can make a difference to any *actual* enquiry. "Putnam's notion of truth makes no difference to the inquirer," he says; "Putnam's is not a conception of truth that allows us to aim for truth." I may be being obtuse, but I confess that I cannot see why not. We indeed aim for what we may achieve, or what others may achieve after us: it is of little use aiming for what we know we cannot achieve. If something hampers us that we cannot overcome, we do the best we can to arrive at the truth. If we were told that everyone would agree with our conclusion if the obstacle had been removed, our conviction or hope that we had arrived at the truth would be confirmed. If we held a Putnamian view of truth, and thought that that was by definition the truth, we should be sure that we had attained our goal; if not, we should nevertheless strongly believe that we had done so. I am sorry, but I do not see the force of Bilgrami's argument.

Bilgrami rightly distinguishes between the value of truth and the value of telling the truth. The liar violates the latter, but he may highly respect truth: he simply does not want certain truths to be in the possession of others. One who does not respect truth at all is he whom Bilgrami calls the bullshitter. He is not especially concerned to say what is false: he has other ends, to which truth and falsity are irrelevant. Into this category would go a police force concerned only to make an arrest and wipe a case off as solved, rather than to catch the true criminal; this may involve them in lying, but they will do so because they have other ends than truth. They make an investigation, indeed, but the investigation is not aimed at truth. It may be profitable here to consider what it is to have a love of truth. A rigorously truthful person may not be much inclined to seek the truth; he merely tells the truth as he understands it whenever he is required to speak. Any enquirer seeks the truth about something; he manifests a love of truth yet he resists all temptation to pretend that he has found it; if, for example, a lingering doubt makes him press on when everyone else would say that his enquiry was completed; or if he declines to conceal or minimise some counter-evidence that comes to light after he has hit on and published a solution to his problem. Love of truth is not the same as truthfulness; but they are very closely allied.

In the last section of his essay, Bilgrami criticises Davidson's response to Frege's celebrated puzzle about statements of identity. Davidson is content to treat the meaning both of "Phosphorus" and of "Hesperus" as consisting in their denoting the same planet, explaining a speaker's assent to "Hesperus is bright" and to "Phosphorus is not bright" as due to his disbelief that Phosphorus is the same as Hesperus: appeal to beliefs renders otiose the introduction of Fregean senses. Bilgrami is entirely correct, as I see the matter, in arguing that one prepared to deny, as such a speaker must be prepared, that Phosphorus is the same as Hesperus "*must* be understanding the *meanings* of the two terms . . . *differently*." In other words, Davidson's notion of meaning is not correlative with understanding: to understand a word is not to know its meaning. There is no point in a concept of meaning that is not correlative with understanding; a theory of meaning is pointless if it does not enable us to explain what it is to understand a sentence or to know the language. What is it for someone to believe a statement (or believe-true a sentence) if its meaning is given in accordance with a theory that does not guarantee that he understands it, in the everyday sense of "understanding"?

Bilgrami refers to "a speaker's conceptions of things" and also of "our conceptions of things." It is important to distinguish between the sense a word has in the language and the sense it has for an individual speaker. This distinction is by no means only to be drawn when a speaker misunderstands a word and attaches an incorrect sense to it. To know the sense the word has in the language is to know enough about its conventional use to qualify as knowing what the word means. One who supposes that the sky is an inverted bowl above the earth may still know enough about the phrase "the sky" to be said to know what it means; but it has a very different resonance for him from that it has for someone who knows that the sky is immaterial, and there are questions he would think to have a sense and to have an answer that the other would not, such as "How far away is the sky?" Indeed, unless he thinks of the sky as the interior of a sphere, he will understand the very phrase "above the earth" rather differently from others. Likewise, the word "crusade" has a very different resonance for President George W. Bush from that it has for Osama bin Laden. The resonance a word has for an individual speaker of the language results from his experience and his beliefs, and from the associations he attaches to the word because of phrases containing it with which he is familiar. The sense an individual attaches to a word, and the resonance it has for him, bear on the content of his beliefs as expressed or reported in language, where the word is used: the content of those beliefs is not to be judged solely by the senses in the language of the words used to formulate them.

As for Bilgrami's concluding remarks, I certainly do not think that my analogy between the concept of truth and the concept of winning a game leads directly to the opposition to a realist notion of truth that I have pressed. It depends in part on whether you believe that the truth is always something to which we might have access, or whether there are truths of which we can understand a formulation but to a knowledge of which we can never attain. The question is not answered by the argument of Bilgrami's essay, and I therefore will not discuss it here. But I thank Akeel Bilgrami for raising some deep and interesting questions.

M. D.

12

Crispin Wright

"WANG'S PARADOX"

I. INTRODUCTION

There is now a widespread accord among philosophers that the vagueness of natural language gives rise to some particularly deep and perplexing problems and paradoxes. It was not always so. For most of the first century of analytical philosophy, vagueness was generally regarded as a marginal, slightly irritating phenomenon,—receiving some attention, to be sure, in parts of the *Philosophical Investigations* and in the amateur linguistics enjoyed by philosophers in Oxford in the 1950s, but best idealized away in any serious theoretical treatment of meaning, understanding and valid inference. Frege, as is well known, had come to be thoroughly mistrustful of vagueness, supposing that a language fit for the purpose of articulating scientific and mathematical knowledge would have to be purified of it. Later trends in philosophical logic and semantics followed his lead, not indeed in setting about the (futile) task of expurgating vagueness from natural language but by largely restricting theoretical attention to artificial languages in whose workings vagueness was assigned no role.

During the 1970s this broadly Fregean disdain for vagueness was completely turned about. The thirty years since have seen a huge upsurge in interest in the topic and publications about it, most of them by philosophers with not one iota of sympathy with the approach of "Ordinary Language Philosophy" or the seemingly haphazard and anti-theoretical remarks of Wittgenstein. The reasons for the sea change are no doubt complex but my own belief is that a crucial impetus was provided by a single publication: the 1975 special number of *Synthese* in which a number of subsequently influential papers were published for the first time but in which the single most important contribution—the paper one would recommend to a philosopher who was only ever going to read one essay on the topic—was Michael Dummett's "Wang's Paradox."[1]

Dummett's paper was actually written some five years earlier and had already had a significant degree of circulation.[2] It focuses only partially on vagueness, giving as much or more attention to strict finitism as a rival to the intuitionist philosophy of mathematics—arguably, indeed, as the proper logical conclusion of the intuitionistic tendency—and to the nature of observational language. The impact of the paper was in no small measure due to these simultaneous concerns: to the connections it made among topics—vagueness, observationality, and finitism in the philosophy of mathematics—which had received no systematic concerted discussion before. But it also contained a strikingly clear display, unmatched in any previous discussion of which I am aware, of the simple essential architecture of one form of the Sorites paradox. The form of the paradox in question involves an observational[3] predicate, F, and a finite series of items connecting a first F-element with a final non-F element, but with each element relevantly indistinguishable (at least by unaided observation) from those immediately adjacent to it. Such a series is possible, of course, because and only because observational indistinguishability is not a transitive relation. Since the thought is, at first blush, utterly compelling that an observational predicate cannot discriminate between observationally indistinguishable items, it seems we have to accept that anything in the series that is F is adjacent only to things which are also F (call this principle the Major Premise.) And that, on the stated assumptions, is enough for paradox. I think some foggy notion had prevailed earlier that the antinomy was somehow due to applying to vague expressions principles of reasoning appropriate only to precise ones. Dummett seems to have been the first explicitly to register simultaneously both the *utterly plausible* character of the major premises in a very wide range of examples and the *utterly basic* character of the logic required: if vague expressions are not fit for reasoning involving merely iterated applications of *modus ponens* and universal instantiation, it is hard to see how they can be fit for reasoning at all. I do not think that the depth of the crisis for common sense which this paradox involves had really been properly appreciated before Dummett's discussion.

Dummett's own reaction was dramatic and is worth quoting in some detail. What the paradox should teach us, he writes, is that, "the use of vague predicates—at least when the source of the vagueness is the non-transitivity of a relation of non-discriminable difference—is *intrinsically incoherent*" [my italics].[4] He then elaborates this conclusion in four subsidiary claims:

(1) Where non-discriminable difference is non-transitive, observational predicates are necessarily vague

(2) Moreover, in this case, the use of such predicates is intrinsically inconsistent

(3) Wang's paradox merely reflects this inconsistency. What is in error is not the principles of reasoning involved, nor, as on our earlier diagnosis, the [major premise]. The [major premise] is correct, according to the rules of use governing vague predicates such as 'small'; but these rules are themselves inconsistent, and hence the paradox. Our earlier —[proto-supervaluationist]—model for the logic of vague expressions thus becomes useless: there can be no coherent such logic.[5]

The fourth subsidiary conclusion, in keeping with (2), then dismisses as correspondingly incoherent the conception of mathematical totalities as the extensions of vague predicates advanced by strict finitism.

On first encounter, Dummett's principal conclusion, that vagueness infects natural language with inconsistency, seems desperate. And there would be, to be sure, more than a suspicion of *non sequitur* in the transition from an argument that observational expressions have to be both vague and governed by inconsistent rules to the conclusion that vague expressions *per se* are governed by inconsistent rules. Observationality, understood in a way that suffices for the major premise, entails both vagueness—an observational predicate will fail to draw a line between indistinguishables—and inconsistency, at least whenever Fs can be ancestrally linked with non-Fs via a chain of indistinguishable pairs. That suffices for the conclusion that vague predicates are one and all governed by inconsistent rules only if all vague predicates are observational. And that is not true—recall the strict finitist's predicates of practical intellectual possibility—"intelligible" as applied to numerals, "surveyable" as applied to proofs, and so on—and indeed "small" as applied to numbers. Moreover even in observational cases, it is apparently the observationality itself that directly generates the problem, rather than the lack of sharp boundaries that it enjoins. Dummett, that is to say, has described a paradox of *observationality* and—it is tempting to say—its solution must consist in an improved understanding of what an expression's possessing observational content involves. But he has made no case for saying that *vagueness* is intrinsically paradoxical—which is just as well when one considers that, whether or not there are any purely observational expressions in the sense the paradox exploits, vagueness is the norm for expressions of natural language.

However a little reflection shows that the concern does indeed ramify across vague expressions as a class. It is constitutive of an expression's being vague, surely—or so one might think—that it should fail to draw a sharp boundary in a suitable Sorites series. Consider a column of soldiers marching past their commanding officer, ranging from five feet six to six feet six inches in height and so lined-up that each man is marginally shorter than the man who immediately succeeds him. The *precision* of the predicate, "is more than six feet tall," consists in the fact that, no matter how small the differences in height between one man and the next, there is certain to be a first man to which it applies. Correspondingly, since vagueness is the complement of precision, the vagueness of "short" should consist in the fact that, on the contrary, if the differences in height are sufficiently marginal, there need be no sharp bound on the short men in the march-past: no last man who is short followed by a first man who is not. But if there is no such boundary, then whenever a man is not short, he cannot be immediately preceded by a short man. Since all the men who are not short come relatively late in the march-past and hence do have predecessors, the latter likewise cannot be short. Lack of sharp boundaries *as such* thus does seem to imply paradox. To say that F lacks sharp boundaries in a series of the germane kind is to say, it seems, that there is no element, x, which is F but whose immediate successor, x', is not. That is a claim of the form,

$$\sim(\exists x)(Fx \;\&\; \sim Fx')$$

and is accordingly classically equivalent to the major premise

$$(\forall x)(Fx \rightarrow Fx')$$

for exactly the kind of Sorites that Dummett focused on. In brief, in the presence of classical logic, vagueness apparently *consists in* the holding of the major premise for the Dummettian Sorites. For a predicate to lack sharp boundaries does indeed imply, in that setting, that it is subject to inconsistent rules of application.

Worse, this form of the Sorites paradox—the *No Sharp Boundaries Paradox*—survives even if we drop the classical logical setting. Where k ancestrally succeeds 0, the logic required for eliciting paradox from the trio, $\{F0, \sim Fk, \sim(\exists x)(Fx \;\&\; \sim Fx')\}$ needs nothing to allow conversion between the quantifiers but consists merely in the standard introduction rules for conjunction, for negation (i.e., *Reductio ad Absurdum*), and for '$\exists$'. These principles are intuitively no less constitutive of the content of the constants they govern than are universal instantiation and *modus ponens*. So there is a powerful-seeming line of argument that appears to drive us towards Dummett's—as it appeared initially, overstated—conclusion. Vagueness *per se* does appear to infect natural language with inconsistency.

David Pears once remarked that the characteristic effect of a Dummett intervention in a philosophical conversation was as if to turn on a light which the others had overlooked in a gloomy room. Sometimes, of course, what better lighting shows up is not the solution to a problem but its real contours. That was the kind of illumination shed by "Wang's Paradox." My own thinking about vagueness and finitism and the associated cluster of issues whose connections Michael's paper displayed had benefited from discussions with him going back almost a decade before its publication to when I was a PhD student. My hope is that, in this distinguished volume to debate and celebrate his wonderful contributions to modern philosophy, he will enjoy the spectacle of my still wrestling, almost forty years on, with the same conundrum.

II. VAGUENESS AS SEMANTIC INCOMPLETENESS

Frege's disparaging view of vagueness is seldom explicitly argued for in his writings but the little he says does indeed suggest he thought that the phenomenon threatens the stability of basic logic. However he does not cite the Sorites paradox in support of this complaint. Frege takes it that if a term is vague, that will be tantamount to its being only partially defined—so that it will only be of things of a certain kind that it will make sense to say that it either applies to them or that it does not. But that will give rise to failures not just of excluded middle, but of other laws too—contraposition, for example. Everything to which the predicate applies will be a thing of the presupposed kind; but it will not be correct to affirm, conversely, that everything not of that kind is something to which the predicate does not apply—since the range of cases of which the predicate may significantly be denied is likewise restricted to the kind of thing in question.[6]

The most interesting thing about this line of thought is not its conclusion, but its premise: the equation of vagueness with partial definition. To fix ideas, consider an artificial example of Tim Williamson's: the predicate, "dommal," whose satisfaction conditions are stipulated as met by a creature which is a dog, and failed by a creature which is not a mammal.[7] Nothing else is said by way of determination of its meaning, so the effect is that it is undefined whether "dommal" applies to mammals other than canines. The conception of vagueness in ordinary language to which Frege gives one of the earliest expressions is in effect exactly that it is in general the naturally occurring counterpart of the artificially generated indeterminacy of "dommal." Our training gives us rules for the application of "bald"— roughly, looking sufficiently like certain paradigms—rules for applying "not bald"—again, looking sufficiently like certain paradigms—and these rules once again fail between them to cater for all cases. The exceptions—the borderline cases—are those for which we lack any sufficient instruction. They stand to "bald" essentially as noncanine mammals stand to "dommal."

This idea conditioned virtually all mainstream work on vagueness until quite recently. It has been so widely accepted as to be either unnoticed or received as a datum of the problem. So conceived, vagueness is a matter of *semantic incompleteness*. A vague expression is one for which we have mastered rules for assenting to its application and rules for denying it which between them leave space for a *gap*—a range of cases where the rules simply do not give us any instruction what to do.

I do not know whether this way of thinking about vagueness implicitly originated with Frege, or whether it is much older. In any case it is, undeniably, extremely natural.[8] To be sure, not all writers about vagueness nowadays think of it as a semantic phenomenon at all, but among the majority who still do, the Fregean conception is entrenched. It is, for example, a presupposition of the whole idea that vague expressions allow of a variety of alternative but admissible sharpenings, whose effect will be to include or exclude certain items from their range of application whose status was previously indeterminate. This idea in turn, of course, is presupposed by the widely accepted supervaluational approaches to the semantics and logic of vague discourse.

Natural as it may be, however, the Fregean conception now seems to me to be almost certainly wrong. At the least, it is open to serious objection on two major counts. First, it is a very poor predictor of our actual linguistic practices. It gives the wrong prediction about our responses to—and responses to responses to—borderline cases of standard Sorites-prone predicates. Someone who has mastered "dommal" will know better than to apply it, or its contrary, to noncanine mammals. Asked if a cat is a "dommal," he will, or should, say that he is not empowered to judge—for all there is to go on is a sufficient condition for being a "dommal" and a necessary condition for being a "dommal," and cats neither pass the first nor fail the second. By contrast, what we find in borderline cases of the distinction between, say, men who are bald and men who are not it is exactly *not* a general recognition that there is no competent verdict to return but rather a phenomenon—spreading both among the opinions of normally competent judges and, across time, among the opinions of a single competent judge—of weak but conflicting opinions, unstable opinions and—between different judges—agreement to differ. It is true that sometimes a competent judge may simply be unable to come to a view but it is not a necessary characteristic of the borderline case region that it comprises just—or even any—cases where competent judges *agree* in failing to come to a view; and any case about which a competent judge fails to come to a view may, without compromising his competence, provoke a (weak) positive or negative response from him on another occasion. Moreover, failure to come to a view is not the same as the judgment that there is no competent view to take—and it is the latter that is appropriately made of a cat by someone competent with the use of "dommal."

These considerations are radically at odds with what the Fregean conception would lead one to expect. If someone takes the view that some particular cat is a dommal, then, *ceteris paribus*, he shows that he has misunderstood the explanation of the word. If someone understands the explanation properly, he will not return a verdict about a cat. In contrast, our responses to those who do return verdicts in the borderline area of "bald" is that, provided those verdicts are suitably sensitive and qualified, it is permissible so to do. We are *liberal* about judgments in borderline cases. Our thought is not that they are cases about which one ought to have no view but rather merely that they are cases about which it is probably pointless to try to work through differences of opinion. The psychologist testing the responses of a variety of, by normal criteria, competent subjects down a Sorites series would *expect* divergences in the borderline area—indeed, that is what the borderline area *is*: an area of expectable and admissible divergence. If the "dommal" model were correct, the expectation would be of consensual silence.

The second major area of difficulty for the Fregean conception concerns one of the most arresting and disconcerting features associated with the kind of vagueness that interests us, that of so called *higher order* vagueness. There are various ways of eliciting the impression that the phenomenon is real and needs to be reckoned with. One line of thought is outlined by Dummett: if I was to introduce a new word—say "sparsey"—to apply just to borderline bald men, we would find that the boundary between the bald men and the sparsey men was itself vague.[9] Another line of thought is to observe that, in a typical Sorites series, there will be no determinate first case of which we are content to judge that doing *something other* than returning the initial positive verdict is appropriate. How is this to be explained under the aegis of Fregean conception? According to the Fregean conception, borderline cases are cases in which we have not provided for a verdict—cases that we failed to cover by the relevant semantic rules; so the remaining cases are ones for which we *have* so provided and a negative or positive version is appropriate. How can *this* distinction in turn be one for the drawing of which we could somehow have made insufficient provision? No doubt it is up to us what provision we have made—Williamson might for example have provided even less for "dommal," restricting the sufficient condition to Corgis. But whatever provision is made, it should not then need a *further* provision to settle which cases it does and does not cover respectively. Giving just the provision that he did, Williamson thereby settled that the borderline cases of "dommal" comprise all noncanine mammals. He did not merely settle that *some* kinds of case are

to be borderline for "dommal," leaving it open whether others are borderline or are cases in which a determinate verdict is mandated. That matter
was determined for him by the nature of his omission. It did not need
further determination by him—indeed, it was not for him to stipulate at
all—how far the omission extends.

Of course, a defender of the Fregean conception has possible responses
to this. It is intelligible, for instance, how an expression with a semantic
architecture like that of "dommal" might nevertheless allow vagueness on
the boundary between the things which satisfied its sufficient condition and
the things that neither satisfied its sufficient condition nor failed its
necessary one. These—second-order—borderline cases may precisely be
things for which it was indeterminate whether or not they satisfied the
relevant sufficient condition. Such indeterminacy could arise because the
concept giving that sufficient condition—*dog* in the Williamson example—might *itself* have the same kind of semantic architecture. Similar
possibilities would apply to the concept—*mammal*— that gave the original
necessary condition. Since there seems to be no limit to the extent to which
the pattern might be iterated, it looks as though the Fregean conception
might after all be able to recover some of our preconceptions about higher
order vagueness, to whatever extent they run, provided the relevant
concepts that would be successively invoked are all of the illustrated
semantic-architectural kind.

That is a proposal. But it seems to have very little mileage in it. When
we reflect on the prototypical Sorites-prone predicates—predicates like
"red," "short," "bald," "heap," and so on—the most salient feature about
them is their *immediacy*: it simply is not credible that our conception of
their conditions of proper application is informed by an indefinitely
extending structure of partial definitions, each one deploying novel
concepts distinct from those employed in the sufficient, or necessary,
conditions articulated by its predecessor.

These are serious difficulties. But higher order vagueness poses a
further and I think decisive problem for the Fregean conception. Simply: it
allows of no coherent description in terms of the Fregean template for what
a borderline case is.[10] The borderline cases of "dommal" are cases in which
there is mandate neither to apply "dommal" nor to apply its contrary.
Borderline cases of borderline cases, on this model, will thus be cases in
which there is neither mandate to apply a predicate or to apply its contrary,
nor mandate to regard them as borderline—to regard them as cases in which
neither the predicate nor its contrary is mandated to apply. So they are cases
in which there is no mandate to apply the original predicate (otherwise they
would not be borderline cases at all), no mandate to apply its contrary (for
the same reason), but also no mandate to characterize as cases those in

which there is neither mandate to apply the predicate nor mandate to apply its contrary! That is absurd. Whenever—as the first two conjuncts say—a case is such that there is no mandate to apply the predicate to it and no mandate to apply its contrary, then it will be *true*—and hence mandated—to say just that; but that is exactly what the third conjunct denies.

In sum: the Fregean conception—the conception of vagueness as semantic incompleteness—is in tension with our actual sometimes positive or negative reactions to borderline cases, at odds with the liberality of our reactions to others' reactions to them, and, on two counts, can provide no room for the—at least apparent—phenomenon of higher order vagueness.

It may be rejoined in mitigation that we should by now have learned to expect that *any* possible broad conception of vagueness will have problems in accommodating one or another of our preconceptions about the matter, or in respecting certain aspects of the phenomenology of vagueness or our linguistic practice with vague expressions. That, indeed, is what makes the whole issue so hard. Even if resolute prosecution of the Fregean conception is going to require a theory which is indeed in tension with certain aspects of the apparent data, that, it may be said, should be a decisive consideration against it only if some other theory can match the available advantages of such a theory, including those made possible by the apparatus of supervaluation, while causing fewer, or less serious casualties. But I disagree. I think the problems I have just outlined are sufficiently serious to justify persisting in the assumption that the Fregean conception, however natural, is mistaken: borderline cases of vague expressions typified by the "usual suspects"—"red," "bald," "heap," "short," and so on—simply are not to be conceived in terms of the idea of, as it were, one's semantic instructions giving out, of the rules of language failing to provide guidance. But if they are not to be so conceived, what are the alternatives?

III. VAGUENESS AS UNKNOWN PRECISION

If the borderline cases of a vague expression are not to be viewed as cases for which its governing rules fail to prescribe any verdict, then there seem to be just two remaining possibilities: either the rules are inconsistent—Dummett's idea—and thus prescribe conflicting verdicts in every case, or we should swallow hard and accept that *consistent* verdicts are indeed prescribed in every case. In any Sorites series of the normal "monotonic" kind, the latter is tantamount to an acceptance that the rules governing the affected predicate mandate a *sharp cut-off*. Bivalence is therefore assured, and with it classical logic. What is missing, though, is any account of what vagueness is or why it arises.

As we know from the work of Williamson and others,[11] this can be made to be a much more resilient proposal than at first appears. Its proponent—the *epistemicist*—is thinking of our use of vague expressions as broadly comparable to the sorts of judgments we should make about the application of precise predicates like "is more than six feet tall" if excluded from reliance on canonical means of measurement and forced to estimate by eye. There would be cases in which it would be clear that a subject was more than six feet tall, cases in which it was clear that he was not, and cases in which observation left one unable to form a view or where our views were weak and unstable. This model thus predicts something very like our actual patterns of application of vague expressions in borderline cases. Presumably these patterns of reaction would be picked up by someone who was trained in the use of "is more than six feet tall" purely by immersion in the practice of those restricted to visual estimation and to whom no communication was made of the real meaning of the predicate, in virtue of which its extension is actually sharp. We can construct a fantasy around that idea. Call those privy to the real meaning the *Priests* and those kept in the dark the *Acolytes*. We might imagine that, as time goes by, the Priests die out but the practice of the Acolytes survives in more or less stable form, though uninformed by any adequate conception of what determines the extension of "morensicksfittle" as the phrase begins to be written in their dialect.

I do not know if Williamson, or any other defender of the epistemic conception, would take any comfort in this parable. Certainly it is no part of their view that we should think of ourselves as having, over generations, lost touch with earlier fully explicit conceptions of the meanings of vague expressions. What cannot be avoided, however, is the admission that, if the epistemicist view is right, we do not as a matter of fact *have* satisfactory such conceptions and have no idea how to go about recovering them. This is something that epistemicism needs to explain, and—so far as I am aware—no explanation has ever been offered. It is true that Williamson, for one, has worked hard to explain why we cannot know where the (postulated) sharp cut-offs come in Sorites series.[12] But it is not an explanation of that that is being requested. Estimations of the application of "is more than six feet tall" based on unaided observation would indeed be subject to margins of error, and for my present purposes we can grant that Williamson explains why, accordingly, we cannot know by such means where, in a march-past of fifty men beginning at five foot six inches tall and increasing by small variable margins less than one quarter of an inch each time, the first man more than six feet tall is to be found. But that does not explain why I cannot know the alleged principle or principles that stand to my use of "bald" as the condition expressed by the predicate, "is more than six foot tall" stands to the practice—at least according to the suggestion of the parable—of the Acolytes.

The real difficulty, though, is to make anything of the suggestion that the Acolytes' practice is indeed actually so informed. It is only because the Priests understood what it is to be more than six feet tall that they had any inkling about when it is safe to apply the predicate, or to deny its application, under circumstances of unaided observation. The practice so informed may be imitable in a relatively stable and transmissible way, but insofar as it is, there is no longer any motivation for saying that it is driven by the original precise principle. What drives it, rather, is a sense of the patterns of use—in which, for the Priests, the precise principle was once instrumental—purely as patterns *in their own right*. There is no sense in the idea of a continuing additional undertow exerted by an originating principle which nobody any longer grasps. The most fundamental difficulty with the epistemicist proposal is not merely—to put it unkindly—the element of superstition involved in the suggestion that there are indeed, in the case of all vague expressions which contribute to a successful linguistic practice, underlying principles which determine sharp extensions. The charge of superstition might be thought to be addressed, at least to a degree, by the reflection that what at this point may appear to be the only possible alternatives—semantic incompleteness, as in Frege, and incoherentism, as in Dummett—also appear radically unsatisfactory But the more acute problem is that, so long as the epistemicist has to concede that we have no inkling of what the relevant principles are or how they might be ascertained, it is merely bad philosophy of mind to suppose that our linguistic practice consists, in some sense, in their implementation—that it is, in any meaningful sense, *regulated* by them at all.

IV. Vagueness as Incoherence

If both Incompleteness and Epistemicism are unacceptable, then rather than merely dismiss it as "radically unsatisfactory," we should reconsider Dummett's incoherentist response before going any further. The leading thought is that the rules governing a vague expression do indeed provide guidance right through Sorites series, rather as a powerful river current guides items of flotsam over the waterfall! The idea that, in our mastery of natural language, we are governed by inconsistent rules is counterintuitive to be sure. But is there some more fundamental objection? A broadly successful practice *can* be informed by incoherent rules: think of simple division taught to children without any explicit proscription of division by zero, or the game of croquet which, I am told, was for years codified by official rules which contained an inconsistency about the permissibility of iterated roquets. Why should it not be so with linguistic competence?

Well, one crucial question is what explanation the incoherentist can offer of our characteristic patterns of response to borderline cases. Why in a Sorites series do we start out with strong positive opinions, then gradually lapse into weak, defeasible opinions, conflicting opinions, unstable opinions, and failures to come to an opinion, before finally gradually reverting to strong negative opinions? Why does confusion not reign throughout the range? The incoherentist may try to suggest that the deterioration of our linguistic practice from broad consensus into paralysis and conflict is a function of our realization that it is toward disaster that the rules are taking us. But that does not explain the subsequent stabilization of confidence in negative verdicts. And it is in any case a poor explanation of the distinctive patterns of reaction in the borderline area. It is a poor explanation of those patterns for the simple reason that it does not need the context of a Sorites paradox to elicit the characteristic responses involved: they are elicited anyway by confrontation with borderline cases, from thinkers who have no inkling of the Sorites or even—in the case of, say, young children—any capacity to follow the reasoning of the paradox and see its point.

There is more. The suggestion that in our linguistic practice with vague expressions we follow incoherent rules—rules that do indeed actually mandate the application both of an affected predicate and of its contrary to the very same object—is powerless to explain the basic point that, when we do confront a Sorites paradox, we have *not the slightest inclination* to weigh the two limbs of the contradiction equally. There is absolutely no inclination to regard the verdict reached by the Sorites chain as correct. It is utterly dominated by the verdict with which it conflicts, and the paradox initially impresses us as the merest trick. By contrast, where we really do have conflict in the rules governing a concept—for example, the concept of *course of values* introduced by Basic Law V of Frege's *Grundgesetze*—the two components of the paradox are balanced in our esteem, and we have not the slightest sense that one is to be preferred to the other. This is a basic datum which any satisfactory account of vagueness should accommodate and explain, but which, at least on the face of it, the incoherentist view is powerless to explain.

As observed, it is not to be denied that sense can be made of a successful (in certain respects) activity being informed by inconsistent rules. The society that teaches rules of division which are correct except for the detail that they allow division by zero, may get away with it because it never occurs to anyone to attempt a calculation involving a ratio with zero as its denominator. Or it may be that practitioners are aware of the contradiction, but do not exploit it and also manage to avoid situations in which it matters. In any such case, though, the warrant to identify contradiction in the rules is wholly dependent on the way they are officially *explicitly* codified: the character of the informed practice, considered just in its own right, furnishes—and in so far as it is stable, successful and communicable, can furnish—*no* grounds to propose a theory of it which represents its rules as inconsistent. The point is surely equally good for our pervasive and remarkably successful linguistic commerce involving vague expressions. To represent it as the product of inconsistent rules purely on the basis of a paradox which nobody actually accepts provides not merely for poor explanations of linguistic practice, in the respects just noticed, but is empirically entirely unmotivated.

V. VAGUE DISCOURSE AS UNPRINCIPLED

Now, however, we appear to have hit a complete impasse. What are we to think of the rules which govern the use of a vague expression and of what they instruct us to do as we advance down a Sorites series into the borderline area? It seems that there are just three possibilities: either there is no prescription in the borderline area, or the prescription remains the same as it was, or it changes abruptly—semantic incompleteness, incoherentism, and (in effect) epistemicism. Yet we have reviewed serious causes for discontent with each of these three proposals. Each, indeed, comes short in the most basic way, by failing to offer a satisfactory explanation of one or another aspect of competent speakers' linguistic practice with vague expressions. Semantic incompleteness fails to explain, for instance, our tolerance of conflicting verdicts in the borderline region; incoherentism fails to explain, among other things, the disparity in our reaction to the two components of the contradiction; and epistemicism, insofar as it is content to appeal to underlying semantic features transcending any sense that competent speakers have of proper linguistic performance, seems to disclaim any ambition of giving an explanation of our linguistic practice with vague expressions at all.

The puzzle is intense. But we get a pointer to what I have long believed to be the direction in which to find the correct response to it if we consider the so-called "Forced March" variation on the Sorites paradox. The Forced March involves no reasoning to a contradiction from premises, plausible or otherwise. Rather we simply take a hapless subject case-by-case down a Sorites series, ranging from things that are clearly F at one end to things that are clearly not F at the other, and demand a verdict at every point. The subject starts out, naturally, with the verdict, F. And there are just two possibilities for what happens afterwards. Either he goes on returning that verdict all the way down, or at some point he does something different—if only refusing to issue a verdict at all. If he does the former, then eventually he will say something false, and hence will betray *incompetence*. And if he does the latter, then he will draw a distinction by his responses which (i) will have no force of precedent for verdicts in other contexts, and (ii) will correspond to no relevant distinction that he can call attention to between the last case in which he gave the original verdict and the first case in which he changes. So his verdicts will be *unprincipled*. Conclusion: anyone who uses a Sorites-prone expression can be forced to use it in ways that are either incompetent or unprincipled. If we add the plausible-seeming supposition that competent linguistic practice is always essentially principled—always consists in the proper observance of semantic and grammatical rules—then the conclusion, on either horn, is that the use of vague language is bound to be incompetent.

The solution must be to break the tie between "unprincipled" and "incompetent." But that is to say there has to be sense in which competent classification utilizing vague expressions does not consist in the implementation of the requirements of semantic rules. When the question is, what do the semantic rules, subservience to which constitutes competence for a vague expression, require when it comes to borderline cases, the answer we should give is not *any* of the three canvassed. The position is neither that the requirements give out, nor that they remain in force driving us on towards paradox, nor that they mandate a sharp cut-off (of some kind). Rather, it is that competence with basic vague expressions is *not a matter of subservience to the requirements of rule at all*.

This is, indeed, the conclusion to which I came in my paper on the Sorites published in the same volume as "Wang's Paradox."[13] The great difficulty now, as then, is to understand what we are committing to if we accept it—and the difficulty is all the more acute when one reflects that, on at least one way of understanding the issue, to claim that basic classifications effected using Sorites-prone expressions are not rule-governed is simply preposterous. It is preposterous because such classifications are, of course, genuine classifications, apt to be *correct* or *incorrect*. And it seems the merest platitude that correctness, or incorrectness, has to be a matter of fit, or failure of fit, between an actually delivered verdict and *what ought to be said*. There is therefore no alternative but to construe vague classification as *in some sense* subject to norm—and now, if the correctness of our verdicts in general is to be a matter of competence, rather than accident, there seems no option but to concede that we are in some way masters of these norms and follow them in our linguistic practice.

I grant there is indeed no option but to concede that. The point, however, is that such a concession may not amount to very much—in particular, it may not amount to anything which sets up the trilemma we confronted above. In order to illustrate how this may be so, we can invoke a comparison with some thoughts about truth which I have canvassed in other work.[14] To speak the truth is to "tell it like it is," represent things as they are, state what corresponds to the facts. Understood in one way, these phrases are platitudes and incorporate no substantial metaphysics of truth, at variance with, say, coherentist or pragmatist conceptions. The patter of correspondence, platitudinously understood, should motivate no questions about the nature of *facts*—what kind of entities they might be (as it were, sentence-shaped objects?) or how they might somehow be fitted to *correspond* in an appropriate way to beliefs and thoughts. I want to suggest that, in a similar way, the conception of basic classificatory linguistic practice as consisting in learning rules and following them is likewise open to a minimalist, or platitudinous construal, but that the trilemma:

<semantic incompleteness, incoherentism, epistemicism>,

arises only on a richer, nondeflated construal. The proper understanding of the idea that such classificatory competence is unprincipled is exactly that the relevant kind of richer construal is inappropriate.

So: that is the *shape* of a proposal. The question is how to fill it out.

VI. THE *MODUS PONENS* MODEL OF RULE-FOLLOWING

Here is one possible direction—one that takes us to the heart of the agenda of the *Philosophical Investigations*.

Take as a simple, uncontroversial example of a rule-governed practice the case of castling in chess. The rule states (something like):

If the squares between the king and one of its rooks are unoccupied, and if neither the king nor the rook has previously moved in the course of the game, and if the king is not in check, nor would move through or into check, then it may be moved two squares toward the rook and the latter then placed on the adjacent square behind it.

Following this rule involves assuring oneself that the antecedent of the conditional articulating the requirement of the rule is satisfied in the circumstances of a particular game, and then—if one chooses—availing oneself of the permission incorporated in the consequent. Generalizing, what is suggested is a model of rule-following which involves (implicit) *reasoning*, of the form of a *modus ponens*, from a conditional statement whose antecedent formulates the initial conditions of the operation of the rule, and whose consequent then articulates the mandate, permission, or prohibition that the rule involves. We can call this the *modus ponens model of rule-following*.[15]

The qualification, "implicit," is suggested because the appropriateness of the *modus ponens* model is not restricted to cases where rule-following is informed by *self-conscious* inference. Following a familiar rule may be, very often, phenomenologically immediate and unreflective. But the important consideration, as far as the appropriateness of the *modus ponens* model goes, concerns what the rule-follower would acknowledge as justifying his performance. It is enough, in order for the *modus ponens* model to be appropriate, that the explicitly inferential structure of reasons it calls for should surface in that context. A practiced chess player may decide to castle without any conscious thought but that of protecting his king from an attack down the left flank. But if the legality of the move were questioned, he would be prepared to advert explicitly to the relevant pattern of reasons of the *modus ponens* type, whose conditional premise embodied a formulation of the rule for castling.

Plausibly, the *modus ponens* model thus extends a long way into the class of phenomenologically immediate decisions and judgments. How far does it extend? In particular, can the competent application of an expression *always* be conceived as rule-following in accordance with this simple prototype? More specifically still, can we regard the classifications we effect using basic vague expressions, of the kind typified by the usual suspects, as an example of rule-governed activity in accordance with the *modus ponens* model?

The answer, I believe, is no, and the reasons why not are instructive. Suppose, to the contrary, that competent classification using "red," for example, is a rule-governed practice in the sense articulated by the *modus ponens* model. Then there should be a conditional which specifies the conditions under which predication of "red" to an item should be assented to, and such that each competent classification can be seen as (implicitly) inferentially grounded in the recognition, of a presented item, that it fulfills the antecedent. The picture, in other words, is that each informed, competent classification of an item, x, as red is underwritten by a pair of reasons of the form:

If something is X, then it should be classified as "red"

and

x is X

So okay: what is X? What is the property whose instantiation underwrites the proper application of "red" as fulfillment of the antecedent for the rule for castling underwrites the judgment that the particular situation in the game is one in which one is permitted to castle? It seems that we do not know of any plausible candidate answer, apt for all cases, except to identify X with *red*. The same goes for the general run of predicates that make up the usual suspects: basic, vague predicates used to record the results of casual observation. In such cases, the correct answer to the question, "what is the condition common to the minor premise and the antecedent of the conditional for the *modus ponens*?" seems to be irreducibly homophonic.

This observation has a striking consequence. It is that the price of continuing adherence to the *modus ponens* model in these cases is that we are forced to think of grasping the concept of what is to be, say, red as *underlying and informing* competent practice with the predicate "red." If the explanation of competent practice with "red" adverts to the intention to follow a rule the grasp of which demands a prior understanding of what it is for something to be red, then the latter grasp has to stand independent of the linguistic competence. So in effect, we commit ourselves to the picture of language mastery displayed in the quotation from Augustine with which Wittgenstein begins the *Philosophical Investigations*—not, to be sure, in the aspect of that picture which involves thinking of the semantics of expressions generally on the model that of a name and its bearer—but rather the aspect which we find made explicit only later, at §32:

> And now, I think, we can say: Augustine describes a learning of human language as if a child came to a strange country and did not understand the language of the country; that is, as if he already had a language, only not this one. Or again: it is as if the child could already *think*, only not yet speak. And "think" would here mean something like "talk to himself."[16]

Wittgenstein, of course, intends his reader to take on board the thought that Augustine prototypically committed a major philosophical mistake. If we agree with him and simply repudiate the Augustinian picture, then we will have to conclude that, at the level of the basic, casual-observational classifications expressed by the usual suspects, the *modus ponens* model is inappropriate. The classifications effected by means of vague expressions of this basic kind are *not supported by reasons*, for the only possible candidates to constitute their reasons would demand, when so conceived, that we think of grasp of the concepts expressed by the vague predicates in question as something prior to and independent of the mastery of these predicates.

In his "later" work Wittgenstein gives expression to an epistemology of understanding wherein language mastery is systematically conceived not merely as a means for the expression of concepts but as the medium in which our possession of them has its very being. As a reaction against the diametrically opposed view, that thought—at whatever degree of sophistication—may always intelligibly be conceived as constitutively independent of the thinker's possessing means for its expression, Wittgenstein's stance is surely compelling. But neither polar view—that language is merely the means of expression of thought, and that nothing worth regarding as thinking is possible without language, respectively—is correct. The correct view of the matter overall is presumably something more nuanced. There is much possible intelligent activity which, though wordless, would naturally call for explanation by ascription to the agent involved of conceptual—content-bearing—states of varying degrees of sophistication. Imagine, for instance, a chimpanzee who, off his own bat and after many days of manipulations in the corner of his cage, is suddenly able repeatedly to solve Rubik's cube; or the wonderful behavior, even in an unfamiliar city, of a well-trained guide dog. On the other hand there are plenty of concepts—take, for instance, that of a parametric variable in a step of existential elimination—of which it strains credibility beyond breaking point to suppose that they could be fully grasped by someone with no linguistic competence at all. So if its implication of the Augustinian picture when applied to "red," "bald," "heap," and so on is to be sufficient reason to reject the *modus ponens* model of competence in those cases, we need a special consideration as to why. Is there one?

We would need further detailed discussion to fully vindicate the assumption, which I will from hereon make, that Wittgenstein is right, at least about the concepts to which we give expression by basic vague expressions—those for which retention of the *modus ponens* model would demand siding with Augustine. Here let me just gesture at one line of thought. We can certainly imagine a creature without language—the chimpanzee again—exhibiting some sort of concepts of color: he may, for example, manifest a preference, among variously colored but identically smelling and tasting boiled sweets, for green ones. More generally, there are any number of kinds of color-sorting behaviors that could be—and in many cases, are—exhibited by prelinguistic children. But grasping the color concepts *we actually have* is not merely a matter of dispositions of appropriate response to paradigms. To grasp any classificatory concept, one needs not just to learn to respond appropriately to central cases but also to acquire a sense of its *limits*. With the usual suspects, however, it is the very pattern of our *linguistic* practices that sets the limits, imprecise though they may be. We learn by immersion in the language how far one can stretch from paradigm cases of red, or blue, before classification starts to become *acceptably* controversial or difficult. Prelinguistic children no doubt have some sort of grasp of color saliencies. But the raw concepts they have, or could have, do not match the vagueness of color concepts as linguistically captured. The reason is that it is precisely the onset of hesitancy, disorder, and weak conflict in the *linguistic* verdicts of the competent that constitutes the gradual intrusion into the borderline area and sets the limits of the concepts in question. I do not deny that the chimpanzee might behave in ways which went some way toward giving sense to the idea that the concepts he was working with were vague—he might hesitate over a turquoise sweet, for example, while vigorously discarding a blue one. What seems to make no sense, however, is that his concept of green so manifested might be identical, vagueness and all, to the concept which, miraculously endowed with the power of speech and perfect basic English, he went on to display in his uses of "green." Competence with vague concepts is an essentially linguistic competence because the extent of their vagueness is an essentially linguistically manifest, socially constrained phenomenon.

If the broad direction of these remarks is correct, we must abandon the *modus ponens* model if we are to understand the sense in which the exercise of vague classifications is a form of rule-governed activity. One reaction would be to deny that it is, properly speaking, rule-governed at all—that it is sensible to think of an activity as *governed* by a rule only if one could in principle articulate the content of what would be the appropriate rules in such a way that a suitable thinker could *generate* a competence by observing them, and justify his performance by their lights. If I am right, that condition is indeed unattainable where competence with vague classifications is concerned. That competence is, precisely, *not* to be viewed as a product of any possible anterior body of information which, in principle, could be used explicitly to inform the moves that competence requires. But actually, I do not think it matters whether we say that there is, properly speaking, no rule-following in such cases or whether we say merely—as I originally announced—that we need a more minimalistic conception of what in the relevant cases rule-following involves. Certainly, even with judgments involving vague expressions, there are still all of correctness and incorrectness, criticizability, proper responsibility, the intention to get things right, and a wide range of contexts in which it is important to succeed in that intention. But what there is not is a body of information which underlies competence, in a way in which knowledge of the rule for castling together with knowledge of the history of the particular game and the present configuration of pieces enables (what may well be an unreflective) awareness by an expert player that castling is an option here if he wants.[17]

If this is right, then we can see our way around the trilemma. The trilemma arises if, but only if, it is a good question concerning the rules which govern our competence with "red": what do they *really have to say* when our color classifications fall into the complex patterns which show that we are in the borderline area?—what is their message, what would we do if we were to do exactly what they require and nothing else? That the three answers canvassed seem, among them, to exhaust all of the alternatives, yet each to be objectionable, might have made one suspect that there is something wrong with the question. Now we see how that suspicion might be substantiated. There *is* no requirement imposed by the rules—not if we understand such a requirement as something whose character may be belied by our practice in the borderline area and into which there is scope for independent inquiry. There is no such requirement because to suppose otherwise is implicitly to commit oneself to the *modus ponens* model of rule-following for the classifications in question, and hence, as we have seen, to open an—at least locally—unsustainable gap between conceptual competence and the linguistic capacities that manifest it.

VII. THE SORITES PARADOX OF OBSERVATIONALITY

To abandon the *modus ponens* model of competence with vague expressions is to open the way for the thought that the characteristic manifestations of vagueness in linguistic practice are, in a sense, *the whole story*. Vagueness is constituted at the level of use, rather than at the level of explanation of use.

Here are some of the kinds of fact that are salient at the level of use. First, competence with a vague expression is, in the usual run of cases, mastery of a practice which is communicated not by verbal explanations and characterizations but by immersion in that very practice. A large part of the acquisition of competence with a vague expression will typically consist in learning to use it to make judgments which we think of as immediately responsive just to how things strike us. Such judgments impress as, in a sense, undiscussable; we have to hand no repertoire of reasons with which to negotiate about them. Second, there is only such a thing as competence with such expressions because the relevant kind of training does generate, fortunately, a high degree of intersubjective—and cross-temporal intrasubjective—constancy in judgments, both positive and negative. Third, however, the training we receive also results in ranges of cases in which constancy breaks down, wherein otherwise perfectly competent subjects differ, views are characteristically unstable, and we often find it difficult to be moved to a view at all.

My suggestion is that a philosophical account of the nature of vagueness is to be sought in the, by all means properly refined and nuanced, elaboration of facts such as these. There is no scope for an, as it were, information-theoretic standpoint whose goal is to outline rules which we implicitly follow in our use of vague expressions, and thereby to explain what it is about those rules that gives rise to the characteristic manifestations. There is no such legitimate explanatory project. Competence with a vague expression is not the internalization of a set of rules that prescribe the agreed verdicts in cases in which agreement occurs, and whose other features explain the cases in which it breaks down—in any of the ways that incompleteness, epistemicism, and incoherentism respectively offer. The breaking down of constancy has to do not with incompleteness or inconsistency in the rules we tacitly follow, nor with the invisibility to us of the lines they draw, but is a matter of how we naturally respond, without reasons, to cases of significant distance from paradigms.

This shift in perspective provides for a major change in the impression given by Dummett's observational Sorites. Take what is surely the most daunting type of example: the Sorites associated with predicates like "looks red" over a series of pairwise indistinguishable square color patches, running from, say, crimson to orange. Here adjacent patches *look just the same*. And "looks red" is surely an observational predicate in Dummett's sense if anything is. But observationality must require—must it not?—that the meaning of "looks red" enjoins that it is properly applied to both, if to either, of any pair of things which look just the same. So the paradox seems iron-cast. Yet this appearance precisely depends on a tacit construal of the observationality of "looks red" and its kin which rests on the *modus ponens* model of competence in their use. In effect, we are seduced into thinking of competence as involving the internalization of a set of rules which connect appearances with the proper application of the predicate: rules of the form, roughly,

If x appears thus-and-so, then it should be classified as "looks red."

Once into this way of thinking of the matter, it is indeed impossible to understand how things which appear the same could possibly deserve any but the same classification. But the allure of the major premise dies away once the idea is taken on board that the classifications effected by these predicates are, in basic cases, essentially unsupported by any articulatable structure of reasons—more specifically, that they can be and normally are competently made without the mandate of any internalized conditional rule of the schematized kind. Since they need no such mandate, they are not properly regarded as unprincipled, at least not just on that account, when they collectively take a shape over a Sorites series—as they must if they are to be consistent—which would violate such a rule. Competent classification over a Sorites series for "looks red" will, indeed must, at some point involve differential responses to presentations that look exactly alike. The (crazy) idea that competence somehow accordingly involves *disrespecting* the rules is an artifact of a misplaced adherence to the *modus ponens* model at a level where it involves an incoherent overrationalization of our practices. As Wittgenstein (near enough) says, not everything judged rationally is judged for reasons.[18]

I said earlier that the natural reaction to the Dummettian Sorites is to seek "an improved understanding of what an expression's possessing observational content involves." I meant that reaction to be in contrast with one of mistrust of the very notion of an observational predicate. To be sure, if what I have been saying has any truth in it, then we should certainly mistrust the idea of an expression's being governed by rules which prescribe like verdicts about like appearances. But that is no cause for suspicion of Dummett's own working characterization of observational expressions as those: "whose application can be decided merely by the employment of our sense organs."[19] What is wrong is the little piece of theory which, under the aegis of the *modus ponens* model, links the Dummettian notion with governance by rules prescribing like verdicts about things our sense organs cannot distinguish. But the right reaction is not to retain the *modus ponens* model and look to somehow complicate or refine the rules which are characteristic of the competent employment of an observational predicate. The right response is to realize the implications of the point that competence with an *observational* predicate is not, even tacitly or "in principle," an *inferentially-controlled* competence.[20]

Dummett put the spotlight on observational predicates and I too have spoken of the usual suspects as predicates of "casual observation." But if the general drift of the foregoing is correct, vagueness will be an expectable characteristic of a more inclusive class of predicates (or other kinds of expression): all those which give rise to judgments for which competence is not, in basic cases, to be explained in terms of the *modus ponens* model—that is, judgments competence with which is not a matter of sensitivity to inferentially-organized reasons but which are characteristically both rationally and phenomenologically immediate. Observational judgments are a species, but only one species, within this wider genus. My conjecture is that all vagueness of the kind which interests us here— vagueness of the kind which seems to be associated with higher-order vagueness and seems to give rise to Sorites-susceptibility—originates at the level of noninferential judgment.

VIII. DÉNOUEMENT

Unfortunately these considerations do not yet take us out of the wood. They provide the means to address one *motivation* for the major premises in Sorites paradoxes for observational predicates. If they are compelling, and if that (illicitly rationalistic) motive exhausts the field, then we can indeed explain away the plausibility of those premises—an essential part of any solution to a paradox, properly so regarded—and are now free, presumably, to regard each such Sorites simply as a *reductio* of its major premise. But now a new concern surfaces. To deny the major premise in the "looks red" Sorites, for example, is to conclude that it is *not true* that each patch that looks red in the series we imagined is succeeded by a patch that looks red. But *how* is that not true? After all, we precisely so conceived the example that no patch that looks red is succeeded by one that *does not*. Surely no implicit overrationalization of competence with observational predicates is involved in the thought that no pair of indistinguishable patches can be such that one looks red while the other does not.

It would be relevant to observe that treating the reasoning of the paradox as a *reductio* of a major premise of the form:

$$(\forall x)(Fx \rightarrow Fx')$$

is a commitment to affirming the corresponding claim of the form

$$(\exists x)(Fx \ \& \ \sim Fx')$$

only on the assumption that classical logic is good for vague statements. And for what it is worth, I do maintain that something like an intuitionistic logic—at the least, a logic in which double negation elimination does not hold unrestrictedly—will be required in any fully satisfactory treatment (and will say more on this shortly). But someone could agree about that and still have the misgiving just aired. Even if we have disposed of the motivation for the universally quantified form of major premise in the observational Sorites, there still appears to be every motivation for the negative existential major premise for a corresponding observational instance of the No Sharp Boundaries paradox. Again: surely there just *nowhere occurs* in the relevant kind of series any patch that looks red while its immediate successor does not. Is not the negative existential major premise just flat-out true in this case?

The problem is, indeed, more general. Nothing has so far been said to address the overarching motivation, noted at the conclusion of section I, for the major premises in No Sharp Boundaries paradoxes as a class—namely, the simple thought that vagueness *per se* consists in absence of a sharp cut-off in the relevant series, hence in the truth of a statement of the form,

$$\sim(\exists x)(Fx \ \& \ \sim Fx').$$

What *is* vagueness if it is not a truth-conferrer on statements of that form?

These are very awkward looking questions. But I think the work we have done has taken us closer to being able to answer them. Let me conclude by sketching how.

In dropping the *modus ponens* model, we drop the idea that truth for vague statements is a matter of fit with the requirements of semantic rules which competence internalizes. Rather, truth must now be viewed as

grounded in the patterns of linguistic practice which competence, uninformed by any such rules and reconceived purely as the ability to participate
successfully in that very practice, exhibits. There is a temptation to try to
say something detailed and specific about the nature of this grounding—perhaps in the form of a developed account of some sort of response-
dependence. I do not know if any such attempt can be fully successful. But
we can get some mileage out of a theoretically more modest standpoint.
Vagueness, of the kind that interests us, gives rise to definite cases as well
as borderline ones. There are things that definitely look red, and things that
definitely do not. These definite cases are cases which elicit a firm and
stable consensus in judgment from those considered competent in conditions considered as relevantly suitable. And in discarding the *modus ponens*
model we now treat that sociological fact as, in a sense, the whole truth
about the cases in question: there is nothing deeper, in particular no tacitly
understood set of guiding requirements that explain and underwrite the
convergence in verdicts about them, and no sense accordingly in the idea
that the convergence might somehow be defeasible by further standards,
implicit in the meanings of the expressions in question. The way is therefore
open to us to regard such convergence as *unimprovable evidence* of the
truth of the statements in question, and—*pari passu*—inconsistency with
verdicts that enjoy such convergence should be regarded as unimprovable
evidence of falsity.

The immediate effect of that consideration is that there is no option but
to regard the verdicts about the end points of a Sorites series—schematically, F0 and ~Fk—as straightforwardly true. For there is now nothing on
which their truth might depend which is left out of the picture after
competent convergence on them in good enough conditions is factored in.
But that entails that there really is no alternative but to regard the negative
existential major premise

$$\sim(\exists x)(Fx \ \& \ \sim Fx')$$

as false. It must be regarded as false because it is inconsistent with a
consistent pair of statements for whose truth there is unimprovable
evidence. Correspondingly, we have therefore no option but to accept *its*
negation

$$\sim \sim(\exists x)(Fx \ \& \ \sim Fx').$$

This realization sets us two problems. The first is to understand how we
can deny the negative existential major premise without controverting the
fact of the vagueness of F within the relevant series. The second, closely
related, is to explain how, after that denial, we can now avoid an apparently
preposterous—*pace* Williamson—endorsement of the Unpalatable Existential

$$(\exists x)(Fx \ \& \ \sim Fx'),$$

which seems tantamount to an endorsement of F's precision.

First, then, on denying the negative existential: Does the vagueness of F in an appropriate series not just consist in the absence of a sharp cut-off and is that not just what the negative existential directly states? Well, no—or rather "yes" to the second question and "no" to the first. Vagueness, we have to learn, does *not* consist in the absence of sharp cut-offs. What the negative existential states—even in intuitionist logic—is the same as what is stated by

$$(\forall x)(\sim Fx' \rightarrow \sim Fx)$$

which, in the presence of ~Fk, is tantamount to the false statement that there are no Fs in the series. So that *cannot* be the correct way to characterize the vagueness of the boundary between the Fs and the non-Fs in a series that contains both. What *is* a fact is the absence of any pattern of responses that would provide evidence for the *existence* of a sharp cut-off. The relevant pattern of responses would involve convergence on the initial elements of the series up to some last positive verdict, Fi, followed by convergence on the negative verdict, ~Fi', and then sustained convergence on negative verdicts up to the end. What we have instead is just the pattern of judgments distinctive of vagueness: polar constancy flanking the gradual breakdown of convergence in verdicts of any kind in the borderline region. That indeed, on the present perspective, is what vagueness consists in. So it does not consist in anything which makes the negative existential true. Rather, if the existence of a sharp cut-off is identified with the truth of the unpalatable existential, then we should say this: that what is distinctive of a predicate's vagueness is not that there is no sharp cut-off, but rather that there is nothing in our practice with the predicate that grounds the claim that there is a sharp cut-off (and that—again, *pace* Williamson—we have no satisfactory conception of how that claim might be grounded in an independent theoretical way).

So as far as the first problem—that of explaining how we can deny the negative existential without controverting F's vagueness—is concerned, then, I am saying the following: that, so far from the negative existential's being a satisfactory characteristic statement of a predicate's vagueness, our practice with vague expressions provides unimprovable evidence that the negative existential is false, and hence that its negation—the double negation of the statement of the existence of a sharp cut-off—is true. The pattern of practice constitutive of vagueness, so far from providing evidence for the truth of the negative existential, is inconsistent with it and needs to be described quite differently.

As to the second problem, that of avoiding endorsement of the Unpalatable Existential,

$$(\exists x)(Fx \& \sim Fx')$$

we have so far observed merely that nothing in our patterns of judgment about each Fi provides any evidence for it, and that—*pace* Williamson—we have no other theoretical reason for thinking it true. These, on the present, "post–*modus ponens* model" perspective, are constitutive facts: vague expressions are ones for which sharp boundaries are neither drawn by actual competent practice nor posited by any known well-motivated theory. So there is no reason whatever to assert that there are such boundaries.[21] The temptation to think that this adds up to enough to justify *denying* the Unpalatable Existential—and so asserting the negative existential major premise—is very strong. It is of a species with a general tendency to deny things for which we have found absolutely no evidence (the spirit in which we would, many of us, deny that there are leprechauns). Usually these somewhat arrogant denials do no serious harm. In this context, however, their nemesis is the No Sharp Boundaries paradox.

Let me relate these proposals to the specific case of the No Sharp Boundaries paradox for "looks red." We left discussion stalled on the thought that it seems merely to be the simple truth that no patch in the relevant series that looks red is followed by the one that does not. But that is not the simple truth. What *is* simply true is that nobody competent will willingly make a judgment which identifies such a pair of patches. And since none of us will do that singly, there is no question of a convergence on a cut-off. So nothing in our practice provides a ground for the claim that there is a cut-off, nor do we have any defensible conception of how there might be one nonetheless which our practice fails to reflect. On the other hand, the equivalent of the "simple truth," namely that no patch in the series that does not look red is immediately preceded by one that does, entails, when some of the later elements do in fact not look red, that none of them does. So the "simple truth that no patch in the series that looks red is followed by one that does not" is actually inconsistent with the way the elements collectively look and is therefore not a truth of any kind. As before, what has happened is a confusion of the complete absence of grounds for the existence of a cut-off with the possession of grounds for denying one.

But in this case I think there is an additional seductive fallacy. It is that we confuse its *not looking as if there is a sharp cut-off* in the series—which is true: if it did look as if there is a cut-off, we would converge on it—with its *looking as if there is none*. The latter is false. It does *not* look as if there is no cut-off—at least not if that is taken to mean that the series collectively looks as it would if there was indeed no cut-off. For if there were no cut-off, the series would have to look to be uniformly composed of squares that all looked red, or all did not look red. Which by hypothesis it does not.[22]

We are having to draw some quite subtle distinctions. It may help to consolidate a sense of what I am proposing in general if the reader reflects that, assuming "monotonicity" for the series in question, the Unpalatable Existential is equivalent to the principle of Bivalence when restricted in range to each ingredient statement, Fi.[23] The temptation to deny the Unpalatable Existential is thus on all fours with the temptation to think that vagueness should prompt denial of Bivalence. That denial however, at least when truth is disquotational, likewise familiarly leads to contradiction. I am suggesting an attitude to the Unpalatable Existential which I take to be comparable in all essentials to the Intuitionists' attitude to Bivalence in those areas of mathematics where they regard it as unacceptable. It is there regarded as unacceptable because, when the truth of statements to which Bivalence is to be applied is conceived as constrained in ways that are taken to be independently motivated, it *goes beyond all evidence* to suppose that each instance of Bivalence is true. In the case of mathematical statements, the Intuitionists take it that there is independent motive to require truths to be constructively provable. I do not know whether the historical motivation for that thought is wholly independent of what I have proposed about vague statements: that their truth and falsity have to be thought of as determined by our very practice, rather than by principles which notionally underlie it. But the effect is similar. The denial of any instance of Bivalence leads by unexceptionable basic logic (and the usual truth rules) to contradiction. So we must deny any such denial. But when Fi is borderline, the break down in convergence of verdicts leaves us without uncontroverted evidence for its truth or for the truth of its negation. Since we lack convincing theoretical grounds to think that one or the other must be true nonetheless—because such grounds would have to regard the determinants of truth and falsity as constituted elsewhere than in our linguistic practice—we are left with no compelling reason to regard either Fi or its negation as true. We should therefore abstain from unrestricted use of the law of double negation elimination. We do so on the grounds that it is nonconservative of knowledge—exactly the Intuitionistic reservation.

The thought that vagueness might require a nonclassical logic is, of course, hardly original. But it has usually been clothed in broadly semantic proposals about third truth values, truth-value gaps, and degrees of truth. All these proposals see the principle of Bivalence as breaking down where vague statements are concerned. I am suggesting that the correct basic complaint to have about Bivalence where vague statements are concerned is not that it breaks down but that it goes beyond the evidence. I have supported this contention by argument that vagueness is a phenomenon of judgment unsupported by reasons, and that this makes for an especially intimate connection between patterns in competent linguistic practice and truth. It is this intimacy of connection that allows us to rest content with our stable verdicts about the poles of a Sorites series and so to enforce denial of the major premises involved. It is the same intimacy of connection that allows us to say that there is no reason—not merely: no reason provided by our actual patterns of judgment, but no reason whatever—to regard the Unpalatable Existential as true. So double negation elimination is, in this instance, epistemically nonconservative.

There is a lot more that would need to be discussed and developed in a fully explicit treatment but I must draw this particular essay to a close. It is, of course, conspicuous among Michael Dummett's many philosophical achievements to have done more than anyone else to rehabilitate the Intuitionistic outlook and to transform it into a significant contemporary force not just in the philosophy of mathematics and logic but in metaphysics and the theory of meaning generally. If there is anything in what I have been saying, he may, ironically, have overlooked one especially apt and helpful application of it, to the riddle of vagueness.

CRISPIN WRIGHT

UNIVERSITY OF ST. ANDREWS
AND NEW YORK UNIVERSITY
MAY 2005

NOTES

1. [*On the Logic and Semantics of Vagueness*], in *Synthese* 30, nos. 3–4 (1975): 301–24.

2. It was the single most important influence on my own first study of the topic, found in "On the Coherence of Vague Predicates," and also I believe on Kit Fine's prototypical supervaluational treatment of the semantics of vagueness, found in "Vagueness, Truth and Logic," both of which were first published in the same number of *Synthese*, 325–65 and 265–300, respectively.

3. Dummett characterizes an observational predicate as one "whose application can be decided merely by the employment of our sense organs," "Wang's Paradox," 320.

4. "Wang's Paradox," 319.

5. Ibid., 319–20.

6. I take this to be the argument of Gottlob Frege's *Grundgesetze Der Arithmetik* (Hildesheim: George olms Verlagsbuchhandlung, 1962), vol. I, §65. Frege does mention "the Heap" itself at *Begriffschrift*, 27, in the context of his definition of what it is for a property to be hereditary in a series, but remarks on no threat to logic, suggesting merely that, since "heap" is not everywhere sharply defined, we may regard the major premise as indeterminate. (That is no option of

course if we take it that the minor premise, that 0 grains of sand cannot constitute a heap, and the conclusion, that—say—200,000 grains of sand cannot constitute a heap, are, respectively, true and false. An indeterminate statement cannot be inconsistent with the facts! Even Frege, it seems, underestimated the Sorites.)

7. Timothy Williamson, *Identity and Discrimination* (Oxford: Basil Blackwell, 1990), 107.

8. Thus Fine, "Vagueness, Truth and Logic," 265: "I take [vagueness] to be a semantic notion. Very roughly, vagueness is deficiency in meaning."

9. See Dummett, "Wittgenstein's Philosophy of Mathematics," *Philosophical Review* 68 (1959): 324–48, (reprinted in M. Dummett, *Truth and Other Enigmas* [London: Duckworth, 1978]; the cited line of thought occurs at p. 182.)

10. See Crispin Wright, "Vagueness: A Fifth Column Approach," in *Liars & Heaps: New Essays on Paradox*, ed. J. C Beall (Oxford: Oxford Univ. Press, 2003), 89.

11. The leading systematic account of the epistemicist view is Timothy Williamson's *Vagueness* (London: Routledge, 1994). See also ch. 6 of Roy Sorensen's *Blindspots* (Oxford: Oxford Univ. Press, 1988).

12. See especially ch. 8 of Williamson's *Vagueness*.

13. Wright, "On the Coherence of Vague Predicates"; and "Language-Mastery and the Sorites Paradox," in *Truth and Meaning: Essays in Semantics*, ed. Gareth Evans and John McDowell (Oxford: Oxford Univ. Press, 1976), 223–47. (Reprinted in *Vagueness: A Reader*, ed. Rosanna Keefe and Peter Smith [Cambridge, MA: Bradford/MIT Press, 1996].)

14. See, for instance, "Truth: A Traditional Debate Reviewed," in supplementary volume 24 (1998) of the *Canadian Journal of Philosophy* (special issue on Pragmatism, guest edited by Cheryl Misak): 31–74. Reprinted in *Truth*, ed. Simon Blackburn and Keith Simmons (Oxford: Oxford Univ. Press, 1999), 203–38.

15. This idea, and its limitations, are anticipated in section V of my "Wittgenstein's Rule-Following Considerations and the Central Project of Theoretical Linguistics," in *Reflections on Chomsky*, ed. Alexander George (Oxford: Blackwell, 1989), 233–64. Reprinted in Crispin Wright, *Rails to Infinity* (Cambridge, MA: Harvard Univ. Press, 2001), 170–213.

16. Ludwig Wittgenstein, *Philosophical Investigations* (New York: Macmillan, 1953).

17. Additional difficulties for the *modus ponens* model are raised in Paul Boghossian, "Meaning, Rules and Intention," *Philosophical Studies* 124, no. 2 (May 2005): 185–97.

18. Wittgenstein, *Philosophical Investigations* §289.

19. See note 3.

20. The point I am making has, I believe, close connections with what Wittgenstein is driving at when he speaks in the famous passage at *Philosophical Investigations* §201 of "a way of grasping a rule which is *not* an *interpretation*, but which is exhibited in what we call "obeying the rule" and going against it "in actual cases." It would not stray very far from the intent of that passage, in my opinion,

if we gloss it as: there is, and has to be, a kind of rule following in which the ingredient steps are performed without the possibility of an articulated justification in the light of a statement of the rule, and in that sense are performed *blindly*. (See *Philosophical Investigations* §219.)

21. This claim presupposes, of course, that classical logic does not provide well-motivated theoretical reason to affirm the Unpalatable Existential on the ground of our acceptance, just argued for, of its double negation. That is exactly my position. I shall say more about it in a moment.

22. The conflation is comparable to one at work in the idea that one can get an inkling of what experience of disembodied survival of death would be like by suffering total sensory and proprioceptive anaesthesia. The latter might indeed generate experience in which one's body was in no way presented to one. But its not appearing as if one has a body is not the same thing as a pattern of experience which represents one has having none.

23. For if $(\exists x)(Fx \ \& \ {\sim}Fx')$ is true, then monotonicity ensures that each $y < x$ will be F and each $z > x'$ will be non-F. So every element will be determinately either F or non-F. Conversely, if Bivalence holds, and there are both Fs and non-Fs in the series, then there will have to be an adjacent pair, the earlier F and the other not.

REPLY TO CRISPIN WRIGHT

I must thank Crispin Wright both for writing about the issues raised by my article "Wang's Paradox" and for his kind remarks about that article. I agree strongly with his criticisms of the Fregean diagnosis of vagueness as mere semantic incompleteness, the vague predicate being undefined for objects on the borderline, and of the "epistemicist" diagnosis of it as due to our ignorance of the precise line of demarcation of the predicate's application, rather than to the non-existence of that line. What of the conclusion that I reached in "Wang's Paradox," that our language is governed by inconsistent rules? Sometimes in philosophy one appears to be driven by cogent arguments to a conclusion that one knows cannot be true. Is this such a case? Tarski also believed, on the strength of the semantic paradoxes, that natural language is governed by inconsistent rules. He did not reject this conclusion as intolerable; nor did he abjure the use of natural language. One can abide the knowledge of lurking inconsistency, if one knows how to avoid provoking the beast.

But this advice simply to avoid what will lead to flagrant contradiction is unsound. If a theory, or a language, is inconsistent, then you cannot trust its assumptions or rules to lead you into truth whenever you start with true premisses. In the case of the inconsistency observed by Tarski, there is a simple remedy. The semantic paradoxes turn on the use of a few expressions—"true," "false," "apply to," and one or two others, including "say that," which would allow the Epimenedes in the form "Things are not as I am now saying that they are." So, anyone willing to forswear the use of these expressions can feel sure of not running into inconsistency for these reasons. But the inconsistency pinpointed in "Wang's Paradox" is due to the use of vague expressions, and these are almost everywhere; someone who forswore their use would be mute, or at least capable of conversing only with mathematicians. So perhaps the charge of incoherence directed at the practice of using vague expressions is to be taken very seriously.

Crispin Wright argues that the view that our use of vague expressions is incoherent is powerless to explain the actual facts that characterise that use. "Why in a Sorites series," he asks, "do we start out with strong positive opinions, then gradually lapse into weak, defeasible opinions, conflicting opinions, unstable opinions, and failures to come to an opinion, before finally gradually reverting to strong negative opinions?" Well, the thesis of incoherence does not purport by itself to explain such behaviour, which simply exemplifies our usual response to being confronted by such a series and asked successively whether the vague predicate applies to particular terms of the series. I will add something to Wright's description that is merely a guess at an empirical fact for which I do not have observational evidence. My guess is that it makes a difference at which end of the series one makes the subject start: if he starts at the positive end, he will begin to become uncertain closer to the negative end than if he starts at the negative end. If this guess is correct, the presumable reason for it is easy to give. We must suppose that, confronted by an item of the sort to which the predicate can be applied, a speaker of the language is impelled to judge that the predicate holds of it, or that it does not hold, by a certain force, depending on that item. He is also impelled by a constant force to give the same verdict upon two items which he cannot distinguish in the relevant respect; let us call this the indistinguishability force. As he moves from the positive end, he becomes uncertain only when the indistinguishability force becomes significantly weaker than the force impelling him to give the negative verdict that the predicate does not hold of the item at which he has arrived. Likewise, when he moves from the negative end, he becomes uncertain only when the indistinguishability force becomes significantly weaker than the force impelling him to give the positive verdict that the predicate does hold of the item at which he has arrived. It seems reasonable to expect that this second point will be closer to the positive end than the first point.

However this may be, Wright correctly describes how we should react to being asked to judge the application of a vague predicate to the terms of a Sorites series. It is not difficult to explain why we react in that manner. If the predicate is an observational one, then we have been trained to judge of its application to particular objects just by using the relevant sense (sight in the case of colour-predicates). This training is such that each of us is disposed to give quite firm affirmative or negative verdicts in certain cases, but to be hesitant or unsure in others. Thus when we first learn colour words we are given books on each page of which the name of a colour is at the bottom and above it a bright archetypal sample of that colour; we shall always without hesitation apply that colour word to anything of just that shade or close to it. We are not shown a range of colours stretching from red to orange, or red to brown, or red to pink, with lines underneath to show how far one colour extends and how far the other. But we have also a profound inclination to suppose that if two things are indistinguishable to the senses in the relevant respect, then they *are* the same in the relevant respect; that is, if the observational predicate applies to either, then it applies to the other. It is, of course, this principle that generates the Sorites paradox.

It might be argued that if two things are indistinguishable in a given respect, they may not be indistinguishable in Nelson Goodman's sense; that is to say, they may not both be indistinguishable from some third thing. Suppose that we have a succession of coloured surfaces running from bright red to bright orange, any two adjacent surfaces being indistinguishable in colour. Two surfaces sufficiently far apart in the succession will be distinguishable. Let us suppose that the succession has been contrived so that the colour of a surface can just be distinguished, under close scrutiny, from that of another if they are ten places apart, but not if they are any closer in the succession. Then the colour of a surface, say A, cannot be distinguished from that of a surface C nine places away in one direction, while that of the neighbour B of A in the other direction *can* be distinguished from that of C. Though we cannot tell that A and B differ in colour, even minutely, just by looking at them, we can tell that they must do so, minutely, by comparing them both with C. Still, such an appeal to Goodman's criterion is of little help with the Sorites problem. For any D that is beyond C (i.e., such that C is between A and D), A and B will both be distinguishable from D, which gives a good warrant for saying that A and B differ only minutely in colour. It still seems compelling to say that if two surfaces differ only minutely in colour, so minutely that their colours cannot be distinguished by looking only at them, even though they can be distinguished by comparing both with some third surface, then, if one is red, the other must be red, too.

So what is the solution? As Crispin Wright acknowledges, we do not need mathematical induction to yield a paradox. Provided that we can reach a surface that is definitely not red from one that is definitely red in a finite, if large, number of steps from one surface to another that differs from it in colour only minutely, we need only universal instantiation and *modus ponens* applied the same large number of times. Does *modus ponens* cease to be valid when applied too often in succession? How could this be? What would be the rationale for it?

Wright points out that the Sorites paradox differs from, say, the Epimenedes in that the reasoning does not lead to two contradictory consequences which we have equal reason to accept, but simply to a conclusion which we unhesitatingly reject as false. This is true; in this it resembles Zeno's paradoxes: we know very well that Achilles *can* catch the tortoise—not by reasoning, but by observation of similar cases. The contrast drawn by Wright in no way impugns the paradoxical character of the

Sorites. A paradox is generated by apparently valid reasoning to a conclusion known to be false, whether on logical or on empirical grounds. There must therefore be something wrong either with the premises of the argument or with the rules of inference invoked: but we cannot think what can be wrong with either.

Wright's solution of the Sorites paradox is to deny that competence in the use of a vague predicate involves "the internalization of a set of rules." He contrasts the rule governing castling in chess with what governs our application of a colour-word such as "red." In the former case we can articulate what, according to the rules of chess, entitles a player to castle at a given stage of the game. But in the latter, we cannot say, in the normal case, what it is that prompts us to apply the predicate. In abnormal cases, we can do so. If I haven't myself seen the book, and am asked, "Why did you call the book 'red'?", I may say, "I know that all the books in that series are red"; or if I am colour-blind, I may say, "I have heard other people say that it is red." But if I say, "Because it looks red," I am not, as in the abnormal cases, giving a *reason* from which I have inferred that the book is red; I am merely indicating that this is a normal case. I might just as well have said, "Because I have seen it." I am fully in agreement with Wright on this point: the judgement I express by applying a colour-word is not based on an inference.

"Competent classification over a Sorites series for 'looks red'," Wright says, "will, indeed must, at some point involve differential responses to presentations that look exactly alike." "The (crazy) idea," he continues, "that competence somehow accordingly involves *disrespecting* the rules" governing our use of the predicate "looks red" is, he says, "an artifact of a misplaced adherence to the *modus ponens* model," by which he means a conception of rules of use according to which the application of a predicate is governed by an articulable condition. I hardly think that the idea that one who has said that one surface looks red, but hesitates to say that another surface looks red which looks to him exactly like the first, is showing disrespect to a principle governing our use of such predicates as "looks red" can be called "crazy"; it may be mistaken, but it is completely rational. Moreover, there are good grounds for thinking that the use of colour-words which we learn is governed by just such a principle; the fact that a simple judgement of colour in an ordinary situation is not based on an articulable ground does not show that there are no regulative principles that may guide us in special circumstances. We learn that colour-adjectives are observational predicates from the fact that we are never told of any other means of determining colours than by looking at the object in question or by asking others what they would say when they have looked at it; by contrast, we are instructed to appeal to measurement to decide whether something really is square. Furthermore, we learn the process of matching colours; we may be instructed to take a sample to a shop and buy something of just the same shade, which we judge by matching the sample with what we are offered by the shop. In this way we learn that we are expected to be able to tell whether or not two things are exactly the same in colour simply by eye. It is difficult to deny that we do learn as a principle governing our use of colour-words that if two things look to us just the same in colour, then, if we apply a certain colour-word to one, we must apply it to the other.

As someone passes along the Sorites series, beginning at the red end, he is therefore driven to keep saying of successive items in turn that they are red. After a time he begins to feel uneasy about giving this response, and at some stage his uneasiness causes him to hesitate and either say, "I'm not sure," or state rather dubiously that the item before him is red. He has not reacted in the same way as he did to the previous item; but, if he were to be asked if he could see any difference between the present item and the previous one, he would have to say that he did not. Asked why, in that case, he was dubious about the present item, he may say that he should perhaps have said that he was not sure about the previous item. This behaviour manifests the pressure upon him to say the same thing about items which he cannot differentiate in colour. He knows that his responses have flouted a principle which we accept as governing our judgements of colour.

Crispin Wright fastens on the No Sharp Boundaries version of the Sorites paradox—there is not in the Sorites series an item that is or looks red whose successor is not or does not look red. He describes the situation as follows.

> There are things that definitely look red, and things that definitely do not. These definite cases are cases which elicit a firm and stable consensus in judgment from those considered competent in conditions considered as relevantly suitable. And in discarding the *modus ponens* model we now treat that sociological fact as, in a sense, the whole truth about the cases in question. ... The way is therefore open to us to regard such convergence [in judgment] as *unimprovable evidence* of the truth of the statements in question, and—*pari passu*—inconsistency with verdicts which enjoy such convergence should be regarded as unimprovable evidence of falsity.

He subsequently speaks of "polar constancy flanking the gradual break-down of convergence in verdicts of any kind in the borderline region." As a sociological observation this cannot be faulted; let us accept Wright's view that this is the whole truth about our employment of the predicate "looks red" to the items in a Sorites series. (I take it that the convergence in judgement of which Wright speaks does not relate to judgements when the items are arranged in the Sorites series, but when they are presented apart from that series.)

We do not have here a bare sociological observation: it is accompanied by a proposal how to assess the truth-values of ascriptions or rejections of the predicate "looks red" in the light of the sociological facts. When there is convergence in judgement, positive or negative, such statements are to be taken to be true or false accordingly. How much agreement does there have to be for there to be convergence? Does every normally sighted person have to agree that something is red before the statement that it is red can be rated true? Presumably not, since Wright speaks of "inconsistency with verdicts which enjoy convergence." Is it enough, then, that 90 percent say without demur that it is red? As Wright recognises, not only is "is red" vague, but "is definitely red" is vague, too. In any case, what of items in the borderline region?

Wright does not immediately reveal what logic he thinks should hold for vague statements, or what semantic theory applies to them; but it turns out that he believes that we should employ intuitionistic logic for this purpose, as Hilary Putnam had earlier proposed in his paper "Vagueness and Alternative Logic."[1] On this proposal, statements applying a vague predicate to something in its borderline zone correspond to mathematical statements that we have as yet no means either of proving or refuting. At first sight, there seems too great a disanalogy between these classes of statements for Wright's proposal to be correct. A mathematical statement as yet undecided may come to be proved or to be disproved; a colour firmly on the borderline between red and orange will never come to be recognised by all as definitely either one or the other. Yet we must bear in mind that intuitionistic logic works well for applications for which it was not devised; and the proposal of Putnam and Wright works remarkably well. Suppose that, for an arithmetical predicate $A(x)$ which is not effectively decidable, we have proved that, for any n, if $A(n)$, then $A(m)$ for every $m < n$, and further, that $A(100)$ but $\neg A(1000)$. An intuitionist mathematician will refuse to assert that $\exists x\,(A(x)\,\&\,\neg A(x + 1))$ if he cannot identify a number between 100 and 999 for which this is true. But he will not assert that $\neg\exists x\,(A(x)\,\&\,\neg A(x + 1))$, since that would lead to a contradiction; rather, he will for that reason assert that $\neg\neg\exists x\,(A(x)\,\&\,\neg A(x + 1))$. Similarly, a follower of Putnam and Wright will not assert that there is a member of a Sorites series from red to orange which is red but whose successor in the series is orange, because he is unable to identify one. But he will not assert the negation of that statement, because that would lead to a contradiction; rather, he will for that reason assert the double negation of that statement. This seems an elegant resolution of the paradox.

Further reflection raises a doubt, however. The mathematician, asked, of any number between 100 and 999, whether it satisfies $(A(x)$ & $\neg A(x + 1))$, will say that he does not know. But someone, asked of any member of the Sorites series, whether it is red but has an orange successor, will surely say that it is not. According to Wright, he must resist the temptation to add, "I do not think there is one," even though he seems to have an excellent reason for denying that there is any such member. It is precisely because he seems to have a reason to say that that a paradox arises. According to Wright, he ought, rather, to add ingratiatingly, "I do not think there is not one." The mathematician, by asserting the double negation of the statement that there is a greatest number n such that $A(n)$, expresses the view that it remains open that such a number will be found. But Wright does not think it open that a sharp boundary between red and orange will be found. In intuitionistic semantics for mathematical statements, a statement not yet assigned the status of not being true or of not being false is one capable, so far as our knowledge goes, of being proved or disproved; one or the other may later occur. On Wright's account of statements ascribing a vague predicate to an object, such a statement, if not assigned the status of being true or being false, is one ascribing the vague predicate to an object whose colour lies in the borderline region. That colour will always remain in that region. There is nothing further about the statement which it remains for us to find out: of a surface on the borderline between red and orange, for example, when we have looked at it and perhaps compared it with other surfaces, we know everything about its (phenomenal) colour that there is to be known. There is a strong disanalogy between the intuitionist theory of meaning for mathematical statements and Wright's account of the meanings of vague statements. What, on Wright's theory, does the meaning of a statement such as "This curtain is red," applied to a curtain whose colour lies on the borderline between red and orange, consist in? On the intuitionist theory, one understands—knows the meaning of—a mathematical statement of which we have at present neither a proof nor a disproof if one is able to recognise, of any mathematical construction, whether it is or is not a proof of the statement—to tell that it is a proof if it is, and to tell that it is not a proof if it is not. Wright can hardly say that to grasp the meaning of the statement about the curtain is to be able to recognise a demonstration that the colour of the curtain is red, not orange, or that it is orange, not red. Presumably he must say that it consists in an ability to judge that the colour of the curtain is neither definitely red nor definitely orange, but is definitely either one or the other. If so, however, the theory of meaning for vague statements on which Wright wishes to rest intuitionist logic as applying to them interprets disjunction quite differently from the intuitionist theory of meaning for mathematical statements. And what in particular, for Wright, does the double negation of the statement that there is a sharp boundary between red and orange *mean*? Not that it is possible that we might identify one: simply that if we were to maintain that there is no such boundary, we could be driven into saying that something was both red and not red.

For these reasons, I am somewhat sceptical about the use of intuitionistic logic as resolving the problems of vagueness (although there may be other reasons for preferring it to classical logic). Wright himself has changed his mind on the matter: in the paper jointly written by him and Stephen Read,[2] Putnam was criticised for suggesting that intuitionistic logic be used for statements containing vague predicates. Admittedly, this was on the basis that we should *deny* that there is a sharp boundary (in our example, between red and orange), namely that there is a red member of the sequence with an orange successor; now Wright is proposing that we should assert the double negation of the statement that a sharp boundary exists. It is still a marked change of mind. In that paper, Read and Wright thought it problematic how vagueness could be acknowledged without denying the existence of a sharp boundary; pending a solution of this problem, "recourse to intuitionistic logic is no help," they concluded.

It may be that I am simply failing to appreciate that intuitionistic logic may have different applications; that is, that different semantic theories may underlie its use in different contexts. In particular, I am impressed by the strength of the inclination to believe that there is no sharp boundary between red and orange (and analogously for other vague predicates). Crispin Wright denies that there is no sharp boundary. This is not because he believes that there *is* one: he merely thinks that it is not the case that there is not one. His sole reason for regarding the highly plausible principle that there is no sharp boundary as false is that it leads to a contradiction.

Indeed it does; and this is the paradox. It may be claimed that Wright's endorsement of the negation of the thesis that there is no sharp boundary is in total accord with the intuitionistic meaning of negation. But to say that the premises cannot all be true is to state the paradox, not to solve it. A genuine solution ought to show, on *independent* grounds, that one of the premises is false, or at least not assertible; here the only possible candidate is the principle that there is no sharp boundary. If we were given independent grounds for thinking it false, we should be relieved of the discomfort that the paradox caused us. But Wright offers no independent ground. He simply observes that it leads to paradox. He professes to be relying on how we should in practice react to questions involving the vague predicate "looks red." For all that, he gives no weight to our propensity to deny, at every point of the Sorites series, that a sharp boundary has been reached.

A sharp boundary in the Sorites series running from red to orange would be a surface that was red while its successor was orange. If it could be argued that the right response to the question, "Is this a sharp boundary?", asked of a surface whose colour was in the borderline region, was not "No" but "I do not know," then the situation would be the same as in the mathematical example of the predicate "$A(x)$" whose application in the interval from 101 to 999 was unknown. It would be the same, that is, if "I do not know" implied that there might at some time be a means of identifying a sharp boundary. Surely, by rejecting epistemicism Wright has rejected any such possibility. If a sharp boundary were located by means of instruments and a precise criterion stipulated for when a surface was to count as red, the concept *red* would have changed: our concept is one whose application can be judged just by looking. It is true that we can detect differences between two surfaces, just by looking, when we cannot see any difference just by looking at *them*, namely by comparing them both with other surfaces; but that is surely not going to lead to the identification of a sharp boundary. It is a fantasy that we might ever identify one.

I am left, then, with admiration for the beautiful solution of the Sorites paradox advocated by Crispin Wright, clouded by a persistent doubt whether it is correct. I harbour a strong disposition to believe that there is no sharp boundary between red and orange. That belief appears to lead to contradiction; if it is a true belief, my original judgement that our use of vague expressions is incoherent has not yet been shown to be at fault. I do not say that Wright's proposed solution of the Sorites is wrong; I say only that we need a more far-going explanation than Wright has given us of why intuitionistic logic is the right logic for statements containing vague expressions before we can acknowledge it as correct. It is not enough to show that the Sorites paradox can be evaded by the use of intuitionistic logic: what is needed is a theory of meaning, or at least a semantics, for sentences containing vague expressions that shows why intuitionistic logic is appropriate for them rather than any other logic. The supervaluational semantics offers a justification for applying classical logic to such sentences, or at least to sentences applying a vague predicate to some object. Unfortunately that semantics cannot be sustained, because it cannot handle higher-order vagueness. More accurately, it can handle it up to any finite order, but only on the assumption that at that order vagueness evaporates, whereas it surely persists however high we are able to go without losing our grip on meaning. (Do you understand the expression "definitely not definitely not definitely red," that is, do you understand it to the extent of having a grip on when it might be right to apply it? If you do,

MICHAEL DUMMETT

you cannot deny that it is still vague. Wherever in this hierarchy your understanding peters out, you will always still be dealing with vague expressions. And who is to say at what stage understanding must give way?) If Crispin Wright is to persuade us that he has the true solution to the Sorites paradox, he must give a more convincing justification of the use of intuitionistic logic for statements containing vague expressions: a justification, namely, that does not appeal only to the ability of that logic to resist the Sorites slide into contradiction. We need a justification that would satisfy someone who was puzzled about vagueness but had never heard of the Sorites: a justification that would sketch a convincing semantics for sentences involving vague expressions. A semantics for such sentences would be very different from the intuitionistic semantics for mathematics: as we have noted, it would interpret disjunction quite differently. Contrary to the position Putnam adopted in his reply to Read and Wright,[3] it is not a solution to the Sorites paradox simply to adopt intuitionistic logic; if that logic is not grounded on an appropriate semantics, that will necessarily differ from the semantics for intuitionistic mathematics. Without at least a sketch of such a semantics, we do not yet have a resolution of the paradox of the heap.

M. D.

NOTES

1. Hilary Putnam, "Vagueness and Alternative Logic," *Erkenntnis* 19 (1983): 297–314; reprinted in H. Putnam, *Realism and Reason* (*Philosophical Papers* vol. 3), Cambridge, 1983, 271–86.

2. S. L. Read and C. J. G. Wright, "Hairier than Putnam Thought," *Analysis* 45 (1985): 56–58.

3. H. Putnam, "A quick Read is a wrong Wright," *Analysis* 45 (1985): 203.

13

Dag Prawitz

PRAGMATIST AND VERIFICATIONIST THEORIES OF MEANING

A recurring theme in a large part of Michael Dummett's work is the philosophical importance of devising a systematic theory of meaning. He has called this "the most urgent task that philosophers are now called upon to carry out."[1] His visions and discussions of how this task is to be carried out, as a collective enterprise he suggests, have been a great source of inspiration to many of us.[2]

Dummett has considered different directions in which the project might be carried out. His criticism of classical attempts to identify the meaning of a sentence with its truth condition is well known. On the constructive side, he has chiefly suggested two kinds of meaning theories, which he has called verificationist and pragmatist, respectively. The aim of this essay is to discuss these two kinds of meaning theories and how they are related. There is also a third kind of theory, which seems to be favored by Dummett in one of his works. It may be called falsificationist, but, as will be argued here, it is best subsumed under the other ones.

1. SOME BASIC NOTIONS AND IDEAS AND AN OUTLINE OF THE ESSAY

Following Dummett's later terminology, I shall speak of a *meaning theory for a language L* when we have a systematic specification of the meanings of the expressions of the language *L*, and of a *theory of meaning* when it is a question of a philosophical account of meaning, in which among other things the general form of meaning theories is discussed.

The actual use of a language L depends obviously on many factors, among which the meaning of the sentences of L is one. Knowledge of meaning is therefore one, but only one, of the ingredients in explanation of various speech acts, actual utterances of sentences as well as reactions upon them. What is then a meaning theory for a language? A short answer according to a main idea of Dummett's is that it is to contain all that a speaker needs to know implicitly in order to be able to speak the language.

One may think that a meaning theory could meet this demand by describing all regularities in how the expressions of the language are used without employing a notion of meaning. Meaning could then afterwards be introduced, if one likes, simply by declaring that the meaning of an expression is identical with its use, in this way literally satisfying the slogan "meaning is use."

Dummett's main objection to such an idea is that what we are seeking is not an empirical description of how language is actually used, nor a causal theory about this. What we want to know is the conventions or rules that govern the use of the language. Furthermore, there are presumably connections among different features of use. A meaning theory should display these connections. In particular, the theory should respect the principle of compositionality, viz., that the understanding of a complex expression results from an understanding of its parts and the way they are put together.

There are other strong arguments for thinking that meaning of a sentence is not to be identified with all rules for how to use the sentence. Such an identification would also go against common, pre-philosophical experiences of meaning. It is true that the meaning of an expression is often explained by quoting examples of its use, and that the use that is so exemplified may be taken as constitutive of the meaning of the expression. But it is also common that a use of a sentence, for instance, the drawing of a conclusion, is *justified* by reference to the meaning without claiming that the use in question is just a part of what the sentence means. In short, there are uses that are justified or explained by referring to meaning and are not constitutive of meaning.

Instead of identifying the meaning of a sentence with its use, we should expect that there is some feature or aspect of the use that is central in the sense that other aspects can be accounted for in terms of the central one. If we succeed in isolating and describing such an aspect, we have found what Dummett calls a central semantic concept. It may rightly be called meaning and should be the hub around which a meaning theory can be constructed.

To discuss this possibility any further we need to characterize in an appropriate way different aspects of language that are relevant in this connection. In Dummett's writings, two main aspects of the use of a sentence are distinguished, schematically characterized as the *conditions* for uttering the sentence and the *consequences* of uttering it. The first aspect covers the conventions that tell on what occasions it is appropriate to utter the sentence as far as it has to do with the meaning of the sentence. In case the sentence is in the assertive mood it amounts to the grounds I need to have in order to be right in asserting the sentence.

The second aspect is concerned with what reactions are appropriate when the sentence has been uttered, both what the speaker commits himself to and what the hearer has the right to expect. In case the sentence is in the assertive mood it amounts to the conclusions that can rightly be drawn when the assertion is assumed to be correct.

The idea is thus that a meaning theory could take one of these two aspects as starting point for developing a notion of meaning and then can account for other aspects in terms of the first. A *verificationist* meaning theory takes the first aspect as its starting point, while a *pragmatist* meaning theory takes the second.

One could hardly deny that there are unwritten rules of our language that govern the two aspects that Dummett distinguishes. To learn a language is among other things to learn what counts as sufficient grounds for asserting a sentence, and what conclusions one can draw from taking the assertion to be correct. But one can doubt that these aspects can be accounted for systematically by some central semantic concept. Meaning theories of these kinds are therefore to be understood as projects. The philosophical project is not to develop them in detail for entire natural languages, but rather to develop enough of such theories for fragments of languages, natural or formal, to be able to judge whether they meet principal obstacles or whether they may be possible to carry out in principle. A positive answer would cast light upon the concept of meaning. The imagined meaning theory that would result, if the project were fully carried out, could then be said to be what a speaker knows implicitly when he or she knows a language.

In this essay, I shall limit myself to the use of sentences in the assertive mood. To account for the use of sentences in other moods we should also have to reckon with various forces of utterances in addition to the meanings of sentences. The question to which we shall now turn is thus whether the use of assertions can be accounted for in meaning theories of the suggested kind.

As a summary of the essay, I may mention five points that I shall try to argue for. They are points where Dummett may disagree with me and where I am therefore especially interested in his response. First, I think that one has grounds for being optimistic about the possibilities of verificationist meaning theories for constructive mathematics; the project has in this case been carried out to a farther extent than Dummett seems usually to acknowledge. Second, what Dummett calls proof-theoretical justifications of logical laws constitute such a meaning theory for logic; it does not deviate from the usual intuitionistic interpretation of the logical constants. Third, there seem to be principal obstacles for a verificationist meaning theory for empirical discourse; the problems met in empirical context for such a theory are more serious than Dummett has perhaps been willing to see. Fourth, I think that kind of pragmatic meaning theories can be developed for mathematics and that there is a better hope for them than for verificationist ones in empirical context, but some of the pragmatist ideas must then be given up. Fifth, I will offer some comments on Dummett's notion of stability, which I see as a very interesting notion, but which I think should be formulated somewhat differently. Many other and more important things could be said about Dummett's admirable contributions to theory of meaning, with which I am essentially in agreement, but these are some points of possible disagreement, which I have not commented on before and shall concentrate on here.[3]

2. VERIFICATIONISM

2.1. *Some General Problems*

The characterization of verificationist meaning theories given above is to be understood as a first rough indication. On some reflection, the idea of identifying the meaning of a sentence with the condition for asserting it turns out not to be feasible. This is easily seen in the case of mathematics where we normally treat the presence of a proof of a sentence as the condition for asserting it. We may thus test the idea of meaning as assertion conditions by trying to specify the meaning of compound mathematical sentences in terms of what counts as proofs of them.

This is what Dummett does for intuitionistic mathematics in *Elements of Intuitionism*, but it soon turns out that the proofs in question are not the kind of thing we demand as grounds for assertions. For instance, it is said that a proof of a conjunction is anything that is a proof of both conjuncts, that a proof of a disjunction is anything that is a proof of one of the disjuncts, and that a proof of an existentially quantified sentence is anything that is a proof of an instance of the sentence. We have here a recursive specification of what a proof of a sentence is in terms of proofs of the immediate subsentences, which accords well with the principle of compositionality, if the notion of proof is to be taken as the central semantic concept. But Dummett remarks soon afterwards that even in intuitionistic mathematics it is not true that a proof as usually understood is always a proof of subsentences in the way stated in his definition. A proof of a disjunction $A(t) \vee B(t)$ may for instance proceed by first proving $\forall x(A(x) \vee B(x))$ and then deriving $A(t) \vee B(t)$ by universal elimination, in which case the proof is neither a proof of A(t) nor of (Bt), contradicting what was said above. Such a proof is a perfect ground for asserting A(t) ∨ B(t), but not for asserting A(t) or B(t).

If we stay with the given explanation of proof, we thus have to admit that the construction of a proof is not, as is usually thought, a prerequisite for an assertion to be warranted. Hence, if that notion of proof is taken as the central semantic concept, then the meaning of a logical constant is after all not explained in terms of the assertibility of sentences that have the constant in question as its principal sign.[4]

Clearly, the conditions for asserting a mathematical sentence cannot be given recursively. As we know from Gödel, in the case of languages containing arithmetic, they cannot even be given in terms of formal systems.

To indicate the special status of the kind of proofs that Dummett delimits, he sometimes refers to them as *canonical proofs*, and this is how I shall refer to them henceforth. In terms of that notion, taken as the central semantic concept, a general assertion condition can be stated: in order for the assertion of a sentence to be warranted one has to know either a canonical proof of the sentence or a method for finding one. I shall refer to a method of this kind as a *(noncanonical) proof*. Given this general condition for assertibility, one can also formulate a condition for an inference to be correct, viz., that one knows how to find a canonical proof of the conclusion given canonical proofs of the premises. Knowing this we know that the conclusion is assertible given that the premises are. It is easily shown that these conditions agree with ordinary constructive practice in mathematics.

2.2. *A Verificationist Meaning Theory for Arithmetic*

We thus seem to have a meaning theory of a (modified) verificationist kind for at least parts of mathematical language understood intuitionistically. Nevertheless Dummett seems to think that the project to find such a theory is still open; in *Elements of Intuitionism* he says, "no one can at present give a detailed account of canonical proofs even of statements of first order arithmetic."[5] I am uncertain whether he is still of this opinion.

Some problems do remain. To see more clearly what the problems may be, it is suitable to try to state a meaning theory for the language of arithmetic in a little more detail. Assuming that atomic sentences have the form t = u for numerical terms t and u built up in the usual way from 0, the successor ' and the operations for addition and multiplication, we may take the canonical proofs of them to consist in ordinary calculations. If the compound sentences are the ones formed by use of the logical constants of predicate logic, we have already seen how Dummett specifies the canonical proofs of conjunctions, disjunctions, and existential sentences. To specify them a little more stringently one may, for each logical constant, introduce an operation such that, when applied on proofs of the required kind, it produces canonical proofs of sentences that have the constant as its principal symbol. For instance, for conjunction we would introduce a primitive, binary operation $\theta_\&$ that brings together two proofs (pair formation, if one likes), and then say that Π is a canonical proof of a conjunction A & B, if and only if, Π has the form $\theta_\&(\Sigma,\Delta)$, where Σ and Δ are proofs of A and B respectively.

Two more crucial cases arise for implication and universal sentences. Dummett requires of a canonical proof of A $\rightarrow$ B that it is a construction of which we can recognize that, applied to any canonical proof of A, it yields a canonical proof of B. Similarly, a canonical proof of $\forall x A(x)$ is a construction of which we can recognize that, applied to any numeral n, it yields a canonical proof of A(n). The stipulation that we shall be able to recognize the construction to be of the required kind is introduced to guarantee that knowledge of meaning is manifestable. This it will be if the question whether something is a canonical proof or not is decidable. To get this effect it seems that the stipulation ought to be that we *have recognized* that the construction is of the required kind. Provided that we can decide whether we have recognized something, it then follows that we can decide whether something is a canonical proof. Whether we *can recognize* that a construction is of a certain kind is not obviously decidable. Faced with the question whether we can recognize the construction to have the required property, we may try to do so, but as long as the outcome is negative, it may remain open whether continued efforts would succeed.

The effect of requiring some kind of recognition in connection with canonical proofs seems anyhow to be that the property of being a canonical proof of a given sentence is really a binary or threefold relation: something is a canonical proof of the given sentence *for a person P* (or for us) *at a certain time t*. To move the recognition requirement to the condition for an assertion to be warranted is not an alternative since knowledge of meaning may then not be manifestable, which is the main charge that Dummett brings against truth-conditional meaning theories. Notwithstanding that the notion of canonical proof is not a straightforward mathematical notion when it has the recognition stipulation as an ingredient, it seems that we have a verificationist meaning theory for intuitionistic arithmetic essentially formulated by Dummett himself. It takes the notion of canonical proofs, specified recursively in a compositional way, as its central semantic concept, and in terms of that it states assertibility conditions and conditions for the validity of inferences that justify intuitionistic practice within arithmetic.

Proofs, whether canonical or not, conceived of as above do not at first sight look like the kind of proofs that we meet in mathematical practice when we assert a theorem by making a series of inferences that ends with the theorem in question. In this respect, the assertion conditions that were given above in terms of constructions do not seem to reflect actual mathematical practice; at least there seems to be some gap here.

2.3. Another Formulation of a Verificationist Meaning Theory for Arithmetic

What at first sight makes it seem credible that something like a verificationist meaning theory is possible for the logical constant is, I think, not so much the ideas of intuitionism but rather Gentzen's system of natural deduction, which directly connects meanings with proofs as they more or less occur in practice. In particular, the idea that the meaning of a sentence can be defined in terms of a certain special way of inferring the sentence, called introductions by Gentzen, and that other inferences, called eliminations, are justified in terms of this meaning, seems to be an embryo to a verificationist kind of meaning theory for logically compound sentences.

To see how this idea can be developed, we may again consider the language of arithmetic, to whose atomic formulas we now add Nt for numerical terms t, to be read "t is a natural number." To Gentzen's introduction rules we add two introduction rules for N,[6] viz., the axiom N0 and the inference rule

$$\frac{Nt}{Nt'}$$

I leave it unspecified how to formulate introduction rules for identities t = u (or other atomic formulas of corresponding kind). It should be added however that we count the logical constant for falsehood, written ⊥, as an atomic sentence. Particular for ⊥ is that there is no introduction rule for it. The presence of ⊥ allows us to define ¬A as A → ⊥, which is a convenient way to handle negation.

The proofs will now be defined as trees of formulas similar to the proofs in natural deduction but with two modifications. First, the inferences that occur do not need to be instances of any given inference rules but are arbitrary. As in natural deduction, an inference may discharge an assumption, and there may be inferences like universal introduction that put special requirements on variables (sometimes referred to as "eigenvariables"). I shall say that such inferences *bind* the assumptions or the variables in question. If all occurring assumptions and free variables are bound in that way, the proof is said to be *closed*; otherwise it is said to be *open*. Second, to any inference that is not an instance of an introduction, there is to be assigned what we may call an (alleged) justification consisting in a transformation rule, similar to the rules of reduction in natural deduction. These justifications are again arbitrary except for satisfying some of the same formal properties as the ordinary reduction rules for natural deduction. In particular, proofs are to be transformed to other proofs of the same conclusion from the same or fewer hypotheses. This means that we can speak of a proof Π *reducing* to another proof Π^* as in natural deduction, except that the reduction rules employed in carrying out the reductions are now given by the justifications that have been assigned to the inferences of Π.

The constructions just described, that is, arbitrary inferences arranged in tree form, justified by reduction rules assigned to them, need clearly not amount to proofs. Let us call them *arguments* and pose the question what is to be required to make them proofs. The question can be given a first answer by defining what I shall call canonical arguments and valid (non-canonical) arguments.

The definition can be put very simply as follows. An argument is *canonical*, if and only if, it is closed, its last inference is an introduction, and its immediate subarguments obtained by deleting the lowest sentence are valid. A closed argument is *valid*, if and only if, it is either canonical or reduces to a canonical argument. An open argument is *valid*, if and only if, all the results are valid that are obtained by substituting first terms for free variables (not bound in the argument) and then closed valid arguments for free (undischarged) assumptions.[7]

This is a short but almost complete outline of how proof-theoretical normalizations of natural deductions can be generalized so as to provide notions of canonical argument and valid argument not tied to any particular formal systems.[8] The topic is taken up at length by Dummett under the title "Proof-Theoretic Justifications of Logical Laws."[9] Here we are interested in whether it can be embedded in a verificationist meaning theory, which Dummett seems to see as doubtful. I shall argue that what is formulated above is virtually the same meaning theory as was given in the section 2.2 above, or at least, it can easily be extended to such a theory.

The basic idea that certain grounds for an assertion are seen as constitutive of meaning is expressed in the definition of canonical argument, which is characterized first of all with respect to the form of the last inference of the argument. In addition, there is only the obvious requirement that the rest of the argument leading up to the premises of the last inference is correct. To know the meaning of a sentence is hence to know what counts as a canonical argument for it. When faced with an alleged canonical argument for a sentence, such knowledge manifests itself first of all in the ability to decide whether what is presented is of the right form with respect to the last inference, in other words whether this inference is an introduction of the right kind.

When it comes to deciding whether something is a canonical argument, however, the situation is as before: we have to add stipulations about recognition in order to guarantee decidability. It is first when we recognize that something is a canonical or valid argument that it can rightly be called a *proof.*

Proofs as now understood are made up of inferences in the way we normally think of proofs. The only cases in which one may suspect that this makes a real, substantial difference from the proofs we considered in the previous section are when we have a proof of an implication or a universal sentence. A canonical proof of a universal sentence now takes the form

$$\frac{\begin{array}{c} \Pi(x) \\ A(x) \end{array}}{\forall x A(x)}$$

where $\Pi(x)$ is a free variable proof of $A(x)$. One may suspect that this is only a special case of a construction that, applied to a term t, produces a proof of $A(t)$. As Dummett remarks, such a construction, when no restriction is put on it, may yield different proofs for different terms; in arithmetic we would typically define the construction by some kind of recursion with this effect. However, there is in fact no difference here, which may easily be seen by an example where $A(x)$ takes the form $(N(x) \rightarrow B(x))$ and $\Pi(x)$ is the free variable argument

$$\frac{\begin{array}{ccc} & [B(y)] & \\ & \Delta & \Sigma(y) \\ N(x) & B(0) & B(y') \end{array}}{\dfrac{B(x)}{N(x) \rightarrow B(x)}}$$

The penultimate inference of the argument, in which $B(x)$ is inferred, is an instance of the rule of induction, which can be seen as the elimination rule justified by the introduction rules for N.[10] Adding a universal introduction to the end of this argument $\Pi(x)$, we get a valid argument for $\forall x(N(x) \rightarrow B(x))$ provided that Δ and $\Sigma(y)$ are valid arguments and that the right justification is assigned to the inference of $B(x)$. The appropriate justification is the obvious justification of induction, viz., a reduction that is applicable when the conclusion is of the form $B(n)$, for a numeral n substituted for the free variable x, and which then yields an argument consisting of the argument Δ for the induction base $B(0)$ followed by n uses of the argument $\Sigma(y)$ for the induction step, with increasing numerals substituted for the free variable y.[11] It is easily seen that the open argument $\Pi(x)$ is valid when Δ and $\Sigma(y)$ are valid arguments and the induction inference is assigned the justification described, and hence that we get a canonical argument for $\forall x(N(x) \rightarrow B(x))$ when a universal introduction is added to $\Pi(x)$.

Similarly, a canonical argument for a conditional takes the form of a hypothetical argument. This, however, does not impose any new restriction as compared to the previous definition of a canonical proof of an implication requiring a construction ϑ that takes any proof of the antecedent to a proof of the succedent, which can be seen in the following example:

$$\frac{\dfrac{A}{B}}{A \to B}$$

If ϑ takes proofs of A to proofs of B, then assigning ϑ to the inference from A to B in the argument above will make the argument a valid proof.

Taking the notions of a canonical proof and valid proof as they are now defined as the central semantic concept, we thus arrive at substantially the same meaning theory as before. The proofs that are now taken as conditions for asserting sentences resemble a little more what we usually take as such grounds as compared to what we had before. This shows, one could say, that proofs as defined in the previous section 2.2 are not as far removed from our practice as they may first seem to be.

One may object to the identification of the assertibility of a sentence with knowing a valid argument as here defined by saying that normally we do not explicitly convince ourselves that an argument is valid by checking that it reduces to a canonical argument. We simply use inferences of whose intuitive validity we are convinced. Although this may be true, we may agree that the conviction can be articulated. For instance, we would probably answer affirmatively, if we were asked whether our trust in the practice of applying a lemma of the form $\forall x(A(x) \to B(x))$ in a proof does not partly rest on our conviction that we would have got the same result if, instead of applying the lemma, we had used a proof of an instance of the lemma, that is, a hypothetical proof of B(t) from A(t). Replacing the proof of the lemma with a hypothetical proof of B(t) from A(t) is of course nothing else than applying the reductions associated with universal instantiation and *modus ponens* as justifications of those inferences. One may thus argue that the idea of defining the validity of an argument in terms of reductions only makes explicit something that is implicitly involved in our treating some arguments as valid.

This defense seems reasonable only as long as the reductions bring out something in an argument that is in some sense already there, but is not applicable when the reduction replaces one argument with another one without their having any structural affinity. From this point of view the main philosophical weakness in the proposed notion of proof seems to be a too liberal notion of what is to count as justification of an inference.

In his discussion of the viability of the proposed meaning theory,

Dummett takes up another kind of objection under the heading "The Fundamental Assumption,"[12] which is the name Dummett gives to the assumption that a valid argument for a sentence, if it can be given at all, could always be given in canonical form. This is indeed a fundamental assumption. The proposed meaning theory hinges on the assumption that, in our practice, what we take as sufficient ground for the assertion of a sentence could always have been given in canonical form. Here I shall not at all discuss the fact that the proposed meaning theory is revisionary, that is, not faithful to classical practice but to a constructive one, which fact is also not the issue in Dummett's discussion. As far as intuitionistic arithmetic is concerned, the doubts that Dummett brings forward should be dispelled by what has been said above about implications and universal sentences. He has other doubts, however, that are highly relevant to the question whether a verificationist meaning theory of the proposed kind can be had for empirical discourse.

2.4. *Empirical Discourse*

When we pass to empirical discourse, one has to take account of the fact, often pointed out by Dummett, that our grounds for assertions may be based on both observations and inferential procedures. Instead of proofs we may now speak of *verifications*. The problem with extending a verificationist meaning theory of the kind considered for arithmetic to empirical discourse does not so much concern observation sentences but arises for compound sentences. It seems quite appropriate to say that a canonical verification of an observation sentence takes the form of an observation of the relevant kind. In several respects, the situation is similar to that in mathematics. It is not required for asserting an observation sentence that a canonical verification is known; it is sufficient to have an indirect argument. But again, the meaning of the sentence does not have to be given by the assertion condition, which is fortunate since it is impossible to survey all the forms that an indirect argument can take. It seems right to say that the meaning of an observation sentence is given by what counts as the relevant observation, because when we assert such a sentence on indirect grounds we always imagine that it could have been verified by observation.

There are, however, at least two main differences between observation sentences and atomic sentences in mathematics. One concerns their indirect verifications. Whereas in mathematics an indirect proof is supposed to give a method for finding a canonical proof, delivered by the reductions in the case of the meaning theory in section 2.3, an indirect verification of an observation sentence only assures us that we could make the relevant observation if we place ourselves appropriately.

Another main difference arises because observation sentences are tensed. If the content of the observation sentence is to be given by what counts as canonical verification, the verification must have the same tense as the sentence. Hence, the condition for a warranted assertion is that, for a suitable placed observer, a canonical verification of the sentence could have been obtained, could be obtained now, or will be possible to obtain in the future, as the case may be.

When we come to compound sentences, Dummett points out in "The Fundamental Assumption" that a disjunction may be verified by an observation that does not contain a verification of any of the disjuncts. For instance, if Charles and Peter are identical twins, we may see that one of them is over there without seeing which one. Nevertheless, we certainly consider ourselves having verified the sentence "Charles or Peter is over there." To fit this with a verificationist theory, the verification in question can not be counted as canonical but must be possible to classify as an indirect verification. What justifies it is not a straightforward reduction, but our knowledge that a suitably placed observer could have, at the time in question, verified canonically one of the sentences "Charles is over there" and "Peter is over there." What the observer verifies is, we could say, something like "one of the Bergman twins is over there," and from that it is inferred that "Charles or Peter is over there." The rationale for the last inference is that whenever someone verifies the premise, one of the disjuncts could have been verified as well. The problems encountered here for disjunctions are thus connected with features that we already met in the case of observation sentences.

The main problem facing a verificationist meaning theory for empirical discourse is certainly how to handle universal sentences in view of the fact that we commonly assert them on grounds involving empirical induction. As clarified by Dummett, the problem is not that such an argument cannot be put in canonical form, i.e., that the last inference of the argument cannot be universal introduction. When an inductive argument is considered to warrant an assertion of $\forall x A(x)$, it clearly also warrants the assertion of $A(t)$ for any term t. In other words, the result of substituting a term t for the variable x in the immediate open subargument for $A(x)$ is (at least) an equally good ground for asserting $A(t)$, just as is the case in mathematics. The problem is that somewhere—if not for universal sentences, then for some other form of sentences, for example, conditionals—we must weaken either the definition of canonical verification or the assertion condition, if we are to incorporate empirical induction as a ground for assertions. Then the consequences that we are accustomed to draw from an assertion will not be validated any more by the meaning theory.

This seems to be an inevitable consequence of the fact that inductive grounds are not conclusive grounds. What was a good, nonconclusive ground yesterday may not be so today. It is plain that our ordinary usage of universal sentences involves risk-taking—some assertions are made on weaker grounds than is needed to uphold the consequences we draw from them, and as a result it is not ruled out that the consequences we draw come in conflict with other usage. It is unclear whether a verificationist meaning theory can cope with this.

It is sometimes suggested that instead of trying to hope for a verificationist meaning theory for empirical language we should try to develop a *justifcationist* theory.[13] The idea seems to be that it is part of the meaning of some sentences that their assertions are justified by grounds that do not amount to verifications. Certainly, as just said, many assertions about empirical matters are made on inconclusive grounds, and, of course, competent hearers accordingly adjust their trust in the assertions and the consequences that they draw from them. But the question is whether this can be considered part of the *content* of the sentence. One problem with that suggestion is that we then seem to be back to a theory that identifies meaning with assertion condition, which was dismissed in section 2.1 as a possible route. It seems difficult to single out any canonical or typical non-conclusive ground among the many kinds of nonconclusive grounds that we use in our linguistic practice.

But there seem to me to be even more serious problems with a justificationist theory. In a verificationist meaning theory, the content of an assertion is taken to be that a canonical verification could be found (or could have been found or will be possible to find). If one tries the same construction in a justificationist theory and says that the content of the assertion, what is asserted by asserting for instance $\forall x A(x)$, is only that a justification of a certain nonconclusive kind can be given, then it is difficult to explain why the assertion may have to be withdrawn in the light of new information, say some counterexample $\neg A(t)$ to $\forall x A(x)$. The fact that the assertion may have to be withdrawn because of new information seems to show that its content goes above claiming that a certain kind of justification can be had. If nothing more was claimed by making the assertion, it would not have to be withdrawn in the case described, since it is still true that there was this inconclusive ground, which is all that the assertion claimed.

A mathematical assertion may have to be withdrawn because one finds some error in the proof that was given; one says then that what one thought was a proof was not really a proof. Similarly an inductively supported assertion may have to be withdrawn, if the induction turns out to have been done incorrectly or carelessly. But it may also have to be withdrawn in spite of the fact that the induction was made according to all the recognized rules. This withdrawal should not be necessary, if nothing more was claimed by the assertion than the existence of that kind of ground.

There are thus serious obstacles to developing a verificationist meaning theory for empirical language, and it seems to me that they are taken too lightly, if one thinks that they could be overcome by switching to a justificationist theory.

3. PRAGMATISM

3.1. *General Formulation and Problems*

A pragmatist meaning theory was roughly described as a meaning theory in which the central semantic concept is concerned with the consequences of an assertion. The consequences may take various forms. They comprise the speaker's commitments because of his or her assertion as well as the hearer's expectations and reactions because of the utterance. The reactions may consist of the drawing of conclusions from the assertion but also in nonverbal actions. A general formulation used by Dummett, which echoes common sayings within pragmatism, runs, "My understanding of a statement consists in my grasp of the difference it would make to me if I were to believe it."

In a pragmatic theory as understood by Dummett, assertions are seen as guides to actions. As in a verificationist meaning theory, where, in the end, we have to go outside of language to base verifications on observations, pragmatism must move outside of language and take the content of an assertion to consist ultimately in what consequences the assertion has for actions.

At the same time, Dummett points out that to find a central semantic notion along the lines suggested by pragmatism, we must replace the too broad notion of consequence by something we may call *direct* consequence. The reason for that is like the reason we have to restrict ourselves to *canonical* proofs or verifications when defining the central semantic concept in a verificationist theory. The consequences of an assertion, like its grounds, are of so many kinds and forms that it is implausible that they could all be included in the meaning of the assertion, and certainly it is out of question that a recursive specification of the meaning of an assertion could be made in terms of the set of all the consequences of the assertion. Let us therefore pass to the question how the direct consequences of an assertion may be specified. I shall first consider compound sentences and then atomic ones.

3.2. *Direct Consequences of Compound Sentences*

For compound sentences, it is again Gentzen's system of natural deduction, one must say, that inspires hope for the idea that a notion of direct consequence can be specified in such a way that it functions as the central semantic concept. This time we shall of course concentrate on the elimination rules in his system, which for conjunction, universal sentences, and implications are indicated by the schemes:

$$\frac{A_1 \ \& \ A_2}{A_i} \qquad\qquad \frac{\forall x A(x)}{A(t)} \qquad\qquad \frac{A \ \ A \to B}{B}$$

Since the conclusion drawn by an inference according to one of these schemes is a subsentence of the premise or, in the case of implication elimination, a subsentence of the major premise, these rules suggest a recursive specification of the direct consequences of a sentence A, saying that they consist of the conclusions that can be drawn from A by an elimination. In the case of implication, we have to add the proviso that we have access to the antecedent of the implication as a premise.

The idea is thus that the meaning of a sentence is determined by what counts as its direct consequences and the meanings of the immediate subsentences. The content of an assertion is then that we are to enlarge our sets of beliefs with the direct consequences of the assertion. To assert $\forall x A(x)$ is for instance to assert that we may infer $A(t)$ for any term t, and to assert an implication $A \to B$ is to issue an inference license that allows the inference of B from A.

Two crucial questions must now be put: When is an assertion warranted? What is it for an inference in general to be valid? Can we answer them when meaning is construed as now suggested?

The natural answer to the first question is that an assertion A is warranted if one knows that all the direct consequences of A can be rightly asserted. This can be put in the form of a recursive specification of assertion conditions, since the direct consequences of A are less complex than A. Then we also have a general answer to the second question, since the validity of an inference amounts to the assertibility of the conclusion given that we are right in asserting the premises. Hence, an inference of B from premises $A_1, A_2, \ldots, A_n$ is valid, if any direct consequence of B can be obtained already from the premises $A_1, A_2, \ldots, A_n$; in other words, if B is guaranteed to hold given the premises. For instance, conjunction introduction, inferring the conclusion A & B from the premises A and B, is valid because the direct consequences of the conclusion A & B, in other words, A and B, are given with (in fact, are) the premises of conjunction introduction.

A more precise, general account of the validity of inferences has to take into consideration that there are less simple inferences that bind assumptions or variables, where the premises therefore consist not of assertions but of deductions. We have also to consider disjunctions and existential sentences, where the problem is that in Gentzen's elimination rules for these constants there are minor premises that also occur as conclusions (then depending on fewer assumptions), but the minor premises are not structurally related to the major premise. One way to formulate the pragmatist ideas more precisely is in terms of a pragmatist notion of valid argument. This is not to switch to a verificationist perspective but is only a convenient way to handle the problems mentioned. When defining the new notion of valid argument, we shall precisely express the idea that an assertion is seen as issuing an inference license.

3.3. *Pragmatist Arguments*

The idea of a pragmatist theory of meaning is much less worked out than that of verificationist theory. A beginning is made by Dummett in *The Logical Basis of Metaphysics*,[14] where he also defines, as I shall do now, a notion of a valid argument for an assertion. My notion of a valid argument will however be different from Dummett's in several respects although the main idea is the same.[15]

As in section 2.3, arguments are arrangements of arbitrary inferences in natural deduction style, but this time all inferences except the eliminations are to be assigned alleged justifications that determine reductions. As before an *open argument* is *valid* when all its instances obtained by replacing its free variables by terms and its open hypotheses by valid arguments are valid. A *closed argument* for a compound formula is now defined as *valid* if all the results of applying an elimination rule to its last sentence are valid. In case of implication elimination we require that the minor premise in the application is the conclusion of an arbitrary closed and valid argument. Hence, a closed argument Π for $A \to B$ is valid, if and only if for all closed valid arguments Σ for A, the argument

$$\frac{\begin{array}{cc} \Sigma & \Pi \\ A & A \to B \end{array}}{B}$$

is valid. For disjunctions and existential sentences we follow Dummett's idea to restrict applications of the elimination rules to the case in which the minor premises are atomic. The applications have the following forms

$$\frac{\begin{array}{ccc} & [A] & [B] \\ \Pi & \Sigma & \Delta \\ A \vee B & C & C \end{array}}{C} \qquad \frac{\begin{array}{cc} & [A(x)] \\ \Pi & \Sigma \\ \exists x A(x) & C \end{array}}{C}$$

A closed argument Π for $A \vee B$ is valid, if and only if, for any valid argument Σ for an atomic sentence C from A and any valid argument Δ for C from B, the argument shown to the left above is valid. A closed argument Π for $\exists x A(x)$ is valid, if and only if, for any valid argument Σ for an atomic sentence C from A(x), the argument shown to the right above is valid.

Finally we define the negation of a sentence A as before, that is, as the implication $A \rightarrow \perp$.

We have now, for any compound sentence of first order languages, a proposal of a pragmatist account of the content of asserting the sentence, formulated in terms of what is required of an argument for the assertion to be valid. The requirement amounts to demanding that we have valid arguments for the direct consequences of the assertion, and is, as we have seen, formulated in terms of what it is to have a valid argument for sentences of less complexity.

The definition of the validity of an argument hangs in the air until we have specified when a closed argument for an atomic sentence is valid. We shall return to the question what are the direct consequences of atomic sentences in the next subsection, but for the moment let us assume, as also Dummett does in his account, that we are given boundary rules for the atomic sentences. The definition can then be completed by saying that a closed argument for an atomic sentence is valid if it reduces to an argument using only the boundary rules.[16]

Let us say that we have a proof of a sentence when we recognize that we have a valid argument for the sentence as now defined. It is now almost immediate that, in a pragmatic meaning theory that takes this notion of proof as its central semantic concept, we arrive at conditions for asserting a sentence and for the validity of an arbitrary inference: An assertion is warranted when we have a proof of the asserted sentence, and an inference is seen to be valid when we know how to transform any argument for the premises to an argument for the conclusion.

It is an easy exercise to verify that all the usual intuitionistic inference rules of predicate logic are valid in the defined sense. For elimination rules this is immediate by the definition of valid argument, except for disjunction and existence eliminations where we have to verify it by an induction over the degree of the conclusion. For introduction rules the example of conjunction given at the end of the last subsection is now to be generalized to inferences in general. For instance, to verify the validity of implication introduction, which allows us to infer an implication $A \rightarrow B$ given a valid argument Π for B from A, we have to show that we have a valid argument for the direct consequence of the conclusion $A \rightarrow B$, i.e., the sentence B, given any closed valid argument Σ for A. Obviously, the required argument for B is obtained from the valid argument Π for B from A by replacing its assumption A by the valid argument Σ for A, which thus is the reduction that is to be assigned to implication introduction as its justification.

3.4. *Direct Consequences of Atomic Sentences*

There are atomic sentences whose meaning may be given in terms of verbal conclusions that can be inferred from them in the form of other atomic sentences or compound sentences. But there must be a point where this way of meaning explanation stops, and where, following the general pragmatist idea as expounded above, the consequences should be given in terms of actions. Dummett calls such sentences *action sentences*.

We certainly sometimes judge whether people understand the meaning of a sentence by observing how they act in response to being informed that the sentence is true, and it is easy to give examples of assertions that are expected to be followed by specific actions. If I am told "the bicycle is in the cellar" and I understand the sentence, one expects me to go to the cellar if I want to take out the bicycle. This action may perhaps be seen as a direct consequence of the sentence in question. Other examples are tools that are defined in terms of what they are used for. For instance, if we understand by a hammer a tool used for driving in nails, one might think that "this is a hammer" is an action sentence whose meaning could be given by saying that its direct consequences consist of the actions of driving in nails with the help of the object in question.

There are examples like this for which the pragmatist idea of meaning seems natural. However, the problem is, as Dummett points out, that different actions follow upon the acceptance of an assertion depending on the intentions and desires of the agent. Some people do not like to be wet, and therefore upon hearing that it rains they stay at home or bring an umbrella if they have to go out. Others like the refreshing feeling of rain in the face, and they go out without umbrella when informed about the rain. Dummett suggests that this problem could be handled by taking the meaning of an action sentence to be a function that takes actions as values and has two argument places, one being filled by possible desires or intentions and the other by beliefs. But of course there is a myriad of possible arguments and values for such a function. The function to be associated with the sentence "it rains" will on its first argument place have not only likes and dislikes for water but also the desire to collect rain water, to get a good growth for different kinds of vegetation and so on. And the values of the function will be varied correspondingly: the action of putting out buckets, sowing, not sowing, and so on. Functions of this kind are simply too complex and too vast to make it reasonable to think that knowing the meaning of an action sentence is to know them.

There are also reasons to think that a notion of direct consequence of this kind, apart from being unwieldy, is not sufficient as the central semantic concept of a meaning theory. The meaning of a compound sentence was specified above by telling what counts as its direct consequences. Correspondingly, to assert a sentence A was understood as asserting that these consequences, whose complexity is less than that of A, can be inferred from A, and hence that they can be rightly asserted in their turn. This makes the content of asserting A dependent on the content of asserting certain action sentences. Now to explain the meanings of the action sentences in terms of the actions that are their direct consequences does not in the same way determine what it is to assert these action sentences. We cannot say, parallel to the explanation of compound sentences, that to assert an action sentence is to assert the direct consequences of the sentence, because actions are not the kind of thing that one asserts. In what way are the contents of an action sentence determined by the fact that holding an action sentence to be true results in certain kind of actions?

The answer must naturally be given somehow in terms of what it is for the actions in question to be successful or to be possible to carry out successfully. For instance, if using the object to drive in nails is the immediate consequence of the action sentence "this is a hammer," then the meaning of the sentence "this object is a hammer" must be that the object can be used to drive in nails. The condition for asserting the sentence must accordingly be that one has verified that the object can in fact be used in that way.

This means that in the end we must rely on observations to determine the meaning of action sentences. To understand the sentence "this object is a hammer" one must know what it is to use it for driving in nails, and to know this one must know how it looks when one uses the object to drive in nails. Even if one succeeded in explaining what it is to drive in nails in a pragmatist way in terms of what that in turn can be used for, it would not help: one would then have to know what it is to observe that this further aim is satisfied. In the end, it seems, it is observations that count when determining the meaning of an action sentence.

Without wanting to deny for a moment that consequences in the form of actions constitute an important aspect of our use of language, I think that observations as grounds for assertions have priority in the end when it comes to accounting for meaning in a systematic fashion. This is also true for sentences whose meaning is naturally thought of in terms of consequences. When the word "hammer" is defined, as in some dictionaries, as a tool used to drive in nails, we may specify the meaning of the sentence "this object is a hammer" by saying that its direct consequence consists in the *sentence* "this object can be used to drive in nails." It is then the latter sentence that becomes an action sentence. Although the action of using the object to drive in nails is, in a natural sense, a direct consequence of the latter sentence, it is rather the observation that the object can be used in that way which is relevant to determining the content of the sentence.

The observation that a tool can be used in a certain way does not consist in only passive registrations by our sense organs. It can be described as carrying out a test and observing what happens. An observation of that kind can also be classified as an action. Of course it is not an action carried out as a consequence of believing the action sentence to be true, but rather it is the appropriate action to perform when one wonders whether the sentence is true. To think of this action as what determines the meaning of the sentence is thus to give up an ingredient in pragmatism and to adopt instead a verificationist attitude towards such atomic sentences that do not have other sentences as consequences. But this move secures a needed base for what remains of the pragmatist idea.

Failing a viable account of the meaning of action sentences in terms of their consequences, we have to admit that they get their meanings from what it is to carry out the relevant observations. But sentences that have direct consequences in the form of other sentences can be seen as having their meanings determined by these consequences. The result is a kind of semi-pragmatist theory which takes care of some valuable ideas in pragmatism. Its strength is especially its account of the meaning of implications and universal sentences, which accords much better than the verificationist account with our actual use of such sentences in empirical discourse.

In the above we have only considered atomic sentences in everyday language. For mathematical language it is even more obvious that the meaning of, for instance, identities between numerical terms must be explained in terms of calculations rather than in terms of any consequences that they may have. Similarly, although we have both introduction rules and elimination rules for the sentence "n is a natural number" as explained in section 2.3, it is only the former that can be used for a meaning explanation. The elimination rule, which is the same as the rule for mathematical induction, may have a complex minor premise, the so-called induction formula. Unlike the situation for disjunction and universal eliminations, we cannot in the definition of valid argument require that the induction formula be atomic and then validate other applications of the rule that have complex induction formulas.

3.5. *Falsificationism*

Dummett has also considered a third kind of meaning theory, besides verificationist and pragmatist ones. In "What is a Theory of Meaning II"[17] he contrasts a verificationist meaning theory with a theory that takes expectation as a core notion, and he seems to lean toward preferring such a theory to a verificationist one. In the above we have used the notion of expectation for one possible formulation of the pragmatist idea of meaning, but in "What is a Theory of Meaning II," Dummett suggests that the substance of an expectation is brought out by what disappoints it. He therefore proposes that a meaning theory may better take the incorrectness of an assertion or what falsifies the assertion as the fundamental notion, but he leaves it at that and does not develop it further.

There are obvious rules for the falsification of a sentence such as inferring ¬(A & B) from either ¬A or ¬B, ¬(A ∨ B) from the two premises ¬A and ¬B, ¬(A → B) from the two premises A and ¬B and so on.[18] The notion of falsity that results if we take such rules as introduction rules is, however, quite different from our usual one, since ¬(A & ¬A) becomes assertible only if either A or ¬A is assertible.

The standard way of falsifying a compound sentence A is of course to make a series of inferences from the assumption that A holds that finally ends in the assertion (under the assumption A) of a contradiction or of the constant for falsity, ⊥, if we allow ourselves that notion. Such a derivation may take many forms, but we can define a notion of *canonical* refutation or *reductio*.[19] We may define a canonical reductio of a set Γ of sentences inductively as an argument that ends with ⊥ and has at least one undischarged hypothesis A that belongs to Γ, is the major premise of an elimination, and in addition satisfies a number of clauses depending on the form of A.

For instance, if A is B & C, then the result of leaving out all occurrences of this hypothesis from the argument is required to be a canonical reductio from the set Γ^* obtained from Γ by replacing (B & C) by B and C. If A is (B ∨ C), then the minor premise can be required to be ⊥ and the result of leaving out the hypotheses from the argument to yield one canonical reductio from the set Γ_1 obtained from Γ by replacing B ∨ C by B, and one canonical reductio from the set Γ_2 obtained from Γ by replacing B ∨ C by C.

A considerable complication arises when A has the form of an implication B → C. When we leave out all occurrences of this hypothesis from the argument, the argument falls into several parts and we must require not only that the part that now contains occurrences of the hypothesis C instead of B → C is a canonical reductio of the set Γ^* obtained from Γ by replacing B → C by C, but also that the other parts that now end with B are valid arguments for B from Γ.

This rough outline seems to show that a meaning theory that takes a notion of canonical falsification as its central semantic notion resembles a pragmatist theory in being based on elimination rules and the direct consequences that they define. To handle implications we seem, however, to be forced to a complication that did not appear in a pragmatist theory. There the argument for the minor premise of an implication elimination that appears in the inductive definition of valid argument is required to be valid in the pragmatist sense. But here we cannot of course use the notion of a reductio that is being defined to put the right requirement on the argument for the minor premise from the set of assumptions in question. Instead we need a separate notion of validity of an argument, which must be inductively defined simultaneously with the notion of reductio. A falsificationist meaning theory seems thus to have to mix different ideas of meaning in an unfavorable way.

4. STABILITY

It is easy to show, as I have already claimed, that both verificationist and pragmatist meaning theories of the kind considered above validate all usual intuitionistic inference rules that can be stated in the languages in question. The question whether these theories also validate other inferences is much harder to answer, if it can be answered at all. One is strongly inclined to think that Gentzen's elimination rules for the logical constants are as strong as possible in the sense that all elimination rules that are validated by a verificationist theory are deducible from Gentzen's rules, but we do not know how to prove this completeness conjecture.[20] Vice versa, one expects that all introduction rules that are validated by a pragmatist theory are deducible from Gentzen's rules, but again we do not know how to prove that completeness conjecture.

One may consider other logical constants than the usual ones treated here and contemplate different kinds of introduction and elimination rules for them that can serve, like Gentzen's rules, as a basis for a verificationist or a pragmatist meaning theory, respectively. Dummett states certain conditions that an introduction or elimination rule for a logical constant has to satisfy in order to be suitable as a base for such theories.[21] We may take these notions as sufficiently clear to discuss possible relations between verificationist and pragmatist meaning theories based on sets of arbitrary introduction and elimination rules, respectively.

To simplify the discussion I shall assume that we have one arbitrary logical constant c, a sentential operator or a quantifier, for which we have formulated introduction and elimination rules. One may say that for disjunction we have two introduction rules and similarly that for conjunction we have two elimination rules. But, of course, the rules can be formulated as one single introduction or elimination rule, respectively, and I shall now assume that we have formulated one introduction rule for c, called I, and one elimination rule for c, called E. To I there corresponds a verificationist meaning theory, call it V_I, obtained by letting I determine the inductive clause in the definition of what counts as a canonical argument for sentences whose principal operator is c. Similarly, to E there corresponds a pragmatic meaning theory, call it P_E, obtained by letting E determine the inductive clause in the pragmatic definition of valid argument for such sentences.

Note that V_I normally validates many different possible elimination rules for c and also other introduction rules than I, some weaker than I and some deductively equivalent to I, and that the corresponding thing holds for P_E. Let us say that V_I and P_E are *adapted to each other* when they validate exactly the same inference rules. Since an inference rule may be validated in V_I or P_E without being deducible from I and E, we get a stronger relation of adaptation if we demand in addition that all elimination rules validated by V_I are deducible from I and E and that all introduction rules validated by P_E are deducible from I and E. These relations of being adapted to each other involve several phenomena: what Dummett calls harmony, the completeness property mentioned above, and *stability*, a notion introduced by Dummett.[22] This can be seen by noting different ways in which a verificationist and a pragmatic meaning theory may fail to be adapted to each other.

If V_I fails to validate E (and hence does not validate all elimination rules validated by P_E), then there is a lack of harmony between I and E, and the same holds if P_E fails to validate I. If V_I validates some elimination rule that is not deducible from I and E, then the completeness conjecture mentioned above is false; E is not strong enough. The same holds if P_E validates some introduction rule that is not deducible from I and E; I is then not strong enough. If V_I validates E but does not validate some introduction rule that is validated by P_E, then there is lack of a kind of stability. If V_I validates E and there is some introduction rule that is validated by P_E but is not deducible from I and E, then there is a lack of another kind of stability that is closer to the notion of stability introduced by Dummett. In both cases, the same holds if we let V_I and P_E, and I and E change places, since all these relations satisfy this kind of duality.

Dummett considers a set of logical constants and a corresponding set S of introduction rules. He then pays attention to the set $E(S)$ of elimination rules that is validated by V_S, that is, the verificationist meaning theory determined by S, and the set $I(E(S))$ of introduction rules that is validated by $P_{E(S)}$, in other words, the pragmatic meaning theory determined by $E(S)$. Finally, he defines S to be *stable*, if the sets S and $I(E(S))$ are interdeducible. Starting instead with a set S of elimination rules for the constants in question, he similarly pays attention to $E(I(S))$ validated by $V_{I(S)}$ and says that S is stable, if $E(I(S))$ is interdeducible with S.

It should be noted that if we start with just one constant c (instead of a set S of constants) and its introduction rule I and elimination rule E, then we still have to speak of the *set $E(I)$* of elimination rules validated by V_I. There is no such thing as *the* elimination rule validated by V_I. Nor can we assume that there is anything like the strongest elimination rule validated by V_I. It is true that one may introduce a notion of inversion and speak of *the* elimination rule that corresponds to a given introduction rule in the sense of being its converse.[23] But as far as I know, there is nothing that says that all elimination rules that are validated by the verificationist theory determined by a certain introduction rule I are deducible from the elimination rule that is the converse of I. This makes Dummett's definition somewhat cumbersome because we have to understand what verificationist or pragmatist meaning theory is determined, not by one introduction or elimination rule, but by a set of such rules for the *same* constant. The notion "adapted to each other" defined above avoids this problem.

We could also recast Dummett's definition somewhat differently by saying that an introduction rule I for a logical constant c is stable, if any introduction rule I^* validated by P_R, where R is some elimination rule validated by V_I, is deducible from I. Similarly, an elimination rule E is stable, if any elimination rule E^* validated by V_R, where R is some introduction rule validated by P_E, is deducible from E.

Stability, like completeness, is clearly a highly interesting notion. Dummett gives examples of introduction and elimination rules that are not stable. What can we say about Gentzen's introduction and elimination rules? One would certainly guess that they are stable. But as long as we cannot rule out that there is some elimination rule stronger than Gentzen's that is validated by the verificationist meaning theory or some introduction rule stronger than Gentzen's that is validated by the pragmatist meaning theory, we cannot rule out instability either.

DAG PRAWITZ

STOCKHOLM UNIVERSITY
MARCH 2005

NOTES

1.   "Can Analytical Philosophy be Systematic and Ought it to Be?" reprinted in *Truth and Other Enigmas* (London: Duckworth, 1978), 454.
2.   For my part it was a joy to meet Michael Dummett in 1974 and to find in

his work a meaning-theoretical framework for some of Gentzen's ideas, which I had been much working on inside logic. Michael's generalization of some of Gentzen's ideas to general philosophy of language has been very important for me.

3. For other points, see for instance my essays in *Michael Dummett: Contributions to Philosophy*, ed. Barry Taylor (Dordrecht: Martinus Nijhoff Publishers, 1987), 117–65, and *The Philosophy of Michael Dummett*, ed. Brian McGuinness and Gianluigi Oliveri (Dordrecht: Kluwer Academic Publishers, 1994), 79–89.

4. A. Heyting, *Intuitionism* (Amsterdam: North-Holland Publishing Company, 1956) had attempted such an explanation, using formulations similar to Dummett's but with "can be asserted" instead of "proof," which results in assertion conditions that are, for the reasons stated above, not faithful to intuitionistic practice.

5. Michael Dummett, *Elements of Intuitionism* (Oxford: Oxford Univ. Press, 1977), 400.

6. First proposed as introduction rules by Per Martin-Löf, "Hauptsatz for the Intuitionistic Theory of Iterated Inductive Definitions" in *Proceedings of the Second Scandinavian Logic Symposium*, ed. J. E. Fenstad (Amsterdam: North-Holland Publishing Company, 1971).

7. The definition proceeds by a simultaneous recursion over the build-up of the sentences that they are arguments for. As is seen, the notion of canonical argument for a compound sentence A depends on the notion of valid argument for the immediate constituents B of A, which in turns depends on the notion of canonical argument for B. This requires that the premises and bound (discharged) assumptions of an introduction inference always have lower degree than the conclusion.

8. First presented in my papers "Towards a Foundation of a General Proof Theory" in *Logic, Methodology and Philosophy of Science IV*, ed. P. Suppes, et al. (Amsterdam: North-Holland Publishing Company, 1973), 225–50, and "On the Idea of a General Proof Theory" in *Synthese* 27 (1974): 63–77.

9. In his *The Logical Basis of Metaphysics* (London: Duckworth, 1991), chs. 11 and 12. The differences that there are between his and my treatments of the topic are described and discussed in my paper "Meaning Approached Via Proofs" in *Proof-Theoretic Semantics*, ed. R. Kahle and P. Schroeder-Heister, special issue of *Synthese* 148, no. 3 (Feb. 2006): 507–24. They are not taken up here.

10. As first observed by Martin-Löf in "Hauptsatz for the Intuitionistic Theory of Iterated Inductive Definitions."

11. Reductions also have to be supplied for the case when the conclusion is of the form B(t) for a closed term t that is not a numeral, but the point of the example should be clear without going into this case.

12. Dummett, *The Logical Basis of Metaphysics*, ch. 12.

13. See for instance Dummett's paper "Combra Lecture: Meaning and Justification" in *Language Logic and Formalization of Logic*, ed. B. McGuinness (Gaeta: Bibliotheca, 1998), 11–30.

14. See chapter 13. Dummett mentions there "an entire meaning-theory for the

language of mathematics based on the assumption that it is the elimination rules that determine the meaning" which should have been constructed by Per Martin-Löf. It is indeed true that Martin-Löf presented a general pragmatist theory of meaning and an outline of a pragmatist meaning theory for mathematical language in a series of lectures at Oxford in the autumn of 1975. (The label "pragmatist" was not used but the constructions were in the spirit of pragmatist ideas of meaning as described above.) However, it turned out that the theories as then conceived were not workable, and Martin-Löf soon afterwards abandoned the project in favor of work on verificationist theories, which resulted in, among other things, in his paper "On the Meanings of the Logical Constants and the Justifications of the Logical Laws" (in *Atti degli Logica Matematica*, vol. 2, Scuola de Specializzazione in Logica Matematica, Dipartimento de Matematica, Università di Siena, 1985, 203–81. Republished in *Nordic Journal of Philosophical Logic* 1 [1996]: 11–60).

15. There are certain weaknesses in Dummett's core concepts, the two notions *canonical argument* and *valid argument*. A canonical argument is roughly one that in its main branch proceeds by a series of eliminations or applications of boundary rules down to an atomic sentence. It is valid if its noncanonical subarguments for minor premises of the kind that appear in implication elimination are valid and of lower degree than the argument as a whole. An arbitrary argument is valid, if to any instance of each *complementation* of the argument obtained by adding a canonical argument to the end of the argument (i.e., by continuing the argument, using only eliminations), one can find a valid canonical argument for the same sentence from the same hypotheses. The definition of the two notions proceeds by induction over the degree of arguments. The induction has its base when the argument is for an atomic sentence from atomic sentences as hypotheses, and the argument is then valid if one can find an argument for the same sentence from the same hypotheses using only the boundary rules.

The main fault is that in a complementation of an argument, the minor premise of an implication elimination is only assumed. By not considering complementations where the minor premise is the end of an arbitrary argument (which is not possible to do in Dummett's definition, proceeding as it does by induction over the degree of arguments), the notion of validity becomes too weak. In particular, it cannot be shown that inferences by *modus ponens* are valid in general, because given two valid arguments Π and Σ for A $\rightarrow$ B and A, respectively, there is no guarantee that the result Δ of combining them in a *modus ponens* to conclude B is valid. For an actual counterexample, we may let B be atomic, Π be simply A $\rightarrow$ B, which is a valid argument for A $\rightarrow$ B from A $\rightarrow$ B, and Σ to be a valid argument for a nonatomic A from some hypotheses of higher degree than that of A $\rightarrow$ B. Then Δ is a canonical argument and is its own complementation, but it is not valid (Σ being of the same degree as Δ), nor can one find another valid canonical argument for B from the same hypotheses.

16. The resulting definition of validity essentially follows the definition given in appendix A2 of "Validity Based on the Elimination Rules," in Dag Prawitz,

"Ideas and Results in Proof Theory," in *Proceedings of the 2nd Scandinavian Logic Symposium*, ed. J. E. Fenstad (Amsterdam: North Holland Publishing Company, 1971), 235–307. There are at least two important differences, however. First, validity is now, in the present essay, applied not to proofs in a given formal system but to arbitrary arguments. Second, the treatment is now extended to disjunctions and existence sentences.

17. In *Truth & Meaning*, ed. G. Evans, et al. (Oxford: Clarendon Press, 1976), 67–137, reprinted in *The Seas of Language* (Oxford: Clarendon Press, 1993), 34–93.

18. Dummett mentions these rules in the *Logical Bases of Metaphysics*, 258. I have called the negation obtained in that way *constructible falsity*, and developed a system of natural deduction for it with introduction and elimination rules, for which the normalization theorem holds, in Dag Prawitz, *Natural Deduction* (Stockholm: Almqvist & Wicksell, 1965).

19. Neil Tennant considers a somewhat similar notion defined for a system of natural deduction in Neil Tennant, *The Taming of the True* (Oxford: Clarendon Press, 1997).

20. This conjecture was made in my paper "Towards a Foundation of a General Proof Theory." See note 8.

21. See Dummett, *The Logical Bases of Metaphysics*, chs. 11 and 13.

22. See Dummett, *The Logical Basis of Metaphysics*, ch. 13.

23. The elimination rule that in this sense corresponds to an arbitrary introduction rule for a sentential operator is described in my paper "Proofs and the Meaning and Completeness of the Logical Constants" in *Essays on Mathematical and Philosophical Logic*, ed. J. Hintikka, et al. (Dordrecht: D. Reidel, 1979), 25–40.

REPLY TO DAG PRAWITZ

I greatly enjoyed reading Dag Prawitz's review and discussion of three theories of meaning. I enjoyed it particularly because it did not contain what I am most used to, namely an exposition, with more or less pugnacity, of the superior virtues of the truth-conditional theory. That theory Prawitz disrespectfully ignored. (Perhaps we could say with Sam Goldwyn that he did not even ignore it.)

Prawitz rightly considers the application of each theory to the logical constants, the sentential operators and the quantifiers: if a theory of meaning cannot deal successfully with complex statements, it matters little how good it is at explaining the atomic ones. He takes as the basic rules of inference governing the constants to be either the introduction rules for natural deduction as given by Gentzen, for a verificationist theory, or the corresponding elimination rules, for a pragmatist one. These are rules which I classified in *The Logical Basis of Metaphysics* as self-justifying, that is, as capable of serving to fix the senses of the logical constants that they govern.

Prawitz then turns to the application, first of the verificationist, then of the pragmatist, theory to empirical discourse. The justification of other logical laws in terms of those taken as basic (introduction rules in the verificationist case, elimination rules in the pragmatist case) turned on what I had called "the fundamental assumption," the assumption, namely, that every complex statement we regard as assertible could have been derived by means of one of the basic rules. In the empirical case, this seems doubtful for disjunction, well brought out by Prawitz's excellent example of identical twins. Suppose I say, "A little boy or little girl rushed out into the road." The fundamental assumption requires that, if my statement was justified, I was in a position to have said either, "A little boy rushed out into the road," or, "A little girl rushed out into the road." Obviously I need not have been in such a position. It may be said that I was tacitly relying on a premiss that everyone would have accepted, namely that all human beings are either male or female. This then raises the question of the meaning, in empirical discourse, of the universal quantifier. The statement "Every human being is either male or female" is not analytic: the existence of a genuine hermaphrodite or a genuinely sexless person is not conceptually impossible. Such a statement is founded on induction with an exceptionally large base. But induction, with however large a base, is not verification, which requires evidence so strong that no counter-evidence could overthrow it.

This suggests that, for empirical discourse, we should replace verificationism, as our theory of meaning, by justificationism. Verificationism regards the meaning of a statement as consisting in what would establish it conclusively. Justificationism regards its meaning as constituted by what we take as entitling us to assert it. Prawitz objects to justificationist theories on the ground that they cannot explain why a statement which was asserted with full justification may nevertheless have to be withdrawn when we come to know of counter-evidence sufficiently strong to overthrow it. The answer is surely that the theory must envisage this possibility. The meanings of empirical statements are given in terms of what entitles us to assert them. But, in coming to understand a statement, we must learn which grounds for asserting it are conclusive and cannot subsequently be overthrown, and which are defeasible and can be defeated by strong enough counter-evidence, in which case the statement can no longer be accepted and is no longer to be asserted. The criterion for a statement to be true is that there exist grounds that justify its assertion, and that no counter-evidence exists, whether known to us or not, that would compel its withdrawal, whether as false or as not qualifying as assertible. I do not think that I have taken the difficulties of a justificationist theory too lightly, and I do not see that such a theory of meaning would be unmanageable: it after all describes what we do learn when we learn to use empirical statements.

Prawitz has a more general objection to basing meaning on the condition for assertion. In mathematics the possibility of asserting a statement on non-conclusive grounds does not arise; but still we do not want to explain the meanings of mathematical statements directly in terms of the conditions for asserting them. Rather, we explain both the meanings of such statements and the conditions for correctly asserting them in terms of the same things—canonical proofs. The meaning of a mathematical statement is given by what would be a canonical proof of it; the condition for asserting it is that we possess an effective means for constructing a canonical proof of it. The attempt to explain the meanings of mathematical statements directly in terms of the conditions for asserting them would fail.

It does not seem to me that this is a sufficient ground for rejecting justificationist theories of meaning. In such a theory, there must also be a distinction between canonical justifications and indirect ones: an indirect justification will be a ground for believing that a canonical justification could have been given. Thus a canonical justification for stating that an observable event occurred or that an observable state of affairs obtained would be an actual observation of the event or state of affairs; an indirect justification for making that assertion would be grounds for believing that such an observation could have been made. A canonical justification for saying that there are or were such-and-such a number of things of a certain kind would be to have counted them; an indirect justification might be a calculation of some sort. There is indeed a difference between the empirical and the mathematical case, which Prawitz points out very clearly. In the mathematical case, an indirect proof furnishes us with an actual ability, at least in principle, to construct a canonical proof. In the empirical case, an indirect justification will usually not enable us to attain a canonical justification—to make the relevant observation or to do the counting: the opportunity may have gone. That is the outstanding difference between the two realms of discourse. If an effective mathematical procedure is available, it always remains available. The opportunity to carry out an effective empirical procedure may quickly slip away. I do not believe that the evanescence of direct empirical evidence is fatal to the possibility of applying to empirical discourse a verificationist or a justificationist theory of meaning; but, in framing such a theory, this evanescence must be taken into account.

I fully accept Dag Prawitz's correction of my handling of the notion of a valid argument when elimination rules are taken as basic, which is of course what we need for a pragmatist theory of meaning. The problem for the application of such a theory to empirical discourse is, as Prawitz observes, to identify the atomic action sentences which the theory requires. There are of course exclamations, such as "Stop!", "Help!", "Fire!", "Hush!", which call on others to take specific actions; but what we need are sentences which determine the *speaker's* action. There are very few of these: "The restaurant is closed" might be one ("We won't go there"). Prawitz considers sentences which prompt an experiment, so that both action and observation are involved; but on the whole the prospects for a pragmatist theory of meaning seem bleak. What pragmatism overlooks is that our own conclusions and the information relayed by others help us to build up a picture of how things are, *on the basis of which* we regulate our actions. As Prawitz rightly remarks, a pragmatist explanation of universal quantification lies more to hand than a verificationist or even justificationist one; but a pragmatist explanation of the whole of language seems very unlikely to be successful. Still less, as Prawitz says, does it seem probable that it would work as applied to the language of mathematics.

Prawitz does not at this point consider the relation between a verificationist and a pragmatist theory of meaning. The former, if it is to be adequate as an overall theory of meaning, must be able to explain the consequences that we draw from statements we accept; the latter, if it is to be adequate, must be able to explain what grounds we require for accepting or asserting statements. If our language is both harmonious and stable (harmony and stability obtain), then (on the doubtful assumption that a pragmatist theory is feasible) a verificationist and a pragmatist theory of meaning for the language will in a clear sense be equivalent: there will be no real choice to be made between them. So it seems to me; but Prawitz does not discuss this point.

An elegant treatment of a falsificationist theory of meaning is to be found in the essay by Ian Rumfitt in this volume; it validates classical logic without assuming bivalence. Perhaps it may provide a theory of meaning for classical mathematics. If so, instead of speaking of classical and constructive mathematics, we may in future speak of negative and positive mathematics.

When he comes to treat of the notion I introduced under the title of "stability," however, Dag Prawitz is concerned with the relation between a verificationist and a pragmatist meaning-theory, because that is precisely what the notion is about. It surely applies quite generally, but, like harmony, it is best first discussed as it relates to the logical constants. If we are operating with a verificationist meaning-theory, we shall fix the meanings of the logical constants by stipulating that certain introduction rules are to hold. If we are also accustomed to employ particular elimination rules, we want to be sure that we do not, by using them, infer more than the introduction rules entitle us to do. For each logical constant, the introduction rules that we have stipulated fix its meaning by laying down the canonical grounds for asserting a statement of which it is the principal operator. These grounds control what we may legitimately infer from such a statement. We want, therefore, to use only such elimination rules as are validated by our introduction rules. If, in fact, we do use only such elimination rules as so qualify, then harmony prevails.

We want more than this, however. We want to be sure that we infer from statements in which the logical constant in question is the principal operator as much as our introduction rules entitle us to do. I will reiterate an example I used in another of my replies. Suppose that, on the basis of a verificationist meaning-theory, we have laid down the usual introduction rules for disjunction. But suppose also that we are accustomed to use only the restricted rule of or-elimination in which the subordinate deductions are not allowed any side-premisses:

$$
\begin{array}{ccc}
 & [A] & [B] \\
 & \vdots & \vdots \\
 & \vdots & \vdots \\
A \lor B & C & C \\
\hline
 & C &
\end{array}
$$

This rule allows us to prove the commutative law for "or," but not the distributive law of "or" into "and"; it holds in quantum logic, but the full or-elimination rule does not.

Now the standard introduction rules for "or" validate the full or-elimination rule. Therefore, if we are allowing ourselves to use only the restricted rule, we are not inferring as much from disjunctive statements as our introduction rules entitle us to do. Clearly our deductive practice is out of joint, though not so badly as if there were disharmony. We want to recognise as valid every rule that is validated by our introduction rules: we want every such rule to be derivable from the introduction and elimination rules that we recognise.

This is clearly a desirable condition. But what does it have to do with any relation between the verificationist theory and the pragmatist theory, or between taking the meanings of the logical constants as fixed by introduction rules and taking them as fixed by elimination rules? This may be illustrated by our example. Suppose that we had relied on the pragmatist meaning-theory, and had tried to fix the meaning of "or" by stipulating the elimination rule or rules governing it. And suppose the elimination rule we laid down was the restricted or-elimination rule. Well, that would surely have been our right: we are understanding the connective "or" in some sense, whatever that may be, under which only the restricted, not the full, or-elimination is valid. But, now, what introduction rules does restricted or-elimination validate? Why, the standard or-introduction rules. But if our deductive practice was out of joint with this combination of introduction and elimination rules for the connective "or" when we were taking the introduction rules as fixing its meaning, it must still be out of joint when we have the same combination of rules, though we are now taking the elimination rule as fixing its meaning.

When we take the elimination rules as fixing the meaning of a logical constant in accordance with a pragmatist theory of meaning, we want the introduction rules to constitute those methods of establishing a statement that will entitle us to draw from it the consequences we have laid down as following from it. This of course means the introduction rules that are validated by the elimination rules we have stipulated as holding. But, having found the introduction rules so validated, we surely then want to be entitled to use the elimination rules that are validated by those introduction rules. For, if not, there is an imbalance: we are not allowing ourselves to draw all the consequences from a statement that the introduction rules we are taking as governing it entitle us to draw. And just that is what has happened in our example. The restricted or-elimination rule validates the standard or-introduction rules; but the standard or-introduction rules validate the full or-elimination rule. Our deductive practice is imbalanced or unstable. With what right is it to be so judged? Surely if the meaning of a logical constant is to be fixed by the elimination rules we stipulate to hold, then we are entitled to stipulate whatever elimination rules we choose, and that fixes the sense of the logical constant; there can be no argument that we ought to adopt stronger elimination rules unless we abandon our pragmatist theory of meaning in favour of a verificationist one. But we are here making a tacit appeal to the idea that a verificationist theory of meaning and a pragmatist one should be essentially equivalent: they should balance one another, issuing in the same linguistic practice, and in particular the same deductive practice. Thus, to verify that our deductive practice is stable, we must consider the introduction rules validated by a given choice of elimination rules, and then the elimination rules validated by those introduction rules: there is stability if we get back to where we started, *modulo* ordinary derivability of rules from other rules. Equally, we may start with a given set of introduction rules, go over to the elimination rules validated by them, and back to the introduction rules validated by the latter: if we end up where we started, we have stability.

The difficulty with this topic is that we have far less grip on the totality of elimination rules validated by a given set of introduction rules, or conversely, than we have on the totality of rules of either kind derivable from a given set of rules of either kind. Prawitz reiterates the conjecture that he previously made, that the elimination rules validated by Gentzen's introduction rules are just those derivable from all Gentzen's rules for intuitionistic logic, taken together, and makes the dual conjecture that the introduction rules validated by Gentzen's intuitionistic elimination rules are just those derivable from all Gentzen's rules for intuitionistic logic, taken together. These conjectures seem to me overwhelmingly plausible, but we need to *prove* them. When we have done so, the question of stability will be much easier to handle. In the meantime, while we can say for sure that Gentzen's introduction rules validate all the intuitionistically valid elimination rules, and conversely, we cannot say for certain that his introduction rules do not validate some intuitionistically invalid rules. It seems unlikely, but we need to prove it to be impossible.

Is the demand for stability reasonable? What meaning should we be intending to confer on statements of the form "A ∨ B" if we stipulated the restricted or-elimination rule, in the framework of a pragmatist meaning-theory, as governing the connective "∨"? Presumably that every proposition held good that was deducible both from A alone and from B alone. But if that is what "A ∨ B" means, then it follows both from A and from B. We have in effect validated the standard ∨-introduction rules. But if "A ∨ B" follows both from A and from B, then whatever follows from A together with some additional hypotheses and also from B together with other additional hypotheses must follow from "A ∨ B" together with all those additional hypotheses. We have in effect validated the unrestricted ∨-elimination rule.

In a similar way, suppose that, in accordance with a verificationist meaning-theory, you had stipulated the restricted →-introduction rule

as the introduction rule for the connective →. This obviously validates the standard elimination rule for → (*modus ponens*). But, if *modus ponens* holds, then it must be legitimate to assert "A → B" as holding under certain hypotheses when B is derivable from A together with those hypotheses: the *un*restricted →-introduction rule must be valid.

Of what worth are these arguments? It could be argued, "If you have adopted a pragmatist meaning-theory, then you are entitled to lay down whatever elimination rules you choose. These will then validate some introduction rules; but what elimination rules these introduction rules validate in turn is irrelevant and should not affect you. It would be relevant only if you were switching to a verificationist meaning-theory." Likewise, "if you have adopted a verificationist meaning-theory, you are entitled to lay down whatever introduction rules you choose. These will then validate some elimination rules; but what introduction rules these elimination rules validate in turn is irrelevant and should not affect you. It would be relevant only if you were switching to a pragmatist meaning-theory." This argument is perfectly sound, and shows the concept of stability to be valueless, if we believe that the verificationist and pragmatist meaning-theories are *rivals*. If, on the other hand, we regard these two theories of meaning as both founded on actual linguistic practice and hence as essentially equivalent, then the argument has no force: the demand for stability is compelling.

Finally, in the introduction to his essay Dag Prawitz listed five points on which he would like my opinion. In case my responses to these are not clear from what I have written above, I will here answer them *seriatim*.

(1) I whole-heartedly agree that the prospect of a verificationist meaning-theory for constructive mathematics is extremely hopeful.

(2) I agree that what I called proof-theoretical justification of logical laws provides such a meaning-theory for logic (or the part of such a theory that deals with the logical operators); it is wrong to think that because it employs proof-theoretic methods it cannot be a component of a meaning-theory.

(3) I agree that there are great difficulties in constructing a verificationist or justificationist meaning-theory for empirical discourse; I have struggled with some of them myself. But until such difficulties supply a compelling reason for thinking that we must fall back on a truth-conditional theory, I think that we must continue to strive to overcome them. At one time I was strongly attracted by falsificationism, but could not see how to develop it. But even though Ian Rumfitt has now shown the way, I have become too attached to intuitionistic logic to want to adopt a theory of meaning that validates classical logic.

(4) I am somewhat surprised by Dag Prawitz's saying, "I think that kind of pragmatic meaning-theories can be developed for mathematics," in view of the difficulties he later ably expounded. It is not a project I can presently view with great hope.

(5) I am not altogether clear how Prawitz wishes to reformulate the concept of stability, but I very much hope that he will be able to prove the completeness results which he mentions in his essay. I hope so especially because few other people seem to be interested in this topic; if he could prove those results, it would make it far easier to handle the notion of stability.

M. D.

14

Eva Picardi

ON SENSE, TONE, AND ACCOMPANYING THOUGHTS

> *We speak of understanding a sentence in the sense in which it can be replaced by another which says the same; but also in the sense in which it cannot be replaced by any other. (Any more than one musical theme can be replaced by another.) In the one case the thought in the sentence is something common to different sentences; in the other, something that is expressed only by these words in these positions. (Understanding a poem.)*
>
> (Wittgenstein, PI, 531)

I. *TEMERAIRE* OR *TÉMÉRAIRE*?

"The Fighting Temeraire" is one of Turner's finest paintings. It was first exhibited in 1839, and its title in full reads "The Fighting *Temeraire*, tugged to her last berth to be broken up, 1838." The painting was inspired by the fate of the *Temeraire*, a ship that had fought bravely at Trafalgar beside Nelson's flagship *Victory*. In August 1838, after many years spent in harbor, the *Temeraire* was auctioned by the Admiralty together with other warships employed at Trafalgar: the once celebrated "hearts of oak" were sold as timber and broken up. I am not here going to dwell on the many interpretations which have been placed on the *Temeraire* and her tug. Rather, I will confine my attention to an anecdote relating to the ship's name, which I stumbled upon when reading Judy Egerton's book in the Making and Meaning series, *Turner: The Fighting Temeraire.*

In 1845 Turner was told by the engraver J. J. Willmore (who had been informed by what proved to be an unreliable source) that the *Temeraire* was not simply named after her predecessor, but was the *Temeraire* herself. The *Temeraire* originally was part of the French Navy, and she was then called *Téméraire*. In 1759 the *Téméraire* was captured and annexed to the British Navy. In France the name of the ship would have recalled the boldness of Charles le Téméraire; but this name meant nothing to English seamen, who simply dropped the accents and called the prize ship *Temeraire*. Thus "Téméraire = Temeraire" is a true identity statement, and conveys a piece of information concerning the prize ship: it is sufficient to imagine the two names uttered, respectively, with a French pronunciation and with an English pronunciation (of a French word), and one will realize that we are not here dealing with an identity statement of the form "a = a." However, we may suppose that for the English seamen, unaware of the details of French history, no renaming had occurred, but only a trifling orthographical modification. And perhaps not even that, since at the time there was no established convention concerning accents. There was no informative identity statement for them to apprehend. In 1798 a British ship, named *Temeraire* after the *Temeraire* (that is, the *Téméraire*), was launched, and it was this ship, made of solid British oak, that fought at Trafalgar. Perhaps it was the ship's melodious name that struck Turner's imagination. In consequence of Willmore's communication Turner may have thought that a ship that originally had been part of the French Navy was not suited to be turned into an icon of the British fight against "The Scourge of Europe." Be that as it may, Turner was so distressed to learn the content of what he took to be a true identity statement, "Temeraire = Téméraire," that he allowed a steel engraving of his painting produced by Willmore to be published under the title "The Old Téméraire." Thornbury, the author of one of the first biographies of Turner, reports that "he seemed almost in tears when he gave up his pet title, and said: 'Call her, then, The Old Téméraire'" (Egerton 1995, 90). As a consequence of this accident, the accents were later added also to the title of Turner's painting, which for a long time was referred to as "The Fighting Téméraire." To make things worse, Turner's original painting was often referred to with the title of Willmore's steel engraving as "The Old Téméraire." Two different titles for the same painting, one of which with a proper name differently spelled, may well prove confusing. Someone who knew of Turner's fondness for ships could have been led to suppose that the titles named different paintings, relating perhaps to different stages of the ship's career.

This anecdote contains all the ingredients required to generate a family of puzzles along the lines discussed by Frege (e.g., 1891; 1892; 1914) and Kripke (1979). We may suppose that Turner did some research concerning the ship after which the *Temeraire* had been named, and possibly came across drawings of the ship. In the process he may have come to the conclusion that, unlike his darling *Temeraire*, her predecessor *Temeraire* (i.e., *Téméraire)* had not been a well-proportioned ship. The (alleged) discovery that he was confronted with the same ship without realizing it while counting as a competent user of both names would have acquainted Turner with a variant of Kripke's puzzle. Turner's case is especially tricky because it cannot be solved by adverting to his idiosyncratic understanding of the names involved. Turner used the name "Temeraire" in accordance with the standards of his linguistic community, and, as we *now* know, he was right in so doing. What he possibly ignored was that the ship after which the *Temeraire* had been named had originally belonged to the French navy. It was the immense popularity of his painting that prompted an interest in the ship's origin and history, and it was in this process that the (alleged) truth of the identity "Téméraire = Temeraire" was divulged.

Frege would have pointed out to Turner that the very fact that he had formed different beliefs (e.g., "The *Temeraire* is well proportioned," "The *Temeraire* is not well proportioned") added to his failure to realize that the two typographically identical replicas of the same name stood for one and the same bearer. Turner had hit on these names in different contexts: "Temeraire*"* is the name of the ship he had read about, whereas "Temeraire*"* is the name of the ship of whose sad fate he had been (let us suppose) an eyewitness. Yet, when forming the judgment that one of them, unlike the other, was well proportioned, he was visually presented with the ship herself and with a drawing originating from that very ship. Here, we do not have a case of straightforwardly contradictory beliefs, although the sentences, read rightly (i.e., with the proper names designating the same ship), contradict each other, as a thinker who is not under any misapprehension quickly realizes. Turner had not been irrational in his epistemic conduct: for though the demonstrative thought he expressed by means of the sentence "The *Temeraire* is well proportioned" does contradict the demonstrative thought he expressed by means of the sentence "The *Temeraire* (i.e., the former *Téméraire*) is not well proportioned," the senses of two names, and the beliefs he attached to the corpus of sentences to which they belong, are different. However, we cannot rest content with this result. We may suppose that Turner, after he had been alerted by Willmore's communication, would simply suspend judgment on both of his previous assessments, since he had no means any more to improve upon them in a rational way. To insist that there is a verdict on which Turner would have settled had he been placed under suitable circumstances is simply to aver one's commitment to realism—an issue I do not wish to take up in this paper.

In general, however, we are in a position to modify our beliefs on the intake of new information. If the sense of a proper name is something objective, i.e., communicable and shareable, as Frege emphatically stressed, it is essential that a tension among the various aspects of one's belief system be brought to the fore. Otherwise, as he pointed out in the draft of a letter to Jourdain written in the same year as the posthumously published piece *Logic in Mathematics*, we would be forced to the conclusion that the thought that a speaker attaches to a sentence never matches the thought that a different speaker attaches to the same sentence: thoughts would be indistinguishable from representations (*Vorstellungen*), and each of us would have his own thoughts, insulated from the thoughts that other thinkers express by means of sentences belonging to the common language.[1] All contradictions could be explained away by adverting to a difference in the thoughts that different thinkers (or the same thinker at different times) attach to the same words. From this he concluded that "the sense of a name is not something subjective [crossed out: in one's mental life (*Seelenleben*)], that it does not therefore belong to psychology, and that it is indispensable" (Frege 1976, 128; 1980, 80).[2]

The discovery of the (alleged) truth of the identity statement "Temeraire = Téméraire," requires a good deal of belief revision (including suspension of belief) on Turner's part. Arguably, however, even after his stunning discovery, the seemingly inconsistent sentences "Turner was indignant that the *Temeraire* should be bereft of her flag" and "Turner was not indignant that the *Téméraire* should be bereft of her flag" are both likely to mirror Turner's attitude towards the event portrayed in his picture. Plainly, if the steamer tugs the *Temeraire* to her last berth, it tugs the *Téméraire* as well; however, while not disputing this fact and making the necessary adjustments to his beliefs concerning what had turned out to be one and the same ship, Turner's attitude did not stabilize so as to result in a unanimous verdict. The *Téméraire* had fought at Trafalgar all right, but her accented name was an obnoxious reminder of her French origin. Turner's troubled attitude is witnessed by his willingness to consent to a change in the title of the engraving made by Willmore after "The Fighting Temeraire," which, as I said, was published under the title "The Old Téméraire." Some may suggest that the circumstance that the picture was, at least for a while, referred to by different titles could be explained in analogy with situations in which we have different descriptions of the same event. It is not surprising in the least that the same event, apprehended under two different descriptions, may prompt different responses. However, it seems to me that the issue here is more subtle. Perhaps a better account of what goes on when the title of Turner's painting undergoes a change in Willmore's steel engraving can be obtained by adverting to a notion that Frege employed to describe that ingredient of the overall significance of a sentence or word that he called "Färbung" or "Beleuchtung," which has been rendered by Dummett (1973) as "tone." A difference in tone need not, and often cannot, be spelled out by means of a specific description or by adverting to specific pieces of collateral information, and this of itself shows that we are not dealing with a case in which the same event is described differently.[3]

The two metaphors of "Färbung" (coloring) and "Beleuchtung" (lighting, illumination), as Frege employed them, have both to do with vision. The idea of "Färbung" applies also to music, as the notion of tone color (*Tonfarbe*) versus musical form or structure indicates. In the case of Turner's picture, we may say that the two titles cast a different light (*Beleuchtung*) on the portrayed scene: "The Fighting Temeraire," could be captioned with Goethe's words to the effect that these times are "schlecht und modern," "The Old Téméraire" with the dictum "Sic transit gloria mundi." Both captions could be used to remind the viewer of the ineluctability of change and human forgetfulness, but they would do so in a different spirit: resignation in the latter case, indignation in the former. Perhaps one may go so far as to suggest that since the title of a painting is an integral part of it, a difference in title does not merely suffuse the picture with a different light, but also presents us with two different works that have a first-level intentional content in common. I will not explore this alternative here—though not for the reason that I consider authorial intentions irrelevant to the identity of a work of art.

But, one may ask, why apply the notion of tone just to the titles of Turner's painting? Why not say that, as a rule, co-designative proper names differ from each other at most in coloring? According to Stephen Neale (2001), for instance, Frege's mistake was to describe the contribution of proper names to the truth conditions of a sentence by appealing to the notion of sense: a proper name—Neale contends—contributes via its referent to the thought and truth conditions of the sentences in which it occurs, though it often conveys an element of coloring. Neale urges that we adopt a modified version of a proposal once made by Russell, according to which, for example, the name "Hesperus" means "the object called 'Hesperus'." He suggests that we add a sortal (not a small concession to the Fregean!) and render the axiom governing the word "Hesperus" in a truth-conditional account *à la* Davidson by saying that "Hesperus" refers to "the planet called 'Hesperus'." This trivial "descriptive name" gives rise, in contextually specified circumstances, to truth conditions appropriate to a general proposition where proper names are treated descriptively. Such general propositions can give rise, again in contextually specified circumstances, to singular propositions where the proper name behaves rigidly.

Neale suggests that we view a sentence as consisting of a set of instructions for generating a sequence of propositions: which proposition in the sequence is activated depends on the pragmatic features of the communicative situation. Neale's proposal rests on a combination of Gricean and Fregean insights. I myself (Picardi 2001) have drawn a parallel between Frege and Grice in a spirit not too dissimilar from his. However, the conclusion I am inclined to draw from the joint lessons of Frege and Grice goes in the opposite direction. My surmise is that co-designative proper names can differ *both* in sense and tone (coloring), and that the difference in tone survives the discovery that the names in question are co-designative. Even when used as labels, proper names never manage to get rid of their aura—provided they had one to start with, and provided that the linguistic community does not fall prey to amnesia all of a sudden.

The questions I would like to discuss in this essay are: (1) whether in the case of proper names there is room for drawing a distinction between sense and tone or whether in such a case a difference in tone amounts to a difference in sense, and (2) whether there is a uniform way of drawing the sense/tone distinction for various categories of words, as Frege thought one could. This will require a close scrutiny of the items that Frege assembled under the miscellaneous heading of "tone." I will discuss question (2) first.

II. METHODOLOGICAL CONSIDERATIONS

Before embarking on this more detailed investigation, I should like to pause on some methodological considerations. In the literature on propositional attitudes (see e.g., Salmon 1986 and Richard 1997) one often comes across criticisms of Frege's theory of proper names, resting on the claim that his construal of the notion of cognitive significance (informational content) is guilty of blurring the distinction between the proposition expressed by a given sentence in a certain context of use and the proposition(s) communicated by means of it in the same context, or between semantically imparted information and pragmatically imparted information. Semantics has to do with *the* proposition expressed, while pragmatics has to do with the proposition(s) communicated or the information otherwise imparted. The basic idea here is that in the singular proposition, expressed proper names behave rigidly, and not as Frege surmised. Sense plays no role in determining reference but provides at most a mode of presentation of it. The "proposition expressed" admits of a variety of construals, ranging from Russellian propositions to structured propositions, sets of possible worlds, and so on. Pragmatics deals with the proposition(s) "communicated": Grice's work provides the tools for handling this aspect of utterance meaning. Grice's account is naturally wedded to a truth-conditional theory of meaning. The received wisdom until not so long ago was that a sentence which is neither ambiguous nor vague says only one thing, expresses a unique proposition. But recently many have turned against the received wisdom: there is no such thing as *the* proposition that a sentence expresses on a certain occasion of its use, they claim, which does not mean that most sentences are semantically or syntactically ambiguous. Contextualists and relevance theorists of various hues (e.g., Travis 2000, Carston 2002, Recanati 2004) have called into question the entire apparatus that Grice had developed to spell out what a sentence says in his favored sense of "saying" in contextually specified circumstances. Neale's appeal to multiple propositions, too, constitutes a departure from the Gricean model.

The methodological lesson to be drawn from these considerations is not just that the notion of a proposition is hopelessly ambiguous, but that no answer is forthcoming to the question "What proposition does a sentence express in a given context?" that relies solely on intuition (be it metaphysical, syntactical, or epistemological). An answer can be given only in the framework of a theory of meaning, a theory which attempts a systematic reconstruction of the various abilities and pieces of knowledge that a speaker deploys when using language in thought and communication. Consider, for instance, the distinction between assertoric content and ingredient sense put forward by Michael Dummett in the framework of such a reconstruction. Should we say that a proposition is that which is conveyed by an assertion of a sentence or that which is conveyed by the sentence's ingredient sense, namely by its contribution when occurring in the scope of modal operators or complex sentences in which it occurs unasserted? It is only on the assumption that a sentence's semantic contribution is uniform that we can ignore this distinction. But this assumption, characteristic of truth-conditional semantics, requires justification: it is not the delivery of an intuition that can go unchallenged.

Dummett (1991) has argued that assertoric content is the right candidate for elucidating the notion of a proposition as something that can be justified, judged, challenged. It is on this notion that a theory of meaning should concentrate its attention: the notion of ingredient sense is needed to account for the way the sentence contributes to the truth conditions of compound sentences, and it is on this notion that we should concentrate when constructing a semantics for a language. Brandom (1994 and 2000) develops Dummett's suggestion, and describes the issue in terms of inferential potential. Brandom holds that the inferential potential of a sentence may be richer than its inferential potential as an isolated assertion when it serves as the antecedent of a conditional or is imbedded in the scope of a modal operator. Stanley (1997) has applied this distinction to modal discourse, following by and large Dummett's lead. There simply is no answer, in advance of a theory of meaning, to the question what proposition is expressed by a sentence on a given occasion of its use.

The distinction originally put forward by Grice between sentence meaning and speaker meaning was meant to account for the skills that enable a hearer to disentangle the content and force of what is said to him, from what is conventionally conveyed or conversationally suggested by his interlocutor in a specific episode of utterance. Grice viewed communication as an eminently rational activity and aimed at reconstructing the moves that enable a hearer to "calculate" the conversational implicatures of a given utterance on the basis of what the utterance "literally" says. But considerations similar to that concerning the notion of a proposition apply to Grice's distinction between what a sentence literally says and what the speaker who utters it in a given context suggests, intimates, presupposes, and what not. There is no principled distinction to be drawn between an assertion being incorrect because the speaker has no justification for it, because what it says is false, or because the speaker's choice of words is inappropriate. The task of a theory of meaning, as Dummett has emphasized, is to offer a framework in which these distinctions can be evaluated for what they are worth. The merits of different reconstructions must be evaluated on a global, and not on a local, basis.

III. TONE AND ACCOMPANYING THOUGHTS

In an article published in 1897, devoted to a comparison between Peano's conceptual notation and his own, Frege describes what he means by "cognitive significance" as follows:

> We sometimes label the same object with different names without being aware of it. E.g., we speak of astronomer X's comet and astronomer Y's comet, only subsequently discovering that we have been tagging the same celestial body with these two labels. In such a case I say that both designations have the same meaning [*Bedeutung*]—that they denote or stand for or name the same thing—but that they have different senses, *because it requires a special act of cognition [eine besondere Erkenntnistat] to apprehend the coincidence.* (Frege 1984, 241, my emphasis)

That a special act of cognition is required shows, in Frege's opinion, that we are confronted with different thoughts. Actually this is the criterion he adopts for detecting a difference in the thoughts expressed by the respective sentences. As he had pointed out in *Function and Concept*, someone who did not know that the Morning Star and the Evening Star are the same planet, might hold true the thought expressed by the sentence "The Evening

Star is a planet with a shorter period of revolution than the Earth" while rejecting as false the thought expressed by the sentence "The Morning Star is a planet with a shorter period of revolution than the Earth" (Frege [1891] 1984, 145).

The distinguishing mark of tone, as Frege construes it, is that if two sentences differ from each other in tone no such separate act of cognition is required. If a hearer does not perceive the element of tone attaching to a word, he has not thereby failed to grasp the *thought* expressed by a speaker. Frege (1892) mentions three ways in which words may differ; they may differ in *Vorstellung* (idea or representation), in sense, and in reference. He says:

> on account of the uncertain connection of ideas (*Vorstellungen*) with words, a difference may hold for one person, which another does not find. The difference between a translation and the original text should properly not overstep the first level. To the possible differences here belong also the colouring and shading [*Beleuchtung*] which poetic eloquence seeks to give to the sense. Such colouring and shading [*Beleuchtung*] are not objective, and must be evoked by each hearer or reader according to the hints of the poet or the speaker. Without such affinity in human ideas art would certainly be impossible; but it can never be exactly determined how far the intentions of the poet are realized. (Frege 1892, 31; 1984, 161)

That tone may resist translation was taken by Frege as a ground for characterizing a thought as that truth-evaluable core of a sentence that is preserved under translation in different languages. But nontranslatability does not mean unintelligibility or irrelevance. One would have to show that the untranslatable difference of tone makes no difference to the truth of the thought expressed by a given sentence when it undergoes translation from the original language into a foreign language. I will return to this in section IV.

Later on in his article Frege applies the notion of tone to "although" and "and":

> Subsidiary clauses beginning with "although" also express complete thoughts. This conjunction actually has no sense and does not change the sense of the clause but only illuminates it in a peculiar fashion. We could indeed replace the concessive clause without harm to the truth of the whole by another of the same truth-value; but the light in which the clause is placed by the conjunction might then easily appear unsuitable, as if a song with a sad subject were to be sung in a lively fashion. (Frege 1892, 49; 1984, 172–73)

In a footnote Frege adds that the same applies to "but" and "yet": they, too, differ only in tone [*Beleuchtung*] and not in sense from the conjunction "and." In his first *Logical Investigation* Frege returns to this issue and here he writes that the function of the word "but" is "to intimate that what follows it contrasts with what was to be expected from what preceded it. Such conversational suggestions [*solche Winke in der Rede*] make no difference to the thought" (Frege 1918, 64; 1984, 357).

As Dummett (1973, 1991) has pointed out, Frege failed to describe accurately the phenomenon to which he had called attention. Inevitably, perhaps, for Frege's category of tone is a miscellaneous one, and he was more interested in brushing aside this aspect of meaning than in accounting for it. Tone is as much a conventional and objective feature of word meaning as sense is, and Frege erred in confining it to the realm of psychological associations. In fact, tone is a feature of the overall signifi-cance of a word or sentence that the speaker expects his audience to be able to apprehend, or at any rate to respond to, in addition to its sense. Frege might have accepted this emendation, while maintaining that tone, though conventional, plays no role in selecting which thought is expressed by a given sentence, for tone is not capable of affecting its truth or falsity. But then he would have had to offer an explanation of how it comes about that a conventional ingredient of meaning is, as a rule, unable to affect the truth of a thought. The weakness of Frege's explanation is particularly striking in the case of "and" and "but." Not only would one be hard put to find a difference in the mental associations carried by words such as "and" or "but," but we have here a clear case of a difference in a conventional aspect of meaning. In commenting on Frege's characterization of the difference between "and" and "but," Dummett says:

> Frege states this difference incorrectly, declaring that to say "A but B" is to make a statement that is true just in case "A and B" is true, while also hinting that the truth of B is unexpected, given that of A. If this were right, it would be difficult to explain why we should want to distinguish, in such a case, between hinting something and asserting it outright. It is not right, however: a sentence like "She is a brilliant performer, but she never appears for a fee smaller than £200" cannot be explained in Frege's way. 'But' is apposite when a contrast of *any* kind is involved; it is its lack of any precise content that keeps it from contributing to the sense of the sentence. (Dummett 1991, 121)

Dummett's account of the matter is very insightful, and provides a key to understanding other cases, too, in which we are inclined to say that a difference in tone makes no difference to the truth of what is said. It is not as if asserting and hinting were two linguistic acts performed in succession, as Frege (and Grice) would have us believe. It is the "indefiniteness of the contrast, and the vagueness of the notion of relevance, that resolve the mystery of the distinction between asserting and suggesting" (Dummett 1973, 86).

Frege's treatment of "and" and "but," as I have pointed out elsewhere (Picardi 2001), closely resembles Grice's suggestion how we should conceive of the import of the word "but." According to Frege (1918), in using this word the speaker is, as it were, stepping back to consider what he is saying, and dropping a hint of contrast to his audience. The idea of contrast carried by the "but" is considered by Grice as generating a *conventional implicature* and not as an integral part of what the sentence "literally and in the strict sense" says. As is well known, the notion Grice wanted to elucidate throughout his philosophical career was that of *saying*—of what a speaker who utters a sentence literally and strictly says. This central core must be distinguished not only from what the speaker conversationally implicates, but also from what the words he uses conventionally mean.[4] In the case of "but" and "on the other hand" Grice's suggestion is that we conceive of the contribution of these words to what is said in uttering, for example, the sentence "She is poor, but she is honest," as a higher order ("noncentral") speech act, parasitic on a ground-floor or central speech act (Grice 1989, 361–62). In the case of "but" we have a speech act of contrasting grafted onto the main speech act of asserting—better, perhaps, onto the two separate assertions "She is poor" and "She is honest." Grice's basic idea is that to the truth of what is said only that which is conveyed in the ground-floor speech act matters, while the falsity of the proposition conveyed by the higher-order speech act renders the speaker's statement inappropriate, but does not falsify it. But as Dummett has pointed out, "examples of this kind can furnish no foundation for the view that we can assign any *definite* condition as a condition for the appropriateness rather than the truth of a statement" (Dummett 1973, 86).

It is unclear, on Grice's own theory, how this machinery is supposed to work when we embed the sentence in the antecedent of a conditional, for here conceivably "but" is not used in the performance of a higher-order speech act. And as many linguists (e.g., Levinson 2000) and philosophers have pointed out, the number of words for which a similar treatment would be required is pretty high, and it is unclear which specific higher-order speech act is performed each time. This is why Dummett's proposal fares much better than the joint proposals of Grice and Frege. There is no need to postulate a hierarchy of speech acts to account for this phenomenon. "But" literally conveys a very general idea of a contrast whose content, as in the case of conversational implicatures, will have to be "calculated" by appeal to contextual clues and pragmatic principles.

But what about the generalized conversational implicatures carried by words for logical particles, and by "and" in particular? According to Grice, the literal meaning of "and" is that of the truth-functional (logical) "&," but its occurrence may serve conversationally to suggest either the temporal or the causal interpretation. However, there are counterexamples that show that the truth value of a sentence may change when the conjunction features as the antecedent of a conditional.[5] The Gricean may this time find refuge in Dummett's distinction between assertoric content and ingredient sense, and protest that there is no reason why a uniform account should be offered that accommodates "A and B" as an isolated assertion and as the antecedent of a conditional. For this proposal to be acceptable, however, we would have to find independently acceptable the idea that in isolated assertions "and" invariably bears the truth-functional meaning. Carston (1988, 2002), for instance, has argued that the meaning of "and" is given by logical conjunction. The hearer, eager to place a relevant interpretation on it, may construe the conjuncts as causally and temporally related. In the antecedent of a conditional the conjunction will bear the content placed on it by the relevant interpretation. The basic idea of Carston's proposal is to view sentences as providing a *scheme* on which relevant interpretations, keyed both to the speaker's intention and the external context of utterance, can be placed.

On the face of it, Carston's suggestion bears a certain resemblance to a proposal made by Frege in the second part of *Über Sinn und Bedeutung*. There he discusses various exceptions to the truth-functional reading of complex sentences invented by him, and in the context of this discussion he employs the notion of a *Nebengedanke* or accompanying thought. In commenting on the material conditional Frege employs the notion of an accompanying thought to indicate a psychological association, governed perhaps by psychological laws, which invariably accompanies the production and understanding of the "if-then" construction. Frege remarks that almost always "we connect with the main thoughts expressed by us subsidiary thoughts, which although not expressed, are associated with our words, in accordance with psychological laws." At this stage of the article Frege wants to convince the reader that the truth-functional reading of the conditional is appropriate, and that other thoughts evoked in the mind of the hearer are not part of the thought expressed by the sentence. That the triggering of such *Nebengedanken* (subsidiary or accompanying thoughts) may be governed by psychological laws was a concession to the scientific psychology of his day. Frege wanted to allow for the possibility of a psychological law of association, to the effect that every time one comes across an "if-then" construction the *Nebengedanke* of consequentiality (*Grund-Folge*) or of causality (*Ursache-Wirkung*) is activated in the thinker's mind. Although *Nebengedanken* of this sort belong to the realm of the psychological, they differ from contents of consciousness and ideas. For while the latter are conceived by Frege as a part of the individual psychological make-up of people, the almost universal triggering of these associations may be due to a law-like mechanism which operates at a sub-personal level. With this observation Frege confined the category of causality, which according to Kant presides over the synthesis of (certain) judgments, to the realm of the psychological, thus carrying a step further his work of deconstructing Kant's classification of judgments, initiated in his *Begriffsschrift*.

However, there are contexts to which the truth-functional reading may not be appropriate, as the test of substitution *salva veritate* shows. To account for these exceptions to his bald conjecture that the *Bedeutung* of a declarative sentence is a logical object, Frege suggests that sometimes a sentence expresses more thoughts than those it declares on its grammatical surface. Unlike the hints conveyed by "but" and "yet," such accompanying thoughts are not conveyed by the choice of specific lexical items, but are signalled by the *syntactic* mode of composition, in particular, by means of a conditional construction or a relative clause. Whereas such accompanying thoughts, once they are made explicit, have a specific content, tone need not be expressible by means of *a*, let alone *one* specific, full-fledged proposition.

One of the examples discussed by Frege (1892, 47–48) helps to clarify what is at issue. He asks us to consider which thought is expressed by the sentence (a) "Napoleon, who recognized the danger on his right flank, personally led his guards against the enemy position." In certain contexts the answer will be that (a) expresses two thoughts: (i) Napoleon personally led his guards against the enemy position; and (ii) Napoleon recognized the danger on his right flank. How are these two thoughts connected to each other? Is the logical form of the sentence in question to be rendered as "(i) and (ii)" or as "(ii), therefore (i)"? For in listening to or reading (a), one is alerted to the presence of a third thought, namely, (iii) that the realization of the danger *was the reason why* Napoleon led his attack. If (a) may count as true even in case Napoleon had taken his decision *before* the perception of danger, then we can conclude that (iii) is merely suggested. Thus, in such a case, the sentence's logical form would be that of a truth-functional conjunction, with a mere hint as to how the two thoughts stand to each other. But if this third thought is not merely suggested, but forms part of what is expressed, the situation becomes more tricky "as we would have more simple thoughts than sentences." In this case, if we substitute clause (ii) with another which agrees with it in truth value, for example, "Napoleon was already more than 45 years old," we alter not only the second thought but also the third, for the truth value of (iii) would be altered if Napoleon's age had not been the reason why he had led his guards against the enemy's position.

Grice wanted to construe such accompanying thoughts as generalized conversational implicatures triggered by the use of the word "and," as he took it for granted that the falsity of the (conversationally implied) temporal or causal connection renders the sentence inappropriate but not false. But, as we have seen,[6] there are embeddings of the conjunction in the antecedent of a conditional whose truth value is sensitive to such conversational implicatures. Frege is ready to admit that there are cases where the falsity of the suggested *Nebengedanke* makes no difference to the truth of the compound sentence, and in this respect his treatment parallels Grice's. However, sometimes the falsity of the accompanying thought makes a difference to the truth value of the whole, and in such a case we do not have simply an instance of pragmatic impropriety. We have to revise our previous assignment of logical form in such a way that the accompanying thought is reckoned part of the thought expressed by the sentence. Frege summarizes the result of his reflections by saying that this shows "why clauses of equal truth-value cannot always be substituted for one another in such cases. *The clause expresses more through its connection with another than it does in isolation*" (Frege 1892, 47; 1984, 174, my emphasis). The contribution of a sentence to the truth conditions of a compound sentence in which it occurs as a component need not be uniform: using Dummett's terminology we may say that its ingredient sense is richer than its assertoric content. If an ingredient of tone can become part of the thought *expressed*, it cannot be simply brushed aside in terms of psychological associations evoked by the words. Thus, on Frege's own grounds, the notions of tone and accompanying thought must be kept apart.[7]

What is remarkable in Frege's treatment of this problem is the way he connects questions of content and questions of logical form. Contextual ingredients (speaker's intention, extra-linguistic context, sentential context) contribute directly to the thought expressed on a given occasion by the assertoric use of a given sentence, and this is why the (situated) thought should be seen as the proper bearer of semantic value. Whether an accompanying thought forms part of the thought expressed, or merely accompanies it, is not something that can be decided on the mere basis of sentential structure but requires that we take the overall context into account. However, the effects of context are *constrained* by the syntactic structure—in the case in question, by the relative construction. The semantic interpretation must be keyed to linguistic items present in the surface structure.

From this perspective, the effect of context on the logical structure is not as free as many philosophers of language (e.g., Carston, Travis, Recanati) have claimed. Here I do not want to explore any further the controversy between truth-conditional pragmatics and truth-conditional semantics, although I am inclined to agree with Stanley's thesis that "in deriving the semantic interpretation of logical form, every feature of the semantic interpretation must be the semantic value of something in that logical form, or introduced via a context-independent construction rule" (Stanley 2001, 398).

Frege used the notion of a *Nebengedanke* consistently in his writings from 1892 until 1923, in his letters, and also in writings preserved in his *Nachlass*. This notion is also designed to handle certain pragmatic effects brought about by a sentence on a certain occasion of use. At least two different ideas are subsumed under the heading of an accompanying thought: (a) that of the point or ulterior purpose which a speaker may want to achieve by uttering a given sentence; and (b), that of a thought that the audience is induced to form on the basis of a nonlinguistic utterance. In his third *Logical Investigation* Frege considers the statement "Frederick the Great won the battle of Rossbach, or two is greater than three" and remarks:

> But why does the speaker add the second sentence at all? . . . We may certainly assume that he does not want to claim that two is greater than three; and if he had been satisfied with just the first sentence, he would have said more with fewer words. Why, therefore, this waste of words? . . . Whatever may be the speaker's intentions and motives for saying just this and not that, our concern is not with these at all, but solely with what he ways. (Frege 1923, 42–43; Frege 1984, 397)

The obvious falsity of the second disjunct fails to render the sentence inappropriate; perhaps the hearer is supposed to reason (after a Gricean fashion) that since the chief aim of an assertion is to convey a true piece of information, and since one of the disjuncts is obviously false, the assertion can be true only because of the truth of the remaining disjunct. Perhaps this unnecessary detour was motivated by the speaker's desire for emphasis, as when one says "If this is a Vermeer, I am Greta Garbo," in order to suggest that the picture in question is an unmistakable forgery.

To illustrate (b) we may consider an example discussed by Frege in his (posthumously published) *Logic* of 1897:

> If a commander conceals his weakness from the enemy by making his troops keep changing their uniforms, he is not telling a lie; for he is not expressing any thoughts, although his actions are calculated to induce thoughts in others. . . . Naturally things are different if certain actions are specifically agreed on as a means of communicating something. In language common usage takes the place of such agreements. Of course borderline cases can arise because language changes. (Frege 1969, 152; Frege 1979, 140–41)

The purpose of the commander's nonlinguistic utterance is not that of communicating anything, but that of getting the enemy to form a certain *Nebengedanke* on the basis of what he sees. The intention behind the utterance is not supposed to be made overt, for the enemy is expected to form his judgment in virtue of his taking the variety of uniforms as a *natural* sign of the size of the army. If the enemy were to suspect a communicative intention, he would immediately become alert to the possibility of deception. So much for the notion of an accompanying thought.

In his writings after 1892, and especially in his *Logical Investigations*, Frege extends his observations concerning "but" and "yet" to cover predicate words, which he regarded as synonyms. He emphatically stresses his point that by claiming that assertoric force does not comprise tone (e.g., Frege [1918] 1984, 356–57):

> It makes no difference to the thought whether I use the word "horse" or "steed" or "nag" or "prad." The assertoric force does not cover the ways in which these words differ. What is called mood, atmosphere, illumination in a poem, what is portrayed by intonation and rhythm, does not belong to the thought. (Frege 1984, 357)

In his *Introduction to Logic* of 1897, preserved as part of his *Nachlass*, he gives the example of the two words "Hund" and "Köter" translatable into English as "dog" and "cur," and says that "That dog howled the whole night" and "That cur howled the whole night" express the same thought (have the same truth conditions) and differ only in tone (Frege 1969, 152; 1979, 184). Since assertoric force does not extend to tone, the two sentences have not only the same truth conditions, but also the same assertibility conditions. On this picture there is no tension between the truth conditions of the thought expressed by a sentence and the conditions of assertibility or acceptability of a sentence that differs in tone from it. And yet, if someone attributes to me the belief that that cur had howled all night on the basis of my utterance "That dog howled all night," he is not reporting my thought correctly, and I may retort that I neither said nor implied any such thing. The difference between sense and tone is not to be confused with the distinction between the descriptive and the evaluative. The point of describing or referring to things in a certain way is generally to prepare the grounds for drawing the consequences that follow from such a description. The use of a pejorative generally commits a speaker to linguistic and non-linguistic consequences. The fact that if a hearer reports my statement "It is late, but I am used to working at night" by saying that I have said that it is late and that I am used to working at night, I am not going to correct him is due to the circumstance that the word "but" conveys a very generic contrast and that it is hard to see how substituting "but" with "and" can make a substantive difference to the assertoric content of the sentence uttered.

The weakness of Frege's suggestion concerning this specific application of the notion of tone is easily appreciated if one considers the case of racist jargon. If we followed Frege's lead, we would have to say that the words "black" and "nigger" differ only in tone: from the point of view of truth conditions the thought expressed by a sentence in which the word "nigger" occurs does not differ from one in which this ingredient is absent. Frege's way of connecting assertion with truth fails to account for the commitments we undertake in endorsing an assertion made by others or in making it ourselves, and is therefore unsatisfactory. We may abstain from accepting a statement made by others because we are aware of the tacit commitments we would undertake in accepting a certain way of referring to people or actions.

And yet, Williamson (2003) urges that we extend Frege's (and Grice's) treatment of "but" and "and" to account for the meaning and reference of pairs of words such as "German" and "Boche" and, we may add, "black" and "nigger," "Marrano" and either "Jew" or "Muslim" (depending on the context), as used in sixteenth-century Spain, or "meridionale" and "terrone," as used in contemporary Italy. Williamson's suggestion is made in a context where he opposes the proposal put forward by Dummett (1973, 453–55) and elaborated by Brandom (2000) and Boghossian (2003) concerning the meaning of pejoratives.[8] According to Dummett, there are two aspects of the application of a concept or the deployment of a thought. On the one hand, there is the condition that warrants us in applying the concept or in using the word, accepting the thought as true or making an assertion by uttering the sentence. On the other, there are the consequences of accepting the thought or endorsing the statement. In a language free from defects there would be harmony between these two aspects. We ought to draw only those consequences from a statement that we have accepted which the condition that warrants its assertion entitles us to draw; conversely, we ought to have the right to regard prejudice and superstition as obvious examples of sources of disharmony. Dummett writes:

> To a racially prejudiced employer a man's race may count as a reason not to employ him; to a superstitious person the fact that someone is coming downstairs is a reason for not going upstairs. In both cases the consequence drawn fails to match the grounds for the proposition from which it was drawn. These disharmonies are obvious; there surely are others only detectable by deep reflection. (Dummett 2001, 114)

Many inferential connections are implicit in our use of words and concepts and can be made explicit; many inferential connections that usage confronts us with (such as e.g., the use of the word "Boche" mentioned by Dummett [1973]) are simply faulty. How are we to handle the concepts expressed by words such as "Boche," "nigger," or "terrone"? Should we say that the word "Boche" resembles the connective "tonk" invented by Prior (1960), in that it fails to specify a concept much as the connective "tonk" fails to specify a function? It is not at all clear what we should say. Unlike "tonk," pejoratives do not give rise to logical contradictions, and unlike words such as "phlogiston" or "ether," their employment is as a rule crowned with referential success. When Dummett says that we are here confronted with a "disharmony" which requires a reform in our way of thinking and speaking, he does not purport to describe how people actually use these words but to hint at the sort of argument that we may employ in order to criticize a certain kind of linguistic usage. We should point out that the grounds for asserting that someone is of German nationality in no way entitles us to draw the consequence that he or she is more prone to cruelty than other Europeans. Brandom (2000) suggests that the best thing to do is to abstain from using such concepts and words, since we are aware of the commitments which we would endorse in uttering them.

The question under discussion is: how are these commitments to be construed? Whereas inferentialists construe the pejorative ingredient implicit in words such as "Boche" in terms of inferential (material) commitments undertaken by a speaker who uses this kind of word, and consider such inferences as meaning-constitutive, Williamson suggests that the derogatory element is not part of what the sentences in which they occur strictly speaking *say* but resembles Fregean tone, construed as a conventional implicature (in Grice's sense), which, as such, has no effect on truth conditions. However, it is very doubtful that Grice's notion of conventional implicature is a useful tool in this area. Many philosophers and linguists have argued on independent grounds (independent, that is, of the inferentialism / representationalism controversy)[9] that the decision to construe the explicit derogatory ingredient as a conventional implicature rather than as constitutive of word meaning is devoid of any clear rationale. What matters on many occasions—and it is a merit of Williamson's proposal that it stresses this feature—is the sentential and extra-linguistic context in which pejoratives are used. However, as Williams (2004) has pointed out, inferentialists could join forces with contexualists such as Charles Travis, and fill in the clauses for the introduction and elimination policies of concepts (and the commitments undertaken on a specific occasion of utterance) by appeal to contextual considerations.[10] Powerful arguments have been put forward by Travis (2000) that undermine the tenets of Grice's conception of meaning and implicature and underline the paramount role that context plays in determining the content of our utterances.

In our survey of various applications of the sense/tone distinction the only semantic category of expressions which has been left out of account is that of proper names. It is to this question, which I addressed but left hanging in section 1, that I now turn.

IV. The Sense and Tone of Proper Names

In *Über Sinn und Bedeutung* Frege employs the metaphor of *Beleuchtung* not only to elucidate what he means by tone, but also in order to characterize the sense of a proper name, as something that everybody who is sufficiently familiar with the language to which it belongs is able to grasp. He says:

> [The sense of a proper name] serves to illuminate only a single aspect of the thing meant [damit ist die Bedeutung aber, falls sie vorhanden ist, nur *einseitig beleuchtet*], supposing it to have one. Comprehensive knowledge of the thing meant would require us [Zu einer *allseitigen Erkenntnis* der Bedeutung würde gehören] to be able to say immediately whether any given sense attaches to it. To such knowledge we never attain. (Frege 1892, 27; 1984, 158, my emphasis)

The underlying assumption is that a line can be drawn between those ways of illuminating an object that are of cognitive significance, and those that are not. Something in a proper name is of cognitive significance if knowledge of it enables the speaker to pick out an object as its bearer in the context of a sentence. The determination of the referent is conceived by Frege as a preparatory step in the process of determining the truth value of the sentence in which a property is ascribed to the referent of the name. One may master two proper names without realizing that they make the same contribution to the truth conditions of the sentences in which they occur. Once we find out that it is the same object that is given to us under different (cognitive) perspectives, the identity will cease to have information value for the (individual) speaker. However, in the case of two linguistic expressions that differ only in tone Frege held that it is impossible for a speaker who fully understands them both not to realize that the contributions they make to the truth of the sentence in which they occur are the same. Failure to do so shows an imperfect mastery of the words in question, which must not be confused with a (necessarily) incomplete knowledge of all possible ways in which an object may be given to us.

But, one may wonder, are there any proper names that differ *both* in sense and in tone? *Téméraire* and *Temeraire* are two such names, if what I have said in section 1 is correct. In *Über Sinn und Bedeutung* Frege himself involuntarily supplies an example when he refers to the battle of Waterloo as the battle of Belle Alliance. Doubtless he was aware that the battle was referred to also in a different way. In referring to it by means of that name Frege wanted to underline Blücher's contribution in addition to that of Wellington to the victory over Napoleon at Waterloo, thus displaying his patriotic stance. He also took it for granted that none of his contemporary (German) readers would be in doubt as to which battle was meant. As long as familiarity with both names is reasonably widespread in a community a competent speaker can *choose* which one of them to use without fear of misleading his audience. It is conceivable, however, that in the course of time one of the two names will gradually fall into oblivion, and in a such a case it would be misleading for a speaker to use the obsolete name when talking to an audience that he believes not to be in possession of this piece of knowledge. However, if we translate Frege's article into Italian or English there is no way of rendering this element of tone, and one may possibly mislead the reader by preserving Frege's choice of words. It may also happen that the ingredient of tone present in one or both of them dies out, and then the names are used interchangeably.

In *Word and Object* Quine, commenting on the Himalayan explorer who finds out that Everest=Gaurisanker, remarks: "His discovery is painfully empirical and not lexicographic: nevertheless the stimulus meanings of 'Everest' and 'Gaurisanker' coincide for him thenceforword" (§11, 49–59).[11] The example discussed by Quine nicely supplements Frege's example of "Afla" and "Ateb," two invented names designating the same mountain, discussed by him in a draft of a letter to Philip E.B. Jourdain, written probably around 1914 (Frege 1976, 128; 1984, 80). However, one may surmise that, while the stimulus meanings of the two names will coincide, once the truth of the identity statement becomes known, the ingredient of tone (if any) may accompany the respective names at least as long as the memory of their cultural and political origin is alive in the linguistic community.

It is not clear how Frege would have described his own choice of words. It is possible that someone may have mastered both names while failing to realize that the battle of Waterloo and the battle of Belle Alliance are one and the same battle. Such a speaker will attach different thoughts to sentences which differ from one another only as regard the occurrence of those proper names, and hence, according to Frege's criterion, we must say that the two names differ in sense. However, also a hearer who is fully aware that the names are co-designative perceives a difference which goes beyond the mere sound of the words uttered. This hearer grasps the element of tone inherent in the choice of words and is thus led to form a guess at the speaker's political stance. The failure to get this element of tone across to his hearer does not compromise the main communicative intention of a speaker to convey a true piece of information—provided that in that context this was his prevailing intention. There is nothing hidden, inexplicit, or purely subjective in tone. Where tone differs from sense is (a) in the varying degree of *specificity* of the suggested piece of information, and (b) in its high degree of context dependence, as regards both the extent to which this piece of knowledge can be expected to be shared within the linguistic community and the relevance of the conveyed piece of information to a given conversational exchange.

Frege's celebrated example of the Morning Star and the Evening Star lends itself to illustrating another facet of the way in which *Sinn* may differ from *Färbung* and *Beleuchtung*. The reason why most competent adult speakers effortlessly understand Frege's example of the *Morgenstern* and the *Abendstern* is not only due to their being aware of the piece of astronomical information needed to grasp the example, but also to their being familiar with works of poetry or mythological and religious narratives where the star plays a role. Consider, for instance, the incongruity of substituting "Abendstern" for "Morgenstern" in Act III of Wagner's *Tannhäuser*, where Wolfram von Eschenbach asks the *Abendstern* to see Elisabeth "out of this mortal vale": "Ach, du mein holder Abendstern, / wohl grüsst' ich immer dich so gern / vom Herzen, das sie nie verriet / grüsse sie, wenn sie vorbei dir zieht/wenn sie entschwebt dem Tal der Erden / ein sel'ger Engel dort zu werden!"[12] Not only would it be demonstratively incongruous to address the star seen at twilight as "Morgenstern," but given the context, the analogy would be lost between the end of day and the end of life. Also the well-known association of the star with the Virgin Mary should be kept in mind in the context of Wagner's opera. Recall the passage in the prayer of Stephen Daedalus in Joyce's *Portrait of the Artist as a Young Man*:

> And now, thy very face and form, dear mother, speak to us of the Eternal; not like earthly beauty, dangerous to look upon, but like the morning star which is thy emblem, bright and musical, breathing purity, telling of heaven and infusing peace. O harbinger of day! O light of the pilgrim! Lead us still as thou hast led. In the dark night, across the bleak wilderness guide us to our Lord Jesus, guide us home. (Joyce [1916] 1976, 139)

True, it is the Morning Star that bears this association, but given the context of Wagner's opera (the return of the pilgrims to the Wartburg), one may suppose that the symbolic association trumps demonstrative incongruity. To refer to the star as "Venus" or "Lucifer" when commenting on or translating *Tannhäuser* clearly would not do. The variety of names under which the planet Venus is referred to testifies to its symbolic significance brought about, no doubt, also by its perceptual salience at dusk and dawn to us Earthlings. When translating from German into Italian or English we must try to do justice to the symbolic habitat of words as best we can. In short, my suggestion concerning "Abendstern" and "Morgenstern" is that here, too, we are presented with proper names that differ not only in cognitive significance but also in tone, and that this difference may in certain contexts be semantically relevant: proper names differing in tone may not be always substitutable and their occurrence may make a difference to the thought expressed. The fact that often we come across speakers who are, as it were, "color(ing)-blind," does not make this ingredient less objective.

Perhaps it is not by chance that Wittgenstein used the word "Färbung" when discussing certain aspects of meaning blindness which have to do with a failure to perceive an aspect of the word's meaning.[13] The best characterization of what goes on in the case of color(ing)-blindness is the one given in the so-called second part of the *Philosophical Investigations*, where we read:

> The familiar physiognomy [*das vertraute Gesicht eines Wortes*] of a word, the feeling that it has taken up its meaning into itself, that it is an actual likeness of its meaning—there could be human beings to whom all this was alien. (They would not have an attachment to their words.)—And how are these feelings manifested among us?—*By the way we choose and value words*. (PI, II xi, p. 218, my emphasis)

Here Wittgenstein is not merely alluding to the familiar phenomenological experience of the fusion of a word with its meaning. He considers it a remarkable feature of human language that we have this sensitivity to tone and stylistic variation. It is indeed remarkable that different sentences can convey the same thought, and that each of them may retain something peculiar. Equally remarkable is the fact that languages are translatable into each other at all, while comprising much that eludes translation. Dummett (1991) closes his discussion in the section "Sense, force and tone" by acknowledging the importance and complexity of the social aspects of linguistic interchange signalled by our choice of words; at the same time he adds:

> When a dictionary notes, after its definition of a word, 'archaic', 'vulgar', or the like, it is, quite properly, indicating its tone. But this feature, important as it is in our dealings with one another, and complex as it is to describe in detail, is evidently peripheral to the problem of explaining what it is for something to be a language. We can hint only at what we could express; we can adopt one or another style of saying things only because we are able to say them at all. (Dummett 1991, 122)

Now, perhaps Dummett is here conceiving of tone and style in a very specialized sense. Even so, it seems to me that there is no way of speaking, even at ground level, which is utterly devoid of style—what may be lacking, of course, is the conscious intention to adopt this or that style or the awareness that one is doing so. Therefore, I am reluctant, for the reasons given above, to consider tone of secondary importance to explaining what it is for something to be a language.[14] We constantly choose, ponder, and evaluate words; we are sensitive both to their evocative and their expressive aspects—two features that, as Dummett remarks, Frege failed to keep apart. The expressive function requires that the hearer recognize the attitude which the speaker intended to convey, whereas for the evocative effect to take place no such recognition is required. Indeed "the evocative use of language does, therefore, depend, in a way in which no other use of language does, upon the dispositions of the individual hearer to react in certain ways" (Dummett 1973, 88).

Place-names offer what may be the best sort of examples of expressions to which the sense/tone distinction can fruitfully be applied. In a paper of 1984 MacIntyre contends that the meanings of proper names such as "Londonderry" and "Doire Colmcille" (in English and Irish, respectively) may give rise to thoughts that are utterly untranslatable into each other: Doire Colmcille (roughly: St. Columba's oak grove) is the Gaelic name for what was later to become the settlement called "Londonderry" by the English. It would be superficial, according to MacIntyre, to attempt to detach the name from the communal intention of naming in which it is embedded. The presuppositions and implications of the uses of the two names in their respective languages are very different:

> But, it may be asked, are these not simply two names of one and the same place? The answer is first that no proper name of place or person names any place or person *as such*; it names *in the first instance* only *for* those who are members of some particular linguistic and cultural community by identifying places and persons in terms of a scheme of identification shared by, and perhaps partially constitutive of, that community. (MacIntyre [1984] 1989, 185)

Later in the same paper MacIntyre suggests that we may construct a language neutral with respect to the two different schemes of identification: in the course of this process "names, having been Fregean will have become by a process of social change Kripkean" (ibid., 193). MacIntyre's aim is to show, against Davidson, that the philosophical problem of relativism is not so easily dismissed, and that failures of translatability are easy to come by. Not all that is untranslatable is unintelligible.

If we follow MacIntyre's lead, we should incorporate what I have treated so far as an ingredient of tone and kept apart from cognitive significance properly so called into the sense of proper names such as "Londonderry" and "Doire Colmcille," and develop a social theory of proper names which does full justice to the significance of the institution of naming. If MacIntyre is right, someone who is culturally and linguistically able to inhabit both worlds must make a choice as to which of them he or she wants to inhabit "for he or she will not be able to find application for the concepts of truth and justification which are independent of the standards of one community or the other. There is no access to any subject matter which is not conceptualized in terms that already presuppose the truth of one set of claims rather than the other" (ibid., 189). The situation that MacIntyre has in mind was masterfully described by James Joyce in a passage of *A Portrait of the Artist as a Young Man* where Stephen Daedalus is talking to an English priest:

> He felt with a smart of dejection that the man to whom he was speaking was a countryman of Ben Jonson. He thought: "The language in which we are speaking is his before it is mine. How different are the words *home*, *Christ*, *ale*, *master*, on his lips and on mine! I cannot speak or write these words without unrest of spirit. His language, so familiar and so foreign, will always be for me an acquired speech. I have not made or accepted its words. My voice holds them at bay. My soul frets in the shadow of his language." (189)[15]

These grand reflections are triggered by the priest's failure to understand what Stephen means by "tundish," which, as he later finds out, is not the Gaelic word for "funnel," but an (obsolete) English word:

> That tundish has been on my mind for a long time. I looked it up and find it English and good old blunt English too. Damn the dean of studies and his funnel! What did he come here for to teach us his own language or to learn it from us? Damn him one way or the other! (ibid., 251)

Similarly, one can easily imagine someone who insists that it was in Toblach, and not in Dobbiaco, that Mahler retired in summer to write his music. Such insistence may be due not just to a desire for chronological accuracy, but to the intention of conveying a political stance towards the geographic area that Italians call "Regione Alto Adige" (in German: "Region Tiroler Etschland"), which before World War I was part of South Tyrol (and of the Austro-Hungarian Empire). Speakers whose first language is German normally refer to it as "Südtirol."[16]

Despite its initial attractiveness, I find MacIntyre's proposal eventually untenable, for it underestimates the fact that each of us has the experience of belonging all the time to different communities (linguistic as well as cultural), with different and perhaps sometimes conflicting allegiances. A possible response to such a situation is a growing uneasiness and suspicion as regards the lore of inherited tradition(s). Such uneasiness may prompt a search for new ways of self-understanding, including the appreciation of certain basic features of the form of life of human creatures, that makes understanding possible in the first place. Gradually, we all become color(ing)-blind to the aura of certain names and acquire a sensitivity to new shades of color that suffuse new names. To some of us it may happen that we feel at home in no language. A better description of the phenomena to which MacIntyre has called attention can be obtained by deploying the sense/tone distinction, under the construal I have suggested.

Michael Dummett has urged that we should consider place-names as a prime example of Putnam's idea of a division of linguistic labor. His proposal points in a direction different from McIntyre's while acknowledging the importance of the political and cultural dimensions of place names. Dummett's suggestion is that for linguistic communication to succeed it is sufficient that speaker and hearer use place-names with the same reference while being both fully aware of the intricate network to which they belong:

> In the use of place-names, we have an instance of the celebrated phenomenon called by Putnam the "division of linguistic labour" far more thoroughgoing than those cited by him. . . . The use of a place-name is not something that anybody could *know* in its entirety. It is integral to our employment of names of places on the Earth's surface that it is possible, using one or another projection, to draw maps of parts of that surface: and so all the complex techniques of surveying and of map-construction play a part in the web of practices that constitutes our use of place-names. . . . We have here the clearest of all instances in which the use of language exists only as interwoven with a multitude of non-linguistic practices: the existence of roads and shipping routes, and, in our time, of railways and air flights, and even of travel agencies, enters essentially into the language-game, to use Wittgenstein's phrase, that involves the use of place-names.
>
> Here, then, we observe the social character of language at its most prominent. But, when we need to characterise with complete accuracy the belief expressed by a speaker by means of a sentence containing a place-name, our concern will be solely with the connection he personally makes between the name and the place. Normally speaking, of course, we have no reason to trouble to attain such accuracy: it is sufficient that he used the name and that he knows enough to count as able to have a belief about the place. In delicate cases, however, we may need to bother: Kripke's well-known Pierre example provides just such a case. (Dummett 1993, 146–47)

Some may object that there is a difference between the phenomenon described by Dummett and the one to which Hilary Putnam and Tyler Burge have called attention. Whereas in the case of "gold," "tiger," or "arthritis" we can, if the need arises, appeal to experts, in the case of place-names there is no specific authority to which we can defer. If Dummett is right, nobody knows all there is to know about place-names, and this is why we cannot even talk of a partial grasp of the significance of a place-name, for the idea of partial understanding makes sense only if a complete grasp is attainable. But the objection is misplaced. What should be attainable (in fact, what *is* attained) at every given stage of language use is a distinction between information about the bearer of a proper name and the semantic information required for someone to count as a competent user of a proper name (i.e., the piece of knowledge required to understand the proposition expressed by a certain sentence, and not merely what is involved in one containing a metalinguistic formulation of the proper name occurring in it).[17] There is not one identical distinction holding throughout, but there is a kind of distinction that can be drawn whenever such a distinction is useful. The sort of objectivity that Frege required of the senses of proper names, and of thoughts in general, is a chimera. Proper names, like all other words, enjoy the degree of objectivity which is bestowed upon them by the intersubjectively accessible intentions of use on the part of competent speakers of the language. A robust account of the social aspect of meaning should assign to tone the importance it richly deserves.

EVA PICARDI

DEPARTMENT OF PHILOSOPHY
UNIVERSITY OF BOLOGNA
SEPTEMBER 2004

NOTES

1. This problem surfaced again a few years later in *Der Gedanke*, in the section where Frege discusses ordinary proper names. He there opts for the radical solution that speakers who attach different means of identification to the same name speak different languages, whereas what he should have said is that there is a tension between the idiolect and the common language (cf. for a discussion Dummett 1974). In attributing to Frege both a descriptivist theory of names and an idiolectal theory of meaning, Kripke (1979) chooses the most uncharitable reading of Frege's statements on the issue of the sense of proper names.

2. In 1914 Frege characterizes the sense of a proper name by reverting to the terminology he had used in his *Begriffsschrift*, §8, i.e., as encapsulating a way of determination (*Bestimmungsweise*) of an object (in 1879 he had said: "of a content"). The terminology employed in 1914 suggests a parallel with a problem Frege came up against when discussing the issue of definitions. In a formalized language one should avoid laying down different definitions of the same notion, for otherwise a proof would be required to establish that different *definientia* pick out the same *definiendum*. Since ordinary proper names encapsulate ways of determining an object, it is far from obvious that different proper names pick out

the same object, both intersubjectively and intrasubjectively. This is why a "proof" may be required, and where there is proof, there is cognitive effort and, possibly, cognitive gain. As Frege points out in the second footnote to *Über Sinn und Bedeutung*, in a formalized language, proper names should be replaced by canonical names. However, as Frege knew full well (or was about to discover) from his experience with *Grundgesetze* I, §10, this does not mean that no cognitive effort is required to establish that two singular expressions of the formal language stand for the same object.

3. I was not able to find out whether Turner lived to discover that he had agonized in vain over the title of his picture. I doubt that he did.

4. Cf. Carston 2002, section 2.5.4 for a discussion of various interpretations of "what is said."

5. Neale (2001) offers the following examples: (1) If B yells and A hits B, then C will punish A and B; (2) If A hits B and B yells, C will punish A and B. On a natural reading (1) and (2) differ in truth value. However, if Grice were right, a conversational implicature brought about by the order of the conjuncts should not make a difference to the truth values of the two sentences.

6. See the example mentioned in note 5 above.

7. Neale (2001) assimilates the notion of an accompanying thought to that of coloring (tone), but for the reasons given above I think that they should be kept apart.

8. Dummett 1973, 453–55; Brandom 2000.

9. See Picardi 2004.

10. See Willliams 2004 and Travis 2000.

11. The sense in which the identity is informative is explained by Quine as follows: "'Gaurisanker = Everest' is indeed informative, even though both of its singular terms are ostensively learned (in the case imagined in §11). For they are learned not in the primeval manner of 'mama', but only after mastering general terms and the adult scheme of enduring physical objects. Even if our explorer learns each of the names by ostension on the part of natives incapable of supplying the auxiliary demonstrative term 'that mountain', it will be much the same to the explorer as if they supplied it: he is confident that both natives are naming from their respective points of view the enduring solid and not just a current phase of exposed side of it" (*Word and Object*, §23, 115). In *The Foundations of Arithmetic* Frege made a similar point by stressing that a sortal must be implicit in the meaning of a proper name in order for questions of identification and re-identification of its bearer to arise.

12. Wolfram's prayer in full reads: "Like a portent of death, twilight shrouds the earth and envelops the valley in its sable robe, the soul, that yearns for those heights, dreads to take its dark and awful flight. There you shine, o fairest of the stars, and shed your gentle light from afar; your friendly beam penetrates the twilight gloom and points the way out from the valley. O my fair evening star I always gladly greeted thee: from a heart that never betrays its faith greet her when she passes, when she soars above this mortal vale to become a blessed angel in

heaven." (English translation of the libretto by Lionel Salter)

13. For a discussion of this aspect of Wittgenstein's thought see Schulte 1993, chs. 1 and 5.

14. Wittgenstein considers the possibility "there might also be a language in whose use the 'soul' of the words play no part. In which, for example, we had no objection to replacing one word by another arbitrary one of our own invention" (PI, 530). Such a language would be vastly different from ours, and I am not sure that Wittgenstein considers it a genuine possibility at all.

15. These grand reflections are triggered by the priest's failure to understand what Stephen means by "tundish": "That tundish has been on my mind for a long time. I looked it up and find it English and good old blunt English too. Damn the dean of studies and his funnel! What did he come here for to teach us his own language or to learn it from us? Damn him one way or the other!"(ibid., 251). All the same, we may suppose that for Stephen Daedalus the two words will differ in tone also after his lexicographic discovery.

16. Consider, moreover, how strange it must be for a German speaker to listen to the translation into English of the Italian sentence "Da qui puoi ammirare il Catinaccio in tutta la sua gloria" as "From here you can admire the Catinaccio in all its glory." Translated from German into English the sentence would read: "From here you can admire the Rosengarten in all its glory"—where "Rosengarten," taken literally, means "a rose garden" and metaphorically a place of delights, while "Catinaccio" literally means a "bucket," and an ugly one to boot. "Rosengarten" and "Catinaccio" are names of one and the same well-known mountain in South Tyrol, i.e., Südtirol, a.k.a. Alto Adige. On a tourist ignorant of both German and Italian such nuances would be lost.

17. Cf. Dummett (1975 reprinted in Dummett 1978), 140: "Even in the case of proper names, there is room for a distinction between the standard explanation of its reference and the provision of standard information about its bearer: only an obsessive adherence to a *theory* could give us any reason to seek to deny this."

REFERENCES

Beaney, M., ed. 1997. *The Frege Reader*. Oxford: Blackwell.

Boghossian, P. 2003. "Blind Reasoning." *Proceedings of the Aristotelian Society*, 225–48.

Brandom, R. 1994. *Making It Explicit*. Cambridge, MA: Harvard Univ. Press.

———. 2000. *Articulating Reasons*. Cambridge, MA: Harvard Univ. Press.

Carston, R. 1988. "Implicature, Explicature and Truth-Theoretic Semantics." In *Mental Representations*, ed. R. Kempson. Cambridge: Cambridge Univ. Press, 155–81.

———. 2002. *Thoughts and Utterances: The Pragmatics of Explicit Communication*. Oxford: Blackwell.

Dummett, M. 1973. *Frege: Philosophy of Language*. London: Duckworth. Second ed. 1981, Cambridge, MA: Harvard Univ. Press.

———. (1974) 1978. "The Social Character of Meaning." Reprinted in *Truth and Other Enigmas*. London: Duckworth, 420–30.

———. (1975) 1978. Frege's Distinction between Sense and Reference." Reprinted in *Truth and Other Enigmas*. London: Duckworth, 116–44.

———. 1991. *The Logical Basis of Metaphysics*. London: Duckworth.

———. 1993. *Origins of Analytical Philosophy*. London: Duckworth.

———. 2001. *La natura e il futuro della filosofia*. Genova: Il Melangolo.

Egerton, J. 1995. *Turner: The Fighting Temeraire*. Making and Meaning Series. London: National Gallery Publications.

Frege, G. 1879. *Begriffsschrift: Eine der arithmetischen nachgebildete Formelsprache des reinen Denkens*. Halle: Nebert, English trans. in Beaney 1997.

———. 1884. *Die Grundlagen der Arithmetik*. Breslau: Koeber. *Centenarausgabe* ed. Christian Thiel. 1986. Hamburg: Meiner; English trans. in Beaney 1997.

———. 1891. *Function und Begriff*. Jena: H. Pohle. Reprinted in Frege 1984.

———. 1892. *Über Sinn und Bedeutung*. "Zeitschrift für Philosophie und philosophische Kritik." 100, 25–50. Reprinted in Frege 1984; English trans. in Beaney 1997.

———. 1893–1903. *Grundgesetze der Arithmetik*. Vol. 1 1893. Vol. II 1903. Jena: Pohle.

———. 1897. *Über die Begriffsschrift des Herrn Peano und meine eigene*, in "Berichte über die Verhandlungen der königlich sächsischen Gesellschaft der Wissenschaften zu Leipzig. Mathematisch-Physische Klasse," 48. Band. 361–78, in Frege 1967, 220–33.

———. 1918. *Der Gedanke. Eine logische Untersuchung*, in Beiträge zur Philosophie des Deutschen Idealismus, I, 58–77. English trans. in Beaney 1997.

———. 1918/9. *Die Verneinung, Eine logische Untersuchung*, in *Beiträge zur Philosophie des Deutschen Idealismus*, I, 143–57. English trans. in Beaney 1997.

———. 1923–26. *Logische Untersuchungen. Dritter Teil: Gedankengefüge*, in *Beiträge zur Philosophie des Deutschen Idealismus*, III, 36–51. English trans. in Beaney 1997.

———. 1967. *Kleine Schriften*, ed. I. Angelelli. Hildesheim: Olms. Second ed. 1990. English edition by B. McGuinness, *Collected Papers on Mathematics, Logic, and Philosophy*. Oxford: Blackwell, 1984.

———. 1969. *Nachgelassene Schriften*, ed. H. Hermes, et al. Hamburg: Meiner. English trans. by P. Long and R. White, *Posthumous Writings*. Oxford: Blackwell, 1979.

———. 1976. *Wissenschaftlicher Briefwechsel*, ed. G. Gabriel, H. Hermes, F. Kambartel, C. Thiel, and A. Veraart. Hamburg: Meiner. English ed. abridged by B. McGuinness and translated by H. Kaal, *Philosophical and Mathematical Correspondence*. Oxford: Blackwell, 1980.

Grice, H. P. 1989. *Studies in the Ways of Words*. Cambridge, MA: Harvard Univ. Press.

Kripke, S. 1979. "A Puzzle about Belief." In *Meaning and Use*, ed. A. Margalit. Dordrecht: Reidel, 239–83.

Joyce, J. 1916 (1976). *A Portrait of the Artist as a Young Man*. London: Penguin Books.

Levinson, S. 2000. *Presumptive Meanings: The Theory of Generalized Conversational Implicature*. Cambridge, MA: MIT Press.

MacIntyre, A. 1984. "Relativism, Power, and Philosophy." Reprinted in *Relativism, Interpretation and Confrontation*, ed. M. Krausz. Notre Dame, IN: Univ. of Notre Dame Press, 1989, 182–204.

Neale, S. 2001. "Implicature and Colouring." In *Paul Grice's Heritage*, ed. G. Cosenza. Turnhout: Brepols, 138–84.

Picardi, E. 2001. "Compositionality." In *Paul Grice's Heritage*, ed. G. Cosenza. Turnhout: Brepols, 52–72.

———. 2005. "Was Frege a Proto-Inferentialist?" In *Facets of Concepts*, ed. J. J. Acero and P. Leonardi. Padova: Il Poligrafo, 31–46.

Prior, A. 1960. "The Runabout Inference-Ticket." *Analysis* 21, no. 2: 38–39.

Quine, W.V.O. 1960. *Word & Object*. Cambridge, MA: Harvard Univ. Press.

Recanati, F. 2004. *Literal Meaning*. Cambridge: Cambridge Univ. Press.

Richard, M. 1997. "Propositional Attitudes." In *A Companion to the Philosophy of Language*, ed. B. Hale and C. Wright. Oxford: Blackwell, 197–226.

Salmon, N. 1986. *Frege's Puzzle*. Cambridge, MA: MIT Press.

Salmon, N. and S. Soames, eds. 1988. *Propositions and Attitudes*. Oxford: Oxford Univ. Press.

Schulte, J. 1993. *Experience and Expression*. Oxford: Clarendon Press.

Stanley, J. 1997. *Rigidity and Content*. In *Language, Thought and Logic*: *Essays in Honour of Michael Dummett*, ed. R. Heck. Oxford: Clarendon Press, 131–56.

———. 2001. "Context and Logical Form." In *Linguistics and Philosophy* 23, no. 4: 391–434.

Travis, C. 2000. *Unshadowed Thought*. Cambridge, MA: Harvard Univ. Press.

Williams, M. 2004. "Context, Meaning and Truth." *Philosophical Studies* 117: 107–29.

Williamson, T. 2003. "Blind Reasoning: Understanding and Inference." *Proceedings of the Aristotelian Society*, 249–93.

Wittgenstein, L. 1953. *Philosophische Untersuchungen/ Philosophical Investigations*, ed. G.E.M. Anscombe and R. Rhees. Oxford: Blackwell.

REPLY TO EVA PICARDI

My thanks go to Eva Picardi for her bold incursion into a difficult area, largely neglected by philosophers or consigned by them to the ragbag category of pragmatics, but of great interest to literary critics. This is that of what I, perhaps ill-advisedly, labelled "tone" and Frege called "*Färbung*" and "*Beleuchtung*." She comes back from her expedition with a rich booty.

I will not entangle myself in the web which she first spins with the name of the *Téméraire*. About her first section, I shall say only the following. First, Stephen Neale's suggestion that the name "Hesperus" should be explained as meaning "the planet called 'Hesperus'" surely commits a well-known mistake. For the description to apply to anything, there must be some people who call a particular planet "Hesperus"; if no one used the name "Hesperus" save as meaning "the planet called 'Hesperus'," then nobody would call any particular planet "Hesperus."

I applaud Eva Picardi's two "surmises," that co-designative proper names can differ both in sense and in tone, and that the difference in tone survives the discovery that names with different senses are co-designative. The notion of an *aura* of a proper name, or indeed of another word, is very compelling. The problem is to state in what it consists.

Eva Picardi quotes me as distinguishing between the evocative and expressive powers of language by the fact that the latter depends upon the perceived intention of the speaker, whereas to the evocative effect his intention is irrelevant. When someone refers to Mrs. Rosa Parks as "Mrs. Parks," he manifests an intention to accord her respect; when a white Southerner counters by calling her "Rosa Parks," he shows his intention to treat her with disrespect, even though that is what many people nowadays (in Britain, at least) would put on an envelope without intending disrespect. But would it not be better to say that the expressive effect of a form of words depends upon the prevailing social conventions, rather than on the intentions of the speaker?

I said also that the evocative effect of a word or phrase may depend upon the personal associations of the hearer. But it often is common to every hearer or reader, and depends not on his individual experience but on the uses of a word or phrase customary in the language. A bird is not born, but hatched. But if in the line in Keats's "Ode to a Nightingale"

Thou wast not born for death, immortal bird

the word "born" were replaced by "hatched," the effect would be ludicrous. No one could doubt this, but why is it so? It is precisely because of what Eva Picardi calls the "auras" of the two words. The word "hatched" very naturally calls up in our minds the process of hatching—the cracking of the shell, the clumsy emergence of the bedraggled chick. But the word "born" does not ordinarily call up in the same way the messy process of birth. Its aura is given to it by the most familiar contexts in which it is used. We think of being born as the beginning of an individual's life, as in "born 1848," "Unto us a child is born," "A son has been born to them," and also "It would have been better for that man if he had never been born." It is strongly connected with parentage and initial position in the world—"nobly born," "born with a silver spoon in his mouth," "born of Mary." It is connected with the destiny of the individual:

> Every Night & every Morn
> Some to Misery are Born.
> Every Morn & every Night
> Some are Born to sweet delight.[1]

It may even be an unfulfilled destiny, as in "the lad that was born to be king." This is the association Keats exploits in the line from the "Ode to a Nightingale." No dictionary will inform those who consult it of this difference between "hatched" and "born," as it will probably inform them of the insulting, contemptuous, or obscene character of a word. A child who has come across a word having one of these characters and asks what it means will need to be told that it has that character; but you cannot tell anyone the difference between the auras of "hatched" and "born," and you do not need to. "Born" acquires its aura from its most familiar uses, which in no way contradict its literal meaning—its sense—but direct attention towards consequences of a birth rather than its circumstances.

Professor Picardi ends her first section by announcing that she will discuss two questions: Is there a uniform way of drawing the distinction between sense and tone for various categories of words? And is there room for drawing a distinction between the sense and tone of proper names?

She addresses the former question first. Before doing so, she interpolates, in her second section, a methodological observation. It is that there is no way of deciding what proposition a sentence expresses save within the framework of a particular theory of meaning. With this I am in full agreement.

In her third section, Professor Picardi surveys the application of the notion of tone to a large range of expressions other than proper names. She begins by noting Frege's criterion for a difference in sense, namely that "a special act of cognition" is required to recognise that two words have the same reference (*Bedeutung*). If no such act is required, the difference, if any, will be only one of tone. She quotes Frege as saying that tone is a subjective property, and as observing that tone often cannot be preserved in translating from one language to another. She rightly repudiates the former contention, saying that "tone is as much a conventional and objective feature of word meaning as sense is." Although people do sometimes attach personal associations to words, it is by and large true that tone is objective; how could Frege have maintained otherwise when considering the difference in meaning between "and" and "but"? Eva Picardi agrees with me that Frege mischaracterised the difference of tone between "and" and "but" (or "although"): a contrast is indeed hinted at, but it may be a contrast in *any* respect. It is the indefiniteness that makes the difference one of tone rather than of sense. If what was hinted or suggested were a definite proposition, the question would arise how there could be a distinction between what a sentence served to say and what it merely served to suggest.

Does the conjunction "and" of natural language express the connective "&" of formal logic (whether classical or intuitionistic), or does it carry the sense of temporal succession or of causal connection? As Professor Picardi says, Paul Grice wished to take its literal sense to be that of logical conjunction, but to regard it as frequently carrying an implicature of temporal succession or of causal connection. Gricean implicature falls under the head of tone, since it does not contribute to the truth-condition of the sentence. She objects to Grice's analysis on the ground that the truth-value of a conditional sentence of natural language may change according to the order of the conjuncts in the antecedent. The example Professor Picardi uses is taken from Neale: "If B yells and A hits B, C will punish A and B" and "If A hits B and B yells, C will punish A and B" may well have different truth-values. Gricean implicature must attach to the whole sentence, not to a clause within it (though it may be *due* to the presence in the sentence of some word, phrase, clause, or syntactic construction.) Professor Picardi then offers the Gricean an escape from this objection by appealing to my distinction between assertoric content and ingredient sense: he might hold that the assertoric content of a conjunctive sentence of natural language should be taken as that expressed by the logical connective, while its ingredient sense imports a temporal or causal component, at least when it forms the antecedent of a conditional. This proposal is perfectly credible in principle. The assertoric content of a sentence does not determine its ingredient sense, and there is no reason why the latter may not incorporate what only belonged to the tone of the sentence when uttered on its own to make an assertion. But, as Eva Picardi says, the proposal rests on the claim that the assertoric content of a sentence of natural language whose principal operator is "and" is just that of logical conjunction. May it not be that the outright assertions "B yelled and A hit B" and "A hit B and B yelled" have different truth-values? If you judged the second true, would you have to concede the truth of the first as well?

Concerning the implication of temporal succession, I am in full agreement with Professor Picardi: Grice's interpretation, however glossed, will not work. What he takes as the content of an implicature is in fact part of the sense. It is surely right to say that in the context of a narrative, however brief, "and" has the sense of "and then." When its sense is to be reduced to that of conjunction in the logical sense, some phrase cancelling the temporal implication, such as "at the same time" or "meanwhile," must be inserted. It is because we are unfamiliar with the idea that an ingredient of a word's sense can be cancelled, as an implicature can be cancelled, that we are inclined to assign the temporal implication to the tone of the word "and," not to its sense in this type of context. But it can hardly be denied that it is one of the conventions governing narrative discourse that, unless otherwise stated, events are retailed in the order in which they are thought to have happened. No one, accused of having said that B had yelled when A had hit him, could get away with the plea that he had merely said that A hit B and that B yelled.

The causal implication is more tenuous. It is true that one who had said, "A hit B and B yelled," could not convincingly claim that he had not said that B yelled because A hit him; but the correct rejoinder would be, "You didn't say it, but you implied it." We cannot say that it is a convention of narrative that each event is to be considered the effect of the previously recounted one, even if they were separated by no interval. So this is no more than an implicature, if not cancelled by "but not for that reason." It occurs when a causal connection is highly plausible, whether the events are narrated in successive sentences or in a single sentence containing "and." I have here myself adopted Grice's notion of implicature, which I have little doubt describes a genuine phenomenon; but the notion can by no means be made to explain everything falling for Frege under the head of tone.

Professor Picardi introduces Frege's notion of *Nebengedanken* (accompanying thoughts). A *Nebengedanke* is a full-fledged *Gedanke* (thought or proposition) and (normally) has a truth-value. There are two distinct cases. In one this accompanying thought is part of the sense of what is said. Frege cites two clear examples. In a sentence such as "Galileo knew that the Earth went round the Sun," we express two thoughts: that Galileo held that the Earth went round the Sun; and that the Earth indeed goes round the Sun. Both must be true for the whole complex thought to be true. The second of the two thoughts is a *Nebengedanke*; it is conveyed by the use of the verb "to know." (Frege notes that, in accordance with his mechanism for explaining clauses in indirect speech, the clause "the Earth went round the Sun" has to be taken twice over, once with its direct *Bedeutung*, as having a truth-value and expressing the accompanying thought, and once with its indirect *Bedeutung*, as referring to that accompanying thought; but this need not detain us.) The other clear example is that of sentences with causal clauses. The sentence "Ice floats on water because it is less dense than water" expresses *three* thoughts—as Frege says, more thoughts than clauses: the whole sentence is false if any one of these three thoughts is false. They are: that ice floats on water; that ice is less dense than water; and that something's being less dense than water causes it to float on water. (Frege renders this last by a generalised conditional, "If anything is less dense than water, it floats on water"; but there is no need for us, in considering the linguistic point, to involve ourselves in controversy about the notion of causality.) The grammatical conjunction "because" imports the third, accompanying, thought into the sense of the whole.

The other case is that in which the *Nebengedanke* is *not* part of the sense of the whole. Professor Picardi cites an example discussed by Frege: suppose someone says "Napoleon, who recognised the danger to his right flank, personally led his guards against the enemy position." No one hearing such an assertion could avoid thinking that he was being told that it was because Napoleon recognised the danger to his right flank that he personally led his guards against the enemy position—a *Nebengedanke*. Frege raises the question whether the quoted statement could still count as true if it could be shown that Napoleon decided to lead his guards personally against the enemy position before he was aware of the danger to his right flank. If it could, then the *Nebengedanke* is merely suggested by the statement, not included in the thought it expressed. This would then count as an example of tone, and a further instance of implicature.

But what provides room for a distinction between what is asserted and what is merely suggested, implicated, or (in a colloquial sense) implied? If an assertion causes everyone who knows the language and believes what was said to suppose that a certain state of affairs obtains, why do we not count it as a part of what was asserted that that state of affairs obtained? What provides room for the distinction between asserting and suggesting is the phenomenon of cancellation. Suppose a speaker utters a sentence S assertorically, thereby asserting that P and suggesting, as an implicature, that Q. It proves to be true that P but false that Q. It is agreed that the speaker misled his hearers by inducing them to believe that Q. But suppose that we, the hearers, are pressed—say by counsel in a court of law—to say whether or not the speaker told the truth by saying S. The fact that the implicature could have been cancelled, though it was not, and that then the utterance would have been unequivocally judged true or false according to whether it was true or false that P, exerts a strong influence on our judgement of the truth or falsity of *S*, though it contained no cancellation. Whether what the speaker actually *said* was true or false is, we feel, to be judged according to what would have remained if the implicature had been cancelled, even though it was not in fact cancelled. This is the reason for our favouring the judgement that what the speaker actually *said* was not untrue.

For a Gricean this account is back to front. He starts with a hypothesis that the statement is true in such-and-such circumstances and false in such-and-such other circumstances. He notes that most hearers will take the statement as conveying more than that the condition he has hypothesised for its truth is satisfied. He explains this as the hearers' surmising the reason for the speaker's expressing himself as he did, rather than by saying something stronger or simpler. He calls this the implicature of the utterance, and notes that it can be cancelled by a certain type of context in which the statement was made, or by certain additional words that could have been added. But what is the ground for his assigning that truth-condition he hypothesised at the outset? It is precisely that that would be the truth-condition of the statement if the implicature were cancelled. So his analysis after all agrees with that in the foregoing account. The difference is only that the Gricean started with theory whereas I started with practice.

The account does not apply to the cancellation of components of the sense. "The President shouted 'Hooligans' and his wig fell off" is just false if the President's wig fell off before he shouted "Hooligans"; "and" here has the sense of "and then." The temporal sense of "and" could have been cancelled by the insertion of "perhaps before, perhaps afterwards" after "and," but it was not. The sense of the sentence determines the thought it expresses, and it is this we judge true or false. But we can see from this why the cancellation of a component of the sense is a rare phenomenon. It sets up a conflict in our intuitive judgements of truth and falsity.

Eva Picardi remarks that Frege subsumed the notion of the *point* of an utterance under that of a *Nebengedanke*. The thought, "Why did the speaker say just that, rather than this?", is one Grice uses to explain many cases of implicature; but this is a different question from "Why did the speaker say something with that assertoric content at that stage of the conversation/discussion?" The latter question asks what the speaker was driving at—was he giving an example, making a concession, changing the subject, or doing one of many other things? It asks for the point of the utterance at a different level, and surely has little or nothing to do with *Nebengedanken*.

Eva Picardi now comes on to differences in tone that may be said to reflect differences in the auras of words, to use the immensely helpful concept to which she had earlier appealed. As she shows, it is not clear whether "dog" and "cur" have just the same sense, differing only in tone. If someone says, "He's not a cur: he won 'Best Dog in Show' at Cruft's last year," is his objection sound or irrelevant? It is probably irrelevant; people often repudiate by means of a negation the application of a term to themselves or to something to which they are attached. I was told of a woman who said, in this spirit, "I am not a person." Still, it is not clear whether a winner at Cruft's dog show may not properly be called a "cur" or cannot even truly be called a "cur." Frege's test of whether the truth-value is affected by the substitution of one word for another does not always yield unequivocal results.

Eva Picardi extends her doubts about Frege's doctrine to pejorative expressions, in particular those applying to racial, national, and religious groups of people. It seems to me that we need to make a firm distinction between any individual's active and his passive grasp of a language, particularly his mother tongue. The word "Kike" will not belong to the active vocabulary of anyone who abhors racist epithets; but it may well belong to his passive vocabulary—he may well know what it means when used by somebody else. He knows its application—that it applies, namely, to Jews—and he knows the attitude of dislike and contempt it expresses. In that its application is the same as that of "Jew," it must be said to have the same sense as that word. If he were to say, "He is not a Kike," he would not be denying that the person referred to was a Jew: he would be repudiating the use of the term. If he said, "I did not say that he was a Kike," he would be disavowing its use. Here would be a case in which a word in indirect speech did not serve solely to pick out its sense.

How should we characterise pejorative and derogatory expressions? Frege's explanation of the notion of tone is inadequate for the purpose. It is useless to demand of someone who regards a word as unwarrantably offensive that he agree that a sentence S containing it has the same truth-value as some sentence differently expressed. He will not say that S is true: he will simply say, "I should never say that" or "No one should ever say that." The sense/tone distinction can be drawn only within the range of what it is permissible to say.

The use of a pejorative expression certainly cannot be said to affect the truth-value of an utterance; it affects its propriety. But, for the same reason, it also cannot simply be explained as affecting the tone of the utterance, or as attaching an implicature to it. I am not altogether clear about Professor Picardi's conclusion on the matter. But for myself I think that the offensive character of certain terms should be accounted for by the license they give their user to draw inappropriate inferences, thus creating a disharmony between grounds and consequences. If this is right, we need a notion of sense as determined not solely by truth-conditions but also by inferential consequences. This would not obliterate the distinction between sense and tone, or even that between asserting and suggesting implicit in the machinery of implicature; by no means every linguistic phenomenon explained as implicature on the Gricean model creates a disharmony between grounds and consequences.

Words often acquire an offensive or contemptuous aura. Neither the word "Asiatic" nor the word "Chinaman" was originally offensive to anyone. "China" was originally the standard form of the adjective in English, as in "China tea" (the alternative being "Indian tea," not "India tea"). Both words came to seem insulting, and were replaced by "Asian" and "Chinese" (originally denoting only the language). A Chinese-American friend of ours described how he arrived late for an appointment with his (white) girl friend, and offered as an excuse that he had been shopping at the Oriental Supermarket. His girl friend said, "Shh! You mustn't use that word." "But that's what it's called," he protested.

Professor Picardi's final section is devoted to a penetrating consideration of proper names. "Téméraire" and "Temeraire" certainly differ in both sense and tone. I doubt that "Waterloo" and "Belle Alliance," considered as names of battles, differ in more than tone; surely anyone who knows both names knows that they denote the same battle (there was only one battle at which Napoleon was defeated before being sent to St. Helena). But the whole topic of different proper names for the same place, favoured by different people, a topic thoroughly explored by Eva Picardi, is a fascinating one. Here the distinction between people's active and passive vocabulary demands to be invoked. All this applies as much to general words for members of different national or ethnic groups as much as to place-names. There are different names in different languages for particular places (London, Londres, Londra); Italian is particularly rich in native forms of the names of foreign cities (Zurigo, Stoccarda, Francoforte). Now we have the phenomenon of demands by certain nations that everybody else should adopt their names or forms of names for their own countries and cities (Mumbai, Beijing, Myanmar).

Eva Picardi interestingly draws attention to the use of different place-names by different groups of people for essentially political, or perhaps only sentimental reasons. This phenomenon also occurs for names of different national, racial, and religious groups; it calls out for the application of the distinction between active and passive vocabularies. As Professor Picardi points out with her excellent example of "Catinaccio" and "Rosengarten," the names may differ not only in the political allegiance they convey, but also in their auras. Two people's active vocabularies may include neither of the names in their intersection, although the intersection of their passive vocabularies contains both.

I recently heard someone interviewed on television about the value of geography as a school subject. She asked, "Why do I have to know where places are, or how to draw a map showing them? If I want to go to a place, I go to the travel agent and book a flight there." The aeroplane, which lifts us out of the dimension in which we live our lives, has brought about an utterly impoverished understanding of place-names and of a sense of place. Eva Picardi rightly says that we cannot talk of a partial grasp of the significance of a place-name, because there is no such thing as a total grasp of it. But we can talk of a defective grasp of it. What should we say of someone's understanding of the name "Rome" who has never heard of the Roman Empire or of the Roman Church?

"Morgenstern" and "Abendstern" differed in sense, at least until the general realisation that they denoted the same planet; as Eva Picardi brings out in detail, they differ greatly in tone also. As she says, they have different auras. I think the notion of aura more useful than that of evocative effect, which it subsumes; it is not only broader but deeper. Words, including proper names, acquire auras from the uses of them with which we are familiar; differences of aura are often subtle, as with the auras of "born" and "hatched." In her essay Eva Picardi does not do a great deal with the concept of the aura of a word which she there introduces; but it is a notable addition to our repertoire nonetheless.

M. D.

NOTE

1. William Blake, "Auguries of Innocence."

15

Richard G. Heck, Jr.

USE AND MEANING

I. OPENING

Many philosophers have found themselves tempted by the view that meaning is, in some way or other, determined by use—which claim I shall call the Use-Meaning Thesis. Stated in such general terms, of course, the Thesis is merely programmatic. Until it is said what use is supposed to be—that is, in what terms use is to be characterized—and how use is supposed to determine meaning, it can function at most as a framework principle. The Thesis will thus admit of a wide range of specifications, depending upon how the notion of meaning is explained and how use is thought to determine meaning, as well as upon how the notion of use itself is understood. My purpose in the present essay is to begin to clarify the Thesis by focusing on this last issue and, more specifically, upon the questions of what different characterizations of use might be available and how a choice among them might be made.

I intend to approach these questions by considering John McDowell's claim[1] that anyone who would attempt to develop the Use-Meaning Thesis will face a dilemma when forced to answer the question whether use encompasses the *contents* expressed by utterances. If it does, then the right way to describe the use of a sentence will be in terms of what it can be used to say: the sentence 'Snow is white', for example, is used to express the thought that snow is white. But then, although the Thesis will surely be *true*—the meaning of a sentence can be taken to be the thought it is used to express—it will not be particularly likely to have far-reaching philosophical consequences. On the other hand, if the notion of use is not, in this sense, "meaning-laden," it is hard to see how use should be explained, if the use of a sentence is not to be characterized in broadly Quinean terms, that is, in terms of the noises people make and the circumstances under which they make them. But then, the Use-Meaning Thesis will commit us to a behavioristic reduction of meaning, which few nowadays would find appealing. The challenge McDowell poses, and which I want here to take up, is thus to explain how the Thesis can be both substantial and plausible, that is, to identify a notion of use that is non-behavioristic but not meaning-laden.

II. USE AS MEANING: METAPHYSICAL, NOT EPISTEMOLOGICAL

No one has done more to contribute to the development of the Use-Meaning Thesis than Michael Dummett, and it is with Dummett's conception of it, and its significance, that McDowell's reflections begin. According to McDowell, Dummett's refusal to countenance a meaning-laden notion of use is, at bottom, driven by a flawed epistemology of understanding. On this picture, when someone makes an utterance, what are immediately available to other speakers are simply facts about what sounds were produced under what circumstances. The epistemological problem facing speakers is to reconstruct from this meager data the meanings carried by the sounds. One might call this picture of understanding the "sense-datum conception of understanding," for it is, as McDowell emphasizes, analogous to the picture of perception found in sense-datum epistemologies. In that case, what are immediately available to me are but facts about my own experiential states, and my problem is to determine what my having these states might tell me about the external world. It is the corresponding picture, in the case of understanding, that is supposed to motivate Dummett's own conception of use, which must now be the Quinean one mentioned above. The use someone makes of a sentence is to be characterized behavioristically, in terms of the sounds she produces and the conditions under which she does so—in terms that do not involve the notion of meaning, nor any psychological notions at all. For the problem is to show how one can get from the data immediately available in experience, itself conceived along broadly empiricist lines, to knowledge of what is said.[2]

It is worth emphasizing, before we move on, that the analogy between understanding and perception cuts both ways. McDowell wants to argue, in the perceptual case, that once we recognize that we literally *see*, say, that there is a lamp on the desk—that experience provides us with such conceptual contents—we should no longer concern ourselves with questions about what determines perceptual content.[3] McDowell seems to think that one can only take seriously the question what it is for particular experiences to have the contents they do if one thinks that experience *as such*, as it is in itself, is content-free. The problem then becomes to explain how we, as perceivers, can *assign* content to experiences that, in and of themselves, are without it, are mere subjective happenings. But the question what determines perceptual content is independent of the question whether experience *has* content, as it is in itself. We could, so far as I can see, even concede that an experience could not be the very experience it was without having the very content it did, and yet raise the question what determined its content, or what determined that someone had an experience with *that* content rather than some other. The present discussion of the case of understanding may therefore teach us lessons that can also be applied to the case of perception.[4]

McDowell argues in detail that the sense-datum conception of understanding is untenable, and I have no wish to quarrel with him. It is obviously incorrect, phenomenologically speaking, that we simply hear other speakers as making noises. We literally hear them as having *said* certain things, for example, that snow is white.[5] And if the only reason to insist upon a "meaning-free" description of use were epistemological prejudice, such conceptions of use would have to be rejected. But there is an answer to this argument of McDowell's: that a rejection of meaning-laden notions of use need not be founded upon any epistemological doctrine, prejudicial or otherwise, but should rest upon a conception of the *purpose* of the Use-Meaning Thesis. McDowell's discussion makes it seem as if the Thesis is a doctrine about how we, as speakers, are able to determine what others mean. But, properly understood, it proposes a framework for answering the question *what it is* for expressions to mean what they do, what determines what they mean, in a metaphysical sense.

That is to say, the Use-Meaning Thesis is not an epistemological doctrine, but a metaphysical one.[6] So the appropriateness of a particular conception of use for specifying the Thesis needs to be evaluated in terms of the metaphysical purposes for which it is wanted. We are not free to select any conception we please, however phenomenologically or epistemologically appealing it might be. To characterize use in terms that incorporate the notion of what a sentence means is to trivialize the metaphysical project to which the Thesis is intended as a contribution. Obviously, if we use the sentence 'Snow is white' to express the thought that snow is white, no theory that says it means something else can be correct; just as obviously, nothing of metaphysical interest follows. So a conception of use fit to serve the purposes the Thesis is intended to serve cannot help itself to facts about the meanings of sentences or other expressions. (It is another question, of course, what an appropriate notion of use might look like—a question to which I shall turn in the next section.)

Now, McDowell could (and, I think, would) concede that the Use-Meaning Thesis is intended to be a metaphysical principle in this sense. His view, as I understand it, is that the impression that there is a substantial question what it is for words to mean what they do depends somehow upon the sense-datum conception of understanding. And so, he might say, I have done nothing to rebut his argument, since I have not provided any alternative way of motivating this problem, that is, of explaining why one ought to think *there is* a problem about what it is for words to mean what they do. But I find it difficult to understand how liberation from the sense-datum conception is supposed to dissolve this problem—and it is even harder to know how to evaluate a claim of this kind. And, although I believe there is more that could be said to motivate the metaphysical project, one part of me wants simply to say that it is *obvious* that there is a real problem about the nature of meaning and that, if one wants to insist upon assigning the burden of proof here, it is far from clear that it should not go to McDowell.

But this response would miss part of McDowell's point, for he does offer positive reasons to think that the question what it is for expressions to mean what they do need not be taken seriously. What I shall claim in response is that his arguments rest upon a confusion about the nature of "homophonic" theories of truth—theories whose meta-languages include their object-languages—and upon a failure to appreciate the distinction between two different, but intimately related, sorts of questions: *semantic* questions, such as what the reference of a particular expression is, or what logical form a particular sort of sentence should be taken to have; and *meta-semantic* questions, such as what it is for a particular expression to have the reference that it does. As I shall suggest below, part of the problem here is an ambiguity in the term "theory of meaning." I shall use the term "theory of truth" to refer to *semantic* theories and the term "theory of meaning" to refer to *meta-semantic* theories.

It would be wrong to say that McDowell does not recognize this distinction at all, or that he rejects meta-semantic questions as unintelligible (though he does sometimes give that impression). In fact, he does offer an answer to the question of what it is for a sentence to mean what it does, namely: A sentence S means that *p* if and only if the assumption that S means that *p*

> should fit coherently into a wider context, in which the speakers' behavior in general, including both their linguistic behavior, under those descriptions, and their non-linguistic behavior, under suitable descriptions, can be made sufficiently intelligible in light of propositional attitudes . . . whose ascription to them is sufficiently intelligible in light of their behavior, again, and of the facts which impinge on them.[7]

McDowell's answer to the meta-semantic question is thus a *thin* one: To say that 'snow is white' means that snow is white is just to say that taking it to mean that makes speakers "sufficiently intelligible."

Once we recognize this point, though, it becomes somewhat hard to understand how McDowell can make the sorts of epistemological objections he does to Dummett's position. Some of McDowell's writings make it seem that he takes Dummett's claim—that facts about what speakers mean by a given sentence are constituted by facts about how they use it—to be undermined by the observation that our *apprehension* of what speakers mean is in no way dependent upon our *apprehension* of how they use it. But if that were his objection, it would apply equally to his own position. My knowing that some stranger means that snow is white when he says "snow is white" does not seem to depend upon my knowing that he would be made sufficiently intelligible by this hypothesis. The objection McDowell means to raise therefore must be sought elsewhere.

McDowell is impressed by a certain feature of homophonic theories of truth, and he suggests that attention to this feature of them, together with recognition that homophonic theories are as good as any, will encourage the proper attitude towards the ambitions of the theory of meaning.[8] The thought here is that a theory of truth that reports such facts as

(1) 'Snow is white' is true if and only if snow is white

does not invite perplexity about what it might be for it to be correct: it wears its correctness on its face, as it were.[9] For it is obviously a necessary condition on the correctness of a homophonic theory that it prove homophonic T-sentences, that is, theorems like (1). And if, as one might well think,[10] the theory's meeting this condition were not only necessary but sufficient for its correctness, there would be no deep meta-semantic question to be raised about it: the theory will be correct if and only if it proves all homophonic T-sentences; whether it does so is a *formal* matter, something that can be decided simply by looking at its syntax.[11] But if the correctness of the theory is, in that sense, obvious, it is hard to see why the question *what it is* for the theory to assign the right references to expressions should be taken seriously. The sort of meta-semantic question McDowell finds intelligible therefore has a trivial answer.

I do not want to object to McDowell's claim that the correctness of a homophonic theory of truth can, in a certain sense, be purely determined by reflection. It is worth noting, however, that, in establishing the truth of (1) by such reflection, we draw upon information that is not contained in it. One must realize that the sentence named on the left-hand side is the same as the sentence used on the right—and not just that it is the same sentence, in a syntactic sense, but that it has the same meaning. Nothing in the T-sentence tells one that: One could have a perfectly good understanding of the sentence itself and yet not realize that the same sentence is both used and mentioned. One can build this information into the T-sentence this way:

> (2) The sentence on the right-hand side of this very biconditional is true, in the very language I am now speaking, if and only if snow is white.

And it is at least arguable that the truth of (2) will be completely obvious to anyone who understands it, although it is in fact equivalent to the original T-sentence (1), as that sentence is intended to be understood.

Note, however, that the fact reported by (1), and so by (2), is contingent.[12] It is obviously a contingent fact about my idiolect that the sentence 'Snow is white' is true in it if and only if snow is white.[13] It is this sort of fact that a theory of truth will report and partially explain by deriving it from other facts about the meanings of sub-sentential expressions and grammatical constructions; and it is this contingent fact that (1) and (2) report. This would once have been confusing: how can it be *both* that (1) is contingent *and* that its correctness can be determined simply by reflection? But, thanks to Kripke, this is now a familiar sort of puzzle. Consider the sentence 'I am here'. Just by reflecting upon it, one can easily convince oneself that any utterance of it must be true. And yet the fact such an utterance would report would (typically) be contingent. That is to say, any particular utterance of the sentence would provide one with an example of a contingent a priori truth. Whether one really wants to say that T-sentences like (1) and (2) are contingent a priori (perhaps they are not really a priori at all), they are cut from the same cloth: They are sentences whose truth can be determined purely by reflection, and yet the facts they report are contingent ones.

McDowell's view, as said above, is that, once we see that there is no reason not to state a theory of truth as a homophonic theory, and see also that the correctness of a homophonic theory is something that is obvious to anyone who understands it, we ought to realize that there can be no serious question about what it is for it to be correct. But this argument finishes with a non sequitur. If someone asks "Why am I here?" it is no answer to tell her that 'here' conventionally refers to the place of utterance.[14] She knew *that*. She wanted to know why she was in the place she happened to be at that time, which she picked out via the word 'here'. And if someone asks "Why is 'Snow is white' true if and only if snow is white?" it is no answer to tell him that the word 'true' is conventionally used so as to sustain disquotation. He knew *that*. What he wanted to know was why the truth of the sentence 'Snow is white' stands or falls with the whiteness of snow—rather than, say, with the greenness of grass.

These questions should not be confused with the historical question how the sentence 'snow is white' came to mean what it does. That question might be answered etymologically, and, of course, the answer is not likely to be of great philosophical interest. Rather, the question being asked is what it is about an utterance of this sentence that makes it mean anything at all, and what it is that makes it mean the very thing it does. The question, that is to say, is what the relevant difference is between "snow is white" and "blurg is white"; and between "snow is white" and "grass is green."[15] These questions are not themselves philosophical ones. They presumably have answers that will one day be provided by some (perhaps now nonexistent) branch of empirical linguistics. But the problem is not just that we do not know the answers to these questions. It is much worse than that: we do not have even a very good idea what the answers to such questions might look like (which is not to say that no one has any ideas about the matter). We really do not know what properties of the sentence 'snow is white' are semantically significant. And insofar as we do not know that, we do not know how its semantically significant properties, whatever they may be, conspire to fix its meaning. This general ignorance is the source of *philosophical* problems about the nature of linguistic meaning. To ask what properties of an expression contribute to determining its meaning, and how they determine it, is precisely to ask the meta-semantic—that is, the meta-physical—question *what it is* for an expression to mean what it does. The Use-Meaning Thesis, as I understand it, amounts to a rough outline of an answer.

When we raise semantic questions, such as what logical form the sentence 'Snow is white' should be taken to have, we need not simultaneously raise meta-semantic questions, such as what it is for the sentence to have the truth-condition it does. Even if we operate under the assumption that the meta-language extends the object-language, so that the T-sentences the theory proves can be seen to be correct merely by reflection, the problem of constructing a theory of truth (for a natural language) that actually *has* all homophonic T-sentences as theorems is nontrivial. And although no serious semantic theory will be close to homophonic (indexicality already makes this impossible),[16] whatever vocabulary is common to the object- and meta-languages is typically assumed to have the same meaning in each. (That assumption will simplify the task of evaluating the theory's correctness, even if it does not reduce it, in all cases, to a problem in proof theory.) But this assumption about common vocabulary does not imply that meta-semantic questions are not there to be raised, and it does not imply that it is legitimate to appeal to the assumption that the meta-language extends the object-language in the context of *meta-semantic* investigations. To appeal to that assumption, and so to answer the question what it is for 'Snow is white' to be true if and only if snow is white by alluding to disquotation, is to fail to answer the question being asked.

It is instructive here to consider Donald Davidson's early writings on the theory of meaning. Discussing homophonic theories of truth, Davidson writes in "Truth and Meaning" that "the trouble is to get a theory that comes close to working; anyone can tell whether it is right."[17] And yet, he also insists that a theory of truth is supposed to be an empirical theory about the semantic properties of the expressions in a particular language. My point is not that Davidson is contradicting himself: we have seen that these views are compatible (if, by an empirical theory, we mean one that states contingent facts about its subject matter).[18] My point, rather, is that Davidson's expressing both of these views is an indication that he is interested in two different projects. The first is the semantic project of actually developing a theory of truth for a natural language, that is, a theory sufficient to yield theorems stating the semantic properties of all expressions of English (and to systematize that collection of facts by deriving those concerning complex expressions from those about their simpler parts). The second is the *meta-semantic* project of answering the question what it is for English expressions to mean what they do.

The two projects are not always clearly distinguished in Davidson's writings, since, for him, they are intimately related. "Truth and Meaning" is, I think it fair to say, most famous for Davidson's having proposed there that a "theory of meaning" may take the form of a Tarskian theory of truth. But something that is, for the most part, only implicit in the paper is more significant. In 1967, semantics was in its infancy, and its influence on philosophy of language was limited. Quine's discussions of the nature of meaning, for example, are quite independent of anything we would recognize as semantics. And yet, Davidson's whole approach, made more explicit in later writings, rests upon the thought that questions about the nature of meaning should be approached by inquiring into the form that might be taken by a complete "theory of meaning"—that is, a semantic theory—for a natural language.[19]

Since a theory of truth, as Davidson conceives it, is a theory that proves sentences giving the meanings of all significant expressions of a given language, the metaphysical question what it is for an expression to mean what it does may be recast as: what is it for a theory of truth to be correct? Asking the question in this way forces us to base our answers to meta-semantic questions upon a conception of what semantic facts *are*, a conception clear enough, at least, for the purpose of developing a compositional theory of meaning for a complete language.[20] Asking the question in this way also enables us to answer the question what it is for 'Snow is white' to be true if and only if snow is white, by addressing the more specific questions what it is for its semantically significant parts to mean what they do and what it is for the modes of composition to have the significance they do. To put the point crisply, Davidson's proposal is that meta-semantics should be *meta* with respect to *semantics*.

And, in the context of the meta-semantic project—which, as argued above, is the only one within which the Use-Meaning Thesis has any place— Davidson commits himself to a version of the Thesis. His view is that the correctness of a theory of truth is determined by the "data" available to a "radical interpreter" prior to, and independently of, any understanding she might have (or come to have) of the language the theory concerns—that is, that a theory of truth's correctness is determined by how the object-language is used, where the notion of use is explained in terms of the data available to a radical interpreter. Davidson explicitly denies that these data include facts about what particular expressions mean. The reason that he restricts his notion of use in this way, and thereby rejects meaning-laden notions of use, is just the one mentioned earlier: to characterize use—that is, the data—in terms of the meanings of sentences would be to trivialize the claim that the semantic properties of expressions are determined by how they are used and, with it, the meta-semantic project of "Radical Interpretation."[21]

If one runs the semantic and meta-semantic projects together in one's mind, it will indeed seem perplexing how one could be interested in homophonic theories of truth, as Davidson is, and yet think, as he also does, that there is a real question about what it is for a theory of truth to be correct, that is, that there is any problem to which the Use-Meaning Thesis might be the solution. But once the distinction between semantics and meta-semantics has been drawn, McDowell's assumption that homophonic theories have any special relevance to meta-semantics can be seen to rest upon a failure to appreciate the distinction. Only if we assume that the meta-language extends the object-language can we reflectively convince ourselves of the truth of homophonic T-sentences—only then will consideration of such theories seem to cast doubt upon the depth of meta-semantic questions. But one cannot appeal to that assumption in answering the meta-semantic questions to which the Use-Meaning Thesis provides an outline of an answer. (That is just to say that the original, flat-footed response to McDowell, that the Use-Meaning Thesis is a metaphysical principle, and not an epistemological one, stands.)

We are now in a position to return to the question on what grounds Dummett rejects meaning-laden notions of use. Dummett is primarily interested in questions about understanding, that is, in questions about linguistic and, specifically, semantic competence. And his proposal is that a speaker's semantic competence should be explained in terms of her knowing a theory of truth for her language, that is, in terms of knowledge she has about her language's semantic properties. Dummett does not, however, mean to be ignoring questions about the nature of meaning: his view, rather, is that "the key to an account of language . . . is the explanation of an individual speaker's mastery of his language."[22] That is to say, he construes the question whether a theory of truth for a given speaker's language is *correct* as the question whether she knows it—whether the theory correctly states what she knows about the semantic properties of her language insofar as she is a competent speaker.[23]

The suggestion that speakers know theories of truth for their languages raises some very hard problems.[24] It is far from clear what it might mean to ascribe knowledge of such a theory to a speaker, since ordinary speakers obviously do not consciously know theories of truth for their languages.[25] Now, the usual alternative is to suppose that such knowledge is *tacit* or *implicit*. But, even if we assume objections to the very intelligibility of the notion of tacit knowledge to have been answered, and even if we assume that we understand in what it might consist that a speaker has tacit knowledge of the semantic structure, or logical form, of sentences,[26] the question remains what it is for a speaker tacitly to know a *particular* theory of truth. For theories of truth may differ, even if they agree about logical form. They may have different axioms, leading the theories to produce different T-sentences as theorems. The theories might produce T-sentences that differ in truth-value, and it has not *even* been said, at this point, what it might be for one, rather than another, of these theories to be that tacitly known by a speaker.[27] Thus, the meta-semantic problems do not vanish once we assume that speakers know theories of truth for their languages; rather, these problems are transformed into questions about what it is for a speaker to know a particular theory of this sort.

Dummett's answer to such questions is offered in passages like the following:

> The philosophical task of explaining in what a mastery of a language consists is not completed when we have set out the theory of meaning for the language. . . . We have to go on to give an account of what it is to have such knowledge. This account can only be given in terms of the practical ability which the speaker displays in using sentences of the language. . . .[28]

Now, it is tempting to interpret Dummett as claiming that a speaker's knowing a particular theory of truth *consists in* her having certain linguistic capacities. And, in "What is a Theory of Meaning?" he writes that a theory of truth is a "theoretical representation of a practical ability," the implication being that a speaker's knowing the theory—that is, her understanding her language—simply consists in her being able to speak it.[29] On this view, the structure the theory assigns to sentences has little purpose other than to articulate this complex ability into component sub-abilities, possession of which constitute the speaker's understanding of the primitive expressions; these sub-abilities then interact, in a way captured by the deductive structure of the theory, to produce other abilities, constituting the speaker's understanding of sentences (and other complex expressions). Talk of a speaker's *knowing* the theory then becomes idiomatic. Speakers know the theory simply in the sense that it articulates an ability they possess, so that someone who *did* know it *would* be able to speak the langauge.

If a theory of truth amounts to an articulation of a speaker's complex ability to speak her language into simpler abilities that jointly constitute it, it must surely follow that the correctness of the theory lies in its correctly characterizing this ability, in a correspondence between the references the theory assigns to the primitive expressions and aspects of the practice itself. That is to say, for Dummett, a description of the use of an expression will be an account of the ability a speaker must possess to understand that expression. How exactly these abilites are to be characterized remains open, but, as with Davidson, what is motivating Dummett's selection of a notion of use are meta-semantic concerns. This may be obscured by the fact that he argues for the Thesis by arguing that we have an obligation to say what it is for a speaker to know such a theory. But, as said above, on Dummett's view, to state the theory known by competent speakers *is* to say what those expressions mean; to say in what it consists that a particular such theory is that known by competent speakers is to say in what it consists for those speakers to mean what they do. Since, on Dummett's view, to know such a theory is to be able to engage in the practice of speaking the language, the description of the practice—that is, of speakers' use of the language— serves to ground an answer to the question what it is for expressions to mean what they do. To describe use in terms of the meanings of expressions would therefore be to render the Use-Meaning Thesis trivial, and *that* is why Dummett rejects meaning-laden notions of use.

III. LANGUAGE, THOUGHT, AND USE

McDowell's challenge was to explain how the Use-Meaning Thesis can be both substantial and plausible. To this point, my task has been primarily defensive: I have argued only that a rejection of meaning-laden notions of use flows from an interest in meta-semantic questions and need not be grounded upon any particular view about the epistemology of understand- ing. But that argument will not matter much unless there are other notions of use available, besides the Quinean one and the meaning-laden one McDowell offers us, and I have yet to argue that there are any other alternatives. It is to that task that I now turn.

One might have hoped that an alternative notion of use could be extracted from the position with which we left Dummett at the end of the last section, from the idea that to understand a language is to possess a practical capacity to speak it. But McDowell's most important objection to Dummett is that no notion of use so obtainable will be different *enough* from Quine's. As McDowell sees it, and I would agree, the problem with the Quinean notion is that if we conceive of the use of language behavioristically, we will be without any explanation of its *rationality*, without any way of recognizing the fact that the use of language is a rational activity on the part of rational agents.[30] And, as McDowell suggests, a similar problem will afflict Dummett's position, that his notion of use too "can be [no] more than a mere description of outward behavior, with the mental . . . aspect of language use left out of account."[31] McDowell's view, of course, is that the only way of "registering the role of mind" in our use of language is by describing use in terms of the contents of speech acts. But once we have a proper understanding of the significance of McDowell's objection, the way to a better account will be clear—or so I shall argue.

Something like McDowell's objection is familiar from the writings of Noam Chomsky, who has argued repeatedly that Dummett's view, like any that identifies linguistic competence with a practical ability to speak a language, fails to make sufficient room for speakers' *knowledge* of their language.[32] As said earlier, if we conceive understanding as a practical ability, talk of a speaker's knowing a theory of meaning becomes a *façon de parler*, and there is a variety of reasons to think we have to take speakers' linguistic knowledge more seriously than that.

Dummett himself has not been insensitive to such concerns.[33] In some of his discussions he expresses the worry that conceiving of understanding as a practical capacity would prohibit us from giving due recognition to the fact that speakers typically know what they mean. Thus, he notes that, on Grice's explanation of conversational implicature, speakers' intentions play a crucial role; and speakers must know what they are saying, and what is being said to them, if Grice's account is to be correct, since only what a speaker *consciously* knows about the meanings of her words can play a role in the formation of her linguistic intentions. We do not recognize the same implicatures in the speech of those whose knowledge of English is poor— because they have no knowledge of the subtleties of meaning necessary for the formation of the requisite intentions.[34]

I do not want to quarrel with Dummett's, or Chomsky's, claim that we should take a speaker's knowledge of her language more seriously than Dummett was once inclined to take it. But I do not think this sort of observation goes to the root of the problem. The problem, as I understand it, does not concern any specifically *linguistic* knowledge we might have, either tacit or conscious, but general facts about how our use of language is integrated with our conscious mental life.[35]

It is not entirely clear what is meant by saying that understanding is a *practical* capacity, but the essential feature of the view, as Dummett conceives it, would appear to be that a practical capacity to do something can be fully characterized in terms independent of the agent's conscious psychological states. Consider, for example, the ability to swim—an example of a practical capacity, if anything is. To swim is, roughly, to locomote in water, so only something capable of locomotion—a creature, let us say—is capable of swimming. But swimming is not necessarily rational action. Fish can swim, and saying that they can does not commit us to viewing them as conscious—let alone rational—creatures. That is not to say that the ability to swim is not to be explained, empirically speaking, in terms of information-processing states within a creature's mind. But there is no reason such states need be accessible to consciousness.

If the use of language were an exercise of a practical capacity in this sense, *what it was* to use language would be fully characterizable in terms independent of a speaker's conscious psychological states. Now, it is true that, in many respects, our ability to use language depends upon sub-personal information-processing. For example, if contemporary linguistic theory is on anything like the right track, our perception of syntactic structure is due to the functioning of complex, and largely innate, systems of whose workings we ordinarily have no conscious knowledge. But our use of language is not all like that.[36] There is a strong intuition that only rational agents are capable of using language, that one is not *using language* unless what one says is connected, in the right kind of way, with what one thinks.

I do not mean here that one ought only to say what one believes; I mean something much more fundamental.[37] It is one thing to suppose us capable of having thoughts we are unable to express in language; but the converse, that we should be capable of *expressing* a content without also being able to *have thoughts* with that same content, is absurd.[38] If our linguistic abilities were really comparable to the ability to swim, then a sentence's having a particular content would be but a matter of our using it in a particular way, where *what it was* to use it in that way would be something that did not require us even to be able to have any thoughts with the content in question. But our use of language is—and if it is to count as use of language at all, must be—integrated with our conscious mental life, at least in the minimal sense that the contents of our utterances must be able to figure in our thoughts. And the fatal problem with the conception of understanding as a practical ability is that it utterly precludes any account of this integration.[39]

If we are to secure language's integration with thought, we must recognize this integration from the very outset. As James Higginbotham puts a similar point, even if our understanding of our language consists in our capacity to use language, the relevant capacity must involve the capacity to *judge* that such-and-such under particular conditions.[40] This observation might well be used to motivate a quite different conception of understanding, and so a correspondingly different conception of use. On this view, our understanding of language depends upon a prior and independent capacity for thought, in the sense that a prior capacity to have thoughts with particular contents is required if one is to be able to use expressions with those same contents; it is this prior capacity that must be invoked if we are to explain what it is for those expressions to have those contents.

One might, indeed, be attracted to such a position for other reasons. The simplest reason is just that beings without language seem to be capable of having certain sorts of thoughts. Pre-verbal children, for example, seem to be able to have thoughts about their mothers, about the colors of objects, and so forth.[41] And if that is right, it would, to say the least, be surprising if the child's developing understanding of her language did not, in some way, exploit her prior capacity for such thoughts. Moreover, there must be a connection between these thoughts and the sentences that come to express them—that, after all, is the point of the remarks about integration above— and one way to secure this connection will be to insist that what it is for the child to mean *red* by 'red' has to be explained in terms of her prior grasp of that very concept, in terms of a connection between her beliefs (and other attitudes) involving this concept and her use of sentences containing the word.[42]

It is important to recognize that assuming a prior grasp of content does not dispose of the meta-semantic question what it is for an expression to mean what it does. The assumption that Kurt can entertain the *thought* that snow is white does not, of itself, yield any answer to the question what it is for him to express that thought by means of some form of words.[43] Indeed, what Dummett takes to be the fatal objection to such views is precisely that they offer no answer to this question—none more promising, in any event, than is contained in the thought that we manage, somehow or other, to "associate" the content with the linguistic expression.[44]

But Dummett wrongly supposes that such views *can* give no answer to this question because he overlooks the fact that it is possible *both* to accept the priority of thought over language *and* to embrace the Use-Meaning Thesis. To do so, one need only insist that use be characterized in terms of the contents of mental states; we might call such a notion of use a *Gricean* one. Such a specification of the Thesis will not enable one to answer the question what content is, in general. But, on this view, the philosophy of language is not where that question *ought* to be answered, and the Thesis can yet play a role in an explanation of what it is for a *linguistic expression* to mean what it does.[45] The very observation that shows that the meta-semantic questions do not vanish the moment we assume the priority of thought also shows that characterizing use in terms of the contents of mental states does not trivialize the Use-Meaning Thesis. Adopting such a characterization of use does affect the metaphysical force of the Thesis—in particular, the Thesis no longer promises a solution to the problem of inten-tionality—but this characterization does not drain the Thesis of all force.

There are various ways a Gricean conception of use might be devel-oped. The general thought, to put the point in Davidsonian language, is that the data available to the radical interpreter should be characterized, not in terms of the external conditions under which speakers make various utterances, but in terms of the *psychological* conditions (in addition, perhaps, to external ones) under which they make them. One option would be to pursue some form of Grice's program—hence my calling the notion of use in play here a Gricean one—arguing that Kurt's meaning that it was raining consisted in his uttering 'It is raining', with the intention that his audience should come to believe he believed that it was raining, by means of their recognizing his intention that they should, and so on and so forth. Another option would be to pursue a proposal of Ian Rumfitt's, which makes essential use of the thought that speakers know the truth-conditions of utterances, in the sense of knowing T-sentences for them.[46] There are other possibilities, to be sure. But the question how such a position is best developed is not the one I wish to pursue here. The issue I want to discuss is a more abstract one that, I think, troubles Dummett in particular.

One might worry that this way of accommodating the rationality of our use of language will commit us to an implausibly strong version of the claim that thought is prior to language. Let us grant that there are many sorts of thoughts pre-verbal children are capable of having and, moreover, that any explanation of what they mean by their most basic utterances will have to make reference to this prior capacity. It is far from obvious that anything like this is correct in general. Surely it is just false that, for *any* sentence a speaker might come to understand, she must have a prior capacity to entertain the thought it expresses. For example, it is far from clear that speakers acquire a capacity to make reference to arbitrarily distant regions of time before they acquire a capacity to use the past-tense. A similar view is yet more plausible in the case of all but the most basic mathematical notions.[47] And, even if neither of these examples is compelling, it would be unfortunate if answering McDowell's objection required us to place a bet that there are no better ones.

If there are sentences our understanding of which is not to be explained in terms of a prior capacity for thoughts with the same content, some notion of use other than the Gricean one will be needed. But the relevant notion of use need not be entirely meaning-free. It would, of course, undermine the purpose for which the notion of use is wanted if, in characterizing the use we make of past-tense sentences (to take them as an example) reference were made to the meanings of sentences in the past tense (which would trivialize the Use-Meaning Thesis) or to the contents of thoughts about the past (which would return us to a Gricean notion of use). But it would *not* be similarly illegitimate to make reference to the meanings of the *present*-tense transforms of those same sentences. The explanation of what it is for the past-tense sentences to mean what they do will have to advert to the meanings of the present-tense sentences embedded in them, since an understanding of past-tense sentences is surely parasitic upon an understanding of their present-tense transforms. And note too that we need have no qualms about making use of psychological notions, like belief, intention, or what have you, so long as we do not assume that the speaker is *antecedently* able to have thoughts about the past. Such a notion of use—which I shall call a *Dummettian* notion—will thus not be vulnerable to McDowell's objections to the Quinean notion of use. We will be able to recognize the integration of a speaker's understanding of sentences in the past tense with her capacity for thoughts about the past, so long as the description of use makes reference, for example, to a requirement that speakers' beliefs reflect their assertions, and those of others, in an appropriate way.

One way to develop the Dummettian notion of use might be to take as a model Peacocke's use of psychological notions in stating what he calls possession conditions. It is essential to a possession condition that it make reference to the agent's beliefs, for example; but it is just as essential that it not presuppose a capacity for beliefs whose contents contain the concept the possession condition concerns. The same sorts of moves Peacocke uses to resolve the threat of circularity are also available for framing a Dummettian notion of use.[48] Another option might be to formulate the requirement that the use of language be integrated with thought as a general principle that does not enter into the characterization of the use of particular expressions—that is, as a general constraint on what it is for an expression to mean anything at all, rather than as something that enters into specific accounts of what it is for expressions to mean what they do. But let me not pursue this issue further here.

The overall shape of one sort of meta-semantic project based upon the Use-Meaning Thesis may thus be understood as follows: For the most fundamental parts of our language, where we have a prior capacity for thoughts with the contents in question, what it is for sentences to mean what they do will be explained in terms of some version of the Gricean notion of use; for other parts, if there are any, in terms of the Dummettian notion. To decide what notion of use to employ in specifying the Use-Meaning Thesis, we must thus decide whether, and where, thought is prior to language. There is no reason such a decision needs to be made once and for all. Although there are extreme views that merit consideration, the truth may well lie somewhere else.[49]

The availability of the position just described seems to me enough to undermine McDowell's claim that once we recognize that the view that understanding is a practical capacity is unable to account for the rationality of our use of language, our only option is to describe use in terms of the contents expressed by utterances. The Gricean conception of use is *content-laden*, to be sure, but it does not help itself to any notion of *linguistic* content—that is, it is not *meaning*-laden—and the position is designed precisely to allow us to recognize the integration of language with thought. On the other hand, however, even if this point is accepted, McDowell might still be said to have offered a compelling argument against *Dummett*. For Dummett is not prepared to employ a Gricean notion of use *anywhere*, since he rejects the priority of thought, arguing that it is at best useless to appeal to a speaker's prior possession of particular concepts in attempting to explain what it is for her words to express them.

It does not follow, however, that any notion of use Dummett could accept would have to be content-free, or even meaning-free. In particular, in explaining what it is for past-tense sentences to mean what they do, he could deploy a notion of use that was not meaning-free, for the reasons discussed above. In general, whenever a speaker's understanding of one (sort of) sentence depends upon a prior understanding of another, it will be legitimate for Dummett to advert both to what she means by that other sentence and to her capacity for thoughts whose content it serves to express.[50]

But that is all just a sideshow. The real issue concerns what goes on at the most fundamental level. For sentences at that level—sentences our understanding of which does *not* depend upon a prior understanding of any other sentences—the notion of use we employ in explaining what it is for *those* sentences to mean what they do will have to be both meaning- and content-free. One might well worry that, at this point, Dummett is forced to turn back to the conception of understanding as a practical ability and face McDowell's objection anew. He writes that "some [of a speaker's knowledge of her language]—the deepest and most interesting components— [consists] of a complex of acquired practices that together constitute a grasp of content."[51] Dummett does later deny that her understanding consists in the "mastery of a purely external practice," the thought being that the practice has, so to speak, one foot in her mouth and another in her head.[52] But he does not attain a clear conception of what this amounts to.

The reason, I think, is that he fails to distinguish the priority of *thought* from what we might call the priority of *reason*. It is one thing to say that thought is prior to language at the level of *content*, that a prior grasp of the contents of sentences needs to be invoked in explaining our understanding of them. It is entirely another to say that *the general capacity for thought and reason* is prior to any linguistic capacity. If we accept this latter claim, as it seems to me we must, then we are free to characterize use in terms of psychological notions, like those of belief and intention, and yet refuse to appeal to any prior capacity to entertain thoughts with the very contents expressed by our utterances. In that way one might recognize Higginbotham's point—that the practice of speaking a language involves a capacity to *judge*—and yet deny that the practice must be described in terms of *what* is judged.

What Dummett does say about the matter is, I think, also best understood in this light. Dummett says, for instance, that to understand a sentence, I must know what bearing its truth may have on my actions. In the relevant sense, though, the truth of a sentence will affect my actions only insofar as I *believe* it to be true. What I need to know, then, is what I would be believing if I were to accept the sentence as true; obviously, that presupposes that my acceptance of its truth will give rise to a belief with an appropriate content.[53] But if that is the sort of view Dummett envisages, then what he ought to say is that a Dummettian notion of use is to be employed *throughout*; this will yield a notion of use, at the most fundamental level that, although content-free, is still non-behavioristic and, for that very reason, allows us to recognize the integration of language and thought.[54]

If we understand Dummett as I have just suggested we should, then his project survives the objections McDowell brings against him. Of course, one might be skeptical that a Dummettian notion of use, at the most fundamental level, can be developed in detail. I have my doubts myself. My point here, though, is that the charge of behaviorism—which is so often brought against Dummett, with a footnote to McDowell's papers—can not be sustained, at least not on the basis of the sorts of general considerations

McDowell develops. No principled reason has emerged that Dummett should be unable to make room for the rationality of language use.

IV. CLOSING: THE EPISTEMOLOGY OF UNDERSTANDING AND THE PRIORITY OF THOUGHT

As I said at the outset, McDowell suggests that Dummett's rejection of meaning-laden notions of use is motivated by a flawed epistemology of understanding. I have rejected this reading. But there are, of course, several passages in Dummett's writings on which one might reasonably base such an interpretation—passages where Dummett deploys arguments that certainly *look* like epistemological ones in support of the claim that the notion of use should be content-free. In closing, I should like to offer, from our present vantage point, an account of the role these arguments play in Dummett's thought.

Illustrating these arguments, McDowell asks us to imagine that Martians speak a language that sounds like English but differs from it semantically. Expressions in Martian do not always mean what their English homophones mean.[55] Dummett's claim about such a case would be that, if meaning were not determined by use—conceived in uniformly Dummettian terms—it might be impossible for us ever to recognize the semantic differences between the languages. Suppose that the Martians' use of their language, so conceived, was in relevant respects *exactly* like ours,[56] not just actually but also counterfactually. Whatever semantic differences there might be between the languages then *could* never be revealed in anything we could glean from the Martians' speech. A Gricean could reply that the differences would yet consist in differences between the contents of the Martians' thoughts and ours, and that it might still be possible to give an account of that difference.[57] But, by hypothesis, the differences between the contents of their thoughts and ours would be epiphenomenal, as far as their speech is concerned, and Dummett regards that situation as intolerable. Ordinarily, we take ourselves to *know*, on the basis of how someone uses language, what she means by her words. And yet, in this case, no amount of ordinary probing could reveal our mistaken assumption that the Martians mean what we do. Are we not forced to conclude either that the grounds on which we ordinarily judge what someone means are insufficient, or alternatively, "that faith is required if we are to believe that we communicate with one another"?[58] Better, says Dummett, to accept that meaning is determined by use, in his sense.

McDowell's view is that such arguments underlie Dummett's rejection of meaning-laden notions of use. But to say so is to misidentify their target.

The argument we just considered is directed not against *meaning*-laden notions of use, but against *content*-laden notions of use, in particular, against the claim that the right way to specify the Use-Meaning Thesis is in terms of a *Gricean* notion of use.[59] The target, that is to say, is the thesis that thought is prior to language. It is in response to this argument—perhaps surprisingly, an argument for a claim with which he actually agrees—that McDowell's epistemological observations are properly deployed. The case of the Martians is indeed analogous, in relevant respects, to the argument from illusion in the philosophy of perception. And we may follow now familiar responses to the argument from illusion and deny that the mere *possibility* that there could be such a language, one we could not distinguish from English on the basis of the evidence upon which we ordinarily base our beliefs, shows that our ordinary beliefs about what utterances mean do not constitute knowledge.[60] I think that response exactly right. In any event, it is Dummett's rejection of *content-laden* notions of use that is epistemologically driven, not his rejection of meaning-laden ones.[61]

RICHARD G. HECK, JR.

DEPARTMENT OF PHILOSOPHY
BROWN UNIVERSITY
MAY 2002

NOTES

1. I shall draw chiefly on McDowell's "Anti-realism and the Epistemology of Understanding," in *Meaning and Understanding*, ed. Herman Parrett and Jacques Bouveresse (New York: W. de Gruyter, 1981), 225–48. Similar views are expressed in a number of his other writings, to which I shall refer below.

2. John McDowell, "Anti-Realism," 239ff. That there is something wrong with McDowell's interpretation of Dummett is suggested by the fact that Dummett frequently expresses dissatisfaction with Quine's conception of use. See, for example, his "What Do I Know When I Know a Language?" in *The Seas of Language* (Oxford: Clarendon, 1993), 105, where he writes that "the notion of knowledge cannot . . . be extruded from the philosophy of language." For references to others with similar interpretations of Dummett, and criticism of that reading, see Sanford Shieh, "On the Conceptual Foundations of Anti-realism," *Synthese* 115 (1998): 33–70.

3. At least this seems to be part of the force of the argument of *Mind and World* (Cambridge, MA: Harvard Univ. Press, 1994), lecture 3 and the appendix to it: I have in mind McDowell's criticisms of Christopher Peacocke's use of the notion of nonconceptual content, in *A Study of Concepts* (Cambridge, MA: MIT

Press, 1992). For a little more on this, see note 48.

4. I have discussed some of McDowell's reflections on perception in my "Non-conceptual Content and the 'Space of Reasons'," *Philosophical Review* 109 (2000): 483–523.

5. Dummett concedes this point in his "Reply to McDowell," in *Michael Dummett: Contributions to Philosophy*, ed. Barry Taylor (Dordrecht: Martinus Nijhoff, 1987), 257.

6. I should also argue that some of McDowell's discussions of perception run epistemological issues together with metaphysical ones (as do those of some of other recent defenders of direct realist views about perception). On this point, see Peacocke, *A Study of Concepts*, 238, n. 22.

7. John McDowell, "Truth, Bivalence, and Verificationism," in *Truth and Meaning: Essays in Semantics*, ed. Gareth Evans and John McDowell (Oxford: Clarendon Press, 1976), 44–45.

8. The appropriate attitude is what McDowell calls a "modest" one, and what is at issue here is, in a sense, whether a theory of truth need only be modest—that is, need only state *what* meanings the speaker takes expressions of her language to have—or must be full-blooded—that is, must also explain what it is for her words to mean what they do.

The issue I am discussing here has been discussed by Dummett on a number of occasions: see "What Is a Theory of Meaning? (I)," in *Seas of Language*, 1–33; "Reply to McDowell"; and *The Logical Basis of Metaphysics* (Cambridge, MA: Harvard Univ. Press, 1991), ch. 5. While I do not really disagree with his diagnosis, I am not sure it goes deep enough; it has the additional disadvantage that it is given from, so to speak, inside his own position.

9. McDowell, "In Defense of Modesty," in *Michael Dummett: Contributions to Philosophy*, ed. Barry Taylor, Nijhoff International Philosophy Series, 25 (Dordrecht, Holland & Boston, MA: Nijhoff, 1987), 69.

10. There are complications here, but they do not affect the points being made. See note 15.

11. This kind of point is familiar from discussions of Tarksi's theory of truth. See, for example, John Etchemendy, "Tarski on Truth and Logical Consequence," *Journal of Symbolic Logic* 53 (1988): 51–79; and Scott Soames, "What Is a Theory of Truth?" *Journal of Philosophy* 81 (1984): 411–29.

12. The point being made here has its origin in Tarski's distinction between formal and material adequacy and in his separation of the mathematical from the empirical aspects of semantics. For more on this, see my "Tarski, Truth, and Semantics," *Philosophical Review* 106 (1997): 533–54. Compare Dummett, *Logical Basis*, 69–71.

13. I might have used the word 'white' to mean *black*, and then 'Snow is white' would have been true if and only if snow were black—a fact I could then have reported, of course, by uttering (1).

14. I owe this example to Vann McGee. It inspired a much cleaner treatment of

this entire issue. Note that one might also put this point by saying that all that has actually been explained is why an *utterance of the sentence* 'I am here' is true, not why I am here. Insofar as that is right, this sort of point is close to those made by Dummett in his discussions of this issue. See "What is a Theory of Meaning?" 8–12.

15. For some further discussion of these matters, see my "Truth and Disquotation," *Synthese* 142 (2004): 317–52.

16. It is one of the ironies of the subject that there is no agreement at all on how mass terms should be treated, that is, how a T-sentence for 'Snow is white' and other sentences containing 'snow' might actually be derived. Actual semantic theories for such sentences tend to make heavy use of concepts from Boolean algebra, and the T-sentences they deliver are not even close to homophonic. One can, of course, add axioms to force the theories to be homophonic, but doing so does not increase the interest of the theories. Moreover, semantics is interested in saying what different readings might be available for a given sentence. It is important that the sentence 'I almost had my wallet stolen' admits of three different readings; to capture the difference, the theory will have to be non-homophonic. See James Higginbotham, *Sense and Syntax: An Inaugural Lecture Delivered Before the University of Oxford on 20 October 1994* (Oxford: Clarendon Press, 1995), from which I borrow the example just used, which originates with Chomsky.

17. See Donald Davidson, "Truth and Meaning," in his *Inquiries into Truth and Interpretation* (Oxford: Clarendon Press, 1984), 25.

18. Ibid., 24–25, 27. See also Donald Davidson, "Radical Interpretation," in *Inquiries*, 134–35. Davidson might be taken to mean by "empirical" a posteriori, in which case there really is a contradiction—unless the claims are taken to concern different projects, as below.

19. The claim is implicit in Davidson's suggestion, at "Truth and Meaning," 27, that the correctness of the theory can be tested using something like radical translation. It is made somewhat more explicit in "Radical Interpretation," where Davidson argues that a theory of truth can serve as a theory of interpretation. I owe my own appreciation of this point to James Higginbotham, "Is Semantics Necessary?" *Proceedings of the Aristotelian Society* 87 (1988): 219–41.

20. It is this issue of developing a compositional theory of meaning that Davidson's other proposal addresses, for it embodies the suggestion that semantic facts are facts about the references of expressions, in the broad sense in which Frege used that term. His position also reflects a commitment to Frege's context principle, that is, to the priority of sentence-meaning over word-meaning.

21. Davidson, "Radical Interpretation," 134–35.

22. Dummett, "What Do I Know?" 99.

23. It is, as he puts it, "not a description from the outside of the practice of using the language, but . . . an object of *knowledge* on the part of speakers" ("What Do I Know?" 100).

24. These problems do not arise for Davidson. The problem facing the radical

interpreter is to discover a theory the knowledge of which will *make* her a competent speaker. Davidson is free to suppose that the interpreter already understands a language in which the theory of meaning can be formulated. But for that very reason, the project of radical interpretation does not address questions of competence. This, indeed, is Dummett's most fundamental criticism of Davidson's program: See "What is a Theory of Meaning?" 6.

25. In a certain sense, it would not matter if they did know the theories of truth for their own languages. The knowledge that underlies competence *cannot* be conscious, explicit knowledge. Even if Anglophone semanticists should one day give a complete theory of truth for English, it would not be their explicit knowledge of that theory that explained their competence. See "What is a Theory of Meaning?" 21ff.

26. For discussion of this, see Gareth Evans, "Semantic Theory and Tacit Knowledge," in his *Collected Papers* (Oxford: Clarendon Press, 1985), 322–42; Martin Davies, "Tacit Knowledge and Semantic Theory: Can a Five per cent Difference Matter?" *Mind* 96 (1987): 441–62; and Crispin Wright, "Theories of Meaning and Speakers' Knowledge," in his *Realism, Meaning, and Truth* (Oxford: B. Blackwell, 1986), 204–38.

27. Of course, it is also possible for the theories to have different axioms, but for the T-sentences produced to agree in truth-value, even necessarily. This problem, the Foster problem, is part and parcel of the problem I am discussing. For my own preferred resolution of it, see my "Meaning and Truth-conditions," *forthcoming* in *Truth and Speech Acts: Studies in the Philosophy of Language*, ed. Dirk Griemann and Geo Siegwart (London: Routledge).

28. Dummett, "What Do I Know?" 101.

29. Dummett, "What is a Theory of Meaning?" 21.

30. Dummett himself emphasizes this fact: See e.g., "What Do I Know?" 104.

31. McDowell, "In Defense of Modesty," 65. See also John McDowell, "Another Plea for Modesty," in *Language, Thought, and Logic: Essays in Honour of Michael Dummett*, ed. Richard Heck (Oxford: Oxford Univ. Press, 1997), 105–30. Of course, no one is suggesting that this objection would impress Quine.

32. See, for example, Noam Chomsky, *Rules and Representations* (New York: Columbia Univ. Press, 1980), ch. 2.

33. Just a few years after the publication of "What Is a Theory of Meaning?" the objection I am about to rehearse in fact led Dummett to reject the view that to understand a language is to possess a *practical* capacity to speak it. It seems fair to say, however, that Dummett has never settled upon an alternative view. Even the appeal to implicit knowledge is deemed unhelpful by the publication of *Logical Basis*.

34. See Dummett, *Logical Basis*, 91–92. A similar point can be made about speakers with only partial knowledge of meaning. If a rheumatologist were to report that he had arthritis in his thigh, one would presumably wonder what else he actually meant to convey; but someone with only partial understanding of the term

should not be taken so.

35. For further discussion of this matter, see my "Reason and Language," in *McDowell and His Critics*, ed. Cynthia Macdonald and Graham Macdonald (Oxford: Blackwell Publishing, 2006), 22–45.

36. It is for this reason that I think Chomsky's observations, valuable as they are, do not really speak to the fundamental problem. True though it may be that our use of language has to be conceived as resting upon our possession of tacit knowledge, this observation does not address the rationality of language use, for a similar point might be made about such abilities as the ability to swim. Indeed, Chomsky himself makes just that point: See *Language and Problems of Knowledge: The Managua Lectures* (Cambridge, MA: MIT Press, 1988), 11–12.

37. I am indebted here to Dummett's discussion at *Logical Basis*, 90–91, although it is again bound up with questions about whether we know what we mean.

38. I am, of course, ignoring cases in which speakers utter sentences they do not understand. And one should not really say, at this point, that the thoughts need to have the *same* content. On some views, the contents of thoughts are of a different sort from the contents of sentences, and so the right thing to say will be that we must be able to have thoughts with appropriately related contents. See my paper "The Sense of Communication," *Mind* 104 (1995): 79–106.

39. Someone sympathetic with this view might try to answer this objection by making use of the sort of machinery discussed in §4 of this essay. But once that has been done, the claim that understanding is a *purely* practical ability has been abandoned.

40. See James Higginbotham, "Priorities in the Philosophy of Thought," *Aristotelian Society* sup. vol. 68 (1994): 85–106.

41. A common move here is to deny that pre-verbal children have anything properly called "thoughts" at all. Dummett himself makes this move, in "Truth and Meaning," in *Seas of Language*, 148–49. The difficulty is that, even if this is right, it is hard to see why a capacity for proto-thought, if that is what one wants to call it, should not *still* be invoked in explaining our grasp of our most primitive concepts.

42. One version of this view has it that a theory of truth for English is explicitly represented in our minds in the language of thought. See Gabriel Segal, "Priorities in the Philosophy of Thought," *Aristotelian Society* sup. vol. 68 (1994): 107–30; and Richard Larson and Gabriel Segal, *Knowledge of Meaning: An Introduction to Semantic Theory* (Cambridge, MA: MIT Press, 1995), ch. 1. But the means of representation is not crucial here.

43. Even if we grant that Kurt knows that 'Snow is white' is true if and only if snow is white, the question remains how this knowledge is to be deployed, how Kurt's having it gives rise to the linguistic abilities that manifest (even if they do not constitute) his competence. In principle, Kurt could have such knowledge and have no idea what the sentence means. Therefore more needs to be said before even

the view mentioned in the preceding note will be of any help here. For some of what needs to be said, see James Higginbotham, "Truth and Understanding," *Iyyun* 40 (1991): 271–88, and my "Meaning and Truth-conditions."

44. Dummett, "What Do I Know?" 97–99.

45. I thus think that Dummett misunderstands Grice's intent. See "Language and Communication," in *Seas of Language*, 171–73.

46. See Ian Rumfitt, "Truth-conditions and Communication," *Mind* 104 (1995): 827–62.

47. Note that the question in play at this point is the *empirical* one whether we *in fact* have a prior grasp of certain contents. The mere fact that one *might* grasp the contents of certain expressions without having a means for expressing those contents does not decide the question how our *actual* understanding of those expressions is to be explained. Compare Christopher Peacocke, "Concepts Without Words," in *Language, Thought, and Logic*, 1–33.

48. See Peacocke, *A Study of Concepts*, 6–10. McDowell thinks there are serious problems with Peacocke's "non-circularity" condition, a commitment to which amounts, in effect, to a rejection of content-laden notions of use. But I think McDowell's objections can be answered. His discussion overlooks the crucial role played by the requirement that a "determination theory" be provided for any putative possession condition. It is this, and not some need for possession conditions to be given "within the space of reasons," that motivates rejection of the neuro-physiological condition McDowell considers in *Mind and World*, 167–68. It is because it is impossible to provide such a determination theory—short a type-type identity theory for concept possession, which is not even worth discussing—that such an account would have nothing to say about 'what someone thinks when she thinks that something is red'. It is *the determination theory* that specifies the content of the concept (what its semantic value is), not the possession condition on its own.

49. One might wonder whether there is not another notion of use to be explored, one that would allow use to be characterized in terms of the *general notion* of linguistic meaning, but would not appeal to any *particular facts* about linguistic meaning—much as the Dummettian notion appeals to psychological notions, but not to our capacity for *particular thoughts*. Such a notion of use is indeed available, in principle, but one might worry that taking the notion of linguistic meaning for granted would enable us only to answer *specific* questions about what it is for words to mean what they do, and not to answer *general* questions about what it is for words to mean anything at all. But the matter is complex; only a developed proposal would allow us to resolve it.

50. Of course, it is here essential that our language have a certain sort of hierarchical structure—that, *modulo* local holisms, an ordering of the sentences in terms of whether an understanding of the one depends upon an understanding of the other will be a partial ordering.

51. Dummett, *Logical Basis*, 102–3.

52. Ibid., 103.

53. See here "The Sense of Communication," where I argue that this principle is required for different sorts of reasons, namely, that the only argument for the claim that the meaning of an expression determines its reference rests upon it.

54. What obscures this point, I think, is Dummett's acceptance of a broadly Davidsonian, "interpretive" philosophy of mind. If one puts the two views together, use will be described in terms that exclude notions like belief, but instead incorporate the interpretive story about what belief is. Nonetheless, even if one does accept such a view, it is worth separating it out from the view about how use should be characterized. The two are quite independent.

55. McDowell, "Anti-Realism," 244.

56. It won't really be exactly like ours, of course; there may be vocabulary differences, and externalist constraints might imply that their word 'water' means twater. But these kinds of differences are presumably ones that *could* become apparent.

57. Another reply would be that, even on a Gricean view, the case is impossible—i.e., that, though meaning does not *consist* in use, described in Dummettian terms, differences in meaning nevertheless will always lead to potential differences in use. Note that this reply in effect concedes that meaning is, in some sense, *determined* by Dummettian use, a claim that may still be strong enough for the anti-realist challenge to get off the ground. In any event, it is this weaker claim for which I would suggest the name "The Manifestation Constraint," familiar from discussions of Dummett's writings. A speaker's linguistic capacities *manifest* what she means in the sense that her having those capacities demands explanation in terms of her having particular semantic knowledge so that, even if her meaning what she does by her words is to be *explained* in terms of a prior capacity for thought, what she means will still be *fixed* by the use she makes of her language.

58. Dummett, "Language and Communication," 177.

59. The quotation at the end of the last paragraph, for example, is taken from a discussion of the view that understanding consists in tacit knowledge of a theory of truth ("Language and Communication," 174–81). More specifically, the target is Chomsky's view that, as Dummett puts it, "language is primarily a vehicle of thought, and only secondarily an instrument of communication" (ibid., 176).

60. McDowell, "Anti-Realism," 244.

61. Thanks to Alex George, Steve Gross, Chris Peacocke, Ian Proops, Jim Pryor, Alison Simmons, Sanford Shieh, and Crispin Wright for helpful comments on earlier drafts of this paper. Thanks to Jim Higginbotham, Sally Sedgwick, Jason Stanley, and Jamie Tappenden for discussions that contributed to its development.

I benefitted from the opportunity to present this material in a graduate seminar on *The Logical Basis of Metaphysics* given at Harvard University in the Autumn of 1994 (and in various undergraduate courses on the philosophy of language taught since then). Thanks to all the participants for their comments, but especially to

Michael Glanzberg, Ian Proops (again), and Jamie Tappenden. The paper was also read to a colloquium at the Massachusetts Institute of Technology, in January 1997. Thanks to all who were present for helpful questions, but especially to Alex Byrne, Vann McGee, and Bob Stalnaker.

When I first wrote this paper, I found Dummett's position, as I interpret it, more attractive than I do now. This change of view left this paper unpublished for a long time. But various people suggested to me, over the years, that its exposition of Dummett was helpful. Others have even found the position it offers Dummett attractive. Thanks to all of them, especially Ian Proops (yet again) and Michael Rescorla, for their encouragement. Without it, this paper never would have been published.

Finally, thanks to Michael Dummett, for his teaching, when I was studying for my B.Phil. in Oxford, and for his writings, which have been an inspiration.

REPLY TO RICHARD G. HECK, JR.

I am a little disconcerted to find myself criticised for failing to make due allowance for the rationality of the use of language, since that is something I have repeatedly stressed: I think I once called the use of language "*the* rational act."[1] I tried to dissociate my view of language from a behaviourist one by saying that the goal of a theory of meaning should not be one enabling us to make accurate predictions of what people would say in given situations, as if it were a scientific theory of speech behaviour; rather, it should give an account of the activity of using a given language that rendered it intelligible as one in which human beings engage. I had in mind here an anthropologist's account of a ritual performance which on first description appeared utterly pointless, but, as described by the anthropologist, made sense as something human beings—members of that society—did. A theory of meaning would not, on this conception, give a predictive account of the causation of linguistic behaviour, but display that behaviour as the rational activity of rational agents, or at least of rational agents similar in their make-up to ourselves.

This, it may be said, still fails to make that allowance for the rationality of our use of language that Richard Heck demands. It may succeed in differentiating my view of language from *psychological* behaviourism, that is, a Pavlovian theory of the causation of our utterances in terms of a stimulus-response mechanism. But it fails to differentiate it from *philosophical* behaviourism. What, then, is philosophical behaviourism? Does Wittgenstein's thesis that "an 'inner process' stands in need of outward criteria" (*Philosopical Investigations*, §580) constitute philosophical behaviourism? Does Frege's view that we human beings can grasp thoughts only as expressed in words or symbols? Or would Frege's view have been behaviourist only if he had held that no beings whatever could grasp thoughts otherwise than as clothed in words or symbols, as he went out of his way to make clear that he did not?

Philosophical behaviourism is, I think, the view that there is nothing to any mental state or process but the behaviour that manifests it. There is nothing to pain but pain-behaviour; there is nothing to fear but frightened actions. I have certainly never maintained a general doctrine of this form. But how is it with meaning something by what we say? The use of language is, in large part, an observable activity in which we engage co-operatively. What I take someone else to mean by what he says largely depends on the language he is using and on my knowledge of that language: I take him to mean such-and-such because I know that what he said means such-and-such in that language. But if it proves that that was *not* what he meant, but that his utterance was intended in some way that diverged from the standard significance of those words in the language, and if he proves incapable of explaining to me what he meant, because of his inarticulateness or my obtuseness, then all I have to go on, in arriving at the meaning he intended, is his subsequent use of those and perhaps other words—when he uses them, his responses to others' uses of them, and his non-linguistic behaviour that appears to be relevant to his and others' uses of them. I cannot look into his mind in order to read off from its contents the meanings he attaches to his words. I mean, I cannot look into his mind independently of what I see of his facial expressions, what I hear of his utterances, and what I observe of his behaviour. And the same goes for the standard meanings of the words and sentences of the language. The only vindication of any dictionary or other authority that states what those meanings are is the use that the speakers of the language make of them.

It is not just that the only conclusive way any of us has of finding out what others mean by what they say is to observe their linguistic behaviour and other behaviour associated with or consequent upon it. It is that such behaviour is *criterial* for their words' having those meanings; it is what *constitutes* their having those meanings—provided, as noted below, that they were in a normal state when they spoke. It is thus not like estimating someone's intention in acting in a certain way. Often it is obvious what the intention must be; sometimes it is uncertain, and then we form *hypotheses* about the intention behind his actions. The same may happen in trying to understand why someone said what he did. Why did he say something so apparently irrelevant? Was he trying to make a joke? Was he deliberately changing the subject, and, if so, why? Was he lying? Though we may in cases of such perplexity describe ourselves as trying to understand what the speaker meant, the questions do not bear on what his words meant, as he intended them to be understood: we are asking why he should have said something with that meaning. But acting with such-and-such an intention is not a *practice*, as speaking a particular language is a practice; and divining someone's intention in a course of action is not, in general, trying to understand what practice his actions instantiated. (It might be one hypothesis among others that there was some such practice.) So acting in that way does not *constitute* having that intention: it is *explained* by the agent's having had that intention. We may sometimes have to form hypotheses about what a speaker means by the words he uses, when he does not know the language well, or if he habitually uses words wrongly or was evidently doing so on this occasion. But his meaning what he does by the words he utters is *constituted* by his having used those words in a similar way in the past and his disposition to use them in a parallel manner in the future. It does not *explain* his saying what he did: it is what his meaning what he did by what he said consists in.

To deny this is to make meaning something by a word or sentence an inner mental act which others can only guess at, but never know for sure. It is to hold that someone may use a word precisely as if he meant one thing by it, and might always use it as if he meant that by it, and yet in fact—in his innermost soul, as it were—mean something different. We can indeed know for sure what someone intended in acting as he did, namely if he tells us; but if we are uncertain what his words mean, we shall be uncertain of understanding any explanation of their meaning that he gives us. We do not have to make an act of faith to understand what someone means by what he says. We may sometimes make mistakes about this; sometimes our mistakes may never come to light for us. But such mistakes always *could* come to light: if they do so, it will be because of some mismatch between what we have taken the speaker to mean and what he subsequently says or does.

So it seems that all there is to the meanings in a language of the words of that language is that the speakers use them in a certain way. Now I might say to the behaviourist that I *know from my own case* that pain-behaviour is not all there is to feeling pain. Can I say that I know from my own case that using a word in a certain way is not all there is to meaning something by it? No: there is no experience of attaching some meaning to a word or sentence that I utter. We do not, as we speak *confer* particular meanings on our words. As Wittgenstein says, "When I think in language, there aren't 'meanings' going through my mind in addition to the verbal expression: the language is itself the vehicle of thought" (*Philosophical Investigations*, §329). For the most part, while we sometimes need to make an effort to hit on the right way to convey our thoughts or memories, and sometimes recognise that the word we have chosen is not the right one, we experience nothing in particular in selecting the words we utter: we speak without effort in a language that we know. I know what I mean, because it fits into the sequence of my thoughts. I may intend an ambiguous word to be taken in one way rather than the other, often without being conscious of the ambiguity as I speak; but I do not derive that knowledge from the experience of attaching that meaning to the word. I know because only that interpretation fits in with my train of thought.

It seems, accordingly, that the Use-Meaning Thesis is correct, and that a behaviourist account of meaning—a *philosophically* behaviourist account of meaning—is therefore nothing to apologise for. Use is not use solely for communication; it comprises what a subject says when he knows that no one is listening, and what he writes but never shows to anyone. It also comprises what he says silently to himself, and is thus not confined to what is observable by others. But of course the content of the Use-Meaning Thesis depends upon the terms in which use is allowed to be characterised. Obviously the Thesis becomes trivial, and patently ceases to be behaviouristic, if a description of use is permitted to be what Heck calls "meaning-laden," that is, if it invokes the notion of meaning itself or other notions, such as that of *saying that* such-and-such is the case, that plainly involve that of meaning. I thoroughly applaud Heck's account of why meaning-laden accounts of use are not to be allowed in construing the Use-Meaning Thesis. He does so by appeal to his distinction between a semantic theory, which, for each sentence, explains in accordance with its composition under what condition it is true, and a meta-semantic theory, which aims to explain what it is for a sentence to mean what it does. I should myself draw the lines somewhat differently; but his emphasis on the meta-semantic question, and defence of it as a genuine philosophical question, accord very well with my view of the matter.

For me, a semantic theory need not take the form of a theory of truth *simpliciter*. In tense logic, it will be a theory of truth at a time; in intuitionistic semantics, it will be a theory of canonical proof. A theory of meaning for a language will constitute a comprehensive account of the practice of using that language, including what those who know it know; it will have a semantic theory as its core, but no more than its core. I do not see the theory of meaning as containing an outright answer to the question "What is it for a word or sentence of the language to mean what it does?"; rather, the theory, if correct, will *show* what it is for a sentence of the language to mean what it does. That, I think, is the point of philosophers' enquiring what form a theory of meaning for a language should take.

I am very tired both of T-sentences and of homophonic semantic theories; but shall not argue about them here, but will add one remark to Heck's discussion. A T-sentence is a biconditional, which is a conjunction of two conditionals. It is not merely that we need to notice that it is the same sentence that is used in one clause of each conditional and referred to in the other: we need to make sure that that sentence functions in the same way in the clause in which it is used and when used on its own as a complete sentence (which is how we take it when it is quoted). To borrow an excellent example of the late Elizabeth Anscombe: the conditional "If Henry can eat any fish, the sentence 'Henry can eat any fish' is true" is false if Henry can eat salmon but cannot eat red mullet.

If meaning is a behaviourist concept, is the same true of understanding? And is it true also of the knowledge of a language? It seems natural that if the meaning of a word or sentence is to be explained in terms of its use, then knowledge of a language—competence in using that language—must be explained as a practical ability. For a long time I thought that knowledge of a language could be characterised as implicit knowledge, manifested by an ability to speak and understand the language. The understanding of the language is thus reduced to a practical ability and a theory of meaning for that language to a theoretical representation of that ability. But, as Heck notes (note 33), I have for some time abandoned that view, and, with it, the formula "a theoretical representation of a practical ability." Implicit knowledge may be characterised as being able to recognise as correct a verbal formulation of the thing known when offered it, even when unable to formulate it oneself. But what is important about knowledge is how it is delivered when it is to be used; implicit knowledge so explained has not been represented as equipped with any means of delivery. Lewis Carroll made many philosophical jokes; hardly any of P. G. Wodehouse's jokes have this character. But one is profound; I cited it also in my reply to John McDowell. In one of his books, someone asks a lady, "Can you speak Spanish?", and she replies, "I don't know: I've never tried." There is no such thing as trying to speak Spanish if you have never learned it: to speak Spanish, or even to try to do so, there is a great deal you have to *know*. If you do not know Spanish, you do not, strictly speaking, know what it is to speak Spanish, and so you cannot try to do so. Even if you have never learned to swim, you may perfectly well know what it is to swim.

I concluded that the dichotomy between theoretical knowledge and practical ability overlooked an intermediate variety of knowledge: knowledge of how to do something that alone constitutes knowing what it is to do it. In knowing how to dance the tango, I know that a step like *that* must be followed by a step like *this*: I identify the two steps just by my learned ability to execute them, but, in order to dance the tango, I must remember and advert to the proposition that the one step is followed by the other. Knowledge of a language is of this mixed variety: it is neither a mere practical ability nor pure theoretical knowledge. This conclusion does no more than announce a programme: a detailed theory of the understanding of any particular language must explain what the components of a knowledge of it are (and they need not be the same for every speaker).

Knowledge of a language supports both the active ability to speak in that language and the passive ability to understand what others say in it. We know immediately whether or not we understand (though not always whether we have understood aright). If I am listening to someone speaking on the radio in a language I know only imperfectly, and a friend asks, "Did you understand what he just said?", I can answer straight out whether I did or not. Understanding is a conscious process, as is speaking. Understanding is manifested by appropriate responses, but it is not constituted by them alone; meaning something by what one says is not constituted by the appropriateness of the words, either. After a prolonged course of sulphona-mide drugs, I once had the frightening experience of taking an apparently reasonable part in a conversation, but being completely unaware of what either I or my interlocutor was saying. So we must demand of a speaker, if he is to be credited with meaning something by the words he utters, that he know, sufficiently well, the language to which they belong, that he is aware of the words he is using, and that he is saying what he intends to say.

It seems to me that the rationality of using language is sufficiently recognised if the aim of a theory of meaning is conceived as I indicated, if knowledge of a language is treated as of the intermediate type, if linguistic understanding is taken as drawing on this knowledge, and if both issuing and understanding linguistic utterances are required to be conscious activities. Heck, however, worries that the rationality of our use of language has not yet been adequately taken into account. He thinks that for this purpose "our use of language . . . must be . . . integrated with our conscious mental life"; let us call this the integration problem. Now if Frege was right that we can grasp thoughts only as expressed in words or symbols, the integration problem does not arise. Heck believes that infants have basic thoughts before they have learned to express them in words. He presents this as a key to solving the integration problem; it surely is, rather, a condition for there being any such problem. Heck thinks that such infant thoughts must be invoked in explaining our learning the meanings of the words that express them. He quite rightly cautions that the assumption that the child can *have* certain thoughts does not of itself explain what it is for him to be able to express those thoughts in words.

I agree that infants and animals have what resemble thoughts that grown-up people have: I have called them "proto-thoughts." One way they differ from thoughts proper is that they concern only the interpretation and manipulation of the current environment: an infant or animal cannot follow an independent train of thought while walking along or playing with a rattle, or sit or lie musing over something not presently apparent. Acquiring language is a condition for having thoughts unconnected with our present surroundings. As Gareth Evans insisted, with his generality constraint, and as their expression in sentences suggests, our thoughts are complex: they have components. Are proto-thoughts complex? Do they involve compo-nent proto-concepts? One of our eldest child's first words was "pussy"; but when he excitedly exclaimed "Pussy" while watching an earwig crawling over the floor, we realised he had made less progress than we had thought. Did he have the concept *cat* but had attached the word "pussy" to the wider concept *animal*, or did he have only that wider concept? Such questions are important if a child's acquisition of language depends on what concepts he already has; do such questions have determinate answers?

Do infants have only such thoughts as can be expressed in one-word utterances? A Gricean account of meaning, involving the hearer's beliefs, applies in the first instance only to the meanings of whole sentences: can it therefore be used to explain the child's grasp of the meanings of only those one-word sentences which first testify that he is beginning to acquire language? I think in any case that the Gricean model is inappropriate to the first acquisition of language. Children use words to manifest their recognition of what they can see or hear well before they use them to inform others of what they do not know.

Heck acknowledges that there are thoughts one could not have without having learned enough language to express them: our grasp of the meanings of the words in which we can express them has to be explained differently, in what Heck calls a "Dummettian" way. I have often stressed that language must have a hierarchical structure, containing expressions and forms of sentence a grasp of whose meanings depends on a prior grasp of those of other expressions and forms of sentence. I thoroughly agree that we cannot come to understand a sentence in the past or future tense until we know the meaning of the present-tense form.

The question arises why the meanings of all words cannot be explained in a "Dummettian" way, that is, otherwise than by acknowledging the priority of thought over language. I have argued for the priority of language over thought *in the order of explanation*. Which has the *temporal* priority matters only to psychologists; it need not matter to philosophers of language. The use a child makes of a word will manifest his grasp of the concept it expresses, and must be described so that it can be seen as doing so. Whether or not he had the concept before he learned the word is irrelevant. Even if he did, I do not see how that fact can be usefully invoked in describing the use of the word that he must acquire. I do not think that recognition of the rationality of our use of language requires a solution of the integration problem, and I doubt that there is any such problem. As adults, we can have proto-thoughts like those that infants and animals have; I have instanced judgements made by someone driving a car or steering a boat. We also frequently have thoughts not fully expressed by the words that serve as their vehicle, and sometimes thoughts the sole vehicle of which are our bodily actions. Such thoughts can be expressed in language, although we do not express them in language. Among them may be thoughts which Heck would acknowledge as incapable of occurring to beings without language. For all this, an explanation of how we can use language as a vehicle of thought does not require that we assume, of some thoughts, that we can have them before we are capable of expressing them in words.

M. D.

NOTES

1. Or, perhaps, "a rational act *par excellence*." My memory is that I used one or other phrase in print; but I have not been able to find it.

2. Ludwig Wittgenstein, *Philosophical Investigations*, 3rd ed., trans. G. E. M. Anscombe (New York: Macmillan, 1958).

16

Carlo Penco

IDIOLECT AND CONTEXT

ABSTRACT

In this essay I will compare some of Dummett's and Davidson's claims on the problem of communication and idiolects: how can we understand each other if we use different idiolects? First I define the problem, giving the alternative theses of (I) the priority of language over idiolects and (II) the priority of idiolects over language. I then present Dummett's claims supporting (I) and Davidson's claims supporting (II).

In the first three sections, I will provide a reconstruction of the debate between Dummett and Davidson, showing some weaknesses in both programs. In the remaining two sections, I will work on the concept of "convergence." I will try to show that the process of convergence, which is basic in Davidson's theory, needs a level of (formal) analysis of what I call "contextual competence."

The main point of the essay is to show a blind spot in the views of Davidson and Dummett, and to fill the gap. In short, to explain communication, Dummett asks for too much sharing among speakers, and Davidson asks for too little. Even if proposed, for the sake of argument, as a possible supplementation of Davidson's idea of convergence, the suggestion of contextual competence may be used as an extension of Dummett's molecularism.[1]

I. THE IDIOLECT PROBLEM

According to Frege, in everyday language people often attach different senses to the same expression:

In the case of an actual proper name such as "Aristotle" opinions as to the sense may differ. It might, for instance, be taken to be the following: the pupil of Plato and teacher of Alexander the Great. Anybody who does this will attach another sense to the sentence "Aristotle was born in Stagira" than will someone who takes as the sense of the name: the teacher of Alexander the Great who was born Stagira. So long as the [reference] remains the same, such variations of sense may be tolerated, although they are to be avoided in the theoretical structure of a demonstrative science and ought not to occur in a perfect language.[2]

We may call this problem "the idiolect problem": How can we understand each other if we attach different senses to the same words, as if each of us had his own idiolect?[3] By "idiolect" we normally intend "a person's individual speech patterns,"[4] but when we look for a better clarification of the term we encounter a difficulty, given the alternative of two claims about the relation between idiolects and language:

(I) idiolects are defined as deviations from a common standard, deviations from a language intended as a social institution or convention (thesis of the *priority of language over idiolects*)

(II) a language is defined as the result of the way individuals use linguistic expressions in different contexts (thesis of the *priority of idiolects over language*).

Michael Dummett[5] assumes thesis (I) from the start, while Donald Davidson[6] assumes thesis (II). Let us begin with Dummett's position. The first step he takes toward a solution of the idiolect problem is to criticize Frege's conception of everyday language. According to Dummett, Frege reduces everyday language to an overlapping of idiolects.[7] On the contrary, language is basically a social institution and an idiolect is constituted by "the partial and imperfect grasp that a speaker has of a language."[8] Two claims implicitly or explicitly support thesis (I):

(a) Frege is wrong, at least because an overlapping of idiolects is possibly empty (if we think of the intersection of all idiolects of a community) or probably inconsistent (if we think of the union of all idiolects).[9] Given that the Fregean picture of reducing language to an overlapping of idiolects does not work, Dummett claims that we should enrich the picture with the idea of the division of linguistic labor (DLL).[10] Language is a social enterprise, and the correct use of words is checked against the information and knowledge mastered by the disseminated authorities (dictionaries, experts, and so on).[11] DLL is a claim about the determination of meaning and about understanding: on the one hand, the content of the linguistic expressions used by individuals is socially determined (determined by the experts); on the other hand, individuals typically grasp stereotypical representations of the meaning. DLL may therefore be compatible with molecularism, which claims that meanings do not depend on the totality of language, but are constituted by determined fragments of language. These fragments may be either parts of language mastered by the relevant experts or sets of canonical or stereotypical representations conventionally defined.

(b) To give a fundamental role to idiolects in the definition of natural language derives from putting too great an emphasis on language as a tool of communication, disregarding language as the expression of thought.[12] However, the idea itself of language as idiolect (which is strictly connected with a holistic view) brings about a kind of *reductio ad absurdum* concerning the process of communication: actually it reduces communication to a mystery. This last claim is put forward by Dummett in an argument concerning the consequences of the holistic stance held by Quine in "Two Dogmas of Empiricism." We may call it the "Master Argument" (MA):

> (MA) Assume that the meaning of a word depends holistically on the entire system of a speaker's idiolect. Then, no two speakers may reasonably give exactly the same meanings to the same expressions, given that there are no analytic definitions and meaning and belief are inextricable. If speakers cannot give the same meanings to the same words, there will be neither agreement nor disagreement and communication will become impossible.[13]

In a later paper Dummett specifies that denouncing the disastrous consequences of holism does not constitute a knockdown argument against it, but it is at least strong evidence in favor of a methodological stance against holism.[14] Before considering Davidson's alternative against this evidence, in the next paragraph I will show some weak points of the two claims supporting thesis (I).

II. Arguments against Defending Thesis (I)

Argument against the Use of DLL to Solve the Problem of Idiolect

Dummett speaks of "unhappy cases" in which the words of a speaker are understood as in common language, while the speaker means them in an idiolectic use of his own. In these cases, the appeal to "authorities" in language is fundamental for checking a deviant idiolect with respect to socially shared meanings.[15] Therefore Dummett seems to assume the thesis of the social determination of the meanings of a word, a claim much discussed in the literature since Burge 1979.

In a strong version of the social determination of meaning, the content of our belief is fixed by the expressions used, whose meaning is socially determined.[16] This may explain the success of communication grounded in the same contents (following the desiderata of Dummett's master argument), but we explain communication at a high price: counterintuitiveness. In fact, strong social externalism contradicts our intuitions concerning semantic deviance because it makes the mental content of the individual speaker independent of his or her intentions.[17] Dummett's thought cannot be assimilated to this strong version of social externalism because, contrary to Burge, he rejects the appeal to the socially defined meaning to justify ascribing a belief to a speaker.[18] However, his weaker form of social determination of meaning cannot obtain the same result given by the stronger form, which assumes the sharing of the same socially determined contents. In fact, if we cannot appeal to socially defined meaning to justify an ascription of belief, how could we describe how communication works when it happens that we do not share the same contents? It seems that from Dummett's perspective, if two people do not share the same contents, either communication does not succeed or it becomes a mystery. But do we really have to assume that to have successful communication we need a previous sharing of meanings or mental contents? There is at least one way to weaken this attitude strongly held by molecularism. Instead of claiming that there is a set of shared meanings that people must share, we might claim that there must be some meaning shared among two speakers, without having to define it in advance. Is this weakening enough to save the molecularist project?[19] I will not develop this strategy; I am simply remarking on the difficulty of a classic molecularist position (even if supplemented with the idea of weak social determination of meaning) in explaining the actual success of communication.

Besides, DLL is compatible not only with a molecularist position, but also with holism. Meanings within language as a social enterprise governed by the division of linguistic labor may be conceived *of* as depending on the entire system. Actual speakers may not know to what extent the meaning of a word or sentence depends on all the other meanings; but the ideal speaker, or a god, should know the whole system and master the interconnections. The social division of linguistic labor is probably necessary to justify a molecularist stance on language, but it is not sufficient to avoid even a strong form of holism.[20] This may be a problem for Dummett, though not necessarily for thesis (I). In principle, we might accept (I) in a holistic vision in which we define language as what is given by the competence of an ideal speaker. This perspective is not free of problems: first, even experts disagree, thus there might be different ideal competencies; second, actual speakers will never have access to the ideal competence(s), and they will once again be forced into their own idiolects (with some occasional sharing of stereotypes).

DLL does not help Dummett in explaining actual communication in a classical molecularist view, and it is compatible with holism. The main burden of proof is therefore the sustainability of a holistic position and the relevance of Dummett's master argument, which claims that holism reduces communication to a mystery.

Argument against Dummett's Master Argument

Dummett's Master Argument claims that the holistic view, connected with the idea of language as idiolect, makes communication impossible. The criticism is mainly devoted to the problem of holism; Dummett might then give up holism and have another vision of idiolects, considered as molecularistic or atomistic. However, this step would not resolve the problem of priority, because taking a molecularist or an atomistic idiolect as prior to common language seems to assume either a strictly naturalistic view of language or a *reductio* of idiolects to private languages, against Wittgenstein's argument on the publicity of rule-following. Therefore, we are back to the main point of Dummett's criticism, which claims that in order to communicate properly, speakers have to share the same meanings, or at least the same basic or constitutive meanings. The molecularist stance should account for the level of shared meaning grounded in social practice. This is the basic assumption of Dummett's view of communication and deserves further clarification.

Dummett's idea of communication cannot be identified with a simple pattern such as "in order to communicate you have to share a mental reality." As Dummett remarks, the idea that communication is sharing the same thing (for instance, the sense of an expression) in the mind is reinforced by the Fregean heritage.[21] However, this heritage was challenged by Wittgenstein who denounced the tendency to consider the whole point of communication as bringing the sense of the words from one mind to another.[22] We may single out two aspects in Wittgenstein's criticism. The first is against the idea of senses or concepts as something pre-existing language, and to which language gives just a practical way to be transmitted from one mind to the other; the second is against the idea of communication as *sharing* the same things—meanings or inferences or beliefs.

Dummett follows, up to a point, the Wittgensteinian path. He rejects the idea of communication as mental coordination: besides mental coordination, we need an outward and public manifestation showing understanding, consisting of "a complex interplay between linguistic exchange and related actions." The outward manifestation is necessary in order for communication not to rest on faith.[23] This view hinges upon the first aspect of Wittgenstein's criticism; but Dummett seems not to consider the second aspect of Wittgenstein's criticism, at least if we assume that the outward manifestation requires the recognition of canonical inferences shared among speakers. Dummett's view appears to consolidate a picture of communication that presupposes a sharing of meanings—with the *caveat* that it is not just sharing in the heads but a sharing checked in the actual practice of linguistic exchange.

To communicate, you have to understand the sentence the interlocutor pronounces. To understand a sentence, you need to show some abilities verifiable in social practice. First of all, you need to know the sentence's meaning—which can be considered in a *molecularist* view as an intended or canonical or stereotypical set of inferences. In a molecularist view, you need to share the practice to recognize the intended or canonical inferences (or justifications). Hence, you need to share in advance these canonical inferences, as meanings of the sentences.

Certainly, if holism holds, we could find it difficult to explain communication within a picture in which sharing meanings is a presupposition of communication. But there is a point at which this picture begs the question. In fact, Dummett's master argument can be read either as evidence against holism or as evidence against this vision of communication. We then have two possible answers to the so-called "disastrous consequence" of holism: either to reject holism and develop an alternative theory of meaning, or to accept holism and develop an alternative view of communication. Dummett chooses the first horn of the dilemma, but—as we hinted in the previous paragraphs—his molecularist stance seems not to be enough to explain actual communication practice; Davidson chooses the second. If this alternative is viable, Dummett's master argument loses most of its weight. Is the alternative given by Davidson enough to avoid the reduction of communication to a mystery?

III. IDIOLECTS AND COMMUNICATION

Davidson has explicitly attempted an alternative picture of communication. Criticizing Davidson, Dummett has implicitly suggested that insisting on the problem of communication, Davidson's picture of natural language is the most adherent to the Fregean one. In fact, Davidson's theory of communication is an attempt to develop in detail and justify the Fregean attitude towards natural language as an overlapping of idiolects. Communication is explained as the converging of different idiolects toward the same meanings, without making any assumptions about previously shared conventional meanings, concepts, or beliefs.[24] Davidson denies that some "basic" or conventional meanings have to be shared in order for communication to start.[25] However, the final *result* of successful communication must still be a kind of sharing, wherein speaker and hearer assign the same meaning to the speaker's word.[26]

The central aspect of Davidson's approach is the idea of idiolects converging toward a common goal. A clear (even if a bit cumbersome) way to put it, is to speak of a "prior" and a "passing theory." The *prior theory* is a theory that a speaker builds up on his provisional assumptions and expectations on what the other speaker accepts as meanings of the words. The *passing theory* is the one derived by his checking the reactions of the other speaker and individuating the possible differences and lack of consonance with his own inferences.[27] The resulting picture sees communication as a process of *converging* toward the same passing theory, and therefore converging toward the same meanings. There are at least two relevant aspects in this picture: (i) successful communication does not depend on previously shared meanings; (ii) the aim of communication is not the *complete* overlapping of idiolects, but only a local one.

In (i) we may interpret Davidson's claim that much successful communication does not depend on previously shared contents as a suggestion for language learning: learning a language might be viewed as extending the limited idiolect of a child by a larger and larger overlapping with adult language. And we might interpret adult language as a continuous attempt at finding agreement about the use of words, an infinite work of convergence and partial overlappings.

In (ii) Davidson insists that there is no language, if language is intended as a set of conventions. We have to abandon a wrong ideal of a language system, and start with the successful communication realized by convergence of (at least two) idiolects. The two interlocutors will converge toward the same meanings and will eventually end up with a common theory. Taking this process of convergence seriously, the common theory will be local to the dialogue or conversation, and the convergence is a gradual process located in specific settings. The ideal of a *complete* overlapping of idiolects is not to be considered a proper aim of communication.[28]

These two tenets are coherent with the basic step assumed by Davidson in relativizing language to a speaker, a hearer, and a time. Davidson's view of the use of language as local overlappings of idiolects sounds very Fregean in spirit and seems to be an alternative reconstruction of the Fregean attitude regarding the idiolect problem. Moreover, the relativization to speaker, hearer, and time is coherent with the Fregean need to contextualize sentences in order to understand what thought is expressed. In everyday language, not only with indexicals, but also with most of our sentences, we need the context of utterance to understand the thought expressed.

Davidson gives his picture of communication assuming that the speakers already know a language.[29] This step is challenged by Dummett, who claims that by giving priority to idiolects, Davidson leaves unanswered the question of how speakers get their knowledge of their own idiolects.

The shared meanings of the passing theory which is the result of the interaction cannot be the *source* of the knowledge of the idiolects, being a work of convergence of two previously given idiolects (or prior theories).[30] We would have here an infinite regress. To understand how idiolects or prior theories have been developed in us, it is sensible to assert, against Davidson's assumption, that we rely on some previously accepted customs (or basic language games), on some previous practice of rule-following, which are the foundation of a common language. Certainly the practice of rule-following is learned during social interaction and language acquisition, but the ability to develop a passing *theory* cannot found rule-following, but rather presupposes it.

Davidson's answer in later papers is to weaken his picture of the prior and passing theories and describe the development of a dialogue on more general grounds. In an answer to Rorty he says that the basic idea is that a dialogue is based on expectations, which may be thwarted and, in that case, require accommodation.[31] This accommodation may be explained following the very general idea of triangulation. We need to be three in order to have concepts and language: we need two speakers whose lines converge to the same object, which cause the same response in them, who react to their own interaction. The idea of triangulation shows that, in order to converge in language, we do not need any shared routine or rule-following, but just the interaction of at least two speakers/interpreters in front of an object or part of speech.[32] We just need the intention to be understood, and the test of the objectivity of meaning is "the success of the speaker's intention to be understood in a certain way."[33]

However, it is not at all clear how this success is confirmed, if based on intention alone: Wittgenstein's argument of rule-following was devised exactly with the purpose of going beyond the explanation of meaning in terms of intentions alone. Success of the intentions can become mysterious if not grounded in some solid, public core where rules are not only *interpreted as* successfully followed, but are *actually followed* in the same way. Triangulation and intention do not seem to be enough to build a theory of meaning that gives a theoretical expression to the social phenomenon of language. We run the risk of reducing understanding to the claim that the meaning of a word is what we expect other people understand and what we believe or decide they understand. But intention or decision cannot be a criterion of success. I may be happy thinking that the other person has understood me because she behaves in a certain way, but I have no criterion but the provisional happiness of what may be a casual coincidence of action or a simple regularity.[34]

The conclusion given by Dummett discussing the paper on "A Nice Derangement of Epitaphs" seems therefore still valid: the alternative proposed by Davidson leaves out the social and conventional aspect of language and just mimics the attitude toward language taken by Humpty Dumpty in *Alice in Wonderland*. Davidson is wrong, and thesis (I) is the only viable explanation of language.

IV. INTERLUDE IN DEFENSE OF HUMPTY DUMPTY

Dummett's accusation is a little unfair. In fact, the Davidsonian Humpty Dumpty should use the meaning of words according to what he thinks Alice thinks them to be, and not according to his own ideas. He should make himself understood trying to guess Alice's theory of meaning. Therefore, from a Davidsonian viewpoint, he does not behave correctly in chapter 6 of *Through the Looking Glass*, when, after having calculated 364 days in which there is no birthday, he says to Alice, who likes birthday presents instead of unbirthday presents:

"And only one for birthday presents, you know. There's glory for you!"

Alice answers: "I don't know what you mean by 'glory.'"

H.D. replies: "Of course you don't—till I tell you. I meant 'there's a nice knockdown argument for you!'"

Alice objects: "But 'glory' doesn't mean 'a nice knockdown argument.'"

H.D. "When I use a word, it means just what I choose it to mean—neither more nor less."

A. "The question is whether you can make words mean so many different things."

H.D. gives now his famous statement:

"The question is which is to be master—that's all."

Still we may find some reasonable aspects in the attitude of Humpty Dumpty, as already hinted at by Donnellan when he suggested he could end an argument against his opponent saying just "There's glory for you!" Given the background, Donnellan argues he would have been understood.[35] To have a knockdown argument certainly corresponds to having glory in some restricted contexts of intellectuals, especially university professors, who have so little glory in life that they find it in giving knockdown arguments. To Humpty Dumpty, the calculation that there are 364 days for unbirthday presents is a knockdown argument against the idea of preferring birthday presents. And therefore, if we were in an academic environment, he would be justified in using the term "glory."

Is this attitude a really totally unpredictable change in the meaning of "glory"? It does not appear to be completely so. It is an application of the meaning of "glory" in a restricted context, in which Humpty Dumpty would have some right to be the master if we were in an academic situation. The problem is how far he is allowed to "force" the meaning of the words, picking a peculiar set of inferences from a typical academic context and using it in a less restricted situation of dialogue. The problem is, therefore, what the reference community is. If Humpty Dumpty wanted to introduce Alice to the reference community of academics, he would be within his right to do so, and he would be the master of the use of the word as a representative of that restricted community.

Referring to the development of the Echelon system[36] (the system for "monitoring" all communication in European countries), a member of the project, Fred Stock, describes his dismay when, after having spied on Fidel Castro, he began to understand that the Echelon system was spying on the Vatican and generally on Europe. Fred Stock, an American patriot, was at the time very much convinced of the fact that Western countries were allies against the Communist countries, which were the enemies. In 1990, after the fall of the Berlin Wall, it was announced that all the countries of the European Community should have been classified as "enemy." Fred Stock reports that, having asked for clarification from his chief about considering European countries as "enemies" he was answered with something like "You should update the meaning of the word." He found himself in the position of Alice with Humpty Dumpty, where the relevant inferences connected with a word are changed and extended to unpredictable examples or applications. The contemporary Humpty Dumpty, the leader of the Echelon Project, has some right to use the term "enemy" as applied to European countries, including connections with economic competition. A member of the opposite party in economic competition becomes a typical case of enemy, and we may correctly use the term "enemy," just as, if a knockdown argument is considered a typical case of glory, we may use the term "glory" for it.

In the reference community of the Echelon program, it is reasonable to accept a new use of the term "enemy." The problem, as with Alice, is when the meaning of the word has to be accepted by a larger reference community. Meaning depends on who the master is, and normally the master is considered the reference community in which the word is used (this might be considered a way to exemplify the idea that "use" is the master).[37] Which community? What is disturbing in the case of Echelon is different communities coming into contact using apparently contrasting meanings (given that there is not only a difference of beliefs). A difference in meaning is always disturbing for communication. When this difference strikes us, we are disturbed by the realization that other people use an expression in a way that differs from ours.[38] However, once the difference is made explicit, we are faced with two possibilities. Either the stronger community (or individual) imposes its meaning (Humpty Dumpty's arrogant position), or the more intelligent individual, for the sake of conversation, accepts the use of the interlocutor (Davidson's interpreter always makes the other speaker win).[39] But we have another alternative: we might converge through some kind of semantic bargaining.[40] How can this convergence be realized?

Davidson seems to have no answer to that question, as if he did not need it. He is content when a speaker individuates a difference in meaning in the interlocutor; then he will use the word as the interlocutor does. But what if both interlocutors behave in the same way? What if they both simultaneously change the meaning of the words, intending to interpret what the other speaker means? What if, when Davidson begins to use "epitaph" as "epithet," Ms. Malaprop begins to use "epitaph" again as Davidson is supposed to intend (that is, the "right" way)? The process of adjustment or theory building may undergo some restriction given by the interaction of two interlocutors. Davidson gives an example of semantic coordination, but avoids treating more complex cases in which both speakers realize the difference in the use of their words and begin a real process of bargaining.

Restricting his example to semantic coordination, Davidson says that there is something *ineffable* which permits the converging of idiolects. Literally speaking, he says that there is a "mysterious process by which a speaker or hearer uses what he knows in advance plus present data to produce a passing theory."[41] The idea of a mysterious process is reminiscent of the Fregean definition of understanding or grasping a thought: "the most mysterious process," in which the mind, through a subjective process, gets in touch with something objective, a thought or *Gedanke*. The mystery in Frege's assessment is a result of thinking of languages as idiolects, wherein individuals cannot properly share anything but have only subjective individual ways to access the *Gedanke*. In the case of communication, there is no common rule, but only the arbitrariness of a speaker, who tries to grasp the thought grasped by the other speaker. Another interpretation of the Davidsonian call to mystery is to refer to Chomsky, who distinguishes between *problems* (like the architecture of our cognitive structure) and *mysteries* (like the use humans make of cognitive structures).[42] The second cannot be the object of scientific inquiry, but only of intuition and insight.[43]

Davidson's conclusion seems to reduce communication to a mystery, which is exactly what Dummett denounced in his master argument. However the point is different. The appeal to mystery, in Frege as in Davidson, is a rejection of the need to formalize a level of inquiry; the strategy of convergence is a question of practical agreement, which has no

real need of conceptual clarification. At most we might try some psychological or sociological inquiry of this natural ability to converge that we
possess since we belong to the human race. However, given the abundant
recent theorization on the problem of context dependence of meanings, it
seems to me that the appeal to mystery is more similar to the warning about
a new conceptual territory. Here it is still difficult to give clear distinctions:
as the ancient geographers used to say, *"hic sunt leones."* However, we are
not beginning to explore a completely new territory: it is not difficult to find
different attempts at a descriptions of it, even if they are not yet uniform and
well accepted. If we are looking for a theory of meaning which is also a
theory of understanding, we need to look for this level of (formal) analysis,
we need to give the rules governing the process starting from different
premises and still arriving at a (partially) common ground.

V. MYSTERY AND RULES ACROSS CONTEXTS

Attempting a solution to the idiolect problem, Davidson and Dummett
impinge upon different aspects of Wittgenstein's philosophy. Dummett
insists on social practice, rule-following, and the need to have grounds for
defining what is correct and incorrect. Davidson's picture matches the
Wittgensteinian view, which denies that there is an essence of language and
leaves us with a nonordered, open set of a great variety of language games.
Both views have their rationale, but both have a blind spot. Dummett finds
it difficult to explain communication without previously shared contents;
Davidson cannot avoid resorting to mystery to explain communication.
Dummett presupposes too much sharing and Davidson presupposes too
little. What is needed to solve the problem is a third way in between
Dummett's requirement of presupposing conventional meaning sharing for
communication and Davidson's requirement of not presupposing any
previous sharing of conventions to explain communication.

A suggestion for an answer comes from Bilgrami, who claims that we
normally share contents at a local level because we do not import in that
local level all we know about the relevant content.[44] It is true that we do not
import all we know about, let us say, "water" while asking for a glass of
water. It is reasonable to assume that we share some typical contents in
advance in special local settings, where we are expected to do exactly what
we do (to ask for a glass of wine in a bar, for a pint of beer in a pub). This
is what grounds most studies about the use of frames and scripts in
cognitive sciences. However, in many cases we are not completely guided
by the local setting, and we have to build it piece by piece, through
bargaining with our interlocutor and converging toward a locally shared

meaning. If we want to generalize this line of thought, we need to look at which abilities are necessary to work out this process of convergence.

Speaking about the necessity of sharing some manifestable abilities, Dummett implicitly points toward the problem raised and not solved by the Davidsonian view of communication as converging: what must we share in order to converge? Dummett does not enlighten us about the *kind* of abilities we should share. Certainly in our introduction to our first language games, we learn *inferential* and *referential* abilities. But being introduced to language use, we learn at the same time some *reflexive* or *contextual* abilities. With these terms I mean linguistically shaped abilities we form in language learning to individuate conceptual or cognitive spaces or contexts and work on them. An example is the mastery of narrative modes and the ability to enter and exit narrative modes and fiction, from the early stages of language learning.[45] We soon acquire reflexive abilities to treat our descriptions or representations of what is going on ("what is she saying?" or "what does he think?"). These abilities, not necessarily conscious, help us to move across different conceptual spaces and permit us to follow the essential contextual dependence of meaning. If we want a theoretical representation of our mastery of language in communication, we should also give proper space, besides inferential and referential abilities, to contextual ones. These abilities can be theoretically represented as rules on conceptual spaces, and we need to define which kinds of rules are required in our theoretical representation.

It might be objected that we could not use higher order rules to fill the gap of the infinite regress of passing theories: we would put in a higher order theory to block the infinite regress of lower order theories (passing theories). The problem, however, is not about the *source* of our basic theories, but about what we share in communication. We learn to use our inferential and referential abilities *in specific contexts*. Then, even if we do not share the same contexts, we have learned some shared and recognized basic inferential abilities (logical constants).[46] However, learning inferential and referential abilities, we realize that the inferences we use depend on contextual restrictions, on different cognitive situations. We need to master a new kind of ability which governs contextual restrictions (in a novel monkeys are allowed to fly). Even if we do not share the same contents, we share the same abilities, which we may use to bargain the meaning (and the reference) of the linguistic expressions we use.

The main source of difficulty of communication is the difficulty to individuate the kind of context within which we are working. What comes at the end of the process of language learning may come first in the process of understanding and explanation. That is why the contextual abilities we learn at the end of our basic linguistic training are the first tool we use to converge with other people toward the same (kinds of) meanings and contexts.

We may describe these contextual abilities using the idea of cognitive contexts. Here with "cognitive context" I mean the state of mind or the set of beliefs of an individual about a situation.[47] In our description of how communication works, we need to describe the interaction of different cognitive contexts, the way in which they are compatible with one another, and the rules used to converge or to tune toward the same inferences and the same domains of interpretation. We may call these rules "rules of contextual dependence." Anticipating his idea of mystery held in "A Nice Derangement of Epitaphs," Davidson said that "what we cannot expect, however, is that we can formalize the considerations that lead us to adjust our theory to fit the inflow of new information."[48] The formalization of rules governing contextual dependence seems to fill exactly this unexpected gap.

Contextual dependence gives fundamental restrictions to our interactions, and our contextual abilities can be (even formally) described as rules which work *on* contexts and permit us to make explicit the kinds of inferences we attach to the linguistic expressions we use. We may define these rules as different kinds of shifting or moving in the space of cognitive contexts. Following a definition of three dimensions of contextual dependence (partiality, approximation, and perspective[49]), we may speak of shifting *inside* contexts, shifting *on* contexts, and shifting *through* contexts:

(i) A primary way of shifting *inside* contexts is the ability to expand or contract the amount of information needed. In any conversation or problem solving, we need to individuate the right set of information, the language, and the rules used in such a context. To take a flight, one only needs to know departure time and place (it would be impossible to consider *all* information about any possible difficulty, from strikes to accidents). But if one loses the ticket, one needs to enlarge the amount of information needed, still remaining inside the intended cognitive context. To say "I lost the ticket" at the help desk of the airlines is in fact normally intended inside a restricted set of assumptions, and one will certainly be correctly understood. As Bilgrami suggested, meaning or inferences are shared *locally*. The cognitive context needed to face any situation is always partial; still it may always be expanded or specialized when new facts occur.

(ii) Shifting *on* context means *reflecting* or moving the balance of parameters like time, location, and speaker; they can be expressed explicitly inside the context or left implicit as taken for granted. One of the main features of shifting on contexts is given by the ability to pass from explicit to implicit representations of parameters and vice versa. This aspect has been abundantly shown by Perry, while he describes the relevance of passing from a description in which indexicals are "out of the picture," as unarticulated constituents, and in which they are explicitly considered. Saying "it rains" and "it rains here and now" may express the same content, but they are different ways of expressing it, and the difference makes a relevant contribution to the cognitive aspect of our thoughts. In short, I may always *de-contextualize* or re-contextualize what I am speaking about, making a parameter explicit or leaving it implicit. Among the parameters we may have the context itself, if we decide to "enter" a context (like entering a novel) and asserting what is valid, forgetting to give explicit reference to the context. Eventually we may "exit" the context and assert something valid with explicit reference to the context. This reflective ability is a basic tool to disambiguate misunderstandings in communication, when people assume different implicit parameters. Also, bargaining on the domain of quantifiers or on the reference of demonstratives used in a dialogue ("*that*, what? Shape or color?") belongs to this kind of reflexive rules.

(iii) *Shifting through contexts or shifting points of view:* we may change parameters and still have compatibility among our assertions. For instance "I am here" said by me can be shifted to "he is there" said by her. "Yesterday was sunny" said today, can be shifted to "today is sunny" said yesterday. "The book is in front of me" said by me, placed behind you, can be shifted to "the book is behind me" said by you, or "the book is behind you" said by me. "I have seen an enemy" said by the soldier of faction A can be shifted to "he has seen a friend" said by a soldier of faction B. "Epithet" said by you can be shifted to "epitaph" said by me. And so on. I may shift to your point of view using the word (I suppose) you are using. This kind of shifting is essential to semantic coordination, and it is the first step for semantic bargaining.

Semantic bargaining needs something more than understanding the use of the interlocutor and speaking as we think she would. We need a further step, making explicit the points of divergence between the two speakers. The ability to follow and pick the points of divergence of anaphoric chains may be a central pattern of this kind of ability.[50] The ability to shift contexts is basic for disambiguating the intentions that guide our assertions and keep communication going. Think of the example given by Sperber-Wilson: "Would you like some coffee?" Answer: "It will keep me awake." The answer amounts to "Yes" or "No" depending on intended context. Here we have to decide which context to take into consideration, and the interlocutors have to bargain the meaning (it may still be undecided yet!). Bargaining may be done either in an explicit way or in an implicit way, but the two interlocutors are on the same level, while the example given by Davidson always makes the interpreter a conscious onlooker in a practice. In contrast to the Malaprop case, we may also shift context together in order to understand what is really going on in the dialogue.

Davidson's examples of convergence are just one case of a more complex and general kind of shifting. Is it beyond any kind of theoretical analysis or formalization? The answer may be: convergence is guided by contextual abilities, which are basic in helping us to see the compatibility of our assertions and may eventually help us to go toward the same meanings. Different kinds of contextual abilities give the necessary condition of successful communication. We may think of them as an extension of abilities to move in physical surroundings; without these abilities we would be lost. Without contextual abilities; it would be impossible to participate in a conversation because we would not know where we were, in which kind of cognitive context we were operating. The particular format given above is widely discussed in many sectors of artificial intelligence and cognitive sciences; it has produced many formalizations competing with one another. If there is not yet a common and defined theoretical setting, there is clearly the need for a general theory which pictures the space in which the prerequisites of linguistic communication can be localized.[51]

Speaking of cognitive contexts, we do not assume that we share exactly the same contexts or the same theories; sometimes we rely on similarities, and all the time we are guided to check compatibility relations. Our abilities to move through different contexts are, however, something we share, and they help us to check the differences in the others' speech and need to be studied and described as rules defining the work of convergence through which we arrive at sharing contents at a local level.

SUMMARY AND CONCLUSIONS

We started with the problem of idiolects posed by Frege: how can we understand each other if we use different idiolects? We described two alternative theses: Dummett, in favor of the thesis that idiolects are defined after language, claims that we need the division of linguistic labor and molecularism against holism. Davidson, supporting the thesis that language is defined after idiolect, claims that communication requires no previous sharing of meaning, but is a work of convergence. Both positions have serious flaws. Against Dummett we may say that the division of linguistic labor neither explains the problem of idiolect, nor excludes the possibility of holism. Dummett's argument against holism is not a knockdown argument; moreover, it is grounded in a vision of communication, based on previous sharing of meanings, which does not completely account for the phenomena of communication. Against Davidson we may say that his theory of communication as convergence grounded on intention alone is not as convincing as the rule-following consideration strategy used by Dummett. Besides, it makes communication a mystery, even if for different reasons than the ones denounced by Dummett in his original argument against holism.

We said that Dummett imposes too much sharing for communication to work and Davidson requires too little sharing. We have claimed that it is highly implausible to think that what is necessary for communication is a previous sharing of meanings, conceptual contents, and sets of inferences. However, we share abilities concerning mental spaces or conceptual contexts. This level of analysis fills a gap both in Davidson's and in Dummett's theory of meaning. The point does not give a conclusive choice between thesis (I) and thesis (II) defined at the beginning (maybe there is no answer but the old fashioned reflexive equilibrium). We found a space in between idiolects and conventions, showing how idiolects are guided by abilities, which are conventionally shared, and these abilities can be represented as rules to describe the proper working of our communication practices. Davidson's approach might abandon mystery and consider a new level of analysis, where his examples are just one kind of application of a kind of rule, belonging to a more structured set of rules of convergence. Dummett's approach would better elaborate on the intuitive idea of sharing abilities, giving these abilities a more precise status and formal expression.

CARLO PENCO

UNIVERSITY OF GENOA
JULY 2002

NOTES

1. I thank Cesare Cozzo, Marco Santambrogio, and Stefano Predelli for comments on an earlier version of the paper. I have given different versions of the paper at University of Genoa, at Columbia University, at King's College (London), and at the ESAP meeting in Lund. Additional thanks to the audience for their comments; thanks to Marcello Frixione, Gurpreet Rattan, Achille Varzi, Mary Margaret McCabe, and Alberto Voltolini for particular comments. Other suggestions came from Cristina Amoretti, Claudia Bianchi, Paolo Bouquet, Mario De Caro, and Massimiliano Vignolo on various points of the paper. Last but not least, I thank Diego Marconi and Mark Sainsbury for very useful comments on one of the last versions of the paper.

2. Frege 1997, footnote B, 153.

3. The problem can be reframed in a direct reference setting: how can people

understand each other if, even using the same causal chain, they give different criteria of identification to the same name? The problem apparently becomes even more puzzling when predicates are concerned.

4. Definition from *Webster's College Dictionary*. If we take a naturalistic point of view, we may consider idiolects, like human faces or bodies, individual variations on a structure. Each speaker has its own unique idiolect, made up by her vocabulary, rules for sentence formation, accepted inferences. For a confrontation between Chomsky's view of idiolects and Dummett's idea of language as a social entity see Green 2001, 150ff.

5. From the start, but also in Dummett 1994, 265: "the primary unit is still a *shared* language, known to all participants in a conversation; and the prototypical case is that in which they all use that language in the same way."

6. I refer to Davidson's well known proposal of relativizing language to a speaker, a time, and a hearer (see for instance Davidson 1984 and Davidson 1986). Davidson (1999, 307) has expressed very clearly the idea of language as over-lapping of idiolects: "people differ greatly in the scope of their vocabularies and in their conceptual resources. This does not prevent them from communicating in the area of overlap, nor it does stop them from increasing the overlap."

7. Dummett says: "On Frege's theory, the basic notion really is that of an idiolect, and a language can only be explained as the common overlap of many idiolects" (1978, 424).

8. Dummett says: "language is not to be characterized as a set of overlapping idiolects. Rather, an idiolect is constituted by the partial and imperfect grasp that a speaker has of a language" (1991, 87).

9. See for instance Marconi (1997, 56), who elaborates this criticism against the idea of "capturing 'communitarian' inferential competence, or the common core of all individual competences."

10. See Dummett 1978, 427ff. and Dummett 1981, 190, where he says that Frege's neglect of the social aspect of language (reference to authorities, and so on) is a "serious defect" in his treatment of language.

11. Even if dictionaries are not absolute standards, they give useful information a "socially adequate use of the language" (Marconi 1997, 56). In an analogous vein, after having discussed the importance of dictionaries as authorities in the standard use of language Dummett (1991, 85) remarks on this paradoxical aspect of language: "while its practice must be subject to standard of correctness, there is no ultimate authority to impose those standards from without."

12. Dummett (1991, 103) avoids the alternative of which aspect is primary; actually the point about language in this respect is that "acquired by interaction with others, it cannot serve for further successful communication unless it has been made a vehicle of thought." Dummett (1986, 470–71) is even willing to take communica-tion as the primary role of language ("language is a vehicle of thought because it is an instrument of communication, and not conversely"); yet insists on warning about the "error to concentrate too exclusively on communication."

13. Taking the terminology from Tennant 1987 we may say that the Master Argument concerns both constitutive holism and holism from inextricability. *Constitutive holism* can be defined as the claim that the meaning of a word is its role in the linguistic system; *holism from inextricability* can be defined as the claim that meaning and belief are inextricable. See Tennant 1987, 32–33.

14. Dummett 1975, 121; see also 1993, 21.

15. Dummett 1991, 85.

16. Burge claims that "the expressions the subject uses sometimes provide the content of his mental states or events even though he only partially understands, or even misunderstands, some of them" (1979, 114).

17. See for instance Marconi 1997, 98, also discussing the problem of the reference a word has for the individual speaker.

18. See for instance Dummett 1991, 88: "When an utterance is made, what the speaker says depends upon the meanings of his words in the common language. But, if he thereby expresses a belief, the content of that belief depends on his personal understanding of those words, and thus on his idiolect."

19. See Marconi 1997, and Perry 1994. They criticize the strong form of molecularism denounced by Fodor and Lepore and accept a weaker form, which passes the test against holism posed by Fodor and Lepore. In short, they do not accept that there is some property which speakers necessarily share in communication $\forall p \, \exists q \, (q \neq p \, \& \, \square \, (p \text{ is shared} \rightarrow q \text{ is shared}))$. However they accept that it is necessary to communicate that some semantic property is shared (without having decided it a priori or in advance), that is: $(\forall p \, \square \, (p \text{ is shared} \rightarrow \exists q \, (q \neq p \, \& \, q \text{ is shared}))$.

20. Certainly there are different forms of holism, and it is possible to find places for different forms of weak holism, like different forms of molecularism. I have treated this aspect in Penco 2001 and 2002 and I will not discuss this issue here.

21. This picture of Frege given by Dummett should be partially revised. In fact, even if we may have access to the same sense, sharing them is not a precondition of communication. The quotation given at the beginning of this paper shows that for communication to work, Frege considered a sufficient condition to refer to the same objects, even if we do not share the same senses. It is true however that the Fregean tradition did not develop this aspect of Frege, relying more on the idea of grasping the same senses in the mind.

22. Wittgenstein, *Philosophical Investigations*, 363.

23. Dummett 1983, 187. Communication would rest on faith if we accepted the idea that the representative power of language that connects language with sense and thought can be isolated from other features of language.

24. See Davidson 1984, 195.

25. Davidson (1986) considers three tenets concerning "first" or "basic" meanings, as (1) systematic, (2) shared, and (3) governed by conventions of regularities. The point is the connection between (1) and (2) with (3).

26. This is a basic aim of communication for Davidson, since his 1982 essay where he says that "if communication succeeds, speaker and hearer must assign the same meaning to the speaker's word" (Davidson 1984, 277). Davidson later accepts the idea that "what must be shared is the interpreter's and the speaker's understanding of the speaker's words" (1986, 438).

27. See the discussion in Davidson 1986. The holistic part is the following: in the passing theory the role temporarily or locally attributed to an expression should have all the (inferential) "power," given by a recursive (holistic) theory. When I interpret "epitaph" as "epithet," I will use all the "inferences to other words, phrases and sentences" connected with "epithet" in my idiolect to interpret "epitaph" in Ms. Malaprop's idiolect. I wonder whether in Ms. Malaprop's idiolect there will be—*salva* translation—the same inferences with other words, phrases, and sentences!

28. As Davidson remarks, apparently a speaker would not be interested in a complete overlapping with the idiolect of all other speakers. It is not clear how much there will be in common after the process of convergence, except occasional overlaps of meanings and beliefs; Davidson abandons the "ideal" interpreter, who would have access to *all* meanings and beliefs (1999, 307–8). It seems to me that in this way we run the risk of thinking of each interpreter as bound to her *solypsistic* idiolect, with some occasional overlapping with other speakers during dialogues, and we risk the *presumption* of sharing a lot of beliefs.

29. "I want to know how people who already have a language (whatever exactly that means) manage to apply their skill of knowledge to actual cases of interpretation" (Davidson 1986, 441).

30. A Davidsonian passing theory is a "second-order theory" (i.e., a theory of an interlocutor's theory of meaning) and must be grounded on a more basic theory of meaning which gives a theoretical expression to the social phenomenon of language. According to Dummett also the prior theory should have the role of second order theory, putting Davidson in an infinite regress (1986, 470). But it seems to me that the point is not so clearly decided here. In fact Davidson's prior theory is bound to play two roles at one time: on the one hand it is the theory of the speaker, on the other hand it is the theory the speaker projects on the interlocutor. Only because it is the (first level) theory of the speaker can it work as a second level theory about the interlocutor.

31. See Davidson 1999, 598–99.

32. See Davidson (2001, 121) where he attempts, via triangulation an alternative argument against the private language, which bypasses the rule following argument given by Kripke or Wittgenstein.

33. Davidson 1992, 117.

34. If I ask you to "open the window" and you open the window I think my intention to be understood has been successful. However, you might have understood "open the door," and—being angry with me—voluntarily disobeyed my order and opened the window instead. In this case, my intention to be understood

has not been properly fulfilled; I have a chance: I may ask you "Did you open the window because I told you that?" If you answer "yes" I would be satisfied enough to think my intention has been really understood. However, you may answer "yes" because you mean by "that" your own interpretation of my utterance, that is "open the door." We may go on as we can. We cannot fill the gap between *succeeding* to making my intention properly understood and *thinking* to succeed in making my intention properly understood. Rule-following considerations seem to be necessary just to fill this gap. Basing communication and linguistic interaction on rule-following considerations does not mean that communication is always granted (just grounded). On the other hand, accepting defeaseability in principle does not imply accepting a picture of communication as resting on faith, a result that seems to be unavoidable if we ground communication on intention alone.

35. Donellan (1968, 213), quoted in Davidson 1986, 438–42.

36. News about the following exchange appeared in European newspapers in 2001, and has been discussed in the European Community. Apparently I am not interested in the historical truth of the matter here. Therefore I report news taken from newspapers without assuming their truth; their verisimilitude is enough for the case. The name "Fred Stock" is also a name of a famous investigator in the literature. Let us assume that the entire matter is a matter of fiction.

37. Humpty Dumpty might be seen either as a metaphor of use or as a metaphor of the influence of media over use. In this second case, we apparently have to fight Humpty Dumpty, like any fight against bad uses of language imposed by bad masters.

38. A peculiar aspect here is that the smaller community uses its jargon against what is officially shared in public speech and official institutional acts—the (provisional) official view of friendship between the USA and Europe. We might think that the difference is a difference in belief and not in meaning. However, the answer given in the Echelon project ("update your *meaning*") has some right, given that the problem is not only to enlarge the range of application of the term "enemy," but also the kind of relevant inferences linked to the term.

39. Shall the larger community accept the meaning as defined by the smaller one? This problem is normally considered a typical case in the development of the terminology of science. What is defined and used in small groups of researchers may become the standard use in the future. It might be that the Echelon project developed enough and persuaded normal newspapers and the government to accept this use of "enemy." We would need a complex updating of the meaning of the semantic field constituted by terms like "war," "enemy," "fight," "competition," and so on.

40. On an aspect of semantic bargaining (on the domain on quantification or on the reference of indexicals) see Penco 2006.

41. Davidson 1986, 445.

42. I take this suggestion from Gurpreet Rattan.

43. Chomsky says: "Roughly, where we deal with cognitive structures, either

in a mature state of knowledge and belief or in the initial state, we face problems, but not mysteries. When we ask how humans make use of these cognitive structures, how and why they make the choices and behave as they do, although there is much that we can say as human beings with intuition and insight, there is little, I believe, that we can say as scientists" (1976, 138).

44. Bilgrami 1991, 11ff.

45. In psychology much research has been done on the importance of abilities concerning narration: ability to enter a narration with identification with a character, ability to detach from the narration, to enter and exit the context of narration, and so on. A relevant author in this setting is Jerome Bruner, who has given much attention to the importance of mastering narrative abilities and semantic bargaining for the development of intelligence. To check some literature see for instance Campart 2000.

46. This amounts to saying that to communicate we need to share the meanings of the logical constants (sharing inferential abilities), but we do not necessarily share a common set of inferences linked to the lexical entries.

47. I refer mainly to Benerecetti et al. 2000, which relies on a wide literature in artificial intelligence, starting with the works of McCarthy, Giunchiglia, Dinsmore, Fauconnier, Sperber, and Wilson. Most of these theories seem to converge toward some common lines in describing which rules are necessary for a good description of our abilities to deal with context. Certainly there is still some intuitive aspect and the definition of these rules is still a work in progress; yet these results are a novelty which the traditional philosophy of language should take care of. Examples in this direction are also the works of Gauker on the idea of multi-contexts systems and the logical works of Thomason on a type theory about multiagent. Another relevant work in this direction is Bouquet et al. 2006.

48. Davidson 1984, 279.

49. Following Benerecetti et al. 2000, the fundamental dimensions of contextual dependence may be described as partiality, approximation, and perspective. (i) *Partiality*: any assertion or use of language is relative to the minimal amount of information needed to understand it according to the relevant goals. When new information is required, we may import it or shift context to get it. (ii) *Approximation*: any representation of a situation, as Barwise and Perry (1983) have insisted, is approximate. Parameters, which can always be expressed if we want more detail in the discourse, are often left unexpressed. A relevant aspect is the granularity of the description: the kind of representation may always shift to different levels of description. (iii) *Perspective*: as Brandom (1994) has abundantly stressed, we need to recognize the interplay of different perspectives; and any representation is perspectival because it is always given from a point of view, either cognitive or pragmatic. Benerecetti, Bouquet and Ghidini suggest that different kinds of rules should be appropriate for these dimensions. In short, we might put it in the following way: First, we have to realize "where" we are in the space of discourse, which conceptual space we have access to or what we are speaking about. Second,

we have to give the right granularity, making explicit for the audience what is needed and avoiding making explicit what is or should be presupposed. Third, we have to decide which perspective has to be taken, or which shift of perspective is needed to make our assertions compatible with other people's assertions.

50. I have expanded on this aspect of semantic bargaining in the use of demonstratives in Penco 2006.

51. See Benerecetti et al. 2000 and Bouquet et al. 2006.

REFERENCES

Benerecetti, Massimo, Paulo Bouquet, and Chiara Ghidini. 2000. "Contextual Reasoning Distilled." *Journal of Theoretical and Experimental Artificial Intelligence* 12 (3): 279–305.

———. 2006. "On the Dimensions of Context Dependence." In *Perspective on Context*, ed. P. Bouquet, L. Serafini, and R. Thomason. Stanford, CA: CSLI Publications.

Bilgrami, Akeel. 1992. *Belief and Meaning: The Unity and Locality of Mental Content.* Oxford: Blackwell.

Brandom, Robert. 1994. *Making it Explicit: Reasoning, Representing, and Discursive Commitment.* Cambridge, MA: Harvard Univ. Press.

Burge, Tyler. 1979. "Individualism and the Mental." *Midwest Studies in Philosophy* 4: 73–121.

Chomsky, Noam. 1976. *Reflections on Language.* London: Fontana.

Cozzo, C. 2002. "Does Epistemological Holism Lead to Meaning Holism?" *Topoi* 21:25–45.

Davidson, Donald. 1967. "Truth and Meaning." Reprinted in Davidson 1984, from which I quote.

———. 1974. "On the Very Idea of a Conceptual Scheme." Reprinted in Davidson 1984, from which I quote.

———. 1977. "The Method of Truth in Metaphysics." Reprinted in Davidson 1984, from which I quote.

———. 1982. "Communication and Convention." Reprinted in Davidson 1984, from which I quote.

———. 1984. *Inquiries into Truth and Interpretation.* Oxford: Clarendon Press.

———. 1986. "A Nice Derangement of Epitaphs." In *Truth and Interpretation: Perspectives in the Philosophy of Donald Davidson*, ed. E. Lepore. Oxford: Basil Blackwell, 433–46.

———. 1991. "James Joyce and Humpty Dumpty." *Midwest Studies in Philosophy* 16:1–12.

———. 1992. "The Second Person." In *The Wittgenstein Legacy, Midwest Studies in Philosophy* 17:255–67. Reprinted in Davidson 2001, 107–22.

―――. 1994. "The Social Aspect of Language." In *The Philosophy of Michael Dummett*, ed. B. McGuinness and G. Oliveri. Dordrecht: Kluwer, 1–16.

―――. 1999. "Reply to Simon J. Evnine" and "Reply to Richard Rorty." In *The Philosophy of Donald Davidson*, vol. 27 of The Library of Living Philosophers, ed. Lewis E. Hahn. Chicago and La Salle: Open Court, 305–10 and 595–600.

―――. 2001. *Subjective, Intersubjective, Objective: Philosophical Essays*. Oxford: Oxford Univ. Press, 107–22.

Donellan, Keith. 1968. "Putting Humpty Dumpty Together Again." *The Philosophical Review* 77: 203–15.

Dummett, Michael. 1981 [1973]. *Frege: Philosophy of Language*, 2nd ed. London: Duckworth.

―――. 1974. "The Social Character of Meaning." *Synthese* 27:523–34. Reprinted in Dummett, *Truth and Other Enigmas*, London: Duckworth, 1978, from which I quote.

―――. 1975. "What is a Theory of Meaning? (I)." In *Mind and Language*, ed. Samuel Guttenplan. Oxford: Clarendon Press, 97–138.

―――. 1976. "What is a Theory of Meaning? (II)." In *Truth and Meaning*, ed. G. Evans and J. McDowell. Oxford: Oxford Univ. Press. Reprinted also in Dummett 1993, from which I quote.

―――.1978. *Truth and Other Enigmas*. London: Duckworth.

―――. 1986. "A Nice Derangement of Epitaphs: Some Comments on Davidson and Hacking." In *Truth and Interpretation: Perspectives in the Philosophy of Donald Davidson*, ed. E. Lepore. Oxford: Blackwell, 459–76.

―――. 1991. *The Logical Basis of Metaphysics*. London: Duckworth.

―――. 1993. *The Seas of Language*. Oxford: Clarendon.

―――. 1994. "Reply to Davidson." In *The Philosophy of Michael Dummett*, ed. Brian McGuinness and Gianluigi Olivieri. Dordrecht: Kluwer.

Esfeld, Michael. 1998. "Holism and Analytic Philosophy." *Mind* 107:365–80.

Fodor, Jerry, and Ernest Lepore. 1992. *Holism*. Oxford: Blackwell.

Frege, Gottlob. 1997 [1892]. "On Sinn and Bedeutung." In *The Frege Reader*, trans. Max Black, ed. Michael Beaney. Oxford: Blackwell, 151–71.

Marconi, Diego. 1997. *Lexical Competence*. Cambridge, MA: MIT Press.

Penco, Carlo. 1999. "Objective and Cognitive Context." *Lecture Notes in Computer Science* 1688:270–83.

―――. 2001. "Local Holism." *Lecture Notes in Computer Science* 2116:290–303.

―――. 2002. "Holism, Strawberries and Hairdryers." *Topoi* 21:47–54.

―――. 2006. "Context and Contract." In *Perspective on Context*, ed. P. Bouquet, L. Serafini, and R. Thomason. Stanford, CA: CSLI Publications.

Perry, John. 1994. "Fodor and Lepore on Holism." *Philosophical Studies* 73: 123–38.

Tennant, Neil. 1987. "Holism, Molecularity and Truth." In *Michael Dummett: Contributions to Philosophy*, ed. Barry M. Taylor. Dordrecht: Nijhoff, 31–58.

Wittgenstein, Ludwig. 1953. *Philosophical Investigations*. Oxford: Blackwell.

REPLY TO CARLO PENCO

"It seems that in Dummett's perspective, if two people do not share the same contents, either communication does not succeed or it becomes a mystery," Carlo Penco says. This is a gross exaggeration. What he calls "weak social determination" is the view I take, that the *meaning* of what someone says is determined by the meaning in the language he is using of the words he utters, but that the *belief* he is thereby expressing is determined by the interpretation he puts on those words, that is, what he thinks they mean. Now weak social determination can allow that very often speaker and hearer understand the words in accordance with their meanings in the language, and that this is why the one understands the other, but can still account for the fact that although the speaker intends one or another word in a sense contrary to its true meaning in the language, the hearer often grasps what he intended to convey.

Suppose that someone says, "It is perfectly safe to smoke near this: it is inflammable." The remark, literally understood, is so ridiculous that it is obvious something has gone wrong: the speaker cannot be meaning what he says. Evidently, he uses "flammable" to mean "inflammable," as some people do; he thinks that "inflammable" is its contrary and would explain it as meaning "not flammable." He does not mean what he says: what he says is not what he means. What he *says* is that the substance in question is inflammable. That, of course, is not what he *thinks*: he believes that it is *not* inflammable. So what someone *says* is to be estimated by the meanings in the common language of the words he uses; but what *belief* he is aiming to express by the words he uses is to be estimated by what he supposes those words to mean. It is difficult to see how this can be contested. Carlo Penco thinks that I am committed to holding that if speaker and hearer do not attach the same meanings to the words, either communication does not succeed or it becomes a mystery. Well, if the speaker had said merely, "This substance is inflammable," meaning that it was *not* inflammable, communication would probably have failed, his hearer naturally taking him to have meant what he said. Given that he said what he did, however, its obvious absurdity would have warned the hearer that something had gone wrong.

Knowing that some people use "flammable" to mean "inflammable," and that "in-" is frequently a negative prefix, as in "inadvisable," he could easily guess that the speaker meant "not inflammable." There is no mystery in this: it follows our usual way of hitting on what people intend when they fail to say what they mean.

I think that the principal reason that we understand each other's speech, when we do, is that speaker and hearer know some common language and are using it. We often manage to understand someone who is *mis*using the language he is aiming to speak. We can do so because he is aiming to speak a certain language, we know that he is doing so, we know what language that is and we know that language. That we can do so is not mysterious in the least: we go on what he probably intended to convey, on commonly made mistakes, on confusions he is likely to have made, on general facts about the language in question. Our ability to guess, frequently correctly, what someone did mean when he said what he did not mean in no way calls in doubt the view that our understanding one another rests upon our shared but imperfect knowledge of a common language. I repudiate Carlo Penco's charge against me that I presuppose too much sharing of mental contents— that is of the meanings of words. I think that such sharing is the basic reason why we understand one another's speech, when we do; but I think it possible to explain how we often come to understand one another when we do not share the meanings of the words each uses.

What is "the idiolect problem"? No doubt it is entangled with the opposition between a holist and a molecularist account of linguistic meaning and understanding, but it is not the same problem. Penco tacitly acknowledges this when he says that appeal to the division of linguistic labour is not sufficient to avoid holism, but that this is not necessarily a problem for his thesis (I), one of two opposed views of idiolects. He takes the idiolect problem to be that of explaining our ability to communicate with one another by means of language in terms of idiolects. Suppose, that is, that we do not assume the existence of languages shared by a number of speakers (most of them by a large number), or even that, like Davidson, we deny the existence of such languages, and suppose that we assume only that, except for infants, each individual has a set of linguistic propensities which together constitute his idiolect. Then we have a problem to explain how it is that we succeed in communicating with one another by employing these idiolects.

Well, that is a problem, all right. It is analogous to the following. It can be observed that some people can send verbal messages by tapping out a series of long and short sounds by telegraph, and that certain recipients can translate these into a sequence of letters. One explanation of what makes this possible is that there is a standard code by which each letter of the alphabet is represented by a specific short sequence of longs and shorts, and that transmitters and receivers have all learned this code. Some do not accept this explanation, and deny that there is any such code; they say that operators and receivers each have individual long-short propensities, and that a receiver interprets a message as the sender intended if his long-short propensity happens to coincide with that of the sender. Plainly, those who deny the code's existence have a good deal to explain.

This way of posing the problem surely caricatures the idiolect theorist. His thesis about communication is that what makes it possible is an overlap of idiolects. Holding this thesis does not debar him from offering an explanation of the fact that idiolects overlap extensively as often as they do. He can acknowledge that children's linguistic propensities are largely formed by imitation of, and some actual instruction from, their parents and other adults, and that the idiolects of the adults were in turn formed in a similar way. Elaborated, this undeniable fact would go far to explain why idiolects overlap as often and to as great an extent as they do. It may be objected that the elaboration will go far to admit the existence of shared languages; it remains that the idiolect theorist's explanation of the fact of communication is still in place.

The question what makes communication possible is indeed relevant to the dispute between a holistic and a molecularist account of language. But, as I see the matter, it is not the question that is truly at issue between the idiolect theorist and the shared-language theorist. Penco thinks that in part it is, because he holds that the idea of language as idiolect "is strictly connected with a holistic view." This is why he characterises as my "Master Argument" against the idiolect theorist one I gave against Quine's combination of views about language. This combination consisted in three theses: the priority in the order of explanation of idiolects over common languages; linguistic holism; and the inextricability of meaning and belief. But I do not think that the idiolect theorist need embrace either of the last two of these theses. The idiolect theorist may think he can disentangle someone's beliefs from the meanings he attaches to the words of his idiolect; and he can give a molecularist account of that idiolect.

What is primarily at issue is the order of explanation. Ought we to explain an idiolect as an individual's partial and faulty grasp of one or more shared languages, or ought we to explain a shared language as the overlap of a large number of idiolects? In other words, do we favour Carlo Penco's definition (II) or his definition (I)? The question bears heavily on our conception of a theory of meaning apt to serve philosophical purposes. Should it be a theory of meaning for an idiolect or for a language common to many speakers?

Suppose it agreed—as it is between myself and Donald Davidson—that the best way to answer the request for a philosophical account of the concept of meaning, where the word "meaning" is understood as applying to linguistic meaning, the meanings of words and sentences, is to sketch a theory of meaning for a particular tongue. But what should be understood by the word "tongue" here? My answer, which I will call DU, is that a tongue should be a language, in the everyday sense in which we might ask an author of travel books how many languages she speaks. Davidson's original answer, which I will call DA, was that a tongue should be an idiolect. I shall call one who accepts the answer DU a Duist, and one who accepts the answer DA a Daist.

Daists must be able to explain the term "idiolect" without appeal to the concept of a language. For we are engaged in explaining, by illustrative example, the notion of linguistic meaning; and it is of the essence of a language that its expressions mean something. When, by sketching a theory of meaning for an idiolect, the Daist has explained what it is for the words and sentences of an idiolect to have meanings, he can then, but not before, say what a language is, for instance that it is a set of overlapping idiolects. How then, is the Daist to explain what, for him, an idiolect is, before setting about sketching a theory of meaning for one?

He must take an idiolect to comprise the whole of an individual's linguistic propensities. If that individual knows, or knows in part, more than one language, his idiolect must include all that he may say, or can understand, in any of them. The Daist cannot treat the individual's idiolect as circumscribed by what he may say, or can understand, in any particular one of the languages that he knows, for that would require appeal to the notion of a language, which, at this initial stage, the Daist is barred from doing. The idiolect may be partitioned into its active and passive halves: what the individual is liable to say, and what he can understand, but would never say himself. The term "understand" here must be taken as signifying "attach some meaning to": there can be no distinction according as he attaches the *right* meaning or the wrong one. Such notions have to do with what a word means in a language, as when Alice said to Humpty-Dumpty, "But 'glory' does not mean 'a nice knock-down argument'," and are therefore forbidden to the Daist at this stage. The meanings which a theory of meaning for an idiolect must assign to its words are those which the speaker thinks he knows them to have. The idiolect may be characterised by a certain aversion from macaronic sentences (which the Daist must specify piecemeal), but not by a complete prohibition of them, since we sometimes help ourselves out by a word from our own or some third language when we cannot recall the proper word in the language we are speaking; we also quote from other languages or borrow phrases from them when we are speaking our own.

It will be apparent that, when the Daist position is taken seriously, an idiolect becomes a very complicated thing. A theory of meaning for such an idiolect would be very unlike a Davidsonian truth-theory.

So is an idiolect a private language in the sense in which Wittgenstein famously argued that a private language is an impossibility? Wittgenstein's argument was that it is essential to language that there be a right and wrong in the use of words; in particular, a right and wrong in judgements of the truth of statements made in the language. Whereas, for a private language as he intended the concept to be understood, there could be no objective determination of right and wrong, and hence no right and wrong: whatever *seemed* right would *be* right. Well, if an idiolect is to consist of the linguistic propensities of an actual individual, it will *not* be a private language in Wittgenstein's sense. Any actual individual speaker will acknowledge a standard of the right use of words and the correct judgement of the truth of a statement. But the standard he acknowledges will not be founded on his own judgment: it will rest on the judgements of others. He will be prepared to submit to the judgements of others concerning his use and understanding of words and the truth of statements made by himself and others. Of course, he will not always accept a correction. Sometimes he may feel assured that he is right; at other times, he will seek the opinions of others in order to decide whether he or the objector was correct. When the word or concept was a specialised one, he may seek the rulings of experts. The point is, however, that he does not behave as the sole speaker of a private language. He behaves as one engaging in a communal practice, for which there are common standards of correctness, to be discovered by enquiry from others engaged in the same practice.

For this reason, even an idiolect is not a private thing, and cannot be described as if it were a purely private thing. An adequate description would have to include the speaker's propensity to accept correction from others. It would have to introduce the concept of a common language such as French, Turkish, and Mandarin Chinese, because a speaker attempting a language not his mother tongue is more apt to accept correction from a native speaker of that language than from one for whom it is a foreign language as it is for him. A full description would have to include an account of the common language, perhaps in the form of a description of the idiolects of all those whose mother tongue it is, so as to display the corrections to which a speaker of the given idiolect is likely to be subject. In short, an account which takes an idiolect as its starting-point will not escape the need to describe a common language; it will need to describe more than one—all the various common languages which the speaker of the idiolect at different times aims to speak. The Daist has an immensely more complicated task than the Duist, and one that is in no way more economical, since it must incorporate the Duist's account, very often not for just one but for several common languages.

This holds good if we are to interpret the term "idiolect" by reference to some supposed speaker's actual linguistic propensities. If the concept of an idiolect is understood to be an idealisation, under which a speaker utters sequences of sounds with no thought or awareness of the linguistic propensities of his hearers to speak in certain ways and to understand certain ways of speaking, then indeed it is a private language, even if one that is not used by the speaker to address himself alone, but, insanely, to address other people with no ground to expect them to understand him, then it is subject to Wittgenstein's demolition of the whole idea of a private language. It was a pointless idealisation in any case: why should we attempt to explain what a language is in terms of an imaginary one which only one person knows or speaks? But it is also an illusory idealisation: there could not be such a thing.

Carlo Penco sees as my prime error my failure to accept what he takes to be a view of Wittgenstein's. He says that the Fregean heritage,

> was challenged by Wittgenstein who denounced the tendency to consider the whole point of communication as bringing the sense of the words from one mind to another. We may single out two aspects in Wittgenstein's criticism. The first is against the idea of senses or concepts as something pre-existing language, and to which language gives just a practical way to be transmitted from one mind to the other; the second is against the idea of communication as *sharing* the same things—meanings or inferences or beliefs.

Penco allows that I am faithful to the first of these two aspects, but accuses me of disregarding the second. I am uncertain that the second can be attributed to Wittgenstein, at least when so broadly stated. Here are two paragraphs from the *Philosophical Investigations* which seem to me to call in question the attribution:

> 241. "So you are saying that human agreement decides what is true and what is false?"—It is what human beings *say* that is true and false; and they agree in the *language* they use. That is not agreement in opinions but in form of life.
> 242. If language is to be a means of communication there must be agreement not only in definitions but also (queer as this may sound) in judgments. This seems to abolish logic, but does not do so.—It is one thing to describe methods of measurement, and another to obtain and state results of measurement. But what we call "measuring" is partly determined by a certain constancy in the results of measurement.

Holism, he concedes, makes communication hard to explain if it is taken to require that speaker and hearer share the meanings they attach to the words. Against this he contends that my "Master Argument" may be read either as telling against holism or as telling against this conception of communication. If it is read in the second way, an alternative view of communication is needed. This, he says, Davidson has tried to provide.

He is here alluding to Davidson's more recent adaptation of his original view, namely to substitute for the concept of an idiolect that of an individual speaker's propensity to speak in a particular way to a specific hearer. This is a great improvement, because it makes prominent the use of language for communication. It is of course true that we adapt our mode of speaking to our hearer: we speak differently to an adult and to a child, to a compatriot and to a foreigner, and many of us to a superior and to a colleague. Davidson envisages a process of adaptation. We begin with one set of assumptions about how our hearer will understand our words, and modify those assumptions in the course of conversation; and this, too, corresponds with what often happens when we converse with someone whose speech habits differ widely from our own.

With these observations I have no quarrel. They do not in themselves constitute an alternative conception of communication; they are simply descriptions of converse between two people both of whom know only imperfectly the language they are speaking, as everyone knows even his mother tongue imperfectly, and whose partial knowledge happens to match rather badly.

What makes them into an alternative conception is Davidson's denial that there is any such thing as a language. For him, the speaker's initial assumptions about how his hearer will understand him do not rest upon any knowledge he has that the hearer is, say, an Italian speaker, and that he is likely to know this word but not that word: they are just assumptions about the passive idiolect of that particular individual. Penco is quite right to object that he must have come by these assumptions from some source. We are all brought up to speak a particular language (or sometimes more than one language). We are brought up to speak a particular dialect of that language and to speak it with a particular accent. I here mean the word "dialect" in its proper sense, not as denoting a language deemed socially or culturally inferior. A dialect in the proper sense is a way of speaking a certain language, as an accent is a way of pronouncing it: a Scotsman, speaking to an Englishman, may use the phrase "wee bairns" without expecting the other to use it too, any more than to affect a Scots accent. In learning the language, or the particular dialect of it, we pick up much by imitation, but are also instructed, often in response to our questions, and also corrected; this process does not end with childhood. As we grow older, we learn in part to understand other accents and other dialects. It is this knowledge, together with what we know about the person we are speaking to, that determines our initial assumptions about what that person is likely to understand and how he is likely to understand it. All this is obvious; it is hard to suppose that Davidson would actually deny it.

There are two things that he does deny. First, that it is necessary that we should have acquired our initial assumptions in this way. *In principle*, on his view, any two human beings, say a monoglot Lithuanian and a monoglot Japanese, could communicate with one another by modifying their passing theories of each other's idiolects, even if both started with the assumption that the other would speak like him. I find it hard to grasp the theoretical role of this fantastic hypothesis. Davidson's second denial is that there are any languages; for him the concept of a language, in the sense in which it is employed by language schools, is one of those "folk" concepts which contemporary philosophers repudiate. This means that, although there may be linguistic habits which are widespread among certain populations, these habits are regularities, not rules. There are no rules; there is no right or wrong in what anyone says. This is not to say that everything anyone says is true: what someone *means* by what he says may be false, but there cannot be anything wrong in his meaning that by *saying* it.

This, of course, is full-blown idiolect theory. According to it, what someone means by what he says is determined by his own personal idiolect. His idiolect subsists in a meaning-theory that governs his utterances, even if he himself is unable to articulate it. A meaning-theory for a common language gives an account, as from the outside, of a complex social practice. But a meaning-theory for an idiolect is something grasped by the speaker of the idiolect. His grasp of it is what makes it his idiolect; but in what that grasp consists it is baffling to say. I find it equally baffling to decide what are supposed to be the virtues of this theory, so grossly at variance with what we know of the facts of our acquisition of language and our subsequent use of it.

Penco complains that, on Davidson's account, the interpreter always makes the other speaker win. I am not convinced that Davidson does not provide for more convergence than Penco allows. After all, if a dialogue rather than a monologue is in progress, the roles of speaker and interpreter alternate: each is adjusting his theory of interpretation in accord with the other's responses. But I have no wish to decry Penco's exploration of all that is involved in our understanding of each other in the course of linguistic interchange, including what he calls "contextual abilities." The project is undoubtedly interesting; it promises to shed light on our practice of conversing with one another, and possibly to provide a more plausible model of the process than either Davidson or I have succeeded in doing. I cannot agree with his final assessment, however. He thinks that there is no conclusive choice between his thesis (I) and his thesis (II), that is, between taking a common language as the fundamental notion and explaining an idiolect as an individual's imperfect grasp of that, and taking an idiolect as the fundamental notion and explaining a common language as an overlap of idiolects. There is no middle way between these alternatives. Considered as a fundamental notion, to be explained independently of that of a common language, the notion of an idiolect is a confusion with which it is impossible to operate. This is manifest from the impossibility of explaining differences in the force of utterances—assertoric, interrogative, imperative, and so on— save in terms of interaction between conversants. If, like Davidson, you think that the hearer need know only the truth-conditions of the sentence uttered, and that he can then pick up from the circumstances the intention with which it was uttered, this will not worry you; but in my view differences of force depend upon conventions that we all learn as we learn to speak our language. This aside, the notion of an idiolect, considered as subject to Penco's definition (II), can be recognised as confused and impracticable, for the reasons set out in this reply. Definition (I) is the only one in terms of which the notion of an idiolect can properly be explained.

M. D.

17

Bernhard Weiss

MOLECULARITY AND REVISIONISM

To my mind too many discussions of holism and molecularity in the philosophy of language begin with holism and become pretty thoroughly mired in discussion of its content and reasons in its favor or disfavor. I would like here instead to concentrate on molecularity and its motivation; after all it is the molecularist who appears to be advancing a definite thesis about language while holism is simply a denial of this thesis. I will then turn to discuss the implications of the molecularity requirement for theory of meaning and, in particular, its implications for anti-realist or constructive meaning theories. The relationship between Michael Dummett's insistence on molecularity and his distinctive revisionist stance in philosophy is a theme which permeates the essay.

I. MOLECULARITY

Molecularity is the claim that speakers' understanding of language imposes a partial order (or something approaching one) on sentences of the language. Sentence A depends on sentence B just in case an understanding of sentence A presupposes an understanding of sentence B. According to the molecularity constraint, sentences ordered according to this relation of dependence form a partial order. Baldly stated in these terms the claim is reasonably clear. But the bald claim is thoroughly implausible; it becomes plausible only if it is compromised to allow for "local holisms." Of course this raises an issue about how the claim is to be weakened without thoroughly undercutting the motive for or the clarity of the view. But let us set that question aside and move on to consider how the claim might best be motivated.

II. Some Arguments for Molecularity

One sort of argument—one often attributed to Dummett—takes molecularity to be a consequence of the nature of language acquisition. Roughly, the idea is as follows. *Argument one*: Learning a language is a piecemeal process; speakers learn a portion of language which then provides a *stable* base for their passage to increased linguistic competence. So their understanding of more primitive regions of language remains intact as they become more linguistically sophisticated. If this were not the case then we would have a circle of interdependence of competencies into which it is impossible to see how speakers are to enter. The possible epistemological route to linguistic expertise thus reflects an order imposed by the character of speakers' understanding. Since the former relies on a partial ordering of sentences, the latter imposes a partial order on sentences just as molecularity requires.

Argument two: An allied line of argument appeals to a familiar thought about the compositionality of understanding. Linguistic competence involves the ability to understand indefinitely many novel utterances. The ability is, supposedly, explained in compositional terms: one understands the novel sentence because one understands the component expressions and grasps the significance of so combining them in the sentence. So a speaker's understanding of the more complex expression is based on her *prior* understanding of simpler expressions. That prior understanding must thus be complete at the earlier stage; linguistic understanding is a stage by stage process each stage of which involves a complete understanding of a relevant class of expressions.

Some of Dummett's comments support attribution of these arguments to him. Witness the following extracts:

> An understanding of such a sentence as "I'm afraid that I forgot that it was fragile" *builds on* and *requires* an antecedent understanding of the word "fragile" but is not a condition of understanding it. Holistic meaning-theories are in principle incapable of drawing this distinction. For them, it is a condition of understanding any sentence of the language that one be capable of understanding any other sentence of the language. (*LBoM*, 224–25)

> . . . holism must allow for degrees of logical complexity; but since . . . the understanding of an apparently less complex sentence may presuppose that of a more complex one, it is not a stable position. We are thus driven to accept that relations of dependence often hold in one direction only: the understanding of certain expressions or forms of sentence may require a prior grasp of the meanings of others. (Taylor, 251)

Argument three: A rather different sort of argument than these two might take something like the following form. The meaning of a sentence must be surveyable. If, however, we identify the meaning of a sentence with its use, then we seem to have a tension, since the overall set of legitimate uses of a sentence is not surveyable: the sentence can be used to effect a multitude of different sorts of utterance and may be used in an indefinite variety of linguistic and nonlinguistic contexts. Now one might think of the unsurveyable set of uses as *determined by* the sentence's surveyable meaning. But if we think of meaning as use or, better, grasp of meaning as grasp of use, then meaning will have to be identified with a surveyable set of central conditions of use. The overall use of the sentence will then consist in a central set of surveyable uses and the peripheral uses which flow, in some general way (of which speakers are, in some sense apprised), from the central set. (In this way we *explain* speakers' competence in using the sentence.) So the only thing specific to the individual sentence which a speaker needs to learn is its central set of legitimate uses, and these must be capable of being finally cordoned off and specified relative to a proper fragment of language, since otherwise these will be unsurveyable.

I shall refer to the first two arguments as the acquisition arguments and the third as the surveyability argument. Each of these arguments makes an epistemological assumption. In each case we are presented with a capacity—the capacity to use language, the capacity to understand novel utterances and the capacity to use a sentence, respectively—that is, in some sense, intractable. And the assumption is that when we are presented with such a capacity we must be able to see it as a complex product of tractable capacities.[1] There is, of course, much to question here, but the broad thrust of the assumption is that in many cases we have a certain capacity and we crave, not merely a description of the capacity, but an account of how the capacity is gained and/or implemented. Now, though this is by no means an uncontroversial or uniformly uncontroversial craving,[2] to deny the craving outright would be to find all our capacities transparent or to resist explaining our possession of certain capacities. No one who finds any attraction in the business of epistemology will be able to live comfortably with either of these options.

It will take just a little more work to bring out the inadequacy in these arguments but we can quickly see that they cannot be a good reflection of Dummett's considered thought on these matters. Dummett is a revisionist in that he thinks a legitimate linguistic practice must meet certain conditions—for instance, that of being capable of being described by a molecular theory of meaning—which we cannot guarantee that our actual practice fulfills. So our actual practice may be illegitimate in certain respects and for that reason stand in need of revision. Now one thing that is definitely true about our actual practice is that it is acquirable. Thus one could not motivate a revisionary position in the philosophy of language from general considerations about the nature of language acquisition. To put the point slightly differently, if our actual practice cannot be described in molecular fashion then that shows that we can, despite the arguments lately rehearsed, acquire a holistic practice. But then thoughts about the nature of acquisition cannot form the basis of an argument for molecularity.

Dummett is aware of this very point and gives it flesh in the person of Brouwer. How, he asks, could Brouwer have consistently rejected the meaningfulness of classical mathematics while at the same time exhibiting a supreme competence in classical (topological) techniques (*LBoM*, 239)? The answer Dummett gives on Brouwer's behalf is that there is more to learning a language than being able to engage in a practice. It may be that we have a practice but cannot give ourselves an adequate account of how that practice functions. As Dummett says: "A practice may exist, and be learnable, but still open to criticism as failing to achieve the purpose that a linguistic practice should serve. That was precisely what Brouwer believed to be true of the practice of classical mathematics" (*LBoM*, 241).

Dummett claims that we should be able to arrive at a general conception of how language functions and of how content is conferred on individual sentences. Not all conventionally established practices are guaranteed to admit of being seen in this light. But holism simply denies that our linguistic practices should be capable of being portrayed in accordance with this conception. It thus becomes, for Dummett, the denial that we can achieve this clear view of the workings of our own practices and is castigated as a brand of intellectual nihilism. At this stage debate between these two positions peters out and we are left with a conflict between philosophical temperaments; molecularism becomes a methodological constraint redolent of a certain philosophical ambition. Now, though I think something like this position is rightly the destination of our discussion, were we to leave matters here we would have reached that end point prematurely. Molecularity, even construed as a methodological maxim, would be sorely in need of motivation.

We can, I think, move things forward by returning to uncover the inadequacy in our arguments for molecularity. What each of them assumes is that the more primitive competencies on which sophisticated linguistic competence is based are an *understanding* of elements of language. This is clear in the first two arguments and emerges in the third in the assumption that *meanings* must be surveyable. But this is just an assumption. A holist might reply to the acquisition arguments by admitting that there is a partially ordered structure of competencies while denying that these mirror a structure of understanding. Similarly a holist might accept that a speaker's grasp of use must be decomposed into a grasp of surveyable elements but insist that meaning is unsurveyable. Thus a holist might concede the lesson of the acquisition and surveyability arguments without being forced to admit that *understanding* elements of language is a stable base in this process.[3] So our question is: why take the stages of language learning to be stages that are constituted by understanding?

III. THE RATIONALITY OF LANGUAGE USE[4]

Dummett writes, "The use of language is, indeed, the primary manifestation of our rationality: it is *the* rational activity *par excellence*" (*SoL*, 104). "Behaviourism is worse than psychologism, because it leaves out the mind altogether, and so reduces the use of language, which is *the* rational activity *par excellence*, to an affair of stimulus and response. It is because the utterance has a content, or, as we can say expresses a thought, that it is a manifestation of rationality" (Taylor, 256). The first quote comes from the paper, "What do I Know when I Know a Language?" in which Dummett argues that the notion of knowledge is essentially implicated in the theory of meaning. The second quote is from his rejection of McDowell's defense of modesty. McDowell had accused Dummett of collapsing into behaviorism through his insistence on both full-bloodedness and anti-psychologism. McDowell's thought was that only through modesty could one reject both psychologism and behaviorism. Dummett's reply is that behaviorism is not a threat because the notion of knowledge will play an essential role in the theory of meaning.

From the point of view of the present discussion what we need to establish is a result, not so much about the role of knowledge in linguistic competence, but about the objects of such knowledge. What we need to show is that the knowledge involved is not knowledge of certain rules of use, which only when considered as a whole issues in linguistic mastery, but is knowledge of meaning or, as Dummett hints in the second quote, is knowledge of the utterance's content. Now it may seem obvious that if a theory of meaning involves itself with characterizing pieces of knowledge, then those pieces of knowledge are knowledge of meanings. But, in fact, it is far from clear that this is indeed the case since meaning connects both with what speakers know when they understand an expression and with the semantic value of the expression. Frege, in assuming that sense both determines semantic value and specifies the content of speakers' knowledge, committed himself to this view. And Dummett, emulating Frege, shares the assumption. However, again in reflection of Frege, Dummett does not provide much in the way of explicit argument for it. However the crucial consideration can, I think, be found in his writings.

Witness this selection from Dummett's account of the rationality of the setting in which language use occurs.

Usually without conscious self-questioning, we estimate other people's intentions in saying what they do. Why did he see that observation as relevant? What was he driving at? What was the point of saying something so obvious/so obviously false/so embarrassing/apparently so irrelevant? Was he changing the subject, and, if so, why? Was his remark intended as an example of what he was maintaining, or as a ground for it, or as a conclusion from it, or even as a concession to those who were disagreeing? (Taylor, 261)

The point here is that the intentions relating to speakers' utterances are intentions which relate to the content or meaning of the utterance. No doubt it is possible to think of rational agents as simply involved in a practice of manipulating rules. (Think, for instance, of someone, who has no knowledge of the world of commerce, engaged in a bookkeeping exercise whose rules she knows by rote.) And here there would be room for one to set about estimating the agent's intentions by considering her actual practice in relation to the rules governing it. But when we come to the case of language the specific intentions that form the rational setting of language use are intentions which are *unintelligible* if we persist in thinking of speakers as unaware of the content of their utterances and of the meanings of their words. As Dummett says, "A speaker must know what he is saying; if he does not, he is not truly saying anything. For someone to have a reason or motive for his utterance, an intention or purpose in making it, he must know what it, and other things he might have said, mean" (Taylor, 262).

What reason can we give for this view? To focus matters let us start with a misuse of language. Consider Bird's utterance of "We shall now play a tune composed by my worthy constituent, Mr. Dizzy Gillespie." Later Roach asks Mingus why Bird called Dizzy his constituent. Mingus replies that Bird does not know the meaning of "constituent" and thinks it can mean *band member* and that he intended, conceitedly, to draw attention to Dizzy's membership in *his* band. So the thought would be that since in this case an explanation of the act involves knowledge of a nonstandard meaning (or a confusion of meanings) in other cases an explanation would (even if there is not a felt need for an explanation) appeal to or presuppose knowledge of meaning. That is, if Bird had in fact said "We shall now play a tune composed by my worthy band member, Mr. Dizzy Gillespie" (intending to say precisely that) then the intentional explanation of that action would, at the very least, presuppose that Bird knew the meaning of "member": one could not use those words *with* that intention unless one knew their meanings.[5]

Let us sum up the dialectical position. The holist had responded to the molecularist's arguments by conceding the general epistemological point, but had denied that this had a molecularist implication for the nature of linguistic meaning by rejecting the idea that the epistemological point must be applied to understanding rather than to some set of ulterior capacities. The molecularist response is to appeal to the rationality of language use to claim that, since rational appraisal of linguistic acts requires that we ascribe awareness of meaning to speakers, the knowledge implicated in a theory of meaning will be knowledge of meaning.

To be sure it is possible for the holist to accept the point about the rationality of language use and to insist that her aim was never to attack the idea that speakers have knowledge of meaning, but rather that she sees (and continues to see) no reason to take knowledge of meaning, as opposed to the ulterior capacities, as fulfilling any kind of explanatory role in a theory of meaning.

There is clearly room for some further debate here. As it stands the acquisition arguments are inconclusive. The best hope of buttressing these arguments would be to point out that the capacities relevant to knowledge of language are those capacities of which, as teachers and learners, we keep track. But the concept of understanding—of knowledge of meaning—precisely relates to the ways in which we police one another's use. So the relevant knowledge is indeed knowledge of meaning.[6]

But, as I see it, our previous response—or something like it—is always available to the holist. That is, the holist will always be able to say that our ascriptions of understanding and misunderstanding are simply ways of enforcing correct use and that the successful upshot of these practices is to instill the appropriate ulterior capacities in speakers. Given the availability of such a response it is hard to see how a *direct* connection can be forged between our normal practices of ascribing understanding and those states which, on mature reflection, deserve the accolade "understanding." The point could be made by returning to the earlier one about revisionism. Presumably Brouwer's teachers commended him on the ease and thoroughness of his understanding of classical mathematics. Yet, if Brouwer is right, there is no such understanding to be had (though, of course, there is a competence to be gained). So it seems plausible to hold that our ascriptions of understanding are focused on certain competencies that, on (presumably frequent) occasion, reflection will ratify as constituting or delivering understanding, but need not always do so.

Things stand quite differently, however, with our third argument. The acquisition arguments are problematic because it is hard to secure, merely from the fact that speakers have knowledge of meaning, that knowledge of meaning plays the right epistemological role in acquiring linguistic competence. But the third argument is different: its premise is merely that meaning is surveyable. And, if the rationality of language use delivers the conclusion that speakers must be credited with an awareness of meaning, then meaning must, in some sense, be surveyable: we have the premise for the third argument.

It would be wrong to think that this settles matters. Externalists about propositional attitude ascription might well want to question whether rational explanation and rational appraisal of linguistic acts require that speakers be related to meanings in such a way as to guarantee that these are surveyable. Clearly prosecution of this debate will depend, at least in part, on making the notion of surveyability more precise. The externalist will however be forced to demonstrate that the rationality of language can be reconciled with a degree of opacity in our relations to meanings. I will not pursue this issue here.[7]

IV. SYSTEMATICITY

Let us suppose then that some version of the third argument is viable. Does this deliver molecularism, as Dummett conceives of it? What the third argument establishes is that the meaning of a sentence must be determined by reference to a surveyable set of uses and thus by reference to a proper fragment of language. Moreover if these fragments cannot be placed in a partial order then the meanings of sentences will become unsurveyable: tracing the fragment of language with respect to which the meaning of a sentence is given will endlessly ramify or will be circular. But Dummett's molecularist advocates a rather stronger view than this. She does not simply think that there is such an ordered structure to language but she also thinks that this structure can be made fully explicit in a theory of meaning. Thus Dummett is wont to castigate the holist as denying the possibility of a theory of meaning, or as claiming that we cannot obtain a clear view of the workings of our own language. When he construes holism in this way he takes it to be a form of intellectual defeatism, indeed, a kind of nihilism.

> The theory of meaning is concerned only with the general form of a representation of content, but is fundamental for just that reason: linguistic holism, which rejects, wholly or largely, the need for such representation, thus inadvertently runs counter to the entire philosophical enterprise. (Taylor, 252)

Dummett's thought seems to go along the following lines. One of the faults in Quine's picture of language use is that he focuses exclusively on the use of language in making assertions and ignores the practice of elucidating meaning. This means that as speakers we engage in the business of explaining meanings and holding one another to account for our use of language. We ask for and provide justifications of our use of language. Now, as we have remarked in connection with the example of Brouwer, none of this demonstrates that there is a proper subject matter for a systematic theory of meaning.

We have, however, uncovered reason for supposing that, if linguistic acts are to be subject to proper rational appraisal, then these elucidatory practices must fix surveyable meanings, meanings which thus must be capable of being specified. A systematic, molecular theory of meaning extends this practice. The theory extends the practice because the elucidations offered by such a theory are, in essence, no different from those which we provide as speakers. The theory departs from the practice only in aiming at systematicity. In searching for systematicity we force the business of providing justifications well beyond what ordinary speakers would provide. As Dummett says, "One task of systematization, in philosophy, logic, mathematics or science, is the pursuit of questions of justification beyond the point where most people would be able to go. But to do this is merely to extend a procedure which is integral to our use of language" (FPoL, 622).

I said earlier that the molecularity constraint is ultimately a methodological constraint. Its methodological character emerges through its collaboration with the goal of systematization. This receives no justification in terms of the nature of language. Rather systematization is seen as a deep feature of our cognitive architecture: we seek to understand phenomena by incorporating them within the scope of systematic theories. And now given that our argument established that there is prima facie reason for thinking that there is a subject matter for such a theory of meaning and given that the holist has no conclusive arguments in her favor, holism is rightly stigmatized by Dummett as a kind of intellectual defeatism.

With these thoughts about the nature of molecularity in mind I want now to concentrate on the possible form of a constructive meaning theory. Our question will concern how the molecularity constraint should be interpreted by the detailed workings of a constructive theory of meaning.

V. HARMONY AND CONSERVATIVE EXTENSION

Two notions are central to Dummett's imposition of the molecularity constraint: those of *conservative extension* and of *harmony* (or, a technical variation of this idea which need not concern us here, *stability*). The notion of conservative extension is an attempt to ensure that when a new region of language is added to an existing language the meanings of terms in the original fragment of language remain unchanged. So, if we take the meaning of a sentence to be determined by its φ-conditions, then a sentence of the original fragment is φ in the expanded language just in case it is φ in the original fragment. Thus, since its φ-conditions remain unchanged, and since these determine its meaning, its meaning will be unchanged. Of course, in a use-based theory of meaning the sorts of conditions we are likely to focus on are conditions in which a sentence is assertible, or those in which we have evidence in its favor, or those in which it is deniable, or the like.

At first sight the notion of harmony seems to chime well with our third argument for molecularity. Harmony obtains between the grounds and consequences of an assertion. If an assertion's grounds can be derived from its consequences and vice versa, then its grounds and consequences are said to be in harmony. So the notion of harmony seems to be a technical means of unpacking at least part of the idea that the overall use of a sentence should flow from some central meaning-determining or canonical set of uses: by insisting on harmony we might take the meaning of a sentence to be established by fixing the grounds for its assertion and then see the consequences of the assertion as flowing from the meaning as thus established (or vice versa).

The notions of harmony and of conservative extension seem to be linked, at least if we take the meaning of a sentence to be determined by its assertibility conditions. The reasoning is as follows: Suppose that a sentence is introduced into language by means of a conservative extension (relative to assertibility). Suppose the sentence is assertible because grounds expressible in the original vocabulary obtain.[8] Any consequence expressible in the original vocabulary must be such that it would, in these circumstances, have been assertible within the original fragment of language. That is, the consequences of the assertion must obtain whenever the grounds obtain: the consequences of the assertion are thus consequences of the grounds. Thus harmony in one direction holds. To be sure we can only show this in one direction since, from the notion of conservative extension, we can only show that the consequences of an assertion are consequences of its grounds, not that they are the strongest consequences. A sentence whose grounds and consequences exhibited this less grave failure in harmony, might still constitute or be part of a conservative extension. Conversely, if harmony holds, then the consequences of an assertion are consequences of the grounds for assertion. So no sentence could become assertible on the introduction of our sentence, if it was not so before: harmony guarantees conservative extension.

However there is a flaw in this reasoning. An extension of language might be conservative but it might not be demonstrably so. In this case although the consequences of an assertion would obtain only when the grounds obtain this might not be demonstrable. So it may be that there is no deriving the consequences of an assertion from its grounds, as harmony requires. Here I am not imagining a case in which the relation of semantic consequence may outrun the relation of derivability. Rather I am imagining the less imaginatively taxing scenario in which conservativeness holds only as a matter of contingent fact. When we say that the extension is conservative we mean that a sentence of the original language is assertible in the extended language just in case it is assertible in the original language: the "just in case" may only apply to the actual world.[9] The property of harmony, which must be *demonstrated*, will thus fail.

Does molecularity require that language exhibit the strong property of harmony (or demonstrable conservative extension) or merely that one region of language conservatively extend another as a matter of contingent fact?[10] Now the conclusion of the third argument might lead one to believe that we need the stronger, demonstrable property. For our conclusion there was that there must be a canonical set of uses of a sentence from which its other uses flow, and, clearly, the grounds do not flow from the consequences if these form a conservative extension only contingently. But for this argument to work we would have, in addition, to argue that a joint specification of two sets of conditions of use (e.g., grounds and consequences) would be unsurveyable. And there appears to be no reason to suppose that this is the case; indeed, if both sets individually are surveyable then the natural inclination would be to suppose that the combination of the two sets is itself surveyable. Conversely, it is hard to see how a derivation of, say, consequences of an assertion from its grounds guarantees surveyability; since it is thoroughly implausible to ascribe implicit grasp of such a procedure of derivation to speakers, the existence of the derivation will fail utterly to speak to the question of how sense is surveyable from the perspective of speakers. It may seem, however, that the real worry about a failure to *demonstrate* the conservativeness of an extension is that the surveyability of meanings of expressions in the original fragment is compromised. I shall come back to this worry—let us call it "ramification"—below. It seems to me that the worry, if there is a legitimate one, about sticking with the weaker requirement does relate to the rationality of language, but does so in a quite different way to that so far considered.

An assertion furnishes an inferential route from its grounds to its consequences. This route is guaranteed by the very meaning of the assertion, so it is an inferential passage which is given a priori. Of course there is no guarantee that the particular assertive practices into which speakers can be inducted, and thus the inferential passages they can be brought to accept a priori, will be a priori *valid*. So it seems that there is a genuine philosophical task here: we should reflect on our use of language, attempting to ratify it as valid where possible but criticizing it as failing to meet standards of rational appraisal when it cannot be shown to be valid. Here ratification will require that we show that a region of language exhibit the stronger, demonstrable properties of harmony and of conservative extension. So the thought is that our practices of asserting involve the acceptance a priori of a range of inferential transitions. If this a priori acceptance is to be rationally acceptable, these inferential transitions must be shown to be logically valid.

Notice, though, that if this is the picture then what we have is a rather different sort of philosophical revisionism from that envisaged up till now. For previously, the thought was that speakers may be inducted into a practice—they may confer a use on certain linguistic items—but be mistaken in supposing that thereby they had succeeded in conferring meanings on their terms. The present revisionary position is not motivated by general considerations about the natures of meaning and understanding, but instead, claims that there is a failure of rationality in giving a priori endorsement to inferential transitions which cannot be given a purely rational vindication. I will not be able to say much about this new position in the space left to me here. To close, I will make a brief attempt to clarify the issues involved.

Now it would certainly be absurd to suppose that speakers' acceptance of a new linguistic practice awaited an empirical investigation into whether the extension of language in fact constitutes a conservative extension. This would be to deny that the inferential passages we accept in adopting the extended language are given a priori. However the a priori givenness of these inferential passages need not be constituted by their logical validity; rather it might be constituted by speakers accepting the extension as conservative as a matter of *presupposition*.

Let me now address the ramification problem, which I raised a few paragraphs ago. If one clings to the idea that the consequences of an assertion should be derivable from its grounds—that is, if one insists on harmony—then one is bound to see an extension which is not demonstrably conservative as affecting the meanings of expressions in the original fragment of language. For then, the only way of retaining harmony is to see the meanings of consequences expressible in the original vocabulary as having changed. And these ramifying changes in meanings threaten their surveyability. In contrast, on the view I have just mooted, the fact that we make a substantial presupposition in presuming that the extension is conservative depends on the idea that meanings in the original fragment of language are unaltered. So the ramification problem does not arise.

Let me map the shape of things as the proposal would have them. First, the supposition is that conditions of a certain type, by convention, constitute grounds for an assertion A (let us call these G_A), while other conditions of a certain type, by convention, constitute consequences of the assertion (let us call these C_A). Thus an inferential transition from a certain type of condition constituting the grounds to a certain type of condition constituting the consequences is given in accepting the meaning of A and is therefore given a priori (let us call this I_A). Speakers' acceptance of I_A is not constituted by anything other than their preparedness to endorse assertion of A on the basis of G_A and to withdraw that assertion if C_A fail to hold and, perhaps, also to infer that C_A hold, given the assertibility of A. It is not, in other words, a matter of accepting as true a sentence of the form $G_A \rightarrow C_A$. One of the reasons for this is that, though the nature of this inferential transition is, one hopes, capable of some philosophical elucidation, it may not be susceptible to formulation in terms of logical entailment. And clearly speakers are unable to formulate an expression for this inferential connection.

The inferential transition from tokens of G_A to tokens of C_A may fail. In these particular cases in which I_A fails there may or may not be an explanation for the failure. We may, for instance, be able to account for a failure of consequences of an ascription of pain to hold because the pain behavior which warranted that ascription may have been shammed. On the other hand, there may not be such an explanation available: failure of the consequence simply constitutes defeat of the ground for assertion. So for instance, failure to manifest any unfitness for an activity (where such unfitness is taken as a consequence of a warranted ascription of pain) may defeat an ascription of pain made on the basis of an exhibition of pain behavior, without our being able to explain this by appeal to shamming or the like.

So speakers will know how the warrant provided by a token ground for assertion might be empirically investigated, viz., one enquires into whether the consequences of the assertion hold. But, more, in making an assertion we are not indifferent to its defeat, rather we set ourselves against its defeat.[11] Thus, if tokens of G_A are defeated sufficiently often by the failure of tokens of C_A then the assertive practice involving A will be threatened and I_A will be empirically disconfirmed. Moreover if each case of defeat is explicable and these explanations yield a general explanation of the defeat, then speakers will have a clear grasp of the state of affairs which gives rise to an empirical defeat of I_A.[12] For example, we might have a general explanation of the defeat of pain ascriptions in terms of the prevalence of shamming. So, in the most awkward case, what the proposal needs to explain is the a priori endorsability of an inferential transition which can be seen both to be capable of empirical disconfirmation and where the circumstances giving rise to this disconfirmation can, in addition, be envisaged. And now it is apt to seem that some sort of lapse in rationality, or, at least, in intellectual rigor is involved in persisting with such a practice in advance of the empirical investigation.

Two points should be noted. First, as long, as we are only concerned with empirical disconfirmation it is, at least, not obvious that there is a worrying lapse here. Continuing the practice involves a certain risk but, in sticking with the practice, we do not disqualify ourselves from making the empirical discovery. Second, it would thus appear that the gravity of the lapse needs to be made apparent by additional philosophical support. And the source of this support seems clear enough. The inferential transition I_A transmits an *epistemic* entitlement (the exact nature of which we can leave undetermined here) and one's epistemology may well give one reason for rejecting the combination of an a priori acceptance of such a transmission with an awareness of its empirical disconfirmability.[13] So here we *may* have an epistemologically inspired philosophical revisionism[14] but, note, not a meaning-theoretically inspired revision.[15]

VI. CONCLUSION

This essay is inconclusive in a multitude of ways. What I have tried to suggest is that the rationality of language use promotes a view of meanings as surveyable and this can be deployed in an argument in favor of molecularity. Molecular theories of meaning emerge when we bring this view of the nature of meaning and understanding together with an attempt to understand phenomena through construction of systematic theories. This means that molecularity in the philosophy of language is ultimately a methodological position but one which, plausibly, is well motivated. Conversely, I have also suggested that arguments for molecularity based on the acquisition of language are unlikely to succeed because the holist can always deflect general observations about acquisition away from linguistic understanding by focusing them on ulterior capacities which issue in linguistic competence. Finally, I have claimed that molecularity, as motivated by the insistence on surveyability of meanings, will not justify Dummett's insistence on harmony. The alternative position discerns substantial presuppositions built into linguistic practice. Whether it is rational for one reflectively to acknowledge these presuppositions is a question which can only be answered by means of an excursion into the terrain of the epistemology of the a priori.

BERNHARD WEISS

DEPARTMENT OF PHILOSOPHY
UNIVERSITY OF CAPE TOWN
NOVEMBER 2001

NOTES

1. It is a very good question, and one perhaps too often neglected, what makes a capacity tractable.

2. It may, for instance, be less apt in connection with practical than with theoretical knowledge.

3. Consider this analogy. One might think of mastery of chess as accruing through grasp of the powers of the individual pieces (which would correspond to grasp of the meanings of words). The power of the pawn involves the ability to become any other piece (other than the king) when it reaches the eighth rank. So fully to grasp the power of the pawn involves a grasp of the powers of the other pieces. Now suppose that each piece has the power to mutate when it reaches a designated square. In this case a mastery of chess could not accrue through grasp of the powers of the individual pieces since each power depends on the other powers. Rather the rules governing chess would be learnable and would issue in a mastery of the game, which would include grasp of the powers of the individual pieces.

4. Shieh (1997) also points to the importance of the rationality of language use in motivating molecularity. But his focus is rather different; he discusses arguments for the view that logic must be irrevisable if accommodations of empirical evidence are to be rational.

5. The "with" is important. One might have the intention *and* use the words but not know what they meant: choose your own scenario involving, say, drugs or hypnosis.

6. In a similar vein, one might want to say that the communicative role of language depends essentially upon speakers' knowledge of the content of utterances.

7. Recall, however, that the brunt of Dummett's criticism of Kripke's externalism about proper names is that Kripke needs to invoke the intention to preserve reference but that he can give no content to this intention without introducing a notion analogous to sense. Here our use of names, even on Kripke's account, must be explained by reference to speakers' intentions whose content can only be given in terms of the meanings of names (see *FPoL*, 148–51).

8. It seems plausible for us to restrict our attention to grounds and consequences expressible in the original vocabulary since the meaning of the sentences in the extended language will be given by reference to the meanings of expressions in the original fragment of language.

9. To be sure, the standard use of conservative extension refers to the demonstrable property. I see no reason not to weaken this standard meaning in the way I have done.

10. Brandom (1994), though he does not tackle issues relating to molecularity, favors the weaker position.

11. This point is a crucial part of Wright's argument against the "traditional" notion of criteria (see his 1993, essay 13).

12. This point is, I think, important. If there were no such conception then the a priority of the inferential transition might, arguably, be constituted by the fact that speakers have no clear conception of the circumstances that would count as its defeat.

13. See Wright and Hale 2000 for a good discussion of this issue.

14. Whether we do or not would require much more investigation into what seem now to be called a priori entitlements.

15. I would like to thank David Cockburn and Christine Jacobsen for discussion of this material and, for having listened to a somewhat distant ancestor of this essay, audiences at Lampeter and at Cardiff. I would also like here to thank Michael Dummett for having utterly transformed my philosophical landscape—as, of course, I am bound to take it—for the better.

REFERENCES

Brandom, Robert. 1994. *Making It Explicit: Reasoning, Representing, and Discursive Commitment*. Cambridge, MA: Harvard Univ. Press.

Dummett, Michael A. E. 1978. *Truth and other Enigmas*. London: Duckworth.

———. 1981. *Frege: Philosophy of Language*. 2nd ed. London: Duckworth. Cited as *FPoL*.

———. 1991. *The Logical Basis of Metaphysics*. London: Duckworth. Cited as *LBoM*.

———. 1993. *The Seas of Language*. Oxford: Oxford Univ. Press. Cited as *SoL*.

Shieh, S. 1997. "Some Senses of Holism." In *Language, Thought and Logic*, ed. R. Heck, 71–104. Oxford: Oxford Univ. Press.

Taylor, Barry. 1987. *Michael Dummett: Contributions to Philosophy*. Dordrecht: Nijhoff.

Wright, C., and Bob Hale. 2000. "Implicit Definition and the A Priori." In *New Essays on the A Priori*, ed. P. Boghossian and C. Peacocke, 286–319. Oxford: Oxford Univ. Press.

Wright, Crispin. 1993. *Realism, Meaning and Truth*. 2nd ed. Oxford: Blackwell.

REPLY TO BERNHARD WEISS

Bernhard Weiss asks for the ground of my belief in molecularity as the proper form of a theory of meaning. He sets out three arguments for it, the first two of which relate to the process of learning a language. Arguments of that kind must indeed be treated with care, for it is far from being strictly true that the meanings we attach to the words that we first learn remain constant throughout the rest of the process of learning: think, for instance, how a child's understanding of the word "father" changes when he learns what used to be called "the facts of life." Weiss decides that, despite hints of them in my writings, neither of the first two arguments can be my true ground for molecularity. His reason for this is that he attributes to me, and I think adopts for himself, the view that it is possible to master the practice of speaking some given language without really understanding it.

Now this is a view against which I have frequently inveighed. Suppose that you and I are conversing in English. How do I know that you understand what I say as I mean it? Well, first because I am speaking standard English and I judge that you understand English; and secondly because you do not look puzzled or ask me what I mean, but respond sensibly. I judge that you understand English from how you have spoken to me and to others in the past, and from your reactions to what has been said to you in English. To suppose that, despite your apparent mastery of the English language, you do not *really* understand me as I intend is to make understanding an inner mental act hidden from outward view, not manifestable by outward behaviour: I cannot know, but can only have faith, that you understand me.

Weiss attributes to me the view that mastery of a language does not guarantee understanding of it on the basis of observations of mine on the extraordinary career of the great Dutch mathematician L. E. J. Brouwer. Brouwer was the founder of mathematical intuitionism. He was not an intuitionist because he considered it more interesting, or more fruitful, to carry out mathematical proofs in a constructive manner; he was one because he did not think that mathematical statements could be understood in any other than a constructive way. He believed that classical mathematics did not make genuine sense; the illusion that it did was for him due to mistaken metaphysical opinions held by classical mathematicians, which led them to hold a quite different conception of the meanings of mathematical statements—an untenable conception on Brouwer's view. Yet, before Brouwer obtained the chair of mathematics at the University of Amsterdam, he proved a succession of remarkable theorems in classical topology. How could he have done this? Does it not demonstrate that he *did* understand classical mathematics, as he professed not to do? Weiss takes my explanation to be that he had mastered the language of classical mathematics, although he was unable to understand it, and believed such an understanding to be unattainable. If so, it is possible to master a linguistic practice without *really* understanding it.

The plea might be made that it is much simpler to master a mathematical practice than to master the practice of everyday discourse. To master the mathematical practice one has only to learn the forms of reasoning considered valid within that practice; to master the use of language in everyday practice, one has to grasp the point of what is said and how it should affect one's subsequent behaviour. A riposte would be that merely storing up a knowledge of the forms of reasoning admitted by classical mathematicians would be sufficient to enable one to follow classical proofs and check that they were classically valid; but that it would not suffice to enable one to *devise* classical proofs. To do that, it would be necessary to be able to *think* like a classical mathematician: and how could one do that if one did not regard classical mathematics as truly intelligible?

Learning to think as others do is an ability important to historians. It is possible to come to be able to think like those whose views and presuppositions one does not share: that is, not to surrender to their way of thinking, but to grasp what trains of thought they would have had, to conceive of how it would have been to think in those ways. It was the great merit of Isaiah Berlin's lectures that he made his audience understand how to think like the various political theorists of the past whom he discussed. Is it possible for an atheist to understand disputes that have arisen within some theistic religion? Yes, if he has learned to think like a believer in that religion. It does not matter, for this purpose, whether he takes the propositions of that religion, including the existence of God, to be false or to be unintelligible: he can grasp what it would be like to believe them to be meaningful and true.

I have many times given introductory lectures on intuitionism. I was not seeking to convert my hearers to intuitionism; but I was trying to induce them to think like intuitionists: not, in general, to think for themselves in full seriousness like intuitionists, but to think in imagination like intuitionists. A classical mathematician may consider whether a given theorem could be proved intuitionistically; an intuitionist could devise a classical proof, and point out why it was, from his own viewpoint, fallacious. Each is engaging in the difficult but feasible task of thinking in imagination like someone whose mentality differs from his own. This is not adopting an alien practice uncomprehendingly; it is imagining comprehension. Brouwer was thinking in imagination like a classical mathematician when he proved those theorems in topology.

The difficult intellectual exercise of imagining the understanding of what one does not believe to be genuinely meaningful is a sophisticated one: no one could engage in it unless he had first attained a straightforward understanding of some language. A child, when first learning language, could not be merely imagining that he understood it: to imagine understanding of some language—to think like those who use it—one must already genuinely understand some other language. I conclude from this that the arguments for molecularity from the process of acquiring language are not as weak as Weiss supposes. He writes, "it is hard to see how a *direct* connection can be forged between our normal practices of ascribing understanding and those states which, on mature reflection, deserve the accolade 'understanding'." Doubtless our normal practices of ascribing understanding are not proof against the performance of one capable of the feat of thinking like others; but they are good enough to recognise what is either genuine understanding or understanding in the imagination.

Weiss says that "one could not motivate a revisionary position in the philosophy of language from general considerations about the nature of language acquisition." I agree: if the linguistic practice one has learned as a child is defective and requires revision, its defectiveness is not likely to be detectable from the process of learning it. Weiss also argues that to offer grounds for molecularity based on considerations about the acquisition of language conflicts with a revisionist attitude. I indeed have such an attitude. I believe that our various languages are marvellous but imperfect instruments for the expression of thought and communication with one another. I think it possible to detect the defects in a language, some of which may be deep and others superficial, and that their elimination is a necessity for us to attain greater clarity of thought. I even suspect that such revision may require a change in the forms of inference we treat as valid. But I have never suggested that among these defects may be an inability to be described by a molecular theory of meaning. The deepest type of defect is a lack of harmony between accepted grounds for and accepted consequences of a statement, something Weiss subsequently discusses. If harmony is lacking, then, strictly understood, no theory of meaning can give a completely faithful account of the language: whatever is taken as the central notion of the theory, it will either be impossible to derive from the meanings of some sentences the grounds for asserting them, or be impossible to derive the consequences of doing so. But this would not be due to a failure of molecularity as such. It cannot be argued that a revisionist attitude to natural language entails acceptance that it is possible to learn a language that can be understood only holistically.

The third argument for molecularity cited by Weiss, and favoured by him, is expressed by him in terms of the need that the meaning should be surveyable. Although I have never expressed it in this manner, I acknowledge that such an argument can be extracted from what I have written. Weiss regards the argument as justifying treating molecularity—tempered by the admission of local holisms—as a methodological constraint on our accounts of meaning, at least when this is backed by the requirement of systematicity, as being "a deep feature of our cognitive architecture." I am content to accept this as a justification for molecularism: it corroborates my condemnation of linguistic holism as defeatist.

Part of the argument for requiring that harmony should prevail in a linguistic practice—that is, in the whole system of linguistic conventions that the speakers of a language have to learn—is, as Bernhard Weiss very clearly sees, that the use of a sentence must ordinarily be determined by its meaning; the qualification "ordinarily" is needed to guard against irregularities due to particular idioms. A theory of meaning will determine the meaning of each sentence, as given in terms of the central notion of the theory, from the meanings of the words of which it is composed and the way they are put together. If the central notion is that of the accepted grounds for an assertion made by uttering the sentence, then the principle that meaning determines use requires that what are taken as the consequences of such an assertion ought to follow from the accepted grounds for making it. Conversely, if the central notion is that of the consequences of asserting the sentence, then the grounds for such an assertion ought to be determinable from its consequences. And if the central notion is that of the conditions for the truth of an assertion, then both the grounds for and the consequences of the assertion ought to be determinable from its truth-conditions. In all three cases, harmony will prevail.

Weiss raises the question whether it is sufficient that harmony should prevail *as a matter of contingent fact*, or whether it ought to prevail demonstrably. He argues that the demand for the surveyability of meaning cannot sustain a requirement that harmony should be demonstrable unless it can be shown that "a joint specification of two sets of conditions of use (e.g., grounds and consequences) would be unsurveyable" and comments that there is no reason to think this to be so. What he means here is a joint specification whose two components happen to be in harmony, although we cannot recognise the fact. As Arthur Prior is celebrated for having pointed out, a joint specification, say of introduction and elimination rules for a logical constant, whose two parts are *not* in harmony may lead to contradiction; it will render introduction of the item that it specifies a non-conservative extension of the language, and so violate surveyability. From this it is apparent that joint specification is, in general, an illegitimate procedure, which may be allowed when harmony is apparent or at least demonstrable, but not when it is not. I do not think that specifications of meaning that merely happen to preserve harmony but cannot be shown to do so ought to be recognised as conferring a surveyable meaning. It is true enough that ordinary speakers are unfamiliar with technical notions such as harmony, and would flinch at being asked to prove that it obtained in a particular natural or formal language. But I doubt whether much weight should be attached to this consideration. The philosophy of language is concerned to make explicit much that is merely implicitly grasped by ordinary speakers: such speakers typically have an inchoate sense of what does and what does not hang together.

Bernhard Weiss ends by speculating whether linguistic revisionism may be inspired by epistemological rather than meaning-theoretical considerations. The epistemological question at issue is whether we may treat as a provisional ground for a form of assertion what we are aware is defeasible, so that in some special instances the consequences of the assertion may empirically prove to be false. Now we may regard some grounds for making certain assertions as conclusive (which ought to be qualified by "except in quite extraordinary circumstances"); and we may acknowledge certain other grounds as entitling us to make other assertions—perhaps even to claim to know that they are true—and yet as defeasible. Whether we treat them in one way or the other depends on the meanings we attach to the forms of assertion for which they are grounds. Epistemology may challenge our right to accept provisionally as a ground entitling us to make some assertion what we admit may be overturned. Nevertheless, Weiss has not demonstrated that epistemology can supply a primary motivation for modifying our use of our language; he has not *replaced* meaning-theoretical considerations by epistemological ones. All is still governed by the demand for harmony; and this demand is always inspired by the need for meaning to be surveyable, that is, for us to have a firm grasp of what it is that we are saying when we use language. The primary motivation for revisionism remains meaning-theoretical, even if epistemological questions are sometimes relevant.

M. D.

18

Christian Thiel

THE OPERATION CALLED ABSTRACTION

The term "abstraction" has a variety of meanings, a few of which link up with properly Fregean themes. Abstraction in a first sense, that of leaving aside some of the marks comprised in a complex concept, or—much to the same effect—of marking out the others, belongs to the logic of marks (*Merkmalslogik*), a traditional approach to the logic of the concept that for Frege was only a subordinate case of his functional approach to concepts, insufficient to deal with the fundamental problems of the more general case. Frege's criticism is directed less against this limitation than against viewing the deletion or election of marks as a mental operation.

"Abstraction," in a second sense, is used to refer to the change from talk about objects of a certain kind (or as some would say, belonging to some class), given an equivalence relation between or among such objects, to talk about the associated equivalence classes. Finally, a third sense of "abstraction" refers to the restriction of the realm from which the predicators in a predicative sentence are taken, to predicators which are "invariant" with respect to a specified equivalence relation. This is a purely linguistic operation that can be formally described by an "abstraction schema" to be given below. The procedure is obviously related to the second one, but clearly distinct from it by avoiding commitment to new kinds of ("abstract") entities like classes. Indeed, it is the most remarkable feature of abstraction conceived as change to an invariant mode of speaking that talk about classes can itself be introduced, and thus explained, by a process of abstraction in the third sense here mentioned.

Anyone familiar with Frege's principal works will be reminded of the Fregean operation of converting or transforming a generalized equivalence into an equation between abstract objects, first described and tentatively analyzed in *Die Grundlagen der Arithmetik* (henceforth *GLA*), then extended and formalized in *Grundgesetze der Arithmetik* (henceforth *GGA*). This procedure has been the subject of discussion and of disagreement in several, very different contexts for a long time. Viewed as a principle of abstraction, it has given rise to an (as yet unresolved) controversy over Frege's understanding of the process, and to Frege's role in the history of abstraction (emphatically denied by the leading expert in this field, Ignacio Angelelli, and yet affirmed, albeit with qualifications, in my introduction to the centenary edition of *Grundlagen*). In Michael Dummett's *Frege: Philosophy of Language*, as well as in *Frege: Philosophy of Mathematics*, the transformation schema holds a central place, not least for its possible use as a touchstone of the context principle, the significance of which appears from Dummett's appraisal that it is "the most important philosophical statement Frege ever made" (Dummett 1956, 491).

The great diversity of contexts in which Frege's schema has been discussed (contextual definitions, philosophy of language, theories of abstraction, ontology, epistemology, etc.) has led to a variety of perspectives the value of which no one would like to deny. It has, however, also diverted attention from the character of the process itself, and also from Frege's own differing attitudes towards the transformation scheme the structure of which he was the first to analyze. It seems to me that both directions of inquiry deserve to be followed out, even at the price of bypassing more topical debates about the scheme, for instance, on its capacity of opening access to abstract entities the ontological status of which is already taken to be settled. In view of the abundance of systematic and historiographical discussions and analyses of abstract objects, incomplete entities, objects going proxy for others, the transition schema (fundamental law V), Julius Caesar, and so on, I will in this short essay merely touch on three subject areas: first, the adequate description of the method of "modern" abstraction itself; second, the appearance (as I see it) of abstraction in Frege's *GLA* and the development of its enigmas into the no less stupendous problems of *GGA*; and third (illuminating the clash between the linguistic character of the transition schema and Frege's Platonism), the labyrinth of unsaturated entities which allegedly evade every attempt to say something undistorted about them.

(1) Turning to the third of the above-mentioned procedures, dubbed "modern abstraction" by Angelelli in view of its prominent role in Peano, Weyl, and Lorenzen (but not, according to Angelelli, in Frege), it may be helpful to begin with some examples. Suppose we have at our disposal a

certain supply of words, that is, of simple linguistic means of expression, for any two of which we have explained certain relations that are reflexive, symmetric, and transitive, in short: equivalence relations (take, e.g., the relation of being equally long, "is as long as," or the relation of having the same sense due to some set of rules governing synonymy within the language system in question). If A, B, C, . . . are words for which an equivalence relation has been defined, the replacement in certain elementary propositions of a specimen from this stock by another one standing to it in that equivalence relation will yield, in case the proposition is true, another true elementary proposition. If, for example, it is true that A is short (meaning that it contains at most four letters), this is also true of every word standing to A in the equivalence relation "equally long." Likewise, if synonymy has been defined for predicators, and if A is an exemplifiable predicator (which is to say that we can exhibit an object to which it applies), then every predicator which is synonymous to A is also exemplifiable.

There are elementary propositions which do not have this invariance property, for example, "A is disyllabic." The words "fleet" and "fluid" are equally long, and the proposition "the word 'fluid' is disyllabic" is true, but replacing the word "fluid" by the word "fleet" results in the false proposition "the word 'fleet' is disyllabic." This shows that the property of invariance is a special property that may be described as follows: If B is the word occurring in the elementary proposition $A(B)$, and the invariance property obtains, then $A(B)$ implies $A(X)$ for every X that is equivalent to B, i.e.

$$\bigwedge_x (X \sim B \to A(X)).$$

This universal proposition contains as a special case the original elementary proposition $A(B)$: taking B for X, we obtain $B \sim B \to A(B)$, and since $B \sim B$ holds for an equivalence relation by definition, we may detach $A(B)$ alone as true.

What is remarkable about this is not the existence of such cases, but the possibility of exhibiting in our common language a *schema* the purpose of which is just the formation of universal propositions of the type shown. The schema allows the formation of elementary propositions which have the same form as an elementary proposition $A(B)$, but contain, instead of the single word B, a composite expression αB. The additional sign α serves to indicate that by $A(\alpha B)$ we are in the first place told that $A(B)$, but that moreover we are being asked to disregard the fact that B is this particular word from among a whole series of equivalent words. That is, we are required to *abstract* from all properties of B which it does not share with every one of the other words equivalent to it. It is for this reason that additional signs α serving this purpose are called *abstractors*, and the whole process of "translation" is called an *abstraction* process, fixed by the rule of transition:

$$A(\alpha B) \Leftrightarrow \bigwedge_x (X \sim B \to A(X)).$$

To illustrate this, take the concrete geometrical figures in the Euclidean plane as objects, and the relation of similarity as the equivalence relation between them. Then the transition from right to left in the abstraction schema will yield elementary propositions about shapes, that is, about abstract geometrical figures. For example, rotational symmetry turns out to be a property of the (shape of a) square, since it is a property which, if it pertains to some specified square in the Euclidean plane, it pertains to every other square: rotational symmetry is an invariant property with respect to similarity. If we take predicators once more, elementary propositions predicating of some predicator a property invariant with respect to the equivalence relation

$$\bigwedge_x (A(x) \leftrightarrow B(x))$$

between any two predicators A(x) and B(x), can be formulated as elementary propositions $A(\alpha A)$, in this particular case as propositions about the *class* or *set* αA, usually written as $\epsilon_x A(x)$ or $\{x \mid A(x)\}$. If the equivalence relation is that of synonymy of A(x) and B(x) in the sense of mutual derivability within a given system of predicator rules, we get elementary propositions about *concepts*.

The procedure of "modern abstraction" is standard in introductory text-books of constructive philosophy of science where it is studied in more detail. In our context, only two remarks need to be added. First, abstraction may of course be applied not only to elementary propositions, but also to complex propositions—but in that case the initial propositions must first be decomposed into elementary propositions all of which are then submitted to the abstraction process singly, and the results recomposed into the corresponding complex proposition about the new "abstract" objects; otherwise, certain inconsistencies will arise. Second, it is advisable to use the predicator $A(...)$ only on the right side of the abstraction schema and to use another predicator exactly corresponding to it, e.g., $A^\alpha(...)$ or $A^*(...)$, on the left side, to avoid typical confusions. Logical and mathematical usage has followed this advice instinctively: in the example above, we speak of the exemplifiability of a predicator, but we do not call the corresponding concept *exemplifiable*, speaking of a *non-empty* concept instead.

It appears from this sketch that concerning the initial objects and the final objects of an abstraction process, we have not committed ourselves ontologically. We have merely fixed a particular way, or method, of handling certain means of expression syntactically (or linguistically). "Modern abstraction" may thus be characterized as the move from an "old" way of speaking to a "new" way of speaking, from one *façon de parler* to another one. Since the propositions in the new way of speaking were stipulated to have the same sense as the corresponding propositions in the old way of speaking, a move of this kind may also be reversed in the sense of doing the step in the other direction. That is, the newly introduced "words of the third kind"—abstractors, in addition to nominators and predicators—may in principle be eliminated. But their employment makes things easier where the old way of speaking is beginning to get complicated.

So much for the systematic side of a procedure concerning which it is still controversial how much, if anything, it owes to Frege, and also how much it may contribute to elucidating and perhaps avoiding some of the well-known impasses connected with referring to "logical objects" in which Frege found himself caught.

(2) At the end of §65 of *GLA* (p. 77), in order to justify his tentative contextual definition of "The direction of line *a* is equal to the direction of line *b*" by "Line *a* is parallel to line *b*," Frege points out, not only that by Leibniz's substitutability criterion we are allowed to replace the expression "the direction of line *a*" by "the direction of line *b*" *salva veritate* in every proposition about directions if line *a* is parallel to line *b*, but—more important—that we can establish the general rule to admit as propositions about directions only propositions whose truth value remains invariant against replacement of the direction of a line by the direction of another one parallel to it (the "replacement" being, more precisely, that of the *expressions* for directions, as is clear from the beginning of the paragraph). It is astonishing that this passage has received so little attention from interpreters of Frege, in face of the fact that Frege's postulation of the invariance property for propositions about directions with respect to parallelism exactly corresponds to the transition step (from right to left, in our notation) of the modern abstraction schema. It is regrettable, to say the least, that Frege failed to notice the importance—and, most important, the sufficiency—of this invariance for the justification of the "abstract way of speaking" in its full generality (i.e., not only for equations). Avoiding the ill-fated recurrence to extensions of concepts would have saved him the troublesome (and, in the end, equally ill-fated) revision and transformation of the ingenious procedure in *GGA*.

I am convinced that Frege, in discovering the invariance property of statements about "abstract objects" in a special case, gave an essentially correct analysis of the process called modern abstraction; I will not repeat here the meta-analysis given in my introduction to the centenary edition of Frege's *Grundlagen* in 1986. But even granted that I am right in my claim, we have to face a whole series of disquieting questions if we follow Frege on his way from *Grundlagen* to *Grundgesetze*. As it seems, Frege considers the Julius Caesar problem of *GLA* §55 and the reflections of §67 as conclusive evidence that statements about numbers cannot be analyzed by abstraction procedures in a satisfactory manner. Therefore, he proposes to "try another way" (*GLA*, 79; Beaney 1997, 114) and produces his famous explicit definition according to which "the Number that belongs to the concept *F* is | the extension of the concept 'equinumerous to the concept *F*'" (*GLA*, 79f.; Beaney 1997, 115). For our discussion, Frege's additional (and unfortunately rather evasive) remarks in the adjoined footnote (*GLA*, 80; Beaney 1997, 115) are noteworthy. Frege believes that he could simply have said "concept" instead of "extension of the concept" even though "concepts can be of equal extension, without coinciding" (ibid., n^s), and a concept "has always to be completed" (*GLA*, 82), whereas extensions of concepts are complete like numbers after Frege's analysis. Frege thinks that "both objections can be met," but he does not reveal how this could be done, and assumes "that it is known what the extension of a concept is" (*GLA*, 80; Beaney 1997, 115 n^s). Disregarding my one-time complaint about this shirking maneuver and my curiosity how "[Frege] would have answered the directly posed question, 'what is the extension of a concept?'" (Thiel 1965, 43, and 1968, 38), it is clear that the problem must have accompanied Frege permanently on his way from *GLA* to *GGA*, leading him to the insight that identity of the extensions of two concepts ranks equally with identity of the directions of two straight lines, identity of the shapes of geometric figures, and so forth.

But what is the equivalence relation between concepts from which to start the abstraction process? The necessary link is the consistent and formally regimented conception of concepts as functions, and along with it that of extensions of concepts as courses-of-values, first presented in *Function und Begriff* in 1891 and in elaborated form in *Grundgesetze*. In *Function und Begriff*, Frege starts with two mathematical functions given by differing functional terms but describing the same curve; this makes it plausible that he uses the term "course-of-values" (or "value-range," *Wertverlauf*) also in cases in which the terms refer to functions in Frege's now extended sense which have the same course-of-values, that is, yield equal values for every argument inserted into the argument places of the respective functional terms. Writing this relation (in his example) as "$x^2 - 4x = x(x - 4)$," Frege goes on to explain: "if we so understand this equation that it is to hold whatever argument may be substituted for x, then we have thus expressed that an equality holds generally. But we can also say: 'the value-range of the function $x(x - 4)$ is equal to that of | the function $x^2 - 4x$', and here we have an equality between value-ranges" (Beaney 1997, 135). Likewise, when he has expanded the notion of function, Frege declares that "the functions $x^2 = 1$ and $(x + 1)^2 = 2(x + 1)$ always have the same value for the same argument, viz. the True for the arguments $- 1$ and $+ 1$, and the False for all other arguments. According to our previous conventions we shall also say that these functions have the same value-range, and express this in symbols as follows:

$$\dot{\varepsilon}(\varepsilon^2 = 1) = \dot{\alpha}((\alpha + 1)^2 = 2(\alpha + 1)).$$

In logic this is called identity [*Gleichheit*] of the extension of concepts" (*Function und Begriff* 16; Beaney 1997, 139). The parallel passages of *Grundgesetze* (e.g., *GGA* I, 7) are even more widely known, so that further quotations will be superfluous.

What is the nature of this transformation of a general equivalence into an equation between courses-of-values? In *Grundlagen*, i.e., at an earlier stage of his analysis when he still lacked a special notation for abstract terms, Frege had called the procedure "not unheard of" (*nicht unerhört*, *GLA*, 74; Beaney 1997, 110), and in *Grundgesetze* he assured the reader that "what we are doing by means of our transformation is thus not really anything novel" (*GGA* II, 148; Beaney 1997, 278). But this allusion to an established mathematical practice does not answer the question concerning its conceptual or formal characterization. In *Grundlagen*, he calls it an (unusual kind of) definition, but in the second volume of *Grundgesetze*, having expounded a very detailed theory of definition in §§55–67 of volume II, he clearly states that "this transformation must not be regarded as a definition" (*GGA* II, 147; Beaney 1997, 277). Rather, as we learn on the page immediately following, in making the transformation step, we are "appealing to a fundamental law of logic" (*GGA* II, 148; Beaney 1997, 278).

Now this seems to be a rather unusual kind of logical law. In *Function und Begriff*, the transition step is preceded by the words, "we can also say" [*wir können dafür aber auch sagen*] (9; Beaney 1997, 135), or by "we shall also say" [*werden wir also sagen*] (16; Beaney 1997, 139), and in *Grundgesetze* Frege says that he uses the statement of equality of two courses-of-values as *gleichbedeutend* with the statement of the general equivalence of the corresponding functions (*GGA* I, 7; Beaney 1997, 213). Michael Beaney, who translated the passage for his collection, argues that the two statements are intended by Frege to have the same sense, not only the same reference, an explanation with which I agree. With regard to logical laws, we would find it totally inappropriate to claim, for instance, that instead of $\neg\, a$, "we can also say" $a \to \neg\, a$. What Frege wants to express is different, although related, and he is quite clear that the two sides of the transformation schema express "the same sense, but in a different way" (*Function und Begriff*, 11; Beaney 1997, 136), and that "we have expressed what is essentially the same thought" in both cases (*Ausführungen über Sinn und*

Bedeutung, in *Nachgelassene Schriften* I, 132; Beaney 1997, 177). I therefore remain unconvinced by Dummett's strong statement that the interpretation of Frege's *Umsetzung* as a step in the spirit of modern abstraction would run "counter to Frege's evident intentions" (Dummett 1991, 169), although I am fully aware of the passages from Frege's *Nachwort* which he quotes in support of his judgment, and share his assessment of "Frege's hesitancy about contextual definitions . . . as due to an only partly conscious realization of the tension between his 'context' doctrine and his realistic notion of reference" (Dummett 1973, 501). Liberalizing the transformation step (in the sense of *Umsetzung*) to include applications of the abstraction schema described in section (1) would have enabled Frege to answer the question whether a particular course-of-values is identical with Caesar: the transition schema

$$\dot{\varepsilon}\Phi(\varepsilon) = \text{Caesar} \Leftrightarrow \bigwedge_x (X \sim \Phi(\xi) \rightarrow X = \text{Caesar})$$

shows that the statement on the left side of the double arrow is meaningful but false, since the statement on the right side is meaningful but false—provided identity between a predicator and a proper name has been suitably defined so that its statement is not meaningless but false in its turn.

Summing up the earlier reflections, Frege seems to have been the first to see the invariance property of statements about abstract objects (often treated under the heading of "substitutivity") as the essential point of the process of abstraction. But due to his fixation on recognition-judgments in *GLA* (a restriction which, incidentally, we also find in Peano and Weyl), he restricted the abstraction step to the transformation of an equivalence statement into an equation between abstract objects (as, by the way, we find it also in Peano and in Weyl). By this omission of statements about abstract objects that do not have the form of an equation, Frege landed himself in the so-called Julius Caesar problem, from which he did not see any other escape than the introduction of abstract objects of any kind as extensions of concepts, in the form "the extension of the concept 'is equivalent to . . . '" for the equivalence relation under consideration in the particular case.

One should remind oneself of the fact that this is precisely the procedure of constructing equivalence classes in contemporary mathematics (cf. the second sense of "abstraction" in the beginning of this paper). As soon as Frege did no longer content himself with presupposing everybody's acquaintance with extensions of concepts (or classes), but asked for a characterization of extensions, he immediately realized that they are themselves nothing else but abstract objects the identity criterion of which is the general equivalence of the concepts whose extensions they are (in the sense of exactly the same objects falling under these concepts). But now the

Julius Caesar problem returns through just the same back door with the sign "extension" that in *Grundlagen* seemed to offer a way out of the difficulty. Frege was back from his unlucky experiment with the method (?) of "looking-around" (I. Angelelli) or "circumspection" (J. Nubiola), and tried to solve the problem at least for the artificial language of the Begriffsschrift in §10 of *Grundgesetze*, not to everybody's satisfaction.

(3) The close interconnection of language and ontology in Frege's thinking is manifest, with far-reaching consequences, in the dichotomy between objects and functions. Objects are saturated entities to which we can refer by (and only by) saturated expressions of our language, whereas functions and particularly concepts are incomplete, unsaturated entities to which we can refer by (and only by) incomplete expressions, so that inspection of the relevant parts of a sentence often will show what we are talking about. In "On Concept and Object," Frege claims that, if one "needs to say something about a concept," this will usually be done by using a grammatical subject to refer to this concept which, in such cases, does not play its normal predicative role and will therefore not be expressed by a predicate, but by an expression of the form "the concept F" which, according to Frege, is a proper name, in other words, a saturated expression. To become the reference of the grammatical subject of a sentence, "[the concept] must first be converted into an object, or, more precisely, an object must go proxy for it" (Frege 1892, 197; Beaney 1997, 185). In Frege's view, this move is unavoidable since "the words 'the concept *square root of 4*' have an essentially different behaviour, as regards possible substitutions, from the words 'square root of 4' in our original sentence [sc. 'The concept *square root of 4* is realized'], i.e., the *Bedeutungen* of the two phrases are essentially different" (Frege 1892, 201; Beaney 1997, 189).

As is well known, Frege got himself into trouble with the details of this analysis, and interpreters of Frege have had much trouble in defending it in principle. The far-reaching consequences mentioned above include the fact that Frege charged this systematically misleading feature of language with having led to the mistaken belief in sets and to a whole theory of sets, blinding us to the fact that, for example, "the set of fixed stars only seems to be an object [whereas] in truth there is no such object at all" (Letter to Hönigswald, 26 April 1925, PMC 54). The interconnection of language and ontology shows its negative side in Frege's confusion of the transformation of a concept word into a proper name with the "transformation of a concept into an object" (ibid., 55). Since a proper name can never take the place of a concept word in a sentence, special proper names must substitute for concept words, and seemingly, therefore, special objects for concepts, taking us into the muddle of the "representing objects."

It seems to me that this is an ontological pseudo-problem that might have been avoided had one taken the trouble to make a comparison with Frege's procedure in *GGA* where, not unexpectedly, he needs to say much about concepts. In the Begriffsschrift of 1893, we say something about a first-order concept $\Phi(\xi)$ by taking it as the argument of a one-place second-order function $M_\beta(\varphi(\beta))$ where "β" is a binding operator occupying and thereby blocking the argument place of $\Phi(\xi)$ so that in "$M_\beta(\varphi(\beta))$" the letter "φ" is the only free variable ("M" being not a variable but a schematic letter). Obviously, the insertion of "$\Phi(\xi)$" into the argument place of "$M_\beta(\varphi(\beta))$" does not transform $\Phi(\xi)$ into an object; "$\Phi(\xi)$" does not even *occur* in "$M_\beta(\Phi(\beta))$" (otherwise "ξ" would appear as an additional variable, free for object names). For example, we get the expression ⎯⎯ᵅ⎯ a = a by inserting the first-order function name "$\xi = \xi$" into the argument place of the second-order function name "⎯⎯ᵅ⎯ $\varphi(a)$," without transforming the function $\xi = \xi$ into an object or having an object substitute for it.

This shows clearly that here the situation is quite different from that in natural languages: in saying that "the function $\xi = \xi$ is satisfied by any object whatsoever," we would, according to Frege, have transformed the function we are speaking about into an object, whereas in ⎯⎯ᵅ⎯ a = a we are saying something about the function $\xi = \xi$ without having to transform the function name "$\xi = \xi$" into an object name for that purpose. The question whether "$\xi = \xi$," somehow hidden in ⎯⎯ᵅ⎯ a = a, plays or does not play the role of a proper name will not even arise, since the means of the Begriffsschrift make it unambiguously clear that the function $\xi = \xi$ is the subject of the statement (the "object" we are talking about), but has been divested of its normal role as predicate. It is certainly regrettable that natural languages lack the means available in the Begriffsschrift which are exhibited by the binding operator in the schematic representation "$M_\beta(\Phi(\beta))$," and are unable to prevent the formation of pseudo-object names. Frege's successful avoidance of this deficiency in the construction of his Begriffsschrift shows that we do not have an ontological problem here, and that the decisive point in a correct analysis of the situation is the clear separation between the linguistic form and the semantic role of an expression.

Here the circle closes in a felicitous way, since the linguistic form just analyzed coincides with that of the names of abstracta which we considered in the first part of our investigation, like "the concept F," "The number n," "the thought that p," and the like. If Frege is right in claiming that "language has means of presenting now one, now another, part of the thought as the subject," and that it is "not impossible that one way of analysing a given thought should make it appear as a singular judgement; another, as a particular judgement; and a third, as a universal judgement"

(Frege 1892, 199–200; Beaney 1997, 188), then he has also illuminated the transformation processes between the universal judgments on the one hand, and on the other hand, singular judgements about *abstracta* that were the subject of our investigation of the operation called abstraction.

CHRISTIAN THIEL

UNIVERSITY ERLANGEN-NURNBERG
MARCH 2005

REFERENCES

Beaney, Michael, ed. 1997. *The Frege Reader*. Oxford: Blackwell.
Dummett, Michael. 1956. "Nominalism." *The Philosophical Review* 65: 491–505.
———. 1973, 1981. *Frege: Philosophy of Language*. London: Duckworth.
———. 1981. *The Interpretation of Frege's Philosophy*. Cambridge, MA: Harvard Univ. Press.
———. 1991. *Frege: Philosophy of Mathematics*. London: Duckworth.
Frege, Gottlob. *Die Grundlagen der Arithmetik. Eine logisch mathematische Untersuchung über den Begriff der Zahl*. Breslau: Wilhelm Koebner, 1884; Centenarausgabe [...] ed. Christian Thiel, Felix Meiner: Hamburg 1986; *The Foundations of Arithmetic: A logico-mathematical enquiry into the concept of number*, 2nd. rev. ed., trans. J. L. Austin. Oxford: Basil Blackwell, 1959.
———. 1891. *Function und Begriff*. Jena: Hermann Pohle.
———. 1892. "Über Begriff und Gegenstand." *Vierteljahrsschrift für wissenschaftliche Philosophie* 16:192–205.
———. I 1893, II 1903. *Grundgesetze der Arithmetik. Begriffsschriftlich abgeleitet*. Jena: Hermann Pohle.
———. 1976. *Wissenschaftlicher Briefwechsel*, ed. Gottfried Gabriel et al. Hamburg: Felix Meiner, (= *Nachgelassene Schriften und Wissenschaftlicher Briefwechsel*, vol. II); *Philosophical and Mathematical Correspondence* (PMC), ed. Gottfried Gabriel et al., abridged for the English edition by Brian McGuinness, trans. Hans Kaal. Oxford: Basil Blackwell, 1980.
Thiel, Christian. 1965. *Sinn und Bedeutung in der Logik Gottlob Freges*. Meisenheim am Glan: Anton Hain; *Sense and Reference in Frege's Logic*. Dordrecht: D. Reidel, 1968.

REPLY TO CHRISTIAN THIEL

Christian Thiel opens his essay by distinguishing three types of abstraction. First is psychological abstraction, effected, in all the accounts, by not attending to those properties of an object taken to be irrelevant. The alleged result is a conception of an object lacking both the irrelevant properties and their opposites. This psychological operation with a logical outcome was a device much favoured by mathematicians of the later nineteenth century, including even Dedekind and Cantor; but it was ridiculed by Frege as a particularly absurd example of the misguided attempt to achieve logical effects by means of inner mental operations, instead of operations, expressible in language, on concepts to attain new concepts.

Thiel's second type is logical abstraction, illustrated and toyed with by Frege in his *Grundlagen*. We have some range of objects, say specific plane figures, and an equivalence relation $E(\xi, \zeta)$ between them, say similarity. We introduce an operator $\varphi(\xi)$, defined over the same range of objects, subject to the criterion of identity:

$$\forall x \, \forall y \, [\varphi(x) = \varphi(y) \leftrightarrow E(x, y)]$$

The products of the operation φ, denoted by expressions of the form "$\varphi(a)$," are abstract objects of a newly delineated kind, in our example shapes.

Thiel then describes a third type of abstraction, which he calls "modern abstraction." It shares many merits with logical abstraction, but has the additional merit of not inflating our ontology. Using it, we can get on with just the objects we already had; we do not need to recognise any new range of abstract objects such as shapes or directions. We have a range of objects, and an equivalence relation E defined over it, as before; let us use the same example of plane figures under similarity. We now consider predicates that are, in Thiel's terminology, invariant under E; namely those predicates "$F(\xi)$" that apply to any object equivalent (in the sense of E) to an object to which they apply. Symbolically, these are the predicates that satisfy the formula:

$$\forall x \ \forall y \ [E(x, y) \rightarrow (F(x) \rightarrow F(y))]$$

(I am here and subsequently modifying Thiel's symbolism to my own taste.) Thus (Thiel's example) if our range of objects consists of English words, and the relation E is that of having the same number of letters, the predicate "ξ is short" is one of these: since "short" is short, and "flood" has the same number of letters as "short," "flood" is necessarily short also. As Thiel remarks, "ξ is monosyllabic" is not invariant under E. Note that Thiel does not require that if "F(ξ)" applies to a given object, it should apply to another object *only if* it is equivalent to the given object, symbolically:

$$\forall x \ \forall y \ [E(x, y) \rightarrow (F(x) \leftrightarrow F(y))]$$

The word "food" is short, but it does not have the same number of letters as "flood."

We now introduce a symbol α to be prefixed to an individual variable or term. Unlike φ as used above in logical abstraction, α is not an operator mapping objects of our range on to other, abstract, objects: it is simply a logical symbol restricting the application of predicates. The symbol α is explained by the following definition:

$$F(\alpha x) \leftrightarrow \forall y \ [E(x, y) \rightarrow F(y)]$$

By this definition "F(αx)" says that "F(x)" holds and that also "F(y)" holds for any y equivalent to x. If "F(ξ)" is invariant with respect to the equivalence relation E, then "A(αx)" will hold just in case "A(x)" holds. To use Thiel's example, let x be a particular square, and let "F(x)" express "x is symmetrical under rotations of 90°." Since such rotational symmetry is invariant under similarity, "F(αx)" truly says that x is symmetrical under rotations of 90° and that so is any other square. But if "F(ξ)" is *not* invariant under E, "F(αx)" does not hold even if "F(x)" holds.

In these formulas "F(ξ)" is taken to be a primitive predicate. As we noted, the symbol "α" does not really operate on the variable x (or other term), but serves to restrict the application of the predicate, or, more exactly, to transform it into another predicate. For this reason it might seem more perspicuous if it were attached to the predicate-letter. We want, however, that it should also govern predicates expressed by a complex formula. Thiel says that in this case the complex predicate should first be decomposed into the primitive predicates which make it up, and the α-operation applied to each separately; otherwise, he says, certain inconsistencies will arise. I do not see that his recommendation will avoid the difficulty. While the complex predicate as a whole may be invariant under the equivalence relation, some of the component predicates may not be, in which case the application to them of the α-operation will lead to quite unintended results. The correct procedure surely is to express the α-operation by binding the variable of the predicate and adding an argument-place (as with the λ-notation). Thus with a primitive predicate "F(ξ)" we shall write

$$\alpha x \, [F(x)] \, (x),$$

where the second occurrence of "x" is bound, but the third is free. We may use the same notation with a compound predicate, however complex. If, in the formula we wish to use, the complex predicate is subjected to further logical operations, this notation will allow us to make clear to which predicate we are applying the α-operation.

When a complex predicate is decomposed into its component primitive predicates, there will usually be among these two- or more-place predicates. Thiel therefore owed us an explanation of how the α-operation is to be applied to these. We shall need such an explanation in any case, because we shall certainly want to apply it to predicates with more than one argument-place.

Thiel's intention is certainly that "modern" abstraction shall be able to serve all the purposes that logical abstraction can serve. Instead of saying that a certain shape satisfies a given condition, we shall say that every plane figure similar to some specified one satisfies an analogous condition. Instead of saying that there are just two shapes that satisfy some other condition, we shall say that there are two plane figures, not similar to one another, that satisfy a likewise analogous condition, and that any plane figure that satisfies it is similar to one or other of the original two. Thiel does not take the time to expound this, and therefore does not answer the question how far modern abstraction can take the place of logical abstraction. Nor does he make any more distinction than Frege did between abstraction on objects and abstraction on concepts—in Frege's case, between the directions of lines and the numbers belonging to concepts. He appears to envisage the use of expressions of the form "F(ξ)" as terms within formulas, a most unFregean and, I think, improper procedure. What we shall need, in order to apply modern abstraction to concepts under the equivalence relation of equinumerosity, is a higher-order α-operation applicable to second-order predicates; the notation will become very cumbersome. How much arithmetic could be developed in this way must be investigated. What is certain is that it will not make possible Frege's proof of the infinity of the sequence of natural numbers. For the sake of this proof Frege needed numbers to be full-fledged objects, not concepts doing duty for them. Of course, if numbers are taken as full-fledged objects, the Julius Caesar problem cannot readily be evaded.

In his essay, Thiel is most interested, not in promoting the virtues of modern abstraction, but in enquiring how far Frege anticipated the ideas underlying it. He first calls attention to Frege's having introduced in *Grundlagen* the notion of a predicate invariant under some equivalence relation, and then expresses regret that Frege did not see that it could be used as the basis of an abstraction procedure—"modern" abstraction—that avoided the introduction of abstract objects. Thiel reluctantly admits that Frege fell back instead on logical abstraction, by means of which a range of abstract objects is introduced, landing him with the Julius Caesar problem and ultimately with the contradiction. Thiel does not mention that it allowed Frege to give what could be claimed as a purely logical proof that there are infinitely many natural numbers. He then discusses the principle Frege adopted of transforming a statement that two functions had the same values for all arguments into an equation between their value-ranges—the content of the fatal axiom V of *Grundgesetze*. As he remarks, Frege presented this, not as a definition, but as a fundamental logical law; but he thinks it a very odd kind of law. He then criticises me for saying, in *Frege: Philosophy of Mathematics*, that to construe "The number of Fs is the same as the number of Gs" as merely an idiomatic way of saying "There are just as many Fs as Gs," rather than as to be taken at face value, "runs counter to Frege's evident intentions." His criticism of this remark is an expression of his hankering to believe that Frege espoused modern, rather than logical, abstraction. But he cannot maintain this. Frege wanted to take expressions of the form "the number of Fs" as standing for self-subsistent objects. To construe them otherwise *does* run counter to his evident intentions.

Thiel next proceeds to discuss Frege's dichotomy between objects and functions, rightly emphasising the "close interconnection of language and ontology" in his thinking. He dwells on the muddle into which Frege notoriously fell in discussing phrases such as "the concept *square root of 4*." He points out that in Frege's own symbolism a second-order statement about a concept is expressed in a way that allows what stands for the concept to retain the form of a predicate with an argument-place. He concludes that the question about the role of the expression "the concept *square root of 4*" is an ontological pseudo-problem. We repeatedly encounter expressions of this kind in natural language: we have to say *something* about them. But I agree with Thiel if he means that we ought not to ask what they stand for, still less to say that they stand for objects, as Frege slipped into saying in "Über Begriff und Gegenstand." From a Fregean standpoint they are misbegotten expressions, to be explained only as idiomatic means of saying something in which the concept is designated by a predicate and the function by a functor. They are legitimate only when the logically correct formulation can be given. It is not always obvious what that formulation is: what, for example, is the logically correct formulation of the statement "The predicate 'ξ is a square root of 4' stands for a concept"? Perhaps something like "What the predicate 'ξ is a square root of 4' stands for is something which everything either is or is not."

Thiel's concluding paragraph opens with the remark that "the linguistic form just analyzed coincides with that of the names of abstracta which we considered in the first part of our investigation, like 'the concept F,' 'the number n,' 'the thought that p,' and the like." The suggestion is that we have been given the means to eliminate all apparent singular terms standing for abstract objects. But the cases are different. Expressions of the form "the concept F" are by Frege's standards misbegotten: we are bound on his principles to find a way of getting rid of them, or at least of interpreting them not at face value but as going to form sentences to be understood as substituting for ones that are genuinely well formed and to be taken at face value. There is no such objection on Fregean grounds to expressions of the form "the number 9." The pressure on Frege to deny that the concept *horse* is a concept is clear; there was no pressure on him to deny that the number 9 is a number, nor that the thought that the Earth moves is a thought. By means of modern abstraction Thiel may be able to analyse away terms for numbers: we must see how much arithmetic he is able to obtain in this way. But, except for one who is a nominalist on principle, which Frege himself most certainly was not, it is not mandatory to eliminate them; it would certainly be most troublesome to do so. As for expressions of the form "the thought that . . . ," it is not at all evident how Thiel proposes to eliminate *them*, and it in no way follows from Frege's principles that we are under any necessity to do so. Perhaps Thiel proposes to apply modern abstraction to sentences under the equivalence relation of synonymy (for Frege thoughts are expressed by sentences); but that would make it very difficult even to express the question whether animals have thoughts. Thiel is an enemy of abstract objects; I am not. I think that he has here rounded up a miscellany of them, which require varied treatment. I do not think he is entitled to invoke the authority of Frege for doing so.

M. D.

19

Ian Rumfitt

ASSERTING AND EXCLUDING: STEPS TOWARDS AN ANTI-REALIST ACCOUNT OF CLASSICAL CONSEQUENCE

The Michaelmas Term of 1987 ought to have been a bad time at which to embark on graduate study in philosophy at the University of Oxford. Of the three statutory chairs in the modern subject, two were vacant, and it was unclear when the university would be able to afford to fill them. Moreover, some of the tutorial fellows who had been most active in supervising graduate students over the previous ten years had either left to take chairs elsewhere or were known to be on the point of doing so. Michael Dummett, though, responded to the crisis by taking on students far in excess of his contractual requirements; I remember him telling me at one point in the late eighties that he was then supervising thirty people. Many philosophers rightly regret the consequent loss of time for Dummett's own writing. Those of us who were then his students, however, remain forever in his debt for the graduate education that he gave us, which was bestowed quite against the politically determined odds.

And what an education it was. A supervision took place once a fortnight in term, and lasted two hours. The student would have delivered a piece of writing the previous day; this would be returned as he left, with detailed marginal comments. Rarely, however, would it provide the starting point for the supervision. Instead, Dummett would begin by asking a series of philosophical questions, apparently remote from the assigned topic, and strenuous discussion would ensue until that topic returned into view, now approached from a fresh and unexpected angle. In this way, one was brought—almost by magic, it sometimes seemed—to appreciate the wider context in which the topic needed to be situated and to feel the deeper currents bearing upon it. One would leave Dummett's room, frequently exhausted by the intensity of the conversation, but invariably elated by the new perspectives attained on apparently familiar matters and soon re-energized by the enticing new questions raised about them. If there is a better way of teaching philosophy to graduate students, I have no idea what it might be. The method requires, though, a teacher who possesses a quite exceptional mastery of a wide range of philosophical issues.

I. JUSTIFYING LOGICAL LAWS

For the past forty-five years, Dummett has been preoccupied with "the question how, if at all, it is possible to criticize or question fundamental logical laws that are generally accepted."[1] As most readers of the present volume will know, his reflections on this matter have led him to call into question some of the generally accepted laws of the classical propositional calculus—notably the laws of excluded middle and of double-negation elimination.[2] Indeed, they have led him to conclude that only the laws of intuitionistic logic—and not the distinctively classical laws which go beyond those also accepted by the intuitionist—can be given a satisfactory philosophical justification.

Dummett's arguments for this conclusion fall under two heads. First, there are proof-theoretical considerations, which ultimately rest on a perceived lack of "harmony" between the classical introduction and elimination rules for negation. This strand in Dummett's thinking has assumed greater prominence as the years have passed, and it runs right through his 1991 book on the subject, *The Logical Basis of Metaphysics*. I have already explained in print why I do not find these proof-theoretical considerations compelling,[3] and Dummett has been kind enough to reply to my criticisms.[4] Whilst there is, no doubt, a great deal more to be said on each side of that debate, I shall not pursue the matter here.[5]

My topic in this essay is instead a second way Dummett has of calling classical logical laws into question. If a classical logician is asked to justify a primitive rule of his system, he may well respond by giving a proof of the rule's soundness, relative to some semantic specification of the relationship of consequence. As Dummett notes, many philosophers would regard such a response as quite hopeless. On their view,

> a soundness proof for our primitive rules would, if offered as a justification of them, incur just the same charge of circularity as if we attempted to justify each of two sets of primitive rules by showing the derivability of each from the

other. For, in demonstrating soundness, we should be bound to employ deductive argument; and, in doing so, we should probably make use either of those very forms of inference which we were supposed to be justifying, or else of ones which we had already justified by reduction to our primitive rules. And, even if we did neither of these things, so that our proof was not strictly speaking circular, we should have used some principles of inference or other, and the question could then be raised what justified them: we should therefore either eventually be involved in circularity, or have embarked upon an infinite regress.[6]

Although Dummett distinguishes such "rule-circularity"—whereby a rule of inference is applied in proving the soundness of that very rule—from the gross circularity that would be involved in taking the rule's soundness to be a premise in a proof of soundness,[7] he agrees with those who object in the way just sketched that rule-circularity "would be fatal if our task were to convince someone, who hesitates to accept inferences of . . . [a given] form, that it is in order to do so."[8] For this reason, he denies that a rule-circular proof of a law's soundness could be used to persuade someone who is skeptical of the law to accept it. He argues, however, that a justification of a logical rule need not be capable of persuading a skeptic to follow it. A system of logical rules, he thinks, may be said to be justified if their soundness is deducible from the best explanation of a philosophically puzzling phenomenon—even if "deducible" here means deducible by the rules of the system in question.

The philosophically puzzling phenomenon that Dummett has in mind is nothing less than the very possibility of gaining knowledge through deductive inference from known premises. The puzzle is to explain how it is "that, by means of such inferences, we can establish as true a statement that has not been directly so established, that is, which has not been so established by the means for which our method of conferring meaning on it expressly provides."[9] More particularly, "when a statement is established, conclusively but indirectly, by the use of a deductive argument," we need to explain in precisely what sense it would "be right to say that, in accepting it as so established, we have remained faithful to the meaning we originally gave it."[10]

In explaining this puzzle, Dummett predicates truth *simpliciter* of statements, but what exactly does he mean by the term "statement"? He cannot mean the proposition that is expressed by a declarative utterance; for he speaks of statements as *having* meanings or senses, and as belonging to particular languages, speech which would make no sense if applied to propositions. Neither can he mean the particular declarative utterance itself; since the problem is to explain the possibility of establishing a statement conclusively but indirectly through deductive argument it would be too

narrowing to confine attention to actual declarative utterances.[11] Given that
these familiar glosses on the term are excluded, let us consider instead those
ordered pairs whose first element is a meaningful, indeed disambiguated,
declarative type-sentence and whose second element is a possible context
of utterance; by a possible context of utterance, I mean a determination of
all the contextual features which can bear upon the truth or falsity of a
declarative utterance. Some of these ordered pairs will be such that, were
the declarative type-sentence that is the first element uttered in the context
that is the second element, a determinate proposition, or Fregean thought,
would then be expressed. I shall say that a *statement* is an ordered pair that
meets this condition. Not every ordered pair of declarative type-sentence
and possible context of utterance will qualify as a statement in this sense.
For example, an ordered pair of sentence and context whose first member
is 'You are ill' will not count as a statement unless the context provides an
addressee. I cannot claim any direct textual warrant for this gloss on
Dummett's use of the term 'statement,'[12] but it fits the preponderance of
texts better than any alternative I have been able to devise, and it avoids the
difficulties that we found to attend our two previous glosses. First, each
statement will now possess a sense: this will be the thought which would be
expressed by uttering the statement's first element (the declarative sentence)
in the context that is its second element. Second, the quantification over all
possible contexts of utterance means that the class of all statements will
possess the requisite generality. Admittedly, we shall not have determined
the extent of that class until we have enumerated all the features of an
utterance's context that can bear on its truth or falsity. Any indeterminacy
there, however, will not affect the argument to follow, so there is no call to
enumerate the relevant features on this occasion.

   In any event, I think that Dummett is right to perceive the need for
some kind of philosophical explanation of how a thinker can establish a
statement conclusively but indirectly through deductive proof. He is right,
too, in supposing that most classical logicians will try to provide such an
explanation by appealing to what he calls the "realist model of meaning."
According to this model, a statement's logically relevant meaning consists
in the division that it effects between those possible states of affairs in
which it is true and those in which it is false. This division is assumed to be
exclusive and exhaustive even when it is in principle impossible to
determine whether the statement is true or false. Now on this view, when a
thinker conclusively establishes a statement by deduction—that is, when he
correctly deduces it from premises he knows—infidelity to its meaning
would consist in asserting it when it is in fact false. And, given that the
premises are known and hence true, such infidelity is excluded if the rules
applied in the argument are sound. The relevant notion of soundness is itself

explained in terms of truth. As I am using the term, a logical rule is a rule of a natural deduction system, and the rules of such a system are either rules of inference (the Stoics' *schemata*) or rules of proof (their *themata*). If the rule in question is a rule of inference, its soundness will consist in its preserving truth; the conclusion of any application of it is true whenever each of the premises is true. If it is a rule of proof, its soundness will consist in its preserving the preservation of truth. In order, then, to complete the proposed explanation of how a classically valid argument remains faithful to the meaning of its conclusion, it needs to be shown that each of the classical logical rules is (in the relevant sense) sound.

Because the realist model of meaning assumes that each statement will divide all possible states of affairs exclusively into those which render the statement true and those which render it false, the model implies the principle of noncontradiction: "No statement is both true and false." Because the division is also assumed to be exhaustive, it also implies the principle of bivalence: "Every statement is either true or false." In tandem with semantic axioms saying how the truth or falsity of complex statements depends upon the truth or falsity of their parts, these principles suffice to demonstrate the soundness of the classical logical rules. We may take as an example double-negation elimination, a classical deduction rule which the intuitionist logician declines to accept. Since double-negation elimination is a rule of inference, rather than of proof, its soundness may be formulated as the proposition that each statement is true if its double negation is. The demonstration of this proposition is formalized below. The domain of quantification comprises statements; 'T' symbolizes the (unary) truth predicate for statements; 'F' symbolizes the corresponding falsity predicate; and 'neg' symbolizes the functor 'the negation of':

1.	$\forall x \neg (Tx \wedge Fx)$	Premise
2.	$\forall x (Tx \vee Fx)$	Premise
3.	$\forall x (T(\text{neg } x) \leftrightarrow Fx)$	Premise
4.	$Ta \vee Fa$	2, $\forall$-elimination, with 'a' parametric
5.	$T(\text{neg neg } a)$	Assumption
6.	$T(\text{neg neg } a) \leftrightarrow F(\text{neg } a)$	3, $\forall$-elimination, substituting 'neg a' for 'x'
7.	$T(\text{neg neg } a) \rightarrow F(\text{neg } a)$	6, $\wedge$-elimination
8.	$F(\text{neg } a)$	5, 7, $\rightarrow$-elimination
9.	Fa	Assumption
10.	$T(\text{neg } a) \leftrightarrow Fa$	3, $\forall$-elimination, substituting 'a' for 'x'
11.	$Fa \rightarrow T(\text{neg } a)$	10, $\wedge$-elimination
12.	$T(\text{neg } a)$	9, 11, $\rightarrow$-elimination
13.	$T(\text{neg } a) \wedge F(\text{neg } a)$	12, 8, $\wedge$-introduction
14.	$\neg (T(\text{neg } a) \wedge F(\text{neg } a))$	1, $\forall$-elimination, substituting 'a' for 'x'

15. $\neg Fa$ 9, 13, 14, $\neg$-introduction, with discharge
                                 of assumption 9
16. Ta 4, 15, *modus tollendo ponens*
17. $T(\text{neg neg } a) \to Ta$ 5, 16, $\to$-introduction, with discharge
                                 of assumption 5
18. $\forall x \, (T(\text{neg neg } x) \to Tx)$ 17, $\forall$-introduction, since 'a' was
                                 parametric

We have here a proof of the soundness of double-negation elimination from the principles of noncontradiction and bivalence together with the semantic axiom stating that a statement is false if and only if its negation is true. We could prove similarly the soundness of the other classical laws.

The proof just given assumes that the 'or' used in formulating the principle of bivalence sustains inference by *modus tollendo ponens*: from 'A or B' and 'not B', infer A. Dummett, indeed, takes care to secure this by formulating bivalence as the principle that every statement is *determinately* either true or false, where

> the force of 'Determinately, either A or B' is that 'or' is being used as subject to a quite unrestricted application of the rule of or-elimination [or of 'proof by cases']: one may infer any statement 'C' that may be shown to follow both from 'A', together with any other statements accepted as true, and from 'B', together with any other statements accepted as true.[13]

Given *ex contradictione quodlibet*, an occurrence of 'or' that conforms to unrestricted proof by cases will also sustain *modus tollendo ponens*. Given uncontroversial rules for introducing 'and' and 'or,' such an occurrence of 'or' will also distribute over conjunction. Hence, given the premises that a statement A is either true or false, and that a statement B is too, we may infer that there are just four possibilities for the pair of statements: that A and B are both true, that A is true and B is false, that A is false and B is true, and that A and B are both false. So similarly for larger collections of statements. Thus the principle that each statement is (in this sense) determinately either true or false entails what is sometimes called the dissection principle—the principle, namely, that the 2^n cells in a truth table for an n-place connective exhaust the possible assignments of truth and falsity to the propositional variables thereby connected.

In what sense, if any, may our proof of its soundness be said to justify the rule of double-negation elimination? It must be conceded that the proof is unlikely to persuade somebody antecedently skeptical of the rule. Certainly, it will not persuade the intuitionist. For although the proof given is intuitionistically valid—*modus tollendo ponens* and the other rules applied in the course of it are all intuitionistically acceptable—an intuition-ist will not accept its second premise, the principle of bivalence. All the same, it seems to me that the proof may be said to help explain *why* double-negation elimination is sound from a realist perspective. We started from a certain conception of how a conclusive but indirect argument could remain faithful to the meaning of its conclusion. This conception (Dummett's "realist model of meaning") was then crystallized into four axioms: (1) the principle that a valid argument preserves truth; (2) the principle of noncontradiction; (3) the principle of bivalence; and (4) an axiom obtained by conjoining the familiar principles relating the truth or falsity of complex statements of a propositional language to the truth or falsity of their components. Let us call these principles the axioms of *classical proposi-tional semantics*. We were then able to explain why double-negation elimination is sound by deducing its soundness from these axioms. Of course, deducing so much will involve making inferences; this may preclude these axioms—or any others—from serving as a foundation for classical propositional logic, or any other logic. But there is no reason why an adherent of classical logic should abjure classical rules of inference in seeking to explain why those rules are sound. On the contrary: it is at this stage of the discussion quite unclear why he should even consider alternatives. So far from betraying a vicious circularity, then, the fact that the soundness of classical rules follows classically from an apparently attractive general account of the role of deductive argument exhibits the sort of virtuous circularity—the undisturbed internal coherence—that is characteristic of a good philosophical explanation. As Dummett says, "the charge of circularity or of begging the question is not applicable to an explanatory argument in the way that it is to a suasive argument," that is, to an argument designed to persuade somebody of its conclusion.[14]

The realist model of meaning, then, may be said to explain why classical logical laws are sound. Dummett's complaint against it—the reason why it does not really justify those laws—is not that it is viciously circular, but that the explanation is a bad one. The model's adherent supposes that he has explained how deductive argument can remain faithful to meaning, and has thereby provided "a satisfactory explanation of the role of such [deductive] arguments in our use of language."[15] But, Dummett objects, his model invokes a notion—that of a statement's being true in the absence of any possible verification—that is not really intelligible. Dummett allows that we have the idea of a statement's being *justifiable*, or (objectively) *correct*, meaning by this that "there is some [effective] means of verifying it, a knowledge of which by the speaker at the time of utterance would have" justified him, had he asserted the statement in question.[16] He denies, however, that we can apprehend a concept of truth which further transcends the present notion of justifiability or objective correctness. In a recent paper, he records his continuing suspicion that

> the leap required for a tacit attainment of the concept of truth takes us, not on to firm ground, but into a chasm. That is what, for mathematical statements, the intuitionist holds, and what, for statements of all kinds, the verificationist holds: we are under an illusion that we have acquired a genuine concept or have mastered a coherent linguistic practice.[17]

The ground for deeming this notion of truth unintelligible is a strong verificationism whereby "ordinary mastery of a language . . . is a state acquired solely by the acquisition of, and therefore consisting solely in, dispositions to suit one's linguistic behavior to evidence for the truth and falsehood of [statements]."[18] If the statement A says that p, then evidence for the truth of A will *ipso facto* be evidence that p, so that a disposition to suit one's linguistic behavior to evidence for the truth of A will *ipso facto* be a disposition to suit one's linguistic behavior to evidence that p. If mastery of the language consists solely in such dispositions, it is indeed hard to see how a speaker could so much as form the idea of statement A's being true in a case where there was no evidence that p.[19]

Moreover, the notion of correctness that Dummett allows we can attain does not generate any analogue of classical semantics, for it does not sustain any analogue of the principle of bivalence. Bivalence has it that each statement is either true or false, and in tandem with the classical semantical principle for negation (namely, that a statement is false just when its negation is true), it entails that, for each statement, either it or its negation is true. The analogous principle for correctness, then, would say that, for each statement, either it or its negation is correct or justifiably assertible. As Dummett remarks, however, this latter principle has no plausibility whatever. For many statements, there exists neither an effective means of verifying it nor an effective means of verifying its negation. If Dummett is right, then, in holding that we can attain no coherent concept of truth which transcends his notion of objective correctness, then the theory we have called classical propositional semantics is either false—if we re-interpret "true" to mean "objectively correct"—or senseless, if we persist in trying to employ a verification-transcendent notion of truth.

Because it is either false or unintelligible, the realist model of meaning cannot explain anything. In particular, it cannot explain how we remain faithful to a statement's meaning when we deduce it, conclusively but indirectly, from premises we know. In articulating the sense in which we do remain faithful, Dummett proposes, we must instead start from the idea that a statement's meaning is given by certain basic, or *canonical*, conditions for our being entitled to assert it.[20] In the case of empirical statements, these conditions will be the making of appropriate observations. A logical system will be faithful to those meanings only if it ensures that whenever we would have been able to make observations which would have entitled us to assert the premises, we would also have been able to make observations which would have entitled us to assert the conclusion. Thus Dummett regards Euler's famous theorem about the seven bridges of Königsberg as deductively valid insofar as it shows "us, of someone observed to cross every bridge at Königsberg, that he crossed at least one bridge twice, *by the criteria we already possessed for crossing a bridge twice.*" The essence of the proof is that it tells us "what we should observe, were we able to make certain observations, or what we should have observed, if we had chosen to make certain others."[21] Although the matter is delicate, I think that Dummett is right to hold that the rules of intuitionistic logic are the strongest logical principles that can be justified on this conception of what a valid inference must preserve.

Dummett's attack on the realist model of meaning has been scrutinized as closely as anything he has written. In this paper, however, I shall not try to assess its effectiveness, although I note in passing that its force does not depend on the claim that no verification-transcendent notion of truth is so much as intelligible. (Even if we can grasp such a notion of truth, it remains doubtful whether all statements obey the law of bivalence; and if some statements, perhaps vague statements, do not, then the proposed explanatory justification of the validity of double-negation will fail.) Instead I aim to show how, even if no verification-transcendent notion of truth is intelligible, this need have no revisionary consequences for classical propositional logic *per se.*[22] Indeed, I aim to provide a justification of the classical propositional laws of just the kind for which Dummett was looking—namely, a classically valid deduction of their soundness from principles which explain the role of logical laws in our use of language. I have sketched Dummett's objections to the realist explanation, whereby the essence of good deduction is the preservation of verification-transcendent truth. And I have mentioned Dummett's own explanation, whereby the essence of good deduction is the preservation of canonically warranted assertibility. I shall be essaying a third explanation of the role of deductive argument in our use of language. Like Dummett's explanation, this account will avoid appealing to the principle of bivalence; indeed, it will eschew any verification-transcendent notion of truth along with the other allegedly dubious notions of classical propositional semantics. Unlike Dummett's explanation, however, but like the realist model, it will yield natural senses for the sentential connectives which combine with its underlying principles to entail (classically) the soundness of the laws of classical propositional logic.

Other writers have advanced accounts of what classically valid arguments preserve which constitute alternatives to classical semantics. One well-known example is the probabilistic semantics which Hartry Field developed for classical languages on the basis of prior work by Karl Popper.[23] However, the account to be presented here has particular significance for the debate about realism that Dummett's work has inspired, for each of the notions and principles to be employed ought, I think, to be acceptable to a Dummettian anti-realist.[24] Indeed, with one exception, it will use the very same basic notions that Dummett uses in giving his semantics for intuitionistic propositional logic, although these notions will be deployed in a rather different way. For all that, the propositional logic that emerges will be fully classical, not intuitionistic.

Dummett himself supposes that his argument against the realist model of meaning extends to provide a reason for rejecting classical propositional logic *per se* in favor of its intuitionistic rival. "An opponent of a realist model of meaning," he writes, will conclude "that these [classical] forms of reasoning, though generally accepted, are fallacious."[25] The extension of the argument, however, relies exactly upon the assumption that objective correctness—although not subject to the principle of bivalence—will otherwise assume the role that truth plays in classical propositional semantics. A valid argument is taken to be one which preserves objective correctness, or the availability of a canonical verification; and the senses of the connectives will be given by specifying when a complex sentence is canonically verified. But while this may be the most obvious way of constructing a semantic theory using notions acceptable to an anti-realist, it is very far from being the only way.

In fact, the alternative method I shall develop here is founded on an anti-realist analysis of the speech act of asserting which Dummett himself has advanced. It leads to a semantic theory whereby a statement's sense is given, not in terms of the conditions under which it would be canonically verified, but in terms of the conditions under which it would be directly falsified. Admittedly, the axioms of this new semantical theory will validate the full classical propositional calculus only if we are allowed to use some principles of classical logic in deriving theorems from them. As we have seen, however, this point need not detract from the value of a semantic theory in explaining why an argument is valid, and thereby providing "a satisfactory explanation of the role of . . . arguments in our use of language." (Dummett, it may be noted, allows himself the full resources of intuitionistic logic in establishing the soundness and completeness of that logic with respect to his preferred semantics.) It is, though, of some interest that specifically classical resources will not in fact be needed in establishing the validity of the classical inference rule which the intuitionist contests, namely, the rule of double-negation elimination.[26]

II. Assertions and the Content of a Statement

A statement—understood as a particular sort of ordered pair of declarative type-sentence and possible context of utterance—cannot be identified with any particular *saying*, that is, with any particular speech action of uttering a complete declarative sentence. It will be useful, however, to deem a saying to be an *instance* of a statement when the sentence uttered in the saying is the statement's first element and the saying's context is the statement's second element. Statements—when understood in the recommended way—have no particular relation to any one variety of illocutionary force: for sayings issued with different forces may yet be instances of a given statement. One of the leading ideas in Dummett's treatment of these matters, however, is that all the semantical attributes of statements should ultimately be explicated by reference to those possible instances of statements which are assertions.[27] In particular, he holds that a statement's free-standing content should be identified with the content of a possible assertive instance of it: this is why he contrasts a statement's "ingredient sense" (its contribution to the content of more complex statements of which it is a part) with its own "*assertoric* content." Dummett also holds that we should understand the notion of an assertion's content by attending to particular features of the speech act of asserting.

The feature of that speech act which Dummett takes to be crucial to the determination of contents is explained most clearly in his 1976 paper, "What is a Theory of Meaning? (II)." "An assertion," he observes,

> is not, normally, like an answer in a quiz programme; the speaker gets no prize for being right. It is, primarily, a guide to action on the part of the hearers . . . ; a guide which operates by inducing in them certain expectations. And the content of an expectation is determined by what will surprise us; that is, by what it is that is *not* in accord with the expectation rather than by what corroborates it. The expectation formed by someone who accepts an assertion is not, in the first place, characterized by his supposing that one of those recognizable states of affairs which render the assertion correct will come to obtain; for in the general case there is no bound upon the length of time which may elapse before the assertion is shown to have been correct, and then such a supposition will have, by itself, no substance. It is, rather, to be characterized by his *not* allowing for the occurrence of any state of affairs which would show the assertion to have been incorrect; a negative expectation of this kind has substance, for it can be disappointed. The fundamental notion for an account of the linguistic act of assertion is, thus, that of the *incorrectness* of an assertion: the notion of its correctness is derivative from that of its incorrectness, in that an assertion is to be judged correct whenever something happens which precludes the occurrence of a state of affairs showing it to be incorrect.[28]

In order to appreciate the account of asserting that Dummett is proposing here, it may help to explain how it applies to one of the famous examples from his own early paper, "Truth."[29] Suppose, then, that I make an assertion by uttering the sentence "A city will never be built on this spot." Suppose too that a friend understands and accepts my assertion, and on the strength of it buys a field in the place where I made it, in the hope that his sheep may safely graze there. Now when we consider the social importance of acts of assertion, the thought runs, we see that the crucial division of cases is between those recognizable states of affairs in which my assertion is shown to be incorrect and all other states of affairs. For it is precisely in a state of affairs of the first kind that my friend may remonstrate "What you told me has turned out to be false," and perhaps then demand redress from me. As a responsible maker of assertions, the thought continues, my primary concern will be to ensure that I do not find myself facing remonstrations or demands of this kind from hearers who have taken my word. Accordingly, the content of an assertion will be given by the division between those recognizable states of affairs which leave me liable to such remonstrations and all other states of affairs. That is to say, Dummett's analysis of asserting leads to the conclusion that an assertion's content will be defined by the class of recognizable states of affairs which *falsify* it.

It will be clear that this is a distinctively—indeed, paradigmatically— anti-realist account of acts of assertion and their contents. The content of these acts is not explained in terms of their relationship to extra-linguistic reality. Instead, it is explained in terms of the role the acts play in our inter-subjective cognitive economy. I think, moreover, that the feature of the act of asserting upon which Dummett focuses is indeed the crucial one for any anti-realist theory of content. There are, though, a number of respects in which his idea needs glossing and refining.

It may be objected at once that many ordinary assertions *are* like answers in quiz programs, insofar as their speakers get credit for being recognizably right. There are, admittedly, exceptions to this. Cassandra was recognizably right in all of her assertions about the siege of Troy; little good it did her. But in general, it might be said, advantage accrues to those whose assertions recognizably get things right, so we often have an interest in making assertions that will be recognizably verified.

Although this observation is true, it does not seem to me to touch the real insight in the passage just quoted from Dummett. It is equally true that advantage may accrue to those recipients of orders who are seen to obey them. For all that, Dummett is surely right to hold that the content of an order is given by the conditions in which it would be disobeyed. This is because of

the role of commands in our society. The right to a reward is not taken to be an automatic consequence of obedience to a command, as the *right* to reproach is an automatic consequence of disobedience; if a reward is given, this is an act of grace, just as it is an act of grace if the punishment or reproach is withheld.[30]

The primary consequence of issuing a command, as one might put it, is that "one acquires a right to punish or at least reprobate disobedience," always provided one had the right to give the command in the first place (ibid.). And it is in relation to its primary consequence that the content of a command must be identified. Dummett is well aware that the analogy between assertions and commands cannot be pressed too hard. "Assertions," he remarks, "do not have the same kind of relation to determinate consequences that commands . . . do."[31] But it remains the case that the content of an assertion (like that of a command) must ultimately be identified by reference to the role that assertions play in our linguistic practice. Underpinning the argument is a particular conception of what that role is: at least in the central cases of asserting, an asserter invites his audience to rely on his word. Accordingly, an assertion's content is fixed by the difference between those circumstances in which that reliance proves to be misplaced and those in which it does not.[32]

In developing this idea, though, we should reject the suggestion—made early in the passage quoted from "What is a Theory of Meaning? (II)"—that an assertion's content bears any close relationship to the states of affairs whose obtaining might surprise a person who had understood and accepted it, or which might disappoint or dash such a person's expectations. Certainly, states of affairs of these kinds need not be those which falsify the assertion in question. For consider again an assertion of "A city will never be built here." Only the actual construction of a city will falsify this assertion. However, many things short of an actually constructed city will surprise, and disappoint the expectations of, somebody who has understood and accepted the assertion: a city *is* being built; lots of foundations have been laid; planning permission has been granted; the Prime Minister is known to want the scheme promoted; and so on. Philosophers who wish to attach contents to individual assertions at all—rather than to the "webs of belief" that whole systems of assertions might evince—aim precisely at isolating an assertion's content from the various states of affairs that may (given appropriate background knowledge) surprise or disappoint somebody who accepts the assertion. Perhaps the notion of an assertion's being falsified by a state of affairs can be used to effect such isolation; but not if that notion is in turn elucidated in terms of what will surprise or disappoint.

This point, though, brings out the need for a gloss: what *is* a recognizable state of affairs? Although I can claim no warrant for this in the text of "What is a Theory of Meaning? (II)," I suggest that we might helpfully identify this notion with one that looms large in Dummett's own exposition of the semantics of intuitionistic logic—namely, that of a state of information, which

I shall understand to be a set of propositions which might comprise the propositional knowledge of a (human) thinker at a particular time.[33] This identification is certainly consonant with the overarching aim of giving a semantics in terms that a Dummettian anti-realist will understand. Moreover, the proposed identification helps us to make progress on the task of isolating an assertion's content. For we can say that a recognizable state of affairs (i.e., a state of information) *directly* falsifies an assertion if and only if any thinker who is in that state of information, and who understands the assertion, will know immediately that the assertion is false. Clearly, a state of affairs may falsify an assertion without directly falsifying it. A state of affairs in which everybody here is taller than somebody there falsifies the assertion that everybody there is at least as tall as anybody here, but it does not do so directly: some people who understand the assertion will nevertheless need to pause to work out the incompatibility. The idea, then, will be that an assertion's content is fixed by the recognizable states of affairs that directly falsify it.

On this proposal, an assertion will have a determinate content only if it is determinate which recognizable states of affairs—which states of information—directly falsify it. This condition will be met in turn only if it is determinate in which states of information any thinker who understands the assertion will immediately know it to be false. The claim that this matter is determinate is a form of the analytic-synthetic distinction, and it is certainly open to challenge. However, it is plausible that determinacy of content for individual assertions should require it. Admittedly, identifying the direct falsifiers of atomic assertions of various kinds will be a painstaking analytical task, but Dummett himself is ill placed to claim that it could not be completed. As we have seen (in section I), constructing the sort of semantics that he envisages for intuitionistic languages will involve identifying the direct or "canonical" verifiers of various sorts of assertion.[34] Hard as this task may be in some cases, there is no reason to think that identifying direct or canonical falsifiers will be any harder.

The states of affairs which directly falsify an assertion should not be confused with the states of affairs in which that assertion would be unwarranted. Our leading example again makes the difference clear. A state of affairs in which an assertion of "A city will never be built here" is (objectively) unwarranted will be one in which there is no reason for deeming the place in question to be unable to host a city. In order for the assertion to be unwarranted, then, it is not required that a city should already have been built. By contrast, a state of affairs which directly falsifies the assertion must be one in which a city has been successfully constructed in the place in question. All the same, we might explain the notion of a warrant in terms of the notion —direct falsification—which the proposed account of assertion takes to be basic. Specifically, a warrant to make an assertion will consist in a reason to suppose that no circumstance which would directly falsify it will obtain.

In expounding Dummett's proposal, I have set no upper bound upon the length of time which may elapse before an assertion is shown to be wrong. In doing so, I may be deviating from Dummett's claim that an assertion should be understood as "a guide to action on the part of the hearers," which implicitly imposes such a bound—namely, the lifetime of the hearers. It seems to me, however, that we get a simpler and better version of his proposal if we say that an assertion is a guide to action on the part of all those who take the asserter's word, even if they do so by distant report. My friend may tell his children of my assertion "A city will never be built here," and his children may tell their children, so that my assertion induces expectations in people who are twenty generations removed from my actual hearers. But if a city is built there, centuries after I speak, my friend's descendants will be just as entitled to complain "What Rumfitt said all those years ago was wrong" as their ancestor would have been had a city been built during his lifetime. Dummett encapsulates his account of asserting by describing an assertion as a "gamble that the speaker will not be proved wrong."[35] But we shall certainly not attain a satisfactory general account of asserting if we understand the gamble to be that the asserter will not be proved wrong while he and the immediate recipients of his assertion are all alive. For many assertions are made in writing, and are expressly directed to readers unborn at the time of writing. Thucydides expressed the hope that his *History* would be a possession forever; he could entertain that hope only by accepting a strictly open-ended liability to criticism in the event of being shown to be wrong.[36]

I have been writing of the content of assertions, but the theory of content distilled from the excerpt from "What is a Theory of Meaning? (II)" applies equally to statements. The relation which underpins the theory is that between a state of affairs and an assertion which it directly falsifies. But if we can make sense of such a relation to an assertion, we can also make sense of the cognate relation to a statement, for we may call a statement directly falsified just when any assertive instance of it would be directly falsified. Our analysis of asserting, then, issues in the claim that a statement's assertoric content—the content of a potential assertive instance of it—is characterized by the recognizable states of affairs (the states of information) which directly falsify it. Let us label this claim "Thesis α."

III. *TERTIUM NON DATUR* AND BIVALENCE

Why should Thesis α be thought to demand a nonclassical logic? In "Truth," the main argument for this conclusion has the following structure. As it stands, Thesis α strictly concerns the content of statements; it says nothing at all about their truth or falsity. When, however, the appropriate connections are made between the truth and falsity of statements and their contents, Thesis α entails the semantical principle of *tertium non datur*, viz., the claim that no statement is neither true nor false. Philosophical reflection, then, enables us to *know* that no statement is neither true nor false. Now *tertium non datur* classically entails the principle of bivalence. From the premise "No statement is neither true nor false," in symbols $\neg \exists x \, (Sx \wedge \neg \, (Tx \vee Fx))$, one may infer $\forall x \, \neg \, (Sx \wedge \neg \, (Tx \vee Fx))$, thence $\forall x \, (Sx \rightarrow \neg\neg \, (Tx \vee Fx))$, and finally $\forall x \, (Sx \rightarrow (Tx \vee Fx))$, which symbolizes the principle of bivalence. If classical logic could be applied to semantical discourse, then, a simple deduction enables us to move from knowledge that no statement is neither true nor false to knowledge that every statement is either true or false. Dummett argues, however, that other conceptual constraints on the notions of truth and falsity mean that we can know no such thing:

> We are entitled to say that a statement P must be either or false, that there must be something in virtue of which it is true or it is false, only when P is a statement of such a kind that we could in a finite time bring ourselves into a position in which we were justified either in asserting or in denying P; that is, when P is an effectively decidable statement. This limitation is not trivial: there is an immense range of statements which, like 'Jones was brave', are concealed conditionals, or which, like 'A city will never be built here', contain— explicitly or implicitly—an unlimited generality, and which therefore fail the test.[37]

But if *tertium non datur* is knowable while bivalence is not, then classical logic is not applicable to semantical discourse. *A fortiori*, it is not applicable universally. The argument also suggests that within semantics, at least, it ought to be replaced by a logic cast from an intuitionistic mold, for in intuitionistic logic the final step in the deduction fails. The rule for eliminating double negations can be applied only to an effectively decidable statement; but not all of the matrix instances $Ta \vee Fa$ will qualify as such.

As I understand the argument of "Truth," Dummett's statements 'Jones was brave' (said of a man, now dead, who never encountered danger in his life) and 'A city will never be built here' are not advanced as counter-examples to the principle of bivalence *per se*. A counterexample to bivalence would be a statement which was neither true nor false, and the existence of such a thing is what *tertium non datur* excludes. Rather, they are put forward as cases in which we would not be "entitled to say that a statement must be either true or false." Since we are entitled to say what we know, I take it that they are also put forward as statements which we do not know to be either true or false.[38]

How does Dummett try to derive *tertium non datur* from Thesis α? "A statement," he explains,

> so long as it is not ambiguous or vague, divides all possible states of affairs into just *two* classes. For a given state of affairs, either the statement is used in such a way that a man who asserted it but envisaged that state of affairs as a possibility would be held to have spoken misleadingly, or the assertion of the statement would not be taken as expressing the speaker's exclusion of that possibility. If a state of affairs of the first kind obtains, the statement is false; if all actual states of affairs are of the second kind, it is true. It is thus *prima facie* senseless to say of any statement that in such-and-such a state of affairs it would be neither true nor false.[39]

Tertium non datur in turn grounds Dummett's rejection of Strawson's treatment of statements which contain a definite description lacking a unique satisfier. A speaker who asserts 'The present King of France is bald,' while envisaging as a possibility a state of affairs in which there is no unique King of France, would certainly be held to have spoken misleadingly. Accordingly, a state of affairs which Strawson would describe as rendering this statement neither true nor false Dummett describes as rendering it false in a particular way. And while Dummett allows that it may be worth distinguishing this way of rendering the statement false from the way in which it is rendered false when there is a reigning, but hirsute, King of France, "the point of such distinctions," he insists, "does not lie in anything to do with the sense of the statement itself, but has to do with the way in which it enters into complex statements."[40] In the terminology that Dummett was later to adopt, such distinctions lie at the level of a statement's ingredient sense, rather than its assertoric content.

But is the derivation of *tertium non datur* from Thesis α sound? In addressing this question, it will help to make Dummett's argument formally explicit. Let us introduce, then, the notation '$S\xi$' to mean 'ξ is a statement', '$A\xi$' to mean 'ξ is a possible or actual state of affairs', '$O\xi$' to mean 'ξ is a state of affairs which actually obtains', '$R\xi\eta$' to mean 'In the event that the state of affairs ξ obtains, any assertive instance of the statement η would be recognizably falsified, or refuted, and would have to be withdrawn', '$C\xi\eta$' to mean 'The obtaining of the state of affairs ξ is not excluded by an assertive instance of the statement η' or (for brevity) 'The state of affairs ξ is consistent with the statement η', '$T\xi$' to mean 'ξ is true', and '$F\xi$' to mean 'ξ is false'. In this notation, the aim of the argument is to establish *tertium non datur* in the form

$$\neg\, \exists x\, (Sx \wedge \neg\, (Tx \vee Fx))$$

('No statement is neither true nor false'). The method is to reduce to absurdity the contrary supposition that there is such a statement.

Dummett's argument has three substantial premises. The first says that, for any statement, the class of all possible states of affairs divides into those which would recognizably falsify an assertive instance of it and those with which the statement is consistent:

α) $\forall x\,[Sx \rightarrow \forall y\,(Ay \rightarrow (Ryx \lor Cyx))]$.

As my tag for it suggests, this premise derives directly from Thesis α. As we have defined things, each statement has a determinate content: in Dummett's phrase, it will not be "ambiguous or vague." By Thesis α, then, each possible state of affairs will either directly falsify the statement—that is, be such that "a man who asserted [the statement] but envisaged that state of affairs as a possibility would be held to have spoken misleadingly"—or will not directly falsify it, in which case "the assertion of the statement would not be taken as expressing the speaker's exclusion of that possibility." The second premise says that if a state of affairs obtains which would recognizably falsify an assertive instance of a statement, then that statement is false:

β) $\forall x\,[Sx \rightarrow (\exists y\,(Oy \land Ryx) \rightarrow Fx)]$.

The third premise says that if all actual states of affairs are consistent with a statement, it is true:

γ) $\forall x\,[Sx \rightarrow (\forall y\,(Oy \rightarrow Cyx) \rightarrow Tx)]$.

Finally, we need a premise recording the fact that things which obtain are possible or actual states of affairs:

δ) $\forall x\,(Ox \rightarrow Ax)$.

The argument then runs as follows:

1. $\exists x\,(Sx \land \neg\,(Tx \lor Fx))$	Assumption, for reductio
2. $Sa \land \neg\,(Ta \lor Fa)$	1, existential instantiation
3. Sa	2, ∧-elimination
4. $\neg\,(Ta \lor Fa)$	2, ∧-elimination
5. $\neg\,Ta \land \neg\,Fa$	4, by the rule 'From $\neg(A \lor B)$ infer $\neg A \land \neg B$'
6. $\neg\,Ta$	5, ∧-elimination
7. $\varnothing\,Fa$	5, ∧-elimination
8. $Sa \rightarrow \forall y\,(Ay \rightarrow (Rya \lor Cya))$	α, universal instantiation
9. $\forall y\,(Ay \rightarrow (Rya \lor Cya))$	3, 8, →-elimination
10. $Sa \rightarrow (\exists y\,(Oy \land Rya) \rightarrow Fa)$	β, universal instantiation
11. $\exists y\,(Oy \land Rya) \rightarrow Fa$	3, 10, →-elimination

12. $\neg\, \exists y\, (Oy \wedge Rya)$	7, 11, contraposition
13. $\forall y \neg (Oy \wedge Rya)$	12, using the rule 'From $\neg\, \exists y\, \varphi y$ infer $\forall y \neg \varphi y$'
14. $\neg\, (Ob \wedge Rba)$	13, universal instantiation with 'b' parametric
15. $Ob \rightarrow \neg Rba$	14, using the rule 'From $\neg\, (A \wedge B)$, infer $A \rightarrow \neg B$'
16. Ob	Assumption
17. $\neg Rba$	15, 16, $\rightarrow$-elimination
18. $Ob \rightarrow Ab$	δ, universal instantiation
19. Ab	16, 18, $\rightarrow$-elimination
20. $Ab \rightarrow (Rba \vee Cba)$	9, universal instantiation
21. $Rba \vee Cba$	19, 20, $\rightarrow$-elimination
22. Cba	17, 21, using the rule 'From $A \vee B$ and $\neg A$, infer B'
23. $Ob \rightarrow Cba$	16, 22, $\rightarrow$-introduction, discharging assumption 16
24. $\forall y\, (Oy \rightarrow Cya)$	23, universal generalization, since 'b' was parametric
25. $Sa \rightarrow (\forall y\, (Oy \rightarrow Cya) \rightarrow Ta)$	γ, universal instantiation
26. $\forall y\, (Oy \rightarrow Cya) \rightarrow Ta$	3, 25, $\rightarrow$-elimination
27. Ta	24, 26, $\rightarrow$-elimination
28. $\neg\, \exists x\, (Sx \wedge \neg (Tx \vee Fx))$	6, 27, reductio ad absurdum, discharging assumption 1

As we should expect of a reconstruction of Dummett's argument, the reasoning just given constitutes an intuitionistically correct proof of the conclusion $\neg\, \exists x\, (Sx \wedge \neg (Tx \vee Fx))$ from the premises α to δ. The De Morgan law used at step 5 is acceptable to an intuitionist, as are the type of contraposition used at step 12 and the conversion principle used at step 13. So is the form of *modus tollendo ponens* used at step 22: this rule may be derived from $\vee$-elimination together with *ex contradictione quodlibet*. As for the principle used at step 15, perhaps the easiest way to see its intuitionistic acceptability is to apply the familiar equivalence between $\neg A$ and $A \rightarrow \bot$. By $\wedge$-introduction, we have $A, B \vdash A \wedge B$, so that $A, B, (A \wedge B) \rightarrow \bot \vdash \bot$, by $\rightarrow$-elimination. One application of $\rightarrow$-introduction then yields $A, (A \wedge B) \rightarrow \bot \vdash B \rightarrow \bot$, and another yields

$$(A \wedge B) \rightarrow \bot \vdash A \rightarrow (B \rightarrow \bot),$$

which by the equivalence is $\neg\, (A \wedge B) \vdash A \rightarrow \neg B$, as required.

Dummett's argument is, then, intuitionistically valid and *a fortiori* classically valid. But are its premises correct? I have given my reasons for accepting premise α; and premise δ, being no more than an analytic triviality, is unassailable. Moreover, it is hard to conceive how premise β could be seriously contested. If a state of affairs obtains which would force an asserter to concede that he had misled his hearers as to the facts, then the statement of which his assertion is an instance must be false. Premise γ, however, is not similarly compelling. According to it, a sufficient condition for a statement to be true is that all actual states of affairs are consistent with it. That is to say, the absence of any recognizable state of affairs which would directly falsify a statement suffices for that statement's truth. It is very far from obvious that this is correct. Consider, for example, the statement made when somebody says "One day, a city *will* be built here," while leaving the time within which his prediction is to come true completely unbounded. There is no recognizable state of affairs which would directly falsify this statement. But it seems odd to claim on that basis that the statement is true.

How, though, does Dummett argue for premise γ? "Any situation," he writes in "Truth," "in which nothing obtains which is taken as a case of [a statement's] being false may be regarded as a case of its being true, just as someone who behaves so as not to disobey a command may be regarded as having obeyed it."[41] There is, perhaps, a whiff of stipulation here: one would like to know what someone would be losing if he chose not to regard the absence of a recognizable falsifier as sufficient for truth. But in any case, the argument seems to trade upon an ambiguity in the phrase "so as not to disobey." "X behaves so as not to disobey command C" could mean either (a) "The behavior of X does not, as a matter of fact, include any action that would constitute disobeying C" or (b) "X comports himself, successfully, with an eye to not disobeying C." When "X behaves so as not to disobey command C" is taken in sense (b), it is plausible to maintain that the formula entails "X obeys C." When taken in sense (a), however, the formula does not entail "X obeys C." For in this sense, the formula may be true of X even though he has never heard of the command C. Dummett's argument, however, needs the truth of the formula taken in sense (a) to suffice for X's obeying C. He needs, that is, the mere nonoccurrence of any disobedient action to suffice for obedience. For only then shall we have the desired analogy with the way the mere nonobtaining of any recognizable falsifier is supposed to suffice for truth.

Far more importantly for our purposes, though, premise γ does not cohere with what Dummett says about truth later in his article. Our aim is to evaluate the argument in "Truth" for deeming classical logic not to be universally applicable. The nerve of the argument is that, while we know *tertium non datur*, we do not know the principle of bivalence. This combination of knowledge and ignorance is impossible if following a classical deduction from known premises always issues in knowledge of the conclusion, for we have a simple classical deduction of bivalence from *tertium non datur*. Now the mainstay of Dummett's argument that we do not know bivalence is a necessary condition for truth that I shall label principle ε: "a statement cannot be true unless it is in principle capable of being known to be true."[42] More briefly, a statement is true only if we can recognize it as true. If a statement's falsity is understood as the truth of its negation, this will entail a cognate principle for falsehood: a statement is false only if we can recognize it as false. The argument may then be spelled out as follows:

Let A be the statement 'A city will never be built here,' uttered at a place where (i) no city has been built by the time of utterance and there are no plans to build one, but which (ii) is indistinguishable from the locations of actually thriving cities in respect of climate, water provision, communications, and all other respects which best geographical theory suggests are relevant to the viability of a city. Suppose, for reductio, that we do know the principle of bivalence, that is, know that every statement is either true or false. Then, in particular, we know that statement A is either true or false. Now by principle ε, statement A is true only if we can recognize it as true. By the same principle, statement A is false only if we can recognize it as false. Furthermore, we know both these conditionals. Hence, we know that either we can recognize statement A as true or we can recognize statement A as false. Given (ii), however, we cannot exclude the possibility that we shall never be in a position to recognize A as true. While future geographic theory may identify a respect in which the place of utterance is inimical to the viability of a city, we cannot know that it will. So, for all we know, it may be that we cannot recognize A as true. Given (i), however, we also cannot exclude the possibility that we shall never be in a position to recognize A as false: for all we know, it may be that we cannot recognize A as false. For all we know, then, it may be that we can neither recognize statement A as true nor recognize it as false. So we do not after all know that either we can recognize statement A as true or we can recognize statement A as false. This contradiction reduces to absurdity the initial supposition that we know the principle of bivalence. We may conclude, then, that we do not know that principle.[43]

Dummett's argument for our ignorance of bivalence, then, rests on principle ε together with the assumption that there is a possible context of utterance satisfying conditions (i) and (ii). Just these premises, however, fail to cohere with premise γ of our argument for *tertium non datur*. As we have already had occasion to note, a state of affairs which falsifies an utterance of 'A city will never be built here' must be one in which a city has been successfully constructed in the place in question. Accordingly, since the context of statement A satisfies condition (i), "nothing obtains [in that context] which is taken as a case of [A's] being false." By premise γ, then, statement A is true. By the necessary condition for truth which is Dummett's postulate ε, however, the truth of A entails that A is in principle capable of being known to be true. And this entailment contradicts the supposition that the context of A satisfies condition (ii). For nobody can know that a city will never be built in a given spot unless he has identified a feature of the place in which it relevantly differs from the locations of thriving cities. The trio of propositions comprising premise γ, principle ε, and the supposition that a possible context of utterance meets conditions (i) and (ii) is, then, inconsistent; so at least one of them must be rejected. We must, in other words, reject either a premise crucial to Dummett's argument for *tertium non datur* (viz., γ), or one of the premises of his argument for our ignorance of bivalence (viz., ε and the supposition about contexts). The present argument against classical logic, however, was that we know *tertium non datur* while being ignorant about bivalence. So that argument fails.

IV. Semantics without Truth

The failure of Dummett's argument in "Truth" leaves us with no reason to suppose that Thesis α cannot cohere with classical logic. More problematically, it also leaves us without the sort of explication of truth which Dummett hoped to find—one, namely, which directly connects the truth of a statement with notions that are more immediately applicable in assessing particular speech actions. Important, however, as finding such an explication may be to the construction of a fully viable anti-realism, it is, for present purposes, a side issue. We did not set out to explicate the concept of truth. Rather, we wanted to investigate whether there is an anti-realist account of consequence which validates the laws of classical propositional logic, and such an enterprise need tangle with the explication of truth only if the notion of truth is implicated in the notion of consequence. It is commonly assumed, of course, that it is so implicated: consequence is often explained as the necessary preservation of truth. In the following two sections, however, I shall develop a semantical theory which reflects what I take to be the insight in Dummett's Thesis α, and which leads to explications of notions of entailment and of consequence, but which eschews altogether the concept of truth.

In a footnote to "What is a Theory of Meaning? (II)," Dummett himself essays a semantical theory of this kind:

Let us write f_A for the set of recognizable states of affairs in which A is falsified, and $f^\perp$ for the set of recognizable states of affairs which preclude the occurrence of any state of affairs in f. Plainly, $f \cap f^\perp = \varnothing$, $f \subseteq f^{\perp\perp}$ and, if $f \subseteq g$, then $g^\perp \subseteq f^\perp$; hence $f^\perp = f^{\perp\perp\perp}$. We may also assume that $(f \cup g)^\perp = f^\perp \cap g^\perp$ and that $f^\perp \cup g^\perp \subseteq (f \cap g)^\perp$. It seems reasonable to take $f_{\neg A} = f_A{}^\perp$, $f_{A \vee B} = f_A \cap f_B$, $f_{A \wedge B} = f_A \cup f_B$ and $f_{A \to B} = f_B \cap f_A{}^\perp$, and to define $A_1, \ldots, A_n \vdash B$ as holding when $f_B \subseteq f_{A_1} \cup \ldots \cup f_{A_n}$, so that $\vdash B$ holds just in case $f_B = \varnothing$; on this definition, however, $\vdash A \to B$ may hold when $A \vdash B$ does not. On this basis, we have $\neg\neg A \vdash A$ and $\vdash A \to \neg\neg A$, but not $A \vdash \neg\neg A$. We also have $\vdash A \vee \neg A$, $\vdash \neg(A \wedge \neg A)$, $\neg(A \wedge B) \dashv \vdash \neg A \vee \neg B$ and $\neg(A \vee B) \vdash \neg A \wedge \neg B$, but not $\neg A \wedge \neg B \vdash \neg(A \vee B)$. However, I do not feel at all sure that this approach is correct.[44]

The doubt that Dummett expresses in the last quoted sentence is understandable: it is hard to attach intuitive senses to the sentential connectives which would validate precisely these entailments. But I wish to show that, when the semantical theory he adumbrates here is developed so as to conform fully with Thesis α, it yields a more familiar logic.

At the core of the proposed semantics is a relation—that of falsifying —which obtains between a "recognizable state of affairs" and a statement. Earlier, I suggested that we should understand a recognizable state of affairs to be a state of information, and that we should gloss "falsifies" as meaning "directly falsifies": a state of information directly falsifies a statement when any thinker in the state who understands the statement will know directly— in other words, without needing to make inferences, or to invoke ancillary information—that it is false. On the semantic theory being considered, then, the meaning of an atomic statement will be given by specifying which recognizable states of affairs (i.e., which states of information) directly falsify it.

In saying which states of affairs falsify negated and conditional statements, Dummett invokes the notion of a set, labeled $f^\perp$, which comprises all and only those recognizable states of affairs which preclude the occurrence of any state belonging in the set f. How, though, should we understand "preclude" here? Since the semantics is supposed to encapsulate the idea that "an assertion is to be judged correct whenever something happens which precludes the occurrence of a state of affairs showing it to be incorrect," and since, for Dummett, the notion of correctness is an epistemic one, we should try to explain preclusion in epistemic terms. In doing so, however, we need to take care. It might be suggested that the state of information s will belong to $f^\perp$ if and only if any thinker who is in state s knows that no state of information in f will occur, but this condition for membership in $f^\perp$ is not well defined. It may be true that any thinker in state s knows that no state of information will obtain whose subject knows that

Anna will be on time for dinner. Yet it may at the same time be false that any thinker in state s knows that no state of information will obtain which meets the condition specified on the piece of paper hidden in Bernard's breast pocket. For all that, the condition on a state of information there specified may be precisely that its subject should know that Anna will be on time for dinner. This example brings out how, in the suggested condition for s to belong to $f^\perp$, the letter 'f' falls within the scope of the intensional verb "knows," so that the way in which the set $f^\perp$ is described (or is otherwise identified) affects whether the condition is met. But in that case, and contrary to Dummett's manifest intentions, the membership of the set $f^\perp$ will not be determined simply by the membership of the set f.

The sets in question here are sets of propositions, and we can see our way round the problem if we remark that certain expressions that designate propositions have a special, or canonical, status. A proposition is, essentially, something expressed by certain statements all of which "say the same"; so if A is one of these statements, the corresponding clause "that A" may be taken to designate canonically the proposition in question. We may then say that a state of information *leaves open* this proposition if a thinker in the state is not in a position to know that not A. Equivalently: if, for all such a thinker knows, A. (It is assumed that the notion of "saying the same" is explicated so that whether a state of information leaves a proposition open does not depend on the particular choice of clause to serve as the proposition's canonical designator.) We may then define a relation $\leq$ between states of information so that $s \leq t$ if and only if (i) $s \subseteq t$; (ii) if s is a subject's state of knowledge at one time, then t may be his state of knowledge at some future time; and (iii) s leaves open every proposition in $t \setminus s$ (i.e., every proposition which belongs to t but not to s). When $s \leq t$ we shall say that the state of information t is an epistemically possible expansion of the state of information s. We may then define $f^\perp$ by the principle

$$s \in f^\perp \leftrightarrow \neg \exists t\, (s \leq t \wedge t \in f).$$

Given the definition of the $\leq$-relation, we shall have that $\exists t\, (s \leq t \wedge t \in f)$ precisely when a state of information belonging to f is an epistemically possible expansion of the state of information s. Accordingly, the set $f^\perp$ is defined as comprising precisely those states of information which have no epistemically possible expansions that belong to f. This is surely one way of explicating Dummett's definition of $f^\perp$ as "the set of recognizable states of affairs which preclude the occurrence of any state of affairs in f." Since we are assuming that classical logic regulates inferences in the metalanguage, the principle that defines $f^\perp$ is equivalent to

$$s \in f^\perp \leftrightarrow \forall t\, (s \leq t \rightarrow t \notin f).$$

I shall call $f^\perp$ the *exterior* of set f.

Readers of Dummett will recognize the $\leq$-relation. In developing his semantics for intuitionistic logic, he gives a central role to the relation that obtains between two states of information when the first state "may subsequently be improved upon by achieving the" second.[45] This is just an alternative description of the $\leq$-relation.[46] The character of the relation between a set of states of information and its exterior depends crucially upon the logical properties of the $\leq$-relation. But what are those properties? In developing the semantics of intuitionistic logic, Dummett assumes that there is never a "guarantee that we shall ever advance to a state" of information which is strictly larger than the one we are in.[47] I shall also make this plausible assumption, so that, for any state of information s, s itself may—for all that anybody in that state knows—constitute his (propositional) knowledge at some future time. Since, for any state s, we also have that $s \subseteq s$, and since $s \setminus s$ is empty, it follows directly from its definition that the $\leq$-relation is reflexive: $\forall s\; s \leq s$. Moreover, since $s \leq t$ only if $s \subseteq t$, and ($s \subseteq t$ and $t \subseteq s$) only if $s = t$, the $\leq$-relation is anti-symmetric: $\forall s\, \forall t\, (s \leq t \wedge t \leq s \to s = t)$. The $\leq$-relation is also transitive. If state s may be improved upon by attaining state t, and state t may be improved upon by attaining u, then state s may be improved upon by attaining state u.[48] Given any set of states of information, then, $\leq$ will be a reflexive, anti- symmetric, and transitive relation on that set. That is to say, it will be a *partial order* on that set.

The $\leq$-relation, and its field, constitute a simple model of the way in which a thinker's knowledge might grow: since $\leq$ was defined so that $s \leq t$ only if $s \subseteq t$, when $s \leq t$ a thinker in state t knows everything that is known by a thinker in state s. Since every individual forgets things, and since even the collective knowledge of a group or society undergoes loss, this is a highly idealized model of the way people's knowledge actually changes. Moreover, this kind of idealization is not that found (for example) in accounts of the motion of bodies on frictionless planes. In such accounts, the idealization exposes more clearly than would otherwise be possible how basic scientific laws, such as the laws of gravity, apply to the system. But there is no basic scientific law guaranteeing the retention of knowledge, whose operation is somehow compromised by various more-or-less incidental frictional effects. On the contrary, the knowledge available in a system may be assumed to vary inversely with its entropy, so that the relevant basic law—namely, the Second Law of Thermodynamics—posits an ineluctable loss of knowledge with time. For present purposes, however, this deviation from the laws of physics does not matter. The challenge we are addressing is to find some account of the classical consequence relation that is *intelligible* to the anti-realist, it being assumed for the sake of argument that the notion of verification-transcendent truth is not intelligible. The model of how a subject's knowledge might grow without loss is surely intelligible, even if a law of nature precludes its ever being exemplified. Certainly, a revisionary anti-realist—or, at least, a revisionist of Dummett's ilk, who excises from classical logic those laws that are not also acceptable to an intuitionist—is in no position to deem this model unintelligible. For he uses it to explain the meanings he wishes to attach to the logical connectives, and to explicate the notion of consequence to which his preferred logical laws are supposed to be faithful. He cannot complain, then, if we use the same conceptual resources in explicating a notion of consequence to which the laws of classical logic are faithful.[49]

Let us now return to the special case where the set f comprises those states of information which would directly falsify a statement A; in Dummett's notation, this will be a case where $f=f_A$. Our definition entails that set $f_A{}^\perp$ will comprise precisely those states of information which may not be expanded to form a state of information which would directly falsify A. We may say that a state of information which may not be so expanded is one in which statement A is *safely assertible*. In these terms, the set $f_A{}^\perp$ will comprise precisely those states of information in which the statement A is safely assertible. For this reason, I shall sometimes use the notation 'ass (A)' as an alternative to '$f_A{}^\perp$'. This involves no departure from our basic idea that it is the circumstances which directly falsify a statement that determine its content; for each set ass (A) is defined in terms of the states of information which falsify A.

Let us further assume that if a statement is directly falsified in any state of information, then that falsification is *indefeasible* in that the statement will remain directly falsified under any possible expansion of the state of information. Given the partial ordering $\leq$ on the states of information, we may formulate this assumption as the axiom that, for any statement A, the set f_A of states of information which directly falsify A will meet the following condition:

$$\forall s \, \forall t \, (s \in f_A \wedge s \leq t \to t \in f_A).$$

This assumption has important consequences for the formal development of the semantics. Let us say that a set X of states of information is *open* (with respect to the relation $\leq$) if and only if

$$\forall s \, \forall t \, (s \in X \wedge s \leq t \to t \in X).$$

In these terms, the assumption of indefeasibility is the assumption that the set f_A will be open for any statement A. This shows how to construct a semantic theory based upon the notion of a state of information's directly falsifying a statement. The core of such a theory will systematically associate with each statement A that could be made in the language in question an open set f_A comprising all and only those states of information which directly falsify A. The association will be systematic in the sense of being recursively determined by the construction of the statement from its parts.

As the choice of terminology will already have suggested, the significance of the definition of openness is that, given any set T which comprises the totality of states of information that are "possible" in a given context, the class $\mathfrak{I}$ of subsets of T that are open (with respect to a given partial ordering $\leq$) constitutes a topology on T. Clearly $\varnothing \in \mathfrak{I}$ and $T \in \mathfrak{I}$; and arbitrary unions of open sets are open. That is to say, if each of the sets in a family $\{S_i\}$ is open then so will be their union $\bigcup_i S_i$. For suppose that $s \in \bigcup_i S_i$ and that $s \leq t$. By the first supposition, there is some open set S_j such that $s \in S_j$; and since S_j is open and $s \leq t$, it follows that $t \in S_j$ so that $t \in \bigcup_i S_i$. Finally, finite intersections of open sets are open; in fact, arbitrary intersections of open sets are open. For suppose that each of the sets S_i is open, that $s \leq t$ and that $s \in \bigcap_i S_i$. Since $s \in \bigcap_i S_i$, we have that $s \in S_j$ for all j; and since each S_j is open and $s \leq t$, $t \in S_j$ for all j so that $t \in \bigcap_i S_i$, as required.

As is usual in topology, we define the *interior* Int (S) of a set $S \subseteq T$ to be the union of all the open subsets of S. Int (S) is always open, and in the present case it is easy to verify that

Int $(S) = \{s : \forall t (s \leq t \rightarrow t \in S)\}$.

Thus, where $T \setminus S$ is the complement of a set S in the background total set T, we have that

$f^\perp = \text{Int} (T \setminus f)$.

We also may define a *closed* set (in $\mathfrak{I}$) to be one whose complement is open, and define the *closure* Cl(S) of a set $S \subseteq T$ to be the intersection of all the closed sets that contain S. Since

$x \notin \text{Cl}(S)$ iff $\exists Y (S \subseteq Y \land Y$ is closed $\land x \notin Y)$,

we have (assuming classical logic in the metalanguage) that

$x \notin \text{Cl}(S)$ iff $\exists Y (T \setminus Y \subseteq T \setminus S \land T \setminus Y$ is open $\land x \in T \setminus Y)$,

whence

$x \notin \text{Cl}(S)$ iff $\exists Z (Z \subseteq T \setminus S \land Z$ is open $\land x \in Z)$,

so that $T \setminus \text{Cl}(S) = \text{Int} (T \setminus S)$ and hence Cl$(S) = T \setminus \text{Int} (T \setminus S)$. On the same assumption, it may further be verified that

Cl$(S) = \{s : \exists t (s \leq t \land t \in S)\}$.

Since in any topological space, Int $(T \setminus f) = T \setminus \text{Cl}(f)$, we have $f^\perp = T \setminus \text{Cl}(f)$: a set's exterior is the complement of its closure.[50] It is also noteworthy that

$f^{\perp\perp} = \text{Int} (T \setminus f^{\perp}) = \text{Int} (T \setminus \text{Int} (T \setminus f)) = \text{Int} (\text{Cl}(f))$: a set's double exterior is the interior of its closure.

The definition of $f^{\perp}$ as $\text{Int} (T \setminus f)$ enables us to prove the inclusions and identities which Dummett enumerates as axioms in the footnote quoted from "What is a Theory of Meaning? (II)." Since $f^{\perp} = \text{Int} (T \setminus f)$, we certainly have that $f \cap f^{\perp} = \varnothing$. Since $f \subseteq \text{Cl}(f)$, and since f is open, $f \subseteq \text{Int} (\text{Cl}(f))$, i.e., $f \subseteq f^{\perp\perp}$. If $f \subseteq g$, then $T \setminus g \subseteq T \setminus f$, so that

$\quad \text{Int} (T \setminus g) \subseteq \text{Int} (T \setminus f)$, i.e., $g^{\perp} \subseteq f^{\perp}$.

Again,

$\quad (f \cup g)^{\perp} = \text{Int} (T \setminus (f \cup g)) = \text{Int} ((T \setminus f) \cap (T \setminus g))$
$\quad\quad = \text{Int} (T \setminus f) \cap \text{Int} (T \setminus g) = f^{\perp} \cap g^{\perp}.$

(In any topological space, $\text{Int} (A \cap B) = \text{Int} (A) \cap \text{Int} (B)$.) Finally, since $T \setminus f \subseteq T \setminus (f \cap g)$, $\text{Int} (T \setminus f) \subseteq \text{Int} (T \setminus (f \cap g))$, i.e., $f^{\perp} \subseteq (f \cap g)^{\perp}$. By parallel reasoning, $g^{\perp} \subseteq (f \cap g)^{\perp}$, showing that $f^{\perp} \cup g^{\perp} \subseteq (f \cap g)^{\perp}$.

Dummett's identity for $(f \cup g)^{\perp}$ and his lower bound for $(f \cap g)^{\perp}$ extend by induction to yield an identity for the exterior of any finite union of sets and a lower bound for the exterior of any finite intersection of sets. Our analysis, however, yields in addition the expected generalizations of his results to the infinite case. We have, in other words, the following two lemmas:

LEMMA 1. $(\bigcup_i f_i)^{\perp} = \bigcap_i f_i^{\perp}$.

PROOF. By definition, $(\bigcup_i f_i)^{\perp} = \text{Int} (T \setminus \bigcup_i f_i) = \text{Int} (\bigcap_i (T \setminus f_i))$, given classical logic in the metalanguage. Now

$\quad s \in \text{Int} (\bigcap_i (T \setminus f_i))$ iff $\forall t \, (s \leq t \rightarrow t \in \bigcap_i (T \setminus f_i))$
$\quad\quad\quad\quad\quad\quad\quad\quad\quad$ iff $\forall t \, (s \leq t \rightarrow \forall i \, (t \in (T \setminus f_i)))$
$\quad\quad\quad\quad\quad\quad\quad\quad\quad$ iff $\forall i \, \forall t \, (s \leq t \rightarrow t \in (T \setminus f_i)),$

since '$s \leq t$' is free for the variable 'i'. However,

$\quad \forall i \, \forall t \, (s \leq t \rightarrow t \in (T \setminus f_i))$ iff $s \in \bigcap_i \text{Int} (T \setminus f_i)) = \bigcap_i f_i^{\perp}.$

Thus $(\bigcup_i f_i)^{\perp} = \bigcap_i f_i^{\perp}$, as required. □

LEMMA 2: $\bigcup_i f_i^{\perp} \subseteq (\bigcap_i f_i)^{\perp}$.

PROOF. Suppose, for a contradiction, that (a) $s \in \bigcup_i f_i^{\perp}$ while (b) $s \notin (\bigcap_i f_i)^{\perp}$. By (a) there is a j such that $s \in f_j^{\perp}$, i.e., such that $s \in \text{Int} (T \setminus f_j)$. Let us call such a j 'k'. Then $\forall t \, (s \leq t \rightarrow t \notin f_k))$. By (b), however, we have

$\quad s \notin \text{Int} (T \setminus \bigcap_i f_i)$, whence $\neg \forall t \, (s \leq t \rightarrow t \in (T \setminus \bigcap_i f_i)),$

whence $\exists t \, (s \leq t \wedge t \notin (T \setminus \bigcap_i f_i))$, i.e., $\exists t \, (s \leq t \wedge t \in \bigcap_i f_i).$

Let us call such a t 'u'. Then $s \leq u$ and $u \in \bigcap_i f_i$, so in particular $u \in f_k$. Since, though, $\forall t \, (s \leq t \rightarrow t \notin f_k)$, we have $s \leq u \rightarrow u \notin f_k$ and hence $u \notin f_k$.

This contradiction shows that whenever $s \in \bigcup_i f_i^\perp$ then $s \in (\bigcap_i f_i)^\perp$, i.e., that $\bigcup_i f_i^\perp \subseteq (\bigcap_i f_i)^\perp$, as required. $\square$

These two lemmas combine to yield

LEMMA 3. $(\bigcap_i f_i)^{\perp\perp} \subseteq \bigcap_i f_i^{\perp\perp}$.

PROOF. By (2), $\bigcup_i f_i^\perp \subseteq (\bigcap_i f_i)^\perp$ and since $f \subseteq g$ only if $g^\perp \subseteq f^\perp$, this gives $(\bigcap_i f_i)^{\perp\perp} \subseteq (\bigcup_i f_i^\perp)^\perp$. By lemma (1), however, $(\bigcup_i f_i^\perp)^\perp = \bigcap_i f_i^{\perp\perp}$, whence the desired result. $\square$

What of the converse inclusion? In this regard, two further lemmas will be useful:

LEMMA 4.   If f and g are any open sets, then $(f \cap g)^{\perp\perp} = f^{\perp\perp} \cap g^{\perp\perp}$.

PROOF. The inclusion $(f \cap g)^{\perp\perp} \subseteq f^{\perp\perp} \cap g^{\perp\perp}$ is immediate from lemma (3). Or, more directly, note that $f^\perp \cup g^\perp \subseteq (f \cap g)^\perp$ so that

$$(f \cap g)^{\perp\perp} \subseteq (f^\perp \cup g^\perp)^\perp = f^{\perp\perp} \cap g^{\perp\perp}.$$

For the reverse inclusion, recall that a set U is said to be a *neighborhood* of a point x in a topological space T iff it is an open set containing x, and that a point x belongs to the closure of a set Y in T iff every neighborhood of x meets Y (that is, has an nonempty intersection with Y). Now take any two open sets f and g and consider the set $f \cap \text{Cl}(g)$. If x is any point in $f \cap \text{Cl}(g)$, and U is any neighborhood of x, then $U \cap f$ is also a neighborhood of x, and this implies that $U \cap f$ meets g, or equivalently, that U meets $f \cap g$. That is to say, any neighborhood of any point in $f \cap \text{Cl}(g)$ meets $f \cap g$, so that

$$f \cap \text{Cl}(g) \subseteq \text{Cl}(f \cap g).$$

Taking complements then gives

$$(f \cap g)^\perp \subseteq (T \setminus f) \cup g^\perp,$$

whence

$$\text{Cl}(f \cap g)^\perp \subseteq \text{Cl}[(T \setminus f) \cup g^\perp] = \text{Cl}(T \setminus f) \cup \text{Cl}(g^\perp) = (T \setminus f) \cup \text{Cl}(g^\perp)$$

since $(T \setminus f)$ is closed. Taking complements again gives:

$$f \cap (T \setminus \text{Cl}(g^\perp)) \subseteq T \setminus \text{Cl}(f \cap g)^\perp$$

that is,

$$(*) \; f \cap g^{\perp\perp} \subseteq (f \cap g)^{\perp\perp}.$$

Now the set $f^{\perp\perp}$ is always open, so an application of (*) is

$$f^{\perp\perp} \cap g^{\perp\perp} \subseteq (f^{\perp\perp} \cap g)^{\perp\perp}.$$

Another application of (*) reverses the roles of f and g, giving

$$(f^{\perp\perp} \cap g) \subseteq (f \cap g)^{\perp\perp},$$

whence

$$(f^{\perp\perp} \cap g)^{\perp\perp} \subseteq (f \cap g)^{\perp\perp\perp\perp}.$$

Combining these inclusions gives, then,

$$f^{\perp\perp} \cap g^{\perp\perp} \subseteq (f \cap g)^{\perp\perp\perp\perp}$$

and hence

$$f^{\perp\perp} \cap g^{\perp\perp} \subseteq (f \cap g)^{\perp\perp},$$

as required. This completes the proof of lemma 4.   □

A corollary is

LEMMA 5.   If f and g are open sets, then $(f \cap g)^{\perp} = (f^{\perp} \cup g^{\perp})^{\perp\perp}$.

PROOF. Suppose that f and g are open sets. Then so is their intersection so that $(f \cap g)^{\perp} = (f \cap g)^{\perp\perp\perp}$. Now by lemma 4, $(f \cap g)^{\perp\perp\perp} = (f^{\perp\perp} \cap g^{\perp\perp})^{\perp}$. Since, however, $(f \cup g)^{\perp} = f^{\perp} \cap g^{\perp}$, we have $f^{\perp\perp} \cap g^{\perp\perp} = (f^{\perp} \cup g^{\perp})^{\perp}$, so that $(f^{\perp\perp} \cap g^{\perp\perp})^{\perp} = (f^{\perp} \cup g^{\perp})^{\perp\perp}$, giving $(f \cap g)^{\perp} = (f^{\perp} \cup g^{\perp})^{\perp\perp}$, as required.   □

Lemma 4 entails that the operation of forming a set's double exterior distributes over finite intersection whenever the sets involved are all open. Let us say that a set f is *regular open* if $f = f^{\perp\perp}$.[51] Then we have the following infinitary analogue of lemma 4:

LEMMA 6.   If all the sets f_i in some possibly infinite collection are regular open, then $(\bigcap_i f_i)^{\perp\perp} = \bigcap_i f_i$.

PROOF. By lemma 3, $(\bigcap_i f_i)^{\perp\perp} \subseteq \bigcap_i f_i^{\perp\perp}$. But if all the sets f_i are regular open, then for all i, $f_i^{\perp\perp} = f_i$. Thus, given the hypothesis, we have $(\bigcap_i f_i)^{\perp\perp} \subseteq \bigcap_i f_i$.

For the converse inclusion, we know that whenever f is open $f \subseteq f^{\perp\perp}$, so it suffices to prove that the intersection of an arbitrary collection of regular open sets is itself open. But we noted above that the intersection of an arbitrary collection of open sets was open, so we certainly have $\bigcap_i f_i \subseteq (\bigcap_i f_i)^{\perp\perp}$.   □

V. ENTAILMENT AND LOGICAL CONSEQUENCE

How should the notions of entailment and of logical consequence be explained within this semantic theory?

In the passage quoted from "What is a Theory of Meaning? (II)," Dummett suggests "defining $A_1, \ldots, A_n \vdash B$ as holding when $f_B \subseteq f_{A_1} \cup \ldots \cup f_{A_n}$, so that $\vdash B$ holds just in case $f_B = \varnothing$." I think, however, that this definition betrays the original insight into the nature of assertion that underpins the present semantics. The condition $f_B \subseteq f_{A_1} \cup \ldots \cup f_{A_n}$ obtains if and only if a state of information s directly falsifies one or other of the statements $A_1, \ldots, A_n$

whenever it directly falsifies the statement B. The suggestion, then, is that some premises entail a conclusion if and only if, whenever the conclusion is falsified, one of the premises should *then* be falsified as well. As we saw, however, Dummett's account of asserting rests on the insight that, in making an assertion, a speaker incurs an *open-ended* liability to criticism for having misled those people who have taken his word. As the example of "A city will never be built here" showed, the people who take an asserter's word are in no way confined to his immediate audience, so that an assertion may be criticized for having got things wrong indefinitely long after it has been made. For this reason, the crucial requirement for an entailment is not that, whenever the conclusion is falsified, one or other of the premises should *then* be falsified. Rather, the condition for some premises to entail a conclusion should be that a speaker who asserts the conclusion incurs no additional exposure or liability to future criticism or remonstration that he has not already incurred by asserting the premises. Now a speaker is exposed to criticism, or liable to be criticized, for an assertion of a statement A if and only if he may, for all he knows, find himself in a state of information which would directly falsify A. That is to say, in a state of information s, he is exposed to criticism, or liable to be criticized, for asserting a statement A if and only if $\exists t \, (s \leq t \wedge t \in f_A)$. This in turn means that the state of information s leaves one exposed to such criticism if and only $s \in \mathrm{Cl}(f_A)$. Accordingly, the inference '$A_1, \ldots, A_n$; so B' will meet the condition of not increasing one's exposure to criticism if and only if

$$\mathrm{Cl}(f_B) \subseteq \mathrm{Cl}(f_{A_1}) \cup \ldots \cup \mathrm{Cl}(f_{A_n}).$$

This, I propose, is the correct criterion for $A_1, \ldots, A_n$ to entail B.

Assuming classical logic in the metalanguage, this criterion for entailment is equivalent to the complementary condition

$$(T \setminus \mathrm{Cl}(f_{A_1})) \cap \ldots \cap (T \setminus \mathrm{Cl}(f_{A_n})) \subseteq T \setminus \mathrm{Cl}(f_B);$$

and since $T \setminus \mathrm{Cl}(X) = \mathrm{Int}\,(T \setminus X)$, this in turn is equivalent to

$$\mathrm{Int}\,(T \setminus f_{A_1}) \cap \ldots \cap \mathrm{Int}\,(T \setminus f_{A_n}) \subseteq \mathrm{Int}\,(T \setminus f_B),$$

that is, to

$$f_{A_1}{}^{\perp} \cap \ldots \cap f_{A_n}{}^{\perp} \subseteq f_B{}^{\perp}.$$

Now we noted earlier that a state of information belongs to $f_A{}^{\perp}$ just in case the statement A may be safely asserted in that state of information. So another way of putting our criterion is that $A_1, \ldots, A_n$ entail B if and only if

$$\mathrm{ass}\,(A_1) \cap \ldots \cap \mathrm{ass}\,(A_n) \subseteq \mathrm{ass}\,(B).$$

That is to say, some premises entail a conclusion if and only if any state of information in which all of the premises are safely assertible is one in which the conclusion is safely assertible. As one might put it for brevity, entailment preserves safe assertibility.

How does this definition of entailment relate to Dummett's? Whenever $f_B \subseteq f_{A_1} \cup \ldots \cup f_{A_n}$, then $(f_{A_1} \cup \ldots \cup f_{A_n})^\perp \subseteq f_B^\perp$ (since if $f \subseteq g$ then $g^\perp \subseteq f^\perp$), and thence $f_{A_1}{}^\perp \cap \ldots \cap f_{A_n}{}^\perp \subseteq f_B{}^\perp$ (since $(f \cup g)^\perp = f^\perp \cap g^\perp$). So any entailment that is good by Dummett's criterion is also good by this one. The converse, however, does not hold. Suppose, for example, that we accept the clause that Dummett proposes for the conditions in which a negated statement is directly falsified. As Dummett himself notes, under his definition of entailment, a statement A will not in general entail its double negation $\neg\neg A$. Since, however, $f_A{}^\perp = f_A{}^{\perp\perp\perp} = f_{\neg\neg A}{}^\perp$, we have ass $(A) = $ ass $(\neg\neg A)$, so that A and $\neg\neg A$ entail each other under the revised criterion. That criterion, then, identifies a relation of entailment that strictly includes Dummett's.

How might this definition of entailment be extended to produce a definition of logical consequence for the language of the propositional calculus? Let us suppose that L is a sentential language whose well-formed formulae are got from a denumerable stock of sentence letters by freely applying the connectives '$\wedge$', '$\vee$', '$\rightarrow$' and '$\neg$'. Our problem is then to define a relation of logical consequence $X \models A$ for the case where the first element of each of the statements in $X \cup \{A\}$ is a well-formed formula of L, and where the second element (the context) is the same for all the members of $X \cup \{A\}$.

In framing such a definition, we need somehow to generalize over all the admissible interpretations of the nonlogical vocabulary; as before, the semantics for intuitionistic logic gives us a template for doing so. Given a partial ordering $\leq$ on a set T, a subset $S \subseteq T$ may be deemed to be open just in case $\forall x\, \forall y\, (x \in S \wedge x \leq y \rightarrow y \in S)$; for the reasons given in section V, the resulting *PO-space* is a topology. If the elements of T are states of information, an intuitionist may think of an open subset of T as the set of states of information in which a statement is assertible. Given a PO-space $\wp$, then, it is open to him to take any function φ which associates an open set in $\wp$ with each atomic sentence of L to be an (intuitionistic) *assignment* for L. We may think of this set as comprising those states of information which would directly verify the statement that would be made (in the given, fixed, context) by affirming the atomic sentence. When the points of a PO-space are conceived as states of information, moreover, we may define operations on the open sets in that PO-space which capture the intuitionistically intended senses of the logical connectives.[52] By appeal to those operations, our intuitionist may extend any assignment φ to produce a *valuation* v_φ which associates an open set in $\wp$ with each well-formed formula of L. And he may then say that

$X \models_{IL} A$ iff, for any assignment φ on any PO-space deriving from any finite partially ordered set, $\bigcap_{B \in X} v_\varphi(B) \subseteq v_\varphi(A)$.

The restriction to partial orderings on finite sets is needed to ensure that this definition of consequence for an intuitionistic sentential language coincides with the more familiar definitions in terms of Heyting lattices, Kripke trees, and Beth trees.[53]

We may take a similar tack to produce a definition of consequence founded on our falsificationist semantics for statements made (in a given context) using our sentential language L. Given a PO-space $\wp$, we may identify a (falsificationist) assignment for L to be any function φ which associates an open set in $\wp$ with each atomic sentence of L. This time, the open set is taken to comprise those states of information which directly falsify the statement consisting of the atomic sentence, and the context (which is again held fixed). Let us suppose that we can specify the states of information which would directly falsify the complex statements made in L in terms of the states of information which would directly falsify the parts of those statements. In that case, we shall be able to extend any (falsificationist) assignment φ to produce a (falsificationist) valuation f_φ which associates an open set in $\wp$ with each statement that could be made in L. This open set will comprise those states of information which would directly falsify the statements in question, under the assignment φ. One may then say that

$X \models A$ iff, for any falsificationist assignment φ on any PO-space deriving from any partially ordered set, $\bigcap_{B \in X} f_\varphi^\perp(B) \subseteq f_\varphi^\perp(A)$.

Or, equivalently,

$X \models A$ iff, for any falsificationist assignment φ on any PO-space deriving from any partially ordered set, $\bigcap_{B \in X} \mathrm{ass}_\varphi(B) \subseteq \mathrm{ass}_\varphi(A)$.

In words: A is a logical consequence of X if and only if, no matter what a the conditions under which the atomic statements of L are directly falsified, in any state of information in which all the statements in X may be safely asserted, statement A may be safely asserted too.

Until it is completed with principles relating the direct falsification of a complex statement to that of its parts, this definition remains schematic. No matter what those principles may be, however, the definition validates the three familiar structural principles—of reflexivity, dilution, and cut— which we expect any well-defined relationship of consequence to obey. The validity of the principle of reflexivity—viz., $A \models A$—is trivial. And if $\bigcap_{B \in X} \mathrm{ass}_\varphi(B) \subseteq \mathrm{ass}_\varphi(A)$ then certainly $\bigcap_{B \in Y} \mathrm{ass}_\varphi(B) \subseteq \mathrm{ass}_\varphi(A)$ for any set

Y for which $X \subseteq Y$, so that if $X \models A$ and $X \subseteq Y$ then $Y \models A$. Finally, the cut principle states that if $X \models A$ for all $A \in Y$ and $Y \models B$ then $X \models B$. Suppose, then, that $X \models A$ for all $A \in Y$ and $Y \models B$, and consider an arbitrary PO-space $\wp$ and an arbitrary falsificationist assignment φ into $\wp$. By the first supposition we have that $\bigcap_{C \in X} \mathrm{ass}_\varphi (C) \subseteq \bigcap_{A \in Y} \mathrm{ass}_\varphi (A)$ and by the second we have that $\bigcap_{A \in Y} \mathrm{ass}_\varphi (A) \subseteq \mathrm{ass} (B)$, so that $\bigcap_{C \in X} \mathrm{ass}_\varphi (C) \subseteq \mathrm{ass}_\varphi (B)$. Since $\wp$ and φ were chosen arbitrarily, this shows that $X \models B$, as the cut principle requires.

By the dilution principle, if $\varnothing \models A$ then $Y \models A$ for any set of statements Y. Accordingly, we shall have $\models A$ iff, for any falsificationist assignment φ on any PO-space deriving from any partially ordered set $<T, \leq >$, $\mathrm{ass}_\varphi (A) = T$. That is to say, a statement A counts as a logical truth if, no matter what the states of information might be, and no matter which states of information are taken as directly falsifying the atomic statements, A may be safely asserted in any state of information. This does not commit us to counting the open-ended prophecy 'One day, a city will be built here' as a logical truth. This statement owes its irrefutable status to the fact that no bound is placed upon the relevant range of days, rather than to the senses of the connectives or quantifiers, so that on the present approach it will not qualify as a logical truth of either the propositional or the predicate calculus. We might liken its status in relation to our definition of logical truth to the status that 'This sphere is not red and green all over' enjoys in relation to the more familiar, realist definition of logical truth. There is no logical possibility that the statement 'This sphere is not red and green' should be false; though since this possibility is excluded by a relationship of meaning between 'red' and 'green,' the statement does not instantiate any logical form, all of whose instances are true. Similarly, there is no state of information which could directly falsify 'One day, a city will be built here'; though since the existence of any such state of information is excluded by the unboundedness of the range of days, the statement does not instantiate any logical form, all of whose instances are safely assertible in any state of information.

On the present account, however, there is a sense in which an affirmation of a logical truth is at best a degenerate case of an assertion. Dummett describes an assertion as a gamble that the speaker will not be proved wrong. And in the case where a speaker affirms a logical truth—as in the case of 'One day, a city will be built here'—there is no gamble, for there is no possibility of his being proved wrong. We glimpse a possible ground here for the Tractarian doctrine that "the propositions of logic say nothing."[54]

VI. Clauses for the Connectives

Our definition of consequence remains schematic, pending a specification of the principles that relate the direct falsification of a complex statement to the direct falsification of its parts. What should those principles be?

I wish to defend the clauses which Dummett proposes for the sentential connectives. A conjunctive sentence is directly falsified by all and only those states of information which directly falsify one or other of its conjuncts; thus $f_{A \wedge B} = f_A \cup f_B$. A disjunctive saying is directly falsified by all and only those states of information which directly falsify both of its disjuncts; thus $f_{A \vee B} = f_A \cap f_B$. However it may relate to conditionals in natural languages, the logician's understanding of the arrow conforms to the principle that a state of information directly falsifies $A \rightarrow B$ if and only if it directly falsifies B but renders A safely assertible; thus $f_{A \rightarrow B} = f_B \cap f_A^{\perp}$. Finally, it is plausible to take those states of affairs which directly falsify $\neg A$ to be precisely those in which A itself may be safely asserted; thus $f_{\neg A} = f_A^{\perp}$. (These last two clauses secure the equivalence between $\neg A$ and $A \rightarrow \perp$, where $\perp$ is a sentence directly falsified in every state of information whatever.) Under these specifications, the set f_A of states of information which directly falsify A will be open no matter what formula A might be, as the theory of assertion which underpins the semantics requires.

We can best appreciate the merits of these clauses for the sentential connectives by deriving the principles that they entail for when complex statements are safely assertible. Earlier, we identified $f_A^{\perp}$, the exterior of f_A, as the set of states of information in which statement A is safely assertible. And the lemmas of section V yield the following principles relating the conditions for safely asserting a complex statement to the conditions for safely asserting its parts:

$$\text{ass } (A \wedge B) = (f_{A \wedge B})^{\perp} = (f_A \cup f_B)^{\perp} = f_A^{\perp} \cap f_B^{\perp} = \text{ass } (A) \cap \text{ass } (B)$$

$$\text{ass } (A \vee B) = (f_{A \vee B})^{\perp} = (f_A \cap f_B)^{\perp} = (f_A^{\perp} \cup f_B^{\perp})^{\perp\perp}, \text{ by lemma (5) above}$$
$$= (\text{ass } (A) \cup \text{ass } (B))^{\perp\perp}$$
$$= \text{Int Cl(ass } (A) \cup \text{ass } (B))$$

$$\text{ass } (A \rightarrow B) = (f_{A \rightarrow B})^{\perp} = (f_A^{\perp} \cap f_B)^{\perp} = (f_A^{\perp\perp} \cup f_B^{\perp})^{\perp\perp}, \text{ by lemma (5) again}$$
$$= \text{Int Cl [ass } (A)^{\perp} \cup \text{ass } (B)]$$
$$= \text{Int Cl [Int } (T \setminus \text{ass } (A)) \cup \text{ass } (B)]$$

$$\text{ass } (\neg A) = f_{\neg A}^{\perp} = f_A^{\perp\perp} = \text{Int } (T \setminus f_A^{\perp}) = \text{Int } (T \setminus \text{ass } (A)).$$

In connection with the last clause, it may be noted that, while there may be states of information which directly falsify neither A nor $\neg A$, since $f_A^{\perp} \cap f_A^{\perp\perp} = \varnothing$ there is no state of information in which both A and $\neg A$ are safely assertible.

Further lemmas about regular sets lead to a more tractable specification of ass $(A \to B)$. Recall that a set X in a topological space T was said to be regular open iff $X = \text{Int Cl}\,(X)$; we may say dually that a set X in space T is *regular closed* iff $X = \text{Cl Int}\,(X)$. We then have

LEMMA 7.   (a) If X is a regular open set, then its complement in T is a regular closed set.

(b) If X is a regular closed set, then its interior is a regular open set.

PROOF.   (a) If X is a regular open set, then $X = \text{Int Cl}\,X$. Let $Y = T \setminus X$. Y is certainly closed. Moreover,

$$\text{Cl Int}\,Y = T \setminus \text{Int}\,(T \setminus \text{Int}\,Y) = T \setminus \text{Int}\,(T \setminus \text{Int}\,(T \setminus X)) = T \setminus \text{Int Cl}\,X = T \setminus X = Y,$$

so Y (i.e., $T \setminus X$) is regular closed, as required.

(b) If X is a regular closed set, then $X = \text{Cl Int}\,X$. Let $Y = \text{Int}\,X$. Y is certainly open. Moreover, $\text{Int Cl}\,Y = \text{Int Cl Int}\,X = \text{Int}\,X = Y$, as required.   □

We also have

LEMMA 8.   Any set of the form ass (A) is regular open.

PROOF. For any formula A, ass $(A) = f_A^{\perp}$, and since $f^{\perp} = f^{\perp\perp\perp}$, we have that for any formula A, ass $(A) = $ ass $(A)^{\perp\perp}$, whence the result.   □

LEMMA 9.   ass $(A \to B) = [(T \setminus \text{ass}\,(A)) \cup \text{ass}\,(B)]^{\perp\perp}$.

PROOF. It follows from lemmas 8 and 7 (a) that any set of the form $(T \setminus \text{ass}\,(A))$ is regular closed. Then

	ass $(A \to B)$	
$=$	Int Cl $[$ Int $(T \setminus \text{ass}\,(A)) \cup \text{ass}\,(B)]$	see above
$=$	Int $[\text{Cl Int}\,(T \setminus \text{ass}\,(A)) \cup \text{Cl ass}\,(B)]$	since $\text{Cl}(A \cup B) = $ $\text{Cl}(A) \cup \text{Cl}\,(B)$
$=$	Int $[(T \setminus \text{ass}\,(A)) \cup \text{Cl ass}\,(B)]$	since $(T \setminus \text{ass}\,(A))$ is regular closed
$=$	Int $[\text{Cl}\,(T \setminus \text{ass}\,(A)) \cup \text{Cl ass}\,(B)]$	since $(T \setminus \text{ass}\,(A))$ is closed
$=$	Int Cl $[(T \setminus \text{ass}\,(A)) \cup \text{ass}\,(B)]$	since $\text{Cl}(A \cup B) = $ $\text{Cl}(A) \cup \text{Cl}\,(B)$
$=$	$[(T \setminus \text{ass}\,(A)) \cup \text{ass}\,(B)]^{\perp\perp}$. □	

These falsificationist specifications of the senses of the connectives avoid some of the problems that attend the standard verificationist specifications. The mathematical intuitionists specify the intended sense of the sign of disjunction by saying that a disjunctive statement is canonically provable if and only if one or other of the disjuncts is. And the generalization of this to cover other forms of verification will say that a disjunctive statement is directly verifiable if and only if one or other disjunct is. This claim seems to conflict, however, with our ordinary understanding of 'or'. As Dummett himself has pointed out, once we have the concept of a disjunction, the content of our perceptions may take an irremediably disjunctive form, and thus perceptual knowledge might be irreducibly disjunctive. Thus Hardy may have been unable to hear whether Nelson said 'Kismet, Hardy' or 'Kiss me, Hardy,' even though he heard him say one or the other.[55] And, we may assume, nobody—even with the sharpest hearing—could have done better. But if that is right, then it may be directly verifiable (by listening) that Nelson's last words were either 'Kismet, Hardy' or 'Kiss me, Hardy,' even though neither disjunct is (or ever was) directly verifiable.[56] No analogous problem, however, attends the proposed falsificationist explanation of 'or'. Neither, it seems, do we have a dual problem for the proposed explanation of 'and'. It does not seem as though there are any conjunctive statements which are plausibly described as being directly falsified by a perceptual state which nevertheless does not directly falsify either one conjunct or the other.

All the same, the theory has some perplexing consequences. Since I have been concerned in this paper only with the *logic* of safe assertibility, I have not said anything about the conditions under which statements about different sorts of subject matter might be directly falsified. For the sake of an example, however, let us suppose that a statement 'The number of stars in the universe is odd' could be directly falsified only by counting the number of stars present in the universe at the time of the statement, and ascertaining that that number was even. Let us also assume that a statement 'The number of stars in the universe is even' could be directly falsified only by counting the number of stars present in the universe at the time of the statement and ascertaining that that number was odd. Let us then consider a statement, O, of 'The number of stars in the universe is odd' made shortly before the end of the universe, and a contemporaneous statement, E, of 'The number of stars in the universe is even.' And let us consider a state of information s in which it is known that the universe will end before there is time to count the stars in it. Now somebody in state s knows that there is no chance of anybody's directly refuting statement O before the universe comes to an end. Accordingly, O is safely assertible in state s, that is, $s \in \text{Ass}(O)$. Similarly, somebody in state s knows that there is no chance of anybody's directly refuting statement E before the universe comes to an end. Accordingly, E is safely assertible in state s, that is, $s \in \text{Ass}(E)$. Thus $\text{Ass}(O) \cap \text{Ass}(E)$ is nonempty, and by our principle concerning the safe assertibility of conjunctions, the conjunctive statement, $O \wedge E$, that is, 'The number of stars in the universe is both odd and even,' is safely assertible in some circumstances (for example, state s).[57]

This conclusion reflects the anti-realist character of the underlying theory of assertion, whereby an assertion's content is determined by its role in the intersubjective linguistic economy, rather than by reference to any putative extralinguistic facts. More exactly, it reflects the fact that Thesis α is an example of what Dummett has called a pragmatist theory of meaning: "the content of a statement should be regarded as determined by its *consequences* for one who accepts it as true."[58] A theory of this kind is liable to generate odd results when, so to say, an assertion is made near the edge of the relevant space of states of information—in particular, when the linguistic economy which determines content faces imminent extinction. However, since we do not know how we should react to such a predicament, the defender of Thesis α may deem our sense of the oddity of such cases to be the product of years of realist indoctrination.

Certainly, the oddity in question here—namely, the safe assertibility of $O \wedge E$ in state of information s—does not extend to the safe assertibility in s of the formally contradictory statement $O \wedge \neg O$. To reach that conclusion, the statement E would have to entail $\neg O$, but when entailment is understood to mean the preservation of safe assertibility, there is no entailment. As we have seen, $s \in \mathrm{Ass}\,(E)$. Equally, however, $s \in \mathrm{Ass}\,(O)$, so that $s \notin (T \setminus \mathrm{Ass}\,(O))$ and $s \notin \mathrm{Int}\,(T \setminus \mathrm{Ass}\,(O))$; that is to say, $s \notin \mathrm{Ass}\,(\neg O)$. Thus E can be safely asserted in circumstances where $\neg O$ cannot. This brings out how strong is the condition for safely asserting a negated statement: in order safely to assert $\neg A$, a speaker needs to know that no state of information will obtain in which A could be safely asserted. In a state of affairs such as s, where many statements may be safely asserted on account of the lack of time to ascertain their falsity, this condition will not be met, so that the negations of those statements will not be safely assertible. It is in this way that the semantics ensures that a statement and its negation will never be safely assertible in the same state of information.[59]

VII. SOUNDNESS

When it is combined with these clauses for the sentential connectives, our definition of logical consequence validates all the introduction and elimination rules of the standard classical propositional calculus. I shall show this by proving theorem 1.

THEOREM 1 (SOUNDNESS).

Let us say that $X \vdash A$ if and only if the statement A is deducible from the set of statements X using the introduction and elimination rules of the standard natural deduction formalization of the classical propositional calculus. And let $X \vDash A$ be defined as in section V with the clauses for the connectives as specified in section VI. Then $X \vdash A$ only if $X \vDash A$.

PROOF.

We saw at the end of section V that $\vDash$ has the structural properties of a consequence relation. Given that fact, it suffices to show that each of the rules of inference among the standard deduction rules is sound in the sense of preserving safe assertibility, and that each of the rules of proof preserves soundness. The result then follows by induction on the length of a deduction of A from X. For the rules enumerated below, the fact that needs to be established to show that the rule is sound, or preserves soundness, is stated in the first line. In the proofs that follow, formulae such as "ass (A)" "ass (B)," "ass $(A \wedge B)$," and so on, are to be understood as abbreviating "ass$_\varphi (A)$," "ass$_\varphi (B)$," "ass$_\varphi (A \wedge B)$," and so on, where φ is an arbitrary falsificationist assignment on the PO-space deriving from an arbitrary partially ordered set.

$\wedge$-INTRODUCTION. $A, B \vDash A \wedge B$
ass $(A) \cap$ ass $(B) =$ ass $(A \wedge B)$, so *a fortiori* ass $(A) \cap$ ass $(B) \subseteq$ ass $(A \wedge B)$, showing that $A, B \vDash A \wedge B$.

$\wedge$-ELIMINATION. $A \wedge B \vDash A$ $A \wedge B \vDash B$
ass $(A \wedge B) =$ ass $(A) \cap$ ass $(B) \subseteq$ ass (A), showing that $A \wedge B \vDash A$.
The proof that $A \wedge B \vDash B$ is similar.

$\vee$-INTRODUCTION. $A \vDash A \vee B$ $B \vDash A \vee B$
ass $(A) \subseteq$ ass $(A) \cup$ ass (B), so Cl ass $(A) \subseteq$ Cl (ass $(A) \cup$ ass (B)), so Int Cl ass $(A) \subseteq$ Int Cl (ass $(A) \cup$ ass (B)). But Int Cl ass $(A) =$ ass (A) and Int Cl (ass $(A) \cup$ ass $(B)) =$ ass $(A \vee B)$ so that ass $(A) \subseteq$ ass $(A \vee B)$, showing that $A \vDash A \vee B$. The proof that $B \vDash A \vee B$ is similar.

$\vee$-ELIMINATION.   If $X, A \vDash C$ and $Y, B \vDash C$ then $X, Y, A \vee B \vDash C$.
By dilution, $X, A \vDash C$ only if $X, Y, A \vDash C$ and $Y, B \vDash C$ only if $X, Y, B \vDash C$, so it suffices to show that if $Z, A \vDash C$ and $Z, B \vDash C$ then $Z, A \vee B \vDash C$. Suppose, then, that $Z, A \vDash C$ and that $Z, B \vDash C$. In that case, we shall have

$$\bigcap_{D \in Z} \text{ass } (D) \cap \text{ass } (A) \subseteq \text{ass } (C)$$

and

$$\bigcap_{D \in Z} \text{ass } (D) \cap \text{ass } (B) \subseteq \text{ass } (C)$$

so that

$$[\bigcap_{D \in Z} \text{ass } (D) \cap \text{ass } (A)] \cup [\bigcap_{D \in Z} \text{ass } (D) \cap \text{ass } (B)] \subseteq \text{ass } (C).$$

One of De Morgan's Laws then yields

$$\bigcap_{D \in Z} \text{ass } (D) \cap (\text{ass } (A) \cup \text{ass } (B)) \subseteq \text{ass } (C),$$

so that

$$[\bigcap_{D \in Z} \text{ass } (D) \cap (\text{ass } (A) \cup \text{ass } (B))]^{\perp\perp} \subseteq (\text{ass } (C))^{\perp\perp}.$$

Now the sets $\bigcap_{D \in Z} \text{ass } (D)$ and $(\text{ass } (A) \cup \text{ass } (B))$ are both open, so by lemma 4 of section IV, it follows that

$$[\bigcap_{D \in Z} \text{ass } (D)]^{\perp\perp} \cap [(\text{ass } (A) \cup \text{ass } (B))]^{\perp\perp} \subseteq (\text{ass } (C))^{\perp\perp}.$$

Moreover, since ass (C) and all the ass (D) are open and regular, it follows by lemma 6 of section IV that

$$\bigcap_{D \in Z} \text{ass } (D) \cap [(\text{ass } (A) \cup \text{ass } (B))]^{\perp\perp} \subseteq \text{ass } (C).$$

However, $[(\text{ass } (A) \cup \text{ass } (B))]^{\perp\perp} = \text{ass } (A \vee B)$, so we have

$$\bigcap_{D \in Z} \text{ass } (D) \cap (\text{ass } (A \vee B)) \subseteq \text{ass } (C),$$

which shows that $Z, A \vee B \models C$, as required.

$\rightarrow$-INTRODUCTION. If $X, A \models B$ then $X \models A \rightarrow B$.
Suppose that $X, A \models B$. Then

$$\bigcap_{D \in Z} \text{ass } (D) \cap \text{ass } (A) \subseteq \text{ass } (B).$$

It follows that

$$\bigcap_{D \in Z} \text{ass } (D) \subseteq \text{ass } (B) \cup (T \setminus \text{ass } (A)),$$

so that

$$\bigcap_{D \in Z} \text{ass } (D))^{\perp\perp} \subseteq ((T \setminus \text{ass } (A) \cup \text{ass } (B))^{\perp\perp}.$$

Now all the sets ass (D) are regular open; so by lemma 6 of section IV, we have

$$\bigcap_{D \in Z} \text{ass } (D) \subseteq ((T \setminus \text{ass } (A) \cup \text{ass } (B))^{\perp\perp}$$

and thence

$$\bigcap_{D \in Z} \text{ass } (D) \subseteq \text{ass } (A \rightarrow B),$$

by lemma 9 of section VI. This shows that $X \models A \rightarrow B$, as required.

$\rightarrow$-ELIMINATION. $A, A \rightarrow B \models B$

$$\text{ass } (A) \cap \text{ass } (A \rightarrow B)$$

$= \quad \text{ass } (A) \cap \text{Int Cl}((T \setminus \text{ass } (A)) \cup \text{ass } (B))$ \quad by lemma 9 of section VI

$= \quad \text{Int ass } (A) \cap \text{Int Cl}((T \setminus \text{ass } (A)) \cup \text{ass } (B))$ \quad since ass (A) is open

$= \quad \text{Int } [\text{ass } (A) \cap \text{Cl}((T \setminus \text{ass } (A)) \cup \text{ass } (B))]$ \quad since $\text{Int } (A \cap B) = \text{Int } (A) \cap \text{Int } (B)$

$= \quad \text{Int } [\text{ass } (A) \cap (\text{Cl}(T \setminus \text{ass } (A)) \cup \text{Cl ass } (B))]$ \quad since $\text{Cl } (A \cup B) = \text{Cl } (A) \cup \text{Cl } (B)$

$= \quad \text{Int } [\text{ass } (A) \cap ((T \setminus \text{ass } (A)) \cup \text{Cl ass } (B))]$ \quad since $T \setminus \text{ass } (A)$ is closed

$=$ Int $[($ass $(A) \cap (T \setminus$ ass $(A))) \cup ($ass $(A) \cap$ Cl ass $(B))]$ by De Morgan

$=$ Int $[$ass $(A) \cap$ Cl ass $(B)]$ since ass $(A) \cap (T \setminus$ ass $(A)) = \varnothing$

$\subseteq$ Int Cl ass $(B) =$ ass (B).

That is to say, ass $(A) \cap$ ass $(A \to B) \subseteq$ ass (B), showing that $A, A \to B \models B$.

$\neg$-INTRODUCTION.   If $X, A \models B$ and $X, A \models \neg B$ then $X \models \neg A$.

Suppose that $X, A \models B$ and that $X, A \models \neg B$. In that case,

$$\bigcap_{C \in X} \text{ ass } (C) \cap \text{ ass } (A) \subseteq \text{ ass } (B)$$

and

$$\bigcap_{C \in X} \text{ ass } (C) \cap \text{ ass } (A) \subseteq \text{ ass } (\neg B).$$

It follows that

$$\bigcap_{C \in X} \text{ ass } (C) \cap \text{ ass } (A) \subseteq \text{ ass } (B) \cap \text{ ass } (\neg B) = \text{ ass } (B) \cap \text{ Int } (T \setminus \text{ ass } (B))$$
$$= \varnothing.$$

We have, then, that

$$\bigcap_{C \in X} \text{ ass } (C) \subseteq (T \setminus \text{ ass } (A)).$$

The set $\bigcap_{C \in X}$ ass (C), however, is open, so

$$\bigcap_{C \in X} \text{ ass } (C) \subseteq \text{ Int } (T \setminus \text{ ass } (A)) = \text{ ass } (\neg A)$$

Thus $X \models \neg A$, as required.

$\neg$-ELIMINATION. $\neg \neg A \models A$

ass $(\neg \neg A) = $ Int Cl ass $(A) = $ ass (A) so certainly ass $(\neg \neg A) \subseteq$ ass (A), showing that $\neg \neg A \models A$, as required.

This shows that each rule of inference in the standard natural deduction formalization of the classical propositional calculus is sound and that each rule of proof in that formalization preserves soundness. The proof that $\vdash$ is sound with respect to $\models$ is therefore complete. $\square$

     This result has great significance for our inquiry. We saw how a soundness proof—although it cannot provide a foundation for a logical system—may yet provide a rationale for it by showing how arguments that conform to the system's laws preserve some property in whose preservation we have an interest. And we noted how Dummett's attacks on the intelligibility of a verification-transcendent notion of truth seek to deprive the classical propositional calculus of its standard rationale. Even if those attacks are successful, however, our soundness theorem opens the door to an alternative explanatory justification. For we have a clear interest in arguments which preserve safe assertibility, and which thereby do not increase our exposure to direct falsification. Because it shows that arguments conforming to the laws of the classical propositional calculus preserve safe assertibility, our soundness theorem provides a rationale for that calculus which makes no use of any verification-transcendent notion of truth—which invokes, indeed, notions that are surely intelligible to (because they are used by) an anti-realist of Dummett's stripe. In this way, the soundness theorem provides an anti-realist rationale of classical propositional logic.

VIII. COMPLETENESS

Although the philosophical argument of this paper does not require it, the formal materials needed to prove a converse of the soundness theorem lie to hand.

As was noted in section VI, every set of the form ass (A) is regular open. What is more, if A is regular open, then

$$A = \text{Int Cl } A = \text{Int } (T \setminus \text{Int } (T \setminus A)) = (\text{Int } (T \setminus A))^{\perp},$$

so that every regular open set is the exterior of some open set (namely, the interior of its complement). Hence, our definition of logical consequence for a propositional language L, namely

$X \vDash A$ iff, for any falsificationist assignment φ on any PO-space deriving from any partially ordered set, $\bigcap_{B \in X} \text{ass}_\varphi(B) \subseteq \text{ass}_\varphi(A)$,

is equivalent to

$X \vDash A$ iff, for any regular assertibility assignment ψ on any PO-space deriving from any partially ordered set, $\bigcap_{B \in X} \text{ass}_\psi(B) \subseteq \text{ass}_\psi(A)$.

Here, a regular assertibility assignment for L is a function ψ which associates a regular open set in $\wp$ with each atomic sentence of L; the regular open set is taken to comprise those states of information in which it would be safe to assert the statement that would be made (in the given context) by affirming that atomic sentence. This function may be directly extended to produce a regular assertibility valuation ass_ψ which associates a regular open set in $\wp$ with each sentence of L as follows:

$\text{ass}_\psi (A \wedge B) = \text{ass}_\psi (A) \cap \text{ass}_\psi (B)$
$\text{ass}_\psi (A \vee B) = \text{Int Cl } (\text{ass}_\psi (A) \cup \text{ass}_\psi (B))$
$\text{ass}_\psi (A \rightarrow B) = \text{Int Cl } [(T \setminus \text{ass}_\psi (A)) \cup \text{ass}_\psi (B)]$
$\text{ass}_\psi (\neg A) = \text{Int } (T \setminus \text{ass}_\psi (A))$.

These conditions for complex sentences to be safely assertible are of course exactly those which we derived in section VI from Dummett's conditions for complex sentences to be directly falsified, save that we use the more tractable form for $\text{ass}_\psi (A \rightarrow B)$ established in lemma 9.

Let us now consider the set $O(T)$ of all regular open subsets of a given set T, and let X and Y be members of $O(T)$. Let the binary operations $\wedge$ and $\vee$ be defined on members of $O(T)$ as follows:

$X \wedge Y = X \cap Y$

$X \vee Y = \text{Int Cl} (X \cup Y)$.

Then we have theorem 2.

THEOREM 2.
The structure $<O(T), \wedge, \vee>$ is a distributive lattice. That is to say, for any sets X and Y in $O(T)$, $X \wedge Y$ and $X \vee Y$ are also in $O(T)$, and for any sets X, Y, and Z in $O(T)$ we have

L1. $X \wedge X = X \vee X = X$

L2. $X \wedge Y = Y \wedge X$ $\qquad\qquad$ $X \vee Y = Y \vee X$

L3. $X \wedge (Y \wedge Z) = (X \wedge Y) \wedge Z$ $\qquad$ $X \vee (Y \vee Z) = (X \vee Y) \vee Z$

L4. $X \wedge (X \vee Y) = X \vee (X \wedge Y) = X$

D1. $X \wedge (Y \vee Z) = (X \wedge Y) \vee (X \wedge Z)$

D2. $X \vee (Y \wedge Z) = (X \vee Y) \wedge (X \vee Z)$.

PROOF.
To show that $X \wedge Y$ is regular open when both X and Y are, we apply lemma 4 of section V. If X and Y are both regular open, then they are certainly both open, so by lemma 4 we have that $(X \cap Y)^{\perp\perp} = X^{\perp\perp} \cap Y^{\perp\perp}$. Since X and Y are regular open, though, $X^{\perp\perp} = X$ and $Y^{\perp\perp} = Y$ so that $(X \cap Y)^{\perp\perp} = X \cap Y$, showing that $X \cap Y$ is regular open.

Given the definition of $\vee$, it is trivial to show that $X \vee Y$ is regular open. This is because, for any set Z, $Z^{\perp\perp\perp\perp} = Z^{\perp\perp}$. Note that when both X and Y are regular open, it is not in general true that $X \cup Y$ is.[60] However, if Z is regular open and $X \cup Y \subseteq Z$, then $\text{Int Cl}(X \cup Y) \subseteq \text{Int Cl } Z = Z$, so that $X \vee Y$ is the smallest regular open set which includes X and Y.

It is trivial to show that the operations $\wedge$ and $\vee$ satisfy **L1, L2** and the first half of **L3**. For the second half of **L3**, we need to show that whenever X, Y and Z are regular open, $[X \cup (Y \cup Z)^{\perp\perp}]^{\perp\perp} = [(X \cup Y)^{\perp\perp} \cup Z]^{\perp\perp}$. Now

$[X \cup (Y \cup Z)^{\perp\perp}]^{\perp\perp}$

$= [X^{\perp\perp} \cup (Y \cup Z)^{\perp\perp}]^{\perp\perp}$ $\qquad$ since X is regular open

$= [X^{\perp} \cap (Y \cup Z)^{\perp}]^{\perp}$ $\qquad$ by section IV lemma 5, since $X^{\perp}$ and $(Y \cup Z)^{\perp}$ are open

$= [X^{\perp} \cap (Y^{\perp} \cap Z^{\perp})]^{\perp}$ $\qquad$ since $(Y \cup Z)^{\perp} = Y^{\perp} \cap Z^{\perp}$

$= [(X^{\perp} \cap Y^{\perp}) \cap Z^{\perp}]^{\perp}$ $\qquad$ since $\cap$ is an associative operation on sets

$= [(X \cup Y)^{\perp} \cap Z^{\perp}]^{\perp}$ $\qquad$ since $X^{\perp} \cap Y^{\perp} = (X \cup Y)^{\perp}$

$= [(X \cup Y)^{\perp\perp} \cup Z^{\perp\perp}]^{\perp\perp}$ $\qquad$ by section IV lemma 5, since $(X \cup Y)^{\perp}$ and $Z^{\perp}$ are open

$=\ [(X\cup Y)^{\perp\perp}\cup Z]^{\perp\perp}$ since Z is regular open.

For **L4**, we need to show that whenever X and Y are regular open, $X\cap (X\cup Y)^{\perp\perp}=X$ and that $(X\cup (X\cap Y))^{\perp\perp}=X$. Now

$$X\cap (X\cup Y)^{\perp\perp}$$
$=\ X^{\perp\perp}\cap (X\cup Y)^{\perp\perp}$ since X is regular open
$=\ (X\cap (X\cup Y))^{\perp\perp}$ by lemma 4 of section IV, since X and
                              $(X\cup Y)$ are open
$=\ X^{\perp\perp}$ by elementary set theory
$=\ X$ since X is regular open.

For the second equation, note that $(X\cup (X\cap Y))=X$, so that $(X\cup (X\cap Y))^{\perp\perp}=X^{\perp\perp}=X$, since X is regular open.

For **D1**, we have that
$$X\wedge (Y\vee Z)$$
$=\ X\cap (Y\cup Z)^{\perp\perp}$ by the definitions of $\wedge$ and $\vee$
$=\ X^{\perp\perp}\cap (Y\cup Z)^{\perp\perp}$ since X is regular open
$=\ (X\cap (Y\cup Z))^{\perp\perp}$ by lemma 4 of section IV, since X and
                              $Y\cup Z$ are open
$=\ [(X\cap Y)\cup (X\cap Z)]^{\perp\perp}$ by De Morgan
$=\ (X\wedge Y)\vee (X\wedge Z)$ by the definitions of $\wedge$ and $\vee$.

For **D2**, we have that
$$(X\vee Y)\wedge (X\vee Z)$$
$=\ (X\cup Y)^{\perp\perp}\cap (X\cup Z)^{\perp\perp}$ by the definitions of $\wedge$ and $\vee$
$=\ [(X\cup Y)\cap (X\cup Z)]^{\perp\perp}$ by lemma 4, since $X\cup Y$ and $X\cup Z$
                              are both open
$=\ [X\cup (Y\cap Z)]^{\perp\perp}$ by De Morgan
$=\ X\vee (Y\wedge Z)$ by the definitions of $\wedge$ and $\vee$. $\square$

The natural ordering relation on this lattice is the set inclusion relation $\subseteq$. The empty set $\varnothing$ and the total set T are regular open sets so that $\varnothing$ is the least element, or *zero*, of the lattice $<O\ (T),\ \wedge,\ \vee>$ and T is its greatest element, or *unit*.

Now where X is a member of $O\ (T)$, let the unary operation $\neg$ be defined as follows:

$$\neg X = \text{Int}\ (T\setminus X).$$

We then have theorem 3.

THEOREM 3.

The lattice $<O\ (T),\ \wedge,\ \vee>$ is complemented by $\neg$. That is to say, for any set X in $O\ (T)$, $\neg X$ is also in $O\ (T)$, and we have

C1. $X \wedge \neg X = \varnothing$
C2. $X \vee \neg X = T.$

PROOF.

To show that $\neg X$ belongs to $O(T)$ when X does, suppose that X is regular open. Then $T \setminus X$ is regular closed by lemma 7 (a) and thus Int $(T \setminus X)$ is regular open by lemma 7 (b).

To establish **C1**, note that if $x \in$ Int $(T \setminus X)$ then certainly $x \in T \setminus X$, so $x \notin X$. Hence $X \cap \neg X = \varnothing$, showing that $X \wedge \neg X = \varnothing$.

For **C2**, note that

$\qquad X \vee \neg X$
$=$ Int Cl $(X \cup$ Int $(T \setminus X))$ by the definitions of $\vee$ and $\neg$
$=$ Int $($Cl $X \cup$ Cl Int $(T \setminus X))$ since Cl $(A \cup B) =$ Cl $(A) \cup$ Cl (B)
$=$ Int $($Cl $X \cup (T \setminus X))$ since $T \setminus X$ is regular closed by lemma
$\qquad\qquad\qquad\qquad\qquad\qquad$ 7 (a)
$=$ Int T since every member of T is either in X
$\qquad\qquad\qquad\qquad\qquad\qquad$ (and hence in Cl X) or in $T \setminus X$
$=$ T since T is open. $\square$

Putting these results together gives theorem 4.

THEOREM 4 (TARSKI).[61]

The family $O(T)$ of regular open subsets of a given set T, together with the operations $\wedge$, $\vee$, and $\neg$ satisfy the postulates of Boolean algebra with set inclusion as the underlying ordering relation, with the empty set as the algebra's zero and with T itself as its unit.

PROOF. Immediate from the preceding theorems, given the definition of a Boolean algebra as a distributive complemented lattice. $\square$

Let us further introduce the binary operation $\rightarrow$ on regular open sets according to the definition

$\qquad X \rightarrow Y =$ Int Cl $[(T \setminus X) \cup Y]$.

Then $\rightarrow$ is *material* with respect to $\wedge$, $\vee$, and $\neg$ in the sense that for any regular open sets X and Y,

$\qquad X \rightarrow Y = \neg X \vee Y = \neg (X \wedge \neg Y).$

This is because

$\qquad X \rightarrow Y$
$=$ Int Cl $[(T \setminus X) \cup Y]$ by definition of $\rightarrow$
$=$ Int Cl $[$Int $(T \setminus X) \cup Y]$ by lemma 9 of section VI
$=$ Int Cl $[\neg X \cup Y]$ by definition of $\neg$
$=$ $\neg X \vee Y$ by definition of $\vee$

Also

$$X \to Y$$
=	Int Cl [Int $(T \setminus X) \cup Y]$	as above
=	Int [Cl Int $(T \setminus X) \cup$ Cl $Y]$	since Cl $(A \cup B) =$ Cl $(A) \cup$ Cl (B)
=	Int $[(T \setminus X) \cup$ Cl $Y]$	since $T \setminus X$ is regular closed
=	Int $[T \setminus (X \cap (T \setminus$ Cl $Y))]$	by De Morgan
=	Int $[T \setminus (X \cap$ Int $(T \setminus Y))]$	since $T \setminus$ Cl $Y =$ Int $(T \setminus Y)$
=	$\neg (X \wedge \neg Y)$	by definitions of $\neg$ and $\wedge$.

The significance of these results is as follows. Let us consider the family of valuation systems of the form

$$M = <O\,(T),\, \wedge,\, \vee,\, \to,\, \neg,\, \subseteq >$$

in which T is an arbitrary set and $O\,(T)$ is the set of regular open subsets of T; in which an assignment ψ is made by associating an arbitrary member of $O\,(T)$ with the atomic sentences of a propositional language, and in which the assignment ψ is extended to a valuation v_ψ of the class of all sentences by interpreting the connectives '$\wedge$', '$\vee$', '$\to$', and '$\neg$' as the operations $\wedge$, $\vee$, $\to$, and $\neg$ defined above (that is, we have $v_\psi (A \wedge B) = v_\psi (A) \wedge v_\psi (B) = v_\psi (A) \cap v_\psi (B)$, and so on). What we have shown is that any such matrix is a Boolean algebra for $\wedge$, $\vee$, and $\neg$, and that $\to$ is material with respect to $\wedge$, $\vee$, and $\neg$. By a well-known theorem in the algebra of logic, this entails that this family of valuation systems is *characteristic* for the classical propositional calculus.[62] That is to say, where '$X \vdash_c A$' means that formula A is deducible from the set of formulae X by the rules of the classical propositional calculus, we shall have, for any M of this form,

$X \vdash_c A$ iff, for any M of this form and for every assignment ψ in M, $\bigcap_{B \in X} v_\psi (B) \subseteq v_\psi (A)$.

Now where $X \models A$ is defined as in section V with the clauses for the connectives as specified in section VI, we saw that

$X \models A$ iff, for any regular assertibility assignment ψ on any PO-space deriving from any partially ordered set, $\bigcap_{B \in X} \mathrm{ass}_\psi (B) \subseteq \mathrm{ass}_\psi (A)$.

Since the regular assertibility assignments on any PO-space deriving from any partially ordered set will meet the conditions for belonging to this family of valuation systems, we have that

$X \vdash_c A$ iff $X \models A$.

That is to say, the rules of the standard formalization of the classical propositional calculus are both sound and complete with respect to the relation of consequence that was defined on the basis of Thesis α, using

Dummett's falsificationist clauses for the sentential connectives.

The observation that the algebra of regular open sets in a topological space provides a family of valuation systems characteristic for the classical propositional calculus is again due in all essentials to Tarski.[63] However, he made no effort to relate the topological operations thereby associated with the connectives to their ordinary meanings.[64] For his purposes, he had no reason to do so. As Dummett himself has observed, in the work of the Polish school,

> valuation systems were largely employed as a technical device for proving the independence of axioms in axiomatic formalizations of classical and modal logic. . . . In such applications, the valuation systems considered need have no manifest relation to the intended meanings of the logical constants . . . or the intended interpretations of the formulas.[65]

For our purposes, however, it is highly significant that we have been able to reach a characterization of the classical propositional calculus on the basis of a general theory of assertoric content (namely, that encapsulated in Thesis α) together with semantic clauses which plausibly reflect the meanings of the sentential connectives. I began this essay by noting that Dummett has sometimes attacked classical logic by attacking the semantic theory—classical propositional semantics—which is usually invoked to explain the meaning of the sentential connectives and thereby to character-ize the relationship of classical consequence. That semantic theory corresponds—in a way that is probably too familiar to need spelling out[66] —to the two-element Boolean algebra of the two classical truth values. If Dummett's attack on classical propositional semantics succeeds, then we shall not be able to explain the meanings of the classical connectives by reference to that very simple algebra. Provided that Thesis α is accepted, however, we shall be able to characterize those meanings perfectly satisfactorily by reference to the algebra of regular open sets on an arbitrary space of states of information ordered by the $\leq$-relation. So far from casting doubt on classical propositional logic *per se*, then, Dummett's attack may show only that classical logicians have standardly tried to convey the intended meanings of their connectives by reference to the wrong Boolean algebra.

IX. CONCLUSION

Even if Thesis α is accepted, the soundness proof given in section VII will not persuade everybody that the introduction and elimination rules of the classical propositional logic really are sound. At a number of points, the proof appeals to classical rules which have been seriously controverted. This metalogical deployment of classical rules deprives the soundness proof of suasive power. For the reasons Dummett gives, however, it does not disqualify the proof from forming part of an explanation of what classical consequence preserves, and hence forming part of a rationale for classical logic.[67] It does, though, inspire a question. Let us a say that a logic L *coheres* with a semantic definition of consequence if the soundness and completeness of the rules of L are derivable from that definition using the rules of L themselves. By extending the argument of sections VII and VIII to the case of the classical first-order predicate calculus, it is possible to show that classical first-order logic coheres with our definition of consequence based upon the notion of direct falsification. It remains an open question, however, whether there are weaker logics which also cohere (in the specified sense) with the present semantic definition of consequence.

I shall not address this question systematically here. It is clear, however, that intuitionistic logic does not cohere with the proposed definition of consequence. To see this, observe first that, even if we restrict ourselves to intuitionistic logic in the metalanguage, the inference from $f \subseteq g$ to $(T \setminus g) \subseteq (T \setminus f)$ and thus to Int $(T \setminus g) \subseteq$ Int $(T \setminus f)$ still goes through. Even under that restriction, then, we have $f \subseteq g$ implying $g^\perp \subseteq f^\perp$. Similarly, we can show intuitionistically that $f \subseteq f^{\perp\perp}$. For suppose that $s \in f$, that $s \leq t$, and that $\forall u(t \leq u \rightarrow \neg u \in f)$. Since f is open, it follows from the first two suppositions that $t \in f$. If we use 't' to instantiate the variable 'u' in the third supposition, however, we obtain $\neg t \in f$. The resulting contradiction means that $s \in f$ intuitionistically entails $\forall t(s \leq t \rightarrow \neg \forall u (t \leq u \rightarrow \neg u \in f))$, that is, $s \in f^{\perp\perp}$. These two lemmas together intuitionistically entail that $f^\perp = f^{\perp\perp\perp}$. Given the explanation of negation whereby $f_{\neg A} = f_A^\perp$, we shall have, then, that $f_A^\perp = f_A^{\perp\perp\perp} = f_{\neg\neg A}^\perp$ and hence that ass (A) = ass $(\neg\neg A)$. Given the present definition of consequence, then, we shall have $\neg\neg A \models A$ even with intuitionistic logic as the metalogic. Where $\vdash_I$ signifies intuitionistic deducibility, however, we certainly do not have $\neg\neg A \vdash_I A$. Hence, intuitionistic logic does not cohere with the present definition of consequence.

It is, moreover, hard to envisage any alternative falsificationist specification of the meaning of the negation operator, or any alternative falsificationist definition of consequence, which will possess the slightest intuitive plausibility and which will combine to generate the characteristically intuitionistic pattern whereby $A \models \neg\neg A$ is sound while $\neg\neg A \models A$ is in general unsound. (Recall that Dummett's own falsificationist definition of consequence in "What is a Theory of Meaning? (II)" invalidated the first inference while validating the second.) That is to say, it is hard to see how Dummett's Thesis α could be parlayed into a definition of consequence with which intuitionistic logic might cohere.

Since he is attached to intuitionistic logic, as well as to Thesis α, the apparent impossibility of constructing such a definition presents a problem for the overall coherence of Dummett's position. For those of us who accept classical logic, however, the results of sections VII and VIII offer the prospect of anti-realism without the tears of an unfamiliar logic. The semantic theory that has been constructed on the basis of Thesis α is recognizably anti-realist. It makes no assumption of bivalence: indeed, it does not invoke the notion of truth. *A fortiori*, it does not try to fix expressions' senses by specifying how they contribute to the truth conditions of statements which contain them. Rather, it specifies the senses of the sentential connectives in the general manner that Dummett himself recommends for intuitionistic logic—namely, by reference to a model (admittedly idealized) of the possible ways in which human knowledge might grow. It differs from intuitionistic semantics chiefly in according pride of place to Dummett's own Thesis α. As we have seen, however, that thesis combines with perfectly intuitive clauses for the connectives to generate a family of valuation systems that is characteristic for classical logic. To those of Dummett's readers who have been impressed by the power of his criticisms of classical semantics, but who cannot stomach the loss of classical logic, this outcome may be attractive. It shows how anti-realism might yield, not an alternative to classical logic, but an alternative rationale for it. We now have two radically different reasons for accepting classical propositional logic: first, that its laws preserve verification-transcendent truth; second, that they preserve safe assertibility in every appropriately structured space of states of information. "The last temptation is the greatest treason: To do the right deed for the wrong reason." For a classical logician, the deep question raised by Dummett's attack on the realist model of meaning is which (if either) of these reasons for accepting classical logic is the right one.[68]

IAN RUMFITT

UNIVERSITY COLLEGE
OXFORD
JUNE 2002

NOTES

1. Michael Dummett, *Truth and Other Enigmas* (London: Duckworth, 1978), xix.

2. Like Dummett, I think that logical systems are best formalized as systems of natural deduction or as sequent calculi. (For Dummett's views on this matter, see, for example, *Frege: Philosophy of Language*, 2nd ed. [London: Duckworth, 1981], 434–35.) So when I write of logical "laws" or "rules," I mean to refer to the rules of such systems. A schema such as the law of excluded middle may be regarded as a rule of inference having a null set of premises.

3. Ian Rumfitt, "'Yes' and 'No'," *Mind* 109 (2000): 781–823.

4. Dummett, "'Yes', 'No', and 'Can't Say'," *Mind* 111 (2002): 289–95. See also Rumfitt, "Unilateralism Disarmed: A Reply to Dummett and Gibbard," *Mind* 111 (2002): 305–21.

5. There is also much to be said about how the arguments I gave in "'Yes' and 'No'" relate to the semantical theory that I am about to develop here. But that, too, must await another occasion.

6. Dummett, "The Justification of Deduction" (London: The British Academy, 1973). My page references will be to the reprinting of this lecture in *Truth and Other Enigmas*, 290–318, where the passage just quoted appears on pp. 291–92.

7. Ibid., 295. I take the terminology of "rule-circularity" from Paul Boghossian, "Knowledge of Logic," in *New Essays on the A Priori*, ed. Paul Boghossian and Christopher Peacocke (Oxford: Clarendon Press, 2000), 229–54 at 231.

8. "The Justification of Deduction," 295–96.

9. Ibid., 299.

10. Ibid., 299–300.

11. For these two senses of "statement," see P. F. Strawson, "Truth," *Proceedings of the Aristotelian Society*, supplementary vol. 24 (1950): 129–56, at 129: "'My statement' may be either what I say or my saying it. My saying something is . . . an episode. What I say is not."

12. Dummett does make it clear, however, that his use of the term is intended to help overcome the problems that the phenomenon of context-dependence creates for the formulation of semantical principles. See e.g., Dummett, "What is a Theory of Meaning? (II)" in *Truth and Meaning: Essays in Semantics*, ed. Gareth Evans and John McDowell (Oxford: Clarendon Press, 1976), 67–137 at 67, n.*. Since this paper is rather long, when citing it I shall also give page references to its reprinting in Dummett, *The Seas of Language* (Oxford: Clarendon Press, 1993), 34–93, where the relevant footnote appears on 34. [Hereafter, cited as *TSOL*.]

13. Dummett, *The Interpretation of Frege's Philosophy* (London: Duckworth, 1981), 436.

14. Dummett, "The Justification of Deduction," 296.

15. Ibid.

16. Dummett, "What is a Theory of Meaning? (II)," 119 (*TSOL*, 78).

17. Dummett, "The Source of the Concept of Truth" in *Meaning and Method: Essays in Honour of Hilary Putnam*, ed. George Boolos (Cambridge: Cambridge Univ. Press, 1990), 1–15 at 15; reprinted in Dummett, *TSOL*, 188–201, at 200.

18. I take this useful encapsulation of this element in Dummett's thinking from McDowell. See John McDowell, "Truth Conditions, Bivalence and Verificationism," in *Truth and Meaning*, ed. Evans and McDowell, 42–66, at 47–48.

19. Equally, it is hard to see how a speaker could so much as form the idea of statement A's not being true in a case where there was evidence that p. No doubt this is part of the reason why Dummett formulates his verificationism in terms of *conclusive* evidence.

20. For the notion of a canonical warrant for an assertion, see e.g., Dummett, *The Logical Basis of Metaphysics* (London: Duckworth, 1991), 177–78.

21. *The Logical Basis of Metaphysics*, 219, emphasis in the original.

22. I do not think that it has any revisionary consequences for first-order predicate logic either, but for ease of exposition I shall in what follows restrict attention to propositional logic. Substantial as this restriction is, it does not deprive my conclusion of interest, for Dummett himself certainly supposes that his semantical considerations have revisionary consequences even within propositional logic. In particular, he supposes that they demand revision in the classical rules for the negation operator.

23. Hartry Field, "Logic, Meaning, and Conceptual Role," *The Journal of Philosophy* 74 (1977): 379–409. Field acknowledges (380) the impetus provided by appendices IV and V of Popper's *The Logic of Scientific Discovery* (London: Routledge and Kegan Paul, 1959).

24. This marks an important difference between my goal and Field's. He also aims to disprove Dummett's suggestion "that, unless one believes that sense can be made of the notion of [verification-transcendent] truth, one should not accept the laws of classical logic" (Field, "Logic, Meaning, and Conceptual Role," 379). He does this by constructing "a semantics in terms of a purely epistemic notion, viz., subjective probability" and showing "that, with respect to such a probabilistic semantics, classical logic is both sound and complete" (ibid.). But he does not try to show that his semantic axioms concerning subjective probabilities would be acceptable to a Dummettian anti-realist.

25. Dummett, "The Justification of Deduction," 318.

26. This is a further point of contrast with Field. He gets his propositional logic to be classical only by assuming the transparently classical postulate that $\text{Prob}\,(\neg B \mid A) = 1 - \text{Prob}\,(B \mid A)$ (Field, "Logic, Meaning, and Conceptual Role," 382). (Here, $\text{Prob}\,(B \mid A)$ is the conditional probability of B, given A.)

27. See especially Dummett, *Frege: Philosophy of Language*, 2nd ed., 413–17, and *The Origins of Analytic Philosophy* (London: Duckworth, 1993), 11–13.

28. "What is a Theory of Meaning? (II)," 124 (*The Seas of Language*, 82).

29. Dummett, "Truth," *Proceedings of the Aristotelian Society* 59 (1959): 141–62; page reference will be to the reprinting in *Truth and Other Enigmas*, 1–19, where the example appears on 16.

30. Ibid., 9.

31. Postscript to "Truth," *Truth and Other Enigmas*, 19–24, at 23.

32. In "Truth," Dummett seeks to buttress this conclusion with an argument about conditionals. The case of conditionals, he observes in the Postscript, "shows so clearly why . . . [a characterization of an assertion's content in terms of what it excludes] is better [than one in terms of what would establish it as correct]" (22).

Anybody who has taught logic to beginners will appreciate why Dummett chooses this example. It is much easier to get tyros to agree that a conditional statement with a true antecedent and a false consequent is false than it is to settle on when such a statement is true, or on the conditions in which it may be correctly affirmed. It is far from obvious, however, that considerations of this kind add much to the case for explicating content in terms of recognizable falsifiers. For, in the first place, it is not clear that a speaker who affirms a conditional statement is asserting a content outright. Notwithstanding Dummett's arguments to the contrary, some would hold that a speaker who affirms a conditional *conditionally* asserts the content of the consequent—the condition for his doing so being the truth of the antecedent.

On this view, the analysis of conditional statements can tell us nothing directly about the contents of straightforwardly assertoric statements. (For a critical analysis of Dummett's arguments against this view, see especially Dorothy Edgington, "On Conditionals," *Mind* 104 [1994]: 235–329, at 289–91.) In the second place, the general claim that an assertion's content is to be explained by reference to recognizable falsifiers needs to be grounded in a general analysis of the act of asserting. Even if conditionals are straightforwardly assertoric, why should we assume that a theory which works well for them will work equally well across the board?

33. For the role this notion plays in Dummett's account of intuitionism, see especially *Elements of Intuitionism*, 2nd ed. (Oxford: Clarendon Press, 2000), 132ff.

34. For the role this notion plays in Dummett's preferred semantics for intuitionistic logic see *Elements of Intuitionism*, 2nd ed., 139 and 277ff, where the canonical/ noncanonical distinction appears as the distinction "between the *verification* of an atomic statement in a given state of information, and its being *assertible*" (139).

35. "What is a Theory of Meaning? (II)," 126 (*TSOL*, 84).

36. For this example, and for very helpful discussion of the issues treated in this paragraph, I am indebted to conversation and correspondence with David Charles.

37. "Truth," 16–17.

38. This consequence is stressed by McDowell, who notes that Dummett's position "implies not that the principle of bivalence is false but, at most, that it is not known to be true" ("Truth-conditions, Bivalence, and Verificationism," 59.)

39. "Truth," 8.

40. Ibid., 12.

41. Ibid., 10–11.

42. I take principle ε from the Postscript to "Truth" (23–24), where it replaces an unsatisfactory formula adopted in the main text—namely, that if a statement is true, "it must be true in virtue of the sort of fact we have been taught to regard as justifying us in asserting it" (16). I agree that the original formula is unsatisfactory. There is no good reason to confine our modes of justification to those we have been taught, as opposed to those we have invented for ourselves, for example. I do not see, however, that principle ε is strictly weaker than its predecessor, as Dummett claims ("Postscript," 23). Consider the statement (made now) 'There was an odd number of geese on the Capitol at the moment of Julius Caesar's death.' Assuming that nobody present thought to count them at the time, and that traveling back in time is impossible in principle, the statement is, now, in principle incapable of being known to be true, and so by principle ε cannot be true. All the same, it may be said to be true in virtue of the *sort* of fact we have been taught to regard as justifying us in asserting it—namely (let us suppose) that there were precisely seventeen geese there then. Somebody who thinks that we do know that such a statement is either true or false, even when we cannot know which it is, may wish to exploit the point that it can be true, or false, in virtue of a fact which belongs to a *sort*, many of whose instances are knowable, even if (as a result of historical contingencies) the particular instance relevant to the statement is not knowable. See John McDowell, "On 'The Reality of the Past'," in *Action and Interpretation: Studies in the Philosophy of the Social Sciences*, ed. Christopher Hookway and Philip Pettit (Cambridge: Cambridge Univ. Press, 1978), 127–44, esp. §9.

43. Dummett holds that "we are entitled to say that a statement P must be either true or false . . . only . . . when P is an effectively decidable statement" ("Truth," 16–17). On my reconstruction of Dummett's argument concerning 'A city will never be built here,' we shall be entitled to say that a statement must be either true or false only when we know that either we can recognize it to be true or we can recognize it to be false. The reconstruction suggests, then, a gloss on Dummett's use of the term "effectively decidable" whereby it applies to a statement if and only if we can know that either we can recognize it to be true or we can recognize it to be false. Sanford Shieh has argued for this gloss on more general grounds in his "Undecidability in Anti-Realism," *Philosophia Mathematica* 6 (1998): 324–33.

44. "What is a Theory of Meaning? (II)," 126 (*TSOL*, 83–84). I have altered Dummett's notation; he writes '$\overline{f}$' where I write '$f^{\perp}$'. For the reasons for this change, see n. 50 below.

45. Dummett, *Elements of Intuitionism*, 2nd ed., 132.

46. Dummett himself uses the same notation, but in the opposite sense. "That the state of information represented by a may subsequently be improved upon by achieving the state represented by a point b," he explains, "is represented by the fact that $b \leq a$" (ibid.). I prefer, however, to align the direction of the $\leq$-relation with that of the passage of time.

47. Ibid.

48. More rigorously, suppose that $s \leq t$ and that $t \leq u$. Since conditions (i) and (ii) in the definition of the $\leq$-relation are clearly transitive, we immediately have (i) $s \subseteq u$ and (ii) if s is a subject's state of knowledge at one time, then u may be his state of knowledge at some future time. For (iii), we are given that for all P in $t \setminus s$, $\neg K_s \neg P$, and for all Q in $u \setminus t$, $\neg K_t \neg Q$; we need to show that for all R in $u \setminus s$, $\neg K_s \neg R$. (Here '$K_s P$' is to be read 'A thinker in state of information s is in a position to know that P.') Suppose for a contradiction that for some R in $u \setminus s$, $K_s \neg R$. Call such an R, 'R_0'. Then $R_0 \in u$ but $R_0 \notin s$. Since $K_s \neg R_0$ and $\neg K_s \neg P$ for all P in $t \setminus s$, we have that $R_0 \notin t \setminus s$, so that either $R_0 \notin t$ or $R_0 \in s$. Since $R_0 \notin s$ we must have $R_0 \notin t$. So $R_0 \in u \setminus t$, whence $\neg K_t \neg R_0$. But $K_s \neg R_0$ and since $s \subseteq t$, $K_t \neg R_0$. This contradiction shows that for all R in $u \setminus s$, $\neg K_s \neg R$, as required.

49. In this paragraph, I am indebted to discussions with John Campbell and Wolfgang Künne.

50. This is why I substituted my notation '$f^{\perp}$' for Dummett's '$\overline{f}$' (see n. 44 above). Topologists will read the symbol '$\overline{f}$' as referring to the closure of f; $f^{\perp}$, by contrast, is the complement of f's closure. I take the '$\perp$' symbol, which may be read as amalgamating the overscore of topological closure with the $'$ of set-theoretic complementation, from Halmos: see Paul R. Halmos, *Lectures on Boolean Algebras* (Princeton, NJ: Van Nostrand, 1963), 13.

51. In geometric terms, an open set is regular open if there are no cracks in it.

52. For these definitions, see e.g., Dummett, *Elements of Intuitionism*, 2nd ed., 133.

53. See ibid., 213–14.

54. Ludwig Wittgenstein, *Tractatus Logico-Philosophicus* (London: Routledge and Kegan Paul, 1922), 6.11. See also 6.121: "The propositions of logic demonstrate the logical properties of propositions by combining them so as to form

propositions that say nothing."

55. Dummett's own example: see *The Logical Basis of Metaphysics*, 267.

56. A theorist ambitious to construct a verificationist semantics is not obliged to follow the intuitionistic model, and Dummett has toyed with an alternative whereby '*A* or *B*' is verifiable when the verifiability of 'not *A*' suffices for that of *B*, and the verifiability of 'not *B*' suffices for that of *A*. (See Dummett "The Source of the Concept of Truth," 7). There is, however, a problem for this proposal. As Dummett says, it "in effect equates '*A* or *B*' with 'If not *A*, then *B*, and, if not *B*, then *A*', understood intuitionistically, a rendering of course weaker than the ordinary intuitionistic interpretation of '*A* or *B*'" (ibid.). Weaker it certainly is. The fact that we can transform any refutation of *A* into a proof of *B* and transform any refutation of *B* into a proof of *A* in no way implies that we can get either a proof of *A* or a proof of *B*. Just for this reason, however, the interpretation proposed for 'or' fails to validate the rule of 'or-elimination—that is, the rule of "proof by cases" —even in its form without side premises. That form of the rule says that where a conclusion is deducible from each of two sentences taken as assumptions, it is deducible from their disjunction. So if the present interpretation of 'or' is to validate the rule, we must have $(\neg A \to B) \wedge (\neg B \to A) \vdash C$ whenever $A \vdash C$ and $B \vdash C$. (Here $X \vdash A$ signifies that A is intuitionistically deducible from the set X.) However, while $A \vdash A \vee B$ and $B \vdash A \vee B$, we have just seen that not $(\neg A \to B) \wedge (\neg B \to A) \vdash A \vee B$. Since arguing by cases is an important element in our ordinary use of disjunctive sentences, this result will count heavily against any claim that Dummett's explanation might have to capture the ordinary sense of 'or'.

57. In this paragraph, I am grateful for discussion with Timothy Williamson.

58. *The Logical Basis of Metaphysics*, 211.

59. Some readers may still balk at calling 'The number of stars is both even and odd' safely assertible, so it is worth noting that we may avoid this consequence by slightly adjusting the semantic theory. In order to make it as palatable as possible to an anti-realist, I have taken the key notions of that theory (notably, the concept of a state of information) from Dummett's semantics for intuitionism. But the original discussion in "Truth" suggests a subtly different approach. There, Dummett says that a statement excludes a *possible state of affairs* if the statement's assertion would "be taken as expressing the speaker's exclusion of that possibility": falsification may then be taken as the converse relation between a state of affairs and a statement. For any possible state of affairs *s*, we may require it to be decidable (in principle) whether *s* obtains. It makes sense to speak of one possible state of affairs' including another: a city's having been built within ten years includes its having been built within twenty. This relation of inclusion will be a partial order, and the set of falsifiers of any statement will be open with respect to it: if *s* falsifies a statement then so does any possible state of affairs that includes *s*. As above, we may explain preclusion in terms of the partial order: *s* precludes the obtaining of any state of affairs in *f* if no possible state of affairs in *f* includes *s*. This time, though, 'ass (*A*)' plausibly means '*A* is true' rather than just '*A* is safely assertible': if *s* actually obtains and precludes the obtaining of any possible falsifier of *A*, then *s* renders *A* true. My revised condition for consequence then ensures preservation of truth. Dummett's premise (γ), and his argument for *tertium non datur*, still fail: *A*'s not having been falsified does not entail

that some state of affairs obtains that precludes its being falsified. But his counter-example to bivalence is powerful: there is no guarantee that either a state of affairs will obtain which renders 'A city will never be built here' true, or that one will obtain which renders that statement false. (The quantifier in the definition of 'ass (A)' means that truth need not be decidable even if the obtaining of any given state of affairs is.) At any rate we avoid entirely the problem over 'and'. Suppose that N is the actual number of stars, so that s, the state of affairs of there being N stars, actually obtains. If N is odd, then s falsifies statement E, and if N is even, s falsifies statement O. Since N is either odd or even, s will belong either to f_E or to f_O, so that s belongs to $f_O \cup f_E$, which is $f_{O \wedge E}$. So, on the revised approach, '$O \wedge E$' comes out falsified after all.

60. For example, take X to be the open left half-plane and Y to be the open right half-plane. X and Y are both regular open, but the interior of the closure of $X \cup Y$ is the interior of the whole plane, which is the whole plane; this strictly includes $X \cup Y$. As we have noted, a regular open set may be visualized as an open set with no cracks in it. But there may be two regular open sets with a crack between them.

61. See Theorem B of Alfred Tarski, "Les fondements de la géometrie des corps," in the supplement to *Annales de la Société Polonaise de Mathématique* (Krakow, 1929), 29–33; translated by J. H. Woodger as "Foundations of the Geometry of Solids" in Alfred Tarski, *Logic, Semantics, Metamathematics* (Oxford: Clarendon Press, 1956), 24–29 at 29.

62. For a proof of this theorem, see now J. M. Dunn and G. M. Hardegree, *Algebraic Methods in Philosophical Logic* (Oxford: Clarendon Press, 2001), §9.2.

63. See the remarks at the end of §4 of Tarski, "Der Aussagenkalkül und die Topologie," *Fundamenta Mathematicae* 31 (1938): 103–34; translated as "Sentential Calculus and Topology" in *Logic, Semantics, Metamathematics*, 421–54, esp. 448–49.

64. See again *Logic, Semantics, Metamathematics*, 448–49.

65. Dummett, *Elements of Intuitionism*, 2nd ed., 120–21.

66. For a good exposition, though, see Dunn and Hardegree, *Algebraic Methods in Philosophical Logic*, §5.4.

67. See again the passages quoted from "The Justification of Deduction" in section I.

68. This essay originated in a seminar I gave in the Fall Term of 1995, in the course of which I undertook to explain the argument of Dummett's "Truth" to a group of talented and receptive graduate students at the University of Michigan at Ann Arbor who had, all the same, been baffled by it. Two of my then colleagues, Mark Crimmins and Stephen Everson, were kind enough to attend the seminar, and the genesis of the essay owes much to their acute requests for further explanations.

In addition to the particular debts recorded in the footnotes, I should like to thank Jonathan Barnes, Wolfgang Künne, Christopher Peacocke, James Walmsley, and David Wiggins for their comments on complete drafts, and the Leverhulme Trust for its financial support during the composition of the final version. I have presented parts of the paper on many occasions, including a meeting of the Tuesday Group at Oxford held in February 1999, which marked the fortieth anniversary of the original publication of "Truth." I am particularly grateful for the comments and encouragement on that occasion of Sir Michael Dummett himself.

REPLY TO IAN RUMFITT

I have much enjoyed reading Ian Rumfitt's well-reasoned essay. I was, naturally, overwhelmed by the first two paragraphs. Since I have spent a large proportion of my professional career in teaching, I am delighted by the comments of someone who thought I did it well. The substance of the essay is as perceptive and well thought out as I should have expected from its author.

I am particularly grateful to Ian Rumfitt for taking seriously the strong falsificationist strain in my article "Truth," as scarcely anyone else has done. It is a line of thought I subsequently neglected, and I am very glad that Rumfitt has developed it much further than I ever did.

His first disagreement with me is over the argument that we can assert the principle of *tertium non datur*—the principle that no statement can be neither true nor false. Its interest for him lies in the possibility of classically deriving from it the principle of bivalence, that every statement is either true or false; if I am right that we cannot assert the principle of bivalence, but that we can assert that of *tertium non datur*, classical logic must be erroneous. Rumfitt allows that my (tacit) derivation of *tertium non datur*, which he reconstructs, is (intuitionistically) correct, but challenges the thesis concerning truth that forms one of the premises of that derivation. This premiss he formalises as the formula (γ):

$$\forall x \, [Sx \rightarrow (\forall y \, (Oy \rightarrow Cyx) \rightarrow Tx)],$$

where 'Sx' means 'x is a statement', 'Tx' means 'x is true', 'Oy' means 'y is a state of affairs that actually obtains' and 'Cyx' means 'the state of affairs y is consistent with the statement x'. (γ) encapsulates the thesis which Rumfitt quotes me as propounding in "Truth," that if all actual states of affairs are consistent with a statement x, then x is true. Rumfitt rightly objects to this thesis, both as implausible in itself and as incompatible with what I later say in the article about truth. My error had been to think classically: I had understood the quantification 'all actual states of affairs' classically, and had meant it to be understood classically. The thesis that I ought to have propounded may be symbolised by the formula (γ^*):

$$\forall x \, [Sx \rightarrow (\forall y \, (Oy \rightarrow \neg Ryx) \rightarrow Tx)],$$

where (as in Rumfitt's notation) 'Ryx' means 'the state of affairs y falsifies the statement x'. At first glance (γ^*) says essentially the same as (γ); but my intention is that the logical constants in (γ^*) be interpreted intuitionistically. So interpreted, the hypothesis '$\forall y \, (Oy \rightarrow \neg Ryx)$' may be asserted only if we have a general method of deriving, for any y, y's not falsifying the statement x from y's being an actually occurring state of affairs. So understood, (γ^*) is plausible and consonant with my subsequent remarks about truth. It is plausible that, if we know a systematic means of rebutting any claim to falsify x, then x may be safely asserted and is true. From an intuitionistic, that is, a verificationist, standpoint, we might be thought entitled to assert only the double negation of x; but we are here attempting to give a criterion for truth from a falsificationist standpoint, and this seems as plausible a criterion as could be proposed. The subsequently enunciated principle concerning truth cited by Rumfitt from a postscript to "Truth" is that a true statement must be capable of being known to be true; and, if we are in possession of a means of refuting any alleged falsification of x, then we certainly know that, by this criterion, x is true: intuitionistically, we are entitled to assert a universally quantified statement only if we know how to establish any given instance of it.

It will now be possible to set out a revised derivation of *tertium non datur*. We shall no longer need the predicates '$A\xi$' ('ξ is a possible or actual state of affairs') and '$C\xi\eta$'. The premises of the derivation will be formula (γ^*) and formula (β), as formulated by Rumfitt:

$$\forall x \, [Sx \rightarrow (\exists y \, (Oy \wedge Ryx) \rightarrow Fx)],$$

where 'Fx' means 'x is false'; (β) states the obvious fact that if some actual state of affairs falsifies x, then x is false. Lines (1) to (7) of the revised derivation will be as in Rumfitt's derivation. Line (7) will be followed by lines (10) to (15) of Rumfitt's derivation, renumbered as lines (8^*) to (13^*), and then by

14^*. $\forall y \, (Oy \rightarrow \neg Rya)$	13^*, universal generalisation, since 'b' was parametric
15^*. $Sa \rightarrow (\forall y \, (Oy \rightarrow \neg Rya) \rightarrow Ta)$	γ^*, universal instantiation
16^*. $\forall y \, (Oy \rightarrow \neg Rya) \rightarrow Ta$	3, 15^*, $\rightarrow$-elimination
17^*. $\neg\forall y \, (Oy \rightarrow \neg Rya)$	6, 16, contraposition

We now have, in lines 14^* and 17^*, a contradiction, whence we may infer by reductio the desired conclusion (18^*) = (28), the principle *tertium non datur*.

*   *   *

The foregoing is what I wrote as an opening part of a reply to Rumfitt's essay, having read with care its first three sections and only very lightly skimmed the rest. Having now read attentively the whole of Rumfitt's essay, I have decided to allow my initial remarks to stand, rather than revising them to integrate them into a single response. I have the greatest admiration for Rumfitt's development, in his sections IV–VIII, of a falsificationist semantics for sentential logic, and warmly thank him for so elegantly carrying it out. His development takes its starting-point from an abortive attempt of my own to do the same, my report of which he quotes from a footnote to my "What is a Theory of Meaning? (II)." He equates the notion of a recognisable state of affairs that I used there with that of a state of information, which he takes from my *Elements of Intuitionism*. That notion is essential to the semantics for intuitionistic logic provided by Beth trees and by Kripke trees, and Rumfitt gives a perspicuous explanation of it. He defines on such states the standard partial ordering $\leq$: if s and t are states of information, $s \leq t$ if s is capable of being succeeded, at once or later, by the expanded state of information t (it is of course a matter of taste if we so define $\leq$ or $\geq$). This partial ordering enables Rumfitt to use the PO-space topology employed in *Elements of Intuitionism*. He borrows from my footnote to WTM(II) the operator $f^{\perp}$, adopting this better notation and giving it a more precise explanation. If f is a set of states of information, $f^{\perp}$ is the set of all those states of information s such that $s \leq t$ for no state of information $t \in f$; in a state of information belonging to $f^{\perp}$, the possibility of being in a state of information belonging to f is forever foreclosed. $f^{\perp\perp}$ is then the set of states of information which, in intuitionist terminology, are barred by f, that is, which are such that they may always be extended to a state of information in f. I was pleased to see that in his section VI Rumfitt agrees with my clauses for the falsification-conditions of complex statements formed by means of the sentential operators, as given in the footnote to WTM(II). Where f_A is the set of states of information in which the statement A is falsified, $f_A^{\perp}$ is the set of states of information in which A is secure from ever being falsified. Then:

$$f_{A \wedge B} = f_A \cup f_B, \ f_{A \vee B} = f_A \cap f_B, \ f_{A \to B} = f_A^{\perp} \cap f_B \text{ and } f_{\neg A} = f_A^{\perp}.$$

However, in his section V Rumfitt rejects my tentative characterisation of logical consequence in favour of an emended one. I fully accept his emendation, which allows him to construct so convincing a falsificationist semantics. Without doubt it was my faulty notion of the falsificationist relation of logical consequence that led to my becoming discouraged about the whole enterprise, and so abandoning the falsificationist line of thought that I had argued for in "Truth" and ought thereafter to have pursued.

In the preliminary part of this reply, I used the concept of its being safe to assert a given statement, namely when we have the means to rule out the possibility of its being falsified. I had not then spotted, and hence was unaware, that this concept would play a salient role in Rumfitt's falsificationist semantics. He explains the statement A as being safely assertible in the state of information s if $s \in f_A{}^{\perp}$, the set of states of information that cannot be expanded to one in which A is falsified; he therefore defines the set ass (A), the set of states of information in which A is safely assertible, as $f_A{}^{\perp}$. In my preliminary comments to this reply, I proposed safe assertibility as a plausible notion of truth in a falsificationist setting. My article "Truth" opposed the conception that truth and falsity have equal rights in explanations of meaning; but failed to determine whether truth or falsity should be the primary notion. If we take falsity as the primary notion, we shall still want a notion of truth; safe assertibility seems to me the best notion of truth that can be attained within a falsificationist theory of meaning.

It is of interest to formulate Rumfitt's clauses for the safe assertibility of sententially complex statements in this terminology, writing 'A is true in s' for '$s \in$ ass(A)' and 'A is false in s' for '$s \in f_A$'. If $s \in f^{\perp}$, then, however s may be expanded, the possibility of expanding it still further (if necessary) to a state of information in f will always obtain—s is barred by f: we may therefore say that in s we may always come to f, meaning thereby that a state of information in f will always remain a possibility. If $f =$ ass (A), we shall say that in s A always may come true, and if $f = f_A$, that in s A always may turn out false. Using this terminology, and using Rumfitt's Lemma 9 for the conditional, we have:

$A \wedge B$ is true in s iff A is true in s and B is true in s

$A \vee B$ is true in s iff in s it may always be that either A comes true or B comes true

$A \rightarrow B$ is true in s iff in s it may always be that either A does not come true or B comes true

$\neg A$ is true in s iff A may always turn out false

It should also be noted that Rumfitt's criterion for B to be a logical consequence of $A_1, \ldots, A_n$ is that, for every s, B is true in s if every A_i is true in s.

It is of interest to consider what, under this semantic theory, is the condition for the safe assertibility of a statement of the form $A \vee \neg A$. By the falsification-condition for disjunction, $f_{A \lor \neg A} = f_A \cap f_{\neg A}$. But $f_{\neg A} = $ ass (A) $= f_A \perp$, so that $f_A \cap f_{\neg A} = \emptyset$; hence ass $(A \lor \neg A)$ comprises all possible states of information. Thus, whatever our state of information, $A \lor \neg A$ is true in it. This is not because A is of necessity either true or false, but because nothing can falsify both it and its negation, in other words, because *tertium non datur* holds.

It is not in the least surprising that a falsificationist semantics should yield classical logic, as Rumfitt demonstrates that it does. Intuitionistically, A and $\neg\neg A$ have the same negation, namely $\neg A$; in fact, $\neg\neg A$, understood intuitionistically, says essentially that A is safely assertible, that is, can never be falsified, which is as close as we can get from a falsificationist standpoint to A's being true. In Rumfitt's semantics, the falsification-condition for $\neg\neg A$ is closely allied to that for A: $f_{\neg\neg A} = f_A \perp\!\!\perp$. By his Lemma 8, ass $(A) = $ ass $(\neg\neg A)$, so that a statement is true in any state of information if and only if its double negation is.

I congratulate Ian Rumfitt on his masterly and convincing construction of a falsificationist semantics, which it remains to extend to one for full first-order logic. I agree with Rumfitt that the intuitionistic interpretation of disjunction is unsatisfactory in empirical contexts, and wish I knew how to give a better one for an empirically applicable justificationist semantics; I believe that it would still sustain intuitionistic logic. I think that Rumfitt's falsificationist semantics, which is constructed from an anti-realist standpoint, should be considered seriously by everyone who is inclined to that standpoint. The question is whether, from that standpoint, we can really attain a stronger conception of truth than safe assertibility, in which case truth rather than falsity should be the primary notion. More starkly expressed, ought we to consider the content of an assertoric utterance to be determined by what shows it to be true or by what shows it to be false? On this question it hangs whether anti-realism demands a justificationist or falsificationist semantics, and hence whether it supports intuitionistic or classical logic. I leave Rumfitt's readers and mine to ponder the question.

M. D.

20

Marco Santambrogio

BELIEF AND DEDUCTIVE INFERENCE

Deductive inference raises a problem for any theory of belief and belief ascription. Michael Dummett stated it with unsurpassed clarity:

> The existence of deductive inference is problematic because of the tension between what seems necessary to account for its legitimacy and what seems necessary to account for its usefulness. For it to be legitimate, the process of recognising the premisses as true must already have accomplished whatever is needed for the recognition of the truth of the conclusion; for it to be useful, a recognition of its truth need not actually have been accorded to the conclusion when it was accorded to the premisses. Of course, no definite contradiction stands in the way of satisfying these two requirements: recognising the premisses as true involves a possibility of recognising the conclusion as true, a possibility which will not in all cases be actualised. Yet it is a delicate matter so to describe the connection between premisses and conclusion as to display clearly the way in which both requirements are fulfilled.[1]

That a deductive inference can be useful depends upon (even though it is not quite the same as[2]) that inference's being possibly informative. This in turn amounts to it being possible to believe the premisses without believing the conclusion. Belief is involved also in the notion of legitimate inference: if recognition of the truth of the premisses, which is the same as believing in them, is to suffice for believing the conclusion, then and only then, some *a priori* links must exist between beliefs, which we ought to be able to spell out. The very existence of deductive inference raises, therefore, a problem—or, rather, a pair of symmetrical problems—with which any theory of belief, and more generally of propositional attitudes, must grapple. I shall claim that the beginning of a solution can be found by re-examining the ordinary notion of belief.

Surprisingly, that deductive inferences can be both useful (hence informative) and legitimate seems to go unnoticed most of the time. Let us

consider possible informativeness first. In order to see how easy it is to
ignore it, one has only to be reminded of the attempts made by Carnap and
others in the sixties to measure the information values of the statements of
some artificial languages. In a nutshell, Carnap's intuitive idea was that the
information value of a statement was given by suitably weighting the set of
all state descriptions in which the statement was false. No reference was
made to anyone's *believing* a statement to be true or false. I conjecture that,
by keeping belief completely out of the picture, Carnap thought that the
notion of informativeness could be taken to be entirely objective and freed
from the subjective vagaries of belief. As an immediate consequence of that
intuitive idea, logically and mathematically true statements turned out to be
utterly uninformative, and any statement whatever was as informative as
any other statement logically equivalent to it. Carnap did not demur at that
consequence, for he took himself to be explicating only what he termed
"empirical" informativeness. (He never went so far as to claim that logic
and mathematics are uninformative *simpliciter.*) Unfortunately, as far as I
know, he never offered any satisfactory account of what empirical
informativeness amounts to and how it differs from the nonempirical
variety. In the absence of such clarification, the functions he offered,
allegedly measuring information, were just that: ways of weighting, for
every statement in the language, the set of all state descriptions in which it
was false. Obviously, whether or not this amounts to denying that deduction
can be informative, no solution to our problem, as set out by Dummett, is
likely to be found in Carnap's theory.

It can be supposed that it was the divorce between informativeness and
belief that was responsible for the dim view Carnap took of the informativeness of deduction. Surprisingly, however, not much progress has been
achieved by tightly securing informativeness to belief, as we now tend to
do. Much the same problems Carnap had with the informativeness of
deduction are still there for us to solve as we fumble at directly accounting
for belief in logical truths and for the inferential links that hold between
beliefs. Let us see how contemporary theories fare in this respect. Most of
the theories of belief ascription now available fall into one or the other of
two large classes, diametrically opposite on the issue of deductive inference.

On the one hand, we have those theories which base their account of the
proper objects of belief and other propositional attitudes, namely propositions, on the apparatus of state descriptions and possible worlds. The
resulting notion of proposition is of the nonstructured kind, in the sense that
a number of structurally dissimilar statements can express the same
proposition, and accordingly, the structure of the proposition itself (if it has
one) bears no resemblance to the structures of the statements that express
it. From the assumption that believing that *p* amounts to being in some

relation with the proposition expressed by p, it follows that anyone who believes that p also believes that q, for any q equivalent (in the sense of expressing the same proposition) to p.[3] In most theories in this class, logically equivalent statements, being true in the same worlds, express the same proposition. Together with the entirely natural assumption that belief distributes over conjunction—that is, that the following rules are truth preserving:

$(B\&\text{-}elim)$ $\quad \dfrac{S \text{ believes that } p \text{ and } q}{S \text{ believes that } p} \quad , \quad \dfrac{S \text{ believes that } p \text{ and } q}{S \text{ believes that } q}$

—this entails logical omniscience, in other words, the thesis that anyone entertaining a belief also believes all its logical consequences. In order to see this, let a subject S believe that p, and let q be any statement validly following from p; p is then equivalent to p and q. It follows that S believes that p and q, and (by $B\&\text{-}elim$) that S believes that q, that is, that S is logically omniscient.[4] Thus, according to the theories in the first class, which are based on nonstructured propositions, a great many inferences involving belief turn out to be truth preserving on logical grounds alone. In particular, holding as they do that no one can believe the premises of a deductive inference without thereby also believing its conclusion, these theories flatly deny that deductive inference could ever be informative. The notion of informativeness referred to here, unlike the Carnapian notion, involves belief essentially.

More than one way has been suggested of reconciling such theories with the fact that people do not believe all the logical consequences of their beliefs. For example, one might either take these theories to involve some kind of idealization of the believers or take the notion of belief they model in some special technical sense.[5] Attempts have also been made at fine-graining the notion of proposition (while leaving it unstructured) in such a way that logically equivalent sentences no longer say the same thing or express the same proposition. All of these strategies have been confronted with powerful objections, and I shall not dwell on them.

Having witnessed the difficulties that confront the theories of belief ascription in the first class, those in the second class overreact and go to the other extreme of taking deductive inference to be so informative as to make one seriously doubt that it can ever be legitimate. Their starting point is a different view of propositions: they take propositions as mirroring in their structures the structures of the statements that express them, while still maintaining that propositions are the proper objects of belief and other attitudes. Russellian theories, resorting to singular Russellian propositions, belong in this class, as well as those theories which build on the Carnapian notion of structured intension. As to the inferential links between beliefs, these theories take the extreme view that *no* inference of the form

(Bel)

$$\frac{S \text{ believes that } p_1, \ldots, \quad S \text{ believes that } p_n}{S \text{ believes that } q}$$

is truth preserving on logical grounds alone, for p_i and q that differ, however slightly, in structure, since the propositions expressed by p_i and q are different. In itself, this does not yet amount to a criticism of such theories, since one might reply either that these theories are not at all concerned with accounting for the transitions between beliefs or that, in any case, they can be supplemented with further principles. This might very well be true, even though no suggestion as to how to achieve this has emerged so far. Once content is so finely individuated that no two statements that differ in structure can express the same content, it is no easy matter to find an a priori basis on which any belief state (which, of course, is partly individuated by its content) follows from other belief states. It is, however, an objection to such theories that it surely is possible to recognize the First Law of Thermodynamics or the Axiom of Choice as being true, in other words, to believe them. From the assumption that propositions are the proper objects of belief it follows that each of these must be some proposition or other. But which one? There are infinitely many structurally different but logically equivalent sentences, none of which has any special right to be singled out as being *the* proper formulation of either the First Law of Thermodynamics or the Axiom of Choice. Correspondingly, there are infinitely many distinct propositions, according to the theories of structured propositions, none of which can be taken to be either *the* First Law or *the* Axiom of Choice. Furthermore, some positive reason will emerge later for doubting that any theory of structured propositions could ever be supplemented with principles accounting for a priori transitions between beliefs.

Surely, blocking all inferences from premises of the form 'S believes that p' is an overreaction to the difficulty raised for the theories in the first class—unstructured propositions—by logical omniscience. *Some* inferential links between beliefs seem to hold a priori. The rule (*B&-elim*) above is a case in point. Clearly, there is some intuitive difference between it and a rule such as the following:

(*B&-intr*)

$$\frac{S \text{ believes that } p \quad , \quad S \text{ believes that } q}{S \text{ believes that } p \text{ and } q}$$

which is definitely *not* truth preserving. Any satisfactory theory of belief ascription ought to account for this difference somehow.

Let us go back to our original problem, which was to explain how deduction could be both informative and legitimate at the same time. Any theory of belief ascription that is unable to account for transitions between belief states is vulnerable to a peculiar form of skepticism. To claim that *no* deductive inference is *ever* legitimate, so that one is perfectly free to reject its conclusion even after accepting its premises, is a form of skepticism, an answer to which must consist in some general account of transitions, a priori and otherwise, between beliefs. The Tortoise, in Lewis Carroll's famous paper "What the Tortoise said to Achilles," is precisely such a skeptic.

> "That beautiful First Proposition of Euclid!" the Tortoise murmured dreamily.
> "You admire Euclid?"
> "Passionately! So far, at least, as one *can* admire a treatise that won't be published for some centuries to come!"
> "Well, now, let's take a little bit of the argument in that First Proposition—just *two* steps, and the conclusion drawn from them. Kindly enter them in your notebook. And in order to refer to them conveniently, let's call them A, B, and Z:
>
> (A) Things that are equal to the same are equal to each other.
> (B) The two sides of this Triangle are things that are equal to the same.
> (Z) The two sides of this Triangle are equal to each other.
>
> Readers of Euclid will grant, I suppose, that Z follows logically from A and B, so that any one who accepts A and B as true, *must* accept Z as true?"
> "Undoubtedly! ....
> ....
> "Well, now, I want you to . . . force me, logically, to accept Z as true."[6]

The Tortoise claims (or pretends) that it cannot believe a proposition that is the conclusion of an application of *modus ponens* to a pair of propositions, both of which are believed by it—as it is perfectly willing to admit.[7] It challenges Achilles to force it to accept the conclusion. Were Achilles to succeed, he could even convince the Tortoise of the validity of *modus ponens* in general. But it would be hopeless to appeal to *modus ponens* in an argument aiming at convincing the Tortoise, who does not accept it, to accept the conclusion of a particular application of it. For instance, were Achilles to argue as follows: the truth table for *if . . . then* shows that if both p and *If p, then q* are true, then q is also true; now you, Tortoise, have already acknowledged that both p and *If p, then q* are true; then q too must be true—he would be taking one step in accord with *modus ponens*. As the Tortoise is not yet convinced to accept *modus ponens*, Achilles would have achieved nothing. Circularity is to be avoided at all cost in an argument aiming at persuading someone.

Now, the theories of belief ascription that take content to consist of structured propositions, unless a way is found of supplementing them with some principles governing transitions between beliefs, would find the Tortoise's refusal to accept the conclusion of an application of *modus ponens* perfectly in order. Surely, the inference

$$(B\supset\text{-}elim) \quad \frac{S \text{ believes that } p \quad , \quad S \text{ believes that } if\, p \text{ then } q}{S \text{ believes that } q}$$

is not truth preserving. The structural difference in the that-clauses involved and *therefore*—this step is what the theories of structured propositions properly contribute—in the propositions expressed, explains well enough why *S* might be unable to proceed from the premises to the conclusion. And it looks as if the same reason could be appealed to by the Tortoise itself in order to account for its own purported inability to take that step. Whether it is a third person or *S* itself, as in the Tortoise's case, reporting about its own inability to accept the conclusion, makes no difference that those theories can take to be significant. But let us now put aside the existing theories of belief ascription, which were brought in only to show how little attention has been given to our original problem so far, and concentrate on the skepticism voiced by the Tortoise.

If the Tortoise was right and Achilles could do nothing to persuade it, no inference would ever be justified. Of course, *modus ponens* is only one among many rules of inference, but no doubt the Tortoise's skepticism could work just as well for all of them, if it works for *modus ponens*. Before answering the Tortoise's challenge, let us get a little clearer about what exactly it is that its skepticism amounts to. Questioning that it is under any obligation to believe that *q*, given that it believes that *p* and also that *If p then q*, the Tortoise is not raising any doubt as to the meaning of the words 'if . . . then . . .'. On the contrary, it says that it firmly believes that *if p then q*. In saying that one believes that *p*, one is not questioning the meaning of the words occurring in '*p*'. Conversely, not grasping the meaning of '*p*' has nothing to do with doubting that *p*. For example, one might doubt that the Italian word "atteggiamento" means the same as the English "attitude"; if so, one does not know what exactly "La credenza è un atteggiamento proposizionale" means. This is not at all the same as doubting that belief is a propositional attitude. An English-speaking philosopher ignorant of Italian might doubt the former thing while feeling perfectly confident that belief *is* a propositional attitude. Conversely, any Italian with a good command of English knows that "La credenza è un atteggiamento proposizionale" means the same as "Belief is a propositional attitude"; however, this will not assuage any doubt he might have concerning the nature of belief.

Now, if we believe the Tortoise, we do not have to explain to it what the words 'if ... then' mean, for its doubts are not about the meaning of the connective. However, it is possible that the Tortoise is confused and thinks it knows what they mean, but really does not. Can we hope then that, by carefully explaining the meaning of the connective, we would stand a better chance of answering the Tortoise's doubts and persuading it that *modus ponens is* truth-preserving and that the conclusion of the inference in point is in fact true? One might hope that, perhaps, a satisfactory theory of meaning in general, together with a full explanation of the meaning of the logical connectives, would leave no doubt as to the validity of the standard rules of inference in which they figure and would thus convince the Tortoise to accept the conclusion of our inference. I am afraid, however, that our hopes of convincing the Tortoise by these means are dim. The problem of knowing how meaning is conferred upon the logical connectives is as difficult as it is profound, but it is only loosely related to the issue at hand.

If the Tortoise's doubts were due to some misunderstanding of the meaning of a connective, the misunderstanding would be either trivial or nontrivial. It would be trivial if the Tortoise had, e.g., mistaken one connective for another—'if...then' for 'or', say—and things could be straightened up by some explanation. But suppose that, after an explanation has been given, the Tortoise still insists that it cannot see that the conclusion of the inference in question is true. The misunderstanding would then be of a nontrivial kind: the Tortoise accepts our explanation, but must be taking it in some odd sense that does not entail the validity of *modus ponens*. What could we do at this point—apart from trying some other explanation, which will be no better than the previous one, unless the misunderstanding was, after all, trivial? (Of course, it is possible that the skeptic's doubts are due to a poor grasp of the meaning of some word other than 'if...then'. Then again our disagreement would be trivial, and it could be settled by resorting to a different vocabulary, *unless* it is the term "belief" itself that is in question. This would be far from trivial. It will be taken up shortly). Suppose then that we *stipulate* the meaning of 'if ... then' as follows: 'if ... then' is that unique connective which makes *modus ponens* (and some other rules) truth preserving.[8] In order to leave no doubt as to what is being stipulated, let us rename the connective as "that-connective-which-makes-*modus-ponens*-(*inter-alia*)-truth-preserving." Would it still be possible for the Tortoise to use the connective so defined without having to recognize that the conclusion of the inference is true? It seems to me that it would. The Tortoise can say: "After your explanation, I no longer doubt that *modus ponens* in general preserves truth. I also accept that if *modus ponens* preserves truth in general then, in this particular application of it, if the premises are true then so is the conclusion. And I also believe that the premises are true. Still, I cannot bring myself to believe that the conclusion is true. Applying *modus ponens* to this particular case is no easier for me than it was before."

There is perhaps another argument the Tortoise could use. Once the meaning of an expression is fixed, a supplementary argument is needed to show that, every time that expression is used, the use is faithful to the meaning as so fixed. For instance, there is a sense in which the name "Dartmouth" *means* "the city that lies at the mouth of the Dart," but it ought not to be taken for granted that it is this description that fixes the referent of the name every time it is used (as a matter of fact, it usually does not). It is a priori possible that the same happens with our connective, that is, with "that-connective-which-makes-*modus-ponens*-(*inter-alia*)-truth-preserving." It must be shown that this is not in fact the case, at least in that particular application of *modus ponens* we happen to be interested in. What needs to be shown is that *modus ponens* is not just *said* by its very name to be truth preserving—as the name "Dartmouth" says that the city so named lies at the mouth of the Dart—but it really *is* truth preserving *in the particular case at hand*. The Tortoise, however, has already refused once to recognize that *modus ponens* takes us from true premises to a true conclusion. It is unlikely that we shall be able to convince it this time.

I conclude that, in itself, a satisfactory theory of how the connectives get their meanings is useless as an instrument to force the skeptic into believing what we want him to believe. The only meaning that has to be clarified here is that of the word "belief" itself.[9]

Let us now examine a little more closely what is involved in an inference's being useful and legitimate, in order fully to grasp the import of the Tortoise's challenge. Given such an inference, what is involved in persuading someone of its validity? Is it like making an appeal to her will to believe, or is it more like forcing her to believe its conclusion? According to a number of philosophers, it is entirely inappropriate to appeal to anyone's will to believe, since belief has nothing to do with the will.[10] And in any case, is it not perfectly obvious that the Tortoise is quite *un*willing to take any appeal of ours into consideration? Thus, it seems that our only hope of answering its challenge must lie in our ability to force it. Unfortunately, there are general reasons for despairing that we shall ever be able to force anyone into believing anything.

It is far from clear that the will really has nothing to do with belief. Surely, no one is able to believe at will whatever he would like to believe. But refusing to believe is not so difficult. To some extent, we can decide to suspend belief and succeed in so doing. Sometimes, even if confronted with strong visual evidence, we can decide not to believe our own eyes and force ourselves to suspend the assent we are inclined to give to what we seem to be seeing. This can happen even in the absence of any clear evidence to the contrary. It is—surely not always, but sometimes—within our power to adopt an attitude of cautiousness or even overcautiousness. I am not just saying that we can refuse to admit that we believe something, even though the evidence for it is overwhelming. I mean that we can have the psychological experience of doubt and disbelief if, by a voluntary decision of ours, we put ourselves in an attitude of cautiousness and, as a consequence of this, undergo an arrest in our spontaneous propensity to believe. For instance, it is entirely within our powers to decide to put all our efforts into detecting the slightest clue against what we are inclined to believe. It is easier to put oneself in this state of mind if the practical consequences of either belief or disbelief are serious. But even the experience of Cartesian doubt can be undergone voluntarily, if we are to believe Descartes himself.

That it is possible to doubt or to suspend belief at will seems to make life more difficult for us, since we can no longer hope to force the Tortoise, or anyone for that matter, into believing what we want it to believe, for it is (almost) always open to anyone to suspend belief and simply refuse to go any further.

Fortunately we do not have to force anyone, as we shall presently see. I now begin sketching an argument to the effect that the Tortoise's skepticism is ungrounded and its challenge is void. The Tortoise—so I want to claim—is only pretending that it does not believe what it cannot help believing, if it understands its own words. The first step in the argument consists in showing that the inference the Tortoise pretends to be unable to draw is not of the form ($B\supset$-$elim$), but has a slightly different form instead, namely:

$$(I\text{-}B\supset\text{-}elim) \quad \frac{\text{I believe that } p \text{ and that if } p \text{ then } q}{\text{I believe that } q}$$

A crucial difference with respect to ($B\supset$-$elim$) is that, whereas the latter is in the third person, (I-$B\supset$-$elim$) is in the first. The letters 'p' and 'q' in (I-$B\supset$-$elim$) are abbreviations used by the speaker for some sentences he has in mind.

All the theories of belief ascription I am aware of seem not to perceive any difference between (I-$B\supset$-$elim$) and ($B\supset$-$elim$). Let us call a theory that does take (I-$B\supset$-$elim$) and ($B\supset$-$elim$) apart, "subjective." It is at a subjective theory that I am now aiming. We know of course that it is not rare that statements in the first person can behave quite differently from the corresponding statements in the third person: a well-known case in point is that of "It is raining, but I don't think it is," which is (Moore-) paradoxical, whereas "It is raining, but he does not think it is" is not. Now, in challenging Achilles, the Tortoise is in effect asserting something along the following lines: "No matter how much I try, I cannot believe the conclusion of that inference by *modus ponens*, of which I firmly believe the premises. There is nothing I can do about it. I am simply unable to see that the conclusion is true." I want to claim that, even though it is not an instance of Moore's Paradox, this is just as paradoxical and, like any Moore-paradoxical statement, fails to make any clear sense. That Moore-paradoxical statements are, strictly speaking, nonsensical has been claimed, e.g., by Rogers Albritton:

> *Is* it only hard to credit . . . that a thinking creature, say a male human being relevantly *un*like us, should honestly insist that although it's raining, he doesn't believe any such thing? He wishes he did. He thinks he must be going mad. But there it is. Look at him, he says. He's drenched. It is *of course* raining. And yet he *doesn't think so*. He just doesn't. Not for a minute. Isn't that strange? Perhaps he should drop in on Oliver Sacks! Well, perhaps he should. But what he has to offer, if he talks like that and obviously isn't kidding, is a *linguistic* disorder, to begin with. Isn't it? Is it really a question whether or not he believes what he's saying? Or is he on reflection, not saying anything, except around the edges, interesting as *that* phenomenon should prove to neurological connoisseurs? I am inclined to think, as I've confessed, that he is not making sense, profoundly not, and that the utter nonsense of what he seems to be saying is not merely "pragmatic." It sounds awfully semantic to me.[11]

Similarly, I want to claim that the Tortoise is not making sense. If I am right, the challenge posed by it is empty and neither Achilles nor we owe it any argument to persuade it to accept the statement in question. But I cannot suppose that the paradoxical character of what the Tortoise is saying is immediately obvious—in fact, it seems to have escaped notice entirely.[12] The subjective theory of belief I am about to offer is meant to help the reader to see it. It will also point the way to a solution of our original problem.

Now I shall proceed as follows. First, I shall put forward an intuitive picture of what belief is like—a picture at variance with the usual picture, which takes entertaining a belief to be like having a proposition stored in some box in the mind. The alternative idea will be that believing that *p* is very much like *seeing that p is true*—belief being a sort of intellectual vision, modelled on ordinary vision and sharing with it some structural properties.[13] I shall then define two notions of belief: actual belief and belief *simpliciter*. The main task I shall have to discharge will be to show that, under certain conditions, actual belief is closed under *modus ponens*, whereas belief *simpliciter* is not. The gap between the two notions will answer most of the questions that have been raised so far.

The Tortoise itself, quite appropriately, uses the metaphor of vision.[14]

We commonly say that we see that a proposition is true in case we believe it on the basis of overwhelming evidence. We say, for instance, that we see that a mathematical proposition is true when we have grasped a proof for it. The appropriateness of the metaphor comes from the fact that seeing, in the nonmetaphorical sense, that something is the case is already to believe it.

Here and in the following sections I shall be mainly considering vision in a narrow sense—let us call it "primary vision." Even though we can commonly say both that we see that a patch is yellow and that we see that a person is elderly, there is a clear difference between these two things: we do not need to draw any inference in order to see that the patch is yellow, nor do we need to have any previous belief; this vision is primary. Even brutes, lacking any language and lacking the ability to draw inferences, can see such a thing. In contrast, in the case of the elderly person, we cannot directly see her age; all we can do is see, for example, that her hair is white or that she has other traits from which we infer that she is elderly. For this, we need to have a certain number of beliefs concerning the relationship, causal or otherwise, between age and physical appearance. I do not have to give here a precise definition of "primary vision"; nor do I need to be able to distinguish with any confidence between instances of primary vision and instances of nonprimary vision. The notion is needed here only in order to give an intuitive picture of what it is like to have a belief.

If I had time, I would expand on the analogy between seeing and believing, which is in fact quite strict. There seem to be exceptions to the principle that "seeing (in the primary sense) is believing," for example, in those cases in which we see something but we do not believe our own eyes, either because we are not aware of what we are seeing (the focus of our attention being elsewhere) or because we have independent reasons for not assenting to what we seem to be seeing. One might then conclude that believing is more than seeing, that some further condition involving attention, reasons, judgment, or a supplementary assent, must be satisfied. Or equivalently, that vision yields only a "prima facie inclination to believe," whereas belief proper is a far more sophisticated cognitive state.[15] This might well be true in the third person, but it is not how the subject himself would describe his own experience. One cannot say, in the first person and in the present tense, that one sees, for instance, that Mary is in the audience (at a conference, say) but one does not realize it; and one cannot assert "I see that the stick is broken, but I do not believe it"—the verb "seeing" being employed here in the veridical sense, which is the only sense available in the first person.[16] In such cases it is mandatory to say, "I seem to be seeing that the stick is broken, but I do not believe it." Properly developed, such considerations as these can (I believe) establish that seeing does indeed entail believing, at least in the first person. In any case, that seeing and believing are related somehow is undisputable.[17] In a while, I shall say something more specific concerning their connection.

Two traits of (primary) vision are relevant here. First, we are able to see not just that a patch is red, but also that some patch is more or less red than another, that this dog is bigger than that dog, that an object is farther away than another object. That is, we are able to see not only that objects instantiate properties, but also that relations hold between objects, without resorting to inferences. Some animals, presumably unable to draw inferences, can very well see any one of the things just mentioned. Second, primary vision is transitive, at least with respect to some relations, in the following sense. Suppose that a person S is seeing that Bill is taller than Adam and, simultaneously, also that Chris is taller than Bill; then S is simultaneously seeing that Chris is taller than Adam. The crucial point, of course, is that S is seeing this without any inference being involved—provided that Bill is not given to S in two different ways, so that it can only be inferred that the same person is involved in both cases.

It is possible that primary vision is not transitive with respect to *all* relations, instances of which can be seen in the primary sense to hold. Some cases might be debatable. For example, *prima facie* it looks as if seeing that A is to the left of B and B is to the left of C is also seeing that A is to the left of C. Suppose, however, that S is looking at A and B through a telescope (or a monitor), and at B and C through a different telescope. Suppose that the former telescope is to the right of the latter. Then some inference might be needed in order to see that A is to the left of C. It is not quite clear, however, whether this really amounts to a counterexample to the claim that primary vision is transitive with respect to the relation of being to the left of, both because it is not clear whether B is given as being the same in both cases, and also because A, B, and C (unlike their images in the telescopes) are perhaps not seen in the primary sense. Be that as it may, I do not need to claim that primary vision is transitive with respect to *all* the relations instances of which can be primarily seen to hold.

Taking primary vision as a model, I shall now *define* the notion of *actual belief* in two steps. First step: a subject S *actually believes that p*, if S is in such a state that it would be correct for S to assert in the first person (whether or not S actually asserts it), "It now appears to me, all things considered, that p," or "I now judge that it is true that p," or even "I now see that p." ('See' need not be taken here in its primary sense. Any kind of seeing will do.) It might be objected that this cannot be really interesting: judging, for instance, that a proposition is true comes so close to entertaining the corresponding belief that no clarification at all has been effected. This is entirely correct, but my aim here is not to define belief from scratch, that is, in terms of entirely different notions. Rather, I intend to isolate within the general notion of belief a more restricted notion—actual belief—and then to ascribe to it some traits (this I shall be doing in a minute). Finally I shall examine how the general notion of belief and the restricted one are related. It is the gap between them that is explanatory of the phenomena we are mainly interested in.

Right now, for instance, I actually believe that I am late for dinner, because I realize from various clues (not all visual in kind) that it is almost nine in the evening and we dine at eight thirty. I do not just have a disposition to believe this, as would be the case if my attention were focused on something else, but I would be able to realize that it is late if my attention were appropriately redirected (for example, by someone's calling). No, I am actually entertaining, and assenting to, the thought that I am late. This is what makes it correct for me to say, "It now appears to me that I am late." Actual beliefs are *conscious*—the subject is aware of having them—and *occurrent*.[18]

Let it be noted that if S actually believes that *p and q*, that is, if it is correct for S to assert that the conjunction *p and q* actually appears to him to be true, then it is also correct for S to assert that *p* so appears to him, and also that *q* does—that is, S actually believes that *p* and also actually believes that *q*. Actual belief is therefore such as to make (*B&-elim*) truth-preserving.

Now consider the relation of *being no less true than*. Clearly, S actually believes that *if p then q* iff *q* appears to S as being no less true than *p*. Now suppose that it is correct for S to assert that *q* actually appears to him as being no less true than *p*, and simultaneously that *r* actually appears to him as being no less true than *q*. Here, '*p*', '*q*', and '*r*' abbreviate some propositions S has in mind. *In such a case it seems to me that it would be impossible that r does not appear to* S *as being no less true than p*—that is, it must appear to S that *if p then r*. In other words, if S actually believes that *if p then q*, and simultaneously that *if q then r*, then S actually believes that *if p then r*. It follows from this as a special case, taking '*p*' to abbreviate the proposition that 1=1 or any other obviously (for S) true proposition, that if S actually believes that *q* and also (simultaneously) actually believes that if *q* then *r*, then S (simultaneously) actually believes that *r*.

As I said, this is how I see things. But I have no argument to offer showing that this is how they are. What I must do at this stage, then, is to *assume*—this is the second of the two steps in the definition of actual belief mentioned above—that actual belief is transitive with respect to the relation of *being no less true than*. Later on we shall consider whether this assumption is borne out by its consequences.

Let it be noted that the notion of primary vision was not mentioned in the definition we gave of actual belief. Instead, it was used as an intuitive model. The close intuitive connection between vision and belief was what motivated us to assume that the latter shares with the former some structural traits—namely, that it is possible to actually believe (respectively, see) that some relations hold without resorting to inferences, and that actual belief, like primary vision, is transitive with respect to some relations (in particular, the relation *being no less true than*).

Actual belief clearly is a special case of the general notion of belief as ordinarily understood, for it is possible to believe something without believing it actually. For instance, if one is in one's right mind one believes that a cat is smaller than a cloud, but usually this is not due to the fact that one has ever given any particular thought to the matter. This example would generally be taken as an instance of tacit belief, which is in turn explained as what follows as a consequence (or, according to some authors, as an *easy* consequence) from the beliefs one explicitly entertains. Without denying that it is possible to derive the content of that belief from others that most of us have, it seems to me that we have that belief in the sense that we have a *disposition* (in some circumstances at least) to *actually* believe it. Here too, vision provides a model: we have a clear grasp of what it means to say that in certain circumstances we have a disposition to see something. If appropriately positioned, with the visual apparatus in good order, in good light conditions, we have a disposition to see what there is to see. In other circumstances, we have a disposition to see (in the nonveridical sense of the word) what is not there.

Belief as ordinarily understood—belief *simpliciter*—is the disposition to have actual belief. Just as in the case of vision, however, such a disposition is something we have not absolutely, but only relative to a number of factors. For example, we ascribe to a person the disposition to answer "125" to the question "What is $67 + 58$?"—and so grant her some mathematical knowledge—only if she is allowed enough time to answer. If an immediate answer is required, then we might have to deny her that knowledge. The time allowed to answer the question "What is the square root of 87?" is usually longer. A number of parameters have to be fixed before one can meaningfully ask what dispositions a given subject has. What parameters are relevant—in what conditions of attention, given what stimuli, in the absence of what disturbing factors—for ascribing a disposition to actually believe anything, is too variable a matter to be decided once and for all. For instance, to stay within mathematics, it is quite relevant that a subject be given appropriate hints instead of being left unassisted. This example is due to Stalnaker: the answers to the two questions "What are the prime factors of 1591?" and "Are 43 and 37 the only two prime factors of 1591?" have the same content, but it is unlikely that it will take any subject the same amount of time and effort to figure them out. So the questions themselves have a supplementary role to play in fixing a subject's dispositions to actual belief, over and above what is already stored in her memory. (Addressing the same point in *Meno*, Plato made unnecessarily heavy weather of it). We must conclude that dispositions to actual belief are relative to circumstances and to all sorts of factors.

That belief *simpliciter* is the disposition to have an actual belief—it has to be borne in mind that actual belief was introduced as a theoretical concept—is a conjecture, which would be disconfirmed if cases were found where a subject could be ascribed a belief that is neither an actual belief nor a disposition to have an actual belief. I have been unable to find any such case.

Some of the traits proper to actual belief are missing from belief *simpliciter*. For instance, if S nonactually believes that p and also, simultaneously, that q, it is quite possible that S has no disposition to believe p *and* q. Sitting in a theater, we have a disposition to see the person next to us on the left (turning our head to the left), and also the person next to us on the right; but we have no disposition to see them both simultaneously. Or again, we might be disposed to see each one of the pages of a given book, without being disposed to see them all together at the same time. The same holds for belief: one can be disposed to actually believe each one of the propositions making up a book, without being disposed to believe them all together and therefore to believe their conjunction.[19] A further example is this: there are numbers so big that a given memory (e.g., of a computer) can take them in only one at a time. Let n and m be two such numbers; consider "n is odd" and "m is even." The owner of that memory can have a disposition to believe either proposition separately, but not both of them together. We shall soon have to consider a different example to the same effect (the undecided smoker).[20] It ought to be clear by now why the *(B&-intr)* rule is *not* truth preserving, while *(B&-elim)* is.

Now we are in a position to answer at least some of the questions raised in the first part of this paper. A subject who asserts that she believes that p and that *if p then q*, is asserting that she actually (since the assertion is in the first person and in the present tense) and simultaneously (since she is asserting a conjunction) believes both that p and that *if p then q*. This is precisely the case with the Tortoise. By transitivity (assumed to hold for actual belief), it is impossible that the subject does not believe the conclusion, that q, of an application of *modus ponens* to the two premises. Were it otherwise—that is, if that p, but not that q, appeared to her as being true—how could it appear to her that *if p then q*, i.e., that q is no less true than p? Of course, we are assuming here that the subject understands what she is asserting, and in particular that she can grasp the meaning of 'if …then'. Let it be noted that it is the Tortoise itself who employs here the abbreviations 'p' and 'q', thereby showing that it is aware that one of the two premises is the same as the antecedent of the other. This is crucial for the transitivity of actual belief to apply.[21]

The same does *not* hold either for the corresponding assertion in the third person, "*S* believes that *p* and that *if p then q*" or for the corresponding assertion in the past tense. It does not follow from either of them that *S* believes those two things actually and simultaneously, since *S* might have a disposition to believe them at different times. Here too, the parallel with vision is useful: someone might see on Monday that Adam, standing next to John Wayne, is tall and then the following Tuesday (in a picture, say) that Ben is taller than Adam, without seeing either on Monday or on Tuesday that Ben is tall. It is the same with belief: if the premises of an application of *modus ponens* are actually believed at different times, there is no reason that the conclusion must be believed. Only (*I-B⊃-elim*), but not (*B⊃-elim*), is truth-preserving. As a further example, consider *If p then (if not-p then 0=1)*. Let *p* abbreviate "I shall give up smoking" as asserted by *S*, a subject who changes his mind every single day about the strength of his own will. There is a sense in which he has both a disposition to actually believe that *p* (on some day) and a similar disposition to actually believe that *not-p* (the next day), so that it would not be incorrect to say that he believes both that *p* and that *not-p*. However, this is not to charge him with being incoherent, as he has no disposition to believe either that *p and not-p*, or that 0=1.

This then is our answer to the Tortoise. Since it believes both premises actually and simultaneously, because of the nature of actual belief, it must also *already* believe (without any further step being required) the conclusion of an application of *modus ponens*. Of course, it pretends otherwise, but we do not know what to make of its words. Its skeptical challenge for us to justify *modus ponens* without circularity is unintelligible. (Of course, this is not to say that the same holds for all valid rules of inference, and that believing their premises already is to believe their conclusions—just think of ∀-introduction.)

The fact that the Tortoise, believing that *p* and also that *if p then q*, also believes that *q*, without having to take any extra step, does not mean that it is logically omniscient. This, of course, is no secondary matter: we rejected the theories of belief ascription based on the notion of unstructured propositions just because they turn out inevitably to ascribe logical omniscience to every believer. Now, we have already seen that ordinary belief is not closed under *modus ponens*. Actual belief, however, *is* closed under *any* number of applications of *modus ponens*, provided that the premises are believed simultaneously. This, however, still does not yield logical omniscience, because, first, no one can actually believe simultaneously more than finitely many propositions and, second, by applying *modus ponens* to finitely many premises one can reach only finitely many different conclusions. It can be added that, having accepted the axioms of, say, Peano arithmetic, we have a disposition to actually believe any one of their deductive consequences *in suitable circumstances* (e.g., if we are given a proof of it) and *in this sense* we believe it *simpliciter*. Plainly, reference to suitable circumstances cannot be dropped.

Let us now go back to our original problem. As remarked by Dummett, some explanation must be given of why, for an inference to be legitimate, the process of recognizing the premises as true must already have accomplished whatever is needed for the recognition of the truth of the conclusion, even though, for it to be useful, a recognition of its truth need not actually have been accorded to the conclusion when it was accorded to the premises. Let us consider once again our usual visual example: in order to see that Bill is tall, it is sufficient to see that Adam is tall and that Bill is taller than Adam. Of course, one can see the two things separately (e.g., in two different days), but then one does not *see* that the conclusion holds. It is the same with belief with respect to *modus ponens*: what is needed to go from the premises to the conclusion is not some supplementary information, that is, other beliefs beyond those expressed by the premises. What is needed is that they be put together, in other words, that the subject believe them actually and simultaneously. This is not the general case, however, as witnessed by other rules of inference, such as universal generalization, which must be treated otherwise. This issue is left for another paper to consider.

A general conclusion to be drawn from what we have seen so far is that a model widely employed to represent belief states and other propositional attitudes is likely to be wrong, namely, the model of the belief box. This model depicts the mind as composed of several boxes in which, respectively, the propositions believed, hoped for, and so on, are stored. If belief resembles vision in some respects, as I have been arguing, then the belief box is bound to appear as preposterous as the notion of a box in which are kept all the images that we are likely ever to see. Seeing something is not at all like accessing an image stored in memory and looking at it. Similarly, believing that p is not at all like accessing the proposition that p, stored in a box or in memory. This is not to deny, of course, that memory does keep traces both of beliefs and of images seen in the past. An examination of the belief box model, however, has to be left to be dealt with in another essay.

MARCO SANTAMBROGIO

DEPARTMENT OF PHILOSOPHY
UNIVERSITY OF PARMA—ITALY
FEBRUARY 2004

NOTES

I am grateful for valuable comments from Paolo Casalegno, and from the participants at the Summer School in Analytic Philosophy, Parma, Italy (July 2000).

1. Michael Dummett, "The Justification of Deduction," in *Truth and Other Enigmas* (London: Duckworth, 1978), 297.

2. It is definitely not the same. Some deductive inferences are also useful in that they can *convince* someone who believes their premises to believe their conclusion. Of course, most contentful statements, as well as most inferences, are informative without being convincing.

3. Here and in the sequel I shall let myself be lax in matters of use and mention, whenever context can be depended upon to make it clear whether an expression is being used or mentioned.

4. A further (and immediate) corollary to this is that no one ever believes anything that could not be true (in any possible world): since every q is a consequence of an impossible p, anyone who believes that p believes everything. But no one could do that.

5. See Robert Stalnaker, "The Problem of Logical Omniscience, I," in *Context and Content* (Oxford: Oxford Univ. Press, 1999), 241–54, for a clear statement of these alternatives.

6. Lewis Carroll, "What the Tortoise Said to Achilles," *Mind*, n.s., 4, (1895): 278–80.

7. As a matter of fact, besides *modus ponens*, an application of universal instantiation is also involved in the inference discussed by Achilles and the Tortoise. I shall ignore this little complication and assume that the example is modified accordingly.

8. This is not to mean that I am endorsing here a conventionalist theory of logical truth, or any other theory for that matter. What I mean is: let the Tortoise explicitly *agree with us* that the meaning of 'if … then' is such that *modus ponens* is truth preserving. The argument in the text bears an obvious resemblance to one of Quine's objections to conventionalism, but it seems to apply no matter what theory we and the Tortoise (independently) adopt concerning logical truth. This point is in need of further thought, for it has some tendency to show that the scope of Quine's criticism might go well beyond the conventionalist theory of logical truth.

9. Thomas Nagel has clearly seen this point: "What I deny is that the validity of the thoughts that language enables us to express, or even to have, depends on those conventions and usages." (*The Last Word* [Oxford: Oxford Univ. Press, 1997], 40). Also, "The fact that contingencies of use make 'and' the English word for conjunction implies absolutely nothing about the status of the truth that p and q implies p. What is meant by a set of sentences is a matter of convention. What follows from a set of premises is not. This is just another case where relativism is inconsistent with the content of the judgments under analysis" (ibid.).

10. See e.g., Bernard Williams, "Deciding to Believe," in *Language, Belief,*

and Metaphysics, ed. H. Kiefer and M. Munitz (Albany: State Univ. of New York Press, 1970).

11. Rogers Albritton, "Comments on 'Moore's Paradox and Self-Knowledge'," *Philosophical Studies* 77 (1995): 238.

12. Among those who seem to think that the Tortoise's statements about its own inability to believe are straightforwardly true are Simon Blackburn, "Practical Tortoise Raising," *Mind* 104, no. 416 (1995): 695–712, and G. F. Schueler, "Why 'Oughts' are not Facts," *Mind* 104, no. 416 (1995): 713–24.

13. The notion of rational intuition as a quasi-perceptual faculty, albeit quite obscure, has been historically influential. I shall claim that, in a sense, belief itself is such a faculty (and we need no other).

14. "And, if I failed to *see* [my italics] its truth, I might accept A and B and C, and *still* not accept Z, mightn't I?" Lewis Carroll, "What the Tortoise said to Achilles," 45.

15. See, e.g., Gareth Evans, *Varieties of Reference* (New York: Oxford Univ. Press, 1982), 120 ff. See also John McDowell, *Mind and World* (Cambridge: Harvard Univ. Press, 1994), 60.

16. There are some apparent counterexamples to this claim (which of course is in need of extensive examination), but it can be shown, I am convinced, that in fact they are just instances of pretense.

17. Well, maybe I am wrong about this, as it is not at all undisputed. Galen Strawson for one has remarked: "The tendency of the last fifty years of analytic philosophy has been to separate the notion of conceptual content sharply from the notion of experience, and this fact, combined with the diaphaneity property of conscious thought may make it seem odd to many to say that the experience of seeing red and the experience of now seeming to understand this very sentence, and of thinking that nobody could have had different parents, are alike in respect of having a certain qualitative character" (Galen Strawson, *Mental Reality* [Cambridge: MIT Press, 1994], 194). Whatever the tendency of mainstream analytic philosophy, my goal here is tightly to connect the notion of experience (in particular, vision) with propositional attitudes. But I am more interested in their structural similarities than in any qualitative character they might share.

18. The phrase "occurrent belief" has been given slightly different meanings. Gilbert Harman for instance defines it as follows: "we can say a belief is occurrent if it is either currently before one's consciousness or in some other way currently operative in guiding what one is thinking or doing" (*Change in View*, Cambridge, MA: MIT Press, 1986, 14). Harman's occurrent belief can therefore be unconscious, unlike actual belief as I have characterized it.

19. This is related with the Paradox of the Preface, but a more extensive discussion than is allowed here would be needed.

20. Another source of counterexamples to the rule of conjunction introduction in belief contexts is the fact that dispositions to believe are relative to a number of factors.

21. This also raises a serious problem—it seems to me—for any theory of belief

that takes propositions to be the objects of belief. What is the content of the Tortoise's self-ascription of belief? If we take it to be the pair of propositions expressed by the that-clauses abbreviated by 'p' and '*If p then q*', then we leave it open that the Tortoise might not be aware that they are related as we just said they are. The inference we are interested in would therefore not have been validated.

REPLY TO MARCO SANTAMBROGIO

I am generally sympathetic to Marco Santambrogio's method of reconciling the validity of deductive inference with its capacity to provide us with new information that we did not have before. He does so by examining the concept of belief. In the passage from me which he begins by quoting, I spoke of recognising the premisses as true and of recognising the truth of the conclusion, but he is right to say that recognising the premisses as true is the same as believing them (save that it suggests, if not strictly implies, that they *are* true). Belief is certainly the right notion to examine in this connection. Marco is right to say, in a footnote, that the usefulness of deductive inference is not exhausted by its yielding new information to the one who devises and propounds the inference: it may be used to persuade someone of the conclusion. Even in this case, the hearer, if he is convinced, acquires new information.

Marco is also entirely in the right in arguing that one who takes belief to be a relation of a subject to a proposition, and then adopts what he, Santambrogio, calls a non-structured notion of a proposition, such as the set of possible worlds in which it is true, or the set of state-descriptions in which it is false, commits himself to attributing logical omniscience to all who have any beliefs. The relevant notion of informativeness is tied to that of belief—the speaker or hearer's beliefs. The notion of informativeness (cognitive value—*Erkenntniswert*) Frege used in posing his problem of true statements of identity has explicitly to do with knowledge; in the general case, in which we do not assume the truth of the statement, we must make it turn on the notion of belief, counting misinformation as information. In any case, the notion of the informativeness of a statement has nothing to do with its empirical or contingent character, as Frege saw by citing his geometrical example; it could have been an arithmetical one. Indeed, those who treat of metaphysical necessity would count "Phosphorus is (the same celestial body as) Hesperus" as metaphysically necessary.

Santambrogio thinks that the adoption of the extreme opposite view, that of regarding propositions to be as finely structured as their linguistic expressions in sentences, leads to the opposite difficulty: it calls in question, not the informativeness of deductive inference, but its validity. This structured view of propositions—of what he called "thoughts"—was Frege's. His last published essay "Gedankengefüge" opens with the observation that language allows us to express thoughts that have never previously been grasped by anyone on earth. This, he says, "would not be possible if we could not distinguish parts within the thought that correspond to the parts of the sentence, so that the structure of the sentence could serve as a picture of the structure of the thought." Many similar remarks are to be found in his unpublished writings. The first reason given by Santambrogio for rejecting this view is that there are many different though equivalent formulations of celebrated propositions such as the Axiom of Choice or the First Law of Thermodynamics. This seems to me a point about the looseness of our nomenclature (the name "Zorn's Lemma" is undoubtedly more precise): what prohibits us from admitting that the variant formulations express distinct propositions?

Santambrogio also suggests that a fully structured notion of propositions, taking their structure to be roughly mirrored by that of the sentences expressing them, runs the risk of calling in doubt the possibility that any principles could be framed that accounted for a priori transitions between beliefs. I do not see that he makes this out; and I do not see why it should be so. Let us consider Santambrogio's favourite example, inference by modus ponens. Suppose that the letters "p" and "q" abbreviate two English sentences devoid of demonstratives and of indexicality; and let the letter "r" abbreviate the sentence "If p, then q." A certain subject Vittorio (whose name we may abbreviate by "V") understands the sentences "p" and "r," and is disposed to regard them as true. He perceives that, taking both "p" and "r" to be true, he must acknowledge "q" to be true also. Why should this become inexplicable when expressed in the terminology of propositions? We surely need to recognise some similarity of structure between the propositions and the sentences expressing them. In virtue of understanding the sentence "p," V grasps the proposition it expresses, which we may reasonably call the proposition that p; in virtue of his taking the sentence to be true, he takes the proposition to be true. In virtue of his understanding the sentence "r," he grasps the proposition *it* expresses, which we may reasonably call the proposition that if p, then q, and which he also takes to be true. Should we not, *must* we not, call r a conditional proposition? If we are to speak of propositions at all, must we not admit that there are conditional propositions, and that the sentence "If p, then q" expresses such a proposition?

Admittedly, that proposition can be expressed in other ways, such as "q, provided that p"; Frege of course allowed that the same thought can be expressed verbally in different ways. Sentences of natural language need some regimentation before they can be claimed to mirror in structure the propositions they express. (Perhaps they need to be expressed with quantifiers and variables rather than with the devices of natural language for expressing generality before the reflection is perfected or at least improved.) In any case, it was not trivial reformulations of this kind that Santambrogio had in mind with his examples of the Axiom of Choice and the First Law of Thermodynamics. Now V perceives that the truth of the proposition that p constitutes the condition for the truth of the proposition that q which the conditional proposition that if p, then q lays down. He therefore perceives that, taking the proposition that p and the proposition that if p, then q to be true, he must take the proposition that q to be true also. The only assumptions concerning the structure of propositions that we have had to make, in thus representing in terms of propositions the inferential step that V takes, have been that there are conditional propositions, and that one who grasps them can discern the propositions that serve as their antecedents and consequents: assumptions surely inescapable if we are to entertain the concept of propositions at all.

Santambrogio proceeds to examine Lewis Carroll's famous essay, "What the Tortoise said to Achilles." The tortoise refuses to accept the conclusion of an inference by modus ponens, though he accepts its premisses. Santambrogio asks whether we can force it to accept the conclusion. This he denies, because he disputes the contention that belief has nothing to do with the will. I warmly welcome his repudiation of this contention. Suppose someone in the public eye is accused of some utterly disreputable and dishonourable, though not actually illegal, action. He denies having done it; but the evidence appears incontrovertible. He is pilloried in the Press, and most of his friends desert him. His closest friend at first stands by him, but eventually gives way and concedes that the accusation must be true. Then new evidence turns up which vindicates him. He now reproaches that closest friend for his disloyalty in failing to stand firm in his initial belief that he was innocent: "You ought never to have believed that of me," he says. The friend pleads the strength of the evidence against him: "It was just because of that that I needed you to hold on to your faith in me," he replies. Is he not justified in his reproach? The friend's failure was not that of not paying due attention to all the rational grounds for forming his opinion: it was a failure of the will in not hanging on to a conviction of the accused man's innocence when he so desperately needed someone to believe in him and when, if anyone was to do so, it was that friend who must. He could not be reproached for not having done so if doing so were not subject to his will.

Should we form our beliefs by considering only the strength of the grounds for and against? In the great range of indifferent matters, yes. But on certain questions we need to take heed of the consequences, including the moral consequences, of being wrong one way or the other. In such cases we are not merely the passive subject of the pressures on us of the pieces of evidence with their different weights; we have to decide what we shall believe, when this does not consist solely of evaluating the evidence. We must evaluate the consequences of adopting one belief or the other. Our wills are involved as much as in deciding what to do.

Conceding that we cannot force the tortoise to accept the conclusion of the modus ponens, Santambrogio argues that we do not need to. The tortoise's claim to accept the premises but not the conclusion makes no more sense than Moore's paradoxical utterance, "It is raining but I do not believe that it is." The difference between the first person and the third is as significant in the tortoise's case as in Moore's. Santambrogio maintains that while "S believes that q" does not follow from "S believes that p" and "S believes that if p, then q," "I believe that q" *does* follow from "I believe that p" and "I believe that if p, then q." The reason is that the first-person present-tense statement can be used only as an avowal of what Santambrogio calls "actual belief," whereas the third-person statement expresses only what he calls "belief *simpliciter*." Actual belief is conscious and occurrent; belief *simpliciter* is a disposition to have an actual belief. By requiring it to be conscious, Santambrogio disallows as an instance of actual belief the case Gilbert Harman accepts as one of an occurrent belief, namely one that is not currently before one's consciousness but in some other way is currently guiding what one is thinking or doing. I go upstairs to fetch a comb. I believe there is a comb on top of my chest of drawers, and this belief guides my action of going to my chest of drawers. But I am not thinking to myself that there is a comb on top of my chest of drawers; I am taking that for granted, and, in opening the door of the bedroom and going to the chest of drawers I am on auto-pilot. However we ought to understand the phrase "occurrent belief," this is not actual belief in Santambrogio's sense.

Santambrogio's distinction is entirely sound. Knowledge, like his belief *simpliciter*, is a dispositional concept: to know something is to be able to bring it to mind when it is called for. There is ambiguity about how much prompting the "calling for" may involve, and how much reflection the subject may be allowed. When someone else states something to which I have previously concluded, I may legitimately say, "Yes, I know"; but it does not follow that if I had been asked what I knew about the matter, I should have said just that. Not having reflected about the subject lately, I may for the moment have forgotten the conclusion I had previously come to. Everyone is familiar with hearing a question asked, perhaps of someone else, and thinking, "I know that," and yet being unable, just then, to call it to mind. As Santambrogio rightly remarks, the same applies to belief in the dispositional sense; when being asked a question prompts an avowal of a belief, the very form of the question may, as he says, affect how much thought the answer requires. The question, "What do you think about . . . ?" is ambiguous between asking after an opinion already formed and calling for a decision to be made; but whether the answer testifies to a belief previously held depends upon how much reflection it required, and of what kind. As Santambrogio's example of the cat and the cloud demonstrates, we cannot say that it expresses a belief already held only if the subject has previously considered the matter and arrived at that conclusion; but we also cannot say that it does so whenever it holds good that he would have given that answer at any time that he had been asked.

The concept of belief as a disposition is thus moderately problematic; that of what Santambrogio calls "actual belief" is much less so. I have an actual belief when I reach some conclusion, when I note something with interest or surprise, when I recall or realise something bearing on what I am engaged in doing: in all such cases the proposition is before my mind, and I should assert it if there were occasion to do so.

Santambrogio uses the distinction between actual belief and belief *simpliciter* to resolve the tension between the validity of deductive inference and its informativeness. Presented with a sufficiently evident deductive step whose premisses he understands and has accepted, no one can but believe the conclusion: actual belief is here involved. Santambrogio concedes that this does not hold good of all deductive steps. Indeed it does not: recall the story of the mathematics lecturer who, in expounding a proof, said at one stage, "It is therefore obvious that . . . ." A member of the audience asked, "Sir, is that obvious?" The lecturer pondered for a notable length of time, and then looked up and said, "Yes, it is obvious." I am surprised that Santambrogio classes the ordinary rule of ∀-introduction among those which, unlike and-introduction and modus ponens, do not compel actual belief in their conclusions. When someone wishing to prove something about all triangles begins, "Let ABC be a triangle," it will normally be apparent to all his hearers that he has indeed proved that his conclusion holds of all triangles. True, someone unfamiliar with reasoning of this kind might object, "You have proved it only of *that* triangle." It will then have to be pointed out to him that nothing was assumed of ABC save that it *was* a triangle. He will then have grasped the principle of ∀-introduction; next time it is used, he will feel unable not to accept the conclusion.

It is different with belief in the dispositional sense. Even if someone, presented with a compellingly evident deductive step, had always believed the premises, the conclusion may come to him as a surprise: he may never have had both premises in mind at the same time. This is characteristic of mathematical proofs: think of a construction in the proof of a theorem in Euclid, which forces us to consider simultaneously propositions that it had never occurred to us to put side by side; proofs in other branches of mathematics often involve similar steps.

I think that Marco Santambrogio is quite right in thinking that the distinction between occurrent and dispositional belief is central to dissolving the tension between the validity of deductive inference and its capacity to advance our knowledge.

A deductive step that may seem evident to some fails to be immediately compelling; that is, in Santambrogio's terminology, the avowal that results from prefixing "I believe that" to the conclusion cannot be inferred from the statements that result from prefixing "I believe that" to each of the premises. This may be because the step is too great: it could be broken down into a sequence of shorter steps each of which was immediately compelling; we seldom argue informally solely in steps admissible in a formalised natural-deduction proof. But it may also be due to the fact that, for inferential purposes, a statement may admit of several distinct analyses (better, decompositions). Recognition of the validity of an inference may depend upon discerning the same complex predicate in each of two statements, something not always easy to do. Such discernment is an intellectual act which makes not only devising a deductive argument, but following it—perceiving it to be valid when it is presented—a creative activity. Marco Santambrogio does not mention this. But he is entirely right to draw his distinction between actual belief and belief *simpliciter* and to see in it the key to resolving the tension between the legitimacy of deductive inference and its usefulness.

M. D.

21

Pascal Engel

DUMMETT, ACHILLES, AND THE TORTOISE

What is the relationship between the meaning of logical words and their use in particular inferences? What is an inference and what does our knowledge of logical deductive rules consist in? How can we be justified in following these rules? Much of Michael Dummett's work has been devoted to an investigation into such questions in the epistemology of logic, and he has illuminatingly shown how they connect with basic issues in the philosophy of language, in the theory of knowledge, and in metaphysics. Quite often, his discussions of these issues have taken their start from one or another of the many puzzles and paradoxes which pervade the philosophy of logic more than in any other field of analytic philosophy. I have, however, always been surprised that—as far as I know—he did not discuss at some length, or at least directly, Lewis Carroll's paradox of Achilles and the Tortoise, which is often called the "paradox of inference."[1] It seems to me to raise many issues which are relevant to his concerns. In what follows, I shall review some of these issues, and I shall try to show that although many of Dummett's views provide an answer to them, it is not so clearly the case for a particular kind of skepticism that one can draw from Carroll's tale, about the normative force of logical reasons.

I

Lewis Carroll's enigmatic piece "What the Tortoise said to Achilles" (1895) stages Achilles presenting to the Tortoise three propositions:

(A) Things that are equal to the same are equal to each other
(B) The two sides of this triangle are things that are equal to the same
(Z) The two sides of this triangle are equal to each other

The Tortoise accepts A and B, but does not accept Z, although she[2] accepts the proposition that Achilles presents to her:

(C) If A and B are true then Z must be true

As Achilles insists, the Tortoise is also prepared to accept that if A and B and C are true, then Z must be true, but she still refuses to accept Z, and the story suggests that the regress never ends.

There are two striking features of this story. The first is that the Tortoise accepts C, and does so because she agrees that C expresses a logical truth.[3] The second is that the Tortoise makes her acceptance conditional on C being entered as a further premise. The puzzle is: how, given these facts, can she fail to accept Z?

It is not easy to say what the meaning of the tale might be. At least four kinds of morals have been drawn, whether or not they were actually intended by Carroll himself.

(1) The most usual interpretation focuses on the second feature: the fact that the Tortoise needs to add the conditional C as a supplementary premise shows that she fails to make a distinction between the propositions A and B on the one hand and the logical truth C on the other, and more generally between a premise and a rule of inference.[4] This is Carroll's own diagnosis when he explains his article to the editor of *Mind*: "My paradox turns on the fact that in an Hypothetical, the truth of the Protasis, the truth of the Apodosis, and the *validity of the sequence* are three distinct propositions."[5] In other terms, we can neither treat a rule of inference, such as *modus ponens* (MP), as conditionals, nor as premises. Once we respect this distinction, Carroll's regress cannot start.

(2) The second interpretation has to do with the *epistemology of understanding*. It can be formulated thus: "Understanding and accepting premises of the form P, and if P then Q, but not accepting the corresponding proposition of the form Q describe nothing at all" (Black 1970, 21).[6] Either the person in question does not understand the meaning of these sentences or of the words which they contain (in particular the logical word *if*), or her acceptance of the premises is not sincere or faked. The same point can be put in terms of the notion of knowledge: "A man knows that if P, then Q if, when he knows that P, he is able to see that, consequently, Q. If a man knows that P, but cannot see that Q, this is just what shows him not to know that if P, then Q" (Brown 1954, 175). The Tortoise seems to be a person of this kind. Hence she does not know what "if P, then Q" means, or does not understand it.

A more specific way of making a similar diagnosis consists in saying that the Tortoise's predicament illustrates that the kind of knowledge involved in this case cannot be expressed by a *proposition* like C. Our knowledge of the rule is not a form of knowledge *that* or propositional knowledge but a form of knowledge *how*, or of practical knowledge. This was indeed Ryle's reaction to the paradox, closely related to his 1954 article mentioned above.[7]

One could also read the tale as a version of Wittgenstein's "skepticism" about rules, as it is interpreted by Kripke (1981). What the Tortoise's refusal to accept the conclusion suggests, on this view, is that there is no principled reason to interpret the sequence A-B-Z as an ordinary instance of *modus ponens* rather than as an instance of a deviant rule of *schmodus ponens* (e.g., "from P and if P and Q infer Q, unless P and Q are propositions about geometry, in which case do not accept Q"). Of course given that neither Carroll nor the Tortoise had heard about Kripke, this interpretation is far-fetched, but there are clear similarities with Wittgenstein's problem. Wittgenstein points out that following a rule is not an interpretation. Adding successive, possibly indefinite, interpretations of the rule as conditionals cannot fix its meaning.

(3) The third kind of interpretation concerns the *justification of logical laws*. Although it is clear that this is an extrapolation from Carroll's tale, we could read it as making a point about the justification of logical rules: suppose that logical rules could be justified by the fact that we have accepted general conventions. Suppose, in particular that such conventions took the form: for any x, y, and z, if x and y stand in the MP relation to z, then x and y imply z. Now suppose that the particular sentences 'P' and 'If P then Q' stand in the MP relation to 'Q'. Do 'P' and 'if P then Q' imply 'Q'? If we reason thus :

(a) 'P' and 'if P then Q' stand in the MP relation to 'Q'
(b) if ' P' and 'If P then Q' stand in the MP relation to 'Q', then 'P' and 'If P then Q' imply 'Q'
(c) hence 'P' and 'if P then Q' imply 'Q'

But the question whether (c) can be inferred from (a) and (b) turns out just to be the question whether it is true that for any x, y, and z, if x and y stand in the MP relation to z, then x and y imply z. In other words, if we want to explain the nature of logical truths or rules from the existence of conventions, we must presuppose these logical truths and rules to derive them from conventions, and our derivation is thus circular. This is indeed Quine's famous argument against Carnap's conventionalism about logic in "Truth by Convention." Quine explicitly refers to Lewis Carroll's regress when he mounts his argument.[8]

A stronger reading along these lines would be that the Tortoise is not so much rejecting a particular account of the justification of logical rules as expressing skepticism about *any* sort of justification of them. As we have already noted, she neither disputes the validity of the "sequence" C nor the validity of the inference from A and B to Z. But her refusal to accept the conclusion C might be the expression of her skepticism about logical truths or logical rules in general. In other words the Tortoise would be a radical skeptic about deduction, just as Hume is skeptical with respect to induction.

(4) The fourth interpretation, unlike the others, does not focus on the second feature of the story—the insertion of an additional premise—but on the first: the Tortoise *accepts* C. Given this, why does she not accept Z? Again she perfectly agrees that C is a logical truth. So the problem is: how can someone who accepts a logical truth or a logical rule fail to infer accordingly? One answer could be that she actually does not really accept the logical truth C, because she does not really understand the meaning of C. This would bring us back to interpretation (2). Another answer would be that the Tortoise accepts C, fully understands what it means, but still *cannot*, or possibly *refuses* to, draw the appropriate conclusion. She would thus intend to convey another form of skepticism, which would bear upon the *normative force* of the logical laws or rules. On this reading the Tortoise is fully aware that C is a logical truth or a valid rule of inference. But she fails to draw the conclusion because she does not take the rule or law as binding and as being able to *move* her to the appropriate conclusion. Either she is a sort of akratic in the domain of logical inference, seeing what she ought to infer, but failing to comply, or she explicitly questions the normative power of the *logical must*. The Tortoise recognizes that Z follows from A and B by "logical necessity." She recognizes that "any one who accepts A and B as true, *must* accept Z as true," and that "The youngest child in High School . . . will grant that." For all that, she still refuses to accept Z, and challenges Achilles "to force [her], logically, to accept Z as true." This is why her acknowledgment of the authority of logic is somewhat ironic: "Whatever *Logic* is good enough to tell me is worth *writing down*." She writes it down, but does not act accordingly. Hume is often presented as a skeptic about practical reason: reason, or belief, as such, cannot move us to act, only passions or desires can do so.[9] In parallel fashion, the Tortoise would be a sceptic about the power of logical reasons to force us to believe any sort of conclusion. She would be a skeptic about *the force of logical reasons*. The question is: "How can logic move the mind?"[10]

II

Although there are very few allusions to Carroll's paradox in Dummett's writings, it is obvious that they are relevant to a number of the issues just mentioned. Dummett's diagnosis is very much along the lines of (1) above:

> In *Principles of Mathematics* Russell falls into confusion through a desire to say both that, e.g, "Peter is a Jew" is the same proposition when it occurs alone and when it occurs in "If Peter is a Jew, then Andrew is a Jew," and that it is not. It must be the same, because otherwise *modus ponens* would not be valid; it cannot be the same, because then "Peter is a Jew; if Peter is a Jew, Andrew is a Jew; therefore Andrew is a Jew" would be the same as "If both Peter is a Jew and if Peter is a Jew, then Andrew is a Jew, then Andrew is a Jew" and it was precisely Lewis Carroll's discovery (in "What the Tortoise said to Achilles") that it was not. Frege provides a solution by saying that the sense of the two occurrences of "Peter is a Jew" (the thought expressed by them) is the same, but that the assertoric force is present in one and lacking in the other. (Dummett 1973, 304)

There are actually two points here, although intimately related. The first is what Geach (1965) calls "the Frege point": that one should distinguish two occurrences of the same sentence when the one is asserted and the other not (hence that the assertion sign, and the assertoric force that it conveys, should be applied to a sentence as a whole, and not to its constituents).[11] The second is that one should distinguish a *logically true proposition*, such as "If A, and if A then B, then Z" not only from a premise in an argument, but also from a *rule of inference*. The regress cannot start if one recognizes that A and B do not have the same status as C.[12] These distinctions are undoubtedly of first importance, and Dummett emphasizes them in many places, for instance when he contrasts Frege's conception of logic as a science of *truth* with Gentzen's conception of logic as a science of *inference*.[13]

They are also quite relevant to Dummett's (1973a, 1991) treatment of the problem of the justification of deduction, which can be considered as a direct answer to the skeptical Tortoise (3). Dummett characterizes the problem of deductive inference through the

> tension between what seems necessary to account for its legitimacy and what seems necessary to account for its usefulness. For it to be legitimate, the process of recognising the premises as true must already have accomplished whatever is needed for the recognition of the truth of the conclusion; for it to be useful, a recognition of its truth need not actually have been accorded to the conclusion when it was accorded to the premises. (1973a, 297)

As Dummett notes further, "on the ordinary notion of proof, it is *compelling* just because, presented with it, *we cannot resist* the passage from premises to conclusion without being unfaithful to the meanings we have already given to the expressions employed in it"(ibid. 301, [my italics]). Carroll was certainly familiar with Mill's view, discussed by Dummett, that deductive inference is a *petitio principii* and hence useless. Thus the Tortoise's refusal to draw the conclusion might be interpreted as an acknowledgment of the tension between the usefulness and the legitimacy of deductions.

Dummett describes two views which attempt to solve this problem. The first is Wittgenstein's, who, in claiming that when we move from premises to conclusion we are giving a new meaning to the expressions we employ in it, denies that the connection between premises and conclusion is necessary and therefore that the proof is compelling. Again Carroll's Tortoise had not read Wittgenstein, but her reluctance to grant the "hardness of the logical must" is strikingly similar: she denies that "logic is going to take you by the throat and *force* you to do it." The second view is the holistic conception, according to which deduction is justified, but only against the global background of our inferential practices. Justification, on this view, can only be circular.[14] This is quite in line not only with Quine's argument in "Truth by Convention," but also with his holistic conception of meaning. Dummett explicitly rejects both. Quine's refutation of Carnap's conventionalism does not involve any distinction between logical laws and rules,[15] and his own holistic conception of the justification of logical laws prevents him from making it:

> Quine's thesis [that nothing is immune to revision] involves, however, that the principles governing deductive connections themselves form part of the total theory which, as a whole, confronts experience. Presumably, in order to avoid Achilles and the Tortoise troubles of the Lewis Carroll type, we must recognise the total theory as comprising rules of inference as well as logical laws in the form of valid schemata and their instances: but there is no reason to suppose that Quine draws a distinction between the status of such rules as against laws like Excluded Middle; they too must be equally liable to rejection under a heavy enough impact from without. (1973, 596)

Justification can be justified only on the basis of a conception of logic in which the primary concept is that of inference and not that of logical truth, and on the basis of a molecularist theory of meaning according to which each sentence possesses a determinate content which can be grasped independently of our knowledge of the whole language. For logical constants, this implies that their meaning be determined directly by the deductive rules associated with them, and that they satisfy the requirement of harmony and conservative extension. When we derive a given logical law from others, we have what Dummett calls a "proof-theoretic justification of the first grade." But such a justification is only "relative," for the derivation already assumes the validity of certain other laws (or, in a justification of the form (a)–(c) above, of the very same law that is meant to be justified). In order to have a nonrelative justification, certain laws must be "self-justifying," and they are such when they satisfy the requirement of harmony.[16] Dummett's views have attracted a lot of discussion,[17] and it is clear that if the main issue raised by Carroll's paradox is that of skepticism about the justification of deduction, they are among the most forceful responses to this challenge.

I do not, however, intend to discuss here Dummett's conception of the justification of deduction. For I do not believe that an answer to a skeptic's challenge about justification can provide an answer to the other form of skepticism raised by Carroll's paradox, that is, (4), about the force of logical reasons. For this skepticism can arise even when we have a philosophically satisfactory account of the justification of logical rules. There are three things to distinguish in the story:[18]

   (i)   Do the two premises A and B imply the conclusion Z?
  (ii) Given that one has good reasons to believe that A and B are true, is it reasonable to believe that Z is true?
 (iii) Supposing it is reasonable for me to believe Z on the basis of A and B, what is supposed to move our mind to believe that Z?

Item (i), as we saw, is not in question. Neither is (ii), if we are equipped with an appropriate—let us suppose—molecularist justification of our rules of deduction. The point of skepticism about the force of logical reasons is that neither a positive answer to (i) nor a positive answer to (ii) can yield a positive answer to (iii). However willing to recognize the validity of the inference, and however well equipped with a full justification of deduction in general, this kind of skeptic will not be moved.

As I have already suggested above, in order to understand the challenge, it is interesting to compare it to a parallel kind of challenge for practical reasoning. Simon Blackburn (1995) in particular, in his essay for the centenary of Carroll's piece in *Mind*, shows that a similar problem to Carroll's arises when we consider an instance of practical reasoning:

(P) I would prefer lettuce to souvlaki
(B′) The moment of decision is at hand,
(Z′) Let me choose to eat lettuce rather than souvlaki!

However many premises of the form

(P*) It is right (good, desirable, rational, etc.) to prefer lettuce to souvlaki are added, the Tortoise still does not act. Blackburn argues for a "Humean conclusion" to the problem of skepticism about practical reasons: "there is always something else, something that is not under the control of fact and reason, which has to be given as a brute extra, if deliberation is ever to end by determining the will" (1995, 695).

There are, of course, strong differences between practical reasoning on the one hand, and logical reasoning and theoretical reasoning on the other hand: on the standard account, the former goes from beliefs and desires to intentions or actions, whereas the latter goes from beliefs to beliefs; desires do not have the same "direction of fit" as beliefs and desires are not, in general, under the control of the will, unlike actions. But the form of the skeptic's challenge about the force of logical reason is very close to the one which affects the practical case. For suppose that the Tortoise had accepted not only C but the apparently stronger:

(C*) It is a norm of correct deductive reasoning that if one accepts that MP kind of inferences are valid, one should in the presence of a particular instance of MP, accept the conclusion.

Suppose also that the Tortoise had recognized that

(I) The propositions A, B, and Z stand in the MP relation.

Would she not be bound to accept Z? No. (I) here plays the same role as the minor premise of the practical syllogism (P)–(Z′) above. But even though the Tortoise sees its truth, and accepts (C*), she is not moved. Neither would she if we reinforced again (C*) into :

(C**) There are absolute rational justifications for the norm of correct deductive reasoning that if one accepts that MP kinds of inferences are valid, one should in the presence of an instance of MP, accept the conclusion.

And so on. Whether we say that our norms of reasoning are justified because they are metaphysically necessary, or because they correspond to what ideal agents would believe in ideal circumstances, they would not be able to *force* us to reason according to them.

It is important to distinguish this (type (4)) skepticism raised by the Tortoise's resistance to accept the obvious conclusion from the type-(3) skepticism about justification. The skeptic about the force of logical reasons grants that we do have good reasons and justifications to infer according to a given rule of inference. Following the terminology which is common in the literature on practical reasoning, let us call these reasons *normative reasons*.[19] Now to say that they are normative is to say that, at least *prima facie*, they are such that a subject who recognizes them as reasons would be ready to act, or in the case at hand, to infer, according to them. A subject can, however, have good reasons to do an action, or to have a certain belief, but still not act upon this reason, and act upon other reasons, which might not be good ones. Such reasons will explain our action, and motivate it, but they will not necessarily coincide with the normative reasons that we have. They can be called *motivating reasons*. Of course the distinction between normative and motivating reasons does not imply that they cannot be identical. In the normal case, when, so to say, everything goes right, the reasons *for* acting or believing in a certain way just are the reasons *why* the agent acted or believed in that way. But the two can diverge. Cases of *akrasia* are a well-known example where normative reasons fail to be motivating, but there are simpler examples of the distinction. To use a well-worn example, I have reasons not to drink the glass of transparent liquid that is before me, because, unbeknownst to me, it is a glass of petrol, although I have a reason to drink it if I believe that it is a glass of water. In the case of having reasons for inferring a certain conclusion from certain premises which concerns us here, the situation is similar. Someone who believes that P and believes that if P then Q, has a normative reason to believe that Q—since the latter belief follows logically from the two others —but he still might not believe that Q. For he might, for other reasons, happen to believe that not Q (for instance, he has sworn to his mother that he would never believe Q). He might also believe that Q, as expected, but for other reasons, completely unconnected with P (Q is his favorite proposition: every time he encounters it, he asserts it). The *modus ponens* rule is a proposition of logic. As such it is worth being written down. But it does not tell you in itself anything about your beliefs. It tells you that if P, and if P then Q, imply Q, but it does not tell you that if you *believe* that P, and if you believe that if P then Q, then you *believe* that Q.[20] Similarly when we open a logic book, we just see a number of propositions written. The fact that they are in the book does not in itself move us to reason logically. We might nevertheless want to formulate the MP rule as a normative requirement of reasoning and belief. Then we would formulate it as a normative reason for belief, using the deontic term "ought":

(O1) You ought (to believe Q, if you believe that P, and that if P then Q)

This is just a reformulation of (C*) above. But the "ought" which figures in this proposition has a wide scope: it governs a conditional. (O1) does not allow you to infer or detach that

(O2) You ought to believe that Q[21]

for the reason that we have just noted. Your normative belief O1 does not tell you what particular belief you have to adopt relative to Q, it just tells you that your recognize O1 as a normative reason. On the present interpretation of the paradox, the Tortoise intends to remind us of this simple, but very important, point.

If we take this lesson of Carroll's tale seriously, the important question becomes: what is the relationship between the normative and the motivating reasons when it comes to having particular beliefs? Normally we should expect the normative reasons to be in some sense able to move us to having certain beliefs and to make certain inferences, that is to enter into certain kinds of psychological states. It is natural, therefore, to think of this relationship as a causal one. But how can normative reasons, which are supposed to be objective and independent of the agent's specific mental states, be able to move our minds in a particular way?[22]

<h1 style="text-align:center">III</h1>

If we interpret Carroll's story in this way, what kind of answer shall we adopt? The answers lie between two extremes.

One extreme view consists in adopting a form of Platonism about logical reasons. It was Frege's view: once we grasp that a certain proposition is a truth of logic, a "law of Being-True," we cannot but infer accordingly. Logical laws *as such* are normative, not only in the sense that they are absolutely correct, but also in the sense that they motivate us to infer in conformity with them. Being eternal laws of truth, the logical laws do not tell us anything about our psychology or about mental representations. But we have nevertheless a certain kind of relationship with them, which Frege, as most Platonists, conceives as a kind of intuitive grasp (*Fassung*).[23] So it is the direct, intuitive apprehension of the validity of *modus ponens* that is sufficient to move our minds to infer accordingly. In the field of practical rationality, this kind of view has been revived by writers who construe normative reasons as certain objective *facts*, the intuitive recognition of which is supposed to move the agent directly into doing the appropriate action. The view can be transposed to logical reasons.[24] The obvious problem with this view is precisely what the Tortoise, on our present interpretation of the story, is meant to remind Achilles of (who, for that matter, seems to be a straight Platonist): a Fregean Thought or a Platonic fact does not have any causal impact upon our minds, and intuition of Platonic fact seems even more mysterious than the idea of causal contact between laws of being true and our minds.

The other extreme view lies at the opposite end. It says that only a *psychological* state can play the *causal* role of moving the mind. This is an equivalent of the Humean solution that Blackburn suggests for the practical case. On such a view the existence of objective reasons for inference will never "move the mind." The mind, when it comes to ending a deliberation by an action, or a reasoning by the assertion of a conclusion, is always moved by some "brute extra." In the case of action, it must be, for a Humean, a desire or a passion, which is the only psychological state which can motivate one to act. In the case of reasoning from beliefs to beliefs, it also has to be some psychological state. But it cannot be a belief, for beliefs, at least on the official Humean doctrine, do not in themselves cause us to act. They cannot be motivating reasons. Hence the "brute extra" must consist in something else. The most plausible view would be that it is a *habit*. We could understand this in the way Hume gives a "sceptical solution" to his skeptical doubts about induction, by pointing out the force of habit and custom, or in a Wittgensteinian fashion, by saying that at some point, reasons must come to an end, and that drawing a conclusion from premises according to a rule of inference is "simply what we do." It is a brute fact of our practices that we reason *that* way.[25]

The problem with this is that it seems to give us a plausible answer to the causal question about the normative force of reasons at the expense of the justificatory nature of reasons. We lose sight, on this view, of why logical reasons are good reasons, and of how they can be objective. As Dummett says, to be told that we have the practice or habit of inferring in a certain way, and that *modus ponens* kinds of inferences belong to these practices, does not tell us whether we should maintain this practice if we believed the theory according to which the force of reasons consists in nothing but the existence of this practice.[26] Wittgenstein's kind of answer consists simply in questioning the normativity of logical reasons. He says, famously:

> F. P. Ramsey once emphasised in conversation with me that logic was a "normative science." I do not know exactly what he had in mind, but it was doubtless closely related to what only dawned on me later: namely, that in philosophy we often *compare* the use of words with games and calculi which have fixed rules, but cannot say that someone who is using language *must* be playing such a game. (Wittgenstein 1958, 38)

But this leaves us with a mystery: why is it that we find the reasons for our beliefs, and especially our inferential reasons, satisfactory and even compelling? I agree here with Dummett when he says, about Wittgenstein, that "we ought not to rest content with saying, of any feature of our linguistic practice, 'That is simply what we do'."[27] Not only does this view deprive logical reasons of any normativity, but also it does not tell us what they *do*.

But there are intermediate answers between these two extremes. The most natural one, if we agree that there must be some psychological state to cause the mind to infer a conclusion, would be that the state in question is a *belief* about the validity of the rule. But it is precisely this view which is the target of Carroll's paradox. Let us call this *reflective internalism*.[28] According to it, the subject would be reasoning by entertaining beliefs to the effect that a given rule is valid, and that he is presented with a particular instance of this rule, by reasoning in the following way:

> (*i*) Any inference of the form MP is valid
> (*ii*) This particular inference (from A and B to Z) is of MP form
> (*iii*) Hence this particular inference (from A and B to Z) is valid

Not only would such beliefs be reflective, in the sense that they would be beliefs about beliefs, but they would also be inferential, since (*i*)–(*iii*) is an inference. But the point of Carroll's story is that this kind of reflective belief would lead us to the familiar regress. This does not mean that we cannot have, when we reason from P to Q, such beliefs as *that if P were true, Q would be true*, or *that P implies Q*, but only

> that even if the person is said to believe or accept some statement R linking things he already believes with his conclusion we still must attribute to him something else in addition if we are to represent his belief in that conclusion as based on those other beliefs. That additional factor cannot be identified as simply some further proposition he accepts or acknowledges. There must always exist some "non propositional" factor if any of his beliefs are based on others. (Stroud 1979, 188–89)

Here Stroud's diagnosis is quite close to Blackburn's Humean view. He does not dispute that some beliefs are based on others, nor that there can be a "linking" belief of the reflective kind,[29] but denies that the belief in question is part of the content of the reason. Reflective internalism is the psychological counterpart of the Carroll story. Reflective beliefs about the validity of our inference rules can no more move our minds than the fact that further premises are added to the initial ones in the tale. As Paul Boghossian says, discussing this point:

> At some point it must be possible to use a rule in reasoning in order to arrive at a *justified* conclusion, without this use needing to be supported by some knowledge about the rule one is relying on. It must be possible simply to *move* between the thoughts in a way that generates justified belief, without this movement being grounded in the thinker's justified belief about the rule used in the reasoning. (Boghossian 2002, 37)

Reflective internalism says that our belief in the validity of the rule is the product of an inference, (*i*)–(*iii*). But we might still accept the idea that we must have in some sense an access to the thought that the inference is valid without this access being *inferential* or even reflective. We could say that this access is a direct access, which allows us to go from premises to conclusion through some insight or intuition, rather than through an act of reflection and an inference. For instance, Laurence Bonjour describes it in the following way (about disjunctive syllogism, but the latter is of course equivalent to MP in the form *not P or Q, not not P therefore Q*):

> I am invited to assess the cogency of inferring the conclusion that David ate the last piece of cake from the premises, first, that either David ate the last piece of cake or else Jennifer ate it and, second, that Jennifer did not eat it. . . . The obvious construal of this case from an intuitive standpoint is that if I understand the three propositions involved, I will be able to see or grasp or apprehend directly and immediately that the indicated conclusion follows from the indicated premises, that is that there is no way for the premises to be true without the conclusion being true as well. It is obvious, of course, that I might appeal in this case to a formal rule of inference, namely the rule of disjunctive syllogism. But there is no good reason to think that any such appeal is required in order for my acceptance of the inference as valid to be epistemically justified. Nor . . . is there any reason to think that such a rule would not itself have to be justified either by appeal to the same sort of apparent *a priori* insight at a more abstract level or else to other rules or propositions for which an analogous sort of justification would be required. (Bonjour 1998, 105–6)

Here Bonjour insists on the fact that rational insight does not depend "on any further ratiocinative process," nor on any reflective apprehension of the rule. Let us call this *nonreflective internalism*. Of course, in our post-Wittgensteinian times, a likely reaction to such a proposal may be to reinstate Wittgenstein's qualms about intuition: if it can lead me in one way, it can lead me in another, and it does not give me the possibility of distinguishing between what seems right and what is right. But the proponent of the idea of rational insight has a point, if he means that the kind of mental state involved in the recognition of a certain pattern as instantiating validity is neither reflective nor inferential: if it is not, then a regress like the Carrollian one does not seem to arise.[30] We may grant this point without finding this kind of description of what happens when one makes simple inferences less problematic than the Platonist's appeal to a faculty of intuition.[31]

None of these solutions—Platonism, Humcanism, reflective internalism, nonreflective internalism—is satisfactory. But the following points emerge. First, reasoning in the deductive manner from premises to conclusion does not involve any sort of belief about the normative rules that one follows. When we reason, we do not move from beliefs to beliefs through some linking proposition *about* the link between our beliefs, but we move directly from the content of certain beliefs to other contents. In this sense, our reasoning (at least for simple kinds of inference) is nonreflective and "blind."[32] But second, for all that, our reasoning is not blind, in the sense in which it would be simply a causal process leading us from certain beliefs to other ones. It has to be, in some sense, the exercise of a rational capacity, not a brute causal fact.

IV

Dummett's approach to the issues raised by Carroll's paradox as I described them in the previous section has been only indirect. It is not difficult to see why. In the first place, the chief problem which interests Dummett is that of the justification of deduction. It is then normal that he has no interest for the problem about the *force* of reasons as I have formulated it. In the second place, Dummett would probably remind me here about Wittgenstein's distinction between reasons and causes. The problem of finding an appropriate causal factor which would play the appropriate explanatory role in an account of how minds can be moved to infer would probably seem to him to imply some form of category mistake or a reversion to psychologism. Actually I do not think that psychologism is *always* irrelevant in the philosophy of thought, but this is not the place to argue for this.[33] But I am sure that Dummett would agree that we must at least give some plausible philosophical account of the kind of knowledge that is involved, which would allow us to understand not only why the Tortoise is justified to infer her conclusion, but also compelled to do so. And indeed Dummett's work gives us a number of clues to answer these questions.

It seems quite clear that the natural place to look for an answer to our problem is in an account of the way in which our *understanding* of the premises relates to our inferring the conclusion, as suggested by the second interpretation that we drew from the paradox suggests. In the first place, as Stroud (1979) has shown convincingly, Carroll's puzzle reminds us that to actually believe a certain proposition, especially on the basis of others, is not to have more propositions "written," either in one's notebook or some place in our minds.[34] To actually believe a certain proposition requires understanding it, where understanding is a complex kind of state. Our paradox obviously turns upon this, as Black's quotation above reminds us. If the Tortoise really understands the meaning of *if*, it seems absurd to say that she fails to perform a simple MP kind of inference. But precisely, in what does the meaning of a logical constant such as *if* consist? But, for the very same reason that believing that P is not simply to possess some sort of representation of P stored somewhere in a place where we could retrieve it, but actually understanding it, to have a certain account of the meanings of logical constants will not be sufficient to provide a speaker with an adequate understanding of their meanings, at least if this account is formulated in a certain way. Dummett has forcefully argued, in particular against Davidson's truth-theoretic version of what a theory of meaning could be, that such a theory, conceived as an abstract representation of the truth conditions of a language, would not suffice to give us a genuine, "full-blooded" understanding of this language. A distinction that the Tortoise needs is that between knowing that a sentence is true and knowing what proposition the sentence expresses. In this sense, she might be said not to understand the sentence C that she adds to her premises. Similarly, knowledge of what a sentence *s* means cannot simply consist in knowing a set of T-sentences of the form "*s* is true iff P," for one must also understand the biconditionals themselves. A regress looms here too.[35] But what would the Tortoise understand if she knew what the words presented to her mean? Does it consist in the canonical rules of inferences associated with the words? Dummett's molecularism rests upon a view of this kind, when he associates the assertion and justification conditions of logical constants with their meaning. Other writers, such as Peacocke and Boghossian, have proposed versions of the view according to which the meaning of logical constants is constituted by their canonical inferential rules.[36] But, as I said above regarding the problem of the justification of deduction, I do not think that a theory about the meaning of logical constants and a theory of the transfer of warrant from premises to conclusion can *by itself* solve the problem of the force of logical reasons. For the latter problem, to repeat, is not the question whether we are justified in our inferences, but the question of *how*, given that we are justified, we can account for our *actually* performing the inferences in question. Certainly the *shape* of the account of the meaning of logical words that we give affects the kind of account that we can give of how logic can move our mind, but it is certainly not sufficient.[37] So let us suppose that an account of logical constants is correct. It still would not tell us how one infers.

The obvious suggestion to answer this question is to try to characterize the kind of knowledge that one can have of a word like *if.* And the natural answer would seem to be Ryle's, in other words, that it is a piece of practical knowledge, of knowledge how, and not of propositional knowledge, knowledge that. This kind of knowledge would, moreover, be implicit or tacit, and not explicit. But, as Dummett has pointed out quite often in his discussion about knowledge of language, although the kind of knowledge that we have of the rules which govern the words of our language (and therefore of logical words as well) is implicit in the sense that it manifests itself partly through a form of practical ability and partly by readiness to acknowledge its content when presented, neither is it correct to characterize it as a form of practical knowledge nor is it sufficient to characterize it as a form of implicit knowledge.[38] Knowing a language, Dummett insists, is neither like knowing how to swim nor like knowing explicitly a set of propositions. To say that it is implicit knowledge in the sense of its being susceptible to conscious access in certain circumstances does not tell us much, unless we can state how this access can occur and how the knowledge in question is applied. For the same reason, Dummett considers that characterization of our knowledge of meaning in terms of tacit knowledge in the psychological style is just idle, and "does nothing to explain how it is delivered—how possession of the unconscious knowledge operates to guide, prompt, or control the speaker's utterances" (Dummett 1993, xi).

Dummett tells us that it is not enough to say that knowledge of meaning is implicit. It has to be manifested in the *use* that speakers make of the language. But this "manifestation requirement" is again in itself not sufficient. For the use in question must be such that the speaker is also *aware* of what this use amounts to. Dummett tells us that being aware of the meaning of one's word does not necessarily involve "having it in the forefront of one's consciousness," but this kind of knowledge must involve some sort of recognitional activity. What kind of recognition? The obvious answer is: recognition of fulfillment of the conditions which establish that a given sentence is true (1991, 317; 1993, 45). In other words, recognition of the assertability conditions of the sentence. On Dummett's account, then, what is missing in the Tortoise is the appropriate recognition of the assertability conditions of sentences of the *if P then Q* form.

The problem is that it is hard not to assimilate this view to what I have called above a form of reflective internalism. Even though the kind of knowledge that we manifest when we make elementary inferences such as A–Z is implicit, and when manifested not "in the forefront of our consciousness," it seems clear that what Dummett requires of knowledge of meaning is that such knowledge be, in Williamson's phrase, "luminous." What one must know in order to know that a certain connective has certain assertion-conditions, is that one *knows that one knows it*, or at least one must be in a position to know that one knows it (Williamson 2000, 111). My point here is not, unlike Williamson, to argue that the thesis that knowledge is "luminous" is false, that is, to argue against the thesis that to know that P one must know that one knows that P. It is just that if one accepts this thesis, or even the weaker thesis that to believe one must believe that one believes, or that one has a reflective awareness of what one believes, it is not clear that we move further than reflective internalism. The way in which Dummett describes our awareness of meaning also suggests that he might be close to what I have called above nonreflective internalism. But I doubt he would accept here the notion of rational intuition that this view presupposes. So it is not obvious that the Tortoise's challenge about the force of logical reasons has been appropriately answered. In any case, an externalist reading of the relationship between our logical reasons and our particular inferences seems to be required.[39]

This is not the place to attempt to describe what a possible solution to the problem of the force of logical reasons could be and I would not pretend to have one. I agree, however, with Dummett that one must give an account of our implicit knowledge of rules, and of the dispositions which are associated with their use. I also agree with him that there must be some sort of explanation of how these dispositions are manifested and how they can be prevented from being manifested in some cases. But I disagree with him that we must impose strong internalist requirements about our knowledge of rules, and I am less confident that the explanation in question can proceed at the level of the description of a practice in which everything is manifest and open to view, and that it can be completely free from causal considerations. Unless we answer these questions the Tortoise's challenge might well be still with us.

PASCAL ENGEL

UNIVERSITY OF PARIS SORBONNE
CENTRE FOR ADVANCED STUDY, OSLO
APRIL 2004

NOTES

This article was written while I was a member of the Centre for Advanced Study of the Norwegian Academy of Sciences in Oslo. I thank warmly the Center for its hospitality, and Olav Gjlesvik, Peter Pagin, Dag Prawitz, and Åsa Wikforss for fruitful discussion and help. My debt towards Michael Dummett is deep and long standing. I want to express here all my admiration and gratitude.

1. As it is named, for instance, in a recent collection of paradoxes, Clark 2002. It is not clear, however, that this puzzle is a genuine paradox, in the ordinary sense of a set of acceptable premises leading to an unacceptable conclusion through apparently acceptable rules of inference, for in the case at point precisely nothing is inferred from the premises.

2. Some writers (Stroud 1979) take the Tortoise's gender to be masculine, others (e.g., Smiley 1995, Simchen 2001) as neutral. My Harrap's Dictionary tells me that it is a feminine noun. Hence I shall adopt the feminine "she."

3. See Simchen 2001. The Tortoise agrees that (Z) "follows logically" from (A) and (B), and that "the sequence [expressed by (C)] is a valid one" (Carroll 1895, 691).

4. Among the reactions to Carroll's paradox along these lines, see: Peirce 1902 (*Collected Papers* 2.27); Russell 1903, 35, note; Ryle 1945–46; Brown 1954; Geach 1965; Thomson 1960; Smiley 1995.

5. Dogson 1977, 472. Quoted by Smiley 1995.

6. Quoted by Stroud 1979: this is also, basically, the moral that Stroud derives from the paradox.

7. Ryle 1945–46, Ryle 1949.

8. Quine 1936 (in 1976, 104, n. 21). The presentation above is from Harman 1996, 395.

9. See Korsgaard 1986.

10. Blackburn 1995, Engel 1998.

11. This is also Russell's diagnosis: according to him the solution to Carroll's puzzle resides in the distinction between the relation of (implies) which holds between two propositions, and which can be considered without being asserted, and the relation of consequence (*therefore*) which holds between two *asserted* propositions. Russell explicitly mentions Frege in this respect.

12. Ryle 1954, although he notoriously takes the *modus ponens* rule to be an "inference ticket" to the conclusion, to which Geach (1965) objects that if the inference from the premises to the conclusion is valid, there is neither need of a supplementary premise nor of a license for going from the premises to the conclusion.

13. See Dummett 1973, 434; 1991, ch. 11.

14. Goodman's and Rawls' notion of "reflective equilibrium" would be here the appropriate kind of justification, as Dag Prawitz reminded me. See his 1978 article on this point.

15. See Tennant 1986, 76–80. Quine's presentation of the regress of justification to which the derivation of logical truths from conventions leads explicitly employs axioms and their instances. Tennant argues that once *modus ponens* is conceived as a natural deduction rule (conditional elimination), the regress cannot start.

16. Dummett 1973a; 1991, chs. 10, 11.

17. See, for example, Haack 1982, Tennant 1986, Engel 1991.

18. See Schueler 1995.

19. See for instance Dancy 2000. For a more elaborate parallel between the practical case and the theoretical case, see Engel 2005.

20. Harman 1986 makes this point.

21. Broome (2000 and 2002) emphasizes this point.

22. Simchen 2001 formulates well this form of skepticism, but his analysis of the paradox focuses on the question whether a rule can be action guiding, especially when it is quoted. I cannot deal here with this specific interpretation of the paradox.

23. In the preface to the *Grundgesetze der Arithmetik*, Frege tells us that we should distinguish two senses of "law" when we talk about the laws of thought: the normative and the causal. Psychologism confuses these two senses. For Frege, the laws of thought are normative insofar as they are descriptive of a Third Realm. See Dummett, "Frege's Myth of the Third Realm" in Dummett 1991a.

24. See Engel 2005. The Platonist view in the practical case is defended by Dancy 2000.

25. This would in some sense harmonize with what Kripke (1981) calls Wittgenstein's "skeptical solution" to his "skeptical paradox" about rules. Dummett hints at this "brute fact" when he describes Wittgenstein's position: "We do, by and large, agree on what the consequences are, what follows from what, what is a valid proof and what is not. . . . On Wittgenstein's view, it is a *brute* fact: nothing explains it." ("Wittgenstein on Necessity: Some Reflections," in Dummett 1993, 449). On Wittgenstein's views on logic, see also Lear 1982, 387 (who defends an interpretation quite distinct from Dummett's), and Railton 1999.

26. Dummett "Wittgenstein on Necessity: Some Questions," in Dummett 1993, 446.

27. Dummett 1973a, 309.

28. The view described is quite close to what Boghossian (2003) describes as "simple inferential internalism" (2003, see also his 2002 article, where he adopts slightly different formulations). I here only *partly* use Boghossian's formulation for he is concerned, in his paper, with the question of the *justification* of the rules of reasoning, and not with the question of their normative force.

29. The notion of a "linking" belief is also the one used by Broome op. cit.

30. Crispin Wright suggests something of that sort in his commentary on Boghossian 2002 (Wright 2002, 83). He calls it "simple internalism." Wright also suggests (78–79) that the regress as presented by Boghossian might not be vicious. I cannot deal with this point here, which has more to do with the problem of justification, which is not my direct concern. Something like this view is suggested by Bill Brewer. "There is more to grasping the laws of logic or mathematical argument than simply being disposed to have one's beliefs mirror the moves they prescribe. Epistemologically productive reasoning is not a merely mechanical manipulation of belief, but a compulsion in thought *by reason*, and as such involves conscious understanding of why one is right in one's conclusion" (Brewer 1995, 242). Brewer talks of "causation in virtue of rationalisation." But this seems to me just to give a label to the problem, not to give a solution to it.

31. Boghossian 2003, 235–36.

32. Boghossian 2003, an elaboration of Wittgenstein's famous remark: "I obey the rule blindly."

33. See Engel 1996, and Engel 1998a.

34. Dennett 1978; Stroud 1979, 194. A certain version of the thesis that there is language of thought is open to the Carrollian objection.

35. Dummett, "What is a Theory of Meaning" I (1975), and II (1976).

36. Peacocke 1992; Boghossian 1999, 2002, 2003. For an opposite view, see Williamson 2003.

37. For instance Boghossian (2003) gives the following account: "A deductive pattern of inference P may be blamelessly employed, without any reflective appreciation of its epistemic status, just in case inferring according to P is a precondition for having the concepts ingredient in it." Boghossian speaks of a blind, but blameless (entitling) inference. This mixes psychological characteristics (blindness, nonreflectivity) with a justificatory one (blamelessly). But my problem

is with the former. Boghossian's (2002) formulation is: "If fundamental inferential dispositions fix what we mean by ours words, then we are entitled to act on these dispositions prior to and independently of an explicit justification for them." But for the purpose (which is not Boghossian's, but mine) of spelling out what the dispositions are—which is certainly part of the answer to the psychological problem of how we can causally be moved to infer—it presupposes an answer to this problem.

38. See in particular "What is a Theory of Meaning? (II)" and "What do I Know when I Know a Language?" in Dummett 1993, chs. 2 and 3.

39. Olav Gjelsvik pointed this out to me, suggesting that at this point the epistemology of logical knowledge might benefit from virtue epistemology. In discussion Peter Pagin has also suggested to me a very interesting way to relate interpretations (1) and (4) of the paradox. We always have to formulate rules of inference so that they do not become other propositions. So we formulate them in a metalanguage. Rules in this sense are always general, whereas their applications are always particular. One always has to have variables. Hence there is always a gap. This gap is related to the causal gap between normative reason and motivation reason. I have given some hints of a solution in Engel 2001 and 2005. In Engel 1994, I argued that some notion of tacit knowledge of a theory of meaning is legitimate.

REFERENCES

Bermúdez, José, and Alan Millar, eds. 2002. *Reason and Nature*. Oxford: Oxford Univ. Press.

Black, Max. 1951. "Achilles and the Tortoise." *Analysis* 11:91–101.

———. 1970. "The Justification of Logical Axioms." In *Margins of Precision*. Cornell: Cornell Univ. Press.

Blackburn, Simon. 1995. "Practical Tortoise Raising." *Mind* 104:695–711.

Boghossian, Paul. 1999. "Knowledge of Logic." In Boghossian and Peacocke 2000.

———. 2002. "How are Objective Reasons Possible? In Bermúdez and Millar 2002.

———. 2003 "Blind Reasoning." *Supplement to the Proceedings of the Aristotelian Society* 77, no. 1 (July 2003): 225–48.

Boghossian, Paul, and Christopher Peacocke, eds. 2000. *New Essays on the A Priori*. Oxford: Oxford Univ. Press.

Bonjour, Laurence. 1998. *In Defense of Pure Reason*. Cambridge: Cambridge Univ. Press.

Brewer, Bill. 1995. "Compulsion by Reason." *Proceedings of the Aristotelian Society*, supp. vol. 69:237–54.

Broome, J. R. 2000. "Normative Requirements." In Dancy 2000.

———. 2002. "Practical Reasoning." In Bermúdez and Millar 2002.

Brown, D. G. 1954. "What the Tortoise Taught Us." *Mind* 63, no. 250: 170–79.

Carroll, Lewis (C. L. Dogson). 1895. "What the Tortoise said to Achilles." *Mind* 1:278–80.

Clark, Michael. 2002. *Paradoxes, from A to Z*. London: Routledge.

Dancy, Jonathan. 2000. Practical Reality. Oxford: Oxford Univ. Press.

———, ed. 2000a. *Normativity*. Oxford: Blackwell.

Dennett, Daniel. 1978. "Brain Writing and Mind Reading." In *Brainstorms*. Cambridge, MA: MIT Press.

Dogson, C. L. 1977. *Lewis Carroll's Symbolic Logic*, ed. W. Bartley III. New York: Clarkson Potter.

Dummett, Michael. 1973. *Frege, Philosophy of Language*. London: Duckworth.

———. 1973a. "The Justification of Deduction." In Dummett 1978.

———. 1975. "What Is a Theory of Meaning? (I)." In *Mind and Language*, ed. S. Guttenplan. Oxford: Oxford Univ. Press. Reprinted in Dummett 1993.

———. 1976. "What Is a Theory of Meaning? (II)." In *Truth and Meaning*, ed. G. Evans and J. McDowell. Oxford: Oxford Univ. Press. Reprinted in Dummett 1993.

———. 1978. *Truth and Other Enigmas*. London: Duckworth.

———. 1991. *The Logical Basis of Metaphysics*. Harvard: Harvard Univ. Press.

———. 1991a. *Frege and Other Philosophers*. Oxford: Oxford Univ. Press.

———. 1993. *The Seas of Language*. Oxford: Oxford Univ. Press.

Engel, Pascal. 1991. *The Norm of Truth*. Harvester: Hemel Hamstead.

———. 1994. *Davidson et la philosophie du langage*. Paris: Presses universitaires de France.

———. 1996. *Philosophie et psychologie*. Paris: Gallimard.

———. 1998. "La logique peut elle mouvoir l'esprit?" *Dialogue* 37:35–53.

———. 1998a. "L'antipsychologisme est-il irrésistible?" In M. Marion and A. Voizard, *Frege, logique et philosophie*. Paris: l'Harmattan.

———. 2001. "Logica, ragionamento e constanti logische." In *Ragionamento, psicologia e logica*, ed. P. Cherubini, P. Giaretta, and A. Mazzocco. Florence: Giunti, 108–27. Published in English as "Logic, Reasoning and the Logical Constraints" (*Croatian Journal of Philosophy* 6, no. 17 [2006]: 219–35).

———. 2005. "Logical Reasons." *Philosophical Explorations* 8, no. 1: 21–38.

Geach, Peter T. 1965. "Assertion." *Philosophical Review*. Repr. in *Logic Matters*. Oxford: Blackwell, 1972, 254–69.

Haack, Susan. 1976. "The Justification of Deductions." *Mind* 85:112–19.

———. 1982. "Dummett's Justification of Deduction." *Mind* 91, no. 362: 216–39.

Harman, Gilbert. 1986. *Change in View*. Cambridge, MA: MIT Press.

———. 1996. "Analyticity Regained?" *Nous* 30 (1996): 392–400.

Korsgaard, C. 1986. "Scepticism about Practical Reasoning." *Journal of Philosophy* 83: 5–25.

Kripke, Saul. 1981. *Wittgenstein on Rules and Private Language*. Oxford: Blackwell.

Lear, Jonathan. 1982. "Leaving the World Alone. "*Journal of Philosophy* 79, no. 7: 382–403.

Peacocke, Christopher. 1992. *A Study of Concepts*. Cambridge, MA: MIT Press.

Peirce, C. S. 1935–1962. *Collected Papers*. Ed. C. Hartshorne, A. Burks, and P. Weiss. 8 vols. Harvard: Harvard Univ. Press.

Prawitz, Dag. 1978. "Om moraliska och logiska satsers sanning." In *En filosofibok*, ed. L. Bergström et al. Stockholm: Bonniers, 145–55.

Railton, Peter. 1997. "On the Hypothetical and the Non-Hypothetical in Belief and
    Action." In *Ethics and Practical Reason*, ed. G. Cullity and B. Gaut. Oxford:
    Oxford Univ. Press.
————. 2000. "Wittgenstein on the Normativity of Logic." In Boghossian and
    Peacocke 2000.
Russell. Bertrand. 1903. *The Principles of Mathematics*. London: Allen and Unwin.
Ryle, Gilbert. 1945-46. "Knowing How and Knowing That." *Proceeedings of the
    Aristotelian Society*. 1949, in *The Concept of Mind*, London: Hutchninson.
————. 1954. "If, So and Because." In G. Ryle, *Dilemmas*, Oxford: Oxford Univ.
    Press.
Schueler, G. F. 1995. "Why 'Oughts' are not Facts." *Mind* 104:712–23.
Simchen, Ori. 2001. "Rules and Mentions." *Philosophical Quarterly* 51, no. 205
    (Oct.): 455.
Smiley, Timothy. 1995. "A Tale of Two Tortoises." *Mind* 104:725–36.
Stroud, Barry. 1979. "Inference, Belief and Understanding." *Mind* 88:179–96.
Tennant, Neil. 1986. *Anti-Realism and Logic*. Oxford: Oxford Univ. Press.
Thomson, J. F. 1960. "What Achilles Should Have Said to the Tortoise." *Ratio* 3:
    95–105.
Williamson, Timothy. 2000. *Knowledge and its Limits*. Oxford: Oxford Univ. Press.
————. 2003. "Understanding and Inference." *Proceedings of the Aristotelian
    Society* 77:249–93.
Wittgenstein, Ludwig. 1958. *Philosophical Investigations*. Trans. G. E. M.
    Anscombe. Oxford: Oxford Univ. Press.
Wright, Crispin. 2002. "On Basic Logical Knowledge." In Bermúdez and Millar
    2002, 49–84.

REPLY TO PASCAL ENGEL

I much enjoyed Pascal Engel's inconclusive discussion of what was wrong with the Tortoise of Lewis Carroll's one brilliant incursion into philosophy, and his instructive survey of the many inconclusive attempted solutions to it, although I appreciated less his challenge to me to give a conclusive diagnosis.

So what *is* wrong with the Tortoise? Let us change the story a little. Achilles and the Tortoise are sheltering under a tree. Achilles says, "There's going to be a thunderstorm." "I think you're right." says the Tortoise. "If there's a thunderstorm, this tree will be struck by lightning," Achilles goes on. "Yes, I'm sure that in that event, it will be," agrees the Tortoise. "So the tree is going to be struck by lightning, and we'd better get out from under it," Achilles concludes. "I don't see that," the Tortoise says. There *is* a thunderstorm; Achilles runs out into the open, but the Tortoise remains for a bit sheltering under the tree. The tree *is* struck by lightning, and falls on the Tortoise; perhaps she was just coming out from under it. The poor Tortoise is killed.

What is the moral of this story? One moral is that elementary logic can save your life. But what mistake did the Tortoise make? Let us suppose that Achilles is a kindly man and wishes to save the Tortoise's life: so he engages in some more dialogue with the Tortoise before the thunderstorm breaks. When the Tortoise says, "I don't see that," he says, "Well, if it's true to say, 'If there's going to be a thunderstorm, the tree will be struck by lightning,' then if 'There's going to be a thunderstorm' is true, then 'The tree is going to be struck by lightning' is true." "I suppose that's right," the Tortoise concedes. "You agreed that 'If there's going to be a thunderstorm, the tree will be struck by lightning' is true," Achilles goes on. "Not in so many words, but I do agree," says the Tortoise. "And you agreed that 'There's going to be a thunderstorm' is true," Achilles continues. "Again, not in so many words," says the Tortoise cautiously. "But you do agree?" asks Achilles. "Yes," says the Tortoise. "So it follows that 'The tree is going to be struck by lightning' is true," Achilles triumphantly concludes. "That's just what I don't see," says the Tortoise; "I can't accept it." "But you *must* accept it," says Achilles. "Why must I? Show me that I must," the Tortoise challenges.

"Very well, let us discuss the matter in terms of accepting propositions," Achilles responds. "For our purposes," he goes on, "we may understand the statement that some given proposition, say 'Zeus is more powerful than Apollo,' is true as meaning that it is right to accept it, and would be wrong to reject it." "Very well," says the Tortoise, "for the purposes of our discussion I agree to assume that that is what the word 'true' means." "Very well, then," says Achilles, "you agree that it is right to accept the statement 'If there's going to be a thunderstorm, the tree will be struck by lightning,' and that it would be wrong to reject it." "Not only do I agree with that, but I do accept that statement," the Tortoise replies. "And," Achilles continues, "you also agree that it is right to accept the statement 'There's going to be a thunderstorm,' and that it would be wrong to reject it." "I agree, and I accept that statement too," answers the Tortoise. "So you must acknowledge that it is right to accept the statement 'The tree is going to be struck by lightning,' and that it would be wrong to reject it," Achilles declaims. "I still ask, why must I? I don't see that you have shown me that I must, at all," the Tortoise plaintively responds.

What can Achilles say now? If he is as wise as he is kind, he will decline to be launched on an infinite regress; but what *can* he say? He might try asking the Tortoise what he thinks is involved in accepting a statement. The dialogue might proceed as follows:

Achilles: What do you think constitutes accepting a statement, say the statement "A thunderstorm is taking place," said perhaps at a moment at which you have not yet heard any thunder or seen any lightning?

Tortoise: Well, if someone else said, "It's a thunderstorm," I should agree with him, but if someone said, "It's only an ordinary rainstorm," I should contradict him, saying, "No, it's a thunderstorm." And if someone asked me on the telephone, "What's the weather like with you?" I should reply, "There's a thunderstorm going on."

Achilles: So it would be just a matter of your verbal behaviour, would it?

Tortoise: We are talking about my accepting a linguistic utterance, so this would naturally consist in my propensity to linguistic behaviour.

Achilles: Surely accepting a statement may affect your conception of how things are, have been, or are going to be?

Tortoise: I don't have a *conception*, as you call it, of how things are, were, or will be. My verbal behaviour is not guided by any 'conception'.

Achilles: But you surely have expectations about what will happen, and about what you will find out about what is happening or has happened. What you were expecting is shown by what surprises you.

Tortoise: Of course I have expectations.

Achilles: In that case you at least have a tacit conception of how things are.

Tortoise: The phrase "a tacit conception" sounds to me like a contradiction in terms.

Achilles: I don't mean that a tacit conception may *guide* you in what you say and do. The tacit conception is *constituted* by the expectations you have.

Tortoise: Very well, if that's all you mean, I have a tacit conception of how things are.

Achilles: And surely accepting a statement affects your expectations.

Tortoise: I suppose it may.

Achilles: So accepting the statement, "A thunderstorm is taking place," may lead to your taking appropriate action—I mean the action you would take if you yourself could observe the thunderstorm. For instance, if your dog, like most dogs, was frightened by thunder, you might call it over to you and comfort it.

Tortoise: I suppose it might have that effect on me.

Achilles: So your accepting a statement may be manifested in your non-verbal actions as well as in your verbal ones.

Tortoise: It seems so.

Achilles: Now what would your accepting the statement "There will be a thunderstorm soon" involve?

Tortoise: I should thereupon form an expectation of a thunderstorm in an hour or so.

Achilles: And would not this expectation result in your taking suitable precautions, such as coming indoors to be out of the rain?

Tortoise: Yes, it would.

Achilles: Now what about your accepting the statement, "If there is a thunderstorm, the tree will be struck by lightning"?

Tortoise: I should form a conditional expectation.

Achilles: What do you mean by that?

Tortoise: Well, if a thunderstorm took place, I should then form the *unconditional* expectation that the tree would be struck by lightning. It's just as if I had been handed an envelope on which was written, "Open only in the case of a thunderstorm," and inside was a piece of paper saying, "The tree will be struck by lightning."

Achilles: I don't think it's quite like that. If I accepted the conditional statement, and there was a storm, but at the end of it the tree had not been struck by lightning, I should conclude that it had not been a thunderstorm.

Tortoise: I think that a conditional statement is operative—has an effect on what one thinks—only if the antecedent is fulfilled.

Achilles: And if there was a thunderstorm, and you accordingly expected that the tree would be struck by lightning, what would you do?

Tortoise: I should take avoiding action by coming out from under the tree, just as you would.

Achilles: It might be too late once the thunderstorm had actually started.

Tortoise: It might: you must remember that I cannot run as fast as you.

Achilles: But what if you had also previously accepted the statement "There will be a thunderstorm shortly"?

Tortoise: How does that alter the case? My acceptance of the conditional statement can only become operative once a thunderstorm starts.

Achilles: Why should that be? Did you not agree that accepting the statement "A thunderstorm is going on" involved your acting just as you would if you yourself could perceive the thunderstorm?

Tortoise: I did.

Achilles: And you also agreed that accepting such a statement as "There will be a thunderstorm soon" would involve your taking actions in accordance with the expectation you would thereby form.

Tortoise: Yes; but present actions are not in question: the tree gives quite good shelter from the rain.

Achilles: Present actions *are* in question, when you have also accepted the conditional statement "If there is a thunderstorm, the tree will be struck by lightning," just because you cannot run as fast as I.

Tortoise: But acceptance of the conditional statement only becomes operative when the antecedent is fulfilled.

Achilles: Why should that be? Suppose that you had become convinced, not from anybody else's say-so, but from your own observations, that there would be a thunderstorm. Would that not make your acceptance of the conditional statement operative? Would that not lead you to open the envelope?

Tortoise: No, it wouldn't. To do so would violate a trust that the maker of the conditional statement had placed in me.

Achilles: That is ridiculous. I am sure that the maker of that statement did not mean it in that way. Why should he?

Tortoise: Don't you think that I know Greek as well as you?

Achilles: You do not seem to.

[This dialogue has been translated, as was Carroll's, from the original Greek.]

So what does this dialogue show to have been the Tortoise's mistake? At first it seems that she is unaware of what accepting a statement should involve. But then it seems that it is, as on Black's view, a case of her having a bizarre interpretation of the word "if." Perhaps we may generalise this: the Tortoise does not properly understand what it is to believe something on testimony. So she does not speak our language—not in a salient respect.

It might, however, have been that the Tortoise had not accepted the statement "There will be a thunderstorm soon," because Achilles or someone else had told her so, but because, being something of a meteorologist herself, she had worked it out for herself. So it comes back to our earlier original diagnosis: the Tortoise fails to understand what is involved in accepting a statement. If she had done, then, upon accepting, for whatever reason, the future-tensed statement, she would have acted, and thought, as she would have acted and thought when she felt the raindrops, saw the lightning and heard the thunder—or as she would have wished, when she felt the raindrops, saw the lightning and heard the thunder, to have acted and thought beforehand. And this includes her acting on her acceptance of the conditional statement; that is, 'opening the envelope' just as she would have done if she were experiencing the thunderstorm, and in consequence accepting the apodosis "The tree will be struck by lightning"—the contents of the envelope—and acting on it. The tortoise does indeed interpret conditionals—the word "if"—in a peculiar way: she could never infer by *modus tollendo tollens*. But, even granted her interpretation of them, that is, of the word "if," her fundamental mistake remains that of not appreciating what is involved in accepting a statement.

But in what respect does the Tortoise fail to appreciate it? She has acknowledged, grudgingly, that her acceptance of a statement is liable to be manifested not only by what she says but by what she does; so we cannot convict her of supposing that accepting a statement can affect only the subject's verbal behaviour. In any case, it is in the first place in her verbal behaviour that the Tortoise manifests her eccentricity: she will not accept that the tree will be struck by lightning. Why can she not see that acceptance of a conditional statement may, in her words, be operative before the antecedent is fulfilled? It is not a matter of her idiosyncratic understanding of the word "if": it is that she does not conduct herself in accordance with a picture of the world that is constantly modified by the new things she learns (and old things she unlearns)—new things encapsulated in new statements she accepts, whether or not she explicitly formulates them. Acceptance of a statement is for her a readiness to make certain specific responses, verbal and non-verbal, rather than a modification of a comprehensive conception of how things are about her (and within her), in the light of which she acts, and speaks, and thinks. If it were the latter, as it is for all normal human speakers, then accepting the statement "There will be a thunderstorm" would automatically affect her response when she came also to accept a conditional statement of which that was the antecedent: there would be no envelope to be opened.

This discussion has proceeded as if accepting a statement were an all-or-nothing affair. Of course it is not: there are degrees of acceptance. Even if the Tortoise had worked it out for herself, she still might have accepted the statement "There will be a thunderstorm" only with reservations: she feels pretty certain her calculations were right, but she could have made a mistake. Acting on a statement accepted with reservations is a matter for nice judgement: the subject must weigh the cost of acting in accordance with it if it is wrong against the cost of not doing so if it is right. In the present case, the cost of unnecessarily moving out from under the tree is slight in comparison with that of having the tree fall on you; but it will not always work out in the same way.

I do not believe, with Blackburn, that any brute extra, responsive neither to reason nor to fact, is needed for someone to draw a valid conclusion from premisses he accepts. But, equally, I do not think that it is always irrational to refuse to draw a conclusion from premisses which one is disposed to accept and from which one cannot deny that it follows. If it were, there would be no paradoxes. There is such a thing as a gut feeling that such-and-such simply *can't* be true, and it is not infrequently justified. And it may yet be that, in the face of such a feeling, one cannot see what is wrong with the argument—where the inference went wrong, or where the premisses failed. What is irrational is to insist that the premisses *were* true and that the reasoning *was* valid. If one has to be content with saying, "There must be something wrong somewhere," that is enough to certify one as rational.

I hope that Pascal Engel will find my account of the matter more satisfactory than he has found the others he discusses. But I dare not expect that he will.

M. D.

22

Peter M. Sullivan

DUMMETT'S CASE FOR CONSTRUCTIVIST LOGICISM

S elf-evidently the standard work on the topic its whole title defines, Sir
Michael Dummett's *Frege: Philosophy of Mathematics* (*FPM*), is also
the most profound and creative discussion in recent decades of the problems
confronting the philosophy of mathematics in general. Chapters 14–18 and
23–24 of this book constitute a continuous and challenging diagnosis of
these problems.[1] They culminate in the proposal that these problems present
an impasse that can be escaped only by adopting a constructivist understanding of mathematical generality. Dummett's case for that conclusion is
no less complexly over-layered than the problems themselves. By contrast
my aims in this discussion of his case are limited in various ways, and three
of these should be mentioned straightaway. In the first place, I will aim to
consider a case that, if sound, would warrant a constructivist understanding
of generality in mathematics generally (and so I will not be considering
lines of argument specific to set theory, or to those parts of mathematics
plausibly dependent on notions intrinsic to set theory). Secondly, I aim to
consider a case which, while general in its application within mathematics,
is not more general than that (and so would not warrant a broader anti-
realism). Reasons for these first two limitations are discussed in section I.
A third limitation is that I will aim only to understand Dummett's case, and
not to assess it. Perhaps some will think this third limitation calls for
explanation or excuse. I think it needs no excuse and that the explanation
is obvious. When we are dealing with fundamentally important work by a
great philosopher, understanding is often ambition enough. In Michael
Dummett's work, that is what we are dealing with.

I. The Kind of Case to Be Considered

Several writers have questioned Richard Heck's claim that in the concluding chapters of *FPM* Dummett presents us with a "new" case for
constructivism, distinct from his earlier meaning-theoretic argument.[2] On
the face of it Heck is clearly right. The earlier meaning-theoretic argument
turned on the challenge to explain how we could possibly acquire or
manifest grasp of a kind of meaning that fixes as the norm for the correct
use of an expression a condition whose obtaining we are not in general
capable of recognizing. As Dummett immediately observed on formulating
this argument in "The Philosophical Basis of Intuitionistic Logic," it has
nothing specially to do with "the *mathematical* character" of the statements
he was there particularly concerned with (Dummett 1978, 226): a theory
falls within the scope of this argument as soon as not all of its statements
are effectively decidable, a condition at least as soon met in history or
astronomy as in arithmetic. The approach in *FPM* appears to be very
different. The general acquisition and manifestation challenges are not made
prominent there; also, the argument seems crucially to depend on features
of mathematical concepts and statements that are explicitly contrasted with
those of such empirical disciplines as history or astronomy—for instance,
their unrestricted applicability, their necessity and apriority.

Those observations give us some reason to think that Heck's claim is
right. In addition I think we have reasons of three kinds to hope that it is
right, or at least to see how far we can get in reconstructing Dummett's case
on the assumption that it is right.

The first kind of reason is that we do not want the case considered to be
too general. Constructivism in mathematics presents a seriously considered
and developed alternative to classical methods. In sharp contrast with that,
few would claim to have any secure grasp of what anti-realism about the
past actually amounts to. Since there is always reason to consider the
strongest case that can be given for a position, our aim should be to consider
a case for the first that is not weakened by being simultaneously a case for
the second.

To meet that aim the case we consider has to be, not just distinct from
the general meaning-theoretic argument in making essential reference to
features specific to mathematics, but independent of it. Now those I
mentioned, who suspect Dummett's new and specific argument of resting
at bottom on the old and general one, locate that suspicion in the use the
new argument makes of the notion of an indefinitely extensible concept. An
indefinitely extensible concept is defined as one associated with a principle
by which any definite conception of a totality of objects falling under it
provides for the framing of a more inclusive such conception. From that

definition it immediately follows that we can have no definite conception of *all* the objects falling under an indefinitely extensible concept. A classical generalization is conceived as the product or sum of all its instances. So we cannot claim to grasp such a generalization when we lack any definite conception of which instances those are. This constitutes a short argument to the effect that generalization over the objects falling under an indefinitely extensible concept cannot be construed classically. The argument is valid, but as yet it remains to be connected with any of the generalizations attempted in mathematics.[3] Concepts giving the range of some of those generalizations, centrally the concepts of *set* and *ordinal*, do indeed have a feature, that following Russell we can call *self-reproductiveness*, a feature that bears an obvious structural parallel to the feature by which indefinite extensibility was defined: by reference to, so exploiting a conception of, the sets up to a certain rank, we are able to define what are demonstrably new sets, so to frame a more inclusive conception of the kind we began with. Similarly, any initial segment of the sequence of ordinals yields to us their successor. For all the parallel, though, self-reproductiveness is not without further argument indefinite extensibility. The needed further argument would have to establish that only conceptions of totalities destined to be outstripped in the self-reproductive process can qualify as *definite* conceptions, and that therefore the concepts of *set* and *ordinal* are indefinitely extensible. This would need to be established against the natural alternative, that grasp of the self-reproductive feature of these concepts precisely constitutes a definite conception of the sets or the ordinals, on which view the notion of an indefinitely extensible concept, while clearly enough defined, may be, for all that consideration of mathematics shows us, empty. However the argument here is imagined to run, it must surely turn centrally on what it is for a conception to be definite, and thus on broader meaning-theoretic considerations as to what in general is required for grasp of a definite concept. An argument from indefinite extensibility could not, then, be the independent argument for constructivism that it is reasonable to hope for, since it would take general meaning-theoretic argument to establish the premise that any of the relevant concepts is in fact indefinitely extensible. For that reason indefinite extensibility will play no role as premise in the case to be considered here (though of course it remains an importantly illuminating way of formulating the intended conclusion).

The second reason is that the case we consider should not be too restricted in its application, or not general enough. In *FPM* Dummett argues that the concept of natural number is indefinitely extensible (1991, 318). In "The Philosophical Significance of Gödel's Theorem" the "lowest" concept clearly held to be indefinitely extensible had been that of a well-defined property of all the natural numbers (1978, 198). When the notion of indefinite extensibility is motivated by a diagnosis of the paradoxes, it becomes at least contentious whether the concept of real number can be argued to be indefinitely extensible (Clark 1998), and all the more so whether natural number can be. Our best hope of avoiding these problems is by considering a case based on features clearly shared by the concepts defining all the fundamental mathematical domains, and that will be my approach here. (In line with that approach, and for ease and simplicity, I will often state aspects of the case as applying primarily to arithmetic.)

A third reason comes from what I think is a natural and unbiased reading of the final section of *FPM*, where Dummett presents his case in summary form. One passage (315–17) of this section relates specifically to the paradoxes and the role that the notion of indefinite extensibility can have in resolving them. It is introduced, "This does not apply only to concepts like *set* and *ordinal* . . ."; and at its close the theme of the preceding paragraph is taken up again with the words, "One reason why the philosophy of mathematics appears at present to be becalmed. . . ." The passage reads, in other words, as an explanatory interlude designed to make clear the intended scope of the main argument, rather than to contain the main argument. If that impression is accurate, then we should look for the basis of Dummett's case in the passages that surround this interlude. What one finds there, especially at pages 314 and 318–19, is a striking emphasis on the profound contrasts between empirical and mathematical investigation, and in particular on what is required for understanding a generalization in mathematics in contrast to one involving an empirical concept. My aim here is to consider a case that gives to these contrasts the centrality they seem to deserve.

Together, then, the three reasons mentioned encourage us to look for a case that starts from fundamental contrasts between mathematics and empirical science, that is motivated independently of the paradoxes (though yielding an approach to them), and that applies as much to arithmetic as to set theory. These together do not, of course, guarantee that there is a compelling case of this kind to be found (and towards the close I will express a reservation about whether we can, after all, hope to embrace arithmetic). I believe, though, that it is possible to get further along this road than many would imagine; also, that the case that emerges, even if it is no more than part of what Dummett intended, is one of real importance.

In the following section I will first set out the case bluntly as a simple two-premise argument, and then explain how this argument relates to the rather different presentation Dummett offers in the concluding chapter of *FPM*. In subsequent sections I will discuss in turn the meaning and motivation of the two premises.

II. The Argument Bluntly Presented

What I take to be Dummett's best case for constructivism, stated for the case of arithmetic, runs as follows.

(1) It is incoherent to suppose that anything might make for the truth of any statement of arithmetic save the conception we have of the objects it concerns. Arithmetical truth, that is, cannot outrun what is settled as true by our conception of the numbers.

(2) It would be hopelessly heroic to lay claim to a conception of the numbers determinate enough to fix as true or as false every statement in the language of arithmetic.

(3) So we must claim less: a conception that does not pretend to embody a full or final determination of the system of numbers, but only an originating principle of it. Then whatever is implied by this principle may be asserted of all the numbers, and whatever is shown to contradict the principle may be denied of any; but there can be no commitment to there being, for every statement of arithmetic, a determinate truth to the effect either that it holds or that it does not.

While my title speaks of a case for constructivist logicism, this argument might have been better called a case for constructivism from logicism. This is because premise (1) here is intended to capture what is most central in Dummett's endorsement of logicism as the most convincing general account of the nature of mathematics that has ever been given (1991, 310). Postponing discussion of what this premise retains from older versions of logicism and what it surrenders, it might help at this stage to recast the premise as the requirement that mathematical truth *must be* broadly analytic. What drives Dummett's constructivism is the stringency of that requirement—the impossibility, in his view, of satisfying the requirement on a classical basis.

Dummett's grounds for that view, and so in effect his grounds for premise (2), are dispersed through his criticisms of Fregean and neo-Fregean versions of logicism in chapters 14–18 and 23–24 of *FPM*, and can hardly be distilled into a convenient slogan. What matters most at this stage, though, is to stress that those are criticisms of a Fregean attempt to satisfy the requirement set down in premise (1), and must be read in the context of Dummett's own endorsement of that requirement. This is apparent in the following crucial passage.

> The important claim Frege made is that there exists a method of characterizing a system of mathematical objects which serves to confer senses upon the statements of that mathematical theory of which the system is a model in the

light of which the context principle guarantees that we do make genuine reference to those objects. The existence of that system is therefore a priori and independent of intuition, and the axioms of the theory may rank, accordingly, as analytic. Frege believed that he could, by introducing value-ranges, thereby introduce all the logical objects that would be required in mathematics; and he had a quite erroneous idea of how to give a coherent and presuppositionless characterization of the system of such value-ranges. These mistakes do not invalidate the general claim; if it can be sustained, we have a highly plausible account of the character of mathematics in general. (1991, 309–10)

Here Dummett says, "*if* [the general claim] can be sustained. . . ." In the summarizing argument that opens *FPM*'s final section, though, the cautious qualification is removed. The original logicist project, we there read, "failed because it combined three incompatible aims: to keep mathematics uncontaminated by empirical notions; to represent it as a science, that is, a body of *truths*, and not a mere auxiliary of other sciences; and to justify classical mathematics in its entirety" (1991, 312). Dummett's rejection of empiricism and nominalist instrumentalism, that would resolve the incompatibility by rejecting respectively the first and second of these aims, amounts again to endorsement of my premise (1): mathematics is to be presented as a pure a priori science. The judgment that this is incompatible with classicism is premise (2).

In broad outline the criticism of Frege that underlies this judgment is familiar enough. Frege's proposed method of introducing a system of mathematical objects so as to substantiate his general claim, which employs quantification over those objects in the course of setting down truth conditions for the most basic sentences referring to them, is fundamentally and irredeemably flawed. The contradiction Frege ran into is just a symptom of the basic circularity in that method, a circularity that is no less ruinous to the project when, as in the neo-Fregean approach championed by Hale and Wright (2001), the symptom is by good fortune absent. Thus, no minor revision to Frege's program that avoids the contradiction without diagnosing or rectifying the underlying circularity can be accepted. Instead, however richly Frege is to be praised, first for refuting empiricist and nominalist objections to his general claim, and secondly for isolating the crucial question of "what constitutes a legitimate method of specifying the intended domain of a fundamental mathematical theory" that must confront any attempt to substantiate this general claim, Dummett's final, if regretful, assessment is that "Frege's philosophy of mathematics contributed precisely nothing to [that question's] solution" (1991, 235).

It is important that Dummett does not present this criticism of the Fregean approach as constituting an apodictic case for premise (2). His summarizing argument explicitly allows for a "heroic" response claiming that we do indeed have conceptions of the systems described in mathematics sharp enough to sustain a classical understanding of quantification over their elements, though of course he counts this claim "far from compelling" (1991, 320). Dummett could not, I think, harden that estimate into a formally conclusive rejection of the "heroic" stance without at the same time excluding his own response to the crucial question. Ideally a response to this question, and thus a legitimate way of substantiating Frege's general claim, should present a patently "coherent and presuppositionless" characterization of a system of mathematical objects that would then be "in effect self-justifying" (1991, 310). The coherence of the conception, though, exceeds formal consistency in being required to sustain grasp of "an intuitive model for the theory that relates to it" (1991, 311), so that in fundamental cases the claim of *any* characterization to convey such a conception will be contestable (1991, 312). Similarly, the ideal of presuppositionlessness, if strictly interpreted, seems certainly beyond reach for those fundamental theories that give us the notions of particular infinite cardinalities. No demonstration can be brought against "a finitist who professes not to understand the conception of any infinite totality: Frege was mistaken in supposing that there can be a proof that such a totality exists which must convince anyone capable of reasoning" (1991, 234). The imprecise distance by which rational suasiveness falls short of proof, or by which coherence exceeds consistency, is a feature of the problem situation set by Frege's general claim: it has to be acknowledged by *any* response to the crucial question, the constructivist response that Dummett recommends as well as the heroic line he rejects. Thus, Dummett is right to adopt traditional, rationalist terms in describing the needed conception as "*self-justifying*," in preference to any positivist *ersatz* that would seek to downplay the suggestion of a need for substantive justification. We can require of the conception that it be transparently coherent in its own terms, and fully satisfying to any thinker who properly engages with it; it would be too much to ask that its coherence be demonstrable on a prior, less committed basis, or that there should be a route by which any thinker whatever might be compelled to engage with it. The choice is between claiming more and claiming less, not between claiming something and claiming nothing.

This point will have consequences for our examination of both premises (1) and (2). One common understanding of "logicism" is as denoting a position requiring precisely what we have just agreed cannot be required: a reduction of the terms of arithmetic to, and a seamless demonstration of its truths from, a prior neutral basis compulsory for any reasoner, so for any thinker whatever. If we were to understand the position in that way then we should have to conclude that, both in Dummett's view and in fact, logicism is false.[4] So, in investigating premise (1), we will need to ask what alternative position Dummett recommends, and why it might still be counted a version of logicism.

The point's relevance to premise (2) is still more immediate. Something "*self*-justifying" is justified by itself, and so something very like circularity—though we might prefer to call it explanatory and epistemological ungroundedness—is to be a feature of an adequate *solution* to the crucial question. Time and again, though, in drawing the moral from his criticism of Frege's response to the question, Dummett suggests that every whiff of circularity has to be cleansed. Most centrally, from his diagnosis of the fundamental problem in Frege's construction, that it attempted to specify the senses of mathematical terms simultaneously with fixing the domain on which they are to be interpreted, Dummett appears repeatedly to draw the requirement that the domain of a mathematical theory must be specified *in advance* of laying down the interpretation of its terms (e.g., 1991, 232, 235–36). But if those are the rules we know straight off that, in fundamental cases, the game cannot be won. In the case of arithmetic, for instance, these rules would require us to exploit a conception of a denumerably infinite totality in specifying a domain on which are to be interpreted the statements of that theory from which we first derive our conception of a denumerably infinite totality—a more obviously and definitively impossible feat than hauling ourselves out of the swamp by our top-knots. A central task for understanding premise (2), then, will be to explain how Dummett can reasonably insist on this requirement. We will find that the needed explanation lies in his understanding of the contrasts between mathematical and empirical concepts that are rightly emphasized in premise (1).

III. PREMISE ONE

I said that my aim was to explore Dummett's case and not to assess it; even so, it might help orient a reader to confirm what the last sentence gave away—namely, that in my view the problems the case encounters all concern premise (2). Premise (1), that is, is clearly and importantly right.

There are various ways to express the central truth in this premise, but perhaps the best of them is Frege's:

> On this view of numbers the charm of work on arithmetic and analysis is, it seems to me, easily accounted for. We might say, indeed, almost in the well known words: the proper object of reason is reason itself. In arithmetic we are not concerned with objects which we come to know as something alien from without through the medium of the senses, but with objects given directly to our reason and, as its nearest kin, utterly transparent to it.

> And yet, or rather for that very reason, these objects are not subjective fantasies. There is nothing more objective than the laws of arithmetic. (1884, §105)

The striking reversal of that last paragraph ("and yet, or rather for that very reason . . ."), along with the implication about transparency, are both clearly echoed in Dummett's valedictory lecture, "Realism and Anti-Realism," at a point where his attention is directed to Brouwer.

> [In mathematics] the gap between the subjective and the objective is there at its narrowest. Brouwer was, notoriously, a solipsist, or something very close to one; but that did not vitiate his development of a theory of meaning for mathematical statements, and a consequent revisionist programme for mathematical practice. The reason is precisely the flagrant untruth of his solipsism. Far from its being the case, as Brouwer maintained, that mathematical constructions are only imperfectly communicable, the very opposite is true: they are *perfectly* communicable. (1993, 471)

To say that the gap between subjective and objective is at its narrowest in mathematics is not to suggest that mathematics is somehow close to being subjective. It is instead to insist that the objectivity of mathematics cannot be conceived through any analogy with what makes for objectivity in empirical matters. The objectivity of an empirical object consists in its independence from perception, which in turn consists in its opacity or externality to any perceptual viewpoint on it: it stands over against every such viewpoint, in that its nature intrinsically outruns that aspect of itself that it presents to any one of them. Inquiry into its nature, while of course guided by and exploiting the conception of it made available in perception, is then not a matter of unfolding or further articulating that conception, but of genuinely adding to it. In contrast to all that, different mathematicians "do not have different viewpoints on mathematical reality" (1993, 472). Brouwer's solipsistic repudiation of every feature of externality that sustains the objectivity of empirical inquiry, including other enquirers and their viewpoints, does no damage to his mathematical thinking, since its objectivity does not depend on those features. His constructions remain "*perfectly* communicable"—communicable, that is, not only in the weak sense, that one can speak *about* them in words, but in the much stronger sense that words can fully *convey* them. (That they are communicable in this strong sense is perhaps what holds together the denizens of Frege's third realm, that otherwise look a bit of an assortment; nothing in the external world can be communicable in this strong sense.)

In the passages just quoted from Frege and Dummett both philosophers contrast the relation of mathematics to its objects with that of sense

762 PETER M. SULLIVAN

perception to its: the objects of mathematics are "given in thought" (Dummett 1991, 240), or "given directly to our reason," and so "utterly transparent to it" (Frege 1884, §105). In "What Is Mathematics About?" Dummett first exploits the contrast in criticism of empiricism (1993, 429–30), but both there and in *FPM* the more important target is a kind of platonism that casts mathematical intuition in a role analogous to perception.[5]

> Uncertainties about the formation of stars . . . do not reflect any haziness in our grasp of the concept of a star, but only a defect in our knowledge of the behaviour of stars. Likewise, if the analogy between physical and ideal objects were sound, our uncertainty about the continuum hypothesis need show no haziness in our *concept* of a set, but only in our knowledge of what sets God has chosen to create; for presumably ideal objects are as much God's creation as physical ones. (1991, 302)

The transparency that this "lame" analogy offends against does not of course require that all of the properties of mathematical objects be immediately apparent to us, nor that investigation can in practice uncover them; in "What Is Mathematics About?" Dummett further allows that it does not of itself rule out properties that we may in some sense be unable even in principle to establish (1993, 431). What it *does* rule out is the kind of understanding of what our ignorance amounts to that would be appropriate in empirical science.

> A physical complex apprehended by the senses may prove to have properties not immediately apparent, just as a mathematical system may prove to have properties not apparent from our initial grasp of it. But, whereas those of the physical system need in no way be implicit in our means of identifying it, those of the mathematical system must be; this would not be true if mathematical intuition were analogous to sense-perception. If the continuum hypothesis, say, is determinately true, that can only be because it follows from principles not yet formulated by us, but *already* inchoately present in our intuitive conception of the intended model of set theory. If that conception were a kind of blurred perception, on the other hand, it might be that it could be filled out, with equal faithfulness to our present grasp of it, however implicit, both so as to verify and to falsify the continuum hypothesis, which nevertheless possessed a determinate truth-value according to the way things happened to be. . . . This supposition is manifestly absurd. . . . (1991, 310)

Dummett's exposition of this absurdity is laced with irony, and that perhaps leads him to understate his case. "Like the empiricist view," he says, "the platonist one fails to do justice to the role of proof in mathematics" (1993, 431); it raises a problem, "why proof is so salient in mathematics" (1991, 301). Surely, though, what is impossible for analogical platonism to explain is not why proof should have such a prominent role in mathematics, but how it can have *any* role. Suppose we allow that there could be a truth about the layout of things in some mathematical domain that was *in no sense* a consequence of the conception we have of it. We should then have to think of this domain as a region of reality where what holds true does so in virtue of something—call it God's creative will—that is independent of that conception. The deductive articulation of that conception could then in no case be sufficient in itself to establish the truth as to how things stood in that region: we should always need the *further* assurance of conformity between the conception articulated and God's creative will. In loose but convenient summary: if any truth about that region is intrinsically unprovable, then every truth about it is unprovable; or contrapositively, if anything about it is provable then everything is.

This argument is so central to Dummett's case that it is worth pausing to defend it against objections.

First, and most simply, in physics not everything is provable, though deduction still has an essential role. This is of course true, but it does not imply that anything in physics is provable. The role of deduction in physics is to extract the consequences of a theory, not to establish its truth; it serves to lay out what would be involved in the existence of a physical system described by the theory, never to prove that such a system exists (cf. 1993, 429).

More seriously, someone might object to the argument's apparent presumption that the layout of mathematical reality is, on the analogical platonist's view, contingent—that things there just "happen" to be as they are intuited as being. The necessity of mathematical statements is, Dummett remarks,

> enough to rule out our possession of a faculty of mathematical intuition conceived in analogy with perception: if this were the source of our mathematical knowledge, the propositions of mathematics would be as contingent as those of astronomy. (1991, 307)

> For, presumably, the supra-sensible realm is as much God's creation as is the sensible one, and conditions in it therefore as contingent as in the latter. (1993, 431)

The objection is, then, that the argument builds in an alignment between epistemological and metaphysical notions that straightforwardly and question-beggingly excludes mathematical intuition as the platonist conceives it. Intuition, like perception, yields knowledge of things "through the manner in which we are affected by them"; but only the way things in fact are, and not that they must be that way, can affect us (there is "no impression of necessity"); so truths of a kind that can be known by intuition cannot be known through proof. With so much baggage from the empiricist tradition on board (the objection concludes), it is small wonder that Dummett cannot accommodate a rationalist notion of intuition, which is to be understood, precisely as it was in Descartes, as an insight into how things *must* be.

The objection fails, first, in its own historical terms. Descartes's (admittedly baffling) doctrine of God's free creation of eternal truths and essences, with its implication that necessities structuring the created world are in some sense only contingently necessary, was not an arbitrary, pious addition to his scheme. And the need that Dummett's argument insists upon, for an assurance of conformity between the deliverances of reasoning and the created domain it seeks to explore, is of course one that Descartes acknowledged. His doctrine sustains, if only in an obscure and etiolated form, a genuine analogy between insight and sight, between intuition and perception, in acknowledging some genuine condition of the existence of those states of affairs to which we are sensitive through this faculty. Without some such condition it is not plain what remains of the supposed analogy.

Second, the objection is wrong in supposing that Dummett endorses a general alignment of epistemological notions with metaphysical modalities. While Dummett plainly has little sympathy with the prominence that recent debate accords to the kind of non-conceptual necessity discussed by Kripke and Putnam, he does not reject the notion. Early in *FPM* it is traced to a contrast Aquinas drew, in holding that God's existence is *per se nota*, metaphysically necessary, although not *nota quoad nos*, knowable a priori (1991, 30); the current argument is prefaced by a cogent explanation of that claim, and of why it does not support a parallel distinction in understandings of mathematical necessity (1991, 307).[6]

Dummett need not in any case presume that the existence and properties of mathematical objects would be, on the analogical platonist's view, in any absolute sense contingent. The argument turns only on their being conceptually opaque, or contingent so far as our conception of these objects goes. That is enough to require that the ground of mathematical truth, or as it may be of mathematical necessary truth, be conceived as independent of, and so as needing to be co-ordinated with, that conception. A physical object, such as the moon, has a dark side; it still would have even if contingency were confined to the sublunary realm. For any object that has a dark side there has to be some story about what sheds light on the side that is visible—and that we have eyes is not story enough. Dummett's contention is that mathematical objects cannot be admitted to have dark sides without rendering it wholly mysterious how any side of them could be discovered by reason alone, or in other words by proof. That contention is sound.

How far, though, does this contention take us towards logicism? In "What Is Mathematics About?" Dummett presents the brilliance of the logicists' answer to the question as lying in its promise to explain simultaneously the most puzzling (and seemingly conflicting) features of mathematics—above all, its necessity and its universal applicability (1993, 432). We can think of this task as having negative and positive parts, the first a matter of removing obstacles to understanding how any body of knowledge can combine these features, the second a matter of characterizing the particular way they are combined in mathematics. In those terms criticism of analogical platonism belongs to the negative part of the agenda. That view tries to preserve the necessity of mathematics by having it relate to a special region of reality; it thereby "leaves it unintelligible how the denizens of this atemporal, supra-sensible realm could have any connection with, or bearing upon, conditions in the temporal, sensible realm that we inhabit" (1993, 430–31). Rejection of that view then opens the way to an alternative according to which mathematics relates equally, though indirectly, to every region of reality, by relating in the first instance to general features of thought: "The laws of number . . . are not laws of nature. They are, however, applicable to judgments holding good of things in the external world: they are laws of the laws of nature" (Frege 1884, §87). Making good on that alternative, the positive part of the agenda, would justify us in counting mathematics a "branch" of logic (cf. Frege 1893, §0). Dummett's central contribution here, I think, is in explaining why this need not amount to the impossible aim of presenting mathematics as a seamless "development" (cf. Frege 1884, §87) out of elementary logic.

The natural way to pursue that latter aim was never Frege's, but that of Russell and Whitehead. Their core system is genuinely continuous with elementary logic in having no objects of its own, consisting entirely of truths that are to hold good whatever objects there are. This core system, as they showed, yields neither arithmetic nor analysis. To extract those theories the generality of the system has to be restricted, and its purity surrendered, by introducing assumptions about the concrete or non-mathematical domains that supply its intended application.

Dummett's comments on this well known part of logicism's history are specially striking:

> Frege had never given any good reason for insisting on the genuine existence of mathematical objects; perhaps the only plausible reason lies in the difficulties encountered by Russell and Whitehead in trying to dispense with them. (1993, 433)

And still more definitively:

> [Russell and Whitehead's] attempt ran against the difficulty that would have
> supplied *the only valid ground* for Frege's insistence that numbers *are* genuine
> objects. . . . (1991, 302, first emphasis mine)

Pulled out of context these remarks might suggest an uncharacteristic appeal
to regressive methods: mathematical objects can be *validly* postulated
because they *have* to be: as we know from *Principia*, there is no way of
constructing arithmetic without them. Put back into context, though, I think
we have a different and more interesting style of argument, one that turns
not just on the fact of *Principia*'s failure to get by without mathematical
objects, but on the character of the assumptions it was forced into by that
attempt.

By Frege's standard of generality, or universal applicability, "the notion
of number is *already* a logical one" (1991, 224), independently of its being
defined by or constructed out of more elementarily logical materials. It
governs "every realm of reality and every degree of reality—the merely
thinkable as well as what in fact exists" (1991, 308; cf. Frege 1884, §3,
§14). Acknowledging Ramsey's observation, that not every truth formulated entirely in logical terms qualifies as a logical truth, it remains a
reasonable demand that the core principles governing a logical notion
should be formulable without impugning its generality, without restricting
its applicability *either* to one rather than another "realm" of reality *or* to any
one "degree" of reality. This second requirement implies that the laws of
number should be formulable so as to be independent of what objects in fact
exist. On the face of it, that appears to recommend the "non-platonist
logicism" (1991, 302) pursued in *Principia*, but the failure of that attempt
shows precisely how that appearance is misleading. Logic, in Wittgenstein's
phrase, "treats of every possibility and all possibilities are its facts" (1922,
2.0121). The logical principles governing the notion of number can be
"adapted for all possibilities" (Dummett 1991, 304)—they can be available
for reasoning about any region of reality, independently of assumptions as
to what objects in fact exist there—only by building in their own supply of
objects to serve, as it were, as the abstract representatives of every concrete
possibility. On this account, then, precisely the motivations of generality
and purity that seemed to demand an "object-free" exposition of the logic
of the notion of number are what warrant its abstract ontology.

> Why, then, does there appear to be a compelling need for mathematical
> objects? The need arises from the concern of mathematics with infinity. It has
> to be concerned with infinity because of the generality of its applications: even
> if we were fully convinced that everything to which mathematics would ever

be applied would be thoroughly finite, we cannot set an upper bound in advance on the number of its elements, or a lower bound on the ratio of its magnitudes. . . . Granted, for a particular application, the mathematical theory might borrow its objects from physics, or whatever other empirical science it was being applied to. . . . This, however, would both violate the purity of the mathematical theory, and offend Frege's principle of generality. . . . This requires that it have its own objects, and not borrow them from different physical theories in turn. (1991, 304)

This way of thinking of the role of a mathematical ontology explains why retreat to a modal formulation of mathematics can be no more than a futile shuffle (1991, 304–5): "actual" mathematical existence is already the existence of a possibility. It also explains the transparency that it has been the main business of this section to insist upon: possibility is a thin, substanceless kind of being; mathematical objects could have features beyond those required by their conception only if they were actual occupants of a further reality, rather than representatives of possibility in this one. It explains these things, however, without backtracking on the acknowledgment that there is no continuous, demonstrative route leading from elementary logic into arithmetic. Admission of the ontology of arithmetic requires no more than, but equally no less than, the recognition that *every* finite possibility is a possibility to be reckoned with. No individual elementarily-logical inference requires that recognition: it arises instead through the general reflective appreciation of the cogency of those inferences.[7]

In summary of this broadly Fregean view Dummett recommends the following.

On this view . . . that part of mathematics that is independent of intuition simply comprises all the deductive reasoning of which we are capable, purged of all that would restrict its application to particular realms of reality. . . . Geometry apart, mathematics therefore simply *is* logic: no distinction in principle can be drawn. Most of the deductive reasoning which it in this way encapsulates requires, for its formulation, reference to abstract objects mathematical or logical objects; we might use this as a criterion, not for demarcating mathematics from logic, but for singling out the mathematical part of logic. . . . (1991, 308–9)

He envisages the complaint that this is not a purely logicist account,[8] because it does not justify us in regarding mathematical objects as logical objects, but dismisses this as "little more than a boundary dispute" (1993, 445). Part of the point, I take it, is that the important boundary is one that separates the approach of Russell and Whitehead, on the one hand, from those of both Frege and Dedekind on the other. Once that boundary is crossed, by the admission of principles not derivable from elementary logic and sufficient to guarantee arithmetic its own infinite ontology, then it really does not much matter whether we formulate those principles in a way that suits the muted "logicist" claims of the neo-Fregean program (e.g., Hale and Wright 2001, 4), or whether we adopt Dedekind's axiomatization outright: either way, we have entered into a branch of logic that is distinctively mathematical.

IV. PREMISE TWO

Dummett presents for comparison an ordinarily realist picture of generalization involving an empirical concept, the concept of a star, for instance. Suppose it is clear what has to hold of an object for the concept *star* to apply to it, and under what circumstances a star is to be counted the same star as one previously encountered—in Dummett's terminology, that criteria of application and identity for the concept are determinate. Then no more is needed to ensure that generalizations involving the concept will be settled as true or as false. In particular, "We do not have to specify which [stars] there are, once we have rendered our concept of a [star] sharp: reality does that for us, and reality therefore determines the truth or falsity of our quantified statements. So, at least, realism assures us" (1991, 197). Reality's contribution to the joint effort of settling truth and falsity is not undermined even by fairly serious uncertainty or unclarity on the part of the other contributor. Whether I vaguely imagine there to be star upon star without end, or cling to some misunderstood popular science about the universe being somehow doughnut-shaped, things will proceed as described. Provided only that criteria of application and identity are clear, "reality dispels all haziness: we need do nothing further to eliminate it" (1991, 314).

Endorsing premise (1) commits us to holding that this cannot be a true picture of generalization involving a mathematical concept. If our conception of the natural numbers (or the real numbers, or the sets) does not settle which things have to be F for it to be true that every natural number (or every real, or every set) is F, then reality cannot step in to settle it for us. Or, to put things the other way around: if, for every suitable well-defined F, it is settled as true or as false that every natural number (or real, or set) is F, then our conception of the naturals (or reals, or sets) of itself settles which naturals (or reals, or sets) there are. The questions for this section are, first, what else we are committed to in holding that; and secondly, whether it would be, as premise (2) maintains, hopelessly heroic to undertake that commitment.

The agreed starting point, then, is that to claim to understand classical generalization over a mathematical domain is to claim determinacy in our conception of that domain or in our grasp of an intuitive model for the theory these generalizations belong to; to fasten on a favorite instance, adopting classicism in set theory involves claiming that our conception of the sets settles whether the continuum hypothesis is true. Many will naturally hear this as a bold claim, but it takes some positive reason to hear it that way. For it can also be heard, and might be defended, as involving no more than a commitment to the ineluctability of mathematical reasoning. So heard it reminds us that nothing could, or should, persuade us of the continuum hypothesis unless it persuades us that the hypothesis is true of the sets as we conceive them; if it did not, we could only think of the hypothesis as contributing to a new conception, and of our acceptance of it as a decision as to what mathematical structure is most fruitfully investigated. Far from its being an impossibly bold claim, then, this construal of our commitment presents it as no more than we *have* to say to acknowledge the objectivity of mathematics, and to sustain an ordinarily, "internally" realist conception of mathematical investigation as directed towards discovering what is so, rather than as a pragmatic negotiation preliminary to deciding what we will take to be so.

Dummett is not alone in holding that this negative construal of our claim cannot exhaust its commitment. The claim we make would indeed not be a bold one if it had only the implication just noted, for that details merely a conditional or future commitment concerning how we should describe our acceptance of or refusal to accept the hypothesis, whichever of these comes to pass; and *that* commitment is one we can fulfill merely by sitting on our hands, and sitting on it, until occasion arises retrospectively to endorse it. If our claim is to have any substance at all, we cannot sincerely defend it on the ground that it need involve more than that: we must think of it as carrying some present and categorical implication for whether we should or should not accept the hypothesis, and it seems that it will do that only if it also carries some *present* obligation to substantiate it.

It thus seems impossible to resist at this first step the conclusion Dummett draws from the contrast between empirical and mathematical generalizations: more is demanded than in the empirical case of someone who frames a classical generalization across a mathematical domain. In different presentations of the contrast Dummett describes the additional burden somewhat differently. It will be helpful to display these in a rough order of strength.

> What mathematical objects there are within a fundamental domain of quantification is supposed to be independent of how things happen to be in the world, and so, if it is to be determinate, *we* must determine it. (1993, 438)

> For a term of this sort we make a further demand: namely, that we should "grasp" the domain, that is, the totality of objects to which the term applies, in the sense of being able to circumscribe it by saying what objects, in general, it comprises. . . . (1993, 438)

> Few suppose . . . that, once these two criteria [of application and identity] have been fixed, statements involving quantification over the real numbers have thereby all been rendered true or false; to achieve that, it would be generally agreed that further specifications on our part were required, in some fashion circumscribing the totality of real numbers and laying down what real numbers there are to be taken to be. (1991, 197)

> In the mathematical realm, reality cannot be left to blow all haziness away: we have to remove it ourselves by contriving adequate means of laying down just what elements the domain is to comprise. (1991, 315)

> [Frege] saw no need for any *prior* circumscription of the domain. Precisely that is what we now take for granted as required. (1991, 315)

That we must, as the first quotations here insist, grasp the domain, in having a conception that settles which objects it contains, and in that sense determine it, is once again the agreed starting point. The suggestion of the last quotation, that understanding a generalization over a mathematical domain demands a *prior* circumscription of it, is one that we saw reason to look askance at in section II. Between these two lie requirements of being "able to say" what objects the domain comprises, in some fashion "laying this down," and, perhaps more demandingly, of "contriving adequate means" to do so. How far along this road are we committed to go? There are understandings of the requirement of being able to say which objects we are generalizing over on which it is clearly unshirkable; the conclusion just now reached, that the claim to a determinate conception is not exhausted by the negative construal canvassed, is an acknowledgment of that. On the other hand, there are understandings of this requirement on which it demonstrably cannot be satisfied on a classical basis. On just how stringent an understanding should we admit this requirement? Two considerations combine to show that Dummett should not enforce this requirement on the most stringent understanding of it, one that that would require us to be able to say with complete explicitness, and in a way invulnerable to a charge of circularity, precisely what objects are to fall within the range of a mathematical generalization.

To appreciate the first of these considerations, consider a simple argument that starts out on Dummettian ground (though it soon veers off):

> A conception of a mathematical system—an intuitive model—cannot transcend the means—necessarily linguistic and symbolic means—by which one person can convey it to another; it exists only in so far as it can be described. (1991, 311)

We frame intuitive models by means of concepts common to us all, and the models have no more content, and are no more definite, than the verbal or symbolic descriptions by means of which they may be communicated. (1991, 311)

Suppose we were to add to these claims that the most definite description we *can* offer of an intuitive model for a mathematical theory is the one we *have* offered in advancing that very theory, and so conclude that an intuitive model cannot be definite in ways that our formal, axiomatized theories are not. This then would yield a simple argument from the claim of transparency (that things not fixed by our conception are not fixed at all), along with whichever of the limitative results suits the instance in hand (for arithmetic, Gödel's theorem), to the rejection of bivalence (the conclusion that some things are not fixed at all). It is clear from Dummett's discussion in "The Philosophical Significance of Gödel's Theorem" that he would *not* endorse this argument. It helps with the present issue to explain why.

Grasp of an intuitive model, Dummett rightly holds, is necessary if we are to have a mathematical theory at all, in contrast to an uninterpreted formalism (1991, 229–30, 311). He has no general suspicion of this notion. The remarks just quoted target only a misconstrual of it, one that "creat[es] the impression that the grasp of an intuitive model for a theory is unmediated by language: that we perceive its structure by direct intellectual apprehension" (1991, 311). Identifying that target already undercuts the simple argument's addition to Dummett's premise. That a model "exists only in so far as it *can* be described" does not imply that it can be no more definite that a formal systematization that *has* been supplied. If reflection persuades us of the consistency of this systematization, and so of the truth of its Gödel sentence, then this *may* be communicated, by that very sentence: there is nothing in this scenario that resembles a wordless stab. Dummett thus has no reason to endorse the simple argument's reduction of the notion of an intuitive model to what is settled by a given axiomatization. More importantly, though, he has every reason to reject it. The central misuse of this notion that he opposes is in giving a pseudo-explanation of our understanding of a mathematical theory, one that says, for instance, that we understand arithmetic *because* we grasp the structure of the standard model for it. The resources presupposed in any ordinary use of the notion of such a model would make this explanation immediately and obviously circular: "a framework within which a model for the natural numbers can be described will itself involve either the notion of 'natural number' or some equivalent or stronger notion" (1978, 193). It is to suppress that obvious circularity that this pseudo-explanation casts the intended model as something grasped "in our mind's eye," or by "direct intellectual apprehension," which is to say, grasped independently of the conceptual understanding we are pretending, poorly, to explain. The relevant point here is that the reductionism of the simple argument misuses the notion of model in just the same way. Whether, optimistically, we portray ourselves as striking out with the laser ray of intellectual intuition to precisely one model, or, pessimistically, as short-sightedly loosing off the blunderbuss of a non-categorical axiomatization in the general direction of many, models are equally playing the role of some kind of target set up independently of any mathematical theory, and standing there ready to supply the theory with whatever content it has by bare association—whether unique or otherwise. Thus the simple argument, for all its seemingly more modest pretensions, is involved in the same pretense of explanation. "The notion of a model," Dummett concluded, "cannot serve to explain what it is to know the meaning of the expression 'natural number'" (1978, 193). Nor, for the same reason, can the plural notion of models; it is incoherent to suppose that our understanding of a theory reduces to what is common among its various models.

The simple argument understands the requirement, that we should be able to say what objects are generalized over by a theory we claim to understand, in the most stringent possible way—as demanding, in effect, that we should lay down certain sentences for which the intended model of the theory provides the only admissible interpretation. Unsurprisingly it concludes that the requirement cannot be met. The argument clearly offers us no reason at all to accept that understanding of the requirement: it simply presupposes it. In doing so it builds in a reductionism that is quite contrary to Dummett's views. Any reasonable understanding of the requirement that we must be able to say what objects we are generalizing about, and any understanding on which Dummett would endorse the requirement, must be one that allows us meaningful words with which to say it.

The second and simpler of these considerations is that we must also be allowed someone to say it *to*. To be able to say what objects the generalizations of our theory concern is to be able to communicate the conception we have of those objects. Since the coherence of this conception suffices for the existence of a system of mathematical objects satisfying it, fully to communicate this conception to another is to give to that other a priori sufficient reason to recognize that this system exists. From the beginning, though, we have, along with Dummett, acknowledged limitations on our ability to provide such reasons: nothing we can say can be guaranteed to demonstrate to a finitist the mistake in his finitism (see section 2 and 1991, 234). It follows that the requirement of being able to say what objects our theory concerns should be understood in a way that recognizes these limitations: our ability to say what we then do will inevitably depend on co-operative uptake.

Dummett gives proper weight to these limitations in his exposition of Frege, as, for instance, when he remarks that "Frege did not suppose that a verbal description of a model for a theory played any essential role in our grasp of the meaning of the language of the theory" (1991a, 5). This point, like the two considerations just outlined, applies only to fundamental theories. For a non-fundamental theory, such as the theory of groups, we can exploit the resources of a more embracing theory to lay down precisely which of the objects recognized by the broader theory are to be the subject matter of the narrower one, and to define its terms. Clearly none of this is feasible for a fundamental theory. Definitions then have to give way to what Frege calls "elucidations," informal prompts whose uptake depends on a meeting of minds. That on which minds then meet can, of course, be given some kind of description (we agreed that it had to be right in some sense that one must be able to say what a theory one understands is about), but this description cannot be held to standards of explicitness and explanatoriness appropriate for a non-fundamental theory. It may of course take the form of a description of the intended model of the theory. If it does so, then we should regard this description, as Dummett says in another connection, as "an account—perhaps one that is not fully explicit, or one that can be fully understood only when the senses of the expressions of the theory have already been understood—of what it is that somebody implicitly knows when he understands the language of the theory" (1991a, 6).

Given that, how should we view the fact that "it is extremely difficult to frame a clear description of a [fundamental] mathematical system," or that attempts to do so "leave some quite unconvinced that any sharp conception is being conveyed, while satisfying others" (1991, 312)? The difficulty is not to be denied, and whether one finds in it cause for "embarrassment" at the "lameness of our attempts" (1993, 442) might be in part a matter of temperament. For Dummett, though, the difficulty transforms itself into an "impasse . . . intrinsically impossible of resolution":

> for fundamental mathematical theories, such as the theory of natural numbers or the theory of real numbers, are precisely those from which we initially derive our conceptions of different infinite cardinalities, and hence no characterization of their domains could in principle escape the accusation of circularity. (1991, 317–18)

The reason given for the transformation is, however, one that we have all along acknowledged: no non-circular reasoning can compel a finitist out of his finitism. Similarly, we have accepted from the beginning that a "self-justifying" conception, while we might hope that it will satisfy anyone "without preconceptions," cannot be required to overcome every kind of skepticism: an elucidation of the conception, we have just noted, calls for co-operative uptake. And the root reason for that, which Dummett himself makes clear, is that the ground for regarding number as a logical notion is not one that renders it obligatory for any thinker whatever. These points all contribute to explaining why the difficulty is a real one, and why, in a sense, it is an essential one: a finitist's skepticism is not a merely practical obstacle, comparable to someone's obtuse inability to follow an elementary logical proof. Precisely by explaining that, however, these points undercut the reason offered for thinking that the difficulty constitutes an impasse. If we were persuaded of that description of the position, then Dummett's proposed escape from the impasse would indeed offer an explanation of it: "The hypothesis that the domains of the fundamental mathematical theories are given by . . . indefinitely extensible concepts explains why we are at such a loss to supply uncontentious characterizations of their domains" (1991, 318). But to the extent that we must acknowledge these characterizations to be contentious, this is *already* explained precisely by the fact that the theories are fundamental.

Our only model for a completely non-contentious explanation of a domain of generalization is one in which the resources of an equally strong or stronger theory are used in the metalanguage to specify this domain.[9] It would clearly involve an impossible regress to hold that *no* generalization can *ever* be understood without the backing of that kind of explanation; and it follows immediately from the account of what a fundamental theory is that the range of its generalizations cannot be specified in that kind of way. Dummett's insistence, in the face of these obvious points, that a classical mathematical generalization *must* be given that kind of explanation thus presents us with the puzzle we anticipated back in section II. It is, of course, quite consistent to hold both that a classical generalization must have, and that it cannot have, the support of a prior specification of its range; together the two contentions would enforce Dummett's conclusion that generalization in mathematics cannot be classically construed. Even so it is puzzling —and nothing we have uncovered in exploring his case makes it less so—that Dummett's clear understanding of why a prior specification is impossible does not at all lessen his conviction that it is necessary.

I think we can only begin to make sense of this by reintroducing some of the non-mathematical background to the issues we have been focusing on, and in particular by re-examining the contrast set out at the beginning of this section between an empirical and a mathematical generalization. Motivation for taking this broader view can be found in an admittedly impressionistic characterization of the puzzle that confronts us. Part of this puzzle is that Dummett seems to be insisting that the generalizations of fundamental mathematical theories be given an explanation that he knows cannot be given just because the theories concerned are fundamental—and in that way, one is almost tempted to say, he seems to be insisting on treating these theories as fundamental and non-fundamental at once. Perhaps there is some explanation of this to be found in the idea that, while the theories we have been considering are indeed fundamental *mathematical* theories, no mathematical theory is fundamental in the broader setting of our total scheme of things. Another part of the puzzle is that the demand that Dummett presses in relation to mathematics, that its generalizations be given a prior supporting explanation, is a demand that it would be plainly inconsistent to press quite generally. Again, perhaps we can understand why Dummett does press this demand in mathematics by attending to the contrast with the broader framework, where he would not.

So, consider in this vein the following central claim.

> [Frege believed] that he could simultaneously fix the truth-conditions of [identity statements about abstracta] and the domain over which the individual variables were to range. This belief was a total illusion. To arrive at an interpretation of a formal language of the standard kind, employing an essentially Fregean syntax, we have *first* to attain a grasp of the intended domain of the individual variables: it is only after that that we can so much as ask after the meanings of the primitive non-logical symbols. (1991, 232)

Although it includes no explicit restriction, it is perfectly obvious that this statement is not intended to apply to our language as a whole (even though we do, according to Dummett, speak a language with a broadly Fregean syntax). If the claim did apply generally it would imply that we must somehow get hold of a range of empirical objects in advance of, and as a necessary preparation for, coming to understand any terms referring to them. Nothing could be clearer from Dummett's general discussions of the context principle than that he completely rejects that picture. A central theme of these discussions is presented in *FPM*:

> There is no such thing as an immediate apprehension of an object: it is only by coming to grasp the use of proper names, or other terms, referring to them that we form any conception of objects as persisting constituents of a hetero-geneous, changing reality and as identifiable as the same again. (1991, 203–4)

In the general case, then, the recognition of objects *is* simultaneous with coming to understand terms referring to them.

Dummett would thus resist the generalization to language as a whole of the claim he makes about the language of a mathematical theory, that we have *first* to grasp the range of objects it concerns. We now need to ask why, or how, he would do so. Any answer must involve the idea that, in the case of empirical objects, the grasp of terms referring to them *does* simultaneously accomplish the thing that, in Dummett's view, needs to be done *first* in mathematics: understanding reference to an empirical object automatically carries with it grasp of a domain of generalization to which it belongs. If this is right, the reason must lie in the basic role in understanding empirical terms that Dummett assigns to "recognition statements," in which the term's reference is singled out demonstratively (1991, 204). The sense of a term for an empirical object locates it in the spatio-temporal framework, roughly speaking as "that thing there now," and it is a compelling thought that this carries with it automatically an understanding of a domain as comprising whatever is anywhere at any time.

This point now forces us to reconsider the contrast we drew between empirical and mathematical generalization. Generalization involving a mathematical concept, Dummett says, requires us to settle criteria of application and identity for the concept, and in addition requires us to circumscribe the domain; for an empirical generalization we need only attend to the first two, leaving reality to sort out the rest. "So, at least, realism assures us" (1991, 197). It must always have seemed odd that Dummett should rest a contrast so central to his case on a realism he does not endorse, and I think we can now see how to remove that oddity. Imagine, to make things vivid, that the heavens are marked out as a giant checkerboard; on some of the squares are stars. A generalization, "Every star is F," has on this assumption a clear and determinate content. But what exactly is reality's role in ensuring this? A first thought is that the contingent layout of reality settles which squares have stars on them, and thereby settles which squares must have something F on them for our generalization to hold: its truth is a product of all those statements "Square X holds something F" where X is the location of a star; and which squares those are is of course reality's business to settle rather than ours. But while this first thought is true enough, its truth seems hardly relevant to our generalization's having a determinate content. For this generalization might instead have been cast (and on a Fregean analysis already was cast) in the form: "Every square, if it has a star on it, has something F on it." It does not matter for the determinate content of this generalization which squares have stars on them, nor therefore which stars there are. What *does* matter, and what supports our conviction that the content of the generalization is clear and determinate, is the celestial checkerboard itself. Now, in terms of this image, the conclusion of the previous paragraph was that the checkerboard is given automatically with an empirical concept, and is implicit in our most basic understanding of terms for objects falling under it. If that is right, our way of framing Dummett's contrast between empirical and mathematical generalization was mistaken. It suggested: (i) that in each case there are three determinants of the content of the generalization to be settled, criteria of application and identity for the concept, and the domain; (ii) that in the mathematical case all three of these are our responsibility; whereas (iii) in the empirical case, our responsibility extends only to the first two, reality being left to take care of the third. This is misleading just because of its presumption that we *could* attend to the first two while leaving the third untouched. The contrast Dummett intends is rather that, in an empirical generalization, to take care of the first two is *already* to take care of the third; whereas, for a mathematical generalization, this is not so.

We now need to ask after the source and significance of this contrast. This resolves into three questions. What role does the checkerboard fill in the empirical case? Why, in Dummett's view, does it have no analogue in a mathematical generalization? And, if it has no analogue there, why does this matter? Answers to at least the first and third of these questions are suggested in the following passage.

> The contrast between mathematical and empirical enquiry concerns not so much the discovery of individual objects as the delineation of the area of search. The astronomer need have no precise conception of the totality of celestial objects: he is concerned with detecting whatever is describable in physical terms and lies, or originates, outside the Earth's atmosphere, and he need give no further specification of this "whatever." In mathematics, by contrast, an existential conjecture, to have definite content, requires a prior circumscription of the domain of quantification. (1991, 228)

We should grant that an existential conjecture will have definite content only if we have at least some general grip on the range of instances that would verify it. As Dummett understands this condition, it can be re-expressed by saying that we can ask a definite question "Is there an F?" only if we know in general what statements, "a is F," would entail a positive answer. Where F is an empirical concept its criteria of application and identity suffice to ensure that this condition is met. Such a concept locates something that it applies to in the spatio-temporal framework, and that in turn circumscribes the ways in which this object might be presented to other locations in that same framework. The role of the checkerboard, that is, is to provide positions, not only for objects that might fall under the concept, but at the same time for other viewpoints that might ground alternative ways of referring to those same objects. It is because it provides both of these that it is a framework both for differentiating and for identifying these objects. It follows that our understanding of the concept F settles, not only the condition that a given object has to meet for the concept to apply to it, but also the range of ways in which a candidate for being F might be given. And so, in knowing how to answer a question, whether a certain object is F, we also know in general which such questions there are to answer.

In the mathematical case, though, criteria of application and identity give us less. It is straightforward to give these criteria in a way that is "adequate to explain what is required of a specified mathematical entity for us to recognize it as a real number." Doing this, however,

> does not suffice as a means of circumscribing a domain of quantification, when such quantification is to yield statements with determinate truth-values. It does not do so, because *it fails to determine the limits of acceptable specification* of something to be acknowledged as a real number: we still need a means of saying which real numbers the domain comprises. (1991, 315, my emphasis)

In the absence of a checkerboard, that is, our understanding of what it is for any given object to be *F* does not include any circumscription of the ways in which a candidate for being *F* might be given. In the mathematical case, then, knowing how to answer a question, "Is so-and-so an *F*?" does not give us even a general grip on which such questions there are.

Grant for a moment the lack of any such general conception (that an answer to the second of our three questions will be forthcoming). This lack could be made good, and it seems could only be made good, by an independent characterization of which objects might be presented to the concept for decision. Yet that would be precisely the kind of prior specification of the domain that we know to be impossible for fundamental mathematical theories. The only option would then be to adjust our understanding of the content of a generalization to make do without it. This is Dummett's constructivist proposal:

> If we choose to explain the concept real number in a Dedekindian manner . . . by saying that a real number is required to have determinate relations of magnitude to rationals, *we say nothing about the manner in which an object having such relations is to be specified*, but simply leave any purported specification to be judged on its merits when it is offered. (1991, 319, my emphasis)

Thus the indeterminacy or open-endedness that we have to recognize and tolerate in a mathematical generalization, and that makes it impossible to construe the generalization classically, relates precisely to the end that the checkerboard closes off in the empirical case—to the range of ways, that is, in which an object perhaps falling under the concept might be *given*.

In following Dummett's case to its conclusion, and thus to his answer to the third of the three questions recently posed, we skipped over the second, which asked why there is no analogue of the checkerboard in mathematics. Less metaphorically, why will a mathematical concept leave open the ways in which an object putatively falling under the concept might be specified? While there is, I think, no full or direct discussion of this question in *FPM*, Dummett's examples—and in particular, the fact that in the two passages just quoted, where this contention is most explicit, the real numbers are chosen to illustrate it—give a clear indication of what he has in mind. Suppose we explain a real number as a set of rationals meeting the conditions on a Dedekind cut. Those conditions, filling here the role of application and identity criteria, will decide of a given set whether it is a real number. But a real number is to be *any* set meeting those conditions, and understanding these conditions does not in itself ensure any general grasp of the conceptual resources by which a set putatively satisfying these conditions might be specified. Alternatively, suppose we think of a real number as represented by its binary expansion, and so determined by any sequence of 0's and 1's however effected. Again, that "*however*" invokes a notion that is not sharpened or settled within the theory of real numbers itself. A natural extrapolation of these illustrations would hold that the resources of stronger mathematical theories provide ways of specifying objects putatively falling under the application condition of the concept determining the range of generalizations belonging to a weaker theory.[10] This source of open-endedness would be closed off if the contours of the stronger theory were implicit, however inchoately, in the grasp we have of the weaker one; but to commit oneself quite generally to that contention, one might well think, really would be hopelessly heroic.

If, though, this suggestion does properly reflect Dummett's understanding of the character and source of the open-endedness of mathematical generalization, that creates a problem for the whole approach adopted in this discussion. This has been to seek a case for a constructivist understanding of generalization over any of the fundamental mathematical domains, and thus a case that turns only on features that are shared by the concepts defining these domains, and by which they equally contrast with a concept giving the range of an empirical generalization. It is clear, however, that the illustrations of the previous paragraph turn essentially on the intrinsically infinite character of the real numbers—of *each* real number, that is, and not only of the totality of real numbers. And that makes it far from clear that any genuinely parallel source of open-endedness could afflict generalization over the natural numbers. At the metaphorical level of the checkerboard, there surely remains some intuitive force in the thought that in this case, too, the grasp of these objects that we attain in understanding arithmetic does not determinately place them in relation to others, nor therefore give us any grip on the question of what other ways there might be of being presented with these same objects. Perhaps Frege's "Caesar problem" can best be seen as a way of scratching away at that thought until it becomes a nagging insecurity. But even if it is effective in that, the insecurity concerns only the account we should give of the application of arithmetic. Unless we can shift the thought from the metaphorical to a properly mathematical level, by considerations genuinely parallel to those that apply to the real numbers, it is very hard to see that it points to any indeterminacy or open-endedness in the content of an arithmetical generalization.

To some who have considered Dummett's case for constructivism this conclusion will come as no surprise. They will have taken it as clear from the beginning that this case cannot be reconstructed without giving a pivotal role to the notion of indefinite extensibility, understood as dictated by a diagnosis of the paradoxes; and also clear, therefore, that the case can extend "downwards" (as it were) at most to the theory of the real numbers, in virtue of the role that the notion of an arbitrary subset plays in that theory. But this is too quick. Even if the case that I have been concerned to explore does prove to be limited as this reaction suggests, the reasons for the limitation are not at all the same; and even if the scope of the two lines of argument is the same—from the real numbers "upwards"—their bases lie in considerations of very different kinds. Most obviously, the contrast between empirical and mathematical generalizations, that I have aimed to present as central to Dummett's case, and which certainly appears to have a central role in the argument of *FPM*, has at most a walk-on part in discussions approaching the issue through the paradoxes (cf. again Oliver 1998 and Clark 1998).

No doubt it is right that an adequate understanding of Dummett's case for constructivism has to accommodate and connect both kinds of approaches. I hope, though, that by pursuing a less familiar aspect of it this discussion might help to make prominent rather different grounds on which one might begin to try to assess this case. Assessment, as I said at the beginning, is more than I can aim at here. But my discussion should include at least a sketch of one such ground.

A feature of the argument of *FPM* that I have so far neglected is that its treatment of the issue between realism and constructivism is at every step bound up with the issue between realism and nominalism. This is particularly true of chapter 18's discussion of "Abstract Objects," where points about the contrast between empirical and mathematical inquiry, whose importance for the first issue I have tried to emphasize, simultaneously play a central role in the second (see especially Dummett 1991, 234–36). In Dummett's treatment the decisive question for that second issue is whether the senses of statements of a mathematical theory can be explained in such a way that ascription of reference to its terms may be *both* legitimated by that explanation in accordance with the context principle *and* robustly construed. A robust construal will be appropriate, he explains, only if the attribution of reference to these terms is "operative within a semantic theory" for the language of the theory, in such a way as "to admit a suitable notion of identifying the referent of the term as playing a role in the determination of the truth-value of a sentence containing it" (1991, 239). For, if that condition were not met, we should have to conclude that "the referents of the newly introduced terms cannot be thought of in any other way than simply as the referents of those terms, and hence the analogy with other cases, that ought to sustain all uses of the notion of reference, [would be] lacking" (1991, 235).

This conception of the issues stands opposed to a straightforwardly internalist understanding of the context principle, one that would content itself with the thought that, if the language-game works, its terms refer. Against that Dummett insists that we need to be able *to say how* the language-game works, and that the notion that its terms have reference is to be taken seriously only if it is appealed to when we say that. But this insistence—like the insistence on a prior specification of the range of a mathematical generalization—is one that immediately threatens to put the goal beyond reach. And again, the reasons for this are obvious enough that the insistence creates the same kind of puzzle we faced before. For, if we are genuinely obliged to explain from outside of it how this language-game works, then in offering that explanation we will either speak of the things that terms of the language are to refer to, and associate terms with them, or we will not. On the first alternative the reference ascribed to terms may be robustly construed but the context principle will have no role in legitimating it;[11] on the second the context principle has a role in legitimating the ascription of reference to terms, but the reference ascribed can be understood only thinly.[12]

This new puzzle has to be resolved, I think, through an approach broadly similar to that adopted above to the puzzle about generalizations. For the demands that generate this puzzle are again ones that Dummett would not insist upon quite generally, and in particular ones that he would not insist upon in relation to levels of empirical discourse that are fundamental to our scheme of things. At that level, reference may be construed *both* robustly *and* in accordance with the context principle (1991, 203). That this combination of views *has to be* possible is clear from the evident fact that whatever explanation we can offer of the functioning of this fundamental part of language cannot coherently be thought of as being offered entirely "from outside" of it, or as exploiting only resources more basic than its own; in consequence of that, when a semantic theory ascribes reference to basic empirical terms, the reference ascribed, to be robust, need not inherit that robustness from the previously established credentials of the metalanguage. In Dummett's account of how, at this level, the combination of views *is* possible—of how basic empirical reference can be robustly

construed in accordance with the context principle—"recognition statements" once again play a key role: the connection with the framework of
perceptual viewpoints that recognition statements establish ensures that,
even without any anchor in the more solid ground occupied by the
metalanguage, the referents of basic empirical terms are not reduced to
things that can be thought of only as the referents of those terms (cf.
Dummett 1991, 204, 235). Whether the same combination of views can be
maintained regarding mathematical reference—whether, that is, we can
view the ascription of reference to the terms of fundamental mathematical
theories robustly yet still as legitimated by the context principle—will then
depend on whether reference to mathematical objects can be understood in
a way that sustains a genuine analogy with that core feature of basic
empirical reference: for only that analogy can, in Dummett's view, deflect
the forced choice between, on the one hand, accepting that the reference
ascribed to mathematical terms is thin and insubstantial and, on the other,
undertaking to bolster and substantiate it from a prior and independent
perspective.

On the account of Dummett's case given above the issue between
realism and constructivism also turns on whether a suitably strong analogy
can be sustained between mathematical and empirical reference. As with the
issue between realism and nominalism just sketchily reviewed, only that
analogy could deflect insistent demands for a prior and independent
specification—of the range of a theory's generalizations in the one case, and
of the objects to which its terms are to refer in the other—demands which
in the nature of the case cannot be satisfied, and which, therefore, if not
deflected, will rule against the realist side of the issue.

Clearly, then, any assessment of Dummett's case against realism in
mathematics must attend to that question of analogy. It seems to me quite
certain that no reasonable assessment could conclude that Dummett is
altogether mistaken in the importance he attaches to it. The very core of the
notion of an object is that of a common focus of distinct representations,
something that provides for the integration of these representations as
offering different viewpoints on a single thing.[13] We therefore cannot think
of our understanding of a mathematical theory as enabling us to grasp a
range of objects, or to refer by its terms to some amongst these objects,
unless we thereby understand how these same objects can be the referents
of distinct representations. But agreement over that core point leaves plenty
of scope for disagreement over precisely how tight an analogy is reasonably
expected between mathematical and empirical reference, and so over
whether the points of disanalogy emphasized in Dummett's case are as
damaging to realism as he contends. To take just one instance, when
thinking primarily of empirical reference we naturally attend to ways of

individuating *particular* objects and of recognizing those objects as the same again. By contrast, the objects that form the subject matter of a mathematical theory are recognized at once, and as a system, if they are recognized at all. The theory itself then provides alternative ways of referring to elements of the system by means of the various relations they bear to others of its elements ('$2 \times 2 = 7 - 3$'). If it leaves us in the dark that will be over how representations provided by the theory are to be integrated with representations of objects grasped independently of the theory. We saw how Dummett's case fastens on to this limitation. His understanding of what is needed for an existential conjecture to have definite content requires that grasp of a range of objects should include a general circumscription of every possible alternative way of representing those same objects (cf. p. 777 above). That requirement is clearly stronger than the core point just agreed. Perhaps, then, it could be argued that while the stronger requirement has an important role in the empirical case—that of determining the bounds within which *a posteriori* inquiry could coherently aim to integrate representations that are not already conceptually connected, and so in one of the needed respects of setting a limit to scientific questions—this is a role that simply has no intelligible analogue in mathematics, where transparency dictates that every integration that is possible at all will be possible a priori.

Perhaps that could be argued. Such argument would belong, though, to the assessment of Dummett's case. My aim has been only to indicate something of the philosophical richness of this case, and therewith both the range and the depth of the issues with which an assessment of it would have to engage.[14]

PETER M. SULLIVAN

UNIVERSITY OF STIRLING
NOVEMBER 2004

NOTES

1. With a degree of arbitrariness this statement casts the discussion in chapters 19–22 of Part III of Frege's *Grundgesetze* in the role of an interlude.

2. For the claim see Heck 1993, 233. For the questioning see Oliver 1994, 387–88; Oliver 1998, 26–29, 33–34; Clark 1998, 60–61.

3. There are terminologically different ways of dividing the distance that Dummett's argument has to cover. Potter (2001), and similarly Clark (1998), understand "indefinitely extensible concept" (IEC) in such a way that *set* and *ordinal* clearly count as IECs; Potter then naturally balks at Dummett's statement that quantification over the objects falling under an IEC "*obviously* does not yield

statements with determinate truth-conditions" (1991, 319, emphasis added). I prefer—because it seems to make for a smoother reading of passages in *FPM*, though perhaps not of Dummett's earlier papers—to understand "IEC" in such a way that this is obvious; compensating for this, it can then no longer be obvious that *set* or *ordinal* is an IEC. There is no difference here beyond terminology: substantive argument is clearly necessary for the conclusion that quantification over sets or ordinals cannot be classically construed, and these are just two different ways of describing the needed argument.

4. This remark includes in its scope constructions based on the kind of "explicative" principles proposed by the neo-Fregean approach that fall short of being definitions. If it did not it would reduce to the triviality that the standardly accepted core of logic will not yield arithmetic.

5. Potter (2001) explains why the kind of platonism that Dummett targets should not be called "Gödelian."

6. Dummett is surely right in his general approach here, as well as about the contrasting details of the two cases. Kripke's and Putnam's arguments do not issue any general licence to declare some species of truths necessary but not a priori: the claim is empty unless we have some specific model of what the supposed necessity consists in.

7. No doubt this is merely to wave a hand towards a region where one knows the truth has to be located, without locating it. It is not news that elementary logic falls short of mathematics while its metatheory already is mathematics. What one needs to explain—somehow—is how the understanding of inferences one conducts in elementary logic *as* valid inferences provides for a reflective appreciation that is then metatheoretically codified, and to explain this without, as Poincaré did, reversing the true order of things: that is, without representing the ground-level acknowledgment of validity as *resting on* an intrinsically mathematical metatheory.

8. The complaint is in fact entered against Dummett's own final proposal, but if it had any force there it would be applicable at this earlier stage of the discussion.

9. Approaching the domain via an index set is for current purposes not significantly different from this; see Dummett 1991, 234.

10. A closely analogous thought would hold within the theory of the hierarchy of sets, in the familiar idea that "width" depends on "height."

11. This runs counter to a passage where Dummett says: "when the intended meanings of the statements of the theory are explained by first laying down what the domain comprises, and then interpreting the terms of the theory as denoting particular elements of that domain, Frege's context principle is entirely correct in pronouncing that there is no further problem of warranting the ontological implications of the theory" (1991, 235). Surely in the case described there *could* be no further problem, independently of any pronouncement by the context principle, since the ontological commitment is already carried by the metalanguage in which the intended meanings are specified.

12. A thin or non-robust construal of the ascription of reference to a range of terms amounts, in effect, only to rebuttal of a nominalist's challenge to our right to

use these terms; see 1991, 236.

13. I have claimed elsewhere (Sullivan 2004, §4.1) that this is as much the core of Frege's notion of an object as it is of Kant's.

14. A version of this paper was presented at a workshop in St. Andrews in October 2004; I am grateful to Peter Clark, Dan Isaacson, Carrie Jenkins, and Crispin Wright for critical points raised then. Michael Potter read and commented on a draft of the paper and offered valuable help in many other ways. The paper was written during research leave funded by the University of Stirling and the Arts and Humanities Research Board; I gratefully acknowledge their support.

REFERENCES

Clark, Peter. 1998. "Dummett's Argument for the Indefinite Extensibility of Set and Real Number." In *New Essays on the Philosophy of Michael Dummett*. Edited by J. L. Brandl and P. M. Sullivan. Amsterdam: Rodopi, 51–64.

Dummett, Michael. 1978. *Truth and Other Enigmas*. London: Duckworth.

———. 1991. *Frege: Philosophy of Mathematics*. London: Duckworth.

———. 1991a. *Frege and Other Philosophers*. Oxford: Clarendon Press.

———. 1993. *The Seas of Language*. Oxford: Clarendon Press.

Frege, Gottlob. 1884. *Die Grundlagen der Arithmetik*. Translated by J. L. Austin as *The Foundations of Arithmetic*. Oxford: Blackwell, 1978.

———. 1893. *Grundgesetze der Arithmetik*, vol. 1. Part translated by M. Furth as *The Basic Laws of Arithmetic*. Berkeley and Los Angeles: Univ. of California Press, 1964.

Hale, Bob, and Crispin Wright. 2001. *The Reason's Proper Study*. Oxford: Clarendon Press.

Heck, Richard. 1993. "Critical notice of M. Dummett, *Frege: Philosophy of Mathematics*." *Philosophical Quarterly* 43: 223–32.

Oliver, Alex. 1994. "Dummett and Frege on the Philosophy of Mathematics." *Inquiry* 37: 349–92.

———. 1998. "Hazy Totalities and Indefinitely Extensible Concepts: An Exercise in the Interpretation of Dummett's Philosophy of Mathematics." In *New Essays on the Philosophy of Michael Dummett*. Edited by J. L. Brandl and P. M. Sullivan. Amsterdam: Rodopi, 25–50.

Potter, Michael. 2001. "Was Gödel a Gödelian Platonist?" *Philosophia Mathematica* 9: 331–46.

Sullivan, Peter M. 2004. "Frege's Logic." In *Handbook of the History of Logic*, vol. 3. Edited by D. M. Gabbay and J. Woods. Amsterdam: Elsevier, 659–750.

Wittgenstein, Ludwig. 1922. *Tractatus Logico-Philosophicus*. London: Routledge and Kegan Paul.

REPLY TO PETER M. SULLIVAN

I thank Peter Sullivan for his penetrating, thoughtful analysis of the argument I gave in *Frege: Philosophy of Mathematics* (*FPM*) for constructive as against classical mathematics. He is of course right to support Richard Heck's judgement that it is a different argument from that I had given previously. As he says, this is sufficiently shown by the fact that the argument of *FPM* applies strictly to mathematical theories, and cannot be generalised, as could the previous argument, to non-mathematical discourse. He has in general understood me very well, and has thought through the issues with great clarity.

Sullivan's avowed aim was to expound and analyse my argument, not to criticise it. Since I had made my argument turn on the indefinite extendibility of the concepts whose extensions were supposed to form the domains of the fundamental mathematical theories, I was therefore disconcerted when, in his very first section, he set aside the notion of indefinitely extensible concepts in favour of a more basic one. The more basic notion was that of a totality of which we can form no definite conception. Certainly we can form no definite conception of the extension of an indefinitely extensible concept, by the very definition of indefinite extendibility. If we form a definite conception of a totality all of whose members fall under the concept, then, by the principle of extendibility, we shall be able to characterise other objects not in that totality that also fall under the concept: so we can never form a definite conception of the totality of all that falls under the concept. Hence the more basic notion subsumes the more specific one; and it was certainly right to infer that we could form no definite conception of the domains of the fundamental mathematical theories from my characterising them as being the extensions of indefinitely extensible concepts.

Russell's Paradox turns on the fact that the concept *class not a member of itself* is indefinitely extensible: if we grasp a totality all of whose members fall under that concept, that totality will again fall under it. I thought that the more general concepts of *ordinal number* and of *set* or *class* were evident examples of indefinitely extensible concepts. The advantage of these examples is that even someone unshakably wedded to classical conceptions must acknowledge them as instantiating the notion of an indefinitely extensible concept, and must therefore acknowledge the existence of such concepts. Such a one must do so, because the supposition that their intuitive extensions form definite totalities (totalities of which we have a definite conception) leads at once to contradiction: the Burali-Forti Paradox in the one case and the Russell Paradox in the other. Indeed, Russell, the inventor of the notion of indefinitely extensible concepts, thought that the use of such concepts explained how the set-theoretic paradoxes arose, and inevitably led to contradiction.

But Sullivan disagrees with me here. He thinks that Russell originated only the notion of what he calls a *self-reproductive* concept, and that the concepts of *ordinal number* and of *set* indeed have this feature; but he thinks that in every case further argument is needed to show that a self-reproductive concept is indefinitely extensible. The further argument would be to the effect that only conceptions of totalities that cannot be extended by the self-reproductive process can qualify as *definite* conceptions. Why is any further argument needed? The intuitive notion of an ordinal number is that of the order-type of a well-ordering. If you claim to grasp the totality of all the ordinals there are—of everything that answers to the intuitive notion of an ordinal—you are claiming to have a definite conception of that totality. You may now be asked whether that totality is not well-ordered by the relation of magnitude. When you agree that it is, it is pointed out to you that the order-type of that well-ordering, which by definition answers to the intuitive notion of an ordinal, cannot be a member of the totality you were envisaging, because it must be greater than all its members: so you were not after all conceiving of the totality of everything that is intuitively an ordinal. Is that not a conclusive argument? What further argument is needed?

Sullivan answers this by proposing that a grasp of the self-reproductive character of the concept may constitute a definite conception of its extension. I entirely disagree. Someone who not only grasps the intuitive concept—that of an order-type of a well-ordering, for example—but has progressed into recognising the principle of extendibility it incorporates, has a clear grasp of the *concept*; but he does not thereby attain a conception of the totality of everything that falls under it. We might grant him such a conception if he was able to form a view of how far the principle of extendibility could be iterated. That, however, is precisely what we do not normally have; we cannot, for example, in any way envisage how often—certainly transfinitely often, and probably more often yet—the process of extending the range of ordinal numbers must be iterated so as to embrace everything which, if described, would be intuitively recognised as an ordinal number. I therefore reject Sullivan's claim that, in any normal case, a further argument is needed to show that a self-reproductive concept is indefinitely extensible.

The analysis of my argument that the fundamental mathematical theories admit only an intuitionistic, not a classical, logic, with which Sullivan opens the second section of his essay, is very well set out. The first premiss is certainly one that I endorse, and on which my argument is based. The second premiss is the crucial one from which, in *FPM*, my conclusion was derived. It certainly applies to the real numbers in my view. Whether or not it applies to the natural numbers is more questionable. I shall revert to this later in this reply.

Sullivan's discussion of the first premiss, in his third section, is exemplary. I have two minor cavils. First, Sullivan believes that my argument against a faculty of intellectual intuition of mathematical structures and mathematical objects analogous to sense-perception of physical objects can be strengthened. He writes:

> Suppose that we allow that there could be a truth about the layout of things in some mathematical domain that was *in no sense* a consequence of the conception we have of it. We should then have to think of this domain as a region of reality where what holds true does so in virtue of something—call it God's creative will—that is independent of that conception. The deductive articulation of that conception could then in no case be sufficient in itself to establish the truth as to how things stood in that region: we should always need the *further* assurance of conformity between the conception articulated and God's creative will. In . . . summary: if any truth about that region is intrinsically unprovable, then every truth about it is unprovable. . . .

I do not follow this reasoning. Suppose that we have correctly characterised a region within mathematical reality. We are aware that there are features of that region that cannot be established by deductive reasoning from our characterisation of it. Nevertheless, we have carried out some valid deductive reasoning from that characterisation that leads to a conclusion that the region has a certain feature. Then that conclusion must stand. We cannot be in need of any further assurance of conformity with God's creative will. For it is impossible that our conclusion should turn out not to be in conformity with how things are in that region: if it did, our reasoning would not have been valid. Some truths about that region may be attainable by deductive reasoning, even though not all are.

In reply to an objection to my criticism of the notion of a faculty of intellectual intuition analogous to sense-perception, Sullivan rightly says that no proposition of physics is provable in the sense that mathematical propositions are provable. The role of deduction in physics is, as he says, to extract the consequences of a theory. Such consequences may form the ground of a prediction, as when physicists say such things as that theory predicts the existence of such-and-such a hitherto unobserved type of particle. The consequences, when not confirmed by observation, may serve to overthrow the theory; they cannot establish it.

Secondly, a small point. Sullivan later alludes to my citation of Aquinas's contrast between the notion of what is *nota quoad nos* and that of what is *per se nota*. As I understand it, the contrast is between what holds in virtue of how we can know it and what holds in virtue of what makes it true. That is a reasonable distinction between metaphysical and epistemic necessity. It is not, I think, to be equated with the Kripkean distinction between the metaphysically necessary and the a priori: the Kripkean necessities of origin and of internal structure do not have the same root. Sullivan says that I argued that the Thomistic distinction has no application within mathematics. I did not argue so much. I certainly claimed that the existence of a mathematical structure (system of mathematical objects), if known at all, could be known only a priori. But Aquinas's distinction can be applied to particular mathematical statements. A platonist believes that such a statement may be true even though it is beyond our reach to prove it. If, say, Goldbach's conjecture is one of these, it will be *per se nota* but not *nota quoad nos*.

Sullivan's discussion of the second premiss in his fourth section is equally percipient. I particularly liked his image of the chequer-board as a means of fastening on the difference between empirical and mathematical generalisation. His development of the argument leads him naturally to question whether what can be said about the real numbers or about sets of natural numbers can be said about the natural numbers themselves, namely that we do not have a definite conception of the totality comprising them. Certainly many mathematicians and philosophers of mathematics have taken it as not at all heroic to suppose that we grasp this totality; they think it immediately apparent that we do. Does not any system of notation for the natural numbers constitute a chequer-board?

It is clear that for a finitist the concept *natural number* must be an indefinitely extensible one. There is in *FPM* a suggestion that we must side with the finitist. On p. 318 there occurs the passage:

> Now what is it for a totality to be infinite? More exactly, what is it for it to be *intrinsically* infinite, that is, for the very conception of that totality to entail its infinity? It is for us always to have a means of finding another element of the totality, however many we have already identified; the new element will be characterised in terms of those previously identified. . . . A denumerable totality . . . is one for which we can find a further element, given any initial

segment of it: the similarity between Frege's proof of the infinity of the sequence of natural numbers and the foregoing demonstration that the concept *class not a member of itself* is indefinitely extensible can hardly escape notice. We have a strong conviction that we *do* have a clear grasp of the totality of natural numbers; but what we actually grasp with such clarity is the principle of extension by which, given any natural number, we can immediately cite one greater than it by 1. A concept whose extension is intrinsically infinite is thus a particular case of an indefinitely extensible one.

This passage is in effect arguing that we can *never* have a definite conception of an intrinsically infinite totality: in other words, that we can never interpret quantification over such a totality as always yielding a statement that is determinately either true or false. That, of course, is something an intuitionist or other constructive mathematician believes: but is the ground given for it in the passage just quoted cogent? Even though the finitist must understand the concept *natural number* as an indefinitely extensible one, can we not attribute even to him a conception of its (infinite) extension? In discussing the general notion of indefinitely extensible concepts, I said above that we might grant one who recognised the indefinite extendibility of a concept a conception of its extension if he was able to form a view of how far the principle of extendibility could be iterated. Can we not credit the finitist with such a view in the case of the concept *natural number*? When we contemplate successive extensions of the sequence of ordinal numbers, they fade away into the utterly hazy distance: we cannot grasp how far they may be carried. Surely it is not like this for the finitist contemplating successive extensions of the sequence of natural numbers: he surely has a quite determinate grasp of how far they may be iterated.

I confess to feeling quite dubious about this question. When I am asked to envisage what, for us, are simply enormous natural numbers—say a number N whose representation in decimal notation would fill as many and as large volumes as the *Encyclopaedia Britannica*, or, larger yet, the number N^N—I think what I said in *FPM* is right, especially when I reflect that N and N^N, like all natural numbers, are small in the sense that most natural numbers are greater than they. Do we really grasp this totality? Or is it that, when we think that we grasp it, we are merely envisaging some finite but vaguely and indefinitely terminating initial segment of it? On the other hand, when I contrast the totality of natural numbers with the totality of real numbers, the sense that we have a perfectly firm conception of the former begins to grip me once more. I shall not argue the point any further here. If what I maintained in *FPM* is wrong, then, as far as the argument of that book goes, we should have to allow the use of classical logic in elementary (first-order) number theory, but only of intuitionistic logic in any higher theory. In principle this would be a large concession to classical mathematics; in practice, it would make hardly any difference. Still, it would be an awkward position to defend.

My argument was for an intuitionistic rather than a classical understanding of the quantifiers, and hence for an intuitionistic logic in general, within fundamental mathematical theories, essentially on the ground that we do not have a sufficiently definite conception of what elements belong to the domains of such theories. Peter Sullivan expounds my argument for that ground, and explores its ramifications. At this point he very naturally raises a doubt whether the argument can apply to elementary number theory. He then turns to consider another question discussed by me in *FPM*, whether reference to mathematical objects, considered as legitimated by the context principle, is necessarily a thin notion, or whether it can be a robust one.

The notion of the reference of a particular singular term or type of singular terms is robust when the meaning-theory provides for that notion to be used in determining the truth-value of a sentence in which the term, or one of that type, occurs; it is weak or thin when the meaning-theory does not so provide. We may seek to illustrate this contrast by opposing the canonical conditions proposed by Husserl with those proposed by Frege for the truth of an identity between empirical assignations of number; or, rather, to make the matter clearer, we may contrast the Husserlian account with the neo-Fregean one propounded by Crispin Wright and Bob Hale. A semantic theory shows the contributions made by the components of a sentence to the determination of its truth-value. Since the theory of sense must rest upon the semantic theory as a base, the semantic theory strongly suggests what the canonical procedure should in practice be for us to ascertain the truth-value of a statement. Thus, if, where s and t are singular terms, we are to decide the truth-value of a sentence of the form "$F(s, t)$," the semantic theory states that the sentence is true iff the referent of s stands in the relation denoted by "$F(\xi, \zeta)$" to the referent of t. This suggests that, given a sentence of that form, say "Titan is the largest satellite of Saturn," we should, in order to determine its truth-value, determine which objects are denoted by "Titan" and by "Saturn," and then discover whether the one stands in the relation denoted by "ξ is the largest satellite of ζ" to the other.

How, then do matters stand with identity-statements? The semantic theory will lay down a general condition for the truth of such statements; but, at least according to the neo-Fregeans, it may allow different explanations for special forms of identity-statement. The general condition is naturally stated as that

(Id)   "$s = t$" is true iff s and t denote the same element of the domain.

This stipulation suggests that we set about discovering the truth-value of an identity-statement by the rather simple-minded procedure of identifying the object denoted by each of the two terms and seeing whether the one object is the same as the other.

It may well be objected that our procedure in determining the truth or falsity of empirical identity-statements, at least of those that have any interest, is very unlike the simple one suggested by the semantic condition for the truth of a statement of identity. We cannot settle the truth of the statement "Phosphorus is the same planet as Hesperus" by fixing on the bright planet we see in the morning and on the bright planet we see in the evening and just checking whether we have got hold of the same planet in each case. Rather, we—or, rather, astronomers—calculate the orbit of each body, calculate where each will be at a given time, and so determine that they are one and the same body. The need for such a complex procedure results from what Frege pointed out: in a true identity-statement the two terms will present the same object under different aspects, which can be connected only by investigation. Such an investigation does not invalidate the semantic stipulation; nor does it make the notion of reference idle. It was not idle: we had to start by identifying the referents of "Phosphorus" and "Hesperus." It is just that the difference of aspect made it unobvious that these referents were the same.

Let us now treat of a statement such as "The number of cups on the table is the same as the number of saucers." Provided that we have laid down truth-conditions for all statements in which it occurs, the context principle licenses us to use such a term as "the number of cups on the table" and to ascribe a reference to it. A Husserlian account of identity-statements of the cited type conforms precisely to the procedure suggested by the semantic proviso, or at least appears to do so. According to it, the canonical way of determining the truth-value of the statement is to count the cups and to count the saucers and then to check whether the number of cups is the same as the number of saucers. The procedure of counting presents itself as the analogue of identifying the referent of a term for a spatiotemporal object. On this account the notion of reference as applied to these terms appears to be robust.

The neo-Fregean account is different. According to it, we do not need to find out what the number of cups or of saucers is: a statement of this form is to be treated by the semantic theory as a special case. The stipulation governing it is:

(Num)   the number of Fs = the number of Gs iff
               the Fs can be mapped one to one on to the Gs.

Thus "the number of cups is the same as the number of saucers" will hold good just in case the cups can be mapped one to one on to the saucers. To determine its truth or falsity, we therefore see whether such a mapping can be effected, say by placing each cup on a saucer as far as can be done. We thus in effect bypass the references of the two terms; the notion of their reference is idle in our procedure, and hence, applied to numerical terms such as these, is thin, or at least will be, provided that other forms of statement involving them are to be handled similarly.

The example seems to provide a vivid contrast between a robust and a thin notion of reference. It is, however, defective. The most obvious objection to the example is that to count the cups on the table and find (say) that there are seven is to set up a one-one map of the cups on to the members of an initial segment of the positive integers (or of the numerals), and that therefore there is no essential difference between Husserl's analysis and the neo-Fregean one: the former simply takes an unnecessary detour. From this it may perhaps be inferred that the distinction between a thin and a robust notion of reference is superficial.

It is not the distinction that is superficial, but the example. The Husserlian account was presented without any analysis of the procedure of counting. When that analysis is supplied, the appearance that it resembles the identification of the referent of a term for a spatiotemporal object evaporates. When we analyse the Husserlian account fully, it is seen to involve a robust notion of reference no more than does the neo-Fregean one.

Though the example was defective, its account of the neo-Fregean analysis of sentences containing numerical terms was accurate. Øystein Linnebo disagrees with both Frege and the neo-Fregeans in thinking, as I do, that the natural numbers should be introduced in the first instance as finite ordinals rather than finite cardinals; but there *are* finite cardinal numbers, and phrases such as "the number of cups on the table" plainly refer to them, so that this is not the issue here. Rather, as against the neo-Fregeans, to whom he rightly objects as flouting the principle of compositionality, Linnebo has argued for a distinction between semantics and "meta-semantics." The equivalence (Num) should not be viewed as an exception to the general semantic stipulation (Id), which applies to numerical terms as it does to others, but as a *meta-semantic* principle. Semantics treats, for Linnebo as for everyone, of the way in which the semantic values of complex expressions, including sentences, depend on those of their simple constituents. Meta-semantics, by contrast, explains what determines the semantic values of expressions. The distinction is valid, but surely coincides with Frege's distinction between the theory of reference (*Bedeutung*) and the theory of sense (though admittedly he said little about the content of the theory of sense). On this view, then, the principle (Num) belongs to the theory of sense. As such, it does not say that the two sides of the equivalence coincide in sense independently, as it were; it says that, given that we understand sentences of the right-hand form, we grasp the sense of a numerical term of the form "the number of Fs" by coming to know that a sentence of the left-hand form is to be taken as true iff the corresponding sentence of the right-hand form is true. (Only those who know some mathematics are familiar with the term "mapping"; but the concept is expressed when we speak of there being just enough to go round.) Linnebo calls objects of a given sort "light-weight" if sentences concerning them admit of a meta-semantic reduction to sentences not containing terms for them. This is equivalent to saying, in my terminology, that the conception of reference to such objects is thin if the explanation of the senses of sentences containing terms for them does not make use of the notion of reference to them. We may adopt this as a revised formulation of the notion of a thin conception of reference.

Sullivan takes me as rejecting "a straightforwardly internalist understanding of the context principle." As a counter to nominalism, I do so understand it. The nominalist argues that, since abstract objects have no causal powers, we cannot know of their existence; moreover, that we can have no reason to believe them to exist, since their existence can have no effect on anything, and so no difference would be made by their non-existence. Against this, the context principle is a complete reply: as Sullivan puts it, since "the language-game works, its terms refer." He rightly says that I insist "that we need to be able *to say how* the language-game works." I do; but, in my eyes, this need is not required in order to vindicate appeal to the context principle, but to distinguish a robust from a thin conception of reference.

Peter Sullivan observes that "the issue between realism and constructivism also turns on whether a suitably strong analogy can be sustained between mathematical and empirical reference." In *FPM* I was primarily concerned with the interpretation of quantification over mathematical objects, and very little with the metaphysical implications of adopting a classical or an intuitionistic interpretation of the quantifiers. Sullivan is right, however, that a fully realist understanding of mathematical propositions demands that we can maintain a robust conception of reference to mathematical objects, as we can of reference not only to material objects but to abstract ones such as the Equator and the Earth's axis. The ringing declarations of realism in Frege's *Grundlagen*—that the mathematician, like the geographer, can only find what is there and give it a name—will sound hollow if it be conceded that we can have only a thin conception of the reference of mathematical terms. Full-blooded realism about mathematics requires a robust conception.

How far, then, are the two issues connected?—whether we have a definite conception of the domain of a mathematical theory, and whether we have a robust understanding of the reference of its terms. Does a classical understanding of the quantifiers require a robust conception of reference to the objects over which we are quantifying? A thin notion of reference will certainly allow of quantification over the referents, when constructively interpreted. For if the ascription of reference to terms of a given range is taken as legitimated by the context principle, the presupposition for an appeal to that principle is that a sense has been provided for sentences containing terms of that range; and an existential quantification over the referents of those terms can be constructively justified only by the production of an instance. As for universal quantification, it is justified by a general means for establishing such instances. That need not mean that we already have a term for every element of the domain; only that we have a means whereby, as soon as anything has been recognised as an element of the domain, we can show that it satisfies the condition in question.

A classical understanding of the quantifiers is often referred to as "objectual quantification," and explained in terms of the application of the predicate to which the quantifier is attached to individual objects. Does it therefore demand a robust conception of reference to the objects quantified over? If these objects can be thought of only as the referents of the terms that denote them, this amounts to explaining the quantified statement in terms of the sentences which are its instances, in other words by substitutional quantification. But provided that truth-conditions for such instances have genuinely been laid down, this does not seem to deprive the classical understanding of the quantifiers of its substance. A classical understanding of the quantifiers, by contrast with a constructive one, demands that we regard every quantified statement as having a determinate truth-value; it therefore requires that, if we do not have a term for each element of the domain, we can at least conceive of having one.

A sharp distinction between substitutional and objectual quantification is in place only when the expressions to be substituted for the bound variable are not thought of as having a reference. When we are quantifying over mathematical objects, what matters is whether we have a determinate range of instances, and whether those instances have determinate truth-values. If the answers to both questions are affirmative, then, even if only a thin notion of reference is in play, there is no reason, among the considerations under review, to deny that the quantifiers may be understood classically.

Can an appeal to the context principle in order to justify the ascription of reference to mathematical terms be reconciled with a robust conception of such reference? Since mathematical objects are not objects of ostension, reference to them can be sustained only by appeal to the context principle, or something resembling it. The qualification is needed because of the great strength of the condition for applying the context principle, as Frege explained it. He required that a truth-value should have been determined for every sentence in which the referring terms occur. Whatever "determined" means here, the impredicativity of his stipulations prevented this condition from being fulfilled in his construction of arithmetic; any more than his "proof" in *Grundgesetze* that every sentence of his formal language had a truth-value established that result. The condition fails equally, and for the same reason, in the neo-Fregean construction. So, insofar as we favour introducing the natural numbers and elements of the domains of other fundamental theories in a Fregean style, we cannot strictly speaking appeal to the context principle as Frege understood it; we can rely only on some vaguer principle, whose condition is that we have a practice of assigning truth-values, according to objective criteria, to statements in which mathematical terms occur. Granted that this entitles us to ascribe reference to such terms, our question is whether we can ever have a robust conception of reference to the mathematical objects they denote.

Sullivan contends that this question turns on whether a suitably strong analogy can be sustained between mathematical and empirical reference. The notion of reference comes into play when we identify a single object as that perceived or conceived under distinct aspects; our conception of reference is robust if such identification can be explained only in terms of features of that object. By a "feature of the object" is meant one that can be attributed to it only by a statement making reference to it. The sense of saying that the number of cups on the table is the same as the number of saucers can be explained without reference to the number 7; so the notion of reference to that number, if confined to such contexts, would certainly be thin. I contrasted the empirical and mathematical cases by arguing that we need to circumscribe the domain of a mathematical theory, whereas no such circumscription of the totality of material objects is required. Sullivan explains this in his chequer-board analogy by the fact that material objects are located in space and time (and visual objects like the constellations in visual space). Their spatiotemporal location accounts for their having different aspects in terms of which they may be referred to in different ways (from different perspectives). In so doing, it fixes the domain of material objects.

Unlike empirical objects, different ways in which a mathematical object may be conceived within mathematics must of course be conceptually connected, that is, they must provably relate to the same object. But this fact does not, in my view, of itself destroy the analogy. The question goes to the principle of individuation of the various sorts of mathematical objects. If we abide by Frege's requirement that these be introduced in such a way as to display the general principle governing their application, this is bound in every case to be what the neo-Fregeans call an "abstraction principle": one determining the condition for the identity of mathematical objects of that sort as the holding of an equivalence relation between things occupying a more basic level within the theory of sense. Thus Frege rejected the strategy of Cantor and Dedekind of first introducing the rational numbers and then defining the real numbers in terms of them. He thought that the real numbers, rational or irrational, positive or negative, should be introduced together, as ratios between quantities of the same kind; the ratio between two quantities of one kind could of course coincide with that between two quantities of some other kind. Of the notion of a "kind" or domain of quantities, Frege offered a purely logical or set-theoretical definition. The condition for one ratio to be the same as another was of course laid down by Eudoxus, as expounded by Euclid, in his theory of proportionality.

Leaving aside the question within what set-theoretical framework the notion of a quantitative domain is to be defined, does this construction of the real numbers satisfy the condition for appeal to the context principle, and is the conception of reference to real numbers robust? The answers to both questions are doubtful, and for the same reason, that the construction is impredicative: Frege wishes to be able to speak of the ratio between two real numbers (a ratio between ratios). The effect of this impredicativity is twofold. First, the stipulation of the condition for the identity between real numbers cannot serve on its own to fix the truth-values of all statements about real numbers; there has to be an independent circumscription of the domain. Hence the condition for appeal to the context principle is not satisfied by the identity-condition for real numbers alone. Secondly, we shall not be able to eliminate terms for real numbers in favour of terms for quantities; the conception of reference to them must therefore be robust if it is justified at all. All this of course applies equally to the cardinal numbers, with their identity-condition that of the equinumerosity of the concepts to which the numerical operator is applied.

It appears at first that the identity-conditions for numbers of different kinds determine the different aspects under which any such number may be presented, as a finite cardinal, as a finite ordinal, or as a ratio. But they do not thus provide a chequer-board, determining the relevant domains: it must still be asked of what they may be the cardinal numbers, of what orderings they may be the order-types, or between what quantities they may be the ratios. The answer is likely to be vague and will almost certainly make explicit the impredicativity of their characterisation. The mathematical theories taking them as their subject-matter supply means of identification quite remote from that original characterisation. When Ramanujan famously picked out 1729 as the smallest number representable as the sum of two cubes in two different ways, he certainly was not thinking of it as the number of objects falling under some concept, or as the number of a house in a very long street. Since there are non-denumerably many real numbers, it is impossible in principle that we should have a comprehensive notation for them, as we do for the natural numbers. Most real numbers are transcendental; we have symbols for only a few particularly interesting ones of these, such as e and π. We have symbols for them precisely because of the multiple connections they have, which yield different ways of picking them out. Think of the different ways in which the function e^x, and hence the number e, can be characterised. The analogy with reference to empirical objects appears strong; but we cannot argue from this that we have a robust conception of reference either to real numbers or to natural numbers. At least we cannot do so in accordance with my characterisation of a robust conception of reference, which implicitly incorporated Frege's strong condition for the application of the context principle. What blocks an appeal to the context principle in the presence of that condition is the impredicativity of the characterisation of the natural and of the real numbers along Fregean lines; we are forced by this to regard our conception of reference to them as robust.

Whether we should characterise the domains of fundamental mathematical theories in a Fregean style is a matter of how the fundamental laws of those theories are to be established. Once the laws of elementary arithmetic are in place, reference to the number of numbers below some bound and having a given property can always be circumvented by summing the characteristic function of the property from 0 to that bound. The only occasion on which it cannot be so circumvented is when it is used, as in Frege's proof, to show the infinity of the sequence of natural numbers. Frege has been applauded, in recent times, by Richard Heck and others, for establishing what they call "Frege's Theorem," extracted from his construction of arithmetic: namely that from the equivalence (Num) alone a set of axioms for arithmetic equivalent to Peano's can be derived in second-order logic. That was indeed a great achievement, and a very interesting one. It does not do what Frege wished to do, however, namely to establish arithmetic on unchallengeable logical foundations. It does not do so, because (Num) (which they misleadingly label "Hume's Principle") characterises the numerical operator impredicatively. It might seem a scandal that after 120 years' study of the foundations of mathematics, no one has succeeded in accomplishing this basic task.

But perhaps it cannot be accomplished. Perhaps there is an inescapable circularity in our understanding of the fundamental mathematical theories. But how can this be? Surely it cannot be that they do not really make sense. Surely it cannot be that, though they make sense, we do not really understand them. The philosophy of mathematics cannot claim, after all this time, to have dispelled these absurd sceptical possibilities. We must certainly not allow empirical concepts, let alone empirical considerations, to intrude into mathematics; nor must we deprive mathematics of the status of a science. Accepting that the domains of the fundamental theories are indefinitely extensible, and hence that they cannot be governed by classical logic, will not wholly solve this problem. But it would make the task less onerous, and so give it a greater chance of eventual success.

M. D.

23

Maurice Salles

MICHAEL DUMMETT ON SOCIAL CHOICE AND VOTING

Michael Dummett worked on the theoretical aspects of aggregation of individual preferences and on the strategic aspects of voting theory. He also extended Black's analysis of single-peaked preferences for majority rule to the case of voting games (majority games), offering a greater flexibility for the expression of voters' preferences. He is also with Donald Saari one of the major advocates of the use of Borda's rule in actual voting. In two books and a paper, he proposed many examples showing the advantages and defects of many voting rules used in the world.

At the beginning of the 1970s, there has been an upsurge of the publications in social choice and voting theory with, for instance, the books of Murakami (1968), Sen (1970), Pattanaik (1971), and Fishburn (1973). On the contrary, the publications in this area were quite rare in the 1950s and the beginning 1960s after the foundational works of Arrow (1951, 1963) and Black (1958). In 1970, I just started my research for my doctoral dissertation. I was particularly interested in the restrictions of individual preferences that could guarantee the transitivity of the social preference and/or the existence of a "best" element generated by some aggregation procedure. I was intrigued by a paper by Michael Dummett and Robin Farquharson published in *Econometrica* in 1961. I was intrigued for three reasons. First, I had never heard of the authors. Second, in the first pages of the paper, what would become, more than ten years later, one of the most famous results of the social choice literature, viz., the Gibbard-Satterthwaite Theorem, was conjectured in passing. Third, the proof technique used was "different."[1] Doing research in social choice theory, I rapidly heard of Farquharson's book (1969) and was very surprised to discover in the book's bibliography that Farquharson published a paper in French on his equilibrium concept in the *Comptes Rendus de l'Académie des Sciences* as early as in 1955.[2] Incidentally, a recent paper by Michael Dummett (2002) is devoted to Farquharson. It took me some time (probably a few years, after I started to develop an amateurish interest in philosophy, particularly in analytic philosophy—surely a major disease for most French *intellectuels*) before I came to know that Michael Dummett was one of the greatest living philosophers.

In 1984, a book by Dummett entitled *Voting Procedures* appeared. I think that this book is one of the main works in voting theory and in the analysis of actual voting procedures—I mean procedures used or usable in real life, political or otherwise. A declared objective of this book was to remedy a "deplorable situation," viz., that the theory of voting "was known only to a small circle of people," excluding "politicians, national and local" as well as, most probably, "experts in political institutions and political theory." *Voting Procedures* was not an easy book. I had the impression from discussions with Michael Dummett that he thought the aforementioned objective had not been reached. On the other hand, it is already a classic even if, precisely because its author is a philosopher, it has not been so far widely read by the so-called "small circle of people." Dummett's *Principles of Electoral Reform* (1997) was surely written to reach the initial objective, and it is, I believe, totally successful. Here is a book easy to read, even for laymen, and full of substance and wit. I am not sure, however, that in these times when electoral reforms are in order in many countries or when groups of countries have to devise procedures (as in the European Union), it has been read by politicians and journalists.

One may wonder why philosophers have been interested at all in social choice and voting theory. On the one hand, social choice theory and welfare economics always had strong links with moral philosophy and it is not a surprise that many philosophers contributed to this area. It has also been the case that some great authors were at the same time philosophers and economists. I can mention without trying to be exhaustive Adam Smith, John Stuart Mill, and Henry Sidgwick. In our time, it is rather difficult to ascertain that Amartya Sen or John Broome are basically economists rather than philosophers. Sen has published many of his recent papers in philosophical journals and some of his books (1987, 2003) are obviously related to moral philosophy. Moreover, important philosophers (professionally they are philosophers because they are or have been academics within departments of philosophy in universities) made major contributions in social choice, from different perspectives. Let me mention Gibbard (1973), Davidson (1986), Gauthier (1986), Griffin (1986), Jeffrey (1992), Suppes (1996), and Nozick (1997). On the other hand, Michael Dummett's work is essentially devoted to social choice theory as a paradigm of voting, in its practical and theoretical guise. In this sense, he is a real heir of another Oxford logician: C. L. Dodgson (Lewis Carroll). It is a fact that today there are several logicians working in this area (such as Moshé Machover, Sven Ove Hansson, or Harrie de Swart) and that meetings are specifically organized to bring logicians together with game theorists and social choice theorists.

In this essay, I will first outline Dummett's theoretical contribution. This includes an original approach to the aggregation of preferences problem and an analysis of strategic voting. It also includes what was the core of his 1961 paper co-authored with Robin Farquharson, where a sufficient condition on individual preferences for the existence of a solution to voting games is given. This condition is related to, but more general than, Duncan Black's single-peaked preferences. Then, I will describe some of Dummett's work on practical voting methods.

I. The Impossibility of Social Welfare Functions

I will first recall the canonical version of Arrow's impossibility theorem. I will use what are now rather standard definitions, notations, and the like.

Let X be a set of alternatives (options, social states, candidates, allocations of standard microeconomic theory, etc.). $\#X$ is the cardinal of X (the number of its elements when X is finite). A binary relation $\succeq$ over X is a set of ordered pairs (x,y) with x and y in X, i.e., $\succeq$ is a subset of the Cartesian product $X \times X$. I use the notation $x \succeq y$ rather than $(x,y) \in \succeq$. Intuitively $x \succeq y$ means in our context 'x is as good as y.' The asymmetric component of $\succeq$, denoted by $\succ$, meaning 'is better than,' is defined by $x \succ y$ if $x \succeq y$ and $\neg y \succeq x$ ($\neg$ is the negation symbol). The symmetric component, denoted by $\sim$, meaning 'there is an indifference between,' is defined by $x \sim y$ if $x \succeq y$ and $y \succeq x$. The binary relation $\succeq$ is reflexive if for all $x \in X$, $x \succeq x$. It is complete if for all $x, y \in X$, $x \succeq y$ or $y \succeq x$ (note that if $\succeq$ is complete, it is reflexive and that, in this case, $x \succ y \leftrightarrow \neg y \succeq x$). It is transitive if for all x, $y, z \in X$, $x \succeq y$ and $y \succeq z \Rightarrow x \succeq z$. A binary relation which is complete and transitive is a complete preorder. With X finite, a complete preorder ranked the alternatives from a most preferred to a least preferred with possible ties.

Let N be a finite set of individuals (economic agents, voters) of cardinal n, i.e., $N = \{1, \ldots, n\}$. Each individual $i \in N$ has a preference over X given by a complete preorder $\succeq_i$. The aggregation question is about the construction of a social (collective, synthetic) preference $\succeq_S$ (or in some cases a social choice) from a list of individual preferences (one preference per individual).

Let $Ord(X)$ be the set of complete preorders over X, $Ord(X)'$ be a subset of $Ord(X)$, and $Bin(X)$ be the set of complete binary relations over X.

DEFINITION 1. An *aggregation function* is a function from $Ord(X)'^n$ into $Bin(X)$, where $Ord(X)'^n$ is the Cartesian product of $Ord(X)'$ n times.

This means that the aggregation function f associates a complete (social) binary relation $\succeq_S$ to a n-list $(\succeq_1, \ldots, \succeq_n)$ of (individual) complete preorders: $f : (\succeq_1, \ldots, \succeq_n) \rightarrow \succeq_S$.

DEFINITION 2. A *social welfare function* is an aggregation function for which $Bin(X) = Ord(X)$.

In this case, the sort of rationality required for the social preference is absolutely identical with the rationality we assumed for individuals. If we consider the simple case where $Ord(X)' = Ord(X)$, $\#X = 3$, and $n = 3$, the number of such functions is 13^{13^3}, which is a number of the order of the positive integer 1 followed by more than 2400 zeros. Of course, some of these functions are unappealing. Some of these unappealing characteristics are excluded by a set of conditions. Arrow's theorem asserts, in a way, that a given set of appealing conditions had so drastically reduced the set of possible social welfare functions that there is no one left! In the standard version of Arrow's theorem there are four conditions.

CONDITION U. $Ord(X)' = Ord(X)$.

This means that the domain of the function is unrestricted or universal (the only restriction being that the individual preferences are given by complete preorders; there is no supplementary rationality assumed from the individuals). This condition will be discussed in section 3.

CONDITION I. Let $(\succeq_1, \ldots, \succeq_n)$ and $(\succeq_1', \ldots, \succeq_n') \in Ord(X)'^n$ and a and $b \in X$. Suppose that for each $i \in N \succeq_i |$ $\{a,b\} = \succeq_i' |$ $\{a,b\}$, then $\succeq_S |$ $\{a,b\} = \succeq_S' |$ $\{a,b\}$ where $\succeq_S = f(\succeq_1, \ldots, \succeq_n)$ and $\succeq_S' = f(\succeq_1', \ldots, \succeq_n')$.

For a simple explanation, suppose that X is finite. Then, in the individual rankings of the alternatives erase all alternatives except a and b. If what is left in the two n-lists coincide, then the social ranking restricted to a and b must also coincide. Many rules, including majority rule or for that matter, all rules where the social preference over two alternatives is defined from the individual preferences over these same two alternatives, will satisfy Condition I. On the other hand, all rules that are based on scores (the simplest one being plurality rule used as a voting procedure in many countries, in particular in the United States and United Kingdom) violate this condition. This condition is often called "independence of irrelevant alternatives," but it is rather unfortunate that a condition of the same name with another meaning is also used in individual decision theory.

CONDITION P. Let $(\succeq_1, \ldots, \succeq_n) \in Ord(X)'^n$ and a and $b \in X$. If $a \succ_i b$ for all $i \in N$, then $a \succ_S b$, where $\succ_S$ is the asymmetric component of $\succeq_S = f(\succeq_1, \ldots, \succeq_n)$.

This says that the social preference respects unanimity. An interesting aspect of the condition is that it excludes that the social welfare function be constant.

CONDITION D^A. There is no individual i such that for any n-list $(\succeq_1, \ldots, \succeq_n) \in Ord(X)'^n$ and any $x, y \in X$, $x \succ_i y \Rightarrow x \succ_S y$, where $\succ_S$ is the asymmetric component of $\succeq_S = f(\succeq_1, \ldots, \succeq_n)$.

Such an individual is called a *dictator*. Note that to be a dictator you have to impose (all) your *strict* preference to the society, i.e., $\succ_i \subseteq \succ_S$.

ARROW'S IMPOSSIBILITY THEOREM. *If $n \geq 2$ and $\#X \geq 3$, there is no social welfare function satisfying Conditions U, I, P, and D^A.*

In his book, Arrow introduced two other conditions. The following conditions are slight modifications of the conditions he introduced in the 1951 version of his book with no consequences on the results.

CONDITION M^A. Let $(\succeq_1, \ldots, \succeq_n)$ and $(\succeq_1', \ldots, \succeq_n') \in Ord(X)'^n$ and $a, b \in X$. Suppose that for each $i \in N$, $a \succeq_i b \Rightarrow a \succeq_i' b$ and $a \succ_i b \Rightarrow a \succ_i' b$. Then $a \succ_S b \Rightarrow a \succ_S' b$, where $\succ_S$ is the asymmetric component of $\succeq_S = f(\succeq_1, \ldots, \succeq_n)$ and $\succ_S'$ is the asymmetric component of $\succeq_S' = f(\succeq_1', \ldots, \succeq_n')$.

This is a monotonicity assumption meaning that if a was socially preferred to b and if a does not decline vis-à-vis b in the preference scale of every individual, then a remains socially preferred to b.

CONDITION NI^A. For all $x, y \in X$, there is an n-list $(\succeq_1, \ldots, \succeq_n) \in Ord(X)'^n$ for which $x \succ_S y$, where $\succ_S$ is the asymmetric component of $\succeq_S = f(\succeq_1, \ldots, \succeq_n)$.

NI^A means "nonimposition." This condition entails that a (strict) social preference cannot be commanded by a moral or religious code. It is not difficult to see that, given Conditions U and I, Conditions M^A and NI^A imply Condition P.

In *Voting Procedures* (1984), Michael Dummett proposes another Arrovian impossibility theorem. He keeps Conditions U and I and introduces variants (strengthenings for the first two and weakening for nonimposition) of Conditions D^A, M^A, and NI^A. The following is a slight modification of Dummett's principle (I) (page 52), taking Condition I into consideration.

CONDITION M^D. Let $(\succeq_1, \ldots, \succeq_n)$ and $(\succeq_1', \ldots, \succeq_n') \in Ord(X)'^n$ and $a, b \in X$. Suppose that for each $i \in N$, $a \succeq_i b \Rightarrow a \succeq_i' b$ and $a \succ_i b \Rightarrow a \succ_i' b$. Then $a \succeq_S b \Rightarrow a \succeq_S' b$ and $a \succ_S b \Rightarrow a \succ_S' b$, where $\succ_S$ is the asymmetric component of $\succeq_S = f(\succeq_1, \ldots, \succeq_n)$ and $\succ_S'$ is the asymmetric component of $\succeq_S' = f(\succeq_1', \ldots, \succeq_n')$.

Dummett's monotonicity assumption differs from Condition M^A only by requiring that if the social preference was $a \sim_S b$, then it must remain so or become $a \succ_S b$.

CONDITION NI^D. There are two alternatives $a, b \in X$ and an n-list $(\succeq_1, \ldots, \succeq_n) \in Ord(X)'^n$ for which $a \succ_S b$, where $\succ_S$ is the asymmetric component of $\succeq_S = f(\succeq_1, \ldots, \succeq_n)$.

This condition is quite weak and its violation means that for every n-list and every x and y the function socially ranks x and y at the same level: whatever the individual preferences, there is a general social indifference.

CONDITION D^D. There is no individual i such that for some $a,b \in X$, for any n-list $(\succeq_1, \ldots, \succeq_n) \in Ord(X)'^n$, $a \succ_i b \Rightarrow a \succ_S b$, where $\succ_S$ is the asymmetric component of $\succeq_S = f(\succeq_1, \ldots, \succeq_n)$.

Such individuals could be called *partial dictators*. It is interesting to note that the condition is quite stronger than Arrow's nondictatorship condition (it is probably very difficult to find a "real" Arrovian dictator; even the worst recent historic figures such as Hitler, Stalin, Amin Dada, Bokassa, or Milosevic were not Arrovian dictators, but one can easily imagine that they were Dummettian partial dictators). Moreover, this kind of condition can be found in Sen (1970) to describe *liberalism* (see Brunel and Salles [1998] and Salles [2000]). Dummett's no-partial-dictatorship condition is somewhere between anonymity and Arrow's no-dictatorship condition. Anonymity means that individuals are treated equally. Mathematically if σ is a permutation over the set N of individuals, $f(\succeq_{\sigma(1)}, \ldots, \succeq_{\sigma(n)}) = f(\succeq_1, \ldots, \succeq_n)$.

DUMMETT'S IMPOSSIBILITY THEOREM. *If $n \geq 2$ and $\#X \geq 3$, there is no social welfare function satisfying Condition U, I, NI^D, M^D, and D^D.*

A very nice feature of Dummett's impossibility theorem is the simplicity of its proof. There is no need to prove what Sen (1985) calls the field expansion lemma, that is, the neutrality (equal treatment of alternatives) property generated by decisive sets (a subset of N is decisive for a against b if $a \succ_S b$ whenever we have $a \succ_i b$ for all i in the subset).

II. STRATEGY-PROOF VOTING PROCEDURES

In my view, the six major pieces of modern social choice theory are at this time Arrow's theorem, Black's single-peaked preferences analysis, Nash's bargaining solution, Harsanyi's utilitarianism (1955), Sen's liberalism theorem, and Gibbard-Satterthwaite's strategy-proofness theorem (1973, 1975). Regarding this last theorem, a remarkable feature is that it was very clearly stated (conjectured) in the *Econometrica* (1961) paper of Dummett and Farquharson. Precisely, one can read

We cannot assume that each voter's actual strategy will be determined uniquely by his preference scale. This would be to assume that every voter votes "sincerely," whereas it seems unlikely that *there is any voting procedure in which it can never be advantageous for any voter to vote "strategically," i.e., non-sincerely.* (34, my emphasis)

A general proof of this conjecture was given by Gibbard only in 1973 and by Satterthwaite in 1975. In *Voting Procedures*, Dummett provides a very interesting and (again) "different" proof of this major result. I will give here the standard version of the theorem and indicate how Dummett's version differs from it.

First, X will be assumed to be finite and to simplify the presentation, I will consider that the individuals' preferences are given by linear orderings over X rather than complete preorders. A linear order is an anti-symmetric complete preorder. $\geq$ is anti-symmetric if for all $x, y \in X$, $x \geq y$ and $y \geq x \Rightarrow x = y$. This means that the alternatives are ranked by the individuals without ties, like points on a line. Let $Lin(X)$ be the set of linear orderings over X.

DEFINITION 3. A *social choice function* is a surjective function f from $Lin(X)^n$ to X.

The problem here is the selection of a single alternative. I need not in this essay introduce any restriction on the linear orderings that the individuals will indicate in the selection procedure. The fact that f is surjective means that $f(Lin(X)^n) = X$, in other words, for any alternative there is a n-list $(\succ_1, \ldots, \succ_n) \in Lin(X)^n$ whose value is this alternative.[3] Surjectivity is only here to remain as simple as possible. It is not a necessary condition. Incidentally, the absence of surjectivity is rather difficult to interpret in a voting context.

DEFINITION 4. Individual i *manipulates* the social choice function in $(\succ_1, \ldots, \succ_n) \in Lin(X)^n$ if there exists $\succ_i'$ over X such that $f(\succ_1, \ldots, \succ_{i-1}, \succ_i', \succ_{i+1}, \ldots, \succ_n) \succ_i f(\succ_1, \ldots, \succ_n)$.

If we suppose that the linear preferences $\succ_1, \ldots, \succ_i, \ldots, \succ_n$ are sincere, the definition means that i by reporting a nonsincere preference can make the outcome be preferable to him according to his sincere preference to the outcome that would have been selected had he reported his sincere preference.

CONDITION *NM*. A social choice function f is said to be *nonmanipulable* if there is no i and no n-list $(\succ_1, \ldots, \succ_n) \in Lin(X)^n$ such that i manipulates f in $(\succ_1, \ldots, \succ_n)$.

CONDITION D^G. There is no individual i for which for all n-list $(\succ_1, \ldots, \succ_n) \in Lin(X)^n, f(\succ_1, \ldots, \succ_n) \succ_i x$ for all $x \in X - \{f(\succ_1, \ldots, \succ_n)\}$.

Such an individual could be called a Gibbardian dictator. In the case of a Gibbardian dictator, the function selects systematically the alternative ranked first by the dictator (whatever the others' preferences are).

GIBBARD-SATTERTHWAITE'S THEOREM. *If $n \geq 2$ and $\#X \geq 3$, there is no social choice function satisfying conditions NM and D^G.*

Dummett introduced a stronger form of nondictatorship, again somewhere between anonymity and the Gibbard-Satterthwaite's version.

CONDITION $D^{D'}$. There is no individual i and no alternative a such that for all n-list $(\succ_1, \ldots, \succ_n) \in f^{-1}(\{a\}), f(\succ_1, \ldots, \succ_n) \succ_i x$ for all $x \in X - \{f(\succ_1, \ldots, \succ_n)\}$.

$f^{-1}(\{a\})$ is the inverse image of $\{a\}$ under f. Essentially, in the Gibbard-Satterthwaite framework, a dictator imposes as the collective choice the alternative that is ranked first in his preference ordering, whatever this alternative is. Dummett excludes this possibility even for a single alternative, that is, for every i and every alternative x, i is not able to impose x on the society.

DUMMETT'S STRATEGY-PROOFNESS THEOREM. *If $n \geq 2$ and $\#X \geq 3$, there is no social choice function satisfying conditions MN and $D^{D'}$.*

A remarkable characteristic of Dummett's version is the proof. It is rather surprising that, coming from a logician, this proof has a geometrical (more precisely, graph-theoretical) and topological aspect, with notions such as 'region,' 'boundary,' 'path' being defined and used systematically.

III. THE CORE OF VOTING GAMES

As mentioned previously, the modern rebirth of social choice theory in the 1940s is due to the works of Arrow and Black. The main result due to Black concerns the majority rule and the existence of a transitive social preference generated by this rule when the individual preferences are appropriately restricted.

DEFINITION 5. The majority rule is an aggregation function for which for all $x, y \in X$ and all n-list $(\succeq_1, \ldots, \succeq_n) \in Ord(X)'^n$, $x \succ_S y \Leftrightarrow \#\{i : x \succ_i y\} > \#\{i : y \succ_i x\}$ and $y \succeq_S x$ otherwise.

Suppose there are three individuals 1, 2, and 3, and three alternatives a, b, and c with the following preferences: $a \succ_1 b \succ_1 c, b \succ_2 c \succ_2 a$, and $c \succ_3 a \succ_3 b$. This means that individual 1 prefers a to b, b to c, and a to c. It is obvious that the majority rule generates $a \succ_S b, b \succ_S c$, and $c \succ_S a$. This is the Condorcet paradox. It indicates that the majority rule is not a social welfare function if Condition U is satisfied (all the other conditions introduced in section I are obviously satisfied). Black introduced a condition on the set of individual preferences called *single-peakedness*. Black considered that the set of alternatives was the real line (or more exactly a part of it). Individuals had a preference represented by a curve with a unique maximum strictly increasing up to the maximum and strictly decreasing from the maximum. He demonstrated that the median maximum was the alternative selected by the majority rule, in other words, using this rule, was a point socially preferred to every other point. This is a famous result of *Public Choice* called "the theorem of the median voter" (not always attributed to Black!). Arrow translated this condition in his set-theoretic framework.

DEFINITION 6. Let $\{a, b, c\} \subseteq X$. A set of complete preorders $\succeq$ over X satisfies the condition of single-peakedness over $\{a, b, c\}$ if either $a \sim b$ and $b \sim c$ or there is one of the three alternatives, say b, such that $b \succ a$ or $b \succ c$.

Let $BL(X)$ denote the set of complete preorders over X such that the condition of single-peakedness is satisfied for all $\{x, y, z\} \subseteq X$.

BLACK'S THEOREM. *If $Ord(X)' = BL(X)$ and if, for any $\{x, y, z\} \subseteq X$, the number of individuals for which $\neg(x \sim_i y$ and $y \sim_i z)$ is odd, the majority rule is a social welfare function.*

This only means that the social preference is transitive.[4] With three alternatives, there are 13 complete preorders and 8 single-peaked complete preorders. Single-peakedness essentially means that among the three alternatives there is one which is never the (strictly) worst. There is an interesting and intuitively meaningful geometrical representation. If the three alternatives a, b, and c are on a line with b between a and c, we have the following possibilities:

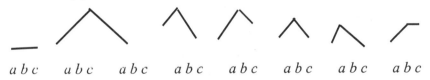

$a\;b\;c$ $a\;b\;c$ $a\;b\;c$ $a\;b\;c$ $a\;b\;c$ $a\;b\;c$ $a\;b\;c$ $a\;b\;c$

Figure 1. Black's single-peakedness condition over $\{a, b, c\}$.

When the alternatives a, b, or/and c are at the same horizontal level, this means that there is an indifference between them, and when one of the alternatives $x \in \{a, b, c\}$ is vertically above $y \in \{a, b, c\}$, this means $x \succ y$. a, b, and c are linearly ordered, a being on the left, b in the center and c on the right. It is then very easy to interpret the admissible (single-peaked) preferences from a political viewpoint, for instance when a, b, and c are candidates to an election.

In voting games, coalitions, that is, nonempty subsets of the set of individuals N, are a priori endowed with power. This power can be, as in the case of symmetric (anonymous) games, defined by a number of individuals, called a quota q (for instance $q > n/2$).

DEFINITION 7. A *voting game* is an ordered pair $G = (N, \mathbf{W})$ where $\mathbf{W} \subseteq 2^N - \emptyset$ and $\mathbf{W}$ satisfies the following monotonicity property:

$$C_1 \in \mathbf{W} \text{ and } C_1 \subseteq C_2 \Rightarrow C_2 \in \mathbf{W}.$$

A voting game G is *proper* if $C \in \mathbf{W} \Rightarrow N - C \notin \mathbf{W}$. It is *strong* if

$$C \notin \mathbf{W} \Rightarrow N - C \in \mathbf{W}.$$

$\mathbf{W}$ is the set of winning (powerful) coalitions. A voting game with quota $q \leq n$ (or q-game) is defined by $C \in \mathbf{W}$ if $\#C \geq q$. With $n = 9$, the q-game with $q = 5$ is proper and strong and the q-game with $q = 6$ is only proper.

We can associate to a voting game G an aggregation function f.

DEFINITION 8. A *voting game of aggregation* is an aggregation function f for which for all $x, y \in X$ and all n-list $(\succeq_1, \ldots, \succeq_n) \in Ord(X)^n$, $x \succ_S y \Leftrightarrow$ there exists a $C \in \mathbf{W}$ such that for all $i \in C$, $x \succ_i y$, and $y \succeq_S x$ otherwise.[5]

Given a voting game of aggregation, we can now define the core associated with a n-list $(\succeq_1, \ldots, \succeq_n)$.

DEFINITION 9. The core of the voting game of aggregation f associated with the n-list $(\succeq_1, \ldots, \succeq_n) \in Ord(X)^n$, denoted $Cor(f,(\succeq_1, \ldots, \succeq_n))$, is the set of the maximal elements of X for the binary relation $\succ_S$, that is,

$$Cor(f,(\succeq_1, \ldots, \succeq_n)) = \{x \in X : (\neg \exists y \in X) y \succ_S x\}.$$

In 1961, Dummett and Farquharson introduced an extended version of single-peakedness.

DEFINITION 10. Let $\{a, b, c\} \subseteq X$. A set of complete preorders $\succeq$ over X satisfies the condition of extended single-peakedness over $\{a, b, c\}$ if there is one of the three alternatives, say b, such that $b \geq a$ or $b \geq c$.

Let $DF(X)$ denote the set of complete preorders over X such that the condition of extended single-peakedness is satisfied for all $\{x, y, z\} \subseteq X$.

DUMMETT AND FARQUHARSON'S THEOREM. *Let X be finite and f be any proper voting game of aggregation. Then for all n-list $(\succeq_1, \ldots, \succeq_n) \in DF(X)^n$, $Cor(f,(\succeq_1, \ldots, \succeq_n)) \neq \emptyset$.*[6]

As seen in figure 2, for a three-alternative subset, the extended single-peakedness condition adds two complete preorders to the eight complete preorders of figure 1. This could appear as only a slight amelioration, contrary to what Dummett and Farquharson wrote in the abstract of their paper: "A condition on the preferences, *substantially weaker* than one postulated by D. Black, is shown to be sufficient for 'stability' in such games" (my emphasis).

But I can explain why they wrote this. First, a reduction from 13 to 8 is quite different from a reduction from 13 to 10. Second, when we try to give an intuitive meaning to single-peakedness, as in the case of the left-right political spectrum mentioned above, the elimination of these two complete preorders is totally unrealistic. These two preferences do make sense in a political context.

a b c   *a b c*

Figure 2. Supplementary preferences for extended single-peakedness.

On the other hand, the three missing complete preorders, as shown in figure 3, do not really make sense, in this political context, unless we imagine that the voters can be totally irrational.

a b c   *a b c*   *a b c*

Figure 3. Excluded preferences.

IV. VOTING PROCEDURES IN PRACTICE

Nowadays, social choice theorists favor two voting methods that are rarely used in practice: the *Borda count* and *approval voting*. Both have interesting features and both have active and famous proponents, Steve Brams and Peter Fishburn for approval voting (see Brams and Fishburn [1983]), Peter Emerson, Donald Saari, and (may I venture?) Michael Dummett for the Borda count (see Emerson [1998], Saari [1995, 2001]). Both procedures are simple (can be easily understood by the voters) and need no difficult computations. In the most satisfying theoretical version of the Borda count, the voters give in their ballot paper a complete ranking of the candidates with no ties. If there are k candidates, $k - 1$ points are given to the candidate ranked first, $k - 2$ to the candidate ranked second, and so on, and no point to the candidate ranked last. For each candidate, the points are added and the social preference is based on the points attributed by the voters to the candidates: the candidate ranked first is the candidate who has obtained the greater total of points, and so forth. With approval voting, voters vote for as many candidates as they wish. If there are k candidates they can vote for all k candidates (though this will have no effect on the collective result, exactly as if they voted for none), or for $k - 1$ candidates or . . . for only one candidate. The candidates are then collectively ranked according to the total number of votes they got. Of course, as these procedures give a collective ranking, they can easily be used to select one or more candidates. Surprisingly, many people interested in voting procedures, believing that it is a rather easy mathematical exercise and imagining that they are good at elementary mathematics, either do not know these procedures—but I cannot believe it—or have the greatest contempt for them. Many of these people are actively trying to impose the *alternative vote* in the case of the selection of a single outcome or the *single transferable vote* in the case of the selection of several outcomes.[7]

When voters have to rank all the candidates, the alternative vote is similar with the positive elimination procedure. In the case of positive voting, an outcome is eliminated at the first stage if it stands at the head of the ranking on the fewest ballots. Then, the rankings are reduced by deleting the eliminated candidate and the same process is used for the reduced rankings. The process is continued until we are left with a unique outcome. In case of equality at some stage, some tie-breaking procedure is used (for instance, the eliminated outcome is that which stands lowest on some individual's list). A dual procedure, the negative elimination procedure, eliminates outcomes which most frequently stand at the bottom of a ranking. Advocates of the alternative vote procedure generally favored it on the grounds of fairness to the voters (these advocates speak of *wasted vote* [Dummett 1997, ch. 10]). Incidentally, Dummett emphasizes the fact that the fairness criteria should concern first outcomes, rather than voters. Regarding fairness to the outcomes, he considers three principles. (1) If x is a unique majority maximum (considered as least as good as every other outcome by a majority), x is the fairest outcome. (2) If there is a maximum, no outcome can be fair unless it is a maximum. (3) No outcome can be fair if it has a lower majority number than some other outcomes (the majority number of any outcome x is the number of other outcomes y for which a majority considers x as least as good as y). Consider the following example: there are three candidates a, b, and c; 35% of the voters ranked them acb (meaning a first, c second, and b third), 33% ranked them bca, and 32% cab. Under the alternative vote procedure (and the French run-off system), c is eliminated. But in pairwise contests, we can see that c is preferred to a (the winner) by 65% of the voters, and preferred to b by 67%. It is a very large "Condorcet winner" (a maximum in my previous terminology, or a top in Dummett's words). Furthermore, the alternative vote procedure (and again the French run-off system) is a nonmonotonic procedure. Consider the same kind of example. Suppose 35% of the voters rank the three candidates *abc*, 33% *bca*, and 32% *cab*. Candidate *a* is the winner. Now suppose that for some reason (for instance, an irregularity), the vote has to be started again and the ranking are 37% *abc*, 31% *bca*, and 32% *cab* (there has been, for instance, a change of mind of some of the people who had previously the ranking *bca* in favor of the ranking *abc*. Then the winner is *c* in spite of the fact that more voters ranked *a*, the former winner, first [Dummett 1997, 99–103]). One might wonder how the alternative vote procedure can still have advocates, once these major flaws are revealed.

Regarding the supposed fairness to the voters of the alternative voting procedure, Dummett (1984, 173–74) rightly observes:

> It is no excuse for having ignored the later choices of the supporters of the eventually successful outcome that those supporters can have no complaint. . . . The second and later choices of a voter who has the misfortune to rank first an outcome that remains live up to the final stage of the assessment, but is then defeated, are likewise neglected; and in this case there is not even a fallacious argument to be offered in justification.

The Borda count has a major drawback (or has it?): it is not a majority procedure. This is related to the fairness mentioned above and to the condition of independence of section I. Though this condition is implicitly included in the fairness to the outcomes I just described, Dummett is not certain of its relevance. He writes, "All but one of (Arrow's) conditions is a minimal requirement for the rule embodied in the social welfare function to be in the least reasonable. One of them, however, is not: Arrow calls it the principle of "independence of irrelevant alternatives" (Dummett 1984, 52).

Consider an election with ten candidates $x_1, \ldots, x_{10}$ and suppose that 50.0001% of the voters ranked these candidates from x_1 to x_{10} in the natural order and 49.9999% ranked them x_2 first, then $x_3, \ldots$, then x_{10}, the last being x_1. According to the fairness criteria x_1 must be chosen. But it is rather obvious (at least to me) that x_2 is the best candidate. Among the new rules proposed by Dummett, one is a composite which he calls the *majority number procedure*:

> The tellers will compute, from the voters' lists, the majority numbers of all the outcomes. . . . Having announced these, they will declare successful an outcome having a higher majority number than any other. If two or more outcomes tie as having the highest majority number, they will then compute and announce the preference scores of these outcomes, that one with the highest preference score being declared successful. (Dummett 1984, 178)

On the one hand, given the fairness criteria, this procedure is the best that one can imagine. On the other hand, it has the same drawback as the preference score procedure (the Borda count): it can select a majority-dominated outcome. Furthermore, in this case, if the tellers have to divulge all the information, the voters will know that the chosen outcome is majority-dominated. Consequently, Dummett thinks that the majority number procedure is to be avoided, "except by voters who are highly self-disciplined and appreciate the importance of knowing no more about how the voting has gone than they need to know" (ibid., 181).

It is well known and easy to see that the Borda count is highly manipulable. But, of course, in large elections, manipulation by a single individual (i.e., the successful misrepresentation of his preference) is nearly null, and manipulation by a group necessitates transfers of information by communication that are rather hypothetical. Dummett (1998) addresses another type of manipulation with the Borda count: the agenda manipulation. A classical example is the introduction, in order to favor a candidate x, of a new candidate y ranked on every voter's preference scale immediately below x. Dummett proposes two ways to correct this.

In the case of elections with many possible outcomes, Dummett (1984, 1997) proposes new procedures. He is particularly interested in rules insuring the representation of minorities. He is rather critical of the single transferable vote procedure (STV). This procedure is in use in Eire, Northern Ireland, Malta, and, I must add, the American Mathematical Society. The rationale for this procedure rests again on the notion of wasted vote. But Dummett clearly explains why. "Most of the advantages advertised for STV are illusory. . . . Its disadvantages are great: it is complex for the tellers to operate, it is almost impossible to explain accurately, and its effects upon the outcome are often arbitrary. Its outstanding merit is the protection that it gives to minorities" (Dummett 1984, 284).

He then proposes a new method called QPS (Q for quota, and PS for preference score). Voters have not to rank all the candidates, but they do provide a ranking. A voter is said to be solidly committed to a set of candidates if he includes every candidate in the set in his ranking, and ranks each of them higher than any candidate not in the set. The assessment proceeds by stages and will terminate as soon as k seats are filled.

> At stage 1, the tellers will determine whether there are any candidates listed first by more than $1/(k + 1)$ of the total n of voters: if so, they immediately qualified for election. If seats remain to be filled, the preference scores of all candidates not qualifying at stage 1 will then be calculated. At stage 2, the ballot papers will be scrutinized to see if there is any pair of candidates, neither

of whom qualified at stage 1, to whom more than $n/(k + 1)$ voters are solidly committed: if so, that member of the pair with the higher preference score now qualifies for election. If seats remain to be filled, the tellers will proceed to stage 3, at which they will consider sets of three candidates, none of whom has already qualified. If more than $n/(k + 1)$ voters are solidly committed to such trio, that one with the highest preference score qualifies for election. . . . If there still remains seats to be filled after all the qualifying stages have been completed, they will be filled at the final stage by those candidates having the highest preference scores out of those who have not yet qualified. (Dummett 1984, 284)

Dummett shows that QPS retains the quality of STV in minorities representation, but is superior to STV in every other respect, in particular, simplicity and fairness. He does not pretend it is the best voting method, but that it is better than STV. "The question what is the best electoral system is of great complexity, and does not belong exclusively to the theory of voting" (Dummett 1984, 292).

V. Conclusion

It is very difficult to convey the richness of the contribution of Michael Dummett to social choice and voting theory and to the practical voting procedures. This essay is only a brief assessment of this richness. What I think is particularly remarkable is that he contributed to three of what I considered above are the six main topics in the area and that he is mainly, after all, a great philosopher and not primarily a social choice theorist. In French "hobby" is *violon d'Ingres*. I do not know whether Ingres, surely a great painter, was a good violinist. However, I am sure that Michael Dummett is a great social choice theorist.

Maurice Salles

CREM, University of Caen and
CPNSS, London School of Economics
December 2002

NOTES

1. The originality of the proof technique is reminiscent of the proof used to show, given an acyclic binary relation over a finite set of elements, the existence of maximal elements in this finite set. To the best of my knowledge this was first

proved in von Neumann and Morgenstern (1944, 1953) and rediscovered by Sen (1970) and Pattanaik (1971).

2. It was not exceptional at that time that important papers by English- speaking natives (and, for this matter, also by Germans and Japanese), particularly in mathematics, be published in French. These days are, alas for me, over.

3. Since indifference is excluded in linear orderings, I use the notation $>$ rather than $\succeq$.

4. Incidentally, we can avoid this condition of oddity if we only require that the asymmetric component of $\succeq_S$, $\succ_S$, be transitive (see Sen 1970 and Sen and Pattanaik 1969).

5. There is no need to have a *complete* social preference. It is supposed here mainly because we previously defined aggregation functions as having values that are complete binary relations.

6. In fact, Dummett and Farquharson considered a majority game defined by $x \succeq_S y$ if $\#\{i \in N : x \succeq_i y\} > n/2$ or $\#\{i \in N : x \succeq_i y\} = n/2$ and $x \succeq_1 y$. In case of equality, individual 1 plays a specific role (like a president in a committee, for instance). This defines a proper and strong voting game of aggregation with $\succeq_S$ obviously complete. Then they proved the existence of a maximum element (called a top), i.e., the existence of a x such that $x \succeq_S y$ for all $y \in X$. The formulation I gave is essentially due to Nakamura (1975). Salles and Wendell (1977) used the similarity between Dummett and Farquharson's condition and quasi-concavity of utility functions in dimension 1 to extend some of Nakamura's results. On the other hand, Pattanaik (1971) used an analysis very similar to Dummett and Farquharson's analysis, with the same kind of proof method, for conditions extending Black-type of conditions—for instance look at figure 1 upside down.

7. After the April and May 2002 presidential elections in France, several articles appeared in *Le Monde* in which a French economist at MIT whom I had never heard of proposed a variant of the alternative vote as a solution to the voting problems met in France. He apparently did not notice the major defects of alternative vote, which are comparable with the major defects of the procedure used by the French (majority with a run-off).

REFERENCES

Arrow, K. J. 1951, 1963. *Social Choice and Individual Values*. New York: Wiley.

Black, D. 1958. *The Theory of Committees and Elections*. Cambridge: Cambridge Univ. Press.

Brams, S. J., and P. C. Fishburn. 1983. *Approval Voting*. Boston: Birkhäuser.

Brunel, A., and M. Salles. 1998. "Interpretative, Semantic and Formal Difficulties of the Social Choice Rule Approach to Rights." In *Freedom in Economics: New Perspectives in Normative Analysis*, ed. J-F Laslier, M. Fleurbaey, N. Gravel and A. Trannoy. London: Routledge.

Davidson, D. 1986. "Judging Interpersonal Interests." In *Foundations of Social Choice Theory*, ed. J. Elster and A. Holland. Cambridge: Cambridge Univ. Press.

Dummett, M. 1984. *Voting Procedures*. Oxford: Oxford Univ. Press.

———. 1997. *Principles of Electoral Reform*. Oxford: Oxford Univ. Press.

———. 1998. "The Borda Count and Agenda Manipulation." *Social Choice and Welfare* 15: 289–96.

———. 2002. "The Work and Life of Robin Farquharson." Paper presented at the conference "The History of Social Choice from Condorcet to Arrow and Beyond," Caen, October 2002. Published in *Social Choice and Welfare* 25 (2005): 475–83.

Dummett, M., and R. Farquharson. 1961. "Stability in Voting." *Econometrica* 29: 33–43.

Emerson, P. J. 1998. *Beyond the Tyranny of the Majority*. Belfast: The de Borda Institute.

Farquharson, R. 1969. *Theory of Voting*. New Haven: Yale Univ. Press.

Fishburn, P. C. 1973. *The Theory of Social Choice*. Princeton: Princeton Univ. Press.

Gauthier, D. 1986. *Morals by Agreement*. Oxford: Oxford Univ. Press.

Gibbard, A. 1973. "Manipulation of Voting Schemes: A General Result." *Econometrica* 41: 587–601.

Griffin, J. 1986. *Well-Being: Its Meaning, Measurement and Moral Importance*. Oxford: Oxford Univ. Press.

Jeffrey, R. 1992. *Probability and the Art of Judgment*. Cambridge: Cambridge Univ. Press.

Harsanyi, J. C. 1955. "Cardinal Welfare, Individualistic Ethics, and Interpersonal Comparisons of Utility." *Journal of Political Economy* 63: 309–21.

Murakami, Y. 1968. *Logic and Social Choice*. London: Routledge and Kegan Paul.

Nakamura, K. 1975. "The Core of a Simple Game with Ordinal Preferences." *International Journal of Game Theory* 4: 95–104.

Nozick, R. 1997. *Socratic Puzzles*. Cambridge, MA: Harvard Univ. Press.

Pattanaik, P. K. 1971. *Voting and Collective Choice*. Cambridge: Cambridge Univ. Press.

Saari, D. G. 1995. *Basic Geometry of Voting*. Berlin: Springer.

———. 2001. *Chaotic Elections! A Mathematician Looks at Voting*. American Mathematical Society.

Salles, M. 2002. "Amartya Sen: droits et choix social." *Revue Economique* 51: 445–57.

Salles, M., and R. Wendell. 1977. "A Further Result on the Core of Voting Games." *International Journal of Game Theory* 6: 35–40.

Satterthwaite, M. A. 1975. "Strategy-proofness and Arrow's Conditions: Existence and Correspondence Theorems for Voting Procedures and Social Welfare Functions." *Journal of Economic Theory* 10: 187–217.

Sen, A. K. 1970. *Collective Choice and Social Welfare*. San Francisco: Holden-Day.

———. 1986. "Social Choice Theory." In *Handbook of Mathematical Economics*, vol. 3, ed. K. J. Arrow and M. D. Intriligator. Amsterdam: North-Holland.

————. 1987. *On Ethics and Economics*. Oxford: Blackwell.

————. 2003. *Rationality and Freedom*. Cambridge, MA: Harvard Univ. Press.

Sen, A. K., and P. K. Pattanaik. 1969. "Necessary and Sufficient Conditions for Rational Choice under Majority Decision." *Journal of Economic Theory* 1: 178–202.

Suppes, P. 1996. "The Nature and Measurement of Freedom." *Social Choice and Welfare* 13: 183–200.

von Neumann, J., and O. Morgenstern. 1944, 1953. *Theory of Games and Economic Behavior*. Princeton: Princeton Univ. Press.

REPLY TO MAURICE SALLES

I have once more to thank a contributor for his kind remarks about me; I most heartily thank Professor Maurice Salles for his. My engagement with social choice theory has been desultory, although prompted by intense interest; and praise from Maurice Salles, the leader of this small band of enquirers, is a rich reward for what little I have contributed. Writing replies to contributions to one's LLP volume is sometimes like an experience we are all denied, writing thank-you letters for favourable obituaries.

As Professor Salles supposes, I am indeed a supporter of the Borda count; more exactly, as a criterion for a fair outcome. One of the prime requirements for a voting procedure is that it should, as often as possible, deliver a fair outcome; and I believe that, in considering what voting procedure to use, we ought first to ask ourselves what we consider to be a fair outcome. Our preliminary question ought, that is, to be: judged from the voters' true preferences, what should the outcome be? We cannot always be sure of the voters' true preferences: but we need to ask ourselves what, if we knew them, we should take the fairest outcome to be. If we do not ask ourselves this question, we cannot judge whether the result of strategic voting under a given voting procedure will be a less fair or a fairer outcome. The question what is or would be the fairest outcome, given the voters' true preferences, is of course not susceptible of a demonstrable answer, since we have no independent criterion for fairness of outcomes. I am nevertheless fully convinced that the Borda count yields the best achievable criterion. Use of the Borda count is impracticable when the number of possible outcomes is too large. If there are twelve candidates in a constituency which is required to return two, there will be 66 possible outcomes, and one cannot ask electors to list 66 pairs of candidates in order of preference. Besides, in an election in a multi-member constituency, there is another requirement that ought to be satisfied: the due representation of minorities. But, in an election to a single-member constituency, or in a vote in a committee between a small number of alternative courses of action, the Borda count is the best criterion for a fair outcome. It selects the outcome that is most generally acceptable. It could be improved upon if we had a practicable method of arriving at numerical valuations of the strengths of voters' preferences; but in practice, when a voter i prefers the possible outcome a to the possible outcome b, the number of possible outcomes i thinks no worse than b and to which he prefers a is a reasonable measure of the strength of his preference for a over b. This is the rationale for Professor Salles's instinctive belief that the x_2 of his example in his section IV concerning the Borda count is a better candidate than x_1.

Is it a demerit of the Borda count that it is not a majority game—that, for example, it will not select the "top" or Condorcet winner even when there is one, or even, as Salles's example just mentioned illustrates, a candidate who has an absolute majority of first preferences? As a practical voting procedure, its not being a majority game is a demerit when there is a possibility of a subsequent vote to overturn the result (which there cannot be in an election). If a committee decides by use of the Borda count to adopt a course of action a, but there is another possible course of action b which a majority prefers to a, then, in such a case, the decision will be overturned if anyone proposes a vote to reverse it. In this sense, the Borda count procedure is unstable: only when the outcome is the Condorcet winner is it stable in this sense. But, as a criterion for a fair outcome, the fact that the Borda count does not respect majorities is no defect. The mystique of the majority is a superstition: the belief that democracy consists in doing what the majority wants is a distorted conception of democracy. Whether doing what the majority wants is democratic or not depends upon how oppressive it is to the minority, compared with how oppressive to the majority is what the minority wants, or how oppressive to either is some compromise. The truly democratic course is to do what is most generally acceptable: and that is the course of action which the Borda count selects.

When we have decided the best criterion for the fairest outcome, judged on the voters' true preferences, we must ask, of any proposed voting procedure, two questions: first, how often it will yield the fairest outcome when all vote sincerely; and secondly, how much incentive it offers for insincere strategic voting. In this latter respect, I feel highly uncertain about the Borda count as a practical procedure. I am not of the opinion that voting "insincerely" is dishonest, as Borda himself famously thought. A ballot paper does not impose upon a voter an oath that what he writes on it will express his true preference: it invites him to write whatever he thinks most likely, under a procedure he understands, to result in an outcome more in accordance with his wishes than would have resulted if he had voted in any other way. The objection to strategic voting is that, for it to be successful, a voter must be both astute and well informed about how others are likely to vote; and it is contrary to the principle of democracy that the astute and well informed should have more voting power than the dull and ignorant. "One man, one vote" is a democratic slogan; "a knowledgeable man, one and a half votes, an ill-informed man, half a vote" is not.

For the same reason, I cannot feel any enthusiasm for approval voting. For very few voters indeed would there be any such thing as a sincere vote under approval voting. The system forces every voter to consider for how many candidates to cast positive votes: essentially, this is to compel everyone to vote strategically. As with all strategic voting, the voter who is both astute and well informed will have an advantage: the outcome will depend upon how many voters possess these qualities. The outcome of a vote ought as far as possible to depend upon the voters' true preferences; hence a good voting procedure ought to offer as little incentive as possible to depart from a sincere vote. A procedure under which it is impossible to say what constitutes a sincere vote cannot be reckoned a good one.

As Professor Salles remarks, the Borda count is open to what is called "agenda manipulation." To favour a particular candidate a in an election, it will be necessary to find some individual b to whom almost every elector will prefer a, but whom almost every elector will prefer to any candidate to whom he prefers a, and then to persuade b to stand. If this can be done, a's Borda score will be increased by the number of electors (or the number of those who prefer a to b), while the score of any other candidate c will be increased only by the number of those who prefer c to a. It will, however, be virtually impossible to find a candidate of the right type who is willing to stand. But when a committee is voting by the Borda method between a number of rival proposals, the analogous device will be much easier to accomplish.

Even when the list of candidates or proposed courses of action has been fixed, there is scope for manipulation in the casting of the votes, as Professor Salles also observes. The best way to fill in the ballot paper to obtain the highest Borda score for that candidate a whom a voter prefers, out of those he considers to have a reasonable chance, is to list a highest, followed by any he prefers to a but thinks unlikely to win, followed in turn by all others in inverse order of their chances of winning, as that voter estimates them. As Professor Salles says, such a strategic vote by a single voter is unlikely to have much effect. If a large group of voters who favour a do this, while the rest all vote sincerely, they may bring about a's election, which would not have occurred had everyone voted sincerely. Such a result will almost certainly involve collusion. But if several different groups were to act in this way, for the benefit of different candidates favoured by them, or if each individual voter were to follow this tactic, the result might bear no discernible relation to the voters' true preferences. This is because the tactic involves the voters' placing high on their lists candidates whom they believe to have a poor chance of winning. Even if their estimates of these chances, given that most voters voted sincerely, were highly accurate, those estimates will become completely wrong if many voters are adopting strategies that involved giving a high ranking to candidates believed to have poor chances. The result may well be that it is one of these supposedly hopeless candidates who obtains the highest Borda score.

It follows that strategic voting under the method of the Borda count is especially deleterious to the prospect of that procedure's yielding the fairest outcome. It also follows that it is very dangerous for anyone to adopt: he has to be sure that sufficiently many other voters will adopt that strategy in favour of the same candidate, and that very few voters will adopt it in favour of different candidates. I simply do not know how in practice things are likely to work out. Will a large number of voters be tempted to vote strategically in favour of their preferred candidate? Or will most perceive the risk they run in doing so, and vote sincerely for safety? This is an empirical question to which we have too few data to hazard an answer.

I should like to add a few comments on the paper I published with Robin Farquharson in 1961, of which Professor Salles treats in his section III, since it contained a little more meat than he mentions. Why did we call our paper "Stability in Voting"? We were interested in the condition for a course of voting, under a given voting procedure, to be *stable* in the sense that no body of voters could, by voting differently, have obtained an outcome they all preferred, the other voters voting as before; this was Farquharson's generalisation of Nash's notion of an *equilibrium point*. The course of the voting would be *strictly stable* if no body of voters could have obtained an outcome they all thought equally good, and at least one of them preferred. We confined our attention to what we called *majority games* (see Salles's note 6 for our possibly eccentric definition, which followed Duncan Black in allowing for a voter with a casting vote). An *outcome* is stable if there is no body of voters who by voting differently could have ensured an outcome they all preferred. In a majority game, there will, for any stable outcome, be a stable course of the voting that will produce it; but we showed by a simple example that a stable outcome may be produced by an unstable course of voting, in which all voters vote sincerely. Plainly, in a majority game, an outcome is stable if and only if it is a top (maximum, Condorcet winner, belongs to the core).

Black's original formulation of single-peakedness did not allow the first case or the last two in Salles's figure 1.[1] Arrow's formalisation of it was as in Salles's definition 6, without the clause permitting the voter to be indifferent among all three alternatives (candidates or possible outcomes); it thus allowed the last two cases in figure 1, but not the first. Arrow's condition implies the transitivity of majority preference, from which the existence of a top follows immediately from the fact that the set of alternatives is finite. It does not, however, guarantee the existence of a strictly stable outcome, as we showed by an example, although Black's original formulation did, but ceases to do so if weakened in any way. Likewise, if Arrow's condition is weakened in any way, transitivity of majority preference no longer follows. Black operated with a linear ordering of *all* the alternatives, which fits very well with their ranging across a left/right spectrum. The diagrams in Salles's figure 1 would be excerpts from a complete diagram of all alternatives; in figure 1, *b* would come between *a* and *c* in the overall ordering. I believe that Farquharson and I were the first to dispense with the linear order. We showed by an example that definition 10 (extended single-peakedness) could be satisfied even though the alternatives could not be linearly ordered in such a way that, whenever y lay between x and z, $y \succeq x$ or $y \succeq z$. So if we know that the preferences of the voters as between the candidates in some political election satisfy extended single-peakedness, we cannot infer that the candidates can be arranged on a scale from left wing to right wing.

All these points are made in "Stability in Voting." They are all minor points, but they all have some interest. I was moved to mention them here, so as to show that that article was not just a proof that extended single-peakedness implies the existence of a top. It was my first, and, until I wrote *Voting Procedures*, my only incursion into social choice theory. I wish I had followed it up by trying to prove our conjecture. I should like to dedicate this reply to Professor Salles to the memory of Robin Farquharson, who was so brilliant, led so tormented a life, and died so tragically.

M. D.

NOTE

1. In speaking of Black's condition of single-peakedness, we were referring to his articles "On the Rationale of Group Decision-making," *Journal of Political Economy* 56 (1948), and "The Decisions of a Committee Using a Special Majority," *Econometrica* 16 (1948). In his *Theory of Committees and Elections* (Cambridge, 1958) he first gives his original definition on p. 7, and subsequently generalises the notion on pp. 25–26 to cover preference curves with a plateau of two or more alternatives (such a plateau occurring only at the top of the curve, i.e., consisting of alternatives which the voter thinks at least as good as any other); he did not consider ones with indifference below and at the same side of the top. Later still (pp. 32–35) he went on to consider a much wider class of curves.

24

Kwame Anthony Appiah

IMMIGRANTS AND REFUGEES: INDIVIDUALISM AND THE MORAL STATUS OF STRANGERS

Much of contemporary political philosophy in the anglophone world is about the demands that morality places on states in their dealings with citizens. It takes for granted the existence of a national community—a group of persons living together through the generations in a geographical region—and asks what principles should govern the way the members of that community should relate to one another as fellow citizens; most particularly, when the state, acting in their name, takes actions that affect the lives of some or all of them. Such questions are, of course, important in the actual world. Many states treat some of their citizens in ways they clearly ought not to and fail to treat others as they should. Almost all have political debates about the extent of state obligation to the least advantaged of their citizens. Understanding how we should decide such questions is not only, therefore, of the greatest intellectual interest, it is a matter of urgent practical significance.

But pursuing these questions without first inquiring into the normative basis of the constitution of a group of people as a community—without, that is, asking on what basis we should decide who belongs to that community and why—opens us up to theoretical and practical problems. On the theoretical side, if we do not have an account of membership and its moral basis, we are ill equipped to understand the obligations of states to two kinds of strangers (as we might dub those who are not citizens): namely those living outside the national territory, whose lives a state's actions may obviously affect in ways both trivial and profound, and, even more urgently, perhaps, those strangers who live among us. On the practical side, we leave ourselves without grounds for settling some of the most urgent questions of modern politics, which are precisely about the morality of membership: immigration and refugee policy and questions of national self-determination most prominent among them. That such questions have been among the most troublesome in the politics of the last hundred years makes it all the more urgent to have some moral understanding of how they should be answered.

This failure to place questions of national membership at the center of political philosophy is, I think, rather odd, given the political history of the West since the Enlightenment. The first modern Western constitutions—the French and the American—were produced in a great ferment of ideas about the rights not just of citizens but of human beings as such: the title of the *Declaration of the Rights of Man and Citizen* mentions the human first; and the American Declaration of Independence enunciates the fundamental truths from which its politics are to be derived as truths about "all men." I concede that once it comes to constitutions the American Founders speak of "we, the people," cheerfully avoiding the question of how the people are to be constituted; but then they pretty immediately went on to pass a Bill of Rights that, once more, focuses on the rights of human beings not of citizens. (It is worth recalling, as well, that alien suffrage was common in the United States in the early republic in local elections.) Against this background, it is, as I say, odd how little attention has been paid to the obligations of states to strangers, whether resident or not, or to questions about when or how strangers ought to be able to become citizens.

It is odder still, when we reflect, that much of modern political theory is resolutely *individualist*, by which I mean, as Thomas Pogge does, that it begins from the premise that "the ultimate units of concern are human beings, or persons—rather than, say, family lines, tribes, ethnic, cultural, or religious communities, nations, or states."[1] If there were some reason to think that national communities were themselves ultimate units of concern, then the fact that we distinguished between members and nonmembers would, perhaps, be easy enough to justify: for on such a view members and nonmembers would contribute differently, no doubt, to the nation's well-being. But if all morality begins with people and not with peoples, then the making of distinctions between one kind of person and another will always have to be justified: and it will have to be justified in terms of what it means for people, for individuals, and not for peoples, for nations or communities of other sorts.

Despite this theoretical individualism, "common-sense moral thought" supposes, as Charles Beitz correctly observed some time ago, both (a) "that a government may legitimately restrict immigration in order to protect the stability and cohesion of domestic political life," and (b) "that a government may give greater weight in redistributing income to improving the welfare of the domestic poor than to improving that of the poor elsewhere—even if the domestic poor are already better off than the foreign poor."[2] To make these suppositions consistent with individualism, we should have to show that these principles (each of which expresses moral partiality for the citizen over the stranger) are somehow justifiable in terms of the way they work out for individuals. Professor Beitz is not alone in thinking that the burden of justification is not easily met.

That these questions are not at the center of political philosophy does not, of course, mean that they have been entirely avoided. Questions of the obligations of states to the foreign poor have been the focus of much attention since Henry Shue's *Basic Rights: Subsistence, Affluence, and American Foreign Policy*,[3] to give only one prominent example; and Michael Walzer's justly well-regarded *Spheres of Justice*[4] prompted a lively literature on the political morality of membership. And I have already quoted Charles Beitz and Thomas Pogge, who have carried on eloquent campaigns for many years for ways of thinking of international justice that are not only individualist, in the way Pogge defined the term in the passage I cited earlier, but also *cosmopolitan*, as he would define that term, in that they combine individualism with *universality* (individuals are all equal units of concern) and *generality* (they are equal units of concern for everyone).[5] Still, there is a great deal more to be said on these questions than has been said: and we should be grateful that a philosopher of Michael Dummett's imagination and intellectual power has entered the lists.

In this essay, I shall try to outline the account of why membership matters morally that Michael Dummett presupposes (and, from time to time, sketches) in his book *On Immigration and Refugees*.[6] I shall discuss some difficulties that I identify in that theory and his application of it. My aim, here, then, is to assess what is most philosophical in this book—the principles and the arguments. But I need to preface this discussion with two observations.

First, to treat the book in this way is, to some extent, to miss its major aim. For the thrust of the book is to establish the injustice of current immigration policy, especially in Europe, and to argue for an international regime governing state treatment of asylum-seekers, refugees, and aspiring immigrants that is more just. The book does show, I think quite conclusively, that European immigration policy in general, and British policy most particularly, is at root plain racist. I find Dummett's assembling of the historical evidence for this conclusion quite compelling; and since he has been for over a generation one of the leading activists in the losing battle to protect the rights of strangers at Britain's borders, he is extremely well informed on the details of that history. Even if the injustice to immigrants and asylum-seekers were not racist, it would, of course, still be wrong. And

Dummett is equally compelling in demonstrating that it is, in fact, unjust. Whatever the merits or defects of the philosophical principles within which Dummett has embedded this critique of current immigration and asylum policies, I respect the decency of the proposals he makes and agree with him as to the wickedness of those policies. Though I am now an American, I was born British; and one contrast I would draw between my erstwhile fellow citizens and my present ones is that many people in England seem unable to grasp the presence of racism in British culture at every level, while most Americans are, on the other hand, able to recognize that our country has a long-standing race problem. I find it particularly refreshing, therefore, to hear a sane and reasonable English voice insisting on this point; and nothing I am going to say in this essay is intended to distract from that truth or the importance of his acknowledgment of it.[7]

My second prefatory observation, then, is that everything I say here by way of philosophical criticism should be seen against the background of a deep sympathy with Dummett's fundamental aims. Both this theoretical work and his long years of practice with the Campaign Against Racial Discrimination and the Joint Council on the Welfare of Immigrants demonstrate Michael Dummett's genuine and laudable commitment to the idea that intellectuals ought to "engage in any matter of social importance to which they can contribute."[8] Both reflect as well a rare and honorable degree of commitment to a practical humanity. In a book that celebrates his philosophy, it is not out of place, I hope, to express admiration for the man, even if, as he says, "philosophy has not driven" him in his work on this matter of the greatest social importance.

The major difficulty that faces the task of examining the philosophical theory that underlies Dummett's approach is that, despite the fact that the book is divided into two sections, the first labeled "Principles" and the second "History," the focus throughout is on the practical question of just immigration policy and the proper treatment of refugees. To lay out a philosophical theory explicitly and technically in this context would be to lose the general audience to which the book is addressed. As a result, Dummett adumbrates his principles in the course of exploring current practice and the arguments of its defenders.[9] Nevertheless, certain general features of the approach can be identified through his arguments.

Let me begin by saying that I understand Dummett's approach to be, occasional appearances notwithstanding, individualist in Pogge's sense. I say "appearances notwithstanding" because in a couple of places he enunciates rights that apparently belong not to individuals but to groups. Thus, in particular, when discussing early on the question whether the need to protect a national identity justifies limitations on the immigration of strangers without that identity, he concedes, "a self-governing nation indeed needs an identity."[10] And he adds a little later that "groups united by race, religion, language or culture . . . have a right not to be submerged."[11] But when he comes to explain the basis for these rights—of the nation or the group—he makes it plain that these collective rights are grounded in what they make possible for the individual members of the groups:

> Why does a nation have a right not to be submerged? Each person's sense of who he is derives from many circumstances: his occupation, his ideals and his beliefs, but also from the customs and language he shares with those about him. If he himself has immigrated to the country in which he is living, and is one of a number of immigrants from the same place, but has been made sufficiently welcome in his new country, he will think of himself as having thrown in his lot with the people of that country; but he will share with those other immigrants some customs and perhaps a mother tongue different from the native majority.[12]

One might wish for more explicitness in making the connection between the fact that each of us has an identity in which language and customs are important, on the one hand, and the rights of groups not to be submerged, on the other. One might wish too, and this is a point to which I shall return, for a more explicit account of what submergence consists in. But an argument can nevertheless be inferred, especially if we take into account a few other observations. Dummett also says, for example, "Most human beings feel some attachment to the place where they live; those who do not are deprived of a natural human sentiment, and are usually conscious of their deprivation."[13]

And again, a little later:

> Many people, probably most, have at least a dual identity: Catalan as well as Spanish, Welsh as well as British, Bengali as well as Indian, Syrian as well as Arab. People vary in which of their identities, the wider or the narrower, is the more important to them, the more definitive of who they feel themselves to be. But in all these cases, the attachment is not only to a body of people with whom they share a language and a culture, but also to a land, the land where those people live.[14]

Taken together, these passages suggest an argument like this:

> People value and profit from a sense of place and the consolations of being surrounded by people speaking a familiar language and following customs they understand and think of as their own. (Let us call these goods "the comforts of home.") As a result, people are harmed—or, at any rate, deprived of something worth having—when they are deprived of the comforts of home; and it would be best, therefore, if it is possible, to create a regime that allows them to maintain them.

This argument is essentially individualist. The comforts of home—as is evident from their very conception—can only be experienced in common: they are, in that sense, essentially social. But their value is nevertheless just their value to the individuals who have access to them; the existence of a group with these properties does not have to be seen as having some further value of its own.

Dummett's individualism is evident too in his discussion of the "principle . . . of national self-determination: every nation deserves to inhabit a state exclusively reserved for it."[15] He points out, by reference to cases, that the principle's application has turned out, in practice, to be largely circular: "if we recognise a group of people as forming a nation according to whether it has a territory it can call its own, the principle that a group is entitled to belong to a separate state if it constitutes a nation is no guide at all."[16] But he goes on to say this.

> The truth within the principle of national self-determination is that everyone has the right to live in a country in which he and others of a group to which he belongs are not persecuted, oppressed or discriminated against, in which his religion, language, race and culture are not reviled or held up to contempt and in which he can fully identify himself with the state under whose sovereignty that country falls.[17]

Notice, once more, that he has reinterpreted a collective right (this time to self-determination) as something owed to individuals in virtue of the role that their identifications with the groups to which they belong play in shaping one's "sense of who one is."

Dummett's position is not just individualist; it is, in a deep way, liberal. It is committed not just to the insistence that what matters first and foremost is what happens to individual persons, but also to a view that assigns to each person an equal presumption of liberty in the management of his or her life. This is most evident, I think, in his discussion of the general logic of the justification of rights-claims that occurs towards the end of his discussion, in chapter 3, of "The Duties of a State to Immigrants." He first introduces the idea of a "conditional right," a right "to do such-and-such a thing if one wishes and if one can."[18] And then, a little later, he proposes the following picture of where the burden of proof lies in claims to rights by individuals and by states:

> There are many things we have no right to do: but a ground must always be given for denying anyone a right to do something. No positive ground need ever be given for claiming a conditional right to do something or ascribing a conditional right to do it to someone else: the only argument that can be required is a rebuttal of a purported reason for denying that right. It is not so with the rights of a state; the presumption is never that it has a right to do what

it likes. The rights of a state are rights over individuals, those who are its citizens and those who are not. . . . There must be a particular ground why any state is entitled to curtail that freedom, if indeed it is.[19]

Distributing the burden of proof this way does not entail individualism in the technical sense I have been relying on: for the state's legitimate grounds might, so far as anything Dummett says here goes, refer to ends other than the good of individuals. What it does, instead, is to insist that each of us is prima facie entitled to do anything we wish to and are able to do, while at the same time insisting that the state, per contra, is not prima facie entitled to do anything. Of course, what rights individuals are left with by these procedures will depend on what counts as a good reason for denying a conditional right, how easily arguments based on such reasons are rebutted, and what grounds justify state limitations on freedom. Still, looking at matters this way surely predisposes one to allow rather extensive individual liberty: this is individualism in a familiar and less technical sense, and it is a feature of Dummett's position that I think quite attractive.

The passage I have just discussed is essentially about liberties—being left to do what you want to do if you can do it—not about the sorts of positive rights that Dummett thinks that refugees have from persecution, for example, which require others not merely to keep out of the way but to take affirmative action to provide aid. These unconditional rights Dummett ascribes to all people can usually be justified by an argument of the following form:

All normal human beings have a certain need, N, if they are to have decent lives.

In a world in which people and states observed the rule:

Everybody has a right to do D (or have H),

(it is likely that most) people will be able to satisfy N.

So, R: Everybody has a right to do D (or have H).

I shall call arguments of this form "rights-grounding arguments."[20] (Readers of *On Liberty* will recognize here the form of Mill's arguments for rights of free expression.)

It is possible to read the conclusion here in a more explicitly programmatic way as saying, in effect,

So, R': We ought to create an international legal regime in which all states recognize and conform to the rule: Everybody may do D (or must have H).

Dummett often says something of the form of R and then goes on to say something of the form of R' that gives practical meaning to R. Thus, for example, he says that we all have a right to "refuge from persecution";[21] and then says that the Convention on the Status of Refugees should be amended to make it "explicit that the persecution which is offered as a ground for asking for asylum need not be persecution from state authorities."[22] This is a proposal to create an international regime that gives practical effect to the idea that we each have a right to have refuge from persecution.

Dummett outlines the general form of such arguments pretty explicitly in discussing the foundations of human rights. "There are some things which are everybody's due. The basic conditions that enable someone to live a fully human life are the due of every human being, just in virtue of being human: there are what are nowadays called 'human rights'."[23] (Replace "decent" above with "fully human.") A rights-grounding argument can be made for many of the rights Dummett suggests we all have.

Take his fundamental argument against the widespread view that it is proper for citizenship to be defined by descent, religion, or language. German immigration law gives special status to people who are ethnically German, whatever their place of birth; Malawi limits its citizenship to black Africans, as Australia once attempted to define itself as white; Israel and Iran define membership in some measure by religion; France and Quebec make the French language central to their self-definition. Dummett's objection to all this begins with the fact that modern states are all irreducibly plural in at least one of these respects.

> We can therefore say with assurance that, in the world as it now is, and as it will doubtless be for many centuries yet, no state ought to take race, religion or language as essential to its identity. If it does, it will inevitably find living within its borders minorities not of the favoured race, practising religions other than the favoured one, speaking languages different from the majority tongue. These minorities will be liable to persecution or discrimination, whether by the laws of the state itself or by the actions of those who belong to the dominant group (usually, but not always, the majority). Whether or not such discrimination is severe, members of these minorities will feel themselves to be 'second class citizens', when they are allowed to be citizens at all.[24]

I take it that the point in this passage—which should be read along with the remarks about one's sense of who one is and identifying with one's state that I have already cited—is that being a first class citizen is empirically necessary to leading a fully human life. And if that is true, then we have a right to first class citizenship by way of a rights-grounding argument.

It is particularly important, I think, to recognize that rights-grounding arguments rely on claims about our social natures. These claims themselves are about what social conditions are necessary for human beings to flourish; or, to put it another way, about how the satisfaction of human needs depends on social arrangements. It is not surprising, if I am right in understanding the arguments behind Dummett's rights ascriptions, that he does indeed make many such claims about our social natures. Here are two such claims:

> A self-governing nation indeed needs an identity; and this identity will always be in part informed by its history.[25]

> But the identity of a state cannot be grounded solely on the territory over which its dominion extends. If it is not to be grounded in a common ethnicity, religion or language, it must be grounded in shared ideals, a shared vision of the society it is striving to create.[26]

I do not know how controversial these claims will seem, but it strikes me that someone (unlike myself) who was unsympathetic with Dummett's conclusions or even someone (like me) of a generally skeptical disposition, might want to question one or other of these claims, or at any rate, to explore them more fully.

Thus, for example, the second claim strikes me as ignoring a possibility that I think is realized in many settled constitutional orders, such as prevail in Britain, Scandinavia, Switzerland, and the United States. And that is a state grounded in an acceptance of certain legal and political arrangements. What fellow citizens need is a mutual commitment to the organization of the state, a willingness to work within the institutions that provide the overarching order of a common life. But this does not require that we have the *same* commitment to those institutions, in the sense that the institutions must carry the same meaning for all of us, and so in particular, I do not think it is an empirical precondition of a stable liberal society that its citizens should share a "vision of the society it is striving to create."[27] I doubt, in fact, that a state needs to be conceived of by its members as striving to create a society at all. But this is, of course, an empirical, socio-political disagreement, not a moral one.

Similarly, Dummett anticipates and rejects rights-grounding arguments for the view that the people of a particular state may have the right to exclude others because their exclusion is necessary to their experiencing what we have dubbed "the comforts of home," which he has allowed to be an important element of human flourishing. So he rejects a familiar argument, made by many across the political spectrum, that the need to avoid submergence entails a right to limit immigration. The form of the rights-grounding argument shows, I think, what the content of the claim about submergence needs to be, if it is to get off the ground. It has to be that the arrival of a group of immigrants of a certain character and number would undermine the native's ability to flourish, to live fully human lives.[28]

And so Dummett argues, in effect, against the rights-grounding argument for the right-to-exclude on essentially empirical grounds.

> But an immigrant presence will only have a faint, and usually beneficial, effect unless the number of immigrants is very large, or their culture powerfully dominant. British eating habits have been considerably affected by the Bangladeshi, and to a lesser extent the Chinese, presence; and there has been a slight, but invigorating, influence of Caribbean and Asian minorities on British popular music; for the rest, British culture has evolved much as it would have done without the immigration that the lady [Mrs. Thatcher] professed to see as threatening it.[29]

This point would be most important, of course, if it were true that,

E: were the introduction of new strangers to change the character of a country in such a way as to make the natives largely unable to feel at home there, it would be morally permissible to exclude those strangers.

Since many politicians, newspaper pundits, and ordinary citizens would probably give assent to E, it is certainly worth pointing out that the antecedent of this conditional is not anywhere satisfied for the sorts of scale of immigration that would, for example, allow all asylum-seekers and many more migrants seeking a better life entry to European societies. But E presupposes, I think, that the interests of natives trump those of strangers: indeed, as stated here, E seems to give the interests of the strangers astonishingly little weight. If, as is actually the case for many refugees, exclusion would produce a life of suffering or even death, and if there are (as there are) hundreds of thousands of them, then E appears to allow that the comforts of home for natives trump any stranger interests, even such much more fundamental interests as life and basic physical security. Dummett, as we shall see, does not believe that this way of looking at things gives proper weight to the strangers' interests; and I shall return to this issue later.

But discussion of E raises the more fundamental question of whether the comforts of home are in fact, for most normal human beings, a condition of a decent human life. If they are not, then a rights-grounding argument for them cannot be mounted. The comforts of home may certainly be something that most people value; but a large number of people value, for example, sugar and soccer, caring about them a very great deal, and we do not normally hear it proposed that we have an unconditional right to either of these.

Part of the difficulty here is that it seems morally important to think about *why* the presence of significant numbers of people of a certain sort, different in some way in appearance or belief or behavior from us, deprives us of the comforts of home. For example, as I understand it, some English people feel that being surrounded by brown people—even Anglican brown people with knowledge of British history and a taste for scrumpy and Yorkshire pudding, speaking English with an accent indistinguishable from the natives—makes a village or town un-English. The land is still English, but it is, they feel, no longer possible to feel at home in it.[30] I should be inclined to call such sentiments racist; and I should be inclined to add that such people are, in effect, facing a problem of their own making and that depriving immigrants of the right of entry in order to solve that problem would be to give an unwarranted weight to immoral sentiments. But I find such color-based unease, at all events, less sympathetic than, say, the thought that replacing all the churches with mosques would radically alter the feel of the country, or the idea that having to learn Urdu in order to do one's grocery shopping is something of an imposition.[31]

All of these objections to immigration, however, presuppose that our native life-style is something we are entitled to protect from the alterations that strangers would bring: and for that to rise to the level of a right, so it seems to me, we should have to show that living with such change would deprive us of a fundamental human need. I am inclined to doubt that this is true. And, if I am right, Dummett concedes too much to the defenders of the significance of the comforts of home.

But how much his concession amounts to depends on the issue, to which I promised earlier I would return, of what exactly Dummett means by "submergence." If I am right, what he ought to mean by it is: a change in the circumstances of life of the citizens that denies them those of the comforts of home that meet fundamental human needs. I have already expressed skepticism that most of the comforts of home are that fundamental. I think the best argument against that skepticism is the sort of argument made by many communitarians of a liberal stripe, who think that people are only willing to sustain the moral burdens of citizenship, if they identify with their society and the state that governs it. If the loss of (some of) the comforts of home made the liberal state unsustainable—and this would be an empirical socio-psychological claim—then allowing submergence of those comforts would undermine the very framework that sustains all our rights. It would therefore threaten the satisfaction of many of our basic needs. If that were so then, plainly, we would have the basis of a rights-grounding argument for immigration restrictions.

Dummett's fundamental position is, at any rate, inconsistent, I think with allowing the comforts of home to count for very much, especially when dealing with those seeking asylum. And, indeed, he offers consider-ations in favor of the view—which is the natural one for someone whose fundamental ideas are what I have called cosmopolitan—that, *ceteris paribus*, strangers should have the right to cross borders pretty much at will.

> What duties and what rights does a state have towards individuals seeking to enter the land over which it rules? The initial answer has to be that it must deal with them justly: it must give them their due.[32]

> But if everyone has a right to live in the country of his citizenship, then a fortiori everyone has the right to live *somewhere*. If it is unjust for a state to deny someone the more particular of these rights, it is unjust for the other states to deny him the more general: someone unjustly expelled from the country to which he belongs by right of being one of its citizens must have a valid claim that some other country should take him in.[33]

In a just world, there would be no refugees from injustice. There is no doubt a rights-grounding argument that everyone is entitled to citizenship somewhere. But suppose C is not the country to which the current scheme of things assigns some refugee, R. One possibility is that the current scheme is unjust. In that case C ought not to participate in it. But nothing yet follows about what C should do affirmatively for R, except work towards a scheme that is just. C has no greater obligation in this respect to R than any other country. Suppose the scheme is just, but R's original country, O, has unjustly expelled him. Then, once again, all that follows is that O has acted unjustly. What C does about this is not yet clear, except that C, like every other country, ought to make sure that R gets a place somewhere. To say this is to say that countries have duties to strangers, as Dummett does, but to allow that the duties may be weaker than Dummett sometimes claims. And, in fact, so it seems to me, Dummett's solutions can usefully be seen as falling into two kinds.

One is of the rights-grounding sort. What scheme of international regulation of rights of movement makes it possible for (most) human beings to lead fully human lives? The answer is, in general, that many such schemes are possible, and that we all (all people and all nations) need to work to set up one of them; evidently the current scheme is not one that meets this condition.

But Dummett also makes other arguments that cannot be so easily fit into this framework. And it is to one of the most interesting of these that I turn in closing.

> It would be wrong to think that, while *individuals* have such a duty towards strangers, the *state* need concern itself only with its own citizens. The state is the representative of its nationals, and acts in their name; in a democratic society it acts at their behest. It must therefore act collectively in accordance with the moral duty laid on its citizens as individuals. It follows that the claim

for refuge of those who flee from persecution should be universally recognised.[34]

The idea that its duty is only to the citizens stems from a faulty conception of the purpose of the state's existence—its mission, in today's jargon. The reason for which the state exists is most usually said to be to promote the welfare of its citizens and to protect them against attack from without. These are among its purposes, indeed: but its further purpose is to *represent* the body of its citizens to the outside world.[35]

Dummett goes on to argue that the state inherits the collective moral responsibilities of the citizens it represents. Citizens "have individual moral obligations to any other human beings whom their actions or failures to act may affect: they therefore have, as a body, collective moral obligations to citizens of other countries. Since the state to which they belong represents them to the outside world, it has, in that capacity, moral obligations to other states and to individuals belonging to those states."[36] It is, Dummett thinks, because we each have duties to aid strangers who are being persecuted that our states inherit our collective obligation to help them.

This argument justifies something weaker than the free movement of persons across borders that is Dummett's actual ambition. For obviously not everyone is being persecuted in the place of his or her current citizenship. But it establishes the need for an international regime that is a good deal more generous to asylum seekers than any that currently exists in Europe, and if the argument is sound, its moral premise—that we each have duties to strangers in distress—is one that would be granted by most of those politicians and pundits who nevertheless advocate immigration and refugee policies that are prima facie (and, I think, not just prima facie) inconsistent with it.

Its philosophical interest lies, I believe, in the notion of representation that Dummett himself italicizes in the passage I quoted a little while ago. And though he says relatively little about it, it is, I believe, very much in the spirit of the fundamental individualism of Dummett's proposals. For it suggests that the moral status of state action in such spheres as foreign and immigration policy derives from the fact that these actions are taken in behalf of citizens and that their results are thus, in a certain sense, the citizen's responsibility. This is more particularly so in a democracy in which the citizen has the power, through advocacy and through the franchise, to make known what state policies he or she believes to be right. State actions matter both because they affect the prospects of persons, both citizens and strangers, and because they are the responsibilities of citizens. They matter then, in both cases, because individuals matter.

Dummett's position in *On Immigration and Refugees* is, by the standards of our actual politics, quite radical in its policy consequences. But it is also philosophically radical in its implications for theories of what I called the moral basis of membership. I have considered two grounds he offers for supposing that membership matters, and in particular, that states are entitled to be partial to citizens, and thus, limited in their generosity to strangers.

One ground is that membership matters because humans need the comforts of home. But this turns out to be a relatively weak basis for limiting the responsibilities of citizens and states to strangers.

The other, which I have discussed most recently, is that we are responsible for the acts states take in our names: citizenship makes a difference here because it is for the citizen that the state acts. If citizens have different responsibilities to fellow citizens from the ones they have to strangers, then the state can inherit their entitlement to partiality. Those who think we are entitled to such partiality have usually argued that it is because of the special character of the relationship we have with our fellow citizens, a historical density, so to speak, that it shares with, say, our relationships with our families or our co-religionists.[37]

Dummett might say to these people that this sort of relationship-grounded partiality has two obvious problems. One—which is relevant to immigration and refugee policy—is that we can only exercise such partiality once we have met our moral duties to all people; so even if relationship-grounded partiality is justified, it cannot trump the *rights* of strangers. A second, is that the relationships we have with fellow citizens in the modern world seem simply too thin—too lacking in density—to bear much ethical weight. Precisely because modern states are, as we saw Dummett insisting earlier, racially, linguistically, culturally, and religiously, plural, their citizens are not like members of a family, a tribe, or the sort of national community imagined in romantic Herderian celebrations of the *Sprachgeist* of the *Volk*. But whatever he would say, he would not think that it provided an excuse for the wickedness that currently passes for sound immigration and refugee policy in the West.

KWAME ANTHONY APPIAH

PRINCETON UNIVERSITY
AUGUST 2002

NOTES

Kwame Anthony Appiah is the Laurance S. Rockefeller University Professor of Philosophy and the University Center for Human Values at Princeton University and co-author, with Amy Gutmann, of *Color Conscious: The Political Morality of Race.*

1. Thomas W. Pogge, "Cosmopolitanism and Sovereignty," *Ethics* 103 (October 1992): 48. I think it is a little unfortunate that the term "individualism," which has, in ordinary usage, a whiff of unsociability about it, should have come to be the technical philosophical label for this position. So it is perhaps worth saying at the start that, as this essay will indicate, individualism of this sort is the basis for an extensive concern for others.

2. Charles R. Beitz, "Cosmopolitan Ideals and National Sentiment," *Journal of Philosophy* 80, no. 10 (1983): 592.

3. Henry Shue, *Basic Rights: Subsistence, Affluence and American Foreign Policy* (Princeton, NJ: Princeton Univ. Press, 1980).

4. Michael Walzer, *Spheres of Justice* (New York: Basic Books, 1983).

5. Pogge, "Cosmopolitanism and Sovereignty," 48–49. I would have preferred to call universality "equality" and generality "universality," but I shall stick with Pogge's terminology.

6. Michael Dummett, *On Immigration and Refugees* (London and New York: Routledge, 2001).

7. In the literature that seeks to define "racism" there are many views currently in contention. But on any reasonable definition a policy that treats people worse than they should be treated, and does so at least in part in virtue of their race, will be racist. Dummett shows that current immigration policy in the United Kingdom does just that. For a useful survey of the positions currently on offer see Jorge Garcia, "The Heart of Racism," in *Racism*, ed. Leonard Harris (Atlantic Highlands, NJ: Humanities Press, 1998).

8. Dummett, *On Immigration and Refugees*, xii.

9. Since these arguments are often dishonest—Dummett correctly points out, for example, that "because everyone recognises that it would be shameful, race is nowadays never offered as an explicit ground for excluding would-be immigrants, even though it is often the true motive" (ibid., 62)—he needs sometimes to make explicit the real bases of current policy.

10. Dummett, *On Immigration and Refugees*, 7.

11. Ibid., 14.

12. Ibid.

13. Ibid., 18.

14. Ibid., 19.

15. Ibid., 9.

16. Ibid., 9–10.

17. Ibid., 10.

18. Ibid., 55.

19. Ibid., 57.

20. I do not mean to imply that there are no other forms of argument that might ground rights.

21. Dummett, *On Immigration and Refugees*, 32.

22. Ibid., 37.

23. Ibid., 26.

24. Ibid., 6.

25. Ibid., 7.

26. Ibid.

27. I made essentially this argument in "Cosmopolitan Patriots," *Critical Inquiry* 23 (Spring 1997): 617–39.

28. Dummett actually rejects this argument on two grounds. One is that some immigrants must be admitted because: "Every human being has a right to refuge from persecution: to deny refuge to the persecuted is to deny them their due; it is a manifest injustice" (*On Immigration and Refugees*, 32). And he adds: "To refuse help to others suffering from or threatened by injustice is to collaborate with that injustice, and so incur part of the responsibility for it" (ibid., 34). But this argument only suggests a rather limited right of entry; indeed, it suggests only that every state ought to agree to participate in a scheme that guarantees refugees from persecution a place of sanctuary somewhere or other. What Dummett argues, however, is that "If aliens should normally be admitted and allowed to reside, and if, in an ideal world, they should be allowed to vote as soon as they establish residence, or if, under existing conditions, they should be speedily enabled to become citizens without any great difficulty, what difference would remain between citizens and resident aliens?" (ibid., 84.) And it is this argument that is supported by the considerations I discuss in the text.

29. Dummett, *On Immigration and Refugees*, 15.

30. They may claim that they feel this way about any foreigners, whatever their race; but if they do, they are either ignorant or dishonest. For many of their white neighbors have ancestors from Ireland, Scotland, France, Poland, Spain, or Italy; many escaped oppression (like the Huguenots) or poverty (like the Irish) elsewhere. And how long must one's ancestors have been in England (and what proportion of them) for them to confer true Englishness upon one?

31. These predilections are biographically unsurprising: I am brown and anglophone and went to Anglican schools!

32. Dummett, *On Immigration and Refugees*, 27.

33. Ibid., 28.

34. Ibid., 34–35.

35. Ibid., 46.

36. Ibid.

37. Avishai Margalit's *The Ethics of Memory* (Cambridge, MA: Harvard Univ. Press, 2002) makes an eloquent recent case for such a view. But his humane view would certainly not lead to immigration and refugee policies as cruel as those Dummett is attacking.

REPLY TO KWAME ANTHONY APPIAH

Imuch enjoyed reading Kwame Appiah's essay on my little book, *On Immigration and Refugees*. He and I are not far apart on these matters. He makes a perceptive and for the most part accurate diagnosis of the position underlying my arguments. I do not apologise for the individualism, understood according to the definition of Thomas Pogge, which Appiah makes his own, though perhaps I ought to apologise for failing to make it an explicit premiss of my reasoning. To many things beside organisms can benefit or harm be done: to nations, states, institutions of all kinds, to languages and many other practices. But only individual human beings and other animals literally enjoy such benefit or suffer such harm. What enhances or impairs their lives or their functioning has moral significance of itself; benefit or harm to other things has only instrumental importance. The extinction of a species, for example, matters only if human beings enjoyed looking at those animals or plants, if biologists could have gained information by studying them, if their absence affects the ecology of some region, or similar reasons; the exhortation, "If we don't do so-and-so, the species may die out," has in itself no moral force.

Where Appiah and I principally differ is, I think, that in my view he does not distinguish sharply enough between refugees and would-be immigrants. We owe to those fleeing persecution or similar intolerable conditions of life an absolute obligation to offer them sanctuary or, when we really cannot do so, to ensure that some other state will grant it to them and will not send them back to the countries from which they had escaped. The question "In what circumstances are we entitled not to do this?" simply does not arise. But would-be immigrants, who wish to enter our country for one reason or another, thinking it would offer them a better life, but not because their former circumstances were unendurable, pose a quite distinct problem. In their case we are fully justified in asking "Do we have reasonable grounds for refusing them?" I think that, in a world in which most major states abided by what I believe to be principles of justice, there would be few occasions for an affirmative answer to this question; but I also believe that, since we do not live in such a world, more such occasions exist. This is to say that the fact that other countries pursue policies that lead to the exclusion of many applicants to live and settle in those countries is of itself a reason to limit the number of those our own country admits. Stated thus, this seems unreasonable and unjust; but the fact is that it would simply be impracticable for a single country to practise a principle of admitting the majority of applicants while other countries continue with policies of harsh exclusion. But, independently of these beliefs, it appears to me undeniable that a question whether a state does or does not do right to refuse admission to particular people applying for entry to its territory presents itself to be answered in the general case of mere putative immigrants. It is equally incontestable that such a question does not arise at all when the applicants are refugees from persecution.

I say that Appiah does not distinguish sharply enough between refugees and ordinary applicants for admission as immigrants because in various passages he treats of both together in a manner I regard as confusing. Thus he remarks that my argument that the state must represent its citizens to the outside world implies that it inherits the collective moral responsibilities of those citizens but "justifies something weaker than the free movement across borders" that I take to be the ultimate goal of immigration policy, since "not everyone is being persecuted" in his native land. No, indeed; but the argument was intended only to establish the duty of states to admit refugees: it did not purport to ground immigration policy generally. Again, in his note 28 he cites my defence of the right of refuge from persecution as a ground of objection to an exclusionist policy founded on claims about submergence. As he says, "this argument only suggests a rather limited right of entry." But, again, exclusionist arguments appealing to notions of submergence deserve no rebuttal when aimed at excluding refugees; they should be dismissed out of hand. Such arguments need to be countered only if they are used to advocate restricting the admission of immigrants, when invoking the right of refuge would be irrelevant.

I think that this divergence between us is a mere matter of presentation, and does not rest on a genuine disagreement. The preceding example raises, however, a question which Appiah explicitly asks, and directs some attention to, namely what I mean by "submergence." I am, as he makes clear, vividly aware of what he engagingly calls the "comforts of home"; but I did not intend to equate submergence with the loss of those comforts. I was well aware that, in introducing the notion of submergence, I risked supporting a ground to which opponents of immigration frequently appeal. They speak, not of being submerged, but of being swamped, as Mrs. Thatcher (as she then was) did in a notorious utterance shortly before, in the 1979 election, she gained power. As I said, it is ludicrous to speak of British culture as being swamped by the entry of people from elsewhere. But I thought it only honest to mention the danger of submergence, since I sincerely believed this to be a legitimate ground for restricting immigration; it is better to acknowledge the grain of truth in your opponents' arguments than to pretend them to be fallacious through and through.

I put forward the danger of submergence, along with that of serious overpopulation, as one of the two admissible grounds, in a just world, for curtailing the entry of immigrants—not, of course, that of refugees, whose entry, or, in dire cases, transfer to some other country of refuge, there is never any admissible ground for curtailing. By "in a just world" I mean "in a world in which most other countries pursue the same policy." It would not be practicable, as I have already said, for any one reasonably-sized country to declare its borders open, or virtually open, while other countries fiercely defended theirs against the entry of strangers. What I had in mind in speaking of submergence was, I had hoped, plain from the examples I gave. It occurs when a whole culture is in danger of being destroyed. There are plenty of instances of an imperialist state's attempting to destroy the culture of a subject territory; and the forced or encouraged entry of an alien population is one of the instruments of this attempt. A salient modern case is that of Tibet; it cannot be contested that the Chinese wish to destroy Tibetan culture, and the importation of people from China proper is one means they employ. Another recent example is the settlement of Indonesian people in East Timor, and, longer ago, the encouragement of Russian people to make their homes in the Baltic states. I cited two examples from British imperial policy. One was the bringing of Indians in large numbers to Fiji, making Fijians for a time a minority in their own country and having very recent repercussions; the other was the very large-scale Chinese immigration to Malaya, which has altered the whole map of the region by separating Singapore from the rest of Malaya and by incorporating parts of Borneo in the new state of Malaysia.

Cultures vary in how robust they are, in the sense of being able to withstand the impact of other cultures. Some, such as the culture of the United States, have at a given time great prestige, seducing others to imitate or try to adopt them; others are fragile, because while those to whom they belong value them as being theirs, they have been induced to suspect them of being inferior. A person's culture is as much a part of that person's make-up and identity as his language; indeed, attempts to suppress a culture are frequently accompanied by attempts to suppress the language that goes with it. The influx over a relatively short period of a number of people of an alien culture in numbers large enough to threaten the survival of the indigenous culture *does* deprive the native population of a fundamental human need, as Appiah maintains that my argument requires: it robs them of something integral to their personal identity.

But the consideration about submergence will only very rarely apply. It is of course a gross injustice when an imperialist state sets out to stamp upon the culture of some small territory it, usually unjustly, occupies; it may rightly be said to be an infringement of human rights. That, however, is not what we are directly concerned with: we are concerned with the question when a sovereign state may legitimately invoke the danger of submergence to justify its limited admission of would-be immigrants. This will happen only when so large number of people of a different, and particularly of a dominant, culture apply for such admission as to threaten the survival of the indigenous culture; and this will not happen very often. So I think that Appiah is unfair to me when he says that I concede "too much to the defenders of the significance of the comforts of home."

There is one matter over which we are in definite disagreement, the foundation of national identity. I said that this ought not to consist of a common ethnicity, religion, or language, because any one of these will in any modern state lead to the formation of one or more minorities of second-class citizens who do not share whatever is proclaimed as the basic core of the state's identity. I concluded that the identity of the nation must be grounded in shared ideals, which I characterised as a shared vision of the society the citizens were striving to create. Appiah objects that it may be grounded in something much weaker than this, "an acceptance of certain legal and political arrangements." This, he says, obtains in Britain, Scandinavia, Switzerland, and the United States. I agree that such an acceptance is enough to make someone content to live in a given country, whether a native or an adopted country. But people need to be able to be proud of their country. Sometimes recent history can make this very difficult; often a country's history may give reason to be proud of it. That they *accept* the legal and constitutional arrangements that prevail in the country in which they live is not enough for them to feel pride in it, even if they think those arrangements admirable. I think they need something more: to feel that their country is going in the right direction, or at least that it can be made to do so. In some cases they cannot feel this: they are at odds with the prevalent trends or the existing set-up. They then have only hope: hope that the country they love or want to love can be brought to move along a better path. But, however people are placed, I do not think that mere acceptance of the way things are run is enough to constitute a sense of what the nation stands for in their eyes and in the world.

Most of my books have been for specialist readerships. It is true that *On Immigration and Refugees* was written for the general public. Yet I consider that Part I of that book is a work of philosophy. From what I can judge, few professional philosophers have treated it as such. I am grateful to Professor Appiah for considering it seriously as a philosophical work.

M. D.

25

Ann Dummett

WORK AGAINST RACISM

On April 23, 1979, the National Front, an extreme right-wing organization, held an election meeting in Southall Town Hall. The violent events which followed were the subject of an unofficial inquiry (the government having refused any official inquiry) set up by the National Council for Civil Liberties and chaired by Michael Dummett. "Of all the events which have . . . caused a sudden deterioration in race relations," he wrote in his introduction, "we think that the disturbance in Southall is the gravest so far."[1]

The report illustrates very well Michael's approach to racism, his particular talents in combating it, and his clarity of vision. There is no jargon in it. It is scrupulous in attempting a fair account of all sides: for example, although the police were the one body of people asked to give evidence who refused to do so, every effort was made to find out the police version of events by studying the testimony of police witnesses in court cases, the remarks of the Metropolitan Police Commissioner in a television interview, and a memorandum laid by the Home Secretary in the House of Commons library and based on a report by that Commissioner. The police stood accused by numerous witnesses (including the local Community Relations Officer) of driving vehicles into the crowd, also of random attacks with batons and even with illegal weapons on bystanders, some of which caused serious head injuries and in one case a death. All available testimony was soberly documented in the report and its effect reinforced by a cumulative weight of careful argument.

Michael's conduct of this inquiry, and in particular his writing of the report, were characteristic of his work against racism in Britain. The arguments included reflections which few white people would have made at the time. For example:

not one [person] appears to have perceived the necessity for saying something to allay the feelings of alienation produced in the Southall community or even to express an understanding of the affront which the day's events had caused."[2] And "We strongly deprecate the use of the word extremists [to label the instigators of the violence] in this connection. Non-pejoratively employed, it would apply to anyone whose opinions on some matter stood at one end of some spectrum. . . . [But] there is no general ground for associating opinions at the end of some scale with irrationality, still less with violence."[3]

More will be said of Southall below. Here, I want to contrast the tone of those remarks, a tone which will be familiar to philosophers, with some of Michael's other activities. He first became involved in work against racism in England in 1964, when a general election was impending. Reading in the news of extreme-Right activities in the Birmingham area (a rare example in those days of reporting about anything to do with race) he became concerned about what might be happening to the minorities in Oxford. These were not visible then, and indeed not numerous, but there were a few thousand West Indians and south Asians working as postmen, bus conductors, nurses, foundry, and bakery workers among others. He had no personal acquaintance with any of them, but managed to find out one or two names and addresses and simply went to call on individuals to ask them about any problems they faced and what he might be able to do to help.

This unexpected visitor must have seemed bizarre, when there was scarcely any contact between university and town. (I remember going to give a talk myself at Cowley Community Centre, on the east side of the city, not long after, where a tutor from Balliol College was also giving a talk, and finding him bemused: he had never been beyond Magdalen Bridge into what for most Oxford residents was the main part of the city, and said to me, "You know, I never knew all this was *here*.") But Michael was not greeted with suspicion. I did not witness any of these meetings, but he evidently found people enthusiastic about forming a co-operative local organization to combat racial discrimination. The local Labour Party Parliamentary candidate, Evan Luard, had been canvassing at the same time and discovered some of the problems. His efforts and Michael's came together in the formation of a local, multiracial organization, the Oxford Committee for Racial Integration (OCRI).

"Integration" was then a good word, and the name of the organization was actually suggested by a Jamaican undergraduate, a former President of the Oxford Union, who was among the first members. These included representatives of the local immigrant organizations, such as the Pakistan Welfare Association, and of trade unions, the churches, local voluntary organizations, and others. These were not representatives in the sense of having been nominated or formally accredited by their organizations: they had been invited as individuals known to be sympathetic to the cause and therefore likely to be active and helpful. Some other cities, which formed similar committees over the next couple of years, sought formal representation sometimes with very unhappy results. I was told, for example, of one place where a nominated member had objected to having upholstered chairs in the office waiting room because "with immigrants, questions of hygiene were involved."

OCRI had no office to begin with: it had only a grant of a hundred pounds from the City Council. I became its honorary secretary. From the start, it was OCRI policy (one of Michael's suggestions) that all approaches on the committee's behalf should be made jointly by a majority and a minority member. Thus, meeting one of the many small-scale requests we dealt with, I went with a Pakistani to ask for a Muslim burial-ground in the city, as none then existed. This was easily solved by a polite official. Rather more difficult was struggling with the local council's municipal housing policy: there was no lack of goodwill but the Council then was unable to comprehend the Asian definition of a family and moreover was hopelessly confused by Muslim and Hindu names. But the most intractable and important problem to be faced was racial discrimination in employment, which was particularly important at the city's two major factories in Cowley, which between them employed well over 20,000 people. This problem was tackled by Michael with the help of trade union members.

Before 1968 there was no law against discrimination in employment, and even the 1968 Act was very limited in scope, relying on complaints from individuals to be dealt with by voluntary conciliation procedures. So OCRI had no bargaining power except the threat of publicity together with its own persuasiveness. Michael spent about six months of effort before the color bar at the two big factories was broken down. He obtained the alliance of the manager of the local employment exchange as well as that of two major trade unions; he went knocking on individuals' doors again, and took part in dozens of meetings. These were not occasions for academic-style argument but for hard-edged bargaining.

In 1965, some of Michael's work moved from the local to the national stage after Campaign Against Racial Discrimination (CARD) was founded. He pressed for OCRI to affiliate to CARD, and was soon elected to the latter's national executive committee, alongside people from various national and local organizations, including multiracial groups, immigrant organizations, and white radicals. From the beginning, there were many

tensions within CARD, partly because of widely varying political affilia-
tions, partly because of rivalries within and between supporting organizations. Working within it was not easy. The problems were exacerbated by
the government's White Paper of summer 1965.

The White Paper came as a terrible shock to immigrants, who had
expected the Labour government elected in autumn 1964 to be their ally.
Parts I and II introduced swingeing new controls over "Commonwealth"
(namely, nonwhite) immigration, while Part III, entitled "Integration"
contradicted the arguments in I and II with a favorable account of the
benefits of immigration and then introduced a new, government-sponsored
structure for local committees' work. Briefly, the proposals sought to fit the
variety of local groups which then existed (including OCRI) into one
pattern under the leadership and grant-giving authority of the National
Committee for Commonwealth Immigrants (NCCI), a small body which up
to then had lacked powers and resources. Conditions were set on the making
of grants to local committees: their constitutions were to be standardized
and the support of their local authorities given to their activities. These
conditions excluded immigrant organizations and the more militant
campaigning groups. Michael argued that the government's "fundamental
aim is to keep the black minority under control, not to give them a part in
how things are run." The local groups, known as Voluntary Liaison
Committees (VLCs), were dominated by respected white people's
institutions, whose presence was supposed to create respectability and
recognition for minorities. Michael wrote later that most of them "have no
conception of what an adequate response to the current racial situation
would constitute; further, even if individually effective in their local areas,
collectively they have lost all resolution or capacity for initiative."[4]
Similarly Dipak Nandy, another CARD executive member complained that
"very few of the VLCs command the confidence of the immigrant
communities . . . the dominant attitude to race relations is one of paternal-
ism."[5]

CARD was badly damaged early in its existence by a rift over relations
with the government's National Committee for Commonwealth Immigrants,
after the publication of the White Paper. Both the Chairman and Vice-
Chairman of CARD, David Pitt and Hamza Alavi, agreed to join NCCI,
without consulting CARD members. One of CARD's largest supporting
national organizations, West Indian Standing Conference, withdrew from
the organization in protest. Michael believed Pitt and Alavi to have made
an irretrievable error. CARD produced a viable plan, drafted by Anthony
Lester and Dipak Nandy, for an anti-discrimination law. Then, in 1967,

CARD fell apart. Its annual convention was wrecked by hundreds of groups which had affiliated the night before the meeting began: an assortment of Maoist, Trotskyite, and West Indian Black Power groups which claimed that CARD was being run by and for Whites and Asians. Lester and Nandy, alongside other individuals and some local organizations, resigned. CARD never recovered and its activities virtually came to a halt. However, its lobbying had had some effect: in 1968 a Race Relations Act covering employment was passed, albeit in a much weaker form than CARD had proposed.

The new immigration restrictions introduced by the White Paper, which were enforceable without new legislation because of the enormous discretion given to the Home Secretary under the 1962 Commonwealth Immigrants Act, not only made entry difficult. They also created many problems for existing residents, making it hard or impossible to bring in family members: they sent out a message to the public at large that black people were undesirable. The code words "immigrant" and "immigration" were intended and taken to refer only to people of color, although alien white entry increased, as did white Commonwealth immigration (particularly from Australia) to meet Britain's continuing labor shortage, while Irish entry was never controlled at all. White people were never called immigrants. From this time onward, Michael's efforts were increasingly devoted to campaigning on the immigration issue. He played a central role in founding the Joint Council for the Welfare of Immigrants (JCWI) in 1967. Learning from the experience of wide ideological differences inside CARD, he decided that it was best to campaign on a single issue, one where all the minorities agreed with one another regardless of political opinion and other differences. So JCWI was a specifically anti-racist body, but its work was all concentrated on immigration.

Learning too from the experience of local voluntary liaison committees, which had become ever more subservient to government policies under threat of having their grants withheld, Michael was insistent that JCWI should never, as a matter of principle, accept any government money. This meant the organization was constantly in financial crisis: sometimes it was unclear where the current month's salaries were going to come from. Just two dedicated employees, Vishnu Sharma and Mary Dines, kept it going with the help of volunteers in a run-down office near Kings Cross. Later it was able to expand with the help of donations, but it did not charge for helping individuals. JCWI still exists after thirty years and has remained an important public voice. Michael has always maintained a connection with it.

From 1964 to 1968, Michael did no work in philosophy except to fulfill the formal requirements of his academic post. All his time apart from teaching and lecturing was devoted to anti-racist work, including frequent visits to London Airport at any hour of the day or night to argue individuals' cases with immigration officers before JCWI was set up. It was an exhausting period, with little sleep and hardly any leisure. The year 1968 was a terrible one. In Britain in March a new law withdrew right of entry from thousands of UK citizens, mostly of Indian descent, who had no other nationality and so became effectively stateless, with no right to be anywhere. There followed swiftly the first of Enoch Powell's violently anti-immigrant speeches, which got massive publicity and was followed in turn by a number of racial attacks within the country. Michael was away for several months in the United States, arriving just before Martin Luther King's assassination and leaving just after Robert Kennedy's. On his return to England, he continued to work within OCRI and CARD but not nearly so intensively. The atmosphere surrounding all such work had become disillusioned and pessimistic. His main efforts were reserved for JCWI, where he believed he could still play a useful part: in anti-racist work generally he had come to believe, partly under the influence of Black Power in the United States, that white people's role in the anti-racist movement had only limited usefulness.

In 1969, Michael returned to original work in philosophy. He had for many years made a series of attempts to write a book on Frege but, constantly dissatisfied, abandoned one draft after another. Early in 1969 Colin Haycraft of Duckworth's came to Oxford in search of new manuscripts, saw Michael, and persuaded him to persevere. By the simple tactic of taking one chapter away at a time and refusing to return it to Michael for revision until the whole work was completed, he acquired the manuscript of "Frege: Philosophy of Language," which was published in 1973. From then on, Michael continued to write voluminously.

In the 1970s, work against racism in Britain was attracting new support. Very few people had been involved in it during the 1960s, but the numbers were growing and so was the pressure for a more comprehensive Race Relations Act than that of 1968. Such an act was achieved in 1976, the Labour Party government elected in 1974 having preceded it by a law on equal opportunities for men and women, whose terms could be readily adapted for a race measure.

But this positive development was offset by continually tightening controls over immigration and by rhetoric surrounding these. Both major parties had, since the 1960s, taken the line that immigrants must be prevented from coming but that, once arrived, they should be treated fairly.

The central problem with this approach was summed up by an employer at a meeting I attended on the prohibition of racial discrimination in employment: "If it's all right for the government to say, 'We don't want you in this country' why can't I say, 'I don't want you in my firm'?" With white immigration always ignored and only black immigration the target of hostility, official policy was quite clearly racist, though everyone in favor of controls vehemently denied the fact.

Even the extreme-Right organization, the National Front (NF), denied publicly that it was racist. Its propaganda concentrated heavily on stopping immigration—indeed very few people knew what other policies it had—but the NF argued it was not blaming immigrants for anything, but only blaming those politicians who had let these people into our overcrowded little island. The NF overlapped with, and recruited for, many small racist groups such as the Racial Preservation Society, which were virulently anti-Semitic, blamed all Britain's problems on blacks and Jews, and acclaimed Hitler's national socialism. The extreme rightists encouraged violent attacks on their opponents, ran military training camps for supporters, and maintained a network of contacts with pro-Nazi parties in other European countries as well as with some "respectable" and established individuals within Britain.

However, with the main political parties emphasizing the need to curb immigration, and with the popular press reinforcing the message by publicizing on the front page every incident where half a dozen people in a small boat tried to enter Britain clandestinely, the NF gained some support and did spectacularly well in the 1976 local elections. The reaction of mainstream politicians was not to denounce the hysteria which had developed over immigration but to try to win back voters with policies of even tougher controls. Reaction among anti-racists resulted in the formation of the Anti-Nazi League, a coalition of groups and individuals ranging from center-Left to far Left, which used street demonstrations and rock music to spread its message. It did not concentrate entirely on immigration but pressed for a number of other policies, with its more vocal members urging easier abortion laws and abolition of the House of Lords. Opposition to current immigration controls then came to be seen as part of a strongly left-wing agenda. Not all immigrants wanted this agenda as a whole.

Michael argued his own case in a series of pamphlets, articles, letters to the press, and speeches at meetings. He did not support any political party and avoided statements on issues other than immigration and race. (He had belonged briefly to the Labour Party, but cancelled his membership when the 1965 White Paper appeared.) He and I had written jointly in 1969 a paper called "The Role of Government in Britain's Racial Crisis,"[6] which claimed that the Labour government's Commonwealth Immigrants Act of 1968 had made possible the famously racist speech of Enoch Powell, then a senior Conservative politician whose intellectual eminence and distinguished career guaranteed him maximum publicity for saying what, it was widely claimed, everyone really thought but did not say openly. Michael wrote two long pamphlets, in 1978[7] and 1984,[8] analyzing the assumptions and combating the arguments of anti-immigration politicians. For example, in Mrs. Thatcher's 1978 remarks on television, she had asserted that prominent politicians had long been afraid to discuss the issue of immigration and ought to put this fear aside and bring the matter out into the open. "Nothing could be more untrue," wrote Michael.

> Since 1961 there has been endless public discussion of immigration. . . . No one subject—not the Common Market, or unemployment, or inflation, or housing, or the Trade Unions, or education—has been so persistently, repeatedly and repetitively discussed. . . . And yet, without doubt, many people responded to Mrs. Thatcher's observation. . . . The explanation is that the words "discussing the question" are an easily understood code. Mrs. Thatcher did not mean that politicians had been afraid to discuss immigration; she meant that they had held back from giving vent to feelings quite as violent, quite as hostile to black people, as those of that section of the electorate to whom she was aiming to appeal.[9]

Nowadays, such an interpretation of her remarks may seem obvious enough: then, it was an unusually forthright and clear description.

The one thing that saved us all from greater success for the extreme Right at this period, apart from Mrs. Thatcher's successful bid for an anti-immigration vote, was a series of quarrels and splits among the extreme-Right organizations themselves. Their successes were to be in local manifestations of violence and hostility, not at the polls. They did badly in the 1979 Parliamentary election, but had a considerable, malign effect in other ways, notably in the Southall affair mentioned at the beginning of this chapter. Southall, on the western edge of London, had a large Indian population and a smaller Caribbean one. The NF booked a hall there for an election meeting—but it was the Town Hall, a symbolic site to the local population, and NF officials admitted only five members of the general public. Nearly three thousand police were drafted in for the morning of the day on which local residents had planned a march and peaceful demonstration in the afternoon and evening. The heavy-handed tactics of the police, their brutality, and the ensuing public disorder had a disastrous effect on both black and white opinion.

With the newly-elected Conservative government firmly refusing an official inquiry into the day's events, Michael agreed to chair the unofficial inquiry set up by the National Council for Civil Liberties. This involved numerous meetings with individuals who had been involved and attendance at Court proceedings when those arrested for public order offenses were tried. The committee, which included an Anglican bishop, a well-known Methodist, an academic lawyer, trade unionists, and others, agreed on a report which Michael wrote up.

The result was a rare piece of documentary evidence for the kind of work Michael had been doing for years past. Most of his efforts had lain in interviews, deputations, informal conversations, and committee work for which no—or very few—records exist. It has therefore been impossible, in this brief chapter, to give a full account of his work against racism. One can only say: he made a difference.

Most recently, a short book he produced in 2001, *On Immigration and Refugees* [10] has had more publicity and a wider circulation than any of his earlier writings. In it, he has used his earlier experiences to explain to younger people how deeply rooted in the history of British racism are today's attitudes to asylum seekers. Moreover, "I have tried in this book," he says in the preface, "to bring together two things that interest me: philosophy and the politics of race, something I had never thought of doing before." The book therefore deals with general principles as well as with specific events. One does not, however, have to be a philosopher to understand it: it is very simply written. The views expressed in it are no less passionate than the opinions in his earlier writings on race; the arguments are more searching and more clearly stated than in much of the voluminous literature that now exists on racism in Britain.

Since 1979, the situation in Britain has gone through many changes. Anti-racism has become a fashionable cause though not always a well-understood one. Superficially, much has improved, with black people represented in many fields that were closed to them in the 1960s and 1970s: we have a black cabinet minister and a handful of black Members of Parliament; black television presenters, city financiers, insurance salesmen, bank workers, head teachers, lawyers, and so on. For those of us who remember how impossible it used to be for a black person to get a job as a baker's deliveryman on the ground that the public would object, this is great progress. But fundamentally the situation is in some ways worse than it was. Racial violence and harassment have actually increased. Discrimination in employment is still widespread, despite anti-discrimination legislation. With widening economic inequality in society as a whole, black people are over-represented in the poorest areas. Moreover, the progress there has been patchy: we have millionaires of Indian origin but this fact is of no help to the wretchedly poor Bangladeshi communities of east London or the unemployed textile workers of Lancashire or the Caribbean and African populations of big cities where crime is endemic and distrust of the police as strong as it ever was.

Furthermore, to speak of "black" and "white" is now an oversimplification. From the early 1970s onward there was significant Chinese immigration; some Vietnamese came in the mid-70s; and since then there have been asylum-seekers from dozens of countries including Iran and Iraq, Turkey, former Yugoslavia (notably Kosovo), Algeria, Sri Lanka, and the Czech Republic. At the same time, xenophobia as well as black/white racism has been on the increase, finding an outlet not specifically against the refugees' nationalities but in hostility to the European Union and its supranational powers. The asylum-seekers have for some years now been the targets of exactly the same hostility that used to greet ordinary immigrants: they too have suffered racial or xenophobic attacks, misrepresentation about their motives and characters, and, most important of all, government policies designed to exclude as many as possible and to harass those who manage to enter by detaining them on the charge of being possibly "illegals" and without any term set to their detention. Michael's book describes this situation and links it to earlier events. But here again, his writing does not indicate the work he has undertaken personally and without publicity on behalf of some of the asylum-seekers in the Oxford area and elsewhere. Many people, locally and across the country, have given enormous voluntary effort on behalf of asylum-seekers in detention in Britain or subsisting on inadequate allowances: he would not claim any particular merit here. Over the years however, he has certainly helped numerous individuals with a great variety of racial problems and influenced ways of thinking and speaking about race. His contribution has been, as he puts it, "to bring together philosophy and the politics of race," and in this respect his contribution is surely unique.

ANN DUMMETT

OXFORD, ENGLAND
JULY 2002

NOTES

1. Unofficial Committee of Enquiry of the National Council for Civil Liberties, *Southall: 23 April 1979: The Report of the Unofficial Committee of Enquiry*

(London: National Council for Civil Liberties, 1980), 9.

2. Ibid., 14.

3. Ibid., 16.

4. Michael Dummett, "Immigrant Organizations" (background paper for a talk given at the Third Annual Race Relations Conference, Queen Elizabeth College, London, 19–20 September 1968) quoted in *Community Action and Race Relations: A Study of Community Relations Committees in Britain*, by Michael J. Hill and Rush M. Issacharoff (London: Oxford Univ. Press, 1971), 31.

5. Dipak Nandy, "An Illusion of Competence" in *Policies for Racial Equality*, ed. Anthony Lester and Nicholas Deakin, no. 262 in Fabian Research Series (London: Fabian Society, 1967), 38; quoted in Hill and Issacharoff, 29.

6. Michael and Ann Dummett, "The Role of Government in Britain's Racial Crisis," in *Justice First*, ed. Lewis Donnelly (London: Sheed and Ward, 1969), 25–78.

7. The 1978 pamphlet was entitled *Immigration: Where the Debate Goes Wrong* and was written for the Action Group on Immigration and Nationality. Issued by JCWI, it has long been out of print.

8. The 1984 pamphlet was entitled *Immigration: The Code that Everyone Knows*. It was written for and issued by JCWI and is also out of print.

9. Dummett, *Immigration: Where the Debate Goes Wrong*.

10. Michael Dummett, *On Immigration and Refugees* (London: Routledge, 2001).

REPLY TO ANN DUMMETT

My wife Ann has told the history of race in Britain through my eyes. I really ceased my active involvement in the combating of racism in Britain in 1981, after the publication of the report by our unofficial enquiry into the disturbances in Southall on St. George's Day, 1979, and its supplement on *The Death of Blair Peach*, the innocent demonstrator killed by a police baton. For many years I remained a member of the executive committee of the Joint Council for the Welfare of Immigrants (JCWI), the body I had helped to set up and of which for a term I had been Chairman, but since 1971 I no longer took part in any active work. Ann has been involved until far later than I was, in fact until quite recently when a series of illnesses forced her to give up work. She has been kind enough to describe some of my participation in the struggle for racial equality. Since she has contributed so much to it herself, I have in this reply sketched what she has done.

From Honorary Secretary of the Oxford Committee for Racial Integration (OCRI), Ann became in 1966 its first paid Community Relations Officer (not paid very much) from a grant by the National Committee for Commonwealth Immigrants (NCCI). It was in this capacity that she organised OCRI's picket of an Oxford ladies' hairdresser's, Annette's, which, despite remonstrances by more than one member of OCRI, refused either to serve or to employ Asian or West Indian people. This must have been in 1966: at that time such discrimination was not illegal. Ann had notified the police of our intention, and the picket had not long begun before an immense number of police irrupted, like the Keystone cops, from a tiny police kiosk. Eight of us were arrested, including a Methodist minister, a future Lord Mayor of Oxford, the West Indian ex-President of the Oxford University Union mentioned by Ann in her essay, and myself. Ann was not arrested because she was escorting home an Indian woman participant in the picket who was scared by the appearance of the police. We were driven to Cowley police station, where our placards were piled face to the wall, and subjected to a furious harangue by a Superintendent. Ann had been careful to make the wording of the placards as innocuous as possible, and this led to a comic incident. The Superintendent denounced us for displaying "inflammatory placards," and picking one up at random turned it around towards us: it said "Oxford citizens ask for fair play." We were shut up in police cells, two to a cell, and let out, one from each pair at a time, to telephone a solicitor; it was remarkable that we got only two different solicitors.

Ann and the eight who had been arrested were charged under the Public Order Act and the (first) Race Relations Act and appeared before three Oxford magistrates. It was rumoured that the Director of Public Prosecutions wanted us to be bound over to keep the peace; if we had been, I think most of us would have gone to prison, since few, if any, would have agreed to promise never to "disturb the peace" in that manner again. A friend from undergraduate days, Peter Weitzman, who had become a distinguished barrister, offered his services free: not surprisingly, his cross-examination was far more skilful than that of the Oxford law professor briefed by the other solicitor. Another comic moment occurred when Peter asked one of the police witnesses whether the public could pass freely along the pavement. "Not really," he replied. "Why not?" Peter asked. "Well, there were so many policemen," he blurted.

At the conclusion of the prosecution evidence, Peter submitted that there was no case to answer. After retiring briefly, the magistrates agreed. Oxford City Council passed a resolution rebuking the police for arresting and charging us. Later Roy Jenkins, then Home Secretary—the only Home Secretary in our lifetimes with a humane and rational attitude to race—had us all up to the Home Office to apologise to us for what had happened, a most gracious act. We were surely vindicated. But we were informed by Dr. David Pitt, chairman of the Campaign Against Racial Discrimination (CARD) and a member of the NCCI, that the NCCI as a whole disapproved of our action. They were opposed to confrontation, believing instead in peaceful persuasion; they never explained what they thought you should do when peaceful persuasion failed.

CARD's annual Convention of 1967, which Ann mentions, was indeed a traumatic experience. The principal engineer of the revolt was Johnny James, a member of CARD's executive and a Maoist; since the disaffiliation of West Indian Standing Conference, the Chairman, Dr. David Pitt (later Lord Pitt), himself a West Indian, had relied on him for contact with the West Indian community. It was an ill-advised alliance, since Johnny James had little interest in combating racial discrimination in Britain, CARD's principal objective, but thought that the important task was to persuade West Indians to return home to take part in the revolution he was confident would take place in the Caribbean. He was a clever man, who made at least one witty remark when he referred to the Communist Party of Great Britain as "Her Majesty's Communist Party." He prepared the take-over with great skill, and, I am sure deliberately, generated a mass hysteria I have never experienced before or since. The conspiracy theory to which Ann referred, that whites and Asians bent on excluding West Indians had seized control of CARD, was widely and excitedly believed; I argued with two normally very sensible young West Indian women with whom I had worked and who, in that heated atmosphere, had acquired a passionate belief in the theory. David Pitt, evidently anxious to remain Chairman, played a questionable role, putting the knife into those who had been his principal lieutenants. After it was over, I remained a member of CARD, and indeed of its National Council, and persuaded OCRI to remain affiliated, while multi-racial organisations all over the country were breaking away. But it was evident, from an executive meeting I was allowed to attend, and from the general inactivity of the organisation, that those who had captured CARD had no interest in doing anything with it. The only national organisation dedicated to combating racism in every sphere had ceased to function; and this was known to the press and the general public. But we still had JCWI, founded the previous September to fight against the most serious manifestation of British racism, our iniquitous immigration laws and regulations, and the manner in which they were put into effect.

As Ann describes, in 1968, with Callaghan having replaced Jenkins as Home Secretary, the infamous Commonwealth Immigrants Act was passed, which denied Asian holders of British passports from independent East African countries the right of entry to Britain. Since there is widespread confusion about their status, readers may be glad of some clarification. The original Commonwealth Immigrants Act of 1962 is sometimes represented as merely denying right of entry to citizens of independent Commonwealth countries such as Canada and Australia. By no means: it also denied entry to citizens of the UK and Colonies living in British colonies. This was already a piece of legal fiction. The pretext was that the passports of such people—which differed from those of people living in Britain only in the line saying "Where issued"—were granted, not by the British government, but by the colonial government, and that they were citizens only of their respective colonies. It is obvious that a colony has no power to grant a passport. It has no representation abroad; and cannot protect anyone travelling to another country.

The 1968 Act relied on no such dishonest pretence: it straightforwardly transgressed international law by denying to British citizens the right of entry to their country of citizenship, and hence the legal right to live anywhere on the globe. As Callaghan said in introducing the Bill, it violated solemn obligations. He did not mean that we were bound to honour such obligations: he meant that it was so urgent to prevent these people from coming to Britain that we must dishonour solemn obligations in order to prevent that. When Kenya had become independent, a choice for people of Asian descent living in that country had been negotiated: they could under the Kenya Independence Act of 1963 either retain citizenship of the UK and

Colonies or opt to become citizens of the newly independent country. The same option had been offered to Asian residents of Tanganyika when it became independent in 1961 and of Uganda upon its independence in 1962 (Tanganyika united with Zanzibar to become Tanzania in 1964); in Malawi they had no choice, because Malawi granted citizenship only to those of African descent. In Uganda and Kenya, and hence implicitly in Tanzania, this choice was offered to people of Asian descent on the explicit understanding that, if they chose to remain citizens of the UK and Colonies, they would have the right to enter Britain freely: their passports would have been issued, not by any colonial government, but by the direct representative of Britain, the British High Commission to an independent African state. Hardly anybody made an attempt to pretend that it was otherwise. Many of the people that the Act kept out had opted to retain their citizenship of the UK and Colonies precisely because they wished to be sure of being able to come to Britain if they found themselves discriminated against in favour of people of African descent. The Act violated principles of international law as well as a promise we had been understood, and had meant to be understood, as making. It was an utterly shameful action, manifestly a state act of racial discrimination. It was rushed through Parliament in record time, because a hysteria had been whipped up about the urgency of stopping these people coming to Britain. It casts great discredit on the Labour Government which introduced it and the majority of Conservative M.P.s who voted for it; and honour on the minority who withstood the hysteria and voted against. It remains to this day a stain on the country's honour. Under the Nationality Act of 1981, Asians living in independent countries such as Kenya and holding UK and Colonies passports have been reclassified as British Overseas Citizens, along with thousands of people of Indian descent in Hong Kong, giving them no right of entry into Britain, although those living in the few remaining British colonies have now been given full British citizenship.

Members of the NCCI were greatly affronted by the 1968 Commonwealth Immigrants Act, but only the two Indian members resigned, the upright Dr. Prem and our friend and colleague the late Vishnu Sharma; the other members were placated by an invitation to tea with the Prime Minister. The NCCI then sent an emissary to visit the local community liaison committees to explain to them the Government's great contribution to racial harmony by introducing the 1968 Act, thus taking the wind out of the sails of the racists campaigning for the exclusion of the East African Asians. The members of OCRI did not find the argument persuasive. I doubt if many people did.

After the passing of the 1968 Act and the widely supported racist campaign of Enoch Powell which followed it, as a sop to liberal opinion the Government introduced and succeeded in getting Parliament to pass a second Race Relations Act. The first one, with a very limited scope (essentially only places of public resort) had been passed in 1965, and set up the Race Relations Board, with local branches, to administer complaints of such racial discrimination as were covered by the Act. The 1968 Act greatly extended the scope of the first one by rendering illegal racial discrimination in employment and housing, but still provided a very feeble mechanism of enforcement. The Act replaced the NCCI by the Community Relations Commission (CRC), which was made responsible to the Home Secretary. The CRC sent an official to the community relations councils, as they were henceforward to be called, to instruct them that they should no longer concern themselves with racial discrimination, since that was the business of the Race Relations Board. This was equivalent to telling the police not to bother about crime, since the lawcourts dealt with that. It was not until 1976 that the then Labour Government brought in a third Race Relations Act which approached effectiveness. It was largely modelled on proposals previously drafted by two members of CARD, Anthony (now Lord) Lester and Dipak Nandy (both had resigned from CARD after the 1967 Convention). The 1976 Act merged the Race Relations Board with the CRC to form the Commission for Racial Equality (CRE).

After resigning in 1969 from her post as OCRI's Community Relations Officer, Ann wrote a wonderful book, *A Portrait of English Racism*, based on her knowledge and experience. It was published by Penguin in 1973. In it she alternated the history of Government policies and their effects with vivid, moving descriptions of the impact of racism on individual lives. It is the best book on racism of the many I have read. I would rather have written it than any of the many books I have written; but I am not and have never been capable of doing so. It sold 15,000 copies, but Penguin did not reprint. The book was republished in 1984 by Christians Against Racism and Fascism, a small voluntary group.

After writing *A Portrait of English Racism*, Ann continued to work for racial equality, from 1971 onward for the rest of her career until a series of illnesses from late 1998 on forced her to give up regular work. 1971 was about the date at which I abandoned any active involvement in work against racism; all that I did after that was to act as chairman of the unofficial enquiry into the events in Southall in 1979 and to attend meetings of JCWI's executive committee, helping to decide its policy and organise its functioning. The work Ann did from that time on was under the auspices of several organisations, the first of them the Institute of Race Relations. Her work from the 1970s onwards was divided between helping individuals with problems to do with immigration and nationality, doing research, campaigning and lobbying for changes in the law and its administration. She spoke at public meetings in cities all over Britain, and, at a later date, at meetings in various parts of Europe; in the days before videotapes, she produced a slide-tape presentation on nationality for use at meetings she could not reach. She lobbied political parties and took part in deputations to Ministers. She wrote a stream of pamphlets, reports, articles, and chapters in various symposia, on government policies, the reform of immigration law, nationality law, racial violence and policing, refugee policy, church schools and racial issues, and European Community law and policy on minorities. She has been a member of various Catholic bodies on race.

For the Runnymede Trust, a body established in 1968 to collect and disseminate information on race and immigration, she produced two pamphlets, *Citizenship and Nationality* in 1976 and, in 1978, *A New Immigration Policy*. In the latter, unusually, she not only described the faults of existing systems, but made specific proposals for change. But her work was ahead of its time; later, many of her proposals were taken up by churches and other voluntary groups.

From 1978 to 1984 Ann worked for JCWI, and represented it on the Action Group on Immigration and Nationality (AGIN), becoming the secretary of the Group. During the passage of the Nationality Act of 1981, she underwent an endurance test, sitting though all the debates and committee discussions. She provided copious notes for opposition speakers and helped them write amendments, some of which were successful; Lord Pitt, as David Pitt had now become, was particularly helpful in this regard. The Bill created five different types of British citizenship, only one of which carried a right of abode in the UK

From 1979 to 1984 Ann was a member of a government committee enquiry into the education of ethnic minority children in England and Wales, which culminated in the Swann Report. From 1984 to 1987 she was Director of the Runnymede Trust, which under her direction produced a number of valuable reports.

From the expertise she had gained on immigration and nationality law, Ann had become a kind of honorary lawyer, and had been invited to take part in more than one conference otherwise attended only by lawyers. She now devoted herself to writing, with Andrew Nicol, a large book in the Law in Context series, *Citizens, Subjects, Aliens and Others*. It took a long time to write; much of it was done while we were in California, when I was at the Stanford Center for Advanced Study in the Behavioral Sciences. The book is a history, going back over many centuries, of British nationality and immigration laws and the political theories on which they were based.

After we returned from California, Ann worked from 1990 to 1998 for the CRE. She acted as their adviser on their policies concerning the European Union, and in this capacity was active in forming and taking part in the Starting Line Group, composed of experts from different European countries. The Group drafted a model directive to outlaw racial discrimination, and a model Treaty amendment for the same purpose. When each of these was eventually realised, its wording was close to what the Group had proposed.

A series of illnesses has prevented Ann from doing any more regular work; but she has laboured in that vineyard for far longer than I did. As she briefly indicates in her essay, race relations in Britain have changed profoundly since she and I were first involved. Then racial prejudice was unashamedly expressed by the majority of white people; now racism is socially unacceptable in most circles, except, alas, when directed towards refugees, called invariably "asylum-seekers." It is possible, though rare, for someone who is not white to grow up in the country without ever encountering racism in speech or action. But it is also possible for such a person to be murdered on the street or to die "accidentally" in a police station. The once widespread low-level prejudice is now concentrated into vicious and often violent hatred on the part of a small number of murderous psychopaths, and diffused as a bullying hostility in certain circles, notably the police. But there are stronger grounds for hope for the future of multi-racial Britain than there are in other major European countries. France is triumphantly prohibiting the wearing of headscarves by Muslim schoolgirls, and the German Länder are doing the same. There is general agreement in France that an appearance of equity must be maintained by banning Christian and Jewish items of wear if of comparable size to headscarves (but not if significantly smaller); but some Frenchmen and many Germans dissent from this, arguing that a headscarf is an aggressive political symbol whereas a monastic habit is not. I grieve to say that the Catholic Bishop of Mainz, Cardinal Karl Lehmann, is among those putting forward this argument. If anything deserves to be called aggressive, it is such a ban. It vividly illustrates the intolerance still rife in those countries, being obviously motivated by hostility to Muslims as such; I think sadly of the contrast with those schools in Britain in which they celebrate the feastdays of all the religions to which their pupils adhere. The ban on headscarves also violates a fundamental principle of justice, not to prevent people from doing what they believe they have a duty to do if it does others no harm. It is hypocritical for non-Muslims to argue that the Koran does not enjoin the wearing of headscarves; these girls believe their religion obliges them to wear them, and to make it illegal to do so is a gross injustice that puts them into an unbearable dilemma. It is cruelty of a kind of which I would until very recently have said that very few head teachers, let alone the State, would think of inflicting in Britain, any more than in the United States. I am sad to say, however, that, in thoughtless imitation of France and Germany, there is a move afoot to ban headscarves in British schools; I am hopeful that the tolerance of new cultural and religious traditions that we have gained will withstand this move and hold it back from making any serious headway.

M. D.

26

Andrew Beards

DUMMETT: PHILOSOPHY
AND RELIGION

No doubt there are many professional philosophers with an interest in Michael Dummett's work who know nothing of his commitment to Roman Catholicism, nor of his essays and lectures manifesting this commitment which are of philosophical interest. On the other hand, I would be surprised if there are many among the Catholic academics who come across the occasional contribution of Dummett to Catholic publications such as *New Blackfriars* and the *Tablet* who have read very much of his philosophical work. It appears then that Dummett's work is divided between two worlds which have little to do with each other, and one may wonder why this is so. The most fundamental reason is that Dummett's philosophical work has been concerned primarily with issues in the philosophy of language, and therefore he has not caught the attention of theologians in the way he would have done were he to have written extensively on the philosophy of religion or theological topics. Another reason why Catholic theologians have not given a great deal of attention to Dummett's philosophy may be that there are not many such theologians around with the requisite philosophical background to appreciate it. Catholic philosophical studies in Dummett's native land have declined in the last thirty years or so with the general decline in Catholic practice and culture. Turning one's attention to other parts of the English-speaking Catholic world one may note in the same period a decline in interest in philosophy in general among theologians; a fact lamented in Pope John Paul II's important encyclical on philosophical studies, *Fides et Ratio*. In addition one should also note that the trend among theologians with an interest in philosophy has been to turn for inspiration to continental rather than analytical thought.

Dummett's theistic commitments, however, have on occasion manifested themselves in works which have been the focus of attention of other
analytical philosophers. In his contribution to the 1994 collection of essays
he edited with G. Oliveri, "Time, Truth and Deity," Brian McGuinness
drew attention to remarks in unpublished lecture material in which
Dummett had hinted at the idea of the need for God if a realistic conception
of the world were to be grounded, and in his response to McGuinness
Dummett argued that the naturalistic attempt to do without God will not
work as an explanation.[1] Even from a purely philosophical standpoint
Dummett's concern with the question of God is understandable since his
philosophical program is one which aims to move forward from an
investigation into the intelligent propositional attitudes embedded in the
linguistic expressions of human beings, to a reflection upon the realities of
the world which human beings attempt to know and describe in language.
It is clear to any student of Dummett's thought, therefore, that his philosophy has as its aim an account, as far as this is possible, of the metaphysical
features of the world insofar as these provide a basic semantics for
intelligent language use. It would appear, then, that the question as to
whether reality includes God is a legitimate one for a philosophy concerned
with metaphysics such as Dummett's. Certainly such a question has been
raised in the traditions of metaphysical speculation in both East and West,
and if we take into account the tastes of some of the analytical followers of
David Lewis for multiple real other (possible) worlds, the notion of God can
hardly be ruled out as a metaphysical extravagance even by current
analytical standards!

However, one should also make clear straight away that because of the
intimate connection that exists in Dummett's philosophy between language
and thought, on the one hand, and the metaphysical structures and features
of the world known by us, on the other, the notion of God is also important
as one wrestles with epistemological and logical issues. Someone inspired
by Dummett's work may wish to argue that even for the philosopher
without religious faith the notion of God is an important one if only as a
factor in metaphysical thought experiment. Given the intimate links among
language, thought, logic, and metaphysics which Dummett's thought labors
to elucidate, one at once has to understand that for Dummett the idea of God
is important for the proper resolution of a number of key philosophical
problems. So, for example, Dummett invites us to reflect upon the idea of
the past and the future by thinking through the implications of what it
would mean for there to be a timeless knower. And he asks us to consider
whether the knowledge of such a Divine knower would have further
implications for the notion of bivalence with regard to future-tensed
statements.

Both Brian McGuinness and Karen Green have drawn attention to the theistic themes which have appeared at the margins of some of Dummett's work, both published and unpublished.[2] One way in which I will attempt to throw a little more light on the importance of the notion of God for Dummett's philosophy in the present essay is by commenting upon Dummett's Gifford Lectures given at St. Andrews University in 1997.[3] Professor Dummett has been kind enough to provide me with a copy of these lectures prior to their publication, although he has some reservations about their content. After outlining the content of the lectures and offering some comment upon them, I will move on to discuss examples of Dummett's work, which are, I believe, of interest to philosophers but which treat of issues that are the concern of Catholic theology. These include writings on scriptural interpretation, transubstantiation (the Catholic belief in the *real presence* of Christ in the Eucharist), and ethics. My aim in offering some account and critical discussion of these contributions is to show something of Dummett's philosophical vision as a whole; to show something of a philosopher who is also a man of religious faith, who brings to bear the tools of philosophical reflection upon that faith, and who takes seriously the implications of the doctrines of a religious faith for philosophy.

While in his essay on the Eucharist Dummett shows himself sympathetic to some aspects of St. Thomas Aquinas's approach to philosophical and theological questions, he also demonstrates critical reserve with regard to certain forms of "degenerate" Aristotelian scholasticism and is also critical of some of the notions adopted by classical Thomism.[4] In attempting to appreciate the relationship between Dummett's Catholic beliefs and his philosophy one should bear in mind that the official position of the Catholic Church (reiterated in the encyclical of Pope John Paul II, *Fides et Ratio*) is that there is no one philosophy to which a Catholic is required to adhere. There are, of course, philosophical positions which are contrary to certain Catholic beliefs and these the Catholic is required to reject. The Catholic Church holds the Thomistic approach in high esteem, and encourages study of it, because it is an approach which appears particularly congruent with Catholic beliefs and has contributed much to the development of Catholic theological positions, some of which have been adopted into the official teaching of the Catholic Church. But Catholic teaching also recognizes that there are a number of different philosophical approaches which are congruent with Catholic belief and which may enrich theological reflection.

One philosophical approach, adopted by certain Catholic philosophers who played a role in Dummett's own development, involves combining in some fashion elements of Thomistic and analytical thought. One sees this, to a certain extent, in the writings of Elisabeth Anscombe and Peter Geach. This option, however, does not appear to have commended itself to

Dummett, for whom Frege and Wittgenstein (and as time went on, Frege rather than Wittgenstein) were the seminal influences.

While recognizing these facts concerning philosophical influences on Dummett and how they affect the approach he takes to questions in the philosophy of religion and philosophical theology, it may be worth noting that when we move back upstream historically there is less of a clear demarcation between such philosophical approaches than was once thought. Indeed, in recent work Dummett has drawn attention to the importance of becoming more historically aware of the origins of analytical philosophy within the nineteenth-century European context.[5] This heightened historical awareness on his part has grown out of his own detailed scholarly studies of the development of Frege's thought, and his call for a more open dialogue between analytical and continental perspectives comes at a time when a number of philosophers, for various reasons, are seeking to overcome barriers erected during the "Cold War" stand-off between philosophical traditions which characterized much of the twentieth century.

Dummett believes that the study of the origins of philosophical traditions is important both for opening up those traditions to fresh perspectives and in order better to understand what is unique to a tradition; for the analytical tradition this uniqueness lies in language as the philosophical point of departure. This study of origins should serve, I believe, not only to demonstrate that there are philosophical interests common to analytical and continental philosophy, but also to highlight the way in which the Thomistic or neo-Scholastic tradition has had some influence upon these traditions and has not been hermetically sealed off from them. For no one, surely, would deny the importance of the nineteenth-century Austrian philosophical scene for later developments, and the key figures here, Bolzano and Brentano, also played an important part in the revival of scholasticism.

It may also be of interest to students of Dummett's thought to note that his awareness of continental philosophy is not only mediated to him via study of Frege and Husserl. His essays on Catholic theological questions, while not demonstrating extensive study in the thought of Catholic continental theologians, nevertheless manifest the way he has absorbed a good deal of continental theological philosophy from his reading of Catholic theological literature.

THE GIFFORD LECTURES

Turning to Dummett's 1997 Gifford Lectures it may at once be observed that if one is expecting to find something akin to the celebrated 1902

Edinburgh lectures with the same title by William James, one will be disappointed. That is, Dummett's four lectures do lead up to a philosophical discussion of God, but they are not lectures preoccupied with discussion of issues that are standard in works of philosophical theology. Apart from a brief reference to God in Lecture One, which occurs in a passage in which we are invited to reflect on the limitations of our knowledge and thus feel humbled before God's limitless wisdom, discussion of God is reserved for the second half of the final, fourth lecture. The approach adopted by Dummett in the four lectures is, rather, to present some of the key ideas of his philosophy, ideas central to his philosophy of language, logic, and metaphysics, and show how his general philosophical approach leads to the idea of God. When we have reached the idea of God in Lecture Four, we are then presented with some brief remarks concerning the way the type of knowledge God must have has implications for logical issues to do with bivalence, especially with regard to statements regarding knowledge of the future.

Students of Dummett's thought, then, will find in the four Gifford Lectures much that is familiar to them, although, no doubt, they will discover nuances and emphases in the argument of the lectures that will enhance their appreciation of Dummett's philosophy as a whole. Dummett is resolved to publish the lectures without significant alteration in due course.

While I understand my primary task here to be a treatment of Dummett's thought on philosophical issues concerning religion, it will not be possible for me to proceed without some account of the contents of the lectures as a whole. They outline the general philosophical position within which Dummett's thoughts on God and religious doctrine have their place. As well as attempting to provide a brief outline of the philosophy adumbrated in the lectures I will offer some comments by way of critical evaluation. My own philosophical position owes a good deal to the thought of St. Thomas Aquinas and to some twentieth-century exponents of his philosophy, and I shall therefore occasionally offer points of comparison and contrast between what I understand to be Dummett's position and a position which owes more to Thomistic philosophy. My hope is that this will further serve to throw light upon Dummett as a religious and Catholic thinker. For while Thomistic thought can in no way be understood as possessing exclusive territorial rights with regard to the Catholic intellectual tradition it has, nevertheless, played a conspicuous role in that tradition during the last seven centuries.

In the first of the Gifford Lectures Dummett makes it clear that on his view a philosopher like himself, who is committed to a philosophical program for which the point of departure is language, should also be committed to the exploration of metaphysical questions. The work of the philosopher entails making explicit or clear what is only implicit or obscure in the intuitions of ordinary, intelligent language users. Since such language users are committed to a robust realism, such that they take it that their discourse is about real states of affairs in the world, the philosopher of language must accept this commitment and attempt to give an explicit account of the world that ordinary language users describe in some partial way, at least, in discourse. As Dummett argues in Lecture Four, a "justificationist" theory like his, which emphasizes our ability or inability to affirm some proposition in a given instance, does not lead to dropping truth out of the picture. For such a position would fail to attribute "to speakers of the language any conception of the reality about which they speak" (21). And the philosopher, on Dummett's view, must appreciate the fact that, "metaphysics is not the specialised interest of metaphysicians, but, in however confused or inchoate a form, part of everybody's mental equipment" (22). What Dummett rejects is not realism but an extravagant realism, which he identifies with what he terms "classical logic." It is a view that would pretend to prescind entirely from the fact that we must approach knowledge of reality from the particular, limited perspective, which we have as human beings, who develop in knowledge over time. Our limitations, on Dummett's view, include our inability to know in advance whether a proposition can in any way be affirmed as true or false, or whether the matter has to be reformulated or the investigation ultimately abandoned since there is no "true or false" about it. This is, of course, the area of "limitation" which has preoccupied Dummett in his writing on bivalence and the limitations of the logical principle of excluded middle. Another conspicuous limitation to our knowledge is one brought home to us, ironically, by our achievements in scientific progress: from the scientific world view arises the question as to how much we really know of "things in themselves."

Some philosophers in ancient, medieval, and modern times have, when faced with similar considerations, taken the path to skepticism, idealism, relativism, or more recently, some form of social constructivism. But, as we have noted, these are not viable options for Dummett since they do not do justice to our reasonable commonsense conviction that we do know the world and that our knowledge of the world has been increasing over time. Dummett also argues, with a nod in the direction of the eighteenth-century debates which led to Kantian thought, that it is illegitimate to push beyond reasonable limits the analogy of human knowing as the comparing of a picture with the original in such a way as to suggest that all our pictures, or concepts, fail to inform us of the "originals" or facts about the real world.

Dummett notes that some of his predecessors in the tradition of analytical philosophy such as A. N. Prior were concerned to move from the intuitions of ordinary language to an investigation of the metaphysical reality to which that language referred, and like Prior, Dummett has been preoccupied with the nature of time and the access we may or may not have via our tensed propositions to this facet of the metaphysical make-up of the world.

What has been said of Dummett's position so far, then, makes it evident that he does not share the suspicion of metaphysics of the twentieth-century verificationists, nor the coyness of earlier analysts with regard to the subject. Rather his work can be seen as a contribution to the renewal of interest in metaphysics on the part of many analytical philosophers. Given that the purpose of the present essay is to highlight connections between Dummett's religious commitments and his philosophy, we can also note that his work on metaphysics is in line with Pope John Paul II's call in *Fides et Ratio* for a renewed philosophical effort in the domain of metaphysics.[6]

If in some way Dummett's endeavor to pursue a philosophical program which includes a metaphysical dimension departs from the prejudices of a number of significant earlier analytical philosophers, his explicit repudiation of a type of analytical philosophy that would deny the obvious facts of human consciousness and intentional, mental acts also marks out the difference between his position and those of philosophers still committed to the ideals of the later Wittgenstein. This aspect of Dummett's philosophy is also evident in the Gifford Lectures. If the way to metaphysics is via a clarification of the sometimes obscure and confused intuitions expressed in language, then the first task of the philosopher is an explication of the meaning expressed in language. This commitment to the priority of language as the philosopher's starting point is central to the approach of the analytical tradition, which in some way was initiated by Frege, Dummett believes, and it marks off Dummett's approach from that of the new group of philosophers of thought in Anglo-Saxon philosophy represented by Christopher Peacock and the late Gareth Evans, a philosopher whose legacy Dummett continues to find stimulating, albeit major differences between the two thinkers are evident.

While an investigation of thought "prior" to language is not the way to proceed in understanding the meaning enshrined in language use, equally problematic for Dummett are deflationary accounts which aim at determining linguistic meaning by taking ordinary discourse to be, at root, a kind of self-sufficient set of mutually conditioning terms and relations on the model of the artificial languages devised in modern symbolic systems. For Dummett this amounts to a meaningless abstraction from the fact that language is the way of expression for intelligent human beings. "Truth," for instance, cannot be understood apart from the place it has in the human activity of trying to justify some proposition or other as true or false. Dummett also reaffirms his commitment to the view that we cannot understand meaning without reference to truth, and truth without reference to meaning. In order to understand linguistic meaning we must, on Dummett's view, begin in a certain sense with the words that constitute the sentences we use, but we must also, in order to appreciate the nature of language as a multifaceted tool devised by human beings, take into account what Frege termed "force" and "tone." Dummett remarks of the latter that modification of Frege's notion is required, but that the notion of "force" is vital to our grasp of linguistic meaning he has no doubt. For "force" is seen in, for example, the assertoric or interrogative way in which intelligent language users utter speech acts. Clearly, by "force" is meant what in other terms is referred to as the conscious intention with which a language user utters a given expression. Here a question arises for me from Dummett's philosophical method. It appears to me that Dummett says that we move from language to study the conscious mental acts of human beings, but when we reflect on what "force" is, our conscious intention in uttering an expression, it seems to me that we cannot begin to understand the meaning of language without reference to conscious thought as intentional "force."

In Lecture Two Dummett employs the results of his own reflections on the varieties of human expression and thought to solve a puzzle which he believes neither the linguistic minimalist nor a philosopher of thought such as Evans can solve: how can the intelligent language user *know* the propositions that express the conditions under which a proposition is to be assessed as true or false prior to knowing that these propositions hold good? Evans admitted that he had no answer to this, and Frege, whom other analysts have followed, attempted a solution which artificially created a world of propositions floating free of human language users in their own metaphysical realm. Dummett's answer is to point to a kind of human knowing which, he says, is a half-way house between knowing *how* and knowing *that*. Many of our ordinary types of practical knowledge are of this kind, he points out. And he gives as an illustration the knowledge someone has when he/she knows how to dance the rumba. This person, when asked for an account of how to perform the dance, will respond with a mixture of gestures and, perhaps some words. Dummett's point here calls to mind John Searle's use of Wittgenstein's distinction between "saying" and "showing."[7] We may not be able to state, to say, what we understand, but we may be able to show it. Dummett resolves the puzzle, then, by arguing that our assessment conditions for accepting or rejecting a proposed proposition as true are known in this way.

The use Dummett makes of the case of the person who is more able to show than to say what he/she understands illustrates Dummett's interest in the wide variety of types of human understanding manifest in language use. In more recent works, such as the *Origins of Analytical Philosophy*, he has expressed some sympathy for insights into human understanding and thought to be found in Evans's work and in the philosophy of Husserl.[8] Dummett is intrigued by this variety of forms and indicates that further work is needed if we are to deepen our understanding of, say, how human insight and concept formation differs from that of animals. In the Gifford Lectures he refers to that "mysterious" phenomenon which is the growth and development of language (Lecture 4, 21). Such growth in language, Dummett remarks, is not to be characterized in some nominalist fashion that fails to recognize that new concepts and linguistic forms arise from genuinely new insights in the worlds of mathematics, science, art, religion, and ordinary discourse. In recognizing the need for further investigation into these diverse aspects of human thought, including the dynamic way in which language develops with creative thinking, Dummett, I believe, contributes to a shift away from a rather static kind of conceptual analysis prevalent in much analytical philosophy in the latter part of the twentieth century. This rather static, ahistorical view of concepts and their role in language games was something that continental philosophers like Jürgen Habermas and Hans-Georg Gadamer found unacceptable in the later Wittgenstein, many of whose insights they otherwise found illuminating. Emphasis on dynamic development within language and conceptual use also serves to draw attention to the creative thinking of human individuals, and therefore draws attention to the intimate interrelationship between language and conscious thought.

In Lectures Three and Four Dummett proceeds to look at what he takes to be the implications for philosophy of the rejection of the truth-conditional theories of Frege and early Wittgenstein which fail, he believes, to take into account our linguistic practice of "recognizing-as-true," "accepting-as-true," "acting on the truth of." He outlines some of the principal features of his own justificationist theory which holds that a statement is justified if we have effective means in principle of coming to recognize its truth (19). In learning a language we gain familiarity and mastery in ordinary situations in which matters are decidable. But errors arise when we attempt to extrapolate from these ordinary cases and pretend to have the same kind of decision procedures for truth and falsity of propositions with regard to realms which are not subject to the same surveyability on our part. As a consequence the logical principle of excluded middle is found to have only limited validity. That such realms or domains include those of putative mathematical proof beyond our powers of surveyability and past and future states of affairs will be no surprise for students of Dummett's thought.

One of the errors of what Dummett names "classical logic" is to fail to understand the indeterminacy of the future, and thus the inapplicability of bivalence to future-tensed statements. Since the future is indeterminate, philosophical determinism is nonsense. One must recognize, he argues, that the scattering of causal connections across space and time implies indeterminism. However, this indeterminism does not extend to basic properties that are the constituents of things. Just as the fact of how many apples there are in a given collection is determinate, so it is true that "If it is always determinable whether an object has a dependent property, then it must be always determinate whether an object has a basic property." And to think otherwise, Dummett avers, is senseless.

On the justificationist view that Dummett defends there is no notion of truth for inaccessible propositions *other than their having been established as true*. What does this imply for our knowledge of the past? On the justificationist view is the past as indeterminate as the future? Dummett's position is that our knowledge of both is in some way indeterminate. He insists, against some extreme forms of idealism, that we do not create the world (20). However, the justificationist view of the matter is illustrated by the image of a blindfolded person exploring and encountering objects that only come into existence as they are found. We cannot talk, therefore, of what is "already there to be discovered" in the future. This is misleading "picture-thinking" of the future as an already existing state of affairs. But for the justificationist this is also true of the past. At best we are entitled to say, we are only justified in saying, that something happened in the past when and if we discover this to be true.

It is in the latter part of Lecture Four that Dummett's concerns become explicitly theological. However, as was pointed out above, what Dummett argues for in this part of the lectures develops out of the general position outlined thus far, a position which is well known among many philosophers. It is Dummett's view, clearly, that the theological part of the lectures follows from his overall philosophical approach. However, it should be borne in mind that, as was remarked above, Dummett is not completely happy with a number of ideas expressed in the lectures and feels that some of these many need further refinement.[9]

In Lecture Four Dummett makes a case for accepting the existence of God, and also offers some remarks on the nature of God's knowledge. It is difficult, given the style of presentation, to determine what weight Dummett gives to each of the considerations he puts forward in order to persuade the metaphysician to accept the hypothesis of God's existence. He begins by pointing out that we are faced with a number of problems: the world as we experience it overlaps with the way animals experience it, but there is an absence of the kind of unity which should characterize one world. Further, science aims at reaching knowledge of things in themselves, and there are problems that arise from this move beyond ordinary commonsense knowledge of things for us, as we describe them from our perspective. First, science knows little of how things really are in themselves—its achievement is limited. Second, there is the problem of unifying the different levels of truth, or description. This is manifest with regard to such questions as the ontological status of consciousness. Third, the knowledge of things in themselves that science does achieve seems to present us with an insubstantial and skeletal mathematical model of things; it does not appear to give us the whole picture of these things and their interrelations.

Dummett suggests that if we accept the hypothesis of God's existence these problems are resolved. For God alone can provide that which is required—the unified knowledge of the whole, and of the parts of the whole in their interrelation. God's knowledge is not from within the world and so is not perspectival like ours. In saying that God is all knowing, however, we do not intend to state that God knows the truth of propositions which are in principle undecidable for us. When propositions are in principle undecidable we are not simply referring to our present limitations. Since God's knowledge of things in themselves constitutes what these things are, we can say that He is the creator of the world. Here, Dummett adds, we should avoid Newtonian picture-thinking of God as dropping a world into time and space as a human person drops a ball into an already flowing river. In making such remarks, one may note, Dummett appears to be close to the classical theism of St. Augustine and St. Thomas Aquinas. For the former insists that God does not create *in* time but *with* time. That is, in holding that space and time are themselves creatures, rather than some prior "receptacle" of creation, St. Augustine and St. Thomas in some fashion anticipate the insights of Einstein.

If I understand Dummett correctly it appears, however, that these reasons offered in support of accepting the existence of God do not constitute the principal argument for God's existence in the lecture, although they are interwoven with the presentation of the principal argument. That argument is to the effect that reality and mind cannot really be thought as so independent, one from the other, that the world could be without being known. Since our knowing cannot perform the task of knowing reality adequately we come to the idea that God is required; for He alone can perform this task.

There would be no point, Dummett maintains, in God creating a creatureless universe. But the further point that he urges is that thought of a universe without the God who knows it as it is in itself is meaningless. One might object here that surely science has good evidence to show that a mindless universe existed before human minds came into being at a certain point in time. In response Dummett argues that just because this was true at one time is not proof that it always was so and always will be so (27). He goes on to argue that we cannot talk of what the world is like without minds to know it, without implying by the use of words such as "like" that we are speaking from our conceptual framework. Therefore we cannot prescind from mind and speak of a mindless universe. Nor can we ask "How is the world to be described in itself independent of all knowers?" For we are seeking an account of the world not framed in any conceptual description. Dummett writes:

> Since it makes no sense to speak of a world, or the world, independently of how it is apprehended, this one world must be the world as it is apprehended by some mind, but not in any particular way, or from any one perspective rather than any other, but simply as it is: it constitutes the world as it is in itself . . . how God apprehends things as being must be how they are in themselves. (Lecture 4, 34)

At the conclusion of the Gifford Lectures Dummett brings a theological perspective to bear on questions arising from intuitionist logic. He observes that if we take it that in the affirmation "God is" the "is" is tenseless, as Frege thought possible, this implies that God can always distinguish between those of our thoughts which we shall later recognize as true or false, and those that will never be verified or falsified (40). This introduces a notion of the truth of a proposition as God's knowing that we shall recognize the proposition as true. This, in turn, implies a principle of trivalence at odds with intuitionist logic. By reference to God's knowing we can divide propositions into those that are or will be true, those that are or will be false, and those forever indeterminate. For God cannot determine propositions that are truly indeterminate. Thus a three-valued logic is required.

COMMENT

In offering a brief evaluation of the lectures one must bear in mind, as remarked above, the tentative way in which some of the points are put forward by Dummett.

If I may begin with the final theological considerations: I believe a number of Dummett's observations on the existence and nature of God harmonize quite well with the classical theological position of thinkers such as Aquinas, particularly with regard to God's timelessness and knowledge. Here, it seems to me, there is an invitation to other philosophical theologians to develop further Dummett's approach to these theological issues. However, I wonder how well some of Dummett's arguments would be received by nontheistic philosophers, and whether they amount to arguments forceful enough to offer a genuine challenge to the positions of such philosophers.

I have no doubt that Dummett is correct in responding to those who point to the history of the cosmos before the emergence of intelligent life as a counterexample to the claim that the world cannot be without mind, that this does not prove that this was always so or will always be so. However, this does not amount to a proof that the world cannot exist without mind. It is also without doubt true that in saying what the world is like we use a conceptual scheme and therefore demonstrate at once that we and our minds are involved in such a description. But in response one can point out that because someone says "I might not have been born," and thereby shows that the person knowing this fact does exist, has been born, this does not invalidate the correctness of the claim. That one knows and exists does not entail that one necessarily exists and knows. In this regard it is surely relevant to recall that Dummett himself does not espouse an idealist or relativist position such that we never truly give a correct description of reality independent of us. Does Dummett really show that the world could not exist without anyone to know of its existence, given that the existence of creatures like us who discuss the matter is only contingent? The skeptical philosopher might also, I think, question Dummett's insistence upon the need to find in God a nonperspectival knowing which gives unity to the world. Is there an argument to show, such a philosopher might ask, that the putative metaphysical and semantic desire for unity is one that can be satisfied?

I agree that if one accepts God's existence one does have a way of talking of a unified intelligent grasp of all there is. Science, and other cognitive disciplines, abstract in their laws, explanations, and statistical evaluations from knowledge of each and every concrete situation in the universe, and these disciplines are at best on the way to reaching their goal. And I agree with Dummett that the diverse perspectives of common sense and these cognitive disciplines may equally reach the truth. Both descriptive judgments and explanatory judgments may be either true or false. God's knowledge would in some respects be a unification of these related but diverse ways of knowing the world which, it should be added, cannot be shown to be the only ways of coming to know aspects of the universe.

However, Dummett's position goes further than this. He states that all we have in an explanatory, scientific account of things in themselves is a skeletal, insubstantial, mathematical account. He believes that even if we hold to a nonreductive view that allows for true statements from the perspectives of science and common sense, we are still left with the problem of harmonizing these accounts. He asks, is hearing the experience of sound, or is it a certain kind of scientifically determined wave phenomenon? Only God's knowledge can resolve this problem of harmonization, he believes. However, I am not convinced that once we do reject reductive accounts that a problem of harmonization remains. Why is it not legitimate to say that the phenomenon of "sound" is both a matter of a description of experience and a scientific account in terms both of physiological states and electromagnetic waves and the like? A scientific account strives to explain why chocolate ice cream tastes different to me from strawberry ice cream, and no doubt it is already possible, or will be in the near future, to stimulate my brain in such a way that these tastes are experienced without eating the respective ice creams. However, if these accounts do not purport to tell me *what* a certain flavor of ice cream tastes like but *why* it tastes different from another flavor, I do not see there need be conflict between the descriptive account and the purportedly explanatory one. With regard to human consciousness as a whole I think things become a little more complicated. For when one goes on to describe the interrelationship between the various acts of thought, one is in the realms of both description and explanation. That is, when one describes and relates such conscious acts as inquiry into sensation, and attention to the same, insight, the forming of hypotheses, and attempts to judge the truth or probability of one's concepts or theories, one is giving some kind of explanatory account. Indeed Frege's account of "force," and Dummett's analyses of the intelligent operations of the language user contribute not a little to such an account.[10] At the very least it is difficult to see what *else* Dummett thinks God would know beyond what is included in the scientific and commonsense ways of describing the world.

While I wonder, therefore, whether Dummett's theological reflection would convince a nontheist philosopher, even one who in other ways was influenced by Dummett's philosophy, I believe there is something to the point he makes concerning the intimate connection between mind and reality. For I think that at root most of the cosmological arguments for God's existence, including those found in Aquinas's work, revolve around the insight that since the universe is knowable in its existence and essence, and is therefore intelligible, there is an intelligible dependence of the universe on mind, on God. In a short contribution such as this, however, I cannot develop these points further nor examine the ways in which such a position might relate to that outlined by Dummett.

Moving on to some of Dummett's other views put forward in the lectures, views characteristic of his philosophy as a whole, I should like, briefly, to offer some comments from the perspective of a philosophical position that is Thomist in inspiration.

To begin with, Dummett's interest in conscious mental activity and his rejection of positions that would deny the importance or even existence of such activity is naturally welcome from a Thomist perspective. Further, I believe Dummett's insistence that the way to investigate intelligent thought is through the study of language is, in fact, not at variance with the Thomist viewpoint. Karen Green has pointed out that the intimate association between language and thought upon which Dummett insists is also asserted by thinkers such as Nietzsche, and I think one should also regard Aquinas as a thinker sympathetic to this perspective.[11]

In fact, in very broad terms one can view Dummett's emphasis on the intimate relationship between thought and language as representing a philosophical option in the tradition which stands in contrast to the Platonic or Cartesian notion of a direct and unmediated approach to thought. On Aquinas's view human thinking in this life must begin with insight into "phantasm" or mental imagery, and this also holds for insight into one's own mental activity. Such mental imagery naturally includes words and language as well as perceptual and other sensory data. The way to come to study our own thinking involves, for Aquinas, attention directed first to the objects aimed at in our mental acts, then attention to those acts themselves, and then to the "faculties" or dispositions they manifest.[12] Such an approach, therefore, emphasizes that our mental acts are manifest in linguistic acts, and thus attention to them is had only through attention to language. That being said, one must also realize that to understand the acts at all involves at once recognizing, as an aspect of what they are, what Frege calls the "force," or intentional aim, with which they are expressed. Even when our conscious insights are not expressed in fully articulate linguistic concepts, as in the case of the person in Dummett's example who knows how to dance the rumba, but not how to give an articulate account, the insight is still into "imagery": into the images and sensations of the dance and its patterns and into the various words spoken regarding directions to be followed.

The way in which Dummett draws attention to the "mysterious" process of language growth going forward together with the growth in knowledge, would also be welcome from this perspective. As I mentioned above, it appears to offer the possibility of enriching the perspectives of analytical philosophy by encouraging analysts to reflect at greater length upon concept formation, and the process by which we revise and reject concepts and hypotheses. If this invitation is taken up, analytical philosophers will no doubt find some helpful insights in other philosophical traditions, and I would include among these the Thomist tradition.[13]

I would also point out that Dummett's attack on what he terms "classical logic," and the use he makes of approaches taken over from intuitionist logic to identify the scope and limits of the application of the principle of excluded middle are cognate with what I believe to be the

Thomistic viewpoint. Bernard Lonergan, a philosopher of Thomistic inspiration, writes of the principle of excluded middle:

> The principle of excluded middle possesses ultimate but not immediate validity; it possesses ultimate validity because, if a judgement occurs, it must be either an affirmation or a denial; it does not possess immediate validity, for with respect to each proposition, rational consciousness is presented with the three alternatives of affirmation, of negation, and of seeking a better understanding and so a more adequate formulation of the issue.[14]

And Lonergan points out that this reserve with regard to excluded middle is manifest in the "logic" of scholastic dialectic in which one always reserved the right to seek further clarification of terms.[15] In his writing on Aquinas in the 1940s Lonergan made the further point that Aquinas's approach to the analysis of mind sought insight into the development of intelligence as it moved from attention to sensation, to understanding, to judgment, and therefore Aquinas's was not the way of many modern works on philosophy of mind which seek to encapsulate the workings of human intelligence in a few well-formulated principles of logic (important as such principles are).[16]

With regard to his position on metaphysics there is an area where I would seek further clarification from Dummett. Dummett holds that in learning a language we acquire familiarity and mastery in a certain domain but then may go astray when in a naive fashion we attempt to extrapolate and make general or universal claims which, in truth, we are in no position to confirm nor deny. The question of surveyability with regard to proof has been at the center of debates which have raged during the last one hundred years over our ability to quantify across domains and our capacity to establish validity and consistency in logical and mathematical systems.

I have no doubt that there are cases in which there occurs an illegitimate extrapolation from insights had in a particular area to claims regarding a more general domain. A notorious example in the history of philosophy is, of course, the insistence of Kantian thought on the uniqueness of Euclidean geometry. However, the question I would ask of Dummett's position is whether there are not still general principles, be these logical or principles of intelligibility, which we bring to the localized situations over which we do come to have cognitive mastery. Upon reflection we note that such principles operative in our thinking are not determined by localized conditions but are rather a priori insofar as they enter into our knowledge of the localized phenomena (and even allow us to make the judgment that these phenomena are local as opposed to nonlocal). If we deny outright that there are such, we seem to land in a crude form of empiricism, a kind of Russellian knowledge by acquaintance, and I do not think Dummett's position is implicated in such empiricism, particularly when we are talking of properly formulated and verified human knowing. In fact, Dummett, in the lectures, does make mention of a priori elements that enter into our evaluation of the truth or falsity of a proposition, but I am not sure what such a priori elements include on Dummett's view. Perhaps it is the case that Dummett has dealt with this somewhere else at length, but I have not come across such a treatment in the works by him that I have read. I would agree with philosophers such as Richard Cartwright that there remains the possibility of formulating certain general principles of intelligibility and logic which are operative in the particular case of knowing but cannot be limited in their validity to the particular case.[17] As I understand it, Dummett's justificationist position is opposed to crude empiricism and naive realism precisely because these positions fail to understand that reality is nothing other than that which is known through the use of intelligence and reason. This surely implies the a priori principle, implicit in all our attempts to know what is the case, that reality is the intelligible and reasonable.

One final matter I would wish to comment upon regarding Dummett's position as outlined in the Gifford Lectures is his view of the past and our knowledge of it. As I mentioned above, Dummett's argument that the future is undetermined, and that therefore one cannot demand that a future-regarding proposition must be either true or false as it stands, would be one welcome to some earlier philosophers in the Western tradition, including Christian ones. However, the view he takes of the nature of the past is, I think, more controversial.

Dummett is clear that our notion of what it is for something to be in the past is in some ways basic, and yet there are naive expectations about both past and future that may need to be challenged through philosophical analysis. I have already mentioned the thought experiment he gives of the blindfolded person searching for objects in a darkened room, in order to point to a naive way of understanding the future; we imagine that the future is the sum of things that are already there just waiting to be discovered by the blindfolded person. However, Dummett also indicates that we are wont to extend similar naive anticipations in the other direction, to the past. On the justificationist view, on the contrary, all we can say is that the objects taken to be from the past can only be said to be such when, and if, the blindfolded researcher discovers them. We could say that they come into existence at the moment of discovery.

Does such a tale do justice to our intuitions concerning the past? The abandonment of certain fundamental intuitions concerning the past means the abandonment of the notion of the past altogether, and it appears to me that Dummett's position is in danger of threatening such fundamental intuitions. I think there are perhaps other lessons to be learned from the story, lessons at variance with the point Dummett wishes to make. For the blindfolded researcher not only derives a notion of past and future from encounters along the journey of discovery, but also from the inner history of his or her own experience of journeying. Thus, in a way that substantiates Dummett's views on the indeterminacy of the future, the blind researcher at time t_2 does not know definitely what will be the case with regard to possible discoveries, *nor* with regard to him or herself at future time t_3; the future is essentially open. But with regard to the past, things are different. At time t_2, the "now" of the researcher's experience, the researcher is aware of some experiences, of discovery or disappointment in that regard, as having been in the past, as having occurred at time t_1. I would suggest that the notion of the past that the researcher has involves the idea that the past was what was true of him or her at time t_1, and of what was true, what was the case, with regard to anything else at that same time t_1. I do not think one can depart from this heuristic notion, of *whatever was definitely the case just as "such and such" was definitely the case with me*, a notion guiding future discovery of what happened in the past, without departing from our basic notion of the "past" altogether.

HERMENEUTICS, THE EUCHARIST, AND ETHICS

Mention of Michael Dummett's name to anyone familiar with the recent literature of English-speaking Catholic theology will invariably lead to mention of the debate he initiated in the pages of *New Blackfriars* in the late 1980s.[18] In his article "A Remarkable Consensus" Dummett outlined and attacked what he considered to be the deplorable state of so-called Catholic theological education in many seminaries and institutions of learning in the United States.[19] He argued that theological liberalism was rife in such institutions and that such liberalism, which denied dogmas of faith such as the Virgin Birth and the Resurrection, threatened to make Catholicism an object of ridicule before the world. The denial of such doctrines implies that one can no longer be considered a Catholic in the sense in which the Church understands the word, and the denial of doctrines on the part of those responsible for teaching the young entails that such teaching is fraudulent. Dummett's forthright objections to what was going on gained him both supporters and opponents in the pages of the journal. In the opinion of the present writer, none of Dummett's detractors came anywhere near to showing that his arguments as to the incoherence and irresponsibility of such liberal dissent were unfounded.

One of Dummett's preoccupations in the debate was with the dubious validity of much modern New Testament scholarship—scholarship which claims that the dogmas concerning Christ and the Church should now be rejected as intellectually flawed. Dummett later expanded on some of the points he had made against this kind of theology in the *New Blackfriars* debate in a contribution to a volume on philosophy and scriptural scholarship edited by Elenore Stump.[20] Dummett argued that in many instances of such revisionary scholarship one encounters a crippling naïveté with regard to the philosophical background assumptions that are tacitly present in the arguments put forward. Dummett is certainly not a lone voice, and there are many philosophers and theologians working in the area of hermeneutics or historiography who would share his point of view. Indeed, the more one becomes familiar with the history of the changing fashions that have occurred in the area of scriptural scholarship over the last two and a half centuries, and with the way these have been linked to phases in the history of German philosophy and theories of historical knowing during this period, the more one may be tempted to an out and out skepticism with regard to the deliverances of the New Testament scholar. However, I do not think one need arrive at this point of hyperbolic doubt as to the validity of the results of any such scholarship (Dummett does not do so), and I believe that it is precisely scholars who are aware of the importance of philosophical background issues, scholars like N. T. Wright and Ben F. Meyer for example, who appear more likely to arrive at sober and sound conclusions which are, in fact, in harmony with the historic doctrines of Christianity.[21]

During the same period as the *New Blackfriars* debate Dummett contributed an essay on the Eucharist to a *Festschrift* for the Oxford philosopher of religion Basil Mitchell.[22] The essay covers a number of topics and makes clear Dummett's familiarity with writing in the area of Catholic dogmatic theology and liturgical history. He offers some interesting insights into the way the Eucharist (the Sacrament which Catholics believe is the body and blood of Christ under the forms of bread and wine), differs from the other six sacraments of the Catholic religion. Naturally from a philosophical perspective the most interesting part of the essay involves a philosophical exploration of the intelligibility of the Catholic belief that after the words of the consecration uttered by the priest at the sacrifice of the Mass, the bread and wine become, in reality, Christ's body and blood. This is referred to as transubstantiation.

Dummett is well aware that Catholic dogma on this matter, as defined at the Council of Trent, affirms certain truths that a Catholic must hold, but leaves other questions open. Thus, as Dummett points out, a Catholic must hold that the "what it is" has in reality changed from bread and wine into the glorified body of Christ. Dummett does not wish to follow either Aquinas's account of how we can understand this change, nor that of the seventeenth-century Cartesians. Instead he takes as his starting point recent theories of "transignification," while identifying the shortcomings of these theories and indicating a way of developing the idea so as to render it satisfactory from an orthodox Catholic perspective. It is true that there is a change when we use certain things in a new way and a new meaning is conferred upon them, a band of metal becomes a wedding ring when we use it as such. But Dummett points out that proponents of transignification fall into error when they fail to see the limitations of their viewpoint. For we cannot change the real nature of many things just by different use, and indeed, we should rightly see it as morally reprehensible *ab*use if we should deem other human beings or even animals mere things to be used by us as we please. However, Dummett does believe that if we push the notion of "deeming" further we may arrive at a satisfactory account of the doctrine. In all our use of the idea of "deeming" that something is to be seen or understood in some modified way there remain ways in which we can say the thing is not truly totally transformed into something different. However, if we understand the transformation of the bread and wine into the body and blood of Christ as God's "deeming" that the bread and wine are now such, then, in this case, no such reservation may be expressed. For since God's knowledge constitutes what a thing in itself really is, it cannot but be true that the bread and wine are now transformed into Christ's body and blood.[23] The use of the notion of "deeming" in this special sense, Dummett thinks, does help us to make sense of the Catholic doctrine.

I have the impression that some of the same Catholic theologians who applauded Dummett's stand and arguments in the *New Blackfriars* debate may have felt a little uneasy with his views on the Eucharist. I would point out, however, that in the essay it is clear that Dummett strives to express a position in accord with Catholic dogma on the Eucharist, and, clearly, believes that he does so. I believe the matter is clarified somewhat if one focuses on Dummett's brief remarks in the essay concerning the fact that only God knows the true nature of certain things in themselves, and that since His knowledge constitutes these things it is infallible.[24] When one sees these remarks in the wider context of the position Dummett outlines in the Gifford Lectures, I have the sense that it is this idea that is doing the real work in the Eucharist essay rather than the "deeming" notion. That is, since we do not know the true nature of things in the world, and God does, it is not unintelligible to say that data which appears to suggest the presence of one reality may, if God wishes it, really be data on another reality. In fact, I am not sure how helpful the idea of "deeming" is, or what it contributes further to the argument. For Dummett, as we have seen, tells us that in the case of God's "deeming" there is no gap, as in human deeming, between the thinking of something *as if* it were something other, and the way the thing really is. It is hard to see how, in that case, God's deeming bears a significant resemblance to human deeming and how it is not, on the contrary, a straightforward knowing and constituting a reality as it is. If the notion of deeming is not really essential to Dummett's position, I think that his view and that of a modern Thomist are not at all far from each other.

For St. Thomas, as for even the boldest advocate of scientific realism in our day, our knowledge of the essences or natures of things is limited and is hard to come by.[25] Hume brought home to us the fact that knowledge of causes is largely (I think there are exceptions) an inferential affair, and this, I believe, applies as much to "formal" causes as it does to others. Thus, on a view which recognizes the, in principle, revisability of science, but which allows that certain scientific positions are at least probable, one can grant that while the formal cause, the *what* of a thing, may, given the data be said in all probability to be an x, one cannot rule it out that similar data may have a different formal cause, may be data of a different thing, a y. In the case of the Eucharist, then, since, as Dummett says, God alone knows definitively what each thing in itself truly is, it is not unintelligible to hold that in a particular case the data before one are not data on whatever bread and wine may, in the normal course of things, be, but have as their formal cause, their explanatory *what*, the body and blood of Christ. And one holds this because one believes one has on God's authority that it is true.

I turn, finally, to comment on three papers on ethics in which Dummett's Christian and Catholic commitments are, in varying degrees, evident. In 1969 Dummett published a paper on the Catholic Church's teaching on contraception at the height of the controversy raging in the aftermath of the publication of Pope Paul VI's encyclical *Humanae vitae*, an encyclical which reaffirmed Catholic doctrine on the matter.[26] The Pope followed the advice of a minority committee which urged fidelity to the perennial stand of the Church against contraception, while the report of a majority of advisors in favor of change was rejected. Dummett examined the arguments of the majority in favor of change and found their position flawed. The majority had argued that a change in the area of the Church's teaching rendering contraception morally licit would in no way alter the perennial teaching of the Church concerning other areas of sexual morality. Dummett rejected this position, writing that such a change would imply that the Church's constant teaching on the immorality of sexual intercourse outside marriage would also need revision. The traditionalist minority, whose views the Pope endorsed, had the stronger arguments according to Dummett. One may well feel that there was an element of prophecy in the position taken by Dummett at the time, since within a decade or so noted theologians like Charles Curran, who had followed the majority view and had dissented from the Papal teaching on contraception, were arguing not only for a rejection of Papal teaching on this matter but that virtually all of the Church's teaching on sexual morality required radical revision.[27] However, in the article Dummett also concluded that the arguments brought forward to defend traditional Church teaching on the immorality of certain sexual acts needed development, since they did not appear to him to be compelling. Commenting on the views Dummett put forward in the article of 1969, Professor Janet Smith has suggested that it is in the teaching and writing of Pope John Paul II on marriage and human sexuality that one may find a more satisfactory defense and exposition of the traditional teaching in this area than that which Dummett found wanting.[28] Whether Dummett would agree with her judgment I do not know.

Two articles that appeared in the 1980s on the immorality of nuclear deterrence also manifest Dummett's Christian background and concerns.[29] In "Nuclear Warfare" and "The Morality of Deterrence" Dummett argues that the use of weapons of mass destruction and the threat to use them are both gravely immoral. In both essays he suggests that in the past both the code of chivalry and the tradition of just war theory developed by Christian theologians placed limits upon what was justified in war. War is always a terrible evil to be avoided, but in a society in which Christian just war theory exerted some influence there were at least attempts to lessen the barbarities unleashed in violent conflict. It is questionable, Dummett maintains, whether some of the prescriptions of just war theory could ever obtain in all circumstances on the battlefield. But at least there was an attempt to draw the line between what might be permitted in conflict and what was seen as utterly without justification. He goes on to argue, however, that in an historical trend which accelerated during the Second World War there occurred a more or less conscious abandonment by Western leaders of the old Christian theoretical constraints upon bellicose actions. These leaders, including those in the democracies, employed various propaganda techniques, during the war and in the cold war period, in order little by little to erode the commitment of the people of their countries to these older, and now held to be outmoded, views. Pretty much anything could now be justified in defending "our way of life" from the threat posed by the Nazis and Communists, including the mass bombing of noncombatants and the obliteration of entire cities through fire bombing or nuclear attack.

Reading "Nuclear Warfare" without reference to "The Morality of Deterrence," one may have the impression that Dummett is ruling out the morality of nuclear deterrence as implicated in a false consequentialist ethic. However, writing in the former essay he claims "If the obliteration of whole cities, or whole populations, is not murder, there is no such thing as murder; if it is not wrong, then nothing is wrong,"[30] and it is clear that on his view the immorality of such mass destruction is grasped in a moral intuition which is fundamental. Therefore, as he argues in "The Morality of Deterrence," the act or rule consequentialist should also feel the moral repugnance any sane person should feel at the prospect of our nations launching a nuclear attack. Nevertheless, it seems to me that the view he puts forward in the two essays has an anti-consequentialist flavor to it insofar as the essays offer a historical sketch of how our societies moved from a moral position which held that some things done in the name of national self-defense are always prohibited, to the acceptance of a moral code according to which any kind of violent act can be justified as a means to the end of defending "our way of life." As such, it appears to me that Dummett shares the concerns expressed in Pope John Paul II's encyclical letter on morality *Veritatis Splendor* in the closing sections of which the Pope put forward the view that the only way of life worth pursuing is one in which certain moral absolutes regarding the rights of persons in community prohibit the use of evil means in the attempt to defend that way of life.[31]

From the viewpoint of not a few observers, Dummett's defense of the minority viewpoint on the immorality of contraception, that endorsed by Pope Paul VI, on the one hand, and, on the other, his passionate attack on nuclear defense as ethically indefensible, might appear paradoxical. Does he not appear to want to side both with the moral Left and with the moral Right? However, the Catholic thinker may hold that such evaluations, based upon dichotomies taken for granted in popular Western culture, are wide of the mark. Dummett is not alone in holding these moral views. The influential moral theologians Germain Grisez and John Finnis are well known both as supporters of the Church's position on contraception, and as advocates of the view that nuclear defense is immoral.[32] Indeed, Dummett's views on these issues, as on other ethical issues with which he has been preoccupied, such as the rights of refugees and immigrants,[33] are quite consistent from the perspective of the tradition of Catholic teaching on family and social life, as is clear if one examines the writings of the Popes during the last century and a half.[34]

I began this essay by drawing attention to the fact that Michael Dummett's work seems to be divided between two worlds which have little to do with one another. Those conversant with his contributions to the world of professional analytical philosophy appear, for the most part, to be unaware of his published writing in the area of Catholic theology, and the Catholic theologians who know of his work in their field may know little concerning the details of his overall philosophical position. In this essay I hope to have drawn attention to ways in which Dummett's theological writing connects with his philosophical work. If one is to have an appreciation of his thought as a whole one cannot ignore his contributions to theological discussion. Indeed his theological writing cannot be ignored by anyone wishing to evaluate his philosophical work, for, as we have seen, his contributions to Catholic theology also involve philosophical exploration. This is the case if one examines his thought on the metaphysical question of the real Presence of Christ in the Eucharist, or on issues to do with historical method as these have a bearing on scriptural studies. Further, as I have attempted to make clear in my discussion of the Gifford Lectures one cannot understand the question of God's existence as something extraneous to Dummett's overall philosophical vision. For it is Dummett's contention that the philosopher's task of rendering explicit what is implicit in the language of human beings must inevitably result in the philosopher grappling with metaphysical questions and, he believes, fundamental among such questions is that of the existence of God.

ANDREW BEARDS

MARYVALE INSTITUTE
OCTOBER 2002

NOTES

1. B. McGuinness and G. Oliveri, eds., *The Philosophy of Michael Dummett* (Dordrecht: Kluwer Academic Publishers, 1994).

2. McGuinness and Oliveri, *The Philosophy of Michael Dummett*; and Karen Green, *Dummett: Philosophy of Language* (Oxford: Polity Press, 2001), 93–94.

3. *Editor's note*: Dummett's Gifford Lectures have appeared as *Thought and Reality* (Oxford: Oxford Univ. Press), but were not available for page references at press time.

4. See "The Intelligibility of Eucharistic Doctrine," in *The Rationality of Religious Belief: Essays in Honour of Basil Mitchell*, ed. W. J. Abrahams and S. W. Holter (Oxford: Clarendon, 1987), 231–61, especially 243–61.

5. See his *Origins of Analytical Philosophy* (London: Duckworth, 1993).

6. Pope John Paul II, *Fides et Ratio* (London: CTS, 1998), 122–24.

7. See John Searle, *Intentionality* (London: Cambridge Univ. Press, 1983), ch. 6.

8. *Origins*, chs. 6, 11, and 12.

9. One idea put forward in the lectures which Dummett now rejects is that of reality as cumulative (Letter to the present author dated 11 October 2001).

10. Of course, reductionist or naturalist attempts to explain these conscious experiences away usually end up with the naturalist arguing in an incoherent fashion that the goal of reasoned argument is not attainable, or cannot be known to have been reached, since the forces which determine the process of thought and argument are other than one's native intellectual and rational capacities.

11. Green, *Dummett: Philosophy of Language*, 200.

12. St. Thomas Aquinas, *In III de Anima*, lect. 9, #724; *In Sent.*, 23, 1.

13. For an analysis of other forms of conscious mental activity beyond those Dummett considers see my article, "Anti-Realism and Critical Realism: Dummett and Lonergan," *The Downside Review* 391 (1995): 119–55.

14. Bernard Lonergan, *Insight: A Study of Human Understanding* (London: Darton: Longman and Todd, 1957), 381.

15. Bernard Lonergan, *Understanding and Being: Collected Works Vol. 5*, ed. F. Crowe (Univ. of Toronto Press, 1990), 116.

16. Bernard Lonergan, *Verbum: Word and Idea in Aquinas*, ed. D. Burrell, (London: Darton, Longman and Todd, 1967), 55.

17. See Richard Cartwright, "Speaking of Everything." *Noûs* 28 (March 1994): 1–20.

18. "A Remarkable Consensus," *New Blackfriars* 68 (1987): 424–43. Dummett responded to contributors to the debate in *New Blackfriars* 68 (1987): 557–66 and in vol. 69 (1988): 237–45, 530–44.

19. That Dummett was right in his estimation of the doctrinal and moral confusion which reigned in a good number of Catholic seminaries and institutions of learning in the United States in the 1980s is borne out by recent well documented studies like that of Michael S. Rose, *Goodbye, Good Men* (Washington, DC: Regnery, 2001). Although many problems remain, Rose and others show that during the 1990s things began to improve as new seminaries and Catholic institutions, with a desire to promote authentic doctrine and moral formation, began to attract increasing numbers of students, while some of the older institutions continued to decline for want of new students.

20. Dummett, "The Impact of Scriptural Studies on the Content of Catholic Belief," in *Hermes and Athena: Biblical Exegesis and Philosophical Theology*, ed. E. Stump and T. P. Flint (Notre Dame, IN: Univ. of Notre Dame Press, 1993), 3–22.

21. See N. T. Wright, *Jesus and the Victory of God* (London: SPCK, 1996); Ben F. Meyer, *Reality and Illusion in New Testament Scholarship* (Collegeville, MN: The Liturgical Press, 1995).

22. Dummett, "The Intelligibility of Eucharistic Doctrine," in Abrahams and Holter, *The Rationality of Religious Belief*, 231–61.

23. Ibid., 252.

24. Ibid., 255.

25. See St. Thomas Aquinas, *In Ioan.*, cap. 1, lect. 1; also *In III Sent.*, d. 23, q. 1, a. 2.

26. "The Documents of the Papal Commission on Birth Control," *New Blackfriars* 50 (1969): 241–50.

27. Charles Curran, *New Perspectives in Moral Theology* (Notre Dame, IN: Univ. of Notre Dame Press, 1976), 20.

28. Janet Smith, *Humanae Vitae: A Generation Later* (Washington, DC: Catholic Univ. of America Press, 1991), 376 n 86.

29. Michael Dummett, "Nuclear Warfare," in *Objections to Nuclear Defense*, ed. N. Blake and K. Pole (London: Routledge & Kegan Paul, 1984), 28–40; "The Morality of Deterrence," *Canadian Journal of Philosophy*, supplementary vol. 12

(1986): 111–27.

    30. Dummett, "Nuclear Warfare," 36.

    31. Pope John Paul II, *Veritatis Splendor* (London: CTS, 1993), 147–52.

    32. See John C. Ford, SJ, Germain Grisez, Joseph Boyle, John Finnis, and William E. May, *The Teaching of Humanae Vitae: A Defense* (San Francisco: Ignatius Press, 1988); John Finnis, Joseph M. Boyle, Jr., and Germain Grisez, *Nuclear Deterrence, Morality and Realism* (Oxford: Clarendon Press, 1987).

    33. See Michael Dummett, *On Immigrants and Refugees* (London: Routledge, 2001).

    34. With respect to modern warfare and the drift to the ethics of "total war" as described by Dummett, one may note the condemnation of the arms race engaged in by Western powers by Pope Leo XIII in his 1889 address *Notis errorem*. Aerial bombing of civilians and noncombatants in the Spanish Civil war evoked condemnation by the official Vatican paper *L'Osservatore Romano* in 1938, and condemnation of this type of military action was reiterated by Pope Pius XII in his 1939 encyclical *Summi Pontificatus* (106). Already in the influential 1912 (Appleton) *Catholic Encyclopaedia* we find the author of the article on "War" (546–50) writing of the immorality of the tactics employed by General Sherman, an advocate of "total war" philosophy, during his march to the South in the American Civil War.

REPLY TO ANDREW BEARDS

Professor Beards is right to say that there has been little connection between my published philosophical writings and my occasional writings about moral and religious topics. This is in large part because I have never attempted to compose a *summa* or expound "my philosophical system"; I have simply tried to tackle such problems as have interested me and on which I believed that I could throw some light. Christian doctrines of the type that are held to rest on revelation, rather than being accessible to the unaided reason, such as the Incarnation, the Trinity, and the Eucharist, frequently call for elucidation by the exercise of analytical thought, of just the same kind as is required by philosophical problems, and in particular by physical theories such as quantum mechanics. Professor Richard Dawkins has complained of religious beliefs that they offer too simple a picture of reality, one that is too easily understood, whereas, he thinks, we should expect to find reality perplexing and hard to understand. As a criticism of Christian belief, this appears to me wildly wide of the mark. I agree that we should expect to find reality perplexing. Physical theories are indeed often perplexing; but so are doctrines of the kind I have just mentioned. It indeed seems to me that it tells in favour of the truth of the Christian creed that it presents reality as intellectually perplexing in the way that it does: that is just how we ought to expect things to be.

The only doctrine of this kind of which I have published any attempted analysis is the Eucharist, as Beards notes. I have written about the Resurrection and the Virgin Birth, but not analytically. Natural theology is that branch of philosophy which enquires, independently of revelation, into the existence or non-existence of God and into what can be said about His nature. Richard Dawkins has argued that theology in general has no subject-matter; but he himself, in arguing against the existence of God, or, more exactly, in rebutting one argument for God's existence, has contributed to natural theology. I originally thought that natural theology could not be tackled by a philosopher until he had answers to a large range of philosophical problems. I no longer think that. My own work has been stimulated by interest in a selection of fundamental questions: the nature of linguistic meaning and the content of thoughts; what truth is; and the basis—that is, the rationale—of logical laws. I should add to this list the many problems about time that philosophical reflection poses, and, of course, the foundations of mathematics and the richness of the a priori which its existence displays. These questions are all fundamental in the sense that thinking about them does not demand the prior solution of a range of other problems. All of them abut on metaphysics; especially so does enquiry into the nature of truth. The world is the totality of facts, not things, and facts are true propositions; so the concept of truth is the hinge upon which the door from the philosophy of thought opens into metaphysics, that is, the range of philosophical problems that concern the general character of reality. Natural theology is a part of metaphysics; so it lies much closer to the most fundamental part of philosophy than does, for example, ethics.

The notion of objectivity, as applied to linguistic statements, bifurcates into that which is independent of *me* and that which is independent of *us*—what is independent of the individual speaker and what is independent of human beings as a whole. The former we may call individually objective, and the latter universally objective. Individually subjective utterances are usually so because of some explicitly indexical ingredient, as in "From where I am standing, the house is hidden by the trees," or by some implicit indexical, as with "The house is hidden by the trees." The dispute between a realist and a justificationist interpretation relates to individually objective statements; it has nothing to do with whether or not they are universally objective. Individually objective statements are objective in virtue of there being a commonly agreed criterion for what requires us to recognise them as true, indefeasibly or defeasibly. The question at issue between the realist and the justificationist is whether we have a conception of what it is for such statements to be true in the absence of any ground accessible to us for recognising them as such.

This question is independent of whether the statement is universally objective or not; the only assumption common to the realist and to his opponent is that there are agreed criteria for what demands that we recognise the statement as true. The principle of bivalence is that every individually objective statement is determinately either true or false; this is tantamount to accepting the classical interpretation of negation. The principle is essential to realism. I may once have thought that a belief in the existence of God underpinned adherence to bivalence. If so, I think so no longer. The thought that God's omniscience entails that He must know, for any statement, whether or not it is true, has no power to deliver bivalence, any more than the thought that Shakespeare must have known the answer to the question whether Hamlet—his Hamlet—parted his hair on the left, in the middle, or on the right. There may be no truth to the matter; and equally, if bivalence fails, there may be no answer to be given to the question whether a particular statement is true or false. An omniscient being must know the answer to every question that has an answer, but need know no answer to a question that does not have an answer.

A universally objective statement is one couched in terms that do not rely for their significance on the position of human beings in the universe, upon human reactions or upon human modes of perception. Such a statement aims at describing things as they are in themselves, independently of the manner in which we apprehend them. Scientific descriptions, particularly those of physics, strive to attain the status of universal objectivity. Physics substitutes wave-length or frequency of a sound-wave or electromagnetic wave for pitch or colour. The concepts of pitch and colour are to be explained in terms of how something sounds or looks to human percipients. Those of wave-length and frequency are not, and hence the replacement of the former by the latter constitutes an advance towards universal objectivity. But complete universal objectivity is difficult to attain. Were it attained, what we should have would be a bloodless mathematical model, of which it would make no sense to say that it constituted the world as it is in itself, that that was what there really is.

Is the conception of a description of the world as it is in itself chimerical, then? It cannot be. There are many different kinds of sentient creatures upon this planet; there may be others, even more different from us, elsewhere in the universe. Their sensory systems, and to a greater degree, their cognitive capacities, differ widely from ours; we can form only a hazy idea of their experience of the world. We may say that theirs are different worlds from ours, though worlds that intersect our own. But we want to claim that we and they inhabit the *same* world. This can be made out if we can explain their and our own experience and conception of the world as the result of the interaction of the world—the world as it is in itself—with creatures with particular sensory and mental capacities. But the notion of the world as it is in itself, considered as the goal of scientific enquiry, has crumbled.

We are seeking a description of reality independent of our own sensory experience, position in the cosmos, and modes of thought, a description of it as it might be if it contained no sentient, let alone rational, creatures. But the conception of a universe devoid of sentient life is a fantasy. What would be the difference between God's conceiving of such a universe and His actually creating it? What would it add to the description of such a universe to say that it *existed*? Matter and radiation can exist only insofar as we, or other sentient creatures, can know—by experience or inference—of their existence. It may be objected that it is certain that, in an early stage, the universe did not yet contain any sentient creatures. It does not follow that it could have been forever devoid of life. We know by inference that there was such an early stage of the universe: its having existed depends upon the possibility of our knowing this.

It makes no sense to speak of a world, or the world, independently of how it is apprehended. The one world which we and other creatures with different sensory and cognitive capacities inhabit must be the world as it is apprehended by some mind, but not *in any particular way*, or from any one perspective rather than any other, but simply as it is: it constitutes the world as it is in itself. God, who stands over against the world, has no particular point of view, no location *in* the world, no perspective contrasted with other perspectives. It is only by adopting this conception that we can allow a place for the idea of the world as it is in itself, an idea which demands that we give a place to it. How things are in themselves consists in the way that God apprehends them. That is the only way in which we can make sense of our conviction that there is such a thing as the world as it is in itself, which we apprehend in certain ways and other beings apprehend in other ways. To conceive of the world as it is in itself requires conceiving of a mind that apprehends it as it is in itself.

We may presume that God knows whatever mathematical theory accounts for the behaviour of physical reality, that is, of matter and radiation: that theory of everything that physics strives to uncover. But His knowledge of the universe cannot be confined to this: He also knows how the different types of sentient creatures will apprehend their physical environment, what their experience of it will be. It is their experience of it that gives substance to its existence, to its being real rather than merely conceived. So the mathematical structure that represents the behaviour of the physical universe cannot be taken to be what there really is, the universe as it is in itself. Reality, as it is in itself, that is, as God knows it, comprises also that experience of it that living things have insofar as they apprehend it; and it would make no sense to say that it could exist if there were no such experience.

Professor Beards asks "what *else* Dummett thinks God would know beyond what is included in the scientific and commonsense ways of describing the world." Well, apart from the mathematical truths that He knows, He knows how various creatures will apprehend the physical world, as I just remarked; and He surely knows what it is like for them so to apprehend it. I am not among those who regard as spurious Tom Nagel's notion of what it is like to have experiences which we can describe only in terms of their physical stimuli and the capacities they confer on those who have them; to wonder how things look to someone with a certain type of colour-blindness is not to ask an empty or an incoherent question. God knows how the world appears to all His creatures, and He knows what it is like to have them appear so.

Professor Beards commends me for acknowledging the changelessness of God; but I fear he has misunderstood me on this point. I have always had great difficulty with the theological tenet that God does not change, for a theological reason and a philosophical one. The Creed says, "For us men and for our salvation He *came down* from heaven; by the power of the Holy Spirit He *became* incarnate from the Virgin Mary, and *was made* man"; I have italicised words that seem to me to make difficulties for that tenet. According to Christian doctrine, before Mary conceived Jesus in her womb, the Second Person of the Trinity had not yet taken on human nature; after she had done so, He had. If that is not a change, I cannot imagine what is.

The philosophical objection is to the thesis that God is not in time, which is possibly stronger than the tenet that God is unchanging: one could perhaps be in time and yet never change, although awareness that one was in time would depend on an awareness of changes outside one, and hence on changes in the content of one's awareness. God must apprehend things as they are; to apprehend things that are in time as being in time it is necessary to apprehend them as changing. It is possible to apprehend things as being in space without oneself being in that space, as we apprehend the constellations as being in the space of the heavens, which we can map, without ourselves being in that space. It is irrelevant that the constellations consist of stars in a space in which we are also located, their apparent unity due only to near coincidence of their lines of sight: we apprehend them as configurations in a space we are not in, and this is enough to establish the point. But we cannot apprehend anything as being in time without ourselves being in that time. Of course, we can watch a representation of something that takes place in time, a cinema film for example, without our watching being contemporaneous with the events represented and conceivably without ourselves being in the time within which those events occurred. This is beside the point, however: we cannot apprehend anything as being in time without being in the time of that process, and we cannot apprehend a representation of something as being in time without ourselves being in the time of that representation. There can, of course, be a representation of something that takes place in time that is not itself in time, and therefore does not represent it as being in time, for instance a strip cartoon. We can apprehend such a representation: but we cannot apprehend the thing itself, as it is, without being in the time within which it takes place. Since God must apprehend temporal processes as they really are, He cannot be outside time. I willingly admit to uncertainty whether this reasoning is conclusive: but it unquestionably demands an answer.

Professor Beards expresses some dissatisfaction with the treatment of the past in my Gifford lectures; I, too, have felt some doubts about it. In my essay of long ago, "The Reality of the Past," I set out to make a case for strong anti-realism about the past, in order to discover whether or not a coherent such case could be made and what it would involve. Since then, I have tended, with some discomfort, to adopt such a view of the past; my failure to publish my Gifford lectures is largely due to my feeling that they probably ought to be revised in this regard, and finding no time to carry out such a revision, with the constant demands to lecture and to give papers on diverse subjects to conferences. Recently I sought in the Dewey lectures I was invited to give at Columbia to expound a version of justificationism that allowed that a statement about the past can be true in virtue of what could have been observed or otherwise known at the time to which it relates, even though no evidence for its truth has survived to the present. I wrote these lectures in something of the same spirit as I had once written "The Reality of the Past," namely to see if such a position could be defended. I remain uncertain where the truth of the matter lies; but I do feel more comfortable with the view set out in the Dewey lectures than with that adopted in the Gifford lectures. Having made the attempt in the Dewey lectures to reconcile the general tenets of justificationism with a more realist view of the past, I think I will now publish the Gifford lectures more or less as they stand, but with warning on this matter.

Professor Beards asks me about our knowledge of a priori general principles. Insofar as he is referring to principles of logic, that is, to the laws that do, or ought to, govern our deductive reasoning, I gave my views on these in my book *The Logical Basis of Metaphysics*. The fundamental laws of logic hold in virtue of acceptable means of determining the meanings of the logical constants: they are not principles that hold because of some necessity external to the way the meanings of those constants are given to us. In my view, to which Professor Beards appears sympathetic, the law of excluded middle is not among the laws that can be justified in this way, and cannot be justified in any other way—unless, indeed, it can be justified by a falsificationist theory of meaning as explained in Ian Rumfitt's masterly contribution to this volume. But in the latter case, the law that every statement of the form "A or not A" is true does not rest upon the semantic principle of bivalence, that every statement is either true or false. As to general principles that belong to semantics—that is, to the theoretical principles that govern and explain our use of language in general—I think that there are indeed some which we can apprehend even before we have anything like a worked out semantic theory. I cannot do better than to cite the two that I mentioned in my early article "Truth": that a statement cannot be true unless there is something in virtue of which it is true; and that a true statement must be—or have been—capable of being known to be true. We can grasp that such principles hold because, on reflection, we see that, without them, the practice of using language becomes unintelligible.

I was astonished by the reaction to my article "A Remarkable Consensus." Professor Beards speaks of my "supporters and opponents" in the long sequence of contributions to *New Blackfriars* that it prompted; but actually I had only one, very welcome, supporter—all the rest were opponents. It was not so much the number of my opponents that amazed me, but the fury which my remarks aroused in some of them and the venom with which the most senior of them attacked me. I experienced the same thing in the conference at Notre Dame whose proceedings were published in the volume to which Professor Beards refers. It called to my mind Chesterton's phrase "the little hiss that only comes from hell."

We are constantly told of the liberation of Catholic scriptural scholars from an oppressively, and indeed ridiculously, conservative authority. But unhappily their liberation had no happy issue: the general tendency of these scholars was to follow blindly the path taken years before by liberal Protestant exegetes. The pronouncements of Catholic New Testament scholars are the principal source for the rejection or "reinterpretation" in senses obviously contrary to their accepted meaning of fundamental doctrines of the Catholic faith: for example, that the Resurrection consists in the fact that the community of Christ's followers became the Body of Christ. This is due to a basic methodological error. Once liberated, Catholic students of scripture were, very rightly, concerned to pursue their *métier* in an objective and scientific spirit. Now when you seek to interpret a text which purports to report real events, your judgements must obviously depend upon your background assumptions. For instance, someone who was convinced, for whatever reason, that it was impossible for human beings to move more than a restricted distance from the Earth, or to cause any object to do so, would have to interpret reports of landings on the Moon quite differently from most people's interpretation of them: he would conclude that some colossal fraud had been perpetrated. Likewise, an atheist must dismiss the veracity of accounts of miraculous occurrences, and choose between regarding them as deluded and as deliberate falsehoods. One who believes in God and supposes that miracles do sometimes occur is free to consider those accounts truthful, though not bound to do so. A Christian is able to take the Gospel accounts of the finding of the empty tomb on the first Easter Sunday at face value (whatever he decides about the angels) and as explained by the Lord's having risen from the dead: one who thinks Jesus Christ to have been a deluded fanatic does not have that option. But the exegetes thought, or, rather, conducted themselves as if they thought, that, to be objective and scientific, they must judge of probabilities as would one who had no religious belief. They had to judge them as if they were atheists. Hence they had never to credit any testimony to the miraculous; any text that purported to testify to it must either be reinterpreted or dismissed as erroneous. Questions of authorship must be judged similarly, that is, as would a critic who had no especial respect for the texts; and the intention of a Gospel passage must be that of the author, rather than of the actors or speakers in the story, even when one of them was Christ himself. We must ask, not what Christ meant in saying this, but what the author of the Gospel had in mind in making Him say it. In order to comply with the requirements of orthodox Catholic belief, it had to be maintained, often with flagrant implausibility, that it was a literary convention of the time to recount events not as warranting that they actually occurred in that way, but with a purely symbolic intent. All this has encouraged progressive theologians to propound wildly distorted versions of basic Christian doctrines, claiming the authority of the exegetes for the concomitant understanding of New Testament texts. But the whole process takes its origin from a methodological mistake. A Christian exegete can do his work quite objectively while judging probabilities in the light of his background beliefs; he is as entitled to do this as an atheist is to judge them in the light of *his* background beliefs. I do not suppose that Catholic biblical scholars have consciously formulated the principle that they must form their opinions of the documents as would one who rejected all religious belief; I do not suppose that they have thought about the matter explicitly at all. But that is the principle upon which they have tacitly acted. It is a mistaken principle which has done much harm.

A modern explanation of the Catholic doctrine of the Eucharist must of course respect defined doctrine; but it must start from the fact that no *physical* change occurs at the consecration of the bread and wine. By saying that there is no physical change I mean that there is no change in the molecules, atoms, and their components. St. Thomas would no doubt have agreed that there was no change detectable by instruments, although he knew nothing of the instruments we have. I think nevertheless that he could not have had the same concept of physical change that we have, since he and people of his time had an entirely different conception from ours of the constitution of matter. An account of transubstantiation that can now be given must be compatible with modern ideas about matter; by "modern ideas" I do not mean ways in which people now choose to think about the subject, but ways of thinking about it that have been forced upon us by what has been discovered. Though I think them inadequate, theories of "transig-nification" have the merit of attempting to do this.

I do not see that Professor Beards has made out that the notion of deeming is inessential to my account of transubstantiation. When adoptive parents deem an adopted child to be their son, there remains a sense in which he is not their son, namely the biological sense. We may say that he is not *really* their son. This is to give the biological sense the priority, which it need not have; the parents may legitimately say, "He is truly our son." It nevertheless remains that there is a sense in which he is not. In the case of the Eucharist, the fact that no physical change has occurred gives a sense to saying that what is there after the consecration is still bread and wine, which is why we need the notion of deeming; perhaps Luther's notion of consubstantiation, properly understood, is not heretical. But the sense in which the elements are still bread and wine cannot have the priority, which is the truth in the scholastic doctrine that only the accidents of bread and wine remain. If *God* deems them to be the Body and Blood of Christ, the sense in which they are so must have the priority. That must be what they *really* are: "Truth Himself speaks truly, or there's nothing true." Just to say that God knows the consecrated elements to be the Body and Blood of Christ suggests that, in perceiving them as bread and wine we are the victims of an illusion, which is not an acceptable account. The notion of deeming *is* essential to my understanding of the matter.

I am not a total defender of Paul VI's encyclical on contraception *Humanae vitae*. The encyclical reaffirmed the traditional Catholic condemnation as immoral of what might be called traditional contraceptive devices. Those in favour of pronouncing the use of such devices morally licit never fully faced the issue of the extent to which this would have entailed that the teaching of the Church on a practical matter touching the lives of very many people, sustained over a long period, could have been woefully mistaken. Indeed, supporters of the traditional view equally failed to examine, let alone to resolve, the crucial question to what degree the Church's teaching on practical questions is capable of going astray by telling the faithful that they must not do what in fact it is all right to do or that they must do what in fact it is wrong to do. How far may a Catholic suppose that such an error has gone? The answer to this question is of pressing importance, and not only in regard to contraception. But the encyclical did more than maintain a teaching of long standing. It condemned as immoral the use for limiting or spacing births of something very new—the pill. This condemnation cannot be called traditional. It was an authoritative pronouncement, though one that did not claim infallibility, on something that had not been considered before.

Why did the pill pose a different problem from the other, "traditional," contraceptive devices? It appears to me that the condemnation of the "traditional" devices is most strongly based if it is subsumed under the strong Catholic insistence on the integrity of the sexual act. It is from this insistence that the condemnation of anal and oral sex acts, and of homosexual congress, flows: the "traditional" contraceptive devices may not unreasonably be seen as violating the integrity of the act. But the use of the pill cannot be so seen: it patently does not violate it. No Catholic authority has thought to condemn all use of the pill whatever. It is agreed that it may licitly be used for the purpose for which it was invented, to regularise menstrual periods. It has been held that it may licitly be used with contraceptive intent by nuns in danger of being raped. Nor is the intention of limiting the number of births or of spacing them out regarded as wrong: on the contrary, doing so is commended as a manifestation of responsible parenthood. So the condemnation of *any* use of the pill with contraceptive intent by married people is ethically bizarre: an act not wrong in itself is held to be wrong if done for a motive not in itself wrong, indeed often laudable. I do not see how this can be correct. To do something that is not in itself wrong for a motive that is not in itself wrong, but may be admirable, cannot be wrong. The ruling was misguided, and has surely done much harm, not least to the authority of the Church and the integrity of many consciences.

I also think that the widely publicised condemnation of the use of condoms in countries where there is great risk of AIDS is morally objectionable. It is possible to think that it is wrong to use condoms, as violating the integrity of the sexual act, and yet acknowledge, and advise others, that it is less wrong than risking infecting one's partner with AIDS. When AIDS is rife, campaigning against condoms manifests a moral blindness that deserves no respect.

The morality of nuclear deterrence depends on whether it can be right to make a conditional threat to do something immoral. I think it can be when there is no intention to carry out the threat; but nuclear deterrence would plainly be ineffective unless the threat was backed by a genuine conditional intention. The question thus becomes whether it can be right to form a conditional intention to do something wrong, in this case something monstrous, the annihilation of whole cities. The standard argument in favour of deterrence is a consequentialist one: the probability that the condition for using nuclear weapons is very small, and rendered small precisely by the making of the threat. This defence rests on the idea that the wickedness of the action threatened is diminished by the low probability of having to perform it: its degree of wickedness is, as it were, to be multiplied by the probability of the antecedent condition, and thus reduced to a very small degree of wickedness.

This is an improper way of looking at the question. What is wrong about forming a conditional intention to do something evil is that one gives one's will to the evil, even if only conditionally. One determines that one will do this terrible thing if the condition is fulfilled; and that—conditionally deciding to do it—is a terrible thing to do. I do not know what the world would be like now if Britain and America had renounced the policy of nuclear deterrence; nor does anyone else. Perhaps it would have been in an even worse state than it is now. Perhaps it would have been, at least on balance, in a better state than it is now; for example, perhaps no other countries would have got hold of nuclear weapons. Or perhaps things would have been much the same as they are now. I know only that we have no right, for fear of any consequences whatever of not doing so, to intend, and plan, if such-and-such were to happen, to repeat, on an even larger scale, the crimes of Hiroshima and Nagasaki. We came very close to a nuclear war at one point that we all know of; God is to be thanked that it never happened. We should not congratulate the policy of deterrence for its never happening; it was the policy of deterrence that brought it so close. But the morality of that policy is not to be argued out on the basis of consequences: it was evil in itself, because it embraced evil.

I owe thanks to Professor Beards for patiently reading my writings on these various topics, as well as the as yet unrevised text of my Gifford lectures, and charitably commenting on them. It is because he covered so wide a range of subjects that this reply to him has been so long.

M. D.

27

Thierry Depaulis

THE FIRST GOLDEN AGE OF THE TAROT IN FRANCE

It may seem strange to find a contribution on the Tarot in this volume. Although it has no direct relationship with his philosophical work, the history of the Tarot is an integral part of Michael Dummett's world. When it appeared in 1980 *The Game of Tarot* was acclaimed as a major contribution to the cultural history of mind games. This thick book—over 600 pages—drastically changed our views on this very special card game and on its no less special cards. With a wealth of impressive documentation Dummett arrived at several conclusions which pulled down old ideas. He first showed that the Tarot was not the "earliest form of playing cards" but that it was, on the contrary, a derivation of the earlier 52-card pack for which evidence exists as early as 1377. He also destroyed an old fancy, namely that the origins of the Tarot lay in divination.

"The Tarot pack," wrote Dummett, "was not invented for use in fortune-telling, but as an instrument of play, and was used only for the latter purpose throughout the fifteenth, sixteenth, and seventeenth centuries."[1] A salutary chapter was devoted to "The Occult": here Dummett revealed how in the end of the eighteenth century the Tarot was diverted towards a new "interpretation" under the influence of Free-Masonry and Egyptomania.[2]

What was the game and when and where was it invented were questions to which Dummett offered sound replies. Starting from a minute classification of the different types of Italian tarots, based on the order of these particular cards called trumps (Italian *trionfi*), Michael Dummett built up a threefold distribution among three main traditions of the Tarot which all rose in Northern Italy. To these three streams the author assigned three birthplaces: Milan, Ferrara, and Bologna. The earliest known packs being illuminated Tarot cards painted for the Visconti and Visconti-Sforza families who reigned in Milan, there is some probability that the Tarot was invented there in the first half of the fifteenth century; however, the Este court of Ferrara cannot be dismissed since the earliest record that bears evidence for the game of Tarot—as *"carte da trionfi"*—is to be found in the Ferrarese account-books of 1442.[3]

The history of the Tarot is not a question of origins only. *The Game of Tarot* went on tracing the diffusion of the game and the evolution of the cards. Born in princely courts the Tarot became more and more popular, and so were the designs too: with the help of woodblock printing and stencil coloring, cardmakers were able to produce "common" tarot packs as early as the second half of the fifteenth century. While the Ferrara tradition seems to have died out in the late sixteenth century, leaving to us only some records and sheets of uncut playing cards, the Bolognese and Milanese branches flourished in the following centuries. From Bologna the Tarot came to Florence then to the rest of Italy, whereas the Milanese designs found their way to Piedmont and outside the Peninsula.

As Dummett puts it: "There can be no doubt that it was in Italy that the Tarot pack was invented, and there that, throughout the fifteenth century, it was chiefly popular; but the question when it first became known in any other country does not admit of so ready an answer. It was certainly in France that it first became known outside its country of origin. . . ."[4] Switzerland was to follow suit some decades later, in the sixteenth century. From Alsace and possibly from Northern Italy the Tarot spread to the German Empire in the late seventeenth century. There a substitution was made in the suit-signs and the trump designs: the traditional "Latin" suit symbols—cups, swords, batons, coins, still to be found in ordinary Italian and Spanish packs of today—were changed for "French" suit-signs—the now universal hearts, spades, clubs, diamonds—while the original trump allegories gave room to more secular subjects like animals, landscapes, theater characters, and so forth.

Thanks to this graphic change—which did not affect the rules and the vocabulary of the game—the Tarot found with the nineteenth century a new life in countries where it had not been known previously: Austria and Hungary, Holland and Denmark, and farther. In the same time the older countries, Italy and France, saw a marked decline. Two European areas were to remain completely void of any Tarot play: the Iberian Peninsula and the British Isles. More recently, the game underwent an unexpected revival in France, which it certainly owes to the substitution for French-suited cards that occurred around 1900.

The Game of Tarot opened many new tracks indeed.[5] It stimulated further research in Germany, Italy, and France. In Paris the present writer organized an exhibition in the Bibliothèque nationale in 1984,[6] while Ferrara housed another exhibition in 1987,[7] all offering new finds that enlarged the range of available Tarot materials. Dummett's theories were amply confirmed but some details had to be revised. Instead of a new edition Michael Dummett was given the opportunity of writing a new book in Italian for the Neapolitan publishing house Bibliopolis, which came out in 1993.[8] Far from being a mere revision of the 1980 volume, *Il Mondo e l'Angelo* was more a linear history of the Tarot, focusing on the evolution of the game in Italy which is so fundamental.

I. THE FIRST AGE OF THE TAROT IN FRANCE

As we have seen, France was the first country outside Italy that welcomed the Tarot. When exactly is a matter of discussion. A document from Avignon, quoted by Hyacinthe Chobaut in 1955 (though with a wrong date),[9] has recently come to light and reveals that *"taraux"* cards were being made in the Papal city in 1505. Since the very word *taraux* is neither Latin, like the rest of the text, nor Provençal, which was the spoken language of Avignon, but French, we can safely conclude that tarot cards were already made northward, most certainly in Lyons, around 1500. By that time Lyons was the French Kingdom's busiest city, attracting Italian capitals, spreading Italian fashions, but also sheltering an impressive number of cardmaking workshops.[10]

It is certain that the Tarot enjoyed a large popularity in France in the sixteenth century. Already in his 1980 book Michael Dummett had brought this to light, writing: "Tarot is likely to have enjoyed its first wave of popularity in France after 1500. In any case, the game has been continuously played in France from its first introduction down to the present day."[11] To the many references given by Dummett some were added in the following years and most are quoted in *Il Mondo e l'Angelo*.[12]

Starting with Rabelais's long list of games in his *Gargantua* (1534) the references to the game of Tarot multiply in the second half of the sixteenth century. To Charles Estienne (*Paradoxes*, 1553) it was clear enough that the Tarot was an Italian invention, but the game was so widespread that in *Le Monstre d'abus* (1558), a pamphlet against the celebrated astrologer Nostradamus, an unknown author writing under the pseudonym of Jean de La Daguenière could utter: "Ce nom [that of Nostradamus, considered as insane] dis-je, duquel jouant aux tarochz on salue reveremment le mat ou le bagat."[13] In 1559 the Protestant physician Rasse des Neux collected a short pamphlet called "Le Tarot des XXII cardinaux," in fact the French adaptation of an Italian pasquinade.[14] It is the earliest complete list of trumps in French.

Other references are quoted in Michael Dummett's two books of 1980 and 1993: Guillaume des Autels's *Mitistoire barragouyne de Fanfreluche et Gaudichon* (1559), an anonymous *Chambriere à louer* of circa 1560, Rabelais again, but in *Book* V (1564), which is only attributed to him, all mention the Tarot together with other fashionable games. More interesting is Lambert Daneau's commentary to the French translation of a Christian pamphlet against gambling which a tradition assigned to St. Cyprian. In this *Contre les jeux et joueurs* (1566), Daneau, a Protestant theologian (ca.1530–1595), remarks: "les premieres cartes estoyent figurées comme sont celles du tarot," so establishing for the first time the (wrong) assumption that the earliest cards were Tarot cards.

Another reference which seems to have been unknown to Dummett is Christoph Plantin's French-Flemish children's dialogue book published in 1567. Entitled *La Première et la seconde partie des dialogues françois pour les jeunes enfans. Het eerste ende tweede deel van de françoische 't samensprekinghen, overgheset in de nederduytsche spraecke*, its Dialogue IIII, "Le meuble commun de la salle et de la chambre / Van den ghemeynen huysraet van der salen ende van de slaepcamer," has: "le livre des Rois, nommé les cartes & les tarots" (the book of Kings, also called cards and tarots).[15]

Another bunch of about twenty more references can be accounted for until the end of the sixteenth century, many of which were unearthed either by Dummett or by the present writer. The game of Tarot and the special cards made by the cardmakers became such an important matter that, following a trend that came from the South of Europe, King Henri III decided on January 21, 1581, to levy an export tax on "aucunes sortes de papier, cartes & tarots" to be carried out abroad. Two years later, on May 22, 1583, a correction to the law was introduced: from now on the tax would be levied on playing and Tarot cards, as well as dice, which were to be sold within the country. Since France was Europe's largest playing-card producer this favored exportations but raised the cost of local purchases so that the law was fiercely resisted by cardmakers.[16] It was in the same time that Paris cardmakers, then called "faiseurs de cartes et tarots," were allowed to organize their craft;[17] this was to give rise to a formal guild of master cardmakers in 1594.

It is a pity that so little survives of the French production of the sixteenth century: the only Tarot cards that have been kept are those, dated 1557, made by Catelin Geofroy, a prominent maker of Lyons, then one of the two largest French cities—with Rouen—where playing cards were manufactured. The thirty-eight cards, out of the usual seventy-eight, that are housed in the Museum für Kunsthandwerk at Frankfurt (Germany), are by no means standard: they use fancy suit-signs (parrots, monkeys, lions, peacocks) but "the trump subjects are standard ones, and, so far as can be told, are arranged in precisely the order later found in the Tarot de Marseille."[18]

Two little pieces, however, bring some more light on the game itself. Claude Gauchet's charming poem *Le Plaisir des champs* (1583) speaks of the pleasure of playing Tarot, naming some of the trumps, while Captain Jacques Perrache, "Provençal Gentleman," in his *Le Triomphe du berlan* (1585), drops hints about the rules. To these we can add a new mention, although unrelated to actual card play, that made by Guillaume Du Bartas in his *Seconde sepmaine* (*ante* 1590):

> un pont de tarots que le soir, pour s'esbatre
> Dessus un verd tapis l'enfant bastit, folastre
> (a bridge of Tarot cards that, in the evening, for amusement,
> the playful child builds up on a green cloth).[19]

With the turn of the century further references to the Tarot have come to light. The popularity of the game in France is evidenced by the Jesuit Father François Garasse who wrote in his *Recherche des recherches d'Estienne Pasquier* (1622) that: "les jeux de tarots, de quille, de courte boule, & autres . . . sont plus en usage parmy les François." (the games of Tarot, of ninepins, of bowling, and such like, . . . are more in use among the French). In English eyes the Tarot was regarded as a French game, witness James Cleland's '*Ηρω–Παιδεια, or the Institution of a Young Nobleman* (1607) referring to "French cardes called Taraux." Taxation on playing cards was resumed after the troubles of the wars of religion. As early as 1605 an agreement was reached between the tax-farmer and the Paris cardmakers in order to fix the amount of the taxes. The price for Tarot cards was set at 48 *sols tournois* per dozen.[20] Although taxation was abandoned in 1609, it was resumed in 1622, and many subsequent edicts establish statutory prices and conditions imposed on the cardmakers until it finally was given up in 1671.[21] Tarot cards were manufactured not only in Lyons and Rouen, but also in Paris, and certainly in other places. However the only Tarot packs that have been kept in a public collection—actually in the Département des Estampes et de la Photographie of the Bibliothèque nationale de France—were all three produced in Paris: one is an anonymous early seventeenth-century set of seventy-eight "nonstandard" cards, much in the Italian manner; a second one, made by Jacques Viéville, must date from around 1650; while the third one, the sole pack which follows a recognized standard pattern, that later known as "Tarot de Marseille" of which it is the earliest example, bears the imprint of Jean Noblet, "Au Faubourg St. Germain," and was probably made in the second half of the seventeenth century.[22]

In his two books Michael Dummett surprisingly makes almost no use of literary references after 1600. They would have brought still more strength to the demonstration. Between 1600 and 1650 such well-known writers as Agrippa d'Aubigné, Tristan L'Hermite, or Scarron mention the Tarot in at least one of their writings, so attesting they were familiar with the game.[23] While French lexicographers, like Jean Nicot, ignored the word, Randle Cotgrave has an entry in his *Dictionarie of the French and English tongues* (1611): "Tarots. A kind of great cards, whereon many several things are figured, which make them much more intricate than ordinarie ones." But the most striking piece of evidence for the popularity of the Tarot in France in the early seventeenth century is the account given by the King's physician Jean Héroard in his diary on November 12, 1615. On his arrival in Bordeaux, where he was to marry his fiancée Anne of Austria, daughter of the King of Spain, the young Louis XIII "se faict monstrer à jouer aux taraults" (let them show him how to play Tarot).[24]

II. THE EARLIEST PRINTED RULES OF THE TAROT

As far as the actual rules are concerned we are fortunate to have now a better source than the 1659 manual *La maison academique contenant les jeux du picquet, du hoc, du tric-trac, du hoca, . . . & autres jeux facetieux & divertissans*, with its "Le plaisant jeu de cartes des taros."[25] Relying on this single source Dummett wrote in 1980: "The description given in the *Maison académique* is very far from being either lucid or exhaustive. . . ."[26] It is in fact quite confused. While preparing the Paris exhibition which took place in 1984, the present writer had the good fortune to discover an anonymous printed pamphlet, though stored in the Département des Manuscrits of the Bibliothèque nationale, entitled *Regles dv iev des tarots* and indeed offering rules for the game in a very clear and elegant style. The pamphlet was kept in a volume of various documents that were gathered by the King's librarian Jacques Dupuy in 1655.[27] These were therefore the earliest printed rules of the game of Tarot, since Italy has nothing to offer before 1747.

In his 1993 Italian book Michael Dummett added a short reference to the *Regles dv iev des tarots* although without any detailed analysis.[28] Since then a further happy research has brought to light new facts that allow us to assign this pamphlet an author, a date, a printer, and an inspiring princess. The key to the whole story lays in the *Mémoires* of Michel de Marolles, who, dealing with his visit to Nevers in 1637, writes:

> Madame la princesse Marie voulut joüer aux Tarots, qui est une sorte de cartes, dont l'usage estoit autresfois plus frequent qu'il n'est à présent, et . . . , comme

les loix de ce jeu ne luy sembloient pas assez belles, ny assez diversifiées, elle trouva bon d'y en faire de nouvelles, & de me charger de les escrire & de les faire imprimer, afin de s'en servir plus commodément, et que personne ne pust abuser. Il est vrai qu'elles rendirent ce jeu beaucoup plus beau. . . .
(Madam the Princess Marie wanted to play with Tarots, which are a kind of [playing] cards whose usage was more common in the past than it is today, and . . . , since the laws of the game did not seem beautiful enough to her, nor varied enough, she saw fit to make new ones, and to put me in charge of writing them and having them printed, so as to use them more conveniently, and so that nobody could cheat. It is true they made the game much nicer.)[29]

The abbé Michel de Marolles (1600–1681) is not unknown to us. Not only do we know him pretty well from his memoirs and his many translations from the Latin, but he amassed such a large number of engravings that, when he published a catalogue of these in 1666, the Sun King got interested and, finally, his minister Colbert bought the whole collection. It was the starting point of the Cabinet des Estampes of the Bibliothèque nationale de France, the world's largest collection of prints and pictures of all sorts.

Marolles was a friend of the Gonzague-Nevers family, a branch of the Gonzagas of Mantua who had come to France with Ludovico Gonzaga (1539–1595), who became Duke of Nevers by his marriage in 1565 and was one of King Henri IV's councillors. Ludovico's son, Charles de Gonzague (1580–1637), was a prominent figure in the Kingdom of France. In 1627, the elder branch of the Gonzagas having died out, he inherited the Duchy of Mantua and reigned there for ten years (not without troubles). The "Princess Marie," Louise-Marie de Gonzague-Nevers to give her her complete name, was one of his two daughters.[30] While her father was in Mantua, she took possession of Nevers with her sister. It was there that she received her guests in summertime. Michel de Marolles was one of them in 1637.

From his own account we can infer Marolles and the Princess were familiar with the Tarot already. This is no surprise: as we have seen the game was then quite popular, probably more with educated than with simple people. But we hear that the Princess was not satisfied with the usual rules and that she devised new "nicer" ones. Here we have to wonder whether Louise-Marie de Gonzague's acquaintance with the Tarot was owed to the game's popularity in France or whether she knew it from family tradition, that is from Mantua. Unfortunately this question remains unanswered for the moment. We know almost nothing of the games played at the Gonzaga court and nothing has come to light from Mantua as far as the Tarot is concerned.[31]

Reading that "she [Louise-Marie] saw fit to make new ones, and to put me in charge of writing them and having them printed" was an invitation to have a fresh look at the *Regles dv iev des tarots*. The text speaks for itself. Three variants of the game are described: successively a standard form for three players, then another game for two with a *"mort"* (dummy), and a third original one for three players again but with sixty-six cards, instead of the usual seventy-eight, twelve small pips being discarded. The elegant and mordant style of the anonymous text agrees with that of Marolles, while the third game would represent the Princess's innovation.

A decisive proof for this identification was found in the initial letter that begins the little pamphlet: a nicely decorated C which belonged to the very collection of such letters used by Jean Fourré, "Imprimeur de Mesdames" at Nevers and his predecessors. Thus the *Regles dv iev des tarots* was printed in Nevers, and there is no doubt they were the rules Marolles was in charge of writing and of having printed. Instead of 1655 we therefore have to assign these rules the date 1637. The author is Michel de Marolles, the printer, Jean Fourré at Nevers. Louise-Marie de Gonzague-Nevers acted as the inspirer.[32]

Once again this must lead us to reconsider the presence of obvious Italianisms in the *Regles dv iev des tarots*: the use of such words as *math* (It. *matto*, "fool"), *bagat* (It. *bagatto*, "mountebank"), *faon* a probable misspelling for **fant* (It. *fante*, "jack"), *brizigole* (It. *verzigole*, "combination[s]") is remarkable. Whereas the first two seem to belong to the common stock of words that have come from Italy with the Tarot and are met with in earlier French texts, *faon/fant* and *brizigole* are not known elsewhere. Whence this insistent question: did they come with the general vocabulary of the game or are they representative of a more specific tradition, that we suspect to have come from Mantua? The question remains open.

Michel de Marolles and Louise-Marie de Gonzague-Nevers were members of the Parisian social elite. Nevers was nothing more than a country house for the Princess. It is not certain that the game of Tarot was played there by the local elite. But many clues lead to a large geographical distribution of the game: we know it was played in Paris, in Lyons, in Rouen, in Grenoble, in Toulouse, in Nancy, in Provence, probably also in Touraine,[33] and we have seen it taught to the King in Bordeaux. The *Maison academique* says it was played "à Lyon, Marseille & autres lieux." The name of Marolles may lead us to think the Tarot was fashionable in some intellectual circles of the French capital.

However, it is remarkable that the Tarot is no longer mentioned after 1650 in any literary source. Although card play and gambling are abundantly reported in and around Paris, none of the writers of the Classical Age of French literature pays attention to the Tarot. The word itself is totally absent from the writings of such careful memoirists as Dangeau, Saint-

Simon, or Madame de Sévigné. Furthermore it seems that even the best lexicographers were ill-informed. Pierre Richelet has no "Tarot" entry in his *Dictionnaire françois* (1680) and Antoine Furetière (d. 1688) offers this poor definition in his *Dictionnaire universel* (1690):

> TARAUDS ou TAROTS, s. m. plur. qui se dit d'une espece de cartes à joüer dont se servent les Espagnols, les Allemans & autres estrangers, qui sont marquées d'autres figures que les nostres, comme *copas*, *diveros* [sic], *espadillas* [sic], *bassos* [sic], &c. Au licu de cœurs, carreaux, piques & trefles, elles ont d'ordinaire l'envers imprimé de divers compartiments.

Not only are the Spanish (!) names of the Latin suit-signs blatantly misspelled but also the gloss is bad: the Spaniards never played Tarot. Surprisingly the *Dictionnaire de l'Académie françoise* (1694) is here much better:

> TAROTS, s. m. plur., Sortes de cartes à joüer, qui sont distinguées par quatre couleurs appellées Deniers, Couppes, Espées & Bastons, & qui sont marquées de rayes noires par dessus. *Jouër aux tarots*.

So it is clear that the Tarot was no longer known in Paris. It was to draw back during the eighteenth century, leaving out the West of France, and concentrating more and more on the eastern strip of the country, including Provence, the Lyonnais, Franche-Comté, Alsace, and probably also a part of Lorraine; by 1860, it seems Provence had forgotten the game.

In his 1980 book Michael Dummett suggested: "It thus appears a plausible conjecture that the game of Tarot was played in Normandy and in Paris from the mid-sixteenth century until the end of the seventeenth ... the game certainly died out in those areas by about 1700. ..."[34]

From what we have put forth above we may conclude the game died out in Paris much earlier. The mid-seventeenth century seems a more reasonable date for the Tarot's disappearance from a large part of France. But we have a decisive confirmation: Michel de Marolles's own words, when he states in his *Mémoires*, published in 1656, that "Tarots, . . . are a kind of [playing] cards, whose usage was more common in the past than it is today." Not only does he feel it necessary to explain to his readers what Tarot cards are, but he also presents them as things of times past. In 1656 nobody, save some old persons like Marolles, would have understood what it was about.

This sudden dying out of the Tarot in Paris—and probably also in other regions—may be a consequence of the Fronde whose disorders turned the country upside down from 1648 to 1652, but particularly in Paris, Rouen, Bordeaux, and Toulouse. These cities, it is to be remarked, are all situated in the west part of France. Burgundy, the Lyonnais, the Dauphiné, and Provence, all homes of the Tarot for the centuries to come, did not seriously take part in the troubles.[35]

THIERRY DEPAULIS
CHAIRMAN OF THE INTERNATIONAL
PLAYING-CARD SOCIETY
DECEMBER 2002

NOTES

1. Michael Dummett, *The Game of Tarot* (London: Duckworth, 1980), 100.
2. For a more comprehensive treatment of the history of the occult Tarot, see: Ronald Decker, Thierry Depaulis, and Michael Dummett, *A Wicked Pack of Cards: The Origins of the Occult Tarot* (London: Duckworth, 1996); Ronald Decker and Michael Dummett, *A History of the Occult Tarot 1870–1970* (London: Duckworth, 2002).
3. Dummett, *The Game of Tarot*, 67.
4. Ibid., 83.
5. In parallel with his major study Michael Dummett has published other books on the Tarot—one specifically dedicated to the Sicilian Tarot: *I Tarocchi Siciliani* (Palermo: Pioppo, 1995; new [revised] ed., Genoa, 2002)—and many articles dealing with the history of card games and of playing cards: see the Bibliography.
6. Thierry Depaulis, *Tarot, jeu et magie* (Paris: Bibliothèque Nationale, 1984).
7. Giordano Berti, Andrea Vitali, eds., *Le carte di corte: I tarocchi. Gioco e magia alla corte degli Estense* (Bologna: Nuova Alfa Editoriale, 1987).
8. Michael Dummett, *Il Mondo e l'Angelo: I Tarocchi e la loro Storia* (The World and the Angel: Tarot Cards and their History) (Naples: Bibliopolis, 1993).
9. Hyacinthe Chobaut, *Les maîtres cartiers d'Avignon du XVe siècle à la Révolution*, Avignon, 1955 (offprint from *Mémoires de l'Académie de Vaucluse*, IV, 1955), 25. See also M. Dummett, *Il Mondo e l'Angelo*, 326, n 2.
10. Thierry Depaulis, "Des 'cartes communément appelées *taraux*,' 1ère Partie," *The Playing-Card* 32, no. 5 (2004): 199–205; and "Des 'cartes communément appelées *taraux*,' 2ème Partie," *The Playing-Card* 32, no. 6 (2004): 244–49.
11. Dummett, *The Game of Tarot*, 202.
12. Dummett, *Il Mondo e l'Angelo*, "Capitolo XIV: I Primi Tarocchi Francesi," 351–57.
13. "This name [that of Nostradamus], I say, with which, playing at Tarot, one greets the *mat* [i.e., the Fool card, Italian *matto*] or the *bagat* [i.e., trump I, Italian *bagatto*]." Jean de La Daguenière is believed by some to be a pseudonym of

Théodore de Bèze (1519–1605).

14. Thierry Depaulis, "Roger de Gaignères et ses tarots," *Le Vieux Papier* 301 (1986): 117–24.

15. Christoph Plantin (1514–1589) was one of the most famous printers of his time. Born in France, settled in Antwerp in 1550, he established there the largest printing office and publishing house of the sixteenth century.

16. See Henri-René D'Allemagne, *Les cartes à jouer du XIVe au XXe siècle*, Paris 1906, I, 293–94; Dummett, *The Game of Tarot*, 202–3; id., *Il Mondo e l'Angelo*, 352–53.

17. Decision of the King's Council of 5th July, 1582 (R. de Lespinasse, *Les métiers et corporations de la ville de Paris (XIVe-XVIIIe siècle)*, I, Paris, 1897, 107).

18. Dummett, *The Game of Tarot*, 203; id., *Il Mondo e l'Angelo*, 353–57. Also Depaulis, *Tarot, jeu et magie*, No. 13.

19. Guillaume de Saluste, seigneur Du Bartas (1544–1590), *Seconde sepmaine*, 'Les capitaines' (*The Works of Guillaume de Salluste sieur du Bartas*, ed. U. T. Holmes, Jr., J. C. Lyons, and R. W. Linker, vol. 3, Chapel Hill, NC, 1940, 313).

20. Archives Nationales, Minutier Central des notaires, CXII, 251, 3-10-1605. The tax-farmer is styled "fermier et adjudicataire général de la ferme des cartes, dez et tarots du royaume de France."

21. Dummett, *The Game of Tarot*, 204; id., *Il Mondo e l'Angelo*, 357–58.

22. Depaulis, *Tarot, jeu et magie*, nos. 33 (Anonymous Parisian pack), 34 (Viéville's Tarot), 35 (Noblet's Tarot); Dummett, *The Game of Tarot*, 205–8; id., *Il Mondo e l'Angelo*, 359–68 with important emendations.

23. For Agrippa d'Aubigné, see his *Lettre* à La Rivière (†1605), VII in *Œuvres complètes*, ed. E. Réaume and F. de Cassade, I, Paris, 1873, 442; Tristan L'Hermite, *Le Page disgracié* (1643), ch. 7; Paul Scarron has two references to the Tarot, one in *Le Virgile travesti* (1648–52), the other in his comedy *Don Japhet d'Arménie* (1652), Act II, scene 1: "Esprit bouché, dy moy, jouë-t'on dans ton bourg aux cartes, aux tarots, aux dez?" (Dull mind, tell me, do they play cards, Tarot, dice in your village?)

24. Jean Héroard, *Journal*, ed. Madeleine Foisil (Paris: Fayard, 1989), 2328. Héroard's diary was not intended for publication. Although a digest had been released in 1868, the whole diary was not published until 1989.

25. Paris, 1659, and later editions in 1665, 1666, 1668, 1674, 1697, 1702. See Thierry Depaulis, *Les loix du jeu: bibliographie de la littérature technique des jeux de cartes en français avant 1800* (Paris, 1994).

26. Dummett, *The Game of Tarot*, 214.

27. BnF, Mss., Dupuy 777; Depaulis, *Tarot, jeu et magie*, no. 36.

28. Dummett, *Il Mondo e l'Angelo*, 374 and 376. Following my own conclusion Dummett assigned it the date of 1655.

29. *Les Mémoires de Michel de Marolles, abbé de Villeloin, divisez en trois parties, contenant ce qu'il a vu de plus remarquable en sa vie depuis 1600; ses*

entretiens avec quelques uns des plus sçavants hommes de son temps, et les genealogies de quelques familles alliées dans la sienne, avec une brieve description de la tres-illustre maison de Mantouë et de Nevers (Paris: A. de Sommaville, 1656), 112–13.

30. Louise-Marie de Gonzague-Nevers was born in 1611. In 1645 she married Ladislas VII, King of Poland, who died in 1648. She later married his brother and successor John II Casimir Vasa (1609–1672). Louise-Marie died in Warsaw in 1667.

31. Laura Romano's doctoral thesis, *Il gioco a Mantova nei secoli XVI e XVII: leggi, disposizioni, strutture di corte*, University of Verona, 1985–86, does not offer much more than a survey of laws on gambling.

32. For a detailed presentation of this find, see Thierry Depaulis, "Quand l'abbé de Marolles jouait au tarot," *Le Vieux Papier* 365 (2002): 313–26.

33. For Grenoble and Toulouse, see Dummett, *Il Mondo e l'Angelo*, 352; for Provence, I infer this from the Tarot being mentioned in the work of the Provençal poet Gaspard Zerbin (†1650), as quoted by F. Mistral, in his *Trésor dóu Felibrige ou Dictionnaire provençal-français,* s.v. 'tarot'. Born in Touraine, Christoph Plantin is unlikely to have learned the game in Antwerp.

34. Dummett, *The Game of Tarot*, 213. I am putting aside the problem of the so-called "Belgian" Tarot in Normandy which would be too long to discuss here.

35. For a general survey of the Fronde, see Orest Ranum, *The Fronde: a French Revolution 1648–1652* (New York: W. W. Norton, 1993); French trans. *La Fronde* (Paris: Éditions du Seuil, 1995). In the mid-seventeenth century the Kingdom of France had not yet integrated such important regions as the North, Lorraine, Alsace, Franche-Comté, and Savoy which were foreign territories, though some—the North, Alsace, Franche-Comté—in the process of being conquered.

REPLY TO THIERRY DEPAULIS

I have no quarrel with anything Thierry Depaulis says in his essay, but I must thank him for his kind remarks about my work on the subject. I think that *The Game of Tarot* did establish a framework for the history of Tarot—the game and the cards. Before that, there had been a tradition of confused statements about it, with frequent references to "the Venetian Tarot," which in fact scarcely, if at all, existed. The framework was consolidated by the great exhibition of Tarot cards at the Bibliothèque Nationale which Thierry organised. I owe the capability of establishing such a framework to the late great playing-card collector, Sylvia Mann. She suggested that I looked into the variations in the order of the Tarot trumps in different traditions. I did so, and quickly realised that these variations supplied an essential clue to the direction of transmission of the game from one locality to another. It turned out, as Thierry says in his essay, that there were three types of trump order, distinguished by the very varying positions of the three Virtues of Fortitude, Justice, and Temperance which figure among the subjects of the trump cards, and by whether the Angel or the World is the highest trump. These three types were associated with Milan, Ferrara, and Bologna, the three cities in which there is the earliest evidence of the use of the cards; the order observed in Florence closely resembled that used in Bologna. Obviously such variations must stem from the earliest origins of the game in these three places, before the practice of numbering the trumps had been adopted. (It was adopted in Ferrara before the end of the fifteenth century, in Milan in the early sixteenth century, but in Bologna not until well into the second half of the eighteenth century; before that, learning the order of the trump subjects was part of learning the game.) To the Bolognese type belongs the trump order observed in Florence and Sicily and probably also Rome; the Milanese type of order was followed in France and Switzerland, and, from them, everywhere outside Italy; and the Ferrarese order was observed in Venice and Trent, though it is not known that Tarot cards were actually manufactured in those cities, and the game was never particularly popular in either. The game had been much practised in Ferrara, in the court and outside it; but in 1598 the d'Este family lost the dukedom of Ferrara, which they held from the Papacy, because the Pope would not recognise the heir, Cesare d'Este, on account of his illegitimacy. The family moved to Modena, of which they held the dukedom from the Emperor, but I have not been able to discover that the game of Tarot, and with it the whole Ferrarese tradition of play, survived there.

The only area indebted to more than one of the three traditions of play is Piedmont/Savoy. This was influenced by neighbouring Lombardy, but also, on the evidence of the practices of play in Piedmont and Savoy, by Bologna; we have no Piedmontese playing cards from before the eighteenth century to show what kind of Tarot pack was originally in use there. To this day, Piedmontese players treat the Angel (numbered 20 in the Piedmontese Tarot pack) as higher than the World (numbered 21), as it is in Bologna and was in Florence but not in Milan or Ferrara. More strikingly yet, players in various parts of Savoy, in Nice as late as 1930 and, as discovered by John McLeod, in the present-day region of Asti, treat the four Papal and Imperial cards as equal in rank, any of them played later to a trick beating one played earlier to it. This is a peculiarity otherwise known only in Bologna. Bologna is a long way from Piedmont. We can surmise only that the game was originally introduced into Piedmont by visitors from Bologna. The most widespread French pattern for the Tarot pack was the celebrated Tarot de Marseille, ancestral to all Italian-suited packs used everywhere in Europe outside Italy, save in what is now Belgium. The quite different pattern used there had also been known in France in the seventeenth and eighteenth centuries, and we may conjecture that it derived from that used in Piedmont/Savoy before the eighteenth century.

I learned one thing from the publication of *The Game of Tarot*, that it is a mistake to publish a book in English on Tarot games or the cards used to play them with the word "Tarot" in the title. I discovered a copy of *The Game of Tarot* in a games shop, of all places, housed in the occult section of the book department. (I have nevertheless included the word in the title of the latest book I have written on the subject with the collaboration of John McLeod, on his insistence that the title ought to say what the book is about; in fact potential readers will take it to be about something quite different.)

The success of the search, prompted by Thierry Depaulis, made by Mme. Esther Moench, curator of the Musée du Petit-Palais d'Avignon, for the document of 1505 containing the words quoted by Chobaut, but incorrectly dated by him to 1507, is a discovery of the highest importance. The document refers (in Latin) to "cards called in the vernacular *taraux*" as being made in Avignon by the cardmaker Jean Fort. Hitherto the earliest French reference to the game of Tarot has been thought to be that by

Rabelais; to learn that the game was known in France, and the cards made there, as early as 1505 makes a salient contribution to our knowledge of the spread of the game from Italy to other parts of Europe. Lyons was indeed a centre for Italian fashions and Italian culture at the time, and it is intrinsically likely that it was there the game of Tarot first spread from Milan. Thierry Depaulis's conjecture that Tarot cards were also made there, and that the word *tarau* stemmed from Lyons, is therefore highly plausible, though as yet we lack actual evidence.

Throughout the fifteenth century, Italian sources referred to the game of Tarot as *trionfi* (trumps); the word is the ancestor of our word 'trumps'. The last documented use of *trionfi* in this sense was from Reggio Emilia in 1500, though it continued often to be used as applying to the trump cards of the Tarot pack. The first documented use of the word *tarocchi* as the name of the game comes from Ferrara in 1505; it was always so called thereafter. The invention of the Tarot pack was indeed the invention of the idea of trumps. Trick-taking games without trumps surely entered Europe from the Islamic world with playing cards themselves in the fourteenth century. The game of Ganjifa, brought to India by the Moghuls, is such a game; trumps are a European invention. The idea was borrowed for games with the ordinary pack by making one of the four suits the trump suit—games such as Triomphe in France (referred to in 1480) and Triumph, the ancestor of Whist, in England (referred to in 1522). The German game of Karnöffel (referred to in 1425) incorporated a presumably independent invention of the idea of trumps, the trump suit being called the *erwelete Farbez* (chosen suit): but that it was from Tarot that the idea was borrowed by other card games is shown not only by etymology, but by the fact that in Karnöffel some members of the trump suit were only partial trumps, for instance being beaten by the King of the suit led but beating all lower cards of that suit—a feature *not* copied by other games.

As Thierry Depaulis says, there is overwhelming evidence that the game of Tarot was popular everywhere in France in the sixteenth century. I based my original supposition that it was towards the end of the seventeenth century that the game of Tarot died out everywhere in France save the eastern parts of the country in part on a 1726 translation, *Les facétieuses nuits*, by Jean Louveau of a book by Giovanni Francesco Straparola, in which the game of Tarot is said to be a *sorte de jeu de cartes aujourd'hui hors d'usage* (see *The Game of Tarot*, 104, n. 12). When I wrote *The Game of Tarot*, Thierry Depaulis had not yet made his great discovery of the *Regles dv iev des tarots*, at first dated to 1655 but now convincingly redated by him to 1637. The only early description of the game of which I knew was that which first appeared in the second edition of the *Maison académique*, published in 1659. The description was reprinted in all editions of the *Maison académique* up to 1702; when the sequence was resumed with the *Académie universelle des jeux* of 1718, the game of Tarot had been dropped. It seemed reasonable with what I knew then to place the disappearance of the game from Paris and eastern and central France to the turn of the century. In his essay, Thierry Depaulis presents strong grounds for believing the decline of the game outside eastern France to be datable to the middle of the seventeenth century. I fully accept this thesis. (He is, however, somewhat unfair to the Italians concerning the earliest statements of the rules of Tarot games. He overlooks the first account of the game of Minchiate by Paolo Minucci in 1676, and the eighteenth-century copy of rules dating from the seventeenth century for Bolognese Partita discovered by Lorenzo Cuppi. Still, 1637 is the earliest specific date for any such compilation of which we know.)

As for why the game went out of practice at that date and came to be forgotten, we have no satisfactory explanation. Depaulis suggests that it could have been a result of the disorders due to the Fronde; but what is the mechanism whereby political disturbances cause a once popular game to go out of favour? We have no theory to explain the swings of fashion that make a social game popular at one time, when everyone seems to be playing it, and out of favour at another time, when few can be bothered with it. Perhaps the same theory would explain the swings of fashion in other matters—dress, music, literature, food, and so on. Or perhaps there is no theory to be had; perhaps such changes are due to random and diverse factors that forbid generalisation. This is not the most important question in the world, but it is interesting. If, as I have long believed, the history of games, playing which is a salient human activity, were treated as a serious subject of academic study, those concerned with it might attempt an answer.

One thing seems certain: it was due to the dying out of the game of Tarot in Paris and central and western France—and especially in Paris—that it was possible for France to give birth to the occultist interpretation of and practices with the Tarot pack that have now infected the entire Western world. A pack of cards bearing unfamiliar and apparently esoteric images is much more plausibly presented as originating in remote antiquity and incorporating mystical or magical significance than one you are accustomed to seeing used for play in the local tavern. It might be objected that divination with Tarot cards appears to have begun in Bologna earlier in the eighteenth century than it did in France. But the history of the practice in Bologna and in France, in both of which localities it has continued to the present day, bears out, rather than refutes, my contention. In France many different Tarot packs were produced, especially designed for esoteric or cartomantic use; elaborate theories were woven around the cards, assigning them an origin in ancient Egypt or associating them with the Cabala so as to integrate them into entire theories of magic. In Bologna nothing of the kind happened. Tarot cartomancy remained just one technique of divining the future, practised with the very same cards that are used for play, just as fortune-telling with ordinary playing cards is done in places where the game of Tarot is unknown. In Bologna no link was made between Tarot cards and any ingredient of magical lore or practice; no fanciful theories of their origin were put forward; no special form of the Tarot pack was devised for divination. Unless Tarot cards are unfamiliar, they cannot be made to appear mysterious or credited with occult significance. It was the dying out of the game in Paris that made possible the rebirth of Tarot as an integral ingredient of the Western magical tradition.

Since 1950 the popularity of the game of Tarot has once more spread throughout France, until now, after three centuries, it is played everywhere in the country. It is not, indeed, played with the traditional cards, with their Italian suit-signs and the original trump subjects, but with packs using the French suits of Spades, Clubs, Hearts, and Diamonds familiar to British and American card-players, and with genre scenes on the trumps. That does not matter: what matters is that a great game enjoys a great revival. Fortune-telling with playing cards was unknown until the eighteenth century. The Tarot pack was not invented for that purpose, but in order to play a new kind of card game which gave to card play the idea of trumps, essential to so many games. That is one of the two great European contributions to card play, the other being bidding, which derives from Ombre, the only card game before Contract Bridge about which whole books were written—an idea borrowed in its turn by many members of the great family of Tarot games.

M. D.

PART THREE

BIBLIOGRAPHY OF
THE WRITINGS OF
MICHAEL DUMMETT

BIBLIOGRAPHY OF THE WRITINGS OF MICHAEL A. E. DUMMETT

A. BOOKS and PAMPHLETS

Appendix to *Tractatus Logico-Philosophicus*, by L. Wittgenstein. Translated by G. Colombo, S. J. Milan, Fratelli Bocca, 1954, "Lo Sfondo Logico del *Tractatus Logico-Philosophicus*," 303–11.

Edited with J. N. Crossley. *Formal Systems and Recursive Functions: Proceedings of the Eighth Colloquium, Oxford 1963*. Amsterdam: North-Holland, 1965.

With Ann Dummett. "The Role of Government in Britain's Racial Crisis." In *Justice First*, edited by Lewis Donnelly. London: Sheed & Ward, 1969.

Frege: Philosophy of Language. London: Duckworth, 1973; 2nd ed., Cambridge, MA: Harvard University Press, 1981. Translated into Italian, 1983.

Elements of Intuitionism. Oxford: Oxford University Press, 1977; rev. ed., Oxford: Clarendon Press and New York: Oxford University Press, 2000.

Immigration: Where the Debate Goes Wrong (pamphlet). London, 1978; 2nd ed., London, 1981.

Truth and Other Enigmas. London: Duckworth, and Cambridge, MA: Harvard University Press, 1978. Partial translation into Italian, 1986; Spanish, 1990; French, 1991.

Catholicism and the World Order: Some Reflections on the 1978 Reith Lectures (pamphlet). London: Catholic Institute for International Relations, 1979.

With Sylvia Mann. *The Game of Tarot: From Ferrara to Salt Lake City*. London: Duckworth, 1980.

Preface to *The City Within the Heart*, by R. C. Zaehner. London: Unwin Paperbacks, 1980.

Southall: 23 April 1979: The Report of the Unofficial Committee of Enquiry. London: National Council for Civil Liberties (N.C.C.L.), 1980, with supplement *The Death of Blair Peach*, 1981.

Twelve Tarot Games. London: Duckworth, 1980.

The Interpretation of Frege's Philosophy. London: Duckworth and Cambridge, MA: Harvard University Press, 1981.

Immigration: The Code that Everyone Knows (pamphlet). London, 1984.

Voting Procedures. Oxford: Oxford University Press, 1984.

The Visconti-Sforza Tarot Cards. New York: Braziller, 1986.

Ursprünge der analytischen Philosophie. Translated from English by J. Schulte. Frankfurt am Main: Suhrkamp, 1987. Translated into Italian 1990, French 1991. Revised English edition, *Origins of Analytical Philosophy.* London: Duckworth, 1993; and Cambridge, MA: Harvard University Press, 1994. Translated into Italian 2001.

Frege and Other Philosophers. Oxford: Oxford University Press, 1991.

Frege: Philosophy of Mathematics. London: Duckworth; and Cambridge, MA: Harvard University Press, 1991.

The Logical Basis of Metaphysics. London: Duckworth and Cambridge, MA: Harvard University Press, 1991. Translated into Italian 1996.

Grammar and Style for Examination Candidates and Others. London: Duckworth, 1993.

Il Mondo e l'Angelo. Naples: Bibliopolis, 1993.

The Seas of Language. Oxford: Oxford University Press, 1993.

I Tarocchi Siciliani. Palermo: La Zisa, 1995; 2nd ed., Genoa: il Melangolo, 2002.

With Ronald Decker and Thierry Depaulis. *A Wicked Pack of Cards: The Origins of the Occult Tarot.* London: Duckworth and New York: St. Martin's Press, 1996.

Principles of Electoral Reform. Oxford: Oxford University Press, 1997.

On Immigration and Refugees. London: Routledge, 2001.

La Natura e il Futuro della Filosofia. Genoa: il Melangolo, 2001.

With Ronald Decker. *A History of the Occult Tarot 1870–1970.* London: Duckworth, 2002.

With J. McLeod. *A History of Games Played with the Tarot Pack: The Game of Triumphs.* Lampeter: Mellen Press, 2004.

Truth and the Past. New York: Columbia University Press, 2004.

Thought and Reality. Oxford: Oxford University Press, 2006.

B. ARTICLES on PHILOSOPHY, LOGIC, SOCIAL CHOICE THEORY, and MATHEMATICS

"Can an Effect Precede its Cause?" *Proceedings of the Aristotelian Society*, Supplementary vol. 28 (1954): 27–44.

Review of *Translations from the Philosophical Writings of Gottlob Frege*, by P. Geach and M. Black. *Mind* 63 (1954): 101–9.

Critical notice of *The Structure of Appearance*, by Nelson Goodman. *Mind* 64 (1955): 101–9.

"Frege on Functions: A Reply." *Philosophical Review* 64 (1955): 97–107.

"Nominalism." *Philosophical Review* 65 (1956): 491–215.

"Note: Frege on Functions." *Philosophical Review* 65 (1956): 229–30.

"Constructionalism." *Philosophical Review* 66 (1957): 47–65.

"Frege's 'The Thought'." *Mind* 66 (1957): 548.

"A Propositional Calculus with Denumerable Matrix." *Journal of Symbolic Logic* 24, no. 2 (June 1959): 97–106.

With John Lemmon. "Modal Logics Between S4 and S5." *Zeitschrift für mathematische Logik und Grundlagen der Mathematik* 5, no. 3 (Sept. 1959): 250–64.

Review of *Studies in Logic and Probability*, by George Boole, edited by R. Rhees. *Journal of Symbolic Logic* 24, no. 3 (Sept. 1959): 203–9.

"Truth." *Proceedings of the Aristotelian Society* 59 (1959): 141–62.

"Wittgenstein's Philosophy of Mathematics." *Philosophical Review* 68 (1959): 324–48.

"A Defence of McTaggart's Proof of the Unreality of Time." *Philosophical Review* 69 (1960): 497–504.

"Oxford Philosophy." *Blackfriars* 41 (1960): 74–80.

Review of articles on presupposition by Strawson, Sellars, and others. *Journal of Symbolic Logic* 25, no. 4 (Dec. 1960): 336–39. Excerpt published as "Presupposition" in M. Dummett, *Truth and Other Enigmas*, 1978, 25–28.

With Robin Farquharson. "Stability in Voting." *Econometrica* 29 (1961): 33–43.

"The Philosophical Significance of Gödel's Theorem." *Ratio* 5 (1963): 140–55. A shorter version, "The Epistemological Significance of Gödel's Theorem," in *Proceedings of the First International Congress on Logic, Methodology and Philosophy of Science*, Amsterdam, 1961.

"Bringing About the Past." *Philosophical Review* 73 (1964): 338–59.

Article on Gottlob Frege, in *The Encyclopaedia of Philosophy*, edited by Paul Edwards, vol. 3. New York, 1967, 225–37. Reprinted as "Frege's Philosophy" in M. Dummett, *Truth and Other Enigmas*, 87–115.

"The Reality of the Past." *Proceedings of the Aristotelian Society* 69 (1969): 239–58.

"Frege's Way Out: A Footnote to a Footnote." *Analysis* 33 (1973): 139–40.

The Justification of Deduction, lecture separately published by the British Academy, 1973; also in *Proceedings of the British Academy* 59 (1975): 201–32.

Article on F. L. G. Frege. In *The New Encyclopaedia Britannica*, 15th ed., vol. 4, 968–69. Chicago: Encyclopedia Britannica, Inc., 1974.

"Postscript." *Synthese* 27 (1974): 523–34. Reprinted as "The Social Character of Meaning" in M. Dummett, *Truth and Other Enigmas*, 420–30.

"The Significance of Quine's Indeterminacy Thesis." *Synthese* 27 (1974): 351–97; "Reply" to Quine's "Comment," in M. Dummett, *Truth and Other Enigmas*, 413–16.

"Frege." In Spanish, *Teorema* 5 (1975): 149–88. Slightly revised version, "Frege's Distinction between Sense and Reference," in M. Dummett, *Truth and Other Enigmas*, 116–44.

"The Philosophical Basis of Intuitionistic Logic." *Logic Colloquium, 1973*, edited by H. E. Rose and J. C. Shepherdson. Amsterdam: North Holland, 1975, 5–40.

"Wang's Paradox." *Synthese* 30 (1975): 301–24.

"What is a Theory of Meaning? " In *Mind and Language*, edited by S. Guttenplan. Oxford: Oxford University Press, 1975, 97–138.

"Frege as a Realist." *Inquiry* 19 (1976): 455–68.

"Frege on the Consistency of Mathematical Theories." In *Studien zu Frege: Studies on Frege*, vol. 1, edited by M. Schirn. Suttgart-Bad Canstatt: Friedrich Fromann/Günther Holzboog, 1976, 229–42.

"Is Logic Empirical?" In *Contemporary British Philosophy*, fourth series, edited by H. D. Lewis. London: Allen & Unwin, 1976, 45–68.

"What is a Theory of Meaning?" (II). In *Truth and Meaning*, edited by G. Evans and J. McDowell. Oxford: Oxford University Press, 1976, 67–137.

"Can Analytical Philosophy be Systematic, and Ought it to Be?" *Ist Systematische Philosophie möglich? – Hegel—Kongreß Stuttgart 1975,* edited by D. Henrich. *Hegel-Studien*, Beiheft Nr. 17. Bonn: Bouvier, 1977, 305–26. In M. Dummett, *Truth and Other Enigmas*. 437–58.

"Platonism" (paper read in 1967). In M. Dummett, *Truth and Other Enigmas*, 202–14.

"Realism" (paper read in 1963). In M. Dummett, *Truth and Other Enigmas*, 145–65.

"Reckonings: Wittgenstein on Mathematics." *Philosophical Quarterly* 28 (1978): 63–68.

What do I Know when I Know a Language? Lecture separately published by Stockholm University, 1978.

"Common Sense and Physics." In *Perception and Identity: Essays Presented to A. J. Ayer*, edited by G. F. Macdonald. London: Routledge & Kegan Paul, 1979, 1–40.

"What does the Appeal to Use Do for the Theory of Meaning?" In *Meaning and Use*, edited by A. Margalit. Dordrecht: D. Reidel, 1979, 123–35.

"Comments on Prawitz's Paper." In *Logic and Philosophy*, edited by G. H. von Wright. The Hague: Martinus Nijhoff, 1980, 11–18.

Reviews of *Gottlob Frege*, by H. Sluga; *Frege's Theory of Judgement*, by D. Bell; *Philosophical and Mathematical Correspondence*, by G. Frege, edited by B. F. McGuinness; and *Translations from the Philosophical Writings of Gottlob Frege*, by P. Geach & M. Black, 3rd ed. In *London Review of Books* 2, no. 18 (1980): 13–15.

"Frege and Wittgenstein." In *Perspectives on the Philosophy of Wittgenstein*, edited by Irving Block. Oxford: Blackwell, 1981, 31–42.

"Frege's Kernsätze zur Logik." *Inquiry* 24 (1981): 439–48.

"Ought Research to be Unrestricted?" *Grazer philosophische Studien* 12 (1981): 281–98.

"Frege and Kant on Geometry." *Inquiry* 25 (1982) 233–54.

"Objectivity and Reality in Lotze and Frege." *Inquiry* 25 (1982): 95–114.

"Realism." *Synthese* 52 (1982): 55–112.

"Existence." In *Humans, Meanings and Existences*, edited by D. P. Chattopadhyaya. Delhi: Macmillan, 1983, 221–58.

"Könnte es Einhörner geben?" *Conceptus* 17 (1983): 5–10. Revised version, "Could there be Unicorns?" in M. Dummett, *The Seas of Language*, 328–48.

"Language and Truth." In *Approaches to Language*, edited by R. Harris. Oxford: Pergamon Press, 1983, 95–125.

"Nuclear Warfare." In *Objections to Nuclear Defence: Philosophers on Deterrence*, edited by N. Blake and K. Pole. London: Routledge & Kegan Paul, 1984, 28–40.

"Rechtsstaat und Meinungsfreiheit. *Rechtstheorie* 15, no. 7 (1984): 1–22.

"An Unsuccessful Dig." Review of *Frege: Logical Excavations*, by G. P. Baker and P. M. S. Hacker. *Philosophical Quarterly* 34 (1984): 379–401. Reprinted in *Frege: Tradition and Influence*, edited by Crispin Wright. Oxford: Blackwell, 1984, 194–226.

"Corrections to Hacking on Frege." *Philosophical Quarterly* 35 (1985): 310.

"Mood, Force and Convention." Written for *Essays on Davidson: Truth and Interpretation*, edited by B. Vermazen and Merrill B. Hintikka, Oxford, due to appear in 1985, but never published. Reprinted in M. Dummett, *The Seas of Language*, 202–23.

"Causal Loops." In *The Nature of Time*, edited by R. Flood and M. Lockwood. Oxford: Blackwell, 1986, 135–69.

"The Ethics of Cultural Property." *Times Literary Supplement* (July 1986): 809–10.

"Frege's Myth of the Third Realm." *Untersuchungen zur Logik und zur Methodologie* 3 (1986): 24–38.

"The Morality of Deterrence." *Canadian Journal of Philosophy*, Supplementary vol. 12 (1986): 111–27.

"'A Nice Derangement of Epitaphs': Some Comments on Davidson and Hacking." In *Truth and Interpretation*, edited by E. LePore. Oxford: Blackwell, 1986, 459–76.

"The Philosophy of Thought and the Philosophy of Language." In *Mérites et limites des méthodes logiques en philosophie*, edited by J. Vuillemin. Paris: Vrin, 1986, 141–68.

With Peter Neumann and Samson Adeleke. "On a Question of Frege's about Right-Ordered Groups." *Bulletin of the London Mathematical Society* 19 (1987): 513–21. Summarized and with final comments in M. Dummett, *Frege and Other Philosophers*, 53–64.

Review of *Foundations of Social Choice Theory*, by J. Elster and A. Hylland. *Economics and Philosophy* 4 (1988): 177–83.

"Second Thoughts." *Philosophical Quarterly* 38 (1988): 87–103. Revised version in M. Dummett, *Frege and Other Philosophers*, 199–216.

"Language and Communication." In *Reflections on Chomsky*, edited by Alexander George.

Oxford: Blackwell, 1989, 192–212.

"More about Thoughts." *Notre Dame Journal of Formal Logic* 30, no. 1 (1989): 1–19.

"The Source of the Concept of Truth." In *Meaning and Method: Essays in Honor of Hilary Putnam*, edited by G. Boolos. Cambridge: Cambridge University Press, 1990, 1–15.

"Thought and Perception: The Views of Two Philosophical Innovators." In *The Analytic Tradition: Meaning, Thought and Knowledge*, edited by D. Bell and N. Cooper. Oxford: Blackwell, 1990, 83–103.

"Does Quantification Involve Identity?" In *Peter Geach: Philosophical Encounters*, edited by H. A. Lewis. Dordrecht: Kluwer Academic, 1991, 161–84.

"Frege and the Paradox of Analysis" (lecture given in 1987). In M. Dummett, *Frege and Other Philosophers*, 17–52.

"The Relative Priority of Thought and Language" (paper delivered 1988). In M. Dummett, *Frege and Other Philosophers*, 1991, 315–24.

Review of *Husserl*, by D. Bell. *Philosophical Quarterly* 41 (1991): 484–88. Extract published as "Frege and Husserl on Reference," in M. Dummett, *The Seas of Language*, 1993, 224–29.

"Which End of the Telescope?" In M. Dummett, *Frege and Other Philosophers*, 1991, 217–36.

"The Metaphysics of Verificationism." In *The Philosophy of A. J. Ayer*, edited by Lewis E. Hahn, Library of Living Philosophers. La Salle, IL: Open Court, 1992, 128–48

"Comments on Dr. Johannes Brandl's Paper." *Philosophy of Mathematics: Proceedings of the 15th International Wittgenstein-Symposium*. Vienna: Hölder-Pichler-Tempsky, 1993, 99–101.

"Comments on Professoressa Picardi's Paper." *Philosophy of Mathematics: Proceedings of the 15th International Wittgenstein-Symposium*. Vienna: Hölder-Pichler-Tempsky, 1993, 86–88.

"Introductory Remarks." *Philosophy of Mathematics: Proceedings of the 15th International Wittgenstein-Symposium*. Vienna: Hölder-Pichler-Tempsky, 1993, 69–76.

"Realism and Anti-Realism." Valedictory lecture, Oxford University, 1992. In M. Dummett, *The Seas of Language*, 462–78.

"Truth and Meaning" (lecture delivered 1985). In M. Dummett, *The Seas of Language*, 147–65.

"Replies." In *The Philosophy of Michael Dummett: Proceedings of Conference on The*

Philosophy of Michael Dummett (September 1991), edited by B. McGuinness and G. Oliveri. Dordrecht: Kluwer Academic Publishers, 1994, 257–369.

"Testimony and Memory." In *Knowing from Words*, edited by B. K. Matilal and A. Chakrabarti. Dordrecht: Kluwer, 1994, 251–72.

"What is Mathematics About?" In *Mathematics and Mind*, edited by A. George. New York and Oxford, 1994, 11–27.

"Wittgenstein on Necessity: Some Reflections." In *Reading Putnam*, edited by Peter Clark and Bob Hale. Oxford: Blackwell, 1994, 49–65.

"Bivalence and Vagueness." *Theoria* 61 (1995): 201–16.

"The Context Principle: Centre of Frege's Philosophy." In *Logik und Mathematik: Frege-Kolloquium Jena*, edited by I. Max and W. Stelzner. Berlin: Walter de Gruyter, 1995, 3–19.

"Force and Convention." In *The Philosophy of P. F. Strawson*, edited by P. K. Sen and R. R. Verma. New Delhi: Indian Council of Philosophical Research, 1995, 66–93.

"Tolérance, vertu de l'état." In *Tolérance, j'écris ton nom*. UNESCO, 1995, 31–45.

"Chairman's Address: Basic Law V." *Proceedings of the Aristotelian Society* 94 (1994): 243–51. Partially reprinted as "Reply to Boolos" in *Frege: Importance and Legacy*, edited by M. Schirn. Berlin: Walter de Gruyter, 1996, 253–60.

"L'intuizionismo." Translated by G. Rigamonti, *La Ricerca filosofica* 9 (1996): 335–53.

"Sense and Reference." In *Sprachphilosophie*, edited by M. Dascal, D. Gerhardus, K. Lorenz, and G. Meggle. Berlin: Walter de Gruyter, 1996, 1188–97.

"Comments on Wolfgang Künne's Paper." In *Bolzano and Analytic Philosophy*, edited by W. Künne, M. Siebel, and M. Textor. Amsterdam: Rodopi, 1997, 241–48.

"Existence, Possibility and Time." *Analyomen 2*, edited by G. Meggle. Berlin: Walter de Gruyter, 1997, 43–67.

Reviews of *Wittgenstein's Philosophy of Mathematics*, by P. Frascolla, and *Wittgenstein on Philosophy and Mathematics: An Essay in the History of Philosophy*, by Christoffer Gefwert. *Journal of Philosophy* 94 (1997): 359–74.

"The Borda Count and Agenda Manipulation." *Social Choice and Welfare* 15 (1998): 287–96.

"Is the Concept of Truth Needed for Semantics?" In *Truth in Perspective*, edited by C. Martinez, U. Rivas, and L. Vellegas-Forero. Aldershot: Ashgate Publishing, 1998, 3–35.

"La existencia de los objectos matematicos." *Teorema* 17 (1998): 5–24.

"Meaning and Justification." In *Language, Logic and Formalization of Knowledge: Coimbra Lecture and Proceedings of a Symposium held in Siena in September 1997*, edited by B. McGuinness. Gaeta: Bibliotheca, 1998.

"Neo-Fregeans: In Bad Company." In *The Philosophy of Mathematics Today*, edited by M. Schirn. Oxford: Oxford University Press, 1998, 369–87.

"The Philosophy of Mathematics." In *Philosophy 2*, edited by A. C. Grayling. Oxford: Oxford University Press, 1998, 122–96.

"Truth from the Constructive Standpoint." *Theoria* 64 (1998): 122–38.

"Of What Kind of Thing is Truth a Property?" In *Truth*, edited by S. Blackburn and K. Simmons. Oxford: Oxford University Press, 1999, 264–81.

"The Source of the Concept of Truth" In *Meaning and Method*, edited by G. Boolos. Cambridge: Cambridge University Press, 1999, 1–15.

"Is Time a Continuum of Instants?" *Philosophy* 75 (2000): 497–515.

"On Frege's Term 'Bedeutung.'" In *Realism: Responses and Reactions: Essays in Honour of Pranab Kumar Sen*, edited by P. K. Sen, D. P. Chattopadhyaya, S. Basu, M. N. Mitra, and R. Mukhopadhyay. New Delhi: Indian Council of Philosophical Research: Sole distributor, Munshiram Manoharlal, 2000, 103–24.

"Sentences and Propositions." In *Logic, Cause and Action*, edited by R. Teichmann. Cambridge: Cambridge University Press, 2000, 9–23.

"Victor's Error." *Analysis* 61 (2001): 1–2.

"What Is a Philosophical Problem?" In *Was ist ein philosopohisches Problem?*, edited by J. Schulte and U. J. Wenzel. Frankfurt: Fischer Taschenbuch, 2001.

"Meaning in Terms of Justification." *Topoi* 21 (2002): 11–19.

"The Two Faces of the Concept of Truth." In *What is Truth?* edited by R. Schantz. Berlin: Walter de Gruyter, 2002, 249–62.

"'Yes', 'No' and 'Can't Say'." *Mind* 111 (2002): 289–95.

"The Nature of Racism." In *Racism in Mind*, edited by M. P. Levine and T. Pataki. Ithaca, NY: Cornell University Press, 2004, 27–34.

"The Justificationist's Response to a Realist." *Mind* 114 (July 2005): 671–88.

"The Work and Life of Robin Farquharson." *Social Choice and Welfare* 25 (2005): 475–83.

"Fitch's Paradox of Knowability." In *New Essays on the Knowability Paradox*, edited by J. Salerno. Oxford University Press, forthcoming.

"Hilary Putnam's New Realism." In *The Philosophy of Hilary Putnam*. Chicago and La Salle, IL: Open Court, forthcoming.

C. ARTICLES ON THE HISTORY OF PLAYING CARDS AND CARD GAMES
(excluding reviews, comments, correspondence)

"Bluff, Counter-bluff." *Games & Puzzles* 5 (1972): 16–17.

"A Note on Cicognara." *Journal of the Playing-Card Society* 2 (1973): 23–32.

"A Note on some Fragments in the Benaki Museum." *Art and Archaeology Research Papers* 4 (1973): 93–99.

"Notes on a 15th Century Pack of Cards from Italy." *Journal of the Playing-Card Society* 1 (1973): 1–11.

With Kamal Abu-Deeb. "Some Remarks on Mamluk Playing Cards." *Journal of the Warburg and Courtauld Institutes* 36 (1973): 106–28.

"Tarock." *Games and Puzzles* 9 (1973): 23–25.

"Terminology." *Journal of the Playing-Card Society* 2 (1973): 34–35.

"The Order of the Tarot Trumps." *Journal of the Playing-Card Society* 2 (1974): 1–17, 33–49.

"Sicilian Tarocchi." *Journal of the Playing-Card Society* 3 (1974): 29–48.

With John McCleod. "Rules of Games: Cego." *Journal of the Playing-Card Society* 4 (1975): 31–46.

———. "Rules of Games: Hachi-hachi." *Journal of the Playing-Card Society* 3 (1975): 26–39.

———. "Rules of Games: Jass." *Journal of the Playing-Card Society* 3 (1975): 21–33.

"More about Cicognara." *Journal of the Playing-Card Society* 5 (1976): 26–34.

"Rules of Games: Trappola." *Journal of the Playing-Card Society* 6 (1977): 1–26; (1978): 129–30.

"A Comment on Mr. Zsoldos' Proposal." *Journal of the Playing-Card Society* 8 (1980): 139–40.

"A Tribute to the International Playing-Card Society." *Journal of the Playing-Card Society* 13 (1980): 109–112.

"Playing Cards found in the Castello Sforzesco in 1908." *The Playing Card* 9 (1980): 33–49; (1981): 89–99.

"On a Thesis of Sylvia Mann's." *The Playing Card* 10 (1981): 11–23.

"Piedmontese Tarocchi with 54 Cards—a Link between Bologna and Belgium." *The Playing Card* 10 (1982): 82–94.

"Some 16th Century Tarot Cards Discovered by Vittoriano Facco." *The Playing Card* 11 (1982): 4–8.

"Dr. Rudolf von Leyden: An Appreciation." *The Playing Card* 11 (1983): 98–100.

"The Tarot Packs of Viéville and de Hautot." *The Playing Card* 14 (1985): 1–14.

"The Earliest Spanish Playing Cards." *The Playing Card* 18 (1989): 6–15.

"The Portuguese Suit-System in the Central Mediterranean." *The Playing Card* 17 (1989): 113–24.

"A Survey of 'Archaic' Italian Cards." *The Playing Card* 19 (1990): 43–51; A Correction: *The Playing Card* 19 (1991): 128–31.

"A Note on the Cimino Family of Cardmakers." *The Playing Card* 20 (1991): 30–32.

"The Tarot and the Occult." In *The Language Game: Papers in Memory of Donald C. Laycock*, edited by T. Dutton, M. Ross, and D. Tryon. Canberra: Pacific Linguistics, 1992, 575–80.

"A Footnote to a Note." *The Playing Card* 21 (1993): 32.

"The History of Card Games." *European Review* 1 (1993): 125–35.

"Obituary of Dr. Hellmut Rosenfeld." *The Playing Card* 23 (1994): 14–15.

"Reply to Trevor Denning." *The Playing Card* 23 (1994): 40–44.

"Sylvia Mann: A Remembrance and an Appreciation." *The Playing Card* 23 (1995): 102–5.

"The Later Pattern for Sicilian Tarots." *The Playing Card* 25 (1996): 90–97.

"A Vietnamese Card Game." *Ludica* 2 (1996): 255–61.

"How Little We Know." *The Playing Card* 31 (2002): 13–16.

"48-Card Packs in Italy." *The Playing Card* 33 (2004): 24–26.

"Where Do the Virtues Go?" *The Playing Card* 32 (2004): 165–67.

"The Sicilian Trumps." *The Playing Card* 33 (2004): 127–31; (2005): 156–60.

"A Brief Sketch of the History of Tarot Cards." *The Playing Card* 33 (2005): 236–46.

D. ARTICLES ON RELIGION

"Our Lady: A Protestant View." *The Old Palace* (1962): 204–7.

"Restoring the Parish Office." *The Old Palace* (1962): 55–56, 60–61.

"The Question of Contraception." *The Clergy Review* 50 (June 1965): 412–27.

"How Corrupt is the Church?" *New Blackfriars* 46 (August 1965): 619–28.

"Church and World." *New Blackfriars* 47 (December 1965): 137–40.

"Racism in the Church." *Janus* (1966): 11–17.

"What is Corruption?" *New Blackfriars* 48 (June 1967): 453–62.

"The Documents of the Papal Commission on Birth Control." *New Blackfriars* 50 (February 1969): 241–50.

"Enforcing the Encyclical." *New Blackfriars* 51 (May 1970): 229–34.

"Eccentric Extraordinary." *The Tablet* (December 1974): 1213–14.

"Biblical Exegesis and the Resurrection." *New Blackfriars* 58 (February 1977): 56–72.

"Holy and Unholy Poverty." *The Tablet* (August 1986): 900–901.

"The Intelligibility of Eucharistic Doctrine." In *The Rationality of Religious Belief: Essays in Honour of Basil Mitchell*, edited by W. Abraham and S. Holtzer. Oxford: Oxford University Press, 1987, 231–61.

"A Remarkable Consensus." *New Blackfriars* 68 (October 1987): 424–31.

"Unsafe Premises." *New Blackfriars* 68 (December 1987): 558–66.

"Theology and Reason." *New Blackfriars* 69 (May 1988): 237–45.

"What Chance for Ecumenism?" *New Blackfriars* 69 (December 1988): 530–45.

"The Virgin Birth." *The New Theologian* 2, no. 2 (Spring 1992): 10–16.

"The Impact of Scriptural Studies on the Content of Catholic Belief." In *Hermes and Athena*, edited by E. Stump and T. P. Flint. Notre Dame: University of Notre Dame Press, 1993, 3–21.

"Response to Collins." In Stump and Flint, *Hermes and Athena*, 31–33.

INDEX

(by Kathleen League)